914.4 Ste 2017
Steves, Rick
Rick Steves France 2017

___ glasses
___ discs/disks
_1_ maps
_1_ bks/pamphs

Rick   ith

2017

CONTENTS

FRANCE . . . . **XIII**

▶ **Introduction** 1

▶ **Paris** 20

▶ **Near Paris** 169
  Versailles. 169
  Chartres 188
  Giverny 198
  Disneyland Paris 204

▶ **Normandy** 207
  Rouen .212
  Honfleur 231
  Bayeux. 247
  D-Day Beaches. 261
  Mont St-Michel 296

▶ **Brittany** 314
  Dinan .317
  St-Malo 332
  Fougères. 344

▶ **The Loire** 345
  East of Tours:
    Amboise and Nearby 355
  West of Tours:
    Chinon and Nearby 402

▶ **Dordogne** 426
  Sarlat-la-Canéda 434
  Best of the
    Dordogne River Valley. . . . 449
  Cro-Magnon Caves 465
  Oradour-sur-Glane. 485
  St-Emilion. 487
  Rocamadour 492
  Lot River Valley. 500

▶ **Languedoc-Roussillon** . . . 504
  Albi. 507
  Carcassonne 521
  Collioure 544

▶ **Provence** 555
  Arles. 565
  Avignon. 596
  Pont du Gard. 620
  Les Baux 625
  Orange 632
  Villages of the
    Côtes du Rhône. 637
  Hill Towns of the Luberon . . 652

▶ **The French Riviera** 663
  Nice 672
  Villefranche-sur-Mer 711

Along the Three Corniches . . 721
Monaco 732
Antibes 743
Inland Riviera. 757

▶ **The French Alps** 764
Annecy 767
Chamonix 783

▶ **Burgundy** 821
Beaune 826
Touring Burgundy's
Wine Villages 848
Between Beaune and
Paris 864
Between Burgundy and
the Loire. 875
Between Burgundy and
Lyon 885

▶ **Lyon** 893

▶ **Alsace** 928
Colmar. 932
Alsace's Route du Vin 955
Strasbourg 979

▶ **Reims & Verdun** 990

▶ **France: Past &
Present** 1031

▶ **Practicalities** 1041
Tourist Information 1041
Travel Tips 1042
Money 1043
Sightseeing 1049
Sleeping 1051
Eating 1062
Staying Connected 1080
Transportation. 1086
Resources from Rick Steves 1110

▶ **Appendix** 1113
Useful Contacts 1113
Holidays and Festivals 1114
Recommended Books
and Films. 1116
Conversions and Climate . . . 1120
Packing Checklist. 1123
Pronunciation Guide for
Place Names. 1124
French Survival Phrases. 1129

▶ **Index**. 1131

▶ **Map Index** 1154

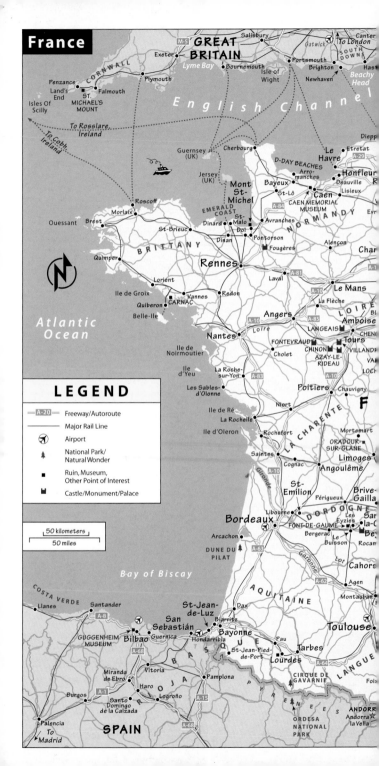

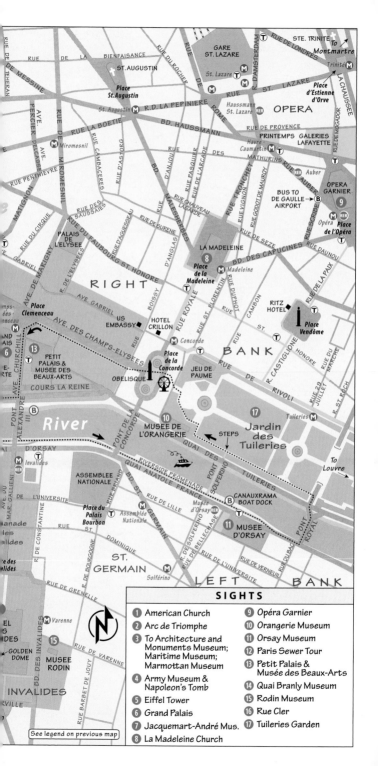

SIGHTS

1	American Church	9	Opéra Garnier
2	Arc de Triomphe	10	Orangerie Museum
3	To Architecture and Monuments Museum; Maritime Museum; Marmottan Museum	11	Orsay Museum
		12	Paris Sewer Tour
4	Army Museum & Napoleon's Tomb	13	Petit Palais & Musée des Beaux-Arts
5	Eiffel Tower	14	Quai Branly Museum
6	Grand Palais	15	Rodin Museum
7	Jacquemart-André Mus.	16	Rue Cler
8	La Madeleine Church	17	Tuileries Garden

See legend on previous map

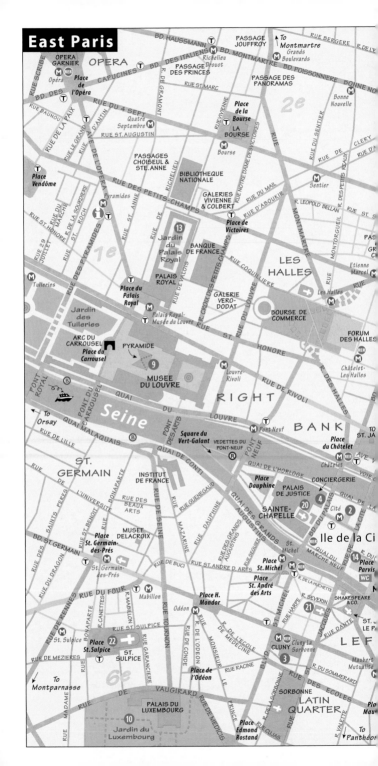

East Paris

LEGEND

- Pedestrian-Friendly Area
- Popular Shopping Area
- Tunnel
- Metro Station, RER Station
- Taxi Stand
- Batobus Boat Stops
- River Tour Boat Stops
- Arrondissement/District
- Landmark or Point of Interest
- Tourist Information Office

500 Meters

500 Yards

SIGHTS

1. Carnavalet Museum
2. Cité Métro Stop & Flower Market
3. Cluny Museum
4. Conciergerie
5. Deportation Memorial
6. Holocaust Memorial
7. Ile St. Louis
8. Jewish Art & History Museum
9. Louvre Museum
10. Luxembourg Garden
11. Notre-Dame Cathedral
12. Opéra Bastille
13. Palais Royal Courtyards
14. Paris Archaeological Crypt
15. To Père Lachaise Cemetery
16. Picasso Museum
17. Place des Vosges
18. Pompidou Center
19. To Promenade Plantée Park
20. Sainte-Chapelle
21. St. Séverin Church
22. St. Sulpice Church

To Gare de l'Est & Gare du Nord

To Place de la République

REAUMUR

Arts et Métiers

RUE DE MALTE

RUE DU PETIT THOUARS

RUE JEAN PIERRE TIMBAUD

BD. RICHARD LENOIR

Oberkampf

RUE DES GRAVILLIERS

Square du Temple

RUE VIEILLE DU TEMPLE

RUE DE BRETAGNE

RUE DU TEMPLE

RUE AMELOT

RUE OBERKAMPF

BLVD. VOLTAIRE

3e

RUE BEAUBOURG

RUE PASTOURELLE

MARCHE DES ENFANTS ROUGES

Filles du Calvaire

RUE DES FILLES DU CALVAIRE

TEMPLE

RUE MICHEL LE COMTE

ARCHIVES

RUE DE POITOU

RUE DE TURENNE

RUE COMMINES

RUE R. FROISSART

RUE ST. SEBASTIEN

Rambuteau

MUSEE DU JUDAISME

RUE RAMBUTEAU

RUE DES 4 FILS

TEMPLE

RUE DU PONT AUX CHOUX

St. Sébastien-Froissart

RUE ST. SEBASTIEN

RUE BAUDIN

CENTRE POMPIDOU

BRAQUE

8

RUE ST. GERVAIS

RUE ST. CLAUDE

RUE PELEE

Place Stravinsky

SIMON

RUE DU TEMPLE

RUE BLANCS MANTEAUX

VIEILLE

RUE DE LA PERLE

16

MUSEE PICASSO

RUE DU PARC ROYAL

RUE ST. GILLES

BEAUMARCHAIS

RUE DU CHEMIN VERTE

BERRI

LA VERRERIE

R. STE. CROIX DE LA BRETONNERIE

RUE ELZEVIR

Place Thorigny

RUE PAYENNE

BD.

Breguet-Sabin

Hotel de Ville

BHV

RUE DE MOUSSY

RUE DES ROSIERS

RUE DES FRANCS-BOURGEOIS

MUSEE CARNAVALET (CLOSED THROUGH 2017)

1

Chemin Vert

RUE AMELOT

HOTEL DE VILLE

RUE DU ROI DE SICILE

MARAIS

RUE DE RIVOLI

RUE DE SEVIGNE

RUE MALHER

RUE DE JARENTE

PL. DES VOSGES

17

RUE DES TOURNELLES

15

BD. RICHARD LENOIR

RUE FR. MIRON

RUE F.-R. MIRON

RUE DES BARRES

RUE GEOFFROY L'ASNIER

RUE DE JOUY

RUE DES NONNAINS D'HYERES

ST. Paul

ST. PAUL

RUE DE TURENNE

Place des Vosges

RUE DE BIRAGUE

VICTOR HUGO'S HOUSE

HOLOCAUST MEMORIAL

6

Pont Marie

RUE CHARLEMAGNE

RUE ST. PAUL

RUE ST. ANTOINE

MONO-PRIX

RUE CASTEX

POST

Bastille

Place de la Bastille

4e

QUAI DES CELESTINS

RUE CHARLES V

RUE BEAUTREILLIS

RUE CASTEX

Bastille

12

QUAI DE BOURBON

PONT MARIE

FAUCONNIER

RUE DU PETIT MUSC

OPERA BASTILLE

RUE ST. LOUIS-EN-L'ILE

QUAI D'ANJOU

RUE DES LIONS

BD. HENRI IV

LA CERISAIE

RUE DE LA ROQUETTE

5

ST. LOUIS EN L'ILE

7

Ile St. Louis

QUAI DE BETHUNE

RUE DE BRETONVILLIERS

Sully-Morland

RUE DE L'ARSENAL

RUE DE LYON

H

D'ORLEANS

QUAI HENRI IV

SULLY

BD. BOURDON

BD. DE LA BASTILLE

RUE DE LYON

LA TOURNELLE

PONT DE SULLY

Bassin de l'Arsenal

RUE CRILLON

RUE MORNAY

RUE LACUEE

19

R. JULES CESAR

12e

ANK

GERMAIN

RUE DES FOSSES ST. BERNARD

CARDINAL LEMOINE

INSTITUT DU MONDE ARABE

QUAI ST. BERNARD

Seine

To Gare d'Austerlitz

To Gare de Lyon

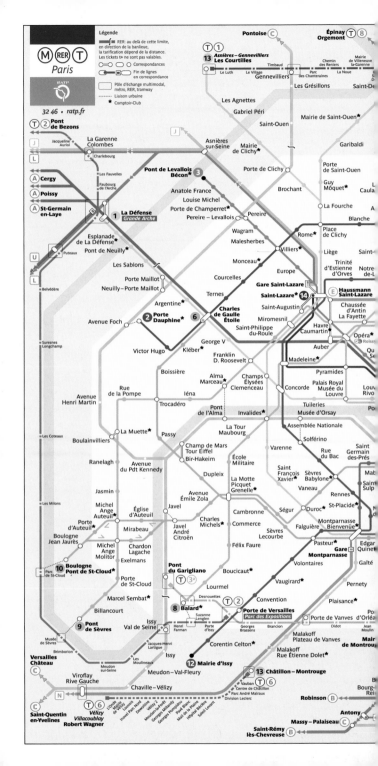

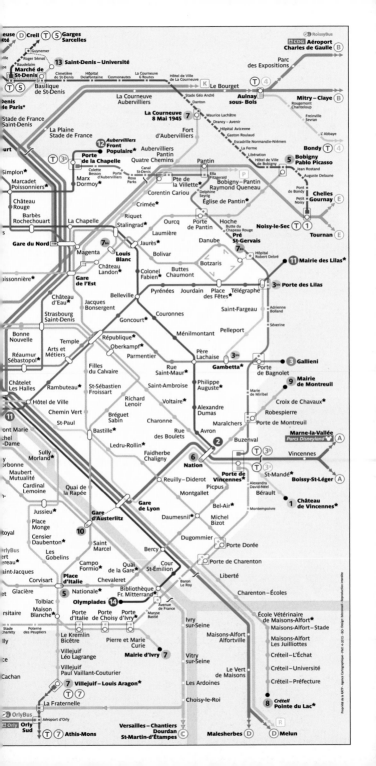

France

Bienvenue! You've chosen well. France is Europe's most diverse, tasty, and, in many ways, most exciting country to explore. It's an intriguing cultural bouillabaisse that will challenge your preconceptions and inspire you to think differently.

France is a place of gentle beauty, where the play of light transforms the routine into the exceptional. Here, travelers are treated to a blend of man-made and natural beauty like nowhere else in Europe. With luxuriant forests, forever coastlines, truly grand canyons, and Europe's highest mountain ranges, France has a cover-girl beauty from top to bottom. You'll also discover a dizzying array of artistic and architectural wonders—soaring cathedrals, chandeliered châteaux, and museums filled with the cultural icons of the Western world.

In many ways, France is a yardstick of human achievement. Here, travelers can trace the whole of European history, from the earliest prehistoric cave paintings to Roman ruins that rival Italy's. In medieval times, France cultivated Romanesque and Gothic architecture, erecting the great cathedrals and basilicas of Notre-Dame, Chartres, Vézelay, and a dozen others. With their innovative designs, French architects set the trends for cities throughout Europe—and with their revolutionary thinking, French philosophers refined modern thought and politics. The châteaux of the Loire Valley and the grand palace of Versailles announced France's emergence as the first European superpower and first modern government. It was France that gave birth to Impressionism and the foundations of modern art. Today's travelers can gaze dreamy-eyed at water lilies in Claude Monet's Giverny, rejoice amid the sunflowers of Provence

that so moved a troubled Vincent van Gogh, and roam the sunny coastlines that inspired Picasso and Matisse. And after all these centuries, France still remains at the forefront of technology, fashion, and—of course—cuisine.

There are two Frances: Paris...and the rest of the country. France's top-down government and cultural energy have always been centered in Paris, resulting in an overwhelming concentration of world-class museums, cutting-edge architecture, historic monuments, and famous cafés. Travelers can spend weeks in France and never leave Paris. Many do.

The other France venerates land, tradition, and a slower pace of life. After Paris, most travelers will be drawn to romantic hill towns and castles, meandering rivers and canals, and oceans of vineyards that carpet this country's landscape. Village life has survived in France better than in most other European countries because France was so slow to urbanize. It was an agricultural country right up until World War II (when a smaller proportion of French citizens lived in cities than Italians did 500 years earlier). And today, even as young people are chasing jobs in the cities, France remains farm country. Even city dwellers venerate the soil *(le terroir)* that brings the flavor to their foods and wines and nourishes a rural life that French people dream about. So although the country's brain resides in Paris, its soul lives in its villages—and that's where you'll feel the real pulse of France.

France offers more diversity than any other nation in Europe; moving from region to region, you feel as if you're crossing into a different country. Paris and the region around it (called Ile de France) is the "island" in the middle that anchors France. To the west are the dramatic D-Day beaches and Tudor-style, thatched-roofed homes of Normandy; to the south lie the river valleys of the Loire and Dordogne, featuring luxurious châteaux, medieval castles, and hill-capping villages. Explore under-the-radar France to the far southwest, in the Spanish-tinged Languedoc-Roussillon region. Closer to Italy, sunbaked and windswept Provence nurtures Roman ruins and rustic charm, while the Riviera celebrates sunny beaches, modern art, and yacht-filled harbors. And to the east, travelers encounter Europe's highest snow-capped Alps, the venerable vineyards and villages of Burgundy, and the Germanic culture and cuisine of Alsace.

The forte of French cuisine lies in its regional diversity. You'll enjoy Swiss-like fondue in the Alps, Italian-style pasta on the Riviera, fresh oysters and mussels in Brittany, Spanish paella in Languedoc-Roussillon, and sauerkraut mixed with fine wine sauces in the Alsace. *C'est magnifique*—you can taste a good slice of Europe without stepping outside of France.

Each region also produces a wine or other drink that complements its cuisine—such as rich Burgundy wines that go perfectly with *coq au vin,* meaty wines from Languedoc-Roussillon to counter heavy cuisine (think cassoulet), fruity Côtes du Rhône wines that work well with herb-infused Provençal dishes, and dry whites in Alsace that meld perfectly with the Germanic cuisine. And in Normandy and Brittany, you'll enjoy apple ciders with crêpes and fresh seafood.

As if that weren't enough, France is also famous for its many pâtés, foie gras, over 350 different cheeses, sizzling escargots, *herbes de Provence,* raw meats, fine wine sauces, French fries, duck and lamb dishes, pastries, bonbons, crème brûlée, and sorbets.

L'art de vivre—the art of living—is not just a pleasing expression; it's a building block for a sound life in France. With

five weeks of paid vacation, plus every Catholic holiday ever invented, the French are obligated to enjoy life. It's no accident that France is home to linger-longer pastimes like café lounging, leisurely dinners, Club Med vacations, barge cruising, and ballooning. You'll run headlong into that mindful approach to life at mealtime. The French insist on the best-quality croissants, mustard, and sparkling water; they don't rush lunch; and an evening's entertainment is usually no more than a lovingly prepared meal with friends.

France demands that the traveler slow down and savor the finer things; a hurried visitor will miss the *"this is what matters"* barge and blame the French for being lazy. One of your co-authors learned this lesson the hard way while

restoring a farm house in Burgundy—and found that it's counterproductive to hurry a project past its "normal pace."

In spite of lavish attention to relaxation, the French are a productive people. French inventors gave us the metric system, pasteurization, high-speed trains, and Concorde airplanes. More importantly, this country rose from the ashes of two debilitating world wars to generate the world's fifth-largest

economy. This is thanks in part to some serious government intervention that continues today (government spending is 48 percent of GDP). Wine, tourism, telecommunications, pharmaceuticals, cars, and Airbus planes are big moneymakers. France is also the European Union's leading agricultural producer and a chief competitor of the US. You'll pass

France Almanac

Official Name: It's officially the République Française, but locals, and everyone else, just call it France.

Population: France has nearly 66 million people (approximately the combined population of California and Texas). They're a mix of Celtic, Latin, and Teutonic DNA, plus many recent immigrants from around the globe—especially North Africa. Two out of three French are (at least nominally) Roman Catholic. Every French citizen is expected to speak French.

Area: At 215,000 square miles, it's Western Europe's largest nation. (But Texas is still 20 percent bigger.)

Latitude and Longitude: 46°N and 2°E (similar latitude to the states of Washington, North Dakota, and Maine).

Geography: The terrain consists of rolling plains in the north and mountains in the southwest (Pyrenees), southeast (Alps), and south-central (Massif Central). Capping the country on both ends are 1,400 miles of coastline (Mediterranean and Atlantic). The Seine River flows east-west through Paris, the Rhône rumbles north-south 500 miles from the Alps to the Mediterranean, and the Loire travels east-west, roughly dividing the country into north and south. Mont Blanc (15,780 feet) is Western Europe's highest point.

Major Cities: Nearly one in five lives in greater Paris (12 million in the metropolitan area, 2.3 million in the city). Marseille, on the Mediterranean coast, and Lyon, in the southeast, both have about 1.5 million people.

Economy: France's gross domestic product is $2.6 trillion (bigger than California's $2 trillion); the GDP per capita is about $41,000 (America's is about $56,000). Though the French are among the world's biggest wine producers, they drink much of it themselves. France's free-market economy is tempered by the government, which collects some of Europe's highest taxes (21 percent of GDP—compared to 11 percent in the US) and invests both in industry and social spending (to narrow the income gap between rich and poor). Despite the three-hour lunch stereotypes, the French work as much as their EU neighbors—that is, 20 percent less than Americans (but with greater per-hour productivity).

Government: President François Hollande, elected by popular vote in 2012, heads a socialist government along with president-appointed Prime Minister Manuel Valls until the spring of 2017 (when elections will likely produce a new president). The upper-house Senate (348 seats) is chosen by an electoral college, the National Assembly (577 seats) by popular vote. Though France is a cornerstone of the European Union, many French are Euro-skeptics.

Flag: The Revolution produced the well-known tricolore, whose three colors are vertical bands of blue, white, and red.

The Average Jean: The average French person is 41 years old and will live 81 years. This person eats lunch in 22 minutes (four times as fast as 20 years ago) and consumes a glass and a half of wine and a pound of fat a day. The average French citizen pops a bottle of Champagne about every four months. The average worker enjoys five weeks of holiday and vacation a year. A dog is a part of one in five French households; cats, one in four.

endless wheat farms in the north, dairy farms in the west, vegetable farms and fruit orchards in the south...and vineyards and sunflowers just about everywhere.

With no domestic oil production, France depends on nuclear power generation, which now accounts for more than 75 percent of the country's electricity production (although renewable energy sources are gaining ground). Electricity is expensive, so the French are careful to turn out lights and conserve—something to remember when you leave your hotel room for the day or evening. Although France's economy may be one of the world's largest, the French remain skeptical about the virtues of capitalism and the work ethic. Business conversation is generally avoided, as it implies a fascination with money that the French find

vulgar. (It's considered gauche even to ask what someone does for a living.) In France, CEOs are not glorified as celebrities—chefs are.

The French believe that the economy should support social good, not vice versa. This has produced a cradle-to-grave social security system of which the French are proud. France's poverty rate is half of that in the US, proof to the French that they are on the right track. On the other hand, if you're considering starting a business in France, think again—taxes are *formidable*. France is routinely plagued with strikes, demonstrations, and slow-downs as workers try to preserve their hard-earned rights in the face of a competitive global economy.

As you travel, you'll find that the most "French" thing about France is the French themselves. Be prepared to embrace (or at least understand) the cultural differences between you and your French hosts. You'll find the French to be reserved in the north and carefree in the sunny south. Throughout the country, they're more formal than you are. When you enter a store, you'll be greeted not simply with a *"Bonjour,"* but with *"Bonjour, Monsieur* (or *Madame)."* The proper response to the shopkeeper is *"Bonjour, Monsieur* (or *Madame)."* If there are others present, you'd say, *"Bonjour, Messieurs* (or *Mesdames)"*—just to make sure you don't leave anyone out. (For more on the French attitude toward language, see page 16.)

The French are overwhelmingly Catholic but not very devout, and are quick to separate church from state. They are less active churchgoers than Americans, whom they find *très* evangelical. And in France you don't go to church to socialize or to help in charitable deeds (that's what taxes are for). France is also Europe's largest Muslim nation, with well over six million followers (there are twice as many Muslims in France as Protestants). The influx of Muslim immigrants has led to considerable problems of assimilation and remains one of France's thorniest issues to resolve.

The French don't seem particularly athletic—unless you consider tossing little silver balls in the dirt (*pétanque,* a.k.a.

boules) a sport. A few jog and exercise regularly, and fewer play on recreational teams—though you will find country lanes busy with bike riders hunched over handlebars on weekends. The French are avid sports-watchers. Soccer is king, bike racing is big, and rugby is surprisingly popular for such a refined place. *Le basket* (basketball) is making a move, with a French league and several French NBA stars, including Tony Parker.

Another passion the French share with Americans is their love of movies. They admire Hollywood blockbusters, but they've also carved out their own niche of small-budget romantic comedies and thought-provoking thrillers.

Today's France will challenge many of your preconceptions. The French have a Michelin Guide-certainty in their judgments and are often frank in how they convey their opinions. (Just ask about the best wine to serve with any given course.)

The French see the world differently than we do. The right to bear arms, the death penalty, minuscule paid vacations, and health care as a privilege rather than a basic human right—these American concepts confound the average Jean. And they don't understand the American need for everyone to be in agreement all the time. Whether it's Iraq, Uber, or globalization, the French think it's important to question authority and not blindly submit to it. Blame this aversion to authority on their Revolution hangover.

For hurried travelers, the French can be a complicated people to understand. But remember where they've come from: In just a few generations, they've seen two world wars destroy entire cities, villages, landscapes, and their self-respect. They've watched as America replaced them as the world's political and cultural superpower. On the bright side, they've seen their country reemerge as a global force, with nuclear weapons, a space program, an international spy network, and their own ideas about geopolitics. Like Americans, they're trying to find their place in an increasingly global, multicultural world. Today, they just don't want to be taken

for granted. And while the French may—or may not—love your country's politics, this has no bearing on how they will treat you as an individual.

As you travel through this splendid country, come with an appetite to understand and a willingness to experience. Welcome new ideas and give the locals the benefit of your doubt. Accept France on its own terms and don't judge. Above all, slo-o-o-ow down. Spend hours in cafés lingering over *un café,* make a habit of unplanned stops, learn what *l'art de vivre* really means, and surrender to the play of light as the Impressionists did.

INTRODUCTION

France is a big country by European standards—and would be one of the biggest states if it ever joined the US (unlikely). Geographically, it's a bit smaller than Texas, but has 66 million people (Texas has 26 million) and over 350 different cheeses (Texas has...not that many). *Diversité* is a French forte. This country features three mountain ranges (the Alps, the Pyrenees, and the Massif Central), two coastlines as different as night and day (Atlantic and Mediterranean), cosmopolitan cities (such as Paris, Lyon, Strasbourg, and Nice), and countless sleepy villages. From the Swiss-like Alps to the *molto* Italian Riviera, and from the Spanish Pyrenees to *das* German Alsace, you can stay in France and feel like you've sampled much of Europe—and never be more than a short stroll from a *bon vin rouge*.

This book covers the predictable must-sees while mixing in a healthy dose of Back Door intimacy. Along with seeing the Eiffel Tower, Mont St-Michel, and the French Riviera, you'll take a minivan tour of the D-Day beaches, pedal your way from village to vineyard in the Alsace, marvel at 15,000-year-old cave paintings, and paddle a canoe down the lazy Dordogne River. You'll find a *magnifique* hill-town perch to catch a Provençal sunset, ride Europe's highest mountain lift over the Alps, and touch the quiet Romanesque soul of Burgundian abbeys and villages. You'll learn about each region's key monuments and cities with thoughtfully presented walking tours and background information. Just as important, you'll meet the intriguing people who run your hotel, bed-and-breakfast, or restaurant. We've also listed our favorite local guides, all well worth the time and money, to help you gain a better understanding of this marvelous country's past and present.

The destinations covered in this book are balanced to include the most interesting cities and intimate villages, from jet-setting

INTRODUCTION

Map Legend

↯ Viewpoint	🚲 Bike Rental/Bike Route	❢ Wine Tasting
↟ Entrance	ⓣ Taxi Stand	▓ Pedestrian Zone
🛈 Tourist Info	+🚋+ Tram & Stop	----- Railway
WC Restroom	⑧ Bus Stop	.... Ferry/Boat Route
🏰 Castle	Ⓟ Parking	
🏠 Church	Ⓡ RER Train	✈ Airport
▪ Statue/Point of Interest	ⓣ Tourist Train	▥▥▥ Stairs
▪	Ⓑ Batobus Stop	------ Walk/Tour Route
🌳 Park	Ⓜ Métro Stop	
◎ Fountain	◮ Vaporetto Dock	------ Trail

Use this legend to help you navigate the maps in this book.

beach resorts to the traditional heartland. This book is selective, including only the most exciting sights and romantic villages—for example, there are hundreds of beautiful châteaux in the Loire region, but we cover only the top 10. And though there are dozens of Loire towns you could use for a home base, we recommend the best two.

The best is, of course, only our opinion. But after spending much of our adult lives writing and lecturing about travel, guiding tours, and gaining an appreciation for all things French, we've developed a sixth sense for what touches the traveler's imagination.

ABOUT THIS BOOK

Rick Steves France 2017 is a personal tour guide in your pocket. Better yet, it's actually two tour guides in your pocket: The co-author of this book is Steve Smith. Steve, who has lived in France on several occasions, now travels there annually (as he has since 1986) as a guide, researcher, and devout Francophile. He restored a stone farmhouse in Burgundy (where he bases himself while updating this book) and today keeps one foot on each side of the Atlantic. Together, Steve and I keep this book current (though, for simplicity, from this point "we" will shed our respective egos and become "I").

This book is organized by destinations. Each is a minivacation on its own, filled with exciting sights, strollable neighborhoods, affordable places to stay, and memorable places to eat. For destinations covered in this book, you'll find these sections:

Planning Your Time suggests a schedule for how to best use your limited time.

Orientation has specifics on public transportation, helpful

Key to This Book

Updates

This book is updated every year—but things change. For the latest, visit www.ricksteves.com/update.

Abbreviations and Times

I use the following symbols and abbreviations in this book:

Sights are rated:

▲▲▲	Don't miss
▲▲	Try hard to see
▲	Worthwhile if you can make it
No rating	Worth knowing about

Tourist information offices are abbreviated as **TI,** and bathrooms are **WC**s. Accommodations are categorized with a **Sleep Code** (described on page 1052); eateries are classified with a **Restaurant Price Code** (page 1063). To indicate discounts for my readers, I include **RS%** in the listings.

Like Europe, this book uses the **24-hour clock.** It's the same through 12:00 noon, then keeps going: 13:00, 14:00, and so on. For anything over 12, subtract 12 and add p.m. (14:00 is 2:00 p.m.).

When giving **opening times,** I include both peak season and off-season hours if they differ. So if a museum is listed as "May-Oct daily 9:00-16:00," it should be open from 9 a.m. until 4 p.m. from the first day of May until the last day of October (but expect exceptions).

A ∩ symbol indicates that a free, downloadable self-guided Rick Steves audio tour is available.

For **transit** or **tour departures,** I first list the frequency, then the duration. So, a train connection listed as "2/hour, 1.5 hours" departs twice each hour and the journey lasts an hour and a half.

---

hints, local tour options, easy-to-read maps, and tourist information.

Sights describes the top attractions and includes their cost and hours. Major sights have self-guided tours.

Self-Guided Walks take you through interesting neighborhoods and villages, pointing out sights and local flavor.

Sleeping describes my favorite hotels and bed-and-breakfasts, from good-value deals to cushy splurges.

Eating serves up a buffet of options, from inexpensive cafés to intimate restaurants.

Connections outlines your options for traveling to destinations by train, bus, and plane. In car-friendly regions, I've included route tips for drivers.

France: Past & Present gives you a quick overview of French history, notable citizens, and current political issues.

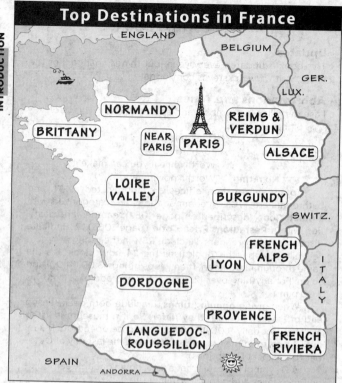

The **Practicalities** chapter near the end of this book is a traveler's tool kit, with my best advice about money, sightseeing, sleeping, eating, staying connected, and transportation (trains, buses, driving, and flights).

The **appendix** has the nuts-and-bolts: useful phone numbers and websites, a holiday and festival list, recommended books and films, a climate chart, a handy packing checklist, a pronunciation guide for place names, and French survival phrases.

Throughout this book, you'll find money- and time-saving tips for sightseeing, transportation, and more. Some businesses—especially hotels and walking tour companies—offer special discounts to my readers, indicated in their listings.

Devour this book, choose your favorite destinations, and link them up. Then have a *très bon voyage!* Traveling like a temporary local, you'll get the absolute most out of every mile, minute, and dollar. And, as you visit places I know and love, I'm happy that you'll be meeting some of my favorite French people.

Please Tear Up This Book!

There's no point in hauling around a big chapter on Normandy for a day in Provence. That's why I hope you'll rip this book apart.  Before your trip, attack this book with a utility knife to create an army of pocket-sized mini guidebooks—one for each area you visit.

I love the ritual of trimming down the size of guidebooks I'll be using: Fold the pages back until you break the spine, neatly slice apart the sections you want with a utility knife, then pull them out with the gummy edge intact. If you want, finish each one off with some clear, heavy-duty packing tape to smooth and reinforce the spine, and/or use a heavy-duty stapler along the edge to prevent the first and last pages from coming loose.

To make things even easier, I've created a line of laminated covers with slide-on binders (available at www.ricksteves.com). With every stop, you can make a ritual of swapping out the last chapter with the new one.

As you travel, throw out the chapters you're done with (or, much better, give them to a needy fellow traveler). While you may be tempted to keep this book intact as a souvenir of your travels, you'll appreciate even more the footloose freedom of traveling light.

Planning

This section will help you get started planning your trip—with advice on trip costs, when to go, and what you should know before you take off.

TRAVEL SMART

Your trip to France is like a complex play—it's easier to follow and really appreciate on a second viewing. While no one does the same trip twice to gain that advantage, reading this book before your trip accomplishes much the same thing.

Design an itinerary that enables you to visit sights at the best possible times. Note festivals, holidays, market days, specifics on sights, and days when sights are closed or most crowded (all covered in this book). To connect the dots smoothly, read the tips in Practicalities on taking trains and buses, or renting a car and driving. Designing a smart trip is a fun, doable, and worthwhile challenge.

Make your itinerary a mix of intense and relaxed stretches.

France at a Glance

These regions and sights are listed (as in this book) looping counter-clockwise around France, starting in Paris and ending in Champagne.

▲▲▲**Paris** World capital of art, fashion, food, literature, and ideas, offering historic monuments, grand boulevards, corner cafés, chic boutiques, cutting-edge architecture, and world-class art galleries, including the Louvre and Orsay.

▲▲**Near Paris** Europe's grandest palace at Versailles, the radiant cathedral of Chartres, Monet's flowery gardens at Giverny, and a mouse-run amusement park.

▲▲**Normandy** Pastoral mix of sweeping coastlines, half-timbered towns, and intriguing cities, including bustling Rouen (Gothic architecture, Joan of Arc sites), the cozy port town of Honfleur, historic Bayeux (remarkable tapestry on the Battle of Hastings), stirring D-Day sites and museums, and the almost surreal island abbey of Mont St-Michel.

▲**Brittany** Windswept and rugged, with a forgotten interior, gorgeous coast, Celtic ties, two notable towns: Dinan (Brittany's best medieval center) and the beach resort of St-Malo, and the sea-swept castle of Fort la Latte.

▲▲**The Loire** Picturesque towns (such as Amboise and Chinon) and hundreds of castles and palaces, including Chenonceau (arcing across its river), the huge Château de Chambord, Villandry (wonderful gardens), lavishly furnished Cheverny, and many more.

▲▲**Dordogne** Prehistoric caves, rock-sculpted villages, lazy canoe rides past medieval castles, and market towns such as pedestrian-friendly Sarlat-la-Canéda, and nearby, for wine lovers, St-Emilion.

▲**Languedoc-Roussillon** Sunny region with a Spanish flair, featuring Albi (fortress-like cathedral and a beautiful Toulouse-Lautrec museum), medieval Carcassonne (walled town with towers, turrets, and cobblestones), remote Cathar castles and villages, vineyards that stretch forever, and the lovely Mediterranean village of Collioure.

▲▲▲**Provence** Home to Arles (Van Gogh sights, evocative Roman arena), Avignon (famous bridge and brooding Palace of the Popes), the ancient Roman aqueduct of Pont du Gard, Orange (Roman theater), the beautiful Côtes du Rhone wine road, and rock-top villages such as Les Baux, Roussillon, and Vaison-la-Romaine.

▲▲▲**The French Riviera** A string of coastal resorts, including Nice (big city with seafront promenade and art museums), romantic Villefranche-sur-Mer and Cap Ferrat, glitzy Monaco (casino), easygoing Antibes (silky-sandy beaches), intriguing inland villages (Vence and St.-Paul-de-Vence), and little hilltop Eze-le-Village, with magnificent Mediterranean views.

▲**The French Alps** Spectacular scenery featuring the drop-dead gorgeous town of Annecy, Mont Blanc (Europe's highest peak), and the world-famous ski resort of Chamonix, with hikes galore and lifts to stunning alpine views.

▲▲**Burgundy** Aged blend of vineyards and spirituality, with the compact town of Beaune (world-famous vineyards), Fontenay (France's best-preserved medieval abbey), Vézelay (magnificent Romanesque church), the one-of-a-kind medieval castle under construction at Guédelon, Cluny's grand medieval abbey, and the modern-day religious community of Taizé.

▲**Lyon** Metropolitan city, located between Burgundy and Provence, with an Italianesque old town, two Roman theaters, a terrific Gallo-Roman museum, the stirring French Resistance Center, an impressive fine arts museum, and delicious but affordable cuisine.

▲▲**Alsace** Franco-Germanic region dotted with wine-road villages, starring half-timbered Colmar and its world-class art, and high-powered Strasbourg and its sensational cathedral.

▲▲**Reims and Verdun** Champagne-soaked Reims with a historic cathedral and cellars serving the sparkling brew, and nearby Verdun, site of horrific WWI battles, with a compelling, unforgettable memorial.

Whirlwind Three-Week Tour of France by Car

While this trip is doable in 22 days, most will appreciate adding an extra day here and there to rest their engine.

Day	Plan
1	Fly into Paris (save Paris sightseeing for the end of your trip), pick up your car, visit Giverny, and overnight in Honfleur (1 night).
2	Morning in Honfleur, afternoon in Bayeux visiting its tapestry and cathedral. Dinner and overnight in Bayeux (2 nights).
3	Spend day touring D-Day sights: Arromanches, American Cemetery, and Pointe du Hoc (and Utah Beach Landing Museum, if you're moving fast).
4	Drive to Dinan and take in its sights. In late afternoon, drive to Mont St-Michel and visit its abbey. Sleep on Mont St-Michel (1 night).
5	Head for château country in the Loire Valley. Tour Chambord, then check in to your Amboise hotel (2 nights). Take my town walk.
6	Do a day trip, touring Chenonceau and Cheverny or Chaumont (or all three if you don't need time later in Amboise). Save time at the end of the day for sights in Amboise if you like.
7	Leave early and head south to the Dordogne region, stopping en route at Oradour-sur-Glane. End in Sarlat-la-Canéda (2 nights) and browse the town late today.
8	Take a relaxing canoe trip, and tour a prehistoric cave.
9	Head to the Languedoc-Roussillon region, lunch in Albi, then dinner and sleep in Carcassonne (1 night).
10	Morning in Carcassonne, then on to Provence with a stop at the Pont du Gard aqueduct. Stay in or near Arles (2 nights).
11	All day for Arles and Les Baux (visit Les Baux early or late).
12	Make a beeline for the Riviera, staying in Nice, Antibes, or Villefranche-sur-Mer (2 nights). Explore your home base this afternoon.
13	Sightsee in Nice and Monaco.
14	Make the long drive north to the Alps, and sleep in Chamonix (2 nights).
15	If the weather is clear, take the mountain lifts up to Aiguille du Midi and beyond.

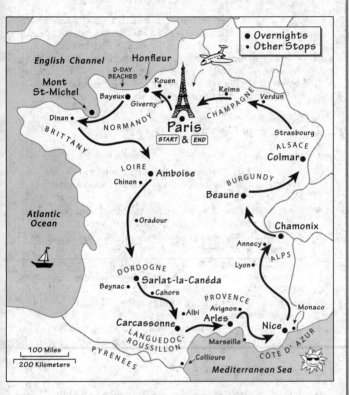

16 Allow another half-day for the Alps (in Chamonix or Annecy). Then head for Burgundy, ending in Beaune for wine tasting. Sleep in Beaune (1 night).

17 Spend half of the day in and around Beaune, then move on to Colmar (2 nights).

18 Enjoy Colmar and the Route du Vin villages.

19 Return to Paris, visiting Verdun or Reims en route. Collapse in Paris hotel (4 nights).

20 Sightsee Paris.

21 More time in Paris.

22 Finish your sightseeing in Paris, and consider side-tripping to Versailles.

Whirlwind Three-Week Tour of France by Train (and Bus)

This itinerary is designed primarily for train travel, with some help from buses, minivan tours, and taxis. It takes 11 days of train travel to complete this trip: Buy a France flexipass with 9 train days and purchase point-to-point tickets for days 5 and 13 (short and cheap trips). Book any TGV train trips as far ahead as possible, particularly if traveling with a rail pass. With only two weeks, end your tour in Nice. *Bonne route* and *bon courage!*

Day	Plan
1	Fly into Paris (3 nights).
2	Sightsee Paris.
3	More time in Paris.
4	Train* and bus to Mont St-Michel via Rennes (4 hours, arrive in Mont St-Michel about 13:00). Afternoon and night on Mont St-Michel (1 night).
5	Train to Bayeux (2 hours, arrive by noon). Afternoon and evening in Bayeux. Sleep in Bayeux (2 nights).
6	All day for D-Day beaches by minivan, taxi, bike, bus, or a combination of these.
7	Train* to Amboise via Caen and St-Pierre des Corps (4.5 hours). Afternoon visit to Amboise sights. Sleep in Amboise (2 nights).
8	All day for touring Loire châteaux (good options by bus, bike, or minivan tour).
9	Early train* to Sarlat-la-Canéda (6 hours, arrive about 13:00). Afternoon and evening in Sarlat. Sleep in Sarlat (2 nights).
10	All day for caves and canoes by train and bike or minivan/taxi tour.
11	Train or bus to Carcassonne via Bordeaux (7.5 hours). Dinner and evening wall walk. Sleep in Carcassonne (1 night).

To maximize rootedness, minimize one-night stands. Every trip—and every traveler—needs slack time (laundry, picnics, people-watching, and so on). Pace yourself. Assume you will return.

Reread this book as you travel, and visit local tourist information offices (abbreviated as TI in this book). Upon arrival in a new town, lay the groundwork for a smooth departure; confirm the train, bus, or road you'll take when you leave.

Even with the best-planned itinerary, you'll need to be flexible. Update your plans as you travel. Though I encourage you to disconnect from life back home and immerse yourself in the French experience, you can get online or call ahead to learn the latest on sights (special events, tour schedules, and so on), book tickets and

12 Train to Arles (4 hours; probable changes in Narbonne and Avignon). Afternoon and evening in Arles. Sleep in Arles (2 nights).

13 Train to Nîmes and connect by bus to Pont du Gard (30 minutes). Tour Pont du Gard, then bus to Avignon (45 minutes) and spend your afternoon/evening there (consider dinner). Return to Arles by frequent train (30 minutes, may require reservation).

14 Morning in Arles or Les Baux (by taxi or tour), afternoon train* to Nice via Marseille (4-5 hours). Sleep in Nice (3 nights).

15 All day for Nice (and maybe Antibes).

16 All day for Villefranche-sur-Mer and Monaco.

17 Morning train* to Lyon (7.5 hours). Afternoon and evening in Lyon. Sleep in Lyon (1 night).

18 Morning in Lyon, then take early afternoon train to Chamonix (4.5 hours), afternoon and evening in Chamonix. Sleep in Chamonix (2 nights).

19 If the weather is clear, take the mountain lifts up to Aiguille du Midi and beyond.

20 Linger in Chamonix or take an early train* to Paris (7 hours) or, closer, Annecy (2 hours). Last afternoon and night in Paris or Annecy (Geneva Airport is 2 hours by train). Or make it a 22-day tour with a night in Burgundy—stay in Beaune, a 6.5-hour train ride from Chamonix—or a 23-day tour with a scenic 6.5-hour train through Switzerland to Colmar, spend two nights there.

21 Fly home.

Indicates TGV train option—book well in advance.

tours, make reservations, reconfirm hotels, and research transportation connections.

Enjoy the friendliness of the French people. Connect with the culture. Learn a new French expression each day and practice it. Cheer for your favorite bowler at a *boules* match, leave no chair unturned in your quest for the best café, find that perfect hilltown view, and make friends with a waiter (it can happen). Most importantly, slow down and be open to unexpected experiences. Ask questions—most locals are eager to point you in their idea of the right direction. Keep a notepad in your pocket for noting directions, organizing your thoughts, and confirming prices. Wear your money belt, learn the currency, and figure out how to estimate prices in dollars. Those who expect to travel smart, do.

TRIP COSTS

Five components make up your trip costs: airfare to Europe, transportation in Europe, room and board, sightseeing and entertainment, and shopping and miscellany.

Airfare to Europe: Paris and Nice have the most convenient flights from the US. A basic round-trip flight from the US to Paris or Nice can cost, on average, about $1,000-2,000 total, depending on where you fly from and when (cheaper in winter). Consider saving time and money by flying into one city and out of another; for instance, into Nice and out of Paris. Most find the easygoing Mediterranean city of Nice far easier than Paris as a starting point for their trip. Overall, Kayak.com is the best place to start searching for flights on a combination of mainstream and budget carriers.

Transportation in Europe: For a three-week whirlwind trip of my recommended destinations by public transportation, allow $800 per person. If you plan to rent a car, allow at least $260 per week, not including tolls, gas, and supplemental insurance. If you'll be keeping the car for three weeks or more, look into leasing, which can save you money on insurance and taxes for trips of this length. Car rentals (if four days or longer) and leases are cheapest if arranged from the US.

Buying train tickets as you go can be fine for short rides but expensive for long ones. To save money, plan ahead, either by buying a rail pass and making seat reservations (rail passes normally must be purchased outside of Europe) or by locking in reserved tickets with advance-purchase discounts. Don't hesitate to consider flying—a short flight can be cheaper than the train (check www.skyscanner.com for intra-European flights). Inexpensive flights can get you between Paris and other major cities (such as Nice, Marseille, Strasbourg, Toulouse, Lyon, and Bordeaux). For more on public transportation and car rental, see "Transportation" in Practicalities.

Room and Board: Outside of Paris, you can thrive in France in 2017 on $145 a day per person for room and board. This allows $15 for breakfast, $18 for lunch, $42 for dinner with drinks, and $70 for lodging (based on two people splitting the cost of a $140 double room). Allow 30 percent more for your days in Paris. Students and tightwads can enjoy France for as little as $60 a day ($30 for a bed, $30 for meals and snacks).

Sightseeing and Entertainment: Figure about $10-15 per major sight (Louvre-$13, Abbey of Mont St-Michel-$11), $7 for minor ones (climbing church towers), $20 for guided walks, and $35 for splurge experiences (concerts in Paris' Sainte-Chapelle or a ride on the Chamonix gondola). An overall average of $30 a day works for most people. Don't skimp here. After all, this category is the driving force behind your trip—you came to sightsee, enjoy, and experience France.

Shopping and Miscellany: Figure $4 per ice-cream cone, coffee, or soft drink. Shopping can vary in cost from nearly nothing to a small fortune. Good budget travelers find that this category has little to do with assembling a trip full of lifelong memories.

SIGHTSEEING PRIORITIES

So much to see, so little time. How to choose? Depending on the length of your trip, and taking geographic proximity into account, here are my recommended priorities:

3 days:	Paris, maybe Versailles
6 days, add:	Normandy
8 days, add:	Loire
11 days, add:	Dordogne, Carcassonne
16 days, add:	Provence, Riviera
19 days, add:	Burgundy, Chamonix
22 days, add:	Alsace, northern France

This includes nearly everything on the map on page 9. If you don't have time to see it all, prioritize according to your interests. The "France at a Glance" sidebar can help you decide where to go (page 6).

For day-by-day itineraries for a three-week trip, see the sidebars (one for drivers and one for people using trains and buses) in this chapter. Note that a car is especially handy for exploring Normandy, the Dordogne, and Provence.

If you have only a week and it's your first trip to France, do Paris, Normandy, and the Loire. For a 10- to 14-day trip that highlights Paris, Provence, and the Riviera, fly into Paris and out of Nice. After touring Paris, take the TGV train to Avignon, rent a car there, and drop it in Nice (or use trains, buses, and minivan tours to get around). This trip also works well in reverse. Travelers with a little more time could add Burgundy and/or the Alps, which are about halfway between Paris and Provence and easy to explore by car or train.

WHEN TO GO

Late spring and fall are best, with generally good weather and lighter crowds, though summer brings festivals, animated villages, reliable weather, and long opening hours at sights.

Europeans vacation in July and August, jamming the Riviera, the coast of Brittany, the Dordogne, and the Alps (worst from mid-July to mid-August), but leaving the rest of the country just lively enough for tourists. And though many French businesses close in

🎧 Rick Steves Audio Europe 🎧

My free **Rick Steves Audio Europe app** is a great tool for enjoying Europe. This app makes it easy to download my audio tours of top attractions, plus hours of travel interviews, all organized into destination-specific playlists.

My self-guided **audio tours** of major sights and neighborhoods are free, user-friendly, fun, and informative. Among the sights in this book, these audio tours include the major sights and neighborhoods in and near Paris (Historic Paris Walk, Louvre, Orsay, and Versailles Palace). Sights covered by my audio tours are marked with this symbol: 🎧. You can choose whether to follow the written tour in this book, or pop in your headphones and listen to essentially the same information—freeing up your eyes to appreciate the sights. These audio tours are hard to beat: The quality is reliable, you can take the tour exactly when you like, and the price is right.

The Rick Steves Audio Europe app also offers a far-reaching library of insightful **travel interviews** from my public radio show with experts from around the globe—including many of the places in this book.

This app and all of its content are entirely free. You can download Rick Steves Audio Europe via Apple's App Store, Google Play, or the Amazon Appstore. For more information, see www.ricksteves.com/audioeurope.

August, the traveler hardly notices. May weekends can be busy anywhere—many French holidays fall in this month—but June is generally quiet (outside of Paris).

Winter travel is fine for Paris, Nice, and Lyon, but you'll find smaller cities and villages buttoned up tight. Winter weather is gray, noticeably milder in the south (unless the wind is blowing), and colder and wetter in the north. Snow is generally not an issue except in the mountains. Sights and tourist information offices keep shorter hours, and some tourist activities (such as English-language tours) vanish altogether. On the other hand, winter travel allows you to see cities and towns through the lens of a local, as hotels, restaurants, and sights are much calmer. See the climate chart in the appendix for an idea of what to expect from the weather.

What's Blooming When

Thanks to France's relatively mild climate, fields of flowers greet the traveler much of the year:

Mid-April-May: Crops of brilliant yellow colza bloom, mostly in the north (best in Burgundy). Wild red poppies *(coquelicots)* begin sprouting in the south.

How Was Your Trip?

Were your travels fun, smooth, and meaningful? You can share tips, concerns, and discoveries at www.ricksteves.com/feedback. To check out readers' hotel and restaurant reviews—or leave one yourself—visit my travel forum at www.ricksteves.com/travel-forum. I value your feedback. Thanks in advance.

June: Red poppies pop up throughout the country. Late in June, lavender blooms begin covering the hills of Provence.

July: Lavender is in full swing in Provence, and sunflowers are awakening. Cities, towns, and villages everywhere overflow with carefully tended flowers.

August-September: Sunflowers flourish north and south.

October: In the latter half of the month, the countryside glistens with fall colors, as most trees in France are deciduous. Vineyards go for the gold.

KNOW BEFORE YOU GO

Check this list of things to arrange while you're still at home.

You need a **passport**—but no visa or shots—to travel in France. You may be denied entry into certain European countries if your passport is due to expire within six months of your ticketed date of return. Get it renewed if you'll be cutting it close. It can take up to six weeks to get or renew a passport (for more on passports, see www.travel.state.gov). Pack a photocopy of your passport in your luggage in case the original is lost or stolen.

Book rooms well in advance if you'll be traveling during peak season (spring through fall) or any major holidays (see page 1114).

Call your **debit- and credit-card companies** to let them know the countries you'll be visiting, to ask about fees, to request your PIN if you don't already know it, and more. See page 1045 for details.

Do your homework if you're considering **travel insurance.** Compare the cost of the insurance to the cost of your potential loss. Also check whether your existing insurance (health, homeowners, or renters) covers you and your possessions overseas. For more tips, see www.ricksteves.com/insurance.

Research your options before buying a **rail pass** (see page 1087 and www.ricksteves.com/rail for specifics).

All **high-speed TGV trains** in France require a seat reservation—book as early as possible, as they fill fast, and some routes

The Language Barrier and That French Attitude

You've probably heard that the French are "mean and cold and refuse to speak English." This is an out-of-date preconception left over from the days of Charles de Gaulle. The French are as friendly as any other people (if a bit more serious), and Parisians no more disagreeable than New Yorkers. Without any doubt, French people speak more English than Americans speak French. Be reasonable in your expectations: French waiters are paid to be efficient, not chatty. And postal clerks are every bit as speedy, cheery, and multilingual as ours are back home.

My best advice? Slow down. The biggest error most Americans make when traveling in France is trying to do too much with limited time. This approach is a mistake in the bustling north, and a virtual sin in the laid-back south. Hurried, impatient travelers who miss the subtle pleasures of people-watching from a sun-dappled café often misinterpret French attitudes. With the five weeks of paid vacation and 35-hour workweek that many French employees consider nonnegotiable rights, your hosts can't fathom why anyone would rush through their vacation. By slowing your pace and making an effort to understand French culture by living it, you're more likely to have a richer experience.

The French take great pride in their customs, clinging to the sense of their own cultural superiority despite the fact that they're no longer a world superpower. Let's face it: It's tough to keep on smiling when you've been crushed by a Big Mac, Mickey-Moused by Disney, and drowned in Starbucks coffee. Your hosts are cold only if you decide to see them that way. Polite and formal, the French respect the fine points of culture and tradition. Here, strolling down the street with a big grin on your face and saying hello to strangers is a sign of senility, not friendliness (seriously). The French think that Americans, while sociable, are hesitant to pursue more serious friendships (and Americans can find the French reserved and moody). Recognize sincerity and look

use TGV trains almost exclusively. This is especially true if you're traveling with a rail pass, as TGV pass-holder reservations are limited, and usually sell out well before other seat reservations. If you're taking an overnight train, and you need a *couchette* (overnight bunk)—and you *must* leave on a certain day—consider booking it in advance through a US agent (such as www.raileurope.com). For more on train travel, see the Practicalities chapter.

To avoid long ticket-buying lines at the **Eiffel Tower,** book an entry time several months in advance using its online reservation system (see page 80). Some **prehistoric caves** in the Dordogne region take online reservations; see page 472. If the greatest cave, Font-de-Gaume, is accepting reservations in 2017, cross your

for kindness. Give the French the benefit of the doubt. When dining, expect reasonable service. If you don't get it, don't tip and move on.

Communication difficulties are exaggerated. To hurdle the language barrier, start with the French survival phrases in this book (see the appendix). For a richer experience, bring a small English/French dictionary and/or a phrase book (look for mine, which contains a dictionary and menu decoder), a menu reader, and a good supply of patience. In transactions, a small notepad and pen minimize misunderstandings about prices; have vendors write the price down.

Though many French people speak English—especially those in the tourist trade, and in big cities—you'll get better treatment if you use French pleasantries. If you choose only five phrases, try these: *bonjour* (good day), *pardon* (pardon me), *s'il vous plaît* (please), *merci* (thank you), and *au revoir* (good-bye). The French value politeness. Begin every encounter with *"Bonjour* (or *S'il vous plaît), madame* (or *monsieur),"* and end every encounter with *"Au revoir, madame* (or *monsieur)."* When spelling out your name, you'll find that most letters are pronounced very differently in French: *a* is pronounced "ah," *e* is pronounced "eh," and *i* is pronounced "ee." To avoid confusion, say *"a,* Anne," *"e,* euro," and *"i,* Isabelle."

When you do make an effort to speak French, you may be politely corrected—*c'est normal* (to be expected). The French are linguistic perfectionists—they take their language (and other languages) seriously. Often they speak more English than they let on. This isn't a tourist-baiting tactic, but timidity on their part about speaking another language less than fluently. To ask a French person to speak English, say, *"Bonjour, madame* (or *monsieur). Parlez-vous anglais?"* They may say *"non,"* but as you continue you'll probably find they speak more English than you speak French.

fingers and book as far ahead as possible (at least six months). A few sights, such as Avignon's synagogue and some wineries, require that you make an appointment and are noted throughout this book.

If you plan to hire a **local guide,** reserve ahead by email. Popular guides can get booked up. If you want a specific guide, reserve as far ahead as possible (especially important for Paris, D-Day beaches, Burgundy's wine country, and Provence).

If you're bringing a **mobile device,** consider signing up for an international plan for cheaper calls, texts, and data (see page 1080). Download any apps you might want to use on the road, such as translators, maps, transit schedules, and **Rick Steves Audio Europe** (see page 14).

Check for recent updates to this book at www.ricksteves.com/update.

Traveling as a Temporary Local

We travel all the way to France to enjoy differences—to become temporary locals. You'll experience some frustrations. Certain truths that we find "God-given" or "self-evident," such as cold beer, ice in drinks, bottomless cups of coffee, "the customer is king," and bigger being better, are suddenly not so true. One of the benefits of travel is the eye-opening realization that there can be logical, civil, and even better alternatives.

With a long history rich in human achievement, France is an understandably proud country. To appreciate its people, celebrate the differences. A willingness to go local ensures that you'll enjoy a full dose of French hospitality. And with an eagerness to go local, you'll have even more fun.

Europeans generally like Americans. But if there is a negative aspect to the French image of Americans, it's that we are loud, wasteful, ethnocentric, too informal (which can seem disrespectful), and a bit naive.

The French place a high value on speaking quietly in public places. Listen while on the bus or in a restaurant—the place can be packed, but the decibel level is low. Adjust your volume accordingly to show respect for the culture, and you'll experience France as it should be.

While the French look bemusedly at some of our Yankee excesses—and worriedly at others—they nearly always afford us individual travelers all the warmth we deserve.

Judging from all the happy feedback I receive from travelers who have used this book, it's safe to assume you'll enjoy a great, affordable vacation—with the finesse of an independent, experienced traveler.

Thanks, and *bon voyage!*

Rick Steves

Back Door Travel Philosophy

From *Rick Steves Europe Through the Back Door*

Travel is intensified living—maximum thrills per minute and one of the last great sources of legal adventure. Travel is freedom. It's recess, and we need it.

Experiencing the real Europe requires catching it by surprise, going casual..."Through the Back Door."

Affording travel is a matter of priorities. (Make do with the old car.) You can eat and sleep—simply, safely, and enjoyably—anywhere in Europe for $100 a day plus transportation costs. In many ways, spending more money only builds a thicker wall between you and what you traveled so far to see. Europe is a cultural carnival, and time after time, you'll find that its best acts are free and the best seats are the cheap ones.

A tight budget forces you to travel close to the ground, meeting and communicating with the people. Never sacrifice sleep, nutrition, safety, or cleanliness to save money. Simply enjoy the local-style alternatives to expensive hotels and restaurants.

Connecting with people carbonates your experience. Extroverts have more fun. If your trip is low on magic moments, kick yourself and make things happen. If you don't enjoy a place, maybe you don't know enough about it. Seek the truth. Recognize tourist traps. Give a culture the benefit of your open mind. See things as different, but not better or worse. Any culture has plenty to share. When an opportunity presents itself, make it a habit to say "yes."

Of course, travel, like the world, is a series of hills and valleys. Be fanatically positive and militantly optimistic. If something's not to your liking, change your liking.

Travel can make you a happier American, as well as a citizen of the world. Our Earth is home to seven billion equally precious people. It's humbling to travel and find that other people don't have the "American Dream"—they have their own dreams. Europeans like us, but with all due respect, they wouldn't trade passports.

Thoughtful travel engages us with the world. It reminds us what is truly important. By broadening perspectives, travel teaches new ways to measure quality of life.

Globetrotting destroys ethnocentricity, helping us understand and appreciate other cultures. Rather than fear the diversity on this planet, celebrate it. Among your most prized souvenirs will be the strands of different cultures you choose to knit into your own character. The world is a cultural yarn shop, and Back Door travelers are weaving the ultimate tapestry. Join in!

PARIS

Paris—the City of Light—has been a beacon of culture for centuries. As a world capital of art, fashion, food, literature, and ideas, it stands as a symbol of all the fine things human civilization can offer. Come prepared to celebrate this, rather than judge our cultural differences, and you'll capture the romance and *joie de vivre* that this city exudes.

Paris offers sweeping boulevards, chatty crêpe stands, chic boutiques, and world-class art galleries. Sip decaf with deconstructionists at a sidewalk café, then step into an Impressionist painting in a tree-lined park. Climb Notre-Dame and rub shoulders with a gargoyle. Cruise the Seine, zip to the top of the Eiffel Tower, and saunter down Avenue des Champs-Elysées. Master the Louvre and Orsay museums. Save some after-dark energy for one of the world's most romantic cities.

PLANNING YOUR TIME

I've listed sights in descending order of importance, filling up to seven very busy-but-doable days in Paris. If you have only one day, just do Day 1; for two days, add Day 2; and so on. When deciding where to plug in Versailles (see next chapter), remember that the main palace is closed on Mondays and especially crowded on Sundays, Tuesdays, and Saturdays (in that order).

Day 1: Follow this chapter's Historic Paris Walk. In the afternoon, tour the Louvre. Then enjoy the Place du Trocadéro scene and a twilight ride up the Eiffel Tower.

Day 2: Stroll the Champs-Elysées from the Arc de Triomphe to the Tuileries Garden. Tour the Orsay Museum. In the evening, take a nighttime tour by cruise boat, taxi/Uber, bus, or retro-chic Deux Chevaux car.

Day 3: Catch the RER suburban train by 7:45 to arrive early at Versailles. Tour the château's interior. Then either sample the gardens or return to Paris for more sightseeing.

Day 4: Visit Montmartre and the Sacré-Cœur Basilica. Have lunch in Montmartre. Continue your Impressionist theme by touring the Orangerie. Enjoy dinner on Ile St. Louis, then a floodlit walk by Notre-Dame.

Day 5: Concentrate on the morning market in the Rue Cler neighborhood, then afternoon sightseeing at the Rodin Museum and the Army Museum and Napoleon's Tomb.

Day 6: Ride scenic bus #69 to the Marais and tour this neighborhood, including the Picasso Museum and Pompidou Center. In the afternoon, visit the Opéra Garnier, and end your day with rooftop views from the Galeries Lafayette or Printemps department stores.

Day 7: See more in Paris (such as Left Bank shopping, Père Lachaise Cemetery, Marmottan Museum), or take a day-trip to Chartres or Giverny.

Orientation to Paris

PARIS: A VERBAL MAP

Central Paris (population 2.3 million) is circled by a ring road and split in half by the Seine River, which runs east-west. If

you were on a boat floating downstream, the Right Bank (Rive Droite) would be on your right, and the Left Bank (Rive Gauche) on your left. The bull's-eye on your map is Notre-Dame, on an island in the middle of the Seine and ground zero in Paris.

Twenty arrondissements (administrative districts) spiral out from the center, like an escargot shell. If your hotel's zip code is 75007, you know (from the last two digits) that it's in the 7th arrondissement. The city is peppered with Métro stops, and most Parisians locate addresses by the closest stop. So in Parisian jargon, the Eiffel Tower is on *la Rive Gauche* (the Left Bank) in the *7ème* (7th arrondissement), zip code 75007, Mo: Trocadéro (the nearest Métro stop).

PARIS

PARIS BY NEIGHBORHOOD

Paris is a big city, but its major sights cluster in convenient zones. Grouping your sightseeing, walks, dining, and shopping thoughtfully can save you lots of time and money.

Historic Core: This area centers on the Ile de la Cité ("Island of the City"), located in the middle of the Seine. On the Ile de la Cité, you'll find Paris' oldest sights, from Roman ruins to the medieval Notre-Dame and Sainte-Chapelle churches.

Major Museums Neighborhood: Located just west of the historic core, this is where you'll find the Louvre, Orsay, Orangerie, and Tuileries Garden.

Champs-Elysées: The greatest of the many grand, 19th-century boulevards on the Right Bank, the Champs-Elysées runs northwest from Place de la Concorde to the Arc de Triomphe.

Eiffel Tower Neighborhood: Dominated by the Eiffel Tower, this area also boasts the colorful Rue Cler, Army Museum and Napoleon's Tomb, and the Rodin Museum.

Opéra Neighborhood: Surrounding the Opéra Garnier, this classy area on the Right Bank is home to a series of grand boulevards and monuments. Along with elegant sights such as the Opéra Garnier, the neighborhood also offers high-end shopping.

Left Bank: The Left Bank is home to...the Left Bank. Anchored by the large Luxembourg Garden, the Left Bank is the traditional neighborhood of Paris' intellectual, artistic, and café life.

Marais: Stretching eastward to Bastille along Rue de Rivoli/Rue St. Antoine, this neighborhood has lots of recommended restaurants and hotels, shops, the delightful Place des Vosges, and artistic sights such as the Pompidou Center and Picasso Museum.

Montmartre: This hill, topped by the bulbous white domes of Sacré-Cœur, hovers on the northern fringes of your Paris map.

TOURIST INFORMATION

Paris' TIs can provide useful information but may have long lines (www.parisinfo.com). While TIs sell Museum Passes and individual tickets to sights, they charge a small fee and

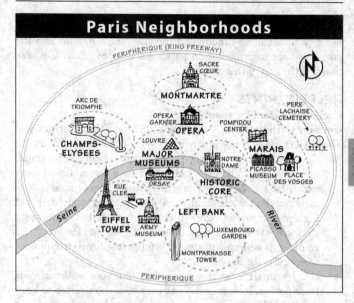

Paris Neighborhoods

may have longer lines than the museums (see "Sightseeing Strategies" on page 42).

Paris has several TI locations, including **Pyramides** (daily May-Oct 9:00-19:00, Nov-April 10:00-19:00, free Wi-Fi, 25 Rue des Pyramides—at Pyramides Métro stop between the Louvre and Opéra), **Paris Rendez-Vous** (a city-sponsored souvenir shop and TI combined, Mon-Sat 10:00-19:00, closed Sun, 29 Rue de Rivoli—located within the Hôtel de Ville city hall), **Gare du Nord** (daily 8:00-18:00), **Gare de l'Est** (Mon-Sat 8:00-19:00, closed Sun), and two in **Montmartre** (21 Place du Tertre, daily 10:00-18:00, covers only Montmartre sights and doesn't sell Museum Passes, tel. 01 42 62 21 21; and at the Anvers Métro stop, full-service office, daily 10:00-18:00). In summer, TI kiosks may pop up in the squares in front of Notre-Dame and Hôtel de Ville. Both Paris **airports** have handy TIs with long hours and short lines.

Event Listings: Several French-only but easy-to-decipher periodicals list the most up-to-date museum hours, art exhibits, concerts, festivals, plays, movies, and nightclubs. The best is the weekly *Pariscope* magazine; *L'Officiel des Spectacles* is similar (available at any newsstand). The *Paris Voice*, with snappy English-language reviews of concerts, plays, and current events, is available online only at www.parisvoice.com.

ARRIVAL IN PARIS

For a comprehensive rundown of the city's train stations and airports, and for information on parking a car, see "Paris Connections" at the end of this chapter.

HELPFUL HINTS

Exchange Rate: €1 = about $1.10

Country Calling Code: 33 (see page 1082 for dialing instructions)

Theft Alert: Paris is safe in terms of violent crime but is filled with thieves and scammers who target tourists. Don't be paranoid; just be smart. Wherever there are crowds (especially of tourists) there are thieves at work. They thrive near famous monuments and on Métro and train lines that serve airports and high-profile tourist sights. Pickpockets work busy lines (e.g., at ticket windows at train stations). Look out for groups of young girls who swarm around you (be very firm—even forceful—and walk away).

It's smart to wear a money belt, put your wallet in your front pocket, loop your day bag over your shoulders, and keep a tight hold on your purse or shopping bag. Watch out for your electronics; pickpockets snatch smartphones and tablets too.

Muggings are rare, but they do occur. If you're out late, avoid the dark riverfront embankments and any place where the lighting is dim and pedestrian activity is minimal.

Paris has taken action to combat crime by stationing police at monuments, on streets, and on the Métro, and installing security cameras at key sights.

Tourist Scams: Be aware of the latest tricks, such as the "found ring" scam (a con artist pretends to find a "pure gold" ring on the ground and offers to sell it to you) or the "friendship bracelet" scam (a vendor asks you to help with a demo, makes a bracelet on your arm that seems like it can't easily be removed, and then asks you to pay for it). Don't be intimidated. They are removed with the pull of a string.

Distractions by a stranger can all be tricks that function as a smokescreen for theft. As you try to wriggle away from the pushy stranger, an accomplice picks your pocket. Be wary of a "salesman" monopolizing your attention, an "activist" asking you to sign a petition (and then bullying you into a contribution), someone posing as a deaf person to show you a small note to read, or a sidewalk hawker inviting you to play shell games (his thuggish accomplices are likely lurking nearby). Be skeptical of anything too good to be true, such as overly friendly people inviting you into impossibly friendly (or sexy) bars late at night.

To all these scammers, simply say "no" firmly and step

away purposefully. For reports from my readers on the latest scams, go to https://community.ricksteves.com/travel-forum/tourist-scams.

Pedestrian Safety: Parisian drivers are notorious for ignoring pedestrians. Paris' popular and cheap short-term electric-car rental program (Autolib') has put many of these small, silent machines on the streets—pay attention. Look both ways and be careful of seemingly quiet bus/taxi lanes. Don't assume you have the right of way, even in a crosswalk. Bikes commonly go against traffic, so always look both ways, even on one-way streets.

Medical Help: There are a variety of English-speaking resources for medical help in Paris, including doctors who will visit your hotel. Try the **American Hospital,** tel. 01 46 41 25 25 (63 Boulevard Victor Hugo, in Neuilly suburb, Mo: Port Maillot, then bus #82, www.american-hospital.org), or **SOS Médicins** (SOS Doctors) at tel. 3624 (www.sosmedecins.fr).

Sightseeing Tips: If you're in Paris on a Monday, be aware that the Orsay, Rodin, Marmottan, and Picasso museums are closed, as are the Catacombs and the Palace of Versailles (but the gardens are open). Many other sights are closed on Tuesdays, including the Louvre, Orangerie, Cluny, and Pompidou museums. Lines at Paris' major sights can be long. Consider the worthwhile Paris Museum Pass, which covers most sights in the city and allows you to skip ticket lines. You can also buy tickets in advance for certain sights. For more on these options, see page 42.

Wi-Fi: You'll find free wireless hotspots at many cafés and in many public areas (including the TI office at Pyramides, parks, squares, and museums). In a café, order something, then ask the waiter for the Wi-Fi ("wee-fee") password (*"mot de passe"*; moh duh pahs).

Select Métro stations offer 20 minutes of free Wi-Fi, and most public parks offer two hours of free Wi-Fi (look for purple *Zone Wi-Fi* signs). The Orange network also has many hotspots and offers a free two-hour pass.

Useful Apps: Gogo Paris reviews trendy places to eat, drink, relax, and sleep in Paris (www.gogocityguides.com/paris). The **RATP** app can help you plan Métro trips (see page 28).

🎧 For free audio versions of some of the self-guided tours in this chapter (the Historic Paris Walk, and Louvre and Orsay museum tours), get the **Rick Steves Audio Europe** app (for details, see page 14).

Bookstores: Paris has several English-language bookstores. My favorites include **Shakespeare and Company** (some used travel books, daily 10:00-23:00, 37 Rue de la Bûcherie, across the river from Notre-Dame, Mo: St. Michel, tel. 01 43 25 40 93); **W. H. Smith** (Mon-Sat 9:00-19:00, Sun 12:30-19:00, 248 Rue de Rivoli, Mo: Concorde, tel. 01 44 77 88 99); and **San Francisco Book Company** (used books only, Mon-Sat 11:00-21:00, Sun 14:00-19:30, 17 Rue Monsieur le Prince, Mo: Odéon, tel. 01 43 29 15 70).

Public WCs: Most public toilets are free. If it's a pay toilet, the price will be clearly indicated. If the toilet is free but there's an attendant, it's polite to leave a tip of €0.20-0.50. Booth-like toilets on the sidewalks provide both relief and a memory (don't leave small children inside unattended). The restrooms in museums are free and the best you'll find. Bold travelers can walk into any sidewalk café like they own the place and find the toilet downstairs or in the back. Or do as the locals do—order a shot of espresso *(un café)* while standing at the café bar (then use the WC with a clear conscience). Keep toilet paper or tissues with you, as some WCs are poorly stocked.

Tobacco Stands *(Tabacs):* These little kiosks—usually just a counter inside a café—are handy and very local. Most sell public-transit tickets, cards for parking meters, postage stamps (though not all sell international postage), and...oh yeah, cigarettes. To find a kiosk, just look for a *Tabac* sign and the red cylinder-shaped symbol above certain cafés. A *tabac* can be a godsend for avoiding long ticket lines at the Métro, especially at the end of the month when ticket booths get crowded with locals buying next month's pass.

Winter Activities: The City of Light sparkles year-round. For what to do and see here in winter months, see www.ricksteves. com/pariswinter.

GETTING AROUND PARIS

Paris is easy to navigate. Your basic choices are Métro (in-city subway), RER (suburban rapid transit tied into the Métro system), public bus, Uber, and taxi. There are also nine tram lines, but few travelers will use these heavily suburban routes. Also consider the hop-on, hop-off bus and boat tours (described under "Tours in Paris," later).

You can buy tickets and passes at Métro stations and at many *tabacs*. Staffed ticket windows in stations are being phased out in favor of ticket machines, so expect some stations to have only machines and an information desk. Most machines accept only credit cards and coins, though there's usually one that will take small bills of €20 or less, and chip-and-PIN cards (no American magnetic-stripe or chip-and-signature cards). If a ticket machine is out of order or if you're out of change, buy tickets at a *tabac*.

Public-Transit Tickets: The Métro, RER, tramways, and

buses all work on the same tickets. You can make as many transfers as you need on a single ticket, except when transferring between the bus or tramway systems and the Métro/RER system (an additional ticket is required). A **single ticket** costs €1.80. To save money, buy a *carnet* (kar-nay) of 10 tickets for €14.10 (cheaper for ages 4-10). *Carnets* can be shared among travelers. Kids under four ride free.

Passe Navigo: The weekly version of this pass covers all forms of transit from Monday to Sunday (expiring on Sunday, even if you buy it on, say, a Thursday). This chip-embedded card costs a one-time €5 fee (plus another €5 for the required photo; photo booths are in major Métro stations). The weekly unlimited pass (Navigo Semaine) costs €21.25 and is good for all zones in the Paris region. You can buy your Passe Navigo at any Métro station in Paris (for more details, visit www.ratp.fr).

Navigo or *Carnet*? The Navigo covers a far greater area than *carnet* tickets, but cannot be shared. It is most worthwhile for visitors who use it for regional trips, or stay a full week (and start their trip early in the week). Two 10-packs of *carnets*—enough for most travelers staying a week—cost €28.20, are shareable, and don't expire, but are only valid in the center of Paris.

The **Paris Visite** travel card is only a good choice over *carnets* if you travel around the city extensively, though they do offer minor discounts at minor sights (1 day-€11.15, 2 days-€18.15, 3 days-€24.80, 5 days-€35.70).

By Métro

In Paris, you're never more than a 10-minute walk from a Métro station. Europe's best subway system allows you to hop from sight to sight quickly and cheaply (runs 5:30-1:00 in the morning, Fri-Sat until 2:00 in the morning, www.ratp.fr). Learn to use it. Begin by studying the color Métro map at the beginning of this book.

Using the Métro System: To get to your destination, determine the closest "Mo" stop and which line or lines will get you

there. The lines are color-coded and numbered. You can tell their direction by the end-of-the-line stops. For example, the La Défense/Château de Vincennes line, also known as line 1 (yellow), runs between La Défense, on its west end, and Vincennes on its east end. Once in the Métro station, you'll see the color-coded line numbers and/ or blue-and-white signs directing you to the train going in your direction (e.g., *direction: La Défense*). Insert your ticket in the turnstile, reclaim your ticket, pass through,

PARIS

Transit Basics

- The same tickets are good on the Métro, RER trains (within the city), and city buses.
- Save money by buying a *carnet* of 10 discounted tickets or a Passe Navigo.
- Beware of pickpockets, and don't buy tickets from people roaming the stations.
- Find your train by its end-of-the-line stop.
- Insert your ticket into the turnstile, retrieve it, and keep it until the end of your journey.
- Safeguard your belongings; avoid standing near the train doors with luggage.

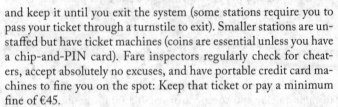

- At a stop, the door may open automatically. If it doesn't, open the door by either pushing a square button (green or black) or lifting a metal latch.
- Transfers *(correspondances)* between the Métro and RER system are free (but not between Métro/RER and bus).
- Trash or tear used tickets after you complete your ride and

and keep it until you exit the system (some stations require you to pass your ticket through a turnstile to exit). Smaller stations are unstaffed but have ticket machines (coins are essential unless you have a chip-and-PIN card). Fare inspectors regularly check for cheaters, accept absolutely no excuses, and have portable credit card machines to fine you on the spot: Keep that ticket or pay a minimum fine of €45.

Transfers are free and can be made wherever lines cross, provided you do so within 1.5 hours and don't exit the station. When you transfer, follow the appropriately colored line number and end-of-the-line stop to find your next train, or look for *correspondance* (connection) signs that lead to your next line.

When you reach your destination, blue-and-white *sortie* signs point you to the exit. Before leaving the station, check the helpful *plan du quartier* (map of the neighborhood) to get your bearings. At stops with several *sorties*, you can save time by choosing the best exit.

Métro Resources: Métro maps are free at Métro stations and included on freebie Paris maps at your hotel. Several good online tools can also help you navigate the public-transit system. The website Metro.Paris provides an interactive map of Paris' sights and Métro lines, with a trip-planning feature and information about each sight and station's history (www.metro.paris). The free RATP

leave the station (not before) to avoid confusing them with fresh ones.

Key Words for the Métro and RER

French	English
station de Métro (stah-see-ohn duh may-troh)	Métro stop/station
direction (dee-rehk-see-ohn)	direction
ligne (leen-yuh)	line
Correspondence (koh-rehs-pohn-dahns)	connection/transfer
sortie (sor-tee)	exit
carnet (kar-nay)	discounted set of 10 tickets
Pardon, madame/monsieur. (par-dohn, mah-dahm/muhs-yuh)	Excuse me, ma'am/sir.
Je descends. (zhuh day-sahn)	I'm getting off.
Rendez-moi mon porte-monnaie! (rahn-day-mwah mohn porte-moh-nay)	Give me back my wallet!

PARIS

mobile app can estimate Métro travel times, help you locate the best station exit, and tell you when the next bus will arrive, among other things (in English, download from Apple's App Store, Google Play, or the Amazon Appstore).

Beware of Pickpockets: Thieves dig the Métro and RER. If your pocket is picked as you pass through a turnstile, you end up stuck on the wrong side while the thief gets away. Stand away from Métro doors to avoid being a target for a theft-and-run just before the doors close. Any jostling or commotion—especially when boarding or leaving trains—is likely the sign of a thief or a team of thieves in action. Make any fare inspector show proof of identity (ask locals for help if you're not certain). Keep your bag close, hang on to your smartphone, and never show anyone your wallet. For more tips, see page 24.

By RER

The RER (Réseau Express Régionale; ehr uh ehr) is the suburban arm of the Métro, serving outlying destinations such as Versailles, Disneyland Paris, and the airports. These routes are indicated by thick lines on your subway map and identified by the letters A, B, C, and so on.

Within the city center, the RER works like the Métro and can be speedier if it serves your destination directly, because it makes fewer stops. Métro tickets are good on the RER when traveling in the city center. You can transfer between the Métro and RER systems with the same ticket. But to travel outside the city (to Versailles or the airport, for example), you'll need a separate, more expensive ticket. The Passe Navigo card covers all RER trips including to the airport and Versailles. Unlike the Métro, not every train stops at every station along the way; check the sign or screen over the platform to see if your destination is listed as a stop (*"toutes les gares"* means it makes all stops along the way), or confirm with a local before you board.

For RER trains, you may need to insert your ticket in a turnstile to exit the system.

By City Bus

Paris' excellent bus system is worth figuring out (www.ratp.fr). Buses require less walking and fewer stairways than the Métro, and you can see Paris unfold as you travel.

Bus Stops: Stops are everywhere, and most come with all the information you need. This includes a good city bus map, route

maps for each bus that stops there, a frequency chart and schedule, live screens showing the time the next two buses will arrive, a *plan du quartier* map of the immediate neighborhood, and a *soirées* map explaining night service, if available (there are even phone chargers at some locations). Bus-system maps are also available in any Métro station (and in the *Paris Pratique* map book sold at newsstands). For longer stays, consider buying the *Paris Urbain* book of transit info, including bus routes.

Using the Bus System: Buses use the same tickets and passes as the Métro and RER. One Zone 1 ticket buys you a bus ride anywhere in central Paris within the freeway ring road *(le périphérique)*. Use your Métro ticket or buy one on board for €0.20 more. These tickets are *sans correspondance*, which means you can't use them to transfer to another bus. (The ticket system has a few quirks—see "More Bus Tips," later.)

When a bus approaches, it's wise to wave to the driver to indicate that you want to be picked up. Board your bus through the

Hop on the Bus, Gus

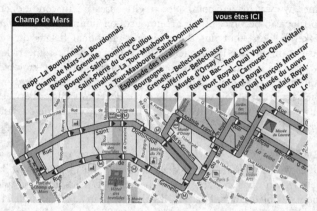

Champ de Mars

vous êtes ICI

Just like the Métro, every bus stop has a name, and every bus is headed to one end-of-the-line stop or the other. This graphic shows the route map posted at the Esplanade des Invalides #69 bus stop. First, find the stop on the chart—it says *"vous êtes ICI"* ("you are HERE") at Esplanade des Invalides. Next, find your destination stop—let's say Bosquet-Grenelle, located a few stops to the west. Now, find out exactly where to catch the bus going in that direction. On the route map, notice the triangle-shaped arrows pointing in the direction the bus is headed. You'll see that Esplanade des Invalides has two different bus stops—one for buses headed east, one for those going west. If you want to go west to Bosquet-Grenelle, head for that street corner to catch the bus. (With so many one-way streets in Paris, it's easy to get on the bus in the wrong direction.) When the bus pulls up, double-check that the sign on the front of the bus has the end-of-the-line stop going in your direction—to "Champ de Mars," in this case.

front door. (Families with strollers can use any doors—the ones in the center of the bus are wider. To open the middle or back doors on long buses, push the green button located by those doors.) Validate your ticket in the machine (stripe up) and reclaim it. With a Passe Navigo, scan it on the pad touchpad. Keep track of which stop is coming up next by following the on-board diagram or listening to recorded announcements. When you're ready to get off, push the red button to signal you want a stop, then exit through the central or rear door. Even if you're not certain you've figured out the system, do some joyriding.

More Bus Tips: Avoid rush hour (Mon-Fri 8:00-9:30 & 17:30-19:30), when buses are jammed and traffic doesn't move.

While the Métro shuts down at about 1:00 in the morning (even later Fri-Sat), some buses continue much later (called *Noctilien* lines, www.vianavigo.com). Not all city buses are air-conditioned, so they can become rolling greenhouses on summer days. *Carnet* ticket holders—but not those buying individual tickets on the bus—can transfer from one bus to another on the same ticket (within 1.5 hours, revalidate your ticket on the next bus). However you can't do a round-trip or hop on and off on the same line using the same ticket. You can use the same ticket to transfer between buses and tramways, but you can't transfer between the bus and Métro/RER systems (it'll take two tickets).

By Uber

Uber works in Paris like it does at home, and in general works better than taxis in Paris (www.uber.com). Drivers are nicer and more flexible than taxi drivers, it's cheaper than a taxi (around €15 for a 20-minute ride, compared to about €25 for a taxi), and you can generally get a car wherever you are within five minutes. Uber drivers can pick you up anywhere so you don't have to track down a taxi stand, and you can text them if you don't see the car. There's no language problem with giving directions, as you can type your destination into the app. Your US app and US Uber accounts will work in Paris as long as you have access to cellular data. The only downside is that Uber drivers can't use the taxi/bus lanes during rush hour, so your trip may take longer at busy times than it would in a cab.

By Taxi

Parisian taxis are reasonable, especially for couples and families. The meters are tamper-proof. Fares and supplements (described in English on the rear windows) are straightforward and tightly regulated.

A taxi can fit four people. Cabbies are legally required to accept four passengers, though they don't always like it. If you have five in your group, you can book a larger taxi in advance (your hotelier can call), or try your luck at a taxi stand. A surcharge may be applied for a fifth rider.

Rates: All Parisian taxis start with €2.60 on the meter and have a minimum charge of €7. A 20-minute ride (such as Bastille to the Eiffel Tower) costs about €25 (versus about €1.40/person using a *carnet* ticket on the Métro or bus, or about €15 via Uber). Taxi drivers charge higher rates at rush hour, at night, all day Sunday, and for extra passengers (see above). There's a standard flat rate for the airport—see page 156. To tip, round up to the next euro (at least €0.50). The A, B, or C lights on a taxi's rooftop sign correspond to hourly rates, which vary with the time of day and day of

Scenic Bus Route #69

Why pay €25 for a tour company to give you an overview of Paris, when city bus #69 can do it for the cost of a Métro ticket? Get on the bus and settle in for a ride through some of the city's most interesting neighborhoods. Or use this line as a handy way to lace together many of Paris' most important sightseeing districts (you'll need a new ticket each time you board the bus).

Handy line #69 crosses the city east-west, running between the Eiffel Tower and Père Lachaise Cemetery, and passing these great monuments and neighborhoods: Eiffel Tower, Ecole Militaire, Rue Cler, Les Invalides (Army Museum and Napoleon's Tomb), Louvre museum, Ile de la Cité, Ile St. Louis, Hôtel de Ville, Pompidou Center, Marais, Bastille, and Père Lachaise.

If you're staying in the Marais or Rue Cler neighborhoods, line #69 is a useful route for just getting around town.

You can board daily until 22:30 (last departure from Eiffel Tower stop). It's best to avoid weekday rush hours (8:00-9:30 & 17:30-19:30) and hot days (no air-conditioning). Sundays are quietest, and it's easy to get a window seat. Evening bus rides are pretty from fall through spring (roughly Sept-April), when it gets dark early enough to see the floodlit monuments before the bus stops running.

In the Rue Cler area, eastbound line #69 leaves from the Eiffel Tower on Avenue Joseph Bouvard (the street that becomes Rue St. Dominique after it crosses the Champ de Mars, two blocks from the tower through the park. Board at one of the first few stops to secure a view seat. The first stop is at the southwestern end of the avenue; the second stop is at the eastern end (just before Avenue de la Bourdonnais).

the week (for example, the A rate of €32.50/hour applies Mon-Sat 10:00-17:00). Tired travelers need not bother with the subtle differences in fares—if you need a cab, take it.

How to Catch *un Taxi*: You can try waving down a taxi, but it's often easier to ask someone for the nearest taxi stand (*"Où est une station de taxi?"*; oo ay ewn stah-see-ohn duh tahk-see). Taxi stands are indicated by a circled "T" on good city maps and on many maps in this book. To order a taxi in English, call the reservation line for the G7 cab company (tel. 01 41 27 66 99), or ask your hotelier or waiter to call for you. When you summon a taxi by phone, a set fee of €4 is applied for an immediate booking or €7 for reserving in advance (this fee will appear on the meter when they pick you up). Smartphone users can book a taxi using the cab company's app, which also provides approximate wait times (surcharge similar to booking by phone). To download an app, search for either "Taxi

G7" or "Taxis Bleus" (the two major companies, both available in English).

If you need to catch a train or flight early in the morning, book a taxi the day before (especially for weekday departures). Some taxi companies require a €5 reservation fee by credit card for weekday morning rush-hour departures (7:00-10:00) and only have a limited number of reservation spots.

By Bike

Paris is surprisingly easy by bicycle. The city is flat, and riders have access to more than 370 miles of bike lanes and many of the prior-

ity lanes for buses and taxis (be careful on these). You can rent from a bike-rental shop or use the city-operated Vélib' bikes. Though I wouldn't use bikes to get around routinely (traffic is a bit too intense), they're perfect for a joyride away from busy streets. Bike-rental shops have good route suggestions. I biked along the river from Notre-Dame to the Eiffel Tower in 15 wonderfully scenic minutes. The Left Bank riverside promenade between the Orsay Museum and Pont de l'Alma is magnificent for biking. The TIs have a helpful "Paris à Vélo" map, which shows all the dedicated bike paths. Many other versions are available for sale at newsstand kiosks, some bookstores, and department stores.

Rental Bikes: The following companies rent bikes to individuals and offer organized bike tours (see "Bike Tours," later) and general tips about cycling in Paris. **Bike About Tours** is your best bet for bike rental, with good information and kid-friendly solutions such as baby seats, tandem attachments, and kid-sized bikes. Their office/coffee shop, called Le Peloton Café, offers bikes, tours, and artisan coffee (bike rental-€15/day during office hours, €20/24 hours, includes lock and helmet; daily 9:00-17:00, closed Dec-mid-Feb; shop/café at 17 Rue du Pont Louis Philippe, Mo: Hôtel de Ville, tel. 06 18 80 84 92, www.bikeabouttours.com). **Fat Tire Bike Tours** has a limited supply of bikes for rent, so call ahead to check availability (€4/hour, €25/24 hours, includes lock and helmet, photo ID and credit-card imprint required for deposit, €2/day rental discount with this book, maximum 2 discounts per book; office open daily 9:00-18:30, May-Aug bike rental only after 11:00 as priority is given to those taking a tour, 24 Rue Edgar Faure—see map on page 81, Mo: Dupleix, tel. 01 82 88 80 96, www.fattiretours.com/paris).

Vélib' Bikes: The city's Vélib' program (from *vélo* + *libre* =

"bike freedom") gives residents and foreigners alike access to more than 20,000 bikes at nearly 1,500 stations scattered around the city at great rates. Use these bikes only for short-term rental (a few hours or less), as pricing is structured to discourage longer use. If you want a bike for longer, rent from one of the companies listed earlier. Vélib' bikes are also very heavy—avoid hills and stairs or rent elsewhere (debit and chip-and-PIN cards accepted, see http://en.velib.paris.fr).

Tours in Paris

𝛀 To sightsee on your own, download my **free audio tours** that illuminate some of Paris' top sights and neighborhoods, including the Historic Paris Walk, Louvre Museum, and Orsay Museum.

BY BUS OR PETIT TRAIN
Bus Tours
City Vision offers bus tours of Paris, day and night. I'd consider them only for their nighttime tour (see page 113). During the day, you'll get a better value and more versatility by taking a hop-on, hop-off tour by bus (described next) or Batobus boat (see "By Boat," later), which provide transportation between sights.

Hop-On, Hop-Off Bus Tours
Double-decker buses connect Paris' main sights, giving you an easy once-over of the city with a basic recorded commentary, punctuated with vintage French folk songs. You can hop off at any stop, tour a sight, then hop on a later bus. It's dang scenic, but only if you get a top-deck seat and the weather's decent. Because of traffic and stops, these buses can be dreadfully slow. (Busy sightseers will do better using the Métro to connect sights.) On the plus side, because the buses move so slowly, you have time to read my sight descriptions, making this a decent orientation tour.

Of the several different hop-on, hop-off bus companies, **L'OpenTour** is best. They offer frequent service on four routes covering central Paris. You can even transfer between routes with one ticket. Look up the various routes and stops either on their website or by picking up a brochure (available at any TI or on one of their bright yellow-and-green buses). Their Paris Grand Tour (green route) offers the best introduction and most frequent buses (every 10 minutes). Other routes run a bit less frequently (every 15-30 minutes). You can catch the bus at just about any major sight (look for the Open Bus icon on public transit bus shelters and signs). Buy tickets from the driver or online and download directly to your smartphone (1 day-€33, 2 days-€37, 3 days-€41, kids 4-11 pay €17 for 1, 2, or 3 days, days must be consecutive, allow 2 hours per

Scenic Buses for Tourists

Of Paris' many bus routes, these are some of the most scenic. They provide a great, cheap, and convenient introduction to the city.

Bus #69 runs east-west between the Eiffel Tower and Père Lachaise Cemetery by way of Rue Cler, Quai d'Orsay, the Louvre, and the Marais.

Bus #24 runs east-west along the Seine riverbank from Gare St.

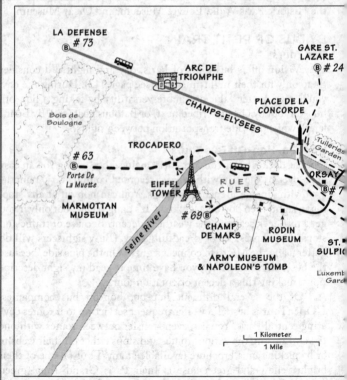

Lazare to Madeleine, Place de la Concorde, Orsay Museum, the Louvre, St. Michel, Notre-Dame, and Jardin des Plantes, all the way to Bercy Village (cafés and shops).

Bus #63 is another good east-west route, connecting the Marmottan Museum, Trocadéro (Eiffel Tower), Pont de l'Alma, Orsay Museum, St. Sulpice, Luxembourg Garden, Latin Quarter/Panthéon, and Gare de Lyon.

Bus #73 is one of Paris' most scenic lines, starting at the Orsay Museum and running westbound around Place de la Concorde, then up the Champs-Elysées, around the Arc de Triomphe, and down Avenue Charles de Gaulle to La Défense.

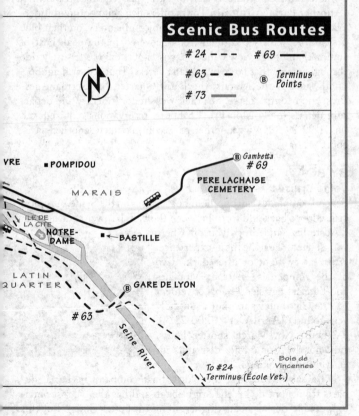

Scenic Bus Routes

# 24 – – –	# 69 ———
# 63 – –	ⓑ Terminus Points
# 73 ———	

route, tel. 01 42 66 56 56, www.paris.opentour.com). A combo-ticket covers the Batobus boats, described later (2 days-€46, 3 days-€50, kids 4-11-€21). L'OpenTour also runs night illumination tours (see page 113).

Big Bus Paris runs a fleet of buses around Paris on a route with just 10 stops and recorded narration (1 day-€33, 2 days-€37, kids 4-12-€16, 10 percent cheaper if you book online, tel. 01 53 95 39 53, www.bigbustours.com).

Paris' cheapest "bus tour" is simply to hop on **city bus #69** and enjoy the sights as they roll by (see sidebar on page 33).

Petit Train Tour

For a relaxing cultural overview of Paris that requires no walking, **"Another Paris" Minitrain Tours** offers five neighborhood itineraries, with simple yet informative audio commentary, on their blue *petit train*. With see-through roofs (covered in the peak heat of summer) and huge view windows, passengers enjoy a leisurely ride through streets that large buses can't access. Tours cover neighborhoods such as the Marais, the Latin Quarter, St. Germain-des-Prés, and Montparnasse. See their website for itinerary and departure details (daily Mon-Fri, 1.5 hours, reservations required; tel. 06 31 99 29 38, www.another-paris.com, contact@another-paris.com).

BY BOAT
Seine Cruises

Several companies run one-hour boat cruises on the Seine. A typical cruise loops back and forth between the Eiffel Tower and the Pont d'Austerlitz, and drops you off where you started. For the best experience, cruise at twilight or after dark. Two of the companies—Bateaux-Mouches and Bateaux Parisiens—are convenient to Rue Cler hotels, and both run daily year-round (April-Oct 10:00-22:30, 2-3/hour; Nov-March shorter hours, runs hourly). Some offer discounts for early online bookings.

Bateaux-Mouches, the oldest boat company in Paris, departs from Pont de l'Alma's right bank and has the biggest open-top, double-decker boats (higher up means better views). But this company caters to tour groups, making their boats jammed and noisy (€13.50, kids 4-12-€5.50, tel. 01 42 25 96 10, www.bateaux-mouches.fr).

Bateaux Parisiens has smaller covered boats with audioguides, fewer crowds, and only one deck. I'd pass on this cruise, as you're stuck inside the boat. It leaves from right in front of the Eiffel Tower (€15, kids 3-12-€7, tel. 01 76 64 14 45, www. bateauxparisiens.com).

Vedettes du Pont Neuf offers essentially the same one-hour tour as the other companies, but starts and ends at Pont Neuf. The boats feature a live guide whose delivery (in English and French) is as stiff as a recorded narration—and as hard to understand, given the quality of their sound system (€14, €12 if you book directly with this book in 2017, discounts for online bookings, kids 4-12-€7, tip requested, nearly 2/hour, daily 10:30-22:30, tel. 01 46 33 98 38, www.vedettesdupontneuf.com).

Hop-On, Hop-Off Boat Tour

Batobus allows you to get on and off as often as you like at any of eight popular stops along the Seine. The boats, which make a continuous circuit, stop in this order: Eiffel Tower, Orsay Museum, St. Germain-des-Prés, Notre-Dame, Jardin des Plantes, Hôtel de Ville, the Louvre, and Pont Alexandre III, near the Champs-Elysées (1 day-€16, 2 days-€18, April-Aug boats run every 20 minutes 10:00-21:30, Sept-March every 25 minutes 10:00-19:00, 45 minutes one-way, 1.5-hour round-trip, www.batobus.com). If you use this for getting around—sort of a scenic, floating alternative to the Métro—it can be worthwhile, but if you just want a guided boat tour, the Seine cruises described earlier are a better choice. Combo-tickets covering the L'OpenTour hop-on, hop-off buses (described earlier) are available, but skip the one-day ticket—you'll feel rushed trying to take full advantage of the bus and boat routes in a single day.

ON FOOT
Walking Tours

For food-oriented walking tours, see page 144.

Paris Walks offers a variety of thoughtful and entertaining two-hour walks, led by British and American guides (€15-20, generally 2/day—morning and afternoon, private tours available, family-friendly and Louvre tours are a specialty, best to check current offerings on their website, tel. 01 48 09 21 40, www.paris-walks. com, paris@paris-walks.com). Tours focus on the Marais, Montmartre, St. Germain-des-Prés and the medieval Latin Quarter, Ile de la Cité/Notre-Dame, the "Two Islands" (Ile de la Cité and Ile St. Louis), the Revolution, and Hemingway's Paris. They also run less-frequent tours to the Puces St. Ouen flea market, in addition to tours on WWI and WWII topics. Reservations aren't necessary for most tours, but specialty tours—such as the Louvre, fashion, or chocolate tours—require advance reservations and prepayment with credit card (deposits are nonrefundable).

Context Travel offers "intellectual by design" walking tours geared for serious learners. The tours are led by well-versed docents (historians, architects, and academics) and cover both museums and specific neighborhoods. They range from traditional topics such as French art history in the Louvre and the Gothic architecture of Notre-Dame to more thematic explorations like immigration and the changing face of Paris, jazz in the Latin Quarter, and the history of the baguette. It's best to book in advance—groups are limited to six participants and can fill up fast (€70-105/person, admission to sights extra, generally 3 hours, tel. 09 75 18 04 15, US tel. 800-691-6036, www.contexttravel.com). They also offer private tours and excursions outside Paris.

Fat Tire Tours offers lowbrow, lighter-on-information but high-on-fun walking tours (run by Fat Tire Bike Tours). Their three-hour Classic Paris Walking Tour covers most major sights and has an option that includes a Louvre ticket (usually Mon, Wed, and Fri at 10:00 or 14:00). They also offer neighborhood walks of Montmartre, the Marais, and the Latin Quarter, as well as a themed walk on the French Revolution. Fat Tire also offers a range of "Skip the Line" tours of major sights, including the Louvre, Notre-Dame Tower, Catacombs, Eiffel Tower, Sainte-Chapelle, and Versailles. Paying more to visit a sight this way is most worthwhile at Sainte-Chapelle, the Eiffel Tower (if you were not able to reserve ahead), and Notre-Dame Tower. Reservations are required and can be made online, by phone, or in person at their office near the Eiffel Tower (€20-40/person for walking tours, €40-90/person for Skip the Line tours, €2 discount per person with this book—two-discount maximum per book; office open daily 9:00-19:00, shorter hours off-season, 36 Avenue de la Bourdonnais, Mo: Ecole Militaire, tel. 01 82 88 80 96, www.fattiretours.com/paris).

Local Guides

For many, Paris merits hiring a Parisian as a personal guide. **Thierry Gauduchon** is a terrific guide and a gifted teacher (€230/half-day, €450/day, tel. 06 19 07 30 77, tgauduchon@gmail.com). **Sylvie Moreau** also leads good tours in Paris (€200 for 3 hours, €320 for 7 hours, tel. 01 74 30 27 46, mobile 06 87 02 80 67, sylvie.ja.moreau@gmail.com). **Arnaud Servignat** is a top guide who has taught me much about Paris (private tours starting at €200, also does minivan tours of the countryside around Paris for more, mobile 06 68 80 29 05, www.french-guide.com, arnotour@me.com). **Elisabeth Van Hest** is another likable and very capable guide (€200/half-day, tel. 01 43 41 47 31, mobile 06 77 80 19 89, elisa.guide@gmail.com). **Sylviane Ceneray** is gentle and knowledgeable (€200/half-day, tel. 06 84 48 02 44, www.paris-asyoulikeit.com).

ON WHEELS
Bike Tours

Run by Christian (American) and Paul (New Zealander), **Bike About Tours** offers easygoing tours with a focus on the eastern half of the city (Marais, Latin Quarter, and Ile de la Cité). Their four-hour tours run daily year-round at 10:00 (also at 15:00 May-Sept). Group tours have a 12-person maximum—reserve online to guarantee a spot, or show up and take your chances (€30, 10 percent discount on this tour with this book, includes helmets upon request, private group tours available). They also offer a day-trip bike tour of Versailles.

Fat Tire Bike Tours offers an extensive program of bike and walking tours (see earlier). Their young guides run four-hour bike tours of Paris day and night (adults-€34, kids-€32 but must weigh at least 100 pounds, €4 discount per person with this book—two-discount maximum per book, reservations recommended but not required, especially in off-season). Kid-size bikes are available, as are tandem attachments that hook on to a parent's bike (tours leave daily rain or shine at 10:30, April-Oct also at 14:30). Livelier night tours follow a route past floodlit monuments and include a boat cruise on the Seine (€44, April-Oct daily at 18:30, less frequent in winter; see listing on page 34).

WEEKEND TOUR PACKAGES FOR STUDENTS

Andy Steves (Rick's son) runs **Weekend Student Adventures** (WSA Europe), offering three-day and 10-day budget travel packages across Europe including accommodations, skip-the-line sightseeing, and unique local experiences. Locally guided and DIY unguided options are available for student and budget travelers in 12 of Europe's most popular cities, including Paris (guided trips from €199, see www.wsaeurope.com for details).

EXCURSIONS FROM PARIS

The following companies offer convenient transportation and a smidgeon of guiding to destinations outside Paris.

Paris Webservices, a reliable outfit, offers day trips with English-speaking chauffeur-guides in cushy minivans for private groups to Giverny, Versailles, Mont St-Michel, D-Day Beaches, and more (figure €90-140/person for groups of 4 or more, use promo code "PWSRS08" and show current edition of this book for discounts of 5 percent—discount valid only for their tours, tel. 01 45 56 91 67 or 09 52 06 02 59, www.pariswebservices.com, contactpws@pariswebservices.com).

City Vision runs tours to several popular regional destinations, including the Loire Valley, Champagne region, D-Day beaches, and Mont St-Michel (tel. 01 42 60 30 01, www.pariscityvision. com). Their minivan tours are pricier, but more personal and given in English, and most offer convenient pickup at your Paris hotel (half-day tour about €100/person, all-day tour about €200/person). Their full-size bus tours are multilingual, mass-marketed, and mediocre at best, but can be worthwhile for some travelers simply for the ease of transportation to the sights (about €80-170, destinations include Versailles, Giverny, Mont St-Michel, and more).

Sightseeing Strategies

If you plan ahead, you can avoid many of the lines that tourists suffer through in Paris. For most sightseers, the best single way to avoid long lines is to buy a Paris Museum Pass. If you decide to forego the pass—or for sights not covered by the pass—you have other options. Note, though, that because of heightened terrorism concerns, there are likely to be slow security checks at most tourist-oriented sights.

PARIS MUSEUM PASS
In Paris there are two classes of sightseers—those with a Paris Museum Pass, and those who stand in line. The pass admits you to many of Paris' most popular sights, and it allows you to skip ticket-buying lines (but not security lines). You'll save time and money by getting this pass. Pertinent details about the pass are outlined here—for more info, visit www.parismuseumpass.com.

Buying the Pass
The pass pays for itself with four key admissions in two days (for example, the Louvre, Orsay, Sainte-Chapelle, and Versailles), and it lets you skip the ticket line at most sights (2 days-€48, 4 days-€62, 6 days-€74, no youth or senior discounts). It's sold at participating museums, monuments, TIs (small fee added; includes TIs at Paris airports), and at some souvenir stores located near major sights. Try to avoid buying the pass at a major museum (such as the Louvre), where the supply can be spotty and lines long. It's not worth the cost or hassle to buy the pass online—you have to either pay dearly for shipping, or print vouchers and redeem them in person at a Paris TI.

To determine whether the pass is a good value for your trip, tally up what you want to see from the following list. Remember, with the pass you skip to the front of most (but not all) lines, which can save hours of waiting, especially in summer. Another benefit is that you can pop into lesser sights that otherwise might not be worth the expense.

Families: The pass isn't worth buying for children and teens, as most museums are free or discounted for those under age 18 (teenagers may need to show ID as proof of age). If parents have a Museum Pass, kids can usually skip the ticket lines as well. A few places, such as the Arc de Triomphe and Army Museum, require everyone—even pass holders—to stand in line to collect your child's free ticket.

What the Paris Museum Pass Covers

Here's a list of key sights and their admission prices without the pass:

Louvre (€15)	Notre-Dame Tower (€10)
Orsay Museum (€11)	Paris Archaeological Crypt (€7)
Orangerie Museum (€9)	Paris Sewer Tour (€4.40)
Sainte-Chapelle (€8.50)	Cluny Museum (€8)
Arc de Triomphe (€9.50)	Pompidou Center (€14)
Rodin Museum (€10)	Picasso Museum (€11)
Army Museum (€11)	Conciergerie (€8.50)
Panthéon (€8.50)	Versailles (€25 total)

Notable sights that are *not* covered by the pass include the Eiffel Tower, Montparnasse Tower, Marmottan Museum, Opéra Garnier, Notre-Dame Treasury, Catacombs, Montmartre Museum, Sacré-Cœur's dome, and the ladies of Pigalle.

Using the Pass

Plan carefully to make the most of your pass. Validate it only when you're ready to tackle the covered sights on consecutive days. Activating it is simple—just write the start date you want (and your name) on the pass. But first make sure the sights you want to visit will be open when you want to go (many museums are closed on either a Mon or Tue).

The pass provides the best value on days when sights close later, letting you extend your sightseeing day. Take advantage of late hours on selected evenings or times of year at the Arc de Triomphe, Pompidou Center, Notre-Dame Tower, Sainte-Chapelle, Louvre, Orsay, Rodin Museum, and Napoleon's Tomb. On days that you don't have pass coverage, plan to visit free sights and those not covered by the pass (see page 56 for a list of free sights).

You can't skip the security lines, though at a few sights (including the Louvre), pass holders may be able to skip to the front. Once past security, look for signs designating the entrance for reserved ticket holders. If it's not obvious, boldly walk to the front of the ticket line, hold up your pass, and ask the ticket taker: *"Entrez, pass?"* (ahn-tray pahs). You'll either be allowed to enter at that point, or you'll be directed to a special entrance. For major sights, such as the Louvre and Orsay museums, I've identified pass holder

Paris at a Glance

▲▲▲**Notre-Dame Cathedral** Paris' most beloved church, with towers and gargoyles. **Hours:** Cathedral—Mon-Sat 7:45-18:45, Sun 7:15-19:15; Tower—daily April-Sept 10:00-18:30, Fri-Sat until 23:00 in July-Aug, Oct-March 10:00-17:30; Treasury—Mon-Fri 9:30-18:00, Sat 9:30-18:30, Sun 13:30-18:40. See page 48.

▲▲▲**Sainte-Chapelle** Gothic cathedral with peerless stained glass. **Hours:** Daily March-Oct 9:30-18:00, Wed until 21:30 mid-May-mid-Sept, Nov-Feb 9:00-17:00. See page 58.

▲▲▲**Louvre** Europe's oldest and greatest museum, starring *Mona Lisa* and *Venus de Milo*. **Hours:** Wed-Mon 9:00-18:00, Wed and Fri until 21:45, closed Tue. See page 63.

▲▲▲**Orsay Museum** Nineteenth-century art, including Europe's greatest Impressionist collection. **Hours:** Tue-Sun 9:30-18:00, Thu until 21:45, closed Mon. See page 72.

▲▲▲**Eiffel Tower** Paris' soaring exclamation point. **Hours:** Daily mid-June-Aug 9:00-24:45, Sept-mid-June 9:30-23:45. See page 80.

▲▲▲**Champs-Elysées** Paris' grand boulevard. **Hours:** Always open. See page 91.

▲▲▲**Versailles** The ultimate royal palace (Château), with a Hall of Mirrors, vast gardens, a grand canal, plus a queen's playground (Trianon Palaces and Domaine de Marie-Antoinette). **Hours:** Château April-Oct Tue-Sun 8:30-19:00, Nov-March 9:00-17:30; Trianon/Domaine April-Oct Tue-Sun 12:00-18:30, Nov-March until 17:30; gardens generally April-Oct daily 8:00-20:30, Nov-March until 18:00; entire complex closed Mon year-round except the Gardens. See the next chapter.

▲▲▲**Picasso Museum** World's largest collection of Picasso's works. **Hours:** Tue-Fri 11:30-18:00 (until 21:00 third Fri of month), Sat-Sun 9:30-18:00, closed Mon. See page 99.

▲▲**Orangerie Museum** Monet's water lilies and modernist classics in a lovely setting. **Hours:** Wed-Mon 9:00-18:00, closed Tue. See page 79.

▲▲**Rue Cler** Ultimate Parisian market street. **Hours:** Stores open Tue-Sat plus Sun morning, dead on Mon. See page 84.

▲▲**Army Museum and Napoleon's Tomb** The emperor's imposing tomb, flanked by museums of France's wars. **Hours:** Daily

10:00-18:00, Nov-March until 17:00; tomb also open July-Aug until 19:00 and April-Sept Tue until 21:00; museum (except for tomb) closed first Mon of month Oct-June; Charles de Gaulle exhibit closed Mon year-round. See page 85.

▲▲**Rodin Museum** Works by the greatest sculptor since Michelangelo, with many statues in a peaceful garden. **Hours:** Tue-Sun 10:00-17:45, Wed until 20:45, closed Mon. See page 86.

▲▲**Marmottan Museum** Art museum focusing on Monet. **Hours:** Tue-Sun 10:00-18:00, Thu until 21:00, closed Mon. See page 86.

▲▲**Cluny Museum** Medieval art with unicorn tapestries. **Hours:** Wed-Mon 9:15-17:45, closed Tue. See page 87.

▲▲**Arc de Triomphe** Triumphal arch marking start of Champs-Elysées. **Hours:** Always viewable; interior daily 10:00-23:00, Oct-March until 22:30. See page 94.

▲▲**Opéra Garnier** Grand belle époque theater with a modern ceiling by Chagall. **Hours:** Generally daily 10:00-16:30, mid-July-Aug until 18:00. See page 96.

▲▲**Pompidou Center** Modern art in colorful building with city views. **Hours:** Permanent collection open Wed-Mon 11:00-21:00, closed Tue. See page 102.

▲▲**Sacré-Cœur and Montmartre** White basilica atop Montmartre with spectacular views. **Hours:** Daily 6:00-22:30; dome climb daily May-Sept 8:30-20:00, Oct-April 9:00-17:00. See page 104.

▲**Panthéon** Neoclassical monument and burial place of the famous. **Hours:** Daily 10:00-18:30, Oct-March until 18:00. See page 89.

▲**Ile St. Louis** Residential island behind Notre-Dame known for its restaurants. **Hours:** Always open. See page 55.

▲**Jewish Art and History Museum** History of Judaism in Europe. **Hours:** Tue-Fri 11:00-18:00, Sat-Sun 10:00-18:00, open later during special exhibits—Wed until 21:00 and Sat-Sun until 19:00, closed Mon year-round. See page 101.

▲**Père Lachaise Cemetery** Final home of Paris' illustrious dead. **Hours:** Mon-Fri 8:00-18:00, Sat 8:30-18:00, Sun 9:00-18:00, until 17:30 in winter. See page 103.

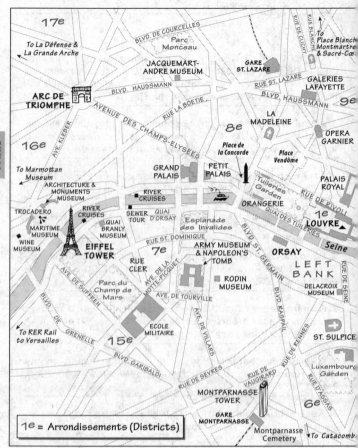

1ᵉ = Arrondissements (Districts)

entrances on the maps in this book. Don't be shy—some places (the Orsay and the Arc de Triomphe, in particular) have long lines in which pass holders wait needlessly.

AVOIDING LINES WITHOUT A PASS

If you don't purchase a Paris Museum Pass, or if a sight is not covered by the pass, there are other ways to avoid long waits in ticket-buying lines.

For some sights, you can buy **advance tickets** either at the official website or through a third party (for a fee). Some tickets require you to choose a specific entry time. An advance timed-entry ticket is essential at the line-plagued Eiffel Tower. You can also buy tickets in advance for many other sights (including the Louvre, Orsay, Picasso Museum, Rodin Museum, and Monet's gardens at Giverny) as well as for activities and cultural events (Bateaux-

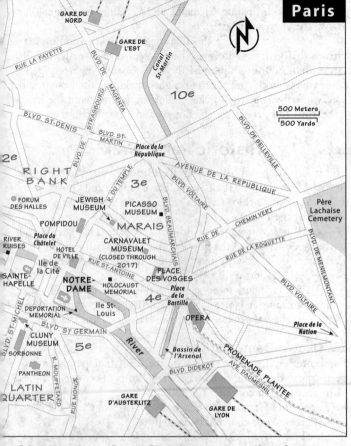

GARE DU
NORD

GARE DE
L'EST

Canal St-Martin

RUE LA FAYETTE

BLVD. DE MAGENTA

10e

BLVD. ST-DENIS

BLVD. DE STRASBOURG

BLVD. ST-MARTIN

Place de la République

500 Meters
500 Yards

BLVD. DE BELLEVILLE

PARIS

2e

RIGHT BANK

AVENUE DE LA REPUBLIQUE

BLVD. DU TEMPLE

3e

BLVD. VOLTAIRE

FORUM DES HALLES

JEWISH MUSEUM

PICASSO MUSEUM

CHEMIN VERT

Père Lachaise Cemetery

POMPIDOU

MARAIS

BLVD. BEAUMARCHAIS

RUE DE LA ROQUETTE

RIVER RUINES

Place du Châtelet

HOTEL DE VILLE

CARNAVALET MUSEUM
(CLOSED THROUGH 2017)

RUE ST-ANTOINE

PLACE DES VOSGES

BLVD. DE MENILMONTANT

SAINTE-CHAPELLE

Ile de la Cité

NOTRE-DAME

HOLOCAUST MEMORIAL

Place de la Bastille

4e

BLVD. VOLTAIRE

DEPORTATION MEMORIAL

Ile St-Louis

OPERA

Place de la Nation

BLVD. ST GERMAIN

CLUNY MUSEUM

5e

River

Bassin de l'Arsenal

PROMENADE PLANTEE

SORBONNE

R. MOUFFETARD

AVE D'AUMESNIL

PANTHEON

RUE MONGE

BLVD. DIDEROT

LATIN QUARTER

GARE D'AUSTERLITZ

GARE DE LYON

Mouches cruises, Sainte-Chapelle concerts, and performances at the Opéra Garnier).

TIs, FNAC department stores, and travel-services companies such as Paris Webservices and Fat Tire Tours sell individual *"coupe-file"* **tickets** (pronounced "koop feel") for some sights, which allow you to use the Museum Pass entrance (worth the extra cost and trouble only for sights where lines are longest). TIs sell these tickets for a small fee, but elsewhere you can expect a surcharge of 10-20 percent. FNAC stores are everywhere (www.fnactickets. com), even on the Champs-Elysées (ask your hotelier for the nearest one); for Paris Webservices, see page 41. Despite the surcharges and often-long lines to buy them, getting *coupe-file* tickets can still be a good idea.

Fat Tire Tours offers **Skip the Line tickets and tours** of major sights, including the Louvre, Notre-Dame Tower, Catacombs, Eiffel Tower, Orsay, Sainte-Chapelle, and Versailles (see page 40 or www.fattiretours.com/paris).

Some sights, such as the Louvre, have **ticket-vending machines** that save time in line. These accept cash (usually no bills larger than €20) or chip-and-PIN cards (many American credit cards won't work). And at certain sights, including the Louvre and Orsay, **nearby shops** sell tickets, allowing you to avoid the main ticket lines (for details, see the Louvre and Orsay listings).

Historic Paris Walk

This information is distilled from the Historic Paris Walk chapter in *Rick Steves Paris*, by Rick Steves, Steve Smith, and Gene Openshaw. (You can download a free 🎧 Rick Steves audio version of this walk; see page 14.)

You'll start where the city did—on the Ile de la Cité, the island in the Seine River and the physical and historic bull's-eye of your Paris map. The closest Métro stops are Cité, Hôtel de Ville, and St. Michel, each a short walk away.

Allow four hours to do justice to this three-mile self-guided walk, beginning at Notre-Dame Cathedral and ending at Pont Neuf; just follow the dotted line on the "Historic Paris Walk" map.

▲▲▲Notre-Dame Cathedral

For centuries, the main figure in the Christian pantheon has been Mary, the mother of Jesus. Catholics petition her in times of trouble to gain comfort, and to ask her to convince God to be compassionate with them. This church is dedicated to "Our Lady" *(Notre Dame)*, and there she is, cradling God, right in the heart of the facade, surrounded by the halo of the rose window. Though the church is massive and imposing, it has always stood for the grace and compassion of Mary, the "mother of God."

Imagine the faith of the people who built this cathedral. They broke ground in 1163 with the hope that someday their great-great-great-great-great-great grandchildren might attend the dedication Mass, which finally took place two centuries later, in 1345. Look up the 200-foot-tall bell towers and imagine a tiny medieval community mustering the money and energy for construction. Master masons supervised, but the people did much of the grunt work themselves for free—hauling the huge stones from distant quarries, digging a 30-foot-deep trench to lay the foundation, and treading like rats on a wheel designed to lift the stones up, one by one.

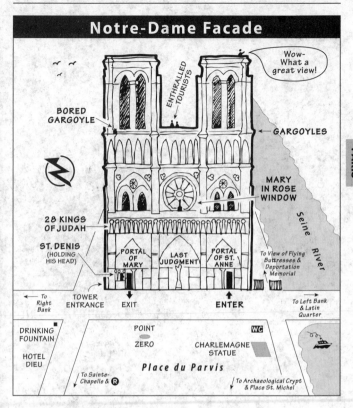

Notre-Dame Facade

Wow– What a great view!

ENTHRALLED TOURISTS

BORED GARGOYLE

GARGOYLES

PARIS

MARY IN ROSE WINDOW

Seine River

28 KINGS OF JUDAH

ST. DENIS (HOLDING HIS HEAD)

PORTAL OF MARY

LAST JUDGMENT

PORTAL OF ST. ANNE

To View of Flying Buttresses & Deportation Memorial

← To Right Bank

TOWER ENTRANCE

EXIT

ENTER

To Left Bank & Latin Quarter

DRINKING FOUNTAIN

POINT ZERO

WC

HOTEL DIEU

CHARLEMAGNE STATUE

Place du Parvis

To Sainte-Chapelle & Ⓡ

To Archaeological Crypt & Place St. Michel

This kind of backbreaking, arduous manual labor created the real hunchbacks of Notre-Dame.

Cost and Hours: Cathedral—free, Mon-Sat 7:45-18:45, Sun 7:15-19:15; **Treasury**—€5, not covered by Museum Pass, Mon-Fri 9:30-18:00, Sat until 18:30, Sun 13:30-18:40; audioguide—€5, free English tours—normally Mon, Tue, and Sat at 14:30, Wed and Thu at 14:00. The cathedral hosts **Mass** several times daily (early morning, noon, evening), plus Vespers at 17:45. The international Mass is held Sun at 11:30. The **Crown of Thorns** is venerated with a service every first Fri at 15:00. Call or check the website for a full schedule (Mo: Cité, Hôtel de Ville, or St. Michel; tel. 01 42 34 56 10, www.notredamedeparis.fr).

The entrance for Notre-Dame's **tower climb** is outside the cathedral, along the left side. You can hike to the top of the facade between the towers and then to the top of the south tower (400 steps total) for a gargoyle's-eye view of the cathedral, Seine, and city (€10, covered by Museum Pass but no bypass line for pass holders; daily April-Sept 10:00-18:30, Fri-Sat until 23:00 in July-Aug, Oct-March 10:00-17:30, last entry 45 minutes before closing; to

PARIS

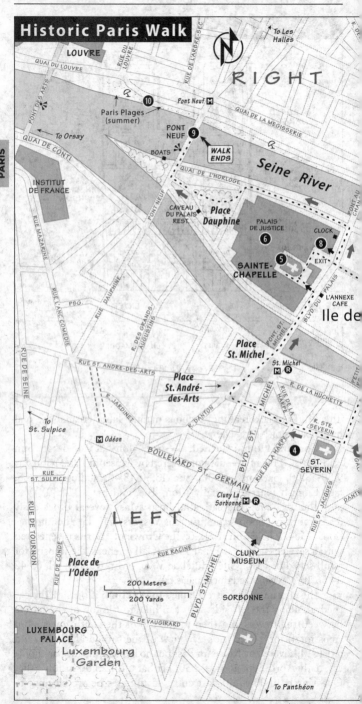

Historic Paris Walk

LOUVRE

QUAI DU LOUVRE

RUE DU LOUVRE

RUE DE L'ARBRE-SEC

R. DE

To Les Halles

RIGHT

PONT DES ARTS

To Orsay

QUAI DE CONTI

10

Paris Plages (summer)

Pont Neuf Ⓜ

QUAI DE LA MÉGISSERIE

PONT NEUF 9

BOATS

WALK ENDS

QUAI DE L'HORLOGE

Seine River

QUAI AU CHARB

INSTITUT DE FRANCE

RUE MAZARINE

RUE DAUPHINE

RUE L'ANCIENNE COMÉDIE

PSG

CAVEAU DU PALAIS REST.

Place Dauphine

PALAIS DE JUSTICE 6

CLOCK 8

EXIT

SAINTE-CHAPELLE 5

L'ANNEXE CAFE

RUE DU PALAIS

Ile de

RUE DE SEINE

RUE DES GRANDS-AUGUSTINS

RUE ST-ANDRE-DES-ARTS

R. JARDINET

Place St. André-des-Arts

PONT ST. MICHEL

Place St. Michel

St. Michel Ⓜ Ⓡ

BLVD. ST. MICHEL

R. DE LA HUCHETTE

PETIT

Ⓜ Odéon

R. DANTON

BOULEVARD ST. GERMAIN

RUE DE LA HARPE

R. STE. SEVERIN

4

ST. SEVERIN

RUE ST. JACQUES

GAL

DANTE

RUE ST. SULPICE

Cluny La Sorbonne Ⓜ Ⓡ

LEFT

RUE DE CONDE

RUE DE TOURNON

RUE RACINE

Place de l'Odéon

CLUNY MUSEUM

200 Meters

200 Yards

BLVD. ST-MICHEL

SORBONNE

R. DE VAUGIRARD

LUXEMBOURG PALACE

Luxembourg Garden

To Panthéon

To St. Sulpice

To Orsay

PARIS

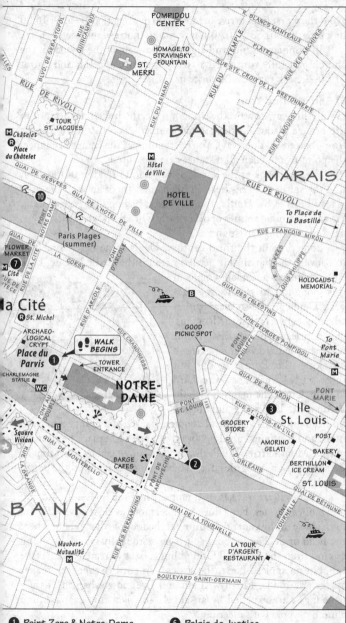

1 Point Zero & Notre-Dame
2 Deportation Memorial
3 Ile St. Louis
4 Latin Quarter
5 Sainte-Chapelle
6 Palais de Justice
7 Cité Métro Stop & Flower Market
8 Conciergerie
9 Pont Neuf
10 Paris Plages (2)

avoid the worst lines arrive before 10:00 or after 17:00—after 16:00 in winter; tel. 01 53 10 07 00, www.tours-notre-dame-de-paris.fr).

In summer, **sound-and-light displays** about the history of the church generally run twice a week (free, usually Thu and Sat at 21:00—check cathedral website or call).

● Self-Guided Tour

"Walk this way" toward the front of the cathedral, and view it from the bronze plaque on the ground marked "Point Zero" (30 yards from the central doorway). You're standing at the center of France, the point from which all distances are measured.

Facade: Look at the left doorway, and to the left of the door, find the statue with his head in his hands. The man with the misplaced head is **St. Denis,** the city's first bishop and patron saint. He stands among statues of other early Christians who helped turn pagan Paris into Christian Paris.

Sometime in the third century, Denis came here from Italy to convert the Parisii. He settled here on the Ile de la Cité, back when there was a Roman temple on this spot and Christianity was suspect. Denis proved so successful at winning converts that the Romans' pagan priests got worried. Denis was beheaded as a warning to those forsaking the Roman gods. But those early Christians were hard to keep down. The man who would become St. Denis got up, tucked his head under his arm, headed north, paused at a fountain to wash it off, and continued until he found just the right place to meet his maker: Montmartre. The Parisians were convinced by this miracle, Christianity gained ground, and a church soon replaced the pagan temple.

Medieval art was OK if it embellished the house of God and told biblical stories. For a fine example, move as close as you can get to the **base of the central column** (at the foot of Mary, about where the head of St. Denis could spit if he were really good). Working around from the left, find God telling a barely created Eve, "Have fun, but no apples." Next, the sexiest serpent I've ever seen makes apples à la mode. Finally, Adam and Eve, now ashamed of their nakedness, are expelled by an angel. This is a tiny example in a church covered with meaning.

Above the arches is a row of 28 statues, known as the **Kings of Judah.** In the days of the French Revolution (1789-1799), these biblical kings were mistaken for the hated French kings, and Notre-Dame represented the oppressive Catholic hierarchy. The citizens stormed the church, crying, "Off with their heads!" Plop—they lopped off the crowned heads of these kings with glee, creating a row of St. Denises that weren't repaired for decades.

Notre-Dame Interior: *Enter the church at the right doorway (the line moves quickly). Be careful: Pickpockets attend church here religiously.*

Notre-Dame has the typical basilica floor plan shared by so many Catholic churches: a long central nave lined with columns

and flanked by side aisles. It's designed in the shape of a cross, with the altar placed where the crossbeam intersects. The church can hold up to 10,000 faithful, and it's probably buzzing with visitors now, just as it was 600 years ago. The quiet, deserted churches we see elsewhere are in stark contrast to the busy, center-of-life places they were in the Middle Ages.

Just past the altar is the so-called choir, the area enclosed with carved-wood walls, where more intimate services can be held in this spacious building. In the right transept,

a statue of **Joan of Arc** (Jeanne d'Arc, 1412-1431), dressed in armor and praying, honors the French teenager who rallied her country's soldiers to try to drive English invaders from Paris.

Join the statue in gazing up to the blue-and-purple, **rose-shaped window** in the opposite transept—with teeny green Mary and baby Jesus in the center—the only one of the three rose windows still with its original medieval glass.

The back side of the choir walls feature scenes of the **resurrected Jesus** (c. 1350) appearing to his followers, starting with Mary Magdalene. Their starry robes still gleam, thanks to a 19th-century renovation. The niches below these carvings mark the tombs of centuries of archbishops. Just ahead on the right is the **Treasury.** It contains lavish robes, golden reliquaries, and the humble tunic of King (and St.) Louis IX, but it probably isn't worth the entry fee.

Notre-Dame Side View: Back outside, alongside the church you'll notice many of the elements of Gothic: pointed arches, the

lacy stone tracery of the windows, pinnacles, statues on rooftops, a lead roof, and a pointed steeple covered with the prickly "flames" (Flamboyant Gothic) of the Holy Spirit. Most distinctive of all are the **flying buttresses.** These 50-foot stone "beams" that stick out of the church were the key to the complex Gothic architecture. The pointed arches we saw inside cause the weight of the roof to push outward rather than downward. The "flying" buttresses support the roof by pushing back inward.

Picture Quasimodo (the fictional hunchback) limping around along the railed balcony at the base of the roof among the **"gargoyles."** These grotesque beasts sticking out from pillars and buttresses represent souls caught between heaven and earth. They also function as rainspouts (from the same French root word as "gargle") when there are no evil spirits to battle.

The Neo-Gothic 300-foot spire is a product of the 1860 reconstruction of the dilapidated old church. Victor Hugo's book *The Hunchback of Notre-Dame* (1831) inspired a young architecture student named Eugène-Emmanuel Viollet-le-Duc to dedicate his career to a major renovation in Gothic style. Find Viollet-le-Duc at the base of the spire among the green apostles and evangelists (visible as you approach the back end of the church). The apostles look outward, blessing the city, while the architect (at top) looks up the spire, marveling at his fine work.

Nearby: The Paris Archaeological Crypt is an intriguing 20-minute stop. View Roman ruins from Emperor Augustus' reign (when this island became ground zero in Paris), trace the street plan of the medieval village, and see diagrams of how early Paris grew. It's all thoughtfully explained in English—pick up the floor plan with some background info—and well presented with videos and touchscreens (€7, covered by Museum Pass, Tue-Sun 10:00-18:00, closed Mon, enter 100 yards in front of cathedral, tel. 01 55 42 50 10, www.crypte.paris.fr).

• *Behind Notre-Dame, cross the street and enter through the iron gate into the park at the tip of the island. (If this gate is closed, you can still enter the park 30 yards to the left.) Look for the stairs and head down to reach the...*

▲Deportation Memorial (Mémorial de la Déportation)

This memorial to the 200,000 French victims of the Nazi concentration camps (1940-1945) draws you into their experience. France was quickly overrun by Nazi Germany, and Paris spent the war years under Nazi occupation. Jews and dissidents were rounded up and deported—many never returned.

Cost and Hours: Free, Tue-Sun 10:00-19:00, Oct-March until 17:00, closed Mon year-round, may randomly close at other times, free but boring audioguide; at the east tip of Ile de la Cité, behind Notre-

Dame and near Ile St. Louis (Mo: Cité); tel. 01 46 33 87 56, www.cheminsdememoire.gouv.fr.

Visiting the Memorial: As you descend the steps, the city around you disappears. Surrounded by walls, you have become a prisoner. Your only freedom is your view of the sky and the tiny glimpse of the river below. Enter the dark, single-file chamber up ahead. Inside, the circular plaque in the floor reads, "They went to the end of the earth and did not return."

The hallway stretching in front of you is lined with 200,000 lighted crystals, one for each French citizen who died. Flickering at the far end is the eternal flame of hope. The tomb of the unknown deportee lies at your feet. Above, the inscription reads, "Dedicated to the living memory of the 200,000 French deportees shrouded by the night and the fog, exterminated in the Nazi concentration camps." The side rooms are filled with triangles—reminiscent of the identification patches inmates were forced to wear—each bearing the name of a concentration camp. Above the exit as you leave is the message you'll find at many other Holocaust sites: "Forgive, but never forget."

• *Back on street level, but before leaving the memorial park, look across the river (north) to the island called...*

▲Ile St. Louis

If Ile de la Cité is a tugboat laden with the history of Paris, it's towing this classy little residential dinghy, laden only with high-rent apartments, boutiques, characteristic restaurants, and famous ice cream shops.

Ile St. Louis wasn't developed until much later than Ile de la Cité (17th century). What was a swampy mess is now harmonious Parisian architecture and one of Paris' most exclusive neighborhoods.

Look upstream (east) to the bridge (Pont Tournelle) that links Ile St. Louis with the Left Bank (which is now on your right). Where the bridge meets the Left Bank, you'll find one of Paris' most exclusive restaurants, La Tour d'Argent (with a flag flying from the rooftop). This restaurant was the inspiration for the movie *Ratatouille*. Because the top floor has floor-to-ceiling windows, your evening meal comes with glittering views—and a golden price (allow €200 minimum, though you get a free photo of yourself dining elegantly with Notre-Dame floodlit in the background).

It's a lovely place for an evening stroll (for details, see page 113). If you won't have time to come back, consider taking a brief detour across the pedestrian bridge, Pont St. Louis, to explore this little island.

• *From the Deportation Memorial, cross the bridge to the Left Bank. Turn right and walk along the river, toward the front end of Notre-*

Affording Paris' Sights

Paris is an expensive city for tourists, with lots of pricey sights, but—fortunately—lots of freebies, too. Smart, budget-minded travelers begin by buying and getting the most out of a **Paris Museum Pass** (see page 42), then considering these frugal sightseeing options.

Free (or Almost Free) Museums: Many of Paris' famous museums offer free entry on the first Sunday of the month, including the Orsay, Cluny, Pompidou Center, Quai Branly, and Delacroix museums. These sights are free on the first Sunday of off-season months: the Louvre, Rodin Museum, and Arc de Triomphe (all Oct-March), and Versailles (Nov-March). Expect big crowds on free days. Some museums are always free (with the possible exception of special exhibits), including the Carnavalet Museum (closed in 2017) and Victor Hugo's House. You can usually visit the Orsay Museum for free right when the ticket booth stops selling tickets. For just €4, the Rodin Museum garden lets you enjoy many of Rodin's finest works in a lovely outdoor setting.

Other Freebies: Many sights don't charge entry, including the Notre-Dame Cathedral, Père Lachaise Cemetery, Deportation Memorial, Holocaust Memorial, Paris *Plages* (summers only), Sacré-Cœur Basilica, St. Sulpice Church (with organ recital), and La Défense mall. Stroll the Left Bank riverside promenade from the Orsay to Pont de l'Alma.

Paris' glorious, entertaining parks are free, *bien sûr*. These include Luxembourg Garden, Champ de Mars (under the Ei-

---

Dame and to the next bridge. Stairs detour down to the riverbank if you need a place to picnic. This side view of the church from across the river is one of Europe's great sights and is best from river level. At times, you may find **barges** housing restaurants with great cathedral views docked here.

After passing the Pont au Double (the bridge leading to the facade of Notre-Dame), watch on your left for **Shakespeare and Company,** an atmospheric reincarnation of the original 1920s bookshop and a good spot to page through books (37 Rue de la Bûcherie). Before returning to the island, walk a block behind Shakespeare and Company, and take a spin through...

▲The Latin Quarter

This area's touristy fame relates to its intriguing, artsy, bohemian character. This was perhaps Europe's leading university district in the Middle Ages, when Latin was the language of higher education. The neighborhood's main boulevards (St. Michel and St. Germain) are lined with cafés—once the haunts of great poets and philosophers, now the hangouts of tired tourists. Exploring a few

PARIS

ffel Tower), Tuileries Garden (between the Louvre and Place de la Concorde), Palais Royal Courtyards, Jardin des Plantes, Parc Monceau, the Promenade Plantée walk, and Versailles' gardens (except when the fountains perform on weekends April-Oct and many Tue).

Reduced Prices: Several sights offer a discount if you enter later in the day, including the Orsay, the Orangerie, and the Army Museum and Napoleon's Tomb. The Eiffel Tower costs less if you're willing to restrict your visit to the two lower levels—and even less if you're willing to use the stairs.

Free Concerts: Venues offering free or cheap (€8) concerts include the American Church, Army Museum, St. Sulpice Church, La Madeleine Church, and Notre-Dame Cathedral. For a listing of free concerts, check *Pariscope* magazine (under the "Musique" section) and look for events marked *entrée libre.*

Good-Value Tours: At €15-20, Paris Walks' tours are a good value. The Seine River cruises (around €14), best after dark, are also worthwhile. The scenic bus route #69, which costs only the price of a transit ticket, could be the best deal of all.

Pricey...but worth it? Certain big-ticket items—primarily the top of the Eiffel Tower, the Louvre, and Versailles—are expensive and crowded, but offer once-in-a-lifetime experiences. All together they amount to less than the cost of a ticket to Disneyland—except these are real.

blocks up or downriver from here gives you a better chance of feeling the pulse of what survives of Paris' classic Left Bank. For colorful wandering and café-sitting, afternoons and evenings are best.

Walking along Rue St. Séverin, you can still see the shadow of the medieval sewer system. The street slopes into a central channel of bricks. In the days before plumbing and toilets, when people still went to the river or neighborhood wells for their water, flushing meant throwing it out the window. At certain times of day, maids on the fourth floor would holler, *"Garde de l'eau!"* ("Watch out for the water!") and heave it into the streets, where it would eventually wash down into the Seine.

Consider a visit to the **Cluny Museum** for its medieval art and unicorn tapestries (see page 87). The **Sorbonne**—the University of Paris' humanities department—is also nearby; visitors can ogle at the famous dome, but they are not allowed to enter the building (two blocks south of the river on Boulevard St. Michel).

Don't miss **Place St. Michel.** This square (facing Pont St. Michel) is the traditional core of the Left Bank's artsy, liberal, hippie, bohemian district of poets, philosophers, winos, and *baba* *cool*s (neo-hippies). In less commercial times, Place St. Michel was a gathering point for the city's malcontents and misfits. In 1830, 1848, and again in 1871, the citizens took the streets from the government troops, set up barricades *Les Miz*-style, and fought against royalist oppression. During World War II, the locals rose up against their Nazi oppressors (read the plaques under the dragons at the foot of the St. Michel fountain). Even today, whenever there's a student demonstration, it starts here.

• *From Place St. Michel, look across the river and find the prickly steeple of the Sainte-Chapelle church. Head toward it. Cross the river on Pont St. Michel and continue north along the Boulevard du Palais. On your left, you'll see the doorway to Sainte-Chapelle (usually with a line of people).*

▲▲▲Sainte-Chapelle

This triumph of Gothic church architecture is a cathedral of glass like no other. It was speedily built between 1242 and 1248 for King Louis IX—the only French king who is now a saint—to house the supposed Crown of Thorns. Its architectural harmony is due to the fact that it was completed under the direction of one architect and in only six years—unheard of in Gothic times. In contrast, Notre-Dame took more than 200 years.

Cost and Hours: €8.50, €13.50 combo-ticket with Conciergerie, free for those under age 18, covered by Museum Pass; daily March-Oct 9:30-18:00, Wed until 21:30 mid-May-mid-Sept, Nov-Feb 9:00-17:00; audioguide-€4.50 (€6 for two), 4 Boulevard du Palais, Mo: Cité, tel. 01 53 40 60 80, www.sainte-chapelle.fr. For info on upcoming church concerts, see page 111.

Getting In: Expect long lines to get in. First comes the security line (all sharp objects and glass are confiscated). No one can skip this line. It can be frustrating, but it's just the way it is. Security lines are shortest first thing (be in line by 9:15, or arrive at 10:00 after the first rush subsides), and on weekends (when the courts are closed). They're longest on Tue and any day around 13:00-14:00 (when staff takes lunch). Once past security, you'll encounter the ticket-buying line—those with combo-tickets or Museum Passes *can* skip this queue.

Visiting the Church: Though the inside is beautiful, the exterior is basically functional. The muscular buttresses hold up the stone roof, so the walls are essentially there to display stained glass.

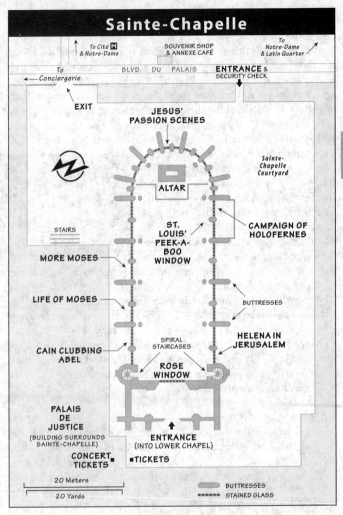

Sainte-Chapelle

↑ To Cité Ⓜ & Notre-Dame

SOUVENIR SHOP & ANNEXE CAFÉ

↗ To Notre-Dame & Latin Quarter

To ← Conciergerie

BLVD. DU PALAIS

ENTRANCE & SECURITY CHECK

EXIT

JESUS' PASSION SCENES

ALTAR

Sainte-Chapelle Courtyard

STAIRS

ST. LOUIS' PEEK-A-BOO WINDOW

CAMPAIGN OF HOLOFERNES

MORE MOSES

LIFE OF MOSES

BUTTRESSES

CAIN CLUBBING ABEL

SPIRAL STAIRCASES

HELENA IN JERUSALEM

ROSE WINDOW

PALAIS DE JUSTICE (BUILDING SURROUNDS SAINTE-CHAPELLE)

ENTRANCE (INTO LOWER CHAPEL)

CONCERT TICKETS ■

■ **TICKETS**

20 Meters

20 Yards

▬ BUTTRESSES

┈┈┈ STAINED GLASS

PARIS

The lacy spire is Neo-Gothic—added in the 19th century. Inside, the layout clearly shows an *ancien régime* approach to worship. The low-ceilinged basement was for staff and other common folks—worshipping under a sky filled with painted fleurs-de-lis, a symbol of the king. Royal Christians worshipped upstairs. The paint job, a 19th-century restoration, helps you imagine how grand this small, painted, jeweled chapel was. (Imagine Notre-Dame painted like this...) Each capital is playfully carved with a different plant's leaves.

Climb the spiral staircase to the Chapelle Haute. Fill the place with choral music, crank up the sunshine, face the top of the altar, and really believe that the Crown of Thorns is there, and this becomes one awesome space.

Fiat lux. "Let there be light." From the first page of the Bible, it's clear: Light is divine. Light shines through stained glass like God's grace shining down to earth. Gothic architects used their new technology to turn dark stone buildings into lanterns of light. The glory of Gothic shines brighter here than in any other church.

There are 15 separate panels of **stained glass** (6,500 square feet—two thirds of it 13th-century original), with more than 1,100 different scenes, mostly from the Bible.  These cover the entire Christian history of the world, from the Creation in Genesis (first window on the left, as you face the altar), to the coming of Christ (over the altar), to the end of the world (the round "rose"-shaped window at the rear of the church). Each individual scene is interesting, and the whole effect is overwhelming.

The **altar** was raised up high to better display the Crown of Thorns, which cost King Louis more than three times as much as this church. Today, the relic is kept by the Notre-Dame Treasury (though it's occasionally brought out for display).

• *Exit Sainte-Chapelle. Back outside, as you walk around the church exterior, look down to see the foundation and take note of how much Paris has risen in the 750 years since Sainte-Chapelle was built.*

Next door to Sainte-Chapelle is the...

Palais de Justice

Sainte-Chapelle sits within a huge complex of buildings that has housed the local government since ancient Roman times. It was  the site of the original Gothic palace of the early kings of France. The only surviving medieval parts are Sainte-Chapelle and the Conciergerie prison.

Most of the site is now covered by the giant Palais de Justice, built in 1776, home of the French Supreme Court. The motto *Liberté, Egalité, Fraternité* over the doors is a reminder that this was also the headquarters of the Revolutionary government. Here they doled out justice, condemning many to imprisonment in the Conciergerie downstairs—or to the guillotine.

• *Now pass through the big iron gate to the noisy Boulevard du Palais.*

Cross the street to the wide, pedestrian-only Rue de Lutèce and walk about halfway down.

Cité "Metropolitain" Métro Stop

Of the 141 original early-20th-century subway entrances, this is one of only a few survivors—now preserved as a national art treasure.

(New York's Museum of Modern Art even exhibits one.) It marks Paris at its peak in 1900—on the cutting edge of Modernism, but with an eye for beauty. The curvy, plantlike ironwork is a textbook example of Art Nouveau, the style that rebelled against the erector-set squareness of the Industrial Age. Other similar Métro stations in Paris are Abbesses and Porte Dauphine.

The flower and plant market on Place Louis Lépine is a pleasant detour. On Sundays this square flutters with a busy bird market.

• *Pause here to admire the view. Sainte-Chapelle is a pearl in an ugly architectural oyster. Double back to the Palais de Justice, turn right onto Boulevard du Palais, and enter the Conciergerie. It's free with the Museum Pass; pass holders can sidestep the bottleneck created by the ticket-buying line.*

Conciergerie

Though pretty barren inside, this former prison echoes with history. Positioned next to the courthouse, the Conciergerie was the

gloomy prison famous as the last stop for 2,780 victims of the guillotine, including France's last *ancien régime* queen, Marie-Antoinette. Before then, kings had used the building to torture and execute failed assassins. (One of its towers along the river was called "The Babbler," named for the pain-induced sounds that leaked from it.) When the Revolution (1789) toppled the king, the building kept its same function, but without torture. The progressive Revolutionaries proudly unveiled a modern and more humane way to execute people—the guillotine. The Conciergerie was the epicenter of the Reign of Terror—the year-long period of the Revolution (1793-94) during which Revolutionary fervor spiraled out of control and thousands were killed. It was here at the Conciergerie that "enemies of the Revolution" were imprisoned, tried, sentenced, and marched off to Place de la Concorde for decapitation.

Cost and Hours: €8.50, €13.50 combo-ticket with Sainte-Chapelle, covered by Museum Pass, daily 9:30-18:00, 2 Boulevard du Palais, Mo: Cité, tel. 01 53 40 60 80, www.paris-conciergerie.fr.

Visiting the Conciergerie: Pick up a free map and breeze through the one-way circuit. It's well-described in English. See the spacious, low-ceilinged Hall of Men-at-Arms (Room 1), originally a guards' dining room, with four big fireplaces (look up the chimneys). During the Reign of Terror, this large hall served as a holding tank for the poorest prisoners. Then they were taken upstairs (in an area not open to visitors), where the Revolutionary tribunals grilled scared prisoners on their political correctness. Continue to the raised area at the far end of the room (Room 4, today's bookstore). In Revolutionary days, this was notorious as the walkway of the executioner, who was known affectionately as "Monsieur de Paris."

Upstairs is a memorial room with the names of the 2,780 citizens condemned to death by the guillotine, including ex-King Louis XVI, Charlotte Corday (who murdered the Revolutionary writer Jean-Paul Marat in his bathtub), and—oh, the irony—Maximilien de Robespierre, the head rabble-rouser of the Revolution, who himself sent so many to the guillotine.

Just past the courtyard is a re-creation of Marie-Antoinette's cell. On August 12, 1793, the queen was brought here to be tried for her supposed crimes against the people. Imagine the queen's last days—separated from her 10-year-old son, and now widowed because the king had already been executed. Mannequins, period furniture, and the real cell wallpaper set the scene. The guard stands modestly behind a screen, while the queen psyches herself up with a crucifix. In the glass display case, see her actual crucifix, rug, and small water pitcher. On October 16, 1793, the queen was awakened at 4:00 in the morning and led away. She walked the corridor, stepped onto the cart, and was slowly carried to Place de la Concorde, where she had a date with "Monsieur de Paris."

• *Back outside, turn left on Boulevard du Palais. On the corner is the city's oldest public clock. The mechanism of the present clock is from 1334, and even though the case is Baroque, it keeps on ticking.*

Turn left onto Quai de l'Horloge and walk along the river, past "The Babbler" tower. The bridge up ahead is the Pont Neuf, where we'll end this walk. At the first corner, veer left into a sleepy triangular square called Place Dauphine. It's amazing to find such coziness in the heart of Paris. From the equestrian statue of Henry IV, turn right onto Pont Neuf. Pause at the little nook halfway across.

Pont Neuf and the Seine

This "new bridge" is now Paris' oldest. Built during Henry IV's reign (about 1600), its arches span the widest part of the river. Unlike other bridges, this one never had houses or buildings growing on it. The turrets were originally for vendors and street entertainers. In the days of Henry IV, who promised his peasants "a chicken in every pot every Sunday," this would have been a lively scene. From the bridge, look downstream (west) to see the next bridge, the pedestrian-only Pont des Arts. Ahead on the Right Bank is the long Louvre museum. Beyond that, on the Left Bank, is the Orsay. And what's that tall black tower in the distance?

• *Our walk is finished. From here, you can tour the Seine by boat (the departure point for Seine River cruises offered by Vedettes du Pont Neuf is through the park at the end of the island—see page 39), continue to the Louvre, or (if it's summer) head to the...*

▲Paris *Plages* (Paris Beaches)

The Riviera it's not, but this string of fanciful faux beaches—assembled in summer along a one-mile stretch of the Right Bank of the Seine—is a fun place to stroll, play, and people-watch on a sunny day. Each summer, the Paris city government closes the embankment's highway and trucks in potted palm trees, hammocks, lounge chairs, and 2,000 tons of sand to create colorful urban beaches. You'll also find "beach cafés," climbing walls, prefab pools, trampolines, *boules,* a library, beach volleyball, badminton, and Frisbee areas in three zones: sandy, grassy, and wood-tiled. (Other less-central areas of town, such as Bassin de la Vilette, have their own *plages.*)

Cost and Hours: Free, mid-July-mid-Aug daily 8:00-24:00, on Right Bank of Seine, just north of Ile de la Cité, between Pont des Arts and Pont de Sully; for information, go to www.quefaire. paris.fr/parisplages.

Sights in Paris

MAJOR MUSEUMS NEIGHBORHOOD

Paris' grandest park, the Tuileries Garden, was once the private property of kings and queens. Today it links the Louvre, Orangerie, and Orsay museums. And across from the Louvre are the tranquil, historic courtyards of the Palais Royal.

▲▲▲Louvre (Musée du Louvre)

This is Europe's oldest, biggest, greatest, and second-most-crowded museum (after the Vatican). Housed in a U-shaped, 16th-century palace (accentuated by a 20th-century glass pyramid), the Louvre is Paris' top museum and one of its key landmarks. It's home to

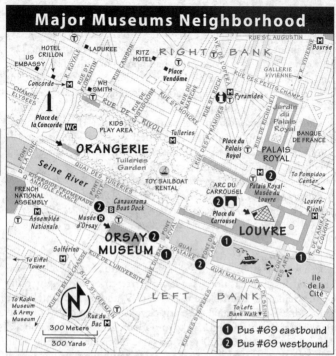

Major Museums Neighborhood

❶ Bus #69 eastbound
❷ Bus #69 westbound

Mona Lisa, Venus de Milo, and hall after hall of Greek and Roman masterpieces, medieval jewels, Michelangelo statues, and paintings by the greatest artists from the Renaissance to the Romantics.

Touring the Louvre can be overwhelming, so be selective. Focus on the Denon wing, with Greek sculptures, Italian paintings (by Raphael and da Vinci), and—of course—French paintings (Neoclassical and Romantic), and the adjoining Sully wing, with Egyptian artifacts and more French paintings. For extra credit, tackle the Richelieu wing, displaying works from ancient Mesopotamia, as well as French, Dutch, and Northern art.

Expect Changes: The sprawling Louvre is constantly shuffling its deck. Rooms close, and pieces can be on loan or in restoration.

Cost and Hours: €15, includes special exhibits, free on first Sun of month Oct-March, covered by Museum Pass, tickets good all day, reentry allowed; open Wed-Mon 9:00-18:00, Wed and Fri until 21:45 (except on holidays), closed Tue, galleries start shutting 30 minutes before closing, last entry 45 minutes before closing; several cafés, tel. 01 40 20 53 17, recorded info tel. 01 40 20 51 51, www.louvre.fr.

When to Go: Crowds can be miserably bad on Sun, Mon (the worst day), Wed, and in the morning (arrive 30 minutes before opening to secure a good place in line). Evening visits are quieter, and the glass pyramid glows after dark.

Buying Tickets: Self-serve ticket machines located under the pyramid may be faster to use than the ticket windows (machines accept euro bills, coins, and chip-and-PIN Visa cards). A shop in the underground mall sells tickets to the Louvre, Orsay, and Versailles, plus Museum Passes, for no extra charge (cash only). To find it from the Carrousel du Louvre entrance off Rue de Rivoli, turn right after the last escalator down onto Allée de France, and follow *Museum Pass* signs.

Getting There: It's at the Palais Royal-Musée du Louvre Métro stop. (The old Louvre Métro stop, called Louvre-Rivoli, is farther from the entrance.) Bus #69 also runs past the Louvre.

Getting In: There is no grander entry than through the main entrance at the **pyramid** in the central courtyard, but lines (for security reasons) can be long. Pass holders have a queue that puts them closer to the head of the security line.

Anyone can enter the Louvre from its less crowded **underground entrance,** accessed through the Carrousel du Louvre

shopping mall. Enter the mall at 99 Rue de Rivoli (the door with the red awning) or directly from the Métro stop Palais Royal-Musée du Louvre (stepping off the train, take the exit to *Musée du Louvre-Le Carrousel du Louvre*). Once inside the underground mall, continue toward the inverted pyramid next to the Louvre's security entrance. Museum Pass holders can sometimes skip to the head of the security line, but if that special line is not obvious, don't bother following signs pointing you to the *Pyramid Passholders* entrance (which is a long detour away).

Information: Pick up the free *Plan/Information* at the information desk under the pyramid as you enter. You'll find explanations throughout the museum. Tel. 01 40 20 53 17, recorded info tel. 01 40 20 51 51, www.louvre.fr.

Tours: Ninety-minute English-language **guided tours** leave twice daily (except the first Sun of the month Oct-March) from the *Accueil des Groupes* area, under the pyramid (normally at 11:15 and 14:00, possibly more often in summer; €12 plus admission, tour tel.

PARIS

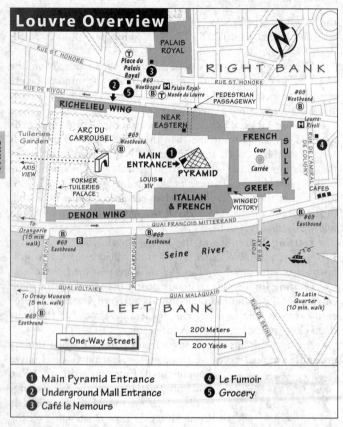

Louvre Overview

1 Main Pyramid Entrance
2 Underground Mall Entrance
3 Café le Nemours
4 Le Fumoir
5 Grocery

01 40 20 52 63). **Videoguides** (€5) provide commentary on about 700 masterpieces.

🎧 Download my free Louvre Museum **audio tour.**

Baggage Check: You can store bags for free in self-service lockers (look for the *Vestiaires* sign). Bigger bags must be checked.

Services: WCs are located under the pyramid, behind the escalators to the Denon and Richelieu wings. Once you're in the galleries, WCs are scarce.

⊘ Self-Guided Tour

With more than 30,000 works of art, the Louvre is a full inventory of Western civilization. To cover it all in one visit is impossible. Let's focus on the Louvre's specialties—Greek sculpture, Italian painting, and French painting. If you don't find the artwork you're looking for, ask the nearest guard for its location.

• *We'll start in the Sully wing, in Salle 16. To get there from the pyramid entrance, first enter the Denon wing, ascend several flights of escalators, and follow the crowds—then get out your map or ask directions to the* Venus de Milo.

The Greeks

Venus de Milo (Aphrodite), late 2nd century B.C.: This goddess of love created a sensation when she was discovered in 1820 on the

Greek island of Melos. The Greeks pictured their gods in human form (meaning humans are godlike), telling us they had an optimistic view of the human race. Venus' well-proportioned body captures the balance and orderliness of the Greek universe. The twisting pose gives a balanced S-curve to her body (especially noticeable from the back view) that Golden Age Greeks and succeeding generations found beautiful. Most "Greek" statues are actually later Roman copies. This is a rare Greek original.

• *Now head to Salle 6, behind* Venus de Milo.

Parthenon Friezes, mid-5th century B.C.: These stone fragments once decorated the exterior of the greatest Athenian temple of the Greek Golden Age. The temple glorified the city's divine protector, Athena, and the superiority of the Athenians, who were feeling especially cocky, having just crushed their archrivals, the Persians. A model of the Parthenon shows where the panels might have hung.

• *About 50 yards away, find a grand staircase. Climb it to the first floor and the...*

Winged Victory of Samothrace (Victoire de Samothrace), c. 190 B.C.: This woman with wings, poised on the prow of a ship, once stood on an island hilltop to commemorate a naval victory. Her clothes are windblown and sea-sprayed, clinging close enough to her body to win a wet T-shirt contest. Originally, her right arm was stretched high, celebrating the victory like a Super Bowl champion, waving a "we're number one" finger.

This is the *Venus de Milo* gone Hellenistic, from the time after the culture of Athens was spread around the Mediterranean by Alexander the Great (c. 325 B.C.). As *Victory* strides forward, the wind blows her and her wings back. Her feet are firmly on the ground, but her wings (and missing arms) stretch upward. She is a pillar of vertical strength, while the clothes curve and whip around her. These opposing forces create a feeling of great energy, making her the lightest two-ton piece of rock in captivity.

• *Facing* Winged Victory, *turn right (entering the Denon wing), and proceed to the large Salle 3.*

PARIS

The Medieval World (1200-1500)

Cimabue, *The Madonna and Child in Majesty Surrounded by Angels (La Vierge et l'Enfant en Majesté Entourés de Six Anges),* c. 1280: During the Age of Faith (1200s), almost every church in Europe had a painting like this one. Mary was a cult figure—even bigger than the late-20th-century Madonna—adored and prayed to by the faithful for bringing Baby Jesus into the world. These holy figures are laid flat on a gold background like cardboard cutouts, existing in a golden never-never land, as though the faithful couldn't imagine them as flesh-and-blood humans inhabiting our dark and sinful earth.

Giotto, *St. Francis of Assisi Receiving the Stigmata (Saint François d'Assise Recevant les Stigmates),* c. 1295-1300: Francis of Assisi (c. 1181-1226), a wandering Italian monk of renowned goodness, kneels on a rocky Italian hillside, pondering the pain of Christ's torture and execution. Suddenly, he looks up, startled, to see Christ himself, with six wings, hovering above. Christ shoots lasers from his wounds to the hands, feet, and side of the empathetic monk, marking him with the stigmata. Francis' humble love of man and nature inspired artists like Giotto to portray real human beings with real emotions, living in a physical world of beauty.

• *Room 3 spills into the long Grand Gallery. Find the following paintings in the Gallery, as you make your way to the* Mona Lisa *(midway down the gallery, in the adjoining Salle 6—just follow the signs and the people).*

Italian Renaissance (1400-1600)

Andrea Mantegna, *St. Sebastian,* c. 1480: Not the patron saint of acupuncture, St. Sebastian was a Christian martyr. Notice the *contrapposto* stance (all of his weight resting on one leg) and the Greek ruins scattered around him. His executioners look like ignorant medieval brutes bewildered by this enlightened Renaissance Man. Italian artists were beginning to learn how to create human realism and earthly beauty on the canvas. Let the Renaissance begin.

Leonardo da Vinci, *The Virgin and Child with St. Anne (La Vierge à l'Enfant Jésus avec Sainte-Anne),* c. 1510: Three generations—grandmother, mother, and child—are arranged in a pyramid, with Anne's face as the peak and the lamb as the lower right corner. It's as orderly as the geometrically perfect universe created by the Renaissance god. There's a psychological kidney punch in this happy painting: Jesus, the picture of childish joy, is innocently playing with a lamb—the symbol of his inevitable sacrificial death. The Louvre has the greatest collection of Leonardos in the world—five of them. Look for the neighboring *Virgin of the Rocks* and *John the Baptist.* Leonardo was the consummate Renaissance Man; a musician, sculptor, engineer, scientist, and sometime painter, he combined knowledge from all these areas to create beauty.

Raphael, *La Belle Jardinière*, c. 1507: Raphael perfected the style Leonardo pioneered. This configuration of Madonna, Child, and John the Baptist is also a balanced pyramid with hazy grace and beauty. The interplay of gestures and gazes gives the masterpiece both intimacy and cohesiveness, while Raphael's blended brushstrokes varnish the work with an iridescent smoothness. With Raphael, the Greek ideal of beauty—reborn in the Renaissance—reached its peak.

Leonardo da Vinci, *Mona Lisa*, a.k.a. *La Joconde*, 1503-1506: Leonardo was already an old man when François I invited him to

France. Determined to pack light, he took only a few paintings with him. One was a portrait of Lisa del Giocondo, the wife of a wealthy Florentine merchant. *Mona* may disappoint you. She's smaller than you'd expect, darker, engulfed in a huge room, and hidden behind a glaring pane of glass. The famous smile attracts you first, but try as you might, you can never quite see the corners of her mouth. The overall mood is one of balance and serenity, but there's also an element of mystery. *Mona*'s smile and long-distance beauty are subtle and elusive, tempting but always just out of reach. *Mona* doesn't knock your socks off, but she winks at the patient viewer.

Paolo Veronese, *The Marriage at Cana (Les Noces de Cana)*, 1562-1563: Venetian artists like Veronese painted the good life of rich, happy-go-lucky Venetian merchants. In a spacious setting of Renaissance architecture, colorful lords and ladies, decked out in their fanciest duds, feast on a great spread of food and drink. But believe it or not, this is a religious work showing the wedding celebration in which Jesus turned water into wine. With true Renaissance optimism, Venetians pictured Christ as a party animal, someone who loved the created world as much as they did.

• *Exit behind* Mona *into the Salle Denon (Room 76). Turn right for French Neoclassicism (Salle Daru, David and Ingres); then backtrack through the Salle Denon for French Romanticism (Room 77, Géricault and Delacroix).*

French Painting (1780-1850)

Jacques-Louis David, *The Coronation of Emperor Napoleon (Sacre de l'Empereur Napoléon)*, 1806-1807: Napoleon holds aloft an imperial crown. This common-born son of immigrants is about to be crowned emperor of a "New Rome." He has just made his wife, Josephine, the empress, and she kneels at his feet. Seated behind Napoleon is the pope, who journeyed from Rome to place the imperial crown on his head. But Napoleon feels that no one is worthy of the task. At the last moment, he shrugs the pope aside...and crowns himself. The traditional setting for French coronations was the ultra-Gothic Notre-Dame cathedral. But Napoleon wanted a location that would reflect the glories of Greece and the grandeur of Rome. So, interior decorators erected stage sets of Greek columns and Roman arches to give the cathedral the architectural political correctness you see in this painting. (The *pietà* statue on the right edge of the painting is still in Notre-Dame today.)

Jean-Auguste-Dominique Ingres, *La Grande Odalisque,* 1814: Take *Venus de Milo,* turn her around, lay her down, and stick a hash pipe next to her, and you have the *Grande Odalisque.* Using clean, polished, sculptural lines, Ingres (ang-gruh) exaggerates the S-curve of a standing Greek nude. As in the *Venus de Milo,* rough folds of cloth set off her smooth skin. Ingres gave the face, too, a touch of *Venus'* idealized features, taking nature and improving on it. Ingres preserves *Venus'* backside for posterior—I mean, posterity.

Théodore Géricault, *The Raft of the Medusa (Le Radeau de la Méduse),* 1819: Clinging to a raft is a tangle of bodies and lunatics sprawled over each other. The scene writhes with agitated, ominous motion—the ripple of muscles, churning clouds, and choppy seas. The bodies rise up in a pyramid of hope, culminating in a flag wave. They signal frantically, trying to catch the attention of the tiny ship on the horizon, their last desperate hope...which did finally save them. Géricault uses rippling movement and powerful colors to catch us up in the excitement. This painting was based on the actual sinking of the ship *Medusa* off the coast of Africa in 1816. About 150 people packed onto the raft. After floating in the open seas for 12 days—suffering hardship and hunger, even resorting to cannibalism—only 15 survived.

Eugène Delacroix, *Liberty Leading the People (La Liberté Guidant le Peuple),* 1831: The year is 1830. Parisians take to the streets once again, *Les Miz*-style, to fight royalist oppressors. Leading them on through the smoke and over the dead and dying is the figure of Liberty, a strong woman waving the French flag. Does this symbol of victory look familiar? It's the *Winged Victory,* wingless and topless.

To stir our emotions, Delacroix uses only three major colors—the

red, white, and blue of the French flag. France is the symbol of modern democracy, and this painting has long stirred its citizens' passion for liberty.

This symbol of freedom is a fitting tribute to the Louvre, the first museum ever opened to the common rabble of humanity. The motto of France is *Liberté, Egalité, Fraternité*—liberty, equality, and brotherhood for all.

• *Exit the room at the far end and go downstairs, where you'll bump into...*

More Italian Renaissance
Michelangelo, *Slaves (Esclaves),* 1513-1515: These two statues by the earth's greatest sculptor are a bridge between the ancient and modern worlds. Michelangelo, like his fellow Renaissance artists, learned from the Greeks. The perfect anatomy, twisting poses, and idealized faces appear as if they could have been created 2,000 years earlier.

The *Dying Slave* twists listlessly against his T-shirt-like bonds, revealing his smooth skin. This is probably the most sensual nude that Michelangelo, the master of the male body, ever created.

The *Rebellious Slave* fights against his bondage. His shoulders rotate one way, his head and leg turn the other. He even seems to be trying to release himself from the rock he's made of. Michelangelo said that his purpose was to carve away the marble to reveal the figures God put inside. This slave shows the agony of that process and the ecstasy of the result.

• *Tour over! But, of course, there's so much more. After a break (or on a second visit), consider a stroll through a few rooms of the Richelieu wing, which contain some of the Louvre's most ancient pieces.*

Nearby: Across from the Louvre are the lovely courtyards of the stately **Palais Royal.** Although the palace is closed to the public, the courtyards are open and free (directly north of the Louvre on Rue de Rivoli). Enter through a whimsical (locals say tacky) courtyard filled with stubby, striped columns and playful fountains (with fun, reflective metal balls). Next, you'll pass into another, perfectly Parisian garden. This is where in-the-know Parisians come to take a quiet break, walk their poodles and kids, or enjoy a rendezvous—amid flowers and surrounded by a serene arcade and a handful of historic restaurants. Bring a picnic and create your own quiet break, or have a drink at one of the outdoor cafés at the courtyard's northern end. This is Paris.

Exiting the courtyard at the side facing away from the Seine brings you to the Galeries Colbert and Vivienne, attractive examples of shopping arcades from the early 1800s.

▲▲▲Orsay Museum (Musée d'Orsay)

The Musée d'Orsay (mew-zay dor-say) houses French art of the 1800s and early 1900s (specifically, 1848-1914), picking up where the Louvre's art collection leaves off. For us, that means Impressionism, the art of sun-dappled fields, bright colors, and crowded Parisian cafés. The Orsay houses the best general collection anywhere of Manet, Monet, Renoir, Degas, Van Gogh, Cézanne, and Gauguin.

Cost and Hours: €11, €8.50 Tue-Wed and Fri-Sun after 16:30 and Thu after 18:00, free on first Sun of month and often right when the ticket booth stops selling tickets (Tue-Wed and Fri-Sun at 17:00, Thu at 21:00; they won't let you in much after that), covered by Museum Pass, combo-ticket with Orangerie Museum (€16) or Rodin Museum (€18). Museum open Tue-Sun 9:30-18:00, Thu until 21:45, closed Mon, last entry one hour before closing (45 minutes before on Thu), Impressionist galleries start shutting 45 minutes before closing, cafés and a restaurant, tel. 01 40 49 48 14, www.musee-orsay.fr.

Avoiding Lines: You can skip long ticket-buying lines by using a Museum Pass or purchasing tickets in advance (available online—see the Orsay website for details); both entitle you to use a separate entrance.

You can also buy tickets and Museum Passes (no mark-up; tickets valid 3 months) at the newspaper kiosk just outside the Orsay entrance (along Rue de la Légion d'Honneur). If you're planning to get a combo-ticket with either the Orangerie or the Rodin Museum, consider starting at one of those museums instead, as they have shorter lines.

Getting There: The museum, at 1 Rue de la Légion d'Honneur, sits above the RER-C stop called Musée d'Orsay; the nearest Métro stop is Solférino, three blocks southeast of the Orsay. Bus #69 also stops at the Orsay. From the Louvre, it's a lovely 15-minute walk through the Tuileries Garden and across the pedestrian bridge to the Orsay.

Getting In: As you face the entrance, pass holders and ticket holders enter on the right (Entrance C). Ticket purchasers enter on the left (Entrance A). Security checks slow down all entrances.

Tours: **Audioguides** cost €5. English **guided tours** usually run daily at 11:30 (€6/1.5 hours, none on Sun, tours may also run at 14:30—inquire when you arrive).

🎧 Download my free Orsay Museum **audio tour.**

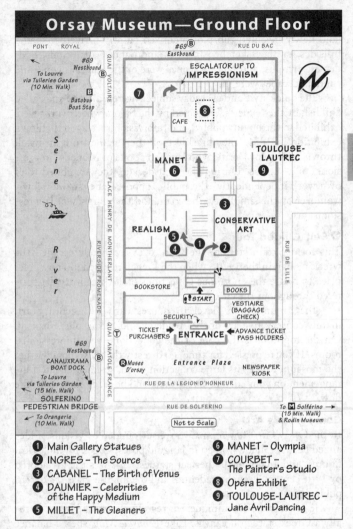

Orsay Museum—Ground Floor

PONT ROYAL

QUAI VOLTAIRE

RUE DU BAC

#69 ⓑ Eastbound

#69 ⓑ Westbound

ⓑ

To Louvre via Tuileries Garden (10 Min. Walk)

ⓑ Batobus Boat Stop

ESCALATOR UP TO IMPRESSIONISM

❼

🖋

❽

CAFE

Seine River

MANET ❻

TOULOUSE-LAUTREC ❾

PLACE HENRY DE MONTHERLANT

RIVERSIDE PROMENADE

❸

REALISM

❺
❹ ❶ ❷

CONSERVATIVE ART

RUE DE LILLE

BOOKSTORE

BOOKS

📍 START

VESTIAIRE (BAGGAGE CHECK)

SECURITY

QUAI ANATOLE FRANCE

TICKET PURCHASERS

ENTRANCE

ADVANCE TICKET PASS HOLDERS

#69 ⓑ Westbound

Ⓣ

CANAUXRAMA BOAT DOCK

Ⓡ Musée D'Orsay

Entrance Plaza

NEWSPAPER KIOSK

To Louvre via Tuileries Garden (15 Min. Walk)

RUE DE LA LEGION D'HONNEUR

SOLFERINO PEDESTRIAN BRIDGE

RUE DE SOLFERINO

To Ⓜ Solférino → (15 Min. Walk) & Rodin Museum

← To Orangerie (10 Min. Walk)

Not to Scale

PARIS

❶ Main Gallery Statues
❷ INGRES – The Source
❸ CABANEL – The Birth of Venus
❹ DAUMIER – Celebrities of the Happy Medium
❺ MILLET – The Gleaners

❻ MANET – Olympia
❼ COURBET – The Painter's Studio
❽ Opéra Exhibit
❾ TOULOUSE-LAUTREC – Jane Avril Dancing

Background

The Impressionist painters rejected camera-like detail for a quick

style more suited to capturing the passing moment. Feeling stifled by the rigid rules and stuffy atmosphere of the Academy (the state-funded art school), the Impressionists took as their motto, "Out of the studio, into the open air." They grabbed their berets and scarves and went on excursions to the country, where they set up their easels (and newly invented tubes of premixed paint) on riverbanks and hillsides, or they sketched in cafés and dance halls. Gods, goddesses, nymphs, and fantasy scenes were out; common people and rural landscapes were in.

The quick style and everyday subjects were ridiculed and called childish by the "experts." Rejected by the Salon (where works were exhibited to the buying public), the Impressionists staged their own exhibition in 1874. They brashly took their name from an insult thrown at them by a critic who laughed at one of Monet's "impressions" of a sunrise. During the next decade, they exhibited their own work independently. The public, opposed at first, was slowly won over by the simplicity, the color, and the vibrancy of Impressionist art.

❍ Self-Guided Tour

This former train station, the Gare d'Orsay, barely escaped the wrecking ball in the 1970s, when the French realized it'd be a great place to house the enormous collections of 19th-century art scattered throughout the city.

The ground floor (level 0) houses early-19th-century art, mainly conservative art of the Academy and Salon, plus Realism. On the top floor is the core of the collection—the Impressionist rooms. If you're pressed for time, go directly there. Remember that the museum rotates its large collection often, so find the latest arrangement on your current Orsay map, and be ready to go with the flow.

Conservative Art

In the Orsay's first few rooms, you're surrounded by visions of idealized beauty—nude women in languid poses, Greek mythological figures, and anatomically perfect statues. This was the art adored by 19th-century French academics and the middle-class (*bourgeois*) public.

Jean-Auguste-Dominique **Ingres'** *The Source* (1856) is virtually a Greek statue on canvas. Like *Venus de Milo,* she's a balance of opposite motions. Alexandre **Cabanel** lays Ingres' *Source* on her back. His *Birth of Venus* (1863) is a perfect fantasy, an orgasm of beauty.

Realism

The French Realists rejected idealized classicism and began painting what they saw in the world around them. For Honoré **Daumier,** that meant looking at the stuffy bourgeois establishment that controlled the Academy and the Salon. In the 36 bustlets of *Celebrities of the Happy Medium* (1835), Daumier, trained as a political cartoonist, exaggerates each subject's most distinct characteristic to capture with vicious precision the pomposity and self-righteousness of these self-appointed arbiters of taste.

Jean-François **Millet's** *The Gleaners* (1867) shows us three gleaners, the poor women who pick up the meager leftovers after  a field has already been harvested for the wealthy. Here he captures the innate dignity of these stocky, tanned women who bend their backs quietly in a large field for their small reward. This is "Realism" in two senses. It's painted "realistically," not prettified. And it's the "real" world—not the fantasy world of Greek myth, but the harsh life of the working poor.

For a Realist's take on the traditional Venus, find Edouard **Manet's** *Olympia* (1863). Compare this uncompromising nude with Cabanel's idealized, pastel, Vaseline-on-the-lens beauty in the *Birth of Venus*. In *Olympia,* the sharp outlines and harsh, contrasting colors are new and shocking. Manet replaced soft-core porn with hard-core art.

Gustave **Courbet's** painting *The Painter's Studio* (1855) takes us backstage, showing us the gritty reality behind the creation of pretty pictures. We see Courbet himself in his studio, working diligently on a Realistic landscape, oblivious to the confusion around him. Milling around are ordinary citizens, not Greek heroes.

Toulouse-Lautrec Detour

The Henri **Toulouse-Lautrec** paintings tucked away on the ground floor (Room 10) rightly belong with the Post-Impressionist works on level 2, but since you're already here, enjoy his paintings incarnating the artist's love of nightlife and show business. Every night, Toulouse-Lautrec put on his bowler hat and visited the Moulin Rouge to draw the crowds, the can-can dancers, and the backstage action. He worked quickly, creating sketches in paint that serve as snapshots of a golden era. In *Jane Avril Dancing* (1891), he depicts the slim, graceful, elegant, and melancholy dancer, who stood out above the rabble. Her legs keep dancing while her mind is far away.

Impressionism

The Impressionist collection is scattered randomly through Rooms 29-36 on the top floor.

In Edouard **Manet's** *Luncheon on the Grass* (*Le Déjeuner sur l'Herbe,* 1863) you can see that a new revolutionary movement was starting to bud—Impressionism. Notice the background: the messy brushwork of trees and leaves, the play of light on the pond, and the light that filters through the trees onto the woman who stoops in the haze. Also note the strong contrast of colors (white skin, black clothes, green grass). Let the Impressionist revolution begin!

Edgar **Degas** blends classical lines and Realist subjects with Impressionist color, spontaneity, and everyday scenes from urban Paris. He loved the unposed "snapshot" effect, catching his models off guard. Dance students, women at work, and café scenes are approached from odd angles that aren't always ideal but make the scenes seem more real. He gives us the backstage view of life. For instance, a dance rehearsal let Degas capture a behind-the-scenes look at bored, tired, restless dancers (*The Dance Class, La Classe de Danse*, c. 1873-1875). In the painting *In a Café* (*Dans un Café*, 1875-1876), a weary lady of the evening meets morning with a last, lonely, nail-in-the-coffin drink in the glaring light of a four-in-the-morning café.

Next up is Claude **Monet** (mo-nay), the father of Impressionism. In the 1860s, Monet (along with Renoir) began painting landscapes in the open air. He studied optics and pigments to know just the right colors he needed to reproduce the shimmering quality of reflected light. The key was to work quickly—at that "golden hour" (to use a modern photographer's term), when the light was just right. Then he'd create a fleeting "impression" of the scene. In fact, that was the title of one of Monet's canvases (now hanging in the Marmottan—see page 86); it gave the movement its name.

One of Monet's favorite places to paint was the garden he landscaped at his home in Giverny, west of Paris (and worth a visit, provided you like Monet more than you hate crowds—see the next chapter). The Japanese bridge and the water lilies floating in the pond were his two favorite subjects. As Monet aged and his eyesight failed, he made bigger canvases of smaller subjects. The final water lilies are monumental smudges of thick paint surrounded by paint-splotched clouds that are reflected on the surface of the pond.

Pierre-Auguste **Renoir** (ren-wah) started out as a painter of landscapes, along with Monet, but later veered from the Impressionist's philosophy and painted images that were unabashedly "pretty."

His best-known work is *Dance at the Moulin de la Galette* (*Bal du Moulin de la Galette*, 1876). On Sunday afternoons, working-class folk would dress up and head for the fields on Butte Montmartre (near Sacré-Cœur Basilica) to dance, drink, and eat little crêpes (galettes) till dark. Renoir liked to go there to paint the common Parisians living and loving in the afternoon sun. The sunlight filtering through the trees creates a kaleidoscope of colors, like the 19th-century

equivalent of a mirror ball throwing darts of light onto the dancers. Like a photographer who uses a slow shutter speed to show motion, Renoir paints a waltzing blur.

Post-Impressionism

Post-Impressionism—the style that employs Impressionism's bright colors while branching out in new directions—is scattered all around the museum. You'll get a taste of the style with Paul Cézanne on the top floor, with much more on level 2.

Paul **Cézanne** brought Impressionism into the 20th century. After the color of Monet, the warmth of Renoir, and the passion of Van Gogh, Cézanne's rather impersonal canvases can be difficult to appreciate (see *The Card Players, Les Joueurs de Cartes*, 1890-1895). Where the Impressionists built a figure out of a mosaic of individual brushstrokes, Cézanne used blocks of paint to create a more solid, geometrical shape. These chunks are like little "cubes." It's no coincidence that his experiments in reducing forms to their geometric basics inspired the...Cubists. Because of his style (not the content), he is often called the first modern painter.

Like Michelangelo, Beethoven, and a select handful of others, Vincent **van Gogh** put so much of himself into his work that art and life became one. In the Orsay's collection of paintings (level 2), you'll see both Van Gogh's painting style and his life unfold.

Encouraged by his art-dealer brother, Van Gogh moved to Paris. He met Monet, drank with Gauguin and Toulouse-Lautrec, and soaked up the Impressionist style. (For example, see how he might build a bristling brown beard using thick strokes of red, yellow, and green side by side.)

But the social life of Paris became too much for the solitary Van Gogh, and he moved to the south of France. At first, in the glow of the bright spring sunshine, he had a period of incredible creativity and happiness. But being alone in a strange country began to wear on him. A painting of his rented bedroom in Arles shows a cramped, bare-bones place (*Van Gogh's Room at Arles, La Chambre de Van Gogh à Arles*, 1889). He invited his friend Gauguin to join him, but after two months together arguing passionately about art, nerves got raw. Van Gogh threatened Gauguin with a razor, which drove his friend back to Paris. In crazed despair, Van Gogh cut off a piece of his own ear.

Vincent sought help at a mental hospital. The paintings he

finished in the peace of the hospital are more meditative—there are fewer bright landscapes and more closed-in scenes with deeper, almost surreal colors.

His final self-portrait shows a man engulfed in a confused background of brushstrokes that swirl and rave (*Self-Portrait, Portrait de l'Artiste*, 1889). But in the midst of this rippling sea of mystery floats a still, detached island of a face. Perhaps his troubled eyes know that in only a few months, he'll take a pistol and put a bullet through his chest.

Nearby are the paintings of Paul **Gauguin,** who got the travel bug early and grew up wanting to be a sailor. Instead, he became a stockbroker. At the age of 35, he got fed up with it all, quit his job, abandoned his wife (her stern portrait bust may be nearby) and family, and took refuge in his art.

Gauguin traveled to the South Seas in search of the exotic, finally settling on Tahiti. There he found his Garden of Eden.

Gauguin's best-known works capture an idyllic Tahitian landscape peopled by exotic women engaged in simple tasks and making music (*Arearea*, 1892). The native girls lounge placidly in unselfconscious innocence. The style is intentionally "primitive," collapsing the three-dimensional landscape into a two-dimensional pattern of bright colors. Gauguin intended that this simple style carry a deep undercurrent of symbolic meaning. He wanted to communicate to his "civilized" colleagues back home that he'd found the paradise he'd always envisioned.

French Sculpture

The open-air mezzanine of level 2 is lined with statues. Stroll the mezzanine, enjoying the work of great French sculptors, including Auguste **Rodin.**

Born of working-class roots and largely self-taught, Rodin combined classical solidity with Impressionist surfaces to become one of the greatest sculptors since the Renaissance.

Like his statue *The Walking Man* (*L'Homme Qui Marche*, c. 1900), Rodin had one foot in the past, while the other stepped into the future. This muscular, forcefully striding man could be a symbol of Renaissance Man with his classical power. With no mouth or hands, he speaks with his body. But get close and look at the statue's surface. This rough, "unfinished" look reflects light in the same way the rough Impressionist brushwork does, making the statue come alive, never quite at rest in the viewer's eye. Rodin created this statue in a flash of inspiration. He took two unfinished statues—torso and legs—and plunked them together at the waist. You can still see the seam.

Rodin's sculptures capture the groundbreaking spirit of much of the art in the Orsay Museum. With a stable base of 19th-century stone, he launched art into the 20th century.

▲▲Orangerie Museum (Musée de l'Orangerie)

Located in the Tuileries Garden and drenched by natural light from skylights, the Orangerie (oh-rahn-zhuh-ree) is the closest

PARIS

you'll ever come to stepping right into an Impressionist painting. Start with the museum's claim to fame: Monet's *Water Lilies*. Then head downstairs to enjoy the manageable collection of select works by

Utrillo, Cézanne, Renoir, Matisse, and Picasso.

Cost and Hours: €9, €6.50 after 17:00, free for those under age 18, €16 combo-ticket with Orsay Museum, covered by Museum Pass; Wed-Mon 9:00-18:00, closed Tue; audioguide-€5, English guided tours usually Mon and Thu at 14:30 and Sat at 11:00, located in Tuileries Garden near Place de la Concorde (Mo: Concorde or scenic bus #24), 15-minute stroll from the Orsay, tel. 01 44 77 80 07, www.musee-orangerie.fr.

Visiting the Museum: Like Beethoven going deaf, a nearly blind Claude Monet (1840-1926) wrote his final symphonies on a monumental scale. Even as he struggled with cataracts, he planned a series of huge six-foot-tall canvases of water lilies to hang in special rooms at the Orangerie.

These eight mammoth, curved panels immerse you in Monet's garden. We're looking at the pond in his garden at Giverny—dotted with water lilies, surrounded by foliage, and dappled by the reflections of the sky, clouds, and trees on the surface. But the true subject of these works is the play of reflected light off the surface of the pond.

Working at his home in Giverny, Monet built a special studio with skylights and wheeled easels to accommodate the canvases. For 12 years (1914-1926), Monet worked on these paintings obsessively. Monet completed all the planned canvases, but he didn't live to see them installed here. In 1927, the year after his death, these rooms were completed and the canvases put in place. Some call this the first "art installation"—art displayed in a space specially designed for it in order to enhance the viewer's experience.

In the underground gallery are select works from the personal collection of Paris' trend-spotting art dealer of the 1920s, Paul

Guillaume. The museum is small enough to enjoy in a short visit, but complete enough to show the bridge from Impressionism to Modernism. And it's all beautiful.

EIFFEL TOWER AND NEARBY
▲▲▲Eiffel Tower (La Tour Eiffel)

Built on the 100th anniversary of the French Revolution (and in the spirit of the Industrial Revolution), the tower was the center-piece of a World Expo designed simply to show off what people could build in 1889. For decades it was the tallest structure the world had ever known, and though it's since been eclipsed, it's still the most visited monument. Ride the elevators to the top of its 1,063 feet for expansive views that stretch 40 miles. Then descend to the two lower levels, where the views are arguably even better, since the monuments are more recognizable.

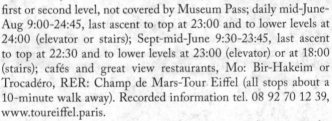

Cost and Hours: €17 to ride all the way to the top, €11.50 for just the two lower levels, €5 to climb the stairs to the first or second level, not covered by Museum Pass; daily mid-June-Aug 9:00-24:45, last ascent to top at 23:00 and to lower levels at 24:00 (elevator or stairs); Sept-mid-June 9:30-23:45, last ascent to top at 22:30 and to lower levels at 23:00 (elevator) or at 18:00 (stairs); cafés and great view restaurants, Mo: Bir-Hakeim or Trocadéro, RER: Champ de Mars-Tour Eiffel (all stops about a 10-minute walk away). Recorded information tel. 08 92 70 12 39, www.toureiffel.paris.

Reservations: Since long waits are common, it's wise to make a reservation well in advance of your visit. At www.toureiffel.paris, you can book a time slot to begin your ascent; this allows you to skip the long initial entry line.

Time slots fill up months in advance (especially from April through September). Online ticket sales open up about three months before any given date (at 8:30 Paris time)—and can sell out for that day within hours. Be sure of your date, as reservations are nonrefundable. When you "Choose a ticket," make sure you select "Lift entrance ticket with access to the summit" to go all the way to the top. You must create an account, with your 10-digit mobile phone number as your log-in. After paying with a credit card, print your tickets. Alternatively, you can have the ticket text-messaged to your mobile phone—click on a link to download and save the ticket bar code to be scanned when you enter. Note that email or

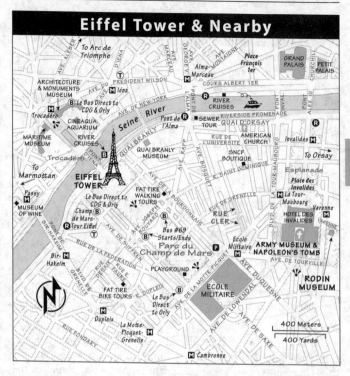

Eiffel Tower & Nearby

text confirmation notices will not get you in; you must have a ticket showing the bar code (print-out or phone version).

If no reservation slots are available, try buying a "Lift entrance ticket with access to 2nd floor" only—you can upgrade once inside. Or, try the website again about a week before your visit—last-minute spots occasionally open up.

Other Tips for Avoiding Lines: If you don't have a reservation, get in line 30 minutes before the tower opens. Going later is the next-best bet (after 19:00 May-Aug, after 17:00 off-season, after 16:00 in winter as it gets dark by 17:00).

You can bypass some (but not all) lines if you have a reservation at either of the tower's view restaurants (Le Jules Verne or 58 Tour Eiffel). Or you can buy a reservation time (almost right up to the last minute) for €40 (or a €59 guided tour) through Fat Tire Tours (see page 40).

When to Go: For the best of all worlds, arrive with enough light to see the views, then stay as it gets dark to see the lights. The views are grand whether you ascend or not. At the top of the hour, a five-minute display features thousands of sparkling lights (best viewed from Place du Trocadéro or the grassy park below).

Getting In: You may encounter a security checkpoint at the base of the tower. Those with reservations may have a special entry. If you have a reservation, arrive at the tower 10 minutes before your entry time and look for either of the two entrances marked *Visiteurs avec Reservation* (Visitors with Reservation), where attendants scan your ticket and put you on the first available elevator. If you don't have a reservation, follow signs for *Individuels* or *Visiteurs sans Tickets* (avoid lines selling tickets only for *Groupes*). The stairs entrance (usually a shorter line) is at the south pillar (next to Le Jules Verne restaurant entrance). When you buy tickets on-site, all members of your party must be with you. To get reduced fares for kids, bring ID.

PARIS

Pickpockets: Beware. Street thieves plunder awestruck visitors gawking below the tower. And tourists in crowded elevators are like fish in a barrel for predatory pickpockets. *En garde*. A police station is at the Jules Verne pillar.

Security Check: Bags larger than 19" × 8" × 12" are not allowed, but there is no baggage check. All bags are subject to a security search. No knives, glass bottles, or cans are permitted.

Services: Free WCs are at the base of the tower, behind the east pillar. Inside the tower itself, WCs are on all levels.

Background

The first visitor to the Paris World's Fair in 1889 walked beneath the "arch" formed by the newly built Eiffel Tower and entered the fairgrounds. This event celebrated both the centennial of the French Revolution and France's position as a global superpower. Bridge builder Gustave Eiffel (1832-1923) won the contest to build the fair's centerpiece by beating out rival proposals such as a giant guillotine.

The tower was nothing but a showpiece, with no functional purpose except to demonstrate to the world that France had the wealth, knowledge, and can-do spirit to erect a structure far taller than anything the world had ever seen. The original plan was to dismantle the tower as quickly as it was built after the celebration ended, but it was kept by popular demand.

The tower, including its antenna, stands 1,063 feet tall, or slightly higher than the 77-story Chrysler Building in New York. Its four support pillars straddle an area of 3.5 acres. Despite the tower's 7,300 tons of metal and 60 tons of paint, it is so well-engineered that it weighs no more per square inch at its base than a linebacker on tiptoes.

Visiting the Tower

There are three observation platforms, at roughly 200, 400, and 900 feet. If you want to see the entire tower, from top to bottom, then see it...from top to bottom.

There isn't a single elevator straight to the top *(le sommet)*. To get there, you'll first ride an elevator to the second level. (For the hardy, there are 360 stairs to the first level and another 360 to the second.) Once on the second level, immediately line up for the next elevator, to the top. Enjoy the views, then ride back down to the second level. When you're ready, head to the first level via the stairs (no line and can take as little as five minutes) or take the elevator down (ask if it will stop on the first level—some don't). Explore the shops and exhibits on the first level and have a snack. To leave, you can line up for the elevator, but it's quickest and most memorable to take the stairs back down to earth.

Top Level: You'll find wind and grand, sweeping views on the tiny top level. The city lies before you (pick out sights with the help of the panoramic maps). On a good day, you can see for 40 miles. Feeling proud you made it this high? You can celebrate your accomplishment with a glass of champagne from the bar.

Second Level: This level has the best views because you're closer to the sights, and the monuments are more recognizable. The second level has souvenir shops, WCs, and a small stand-up café. The world-class Le Jules Verne restaurant is on this level, but you won't see it; access is by a private elevator.

First Level: After a $38 million renovation, this level is decked out with new shops, eateries, and displays. Pop-up restaurants and kiosks appear with every season—even a little playground for kids. In winter, part of the first level is often set up to host an ice-skating rink. The highlight is the breathtaking, vertigo-inducing, selfie-inspiring glass floor. Venture onto it and experience what it's like to stand atop an 18-story building and look straight down.

Back on the Ground: For a final look, stroll across the river to Place du Trocadéro or to the end of the Champ de Mars and look back for great views. However impressive it may be by day, the tower is an awesome thing to see at twilight, when it becomes engorged with light, and virile Paris lies back and lets night be on top. When darkness fully envelops the city, the tower seems to climax with a spectacular light show at the top of each hour...for five minutes.

Nearby, you can catch the Bateaux Parisiens boat for a Seine cruise (see page 38) or hop on bus #69 for a tour of the city (see page 33). The Trocadéro viewpoint, which looks "right there," is a 20-minute walk away. Also nearby are the Rue Cler area (page 84), Army Museum and Napoleon's Tomb (page 85), and Rodin Museum (page 86).

Near the Eiffel Tower
▲Paris Sewer Tour (Les Egouts de Paris)
Discover what happens after you flush. This quick, interesting, and slightly stinky visit (a perfumed hanky helps) takes you along a few

hundred yards of water tunnels in the world's first underground sewer system.

Cost and Hours: €4.40, covered by Museum Pass, Sat-Wed 11:00-17:00, Oct-April until 16:00, closed Thu-Fri year-round, located where Pont de l'Alma greets the Left Bank—on the right side of the bridge as you face the river, Mo: Alma-Marceau, RER: Pont de l'Alma, tel. 01 53 68 27 81.

Visiting the Sewer: Pick up the helpful English self-guided tour, then drop down into Jean Valjean's world of tunnels, rats, and manhole covers. (Victor Hugo was friends with the sewer inspector when he wrote *Les Misérables*.) You'll pass well-organized displays with extensive English information explaining the history of water distribution and collection in Paris, from Roman times to the present.

The evolution of this amazing network of sewers is fascinating. More than 1,500 miles of tunnels carry 317 million gallons of water daily through this underworld. It's the world's longest sewer system—so long, they say, that if it were laid out straight, it would stretch from Paris all the way to Istanbul.

▲Riverside Promenade (Les Berges du Seine)

This one-time busy expressway-turned-riverfront-park runs along the Left Bank of the Seine from the Pont de l'Alma (near the Eiffel Tower) to the Orsay Museum, allowing walkers to experience the Seine at water level. Distractions abound, with loads of kid-friendly activities, gardens, lively cafés, sling chairs, *créperies*, and more. It's part of Paris' grand 21st-century plan to rid the city center of cars and create pedestrian-friendly areas. It's hugely popular in good weather, and a fun place to rub shoulders with Parisians.

▲▲Rue Cler

Paris is changing quickly, but a stroll down this market street introduces you to a thriving, traditional Parisian neighborhood and

offers insights into the local culture. Although this is a wealthy district, Rue Cler retains the workaday charm still found in most neighborhoods throughout Paris. The shops lining the street are filled with the freshest produce, the stinkiest cheese, the tastiest chocolate, and the finest wines (markets generally open Tue-Sat 8:30-13:00 & 15:00-19:30, Sun 8:30-12:00, dead on Mon). I'm still far from a gourmet eater, but my time spent tasting my way along Rue Cler has substantially bumped up my appreciation of good cuisine (as well as the French knack for good living).

▲▲Army Museum and Napoleon's Tomb (Musée de l'Armée)

Napoleon's tomb rests beneath the golden dome of Les Invalides church. In addition to the tomb, the complex of Les Invalides—a

former veterans' hospital built by Louis XIV—has various military collections, collectively called the Army Museum, Europe's greatest military museum. Visiting the different sections, you can watch the art of war unfold from stone axes to Axis powers.

PARIS

Cost and Hours: €11, €9 after 17:00 (16:00 in Nov-March), free for military personnel in uniform, free for kids but they must wait in line for ticket, covered by Museum Pass, special exhibits are extra; open daily 10:00-18:00, Nov-March until 17:00; tomb also open July-Aug until 19:00 and April-Sept Tue until 21:00; museum (except for tomb) closed first Mon of month Oct-June; Charles de Gaulle exhibit closed Mon year-round; videoguide-€6, cafeteria, tel. 08 10 11 33 99, www.musee-armee.fr.

Getting There: The Hôtel des Invalides is at 129 Rue de Grenelle, a 10-minute walk from Rue Cler (Mo: La Tour Maubourg, Varenne, or Invalides). You can also take bus #69 (from the Marais and Rue Cler), bus #87 (from Rue Cler and Luxembourg Garden area), or bus #63 from the St. Germain-des-Prés area.

Visiting the Museum: At the center of the complex, Napoleon Bonaparte lies majestically dead inside several coffins under a grand dome—a goose-bumping pilgrimage for historians. The dome overhead glitters with 26 pounds of thinly pounded gold leaf.

Your visit continues through an impressive range of museums filled with medieval armor, cannons and muskets, Louis XIV-era uniforms and weapons, and Napoleon's horse—stuffed and mounted.

The best section is dedicated to the two World Wars. Walk chronologically through displays on the trench warfare of WWI, the victory parades, France's horrendous losses, and the humiliating Treaty of Versailles that led to WWII.

The WWII rooms use black-and-white photos, maps, videos, and a few artifacts to trace Hitler's rise, the Blitzkrieg that overran France, America's entry into the war, D-Day, the concentration camps, the atomic bomb, the war in the Pacific, and the eventual Allied victory. There's special insight into France's role (the French

Resistance), and how it was Charles de Gaulle who actually won the war.

▲▲Rodin Museum (Musée Rodin)

This recently renovated, user-friendly museum is filled with passionate works by the greatest sculptor since Michelangelo. You'll see *The Kiss, The Thinker, The Gates of Hell,* and many more.

Cost and Hours: €10, free for those under age 18, free on first Sun of the month Oct-March, €4 for just the garden (with several important works on display), €18 combo-ticket with Orsay Museum, both museum and garden covered by Museum Pass; Tue-Sun 10:00-17:45, Wed until 20:45, closed Mon; gardens close at 18:00, Oct-March at 17:00; audioguide-€6, mandatory baggage check, self-service café in garden, 77 Rue de Varenne, Mo: Varenne, tel. 01 44 18 61 10, www.musee-rodin.fr.

Auguste Rodin (1840-1917) was a modern Michelangelo, sculpting human figures on an epic scale, revealing through their bodies his deepest thoughts and feelings. Like many of Michelangelo's unfinished works, Rodin's statues rise from the raw stone around them, driven by the life force. With missing limbs and scarred skin, these are prefab classics, making ugliness noble. Rodin's people are always moving restlessly. Even the famous *Thinker* is moving; while he's plopped down solidly, his mind is a million miles away.

Well-displayed in the mansion where the sculptor lived and worked, exhibits trace Rodin's artistic development, explain how his bronze statues were cast, and show some of the studies he created to work up to his masterpiece, the unfinished *Gates of Hell*. Learn about Rodin's tumultuous relationship with his apprentice and lover, Camille Claudel. Mull over what makes his sculptures some of the most evocative since the Renaissance. And stroll the beautiful gardens, packed with many of his greatest works (including *The Thinker, Balzac,* the *Burghers of Calais,* and the *Gates of Hell*) and ideal for artistic reflection.

▲▲Marmottan Museum (Musée Marmottan Monet)

In this private, intimate, and untouristy museum, you'll find the best collection anywhere of works by Impressionist headliner Claude Monet. Follow Monet's life through more than a hundred works, from simple sketches to the *Impression: Sunrise* painting that gave his artistic movement its start—and a name. The museum also displays some of the enjoyable large-scale canvases featuring the water lilies from his garden at Giverny.

Cost and Hours: €11, not covered by Museum Pass, €18.50 combo-ticket with Monet's garden and house at Giverny (lets you skip the line at Giverny); Tue-Sun 10:00-18:00, Thu until 21:00, closed Mon; audioguide-€3, 2 Rue Louis-Boilly, Mo: La Muette, tel. 01 44 96 50 33, www.marmottan.fr.

Visiting the Museum: Paul Marmottan (1856-1932) lived here amid his collection of exquisite 19th-century furniture and paintings. He donated his home and possessions to a private trust (which is why your Museum Pass isn't valid here). After Marmottan's death, the more daring art of Monet and others was added.

The Marmottan mansion has three pleasant, manageable floors, all worth perusing. The ground floor has several rooms of Paul Marmottan's period furnishings and paintings. Upstairs is the permanent collection, featuring illuminated manuscripts and works by Monet's fellow Impressionists—Edgar Degas, Camille Pissarro, Paul Gauguin, Pierre-Auguste Renoir, and especially Berthe Morisot.

Monet's works—the core of the collection—are in the basement. In this one long room, you'll find some 50 paintings by Monet spanning his lifetime. They're generally (and very roughly) arranged in chronological order—from Monet's youthful discovery of Impressionism, to his mature "series" paintings, to his last great water lilies from Giverny.

LEFT BANK

Opposite Notre-Dame, on the left bank of the Seine, is the Latin Quarter. (For more information on this neighborhood, see my Historic Paris Walk, earlier).

▲▲Cluny Museum (Musée National du Moyen Age)

The Cluny is a treasure trove of Middle Ages (Moyen Age) art. Located on the side of a Roman bathhouse, it offers close-up looks at stained glass, Notre-Dame carvings, fine goldsmithing and jewelry, and rooms of tapestries. The highlights are several original stained-glass windows from Sainte-Chapelle and the exquisite series of six Lady and the Unicorn tapestries: A delicate, as-medieval-as-can-be

PARIS

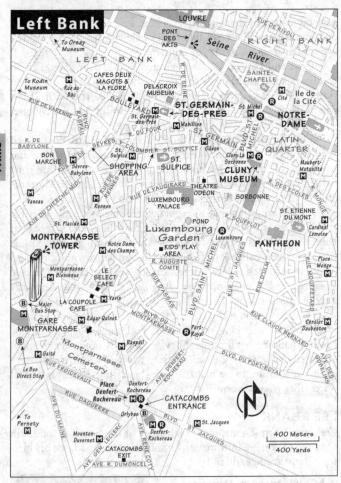

noble lady introduces a delighted unicorn to the senses of taste, hearing, sight, smell, and touch.

Cost and Hours: €8, includes audioguide, free on first Sun of month, covered by Museum Pass (though pass holders pay €1 for audioguide); Wed-Mon 9:15-17:45, closed Tue; near corner of Boulevards St. Michel and St. Germain at 6 Place Paul Painlevé; Mo: Cluny-La Sorbonne, St. Michel, or Odéon; tel. 01 53 73 78 16, www.musee-moyenage.fr.

▲St. Sulpice Church

For pipe-organ enthusiasts, a visit here is one of Europe's great musical treats. The Grand Orgue at St. Sulpice Church has a rich history, with a succession of 12 world-class organists—including

Charles-Marie Widor and Marcel Dupré—that goes back 300 years.

Patterned after St. Paul's Cathedral in London, the church has a Neoclassical arcaded facade and two round towers. Inside, in the first chapel on the right, are three murals of fighting angels by Delacroix: *Jacob Wrestling the Angel, Heliodorus Chased from the Temple,* and *The Archangel Michael* (on the ceiling). The fourth chapel on the right has a statue of Joan of Arc and wall plaques listing hundreds from St. Sulpice's congregation who died during World War I. The north transept wall features an Egyptian-style obelisk used as a gnomon on a sundial. The last chapel before the exit has a display on the Shroud of Turin.

Cost and Hours: Free, daily 7:30-19:30, Mo: St. Sulpice or Mabillon. See www.stsulpice.com for special concerts.

Sunday Organ Recitals: You can hear the organ played at Sunday Mass (10:30-11:30, come appropriately dressed) followed by a high-powered 25-minute recital, usually performed by talented organist Daniel Roth.

▲Luxembourg Garden (Jardin du Luxembourg)

This lovely 60-acre garden is an Impressionist painting brought to life. Slip into a green chair pondside, enjoy the radiant flower beds,

go jogging, play tennis or basketball, sail a toy sailboat, or take in a chess game or puppet show. Some of the park's prettiest (and quietest) sections lie around its perimeter.

Cost and Hours: Free, daily dawn until dusk, Mo: Odéon, RER: Luxembourg.

Other Parks: If you enjoy Luxembourg Garden and want to see more green spaces, you could visit the more elegant **Parc Monceau** (Mo: Monceau), the colorful **Jardin des Plantes** (Mo: Jussieu or Gare d'Austerlitz, RER: Gare d'Austerlitz), or the hilly and bigger **Parc des Buttes-Chaumont** (Mo: Buttes-Chaumont).

▲Panthéon

This state-capitol-style Neoclassical monument celebrates France's illustrious history and people, balances a Foucault pendulum, and is the final home of many French VIPs.

Cost and Hours: €8.50, free for those under age 18, covered by Museum Pass, €2

for dome climb (not covered by Museum Pass); daily 10:00-18:30, Oct-March until 18:00, last entry 45 minutes before closing; audioguide-€5, Mo: Cardinal Lemoine, tel. 01 44 32 18 00, http://pantheon.monuments-nationaux.fr.

Dome Climb: From the main floor, you can climb 206 steps to the colonnade at the base of the dome for views of the interior and a 360-degree view of the city. You're not so much high above Paris—it feels like you're in the middle of it. To visit, join the queue at the meeting spot near the nave. An escort takes groups of about 50 at a time. Visits leave about every hour until 17:30 (or earlier—confirm the schedule as you go in) and take 40 minutes.

Visiting the Panthéon: Stand in the nave, and take in the vast, evenly lit space—360 feet long, 280 feet wide, and 270 feet high. Monuments trace the celebrated struggles of the French people: a beheaded St. Denis (painting on left wall of nave), St. Geneviève saving the fledgling city from Attila the Hun, and scenes of Joan of Arc (left transept). A Foucault pendulum swings gracefully at the end of a cable suspended from the towering dome. It was here in 1851 that the scientist Léon Foucault first demonstrated the rotation of the earth.

A staircase behind the monument leads down to the crypt, where a panoply of greats is buried. Rousseau is along the right wall as you enter, while Voltaire faces him impishly from across the hall. From the small central rotunda, straight ahead are more greats: Victor Hugo *(Les Misérables, The Hunchback of Notre-Dame)*, Alexandre Dumas *(The Three Musketeers, The Count of Monte Cristo)*, and Louis Braille, who invented the script for the blind. To the right of the central rotunda you'll find scientist Marie Curie (follow the glow), and various WWII dead, from Holocaust victims to the hero of the resistance, Jean Moulin.

Montparnasse Tower

This sadly out-of-place 59-story superscraper has one virtue: If you can't make it up the Eiffel Tower, the sensational views from this tower are cheaper, far easier to access, and make for a fair consolation prize. Come early in the day for clearest skies and shortest lines, and be treated to views from a comfortable interior and from up on the rooftop (consider their €5 breakfast with a view). Sunset is great but views are disappointing after dark. Some say it's the very best view in Paris, as you can see the Eiffel Tower clearly...and you can't see the Montparnasse Tower at all.

Cost and Hours: €16, 30 percent discount with this book, not covered by Museum Pass; daily 9:30-23:30, Oct-March until 22:30;

entrance on Rue de l'Arrivée, Mo: Montparnasse-Bienvenüe—
from the Métro, stay inside the station and follow sparse Tour signs
to exit #4; tel. 01 45 38 52 56, www.tourmontparnasse56.com.

▲Catacombs

Descend 60 feet below the street and walk a one-mile (one-hour)
route through tunnels containing the anonymous bones of six million permanent Parisians.

In 1786, health-conscious Parisians looking to relieve congestion and improve the city's sanitary conditions emptied the church
cemeteries and moved the bones here, to former limestone quarries. For decades, priests led ceremonial processions of black-veiled,
bone-laden carts into the quarries, where the bones were stacked in
piles five feet high and as much as 80 feet deep. Descend 130 steps
and ponder the sign announcing, "Halt, this is the empire of the
dead." Shuffle through passageways of skull-studded tibiae, admire
300-year-old sculptures cut into the walls of the catacombs, and
see more cheery signs: "Happy is he who is forever faced with the
hour of his death and prepares himself for the end every day." Then
climb 86 steps to emerge far from where you entered, with white-
limestone-covered toes, telling everyone you've been underground
gawking at bones. Note to wannabe Hamlets: An attendant checks
your bag at the exit for stolen souvenirs.

Cost and Hours: €12, not covered by Museum Pass, Tue-
Sun 10:00-20:30, closed Mon; lines can be long between 10:00
and 16:00; arrive by 9:30 to minimize the wait; ticket booth closes
at 19:30, come no later than 19:00 or risk not getting in; audio-
guide-€5, tel. 01 43 22 47 63, www.catacombes.paris.fr.

Getting There: 1 Place Denfert-Rochereau. Take the Métro
to Denfert-Rochereau, then find the lion in the big traffic circle;
if he looked left rather than right, he'd stare right at the green entrance to the Catacombs.

After Your Visit: You'll likely exit at 36 Rue Rémy Dumoncel,
far from where you started (though this may change in 2017). Turn
right out of the exit and walk to Avenue du Général Leclerc, where
you'll be equidistant from Métro stops Alésia (walk left) and Mouton Duvernet (walk right). Traffic-free Rue Daguerre, a pleasing
pedestrian street, is four blocks to the right on Avenue du Général
Leclerc (a block from where you entered the Catacombs).

CHAMPS-ELYSEES AND NEARBY
▲▲▲Champs-Elysées

This famous boulevard is Paris' backbone, with its greatest con-
centration of traffic. From the Arc de Triomphe down Avenue des
Champs-Elysées, all of France seems to converge on Place de la
Concorde, the city's largest square. And though the Champs-Ely-

sées has become as international as it is Parisian, a walk down the two-mile boulevard is still a must.

In 1667, Louis XIV opened the first section of the street, and it soon became the place to cruise in your carriage. (It still is today.) By the 1920s, this boulevard was pure elegance—fancy residences, rich hotels, and cafés. Today it's home to big business, celebrity cafés, glitzy nightclubs, high-fashion shopping, and international people-watching. People gather here to celebrate Bastille Day (July 14), World Cup triumphs, and the finale of the Tour de France.

● **Self-Guided Walk:** Start at the Arc de Triomphe (Mo: Charles de Gaulle-Etoile; if you're planning to tour the Arc, do it before starting this walk) and head downhill on the left-hand side.

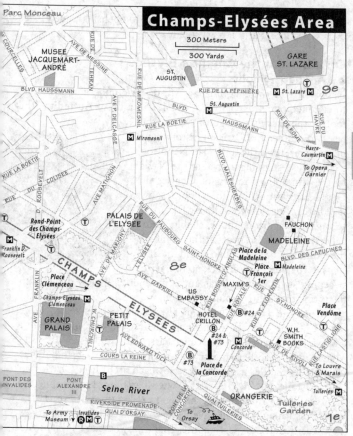

The arrival of McDonald's (at #140) was an unthinkable horror, but these days dining chez MacDo has become typically Parisian, and this branch is the most profitable McDonald's in the world.

Fancy car showrooms abound, including Peugeot (#136) and Mercedes-Benz (#118). The Lido (#116) is Paris' largest burlesque-type cabaret (and a multiplex cinema). Across the boulevard is the flagship store of leather-bag makers Louis Vuitton (#101). Fouquet's café (#99) is a popular spot for French celebrities, especially movie stars—note the names in the sidewalk in front. Enter if you dare for a €10 espresso. Ladurée café (#75) is also classy but has a welcoming and affordable takeout bakery.

Continuing on, you pass international-brand stores, such as Sephora, Nike, Disney, and the Gap. Car buffs should park themselves at the sleek café in the Renault store (#53, open until midnight). The car exhibits change regularly, but the great tables looking down onto the Champs-Elysées are permanent.

You can end your walk at the round Rond Point intersection

(Mo: Franklin D. Roosevelt) or continue to obelisk-studded Place de la Concorde, Paris' largest square.

On and Near the Champs-Elysées
▲▲Arc de Triomphe

Napoleon had the magnificent Arc de Triomphe commissioned to commemorate his victory at the 1805 battle of Austerlitz. The foot of the arch is a stage on which the last two centuries of Parisian history have played out—from the funeral of Napoleon to the goose-stepping arrival of the Nazis to the triumphant return of Charles de Gaulle after the Allied liberation. Examine the carvings on the pillars, featuring a mighty Napoleon and excitable Lady Liberty. Pay your respects at the Tomb of the Unknown Soldier. Then climb the 284 steps to the observation deck up top, with sweeping skyline panoramas and a mesmerizing view down onto the traffic that swirls around the arch.

Cost and Hours: Free and always viewable; steps to rooftop—€9.50, free for those under age 18, free on first Sun of month Oct-March, covered by Museum Pass; daily 10:00-23:00, Oct-March until 22:30, last entry 45 minutes before closing; Place Charles de Gaulle, use underpass to reach arch, Mo: Charles de Gaulle-Etoile, tel. 01 55 37 73 77, www.paris-arc-de-triomphe.fr.

Avoiding Lines: Bypass the slooow ticket line with your Museum Pass (though if you have kids, you'll need to line up to get their free tickets). Expect another line (that you can't skip) at the entrance to the stairway up the arch. Lines disappear after 17:00—come for sunset.

▲Paris Ferris Wheel (Roue de Paris)

The Paris Ferris Wheel, periodically situated on Place de la Concorde or in the Tuileries Garden, offers a 200-foot-high view of Paris. Your ticket covers two slow revolutions, and generally it's two passengers per gondola.

Cost and Hours: €12, open long hours daily in high season.

La Défense and La Grande Arche

Though Paris keeps its historic center classic and skyscraper-free, this district, nicknamed *"le petit Manhattan,"* offers an impressive excursion into a side of Paris few tourists see: that of a modern-day economic superpower. La Défense was first conceived more than 60 years ago as a US-style forest of skyscrapers that would accommodate the business needs of the modern world. Today La Défense is a thriving commercial and shopping center, home to 150,000 employees and 55,000 residents.

For a worthwhile visit, take the Métro to the La Défense Grande Arche stop, follow *Sortie Grande Arche* signs, and climb the steps of La Grande Arche for distant city views. Then stroll about three-quarters of a mile gradually downhill among the glass buildings to the Esplanade de la Défense Métro station, and return home from there. Mall stores are open every day.

Visiting La Défense: The centerpiece of this ambitious complex is the mammoth **La Grande Arche de la Fraternité.** Inaugurated in 1989 on the 200th anniversary of the French Revolution, it was, like the Revolution, dedicated to human rights and brotherhood. The place is big— Notre-Dame Cathedral could fit under its arch. The "cloud"—a huge canvas canopy under the arch—is an attempt to cut down on the wind-tunnel effect this gigantic building creates.

Survey the skyscraping scene. La Défense is much more than its eye-catching arch—it's an international power broker. Wander down the **Esplanade** (a.k.a. "le Parvis"), back toward the city center (and to the next Métro stop).

In France, getting a building permit often comes with a requirement to dedicate two percent of the construction cost to art. Hence the Esplanade is a virtual open-air modern art gallery, sporting pieces by Joan Miró (blue, red, and yellow), Alexander Calder (red), and Yaacov Agam (the fountain with colorful stripes and rhythmically dancing spouts), among others. Near Yaacov's fountain, find *La Défense de Paris,* the statue that gave the area its name; it recalls the 1870 Franco-Prussian war—a rare bit of old Paris out here in the 'burbs.

As you descend the Esplanade, notice how the small gardens and *boules* courts (reddish dirt areas) are designed to integrate tradition into this celebration of modern commerce. Note also how the buildings tend to decrease in height and increase in age as you approach Paris' center. Your walk ends at the amusing fountain of Bassin Takis, where you'll find the Esplanade de la Défense Métro station that zips you out of all this modernity and directly back into town.

OPERA NEIGHBORHOOD

The glittering Garnier opera house anchors this neighborhood of broad boulevards and grand architecture. This area is also nirvana for high-end shoppers, with the opulent Galeries Lafayette and the sumptuous shops that line Place Vendôme and Place de la Madeleine (see page 108 for my self-guided shopping walk of this area).

▲▲Opéra Garnier
(Opéra National de Paris—Palais Garnier)

A gleaming grand theater of the belle époque, the Palais Garnier was built for Napoleon III and finished in 1875. From Avenue de l'Opéra, once lined with Paris' most fashionable haunts, the facade suggests "all power to the wealthy." To see the interior, you have several choices: Take a guided tour (your best look), tour the public areas on your own (using the audioguide), or attend a performance. Note that the auditorium is sometimes off-limits due to performances and rehearsals.

Cost and Hours: €11, not covered by Museum Pass, generally daily 10:00-16:30, mid-July-Aug until 18:00, 8 Rue Scribe, Mo: Opéra, RER: Auber, www.operadeparis.fr/en/visits/palais-garnier.

Tours: The €5 audioguide gives a good self-guided tour. Guided tours in English run at 11:30 and 14:30 July-Aug daily, Sept-June Wed, Sat, and Sun only—call to confirm schedule (€14.50, includes entry, 1.5 hours, tel. 01 40 01 17 89 or 08 25 05 44 05).

Visiting the Theater: For the best exterior view, stand in front of the Opéra Métro stop. The building is huge. Its massive foundations straddle an underground lake (inspiring the mysterious world of *The Phantom of the Opera*). It's the masterpiece of architect Charles Garnier, who oversaw every element, from laying the foundations to what color the wallpaper should be. His cohesive design was so admired that the building came to be known as the Palais Garnier.

Enter, buy your ticket, and make your way (up a small curving staircase) to the foot of the **Grand Staircase.** Gaze up into this vast hall, where the whole building is united by the set of stairs that branches into a Y midway up. Take in the columns, statues, railings, lanterns, chandeliers, and the different colors of marble, as your eye goes up to a ceiling fresco featuring Apollo.

Now enter an open box and take in the view of the **amphitheater.** The red-velvet performance hall seats 2,000. Admire Marc Chagall's colorful ceiling (1964) playfully dancing around the seven-ton chandelier. Now work clockwise around the Grand Staircase to tour the opulent, chandeliered reception rooms, where operagoers gathered for drinks and socializing during intermis-

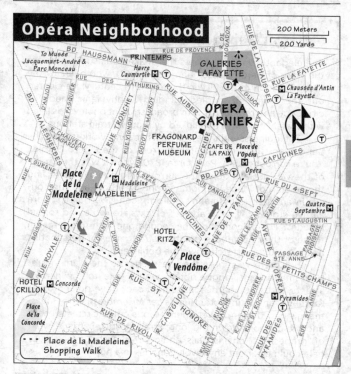

Opéra Neighborhood

200 Meters
200 Yards

To Musée Jacquemart-André & Parc Monceau

BD. HAUSSMANN

RUE DE PROVENCE

PRINTEMPS

Havre Caumartin Ⓜ Ⓣ

GALERIES LAFAYETTE

Ⓣ

RUE LA FAYETTE

Chaussée d'Antin La Fayette Ⓜ

RUE DES MATHURINS

RUE AUBER

OPÉRA GARNIER

RUE TRONCHET

FRAGONARD PERFUME MUSEUM

RUE SCRIBE

CAFÉ DE LA PAIX

Place de l'Opéra

Ⓜ Opéra

CAPUCINES

Place de la Madeleine

Ⓜ Madeleine

LA MADELEINE

R. DES CAPUCINES

BD. DES

RUE DANOU

RUE DU 4 SEPT

Quatre Septembre Ⓜ

RUE ST. AUGUSTIN

HOTEL RITZ

RUE DE LA PAIX

Place Vendôme

Ⓣ

PASSAGE STE. ANNE

HOTEL CRILLON Ⓜ Concorde

RUE ST.

Ⓣ

RUE DES PETITS CHAMPS

Place de la Concorde

RUE DE RIVOLI

RUE ST. HONORÉ

Ⓜ Pyramides

- - - Place de la Madeleine Shopping Walk

sion. Continue straight to the Grand Staircase and turn left, entering the large **Grand Foyer.** This long, high-ceilinged Hall-of-Mirrors-esque space was the main gathering place at intermission. Its golden decor (mostly gold paint, not gilding) features statues, columns, and chandeliers, all set off by colorful ceiling paintings. Look for the **museum,** and browse the long hallway of exhibits, seeing a cutaway model of the stage (with two subterranean levels below and elaborate pulleys above) and many paintings of famous singers, dancers, composers, and set designers. The museum leads into the library, with dioramas of set designs for famous operas, including *Faust,* by Paris's hometown boy Charles Gounod.

Nearby: Across the street, the illustrious Café de la Paix has been a meeting spot for the local glitterati for generations. If you can afford the coffee, this spot offers a delightful break.

High-End Shopping

The upscale Opéra neighborhood hosts some of Paris' best shopping. Even window shoppers can appreciate this as a ▲ "sight." Just behind the Opéra, the **Galeries Lafayette** department store is a magnificent cathedral to consumerism, under a stunning stained-glass dome. The area between **Place de la Madeleine,** dominated by the Madeleine Church (looking like a Roman temple), and the

Baron Georges-Eugène Haussmann

The elegantly uniform streets that make Paris so Parisian are the work of Baron Haussmann (1809-1891), who oversaw the modernization of the city in the mid-19th century. He cleared out the cramped, higgledy-piggledy, unhygienic medieval cityscape and replaced it with broad, straight boulevards lined with stately buildings and linked by modern train stations.

The quintessential view of Haussmann's work is from the pedestrian island immediately in front of the Opéra Garnier. You're surrounded by Paris circa 1870, when it was the capital of the world. Gaze down the surrounding boulevards to find the column of Place Vendôme in one direction, and the Louvre in another. Haussmann's uniform, cohesive buildings are all five stories tall, with angled, black slate roofs and formal facades. The balconies on the second and fifth floors match those of their neighbors, creating strong lines of perspective as the buildings stretch down the boulevard.

But there was more than aesthetics to the plan. In pre-Haussmann Paris, angry rioters would take to the narrow streets, setting up barricades to hold back government forces (as made famous in Victor Hugo's *Les Misérables*). With Haussmann's new design, government troops could circulate easily and fire cannons down the long, straight boulevards. A whiff of "grapeshot"—chains, nails, and other buckshot-type shrapnel—could clear out any revolutionaries in a hurry.

octagonal **Place Vendôme,** is filled with pricey shops and boutiques, giving travelers a whiff of the exclusive side of Paris (for more on shopping in this area, see page 108).

MARAIS NEIGHBORHOOD AND NEARBY

Naturally, when in Paris you want to see the big sights—but to experience the city, you also need to visit a vital neighborhood. The Marais fits the bill, with hip boutiques, busy cafés, trendy art galleries, narrow streets, leafy squares, Jewish bakeries, aristocratic châteaux, nightlife, and real Parisians. It's the perfect setting to appreciate the flair of this great city.

The Marais extends along the Right Bank of the Seine, from the Bastille to the Pompidou Center. The main east-west axis is formed by Rue St. Antoine, Rue des Rosiers (the heart of Paris' Jewish community), and Rue Ste. Croix de la Bretonnerie. The centerpiece of the neighborhood is the stately Place des Vosges. Don't waste time looking for the Bastille, the prison of Revolution fame. It's Paris' most famous non-sight. The building is long gone, and just the square remains.

For a map of this area, see page 126.

Place des Vosges and West
▲Place des Vosges
Henry IV built this centerpiece of the Marais in 1605 and called it "Place Royale." As he'd hoped, it turned the Marais into Paris' most exclusive neighborhood. Walk to the center, where Louis XIII, on horseback, gestures, "Look at this wonderful square my dad built." He's surrounded by locals enjoying their community park. You'll see children frolicking in the sandbox, lovers warming benches, and pigeons guarding their fountains while trees shade this escape from the glare of the big city (you can refill your water bottle in the center of the square, behind Louis).

Study the architecture: nine pavilions (houses) per side. The two highest—at the front and back—were for the king and queen (but were never used). Warm red brickwork—some real, some fake—is topped with sloped slate roofs, chimneys, and another quaint relic of a bygone era: TV antennas.

The insightful writer **Victor Hugo** lived at #6 from 1832 to 1848. (It's at the southeast corner of the square, marked by the French flag.) This was when he wrote much of his most important work, including his biggest hit, *Les Misérables*. Inside this free museum you'll wander through eight plush rooms, enjoy a fine view of the square, and find good WCs (free, Tue-Sun 10:00-18:00, closed Mon; tel. 01 42 72 10 16, http://maisonsvictorhugo.paris.fr).

Sample the razzle-dazzle art galleries ringing the square (the best ones are behind Louis). Ponder a daring new piece for that blank wall at home. Or consider a pleasant break at one of the recommended eateries on the square.

▲Carnavalet Museum (Musée Carnavalet)
The tumultuous history of Paris—starring the Revolutionary years—is well portrayed in this converted Marais mansion (at 23 Rue de Sévigné, closed for renovation throughout 2017 and beyond). The museum contains models of medieval Paris, maps of the city over the centuries, paintings of Parisian scenes, French Revolution paraphernalia—including a small guillotine—and fully furnished rooms re-creating life in Paris in different eras.

▲▲▲Picasso Museum (Musée Picasso)
Whatever you think about Picasso the man, as an artist he was unmatched in the 20th century for his daring and productivity. The Picasso Museum has the world's largest collection of his work—some 400 paintings, sculptures, sketches, and ceramics—spread across five levels of this mansion in the Marais. A visit here walks you through the full range of this complex man's life and art.

Cost and Hours: €11, covered by Museum Pass, free on first Sun of month and for those under age 18 with ID; open Tue–Fri

11:30–18:00 (until 21:00 on third Fri of month), Sat–Sun 9:30–18:00, closed Mon, last entry 45 minutes before closing; video-guide–€4, timed-entry tickets available on museum website but lines generally aren't bad; 5 Rue de Thorigny, Mo: St. Sébastien-Froissart, St-Paul, or Chemin Vert, tel. 01 42 71 25 21, www.musee-picasso.fr.

Visiting the Museum: The core of the museum is organized chronologically. Use this overview to trace Picasso's life and some of the themes in his work.

Early Years and Early Cubism: In 1900, Picasso set out to make his mark in Paris, the undisputed world capital of culture. The brash Spaniard quickly became a poor, homesick foreigner, absorbing the styles of many painters while searching for his own artist's voice. When his best friend committed suicide (look for the painting *Death of Casagemas,* 1901), Picasso plunged into a **Blue Period,** painting emaciated beggars, hard-eyed pimps, and himself, bundled up against the cold, with eyes all cried out (*Autoportrait,* 1901).

In 1904, Picasso got a steady girlfriend, and suddenly saw the world through rose-colored glasses (the **Rose Period,** though the museum has very few works from this time). With his next-door neighbor, Georges Braque, Picasso invented Cubism, a fragmented, "cube"-shaped style. He'd fracture a figure (such as the musician in *Man with a Mandolin,* 1911) into a barely recognizable jumble of facets. Picasso sketched reality from every angle, then pasted it all together, a composite of different views.

Cubist Experiments and *Guernica:* Modern art was being born. The first stage had been so-called Analytic Cubism: breaking the world down into small facets, to "analyze" the subject from every angle. Now it was time to "synthesize" it back together with the real world (Synthetic Cubism). Picasso created "constructions" that were essentially still-life paintings (a 2-D illusion) augmented with glued-on, real-life materials—wood, paper, rope, or chair caning (the real 3-D world). In a few short years, Picasso had turned painting in the direction it would go for the next 50 years.

Meanwhile, Europe was gearing up for war. From Paris, Picasso watched as his homeland of Spain erupted in a brutal civil war (1936-1939), in which a half-million of his countrymen died. Many canvases from this period are gray and gloomy. The most famous one—*Guernica* (1937)—captured the chaos of a Spanish village caught in an air raid (painted in Paris, but now hanging in

Madrid). The Picasso Museum has some of the many studies he did for this monumental canvas. In 1940, Nazi tanks rolled into Paris. Picasso decided to stay for the duration and live under gray skies and gray uniforms.

Later Years: At war's end, Picasso left Paris and all that emotional baggage behind, finding fun in the sun in the south of France. Sixty-five-year-old Pablo Picasso was reborn, enjoying worldwide fame. Picasso's Riviera works set the tone for the rest of his life—sunny, light-hearted, childlike, experimenting in new media, and using motifs of the sea, Greek mythology (fauns, centaurs), and animals (birds, goats, and pregnant baboons). Picasso was fertile to the end, still painting with bright thick colors at age 91.

Rue des Rosiers: Paris' Jewish Quarter

The intersection of Rue des Rosiers and Rue des Ecouffes marks the heart of the small neighborhood that Jews call the Pletzl ("little square"). Once the largest in Western Europe, Paris' Jewish Quarter is much smaller today but still colorful. Lively Rue des Ecouffes, named for a bird of prey, is a derogatory nod to the moneychangers' shops that once lined this lane. The next two blocks along Rue des Rosiers feature kosher *(cascher)* restaurants and fast-food places selling falafel, *shawarma, kefta,* and other Mediterranean dishes (for recommendations, see page 146). Bakeries specialize in braided challah, bagels, and strudels. Delis offer gefilte fish, piroshkis, and blintzes. Art galleries exhibit Jewish-themed works, and store windows post flyers for community events. Need a menorah? You'll find one here.

▲Jewish Art and History Museum (Musée d'Art et Histoire du Judaïsme)

This is a fine museum of historical artifacts and rare ritual objects spanning the Jewish people's long cultural heritage. It emphasizes the cultural unity maintained by this continually dispersed population. You'll learn about Jewish traditions, and see exquisite costumes and objects central to daily life and religious practices. Be aware that the museum is not ideal for the novice. Some visitors may find the displays beautiful and thought-provoking but not especially meaningful. However, those with a background in Judaism or who take the time with the thoughtful audioguide and information (some but not all posted info is in English) will be rewarded.

Cost and Hours: €9, includes audioguide, covered by Museum Pass; Tue-Fri 11:00-18:00, Sat-Sun 10:00-18:00, open later during special exhibits—Wed until 21:00 and Sat-Sun until 19:00, closed Mon year-round, last entry 45 minutes before closing; 71 Rue du Temple, Mo: Rambuteau or Hôtel de Ville a few blocks farther away, RER: Châtelet-Les Halles; tel. 01 53 01 86 60, www.mahj.org.

Holocaust Memorial (Mémorial de la Shoah)

This sight, commemorating the lives of the more than 76,000 Jews deported from France in World War II, has several facets: a WWII deportation memorial, a museum on the Holocaust, and a Jewish resource center. Displaying original deportation records, the museum takes you through the history of Jews in Europe and France, from medieval pogroms to the Nazi era. But its focal point is underground, where victims' ashes are buried.

Cost and Hours: Free, Sun-Fri 10:00-18:00, Thu until 22:00, closed Sat and certain Jewish holidays, 17 Rue Geoffroy l'Asnier, tel. 01 42 77 44 72, www.memorialdelashoah.org.

▲▲Pompidou Center (Centre Pompidou)

One of Europe's greatest collections of far-out modern art is housed in the Musée National d'Art Moderne, on the fourth and fifth floors of this colorful exoskel-etal building. Created ahead of its time, the modern and contemporary art in this collection is still waiting for the world to catch up.

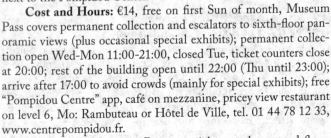

The Pompidou Center and the square that fronts it are lively, with lots of people, street theater, and activity inside and out—a perpetual street fair. Kids of any age enjoy the fun, colorful fountain (an homage to composer Igor Stravinsky) next to the Pompidou Center.

Cost and Hours: €14, free on first Sun of month, Museum Pass covers permanent collection and escalators to sixth-floor panoramic views (plus occasional special exhibits); permanent collection open Wed-Mon 11:00-21:00, closed Tue, ticket counters close at 20:00; rest of the building open until 22:00 (Thu until 23:00); arrive after 17:00 to avoid crowds (mainly for special exhibits); free "Pompidou Centre" app, café on mezzanine, pricey view restaurant on level 6, Mo: Rambuteau or Hôtel de Ville, tel. 01 44 78 12 33, www.centrepompidou.fr.

Visiting the Museum: Buy your ticket on the ground floor, then ride up the escalator (or run up the down escalator to get in the proper mood). When you see the view, your opinion of the Pompidou's exterior should improve a good 15 percent.

The Pompidou's "permanent" collection...isn't. It changes so often that a painting-by-painting tour is impossible. Generally, art from 1905 to 1980 is on the fifth floor, while the fourth floor contains more recent art. Use the museum's floor plans (posted on the wall) to find select artists. See the classics—Picasso, Matisse, Chagall, Braque, Dalí, Warhol—but be sure to leave time to browse the thought-provoking and fun art of more recent artists.

As you tour, remember that most of the artists, including foreigners, spent their formative years in Paris. In the 1910s, funky Montmartre was the mecca of Modernism—the era of Picasso, Braque, and Matisse. In the 1920s the center shifted to the grand cafés of Montparnasse, where painters mingled with American expats such as Ernest Hemingway and Gertrude Stein. During World War II, it was Jean-Paul Sartre's Existentialist scene around St. Germain-des-Prés. After World War II, the global art focus moved to New York, but by the late 20th century, Paris had re-emerged as a cultural touchstone for the world of modern art.

View Art: The sixth floor has stunning views of the Paris cityscape. Your Pompidou ticket or Museum Pass gets you there, or you can buy the €3 View of Paris ticket (good for the sixth floor only; doesn't include museum entry).

Nearby: The studio of sculptor **Constantin Brancusi** is housed in the gray concrete bunker in front of the Pompidou and is free to visit. (Wed-Mon 14:00-18:00, closed Tue, same contact info as Pompidou.)

East of Place des Vosges
▲Père Lachaise Cemetery (Cimetière du Père Lachaise)
Littered with the tombstones of many of the city's most illustrious dead, this is your best one-stop look at Paris' fascinating, romantic past residents. More like a small city, the cemetery is big and confusing, but it holds the graves of Frédéric Chopin, Molière, Edith Piaf, Oscar Wilde, Gertrude Stein, Jim Morrison, Héloïse and Abélard, and many more.

Cost and Hours: Free, Mon-Fri 8:00-18:00, Sat 8:30-18:00, Sun 9:00-18:00, until 17:30 in winter; two blocks from Mo: Gambetta (do not go to Mo: Père Lachaise) and two blocks from bus #69's last stop; tel. 01 55 25 82 10, searchable map available at unofficial website: www.pere-lachaise.com.

Visiting the Cemetery: Enclosed by a massive wall and lined with 5,000 trees, the peaceful, car-free lanes and dirt paths of Père Lachaise cemetery encourage parklike meandering. Named for Father *(Père)* La Chaise, whose job was listening to Louis XIV's sins, the cemetery is relatively new, having opened in 1804 to accommodate Paris' expansion. Today, this city of the dead (pop. 70,000) still accepts new residents, but real estate prices are sky high (a 21-square-foot plot costs more than €11,000).

The 100-acre cemetery, with thousands of graves and tombs crammed every which way, has only a few pedestrian pathways to help you navigate. The maps available from a nearby florist or from street vendors can help guide your way. I recommend taking a one-way tour between two convenient Métro/bus stops (Gambetta and Père Lachaise), connecting a handful of graves from some of this necropolis' best-known residents.

MONTMARTRE

Paris' highest hill, topped by Sacré-Cœur Basilica, is best known as the home of cabaret nightlife and bohemian artists. Struggling painters, poets, dreamers, and drunkards came here for cheap rent, untaxed booze, rustic landscapes, and views of the underwear of high-kicking cancan girls at the Moulin Rouge. These days, the hill is equal parts charm and kitsch—still vaguely village-like but mobbed with tourists and pickpockets on sunny weekends. Come for a bit of history, a getaway from Paris' noisy boulevards, and the view (to beat the crowds, it's best on a weekday or early on weekend mornings). For restaurant recommendations near Sacré-Cœur, see page 151.

▲▲Sacré-Cœur

You'll spot Sacré-Cœur, the Byzantine-looking white basilica atop Montmartre, from most viewpoints in Paris. Though only 130 years old, it's impressive and iconic, with a climbable dome.

Cost and Hours: Church—free, daily 6:00-22:30; dome—€6, not covered by Museum Pass, daily May-Sept 8:30-20:00, Oct-April 9:00-17:00; tel. 01 53 41 89 00, www.sacre-coeur-montmartre.com.

Getting There: You can take the Métro to the Anvers stop (to avoid the stairs up to Sacré-Cœur, use one more Métro ticket and ride up on the funicular). Alternatively, from Place Pigalle, you can take the "Montmartrobus," a city bus that drops you right by Sacré-Cœur (Funiculaire stop, costs one Métro ticket, 4/hour). A taxi from the Seine or the Bastille saves time and avoids sweat (about €15, €20 at night).

Visiting the Church: The Sacré-Cœur (Sacred Heart) Basilica's exterior, with its onion domes and bleached-bone pallor, looks ancient, but it was finished only a century ago by Parisians humiliated by German invaders, who built this as a kind of penitence.

The five-domed, Roman-Byzantine-looking basilica took 44 years to build (1875-1919). It stands on a foundation of 83 pillars sunk 130 feet deep, necessary because the ground beneath was

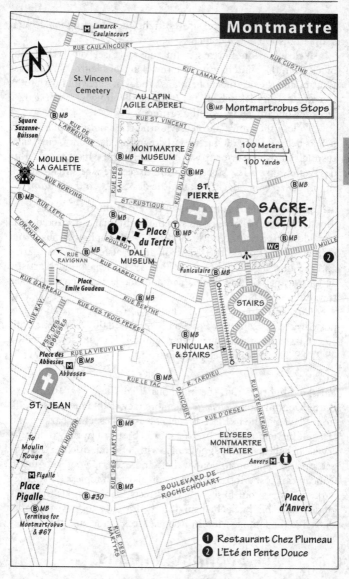

Montmartre

Lamarck-
Caulaincourt

RUE CAULAINCOURT

RUE LAMARCK

RUE CUSTINE

St. Vincent
Cemetery

AU LAPIN
AGILE CABERET

Ⓑ MB Montmartrobus Stops

RUE ST. VINCENT

Square
Suzanne-
Buisson

Ⓑ MB

RUE DE L'ABREUVOIR

MOULIN DE
LA GALETTE

MONTMARTRE
Ⓑ MB MUSEUM

R. CORTOT

Ⓑ MB

100 Meters

100 Yards

Ⓑ MB

RUE NORVINS

RUE DES SAULES

RUE DU MONT CENIS

ST.
PIERRE

SACRE-
CŒUR

Ⓑ MB

Ⓑ MB RUE LEPIC

ST.-RUSTIQUE

Ⓑ MB

RUE
D'ORCHAMPT

Ⓑ MB
Ⓣ Ⓑ MB

Ⓑ MB

WC

MULLE

❶ ⬛⬛
POULBOT

Ⓘ Place
du Tertre

DALÍ
MUSEUM

Funiculaire Ⓑ MB

❷

RUE
RAVIGNAN

Ⓑ MB

RUE GABRIELLE

RUE GARREAU

Place
Emile Goudeau

RUE BERTHE

STAIRS

RUE RAV.

RUE DES TROIS FRERES

Ⓑ MB

PSG. DES
ABBESSES

RUE LA VIEUVILLE

Ⓑ MB

FUNICULAR
& STAIRS

Place des
Abbesses

Ⓜ Ⓑ MB
Abbesses

RUE LE TAC

Ⓑ MB

R. TARDIEU

DANCOURT

RUE STEINKERGUE

ST. JEAN

RUE D'ORSEL

To
Moulin
Rouge

RUE HOUDON

RUE DES MARTYRS

ELYSEES
MONTMARTRE
THEATER

Anvers Ⓜ Ⓘ

Ⓜ Pigalle
Place
Pigalle

Ⓑ MB

Ⓑ #30

BOULEVARD DE
ROCHECHOUART

Place
d'Anvers

Ⓑ MB
Terminus for
Montmartrobus
& #67

RUE DES
MARTYRS

❶ Restaurant Chez Plumeau
❷ L'Eté en Pente Douce

PARIS

honeycombed with gypsum mines. The exterior is laced with gypsum, which whitens with age.

Take a clockwise spin around the crowded interior to see
impressive mosaics, a statue of St. Thérèse, a scale model of the
church, and three stained-glass windows dedicated to Joan of Arc.
Pause near the Stations of the Cross mosaic to give St. Peter's
bronze foot a rub. For an unobstructed panoramic view of Paris,

climb 260 feet (300 steps) up the tight and claustrophobic spiral stairs to the top of the dome.

Nearby: Montmartre's main square (Place du Tertre), one block from the church, was once the haunt of Henri de Toulouse-Lautrec and the original bohemians. Today, it's crawling with tourists and unoriginal bohemians (to beat the crowds, it's best on a weekday or early on weekend mornings).

To lose the crowd and feel Montmartre's pulse, explore a few blocks behind Place du Tertre. Go down Rue du Mont Cenis, then turn left on Rue Cortot (past the Montmartre Museum). At Rue des Saules, take a few steps downhill to see the vineyards that still supply cheap wine. Backtrack up Rue des Saules to the hilltop.

▲Montmartre Museum (Musée de Montmartre)

This 17th-century home re-creates the traditional cancan-and-cabaret Montmartre scene, with paintings, posters, photos, music, and memorabilia. It offers the best look at the history of Montmartre and the amazing period from 1870 to 1910 when so much artistic action was percolating in this neighborhood, plus a chance to see the studio of Maurice Utrillo.

Cost and Hours: €9.50, includes good 45-minute audioguide, not covered by Museum Pass, daily 10:00-18:00, Aug-Sept until 19:00, last entry 45 minutes before closing, 12 Rue Cortot, tel. 01 49 25 89 39, www.museedemontmartre.fr.

Pigalle

Paris' red light district, the infamous "Pig Alley," is at the foot of Butte Montmartre. *Ooh la la.* It's more racy than dangerous. Walk from Place Pigalle to Place Blanche, teasing desperate barkers and fast-talking temptresses. In bars, a €150 bottle of (what would otherwise be) cheap champagne comes with a friend. Stick to the bigger streets, hang on to your wallet, and exercise good judgment. Cancan can cost a fortune, as can con artists in topless bars. After dark, countless tour buses line the streets, reminding us that tour guides make big bucks by bringing their groups to touristy nightclubs like the famous Moulin Rouge (Mo: Pigalle or Abbesses).

Shopping in Paris

Shopping in chic Paris is altogether tempting—even reluctant shoppers can find good reasons to indulge. Wandering among elegant boutiques provides a break from the heavy halls of the Louvre, and, if you approach it right, a little cultural enlightenment. Even if you don't intend to buy anything, budget some time for window shopping, or, as the French call it, *faire du lèche-vitrines* ("window licking").

Before you enter a Parisian store, remember the following points:

- In small stores, always say, *"Bonjour, Madame* or *Mademoiselle* or *Monsieur"* when entering. And remember to say *"Au revoir, Madame* or *Mademoiselle* or *Monsieur"* when leaving.
- The customer is not always right. In fact, figure the clerk is doing you a favor by waiting on you.
- Except in department stores, it's not normal for the customer to handle clothing. Ask first before you pick up an item: *"Je peux?"* (zhuh puh), meaning, "Can I?"
- By law the price of items in a window display must be visible, often written on a slip of paper set on the floor or framed on the wall. This gives you an idea of how expensive or affordable the shop is before venturing inside.
- For clothing size comparisons between the US and France, see page 1121 of the appendix.
- Forget returns (and don't count on exchanges).
- Observe French shoppers. Then imitate.
- Saturday afternoons are *très* busy and not for the faint of heart.
- Stores are generally closed on Sunday. Exceptions include the Carrousel du Louvre (underground shopping mall at the Louvre with a Printemps department store), and some shops near Sèvres-Babylone, along the Champs-Elysées, and in the Marais.
- Some small stores don't open until 14:00 on Mondays.
- Don't feel obliged to buy. If a shopkeeper offers assistance, just say, *"Je regarde, merci."*
- For information on VAT refunds and customs regulations, see page 1047.

DEPARTMENT STORES

Parisian department stores *(les grands magasins)* begin with their showy perfume sections, almost always central on the ground floor, and worth a visit to see how much space is devoted to pricey, smelly water. Helpful information desks are usually located at the main entrances near the perfume section (with floor plans in English). Stores generally have affordable restaurants (some with view terraces) and a good selection of fairly priced souvenirs and toys. Shop at these great Parisian department stores: **Galeries Lafayette** (Mo: Chaussée d'Antin–La Fayette, Havre-Caumartin, or Opéra), **Printemps** (next door to Galeries Lafayette), and **Bon Marché** (Mo: Sèvres-Babylone). Opening hours are customarily Monday through Saturday from 10:00 to 19:00. Some are open later on Thursdays, and all are jammed on Saturdays and closed on Sundays (except in December). The Printemps store in the Carrousel du Louvre is an exception—it's open daily.

BOUTIQUE STROLLS

Give yourself a vacation from your sightseeing-focused vacation by sifting through window displays, pausing at corner cafés, and feeling the rhythm of neighborhood life. (Or have you been playing hooky and doing this already?) Though smaller shops are more intimate, sales clerks are more formal—so mind your manners. Two very different areas to

lick some windows are: Place de la Madeleine to Place de l'Opéra, and Sèvres-Babylone to St. Sulpice.

Most shops are closed on Sunday, which is a good day to head for the **Marais,** where many shops are open on Sunday (and closed on Saturday). For eclectic, avant-garde boutiques in this neighborhood, peruse the artsy shops between Place des Vosges and the Pompidou Center.

Place de la Madeleine to Place de l'Opéra

The ritzy streets connecting several high-priced squares—Place de la Madeleine, Place de la Concorde, Place Vendôme, and Place de l'Opéra—form a miracle mile of gourmet food shops, glittering jewelry stores, five-star hotels, exclusive clothing boutiques, and people who spend more on clothes in one day than I do in a year.

Start at Place de la Madeleine (Mo: Madeleine—for a map of this walk, see page 97). In the northeast corner at #24 is the black-and-white awning of **Fauchon.** Founded on this location in 1886, this bastion of over-the-top edibles became famous around the world, catering to the refined tastes of the rich and famous. **Hédiard** (#21, northwest corner of the square) is older than Fauchon, and it's weathered the tourist mobs a bit better. Wafting the aroma of tea and coffee, it showcases handsomely displayed produce and wines. Hédiard's small red containers—of mustards, jams, coffee, candies, and tea—make great souvenirs.

Step inside tiny **La Maison des Truffe** (#19) to get a whiff of the product—truffles, those prized, dank, and dirty cousins of mushrooms. Check out the tiny jars in the display case. Ponder how something so ugly, smelly, and deformed can cost so much. The venerable **Mariage Frères** (#17) shop demonstrates how good tea can smell and how beautifully it can be displayed. At **Caviar Kaspia** (#16), you can add Iranian caviar, eel, and vodka to your truffle collection.

Continue along, past **Marquise de Sévigné chocolates** (#11) to the intersection with **Boulevard Malesherbes.** When the street officially opened in 1863, it ushered in the golden age of this neighborhood. Cross the three crosswalks traversing Boulevard Malesherbes. Straight ahead is **Patrick Roger Chocolates** (#3), famous for its chocolates, and even more so for M. Roger's huge, whimsical, 150-pound chocolate sculptures of animals and fanciful creatures.

Turn right down **Rue Royale.** There's Dior, Chanel, and Gucci. At Rue St. Honoré, turn left and cross Rue Royale, pausing in the middle for a great view both ways. Check out **Ladurée** (#16) for an out-of-this-world pastry break in the busy 19th-century tea salon, or to just pick up some world-famous macarons. Continue east down **Rue St. Honoré.** The street is a three-block parade of chic boutiques—L'Oréal cosmetics, Jimmy Choo shoes, Valentino, and so on. Looking for a €1,000 handbag? This is your spot.

Turn left on Rue de Castiglione to reach **Place Vendôme.** This octagonal square is *très* elegant—enclosed by symmetrical Mansart buildings around a 150-foot column. On the left side is the original Hôtel Ritz, opened in 1898. The square is also known for its upper-crust jewelry and designer stores—Van Cleef & Arpels, Dior, Chanel, Cartier, and others (if you have to ask how much...).

Leave Place Vendôme by continuing straight, up **Rue de la Paix**—strolling by still more jewelry, high-priced watches, and crystal—and enter **Place de l'Opéra.** You're in the middle of Right Bank glamour. Here you'll find the Opéra Garnier (described on page 96). If you're shopping 'til you're dropping, the Galeries Lafayette and Printemps department stores are located a block or two north, up Rue Halévy.

Sèvres-Babylone to St. Sulpice

This Left Bank shopping area lets you sample smart clothing boutiques and clever window displays while enjoying one of Paris' more attractive neighborhoods. Start at the Sèvres-Babylone Métro stop (take the Métro or bus #87). You'll find the **Bon Marché,** Paris' oldest department store. Continue along Rue de Sèvres, working your way to Place St. Sulpice and making detours left and right as the spirit moves you. You'll pass some of Paris' smartest boutiques and coolest cafés, such as **La Maison du Chocolat** at #19 and **Hermès** (a few doors down, at #17). Make a short detour up Rue du Cherche-Midi and find Paris' most celebrated bread—beautiful round loaves with designer crust—at the low-key **Poilâne** at #8. At the end of your walk, spill into Place St. Sulpice, with its big, twin-tower church. **Café de la Mairie** is a great spot to sip a *café crème*, admire the lovely square, and consider your next move. If you'd like more shopping options, you're in the heart of boutique shopping. As for me, stick a *fourchette* in me—I'm done.

Entertainment in Paris

Paris is brilliant after dark. Save energy from your day's sightseeing and experience the City of Light lit. Whether it's a concert at Sainte-Chapelle, a boat ride on the Seine, a walk in Montmartre, a hike up the Arc de Triomphe, or a late-night café, you'll see Paris at its best.

Music

Jazz and Blues Clubs

With a lively mix of American, French, and international musicians, Paris has been an internationally acclaimed jazz capital since World War II. You'll pay €12-25 to enter a jazz club (may include one drink; if not, expect to pay €5-10 per drink; beer is cheapest). See *Pariscope* magazine under "Musique" for listings, or, even better, the *Paris Voice* website. You can also check each club's website (all have English versions), or drop by the clubs to check out the calendars posted on their front doors. Music starts after 21:00 in most clubs. Some offer dinner concerts from about 20:30 on. Here are several good bets:

Caveau de la Huchette: This fun, characteristic old jazz/dance club fills an ancient Latin Quarter cellar with live jazz and frenzied dancing every night (admission about €15, €10 for those under 25, drinks from €7, daily from 21:30, no reservations needed, buy tickets at the door, 5 Rue de la Huchette, Mo: St. Michel, tel. 01 43 26 65 05, www.caveaudelahuchette.fr).

Autour de Midi et Minuit: This Old World bistro sits at the foot of Montmartre, above a *cave à jazz*. Eat upstairs if you like, then make your way down to the basement to find bubbling jam sessions Tuesday through Thursday and concerts on Friday and Saturday nights (no cover, €5 minimum drink order Tue-Thu; €18 cover Fri-Sat includes one drink; jam sessions at 21:30, concerts usually at 22:00; no music Sun-Mon; 11 Rue Lepic, Mo: Blanche or Abbesses, tel. 01 55 79 16 48, www.autourdemidi.fr).

Other Venues: For a spot teeming with late-night activity and jazz, go to the two-block-long Rue des Lombards, at Boulevard Sébastopol, midway between the river and the Pompidou Center (Mo: Châtelet). **Au Duc des Lombards** is one of the most popular and respected jazz clubs in Paris, with concerts nightly in a great, plush, 110-seat theater-like setting (admission €25-50, €60-90 with dinner, buy online and arrive early for best seats, cheap drinks, shows usually at 19:30 and 21:30, 42 Rue des Lombards, tel. 01 42 33 22 88, www.ducdeslombards.fr). **Le Sunside** is just a block away. The club offers two little stages (ground floor and downstairs): "le Sunset" stage tends toward contemporary world jazz; "le Sunside" stage features more traditional and acoustic jazz (concerts range from free to €25, check their website; 60 Rue des Lombards, tel. 01 40 26 46 60, www.sunset-sunside.com).

Classical Concerts

For classical music on any night, consult *Pariscope* magazine (check "Concerts Classiques" under "Musique" for listings), and look for posters at tourist-oriented churches. From March through November, these churches regularly host concerts: St. Sulpice, St. Germain-des-Prés, La Madeleine, St. Eustache, St. Julien-le-Pauvre, and Sainte-Chapelle.

PARIS

Sainte-Chapelle: Enjoy the pleasure of hearing Mozart, Bach, or Vivaldi, surrounded by 800 years of stained glass (unheated—bring a sweater). The acousti-

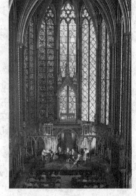

cal quality is surprisingly good. There are usually two concerts per evening, at 19:00 and 20:30; specify which one you want when you buy or reserve your ticket. VIP tickets get you a seat in rows 3-10 (€40), Prestige tickets cover the next 10 rows (€30), and Normal tickets are the last five rows (€25). Seats are unassigned within each section, so arrive at least 30 minutes early to get through the security line and snare a good view.

You can book at the box office, by phone, or online. Two different companies present concerts, but the schedule will tell you whom to contact for tickets to a particular performance. The small box office (with schedules and tickets) is to the left of the chapel entrance gate (8 Boulevard du Palais, Mo: Cité), or call 01 42 77 65 65 or 06 67 30 65 65 for schedules and reservations. You can leave your message in English—just speak clearly and spell your name. You can check schedules and buy your ticket at www.euromusicproductions.fr.

Flavien from Euromusic offers last-minute discounts with this book when seats are available (limit 2 tickets per book). VIP tickets are discounted to €30, Prestige tickets to €25, and Normal tickets to €16. The offer applies only to Euromusic concerts and must be purchased with cash only at the Sainte-Chapelle ticket booth close to concert time.

Concerts on the Seine: Enjoy live classical music while cruising past Paris' iconic monuments (€30-40, summer months only, board at Vedettes du Pont Neuf, Square du Vert Galant, tel. 01 42 77 65 65, http://vedettesdupontneuf.com/concerts-en-seine).

Other Venues: Look also for daytime concerts in parks, such as the Luxembourg Garden. Even the Galeries Lafayette department store offers concerts. Many of these concerts are free *(entrée libre)*, such as the Sunday atelier concert sponsored by the American Church (generally Sept-June at 17:00 but not every week and not in Dec, 65 Quai d'Orsay, Mo: Invalides, RER: Pont de l'Alma, tel. 01 40 62 05 00, www.acparis.org). The Army Museum offers inexpensive afternoon and evening classical music concerts year-round (for programs—in French only—see www.musee-armee.fr).

Opera

Paris is home to two well-respected opera venues. The **Opéra Bastille** is the massive modern opera house that dominates Place de la Bastille. Come here for state-of-the-art special effects and modern interpretations of classic ballets and operas. In the spirit of this everyman's opera, unsold seats are available at a big discount to seniors and students 15 minutes before the show. Standing-room-only tickets for €15 are also sold for some performances (Mo: Bastille).

The **Opéra Garnier,** Paris' first opera house, hosts opera and ballet performances. Come here for grand belle époque decor (Mo: Opéra; generally no performances mid-July-mid-Sept). To get tickets for either opera house, it's easiest to reserve online at www.operadeparis.fr, or call 01 71 25 24 23 outside France or toll tel. 08 92 89 90 90 inside France (office closed Sun). You can also buy tickets in person at their ticket offices, both of which are open Monday-Saturday (Opéra Bastille 14:30-18:30, Opéra Garnier 11:30–18:30) and an hour before the show, and closed on Sunday.

Museum Visits

Various museums are open late on different evenings—called *visites nocturnes*—offering the opportunity for more relaxed, less crowded visits: the Louvre, Orsay, Rodin, Pompidou Center, and Marmottan museums.

Versailles Spectacles: An elaborate sound-and-light show (Les Grandes Eaux Nocturnes) takes place in the gardens at Versailles on some Friday and Saturday evenings in summer (see page 177 for details, www.chateauversailles.fr).

Night Walks

Go for an evening walk to best appreciate the City of Light. Break for ice cream, pause at a café, and enjoy the sidewalk entertainers as you join the post-dinner Parisian parade. (Remember to avoid poorly lit areas and stick to main thoroughfares.)

▲▲▲Trocadéro and Eiffel Tower

This is one of Paris' most spectacular views at night. Take the Métro to the Trocadéro stop and join the party on Place du Trocadéro for a magnificent view of the glowing Eiffel Tower. It's a festival of hawkers, gawkers, drummers, and entertainers.

▲▲Champs-Elysées and the Arc de Triomphe

The Avenue des Champs-Elysées is best after dark. Start at the Arc de Triomphe, then stroll down Paris' glittering grand promenade.

▲Ile St. Louis and Notre-Dame

This stroll features floodlit views of Notre-Dame and a taste of the Latin Quarter. Find your way to the east end of Rue St. Louis-en-l'Ile, stopping for dinner—or at least a Berthillon ice cream (at #31) or Amorino Gelati (at #47). At the end of Ile St. Louis, cross Pont St. Louis to Ile de la Cité, with a great view of Notre-Dame. Wander to the Left Bank on Quai de l'Archevêché, and drop down to the river for the best floodlit views.

After-Dark Tours on Wheels

▲Deux Chevaux Car Tours

If rumbling around Paris and sticking your head out of the rolled-back top of a funky old 2CV car *à la* Inspector Clouseau sounds

like your kind of fun, consider this: The informal student-drivers are not professional guides (you're paying for their driving services), though they speak some English. Appreciate the simplicity of the car. It's France's version of the VW "bug" and hasn't been made since 1985. Notice the bare-bones dashboard. Ask your guide to honk the horn, to run the silly little wipers, and to open and close the air vent—*c'est magnifique!*

They'll pick you up and drop you at your hotel or wherever you choose. **4 Roues Sous 1 Parapluie** ("4 wheels under 1 umbrella") offers several tours with candy-colored cars and drivers dressed in striped shirts and berets (for 2 people it's €40/person for 45 minutes and €70/person for 90 minutes; 10 percent tip appropriate if you enjoyed your ride, longer tours available, maximum 3 people/car, tel. 08 00 80 06 31, mobile 06 67 32 26 68, www.4roues-sous-1parapluie.com, info@4roues-sous-1parapluie.com).

▲Nighttime Bus Tours

City Vision's Paris by Night: City Tour connects all the great illuminated sights of Paris with a 100-minute bus tour in 12 languages. These tours are not for everyone. You'll stampede on with a United Nations of tourists, get a set of headphones, dial up your language, and listen to a recorded spiel. Uninspired as it is, the

PARIS

Floodlit Paris Driving Tour

<u>Stops</u>
1. Notre-Dame View from Pont de la Tournelle
2. Les Invalides View from Place Vauban
3. Eiffel Tower View from Champ de Mars Park
4. Eiffel Tower View from Place du Trocadéro
5. Champs-Elysées View from Place de la Concorde
6. Louvre Museum & Pyramid View

PONT MARIE

Ile St. Louis

PONT DE LA TOURNELLE

PONT DE LA TOURNELLE

HOTEL DE VILLE

CONCIERGERIE

Ile de la Cité

Place St. Michel

NOTRE-DAME

TOUR BEGINS

TOUR ENDS

1

LOUVRE MUSEUM & PYRAMID

6

Tuileries Garden

QUAI DES TUILERIES

ORSAY MUSEUM

NAT'L ASSEMBLY

PONT ALEXANDRE III

Place de la Concorde

5

.5 Kilometer
.5 Mile

CHAMPS-ELYSEES

ARC DE TRIOMPHE

AVE. KLEBER

Place du Trocadéro

4

PONT D'IENA

EIFFEL TOWER

Seine River

BLVD. BOURDONNAIS

Champ de Mars Park

3

Esplanade des Invalides

NAPOLEON'S TOMB

Place Vauban

2

N

Uber & Taxi Instructions

Bonjour, Monsieur/Madame. Nous voulons faire un circuit de Paris illuminé d'une heure, avec quelques petits arrêts. Nous paierons le montant indiqué sur le compteur. Nous voudrions suivre la route suivante—combien cela va t-il coûter approximativement? Ça marche?

Greetings, Monsieur/Madame. We would like a tour of Paris at night for an hour, with a few short stops. We will pay the metered rate. We would like to take the following route—approximately how much will it cost? Can you do it?

1. Notre-Dame
2. Hôtel de Ville
3. Pont Marie
4. **Pont de la Tournelle (arrêt)**
5. Quai de la Tournelle
6. Musée d'Orsay
7. Esplanade des Invalides
8. Invalides
9. **Place Vauban/Eglise du Dôme (arrêt)**
10. **Champ de Mars (Place Jacques Rueff—arrêt)**
11. Tour Eiffel
12. Pont d'Iena
13. **Place du Trocadéro (arrêt)**
14. Avenue Kléber
15. Arc de Triomphe (2 révolutions)
16. Champs-Elysées
17. **Place de la Concorde (1 ou 2 révolutions)**
18. Quai François Mitterrand
19. **Musée du Louvre/Place du Carrousel/Pyramide (arrêt)**
20. Quai du Louvre
21. Notre-Dame

ride provides an entertaining overview of the city at its floodlit and scenic best. Bring your city map to stay oriented as you go. You're always on the bus, but the driver slows for photos at viewpoints (€27, kids-€17, 1.75 hours, departs from 2 Rue des Pyramides at 20:00 Nov-March, at 22:00 April-Oct, reserve one day in advance, arrive 30 minutes early to wait in line for best seats, Mo: Pyramides, tel. 01 44 55 61 00, www.pariscityvision.com). Buy tickets through your hotel (no booking fee, brochures in lobby) or directly at the City Vision office at 214 Rue de Rivoli, across the street from the Tuileries Métro stop.

▲▲▲Do-It-Yourself Floodlit Paris Taxi or Uber Tour

I recommend a loop trip that takes about an hour and connects these sights: Notre-Dame, Hôtel de Ville, Ile St. Louis, the Orsay Museum, Esplanade des Invalides, Champ de Mars park at Place Jacques Rueff (five-minute stop), Eiffel Tower from Place du Tro-cadéro (five-minute stop), Arc de Triomphe, Champs-Elysées, Place de la Concorde, and the Louvre. Use the instructions on page 115 to explain the route to your taxi or Uber driver. Taxis cost more and drivers can be moody; Uber costs less, with drivers who tend to be more fun and flexible. Taxis have a strict meter (figure €38/hour plus about €1/kilometer; taxis start with €2.60 on the meter). This suggested loop costs around €50 (more on Sun) via taxi and around €40 by Uber. If your cabbie was easy to work with, add a 10 percent tip; if not, tip just 5 percent. You don't need to tip with Uber (though you can). Drivers can take up to four people in a cab or regular sedan, though this is tight for decent sightseeing (with three, everyone gets a window).

If you enjoy Uber, this is a far better deal. When ordering your car via the app, you can leave the destination blank, or just choose a random address and then explain your plan when the driver arrives.

Sleeping in Paris

I've focused my recommendations on three safe, handy, and colorful neighborhoods: the village-like Rue Cler (near the Eiffel Tower); the artsy and trendy Marais (near Place de la Bastille); and the historic island of Ile St. Louis (next door to Notre-Dame).

If you're looking on your own for accommodations (beyond this book's listings), other neighborhoods to consider are the classy Luxembourg Garden neighborhood (on the Left Bank) and the less polished, less central, but less pricey Montmartre neighborhood. For lower rates or greater selection, look farther from the river (prices drop proportionally with distance from the Seine), but be prepared to spend more time on the Métro or the bus getting to sights. Those staying at least a week can save on meal costs (if not lodging) by renting an apartment. I also list a few bed-and-break-fast agencies and give suggestions for sleeping near Paris' airports.

Book your accommodations well in advance if you'll be traveling during peak season or if your trip coincides with a major holiday (see page 1114). For information and tips on pricing, getting deals, making reservations, seasonal differences, and chain hotels in France, see page 1051.

RUE CLER NEIGHBORHOOD
(7th arrond., Mo: Ecole Militaire, La Tour Maubourg, Invalides)

Rue Cler is so French that when I step out of my hotel in the morning, I feel like I must have been a poodle in a previous life. How such coziness lodged itself between the high-powered government district, the Eiffel Tower, and Les Invalides, I'll never know. This is a neighborhood of wide, tree-lined boulevards, stately apartment buildings, and lots of Americans. Hotels here are a fair value, considering the elegance of the neighborhood. And for sightseeing, you're within walking distance of the Eiffel Tower, Army Museum, Seine River, Champs-Elysées, and Orsay and Rodin museums.

Become a local at a Rue Cler café for breakfast, or join the afternoon crowd for *une bière pression* (a draft beer). On Rue Cler you can eat and browse your way through a street full of cafés, pastry shops, delis, cheese shops, and colorful outdoor produce stalls. Afternoon *boules* (outdoor bowling) on the Esplanade des Invalides is a relaxing spectator sport. The manicured gardens behind the golden dome of the Army Museum are free, peaceful, and filled with flowers (at southwest corner of grounds, closes at about 19:00), and the riverfront promenade along the Seine (Les Berges du Seine) is a fine place to walk, run, bike, or just sit and watch the river of people stroll by.

Breakfast on Rue Cler: For a great Rue Cler start to your day, drop by **Brasserie Aux PTT,** where Rick Steves readers are promised a *deux pour douze* breakfast special (two "American" breakfasts—juice, a big coffee, croissant, bread, ham, and eggs—for €12; closed Sun, opposite 54 Rue Cler).

Services: There's a handy **SNCF Boutique** at 80 Rue St. Dominique (Mon-Fri 9:00-18:00, Sat 10:00-13:00 & 14:00-18:00, closed Sun). You can buy your Paris Museum Pass at **Tabac La Cave à Cigares** on Avenue de la Motte-Picquet, across from where Rue Cler ends, or at **Paris Webservices** on 12 Rue de l'Exposition (see "Travel Services," later).

Laundry: Launderettes are omnipresent; ask your hotel for the nearest. Here are three handy locations: on Rue Augereau, on Rue Amélie (both between Rue St. Dominique and Rue de Grenelle), and at the southeast corner of Rue Valadon and Rue de Grenelle.

Sleep Code

Hotels are classified based on the average price of a standard double room without breakfast in high season.

$$$$	**Splurge:**	Most rooms over €200
$$$	**Pricier:**	€150-200
$$	**Moderate:**	€100-150
$	**Budget:**	€50-100
¢	**Backpacker:**	Under €50
RS%	**Rick Steves discount**	
*****	**French hotel rating system**	(0-5 stars)

Unless otherwise noted, credit cards are accepted, hotel staff speak basic English, and free Wi-Fi is available. Most hotels have air-conditioning and an elevator; breakfast is usually extra. Comparison-shop by checking prices at several hotels (on each hotel's website, on a booking site, or by email). For the best deal, *book directly with the hotel.* Ask for a discount if paying in cash; if the listing includes **RS%,** request a Rick Steves discount.

Travel Services: Contact the helpful staff at **Paris Webservices** to book *"coupe-file"* tickets that allow you to skip the line at key sights, to buy the Paris Museum Pass, or for assistance with hotels, transportation, local guides, or excursions (office open Mon-Sat 8:00-18:00, closed Sun; available by phone daily 6:00-22:00, 12 Rue de l'Exposition, Mo: Ecole Militaire, RER: Pont de l'Alma, tel. tel. 01 45 56 91 67 or 09 52 06 02 59, www.pariswebservices. com).

Métro Connections: Key Métro stops are Ecole Militaire, La Tsacerour Maubourg, and Invalides. The useful RER-C line runs from the Pont de l'Alma and Invalides stations, serving Versailles to the southwest; the Marmottan Museum to the northwest; and the Orsay Museum, Latin Quarter (St. Michel stop), and Austerlitz train station to the east.

Bus Routes: For stop locations, see the "Rue Cler Hotels" map.

Line #69 runs east along Rue St. Dominique and serves Les Invalides, Orsay, Louvre, Marais, and Père Lachaise Cemetery.

Line #63 runs along the river (Quai d'Orsay), serving the Latin Quarter along Boulevard St. Germain to the east (ending at Gare de Lyon), and Trocadéro and areas near the Marmottan Museum to the west.

Line #92 runs along Avenue Bosquet, north to the Champs-Elysées and Arc de Triomphe (faster than the Métro) and south to the Montparnasse Tower and Gare Montparnasse.

Line #87 runs from Avenue Joseph Bouvard in the Champ de Mars park up Avenue de la Bourdonnais and serves the Sèvres-

Babylone/St. Germain shopping area, St. Sulpice Church, Luxembourg Garden, the Bastille, and Gare de Lyon (more convenient than Métro for these destinations).

Line #42 runs from Avenue Joseph Bouvard in the Champ de Mars park (same stop as #87), crosses the Champs-Elysées at the Rond-Point, then heads to Place de la Concorde, Place de la Madeleine, Opéra Garnier, and finally to Gare du Nord—a long ride to the train station but less tiring than the Métro if you're carrying suitcases.

Taxi: You'll find taxi stands just off Place L'Ecole Militaire and near the intersection of Avenue Bosquet and Rue de Grenelle.

In the Heart of Rue Cler

Many of my readers stay in the Rue Cler neighborhood. If you want to disappear into Paris, choose a hotel elsewhere. The following hotels are within Camembert-smelling distance of Rue Cler.

$$$$ Hôtel Bosquet* is an exceptionally good hotel in an ideal location, with comfortable public spaces and well-configured rooms that are large by local standards and feature effective darkness blinds. The staff are politely formal (RS% but check their Facebook or Instagram pages for other discounts, good but pricey breakfast buffet with eggs and sausage, 19 Rue du Champ de Mars, tel. 01 47 05 25 45, www.hotel-paris-bosquet.com, hotel@relaisbosquet.com).

$$$$ Hôtel du Cadran,* a well-located *boule* toss from Rue Cler, is over-the-top modern for my taste. I prefer their nearby annex, described next (RS% includes big breakfast—use code "RICK" on their website; 10 Rue du Champ de Mars, tel. 01 40 62 67 00, www.cadranhotel.com, resa@cadranhotel.com).

$$$$ Hôtel Valadon* is an annex of Hôtel du Cadran, which is almost across the street (it's also where you'll check in and, if you want, have breakfast). The Valadon's 12 cute-and-quiet rooms are larger than those at the Cadran, with the same comfort, prices, and discounts (family rooms, 16 Rue Valadon, tel. 01 47 53 89 85, www.hotelvaladon.com, info@hotelvaladon.com).

$$$$ Cler Hotel* is a smart boutique hotel with appealing decor, a small outdoor patio, and a great location right on Rue Cler (RS%, 24 bis Rue Cler, tel. 01 45 00 18 06, www.clerhotel.com, contact@clerhotel.com).

$$$ Hôtel de la Motte Picquet,* at the corner of Rue Cler and Avenue de la Motte-Picquet, is an intimate and modest little place with 16 compact yet comfortable rooms. The terrific staff make staying here a pleasure (RS%—use code "STEVE-SMITH," family rooms, good breakfast served in a miniscule breakfast room, 30 Avenue de la Motte-Picquet, tel. 01 47 05 09 57, www.hotelmottepicquetparis.com, book@hotelmottepicquetparis.com).

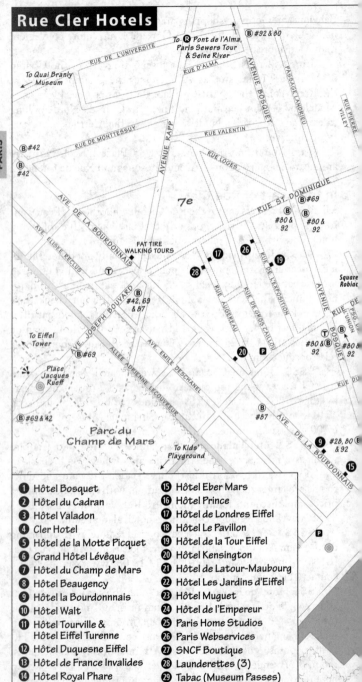

Rue Cler Hotels

PARIS

To Quai Branly Museum

To ® Pont de l'Alma, Paris Sewers Tour & Seine River

RUE DE L'UNIVERSITÉ

RUE D'ALMA

Ⓑ #92 & 80

AVENUE BOSQUET

PASSAGE LANDRIEU

RUE PIERRE VILLEY

Ⓑ #42

RUE DE MONTTESSUY

RUE VALENTIN

RUE LOGES

AVENUE RAPP

Ⓑ #42

7e

RUE ST. DOMINIQUE

Ⓑ #69

Ⓑ #80 & 92

Ⓑ #80 & 92

AVE. DE LA BOURDONNAIS

AVE. ELISEE RECLUS

FAT TIRE WALKING TOURS

Ⓣ

Ⓐ Ⓑ #42, 69 & 87

AVE. JOSEPH BOUVARD

RUE AUGEREAU

RUE DE GROS CAILLOU

RUE DE L'EXPOSITION

AVENUE BOSQUET

Square Robiac

28   17   26   19

To Eiffel Tower

Ⓑ #69

ALLEE ADRIENNE LECOUVREUR

AVE. EMILE DESCHANEL

20   Ⓟ

Ⓣ Ⓑ #80 & 92

Ⓑ #80 & 92

RUE DE L'UNION

RUE DI

Place Jacques Rueff

Ⓑ #69 & 42

Parc du Champ de Mars

To Kids' Playground

Ⓑ #87

AVE. DE LA BOURDONNAIS

9 Ⓑ #28, 80 & 92 Ⓔ

15

Ⓟ

❶ Hôtel Bosquet	⓯ Hôtel Eber Mars	
❷ Hôtel du Cadran	⓰ Hôtel Prince	
❸ Hôtel Valadon	⓱ Hôtel de Londres Eiffel	
❹ Cler Hotel	⓲ Hôtel Le Pavillon	
❺ Hôtel de la Motte Picquet	⓳ Hôtel de la Tour Eiffel	
❻ Grand Hôtel Lévêque	⓴ Hôtel Kensington	
❼ Hôtel du Champ de Mars	㉑ Hôtel de Latour-Maubourg	
❽ Hôtel Beaugency	㉒ Hôtel Les Jardins d'Eiffel	
❾ Hôtel la Bourdonnnais	㉓ Hôtel Muguet	
❿ Hôtel Walt	㉔ Hôtel de l'Empereur	
⓫ Hôtel Tourville & Hôtel Eiffel Turenne	㉕ Paris Home Studios	
⓬ Hôtel Duquesne Eiffel	㉖ Paris Webservices	
⓭ Hôtel de France Invalides	㉗ SNCF Boutique	
⓮ Hôtel Royal Phare	㉘ Launderettes (3)	
	㉙ Tabac (Museum Passes)	

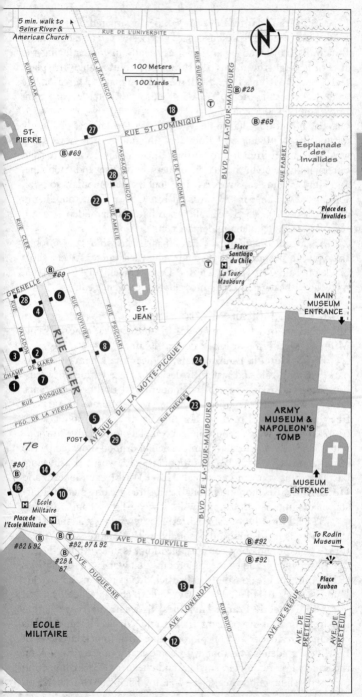

$$$ **Grand Hôtel Lévêque,***** ideally situated on Rue Cler, is all about location. It's a busy place with a sliver of an elevator and thin walls (noise can be an issue, especially in rooms facing the street). Though the rooms are sufficiently comfortable, the place feels in need of some TLC. Still, the location makes it a reasonable value (29 Rue Cler, tel. 01 47 05 49 15, www.hotel-leveque.com, info@hotel-leveque.com).

$$ **Hôtel du Champ de Mars***** is a top choice, brilliantly located barely 10 steps off Rue Cler. This plush little hotel has a small-town feel from top to bottom. The adorable rooms are snug but lovingly kept by hands-on owners Françoise and Stéphane, and single rooms can work as tiny doubles. It's popular, so book well ahead (no air-con, 30 yards off Rue Cler at 7 Rue du Champ de Mars, tel. 01 45 51 52 30, www.hotelduchampdemars.com, reservation@hotelduchampdemars.com).

$$ **Hôtel Beaugency***** has 30 smallish rooms and a lobby that you can stretch out in. It's a fair value on a quieter street a short block off Rue Cler (RS%, 21 Rue Duvivier, tel. 01 47 05 01 63, www.hotel-beaugency.com, infos@hotel-beaugency.com).

Near Ecole Militaire Métro Stop

These listings are a five-minute walk from Rue Cler, near the Ecole Militaire Métro stop or RER: Pont de l'Alma.

$$$$ **Hôtel la Bourdonnais,****** near the Champ de Mars park, is an upscale and tastefully designed place with comfy public spaces and rooms that blend modern and traditional accents. It's run well, with American-style service (elaborate breakfast—free for Rick Steves readers, 113 Avenue de la Bourdonnais, tel. 01 47 05 45 42, www.labourdonnais.com, labourdonnais@inwood-hotels.com). Two sister hotels in the neighborhood—owned by the same company as Hôtel la Bourdonnais—are worth considering, particularly if you can get a deal: **Hôtel Walt** (very modern) and **Hôtel Tourville** (more traditional). All three are top-quality, four-star places in terrific locations (www.inwood-hotels.com).

$$$$ **Hôtel Duquesne Eiffel,***** a few blocks farther from the action, is handsome and hospitable with a helpful staff. It features a welcoming lobby, comfortable rooms (some with terrific Eiffel Tower views), and connecting rooms that work well for families (RS%, big, hot breakfast—free for Rick Steves readers, 23 Avenue Duquesne, tel. 01 44 42 09 09, www.hde.fr, contact@hde.fr).

$$$ **Hôtel de France Invalides**** is a fair midrange option run by a brother-sister team (Alain and Marie-Hélène). It has contemporary decor and 60 rooms, some with knockout views of Invalides' golden dome (but with some traffic noise). Rooms on the courtyard are quieter, smaller, and cheaper (RS%, connecting rooms possible, good breakfast—free for Rick Steves readers, no

air-con, 102 Boulevard de la Tour Maubourg, tel. 01 47 05 40 49, www.hoteldefrance.com, contact@hoteldefrance.com).

$$$ Hôtel Royal Phare* faces the busy Ecole Militaire Métro stop. It's a small place with sharp, well-configured rooms. Courtyard rooms are quieter, but those from the fifth floor up have peekaboo views of the Eiffel Tower (fridges in rooms, 40 Avenue de la Motte-Picquet, tel. 01 47 05 57 30, www.hotel-royalphare-paris. com, hotel-royalphare@wanadoo.fr, friendly manager Hocin).

$$$ Hôtel Eiffel Turenne* is a reasonable bet with good rooms (20 Avenue de Tourville, tel. 01 47 05 99 92, www. hoteleiffelturenne.com, reservation@hoteleiffelturenne.com).

$$$ Hôtel Eber Mars, a few steps from Champ de Mars park, has comfortable, bigger-than-average rooms, an I-try-harder owner (Monsieur Eber), and a very narrow elevator (free breakfast for Rick Steves readers who book directly, 117 Avenue de la Bourdonnais, tel. 01 47 05 42 30, www.hotelebermars.com, reservation@hotelebermars.com).

$$ Hôtel Prince, across from the Ecole Militaire Métro stop, has a spartan lobby and drab halls, but offers good rooms for the price (66 Avenue Bosquet, tel. 01 47 05 40 90, www.hotel-paris-prince.com, paris@hotelprinceparis.com).

Closer to Rue St. Dominique (and the Seine)

$$$$ Hôtel de Londres Eiffel* is my closest listing to the Eiffel Tower and the Champ de Mars park. Here you get immaculate, warmly decorated but tight rooms (several are connecting for families), comfy public spaces, and a service-oriented staff. It's less convenient to the Métro (10-minute walk), but very handy to buses #69, #80, #87, and #92, and to RER-C: Pont de l'Alma (some Eiffel Tower view rooms, 1 Rue Augereau, tel. 01 45 51 63 02, www. hotel-paris-londres-eiffel.com, info@londres-eiffel.com, helpful Cédric and Arnaud). The owners also run a good two-star hotel with similar comfort in the cheaper Montparnasse area: **$$ Hôtel Apollon Montparnasse** (look for Web deals, 91 Rue de l'Ouest, Mo: Pernety, tel. 01 43 95 62 00, www.paris-hotel-paris.net, info@ apollon-montparnasse.com).

$$ Hôtel Le Pavillon* attracts attention with its romantic setting away from the street. Rooms are gray-toned and a tad mod, the comfy breakfast room doubles as a lounge, and the small patio with outdoor tables offers a peaceful refuge (several loft triples, 54 Rue St. Dominique, tel. 01 45 51 42 87, www.hotel-lepavillon.com, lepavillon@green-spirit-hotels.com).

$$ Hôtel de la Tour Eiffel is a terrific value on a quiet street near several of my favorite restaurants. The rooms are well-designed and comfortable, with air-conditioning (but no breakfast). The six sets of connecting rooms are ideal for families (17 Rue de l'Exposition, tel. 01 47 05 14 75, www.hotel-toureiffel.com, hte7@wanadoo.fr).

$$ Hôtel Kensington** is a fair budget value close to the Eiffel Tower and run by formal Daniele. It's an unpretentious place offering classic two-star comfort (RS%, some partial Eiffel Tower views, no air-con but ceiling fans, 79 Avenue de la Bourdonnais, tel. 01 47 05 74 00, www.hotel-kensington.com, hk@hotel-kensington.com).

Near La Tour Maubourg Métro Stop

These listings are within three blocks of the intersection of Avenue de la Motte-Picquet and Boulevard de la Tour Maubourg.

$$$$ Hôtel de Latour-Maubourg** boasts a peaceful manor-home setting with 17 plush, relatively large, and *très* traditional rooms (across from the Métro station at 160 Rue de Grenelle, tel. 01 47 05 16 16, www.latourmaubourg.com, info@latourmaubourg.com).

$$$$ Hôtel Les Jardins d'Eiffel** is a big place on a quiet street, with professional service, a peaceful patio, and a lobby you can stretch out in. The 81 well-configured rooms—some with partial Eiffel Tower views, some with balconies—offer a bit more space and quiet than other hotels (RS%, parking garage, 8 Rue Amélie, tel. 01 47 05 46 21, www.hoteljardinseiffel.com, reservations@hoteljardinseiffel.com).

$$$ Hôtel Muguet** is quiet, well-located, well-run, and reasonable, with tastefully appointed rooms (some view rooms, strict 7-day cancellation policy, 11 Rue Chevert, tel. 01 47 05 05 93, www.hotelparismuguet.com, contact@hotelparismuguet.com).

$$$ Hôtel de l'Empereur** is stylish and delivers smashing views of Invalides from many of its fine rooms. All rooms have queen- or king-size beds, are tastefully designed with hints of the emperor, and are large by Paris standards (some view rooms, family rooms, strict 7-day cancellation policy, tel. 01 45 55 88 02, www.hotelempereurparis.com, contact@hotelempereur.com).

MARAIS

Those interested in a more central, diverse, and lively urban locale should make the Marais their Parisian home. Once a forgotten Parisian backwater, the Marais—which runs from the Pompidou Center east to the Bastille (a 15-minute walk)—is now one of Paris' most popular residential, tourist, and shopping areas. This is jumbled, medieval Paris at its finest, where classy stone mansions sit alongside trendy bars, antique shops, and fashion-conscious boutiques. The streets are an intriguing parade of artists, students, tourists, immigrants, and baguette-munching babies in strollers. The Marais is also known as a hub of the Parisian gay and lesbian scene. This area is *sans* doubt livelier and edgier than the Rue Cler area.

In the Marais you have these major sights close at hand: Carnavalet Museum (closed for renovation through 2017 and beyond), Victor Hugo's House, Jewish Art and History Museum, Pompidou Center, and Picasso Museum. You're also a manageable walk from Paris' two islands (Ile St. Louis and Ile de la Cité), home to Notre-Dame and Sainte-Chapelle. The Opéra Bastille, Promenade Plantée park, Place des Vosges (Paris' oldest square), the Jewish Quarter (Rue des Rosiers), the Latin Quarter, and nightlife-packed Rue de Lappe are also walkable. Strolling home (day or night) from Notre-Dame along Ile St. Louis is marvelous.

Most of my recommended hotels are located a few blocks north of the Marais' main east-west drag, Rue St. Antoine/Rue de Rivoli. For those who prefer a quieter home with fewer tourists, I list several hotels in the northern limits of the Marais, near Rue de Bretagne, the appealing commercial spine of this area.

Services: A busy **SNCF Boutique** is just off Rue St. Antoine at 2 Rue de Turenne (Mon-Fri 8:00-20:30, Sat 10:00-20:30, closed Sun); a quieter SNCF Boutique is nearer to Gare de Lyon at 5 Rue de Lyon (Mon-Sat 8:30-18:00, closed Sun).

Laundry: Launderettes are scattered throughout the Marais; ask your hotelier for the nearest. Here are two that you can count on: on Impasse Guéménée (north of Rue St. Antoine), and on Rue du Petit Musc (south of Rue St. Antoine).

Métro Connections: Key Métro stops in the Marais are, from east to west: Bastille, St-Paul, and Hôtel de Ville (Sully-Morland, Pont Marie, and Rambuteau stops are also handy). Métro connections are excellent, with direct service to the Louvre, Champs-Elysées, Arc de Triomphe, and La Défense (all on line 1); the Rue Cler area, Place de la Madeleine, and Opéra Garnier/Galeries Lafayette (line 8 from Bastille stop); and four major train stations: Gare de Lyon, Gare du Nord, Gare de l'Est, and Gare d'Austerlitz (all accessible from Bastille stop).

Bus Routes: For stop locations, see the "Marais Hotels" map.

Line #69 on Rue St. Antoine takes you eastbound to Père Lachaise Cemetery and westbound to the Louvre, Orsay, and Rodin museums, plus the Army Museum, ending at the Eiffel Tower.

Line #87 runs down Boulevard Henri IV, crossing Ile St. Louis and serving the Latin Quarter along Boulevard St. Germain, before heading to St. Sulpice Church/Luxembourg Garden, the Eiffel Tower, and the Rue Cler neighborhood to the west. The same line, running in the opposite direction, brings you to Gare de Lyon.

Line #96 runs on Rues Turenne and Rivoli, serves Ile de la

PARIS

Marais Hotels

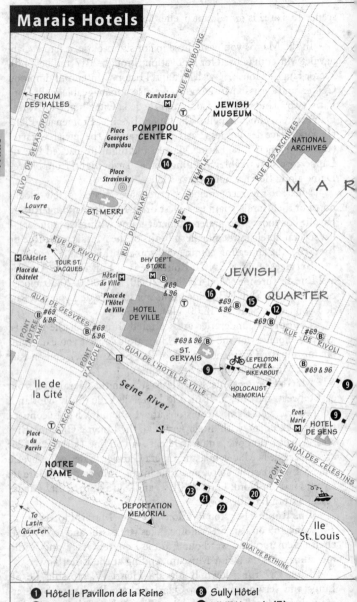

1 Hôtel le Pavillon de la Reine	**8** Sully Hôtel
2 Hôtel Bastille Spéria	**9** MIJE Hostels (3)
3 Hôtel St. Louis Marais	**10** Hôtel Ibis Paris Bastille Opéra
4 Hôtel Jeanne d'Arc	**11** Hôtel Daval
5 Hôtel Castex	**12** Hôtel Caron de Beaumarchais
6 Hôtel de Neuve	**13** Hôtel de la Bretonnerie
7 Hôtel Pratic	**14** Hôtel Beaubourg

PARIS

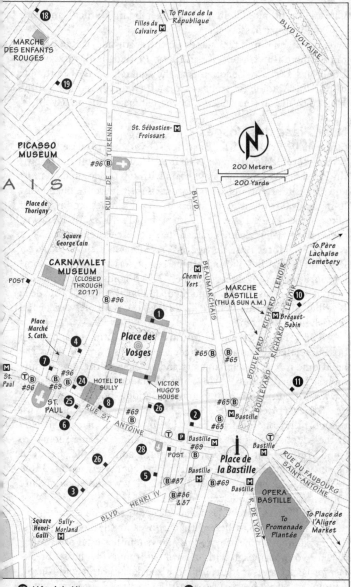

⑮ Hôtel de Nice
⑯ Hôtel du Loiret
⑰ D'Win Hôtel
⑱ Hôtel du Vieux Saule
⑲ Hôtel Saintonge
⑳ Hôtel du Jeu de Paume
㉑ Hôtel de Lutèce

㉒ Hôtel des Deux-Iles
㉓ Hôtel Saint-Louis
㉔ SNCF Boutique
㉕ Monoprix (Grocery)
㉖ Launderettes (2)
㉗ I Love My Blender Book Store

Cité and St. Sulpice Church (near Luxembourg Garden), and ends at Gare Montparnasse.

Taxi: You'll find taxi stands on the north side of Rue St. Antoine (where Rue Castex crosses it), on Place de la Bastille (where Boulevard Richard Lenoir meets the square), on the south side of Rue St. Antoine (in front of St. Paul Church), and behind the Hôtel de Ville on Rue du Lobau (where it meets Rue de Rivoli).

Near Place des Vosges
(3rd and 4th arrond., Mo: Bastille, St-Paul, or Hôtel de Ville)

$$$$ Hôtel le Pavillon de la Reine,***** 15 steps off the beautiful Place des Vosges, merits its stars with top service and comfort and exquisite attention to detail, from its melt-in-your-couch lobby to its luxurious rooms (free access to spa and fitness room, loaner bikes, parking, 28 Place des Vosges, tel. 01 40 29 19 19, www.pavillon-de-la-reine.com, contact@pavillon-de-la-reine.com).

$$$$ Hôtel Bastille Spéria*** is situated a short block off Place de la Bastille, offering business-type service and good comfort in a happening location. The 42 well-configured rooms are relatively spacious, simply appointed, and fairly priced (1 Rue de la Bastille, Mo: Bastille, tel. 01 42 72 04 01, www.hotelsperia.com, info@hotelsperia.com).

$$$$ Hôtel St. Louis Marais*** is an intimate and sharp little hotel that sits on a quiet street a few blocks from the river. The handsome rooms have character...and spacious bathrooms (family rooms, 1 Rue Charles V, Mo: Sully-Morland, tel. 01 48 87 87 04, www.saintlouismarais.com, marais@saintlouis-hotels.com).

$$$$ Hôtel Jeanne d'Arc,*** a lovely if pricey hotel with thoughtfully appointed rooms, is ideally located for connoisseurs of the Marais who don't need air-conditioning. Corner rooms are wonderfully bright in the City of Light. Rooms on the street can be noisy until the bars close (family rooms, some view rooms, 3 Rue de Jarente, Mo: St-Paul, tel. 01 48 87 62 11, www.hoteljeannedarc.com, information@hoteljeannedarc.com).

$$$ Hôtel Castex*** is a well-located place—on a quiet street near Place de la Bastille—with narrow and tile-floored rooms. Their system of connecting rooms allows families total privacy between two rooms, each with its own bathroom (free buffet breakfast for Rick Steves readers, just off Place de la Bastille and Rue St. Antoine at 5 Rue Castex, Mo: Bastille, tel. 01 42 72 31 52, www.castexhotel.com, info@castexhotel.com).

$$$ Hôtel de Neuve*** is a small, dignified place with classical music in the lobby and high tea in the afternoon. Rooms are plush, quiet, and a good value in this pricey area (behind the Monoprix at 14 Rue de Neuve, Mo: St-Paul, tel. 01 44 59 28 50, www.hoteldeneuveparis.com, reservation@hoteldeneuveparis.com).

$$ Hôtel Pratic, just off the quiet and charming Place du Marché Ste. Catherine, works for budget travelers who don't mind squeezing sideways to make it past the bed into the bathroom. The half-timbered interior gives the lobby a trace of character, but also makes for dark hallways. Rooms are clean, but lack charm (some view rooms, no elevator, no air-con, 9 Rue d'Ormesson, tel. 01 48 87 80 47, www.pratichotelparis.com, pratic.hotel@wanadoo.fr).

$ Sully Hôtel, right on Rue St. Antoine, is a basic, cheap dive run by no-nonsense Monsieur Zeroual. The rooms are frumpy, dimly lit, and can smell of smoke, the entry is dark and narrow (need I say more?), but the price fits. Two can spring for a triple for more room (family rooms, no elevator, no air-con, 48 Rue St. Antoine, Mo: St-Paul, tel. 01 42 78 49 32, www.sullyhotelparis.com, sullyhotel@orange.fr).

¢ MIJE Youth Hostels: The Maison Internationale de la Jeunesse et des Etudiants (MIJE) runs three classy, old residences, ideal for budget travelers who are at least 18 years old or traveling with someone who is. Each is well-maintained, with simple, clean, single-sex (unless your group takes a whole room) one- to four-bed rooms. The hostels are **MIJE Fourcy** (biggest and loudest, dirt-cheap dinners available with a membership card, 6 Rue de Fourcy, just south of Rue de Rivoli), **MIJE Fauconnier** (no elevator, 11 Rue du Fauconnier), and **MIJE Maubisson** (smallest and quietest, no outdoor terrace, 12 Rue des Barres). None has double beds or air-conditioning, all have private showers in every room—but bring your own towel (includes breakfast, required membership card-€2.50 extra/person, Wi-Fi in common areas only, rooms locked 12:00-15:00). They all share the same contact information (tel. 01 42 74 23 45, www.mije.com, info@mije.com) and Métro stop (St-Paul). Show up by noon or call to confirm a later arrival time.

East of Boulevard Richard Lenoir
(11th arrond., Mo: Bastille or Bréguet–Sabin)
These cheaper hotels are located a 10-minute walk from Place des Vosges.

$$$ Hôtel Ibis Paris Bastille Opéra*** is well-run and massive, with 300 reasonably priced, modern, comfortable rooms and a lobby with guest computers and room to roam. Amenities include an economical restaurant and private parking (15 Rue Breguet, Mo: Bréguet–Sabin, tel. 01 49 29 20 20, www.ibishotel.com, H1399@accor.com).

$$ Hôtel Daval,** a simple place on the wild side of Place de la Bastille, is handy for night owls. The 23 rooms are small, modest, and clean, with bathrooms like ship cabins, but the rates are good for an air-conditioned place. Ask for a quieter room on the courtyard side (family rooms, 21 Rue Daval, Mo: Bastille, tel. 01 47 00 51 23, www.hoteldaval.com, hoteldaval@wanadoo.fr).

Near the Pompidou Center
(4th arrond., Mo: St-Paul, Hôtel de Ville, or Rambuteau)

These hotels are farther west, closer to the Pompidou Center than to Place de la Bastille.

$$$$ Hôtel Caron de Beaumarchais*** transports you to the 18th century, with a small lobby that's cluttered with bits from an elegant old Marais house. If you want traditional French decor, stay here. Located on a busy street, it's well cared for and filled with character (12 Rue Vieille du Temple, tel. 01 42 72 34 12, www. carondebeaumarchais.com, hotel@carondebeaumarchais.com).

$$$ Hôtel de la Bretonnerie*** makes a fine Marais home. Located three blocks from the Hôtel de Ville, it has a warm, welcoming lobby and helpful staff. Its 29 good-value rooms are on the larger side with an antique, open-beam warmth (family rooms, free breakfast for Rick Steves readers who book directly, no air-con, between Rue Vieille du Temple and Rue des Archives at 22 Rue Ste. Croix de la Bretonnerie, tel. 01 48 87 77 63, www. hotelparismaraisbretonnerie.com, hotel@bretonnerie.com).

$$$ Hôtel Beaubourg*** is a terrific three-star value on a small street in the shadow of the Pompidou Center. The lounge is inviting, and the 28 plush and traditional rooms are well-appointed and quiet (bigger doubles are worth the extra cost, 11 Rue Simon Le Franc, Mo: Rambuteau, tel. 01 42 74 34 24, www.hotelbeaubourg. com, reservation@hotelbeaubourg.com).

$$ Hôtel de Nice,*** on the Marais' busy main drag, features a turquoise-and-fuchsia "Marie-Antoinette-does-tie-dye" decor. This character-filled place is littered with paintings and layered with carpets, and its 23 Old World rooms have thoughtful touches. Rooms on the street come with some noise; bathrooms are tight (reception on second floor, 42 bis Rue de Rivoli, tel. 01 42 78 55 29, www.hoteldenice.com, contact@hoteldenice.com).

$$ Hôtel du Loiret*** feels like the budget place it is when you walk in, but the rooms are surprisingly sharp—though bathrooms are small, and the service lacks a certain *je ne sais quoi* (no air-con, expect some noise, 8 Rue des Mauvais Garçons, tel. 01 48 87 77 00, www.hotel-du-loiret.fr, hotelduloiret@hotmail.com).

$$ D'Win Hôtel** is a rare two-star value in the thick of the Marais, with 40 updated and relatively spacious rooms, no elevator, and red accents everywhere (family rooms, 20 Rue du Temple, tel. 01 44 54 05 05, www.dwinhotel.com, contact@dwinhotel.com).

Near Rue de Bretagne
(3rd arrond., Mo: Filles du Calvaire or Temple)

Called the Haute (upper) Marais, this part of town attracts those wanting easy access to the heart of the Marais and a quieter neighborhood with a more local vibe. Appealing Rue de Bretagne is the soul of this area, with broad sidewalks, a healthy dose of cafés and shops, plus the lively Marché des Enfants Rouges market area. Allow 15 minutes to walk from these hotels to the Marais' main drag, Rue St. Antoine. The hotels themselves are all within a short walk of Rue de Bretagne.

$$$ Hôtel du Vieux Saule,*** well located across from the Marché des Enfants Rouges, offers 26 simple rooms in a good location at fair rates (smoking allowed in rooms on third floor, small sauna free for guests, 6 Rue de Picardie, Mo: Filles du Calvaire or Temple, tel. 01 42 72 01 14, www.hotelvieuxsaule.com, reserv@hotelvieuxsaule.com).

$$$ Hôtel Saintonge*** is a tastefully decorated and well-maintained place with wooden beams and stone floors (16 Rue de Saintonge, Mo: Filles du Calvaire, tel. 01 42 77 91 13, www.saintlouissaintonge.com, saintonge@saintlouis-hotels.com).

ILE ST. LOUIS
(4th arrond., Mo: Pont Marie)

The peaceful, residential character of this river-wrapped island, with its brilliant location and homemade ice cream, has drawn Americans for decades. There are no budget deals here—all of the hotels are three-star or more—though prices are respectable considering the level of comfort and wonderful location. The island's village ambience and proximity to the Marais, Notre-Dame, and the Latin Quarter make this area well worth considering. All of the following hotels are on the island's main drag, Rue St. Louis-en-l'Ile, where I list several restaurants (see page 147). For locations, see the "Marais Hotels" map on page 126. There are no Métro stops on Ile St. Louis; expect a 10-minute walk to the closest stations.

$$$$ Hôtel du Jeu de Paume**** occupies a 17th-century tennis center. Its magnificent lobby and cozy public spaces make it a fine splurge. Greet Lemon (luh-moe), *le chien,* then take a spin in the glass elevator for a half-timbered tree-house experience. The 30 rooms are carefully designed and tasteful, though not particularly spacious (you're paying for the location and public areas). Most rooms face a small garden courtyard; all are pin-drop peaceful (apartments for 4-6 people, 54 Rue St. Louis-en-l'Ile, tel. 01 43 26 14 18, www.jeudepaumehotel.com, info@jeudepaumehotel.com).

$$$$ **Hôtel de Lutèce***** comes with a welcoming wood-paneled lobby and a real fireplace. Rooms are traditional and warm, and those on lower floors have high ceilings. Twin rooms are larger and the same price as doubles; most beds are doubles (no queens). Rooms with bathtubs are on the louder street-side, while those with showers are on the courtyard (65 Rue St. Louis-en-l'Ile, tel. 01 43 26 23 52, www.hoteldelutece.com, info@hoteldelutece.com).

$$$$ **Hôtel des Deux-Iles***** has the same owners, comfort, and prices as the Lutèce (listed above)—but a tad less personality (single rooms available, 59 Rue St. Louis-en-l'Ile, tel. 01 43 26 13 35, www.hoteldesdeuxiles.com, info@hoteldesdeuxiles.com).

$$$ **Hôtel Saint-Louis***** blends character with modern comforts. The sharp rooms come with cool stone floors and exposed beams. Rates are reasonable...for the location (some rooms with balcony, iPads available for guest use, 75 Rue St. Louis-en-l'Ile, tel. 01 46 34 04 80, www.hotelsaintlouis.com, isle@saintlouis-hotels.com).

AT OR NEAR PARIS' AIRPORTS
At Charles de Gaulle Airport

These places are located a few minutes from the terminals, outside the T-3 RER stop, and have restaurants. For locations, see the map on page 153.

$$$ **Novotel***** is a step up from cookie-cutter airport hotels (tel. 01 49 19 27 27, www.novotel.com, h1014@accor.com).

$$ **Hôtel Ibis CDG Airport**** is huge and offers standard airport accommodations (tel. 01 49 19 19 19, www.ibishotel.com, h1404@accor.com).

Near Orly Airport

Two chain hotels, owned by the same company and very close to the Sud terminal, are your best options near Orly. Both have free shuttles *(navettes)* to the terminal.

$$$ **Hôtel Mercure Paris Orly***** provides high comfort for a high price (tel. 08 25 80 69 69, www.accorhotel.com, h1246@accor.com).

$$ **Hôtel Ibis Orly Aéroport**** is reasonable and basic (tel. 01 56 70 50 60, www.ibishotel.com, h1413@accor.com).

APARTMENT RENTALS

Consider this option if you're traveling as a family, in a group, or staying at least a few nights. Intrepid travelers around the world are accustomed to using Airbnb and VRBO when it comes to renting a vacation apartment. In Paris, you also have many additional options among rental agencies, and I've found the following to be the most reliable. Their websites are good and essential to understanding your choices: **Paris Perfect,** www.parisperfect.com; **Adrian Leeds Group,** www.adrianleeds.com; **France Homestyle,** www.francehomestyle.com; **Home Rental Service,** www.homerental.fr; **Haven in Paris,** www.haveninparis.com; **Paris Home,** www.parishome2000.com; **Cobblestone Paris Rentals,** www.cobblestoneparis.com; **Paris for Rent,** www.parisforrent.com; and **Cross-Pollinate,** www.cross-pollinate.com.

BED-AND-BREAKFASTS

Several agencies can help you go local by staying in a private home in Paris. While prices and quality can range greatly, most rooms have a private bath and run from €85 to €150. Most owners won't take bookings for fewer than two nights. To limit stair-climbing, ask whether the building has an elevator. The agencies listed below have a good selection: **Alcôve & Agapes,** www.bed-and-breakfast-in-paris.com; **Meeting the French,** http://en.meetingthefrench.com; and **Good Morning Paris,** www.goodmorningparis.fr.

Eating in Paris

The Parisian eating scene is kept at a rolling boil. Entire books (and lives) are dedicated to the subject. Paris is France's wine-and-cui-

sine melting pot. Though it lacks a style of its own (only French onion soup is truly Parisian; otherwise, there is no "Parisian cuisine" to speak of), it draws from the best of France. Paris could hold a gourmet Olympics and import nothing.

My restaurant recommendations are mostly centered on the same great neighborhoods as my hotel listings; you can come home exhausted after a busy day of sightseeing and find a good selection of eateries right around the corner. And evening is a fine time to explore any of these delightful neighborhoods, even if you're sleeping elsewhere. Serious eaters looking for even more suggestions should consult the always-appetizing www.parisbymouth.com, an eating-and-drinking guide to Paris.

To save piles of euros, go to a bakery for takeout, or stop at a café for lunch. Cafés and brasseries are happy to serve a *plat du jour* (plate of the day, about €12-20) or a chef-like salad (about €10-14) day or night. To save even more, consider picnics (tasty takeout dishes available at charcuteries). Try eating your big meal at lunch, when many fine restaurants offer their dinnertime fixed-price *menus* at a reduced price.

Linger longer over dinner—restaurants expect you to enjoy a full meal. Most restaurants I've listed have set-price *menus* between €20 and €38. In most cases, the few extra euros you pay are well spent and open up a variety of better choices. Remember that a service charge is included in the prices (so little or no tipping is expected).

For details on dining in French restaurants, cafés, and brasseries, getting takeout, and assembling a picnic—as well as a rundown of French cuisine—see the "Eating" section in the Practicalities chapter (page 1062).

RUE CLER NEIGHBORHOOD
On Rue Cler
(Mo: Ecole Militaire)

$ Café du Marché boasts the best seats on Rue Cler. The owner's philosophy: Brasserie on speed—crank out good enough food at

great prices to appreciative locals and savvy tourists. It's high-energy, with young waiters who barely have time to smile...*très* Parisian. This place works well if you don't mind a limited selection and want to eat an inexpensive one-course meal among a commotion of people. The chalkboard lists your choices: good, hearty salads or more filling *plats du jour*. Arrive before 19:30 to avoid long waits (Mon-Sat 11:00-23:00, Sun 11:00-17:00, no reservations, at the corner of Rue Cler and Rue du Champ de Mars, 38 Rue Cler, tel. 01 47 05 51 27).

$$ Tribeca Restaurant, next door to Café du Marché, is less trendy and more family-friendly, serving more varied cuisine. Choose from kid-pleasing Italian dishes or try the roasted Camembert *à la crème* (pizzas, pastas, and salads; daily, tel. 01 45 55 12 01).

$ Le Petit Cler is an adorable and popular little bistro with long leather booths, a vintage interior, tight ranks of tiny outdoor tables, and simple, tasty, inexpensive dishes such as €9 omelets and €7 soup of the moment (delicious *pots de crème,* daily, opens early for dinner, arrive early or call in advance, 29 Rue Cler, tel. 01 45 50 17 50).

$$ Café le Roussillon offers a younger, publike ambience with good-value food. You'll find hearty salads, design-your-own omelets, fajitas, and easygoing waiters (daily, indoor seating only, corner of Rue de Grenelle and Rue Cler, tel. 01 45 51 47 53).

$ Crêperie Ulysée en Gaule offers cheap seats on Rue Cler with crêpes to go. Readers of this book who buy a drink can enjoy

---

Restaurant Price Code

I've assigned each eatery a price category, based on the average cost of a typical main course. Drinks, desserts, and splurge items (steak and seafood) can raise the price considerably.

$$$$	**Splurge:** Most main courses over €25
$$$	**Pricier:** €20-25
$$	**Moderate:** €15-20
$	**Budget:** Under €15

In France, a crêpe stand or other takeout spot is **$**; a sit-down brasserie, café, or bistro with affordable *plats du jour* is **$$**; a casual but more upscale restaurant is **$$$**; and a swanky splurge is **$$$$**.

---

a crêpe at a table for takeaway prices. The family adores its Greek dishes, but their crêpes are your least expensive hot meal on this street (28 Rue Cler, tel. 01 47 05 61 82).

$ Brasserie Aux PTT, a simple traditional café delivering fair-value fare, reminds Parisians of the old days on Rue Cler. Rick Steves diners are promised a free *kir* with their dinner (cheap wine, closed Sun, opposite 53 Rue Cler, tel. 01 45 51 94 96).

Close to Ecole Militaire
(Mo: Ecole Militaire)

$$$ Le Florimond is fun for a special occasion. The setting is warm and welcoming. Locals come for classic French cuisine at fair prices. Friendly Laurent, whose playful ties change daily, gracefully serves one small room of tables and loves to give suggestions. Pascale, his chef of more than 20 years, produces particularly tasty stuffed cabbage, lobster ravioli, and *confit de canard*. The Château Chênaie house wine is excellent (closed Sun and first and third Sat of month, reservations encouraged, 19 Avenue de la Motte-Picquet, tel. 01 45 55 40 38, www.leflorimond.com).

$$$ Bistrot Belhara delivers a delicious, vintage French dining experience in an intimate setting. The chef-owner Thierry cooks up a blend of inventive and classic dishes. Earnest and helpful Frédéric runs the front of the house with a smile (closed Sun-Mon, reservations smart, a block off Rue Cler at 23 Rue Duvivier, tel. 01 45 51 41 77, www.bistrotbelhara.com).

$$ Café le Bosquet is a contemporary Parisian brasserie where you'll dine for a decent price inside or outside on a broad sidewalk. Come here for standard café fare—salad, French onion soup, *steak-frites*, or a *plat du jour*. Lanky owner "Jeff" offers three-course meals and *plats* (closed Sun, corner of Rue du Champ de Mars at 46 Avenue Bosquet, tel. 01 45 51 38 13, www.bosquetparis.com).

$$$ La Terrasse du 7ème is a sprawling, happening café

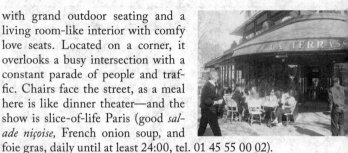

with grand outdoor seating and a living room-like interior with comfy love seats. Located on a corner, it overlooks a busy intersection with a constant parade of people and traffic. Chairs face the street, as a meal here is like dinner theater—and the show is slice-of-life Paris (good *salade niçoise*, French onion soup, and foie gras, daily until at least 24:00, tel. 01 45 55 00 02).

Between Rue de Grenelle and the River, East of Avenue Bosquet
(Mo: La Tour-Maubourg)

$$$$ L'Ami Jean offers authentic Basque specialties in a snug-but-convivial atmosphere with red peppers and Basque stuff dangling from the ceiling. While pricey, portions are hearty and delicious. Parisians detour long distances to savor the gregarious chef's special cuisine and fun atmosphere. For dinner arrive before 19:30 or reserve ahead (€80 eight-course dinner *menu*, a more accessible lunch *menu* for €35, closed Sun-Mon, 27 Rue Malar, tel. 01 47 05 86 89, www.lamijean.fr).

$$$$ Thoumieux is the neighborhood's grand brasserie, with a showy interior lined with red velvet chairs, chandeliers, and fussy waiters. It's a minisplurge for most but designed as an affordable and user-friendly version of the two-star Michelin restaurant upstairs. Come here for a gourmet brasserie experience. Sharing plates is encouraged (enticing tasting menus, daily, 79 Rue St. Dominique, tel. 01 47 05 49 75, www.thoumieux.fr).

$$$ Au Petit Tonneau is a small, authentic French bistro with original, time-warp decor, red-checked tablecloths, and carefully prepared food from a limited menu. Away from the Rue Cler touristic crush, this place is real, the cuisine is delicious, and the experience is what you came to France for (good à la carte choices or three-course *menu* that changes with season, well-priced wines, closed Mon, 20 Rue Surcouf, tel. 01 47 05 09 01, charming owner Arlette at your service).

Between Rue de Grenelle and the River, West of Avenue Bosquet
(Mo: Ecole Militaire unless otherwise noted)

$$$$ 58 Tour Eiffel, on the tower's first level, provides a feast for both your belly and your eyes, with incredible city views. Dinner here is pricey and requires a reservation (two seatings: 18:30 with €85-125 *menus,* and 21:00 with €100-185 *menus;* reserve long in advance, especially if you want a view, no jeans or tennis shoes at dinner). During the day they serve a €42 *picque-nique-chic* lunch, which is packaged in a little basket (€19 for kids, daily 11:30-16:30, reservations are a good idea, Mo: Bir-Hakeim or Trocadéro, RER: Champ de Mars-Tour Eiffel, tel. 01 72 76 18 46, toll tel. 08 25 56 66 62, www.restaurants-toureiffel.com). With a reservation, you ride up for free in the restaurant elevator.

$$$$ La Fontaine de Mars, a longtime favorite and neighborhood institution, is charmingly situated on a tiny, jumbled square with tables jammed together for the serious business of eating. Reserve in advance for a table on the ground floor or square, and pass on the upstairs room (superb foie gras and desserts, daily, 129 Rue St. Dominique, tel. 01 47 05 46 44, www.fontainedemars. com).

$$$ Au Petit Sud Ouest comes wrapped in stone walls and wood beams, making it a cozy place to sample cuisine from southwestern France. Duck, goose, foie gras, *cassoulet,* and truffles are all on *la carte.* Tables come with toasters to heat your bread—it enhances the flavors of the foie gras. Try the *salade* with foie gras or the *cassoulet* (closed Sun-Mon, 46 Avenue de la Bourdonnais, tel. 01 45 55 59 59, www.au-petit-sud-ouest.fr, managed by friendly Chantal).

$$$ Le P'tit Troquet is a petite eatery taking you back to the Paris of the 1920s. Marie serves and José cooks a delicious range of traditional choices prepared creatively. The homey charm and tasty food make this restaurant a favorite of connoisseurs (their €35 three-course *menu* is available for €25 at lunch, dinner service from 18:30, closed Sun, reservations smart, 28 Rue de l'Exposition, tel. 01 47 05 80 39).

$$$ Billebaude, run by patient Pascal, is a small bistro popular with locals and tourists. The focus is on what's fresh, including catch-of-the-day fish and meats from the hunt (available in fall and winter). Chef Sylvain, an avid hunter (as the decor suggests), is determined to deliver quality at a fair price. Skip this place if you're in a hurry (closed Sun-Mon, 29 Rue de l'Exposition, tel. 01 45 55 20 96).

$$$ Pottoka attracts locals willing to crowd into this shoebox for a chance to sample tasty Basque cuisine. Service is friendly, wines are reasonable, and the focus is on food rather than decor (daily, book ahead, 4 Rue de l'Exposition, tel. 01 45 51 88 38, www. pottoka.fr).

$$ Café de Mars is a relaxed place for a reasonably priced and well-prepared meal. It's also comfortable for single diners thanks to a convivial counter (closed Sun, 11 Rue Augereau, tel. 01 45 50 10 90, www.cafedemars.com).

$ Le Royal is a tiny neighborhood fixture offering the cheapest meals in the area. This humble time-warp place, with prices

PARIS

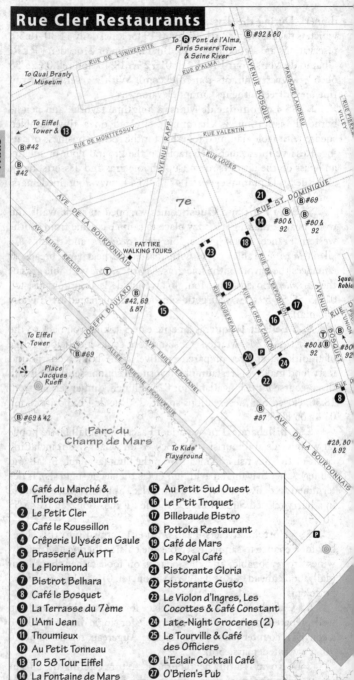

Rue Cler Restaurants

To **R** Pont de l'Alma,
Paris Sewers Tour
& Seine River

B #92 & 80

RUE DE L'UNIVERSITÉ

To Quai Branly
Museum

RUE D'ALMA

AVENUE BOSQUET

PASSAGE L'ANDRIEU

RUE PIERRE...
VILLEY

To Eiffel
Tower & **13**

RUE DE MONTTESSUY

B #42

B #42

AVENUE RAPP

RUE VALENTIN

RUE LOGES

7e

21

RUE ST. DOMINIQUE

B #69

AVE. DE LA BOURDONNAIS

14

B #80 &
92

B #80 &
92

AVE. ELISEE RECLUS

FAT TIRE
WALKING TOURS

23

18

RUE DE L'EXPOSITION

Squa
Robic

T

19

AVENUE

AVE. JOSEPH BOUVARD

B #42, 69
& 87

15

RUE AUGEREAU

17

16

RUE D'PON...
UNION

RUE DE GROS CAILLOU

To Eiffel
Tower

B #69

ALLÉE ADRIENNE LECOUVREUR

AVE. ÉMILE DESCHANEL

20

P

T

B
#80 & 92

B
#80
92

Place
Jacques
Rueff

24

22

RUE D...

8

B #69 & 42

Parc du
Champ de Mars

B
#87

AVE. DE LA BOURDONNAIS

To Kids'
Playground

#28, 80
& 92

P

---

1 Café du Marché &
Tribeca Restaurant

2 Le Petit Cler

3 Café le Roussillon

4 Crêperie Ulysée en Gaule

5 Brasserie Aux PTT

6 Le Florimond

7 Bistrot Belhara

8 Café le Bosquet

9 La Terrasse du 7ème

10 L'Ami Jean

11 Thoumieux

12 Au Petit Tonneau

13 To 58 Tour Eiffel

14 La Fontaine de Mars

15 Au Petit Sud Ouest

16 Le P'tit Troquet

17 Billebaude Bistro

18 Pottoka Restaurant

19 Café de Mars

20 Le Royal Café

21 Ristorante Gloria

22 Ristorante Gusto

23 Le Violon d'Ingres, Les
Cocottes & Café Constant

24 Late-Night Groceries (2)

25 Le Tourville & Café
des Officiers

26 L'Eclair Cocktail Café

27 O'Brien's Pub

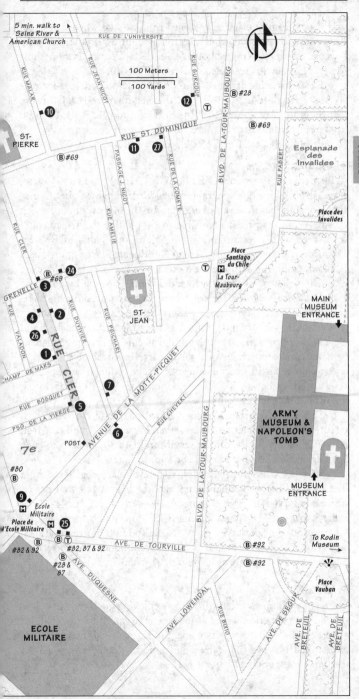

PARIS

5 min. walk to
Seine River &
American Church

RUE DE L'UNIVERSITE

RUE JEAN NICOT

RUE MALAR

RUE SURCOUF

BLVD. DE LA-TOUR-MAUBOURG

(B) #28

(T)

🔟

(T)

1⃣2⃣

ST-
PIERRE

(B) #69

RUE ST. DOMINIQUE

(B) #69

RUE FABERT

Esplanade
des
Invalides

1⃣1⃣ 2⃣7⃣

PASSAGE J. NICOT

RUE DE LA COMETE

RUE AMELIE

Place des
Invalides

RUE CLER

Place
Santiago
du Chile

(T)

GRENELLE

(B) #69 2⃣4⃣

3⃣

(M) La Tour-
Maubourg

RUE DUVIVIER

RUE PSICHARI

MAIN
MUSEUM
ENTRANCE

4⃣ 2⃣

ST-
JEAN

RUE VALADON

2⃣6⃣

1⃣

RUE CLER

CHAMP DE MARS

7⃣

AVENUE DE LA MOTTE-PICQUET

RUE CHEVERT

ARMY
MUSEUM &
NAPOLEON'S
TOMB

RUE BOSQUET

5⃣

PSG. DE LA VIERGE

6⃣

BLVD. DE LA-TOUR-MAUBOURG

7e

POST ♦

MUSEUM
ENTRANCE

#80
(B)

9⃣

(M) Ecole
Militaire

Place de
l'Ecole Militaire

(M) 2⃣5⃣

To Rodin
Museum

(B)
#82 & 92

(B) (T)
#82, 87 & 92

AVE. DE TOURVILLE

(B) #92

(B)
#28 &
87

(B) #92

AVE. DUQUESNE

Place
Vauban

ECOLE
MILITAIRE

AVE. LOWENDAL

RUE BIXIO

AVE. DE SEGUR

AVE. DE BRETEUIL

AVE. DE BRETEUIL

100 Meters

100 Yards

and decor from another era, comes from an age when cafés sold firewood and served food as an afterthought. Parisians dine here because "it's like eating at home." Gentle Guillaume is a fine host (daily, 212 Rue de Grenelle, tel. 01 47 53 92 90).

$$ Affordable Italian: You'll find two good choices for reasonably priced Italian cuisine in the neighborhood. **Ristorante Gloria** is almost elegant (108 Rue St. Dominique, tel. 01 45 56 00 98). **Ristorante Gusto** is more fun, tight, and characteristic (199 Rue de Grenelle, tel. 01 45 55 00 43).

The Constant Lineup
(Mo: Ecole Militaire or RER: Pont de l'Alma)

Ever since leaving the venerable Hôtel Crillon, famed chef Christian Constant has made a career of taking the "snoot" out of French cuisine—and making it accessible to people like us. Today you'll find three of his restaurants strung along one block of Rue St. Dominique between Rue Augereau and Rue de l'Exposition. Each is distinct, offering a different experience and price range. None are cheap, but they're all a good value, delivering top-quality cuisine.

$$$$ Le Violon d'Ingres, where Christian won his first Michelin star, makes for a good excuse to dress up and dine finely in Paris. Glass doors open onto a chic eating scene—hushed and elegant. Service is formal yet helpful; the cuisine is what made this restaurateur's reputation (order à la carte or consider their €110 seven-course tasting menu, cheaper weekday lunch *menu,* daily, reservations essential, 135 Rue St. Dominique, tel. 01 45 55 15 05, www.maisonconstant.com).

$$$ Les Cocottes attracts a crowd of trendy Parisians with its fun energy and creative dishes served in *cocottes*—small cast-iron pots (tasty soups, daily, dinner service from 18:30, go early as they don't take reservations, 135 Rue St. Dominique).

$$ Café Constant is a cool, two-level place that feels more like a small bistro-wine bar than a café. Delicious and well-priced dishes are served in a snug setting. Arrive early to get a table downstairs if you can—upstairs seating is less fun (daily, opens at 7:00 for breakfast, meals served nonstop 12:00-23:00, no reservations, corner of Rue Augereau and Rue St. Dominique, next to recommended Hôtel de Londres Eiffel, tel. 01 47 53 73 34).

MARAIS

The trendy Marais is filled with diners enjoying good food in colorful and atmospheric eateries. The scene is competitive and changes all the time. I've listed an assortment of eateries—all handy to recommended hotels—that offer good food at decent prices, plus a memorable experience.

On Romantic Place des Vosges
(Mo: St-Paul or Bastille)

This square offers Old World Marais elegance, a handful of eateries, and an ideal picnic site until dusk, when the park closes. Strolling around the arcade after dark is more important than dining here—fanciful art galleries alternate with restaurants and cafés. Choose a restaurant that best fits your mood and budget; most have arcade seating and provide big space heaters to make outdoor dining during colder months an option. Also consider just a drink on the square at Café Hugo.

$$$ La Place Royale offers a fine location on the square with good seating inside or out. Expect patient waiters (owner Arnaud prides himself on service), and a family-friendly menu with salads, pizzas, and classic dishes. The cuisine is priced well and served nonstop all day, and the exceptional wine list is reasonable (try the Sancerre white). The €42 *menu* comes with three courses, a half-bottle of wine per person, and coffee (lunch specials, daily, reserve ahead to dine outside under the arcade, 2 bis Place des Vosges, tel. 01 42 78 58 16).

$$ Café Hugo, named for the square's most famous resident, serves salads and basic café fare with a fun energy. The food's good enough, but the setting's terrific, with good seating under the arches (daily, 22 Place des Vosges, tel. 01 42 72 64 04).

Near Place des Vosges
(Mo: Chemin Vert)

$$$ Chez Janou, a Provençal bistro, tumbles out of its corner building and fills its broad sidewalk with happy eaters. Don't let the trendy and youthful crowd intimidate you: It's relaxed and charming, with helpful and patient service. The curbside tables are inviting, but I'd sit inside (with very tight seating) to immerse myself in the happy commotion. The style is French Mediterranean, with an emphasis on vegetables (daily—book ahead or arrive when it opens, 2 blocks beyond Place des Vosges at 2 Rue Roger Verlomme, tel. 01 42 72 28 41, www.chezjanou.com). They serve 81 varieties of *pastis* (licorice-flavored liqueur, browse the list above the bar).

$$$ Le Petit Marché delivers a cozy and intimate bistro experience inside and out with friendly service and a delicious cuisine that blends French classics with a slight Asian influence (daily, 9 Rue du Béarn, tel. 01 42 72 06 67).

Near the Place de la Bastille
(Mo: Bastille)

$$$ Brasserie Bofinger, an institution for over a century, is famous for seafood and traditional cuisine with Alsatian flair. You'll eat in a sprawling interior, surrounded by brisk, black-and-white-

Marais Restaurants

1. La Place Royale
2. Café Hugo
3. Chez Janou
4. Le Petit Marché
5. Brasserie Bofinger
6. Au Temps des Cerises
7. Vin des Pyrénées
8. Chez Mademoiselle
9. Breizh Café
10. Place du Marché
    Ste. Catherine Eateries
11. Les Bougresses
12. Rue St. Antoine Eateries
13. Chez Marianne
14. Le Loir dans la Théière
15. L'As du Falafel
16. La Droguerie Crêperie
17. Au Bourguignon du Marais

PARIS

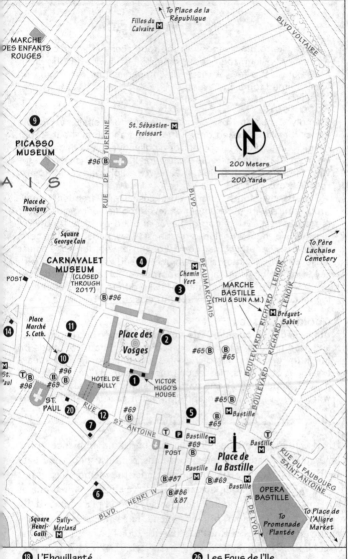

18 L'Ebouillanté
19 BHV Cafeteria
20 Monoprix (Grocery)
21 Late-Night Grocery
22 Au Petit Fer à Cheval &
   La Belle Hortense
23 La Perla Bar
24 Le Pick-Clops Bar Rest.
25 Nos Ancêtres les Gaulois

26 Les Fous de l'Ile
27 La Brasserie de l'Ile St. Louis
28 L'Orangerie & Auberge de la
   Reine Blanche
29 Café Med
30 Bakery & 38 Saint Louis Deli
31 Berthillon Ice Cream
32 Amorino Gelati
33 Good Picnic Spot

The Paris Food Scene

If you'd like to dig deeper into the food scene in Paris, consider a culinary walking tour, cooking school, or a wine-tasting class. These are just a few of the Paris companies that run food- and wine-themed tours and events.

Food Tours

Friendly Canadian Rosa Jackson designs personalized **"Edible Paris"** itineraries based on your interests and three-hour "food-guru" tours of Paris led by her or a colleague (unguided itineraries from €125, guided tours—€300 for 1-2 people, larger groups welcome too, tel. 06 81 67 41 22, www.edible-paris.com, rosa@rosajackson.com).

Paris by Mouth offers more casual and frequent small-group tours, with a maximum of seven foodies per group. Tours are organized by location or flavor and led by local food writers (€95/3 hours, includes tastings, www.parisbymouth.com, tasteparisbymouth@gmail.com). For those who don't like to eat while walking, try their sit-down cheese and wine workshop with seven different wines and an impressive spread of 14 cheeses (€95/3 hours). Given that there are 350 different types of cheese in France, you may need to take this class more than once.

Cooking Classes

At **Les Secrets Gourmands de Noémie,** charming and knowledgeable Noémie shares her culinary secrets in 2.5 hours of hands-on fun in the kitchen. Thursday classes, designed for English speakers, focus on sweets; classes on other days are in French, English, or both depending on the participants, and tackle savory dishes with the possibility of an add-on market tour (€75-105, 92 Rue

attired waiters. Come here for the one-of-a-kind ambience in the elaborately decorated ground-floor rooms, reminiscent of the Roaring Twenties. Reserve ahead to dine under the memorable, grand 1919 *coupole* (avoid eating upstairs). If you've always wanted one of those picturesque seafood platters, this is a good place (open daily for lunch and for dinner, fun kids' menu, fair-value *menus* and reasonably priced wines, 5 Rue de la Bastille, don't be confused by the lesser "Petite" Bofinger across the street, tel. 01 42 72 87 82, www.bofingerparis.com).

$$$ Au Temps des Cerises is a warm place with wads of character and tight inside seating (and a couple of outdoor tables). Come for a glass of wine at the small zinc bar, or stay for a tasty dinner (good cheap wine, daily, at the corner of Rue du Petit Musc and Rue de la Cerisaie, tel. 01 42 72 08 63).

$$$ Vin des Pyrénées is a lighthearted place that feels like Rembrandt's living room—the floor is a mismatch of old tiles,

Nollet, Mo: La Fourche, tel. 06 64 17 93 32, www.lessecretsgour-mandsdenoemie.com, noemie@lessecretsgourmandsdenoemie.com).

Cook'n with Class gets rave reviews for its convivial cooking and wine and cheese classes with a maximum of six students; tasting courses offered as well (6 Rue Baudelique, Mo: Jules Joffrin or Simplon, tel. 06 31 73 62 77, www.cooknwithclass.com).

La Cuisine Paris has a great variety of classes in English, reasonable prices, and a beautiful space in central Paris (2- or 3-hour classes–€65-95, 4-hour class with market tour–€150, gourmet visit of Versailles—see website for details, 80 Quai de l'Hôtel de Ville, tel. 01 40 51 78 18, www.lacuisineparis.com).

Wine Tasting
Olivier Magny and his team of sommeliers teach wine-tasting classes at the Ô Château wine school/bar, in the 17th-century residence of Madame de Pompadour. Olivier's goal is to "take the snob out of wine." At these informal classes, you'll learn the basics of French wine regions, the techniques of tasting, and how to read a French wine label. Classes range from Introductory Tasting (€30, 1 hour) to wine-tasting dinners (€100, about 2 hours). Register online using code "RS2017" for a 10 percent discount (68 Rue Jean-Jacques Rousseau, Mo: Louvre-Rivoli or Etienne Marcel, tel. 01 44 73 97 80, www.o-chateau.com). The same team offers hands-on two-hour workshops in wine blending. You'll leave with a bottle of your very own blend (€75, near the Louvre at 52 Rue de l'Arbre Sec, Mo: Louvre-Rivoli, tel. 01 44 73 97 80, www.cavesdulouvre.com).

knickknacks, and Old World decor. The chalkboard lists a mélange of authentic and nicely presented dishes (two-course lunch special, daily, 25 Rue Beautreillis, tel. 01 42 72 64 94).

In the Heart of the Marais
(Mo: St-Paul)
At **$$$ Chez Mademoiselle,** the country-elegant, candlelit decor recalls charming owner Alexia's previous career as a French *comédienne*. Enjoy a French-paced dinner in a relaxing atmosphere inside or at a sidewalk table. Ingredients are fresh and prepared simply. The tender *château filet* is served all year, but most dishes follow the seasons (good wine list, daily, 16 Rue Charlemagne, tel. 01 42 72 14 16).

$$ Breizh Café is worth the hike for some of the best Breton crêpes in Paris ("Breizh" means Brittany). This simple joint serves organic crêpes—both sweet and savory—and small rolls made for dipping in rich sauces and salted butter. The crêpes run the gamut from traditional ham, cheese, and egg to Asian fusion. They also talk about cider like a sommelier would talk about wine. Try a sparkling cider, a Breton cola, or my favorite—*lait ribot,* a buttermilk-like drink (closed Mon-Tue, serves nonstop 11:30-late, reservations highly recommended, 109 Rue du Vieille du Temple, tel. 01 42 72 13 77, www.breizhcafe.com).

$$ On Place du Marché Ste. Catherine: This small, romantic square, just off Rue St. Antoine, is cloaked in extremely Parisian, leafy-square ambience. It feels like the Latin Quarter but classier. On a balmy evening, this is a neighborhood favorite, with a handful of restaurants offering mediocre cuisine (you're here for the setting). It's also family-friendly: Most places serve French hamburgers, and kids can dance around the square while parents breathe. Survey the square. You'll find three French bistros with similar features and menus: **Le Marché, Chez Joséphine,** and **Le Bistrot de la Place** (all open daily, cheaper for lunch, tight seating on flimsy chairs indoors and out, Chez Joséphine has best chairs). Just off the square, the fun-loving **Les Bougresses** offers less romance but far better food for the price (inside seating only, daily from 18:30, 6 Rue de Jarente, tel. 01 48 87 71 21).

$ On Rue St. Antoine: Several hardworking **Asian fast-food eateries,** great for an inexpensive meal, line this street.

In the Jewish Quarter, Rue des Rosiers
(Mo: St-Paul or Hôtel de Ville)

$$ Chez Marianne is a neighborhood fixture that serves tasty Jewish cuisine in a fun atmosphere with Parisian *élan.* Choose from several indoor zones with a cluttered wine shop/deli feeling, or sit outside. You'll select from two dozen *zakouskis* (hot and cold hor d'oeuvres) to assemble your *plat.* Vegetarians will find great options (takeaway falafel sandwiches, long hours daily, corner of Rue des Rosiers and Rue des Hospitalières-St-Gervais, tel. 01 42 72 18 86).

$$ Le Loir dans la Théière ("The Dormouse in the Teapot"— think Alice in Wonderland) is a cozy, mellow teahouse offering a welcoming ambience for tired travelers (laptops and smartphones are not welcome). It's ideal for lunch and popular on weekends. They offer a daily assortment of creatively filled quiches and bake up an impressive array of homemade desserts that are proudly displayed in the dining room (daily 9:00-19:00 but only dessert-type items offered after 15:00, 3 Rue des Rosiers, tel. 01 42 72 90 61).

$ L'As du Falafel rules the falafel scene in the Jewish quarter. Monsieur Isaac, the "Ace of Falafel" here since 1979, brags, "I've got the biggest pita on the street...and I fill it up." Your cheap meal comes on a plastic plate; the €8 "special falafel" is the big hit, but many enjoy the lighter chicken version *(poulet grillé)* or the tasty and massive *assiette de falafel*. Wash it down with a cold Maccabee beer. Their takeout service draws a constant crowd (long hours most days except closed Fri evening and all day Sat, air-con, 34 Rue des Rosiers, tel. 01 48 87 63 60).

$ La Droguerie, a hole-in-the-wall crêpe stand a few blocks farther down Rue des Rosiers, is a good budget option if falafels don't work for you but cheap does. Grab a stool, or get a crêpe to go (daily 12:00-22:00, 56 Rue des Rosiers).

Near Hôtel de Ville
(Mo: Hôtel de Ville)

$$$$ Au Bourguignon du Marais is a dressy wine bar/bistro for Burgundy lovers, where excellent wines (Burgundian only, avail-

able by the glass) blend with a good selection of well-designed dishes and efficient service. The *œufs en meurette* are mouthwatering, and the *bœuf bourguignon* could feed two (daily, pleasing indoor and outdoor seating on a perfect Marais corner, 52 Rue François Miron, tel. 01 48 87 15 40).

$$ L'Ebouillanté is a breezy café, romantically situated near the river on a broad, cobbled pedestrian lane behind a church. With great outdoor seating and an artsy, cozy interior, it's perfect for an inexpensive and relaxing tea, snack, or lunch—or for dinner on a warm evening. Their €15 *bricks*—paper-thin, Tunisian-inspired pancakes stuffed with what you would typically find in an omelet— come with a small salad (daily 12:00-21:30, closes earlier in winter, a block off the river at 6 Rue des Barres, tel. 01 42 74 70 57).

$ BHV Department Store's fifth-floor cafeteria provides nice views, good prices, and many main courses to choose from, with a salad bar, pizza by the slice, and pasta. It's family-easy (Mon-Sat 11:30-18:00, hot food served until 16:00, open later Wed, closed Sun, at intersection of Rue du Temple and Rue de la Verrerie, one block from Hôtel de Ville).

ILE ST. LOUIS
(Mo: Pont Marie)

These recommended spots—ranging from rowdy to petite, rustic to elegant—line the island's main drag, Rue St. Louis-en-l'Ile (see map on page 142).

$$ Nos Ancêtres les Gaulois ("Our Ancestors the Gauls"), famous for its rowdy, medieval-cellar atmosphere, is made for hungry warriors and wenches who like to swill hearty wine. For

dinner they serve up rustic, all-you-can-eat fare with straw baskets of raw veggies and bundles of *saucisson* (cut whatever you like with your dagger), plates of pâté, a meat course, cheese, a dessert, and all the wine you can stomach for €40. The food is perfectly edible; burping is encouraged. If you want to overeat, drink too much wine, be surrounded by tourists (mostly French), and holler at your friends while receiving smart-aleck buccaneer service, you're home (daily, 39 Rue St. Louis-en-l'Ile, tel. 01 46 33 66 07).

$$ Les Fous de l'Ile is a lighthearted mash-up of a collector's haunt, art gallery, and bistro. It's a fun place to eat bistro fare with gourmet touches for a good price (daily, serves nonstop, 33 Rue des Deux Ponts, tel. 01 43 25 76 67).

$$ La Brasserie de l'Ile St. Louis offers purely Alsatian cuisine (hearty pork and kraut fare—try the *choucroute garnie* or *coq au riesling* for €22), served in a vigorous, hunting-lodge setting with no-nonsense, slap-it-down service on wine-stained paper tablecloths. The front tables make a good, balmy-evening perch for watching the theatrical street scene—

often with live music. If it's chilly, the interior is also fun for a memorable night out (closed Wed, no reservations, faces Ile de la Cité at 55 Quai de Bourbon, tel. 01 43 54 02 59).

$$$ L'Orangerie is an inviting, rustic-yet-elegant place with soft lighting and comfortable, spacious seating. The cuisine is traditional with occasional modern touches (closed Mon, 28 Rue St. Louis-en-l'Ile, tel. 01 46 33 93 98).

$$ Auberge de la Reine Blanche—woodsy, cozy, and tight—welcomes diners willing to rub elbows with their neighbors. Earnest owner Michel serves basic, traditional cuisine at reasonable prices (closed Wed, 30 Rue St. Louis-en-l'Ile, tel. 01 46 33 07 87).

$ Café Med, near the pedestrian bridge to Notre-Dame, is a tiny, cheery *crêperie* with good-value salads, crêpes, and *plats* (daily,

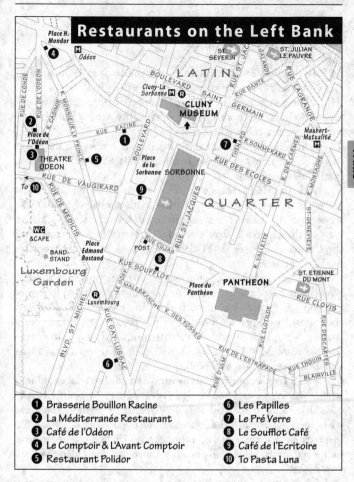

Restaurants on the Left Bank

1 Brasserie Bouillon Racine
2 La Méditerranée Restaurant
3 Café de l'Odéon
4 Le Comptoir & L'Avant Comptoir
5 Restaurant Polidor
6 Les Papilles
7 Le Pré Verre
8 Le Soufflot Café
9 Café de l'Ecritoire
10 To Pasta Luna

77 Rue St. Louis-en-l'Ile, tel. 01 43 29 73 17). Two similar *crêperies* are just across the street.

Ice-Cream Dessert

Half the people strolling Ile St. Louis are licking an ice-cream cone because this is the home of *les glaces Berthillon* (now sold throughout Paris, though still made here on Ile St. Louis). The original **Berthillon** shop, at 31 Rue St. Louis-en-l'Ile, is marked by the line of salivating customers (closed Mon-Tue). For a less famous but satisfying treat, the Italian gelato a block away at **Amorino Gelati** is giving Berthillon competition (no line, bigger portions, easier to see what you want, and they offer little tastes—Berthillon doesn't need to, 47 Rue St. Louis-en-l'Ile, tel. 01 44 07 48 08). Having some of each is not a bad thing.

ON THE LEFT BANK
Near the Odéon Theater
(Mo: Odéon)

$$$ **Brasserie Bouillon Racine** takes you back to 1906 with an Art Nouveau carnival of carved wood, stained glass, and old-time lights reflected in beveled mirrors. The over-the-top decor and energetic waiters give it an inviting conviviality. Check upstairs before choosing a table. Their roast suckling pig (€20) is a favorite. There's Belgian beer on tap and a fascinating history on the menu (daily, serves nonstop, 3 Rue Racine, tel. 01 85 15 21 33, www.bouillon-racine.com).

$$$ **La Méditerranée** is all about seafood from the south served in a pastel and dressy setting...with similar clientele. The scene and the cuisine are sophisticated yet accessible, and the view of the Odéon is *formidable* (daily, reservations smart, facing the Odéon at 2 Place de l'Odéon, tel. 01 43 26 02 30, www.la-mediterranee.com).

$$ **Café de l'Odéon,** on a square with the venerable theater, is a place to savor a light meal with a stylish young crowd (but only in good weather, as it's all outdoors). The menu offers a limited selection of well-prepared dishes at fair prices—you'll feel like a winner eating so well in such a Parisian setting (good salads, reasonable *plats*, May-Oct daily 12:00-23:00, no reservations, Place de l'Odéon, tel. 01 44 85 41 30).

$$$$ **Le Comptoir Restaurant** is a trendy but relaxed splurge where trusting foodies book long in advance to enjoy gourmet dishes with a modern flair. In a lively, street-front setting, you'll eat what the chef cooks—the lone *menu* changes daily based on his inspiration, and there are no other choices (incredible five-course €60 *menu*, daily, book well ahead, 9 Carrefour de l'Odéon, tel. 01 44 27 07 97).

$$ **L'Avant Comptoir,** a stand-up-only hors d'oeuvres bar, serves a delightful array of French-Basque tapas on a sleek zinc counter. With illustrated menu cards hanging from the ceiling, this popular place is designed to make the cuisine from next door's pricey Le Comptoir more accessible. At the walk-up counter outside, you can get top quality sandwiches and crêpes to go (for less and with less commotion). But step inside for the foodie bar and it's another world (daily 12:00-23:00, 3 Carrefour de l'Odéon).

$ **Restaurant Polidor** is the Parisian equivalent of a beloved neighborhood diner. A fixture here since 1845, it's much loved for its unpretentious quality cooking, fun old-Paris atmosphere, and fair value. Noisy, happy diners sit tightly at shared tables, savoring classic bourgeois *plats* from every corner of France (daily 12:00-14:30 & 19:00-23:00, cash only, no reservations, 41 Rue Monsieur-le-Prince, tel. 01 43 26 95 34).

$ Pasta Luna is a deli specializing in porky fare from the southernmost French island of Corsica. The proud owner lovingly and slowly makes €6 sandwiches to order. Try the sheep cheese with fig jam or the cured pork loin (served from 11:00 until the bread runs out—usually about 19:00, closed Sun, 15 Rue Mézières, tel. 01 45 44 32 02).

Between the Panthéon and the Cluny Museum
(Mo: Cluny-La Sorbonne or RER: Luxembourg)
$$$ Les Papilles is a warm, woody bistro where you'll dine surrounded by bottles of wine and eat what's offered...and you won't complain. It's a foodie's dream: one *menu*, no choices, and no regrets. Choose your wine from the shelf or ask for advice from the burly, rugby-playing owner, then relax and let the food arrive. Reserve ahead (€20 daily *marmite du marché*—market stew, bigger and cheaper selection at lunch, closed Sun-Mon, 30 Rue Gay Lussac, tel. 01 43 25 20 79, www.lespapillesparis.fr).

$$ Le Pré Verre, a block from the Cluny Museum, is a chic wine bistro—a refreshing alternative in a part of the Latin Quarter mostly known for low-quality, tourist-trapping eateries. Offering imaginative, modern cuisine at fair prices, the place is packed. The bargain lunch *menu* includes a starter, main course, glass of wine, and coffee (good wine list, closed Sun-Mon, 8 Rue Thénard, reservations necessary, tel. 01 43 54 59 47, www.lepreverre.com).

$$ Le Soufflot, named after the architect of the Panthéon, delivers dynamite views of the inspiring dome. Dine on good-enough café cuisine or just enjoy a drink (16 Rue Soufflot, tel. 01 43 26 57 56).

$$ Café de l'Ecritoire sits on an appealing little square surrounding a gurgling fountain and facing Paris' legendary Sorbonne University—just a block from the Cluny Museum. It's a typical brasserie with salads, *plats du jour*, and good seating inside and out (daily, 3 Place de la Sorbonne, tel. 01 43 54 60 02).

IN MONTMARTRE, NEAR SACRE-CŒUR
(Mo: Abbesses or Anvers)
For locations, see map on page 105.

$$$ Restaurant Chez Plumeau, just off jam-packed Place du Tertre, is touristy yet moderately priced, with formal service but great seating either in a characteristic dining room or on a tiny square under a wisteria arbor (elaborate salads, daily, 4 Place du Calvaire, Mo: Abbesses, tel. 01 46 06 26 29).

$$ L'Eté en Pente Douce is a good Montmartre choice, hiding under some trees just downhill from the crowds on a classic neighborhood corner. It features cheery indoor and outdoor seating, €10 *plats du jour* and salads, vegetarian options, and good wines (daily, many steps below Sacré-Cœur to the left as you leave, 23 Rue Muller, Mo: Anvers, tel. 01 42 64 02 67).

AT GARE DE LYON
$$$$ Le Train Bleu is a grandiose restaurant with a low-slung, leather-couch café-bar area built right into the train station for

the Paris Exhibition of 1900 (which also saw the construction of the Pont Alexandre III). It's simply a grand-scale-everything experience, with over-the-top belle époque decor that speaks of another age, when going to dinner was an event—a chance to see and be seen. Forty-one massive paintings of scenes along the old rail lines tempt diners to consider a getaway. Reserve ahead for dinner, or drop in for a drink before your train leaves (up the stairs opposite track L, tel. 01 43 43 09 06, www.le-train-bleu.com).

Paris Connections

Whether you're aiming to catch a train or plane, budget plenty of time to reach your departure point. Paris is a big, crowded city, and getting across town or from terminal to terminal on time is a goal you'll share with millions of others. Factor in traffic delays and walking time through huge stations and vast terminals. Always keep your luggage safely near you. Thieves prey on jet-lagged and confused tourists on public transportation.

BY PLANE
Charles de Gaulle Airport
Paris' main airport (airport code: CDG) has three terminals: T-1, T-2, and T-3 (see map). Most flights from the US use T-1 or T-2. You can travel between terminals on the free CDGVAL shuttle train (departs every 5 minutes, 24/7) or by shuttle bus (on the arrivals level). Allow 30 minutes to travel between terminals and an hour for total travel time between your gates at T-1 and T-2. All three terminals have access to ground transportation.

When leaving Paris, make sure you know which terminal you are departing from (if it's T-2, you'll also need to know which hall you're leaving from—they're labeled *A* through *F*). Plan to arrive at the airport two to three hours early for an overseas flight, and two hours for flights within Europe (particularly on budget air-

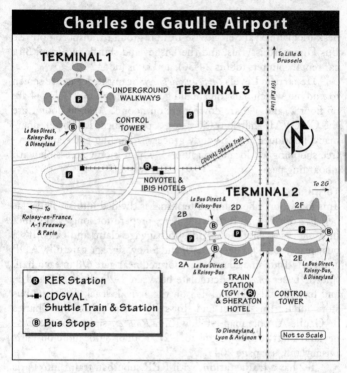

Charles de Gaulle Airport

TERMINAL 1

UNDERGROUND WALKWAYS

TERMINAL 3

CONTROL TOWER

Le Bus Direct, Roissy-Bus & Disneyland

CDGVAL Shuttle Train

NOVOTEL & IBIS HOTELS

To Lille & Brussels

TGV Rail Line

To 2G

TERMINAL 2

Le Bus Direct & Roissy-Bus

2B 2D 2F

2A *Le Bus Direct & Roissy-Bus* 2C 2E *Le Bus Direct, Roissy-Bus, & Disneyland*

TRAIN STATION (TGV + Ⓡ) & SHERATON HOTEL

CONTROL TOWER

To Roissy-en-France, A-1 Freeway & Paris

To Disneyland, Lyon & Avignon

Not to Scale

Ⓡ **RER Station**
↦■ **CDGVAL Shuttle Train & Station**
Ⓑ **Bus Stops**

lines, which can have especially long check-in lines). For airport and flight info, visit www.adp.fr.

Services: All terminals have two types of information desks (both bright orange): Airport Information, or ADP (identified with a large *I*), and Paris Tourisme. ADP counters can help with ground transportation to Paris, bag storage, and airport-related questions. At Paris Tourisme counters you can get city maps, buy a Paris Museum Pass, and get tickets for the RoissyBus or RER train to Paris—a terrific time- and hassle-saver. You'll also find ATMs *(distributeurs)*, free (but slow) Wi-Fi, shops, cafés, and bars. If you are returning home and want a VAT refund, look for tax-refund centers in the check-in area or ask for their location at any ADP information desk.

Terminal 1 (T-1)

This circular terminal has three key floors—arrivals *(arrivées)* on the top floor, and two floors for departures *(départs)* below. The terminal's round shape can be confusing—if you feel like you're going around in circles, you probably are.

Arrival Level *(niveau arrivée):* After passing through customs, you'll exit between doors *(porte)* 34 and 36. Nearby are orange ADP information desks, a snack stand, and an ATM. Walk counterclockwise around the terminal to find the Paris Tourisme desk (door 6). Walk clockwise to find ground transportation: Le Bus Direct, RoissyBus, and the Disneyland shuttle bus (door 34), car rental counters (doors 24-30), and taxis (door 24).

Departure Levels *(niveaux départ):* Scan the departure screen to find out which hall you should go to for check-in. Halls 1-4 are on floor 2, and 5-6 are downstairs on floor 1. Also on floor 1 are the CDGVAL shuttle train, cafés, a post office (La Poste), pharmacy, boutiques, and a handy grocery. Boarding gates and duty-free shopping are located on floor 3, which is only accessible with a boarding pass.

Terminal 2 (T-2)

This long, horseshoe-shaped terminal is divided into six halls, labeled *A* through *F*. If arriving here, prepare for long walks and, in some cases, short train rides to baggage claim and exits. It's a busy place, so take a deep breath and follow signage carefully. ADP and Paris Tourisme counters are located near gate 6/8 in each hall. Shuttle buses *(navettes)* circulate between T-2 halls A, C, and F, and to terminals T-1 and T-3 on the arrivals level. To locate bus stops for Le Bus Direct and RoissyBus—marked on the Charles de Gaulle Airport map—follow *Gare Routière* signs. For the Disneyland shuttle, follow signs to T-2E/F, door 8; for more on Paris Disneyland, see page 204.

T-2 has a **train station,** with RER suburban trains into Paris (described later), as well as longer-distance trains to the rest of France (including high-speed TGV trains). It's located between T-2C/D and T-2E/F, below the Sheraton Hotel (prepare for a long walk to reach your train). Shuttle buses to **airport hotels** leave from above the RER station at T-2.

Car-rental offices, post offices, pharmacies, and ATMs are all well-signed. T-2E/F has several duty-free shopping arcades, and other T-2 halls have smaller duty-free shops. You can stash your bags at Baggage du Monde, located above the train station in T-2, but it's pricey (€14/12 hours, €18/24 hours, daily 6:00-21:30, tel. 01 34 38 58 90, www.bagagesdumonde.com). Some Paris train stations can store for much less.

Getting Between Charles de Gaulle Airport and Paris

Buses, airport vans, commuter trains, and taxis link the airport's terminals with central Paris. If you're traveling with two or more companions, carrying lots of baggage, or are just plain tired, taxis (or Uber) are worth the extra cost. Total travel time to your hotel should be around 1.5 hours by bus and Métro, one hour by train and Métro, and 50 minutes by taxi. Keep in mind that, at the airport, using buses and taxis requires shorter walks than taking RER trains. Also remember that transfers to Métro lines often involve stairs. For more information, check the "Getting There" tab at www.charlesdegaulleairport.co.uk.

By RoissyBus: This bus drops you off at the Opéra Métro stop in central Paris (€11, runs 6:00-23:00, 3-4/hour, 50 minutes, buy ticket at airport Paris Tourisme desk, ticket machine, or on bus, tel. 3246, www.ratp.fr). The RoissyBus arrives on Rue Scribe; to get to the Métro entrance or nearest taxi stand, turn left as you exit the bus and walk counterclockwise around the lavish Opéra building to its front. A taxi to any of my listed hotels costs about €12 from here.

By Le Bus Direct (formerly Air France Bus): Several bus routes drop travelers at different points in and near the city (€17 one-way, runs 5:45-22:30, 2/hour, Wi-Fi and power outlets, tel. 08 92 35 08 20, www.lebusdirect.com). **Bus #2** goes to Porte Maillot (with connections to Beauvais Airport, described later), the Arc de Triomphe (Etoile stop, 50 minutes), the Trocadéro, and ends at the Eiffel Tower/Champ de Mars RER (1.25 hours, see map on page 81). **Bus #4** runs to Gare de Lyon (45 minutes) and the Montparnasse Tower/train station (1.25 hours). **Bus #3** goes to Orly Airport (€21, 1.25 hours). You can book tickets online or pay the driver (see www.lebusdirect.com for round-trip and group discount details).

To return to the airport from Paris, catch Le Bus Direct coaches at any of these locations: Eiffel Tower/Champ de Mars Métro stop, Trocadéro Métro stop, Arc de Triomphe/Etoile (on Avenue Mac Mahon—the non-Champs-Elysées side), Porte Maillot (on Boulevard Gouvion St-Cyr—east side of the Palais des Congrès), Gare Montparnasse (on Rue du Commandant René Mouchotte—facing the station with the tower behind you, it's around the left side), or Gare de Lyon (look for *Navette-Aéroport* signs, and find the stop on Boulevard Diderot across from Café Les Deux Savoies).

By Night Bus: The only bus service late at night is the Noctilien. Route #143 links the airport to Gare du Nord and Gare de l'Est. Buses pick up passengers from Terminal 1 outside door 8, Terminal 2F outside door 2, and at the Terminal 3 bus station (gare routière) every half-hour between midnight and 4:30 (€8, buy ticket on board, www.vianavigo.com/en and select "Noctilien").

By RER Train: Paris' suburban commuter train is the fastest public transit option for getting between the airport and the city center (€11, runs 5:00-24:00, 4/hour, about 35 minutes). It runs directly to well-located RER/Métro stations (including Gare du Nord, Châtelet-Les Halles, St. Michel, and Luxembourg); from there, you can hop the Métro to get exactly where you need to go. The RER is handy and cheap, but it can require walking with your luggage through big, crowded stations—especially at Châtelet-Les Halles, where a transfer to the Métro can take 10-15 minutes and may include stairs.

To reach the RER from the airport terminal, follow *Paris by*

Train signs, then *RER* signs. (If you're landing at T-1 or T-3, you'll need to take the CDGVAL shuttle to reach the RER station.) The RER station at T-2 is busy with long ticket-window lines (the other airport RER station, located between T-1 and T-2, is quieter). To save time, buy tickets at a Paris Tourisme counter or from the green machines at the station (labeled *Paris/Ile de France,* coins required, break your bills at an airport shop). For step-by-step instructions on taking the RER into Paris, see www.parisbytrain.com (see the options under "CDG Airport to Paris RER Trains"). Beware of thieves on the train; wear your money belt and keep your bags close.

To return to the airport by RER from central Paris, allow plenty of time to get to your departure gate (plan for a 15-minute Métro or bus ride to the closest RER station serving line B, a 15-minute wait for your train, a 35-minute train ride, plus walking time through the stations and airport). Your Métro or bus ticket is not valid on the RER train to the airport (but a Passe Navigo is); buy the ticket from a clerk or the machines (coins only) at the RER-B station. When you catch your train, make sure the sign over the platform shows *Aéroport Roissy-Charles de Gaulle* as a stop served. (The line splits, so not every line B train serves the airport.) If you're not clear, ask another rider, *"Air-o-por sharl duh gaul?"* Once at the airport, hop out either at T-2 or T-1/3 (where you can connect to T-1 or T-3 on the CDGVAL shuttle).

By Airport Van: Shuttle vans carry passengers to and from their hotels, with stops along the way to drop off and pick up other riders. Shuttles require you to book a precise pickup time in advance—even though you can't ever know if your flight will arrive exactly on time. For that reason, they work best for trips from your hotel to the airport. Though not as fast as taxis, shuttle vans are a good value for single travelers and big families (about €32 for one person, €46 for two, €58 for three; have hotelier book at least a day in advance). Several companies offer shuttle service; I usually just go with the one my hotel uses.

By Taxi or Uber: Taxis charge a flat rate into Paris (€55 to the Left Bank, €50 to the Right Bank—these mandated flat fees have been recently instituted, so confirm with your driver). Taxis are less appealing on weekday mornings as traffic into Paris can be bad—in that case, the train is likely a better option. Taxis can carry three people with bags comfortably, and are legally required to accept a fourth passenger (though they may not like it; beyond that, there's an extra passenger supplement). Larger parties can wait for a larger vehicle. Don't take an unauthorized taxi from cabbies greeting you on arrival. Official taxi stands are well-signed.

For trips from Paris to the airport, have your hotel arrange it. Specify that you want a real taxi *(un taxi normal),* not a limo service that costs €20 more (and gives your hotel a kickback). For weekday-morning departures (7:00-10:00), reserve at least a day ahead (€7 reservation fee payable by credit card). For more on taxis in Paris, see page 32.

Paris Uber offers airport pickup or drop-off, but since they can't use the bus-only lanes as normal taxis can, expect some added time (€30-80).

By Paris Webservices Private Car: This car service works well from the airport because your driver meets you inside the terminal and waits if you're late (€100 one-way for up to two people, €120-225 round-trip for up to four people, tel. 01 45 56 91 67 or 09 52 06 02 59, www.pariswebservices.com). They also offer guided tours—see page 41.

By Rental Car: Car-rental desks are well signed from the arrival halls. Be prepared for a maze of ramps as you drive away from the lot—get directions from the rental clerks when you do the paperwork. For information on parking in Paris, see page 167.

When returning your car, allow ample time to reach the drop-off lots (at T-1 and T-2), especially if flying out of T-2. Be sure you know your flight's departure hall in T-2 (for example, many Air France and Delta flights for North America leave from T-2E/F). There are separate rental return lots depending on your T-2 departure hall—and imperfect signage can make the return lots especially confusing to navigate.

Orly Airport

This easy-to-navigate airport (airport code: ORY) feels small, but it has all the services you'd expect at a major airport: ATMs and currency exchange, car-rental desks, cafés, shops, post offices, and more (for airport and flight info, see www.adp.fr). Orly is good for rental-car pickup and drop-off, as it's closer to Paris and far easier to navigate than Charles de Gaulle Airport.

Orly has two terminals: Ouest (west) and Sud (south). Air France and a few other carriers arrive at Ouest; most others use Sud. At both terminals, arrivals are on the ground level (level 0) and departures are on level 1. You can connect the two terminals with the free Orlyval shuttle train (well signed).

Services: Both terminals have Paris Tourisme desks in the arrivals area (a good spot to buy the Paris Museum Pass and tickets for public transit into Paris). There are also airport information desks (called ADP, near baggage claim) with information on flights, public transit into Paris, and help with other airport-related questions. Both terminals offer free Wi-Fi.

Getting Between Orly Airport and Paris

Shuttle buses *(navettes)*, the RER, taxis, and airport vans connect Paris with either terminal. Bus stops and taxis are centrally located at arrivals levels and are well signed.

By Bus or Tram: Bus bays are found in the Sud terminal outside exits L and G, and in the Ouest terminal outside exit D.

Le Bus Direct route #1 runs to Gare Montparnasse, La Motte-Picquet, Eiffel Tower, Trocadéro, and Arc de Triomphe/Etoile stops (all except La Motte-Picquet have direct connections to Métro lines). For Rue Cler hotels near the Ecole Militaire Métro stop, take Le Bus Direct to La Motte-Picquet, then walk across the Champ de Mars park to your hotel. Buses depart from the arrivals level—Ouest exit B-C or Sud exit L—look for signs to *navettes* (€12 one-way, 4/hour, 40 minutes to La Motte-Picquet, buy ticket from driver or book online—be sure to print out and bring your tickets with you). See www.lebusdirect.com for details on round-trip and group discounts.

For the cheapest (but slow) access to the Marais area, take **tramway line 7** from outside the Sud terminal (direction: Villejuif-Louis Aragon) to the Villejuif station to catch Métro line 7 (you'll need one Métro ticket for the tram and one for the Métro—buy a *carnet* of 10 tickets at the Paris Tourisme desk in the terminal, 4/hour, 45 minutes to Villejuif Métro station, then 15-minute Métro ride to the Marais).

By RER: These options take you to the RER suburban train line B, with access to the Luxembourg Garden area, Notre-Dame Cathedral, handy Métro line 1 at the Châtelet stop, Gare du Nord, and Charles de Gaulle Airport. The **Orlybus** goes directly to the Denfert-Rochereau Métro and RER-B stations (€7.50, 3/hour, 30 minutes).

The pricier but more frequent—and more comfortable—**Orlyval shuttle train** takes you to the Antony RER-B station (€10, 6/hour, 40 minutes, buy ticket before boarding). The Orlyval train is well signed and leaves from the departure level at both Orly terminals. Once at the RER-B station, take the train in direction: Mitry-Claye or Aéroport Charles de Gaulle to reach central Paris stops.

For access to RER line C, take the bus marked ***Pont de Rungis.*** From the Pont de Rungis station, catch the RER-C to Gare d'Austerlitz, St. Michel/Notre-Dame, Musée d'Orsay, Invalides, and Pont de l'Alma (€7.50, 4/hour, 35 minutes).

By Taxi: Taxis are outside the Ouest terminal exit B, and to the far right as you leave the Sud terminal at exit M. Allow 30 minutes for a taxi ride into central Paris (fixed fare of €30 for Left Bank, €35 for Right Bank).

By Airport Van: From Orly, figure about €23 for one person or €30 for two (less per person for larger groups and kids).

Beauvais Airport

Budget airlines such as Ryanair use this small airport, offering dirt-cheap airfares but leaving you 50 miles north of Paris. Still, this airport has direct buses to Paris and is handy for travelers heading to Normandy or Belgium (car rental available). The airport is basic, waiting areas are crowded, and services are sparse, but improvements are gradually on the way (airport code: BVA, airport tel. 08 92 68 20 66, www.aeroportbeauvais.paris).

Getting Between Beauvais Airport and Paris

By Bus: Buses depart from the airport when they're full (about 20 minutes after flights arrive) and take 1.5 hours to reach Paris. Buy your ticket (€17 one-way) at the little kiosk to the right as you exit the airport. Buses arrive at Porte Maillot on the west edge of Paris (on Métro line 1 and RER-C). The closest taxi stand is at the Hôtel Hyatt Regency.

Buses heading to Beauvais Airport leave from Porte Maillot about 3.5 hours before scheduled flight departures. Catch the bus in the parking lot on Boulevard Pershing next to the Hyatt Regency. Arrive with enough time to purchase your bus ticket before boarding or buy online at http://tickets.aeroportbeauvais.com.

By Train: Trains connect Beauvais' city center and Paris' Gare du Nord (20/day, 1.5 hours). To reach the Beauvais train station, take the Beauvais *navette* shuttle bus (€5, 6/day, 30 minutes) or local bus #12 (12/day, 30 minutes).

By Taxi: Cabs run from Beauvais Airport to the Beauvais train station or city center (€15-20), or to central Paris (allow €150 and 1.5 hours).

Connecting Paris' Airports
Charles de Gaulle and Orly

Le Bus Direct #3 directly and conveniently links Charles de Gaulle and Orly airports (€21, stops at Charles de Gaulle T-1 and T-2 and Orly Ouest exit B-C or Sud exit L, roughly 2/hour 5:45-23:00, 1 hour, www.lebusdirect.com).

RER-B connects Charles de Gaulle and Orly but requires a transfer to the Orlyval train. It isn't as easy as the Le Bus Direct mentioned above, but it's faster when there's traffic (€19, 5/hour, 1.5 hours). This line splits at both ends: Heading from Charles de Gaulle to Orly, take trains that serve the Antony stop (direction: St-Rémy-les-Chevreuse), then transfer to the Orlyval shuttle train; heading from Orly to Charles de Gaulle, take trains that end at the airport—Aéroport Charles de Gaulle-Roissy, not Mitry-Claye.

Taxis take about one hour and are easiest, but pricey (about €80).

Charles de Gaulle and Beauvais

You can connect Charles de Gaulle to Beauvais via train. From Charles de Gaulle, take the **RER-B** to Gare du Nord, catch a train to the town of Beauvais, and then a shuttle or local bus to Beauvais Airport (see earlier).

Taxis between Charles de Gaulle and Beauvais take one hour and cost about €120.

Orly and Beauvais

To transfer from Orly to Beauvais, you can take the Orlybus or Orlyval shuttle train (described earlier, under "Orly Airport") to the RER suburban train station, then hop on the **RER-B** to Gare du Nord. From there, catch a train to the town of Beauvais and then a shuttle or local bus to the airport (see "Beauvais Airport," earlier).

It's about a 1.5-hour **taxi** ride between Orly and Beauvais (about €165).

BY TRAIN

Paris is Europe's rail hub, with six major stations and one minor one, and trains heading in different directions:

- Gare du Nord (northbound trains)
- Gare Montparnasse (west- and southwest-bound trains)
- Gare de Lyon (southeast-bound trains)
- Gare de l'Est (eastbound trains)
- Gare St. Lazare (northwest-bound trains)
- Gare d'Austerlitz (southwest-bound trains)
- Gare de Bercy (smaller station with non-TGV southbound trains)

The main train stations all have free Wi-Fi, banks or currency exchanges, ATMs, train information desks, telephones, cafés, newsstands, and clever pickpockets (pay attention in ticket lines—keep your bag firmly gripped in front of you). Because of security concerns, not all have baggage checks. Any train station has schedule information, can make reservations, and can sell tickets for any destination. Buying tickets can be handier from an SNCF neighborhood office.

Each station offers two types of rail service: long distance to other cities, called Grandes Lignes (major lines, TGV or TER trains); and suburban service to nearby areas, called Banlieue, Transilien, or RER. You also may see ticket windows identified as *Ile de France*. These are for Transilien trains serving destinations outside Paris in the Ile de France region (usually no more than an hour from Paris). When arriving by Métro, follow signs for *Grandes Lignes-SNCF* to find the main tracks. Métro and RER trains, as well as buses and taxis, are well marked at every station.

Budget plenty of time before your departure to factor in ticket

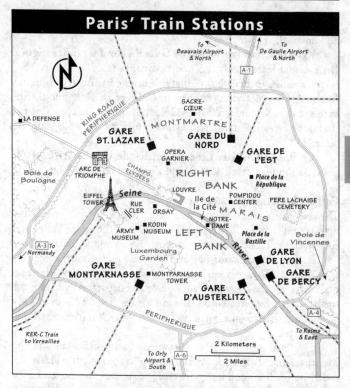

Paris' Train Stations

lines and making your way through large, crowded stations. Paris train stations can be intimidating, but if you slow down, take a deep breath, and ask for help, you'll find them manageable and efficient. Bring a pad of paper and a pen for clear communication at ticket/info windows. It helps to write down the ticket you want. For instance: "28/05/17 Paris-Nord → Lyon dep. 18:30." All stations have helpful information booths *(accueil)*; the bigger stations have roving helpers, usually wearing red or blue vests. They're capable of answering rail questions more quickly than the staff at the information desks or ticket windows. I make a habit of confirming my track number and departure time with these helpers. To make your trip go more smoothly, be sure to review the many train tips on page 1086.

Gare du Nord

The granddaddy of Paris' train stations serves cities in northern France and international destinations north of Paris, including Copenhagen, Amsterdam, and the Eurostar to London.

There's a helpful TI (labeled *Paris Tourisme*) kiosk near track 19 that sells Paris Museum Passes and fast-pass *"coupe-file"* tickets (credit cards only). Baggage check and rental cars are near track 3 and down the steps.

Key Destinations Served by Gare du Nord Grandes Lignes: Brussels (at least hourly, 1.5 hours), **Bruges** (at least hourly, 2.5-3 hours, change in Brussels), **Amsterdam** (9/day direct, 3.5 hours), **Berlin** (4/day, 8.5 hours, change in Cologne or Dortmund), **Koblenz** (4/day, 5 hours, change in Cologne, more from Gare de l'Est that don't cross Belgium), and **London** by Eurostar (1-2/hour, 2.5 hours).

By Banlieue/RER Lines: Charles de Gaulle Airport (4/hour, 35 minutes, track 41-44), and **Pontoise** (2/hour, 50 minutes).

Gare Montparnasse

This big, modern station covers three floors, serves lower Normandy and Brittany, and has TGV service to the Loire Valley and southwestern France, as well as suburban service to Chartres.

Baggage check *(consignes)* and WCs are on the mezzanine *(entresol)* level. Most services are provided on the top level (second floor up, Hall 1), where all trains arrive and depart. As you face the tracks, to the far left and outside are Le Bus Direct buses to Orly and Charles de Gaulle airports (on Rue du Commandant René Mouchotte).

City buses are out front, between the train station and the Montparnasse Tower (down the escalator through the glassy facade). Bus #96 is good for connecting to Marais and Luxembourg area hotels, while #92 is ideal for Rue Cler hotels (both easier than the Métro).

Key Destinations Served by Gare Montparnasse: Chartres (14/day, 1 hour), **Amboise** (8/day in 1.5 hours with change in St-Pierre-des-Corps, requires TGV reservation; non-TGV trains leave from Gare d'Austerlitz), **Pontorson/Mont St-Michel** (5/day, 5.5 hours, via Rennes or Caen), **Dinan** (10/day, 3.5 hours, change in Dol-de-Bretagne, or in Dol and Rennes) (6/day, 4 hours, change in Rennes and Dol), **Bordeaux** (20/day, 3.5 hours), **Sarlat** (4/day, 6-6.5 hours, change in Libourne or Bordeaux), **Toulouse** (8/day, 5-7 hours, most require change, usually in Bordeaux), **Albi** (4/day, 6.5-9 hours, change in Montauban or Toulouse), **Tours** (8/day, 1 hour), **Madrid** (2/day, 13-14 hours, 3-4 changes), and **Lisbon** (2/day, 21-24 hours via Irun).

Gare de Lyon

This huge, bewildering station offers TGV and regular service to southeastern France, Italy, Switzerland, and other international destinations.

Grandes Lignes and Banlieue lines share the same tracks. Platforms are divided into two areas: Hall 1 (tracks A-N, shaded in light blue on signs) and Hall 2 (tracks 5-23, shaded in yellow). Train information booths are opposite tracks A and M in Hall 1 and near track 11 in Hall 2 (others are downstairs). Hall 2 has the best services—including a pharmacy and a good Monop grocery store. You'll find baggage check *(consignes)* in Hall 2 down the ramp, opposite track 17, and in Hall 1, downstairs by track M. Car rental is out the exit past track M (Hall 1).

Don't leave this station without at least taking a peek at the recommended Le Train Bleu Restaurant in Hall 1, up the stairs opposite tracks G-L (see listing on page 152).

Le Bus Direct coaches, to Gare Montparnasse (easy transfer to Orly Airport) and direct to Charles de Gaulle Airport, stop outside the station's main entrance. They are signed *Navette-Aéroport.* To find them, exit Hall 1 with your back to track A. Walk down the ramp with the Café Européen a bit to your right. Turn right at the street (Boulevard Diderot) and find the shelter at the next corner across from Café Les Deux Savoies. (Buses normally depart at :15 and :45 after the hour; see page 155).

Key Destinations Served by Gare de Lyon: Disneyland (RER line A-4 to Marne-la-Vallée-Chessy, at least 3/hour, 45 minutes), **Beaune** (roughly hourly at rush hour but few midday, 2.5 hours, most require change in Dijon; direct trains from Paris' Bercy station take an hour longer), **Dijon** (roughly hourly at rush hour but few midday, 1.5 hours), **Chamonix** (7/day, 5.5-7 hours, some change in Switzerland), **Annecy** (hourly, 4 hours, many with change in Lyon), **Lyon** (at least hourly, 2 hours), **Avignon** (10/day direct, 2.5 hours to Avignon TGV Station, 5/day in 3.5 hours to Avignon Centre-Ville Station, more connections with change—3-4 hours), **Arles** (11/day, 2 direct TGVs—4 hours, 9 with change in Avignon—5 hours), **Nice** (hourly, 6 hours, may require change), **Carcassonne** (8/day, 7-8 hours, 1 change), **Zürich** (4/day direct, 4 hours), **Venice** (4/day, 9.5-11.5 hours with 1-3 changes; 1 direct overnight, 14.5 hours, operated by Thello—which doesn't accept rail passes, important to reserve ahead at www.thello.com), **Rome** (2/day, 10.5-12 hours, 1-3 changes), **Bern** (1/day direct, 6/day with change in Basel, 4-5 hours), **Interlaken** (1/day direct, 4/day with change in Basel, 5-5.5 hours, 8/day more from Gare de l'Est), and **Barcelona** (2-4/day direct, 6.5 hours).

Gare de l'Est

This two-floor station (with underground Métro) serves northeastern France and international destinations east of Paris. All trains depart at street level from tracks 1-30. Most services are down the escalator through the hall opposite tracks 12-20 (baggage lockers, car rental, WC, small grocery store, more shops, and Métro access).

Key Destinations Served by Gare de l'Est: Colmar (12/day with TGV, 3.5 hours, change in Strasbourg), **Strasbourg** (hourly with TGV, 2 hours), **Reims** Centre station (12/day with TGV, 50 minutes), **Verdun** (3/day direct via TGV and shuttle bus, 1.5 hours; 3.5 hours by regional train with transfer in Chalôns-en-Champagne), **Interlaken** (8/day, 6.5-8.5 hours, 1-2 changes, faster trains from Gare de Lyon), **Zürich** (12/day, 5-7 hours, 1-2 changes, faster direct trains from Gare de Lyon), **Frankfurt** (4 direct/day, 4 hours; 3 more/day with change in Karlsruhe, 4.5 hours), **Vienna** (7/day, 11-12 hours, 1-3 changes), **Prague** (3/day, 11 hours, 1-2 changes), **Munich** (1/day direct, 6/day with 1 change, 6 hours), and **Berlin** (3/day, 8.5 hours, change in Frankfurt).

Gare St. Lazare

This compact station serves upper Normandy, including Rouen and Giverny. All trains arrive and depart one floor above street level. Grandes Lignes to all destinations listed below depart from tracks 18-27; Banlieue trains depart from 1-16. This station has no baggage check, but it does have a three-floor shopping mall (Monop grocery store, pharmacy, clothing stores, and more).

Key Destinations Served by Gare St. Lazare: Giverny (train to Vernon, 8/day Mon-Sat, 6/day Sun, 45 minutes), **Pontoise** (1-2/hour, 45 minutes), **Rouen** (nearly hourly, 1.5 hours), **Le Havre** (hourly, 2.5 hours, some change in Rouen), **Honfleur** (13/day, 2-3.5 hours, via Lisieux, Deauville, or Le Havre, then bus), **Bayeux** (9/day, 2.5 hours, some change in Caen), **Caen** (14/day, 2 hours), and **Pontorson/Mont St-Michel** (2/day, 4-5.5 hours, via Caen; more trains from Gare Montparnasse).

Gare d'Austerlitz

This small station currently provides non-TGV service to the Loire Valley, southwestern France, and Spain. All tracks are at street level. Baggage check and car rental are along the side of the station, opposite track 21. You'll find WCs (with €10 showers that include towel and soap) at track 21. To get to the Métro and RER, you must walk outside and along either side of the station. To reach Gare de Lyon on foot (a level 10-minute walk), follow signs opposite track 1.

Key Destinations Served by Gare d'Austerlitz: Orly Airport (via RER-C, 4/hour, 35 minutes), **Versailles** (via RER-C, 4/hour, 35 minutes), **Amboise** (3/day direct in 2 hours, more with transfer; faster TGV connection from Gare Montparnasse), **Sarlat** (1/day, 6.5 hours, requires change to bus in Souillac, 3 more/day via Gare Montparnasse), **Carcassonne** (1 direct night train, 7.5 hours, better day trains from Gare de Lyon), and **Cahors** (5/day, 5 hours; slower trains from Gare Montparnasse).

Gare de Bercy

This smaller station mostly handles southbound non-TGV trains, but some TGV trains do stop here in peak season (Mo: Bercy, one stop east of Gare de Lyon on line 14, exit the Bercy Métro station and it's across the street). Facilities are limited—just a WC and a sandwich-fare takeout café.

Specialty Trains from Paris
To Brussels and Amsterdam by Thalys Train

The pricey Thalys train has the monopoly on the rail route between Paris and Brussels. Without a rail pass, for the Paris-Amsterdam train, you'll pay about €80-205 first class, €35-135 second class (compared to €38-50 by bus); for the Paris-Brussels train it's €65-140 first class, €30-100 second class (€20-30 by bus). Even with a rail pass, you need to pay for train reservations (first class-€30-35, includes a meal; second class-€20-25). Book early for the best rates (seats are limited in various discount categories, www.thalys.com).

Thalys also operates a slower, cheaper Paris to Brussels train called IZY (2-3/day, 2.5 hours, tickets from €10 for standing room to €29 full fare, rail passes not accepted, luggage limits, online only at www.izy.com). For another cheap option, try the Eurolines bus or OuiBus operated by SNCF (see "Paris Bus Connections," later).

Low-Cost TGV Trains to Southern France

A TGV train called OuiGo (pronounced "we go") offers a direct connection from Disneyland Paris to select cities in southern France at rock-bottom fares with no-frills service. The catch: These trains leave from the Marne-la-Vallée TGV station, an hour from Paris on RER-A. So you can hang at Disneyland Paris before (or after) your trip south and connect with a direct TGV. You must print your own ticket ahead of time, arrive 30 minutes before departure, and activate your ticket. You can't use a rail pass, and you can only bring one carry-on-size bag plus one handbag for free (children's tickets allow you to bring a stroller). Larger or extra luggage is €5/bag if you pay when you buy your ticket. If you just show up without paying in advance, it's €20/bag on the train—yikes. There's no food service on the train (BYO), but children under age 12 pay only €5 for a seat. The website explains it all in easy-to-understand English (www.ouigo.com).

To London by Eurostar Train

The Eurostar zips you (and up to 800 others in 18 sleek cars) from downtown Paris to downtown London at 190 mph in 2.5 hours (1-2/hour). The tunnel crossing is a 20-minute, silent, 100-mile-per-hour nonevent. Your ears won't even pop.

Eurostar Fares: The Eurostar is not covered by rail passes and always requires a separate, reserved train ticket. A one-way, full-fare ticket runs about $225 (Standard), $310 (Standard Premier), and $380 (Business Premier). Discounts can lower fares substantially (figure $45-160 for Standard class, one-way) for children under 12, youths under 26, adults booking months ahead or traveling round-trip, and rail-pass holders. You can book tickets as early as four to nine months in advance.

Buying Eurostar Tickets: Because only the most expensive (Business Premier) ticket is refundable, and other rates have exchange restrictions, don't reserve until you're sure of your plans. But if you wait too long, the cheapest tickets will be gone.

You can buy tickets online using the print-at-home eticket option at www.ricksteves.com/eurostar or www.eurostar.com. You can also order by phone through Rail Europe (US tel. 800-387-6782) for home delivery before you go, or through Eurostar (French tel. 08 92 35 35 39, priced in euros) to pick up at the train station. In continental Europe you can buy your Eurostar tickets at any major train station in any country, at neighborhood SNCF offices, or at any travel agency that handles train tickets (expect a booking fee). Discount tickets for rail-pass holders (which can sell out) are available at Eurostar departure stations, through US agents, or by phone with Eurostar, but they may be harder to get at other train stations and travel agencies.

Taking the Eurostar: Eurostar trains depart from and arrive at Paris' Gare du Nord. Check in at least 45 minutes in advance (remember that times listed on tickets are local times—departure from Paris is French time, arrival in London is British time). Pass through airport-like security, show your passport to customs officials, and locate your departure gate (shown on a TV monitor). There's a reasonable restaurant before the first check-in point, but only a couple of tiny sandwich-and-coffee counters in the cramped waiting area.

BY BUS, CAR, OR CRUISE SHIP

Below I've provided some information for travelers not arriving by plane or train.

Paris Bus Connections

The main bus station, Gare Routière du Paris-Gallieni, is in the suburb of Bagnolet (28 Avenue du Général de Gaulle, Mo: Gallieni). Buses provide cheaper—if less comfortable and more time-consuming—transportation to major European cities. The bus is also the cheapest way to cross the English Channel; book at least two days in advance for the best fares.

Eurolines' buses depart from here (toll tel. 08 92 89 90 91 inside France; from the US, dial 011 33 1 41 86 24 21, www.eurolines.com). Look on their website for offices in central Paris. **OuiBus** also offers cheap, Wi-Fi-equipped bus service with an English-speaking driver from Paris to London (6/day, 8 hours), Amsterdam (7/day, 6.5 hours), Cologne (3/day, 8 hours), and other cities, including many in France (toll tel. 08 92 68 00 68 inside France, www.ouibus.com).

Parking in Paris

Street parking is generally free at night (19:00-9:00) and all day Sunday. To pay for streetside parking, you must go to a *tabac* and buy a parking card *(une carte de stationnement),* sold in €15 and €45 denominations (figure €2-4/hour in central Paris). Insert the card into the meter (chip-side in) and punch the desired amount of time, then take the receipt and display it in your windshield. Meters limit street parking to a maximum of two hours.

Underground garages are plentiful in Paris. You'll find them under Ecole Militaire, St. Sulpice Church, Les Invalides, the Bastille, and the Panthéon; all charge about €30-45/day (€60/3 days, €10/day more after that, for locations see www.vincipark.com). Some hotels offer parking for less—ask your hotelier.

For a longer stay, park for less at an airport (about €10/day) and take public transport or a taxi into the city. Orly is closer and easier for drivers to navigate than Charles de Gaulle.

Le Havre Cruise Port

Ships visiting "Paris" actually call at the industrial city of Le Havre, France's second-biggest port (after Marseille), and the primary French port on the Atlantic. Port information: www.cruiselehavre.com.

To reach Paris from Le Havre, it's about a 2.5-hour train ride each way. To get from the port to the Le Havre train/bus station, you can ride a cruise-line shuttle bus, take a taxi, or walk about 35 minutes. From there, trains leave about every 1-2 hours for the 2.5-hour journey to Paris' St. Lazare Station (fewer on weekends).

If you'd rather stick closer to your ship, consider these alternatives: the harbor town of Honfleur (30 minutes by bus); the historic D-Day beaches (an hour or so to the west); and the pleasant small city of Rouen (one hour by train).

For more details on arrival at Le Havre, see my *Rick Steves Northern European Cruise Ports* guidebook.

NEAR PARIS

Versailles • Chartres • Giverny • Disneyland Paris

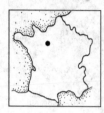

Efficient trains bring dozens of day trips within the grasp of temporary Parisians. Europe's best palace at Versailles, the awesome cathedral of Chartres, the flowery gardens at Giverny that inspired Monet, and a mouse-run amusement park await the traveler looking for a refreshing change from urban Paris.

Versailles

Every king's dream, Versailles (vehr-"sigh") was the residence of French monarchs and the cultural heartbeat of Europe for about 100 years—until the Revolution of 1789 changed all that. The Sun King (Louis XIV) created Versailles, spending freely from the public treasury to turn his dad's hunting lodge into a palace fit for the gods (among whom he counted himself). Louis XV and Louis XVI spent much of the 18th century gilding Louis XIV's lily. In 1837, about 50 years after the royal family was evicted by citizen-protesters, King Louis-Philippe opened the palace as a museum. Today you can visit parts of the huge palace and wander through

acres of manicured gardens sprinkled with fountains and studded with statues. Europe's next-best palaces are just Versailles wannabes.

Worth ▲▲▲, Versailles offers three blockbuster sights. The main attraction is the palace itself, called the **Château.** Here you walk through doz-

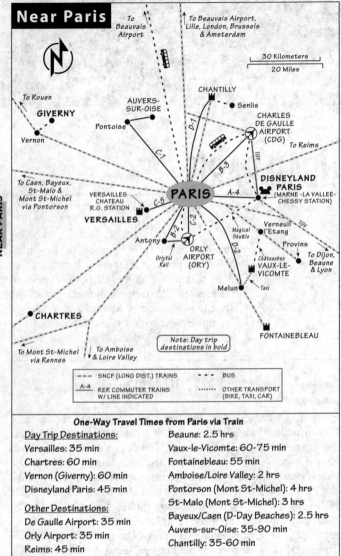

Near Paris

To Beauvais Airport

To Beauvais Airport, Lille, London, Brussels & Amsterdam

30 Kilometers
20 Miles

CHANTILLY
• Senlis

To Rouen

GIVERNY

AUVERS-SUR-OISE

CHARLES DE GAULLE AIRPORT (CDG)

To Reims

Vernon

Pontoise

D-1

C-1

B-3

TGV

DISNEYLAND PARIS (MARNE-LA-VALLEE-CHESSY STATION)

To Caen, Bayeux, St-Malo & Mont St-Michel via Pontorson

VERSAILLES CHATEAU R.G. STATION

PARIS

A-4

C-5

VERSAILLES

C-2

B-2

Verneuil l'Etang

Antony

ORLY AIRPORT (ORY)

Magical Shuttle

Provins

OrlyVal Rail

D-2

Châteaubus **VAUX-LE-VICOMTE**

To Dijon, Beaune & Lyon

Melun •

Taxi

CHARTRES

To Mont St-Michel via Rennes

To Amboise & Loire Valley

Note: Day trip destinations in bold

FONTAINEBLEAU

--- SNCF (LONG DIST.) TRAINS	- - - BUS	
A-4 RER COMMUTER TRAINS W/ LINE INDICATED	······· OTHER TRANSPORT (BIKE, TAXI, CAR)	

One-Way Travel Times from Paris via Train

Day Trip Destinations:
Versailles: 35 min
Chartres: 60 min
Vernon (Giverny): 60 min
Disneyland Paris: 45 min

Other Destinations:
De Gaulle Airport: 35 min
Orly Airport: 35 min
Reims: 45 min

Beaune: 2.5 hrs
Vaux-le-Vicomte: 60-75 min
Fontainebleau: 55 min
Amboise/Loire Valley: 2 hrs
Pontorson (Mont St-Michel): 4 hrs
St-Malo (Mont St-Michel): 3 hrs
Bayeux/Caen (D-Day Beaches): 2.5 hrs
Auvers-sur-Oise: 35-90 min
Chantilly: 35-60 min

ens of lavish, chandeliered rooms once inhabited by Louis XIV and his successors. Next come the expansive **Gardens** behind the palace, a landscaped wonderland crossed with footpaths and dotted with statues and fountains. Finally, at the far end of the Gardens, is the pastoral area called the **Trianon Palaces and Domaine de Marie-Antoinette** (a.k.a. Trianon/Domaine), designed for frolicking blue bloods and featuring several small palaces and Marie's Hamlet—perfect for getting away from the mobs at the Château.

Visiting Versailles can seem daunting because of its size and hordes of visitors. But if you follow my tips, a trip here during even the busiest times is manageable.

GETTING THERE

By Train: The town of Versailles is 35 minutes southwest of Paris. Take the **RER-C train** from any of these Paris RER stops: Gare d'Austerlitz, St. Michel, Musée d'Orsay, Invalides, Pont de l'Alma, or Champ de Mars. Buy your round-trip ticket—ask for "Versailles Château, *aller-retour* (ah-lay ruh-toor)"—from a ticket window or from an easy-to-figure-out ticket machine (€7.10 round-trip, coins only, 4/hour). You can also buy train tickets at any Métro ticket window in Paris—it will include the connection from that Métro stop to the RER at no extra cost. At the RER station, catch any train listed as "Versailles Château Rive Gauche" (abbreviated to "Versailles Chât" or "Versailles RG").

Board your train and relax. On all trains, Versailles Château Rive Gauche is the final stop. Once you arrive, exit through the turnstiles (you may need to insert your ticket). To reach the Château, follow the flow: Turn right out of the station, then left at the first boulevard, and walk 10 minutes. When returning to Paris, catch the first train you see: All trains serve all downtown Paris RER stops on the C line.

By Taxi: The 30-minute ride (without traffic) between Versailles and Paris costs about €60.

By Car: Get on the *périphérique* freeway that circles Paris, and take the toll-free A-13 autoroute toward Rouen. Exit at Versailles, follow signs to *Versailles Château*, and avoid the hectic Garden lots by parking in the big pay lot at the foot of the Château on Place d'Armes (€4/hour).

PLANNING YOUR TIME

Versailles is all about crowd management; a well-planned visit can make or break your experience. Take this advice to heart.

Versailles merits a full sightseeing day and is much more enjoyable with a relaxed, unhurried approach. Here's what I'd do on a first visit:

- Get a pass in advance (explained later, under "Passes").
- In high season, avoid Sundays, Tuesdays, and Saturdays (in

NEAR PARIS

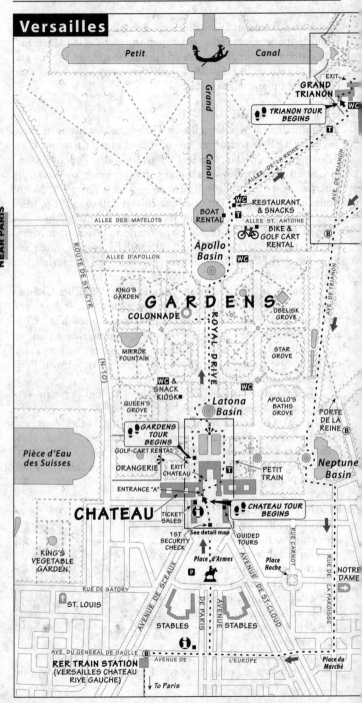

Versailles

Petit Canal — Grand Canal

EXIT
GRAND TRIANON
WC
TRIANON TOUR BEGINS
T
ALLEE DE LA REINE
AVE. DE TRIANON

WC
RESTAURANT & SNACKS
T
ALLEE ST. ANTOINE
BIKE & GOLF CART RENTAL
B

BOAT RENTAL
ALLEE DES MATELOTS
Apollo Basin
WC

ROUTE DE ST. CYR
(N-10)

ALLEE D'APOLLON

KING'S GARDEN
GARDENS
COLONNADE
OBELISK GROVE
AVE. DE TRIANON

MIRROR FOUNTAIN
ROYAL DRIVE
STAR GROVE

QUEEN'S GROVE
WC & SNACK KIOSK
Latona Basin
WC
APOLLO'S BATHS GROVE
PORTE DE LA REINE
B

Pièce d'Eau des Suisses
GARDENS TOUR BEGINS
GOLF-CART RENTAL
ORANGERIE
EXIT CHATEAU
See detail map
T
PETIT TRAIN
Neptune Basin

ENTRANCE "A"

CHATEAU
TICKET SALES
1ST SECURITY CHECK
i
CHATEAU TOUR BEGINS
GUIDED TOURS
RUE CARNOT
RUE DE LA PAROISSE

KING'S VEGETABLE GARDEN
Place d'Armes
P
Place Hoche
AVENUE DE ST-CLOUD
NOTRE DAME

RUE DE SATORY
ST. LOUIS
AVENUE DE SCEAUX
AVENUE DE PARIS
AVENUE
STABLES
STABLES
i

AVE. DU GENERAL DE GAULLE B
RER TRAIN STATION (VERSAILLES CHATEAU RIVE GAUCHE)
AVENUE DE
L'EUROPE
Place du Marché
↓ To Paris

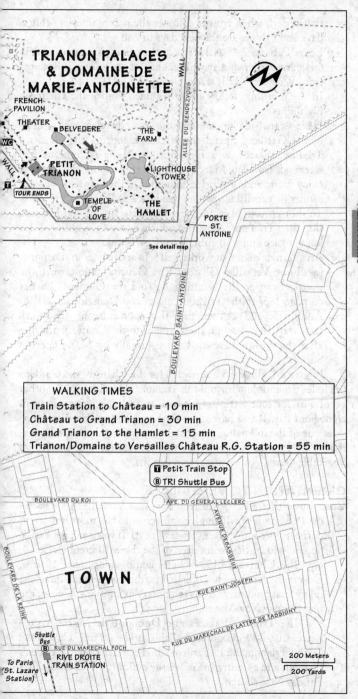

TRIANON PALACES & DOMAINE DE MARIE-ANTOINETTE

FRENCH PAVILION

THEATER

BELVEDERE

THE FARM

WC

WALL

PETIT TRIANON

LIGHTHOUSE TOWER

TOUR ENDS

TEMPLE OF LOVE

THE HAMLET

PORTE ST. ANTOINE

ALLÉE DU RENDEZVOUS

WALL

See detail map

BOULEVARD SAINT-ANTOINE

WALKING TIMES

Train Station to Château = 10 min
Château to Grand Trianon = 30 min
Grand Trianon to the Hamlet = 15 min
Trianon/Domaine to Versailles Château R.G. Station = 55 min

T Petit Train Stop
B TRI Shuttle Bus

BOULEVARD DU ROI

AVE. DU GÉNÉRAL LECLERC

AVENUE DE BASSEUX

T O W N

RUE SAINT-JOSEPH

BOULEVARD DE LA REINE

RUE DU MARÉCHAL DE LATTRE DE TASSIGNY

BOULEVARD DE LA REINE

Shuttle Bus

B RUE DU MARÉCHAL FOCH

RIVE DROITE TRAIN STATION

To Paris (St. Lazare Station)

200 Meters

200 Yards

that order), when crowds smother the palace interior. Thursdays and Fridays are the best days to visit.

- Leave Paris by 7:45 and arrive at the palace as it opens at 8:30 (or leave earlier and have breakfast at the Hôtel Ibis across from Versailles' RER station—see page 187).
- In the morning, follow my self-guided tour of the Château's highlights.
- Have a canalside lunch at one of the sandwich kiosks or cafés in the Gardens. Spend the afternoon touring the Gardens, Trianon Palaces, and Domaine de Marie-Antoinette. On weekends from late March to October (and some Tue and Fri), enjoy music and/or flowing fountains in the Gardens. Stay for dinner in Versailles town, or head back to Paris.
- To shorten your visit, focus on the Château and Gardens and skip the Trianon/Domaine, which takes an additional 1.5 hours to see and a 30-minute walk each way.
- An alternate plan that works well is to arrive later in the morning. From Versailles Château Rive Gauche station, catch the shuttle bus (see the "Getting Around the Gardens" sidebar on page 185) to the Trianon Palaces and Domaine de Marie-Antoinette, and see them first (they open at noon). Then work your way back through the Gardens to the Château, arriving after the crowds have died down (usually by 14:00, later on Sun).

In general, allow 1.5 hours each for the Château, the Gardens (includes time for lunch), and the Trianon/Domaine. Add another two hours for round-trip transit, and you're looking at nearly an eight-hour day. If you have more time to spend at Versailles, consider one of the following, lesser sights near the palace: the Equestrian Performance Academy (www.acadequestre.fr) or the King's Vegetable Garden (www.potager-du-roi.fr).

ORIENTATION TO VERSAILLES

Cost: Buy either a Paris Museum Pass or a Versailles Le Passeport Pass, both of which give you access to the most important parts of the complex (see "Passes," next). If you don't get a pass, buy individual tickets for each of the three different sections.

The Château: €15, includes audioguide, under 18 free. Covers the famous Hall of Mirrors, the king's living quarters, many lesser rooms, and any temporary exhibitions. Free on the first Sunday Nov-March.

The Trianon Palaces and Domaine de Marie-Antoinette: €10, no audioguide available, under 18 free. Covers the Grand Trianon and its gardens, the Petit Trianon, the queen's Hamlet, and a smattering of nearby buildings. Free on the first Sunday Nov-March.

The Gardens: Free, except on Spectacle days, when admission is €9 (see "Spectacles in the Gardens," later).

Passes: The following passes can save money and allow you to skip ticket-buying lines (but not security checks). Both passes include the Château audioguide.

The **Paris Museum Pass** (see page 42) covers the Château and the Trianon/Domaine area (a €25 value) and is the best solution for most. It doesn't include the Gardens on Spectacle days.

The **Le Passeport** pass (€18 for one day, €25 for two days) covers the Château and the Trianon/Domaine area. On Spectacle days, it's €25 for one day, €30 for two.

Buying Passes and Tickets: Ideally, buy your ticket or pass before arriving at Versailles. You can purchase Versailles tickets at any Paris TI, FNAC department store (small fee), or at www.chateauversailles.fr (print out your pass/ticket at home or at your hotel). If you arrive in Versailles without a pass or a ticket, you can buy it at the rarely crowded Versailles TI, not far from the train station (10 percent fee—see "Information," later).

Your last and (usually) worst option is to buy a pass or ticket at the busy Château ticket-sales office (to the left as you face the palace). Ticket windows accept American credit cards. If there's a line, you can use the ticket machines at the back of the room (you'll need a chip-and-PIN card or bills).

Hours: The **Château** is open April-Oct Tue-Sun 8:30-19:00, Nov-March Tue-Sun 9:00-17:30, closed Mon year-round.

The **Trianon Palaces and Domaine de Marie-Antoinette** are open April-Oct Tue-Sun 12:00-18:30, Nov-March until 17:30, closed Mon year-round (off-season only the two Trianon Palaces and the Hamlet are open, not other outlying buildings), last entry 45 minutes before closing.

The **Gardens** are open April-Oct daily 8:00-20:30, Nov-March until 18:00, but may close earlier for special events.

Crowd-Beating Strategies: Versailles is packed May-Sept 9:30-13:00, so come early or late. Avoid Sundays, Tuesdays, and Saturdays (in that order), when the place is jammed with a slow shuffle of tourists from open to close. To skip the ticket-buying line, buy tickets or passes in advance, or book a guided tour. Unfortunately, all ticket holders—including those with advance tickets and passes—must go through the often-slow security checkpoint at the Château's courtyard entry and again at the Château entrance (longest lines 10:00-12:00). Consider seeing the Gardens during midmorning and the Château in the afternoon, when crowds die down.

Skip-the-line tickets from **GuidaTours** are hawked with vigor on your arrival at the Versailles RER station. Their €25 ticket gets you into the Château (but not the Gardens) without a wait (so you're paying an extra €10 to save line time, but you still must go through security). I'd consider it on busy days. Skip their €35 guided tour ticket: You can get the same deal for €22 by booking a tour through the Château directly, with better skip-the-line privileges (see "Tours," below).

Pickpockets: Assume pickpockets are working the tourist crowds.

Information: Check the excellent website for updates and special events—www.chateauversailles.fr. The palace's general contact number is tel. 01 30 83 78 00. You'll pass the city **Tourist Office** on your walk from the RER station to the palace—it's just past the Pullman Hôtel (daily 9:00-19:00, Sun until 18:00, shorter hours in winter, free Wi-Fi, tel. 01 39 24 88 88). The information office at the Château is to the left as you face the Château (WCs, toll tel. 08 10 81 16 14).

Tours: The 1.5-hour English **guided tour** gives you access to a few extra rooms (the itinerary varies) and lets you skip the regular security line (€7, plus €15 palace entry if you don't have it; usually at least five tours in English between 9:00 and 15:00 April-Oct; off-season usually only at 9:30 and 14:00). Book a tour in advance on the palace's website, or reserve immediately upon arrival at the guided-tours office (to the right of the Château—look for yellow *Visites Conferences* signs). Tours can sell out by 13:00, though more are usually available than indicated on the website.

A free **audioguide** to the Château is included in your admission. Other podcasts and digital tours are available in the "multimedia" section at www.chateauversailles.fr.

🎧 Download my free Versailles **audio tour**.

Baggage Check: Free and located just after the Château entry security check. You must retrieve your items one hour before closing (maximum size is same as airlines allow for carry-on bags). Large bags and baby strollers are not allowed in the Château and the two Trianons.

Services: WCs are plentiful and well-signed in the Château. Those in the Gardens are further and fewer between.

Photography: Allowed, but no flash indoors.

Eating: To the left of the Château, the **$** Grand Café d'Orléans offers good-value self-service meals (sandwiches and small salads, great for picnicking in the Gardens). In the Gardens, you'll find several cafés and snack stands with fair prices. One is located near the Latona Fountain (less crowded) and others are in an atmospheric cluster at the Grand Canal (more crowds and more choices, including two restaurants).

Handy McDonald's and Starbucks (both with WCs) are across from the train station. In Versailles town center, the best choices are on the lively Place du Marché Notre-Dame, with a supermarket nearby (listed on page 188), or along traffic-free Rue de Satory, on the opposite (south) side as you leave the Château.

Spectacles in the Gardens: The Gardens and fountains at Versailles come alive at selected times, offering visitors a glimpse into Louis XIV's remarkable world. The Sun King had his engineers literally reroute a river to fuel his fountains and feed his plants. Even by today's standards, the fountains are impressive. Check the Versailles website for current hours and for what else might be happening during your visit.

On nonwinter weekends the Gardens' fountains are in full squirt. The whole production, called **Les Grandes Eaux Musicales,** involves 55 fountains gushing for an hour in the morning, then again for about two hours in the afternoon, all accompanied by loud classical music (€9; late March-Oct Sat-Sun 11:00-12:00 & 15:30-17:00; plus Tue mid-May-June and Fri late March-early May, same hours). Pay at the entrance to the Gardens, unless you've bought Le Passeport—in which case you've already paid (automatically tacked on to Passeport price on Spectacle days).

On most other in-season Tuesdays you get all-day music, but no water, with the **Les Jardins Musicaux** program (€8, April-mid-May and July-Oct Tue 10:00-18:30).

On certain summer weekend nights you get the big shebang: **Les Grandes Eaux Nocturnes,** which presents whimsical lighted displays leading between gushing fountains and a fireworks show over the largest fountain pool (€20-41, mid-June-mid-Sept Sat plus mid-June-mid-July Fri, 20:30-22:40, fireworks at 22:50).

Starring: Luxurious palaces, endless gardens, Louis XIV, Marie-Antoinette, and the *ancien régime*.

◔ SELF-GUIDED TOUR

On this self-guided tour, you'll see the Château (the State Apartments of the king as well as the Hall of Mirrors), the landscaped Gardens in the "backyard," and the

Trianon Palaces and Domaine de Marie-Antoinette, located at the far end of the Gardens. If your time is limited or you don't enjoy walking, I give you permission to skip the Trianon/Domaine, which is a hefty 30-minute hike (each way) from the Château.

This commentary covers the basics. For background, first read

Kings and Queens and Guillotines

• *You could read this on the train ride to Versailles. Relax...the palace is the last stop.*

Come the Revolution, when they line us up and make us stick out our hands, will you have enough calluses to keep them from shooting you? A grim thought, but Versailles raises these kinds of questions. It's the architectural embodiment of the *ancien régime,* a time when society was divided into rulers and the ruled, when you were born to be rich or to be poor. To some it's the pinnacle of civilization; to others, the sign of a civilization in decay. Either way, it remains one of Europe's most impressive sights.

Versailles was the residence of the king and the seat of France's government for a hundred years. Louis XIV (r. 1643-1715) moved out of the Louvre in Paris, the previous royal residence, and built an elaborate palace in the forests and swamps of Versailles, 10 miles west. The reasons for the move were partly personal—Louis XIV loved the outdoors and disliked the sniping environs of stuffy Paris—and partly political.

Louis XIV was creating the first modern, centralized state. At Versailles he consolidated his government's scattered ministries so that he could personally control policy. More importantly, he invited France's nobles to Versailles in order to control them. Living a life of almost enforced idleness, the "domesticated" aristocracy couldn't interfere with the way Louis ran things. With 18 million people united under one king (England had only 5.5 million), a booming economy, and a powerful military, France was Europe's number-one power.

Around 1700, Versailles was the cultural heartbeat of Europe, and French culture was at its zenith. Throughout Europe, when you said "the king," you were referring to the French king—Louis XIV. Every king wanted a palace like Versailles. Everyone learned French. French taste in clothes, hairstyles, table manners, theater, music, art, and kissing spread across the Continent. That cultural dominance continued, to some extent, right up to the 20th century.

Louis XIV

At the center of all this was Europe's greatest king. He was a true Renaissance Man, a century after the Renaissance: athletic, good-looking, a musician, dancer, horseman, statesman, patron of the

the "Kings and Queens and Guillotines" sidebar. For a detailed room-by-room rundown, consider the guidebook called *The Châteaux, the Gardens, and Trianon* (sold at Versailles).

The Château

• *Stand in the huge courtyard and face the palace. The golden Royal Gate in the center of the courtyard—nearly 260 feet long and decorated with*

arts, and lover. For all his grandeur, he was one of history's most polite and approachable kings, a good listener who could put even commoners at ease in his presence.

Louis XIV called himself the Sun King because he gave life and warmth to all he touched. He was also thought of as Apollo, the Greek god of the sun. Versailles became the personal temple of this god on earth, decorated with statues and symbols of Apollo, the sun, and Louis XIV himself. The classical themes throughout underlined the divine right of France's kings and queens to rule without limit.

Louis XIV was a hands-on king who personally ran affairs of state. All decisions were made by him. Nobles, who in other countries were the center of power, became virtual slaves dependent on Louis XIV's generosity. For 70 years he was the perfect embodiment of the absolute monarch. He summed it up best himself with his famous rhyme—*"L'état, c'est moi!"* (lay-tah say-mwah): "The state, that's me!"

Another Louis or Two to Remember

Three kings lived in Versailles during its century of glory. Louis XIV built it and established French dominance. Louis XV, his great-grandson (Louis XIV reigned for 72 years), carried on the tradition and policies, but without the Sun King's flair. During Louis XV's reign (1715-1774), France's power abroad was weakening, and there were rumblings of rebellion from within.

France's monarchy was crumbling, and the time was ripe for a strong leader to reestablish the old feudal order. They didn't get one. Instead, they got Louis XVI (r. 1774-1792), a shy, meek bookworm, the kind of guy who lost sleep over revolutionary graffiti... because it was misspelled. Louis XVI married a sweet girl from the Austrian royal family, Marie-Antoinette, and together they retreated into the idyllic gardens of Versailles while revolutionary fires smoldered.

100,000 gold leaves—is a replica of the original. The ticket-sales office is to the left; guided-tour sales are to the right. The entrance to the Château (once you have your ticket or pass) is marked Entrance A *(where the line usually is). Before entering (or while standing in line at the entrance), take in the Château and the open-air courtyard on the other side of the golden Royal Gate.*

The section of the palace with the clock is the original château, once a small hunting lodge where little Louis XIV spent his happiest boyhood years. Naturally, the Sun King's private bedroom (the three arched windows beneath the clock) faced the rising sun. The palace and grounds are laid out on an east-west axis.

Once king, Louis XIV expanded the lodge by attaching wings, creating the present U-shape. Later, the long north and south wings were built. The total cost of the project has been estimated at half of France's entire GNP for one year.

• *Enter the Château where you'll find an information desk (get a map), bag check, and WCs. Follow the crowds directly across the courtyard, where you'll go back inside, pick up an audioguide, and make your way to the start of our tour.*

On the way to our tour's first stop, the route passes through a dozen ground-floor rooms. The first offers a glimpse through a doorway at the impressive Royal Chapel, which we'll see again upstairs. You'll see rooms with paintings of Louis XIV, XV, and XVI, and models of Versailles at different stages of growth. Climb the stairs, then wander a statue-lined hall to reach a palatial golden-brown room, with a doorway that overlooks the Royal Chapel. Let the tour begin.

Royal Chapel: Dut-dutta-dah! Every morning at 10:00, the organist and musicians struck up the music, these big golden doors opened, and Louis XIV and his family stepped onto the balcony to attend Mass. While Louis looked down on the golden altar, the lowly nobles on the ground floor knelt with their backs to the altar and looked up—worshipping Louis worshipping God. Important religious ceremonies took place here, including the marriage of young Louis XVI to Marie-Antoinette.

• *Enter the next room, an even more sumptuous space with a fireplace and a colorful painting on the ceiling.*

Hercules Drawing Room: Pleasure ruled. The main suppers, balls, and receptions were held in this room. Picture elegant party-goers in fine silks, wigs, rouge, lipstick, and fake moles (and that's just the men) as they dance to the strains of a string quartet.

On the wall opposite the fireplace is an appropriate painting showing Christ in the middle of a Venetian party. The work—by Paolo Veronese, a gift from the Republic of Venice—was one of Louis XIV's favorites, so the king had the room decorated around it.

• *From here on it's a one-way tour—getting lost is not allowed.*

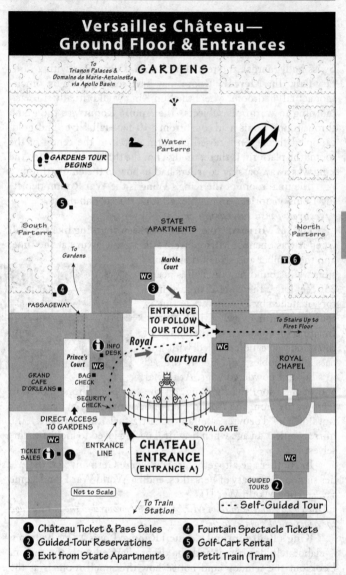

Versailles Château— Ground Floor & Entrances

GARDENS

To
Trianon Palaces &
Domaine de Marie-Antoinette
via Apollo Basin

Water
Parterre

GARDENS TOUR BEGINS

5

South
Parterre

STATE
APARTMENTS

North
Parterre

To
Gardens

Marble
Court

WC **3**

T **6**

4

PASSAGEWAY

**ENTRANCE
TO FOLLOW
OUR TOUR**

To Stairs Up to
First Floor

Royal

WC

i INFO
DESK

Courtyard

**Prince's
Court**

WC

ROYAL
CHAPEL

GRAND
CAFE
D'ORLEANS

BAG
CHECK

SECURITY
CHECK

**DIRECT ACCESS
TO GARDENS**

ROYAL GATE

**ENTRANCE
LINE**

**CHATEAU
ENTRANCE
(ENTRANCE A)**

WC

i **1**

TICKET
SALES

WC

GUIDED
TOURS **2**

Not to Scale

To Train
Station

- - - Self-Guided Tour

1 Château Ticket & Pass Sales **4** Fountain Spectacle Tickets
2 Guided-Tour Reservations **5** Golf-Cart Rental
3 Exit from State Apartments **6** Petit Train (Tram)

The King's Wing: The names of the rooms generally come from the paintings on the ceilings. For instance, the **Venus Room** was the royal make-out space, where couples would cavort beneath the goddess of love, floating on the ceiling. In the **Diana Room,** Louis and his men played pool on a table that stood in the center of the room, while ladies sat surrounding them on Persian-carpet cushions, and music wafted in from next door. Louis was a good pool player, a sore loser, and a king—thus, he rarely lost.

Also known as the Guard Room (as it was the room for Louis' Swiss bodyguards), the red **Mars Room** is decorated with a military flair. The **Mercury Room** may have served as Louis' official (not actual) bedroom, where the Sun King would ritually rise each morning to warm his subjects. The **Apollo Room** was the grand throne room. Louis held court from a 10-foot-tall, silver-and-gold, canopied throne on a raised platform placed in the center of the room (the platform is there, though not the throne). Even when the king was away, passing courtiers had to bow to the empty throne.

The final room of the King's Wing is the **War Room**, depicting Louis' victories—in marble, gilding, stucco, and paint.

• *Next you'll visit the magnificent...*

Hall of Mirrors: No one had ever seen anything like this hall when it was opened. Mirrors were still a great luxury at the time, and the number and size of these monsters was astounding. The hall is nearly 250 feet long. There are 17 arched mirrors, matched by 17 windows letting in that breathtaking view of the Gardens. Imagine this place lit by the flames of thousands of candles, filled with ambassadors, nobles, and guests dressed in silks and powdered wigs. At the far  end of the room sits the king, on the canopied throne moved in temporarily from the Apollo Room. Servants glide by with silver trays of hors d'oeuvres, and an orchestra fuels the festivities. The mirrors reflect an age when beautiful people loved to look at themselves.

In another age altogether, this is where Germany and the Allies signed the Treaty of Versailles, ending World War I (and, some say, starting World War II).

• *Midway down the Hall of Mirrors, you'll be routed to the left through the heart of the palace, to the...*

King's Bedroom and Council Rooms: Louis XIV's bedroom is elaborately decorated, and the decor changed with the season. Look out the window and notice how this small room is at the exact center of the immense horseshoe-shaped building, overlooking the main courtyard and—naturally—facing the rising sun in the east. It symbolized the exact center of power in France.

• *The Queen's Wing of the Château is closed for extensive renovation, so from here you'll walk through several unremarkable rooms as you make your way downstairs to the exit. This ends our tour of the Château, but there is more, all described in the free audioguide.*

The Gardens

Louis XIV was a divine-right ruler. One way he proved it was by controlling nature like a god. These lavish grounds—elaborately

planned, pruned, and decorated—showed everyone that Louis was in total command. Louis loved his gardens and, until his last days, presided over their care. He personally led VIPs through them and threw his biggest parties here. With their Greco-Roman themes and incomparable beauty, the Gardens further illustrated his immense power.

The Gardens are vast. For some, a stroll through the landscaped shrubs around the Château and quick view down the Royal Drive is plenty. But it's worth the ten-minute walk down the Royal Drive to the Apollo Basin and back (even if you don't continue further to the Trianon/Domaine).

As you walk, consider that a thousand orange trees were once stored beneath your feet in greenhouses. On sunny days, they were wheeled out in their silver planters and scattered around the grounds. The warmth from the Sun King was so great that he could even grow orange trees in chilly France.

With the palace behind you, it seems as if the grounds stretch out forever. Versailles was laid out along an eight-mile axis that included the grounds, the palace, and the town of Versailles itself, one of the first instances of urban planning since Roman times and a model for future capitals, such as Washington, D.C. and Brasilia. A promenade leads from the palace to the Grand Canal, where France's royalty floated up and down in imported Venetian gondolas.

Trianon Palaces and Domaine de Marie-Antoinette

Versailles began as an escape from the pressures of kingship. But in a short time, the Château became as busy as Paris ever was. Louis

XIV needed an escape from his escape, so he built a smaller palace out in the boonies. Later, his successors retreated still farther from the Château and French political life, ignoring the real world that was crumbling all around them. They expanded the Trianon area, building a fantasy world of pal-

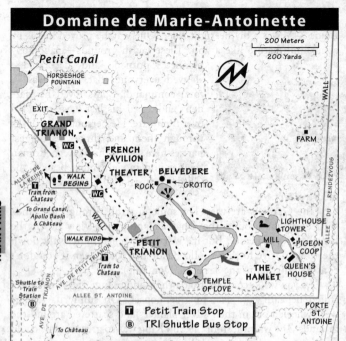

Domaine de Marie-Antoinette

Petit Canal

HORSESHOE FOUNTAIN

200 Meters
200 Yards

EXIT

GRAND TRIANON
WC

FRENCH PAVILION

THEATER   BELVEDERE

ROCK   GROTTO

WALK BEGINS

ALLEE DE LA REINE

Tram from Chateau

To Grand Canal, Apollo Basin & Château

WALK ENDS

WALL

WC

PETIT TRIANON

Tram to Chateau

AVE. DE PETIT TRIANON

Shuttle to Train Station

TEMPLE OF LOVE

ALLEE ST. ANTOINE

AVE. DE TRIANON

To Château

FARM

WALL

ALLEE DE RENDEZVOUS

LIGHTHOUSE TOWER

MILL   PIGEON COOP

THE HAMLET   QUEEN'S HOUSE

PORTE ST. ANTOINE

T Petit Train Stop
B TRI Shuttle Bus Stop

NEAR PARIS

---

aces, ponds, pavilions, and pleasure gardens—the enclosure called Marie-Antoinette's Domaine.

Grand Trianon: Delicate, pink, and set amid gardens, the Grand Trianon was the perfect summer getaway. This was the

king's private residence away from the main palace. Louis XIV usually spent a couple of nights a week here (more in the summer) to escape the sniping politics, strict etiquette, and 24/7 scrutiny of official court life.

Louis XIV built the palace (1670-1688) near the tiny peasant village of Trianon (hence the name) and faced it with blue-and-white ceramic tiles. When those began disintegrating almost immediately, the palace was renovated with pink marble. It's a one-story structure of two wings connected by a colonnade, with gardens in back.

• *To enter the Grand Trianon, you must first pass through its security checkpoint. Pick up the free palace brochure and follow the simple one-way route through the rooms.*

The rooms are a complex overlay of furnishings from many

Getting Around the Gardens

On Foot: It's a solid 45-minute walk from the palace, down to the Grand Canal, past the two Trianon palaces, to the Hamlet at the far end of Domaine de Marie-Antoinette. Allow more time if you stop along the way.

By Bike: There's a bike-rental station by the Grand Canal. A bike won't save you that much time, and you can't take it inside the grounds of the Trianon/Domaine, but it's fun pedaling around the greatest royal park in all of Europe (about €8/hour or €18/half-day, kid-size bikes and tandems available, daily 10:00-18:30).

By *Petit Train*: The very slow-moving tram leaves from behind the Château (north side) and makes a one-way loop, stopping at the Petit and Grand Trianons (entry points to Domaine de Marie-Antoinette), then the Grand Canal before returning to the Château (€7.50, round-trip only, free for kids under age 11, 4/hour, runs Tue-Sun 10:00-18:00, Mon 11:00-17:00, shorter hours in winter). Note that you can hop on and off the train and that the one-way loop only goes from the Domaine de Marie-Antoinette to the Grand Canal (not the other way).

By Golf Cart: This makes for a fun drive through the Gardens, though you can't drive it in the Trianon/Domaine, and there are steep late fees. To go out to the Hamlet, sightsee quickly, and get back within your allotted hour, you'll need to rent a cart at the Grand Canal and put the pedal to the metal (€32/hour, €8/15 minutes after that, 4-person limit per cart, rent down by the canal or just behind the Château, near the *petit train* stop).

By Shuttle Bus: Phébus runs an hourly TRI line shuttle bus between three train stations—Versailles Château Rive Gauche, Rive Droite, and Chantiers—and the Trianon/Domaine (shuttle doesn't stop at the Château). It's ideal if you're visiting the Trianon/Domaine first, before the Château. It also works great if you want to return to the station straight from the Trianon/Domaine (€2 or one Métro ticket, mid-April-Oct only, check current schedule for "Ligne TRI" at www.phebus.tm.fr). Buses depart from Versailles Château Rive Gauche train station Tue-Sun at :40 after the hour 8:40-19:40, and from a stop near the Trianon at :08 after the hour 9:08-20:08 (see map on page 172). Schedules are available at the small Phébus office across from the Versailles Château Rive Gauche train station, near McDonald's (closed at lunch and on weekends).

different kings, dauphins, and nobles who lived here over the centuries. Louis XIV alone had three different bedrooms. Concentrate on the illustrious time of Louis XIV (1688-1715) and Napoleon Bonaparte (1810-1814). Use your map to find the Mirror Room, Louis XIV's Bedchamber, the Emperor's Family Drawing Room, the Malachite Room (Napoleon's living room), and the Cotelle Gallery (Louis' reception hall).

Domaine de Marie-Antoinette: Near the Grand Trianon are the **French Pavilion** (small white building where Marie-Antoinette spent summer evenings with family and a few friends), **Marie-Antoinette's Theater,** and the octagonal **Belvedere** palace.

You'll find the **Hamlet** 10 minutes past the Belvedere palace. Marie-Antoinette longed for the simple life of a peasant—not the hard labor of real peasants, who sweated and starved around her, but the fairytale world of simple country pleasures. She built this complex of 12 thatched-roof buildings fronting a lake as her own private "Normand" village. The main building is the Queen's House—actually two buildings connected by a wooden skywalk. It's the only one without a thatched roof. Like any typical peasant farmhouse, it had a billiard room, library, elegant dining hall, and two living rooms.

After touring the Hamlet, head back toward the Petit Trianon. Along the way, you'll see the white dome of the **Temple of Love.** The gray, cubical **Petit Trianon**  is a masterpiece of Neoclassical architecture. It has four distinct facades, each a perfect and harmonious combination of Greek-style columns, windows, and railings. When Louis XVI became king, he gave the building to his bride Marie-Antoinette, who made this her home base. On the lawn outside, she installed a carousel. Despite her bad reputation with the public, Marie-Antoinette was a sweet girl from Vienna who never quite fit in with the fast, sophisticated crowd at Versailles. At the Petit Trianon, she could get away and re-create the charming home life that she remembered from her childhood. Here she played, while in the cafés of faraway Paris, revolutionaries plotted the end of the *ancien régime.*

• *The TRI shuttle bus stop with service to the RER stations is a few blocks away (see map on page 184).*

TOWN OF VERSAILLES
($$$$ = Splurge, $$$ = Pricier, $$ = Moderate, $ = Budget)
For a less expensive and more laid-back alternative to Paris, the town of Versailles can be a good overnight stop, especially

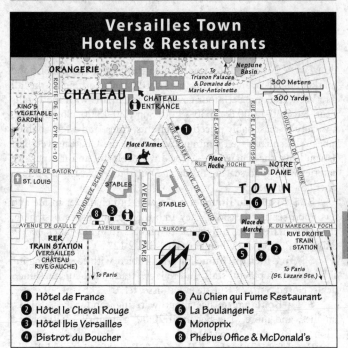

**Versailles Town
Hotels & Restaurants**

1. Hôtel de France
2. Hôtel le Cheval Rouge
3. Hôtel Ibis Versailles
4. Bistrot du Boucher
5. Au Chien qui Fume Restaurant
6. La Boulangerie
7. Monoprix
8. Phébus Office & McDonald's

for drivers. Park in the palace's main lot while looking for a hotel, or leave your car there overnight (see page 171). Get a map of Versailles at your hotel or at the TI.

Sleeping in Versailles: $$ Hôtel de France* is in a 17th-century townhouse a peasant's toss from the palace. It offers Old World class, mostly air-conditioned, traditional rooms with thick tapestries and rugs, a pleasant courtyard, a bar, and a restaurant (just off parking lot across from Château at 5 Rue Colbert, tel. 01 30 83 92 23, www.hotelfrance-versailles.com, hotel-de-france-versailles@wanadoo.fr).

$$ Hôtel le Cheval Rouge,* built in 1676 as Louis XIV's stables, now boards tourists. Tucked into a corner of Place du Marché, this modest hotel has a big courtyard with free parking and sufficiently comfortable rooms connected by long halls (no air-con, all rooms one floor up, no elevator, 18 Rue André Chénier, tel. 01 39 50 03 03, www.chevalrouge-versailles.fr, chevalrouge@sfr.fr).

$$ Hôtel Ibis Versailles* offers a good weekend value and modern comfort, with 85 air-conditioned rooms (good buffet breakfast open to public and served until 10:00 Mon-Thu, until noon Fri-Sun; pay parking, across from RER station at 4 Avenue du Général de Gaulle, tel. 01 39 53 03 30, www.ibishotel.com, h1409@accor.com).

Eating in Versailles: In the pleasant town center, around Place du Marché Notre-Dame, you'll find a thriving open market (food market Sun, Tue, and Fri mornings until 13:00; clothing market all day Wed-Thu and Sat), four covered market halls with food stalls (Tue-Sat 7:30-13:00 & 15:30-19:00, Sun 7:30-13:00, closed Mon), a variety of reasonably priced restaurants, cafés, and a few cobbled lanes. The square—a 15-minute walk from the Château (veer left as you leave the Château)—is lined with colorful and inexpensive eateries with good seating inside and out. Troll the various options or try one of these:

$$$ Bistrot du Boucher reeks with fun character inside and has good seating outside. They like their meat dishes best here, though you'll find a full menu of choices (bargain lunch *menu*, daily, 12 Rue André Chénier, tel. 01 39 02 12 15).

$$ Au Chien qui Fume is a good choice, with cozy seating inside and out, a playful staff, and reliable, traditional cuisine (lunch deals, closed Sun, 72 Rue de la Paroisse, tel. 01 39 53 14 56).

$ La Boulangerie has mouthwatering sandwiches, salads, quiches, and more (Tue-Sat until 20:00, Sun until 13:30, closed Mon, 60 Rue de la Paroisse).

Breakfast: The **Hôtel Ibis Versailles** offers a good buffet breakfast (see listing, earlier).

Supermarket: A big **Monoprix** is centrally located between the Versailles Château Rive Gauche train station and Place du Marché Notre-Dame (entrances from Avenue de l'Europe and at 5 Rue Georges Clemenceau, Mon-Sat 8:30-21:00, closed Sun).

Chartres

Chartres, about 50 miles southwest of Paris, gives travelers a pleasant break in a lively, midsize town with a thriving, pedestrian-friendly old center. But the big reason to come to Chartres (shar-truh) is to see its famous cathedral—arguably Europe's best example of pure Gothic.

Chartres' old church burned to the ground on June 10, 1194. Some of the children who watched its destruction were actually around to help rebuild the cathedral and attend its dedication Mass in 1260. That's astonishing, considering that other Gothic cathedrals, such as Paris' Notre-Dame, took literally centuries to build. Having been built so quickly, the cathedral has a unity of architecture, statuary, and stained glass that captures the spirit of the Age of Faith like no other church.

PLANNING YOUR TIME

Chartres is an easy day trip from Paris (even if you leave Paris in the afternoon and return later in the evening). But with its statues glowing in the setting sun—and with hotels and restaurants much less expensive than those in the capital—Chartres also makes a worthwhile overnight stop. If you'll be here at night, don't miss the light show—Chartres en Lumières—when dozens of Chartres' most historic buildings are colorfully illuminated, adding to the town's after-hours appeal (mid-April–mid-Oct; details at TI). Chartres' historic center is quiet Sunday and Monday, when most shops are closed.

Chartres is a one-hour ride from Paris' Gare Montparnasse (14/day, about €16 one-way; see page 162 for Gare Montparnasse details). Jot down return times to Paris before you exit the Chartres train station (last train generally departs Chartres around 21:30).

Upon arrival in Chartres, head for the cathedral. Allow an hour to savor the church on your own as you follow my self-guided tour. But don't miss the mesmerizing cathedral tour at noon led by Malcolm Miller; also consider the informative tour at 14:45 by Anne-Marie Woods (details on both tours provided later). Take another hour or two to wander the appealing old city. On Saturday and Wednesday mornings, a small outdoor market sets up a few short blocks from the cathedral on Place Billard.

Orientation to Chartres

Tourist Information: The TI is in the historic Maison du Saumon building (Mon-Sat 9:30-18:30, Sun 10:00-17:30, closes earlier Nov-April, 10 Rue de la Poissonnerie, tel. 02 37 18 26 26, www. chartres-tourisme.com). It offers specifics on cathedral tours and also rents audioguides for the old town (€5.50, €8.50/double set, about 2 hours). Skip the Chartres Pass, which is sold here.

The TI has a small map that shows the floodlit Chartres en Lumières sites, and information on the Petit Train you can take to see them all (check the website or ask at the TI for details).

Arrival in Chartres: Exiting Chartres' train station, you'll see the spires of the cathedral dominating the town. It's a 10-minute walk up Avenue Jehan de Beauce to the cathedral. The free minibus, called the Filibus, runs near the cathedral (departs 3/hour Mon-Sat 8:30-19:00), or you can take a taxi for about €7.

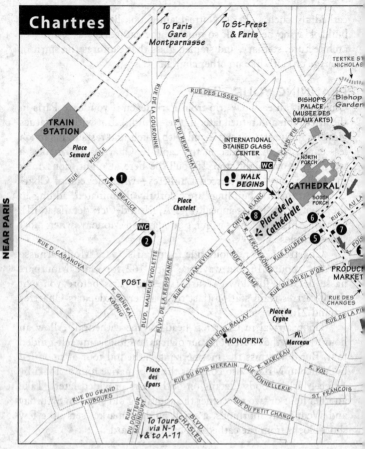

The last train to Paris usually leaves around 21:30 (verify for your day of travel).

If arriving **by car,** you'll have fine views of the cathedral and city as you approach from A-11 autoroute.

HELPFUL HINTS

Exchange Rate: €1 = about $1.10

Country Calling Code: 33 (see page 1082 for dialing instructions)

Wi-Fi: To get online, head to the **TI** (free Wi-Fi and guest computer) or try the **McDonald's** (free Wi-Fi, Place des Epars).

Laundry: A **launderette** is a few blocks from the cathedral (by the TI) at 16a Place de la Poissonnerie (daily 7:00-21:00).

Taxi: If you need to call a taxi, try tel. 02 37 36 00 00.

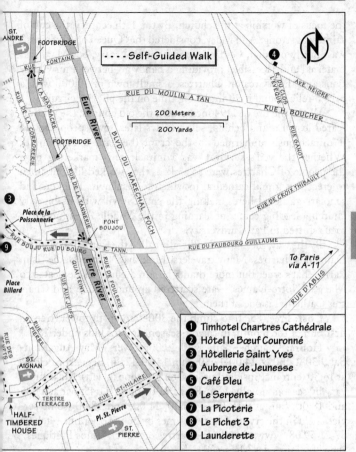

NEAR PARIS

❶ Timhotel Chartres Cathédrale
❷ Hôtel le Bœuf Couronné
❸ Hôtellerie Saint Yves
❹ Auberge de Jeunesse
❺ Café Bleu
❻ Le Serpente
❼ La Picoterie
❽ Le Pichet 3
❾ Launderette

Sights in Chartres

▲▲▲CHARTRES CATHEDRAL

The church is (at least) the fourth one on this spot dedicated to Mary, the mother of Jesus, who has been venerated here for some 1,700 years. There's even speculation that the pagan Romans dedicated a temple here to a mother-goddess. In earliest times, Mary was honored next to a natural spring of healing waters (not visible today).

In 876, the church acquired the torn veil (or birthing gown) supposedly worn by Mary when she gave birth to Jesus. The 2,000-year-old veil (now on display) became the focus of worship at the church. By the 11th century, the cult of saints was strong. And Mary, considered the "Queen of All Saints," was hugely popular. God was enigmatic and scary, but Mary was maternal and accessible, providing a handy go-between for Christians and their Creator. Chartres, a small town of 10,000 with a prized relic, found itself in the big time on the pilgrim circuit.

When the fire of 1194 incinerated the old church, the veil was feared lost. Lo and behold, several days later, townspeople found it miraculously unharmed in the crypt (beneath today's choir). Whether the veil's survival was a miracle or a marketing ploy, the people of Chartres were so stoked, they worked like madmen to erect this grand cathedral in which to display it. Thinkers and scholars gathered here, making the small town with its big-city church a leading center of learning in the Middle Ages (until the focus shifted to Paris' university).

By the way, the church is officially called the Cathédrale Notre-Dame de Chartres. Many travelers think that "Notre-Dame" is in Paris. That's true. But more than a hundred churches dedicated to Mary—"Notre-Dames"—are scattered around France, and Chartres Cathedral is one of them.

Cost: Free, €5.50 to climb the 300-step north tower (free on first Sun of the month, in the off-season, and for kids under 18).

Hours: Church—daily 8:30-19:30; tower—May-Aug Mon-Sat 9:30-12:30 & 14:00-17:30, Sun 14:00-17:30, Sept-April closes at 16:30 (entrance inside church, after gift shop on left). **Mass** times vary by season: usually Mon-Fri at 9:00 and/or 11:45; Sat at 11:45 and 18:00; Sun at 9:15 (Gregorian), 11:00, and 18:00 (some services held in the crypt). Confirm times by phone or online—tel. 02 37 21 59 08, www.cathedrale-chartres.org (click "Infos Pratiques," then "Horaires des Messes").

Restoration: A multiyear restoration is underway, though you should see few signs of it in 2017.

Tours: Malcolm Miller, a fascinating English scholar who moved here almost 60 years ago when he was 24, has dedicated his life to studying this cathedral and sharing its wonder through his guided lecture tours. He's slowing down a bit, but his 1.25-hour tours are still riveting even if you've taken my self-guided tour. No reservation is needed; just show up with cash (€10, €5 for students, includes headphones that allow him to speak softly, Easter-mid-Oct Mon-Sat at 12:00; no tours last half of Aug, on religious holidays, or if fewer than 12 people show up). Tours begin just inside the church at the *Visites de la Cathédrale* sign. Consult this sign for changes or cancellations. He also offers private tours (tel. 02 37 28 15 58, millerchartres@aol.com). Miller's guidebook provides a detailed look at Chartres' windows, sculpture, and history (sold at cathedral).

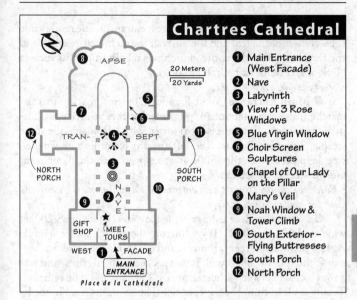

Chartres Cathedral

1. Main Entrance (West Facade)
2. Nave
3. Labyrinth
4. View of 3 Rose Windows
5. Blue Virgin Window
6. Choir Screen Sculptures
7. Chapel of Our Lady on the Pillar
8. Mary's Veil
9. Noah Window & Tower Climb
10. South Exterior – Flying Buttresses
11. South Porch
12. North Porch

Map labels: APSE, 20 Meters, 20 Yards, NAVE, TRAN-SEPT, NORTH PORCH, SOUTH PORCH, GIFT SHOP, MEET TOURS, WEST FACADE, MAIN ENTRANCE, Place de la Cathédrale

Charming American expat **Anne-Marie Woods** is Malcom Miller's understudy and is equally passionate about the cathedral. She leads worthwhile 1.5-hour tours of the cathedral that include the vast crypt (daily at 14:45, tel. 02 37 21 75 02, www.cathedrale-chartres.org).

You can rent **audioguides** inside the cathedral, to the right as you enter. Routes include the cathedral (€4.20, 45 minutes), the choir only (€3.20, 25 minutes), or both (€6.20, 70 minutes). **Binoculars** are a big help for studying the cathedral art (rent at souvenir shops around the cathedral).

Crypt: Beneath the cathedral are extensive remnants of earlier churches, a modern copy of the old wooden Mary-and-baby statue, an amazing 2,000-year-old well, and frescoes from the 12th and 13th centuries. The only way to see the crypt is on a tour. Anne-Marie Woods' tour (see above for details) includes the crypt and helps bring it to life, but I'd avoid the more frequent 30-minute tours in French with English handout (€3, 5/day late-June-mid-Sept, fewer on Sun and off-season, start at the gift shop inside the cathedral's north tower, tel. 02 37 21 75 02).

● **Self-Guided Tour:** Historian Malcolm Miller calls Chartres a picture book of the entire Christian story, told through its statues, stained glass, and architecture. In this "Book of Chartres," the text is the sculpture and windows, and its binding is the architecture. The complete narrative can be read—from Creation to Christ's birth (north side of church), from Christ and his followers up to the present (south entrance), and then to the end of time, when Christ returns as judge (west entrance). The remarkable cohesiveness of the text and the unity of the architecture are due to the fact that nearly the entire church was rebuilt in just 30 years (a blink of an eye for cathedral building).

• *Start outside, taking in the...*

❶ **Main Entrance** (West Facade): Chartres' soaring (if mismatched) steeples announce to pilgrims that they've arrived. Compare the **towers.** The right (south) tower, with a Romanesque stone steeple, survived the fire. The left (north) tower lost its wooden steeple in the fire. In the 1500s, it was topped with the flamboyant Gothic steeple we see today.

• *Enter the church (from a side entrance if the main one is closed) and wait for your pupils to enlarge.*

❷ **Nave:** The place is huge—the nave is 427 feet long, 20 feet wide, and 120 feet high. Try to picture the church in the Middle Ages—painted in greens, browns, and golds (like colorful St. Aignan Church in the old town). It was packed with pilgrims, and was a rough cross between a hostel, a soup kitchen, and a flea market. Taking it all in from the nave, notice that, as was typical in medieval churches, the windows on the darker north side feature Old Testament themes—awaiting the light of Christ's arrival. And the windows on the brighter south side are New Testament.

• *On the floor, midway up the nave, find the...*

❸ **Labyrinth:** The broad, round labyrinth inlaid in black marble on the floor is a spiritual journey. Labyrinths like this were common in medieval churches. Pilgrims enter from the west rim, by foot or on their knees, and wind around, meditating, on a metaphorical journey to Jerusalem. About 900 feet later, they hope to meet God in the middle.

• *Walk up the nave to where the transept crosses. As you face the altar and gleaming choir, north is to the left.*

❹ **The Rose Windows:** The three big, round "rose" (flower-shaped) windows over the entrances receive sunlight at different times of day. All three are predominantly blue and red, but each has different "petals," and each tells a different part of the Christian story in a kaleidoscope of fragmented images.

The brilliantly restored **north rose window** charts history from the distant past up to the birth of Jesus. The **south rose window,** with a similar overall design, tells how the Old Testament prophecies were fulfilled. Christ sits in the center (dressed in blue, with a red background), setting in motion radiating rings of angels, beasts, and instrument-playing apocalyptic elders who labor to bring history to its close. In the center of the **west rose window,** a dark Christ rings in history's final Day of Judgment. Around him, winged angels blow their trumpets and the dead rise, face judgment, and are sent to hell or raised to eternal bliss.

• *Now walk around the altar to the right (south) side and find the window with a big, blue Mary (second one from the right).*

❺ **The Blue Virgin Window:** Mary, dressed in blue on a rich red background, cradles Jesus, while the dove of the Holy Spirit descends on her. This very old window (mid-12th century) was the central window behind the altar of the church that burned in 1194. It survived and was reinserted into this frame in the new church around 1230. Mary's glowing dress is an example of the famed "Chartres blue," a sumptuous color made by mixing cobalt oxide into the glass (before cheaper materials were introduced).

• *Now turn around and look behind you.*

❻ **The Choir Screen—Life of Mary:** The choir (enclosed area around the altar where church officials sat) is the heart *(coeur)* of the church. A stone screen rings it with **41 statue groups** illustrating Mary's life. The **plain windows** surrounding the choir date from the 1770s, when the dark mystery of medieval stained glass was replaced by the open light of the French Enlightenment.

• *Do an about-face and find the chapel with Mary on a pillar.*

❼ **Chapel of Our Lady on the Pillar:** A 16th-century statue of Mary and baby—draped in cloth, crowned and sceptered—sits on a 13th-century column in a wonderful carved-wood alcove. This is today's pilgrimage center, built to keep visitors from clogging up the altar area.

• *Double back a bit around the ambulatory, heading toward the back of the church. In the next chapel you encounter (Chapel of the Sacred Heart of Mary), you'll find a gold frame holding a fragment of Mary's venerated veil. These days it's kept—for its safety and preservation—out of the light and behind bulletproof glass.*

❽ **Mary's Veil:** This veil (or tunic) was supposedly worn by Mary when she gave birth to Jesus. In the frenzy surrounding the fire of 1194, the veil mysteriously disappeared, only to reappear three days later (recalling the Resurrection). This was interpreted by church officials and the townsfolk as a sign from Mary that she wanted a new church, and thus the building began.

• *Return to the west end and find the last window on the right (near the tower entrance).*

❾ **The Noah Window and Tower Climb:** Read Chartres' windows in the medieval style: from bottom to top. In the bottom diamond, God tells Noah he'll destroy the earth. Next, Noah hefts an axe to build an ark, while his son hauls wood (diamond #2). Two by two, he loads horses (cloverleaf, above left), purple elephants (cloverleaf, right), and other animals. The psychedelic ark sets sail (diamond #3). Waves cover the earth and drown the wicked (two cloverleafs). The ark survives (diamond #4), and Noah releases a dove. Finally, up near the top (diamond #7), a rainbow (symbolizing God's promise never to bring another flood) arches overhead, God drapes himself over it, and Noah and his family give thanks.

• *To climb the north tower, find the entrance nearby. Then exit the church (through the main entrance or the door in the south transept) to view its south side.*

⓾ South Exterior—Flying Buttresses: Six flying buttresses (the arches that stick out from the upper walls) push against six pillars lining the nave inside, helping to hold up the heavy stone ceiling and sloped, lead-over-wood roof. The result is a tall cathedral held up by slender pillars buttressed from the outside, allowing the walls to be opened up for stained glass.

⓫ South Porch: The three doorways of the south entrance show the world from Christ's time to the present, as Christianity triumphs over persecution. On the center door, **Jesus** holds a book and raises his arm in blessing. He's a simple, itinerant, bareheaded, barefoot rabbi, but underneath his feet, he tramples symbols of evil: the dragon and lion. Christ is surrounded by his **apostles,** who spread the good news to a hostile world.

The final triumph comes above the door in the **Last Judgment.** Christ sits in judgment, raising his hands, while Mary and John beg him to take it easy on poor humankind. Beneath Christ the souls are judged—the righteous on our left, and the wicked on our right, who are thrown into the fiery jaws of hell.

• *Reach the north side by circling around the back end of the church.*

⓬ North Porch: In the "Book of Chartres," the north porch is chapter one, from the Creation up to the coming of Christ. Imagine all this painted and covered with gold leaf in preparation for the dedication ceremonies in 1260, when the Chartres generation could finally stand back and watch as their great-grandchildren, carrying candles, entered the cathedral.

OTHER SIGHTS IN CHARTRES
Chartres Town
Chartres' old town bustles with activity (except Sun and Mon) and merits exploration. You can rent an audioguide from the TI, or better, just wander (follow the route shown on the map on page 190).

In medieval times, Chartres was actually two towns—the pilgrims' town around the cathedral, and the industrial town along the river, which was powered by watermills. An easy 45-minute loop takes you around the cathedral, through the old pilgrims' town, down along the once-industrial riverbank, and back to the cathedral. Along the way you'll discover

a picnic-perfect park behind the cathedral, see the colorful pedestrian zone, and wander quiet alleys and peaceful lanes.

International Stained Glass Center
(Centre International du Vitrail)

This low-key center on the north side of the cathedral is worth a visit to learn about the techniques behind the mystery of this frag-

ile but enduring art (many are original windows from area churches). Panels describe many displays. Ask at the entrance about the 25-minute video in English describing the process of blown glass and the 10-minute French-only video explaining how it is turned into stained glass (easy to follow for non-French speakers). The center also offers five-day classes; call ahead or email for topics and dates.

Cost and Hours: €6.50, Mon-Fri 9:30-12:30 & 13:30-18:00, Sat 10:00-12:30 & 14:30-18:00, Sun 14:30-18:00, 5 Rue du Cardinal Pie, 50 yards from cathedral, tel. 02 37 21 65 72, www.centre-vitrail.org.

Sleeping in Chartres

($$$$ = Splurge, $$$ = Pricier, $$ = Moderate, $ = Budget)

$$ Timhotel Chartres Cathédrale,*** a block up from the train station, is comfortable and well run. Don't let the facade fool you—inside is a comfy place with a huge fireplace in the lobby and 48 well-kept rooms. Several rooms connect—good for families—and many have partial cathedral views (pricier rooms come with more space and cathedral views, family rooms, good buffet breakfast—extra, but one breakfast per couple free for Rick Steves readers, minibars, air-con, handy and safe pay parking, 6 Avenue Jehan de Beauce, tel. 02 37 21 78 00, www.timhotel.com, chartres@timhotel.fr).

$ Hôtel le Bœuf Couronné*** is more like a vintage two-star hotel, with 17 colorful, good-value rooms and a handy location halfway between the station and cathedral (family rooms, elevator, no air-con, good restaurant with views of the cathedral, reserve ahead for pay parking, 15 Place Châtelet, tel. 02 37 18 06 06, www.leboeufcouronne.com, resa@leboeufcouronne.fr).

$ Hôtellerie Saint Yves, which hangs on the hillside just behind the cathedral, delivers well-priced simplicity with 50 spic-and-span rooms in a renovated monastery with meditative garden areas. Single rooms have no view; ask for a double room with views of the lower town (small bathrooms, good breakfast—extra, 1 Rue

Saint Eman, enter via Rue des Acacias, tel. 02 37 88 37 40, www.hotellerie-st-yves.com, contact@hotellerie-st-yves.com).

Hostel: ¢ **Auberge de Jeunesse,** a 20-minute walk from the historic center, is located in a modern building with good views of the cathedral from its terrace (includes breakfast, dirt cheap meals, 23 Avenue Neigre, tel. 02 37 34 27 64, www.auberge-de-jeunesse-chartres.fr, auberge-jeunesse-chartres@wanadoo.fr).

Eating in Chartres

Dining out in Chartres is a good deal—particularly if you've come from Paris. Troll the places basking in cathedral views, and if it's warm, find a terrace table (several possibilities). Then finish your evening cathedral-side, sipping a hot or cold drink at Le Serpente.

$$ Café Bleu offers a great view terrace and an appealing interior. It serves classic French fare at acceptable prices (closed Tue, 1 Cloître Notre-Dame, tel. 02 37 36 59 60).

$$ Le Serpente saddles up next door to the cathedral, with terrific view tables and an adorable collector's interior. The cuisine is good, basic bistro fare and fairly priced. Simple dishes and to-go food are available from the room at the back (daily, 2 Cloître Notre-Dame, tel. 02 37 21 68 81).

$ La Picoterie serves up a cozy interior and inexpensive fare (omelets, crêpes, salads, and such) with efficient service (daily, 36 Rue des Changes, tel. 02 37 36 14 54).

$$ Le Pichet 3 is run by endearing Marie-Sylvie and Xavier. This local-products shop and cozy bistro make a fun lunch stop. Sit on the quiet street terrace or peruse the artsy inside. Laura serves lots of fresh vegetables and a good selection of *plats*—try the rabbit with plums (Thu-Tue 11:00-dusk, closed Wed and for dinner off-season, 19 Rue du Cheval Blanc, tel. 02 37 21 08 35).

Giverny

Claude Monet's gardens at Giverny are like his paintings—brightly colored patches that are messy but balanced. Flowers were his brush-strokes, a bit untamed and slapdash, but part of a carefully composed design. Monet spent his last (and most creative) years cultivating his garden and his art at Giverny (zhee-vayr-nee), the spiritual home of Impressionism. Visiting the Marmottan and/or the Orangerie museums

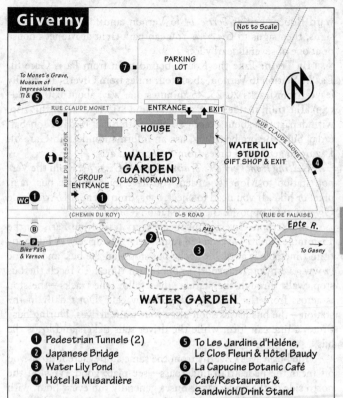

Giverny

Not to Scale

PARKING LOT
P

To Monet's Grave,
Museum of
Impressionisms,
TI & **5**

RUE CLAUDE MONET

7

6

ENTRANCE ↓ ↑ EXIT

HOUSE

RUE CLAUDE MONET

i

RUE DU PRESSOIR

WALLED GARDEN
(CLOS NORMAND)

GROUP ENTRANCE →
1

WATER LILY STUDIO
GIFT SHOP & EXIT

4

WC **1**

(CHEMIN DU ROY)   D-5 ROAD   (RUE DE FALAISE)

B

To Bike Path
& Vernon

Epte R.

Path

2

3

To Gasny

WATER GARDEN

1 Pedestrian Tunnels (2)
2 Japanese Bridge
3 Water Lily Pond
4 Hôtel la Musardière

5 To Les Jardins d'Hèléne,
Le Clos Fleuri & Hôtel Baudy
6 La Capucine Botanic Café
7 Café/Restaurant &
Sandwich/Drink Stand

NEAR PARIS

in Paris before your visit here heightens your appreciation of these gardens.

In 1883, middle-aged Claude Monet, his wife Alice, and their eight children from two families settled into this farmhouse, 50 miles west of Paris. Monet, already a famous artist and happiest at home, would spend 40 years in Giverny, traveling less with each passing year. He built a pastoral paradise complete with a Japanese garden and a pond full of floating lilies.

GETTING THERE

Drivers can get in and out of Giverny in a half-day with ease. The trip is also doable in a half-day by public transportation with a train/bus connection, but because trains are not frequent, be prepared for a six-hour excursion.

By Tour: Big tour companies do a Giverny day trip from Paris for around €70. If you're interested, ask at your hotel, but you can easily do the trip yourself by train and bus for about €40.

By Car: From Paris' *périphérique* ring road, follow A-13 toward Rouen, exit at *Sortie 14* to Vernon, and follow *Centre Ville* signs, then signs to *Giverny*. You can park right at Monet's house or at one of several nearby lots.

By Train: Take the Rouen-bound train from Paris Gare St. Lazare Station to Vernon, about four miles from Giverny (normally leaves from tracks 20-25, 45 minutes one-way, about €30 round-trip). The train that leaves Paris at around 8:15 is ideal for this trip, with departures about every two hours after that (8/day Mon-Sat, 6/day Sun). Before boarding, use an information desk in Gare St. Lazare to get return times from Vernon to Paris.

Getting from Vernon's Train Station to Giverny: From the Vernon station to Monet's garden, you have four options: bus, taxi, bike, or hike. If you need to check bags, drop them at L'Arrivée de Giverny café, opposite the train station (€5/bag).

The Vernon-Giverny **bus** meets every train from Paris for the 15-minute run to Giverny (€8 round-trip, pay driver). A bus-and-train timetable is available at the bus stops, on the bus, and online (www.giverny.org/transpor)—note return times. To reach the bus stop, walk through the station, then follow the tracks—the stop is across from the L'Arrivée de Giverny café. Don't dally in the station—the bus leaves soon after your train arrives. During busy times, a line can form while the driver sells tickets and loads the bus.

The bus leaves Giverny from the same stop where it drops you off (near the pedestrian underpass—see map; good WCs on the north side of the underpass). Buses generally run every hour, with the last one departing at about 19:15 (confirm times by checking schedule upon arrival). Get to the stop at least 15 minutes early to ensure a space. If you miss the return bus and can't wait for the next one, ask any approachable service personnel to call a taxi.

Taxis wait in front of the station in Vernon (allow €15 one-way for up to 3 people, mobile 06 77 49 32 90 or 06 50 12 21 22).

You can also rent a **bike** at L'Arrivée de Giverny café (€14, tel. 02 32 21 16 01) and follow a paved bike path *(piste cyclable)* that runs from near Vernon along an abandoned railroad right-of-way (figure about 30 minutes to Giverny). Get the easy-to-follow map to Giverny when you rent your bike, and you're in business.

Hikers can go on **foot** to Giverny (about 1.5 hours one way) following the bike path (see above) and take a bus or taxi back.

Extension to Rouen: Consider combining your morning Giverny visit with an afternoon excursion to nearby Rouen— together they make an efficient and memorable day trip from Paris (see next chapter). Note that Rouen's museums are closed on Tuesdays. From Vernon (the halfway point between Rouen and Paris), it's about 40 minutes by train to Rouen; the return trip from Rouen back to Paris takes 70-90 minutes. Plan to arrive at Monet's garden when it opens (at 9:30), so you can be back to the Vernon train station by about 13:00. You'll land in Rouen by 14:00 and have just enough time to see Rouen's cathedral and surrounding medieval quarter. If you leave Rouen around 18:00, you'll pull into Paris about 19:15, having spent a wonderful day sampling rural and urban Normandy.

Orientation to Giverny

All of Giverny's sights and shops string along Rue Claude Monet, which runs in front of Monet's house. The **TI** is located at the intersection of Rue Claude Monet and Rue du Pressoir (daily late-March-late-Sept 10:00-17:45, closed off-season, 80 Rue Claude Monet, tel. 02 32 64 45 01). For a Giverny-based taxi, try mobile 06 03 30 85 47.

Sights in Giverny

▲Monet's Garden and House

There are two gardens, split by a busy road, plus the house, which displays Monet's prized collection of Japanese prints. The gardens are always flowering with something; they're at their most colorful April through July.

Cost: €9.50, not covered by Paris Museum Pass, €16.50 combo-ticket includes nearby Museum of Impressionisms, €18.50 combo-ticket with Paris' Marmottan Museum; daily April-Oct 9:30-18:00, closed Nov-March; tel. 02 32 51 90 31, http://fondation-monet.com.

Crowd-Beating Tips: Though lines may be long and tour groups may trample the flowers, true fans still find magic in the gardens. Minimize crowds by arriving a little before 9:30, when it opens, or come after 16:00 and stay until it closes. Crowds recede briefly during lunch (12:00-13:30) but descend en masse after lunch. The busiest months here are May and June.

If you're coming at a busy time, your best bet is to buy advance tickets online or at any FNAC store in Paris, which allows you to skip the ticket line and use the group entrance. Another option, if you also plan to visit the Museum of Impressionisms (described later), is to go there first and buy a combo-ticket (*billet couplé*).

Visiting the House and Gardens: After you get in, go directly into the **Walled Garden** (Clos Normand) and work your way around clockwise. Smell the pretty scene. Monet cleared this land of pine trees and laid out symmetrical beds, split down the middle by a "grand alley" covered with iron trellises of climbing roses. He did his own landscaping, installing flowerbeds of lilies, irises, and clematis. In his carefree manner, Monet throws together holly-

hocks, daisies, and poppies. The color scheme of each flowerbed contributes to the look of the whole garden.

In the southwest corner of the Walled Garden (near the group entrance), you'll find a pedestrian tunnel that leads under the road to the **Water Garden.** Follow the meandering path to the Japanese bridge, under weeping willows, over the pond filled with water lilies, and past countless scenes that leave artists aching for an easel. Find a bench. Monet landscaped like he painted—he built an Impressionist pattern of blocks of color. After he planted the gardens, he painted them, from every angle, at every time of day, in all kinds of weather.

Back on the main side, continue your visit with a wander through Monet's mildly interesting **home** (pretty furnishings, Japanese prints, old photos, and a room filled with copies of his paintings). The gift shop at the exit is the actual sky-lighted studio where Monet painted his water-lily masterpieces (displayed at the Orangerie Museum in Paris). Many visitors spend more time in this tempting gift shop than in the gardens themselves.

Museum of Impressionisms (Musée des Impressionnismes)

This bright, modern museum, dedicated to the history of Impressionism and its legacy, houses temporary exhibits of Impressionist art. Check its website for current shows or just drop in. It also has picnic-pleasant gardens in front.

Cost and Hours: €7, daily April-Oct 10:00-18:00, closed Nov-March; to reach it, turn left after leaving Monet's place and walk 200 yards; tel. 02 32 51 94 00, www.mdig.fr.

Claude Monet's Grave

Monet's grave is a 15-minute walk from his door. Turn left out of his house and walk down Rue Claude Monet, pass the Museum of Impressionisms and the Hôtel Baudy, and find it in the backyard of the white church Monet attended (Eglise Sainte-Radegonde). Look for flowers, with a cross above. The inscription says: *Here lies our beloved Claude Monet, born 14 November 1840, died 5 December 1926; missed by all.*

Vernon Town

If you have time to kill at Vernon's train station, take a five-minute walk into town and sample the peaceful village. Walk between the tracks and the café across the street from the station, and follow the street as it curves left and becomes Rue d'Albuféra. You'll find a smattering of half-timbered Norman homes near Hôtel de Ville (remember, you're in Normandy) and several good cafés and shops—including the killer **$ Boulangerie/Pâtisserie Rose,** which has intense quiche and a good selection of sandwiches (74 Rue d'Albuféra, tel. 02 32 51 03 98).

Sleeping and Eating in Giverny

Sleeping: $ Hôtel la Musardière** is nestled in the village of Giverny two blocks from Monet's home (exit right when you leave Monet's). Carole welcomes you with 10 sweet rooms that Claude himself would have felt at home in (family rooms) and a reasonable and homey **$$ *crêperie*-restaurant** with a lovely yard and outdoor tables (daily with nonstop service, 123 Rue Claude Monet, tel. 02 32 21 03 18, www.lamusardiere.fr, hotelmusardieregiverny@wanadoo.fr).

$ Les Jardins d'Hèléne *chambres d'hôte* is as lovely as a Monet painting, with floral rooms and a terrific garden. Owner Sandrine Chifman goes out of her way to help her guests have a local experience, including free use of her bikes, and cooks dinner on Sunday and Monday evenings when most restaurants are closed—€20, reserve 2 days ahead (includes breakfast, 15-minute walk from Monet's home at 12 Rue Claude Monet, tel. 02 32 21 30 68 or 06 47 98 14 87, www.giverny-lesjardinsdhelene.com, lesjardinsdhelene@free.fr).

$ Le Clos Fleuri is a family-friendly B&B in a traditional house with three fine rooms, handy cooking facilities, and a lovely garden. It's a 15-minute walk from Monet's place and is run by charming, English-speaking Danielle, who serves up a generous included breakfast (cash only, 5 Rue de la Dîme, tel. 02 32 21 36 51, www.giverny-leclosfleuri.fr, leclosfleuri27@yahoo.fr).

Eating: A flowery **café/restaurant** and a **sandwich/drink stand** sit right next to the parking lot across from Monet's home. Enjoy your lunch in the nearby gardens of the Museum of the Impressionisms.

The botanic café by the TI, **$ La Capucine,** is like a self-serve cafeteria, with a pleasant garden and tasty cold or warm soups and quiches (daily 10:00-18:00).

Rose-colored **$$ Hôtel Baudy,** once a hangout for American Impressionists, offers an appropriately pretty setting for lunch or dinner (outdoor tables in front, popular with tour groups, daily, 5-minute walk past Museum of Impressionisms at 81 Rue Claude Monet, tel. 02 32 21 10 03). Don't miss a stroll through the artsy gardens behind the restaurant.

Disneyland Paris

Europe's Disneyland is a remake of California's, with most of the same rides and smiles. The main difference is that Mickey Mouse speaks French, and you can buy wine with your lunch. My kids went ducky for it.

The Disneyland Paris Resort is a sprawling complex housing two theme parks (Disneyland Paris and Walt Disney Studios), a few entertainment venues, and several hotels. Opened in 1992, it was the second Disney resort built outside the US (Tokyo was first). With upwards of 15 million visitors a year, it has quickly become Europe's single leading tourist destination.

Disneyland Paris: This park has cornered the fun market, with classic rides and Disney characters. You'll find familiar favorites wrapped in French packaging, like Space Mountain (a.k.a. *De la Terre à la Lune*) and Pirates of the Caribbean *(Pirates des Caraïbes)*.

Walt Disney Studios: This zone has a Hollywood focus geared for an older crowd, with animation, special effects, and movie magic "rides." The cinema-themed rides include CinéMagique (a slow-motion cruise through film history on a people mover, mixing film clips, audio-animatronic figures, and live actors); Studio Tram Tour: Behind the Magic (another slow-mo ride, this time mostly outdoors, through a "movie backlot"); and Moteurs... Action! Stunt Show Spectacular (an actual movie sequence is filmed with stunt drivers, audience bit players, and brash MTV-style hosts). The top thrill rides include the Rock 'n' Roller Coaster (which starts out by accelerating from a standstill to nearly 60 miles per hour in less than three seconds, all while Aerosmith tunes blast in your ears) and the Twilight Zone Tower of Terror (which drops passengers from a precarious 200-foot-high perch). Gentler attractions include a re-creation of the parachute jump in *Toy Story* and a *Finding Nemo*-themed ride that whisks you through the ocean current.

GETTING THERE

Disneyland is easy to get to, and may be worth a day—if Paris is handier than Florida or California.

By Bus or Train from Downtown Paris: The slick 45-minute RER trip is the best way to get to Disneyland from Paris. Take RER line A to Marne-la-Vallée-Chessy (check the signs over the platform to be sure Marne-la-Vallée-Chessy is served, because the line splits near the end). Catch it from one of these stations: Charles de Gaulle-Etoile, Auber, Châtelet-Les Halles, or Gare de Lyon (at least 3/hour, drops you 45 minutes later right in the park, about €8 each way). The last train back to Paris leaves shortly after midnight. When returning, remember to use the same RER ticket for your Métro connection in Paris.

The all-day Mobilis ticket is a smart purchase for some Disney day-trippers, as it covers your Paris Métro rides for the day and the round-trip train to Disneyland (€16.60 for zones 1-5 ticket). Buy it at any Métro station, fill in your name and date of travel on the ticket, and validate it the day you use it.

Disneyland Express runs buses to Disneyland from several stops in central Paris (including Opéra, Madeleine, Châtelet, and Gare du Nord). A single ticket combines transportation and entrance to Disneyland (€80 for kids 3-11, free for kids 2 and under, €90 for adults; several morning departures to choose from and one return time of 20:00, book tickets online, www.disneylandparis-express.com).

By Bus or Train from the Airport: Both of Paris' major airports (Charles de Gaulle and Orly) have direct shuttle buses to Disneyland Paris (€20; about hourly and takes 45 minutes, www.magicalshuttle.co.uk). Fast TGV trains run from Charles de Gaulle to Disneyland in 10 minutes, leaving hourly (shuttle bus ride required to get from train station to Disneyland).

By Car: Disneyland is about 40 minutes (20 miles) east of Paris on the A-4 autoroute (direction Nancy/Metz, exit #14). Parking is about €15/day at the park.

ORIENTATION TO DISNEYLAND

Cost: A one-day pass to either park—Disneyland Paris or Walt Disney Studios—is about €62 for kids ages 3-11, free for kids 2 and under, €69 for adults. Multiday passes are available. Regular prices are discounted about 25 percent Nov-March, and promotions are offered occasionally (check www.disneylandparis.com).

Hours: Disneyland—daily 10:00-22:00, mid-May-Aug until 23:00, until 20:00 in winter, open later on weekends, hours fluctuate with the seasons—check website for precise times. Walt Disney Studios—daily 10:00-19:00.

Skipping Lines: The free Fastpass system is a worthwhile time-saver for the most popular rides (check map and legend for details; you may have only one Fastpass at a time, so choose wisely). At the ride, check the Fastpass sign to see when you can return and skip the line. Insert your park admission ticket into the Fastpass machine, which spits out a ticket printed with your return time. You'll also save time by buying park tickets in advance (at airport TIs, some Métro stations, or along the Champs-Elysées at the Disney Store).

Avoiding Crowds: Saturday, Sunday, Wednesday, public holidays, and any day in July and August are the most crowded. After dinner, crowds are gone.

Information: Disney brochures are in every Paris hotel. For more info and to make reservations, call 01 60 30 60 53, or try www.disneylandparis.com.

Eating with Mickey: Food is fun and not outrageously priced. (Still, many smuggle in a picnic.) The Disneyland Hotel restaurant Inventions offers an expensive gourmet brunch on Sundays (roughly €60/person) and daily dinners where the most famous Disney characters visit with starstruck eaters.

SLEEPING AT DISNEYLAND

Most are better off sleeping in the real world (i.e., Paris), though with direct buses and freeways to both airports, Disneyland makes a convenient first- or last-night stop. Seven different Disney-owned hotels offer accommodations at or near the park in all price ranges. Prices are impossible to pin down, as they vary by season and by the package deal you choose (deals that include park entry are usually a better value), with most in the $$$$ range. To reserve any Disneyland hotel, call 01 60 30 60 53, or check www.disneylandparis.com. The prices you'll be quoted include entry to the park. **Hotel Santa Fe**** offers a fair midrange value, with frequent shuttle service to the park. Another cheap option is **Davy Crockett's Ranch,** but you'll need a car to stay there. The most expensive is the **Disneyland Hotel,****** right at the park entry, about three times the price of the Santa Fe. The **Vienna House Dream Castle Hotel****** is another higher-end choice, with nearly 400 rooms done up to look like a lavish 17th-century palace (40 Avenue de la Fosse des Pressoirs, tel. 01 64 17 90 00, www.dreamcastle-hotel.com, info@dreamcastle-hotel.com).

NORMANDY

Rouen • Honfleur • Bayeux • D-Day Beaches
• Mont St-Michel

Sweeping coastlines, half-timbered towns, fortified farmsteads, and thatched roofs decorate the rolling green hills of Normandy (Normandie). Parisians call Normandy "the 21st arrondissement." It's their escape—the nearest beach. Brits consider this area close enough for a weekend away (you'll notice that the BBC comes through loud and clear on your car radio).

Despite the peacefulness you sense today, the region's history is filled with war. Normandy was founded by Viking Norsemen who invaded from the north, settled here in the ninth century, and gave the region its name. A couple of hundred years later, William the Conqueror invaded England from Normandy. His 1066 victory is commemorated in a remarkable tapestry at Bayeux. A few hundred years after that, France's greatest cheerleader, Joan of Arc (Jeanne d'Arc), was convicted of heresy in Rouen and burned at the stake by the English, against whom she rallied France during the Hundred Years' War. And in 1944, Normandy was the site of a WWII battle that changed the course of history.

The rugged, rainy coast of Normandy harbors wartime bunkers and enchanting fishing villages like Honfleur. And, on the border Normandy shares with Brittany, the almost surreal island-abbey of Mont St-Michel rises serene and majestic, oblivious to the tides of tourists.

PLANNING YOUR TIME

For many, Normandy makes the perfect jet-lag antidote: A good first stop for your trip is Rouen, which is quick to reach by car or train from Paris' Charles de Gaulle or Beauvais airports. Honfleur, the D-Day beaches, and Mont St-Michel each merit overnight vis-

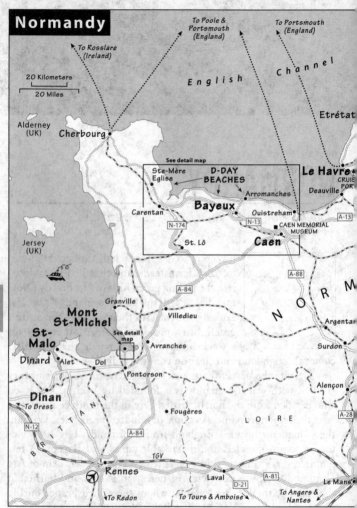

Normandy

20 Kilometers
20 Miles

English Channel

To Poole & Portsmouth (England)

To Portsmouth (England)

To Rosslare (Ireland)

Alderney (UK)

Cherbourg

Etrétat

See detail map

Ste-Mère Eglise

D-DAY BEACHES

Le Havre

CRUISE PORT

Arromanches

Deauville

Carentan

Bayeux

Ouistreham

N-174

N-13

CAEN MEMORIAL MUSEUM

St. Lô

Caen

A-13

Jersey (UK)

A-88

A-84

Granville

Villedieu

N O R M

Mont St-Michel

See detail map

Argentan

St-Malo

Avranches

Surdon

Dinard

Alet

Dol

Pontorson

Dinan

Alençon

To Brest

Fougères

B R I T T A N Y

L O I R E

A-28

N-12

A-84

TGV

Rennes

Laval

A-81

Le Mans

To Redon

To Tours & Amboise

D-21

To Angers & Nantes

its. At a minimum, you'll want a full day for the D-Day beaches and a half-day each in Honfleur, Bayeux, and on Mont St-Michel.

If you're driving between Paris and Honfleur, Giverny (see previous chapter) and Rouen are easy to visit. The WWII memorial museum in Caen works well as a stop between Honfleur and Bayeux (and the D-Day beaches). Mont St-Michel must be seen early or late to avoid the masses of midday tourists. Dinan, just 45 minutes by car from Mont St-Michel, offers a fine introduction to Brittany (see next chapter). Drivers can enjoy Mont St-Michel as a day trip from Dinan.

For practical information about Normandy, see www.normandie-tourisme.fr.

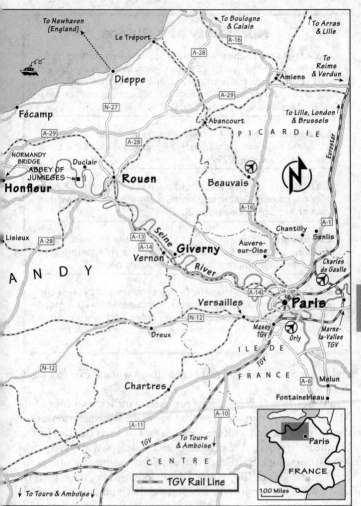

GETTING AROUND NORMANDY

This region is ideal with a **car.** If you're driving into Honfleur from the north, take the impressive but pricey Normandy Bridge (Pont de Normandie, €5.40 toll). If you're driving from Mont St-Michel into Brittany, follow my recommended scenic route to the town of St-Malo (see page 332).

Trains from Paris serve Rouen, Caen, Bayeux, Mont St-Michel (via Pontorson or Rennes), and Dinan, though service between these sights can be frustrating (try linking by bus—see next). Mont St-Michel is a headache by train, except from Paris. Enterprising businesses in Bayeux run shuttles between Bayeux

Normandy at a Glance

▲▲▲**D-Day Beaches** Atlantic coastline—stretching from Utah Beach in the west to Sword Beach in the east—littered with WWII museums, monuments, and cemeteries left in tribute to the Allied forces who successfully carried out the largest military operation in history: D-Day. See page 261.

▲▲▲**Mont St-Michel** Pretty-as-a-mirage island abbey that once sent pilgrims' spirits soaring—and today does the same for tourists. See page 297.

▲▲**Rouen** Lively city whose old town is a pedestrian haven, mixing a soaring Gothic cathedral, half-timbered houses, and Joan of Arc sights. See page 212.

▲▲**Honfleur** Picturesque port town, ideally located where the Seine greets the English Channel, whose shimmering light once captivated Impressionist painters. See page 231.

▲▲**Bayeux** Six miles from the D-Day beaches and the first city liberated after the D-Day landings, worth a visit for its famous medieval tapestry, enjoyable town center, and awe-inspiring cathedral, beautifully illuminated at night. See page 247.

and Mont St-Michel—a great help to those without cars (see page 261).

Buses link Giverny, Honfleur, Arromanches, and Mont St-Michel to train stations in nearby towns (less frequent on Sundays). To plan ahead, visit the websites for Bus Verts (for Le Havre, Honfleur, Bayeux, Arromanches, and Caen, www.busverts.fr), Keolis (for Mont St-Michel, www.destination-montsaintmichel.com), and Tibus or Illenoo (for Dinan and St-Malo, www.tibus.fr or www.illenoo-services.fr). Bus companies commonly offer good value and multiride discounts—for example, Bus Verts offers a 20 percent discount on a shareable four-ride ticket.

Another good option is to use an **excursion tour** to link destinations. **Westcapades** provides trips to Mont St-Michel from Dinan and St-Malo, and **Afoot in France** leads quality tours for small groups or individuals (for details, see page 315).

NORMANDY'S CUISINE SCENE

Normandy is known as the land of the four C's: Calvados, Camembert, cider, and *crème*. The region specializes in cream sauces, organ meats (sweetbreads, tripe, and kidneys—the gizzard salads are great), and seafood *(fruits de mer)*. You'll see *crêperies* offering inexpensive and good-value meals everywhere. A *galette* is a savory

---

Camembert Cheese

This cheap, soft, white, Brie-like cheese is sold all over France (and America) in distinctive, round wooden containers. The Camembert region has long been known for its cheese, but local legend has it that today's cheese got its start in the French Revolution, when a priest on the run was taken in by Marie Harel, a Camembert farm woman. The priest repaid the favor by giving her the secret formula for his hometown cheese—Brie.

From cow to customer, Camembert takes about three weeks to make. High-fat milk from Norman cows is curdled with rennet, ladled into round, five-inch molds, sprinkled with Penicillium camemberti bacteria, and left to dry. In the first three days, the cheese goes from the cow's body temperature to room temperature to refrigerator cool (50 degrees).

Two weeks later, the ripened and aged cheese is wrapped in wooden bands and labeled for market. Like wines, Camembert cheese is controlled by government regulations and must bear the "A.O.C." (Appellation d'Origine Contrôlée) stamp of approval.

---

buckwheat crêpe enjoyed as a main course; a crêpe is sweet and eaten for dessert.

Dairy products are big, too. Local cheeses are Camembert (mild to very strong; see sidebar), Brillat-Savarin (buttery), Livarot (spicy and pungent), Pavé d'Auge (spicy and tangy), and Pont l'Evêque (earthy).

What, no local wine? *Oui*, that's right. Here's how to cope. Fresh, white Muscadet wines are made nearby (in western Loire); they're cheap and a good match with much of Normandy's cuisine. But Normandy is famous for its many apple-based beverages. You can't miss the powerful Calvados apple brandy or the Bénédictine brandy (made by local monks). The local dessert, *trou Normand*, is apple sorbet swimming in Calvados. The region also produces three kinds of alcoholic apple ciders: *Cidre* can be *doux* (sweet), *brut* (dry), or *bouché* (sparkling—and the strongest). You'll also find bottles of Pommeau, a tasty blend of apple juice and Calvados (sold in many shops), as well as *poiré*, a tasty pear cider. And don't leave Normandy without sampling a *kir Normand*, a mix of crème de cassis and cider. Drivers in Normandy should be on the lookout for *Route du Cidre* signs (with a bright red apple); this tourist trail leads you to small producers of handcrafted cider and brandy.

Remember, restaurants serve only during lunch (11:30-14:00) and dinner (19:00-21:00, later in bigger cities); cafés serve food throughout the day.

Rouen

This 2,000-year-old city mixes Gothic architecture, half-timbered houses, and contemporary bustle like no other place in France. Busy Rouen (roo-ahn) is France's fifth-largest port and Europe's biggest food exporter (mostly wheat and grain). Its cobbled old town is a delight to wander.

Rouen was a regional capital during Roman times, and France's second-largest city in medieval times (with 40,000 residents—only Paris had more). In the ninth century, the Normans made the town their capital. William the Conqueror called it home before moving to England. Rouen walked a political tightrope between England and France for centuries and was an English base during the Hundred Years' War. Joan of Arc was burned here (in 1431).

Rouen's historic wealth was built on its wool industry and trade—for centuries, it was the last bridge across the Seine River before the Atlantic. In April 1944, as America and Britain weakened German control of Normandy prior to the D-Day landings, Allied bombers destroyed 50 percent of Rouen. Although the industrial suburbs were devastated, most of the historic core survived, keeping Rouen a pedestrian haven.

PLANNING YOUR TIME

If you want a dose of a smaller—yet lively—French city, Rouen is an easy day trip from Paris, with convenient train connections to Gare St. Lazare (nearly hourly, 1.5 hours).

If you're planning to get a car in Paris, save headaches by taking the train to Rouen and picking up a rental car there (spend a quiet night in Rouen and pick up your car the next morning). From Paris you can also take an early train to Rouen, pick up a car, stash your bags in it, leave it in the secure rental lot at the train station, and visit Rouen before heading out to explore Normandy (for car-rental companies, see "Helpful Hints," later).

Those relying on public transportation can visit Rouen on your way from Paris to other Normandy destinations, thanks to the good bus and train service (see under "Arrival in Rouen, By Train" for bag storage).

NORMANDY

Orientation to Rouen

Although Paris embraces the Seine, Rouen ignores it. The area we're most interested in is bounded by the river to the south, the Museum of Fine Arts (Esplanade Marcel Duchamp) to the north, Rue de la République to the east, and Place du Vieux Marché to the west. It's a 20-minute walk from the train station to the Notre-Dame Cathedral, and everything else of interest is within a 10-minute walk of the cathedral.

TOURIST INFORMATION

The TI faces the cathedral. They rent €5 audioguides covering the cathedral, Rouen's historic center, and the history of Joan of Arc in Rouen (though this book's self-guided walk is enough for most). If driving, get information about the Route of the Ancient Abbeys (May-Sept Mon-Sat 9:00-19:00, Sun 9:30-12:30 & 14:00-18:00; Oct-April Mon-Sat 9:30-12:30 & 13:30-18:00, closed Sun; Wi-Fi, 25 Place de la Cathédrale, tel. 02 32 08 32 40, www. rouentourisme.com).

ARRIVAL IN ROUEN

By Train: Rue Jeanne d'Arc cuts straight from Rouen's train station through the town center to the Seine River. Day-trippers can **walk** from the station down Rue Jeanne d'Arc toward Rue du Gros Horloge—a busy pedestrian mall in the medieval center and near the starting point of my self-guided walk. There's no bag storage at the train station, but the Holibag service lets you store bags at a handful of businesses in central Rouen (tel. 02 35 76 47 80, www. holibag.io).

Rouen's **subway** (Métrobus) whisks travelers from under the train station to the Palais de Justice in one stop (€1.70 for 1 hour; buy tickets from machines one level underground, then validate ticket on subway two levels down; subway direction: Technopôle or Georges Braque). Returning to the station, take a subway in direction: Boulingrin and get off at Gare-Rue Verte.

Taxis (to the right as you exit station) will take you to any of my recommended hotels for about €8.

By Car: Finding the city center from the autoroute is tricky. Follow signs for *Centre-Ville* and *Rive Droite* (right bank). If you get turned around (likely, because of the narrow, one-way streets), aim toward the highest cathedral spires you spot.

As you head toward the center, you should see signs for *P&R Relais*. These are tram stops outside the core where you can park for free, then hop on a tram into town (€1.70 each way). In the city, you can park on the street (metered 8:00-19:00, free overnight), or pay for more secure parking in one of many well-signed underground

NORMANDY

lots (€5/3 hours, €13/day; see map on page 216 for locations). For day-trippers taking my self-guided walk of Rouen, the garage under Place du Vieux Marché is best. For those staying overnight, Parking Cathédrale–Office du Tourism (between the cathedral and the river) is handy.

When leaving Rouen, head for the riverfront road, where autoroute signs will guide you to Paris or to Le Havre and Caen (for D-Day beaches and Honfleur). If you're following the Route of Ancient Abbeys from here, see page 228.

HELPFUL HINTS

Exchange Rate: €1 = about $1.10

Country Calling Code: 33 (see page 1082 for dialing instructions)

Closed Days: Many Rouen sights are closed midday (12:00-14:00), and most museums are closed altogether on Tuesdays. The cathedral doesn't open until 14:00 on Monday, and the Joan of Arc Church is closed Friday and Sunday mornings.

Market Days: The best open-air market is on Place St. Marc, a few blocks east of St. Maclou Church. It's filled with antiques and other good stuff (all day Tue, Fri, and Sat; Sun until about 13:30). A smaller market is on Place du Vieux Marché, near the Joan of Arc Church (Tue-Sun until 13:30, closed Mon).

Supermarket: A big **Monoprix** is on Rue du Gros Horloge (groceries at the back, Mon-Sat 8:30-21:00, Sun 9:00-13:00).

Cathedral of Light: In summer, Rouen's cathedral generally sports a dazzling light show on its exterior after dark (June-Sept at about 23:00).

Wi-Fi: You'll find Wi-Fi at several cafés within a few blocks of the train station on Rue Jeanne d'Arc. Wi-Fi is free (but slow) at the TI.

English Bookstore: **ABC Bookshop** has nothing but English-language books—some American, but mostly British (Tue-Sat 10:00-18:00, closed Sun-Mon, just south of St. Ouen Church at 11 Rue des Faulx, tel. 02 35 71 08 67).

Taxi: Call **Les Taxi Blancs** at 02 35 61 20 50.

Car Rental: Agencies with offices in the train station include **Europcar** (tel. 02 35 88 21 20), **Avis** (tel. 02 35 88 60 94), and **Hertz** (tel. 02 35 70 70 71).

SNCF Boutique: For train tickets, visit the SNCF office at the corner of Rue aux Juifs and Rue Eugène Boudin (Mon 12:30-19:00, Tue-Sat 10:00-19:00, closed Sun).

Rouen Walk

On this 1.5-hour self-guided walk, you'll see the essential Rouen sights (all but the Joan of Arc Museum are free) and experience the city's pedestrian-friendly streets. This walk is designed for day-trippers coming by train, but works just as well for drivers (ideally, park at Place du Vieux Marché, where the walk begins). We'll stroll the length of Rue du Gros Horloge to Notre-Dame Cathedral, visit the plague cemetery (Aître St. Maclou), loop up to the church of St. Ouen, and return along Rue de l'Hôpital. The walk ends at the Museum of Fine Arts, a short walk back to the train station. The map on the next page highlights our route.

• *If arriving by train, walk down Rue Jeanne d'Arc and turn right on Rue du Guillaume le Conquérant (notice the Gothic Palace of Justice building across Rue Jeanne d'Arc—we'll get to that later). This takes you to the back door of our starting point...*

▲Place du Vieux Marché

Stand in the small garden near the entrance of the striking Joan of Arc Church. Surrounded by half-timbered buildings, this old market square houses a cute, covered produce and fish market, a park commemorating Joan of Arc's burning, and a modern church named after her. Find the towering aluminum cross. This marks the spot where Rouen publicly punished and executed people. The pillories stood here, and during the Revolution, the town's guillotine made 800 people "a foot shorter at the top." In 1431, Joan of Arc—only 19 years old—was burned right here. Find her flaming statue (built into the wall of the church, facing the cross). As the flames engulfed her, an English soldier said, "Oh my God, we've killed a saint." Nearly 500 years later, Joan was canonized, and the soldier was proved right.

• *Now step inside...*

▲Joan of Arc Church (Eglise Jeanne d'Arc)

This modern church is a tribute to the young woman who was canonized in 1920 and later became the patron saint of France. The church, completed in 1979, feels Scandinavian inside and out—another reminder of Normandy's Nordic roots. Sumptuous 16th-century windows, salvaged from a church lost during World War II, were worked into the soft architectural lines. The pointed, stake-like support columns to the right seem fitting for a church dedicated to a woman burned at the stake. This is an uplifting place to be, with a ship's-hull vaulting and sweeping wood ceiling sailing over curved pews and a wall of glass below. Make time to savor this unusual sanctuary.

Cost and Hours: Free, Mon-Thu and Sat 10:00-12:00 &

NORMANDY

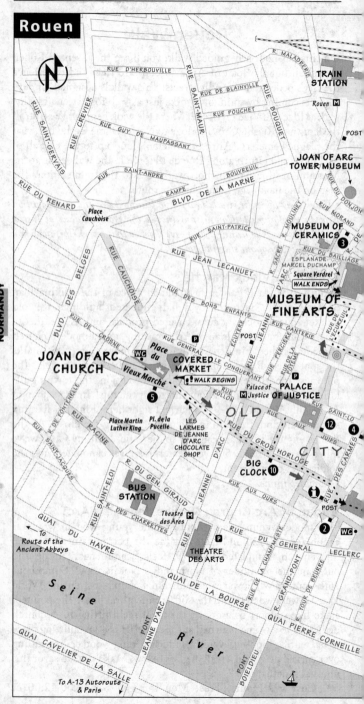

Rouen

TRAIN STATION

Rouen Ⓜ

POST

JOAN OF ARC TOWER MUSEUM

MUSEUM OF CERAMICS ③

R. MALADRERE

RUE D'HERBOUVILLE

RUE DE BLAINVILLE

RUE POUCHET

RUE CREVIER

RUE SAINT-MAUR

RUE BOUQUET

RUE SAINT-GERVAIS

RUE GUY DE MAUPASSANT

RUE SAINT-ANDRE

BOUVREUIL

RAMPE

RUE DU RENARD

BLVD. DE LA MARNE

Place Cauchoise

RUE SAINT-PATRICE

RUE DU DONJON

RUE MORAND

RUE SACRE

RUE MOULINET

ESPLANADE MARCEL DUCHAMP

RUE DU BAILLIAGE

Square Verdrel

WALK ENDS

RUE CAUCHOISE

RUE DES BELGES

RUE JEAN LECANUET

RUE DES BONS ENFANTS

MUSEUM OF FINE ARTS

RUE DE L'...

BLVD. DE CROSNE

RUE DE CROSNE

RUE GENERAL

Place du Vieux Marché

WC

COVERED MARKET

RUE ECUYERE

POST

RUE JEANNE

RUE GANTERIE

RUE PERCIERE

JOAN OF ARC CHURCH

⑤

WALK BEGINS

LE CONQUERANT

RUE ROLLON

Palace of Justice Ⓜ

PALACE OF JUSTICE

RUE POTERNE

RUE DE LA POTERNE

Place Martin Luther King

Pl. de la Pucelle

LES LARMES DE JEANNE D'ARC CHOCOLATE SHOP

OLD

RUE AUX

RUE SAINT-LO

⑫

④

R. DE FONTENELLE

RUE RACINE

RUE SAINT-JACQUES

R. DU GEN. GIRAUD

RUE DU GROS HORLOGE

CITY

RUE DES CARMES

RUE JUIFS

BIG CLOCK ⑩

BUS STATION

RUE SAINT-ELOI

RUE DES CHARRETTES

Theatre des Arts Ⓜ

RUE AUX OURS

Ⓘ

POST

②

WC

QUAI DU HAVRE

To Route of the Ancient Abbeys

RUE JEANNE D'ARC

P

THEATRE DES ARTS

RUE DU GENERAL LECLERC

RUE DE LA CHAMPMESLE

RUE GRAND-PONT

R. TOUR DE BEURRE

QUAI DE LA BOURSE

PONT JEANNE D'ARC

Seine

River

QUAI PIERRE CORNEILLE

QUAI CAVELIER DE LA SALLE

PONT BOIELDIEU

To A-13 Autoroute & Paris

N

NORMANDY

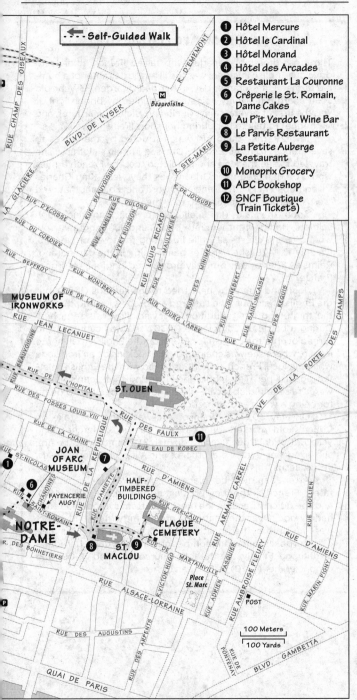

Self-Guided Walk

1 Hôtel Mercure
2 Hôtel le Cardinal
3 Hôtel Morand
4 Hôtel des Arcades
5 Restaurant La Couronne
6 Crêperie le St. Romain, Dame Cakes
7 Au P'it Verdot Wine Bar
8 Le Parvis Restaurant
9 La Petite Auberge Restaurant
10 Monoprix Grocery
11 ABC Bookshop
12 SNCF Boutique (Train Tickets)

NORMANDY

Joan of Arc (1412-1431)

The cross-dressing teenager who rallied French soldiers to drive out English invaders was the illiterate daughter of a humble farmer. One summer day, in her dad's garden, 13-year-old Joan heard a heavenly voice accompanied by bright light. It was the first of several saints (including Michael, Margaret, and Catherine) to talk to her during her short life.

In 1429, the young girl was instructed by the voices to save France from the English. Dressed in men's clothing, she traveled to see the king and predicted that the French armies would be defeated near Orléans—as they were. King Charles VII equipped her with an ancient sword and a banner that read "Jesus, Maria," and sent her to rally the troops.

Soon "the Maid" (la Pucelle) was bivouacking amid rough soldiers, riding with them into battle, and suffering an arrow wound to the chest—all while liberating the town of Orléans. On July 17, 1429, she held her banner high in the cathedral of Reims as Charles was officially proclaimed king of a resurgent France.

Joan and company next tried to retake Paris (1429), but the English held out. She suffered a crossbow wound through the thigh, and her reputation of invincibility was tarnished. During a battle at Compiègne (1430), she was captured and turned over to the English for £10,000. The English took her to Rouen, where she was chained by the neck inside an iron cage while the local French authorities (allied with the English) plotted against her. The Inquisition—insisting that Joan's voices were "false and diabolical"—tried and sentenced her to death for being a witch and a heretic.

On May 30, 1431, Joan of Arc was tied to a stake on Rouen's old market square (Place du Vieux Marché). She yelled, "Rouen! Rouen! Must I die here?" Then they lit the fire; she fixed her eyes on a crucifix and died chanting, "Jesus, Jesus, Jesus."

After Joan died, her place in history was slowly rehabilitated. French authorities proclaimed her trial illegal (1455), and she quickly became the most important symbol of French nationhood. Over the centuries, prominent writers and artists were inspired by her, politicians co-opted her fame for their own purposes, and common people rallied around her idealized image. Finally, the Catholic Church beatified (1909) and canonized her (1920) as St. Joan of Arc.

14:00-18:00, Fri 10:00-12:00, Sun 14:00-17:30, closed during Mass, 50-cent English pamphlet describes the stained-glass scenes. A public WC is 30 yards straight ahead from the church doors.
• *Turn left out of the church.*

Ruined Church and Julia Child

As you leave the church, you're stepping over the ruins of a 15th-century church (it was destroyed during the French Revolution). Just beyond that, in a charming half-timbered building, is the recommended Restaurant La Couronne, reputedly the oldest restaurant in France. It was here, in 1949, that American chef and author Julia Child ate her first French meal, experiencing a culinary epiphany that changed her life (and the eating habits of a generation of Americans). In the lobby are lots of historic photos of happy diners, including Julia (bottom of stairs, just above eye level on the right).

• *Leave the square and join the busy pedestrian street, Rue du Gros Horloge—an important thoroughfare in Roman times, it's been the city's main shopping street since the Middle Ages. A block up on your right (at #163) is Rouen's most famous chocolate shop.*

Auzou and Houses That Lean Out

The *chocolatiers* at Auzou would love to tempt you with their chocolate-covered almond "tears *(larmes)* of Joan of Arc." Although you must resist touching the chocolate fountain, you are welcome to taste a tear (delicious). The first one is free; a small bag costs about €9.

Before moving on, notice the architecture. The higher floors of the Auzou house lean out, evidence that the building dates from before 1520, when such street-crowding construction was prohibited. (People feared that houses leaning over the street like this would block breezes and make the city more susceptible to disease.) Look around the corner and down the lane behind the Auzou building to see a fine line of half-timbered Gothic facades. Study the house just across the lane at #161. You can tell it was built after 1520 (because its facade is flat) and that it's Renaissance (because of the characteristic carved wooden corner-posts). We'll see more houses like this later on our walk.

• *Your route continues past a medieval McDonald's to busy **Rue Jeanne d'Arc**. Pause here and look both ways. With the 19th-century Industrial Age, France expanded its transportation infrastructure. A train line connecting Paris to Rouen arrived in the early 1840s, and major roads like this were built to get traffic efficiently to the station. The facades here date from the 1860s and are in the Haussmann style so dominant in Paris in that era.*

Cross the street and continue straight to the...

The Hundred Years' War (1336-1453)

It would take a hundred years to explain all the causes, battles, and political maneuverings of this century-plus of warfare between France and England. Here's the Hundred Years' War in 100 seconds:

In 1300, before the era of the modern nation-state, the borders between France and England were fuzzy. French-speaking kings had ruled England, English kings owned the south of France, and English merchants dominated trade in the north. Dukes and lords in both countries were aligned more along family lines than by national identity. When the French king died without a male heir (1328), both France and England claimed the crown, and the battle was on.

England invaded the more populous France (1345) and—thanks to skilled archers using armor-penetrating longbows—won big battles at Crécy (1346) and Poitiers (1356). Despite a truce, roving bands of English mercenaries stayed behind and supported themselves by looting French villages. The French responded with guerrilla tactics.

In 1415, with Henry V's big victory at Agincourt, the English took still more territory. But rallied by the heavenly visions of young Joan of Arc, the French slowly drove the invaders out. Paris was liberated in 1436, and when Bordeaux fell to French forces (1453), the fighting ended without a treaty.

▲Great Clock (Gros Horloge)

This impressive, circa-1528 Renaissance clock, the Gros Horloge (groh or-lohzh), decorates the former City Hall. Originally, the clock had only an hour hand but no minute hand. In the 16th century, an hour hand offered sufficient precision; minute hands became necessary only in a later, faster-paced age. The silver orb above the clock makes one revolution in 29 days. (The cycle of the moon let people know the tides—of practical value here as Rouen was a seaport.) The town medallion (sculpted into the stone below the clock) features a sacrificial lamb, which has both religious meaning (Jesus is the Lamb of God) and commercial significance (wool was the source of Rouen's wealth). The clock's artistic highlight fills the underside of the arch (walk underneath and stretch your back), with the "Good Shepherd" and loads of sheep.

Bell Tower Panorama: To see the inner workings of the clock and an extraordinary panorama over Rouen and its cathedral, climb the clock tower's 100 steps. You'll tour several rooms with the help of a friendly, 40-minute audioguide and learn about life in Rouen when the tower was built. The big one- and two-ton bells ring on the hour—a deafening experience if you're in the tower. Don't miss the 360-degree view outside from the very top (€6, includes audioguide; Tue-Sun 10:00-13:00 & 14:00-19:00, shorter hours off-season, closed Mon year-round).

• *Walk under the Gros Horloge and continue straight a half-block, then take a one-block detour left (up Rue Thouret) to see the...*

Palace of Justice (Palais de Justice)

Rouen is the capital of Normandy, and this building is its parliament. The section on the left is the oldest, in Flamboyant Gothic style dating from 1550. Normandy was an independent little country from 911 to 1204, and since then, while a part of France, it's had an independent spirit and has enjoyed a bit of autonomy.

Behind you is the historic Rue aux Juifs (Street of the Jews)—a reminder that this was the Jewish quarter from the 10th century until the early 14th century, when the Jews were expelled from France. Their homes were destroyed and the city took their land. Later, the empty real estate was used for the parliament.

• *Double back and continue up Rue du Gros Horloge. In a block you'll see a stone plaque dedicated to* **Cavelier de la Salle** *(high on the left), who explored the mouth of the Mississippi River, claimed the state of Louisiana for France, and was assassinated in Texas in 1687. Soon you'll reach...*

▲▲Notre-Dame Cathedral (Cathédrale Notre-Dame)

This cathedral is a landmark of art history. You're seeing essentially what Claude Monet saw as he painted 30 different studies of this

frilly Gothic facade at various times of day. Using the physical building only as a rack upon which to hang light, mist, dusk, and shadows, Monet was capturing "impressions." One of these paintings is in Rouen's Museum of Fine Arts; others are at the Orsay Museum in Paris. Find the plaque showing one of the paintings (in the corner of the square, about 30 paces to your right if exiting the TI).

Cost and Hours: Free, Tue-Sun 8:00-19:00 (Nov-March closed 12:00-14:00); Mon 14:00-19:00. The cathedral is closed during Mass (Tue-Sat at 10:00, July-Aug also at 18:00, Sun and holidays at 8:30, 10:30, and 12:00).

Visiting the Cathedral

There's been a church on this site for more than a thousand years. Charlemagne honored it with a visit in the eighth century before the Vikings sacked it a hundred years later. The building you see today was constructed between the 12th and 14th centuries, though lightning strikes, wars (the cathedral was devastated in WWII fighting), and other destructive forces meant constant rebuilding.

Central Facade: Look up at the elaborate, soaring **facade,** with bright statues on either side of the central portal—later, we'll meet some of their friends face-to-face inside the cathedral. The facade is another fine Rouen example of Flamboyant Gothic, and the spire, soaring nearly 500 feet high, is awe-inspiring. Why such a big cathedral here? Until the 1700s, Rouen was the second-largest city in France—rich from its wool trade and its booming port. On summer evenings, there's usually a colorful light show on the cathedral's facade (see "Helpful Hints," earlier).

Above the **main door** is a marvelous depiction of the Tree of Jesse. Jesse, King David's father, is shown reclined, resting his head on his hand, looking nonplussed. The tree grows from Jesse's back; the figures sprouting from its branches represent the lineage of Jesus.

Many statues on the facade are headless. In 1562, during the French Wars of Religion, Protestant iconoclasts held the city for six months—more than enough time to deface the church.

• *Head inside.*

Cathedral Interior: Look down the center of the **nave.** This is a classic Gothic nave—four stories of pointed-arch arcades, the top filled with windows to help illuminate the interior. Today, the interior is lighter than intended because clear glass has replaced the original colored glass (destroyed over the centuries by angry Protestants, horrible storms, changing tastes, and WWII bombs).

Circle counterclockwise around the church, starting down the right aisle. The side chapels and windows, each dedicated to a different saint, display the changing styles through the centuries. Photos halfway down on the right show WWII bomb damage to the cathedral.

At the high altar, look across and up at the north transept **rose window,** which dates from around 1300. It survived a hurricane in 1683. During World War II the glass was taken out, but the stone tracery did not survive. On the right (in the south transept) is a **chapel dedicated to Joan of Arc.** Its focal point is a touching statue of the saint being burned. The chapel's modern 1956 windows replaced those destroyed in the war.

Passing through an iron gate after the high altar, you come to several **stone statues.** Each is "bolted" to the wall—as they originally were in their niches high above the street centuries ago. These figures were lifted from the facade during a cleaning and provide a rare chance to stand toe-to-toe with a medieval statue.

Several **stone tombs** on your left date from when Rouen was the Norman capital. The first tomb is for Rollo, the first duke of Normandy who died about 932 (he's also the great-great-great-

great grandfather of William the Conqueror, seventh duke of Normandy, c. 1028). Rollo was chief of the first gang of Vikings (the original "Normans") who decided to settle here. Called the Father of Normandy, Rollo died at the age of 80, but he is portrayed on his tomb as if he were 33 (as was the fashion, because Jesus died at that age). Thanks to later pillage and plunder, only Rollo's femur is inside the tomb.

And speaking of body parts, the next tomb once contained the heart of English King **Richard the Lionheart,** famous for his military exploits in the Third Crusade (he died in 1199). Over the years, people forgot about the heart, and it was only rediscovered in 1838. It was eventually analyzed by forensic scientists, who concluded that the king had died from a festering arrow wound (not poison, as popularly thought).

Circle behind the altar. The beautiful **windows** with bold blues and reds are generally from the 13th century. Opposite Richard the Lionheart's tomb is a fine window dedicated to St. Julian, patron of hoteliers and travelers (with pane-by-pane descriptions just below).

Continue a few paces, then look up to the **ceiling** over the nave (directly above Rollo's femur). You can see the patchwork where, in 1999, a fierce winter storm caused a spire to crash through the roof.

• *Exit while you can, through the side door of the north transept. (If the door is closed, leave through the main entrance, turn right, then loop back alongside the church.)*

North Transept Facade: Outside, look back at the **facade** over the door of the north transept. The fine carved tympanum (the area over the door) shows a graphic Last Judgment. Jesus stands between the saved (on the left) and the damned (on the right). Notice the devil grasping a miser, who clutches a bag of coins. On the far right, look for the hellish hot tub, where even a bishop (pointy hat) is eternally in hot water. And is it my imagination, or are those saved souls on the far left high-fiving each other?

Most of the facade has been cleaned—blasted with jets of water—but the limestone carving is still black. It's too delicate to survive the hosing. A more expensive laser cleaning has begun, and the result is astonishing.

• *From this courtyard, a gate deposits you on a traffic-free street facing the elegant Art Nouveau facade of the recommended Dame Cakes tea shop. This was originally the **workshop** of the church's lead 19th-century craftsman, Ferdinand Marrou. To showcase his work, he fashioned the wrought iron on this door as well as the fine touches inside.*

Turn right and walk along the appealing Rue St. Romain.

Spire View: In a short distance, look up through an opening above the entrance to the Joan of Arc Museum and gaze back at the cathedral's prickly **spire.** Made of cast iron in the late 1800s— about the same time Gustave Eiffel was building his tower in

Paris—the spire is, at 490 feet, the tallest in France. You can also see the smaller (green) spires—one of which was blown over in that violent 1999 storm and crashed—all 30 tons of it—through the roof to the cathedral floor. Replaced in 2013, you can bet it's now bolted down really good.

• *To learn more about Rouen's most famous figure, consider touring the...*

▲Joan of Arc Museum (Historial Jeanne d'Arc)

Rouen's Archbishop's Palace, where in 1431 Joan of Arc was tried and sentenced to death, now hosts a multimedia experience that tells her story. Equipped with headphones, you'll walk for 75 minutes through a series of rooms, each with a brief video presentation that tries very hard to teach and entertain. Your tour ends in the Officialité—the room where the trial took place. The presentation is creative and dramatic, but it's slow-moving, and both kids and adults may find it boring. You won't see many artifacts, but several interesting rooms at the end display posters and books that illustrate the martyr's impact on modern French culture.

Cost and Hours: €9.50, required tours depart on the quarter-hour Tue-Fri from 11:00, Sat-Sun and July-Aug from 10:00, last tour generally at 17:45 (earlier off-season), closed Mon year-round, 7 Rue St. Romain, tel. 02 35 52 48 00, www.historial-jeannedarc. fr.

• *From the museum, continue down atmospheric Rue St. Romain. A bit farther down the street at #26, find the shop marked...*

Fayencerie Augy

Monsieur Augy and his family welcome shoppers to browse his studio/gallery/shop and see Rouen's earthenware "china" being made in the traditional faience style (Mon-Sat 9:00-19:00, closed Sun, shipping available, 26 Rue St. Romain, www.fayencerie-augy.com). First, the clay is molded and fired. Then it's dipped in white enamel, dried, lovingly hand painted, and fired a second time. Rouen was the first city in France to make this colorfully glazed faience earthenware. In the 1700s, the town had 18 factories churning out the popular product. For more faience, visit the local Museum of Ceramics (see "Sights in Rouen").

• *Before continuing along Rue St. Romain, peek down Rue des Cha-noines for a skinny example of the higgledy-piggledy streets common in medieval Rouen. Back on Rue St. Romain, walk along the massive Archbishop's Palace, which (after crossing Rue de la République) leads to the fancy...*

St. Maclou Church (Eglise St. Maclou)

This church's unique, bowed facade is textbook Flamboyant Gothic. Notice the flame-like tracery decorating its gable. Because this was built at the very end of the Gothic age—and construction took many years—the carved wooden doors are from the next age: the Renaissance (c. 1550). Study the graphic Last Judgment above the doors, and imagine the mindset of the frightened parishioners who worshipped here. If it's open, the bright and airy interior is worth a quick peek.

• *Leaving the church, turn right, and then take another right (giving the little boys on the corner wall a wide berth). Wander past a fine wall of half-timbered buildings fronting Rue Martainville, to the back end of St. Maclou Church.*

Half-Timbered Buildings

Because the local stone—a chalky limestone from the cliffs of the Seine River—was of poor quality (your thumbnail is stronger), and because local oak was plentiful, half-timbered buildings became a Rouen specialty from the 14th through 19th century. There are still 2,000 half-timbered buildings in town; about 100 date from before 1520. Cantilevered floors were standard until the early 1500s. These top-heavy designs made sense: City land was limited, property taxes were based on ground-floor square footage, and the cantilevering minimized unsupported spans on upper floors. The oak beams provided the structural skeleton of the building, which was then filled in with a mix of clay, straw, or whatever was available.

Until the Industrial Age, this was the textile district where cloth was processed, dyed, and sold. When that industry moved across the river in the 19th century, the neighborhood was mothballed and forgotten. After World War II it was recognized as historic and preserved. Eventually rents went up, and gentrification crept in.

• *About 50 yards past the end of the church, on the left at 186 Rue Martainville, a covered lane leads to the...*

▲Plague Cemetery (Aître St. Maclou)

During the great plagues of the Middle Ages, as many as two-thirds of the people in this parish died. For the decimated community, dealing with the corpses was an overwhelming task. This half-timbered courtyard (c. 1520) was a mass grave, an ossuary where the bodies were "processed." Bodies were dumped into the grave (an open pit where the well is now) and drenched in liquid lime to help speed decomposition. Later, the bones were stacked in alcoves above the once-open arcades that line this courtyard. Notice the colonnades with their ghoulish carvings of gravediggers' tools, skulls, crossbones, and characters doing the "dance of death." In this *danse macabre*, Death, the great equalizer, grabs people of all social classes. As you leave, spy the dried black cat (in tiny glass case to the left of the door). Perhaps to overcome evil, it was buried during the building's construction.

Cost and Hours: Free, daily 9:00-18:00.

Nearby: Farther down Rue Martainville, at Place St. Marc, a colorful market is lively Sunday until about 13:30 and all day Tuesday, Friday, and Saturday.

• *Our tour is over. To return to the* ***train station*** *or reach the* ***Museum*** *of Fine Arts, turn right from the boneyard, then right again at the little boys (onto Rue Damiette), and hike up antique row to the vertical St. Ouen Church (a 7th-century abbey turned church in the 15th century; fine park behind). Cross the big square and walk down traffic-free Rue de l'Hôpital (which becomes Rue Ganterie). Turn right on Rue de l'Ecureuil to find the museum directly ahead. To continue to the train station, turn left onto Rue Jean-Lecanuet, then right onto Rue Jeanne d'Arc.*

Sights in Rouen

These museums, all within blocks of one another, are all free, closed on Tuesdays, and never crowded.

NORMANDY

▲Museum of Fine Arts (Musée des Beaux-Arts)

Paintings from many periods are beautifully displayed in this overlooked two-floor museum, including works by Caravaggio, Peter Paul Rubens, Paolo Veronese, Jan Steen, Velázquez, Théodore Géricault, Jean-Auguste-Dominique Ingres, Eugène Delacroix, and several Impressionists. With its free admission and calm interior, this museum is worth a short visit for the Impressionists and a surgical hit of a few other key artists. The museum café is good for a peaceful break.

Cost and Hours: Free, €11 for frequent and impressive special exhibitions—check website; open Wed-Mon 10:00-18:00, closed Tue; bag check available, peaceful café, a few blocks below train station at Esplanade Marcel Duchamp, tel. 02 35 71 28 40, www.musees-rouen-normandie.fr.

Visiting the Museum: Pick up the essential museum map at the info desk as you enter, then climb the grand staircase that divides the museum into two wings.

Turning right when you reach the second floor, you'll pass through a few rooms, then start seeing some names you recognize: Ingres and Jacques-Louis David (Room 2.21) and then a good collection of works by Géricault (Room 2.22—find a small version of his famous *Raft of the Medusa*). Turn left into Room 2.33, with one of Monet's famous paintings of the Rouen cathedral facade. Now loop through this wing to enjoy scenes inspired by Normandy's landscape and works by Impressionist greats (Monet, Sisley, Pissarro, Renoir, Degas, and Corot). Make a point to appreciate beautiful paintings by Impressionists whose names you may not recognize. Room 2.25 showcases a scene of Rouen's busy port in 1855.

Paintings on the other side of the grand staircase are devoted to French painters from the 17th and 18th centuries (Boucher, Fragonard, and Poussin) and Italian works, including several by Veronese. A gripping Caravaggio canvas (Room 2.4), depicting the flagellation of Christ, demands attention with its dramatic lighting and realistic faces.

Stairs at the rear, near the Caravaggio, lead down to an intriguing collection of works by 16th-century Dutch and Belgian artists and a small room of medieval icons. On the other side of the first floor, pass through the bookstore to find a collection of paintings by hometown boy Raymond Duchamp-Villon (brother of the famous Dadaist Marcel Duchamp), several colorful Modiglianis, and a grand-scale Delacroix.

Museum of Ironworks (Musée le Secq des Tournelles, a.k.a. Musée de la Ferronnerie)

This deconsecrated church houses iron objects, many of them more than 1,500 years old. Locks, chests, keys, tools, thimbles, coffee grinders, corkscrews, and flatware from centuries ago—virtually anything made of iron is on display. You can duck into the entry area for a glimpse of a medieval iron scene without passing through the turnstile.

Cost and Hours: Free, no English explanations, Wed-Mon 14:00-18:00, closed Tue, behind Museum of Fine Arts at 2 Rue Jacques Villon, tel. 02 35 88 42 92, www.museelesecqdestournelles.fr.

Museum of Ceramics (Musée de la Céramique)

This fine old mansion is filled with examples of Rouen's famous faience earthenware, dating from the 16th to 18th century. There are also examples of Sèvres and Delft wares—but not a word of English.

Cost and Hours: Free, Wed-Mon 14:00-18:00, closed Tue, 1 Rue Faucon, tel. 02 35 07 31 74, www.museedelaceramique.fr.

Joan of Arc Tower (La Tour Jeanne d'Arc)

This massive tower (1204), part of Rouen's brooding castle, was Joan's prison before her execution. Cross the deep moat and find three small floors (and 122 spiral steps) covering tidbits of Rouen's and Joan's history. The top floor gives a good peek at an impressive wood substructure but no views.

Cost and Hours: Free, Wed-Sat and Mon 10:00-12:30 & 14:00-18:00, Sun 14:00-18:30, closed Tue, one block uphill from the Museum of Fine Arts on Rue du Bouvreuil, tel. 02 35 98 16 21, www.tourjeannedarc.fr.

NEAR ROUEN
The Route of the Ancient Abbeys
(La Route des Anciennes Abbayes)

This driving route—punctuated with medieval abbeys, apples, cherry trees, and Seine River views—provides a pleasing detour for those with cars connecting Rouen and Honfleur or the D-Day beaches. The only "essential" stop on this drive is the Abbey of Jumièges.

From Rouen, follow the Seine along its right bank and track signs for D-982 to Duclair. Fifteen minutes west of Rouen, drivers can stop to admire the gleaming Romanesque church at the **Abbey of St. Georges de Boscherville** (skip the abbey grounds). This perfectly intact and beautiful church makes for interesting comparisons with the ruined church at Jumièges. The café across from the church is good for meals or drinks.

Leaving Duclair, follow D-65 to Jumièges. Here you'll find the **Abbey of Jumièges,** a spiritual place for lovers of evocative ruins (worth ▲). Founded in A.D. 654 as a Benedictine abbey, it was leveled by Vikings in the 9th century, then rebuilt by William the Conqueror in the 11th century. This magnificent complex thrived for centuries as Normandy's largest abbey. It was part of the great monastic movement that reestablished civilization in Normandy from the chaos that followed the fall of Rome (for more about the power of the Benedictines, read about Cluny Abbey on page 888).

The abbey was destroyed during the French Revolution, when it was used as a quarry, and it has changed little since then. Today there is no roof, and many walls are entirely gone. But what remains of the abbey's Church of Notre-Dame is awe-inspiring. Study its stark Romanesque facade standing 160 feet high. Stroll down the nave's center; notice the three levels of arches and the soaring rear wall capped by a lantern tower to light the choir. Find a seat in the ruined choir and imagine the church before its destruction. You'll discover brilliant views of the ruins and better appreciate its importance by wandering into the park (€6.50, helpful English handout, daily mid-April-mid-Sept 9:30-18:30, mid-Sept-mid-April 9:30-13:00 & 14:30-17:30, consider the detailed booklet but skip the unnecessary videoguide, tel. 02 35 37 24 02, www.abbayedejumieges.fr). Decent lunch options lie across the street from the abbey, and there's a TI for the village of Jumièges in front of the parking lot.

From near Jumièges you can cross the Seine on the tiny, free, and frequent car ferry, then connect with the A-13—or continue following the right bank of the Seine and cross at the Pont de Tancarville bridge (free) or the magnificent Normandy Bridge (Pont de Normandie, €5.40). By either route allow 45 minutes from Rouen

---

Sleep Code

Hotels are classified based on the average price of a standard double room without breakfast in high season.

$$$$	**Splurge:** Most rooms over €200
$$$	**Pricier:** €150-200
$$	**Moderate:** €100-150
$	**Budget:** €50-100
¢	**Backpacker:** Under €50
RS%	**Rick Steves discount**
*	**French hotel rating system** (0-5 stars)

Unless otherwise noted, credit cards are accepted, hotel staff speak basic English, and free Wi-Fi is available. Comparison-shop by checking prices at several hotels (on each hotel's own website, on a booking site, or by email). For the best deal, *book directly with the hotel.* Ask for a discount if paying in cash; if the listing includes **RS%**, request a Rick Steves discount.

---

to Jumièges and another 75 minutes to Honfleur, or two more hours to Bayeux.

Sleeping in Rouen

These hotels are perfectly central, within two blocks of Notre-Dame Cathedral.

$$$ Hôtel Mercure*** is a concrete business hotel with a professional staff, a stay-awhile lobby and bar, and 125 well-equipped and thoughtfully appointed rooms. Suites come with views of the cathedral, but are pricey and not much bigger than a double (some rooms with balconies, air-con, elevator, pay parking garage, 7 Rue Croix de Fer, tel. 02 35 52 69 52, www.mercure.com, h1301@accor.com).

$$ Hôtel le Cardinal** is a solid value with 15 sharp, well-designed rooms, most with point-blank views of the cathedral and all with queen-size beds and modern bathrooms (larger but pricier fourth-floor rooms with balconies and great cathedral views; elevator, 1 Place de la Cathédrale, tel. 02 35 70 24 42, www.cardinal-hotel.fr, hotelcardinal.rouen@wanadoo.fr).

$ Hotel Morand,** a five-minute walk from the train station, is a time-warp place with an Old World hunting-lodge feel and simple but good rooms at fair rates (1 Rue Morland, tel. 02 35 71 46 07, www.morandhotel.com, contact@morandhotel.com).

$ Hôtel des Arcades* is bare-bones basic, but as cheap and central as it gets (52 Rue des Carmes, tel. 02 76 27 67 62, www.hotel-des-arcades.fr, hotel_des_arcades@yahoo.fr).

Restaurant Price Code

I've assigned each eatery a price category, based on the average cost of a typical main course. Drinks, desserts, and splurge items (steak and seafood) can raise the price considerably.

$$$$ **Splurge:** Most main courses over €25
$$$ **Pricier:** €20-25
$$ **Moderate:** €15-20
$ **Budget:** Under €15

In France, a crêpe stand or other takeout spot is **$**; a sit-down brasserie, café, or bistro with affordable *plats du jour* is **$$**; a casual but more upscale restaurant is **$$$**; and a swanky splurge is **$$$$**.

Eating in Rouen

To find the best eating action, prowl the streets between the St. Maclou and St. Ouen churches (Rues Martainville and Damiette) for *crêperies,* wine bars, international cuisine, and traditional restaurants. This is Rouen's liveliest area at night (except Sunday and Monday, when many places are closed).

$$$ Restaurant La Couronne is a venerable and cozy place to dine very well. Reserve ahead to experience the same cuisine that Julia Child tasted when she ate her first French meal here in 1948 (31 Place du Vieux Marché, tel. 02 35 71 40 90, www.lacouronne.com.fr).

$ Crêperie le St. Romain, between the cathedral and St. Maclou Church, is an excellent budget option. Gentle Mr. Pegis serves filling crêpes with small salads in a warm setting (tables in the rear are best). The hearty *gatiflette*—a crêpe with scalloped potatoes—is delicious (lunch Tue-Sat, dinner Thu-Sat, 52 Rue St. Romain, tel. 02 35 88 90 36).

$ Dame Cakes is ideal if it's lunchtime or teatime and you need a Jane Austen fix. The decor is from a more precious era, and the baked goods are out of this world. Locals adore the tables in the back garden, while tourists eat up the cathedral view from the first-floor room (garden terrace in back, Mon-Sat 10:30-19:00, closed Sun, 70 Rue St. Romain, tel. 02 35 07 49 31). For more on the history of this place, see page 223.

$ Au P'it Verdot is a lively wine bar-café where locals gather for a glass of wine and meat-and-cheese plates in the thick of restaurant row (no lunch, light meals only, Tue-Sat 18:00-24:00, closed Sun-Mon, 13 Rue Père Adam, tel. 02 35 36 34 43).

$$ Le Parvis, facing St. Maclou Church, is a good bet for classic Norman dishes. You'll get good views of the pretty church from comfortable tables inside and out (ask about their *bouillabaisse* *à la mode Normande,* closed for dinner Sun and all day Mon, 7 Place Barthlémy, tel. 02 35 15 28 80).

$$ La Petite Auberge, a block off Rue Damiette, is the most traditional place I list. It has an Old World interior, reasonable prices, and it's also open on Sunday (closed Mon, 164 Rue Martainville, tel. 02 35 70 80 18).

Rouen Connections

Rouen is well served by trains from Paris and Caen, making Bayeux and the D-Day beaches a snap to reach.

From Rouen by Train to: Paris' Gare St. Lazare (nearly hourly, 1.5 hours), **Bayeux** (14/day, 2.5 hours, change in Caen), **Caen** (14/day, 1.5 hours), **Pontorson/Mont St-Michel** (2/day, 4 hours, change in Caen; more with change in Paris, 7 hours).

By Train and Bus to: Honfleur (6/day Mon-Sat, 3/day Sun, 1-hour train to Le Havre, then easy transfer to 30-minute bus over Normandy Bridge to Honfleur).

Route Tips for Drivers: Those continuing to Honfleur or the D-Day beaches should consider the Route of the Ancient Abbeys, outlined on page 228.

NORMANDY

Honfleur

Gazing at its cozy harbor lined with skinny, soaring houses, it's easy to overlook the historic importance of Honfleur (ohn-flur). For
more than a thousand years, sailors have enjoyed this port's ideal location, where the Seine River greets the English Channel. William the Conqueror received supplies shipped from Honfleur. Samuel de Champlain sailed from here in 1603 to North America, where he founded Quebec City. The

town was also a favorite of 19th-century Impressionists who were captivated by Honfleur's unusual light—the result of its river-meets-sea setting. The 19th-century artist Eugène Boudin lived and painted in Honfleur, attracting Monet and other creative types from Paris. In some ways, modern art was born in the fine light of idyllic little Honfleur.

Honfleur escaped the bombs of World War II, and today offers a romantic port enclosed on three sides by sprawling outdoor cafés.

Long eclipsed by the gargantuan port of Le Havre just across the Seine, Honfleur happily uses its past as a bar stool...and sits on it.

Orientation to Honfleur

Honfleur is popular—expect crowds on weekends and during summer. All of Honfleur's appealing lanes and activities are within a short stroll of its old port, the Vieux Bassin. The Seine River flows just east of the center, the hills of the Côte de Grâce form its western limit, and Rue de la République slices north-south through the center to the port. Honfleur has two can't-miss sights—the harbor and St. Catherine Church—and a handful of other intriguing monuments. But really, the town itself is its best sight.

TOURIST INFORMATION

The TI is in the glassy public library *(Mediathéque)* on Quai le Paulmier, two blocks from the Vieux Bassin (July-Aug Mon-Sat 9:30-19:00, Sun 10:00-17:00; Sept-June Mon-Sat 9:30-12:30 & 14:00-18:30, Sun 10:00-12:30 & 14:00-17:00 except closed Sun afternoon Oct-Easter; free WCs, tel. 02 31 89 23 30, www.ot-honfleur.fr). Here you can rent a €5 audioguide for a self-guided town walk, pick up regional bus and train schedules, and find information on the D-Day beaches.

ARRIVAL IN HONFLEUR

By Bus: Get off at the small bus station *(gare routière)*, and confirm your departure at the helpful information counter. To reach the TI and old town, turn right as you exit the station and walk five minutes up Quai le Paulmier. Note that the bus stop on Rue de la République may be convenient for some accommodations (see map on page 234).

   By Car: Follow *Centre-Ville* signs, then find your hotel and unload your bags (double-parking is OK for a few minutes). Parking is a headache in Honfleur, especially on summer and holiday weekends. Some hotels offer pay parking; otherwise, your hotelier knows where you can park for free. If you don't mind paying for convenience, check first for a space in the small lot directly in front of the TI (€2/hour, €8/24 hours); if that's full, continue a couple of blocks farther to Parking du Bassin (€2/hour, €14/24 hours) or across the short causeway to Parking du Môle (€4/day). Free parking is available farther out at the Naturospace Museum (15-minute walk up Boulevard Charles V, near the beach) and Parking Beaulieu (take Rue St-Nichol to Rue Guillaume de Beaulieu). Street parking, metered during the day, is free from 20:00 to 8:00. See the map on page 234 for parking locations.

HELPFUL HINTS

Museum Pass: The €11 museum pass, sold at participating museums, covers the Eugène Boudin Museum, Maisons Satie, and the Museum of Ethnography and Norman Popular Arts (www.musees-honfleur.fr).

Market Day: The area around St. Catherine Church becomes a colorful open-air market every Saturday (9:00-13:00). A smaller organic-food-only market takes place here on Wednesday mornings, and a flea market takes center stage here the first Sunday of every month and also on Wednesday evenings in summer.

Grocery Store: There's one with long hours near the TI (daily July-Aug, closed Mon off-season, 16 Quai le Paulmier).

Regional Products with Panache: Visit **Produits Regionaux Gribouille** for any Norman delicacy you can dream up (Mon-Tue and Thu-Fri 9:30-12:45 & 14:00-18:30, Sat 9:30-19:00, Sun 10:00-18:00, closed Wed, 16 Rue de l'Homme de Bois, tel. 02 31 89 29 54).

Wi-Fi: Free Wi-Fi is available on the port at **Travel Coffee Shop** and at several other cafés, including the recommended **L'Albatross** and **Le Perroquet Vert** café/bars.

Laundry: Lavomatique is a block behind the TI, toward the port (self-service only, daily 7:30-21:30, 4 Rue Notre-Dame). **La Lavandière** has handy drop-off service (Mon-Fri 9:00-19:00, Sat 10:00-20:00, closed Sun, two blocks from the harbor at 41 Rue de la République).

Taxi: Call mobile 06 08 60 17 98.

Tourist Train: Honfleur's *petit train* toots you up the Côte de Grâce—the hill overlooking the town—and back in about 45 minutes (€6.50, June-Sept daily 10:30-17:30, weekends only rest of year, departures on the hour except at lunchtime, leaves from across gray swivel bridge that leads to Parking du Môle).

Sights in Honfleur

▲▲Vieux Bassin (Old Port)

Stand near the water facing Honfleur's square harbor, with the merry-go-round across the lock to your left, and survey the town. The word "Honfleur" is Scandinavian, meaning the shelter *(fleur)* of Hon (a Viking warlord). This town has been sheltering residents for about a thousand years. During the Hundred Years' War (14th century), the entire harbor was fortified by a big wall with twin gatehouses (the one surviving gatehouse, La Lieutenance, is on your right). A narrow channel allowing boats to pass was protected by a heavy chain.

After the walls were demolished around 1700, those skinny

NORMANDY

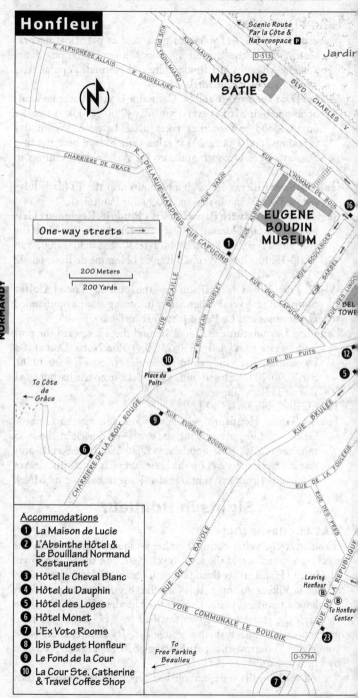

Honfleur

Scenic Route
Par la Côte &
Naturospace

D-513   Jardir

MAISONS
SATIE

BLVD. CHARLES V

R. ALPHONESE ALLAIS

R. TROLMIARD

RUE HAUTE

R. BAUDELAIRE

CHARRIERE DE GRACE

R L DELARUE-MARDRUS

RUE DE L'HOMME DE BOIS

RUE VARIN

RUE ALBERT

EUGENE
BOUDIN
MUSEUM

RUE BOULANGER

RUE CAPUCINS

One-way streets →

RUE DES CAPUCINS

RUE BARBEL

RUE DES LINGO

BEL
TOWE

200 Meters
200 Yards

RUE BUCAILLE

RUE JEAN DOUBLET

RUE DU PUITS

To Côte
de
← Grâce

Place du
Puits

RUE BRULEE

CHARRIERE DE LA CROIX ROUGE

RUE EUGENE BOUDIN

RUE DE LA FOULERIE

RUE DES PRES

RUE DE LA BAYOLE

Leaving
Honfleur

VOIE COMMUNALE LE BOULOIR

To
Free Parking
Beaulieu

D-579A

RUE DE LA REPUBLIQUE

To Honfleu
Center

Accommodations
1 La Maison de Lucie
2 L'Absinthe Hôtel &
   Le Bouilland Normand
   Restaurant
3 Hôtel le Cheval Blanc
4 Hôtel du Dauphin
5 Hôtel des Loges
6 Hôtel Monet
7 L'Ex Voto Rooms
8 Ibis Budget Honfleur
9 Le Fond de la Cour
10 La Cour Ste. Catherine
   & Travel Coffee Shop

NORMANDY

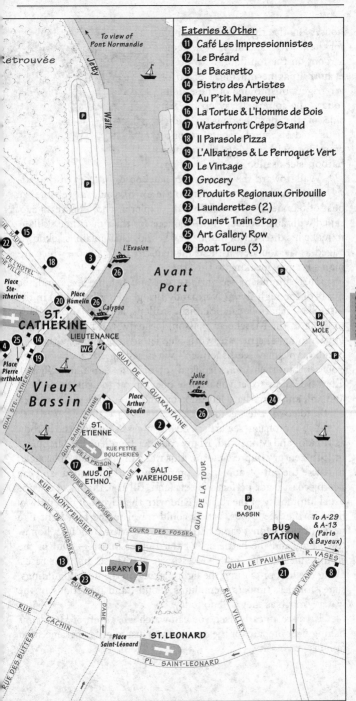

Eateries & Other

11 Café Les Impressionnistes
12 Le Bréard
13 Le Bacaretto
14 Bistro des Artistes
15 Au P'tit Mareyeur
16 La Tortue & L'Homme de Bois
17 Waterfront Crêpe Stand
18 Il Parasole Pizza
19 L'Albatross & Le Perroquet Vert
20 Le Vintage
21 Grocery
22 Produits Regionaux Gribouille
23 Launderettes (2)
24 Tourist Train Stop
25 Art Gallery Row
26 Boat Tours (3)

NORMANDY

houses on the right side were built for the town's fishermen. How about a room on the top floor, with no elevator? Imagine moving a piano or a refrigerator into one of these units today. The spire halfway up the left side of the port belongs to Honfleur's oldest church. The port, once crammed with fishing boats, now harbors sleek sailboats.

Walk toward the Lieutenance gatehouse. In front of the barrel-vaulted arch (once the entry to the town), you can see a bronze bust of Samuel de Champlain—the explorer who, 400 years ago, sailed with an Honfleur crew—famous for their maritime skills—to make his discoveries in the New World. Champlain is acknowledged as the founder of the Canadian city of Quebec—which remains French-speaking to this day.

Turn around to see various tour and fishing boats and the masts of the high-flying Normandy Bridge (described later) in the distance. Fisherfolk catch flatfish, scallops, and tiny shrimp daily to bring to the Marché au Poisson, located toward the river (look for white metal structures with blue lettering). Thursday through Sunday, you may see fishermen's wives selling *crevettes* (shrimp). You can buy them *cuites* (cooked) or *vivantes* (alive and wiggly). They are happy to let you sample one (rip off the cute little head and tail, and pop what's left into your mouth—*délicieuse!*), or buy a cupful to go for a few euros.

You'll probably see artists sitting at easels around the harbor, as Boudin and Monet did. Many consider Honfleur the birthplace of 19th-century Impressionism. This was a time when people began to revere the out-of-doors, and pretty towns like Honfleur and the nearby coast made perfect subjects (and still are), thanks to the unusual luminosity of the region. And with the advent of new railway lines in the late 1800s, artists could travel to the best light like never before. Monet came here to visit the artist Boudin, a hometown boy, and the battle cry of the Impressionists—"Out of the studio and into the light!"—was born. Artists set up their easels along the harbor to catch the light playing on the line of buildings, slate shingles, timbers, geraniums, clouds, and reflections in the water—much as they still do today.

If you're an early riser, you can watch what's left of Honfleur's fishing fleet prepare for the day, and you just might experience that famous luminosity.

Old Honfleur

A chance to study the Lego-style timber-frame houses of Honfleur awaits just off the harbor. On the southern quay, next to the Church of St. Etienne, head up Rue de la Prison (past the Museum of Ethnography; see page 241) and bend around to Rue des Petites Boucheries for some prime examples. The beams of these buildings were numbered so they could be disassembled and moved. Wandering through the stony courtyard of the fancy 15th-century House of the Lord of Honfleur, you'll come to Rue de la Ville with more historic Norman architecture. Across from #16 is one of three huge 17th-century salt warehouses. It's worth entering (often €1 for a local exhibit) to see the huge room with its fine wooden ceiling and imagine the importance of salt as a preservative before refrigeration existed.

Strategically positioned Honfleur guarded Paris from a naval attack up the Seine. That's why the king fortified it with a wall in the 1300s. In the 1600s, when England was no longer a threat, the walls were torn down, leaving the town with some wide boulevards (like the one in front of the TI) and plenty of stones (like those that made the salt warehouse).

▲▲St. Catherine Church (Eglise Ste. Catherine)

St. Catherine's replaced an earlier stone church, destroyed in the Hundred Years' War. In those chaotic times, the town's money

was spent to fortify its walls, leaving only enough funds to erect a wooden church. The unusual wood-shingled exterior suggests that this church has a different story to tell than most. In the last months of World War II, a bomb fell through the church's roof—but didn't explode—leaving this unique church intact for you to visit today.

Cost and Hours: Free, daily July-Aug 9:00-18:30, Sept-June until 17:15, Place Ste-Catherine.

Visiting the Church: Walk inside. You'd swear that if it were turned over, the building would float—the legacy of a community of sailors and fishermen, with loads of talented boat-builders (and no church architect). When workers put up the first (left) nave in 1466, it soon became apparent that more space was needed—so a second was built in 1497 (on the right). Because it felt too much like a market hall, they added side aisles.

The oak columns were prepared as if the wood was meant for a ship—soaked in seawater for seven years and then dried for seven years. Notice some pillars are full-length and others are supported by stone bases. Trees come in different sizes, yet each pillar had to be the same length.

The pipe organ (from 1772, rebuilt in 1953) behind you is popular for concerts, and half of the modern pews are designed to flip so that you can face the music. Take a close look at the balustrade (below the organ) with carved wooden panels featuring 17 musical instruments used in the 16th century.

Find a seat, and enjoy the worshipful ambience of this beautiful space. But don't sit in the box in the center; this was reserved for the local noble lord and his family. If you want to gossip, head to the "cackling zone"—an open-air narthex just outside where historically (and perhaps hysterically) people gathered after Mass.

Bell Tower: The church's bell tower was built away from the church to avoid placing too much stress on the wooden church's roof, and to help minimize fire hazards. Notice the funky shingled chestnut beams that run from its squat base to support the skinny tower, and find the small, faded wooden sculpture of a tiny St. Catherine over the door. Until recently the bell ringer lived in the bell tower (not worth the €2 to enter, but you can peek inside for free to appreciate the ancient wood framing).

HONFLEUR'S MUSEUMS AND GALLERIES

Eugène Boudin established Honfleur's artistic tradition. The town remains a popular haunt for artists, many of whom display their works in Honfleur's many art galleries (the best ones are along the streets between St. Catherine Church and the port). As you stroll around the town taking in its old sights, take time to enjoy today's art, too.

▲Eugène Boudin Museum

This pleasing little museum has three interesting floors with many paintings of Honfleur and the surrounding countryside. The first floor displays Norman folk costumes, the second floor has the Boudin collection, and the third floor houses 20th-century works. (The museum has undergone a major renovation; expect changes to this description.)

Cost and Hours: €6, more during special exhibits, covered by museum pass; May-Sept Wed-Mon 10:00-12:00 & 14:00-18:00, closed Tue, shorter hours off-season; audioguide-€2, elevator, Rue de l'Homme de Bois, tel. 02 31 89 54 00, www.musees-honfleur.fr.

Visiting the Museum: Pick up a map at the ticket counter, tip your beret to Eugène Boudin, and climb the stairs (or take the elevator).

First Floor: Monsieur and Madame Louveau (see their photo as you enter) gave Honfleur this quality collection of local traditional costumes. The hats, blouses, and shoes are supported by

Eugène Boudin (1824-1898)

Born in Honfleur, Boudin was the son of a harbor pilot. As an amateur teenage artist, he found work in an art-supply store

that catered to famous artists from Paris (such as landscapists Corot and Millet) who came to paint the seaside. Boudin himself studied in Paris and his work was exhibited there, but he kept his hometown roots.

At age 30 Boudin met the teenage Claude Monet. Monet had grown up in nearby Le Havre and, like Boudin, sketched the world around him—beaches, boats, and small-town life. Boudin encouraged him to don a scarf, set up his easel outdoors, and paint the scene exactly as he saw it. Today, we say: "Well, duh!" But "open-air" painting was unorthodox for artists trained to thoroughly study their subjects in the perfect lighting of a controlled studio setting. Boudin didn't teach Monet as much as give him the courage to follow his artistic instincts.

In the 1860s and 1870s, Boudin spent summers at his farm (St. Siméon) on the outskirts of Honfleur, hosting Monet, Edouard Manet, and other hangers-on. They taught Boudin the Impressionist techniques of using bright colors and building a subject with many individual brushstrokes. Boudin adapted those "strokes" to build subjects with "patches" of color. In 1874, Boudin joined the renegade Impressionists at their "revolutionary" exhibition in Paris.

paintings that place them in an understandable historical and cultural context. Of special interest are the lace bonnets, typical of 19th-century Normandy. You could name a woman's village by her style of bonnet. The dolls are not toys for tots, but marketing tools for traveling clothing merchants—designed to show off the latest fashions. The men's department is in the back of the room.

Second Floor: Making a right off the stairs leads you into a large room of appealing 20th-century paintings and sculpture created by artists while living in Honfleur (special exhibits sometimes occupy this space). A left off the stairs leads into the Salle Eugène Boudin, a small gallery of 19th-century paintings. Boudin's artwork is shown alongside that of his colleagues and contemporaries (usually Claude Monet and Gustave Courbet), letting you see how those masters took Boudin's approach to the next level. Find the glass display case in the rear titled *Précurseur de l'Impressionisme*, with little pastel drawings, and follow Boudin's art chronologically, as it evolves.

When Boudin and other Honfleur artists showed their work in Paris, they created enough of a stir that Normandy came into vogue. Many Parisian artists (including Monet and other early Impressionists) traveled to Honfleur to dial in to the action. Boudin himself made a big impression on the father of Impressionism by introducing Monet to the practice of painting outside. This collection of Boudin's paintings—which the artist gave to his hometown—shows how his technique developed, from realistic portrayals of subjects (outlines colored in, like a coloring book) to masses of colors catching light (Impressionism). Boudin's beach scenes, showing aristocrats taking a healthy saltwater dip, helped fuel that style. His skies were good enough to earn him the nickname "King of Skies."

Third Floor: Follow the steps that lead up from the Boudin room to the small, enjoyable Hambourg/Rachet collection, which is largely from the mid-20th century. Don't miss the smashing painting of Honfleur at twilight. Also on the third floor is a worthwhile collection of 20th-century works by artists who lived and learned in Honfleur, including the Fauvist painter Raoul Dufy. Be sure to take in the brilliant view of the Normandy Bridge through the windows.

▲Maisons Satie

If Honfleur is over-the-top cute, this museum, housed in composer Erik Satie's birthplace, is a burst of witty charm—just like the musical genius it honors. If you like Satie's music, this is a delight—a 1920s "Yellow Submarine." If not, it can be a ho-hum experience.

Cost and Hours: €6.30, includes audioguide, covered by museum pass; May-Sept Wed-Mon 10:00-19:00, shorter hours offseason, closed Jan-mid-Feb and Tue year-round; last entry one hour before closing, 5-minute walk from harbor at 67 Boulevard Charles V, tel. 02 31 89 11 11, www.musees-honfleur.fr.

Visiting the Museum: As you wander from room to room with your included audioguide, infrared signals transmit bits of Satie's dreamy music, along with a first-person story. As if you're living as an artist in 1920s Paris, you'll drift through a weird and whimsical series of old-school installations—winged pears, strangers in windows, and small girls with green eyes. The finale—performed by you—is the *Laboratory of Emotions* pedal-go-round, a self-propelled carousel where your feet create the music (pedal softly). For a relaxing finale, enjoy the 12-minute movie (plays by request, French only) featuring modern dance springing from *Parade*, Satie's collaboration with Pablo Picasso and Jean Cocteau.

You'll even hear the boos and whistles that greeted these ballets' debuts.

▲Museum of Ethnography and Norman Popular Arts (Musée d'Ethnographie et d'Art Populaire Normand)

Honfleur's engaging little Museum of Ethnography and Norman Popular Arts (pick up English translation at the desk) is located in the old prison and courthouse a short block off the harbor. It re-creates typical rooms from Honfleur's past and crams them with objects of daily life—costumes, furniture, looms, and an antique printing press. You'll see the old yard and climb through two stories of furnished rooms. The museum paints a picture of daily life in Honfleur during the time when its ships were king and the city had global significance. (The adjacent Museum of the Sea is skippable.)

Cost and Hours: €4.20; Tue-Sun 10:00-12:00 & 14:00-18:30, shorter hours off-season, closed mid-Nov-mid-Feb and Mon year-round, Rue de la Prison, www.musees-honfleur.fr. The museum is located in the heart of Old Honfleur (see page 237).

HONFLEUR WALKS AND DRIVES
▲Côte de Grâce Walk (or Drive)

For good exercise and a bird's-eye view of Honfleur and the Normandy Bridge, take the steep 30-minute walk (or quick drive) up to the Côte de Grâce—best in the early morning or at sunset. From St. Catherine Church, walk up Rue du Puits (or drive up Rue Brulée and make a right on Rue Eugène Boudin), then follow the blue-on-white signs to reach the splendid view over Honfleur at the top of the ramp (benches and information plaque). *Piétons* (walkers) should veer right up La Rampe du Mont Joli; *conducteurs* (drivers) should keep straight. Walkers can continue past the view for about 300 yards to the **Chapel of Notre-Dame de Grâce,** built in the early 1600s by the mariners and people of Honfleur (open daily 8:30-17:15). Model boats hang from the ceiling, pictures of boats balance high on the walls, and several stained-glass windows are decorated with images of sailors at sea praying to the Virgin Mary. Find the 23 church bells hanging on a wood rack to the right as you leave the church and imagine the racket they make (the bells ring four times an hour).

Below the chapel, a lookout offers a sweeping view of super-industrial Le Havre and the Seine estuary where the river hits the Manche (English Channel). The Normandy Bridge is just visible to your right.

Jetty/Park Walk

Take a level stroll in Honfleur along the water past the Hôtel le Cheval Blanc to find the mouth of the Seine River and big ships at sea. You'll pass kid-friendly parks carpeted with flowers and grass, and continue past the lock connecting Honfleur to the Seine and the sea. Grand and breezy vistas of the sea and smashing views of the Normandy Bridge reward the diligent walker (allow 20 minutes from the harbor to reach the best views).

NEAR HONFLEUR
Boat Excursions

Boat trips in and around Honfleur depart from various docks between Hôtel le Cheval Blanc and the opposite end of the outer port (Easter-Oct usually about 11:00-17:00). The tour boat *Calypso* takes good 45-minute spins around Honfleur's harbor (€6, mobile 06 71 64 50 46, Jetée de la Lieutenance). Other cruises run to the Normandy Bridge, which, unfortunately, means two boring trips through the locks (€9.50/1.5 hours, choose between *Jolie France*, near Parking du Môle, mobile 06 71 64 50 46, Jetée du Transit; or *L'Evasion* near Hôtel le Cheval Blanc, mobile 06 31 89 21 10, Quai des Passagers).

Normandy Bridge (Pont de Normandie)

The 1.25-mile-long Normandy Bridge is the longest cable-stayed bridge in the Western world (€5.40 toll each way, not worth a detour). This is a key piece of European expressway that links the Atlantic ports from Belgium to Spain. View the bridge from Honfleur (better from an excursion boat or the Jetty Walk described earlier, and best at night, when bridge is floodlit). Also consider visiting the bridge's free Exhibition Hall (under tollbooth on Le Havre side, daily 8:00-19:00). The Seine finishes its winding journey here, dropping only 1,500 feet from its source, 450 miles away. The river flows so slowly that, in certain places, a stiff breeze can send it flowing upstream.

▲Etrétat

France's answer to the White Cliffs of Dover, these chalky cliffs soar high above a calm, crescent beach. Walking trails lead hikers from the small seaside resort of Etrétat along a vertiginous route with sensational views (and crowds of hikers in summer and on weekends). You'll recognize these cliffs—and the arches and stone spire that decorate them—from countless Impressionist paintings, including several at the Eugène Boudin Museum in Honfleur. The small, Coney Island-like town holds plenty of cafés and a TI (Place Maurice Guillard, tel. 02 35 27 05 21, www.etretat.net).

Getting There: Etrétat is north of Le Havre. To get here by car (50 minutes), cross the Normandy Bridge and follow A-29, then exit at *sortie Etrétat*. Buses serve Etrétat from Le Havre's *gare routière*, adjacent to the train station (5/day, 1 hour, www.keolis-seine-maritime.com).

Sleeping in Etrétat: $$$$ Dormy House has a brilliant

NORMANDY

setting and makes a nice splurge (Route du Havre at the edge of Etrétat, tel. 02 35 27 07 88, www.dormy-house.com, info@etretat-hotel.com).

Sleeping in Honfleur

($$$$ = Splurge, $$$ = Pricier, $$ = Moderate, $ = Budget)
Though Honfleur is popular in summer, it's busiest on weekends and holidays (blame Paris). English is widely spoken (blame vacationing Brits). A few moderate accommodations remain, but most hotels are pretty pricey. Only two hotels have elevators (Hôtel le Cheval Blanc and Ibis Budget Honfleur), but Hotel Monet has ground-floor rooms.

HOTELS

$$$$ La Maison de Lucie*** is a fine *Normand* splurge and greets its guests with a garden courtyard, sumptuous lounges, and antique-filled rooms (suites available, 44 Rue des Capucines, tel. 02 31 49 41, www.lamaisondelucie.com, info@lamaisondelucie.com).

$$$ L'Absinthe Hôtel*** offers 11 tastefully restored rooms with king-size beds in two locations. The older rooms in the main (reception) section come with wood-beamed decor and share a cozy public lounge with a fireplace). Five rooms are located above their next-door restaurant and have views of the modern port and three-star, state-of-the-art comfort (air-con in both buildings, private pay parking, 1 Rue de la Ville, tel. 02 31 89 23 23, www.absinthe.fr, reservation@absinthe.fr).

$$$ Hôtel le Cheval Blanc*** is a waterfront splurge with port views from all of its 35 plush and pricey rooms (many with queen beds), plus a rare-in-this-town elevator and a spa, but no air-conditioning—noise can be a problem with windows open (family rooms, 2 Quai des Passagers, tel. 02 31 81 65 00, www.hotel-honfleur.com, info@hotel-honfleur.com).

$$ Hôtel du Dauphin,*** wrapped in a half-timbered shell, is ideally located, with narrow stairs (normal in Honfleur) and

an Escher-esque floor plan. The 30 mostly small rooms (in two buildings) are an acceptable value, though the place could use some work (Wi-Fi in main building only, a stone's throw from St. Catherine Church at 10 Place Pierre Berthelot, tel. 02 31 89 15 53, www.hoteldudauphin.com, info@hoteldudauphin.com). The same owners also run the

$$ Hôtel des Loges*** a few doors up, with larger rooms with Wi-Fi, but less personality). Both hotels offer the first breakfast free for Rick Steves readers in 2017—ask for details when you reserve.

$ Hôtel Monet,** on the road to the Côte de Grâce and a 10-minute walk down to the port, is an overlooked find. This tranquil spot houses 16 good-value rooms, all with private patios that surround a central courtyard. Christophe and Sylvie take fine care of their guests (family rooms, free and easy parking, Charrière du Puits, tel. 02 31 89 00 90, www.hotel-monet-honfleur.com, contact@hotel-monet-honfleur.com). Reception is closed from 13:00-17:00.

$ L'Ex Voto is a small place off a main road with four sweet and simple rooms at good rates (8 Place Albert Sorel, tel. 02 31 89 19 69, www.hotel-honfleur-exvoto.com, honfleurexvoto@gmail.com).

$ Ibis Budget Honfleur is modern, efficient, trim, and cheap, with prefab bathrooms and an antiseptically clean ambience (family rooms, reception closed 21:00-6:00 but automatic check-in with credit card available 24 hours, elevator, across from bus station and main parking lot on Rue des Vases, tel. 08 92 68 07 81, www.ibisbudget.com, h2716-re@accor.com).

CHAMBRES D'HOTES

The TI has a long list of Honfleur's many *chambres d'hôtes* (rooms in private homes), but most are too far from the town center. Those listed here are good values.

$$ Le Fond de la Cour, run by British expats Amanda and Craig, offers a good mix of crisp, modern, and comfortable accommodations around a peaceful courtyard. There's a large cottage that can sleep four, two apartments with small kitchens, and three standard doubles (standard rooms include English-style breakfast, free breakfast for Rick Steves readers who rent an apartment, free street parking, limited private pay parking, 29 Rue Eugène Boudin, mobile 06 72 20 72 98, www.lefonddelacour.com, amanda.ferguson@orange.fr).

$$ La Cour Ste. Catherine, kitty-corner to Le Fond de la Cour, is an enchanting bed-and-breakfast run by the cheery and open-hearted Madame Giaglis ("call me Liliane") and her husband, Monsieur Liliane (Antoine). Their six big, modern rooms—each with a separate sitting area—surround a perfectly Norman courtyard with a small terrace, fine plantings, and a cozy lounge area ideal for cool evenings (includes good breakfast, small apartments and cottage with kitchen available, cash only, ask about free parking when you book, 200 yards up Rue du Puits from St. Catherine Church at #74, tel. 02 31 89 42 40, www.coursaintecatherine.com, coursaintecatherine@orange.fr).

Eating in Honfleur

Eat seafood, crêpes, or cream sauces here. Choose between an irresistible waterfront table at one of the many look-alike places lining the harbor, or finer dining elsewhere in town. It's best to call ahead to reserve (particularly on weekends).

DINING ALONG THE HARBOR

Survey the eateries lining the harbor (all open Wed when other places are closed). The food isn't great, but you'll find plenty of salads, crêpes, and seafood—and a great setting. Heaters and canopies make dining outdoors a good option even in chilly weather. On a languid evening, it's hard to pass up. Along with the restaurant row on the Quai Ste. Catherine, consider **$$$ Café Les Impressionnistes,** with the best afternoon sun, on the other side of the harbor (Place de l'Hôtel de Ville). Even if you dine elsewhere, come to the harbor for a before- or after-dinner drink.

BETTER FOOD, NO VIEWS

While I wouldn't blame you for enjoying a forgettable meal in an unforgettable setting on the harborfront, consider these finer alternatives a couple blocks away.

$$$$ Le Bréard is a nice place to dial it up a little and eat very well for a fair price. The decor is low key but elegant, the cuisine is inventive, delicious, and not particularly *Normand,* and the service is excellent (closed Mon, 7 Rue du Puits, tel. 02 31 89 53 40).

$$$ Le Bouilland Normand hides a block off the port on a pleasing square and offers true *Normand* cuisine at reasonable prices. Claire and chef-hubby Bruno provide quality dishes and enjoy serving travelers (closed Wed and Sun, dine inside or out, 7 Rue de la Ville, tel. 02 31 89 02 41).

$$ Le Bacaretto wine bar-café is run by laid-back Hervé, the antithesis of a wine snob. This relaxed, tiny, wine-soaked place offers a fine selection of well-priced wines by the glass and a small but appealing assortment of appetizers and *plats du jour* that can make a full meal (closed Wed-Thu for lunch and Sun for dinner, 44 Rue de la Chaussée, tel. 02 31 14 83 11).

$$$ Bistro des Artistes is a two-woman operation with a pleasant little dining room (call ahead for a window table). Hardworking Anne-Marie cooks up huge portions; one course is plenty...and maybe a dessert (closed Wed, 30 Place Berthelot, tel. 02 31 89 95 90).

$$$ Au P'tit Mareyeur is whisper-formal, intimate, all about seafood, and a good value. The ground floor and upstairs rooms offer equal comfort and ambience (famous €35 Bouillabaisse Honfleuraise, closed Tue-Wed and Jan, 4 Rue Haute, tel. 02 31 98 84 23, www.auptitmareyeur.fr, Julie speaks some English).

At **$$$ La Tortue,** the owner/chef prepares delicious cuisine, including good vegetarian dishes, and serves it in a pleasing setting (open daily in summer, closed Tue-Wed rest of year, tel. 02 31 81 24 60, 36 Rue de l'Homme de Bois).

$$$ L'Homme de Bois combines way-cozy ambience with authentic *Normand* cuisine (daily, a few outside tables, skip the upstairs room, 30 Rue de l'Homme de Bois, tel. 02 31 89 75 27).

$ Travel Coffee Shop is an ideal breakfast or lunch option for travelers wanting conversation—in either English or French—and good food at very fair prices (April-Sept Thu-Mon 8:00-16:00, closed Tue-Wed; closed Oct-March; 6 Place du Puits).

Breakfast: If it's even close to sunny, skip your hotel breakfast and eat on the port, where several cafés offer *petit déjeuner* (€4-7 for continental fare, €7-14 for more elaborate choices). Morning sun and views are best from the high side of the harbor. If price or companionship matter, head to the Travel Coffee Shop for a good breakfast deal (described above).

Dessert: Honfleur is ice-cream crazy, with gelato and traditional ice-cream shops on every corner. If you need a Ben & Jerry's ice-cream fix or a scrumptious dessert crêpe, find the **waterfront stand** at the southeast corner of the Vieux Bassin.

Nighttime Food to Go: Order a tasty pizza to-go until late from **$ Il Parasole** (2 Rue Haute, tel. 02 31 98 94 29), and enjoy a picnic dinner with port views a few steps away at the Lieutenance gatehouse.

Nightlife: Nightlife in Honfleur centers on the old port. Several bar/cafés line the high-building side of the port, including these down-and-dirty watering holes: pub-like **L'Albatross** (a fun and smoky clubhouse) and **Le Perroquet Vert** (also cool but more existential—"those lights are so..."). **Le Vintage,** just off the port, has live piano and jazz on weekend nights (closed Tue, 8 Quai des Passagers, tel. 02 31 89 05 28).

Honfleur Connections

There's no direct train service to Honfleur, so you must connect by bus or car. The handy, express PrestoBus (line #39) links Honfleur with train service in Caen and Le Havre, but runs only twice a day. Bus #50 runs between Le Havre, Honfleur and Lisieux; the scenic *par la côte* bus #20 connects Le Havre, Honfleur, Deauville, and Caen. Although train and bus service usually are coordinated, confirm your connection with the helpful staff at Honfleur's bus station (English info desk open Mon-Fri 9:30-12:00 & 13:15-18:00, in summer also Sat-Sun, tel. 02 31 89 28 41, www.busverts.fr). If the station is closed, you can get schedules at the TI. Rail-pass holders will save money by connecting through Deauville, as bus fares increase with distance.

From Honfleur by Bus and/or Train to: Caen (express PrestoBus 2/day, 1 hour; bus #20 4/day direct, 2 hours); **Bayeux** (2-3/day, 1.5 hours; first take PrestoBus #39 or bus #20 to Caen, then 20-minute train to Bayeux); **Rouen** (6/day Mon-Sat, 3/day Sun, bus-and-train combo involves 30-minute bus ride over Normandy Bridge to Le Havre, then easy transfer to 1-hour train to Rouen); **Paris'** Gare St. Lazare (13/day, 2-3.5 hours, by bus to Caen, Lisieux, Deauville, or Le Havre, then train to Paris; buses from Honfleur meet most Paris trains).

Route Tips for Drivers: If driving to Rouen, see the Route of the Ancient Abbeys on page 228. If connecting to the D-Day beaches, consider taking the scenic route *"par la côte"* to Trouville and pass sea views, thatched hamlets, and stupendous mansions. From Honfleur, drive to the port, pass Hôtel du Cheval Blanc, and stick to this road (D-513) to Trouville, then follow signs for A-13 to Caen.

Bayeux

Only six miles from the D-Day beaches, Bayeux was the first city liberated after the landing on June 6, 1944. Incredibly, the town was spared the bombs of World War II. The Allied Command needed an intact town from which to administer the push to Berlin. And after a local chaplain made sure London knew that his city was neither strategically important nor a German headquarters, a scheduled bombing raid was canceled—making Bayeux the closest city to the D-Day landing site not destroyed. Even without its famous medieval tapestry and proximity to the D-Day beaches, Bayeux would be worth a visit for its enjoyable town center and awe-inspiring cathedral, beautifully illuminated at night. Its location and manageable size (pop. 14,000) make Bayeux an ideal home base for visiting the area's sights, particularly if you lack a car.

Orientation to Bayeux

Bayeux grew up along the Aure River. Its main street (Rue St. Jean) was a Roman road. The river powered the town's waterwheels and flushed its waste as its industry grew. The TI is located in the old fish market over the river, and the nearby waterwheel was part of the tanning and dyeing industry in the 15th century. Across from the Bayeux Tapestry museum, another waterwheel once powered a flour mill (now a crêpe restaurant); it's lock created a mill pond which did double-duty as the bishop's fish pond.

TOURIST INFORMATION

The TI is on a small bridge two blocks north of the cathedral. Ask for bus schedules to the beaches and inquire about special events and concerts. World War II buffs can buy the D-Day map (about €5) showing troop deployments and more (June-Aug Mon-Sat 9:00-19:00, Sun 9:00-13:00 & 14:00-18:00; April-May and Sept-Oct Mon-Sat 9:30-12:30 & 14:00-18:00, Sun 10:00-13:00 & 14:00-18:00; shorter hours off-season; on Pont St. Jean leading to Rue St. Jean, tel. 02 31 51 28 28, www.bessin-normandie.com).

ARRIVAL IN BAYEUX

By Train and Bus: Trains and buses share the same station (no bag storage). It's a 15-minute **walk** from the station to the tapestry, and 15 minutes from the tapestry to Place St. Patrice. To reach the tapestry, the cathedral, and recommended hotels, cross the major street in front of the station and follow Rue de Cremel toward *l'Hôpital,* then turn left on Rue Nesmond. Find signs to the *Tapisserie* (tapestry) or continue on to the cathedral. **Taxis** usually wait at the station—allow €9 to any recommended hotel or sight in Bayeux, and €21 to Arromanches (€32 after 19:00 and on Sundays, taxi tel. 02 31 92 92 40 or mobile 06 70 40 07 96).

By Car: Look for the cathedral spires and follow signs for *Centre-Ville,* and then signs for the *Tapisserie* or your hotel (individual hotels are well-signed from the ring road). Day-trippers will find pay parking lots in the town center (including at the Hôtel de Ville near the TI, and at Place St. Patrice; €1/hour, 3-hour limit). A few other parking lots are free but require a cardboard clock on your dashboard (buy at any *tabac,* 4-hour limit). Time limits are not enforced from 12:00 to 14:00, allowing you to stretch your stay. To park for longer, find the free, unlimited lots along the southern ring road (along Boulevard Marechal Leclerc and Boulevard Sadi Carnot).

Drivers connecting Bayeux with Mont St-Michel should use the speedy, free A-84 autoroute (from near the train station, follow signs to *Villars-Bocage,* then A-84).

By Airport Transfer from Paris: It's possible to link Paris and Normandy without driving or connecting by train. **Albion** (run by American Adrienne Sion) organizes transfers between Paris airports and Bayeux (1-3 people-€450, up to 8 people-€600, transfers from central Paris possible, extra for stops en route at Giverny or Honfleur, tel. 02 31 78 88 88, www.albion-voyages.com).

HELPFUL HINTS

Market Days: The Saturday open-air market on Place St. Patrice is Bayeux's best, though the Wednesday market on pedestrian Rue St. Jean is pleasant. Both end by 13:00. Don't leave your car on Place St. Patrice on a Friday night, as it will be towed early Saturday.

Grocery Store: Carrefour City, at Rue St. Jean 14, is next to the recommended Hôtel Churchill (daily).

Laundry: A launderette is a block behind the TI, on Rue Maréchal Foch. Two more launderettes are near Place St. Patrice, at 4 Rue St. Patrice and 69 Rue des Bouchers (all open daily 7:00-21:00).

Bike Rental: Vélos Location will deliver to outlying hotels (daily April-Oct 8:00-20:30, closes earlier off-season, inside grocery store across from TI at Impasse de Islet, tel. 02 31 92 89 16, www.velosbayeux.com).

Taxi: Call 02 31 92 92 40 or mobile 06 70 40 07 96.

Car Rental: Bayeux offers a few choices. **Renault Rent** is handiest, just below the train station at the BP gas station. A rental at about €70/day with a 200-kilometer limit is sufficient to see the key sights from Arromanches to Utah Beach—you'll drive about 180 kilometers (16 Boulevard Sadi Carnot, tel. 02 31 51 18 51). **Hertz** is the only agency in town that allows you to drop off in a different city (located west of the city center on Route de Cherbourg, off D-613, tel. 02 31 92 03 26).

Calvados Tasting: For a fun and easy cider sampling, drop by the recommended **Logis les Remparts** B&B (Tue-Sat 10:00-19:00, closed Sun-Mon, 4 Rue Bourbesneur, tel. 02 31 92 50 40).

Tours in Bayeux

Self-Guided Walking Tour: Pick up the map called *Découvrez Vieux Bayeux* at the TI, which corresponds to bronze info plates embedded in sidewalks around town.

Guided Walks of Old Bayeux: For a chatty, anecdote-filled stroll through the historic center—with no interiors but plenty of factoids—join Christèle or Marie-Noëlle for a guided walk (€15, daily April-Sept, 2-hour walk generally at 9:30 and 1.5-hour walk at 17:00, rain or shine, leave from TI, private tours possible year-round, confirm schedule at www.discovery-walks.org).

Touristy Choo-Choo Train: Bayeux's tourist train leaves hourly from the TI for a 35-minute ride through town with recorded English commentary (€6, pay driver).

NORMANDY

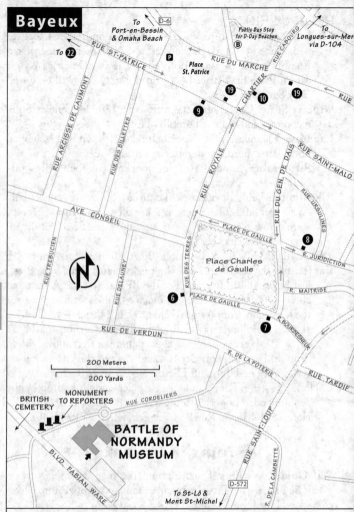

Bayeux

To 22

To Port-en-Bessin & Omaha Beach

To D-6

Public Bus Stop for D-Day Beaches B

To Longues-sur-Mer via D-104

RUE ST-PATRICE

RUE DU MARCHE

RUE CABOURG

RUE

Place St. Patrice

19

R. CHARTIER

10

19

9

RUE ARCISSE DE CAUMONT

RUE DES BILLETTES

RUE ROYALE

RUE SAINT-MALO

RUE DU GEN. DE DAIS

RUE URSULINES

AVE. CONSEIL

PLACE DE GAULLE

8

R. JURIDICTION

RUE TREBUCIEN

RUE DELAUNEY

RUE DES TERRES

Place Charles de Gaulle

R. MAITRISE

6

PLACE DE GAULLE

R. BOURBESNEUR

RUE DE VERDUN

7

200 Meters

200 Yards

R. DE LA POTERIE

RUE TARDIF

BRITISH CEMETERY

MONUMENT TO REPORTERS

RUE CORDELIERS

N

BLVD. FABIAN WARE

BATTLE OF NORMANDY MUSEUM

RUE SAINT-LOUP

R. DE LA CAMBETTE

D-572

To St-Lô & Mont St-Michel

NORMANDY

Accommodations
1. Villa Lara
2. Hôtel Churchill & Carrefour City Grocery
3. Hôtel le Lion d'Or
4. Hôtel Reine Mathilde & Le Garde Manger
5. Hôtel au Georges VII & Café
6. Le Petit Matin B&B
7. Logis les Remparts B&B & Calvados
8. Manoir Sainte Victoire
9. Hôtel d'Argouges
10. Hôtel Mogador

Eateries & Other
11. La Chaumière Deli
12. Le Moulin de la Galette
13. La Rapière
14. Le Volet Qui Penche
15. L'Angle Saint Laurent
16. Le Pommier
17. Au P'tit Bistrot
18. La Fringale
19. Launderettes (3)
20. Bike Rental & Bayeux Shuttle
21. Renault Car Rental
22. To Hertz Car Rental

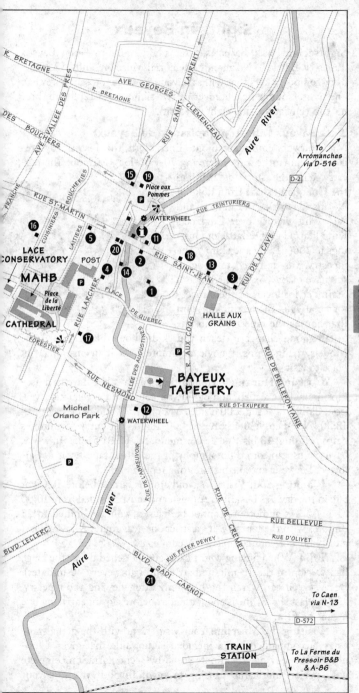

NORMANDY

Sights in Bayeux

Sightseeing Pass: Bayeux's three main museums—the Bayeux Tapestry, Battle of Normandy Memorial Museum, and MAHB—offer combo-tickets that will save you money if you see more than one sight. Combo-tickets covering two sights cost €12; for all three it's €15 (buy at the first sight you visit).

▲▲▲Bayeux Tapestry (Tapisserie de Bayeux)

Made of wool embroidered onto linen cloth, this historically precious document is a mesmerizing 70-yard-long cartoon. The tapestry tells the story of William the Conqueror's rise from duke of Normandy to king of England, and shows his victory over England's King Harold at the Battle of Hastings in 1066. Long and skinny, the tapestry was designed to hang in the nave of Bayeux's cathedral as a reminder for locals of their ancestor's courage. The terrific museum that houses the tapestry is an un-

usually good chance to teach your kids about the Middle Ages. Models, mannequins, a movie, and more make it an engaging, fun place to visit.

Cost and Hours: €9, combo-ticket with other Bayeux museums, includes excellent audioguide for adults and special kids' version; daily May-Aug 9:00-19:00, March-April and Sept-Oct until 18:30, Nov-Feb 9:30-12:30 & 14:00-18:00, last entry 45 minutes before closing; 13 bis Rue de Nesmond, tel. 02 31 51 25 50, www.bayeuxmuseum.com. Photography of the actual tapestry is not allowed, but you can take pictures of a replica.

Planning Your Visit: To avoid crowds, arrive before 10:00 or late in the day. It's busiest in August, and most crowded from 10:00 to 17:00. As audiotours cannot be paused, you are limited to 25 minutes with the tapestry. It's a strict one-way route. Allow at least a full hour for your complete museum visit.

Film: When buying your ticket, get the schedule for the English version of the 16-minute battle film (runs every 40 minutes). Because you can watch the film only after viewing the tapestry, and the last show time is about an hour before closing, arriving late means no film.

Visiting the Museum: Your visit starts with the actual **tapestry,** accompanied by an included audioguide that gives a top-notch, fast-moving, 25-minute scene-by-scene narration complete with period music (no pausing or rewinding—if you lose your

The Battle of Hastings

Because of this pivotal battle, the most memorable date of the Middle Ages is 1066. England's king, Edward the Confessor, was about to die without an heir. The big question: Who would succeed him—Harold, an English nobleman and the king's brother-in-law, or William, duke of Normandy and the king's cousin? Edward chose William, and sent Harold to Normandy to give William the news. On the journey, Harold was captured. To win his release, he promised he would be loyal to William and not contest the decision. To test his loyalty, William sent Harold to battle for him in Brittany. Harold was successful, and William knighted him. To further test his loyalty, William had Harold swear on the relics of the Bayeux cathedral that when Edward died, he would allow William to ascend the throne. Harold returned to England, Edward died...and Harold grabbed the throne.

William, known as William the Bastard, invaded England to claim the throne. Harold met him in southern England at the town of Hastings, where their forces fought a fierce 14-hour battle. Harold was killed, and his Saxon forces were routed. William—now "the Conqueror"—marched to London, claimed his throne, and became king of England (though he spoke no English).

The advent of a Norman king of England muddied the political waters and set in motion 400 years of conflict between England and France—not to be resolved until the end of the Hundred Years' War (1453). The Norman conquest of England brought that country into the European mainstream (but still no euros). The Normans established a strong central English government. Historians speculate that had William not succeeded, England would have remained on the fringe of Europe (like Scandinavia), and French culture (and language) would have prevailed in the New World—which would have meant no communication issues for us in France. Hmmm.

place, find subtitles in Latin). Remember, the tapestry is Norman propaganda: The English (the bad guys, referred to as *les goddamns*, after a phrase the French kept hearing them say) are shown with mustaches and long hair; the French (*les* good guys) are clean-cut and clean-shaven—with even the backs of their heads shaved for a better helmet fit.

Appreciate the fun details—such as the bare legs in scene 4 or Harold's pouting expressions in various frames—and look for references to places you may have visited (like Dinan). Pay strict attention to scene 23, where Harold takes his oath to William; the importance of keeping one's word is the point of the tapestry. Get close and (almost) feel the tapestry's texture.

Next you'll climb upstairs into a room filled with engaging **ex-**

hibits, including a full-size replica of a Viking ship much like the one William used to cross the Channel (Normans inherited their weaponry and seafaring skills from the Norsemen). You'll also see mannequins (find William looking unmoved with his new crown), a replica of the Domesday Book (an inventory of noble's lands as ordered by William), and models of castles (who knew that the Tower of London was a Norman project?). Good explanations outline the events surrounding the invasion and the subsequent creation of the tapestry, and a touchscreen lets you see the back side of the embroidery.

Your visit finishes with a 16-minute **film** that ties it all together one last time (in the cinema upstairs, skippable if you're pressed for time). Just before the theater you reach a full-sized replica of the tapestry (which you are welcome to photograph).

▲Bayeux Cathedral

This massive building, as big as Paris' Notre-Dame, dominates the small town of Bayeux. Make a point to enjoy the cathedral rising over the town after dark, when it's beautifully illuminated.

Cost and Hours: Free, daily July-Aug 8:30-19:00, Sept-June until 18:00, 4 Rue du Général de Dais.

Visiting the Cathedral: To start your visit, find the small **square** opposite the front entry (info board about the cathedral facade in rear corner). Notice the two dark towers—originally Romanesque, they were capped later with tall Gothic spires. The cathedral's west facade is structurally Romanesque, but with a decorative Gothic "curtain" added.

Now step inside the cathedral. The magnificent view of the **nave** from the top of the steps shows a mix of Romanesque (ground floor) and soaring Gothic (upper floors). Historians believe the Bayeux tapestry originally hung here. Imagine it draped halfway up the big Romanesque arches. Try to visualize this scene with the original, richly colored stained glass in all those upper windows. Rare 13th-century stained-glass bits are in the high central window above the altar; the other glass (below) is from the 19th and 20th centuries.

Walk down the nave and notice the areas between the big, round **arches.** That busy zigzag patterning characterizes Norman art in France as well as in England. These 11th-century Romanesque arches are decorated with a manic mix of repeated geometric shapes: half-circles, hash marks, full circles, and diagonal lines. Notice also the creepy faces eyeing you, especially the ring of devil heads lining the third arch on the right.

More 13th-century Norman Gothic is in the **choir** (the fancy area behind the central altar). Here, simple Romanesque carvings lie under Gothic arches whose characteristically tall, thin lines add a graceful verticality to the interior.

For maximum 1066 atmosphere, step into the spooky **crypt** (beneath the central altar), which originally was used as a safe spot for the cathedral's relics. The crypt displays two freestanding columns and bulky capitals with fine Romanesque carving (midway up the nave against the walls). During a reinforcement of the nave, these two columns were replaced. Workers removed the Gothic veneer and discovered their true inner Romanesque beauty. Orange angel-musicians on other columns add color to this somber room.

Nearby: Leaving the church, walk around to the right to a big tree in a little courtyard, and look high on the church's spire to spy a little rectangular stone house. This was the **watchman's home,** from which he'd keep an eye out for incoming English troops during the Hundred Years' War...and for Germans five centuries later (it didn't work—the Germans took the town in 1940). Bayeux was liberated on D-Day plus one: June 7. According to an interesting (but likely false) legend, about the only casualty that day was the lookout, who supposedly was shot while watching from the window of this stone house.

The big tree is a **Liberty Tree.** These were planted in cities throughout France in 1793 (when the king was beheaded) to celebrate the end of the Old Regime and the people's hard-won freedom. When the tree was planted, the cathedral kicked off a decade in which it was not considered a church but a revolutionary "temple of reason."

Place Charles de Gaulle

A block in front of the cathedral (up Rue Maîtrise) is a big, empty-yet-historic square—once the site of a 10th-century castle. The statue in the center is Poppa, the mistress or wife of the Viking conqueror Rollo who, in 911, became first duke of Normandy. The people of Normandy came from this union (not to mention many English royals—Rollo's descendants include William the Conqueror). On June 14, 1944, this square hosted the first public appearance of Charles de Gaulle in newly freed France. The self-appointed leader of the Free French Forces, now with Churchill's endorsement, proceeded to rally the French to rise up and help push out the Germans. This event helped initiate de Gaulle's legitimacy as head of the Free French. And Bayeux later served as the first administrative capital of post-Nazi-occupied France.

River Walk

Join the locals and promenade along the meandering walking path that follows the little Aure River for about 2.5 miles through Bayeux. The path runs both ways from the TI (find the waterwheel behind the TI and keep walking; path marked on city maps).

Lace Conservatory (Conservatoire de Dentelles)

This conservatory offers a chance to watch workers design and weave intricate lace *(dentelle),* just as artisans did in the 1600s, when lace was an important Bayeux industry, competing to break the Venetian monopoly on this required bit of formal wear. Enter to the clicking sound of the small wooden bobbins used by the lacemakers, and appreciate the concentration their work requires. You can also see examples of lace from the past and pick up some nifty souvenirs. The community helps fund this teaching workshop to keep the tradition alive. The conservatory building is nicknamed the "Adam and Eve House" for its carved 15th-century facade (find Adam, Eve, and the snake).

Cost and Hours: Free, Mon-Sat 9:30-12:30 & 14:30-18:00 except Mon and Thu until 17:00, closed Sun, across from cathedral entrance, 6 Rue du Bienvenu, tel. 02 31 92 73 80, http://dentelledebayeux.free.fr.

▲MAHB (Musée d'Art et d'Histoire Baron Gérard)

For a break from D-Day and tapestries, MAHB offers a modest review of European art and history in what was once the Bayeux bishop's palace. The 14 rooms on two floors are laid out in chronological order (prehistory, ancient Rome, medieval, and early modern). You'll see a fine little collection of 18th- and 19th-century paintings donated by Baron Henri-Alexandre Gérard more than a century ago. Notable are an early work—*Le Philosophe (The Philosopher)*—by neoclassical master Jacques-Louis David and, by Antoine-Jean Gros, *Sappho*—a moonlit version of the Greek poetess' suicide that influenced Géricault and Delacroix. In the stern Court of Justice—a courtroom from French revolutionary times (1793)—a bust of Lady Liberty (Marianne) presides over the tribunal like a secular goddess, backed by some Napoleonic stained glass (1806). Lace lovers will enjoy several rooms of exquisite lace with drawers full of bobbins and artful creations. Your visit is capped with an exhibit dedicated to the ceramics of Bayeux.

Cost and Hours: €7, combo-ticket with other Bayeux museums, daily May-Sept 9:30-18:30, shorter hours off-season, near the cathedral at 37 Rue du Bienvenu, tel. 02 31 92 14 21, www.bayeuxmuseum.com.

Battle of Normandy Memorial Museum
(Musée Mémorial de la Bataille de Normandie)

This museum provides a manageable overview of WWII's Battle of Normandy. With its many maps and timelines of the epic battle to liberate northern France, it's aimed at military history buffs. You'll get a good briefing on the Atlantic Wall (the German fortifications stretching along the coast—useful before visiting Longues-sur-Mer), learn why Normandy was selected as the landing site, understand General Charles de Gaulle's contributions to the invasion, and realize the key role played by aviation. You'll also appreciate the challenges faced by doctors, war correspondents, and civil engineers (who had to clean up after the battles—the gargantuan bulldozer on display looks useful).

Cost and Hours: €7, combo-ticket with other Bayeux museums, daily May-Sept 9:30-18:30, Oct-Dec and mid-Feb-April 10:00-12:30 & 14:00-18:00, closed Jan-mid-Feb, last entry one hour before closing, on Bayeux's ring road, 20 minutes on foot from center on Boulevard Fabian Ware, free parking, tel. 02 31 51 25 50, www.bayeuxmuseum.com.

Film: A 25-minute film gives a good summary of the Normandy invasion from start to finish (shown in English May-Sept at 10:30, 12:00, 14:00, 15:30, and 17:00; Oct-April at 10:30, 14:45, and 16:15).

Nearby: A right out of the museum leads along a footpath to the **Monument to Reporters,** a grassy walkway lined with white roses and stone monuments listing, by year, the names of reporters who have died in the line of duty from 1944 to today. Some years have been kinder to journalists than others. The path continues to the **British Military Cemetery,** decorated with 4,144 simple gravestones marking the final resting places of these fallen soldiers. The memorial's Latin inscription reads, "In 1944, the British came to free the homeland of William the Conqueror." Interestingly, this cemetery has soldiers' graves from all countries involved in the battle of Normandy (even Germany) except the United States, which requires its soldiers to be buried on US property—such as the American Cemetery at Omaha Beach.

Sleeping in Bayeux

($$$$ = Splurge, $$$ = Pricier, $$ = Moderate, $ = Budget)
I list hotels in every price range here. Drivers should also see "Sleeping in Arromanches" (page 273).

NEAR THE TAPESTRY
$$$$ Villa Lara**** owns the town's most luxurious accommodations smack in the center of Bayeux. The 28 spacious rooms all have brilliant views of the cathedral, and a few have small terraces. Helpful owner Rima and her attentive staff take excellent care of their guests (pricey but excellent breakfast, elevator, exercise room, comfortable lounges, free and secure parking, between the tapestry museum and TI at 6 Place de Québec, tel. 02 31 92 00 55, www.hotel-villalara.com, info@hotel-villalara.com).

$$$ Hôtel Churchill,* on a traffic-free street across from the TI, could not be more central. Owners Eric and Patricia are great hosts (ask Eric about his professional soccer career). The hotel has 32 plush-and-pricey rooms with wood furnishings, big beds, and convivial public spaces peppered with historic photos of Bayeux's liberation (family rooms, 14 Rue St. Jean, tel. 02 31 21 31 80, www.hotel-churchill.fr, info@hotel-churchill.fr).

$$$ Hôtel le Lion d'Or,*** General Eisenhower's favorite hotel in Bayeux, draws a loyal American and British clientele who love the historic aspect of staying here. It has atmospheric Old World public spaces, 31 stylish rooms, and a responsive staff (no elevator, limited but secure pay parking, restaurant with fair prices, 71 Rue St. Jean, tel. 02 31 92 06 90, www.liondor-bayeux.fr, info@liondor-bayeux.fr).

$ Hôtel Reine Mathilde** is a solid, centrally located value with 16 sharp rooms above an easygoing brasserie, and ten large rooms with three-star comfort in two annexes nearby (family rooms, some rooms with air-con, reception one block from TI at 23 Rue Larcher, tel. 02 31 92 08 13, www.hotel-bayeux-reinemathilde.fr, info@hotel-bayeux-reinemathilde.fr).

¢ Hôtel au Georges VII offers 10 no-star, no-frills rooms (some with only a sink or a shower) with just enough comfort. The rooms are up a tight staircase above a central café, and the bartender doubles as the receptionist (19 Rue St. Martin, tel. 02 31 92 28 53, www.georges-7.com, augeorges7@orange.fr).

CHAMBRES D'HOTES NEAR THE CATHEDRAL

$$ Le Petit Matin, run by friendly Pascal, is a central and handsome bed-and-breakfast with good public spaces, five stylish rooms with big bathrooms, and a *magnifique* back garden (with play toys) on Place Charles de Gaulle (breakfast included, 9 Rue des Terres, tel. 02 31 10 09 27, www.chambres-hotes-bayeux-lepetitmatin.com, lepetitmatin@hotmail.fr).

$ Logis les Remparts, run by bubbly Christèle, is a delightful, three-room bed-and-breakfast situated above an atmospheric Calvados cider-tasting shop. The rooms are big, comfortable, and homey—one is a huge, two-room suite (cash-only if under €200, a few blocks above the cathedral on park-like Place Charles de Gaulle at 4 Rue Bourbesneur, tel. 02 31 92 50 40, www.lecornu.fr, lecornu.bayeux@gmail.com).

$ Manoir Sainte Victoire is a classy, 17th-century building with three top-quality rooms over a small garden at very fair prices. Each has a small kitchenette and views of the cathedral; all come with engaging owner Aitaudia (32 Rue de la Jurisdiction, tel. 02 31 22 74 69, mobile 06 37 36 90 95, www.manoirsaintevictoire.com, contact@manoirsaintevictoire.com).

NEAR PLACE ST. PATRICE

These hotels just off the big Place St. Patrice are a 10-minute walk up Rue St. Martin from the TI (a 15-minute walk to the tapestry).

$$ Hôtel d'Argouges* (dar-goozh) is named for its builder, Lord d'Argouges. This tranquil retreat has a mini-château feel with classy public spaces, lovely private gardens, and 28 standard-comfort rooms. The hotel is run by formal Madame Ropartz, who has had every aspect of the hotel renovated (big family rooms, no elevator, secure free parking, just off Place St. Patrice at 21 Rue St. Patrice, tel. 02 31 92 88 86, www.hotel-dargouges.com, info@hotel-dargouges.com).

$ Hôtel Mogador** is a simple but good 14-room budget value. Choose between wood-beamed rooms on the busy square, or quiet but slightly faded rooms off the street. There are no public areas beyond the small breakfast room and tiny courtyard (20 Rue Alain Chartier at Place St. Patrice, tel. 02 31 92 24 58, www.hotelmo.fr, lemogador@gmail.com).

IN THE COUNTRYSIDE NEAR BAYEUX

$ La Ferme du Pressoir is a lovely, traditional B&B on a big working farm immersed in the Norman landscape about 20 minutes south of Bayeux (see map on page 264). If you've ever wanted to stay on a real French farm yet rest in cozy comfort, this is the place. The five rooms are filled with wood furnishings and decorated with bright garden themes. Guests share a kitchenette, and larger groups can stay in a cottage with its own kitchen. The experience is vintage Normandy—and so are the kind owners, Jacques and Odile (good family rooms, includes good breakfast, Le Haut St-Louet, just off A-84, exit at Villers-Bocage, detailed directions on website, tel. 02 41 40 71 07, www.bandbnormandie.com, lemogador@gmail.com).

Eating in Bayeux

($$$$ = Splurge, $$$ = Pricier, $$ = Moderate, $ = Budget)
Drivers can also consider the short drive to Arromanches for seaside dining options (see page 275). You're smart to book a day ahead for the **$$$**-and-up listings below.

ON OR NEAR RUE ST. JEAN

This traffic-free street is lined with cafés, *crêperies,* and inexpensive dining options.

La Chaumière is the best *charcuterie* (deli) in town; you'll find salads, quiches, and prepared dishes to go (Tue-Sun until 19:30, closed Mon, on Rue St. Jean across from Hôtel Churchill). The grocery store across the street has what you need to complete your picnic.

$ At Le Moulin de la Galette, enjoy tasty crêpes for good prices in a delightful setting right on the small river. There's fine seating inside and out (effective heaters) and a big selection of crêpes, salads, and *plats* (daily, 38 Rue de Nesmond, tel. 02 31 22 47 75).

$$$ La Rapière is a lovely wood-beamed eatery—calm and romantic—filled with locals enjoying a refined meal and a rare-these-days cheese platter for a finale. Reservations are wise (closed Sun, 53 Rue St. Jean, tel. 03 31 21 05 45, www.larapiere.net, charming Linda).

$ Le Volet Qui Penche is a fun-loving, wine-shop-meets-bistro run by gentle, English-speaking Pierre-Henri—a wine lover who clearly has found his niche. He serves salads, escargot, *charcuterie* and cheese platters, and a small selection of à la carte plates to go with a vast selection of wines by the glass (nonstop service until 20:00 most days—making early dinners easy, closed Sun, near the TI at 3 Passage de l'Islet, tel. 03 31 21 98 54).

$$$$ L'Angle Saint Laurent is a tasteful and elegantly simple place run by a husband-and-wife team (Caroline speaks English and manages the spacious restaurant, Sébastien cooks). Come here for a special meal of *Normand* specialties done in a contemporary gourmet style. The selection is limited and changes with the season (good wine list, closed Mon, 2 Rue des Bouchers, reserve in advance, tel. 02 31 92 03 01, www.langlesaintlaurent.com).

$$ Le Garde Manger, a family-friendly eatery, offers basic grub all day (omelets, big salads, pizza) with a marvelous outside terrace and cathedral views (daily 12:00-22:00, a block from Rue St. Jean at 23 Rue Larcher).

$$ Le Pommier, with street appeal inside and out, is a good place to sample regional products with clever twists in a relaxed yet refined atmosphere. Owner Thierry mixes old and new in his cuisine and decor, and focuses on organic food (good vegetarian *menu*, open daily, 38 Rue des Cuisiniers, tel. 02 31 21 52 10, www.restaurantlepommier.com).

$$$ Au P'tit Bistrot is a small, casual eatery with a snappy interior and a good reputation for its carefully prepared food. Warmly run, it's a nice mix of modern and traditional (closed Sun, 31 Rue Larcher, tel. 02 31 92 30 08).

$ La Fringale, well-located on the main pedestrian street, is Bayeux's low-key diner with a big selection of basic café fare (daily, 43 Rue St. Jean, tel. 02 31 22 72 52).

Bayeux Connections

From Bayeux by Train to: Paris' Gare St. Lazare (9/day, 2.5 hours, some change in Caen), **Amboise** (2/day, 4.5 hours, change in Caen and Tours' St-Pierre-des-Corps), **Rouen** (14/day, 2.5 hours, change in Caen), **Caen** (20/day, 20 minutes), **Honfleur** (2-3/day, 20-minute train to Caen, then 1-hour express PrestoBus—line #39—to Honfleur; more with train to Caen and scenic 2-hour ride on bus #20 via the coast; bus info tel. 02 31 89 28 41, www.busverts.fr), **Pontorson/Mont St-Michel** (3/day, 2 hours to Pontorson, then bus to Mont St-Michel; also consider Hôtel Churchill's faster shuttle van—described below).

By Bus to the D-Day Beaches: Bus Verts du Calvados offers minimal service to D-Day beaches with stops in Bayeux at Place St. Patrice and at the train station (schedules at TI, tel. 08 10 21 42 14, www.busverts.fr). Lines #74/#75 run east to Arromanches and Juno Beach (3-5/day, none on Sun Sept-June; 30 minutes to Arromanches, 50 minutes to Juno Beach), and line #70 runs west to the American Cemetery and Vierville-sur-Mer (3/day in summer, 2/day off-season, none on Sun Sept-June; 35 minutes to American Cemetery, 45 minutes to Vierville-sur-Mer). Going round-trip by bus often leaves you stuck with either too much or too little time at either sight; consider a taxi one way and a bus the other (for taxi information, see page 248).

By Shuttle Van to Mont St-Michel: Two services run shuttle-van day trips to Mont St-Michel for €65 round-trip (about 1.5 hours each way, plus at least 3 hours at Mont St-Michel): **Hôtel Churchill** (hotel clients get a small discount; details at www.hotel-churchill.fr) and **Bayeux Shuttle** (www.bayeuxshuttle.com). Either trip is a terrific deal, as you'll get a free tour of Normandy along the way from your knowledgeable driver.

D-Day Beaches

The 54 miles of Atlantic coast north of Bayeux—stretching from Utah Beach in the west to Sword Beach in the east—are littered with WWII museums, monuments, cemeteries, and battle remains left in tribute to the courage of the British, Canadian, and American armies that successfully carried out the largest military operation in history: D-Day. (It's called *Jour J* in French.) It was on these serene beaches, at the crack of dawn on June 6, 1944, that the Allies (roughly one-third Americans and two-thirds British and Canadians) finally gained a foothold in France. From this moment, Nazi Europe was destined to crumble.

> *"The first 24 hours of the invasion will be decisive... The fate of Germany depends on the outcome... For the Allies, as well as Germany, it will be the longest day."*
>
> —Field Marshal Erwin Rommel, April 22, 1944
> (from *The Longest Day*, by Cornelius Ryan)

June 6, 2014, marked the 70th anniversary of the landings. It was a huge deal here, given how few D-Day veterans are still alive. Locals talk of the last visits of veterans with heartfelt sorrow; they have adored seeing the old soldiers in their villages and fear losing the firsthand accounts of the battles. All along this rambling coast, locals will never forget what the troops and their families sacrificed all those years ago. A warm regard for Americans has survived political disputes, from de Gaulle to "Freedom Fries." This remains particularly friendly soil for Americans—a place where US soldiers are still honored and the image of the US as a force for good remains largely untarnished.

PLANNING YOUR TIME

I've listed the prime D-Day sites from east to west, starting with Arromanches (the British sector) and, next, the American sectors (with a stop-by-stop tour of Omaha Beach and its related sights, followed by Utah Beach). Finally, to the far east, I cover the Canadian sector. In the British and Canadian sectors, overbuilding makes it harder to envision the events of June 1944, but the American sector looks today very much as it did 70 years ago. To best appreciate the beaches, avoid visiting at high tide if you can. For more information on touring the D-Day beaches, www.normandie-tourisme.fr is a useful resource.

D-Day Sites in One Day

If you have only one day, I'd spend it entirely on the exciting sites and impressive museums along the beaches and miss the Caen Memorial Museum. (To squeeze in the Caen Memorial Museum, visit it on your way to or from the beaches.) Note that the American Cemetery closes at 18:00 mid-April-mid-Sept and at 17:00 the rest of the year—and you'll want at least an hour there.

If you're traveling by car, begin on the cliffs above Arromanches. From there, visit the Port Winston artificial harbor and the D-Day Landing Museum, then continue west to Longues-sur-Mer and tour the German gun battery there. Spend your afternoon visiting the American Cemetery and its thought-provoking visitors center, walking on Omaha Beach at Vierville-sur-Mer, and exploring the Pointe du Hoc Ranger Monument. With an extra half-day, see the Utah Beach sights (to learn about the paratroopers' role in the invasion).

Canadians will want to start at the Juno Beach Centre and Canadian Cemetery (in Courseulles-sur-Mer, 10 minutes east of Arromanches).

Day-Tripping to the Beaches from Paris: If you're staying in Paris and are considering a day trip to the D-Day beaches in a rental car, think twice. Just getting to and from the D-Day beaches (going by train to Caen, picking up a car, driving to your first stop, etc.) will take about six hours. Also beware that Sunday train service to Bayeux is limited. A better alternative is to book a service that will meet you at a Normandy train station and drive you to the D-Day sights (see "By Taxi Minivan" and "By Minivan Tour," below). Or take a bus tour that starts in Paris.

GETTING AROUND THE D-DAY BEACHES
On Your Own
By Rental Car: Though the minivan excursions listed below teach important history lessons, renting a car is a far less expensive way to visit the beaches, particularly for three or more people (for rental suggestions, see Bayeux's "Helpful Hints" on page 249).

By Bus or Bike: Very limited **bus service** links Bayeux, the coastal town of Arromanches, and the most impressive sites of D-Day (see Bus Verts du Calvados information on page 261)— but it's not practical for anything more than one sight. **Bike riding** is dicey as roads are narrow (no bike lanes), with plenty of blind curves and relentless traffic.

By Taxi Minivan (Unguided)
Taxi minivans shuttle up to seven people between the key sites at reasonable rates (which vary depending on how far you go). Allow €240 for an eight-hour taxi day to visit the top Utah and Omaha Beach sites. No guiding is included; you are paying strictly for transport. Figure about €21 each way between Bayeux and Arromanches, €37 between Bayeux and the American Cemetery, and €100 for a 2.5-hour visit to Omaha Beach sites from Bayeux or Arromanches (50 percent surcharge after 19:00 and on Sun, taxi tel. 02 31 92 92 40 or mobile 06 70 40 07 96, www.taxisbayeux.com, taxisbayeux@orange.fr).

Abbeilles Taxis offer D-Day excursions from Caen (€200/5-hour visit, tel. 02 31 52 17 89, www.taxis-abbeilles-caen.com).

By Minivan Tour (Guided)
An army of small companies and private guides offers all-day guided excursions to the D-Day beaches. Travelers beware: It seems that anyone with passable English wants to guide. Anyone can get you around the beaches, but you should expect your guide to deliver coherent history lessons (not simply orient and disperse you).

NORMANDY

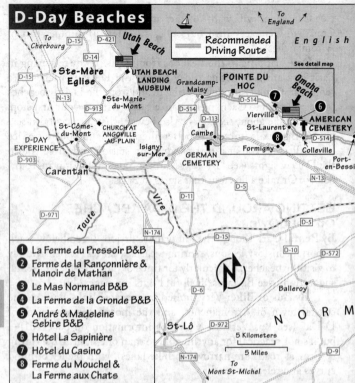

D-Day Beaches

Recommended
Driving Route

To England

English

To Cherbourg — D-15 — D-421 — Utah Beach

D-14

D-15 — Ste-Mère Eglise — UTAH BEACH LANDING MUSEUM — Grandcamp-Maisy

N-13 — Ste-Marie-du-Mont

POINTE DU HOC — Omaha Beach

See detail map

D-913 — D-514 — ❼ — ❻ AMERICAN CEMETERY

St-Côme-du-Mont — CHURCH AT ANGOVILLE-AU-PLAIN — Vierville

D-DAY EXPERIENCE — D-113 — St-Laurent

La Cambe — ❽ — Colleville

D-903 — Isigny-sur-Mer — Formigny

Carentan — GERMAN CEMETERY — Port-en-Bessi

D-971 — Vire — D-5 — N-13

Taute — D-11 — D-5

N-174 — D-15 — D-10 — D-572

❶ La Ferme du Pressoir B&B
❷ Ferme de la Rançonnière & Manoir de Mathan
❸ Le Mas Normand B&B
❹ La Ferme de la Gronde B&B
❺ André & Madeleine Sebire B&B
❻ Hôtel La Sapinière
❼ Hôtel du Casino
❽ Ferme du Mouchel & La Ferme aux Chats

D-6 — Balleroy

St-Lô — D-972 — N O R M

5 Kilometers
5 Miles

N-174 — D-9

To Mont St-Michel

NORMANDY

Many tours prefer to pick up in or near Bayeux, and a few levy a small surcharge for a Caen pickup. Most guides skip Arromanches, preferring to focus on sights farther west: The "classic" itinerary run by most is Ste-Mère Eglise, Utah Beach, Pointe du Hoc, Omaha Beach, and the American Cemetery. The tour companies and guides listed here are people I trust to take your time seriously. Most deliver riveting

commentary about these moving sites. (Most tours don't go inside museums.) To land one of these guides, book your tour in advance (3-6 months is best during peak periods).

These tours are pricey because you're hiring a professional guide and driver/vehicle for the day. To spend less, look for a guide who will join you in your rental car. While you can save by hiring a guide for a half-day tour, a full day on the beaches is more satisfying. (These guides may do half-day trips: Bayeux Shuttle, Nor-

mandy Sightseeing Tours, Vanessa Letourneur, Edward Robinson, Rodolphe Passera, and Mathias Leclere—details for each below.)

Working with Your Guide: When hiring a private guide, take charge of your tour if you have specific interests (some guides can get lost in battle minutiae that you don't have time for). The best route for a one-day tour with a private guide is to start in Arromanches and end at Point du Hoc or the American Cemetery. Request extra time at the American Cemetery to see the excellent visitors center. While some companies discourage children, others (including Dale Booth, Normandy Sightseeing Tours, Mathias Leclere, Sylvain Kast, and Edward Robinson) welcome them.

Tours in a Shared Minivan

A few tour companies offer shared departures, available for individual sign-ups. Figure about €110/person for a day and €65/person for a half-day. (These companies also run private tours.)

Bayeux Shuttle is well-run and user-friendly for individuals. You can visit their office in Bayeux and usually book at the last minute. Their vans have monitors explaining what's out the window, and they offer several all-day and half-day tours with

Countdown to D-Day

1939

On September 1, Adolf Hitler invades the Free City of Danzig (today's Gdańsk, Poland), sparking World War II.

1940

Germany's Blitzkrieg ("lightning war") quickly overwhelms France, Nazis goose-step down Avenue des Champs-Elysées, and the country is divided into Occupied France (the north) and Vichy France (the south, administered by right-wing French). Just like that, nearly the entire Continent is fascist.

1941

The Allies (Britain, Soviet Union, and others) peck away at the fringes of "Fortress Europe." The Soviets repel Hitler's invasion at Moscow, while the Brits (with American aid) battle German U-boats for control of the seas. On December 7, Japan bombs the US naval base at Pearl Harbor, Hawaii. The US enters the war against Japan and its ally, Germany.

1942

Three crucial battles—at Stalingrad, El-Alamein, and Guadalcanal—weaken the German forces and their ally Japan. The victorious tank battle at El-Alamein in the deserts of North Africa soon gives the Allies a jumping-off point (Tunis) for the first assault on the Continent.

1943

More than 150,000 Americans and Brits, under the command of George Patton and Bernard "Monty" Montgomery, land in Sicily and begin working their way north through Italy. Meanwhile, Germany has to fend off tenacious Soviets on their eastern front.

1944

On June 6, 1944, the Allies launch "Operation Overlord," better known as D-Day. The Allies amass three million soldiers and six million tons of *matériel* in England in preparation for the biggest

capable guides (office open daily about 7:45-18:00, across from the Bayeux TI at Impasse de Islet, tel. 09 70 44 49 89, www. bayeuxshuttle.com).

Normandy Sightseeing Tours delivers a French perspective with well-trained guides and will pick you up anywhere you like— for a price (€65 morning tour, €75 afternoon tour, €105 all-day tour, tel. 02 31 51 70 52, www.normandy-sightseeing-tours.com).

Overlord Tours is also good (€65 half-day tour, €100 all-day tour, www.overlordtour.com).

The Caen Memorial Museum runs a busy program of half-day tours covering the American and Canadian sectors

fleet-led invasion in history—across the English Channel to France, then eastward toward Berlin. The Germans, hunkered down in northern France, know an invasion is imminent, but the Allies keep the details top secret. On the night of June 5, more than 180,000 soldiers board ships and planes in England, not knowing where they are headed until they're under way. Each one carries a note from General Dwight D. Eisenhower: "The tide has turned. The free men of the world are marching together to victory."

At 6:30 on June 6, 1944, Americans spill out of troop transports into the cold waters off a beach in Normandy, code-named Omaha. The weather is bad, seas are rough, and the prep bombing has failed. The soldiers, many seeing their first action, are dazed, confused, and weighed down by heavy packs. Nazi machine guns pin them against the sea. Slowly, they crawl up the beach on their stomachs. More than a thousand die. They hold on until the next wave of transports arrives.

Americans also see action at Utah Beach, while the British and Canadian troops storm Sword, Juno, and Gold. All day long, Allied confusion does battle with German indecision—the Nazis never really counterattack, thinking D-Day is just a ruse, not the main invasion. By day's end, the Allies have taken all five beaches along the Normandy coast and soon begin building two completely artificial harbors, code-named "Mulberry," providing ports for the reconquest of western Europe. The stage is set for the eventual end to the war.

1945
Having liberated Paris (August 26, 1944), the Allies' march on Berlin bogs down, hit by poor supply lines, bad weather, and the surprising German counterpunch at the Battle of the Bulge. Finally, in the spring, the Americans and Brits cross the Rhine, Soviet soldiers close in on Berlin, Hitler shoots himself, and—after nearly six long years of war—Europe is free.

NORMANDY

in combination with a visit to the museum (handy for those with limited time—see museum listing on page 295).

Tours with a Private Guide
Costs are about the same for all guides listed here. Private groups should expect to pay €500-650 for up to eight people for an all-day tour and €250-330 for a half-day.

Ex-Pat Guides: These (mostly British) guides, like a band of brothers, are passionate about teaching and offer excellent private tours. All have their own vehicles. While some are happy to ride in your car, let them do the driving. They work together and can help you find a guide if the first one you call is booked.

• **Dale Booth Normandy Tours,** led by Dale Booth (tel. 02 33

71 53 76, www.dboothnormandytours.com, dboothholidays@
sfr.fr).

- **D-Day Historian Tours,** with Paul Woodadge (mobile 07 88
  02 76 57, www.ddayhistorian.com, paul@ddayhistorian.com).
- **First Normandy Battlefield Tours,** offered by Allan Bryson
  (www.firstnormandybattlefieldtours.com, firstnormandy@sfr.
  fr).
- **Normandy Battle Tours,** led by Stuart Robertson (tel.
  02 33 41 28 34, www.normandybattletours.com, stuart@
  normandybattletours.com).
- **Edward Robinson** is Irish, informal, and has the gift of
  gab; he previously guided for the Caen Memorial Museum (www.battleofnormandytours.com, edrobinson@
  battleofnormandytours.com).
- **D-Day Battle Tours,** run by WWII-enthusiast and eccentric D-Day buff Ellwood von Seibold (tel. 02 33 94 44 13,
  mobile 06 32 67 49 15, www.ddaybattletours.com, ellwood@
  ddaybattletours.com).

French Guides: These guides speak fluent English and are excellent teachers.
- **Rodolphe Passera** works as a guide at the D-Day Landing Museum at Utah Beach (mobile 06 30 55 63 39, www.
  normandyamericanheroes.com, normandyamericanheroes@
  gmail.com).
- **Sylvain Kast** has many French family connections to the war
  (mobile 06 17 44 04 46, www.d-day-experience-tours.com,
  sylvainkast@yahoo.fr).
- **Vanessa Letourneur** can guide anywhere in Normandy. She
  worked at the Caen Memorial Museum and offers full and
  half-day tours from Bayeux or Caen (mobile 06 98 95 89 45,
  www.normandypanorama.com).
- **Mathias Leclere** was born four miles from Juno Beach to
  a family with three centuries of roots in Normandy. Mathias leads half-day, full-day, and multiple-day tours (www.
  ddayguidedtours.com).
- **Magali Desquesne** runs good tours at DDay4you (www.
  dday4you.com, mag.ddayguide@gmail.com, tel. 06 88 75 86
  17).
- **Bertrand Soudrais** is a young, flexible, and hardworking
  guide whose American wife gives him an inside track on Yankee interests (www.executived-daytours.com).

HELPFUL HINTS

Good Booklet: A free visitor's guide gives succinct reviews of
D-Day museums and sights with current opening times. It's

available at TIs, but you usually need to ask for it (download-able at www.normandie-tourisme.fr).

TV and Films About D-Day: Local guides recommend some pre-paratory viewing before your visit. The best two movies are *The Longest Day* (for the big D-Day story) and *Saving Private Ryan* (for the most realistic sense of what it was like to land here and battle your way into France). Also consider *Band of Brothers*, a powerful 11-hour HBO miniseries telling the story from D-Day preparations, through the landing, and on to the end of the war.

Food Strategies: The D-Day landing sites are rural, and you won't find a grocery on every corner. Pack ahead if you plan to picnic.

Tides: Tides will affect your experience of the beaches throughout the region, changing what you can see and your access to the sand. Avoid visiting the beaches at high tide if possible. Most TIs have tide tables to help you plan, or consult the easy-to-navigate www.maree.shom.fr (when searching tide charts, the nearest reference point is Port-en-Bessin).

Arromanches

This small town—part of Gold Beach (in the British landing zone)—was ground zero for the D-Day invasion. The Allies decided it would be easier to build their own port than to try to take one from the Nazis. And so, almost overnight, Arromanches sprouted the immense harbor Port Winston, which gave the Allies a foot-hold in Normandy from which to begin their victorious push to Berlin and the end of World War II.

A touristy-but-fun little town that offers a pleasant cocktail of war memories, cotton candy, and trinket shops, Arromanches makes a good home base for touring the D-Day beaches. Here you'll find an evocative beach, rusty hardware with English de-scriptions scattered around town, a good waterfront museum, a bluff with great views, and a theater with a thrilling little video. The town's pleasant seaside promenade is a great place from which to view the port.

Sit on the seawall after dark, listen to the surf, and contem-plate the events that took place here more than 70 years ago.

Orientation to Arromanches

TOURIST INFORMATION

The service-oriented TI in the town center has a free leaflet illus-trating the Port Winston harbor, bus schedules, a listing of area ho-tels and *chambres d'hôtes*, and helpful Mathilde (daily 10:00-12:00 & 14:00-17:00, longer hours in summer—July-Aug 9:30-19:00,

Arromanches

English Channel

More of "Port Winston" artificial harbor in distance

Note: Map shows beach at low tide.

Beach

BEACHFRONT PROMENADE

RUSTED REMAINS OF ARTIFICIAL HARBOR

D-DAY LANDING MUSEUM

Beach

To Longues-sur-Mer via Coastal Path (on foot only)

RUE JOFFRE

Pl. du 6 Juin 1944

RUE DU COL. JOB

RUE COL. MICHEL

BLVD LONGUET

R. PETIT FONT.

R. JOURDAIN

RUE LAURENT

TOWER

PONTOON ROAD

To Courseulles-sur-Mer, Gold, Juno & Sword Beaches

CAMPGROUND

360 THEATER

POST

CHURCH

To Bayeux, Longues-sur-Mer & Omaha Beach

D-514

D-514

D-514

D-22

To Caen

① Hôtel de la Marine
② Hôtel d'Arromanches & Restaurant "Le Pappagall"
③ Ideale Hôtel Mountbatten
④ The Pub Mary Celeste
⑤ Supermarket
⑥ Arromanches Militaria Shop

200 Meters
200 Yards

One-way streets →

NORMANDY

2 Avenue Maréchal Joffre, tel. 02 31 22 36 45, www.ot-arromanches. fr). You may find a seasonal branch TI at the parking lot near the Arromanches 360° theater.

ARRIVAL IN ARROMANCHES
The bus stop is at the top of the town across from the post office. The main parking lot by the D-Day Landing Museum costs €1.50 per hour (free 19:00-9:00). For free parking and less traffic, look for the lot between the small grocery store and Ideale Hôtel Mountbatten as you enter Arromanches.

HELPFUL HINTS
ATM: An ATM is by the post office, across from the museum parking lot.
Groceries: A little **supermarket** is a long block above the beach, across from Ideale Hôtel Mountbatten (closed Sun afternoon and Mon).
Taxi: To get an Arromanches-based taxi, call mobile 06 66 62 00 99.
WWII Paraphernalia Store: Arromanches Militaria sells all sorts of D-Day relics in a tight space (daily 10:00-19:00, 11 Boulevard Gilbert Longuet).

Sights in Arromanches

Arromanches' key sight, the Port Winston artificial harbor, is best seen from two vantage points—above town on the bluff (with the Arromanches 360° theater), and from the seawall in town (near the D-Day Landing Museum).

▲▲▲Port Winston Artificial Harbor

Arromanches is all about its artificial harbor—the remains of which can be seen to this day. Winston Churchill's brainchild, the prefab harbor was made by the British and affectionately nicknamed Port Winston by the troops. To appreciate the massive undertaking of creating this harbor in a matter of days, start on the bluff overlooking the site of the impressive harbor. See the presentation at the cliff-top Arromanches 360° theater, and then head down to the D-Day Landing Museum and a nearby viewing area.

Getting to the Bluff: Drive two minutes toward Courseulles-sur-Mer and pay €3 to park in the big, can't-miss-it lot overlooking the sea. Your other options are to hike 10 minutes up the hill behind the town's D-Day Landing Museum, or take the free white train from the museum (daily June-Sept, Sat-Sun only Oct-mid-Nov and April-May, none in winter, departures on the half-hour timed to arrive for the film at the Arromanches 360° theater).

Viewing the Harbor from the Bluff: Survey the coast from this dramatic perch. To the left is the American sector, with Omaha Beach and then Utah Beach (notice the sheer cliffs typical of Normandy's coastline). Below and to the right lie the British and Canadian sectors.

Along the beaches below, the Allies arrived in the largest amphibious attack ever, launching the liberation of Western Europe. On D-Day +1—June 7, 1944—17 old ships sailed 100 miles across the English Channel under their own steam to Arromanches. Their crews sank them so that each bow faced the next ship's stern, forming a sea barrier. Then 500 tugboats towed 115 football-field-size cement blocks (called "Phoenixes") across the channel. These were also sunk (with the ships and Phoenixes making a semicircle). This created a four-mile-long breakwater about a mile offshore. Finally, engineers set up seven floating steel pierheads with extendable legs; they then linked these to shore with four floating roads made of concrete pontoons. (You can see a segment of pontoon road in the parking lot behind you, by the statue of the Virgin Mary.) Soldiers placed 115 antiaircraft guns on the Phoenixes and pontoons, protecting a port the size of Dover, England. Within just six days of operation, 54,000 vehicles, 326,000 troops, and 110,000 tons of goods had crossed the English Channel. An Allied toehold in

Normandy was secure. Eleven months later, Hitler was dead and the war was over.

▲▲Arromanches 360° Theater

The domed building just off the cliff-top parking lot houses the powerful film *Normandy's 100 Days*. The screens surrounding you show archival footage and photographs of the endeavor to liberate Normandy (works in any language). In addition to honoring the many Allied and German soldiers who died, it reminds us that 20,000 French civilians were killed in aerial bombardments. The experience is powerful—as loud and slickly produced as anything at the D-Day beaches.

Cost and Hours: €5.50, €21.50 combo-ticket with Caen Memorial Museum (see page 293); shows at :10 and :40 past the hour, daily June-Aug 9:40-18:10, April-May and Sept 10:10-18:10, Oct-mid-Nov 10:10-17:40, these are first and last show times, closed most of Jan, Chemin du Calvaire, tel. 02 31 06 06 45, www. arromanches360.com.

• *To return to the town center from the bluff, follow signs to* Musée du Débarquement—*the D-Day Landing Museum.*

▲D-Day Landing Museum (Musée du Débarquement)

This museum, facing the harbor, makes a worthwhile hour-long visit (if you watch the two videos) and is the best way to appreciate how the artificial harbor was built. While gazing through windows at the site of this amazing endeavor, you can study helpful models, videos, and photographs illustrating the construction and use of the prefabricated harbor. Screens over the model show a virtual reconstruction of Port Winston. Those blimp-like objects tethered to the port prevented German planes from getting too close (though the German air force had been made largely irrelevant by this time). Ponder the remarkable task of building this harbor in just 12 days, while battles raged. The essential 15-minute film (up the stairs behind the cashier) uses British newsreel footage to illustrate the construction of the port. Another video (7 minutes, far end of ground floor) recalls D-Day.

Cost and Hours: €8, daily May-Aug 9:00-19:00, Sept until 18:00, Oct-Dec and Feb-April 10:00-12:30 & 13:30-17:00, closed Jan, Place du 6 Juin, tel. 02 31 22 34 31, www.arromanches-museum.com.

Viewing the Harbor from near the Museum: Find the round bulkhead on the seawall, near the entrance to the D-Day Landing Museum. Stand facing the sea. Designed to be temporary (it was used for six months), the harbor was supposed to wash out to sea over time—which is exactly what happened with its twin harbor at Omaha Beach (which lasted only 12 days, thanks to a terrible storm). If the tide is out, you'll see several rusted floats mired on the sand close in—these supported the pontoon roads. Imagine the traffic pouring in past the many antiaircraft guns poised to defend against the invasion.

On the hill beyond the museum, you'll spot a Sherman tank, one of 50,000 deployed during the landings. Behind the museum (not viewable from here) is another section of a pontoon road, an antiaircraft gun, and a Higgins boat, which was used to ferry 30 soldiers at a time from naval ships to the beaches. If you can, walk down to the beach and wander among the concrete and rusted litter of the battle—and be thankful that all you hear are birds and surf.

Sleeping in Arromanches

($$$$ = Splurge, $$$ = Pricier, $$ = Moderate, $ = Budget)
Arromanches, with its pinwheels and seagulls, has a salty beach-town ambience that makes it a fun overnight stop. For evening fun, do what most do and head for the small bar at **Restaurant "Le Pappagall"** (French slang for "parakeet") in the Hôtel d'Arromanches, or, for more of a nightclub scene, have a drink at the **Mary Celeste Pub,** around the corner on Rue Colonel René Michel.

Drivers should also consider my sleeping recommendations near Omaha Beach (see page 287).

$$ Hôtel de la Marine*** has a knockout location with point-blank views to the artificial harbor from most of its 33 comfortable rooms (family rooms, includes breakfast, elevator, view restaurant, Quai du Canada, tel. 02 31 22 34 19, www.hotel-de-la-marine.fr, hotel.de.la.marine@wanadoo.fr).

$ Hôtel d'Arromanches,** on the main pedestrian drag near the TI, is a good value, with nine mostly small, straightforward rooms (some with water views), all up a tight stairway that feels like a tree house. Here you'll find the cheery, recommended Restaurant "Le Pappagall" run by English-speaking Luis (2 Rue Colonel René Michel, tel. 02 31 22 36 26, www.hoteldarromanches.fr, reservation@hoteldarromanches.fr).

$ Ideale Hôtel Mountbatten,*** located a long block up from the water, is an eight-room, two-story, motel-esque place with generously sized, stylish, clean, and good-value lodgings, and welcoming owners Sylvie and Laurent (family rooms, reception closed 14:00-16:00, easy and free parking, short block below the main post office at 20 Boulevard Gilbert Longuet, tel. 02 31 22 59 70, www.hotelarromancheslideal.fr, contact@hotelarromancheslideal.fr).

IN THE COUNTRYSIDE NEAR ARROMANCHES
$$ Ferme de la Rançonnière is a 35-room, country-classy oasis buried in farmland a 15-minute drive from Bayeux or Arroman-

ches. It's flawlessly maintained, from its wood-beamed, stone-walled rooms to its traditional restaurant (good *menus* from €32) and fireplace-cozy lounge/bar (family rooms, bike rental, service-oriented staff, 4.5 miles southeast from Arromanches in Crépon, tel. 02 31 22 21 73, www.ranconniere.fr, ranconniere@wanadoo.fr).

The same family has two other properties nearby: The **$$ Manoir de Mathan** has 21 similarly traditional but bigger rooms a few blocks away in the same village (comparable prices to main building, Route de Bayeux, Crépon). An eight-minute drive away, in the village of Asnelles, are seven slick, glassy, modern seaside **$$ apartments** right along the beachfront promenade (2 Impasse de l'Horizon, www.gites-en-normandie.eu). For any of these, check in at the main hotel. Book directly so they can help you choose the property and room that works best for you.

$$ Le Mas Normand, 10 minutes east of Arromanches in Ver-sur-Mer, is the child of *Provençale* Mylène and *Normand* Christian. Here you get a warm welcome and the best of two French worlds: three lovingly decorated, Provence-style rooms wrapped in 18th-century Norman stone. The place is family-friendly with ample grass (family rooms, ask about their fun, funky, and tight *roulotte*—a Gypsy-style trailer; includes breakfast; drive to the east end of little Ver-sur-Mer, turn right on Avenue de Provence, take another right where the road makes a T, and find the sign at 8 Impasse de la Rivière; tel. 02 31 21 97 75, www.lemasnormand.com, lemasnormand@wanadoo.fr).

$ La Ferme de la Gronde lies midpoint between Bayeux and Arromanches with large traditional rooms in a big stone farmhouse overlooking wheatfields (includes breakfast, 2 apartments ideal for families, well-signed from D-516 on Route de l'Eglise in Magny-en-Bessin, tel. 02 31 21 33 11, www.chambres-gite-normandie.fr, info@chambres-gite-normandie.fr).

¢ At **André and Madeleine Sebire**'s B&B, you'll experience a real Norman farm. The hardworking owners offer four modest, homey, and dirt-cheap rooms in the middle of nowhere (includes breakfast, 2 miles from Arromanches in the tiny Ryes at Ferme du Clos Neuf, tel. 02 31 22 32 34, emmanuelle.sebire@wanadoo.fr, little English spoken). Follow signs into Ryes, then go down Rue de la Forge (kitty-corner from the restaurant). Turn right just after the small bridge, onto Rue Tringale, and go a half-mile to a sign on the right to *Le Clos Neuf.* Park near the tractors.

Eating in Arromanches

You'll find cafés, *crêperies,* and shops selling sandwiches to go (ideal for beachfront picnics). Many restaurants line Rue Maréchal Joffe, the bustling pedestrian zone a block inland. The following hotel restaurants are also reliable:

$$ Restaurant "Le Pappagall" serves basic café fare in a cheery setting (daily in high season, closed Wed and possibly other days off-season, see Hôtel d'Arromanches listing, earlier).

$$$ Hôtel de la Marine allows you to dine or drink in style on the water (cool bar with same views, daily, see hotel listing earlier).

Arromanches Connections

From Arromanches by Bus to: Bayeux (bus #74/#75, 3-5/day, none on Sun Sept-June, 30 minutes), **Juno Beach** (bus #74/#75, 20 minutes). The bus stop is near the main post office, four long blocks above the sea (the stop for Bayeux is on the sea side of the street; the stop for Juno Beach is on the post office side).

American D-Day Sites

The American sector, stretching west of Arromanches, is divided between Omaha and Utah beaches. Omaha Beach starts just a few miles west of Arromanches and has the most important sights for visitors. Utah Beach sights are farther away (on the road to Cherbourg), but were also critical to the ultimate success of the Normandy invasion. The American Airborne sector covers a broad area behind Utah Beach and centers on Ste-Mère Eglise.

Omaha Beach

Omaha Beach is the landing zone most familiar to Americans. This well-defended stretch was where US troops saw their biggest losses. Going west from Arromanches, I've listed four powerful stops (and a few lesser ones): the massive German gun battery at Longues-sur-Mer (which secured the west end of the beach), the American Cemetery, Omaha Beach itself (at Vierville-sur-Mer, the best stop on the beach), and Pointe du Hoc.

• *The D-514 coastal road links to all the sights in this section—just keep heading west. I've provided specific driving directions where they'll help.*

▲Longues-sur-Mer Gun Battery

Four German casemates (three with guns intact)—built to guard against seaborne attacks—hunker down at the end of a country

Omaha Beach Area

RECOMMENDED DRIVING ROUTE

C CALVADOS TASTING

English Channel

Omaha Beach

POINTE DU HOC

VISITORS CENTER

Pointe de la Percée

COASTAL PATH

D-514

To La Cambe via D-113 & Utah Beach

C LEBREC

HOTEL CASINO

ARTIFICIAL HARBOR REMAINS

NAT'L GUARD MEMORIAL

"THE BRAVES" STATUE

Vierville-sur-Mer

D-517

OMAHA BEACH MUSEUM

AVE. DE LA LIBERATION

AMERICAN CEMETERY

VISITORS CENTER

Englesqueville-la-Percée

St-Laurent-sur-Mer

HOTEL LA SAP.

Colleville-sur-Mer

D-514

To La Cambe & Utah Beach

D-125

LA FERME DE LA SAPINIÈRE

OVERLORD MUSEUM

To Longues & Arromanches

LA FERME AUX CHATS B&B

N-13

FERME DU MOUCHEL B&B

BIG RED ONE MUSEUM

Formigny

2 Kilometers

2 Miles

To Bayeux & Caen

---

road. The guns, 300 yards inland, were arranged in a semicircle to maximize the firing range east and west, and are the only original coastal artillery guns remaining in place in the D-Day region. (Much was scrapped after the war, long before people thought of tourism.) This battery, staffed by 194 German soldiers, was more defended than the better-known Pointe du Hoc. The Longues-sur-Mer Battery was a critical link in Hitler's Atlantic Wall defense, which consisted of more than 15,000 defensive structures stretching from Norway to the Pyrenees. These guns could hit targets up to 12 miles away with relatively sharp accuracy if linked to good target information. The Allies had to take them out.

Cost and Hours: Free and always open (and a good spot for a picnic); on-site TI open April-Oct daily 10:00-13:00 & 14:00-18:00. The TI's €5.70 booklet is helpful.

Getting There: You'll find the guns 10 minutes west of Arromanches off D-514 on Rue de la Mer (D-104). Follow *Port-en-Bessin* signs from Arromanches; once in Longues-sur-Mer, turn right at the town's only traffic light and follow *Batterie* signs to the free and easy parking lot (with WC).

Visiting the Battery: Walk in a clockwise circle, seeing the inland gun bunkers first and then the command bunker closer to the bluff before circling back to the parking lot. Enter the third bunker you pass. It took seven soldiers to manage each gun, which could be loaded and fired six times per minute (the shells weighed 40 pounds). Climbing above the bunker you can see the hooks that

NORMANDY

secured the camouflage netting that protected the bunker from Allied bombers.

Head down the path (toward the sea) between the second and third bunkers until you reach a lone observation bunker (look for the low-lying concrete roof just before the cliffs). This was designed to direct the firing; field telephones connected the observation bunker to the gun batteries by underground wires. Peer out to sea from inside the bunker to appreciate the strategic view over the Channel. From here you can walk along the glorious *Sentier du Littoral* (coastal path) above the cliffs and see Arromanches in the distance, then walk the road back to your car. (You can drive five minutes down to the water on this same small road.)

• *Continue west on D-514, passing two small sights of note—Port-en-Bessin and the Big Red One Museum—before arriving at the American Cemetery.*

Near Longues-sur-Mer
Port-en-Bessin

This charming fishing port west of Longues-sur-Mer has a historic harbor, lots of harborfront cafés, and easy, free parking. While the old harbor was too small to be of use during the invasion, this was the terminus of PLUTO (Pipe Line Under The Ocean), an 80-mile-long underwater fuel line from England. This (and an American version that terminated at Ste-Honorine, one town over) kept the war machine going after the Normandy toehold was established.

Big Red One Museum

Just outside humble Colleville-sur-Mer is this museum, a roadside warehouse filled with D-Day artifacts. This labor of love—one of many small D-Day museums in the area—is the life's work of Pierre, who for 30 years (since he was nine) has been gathering D-Day gear. "Big Red One" refers to the nickname of the 1st Infantry Division, the US Army troops in the first wave (with the 29th Infantry Division) to assault Omaha Beach. Pierre is happy to show visitors around. Near the museum, the main street of little Colleville-sur-Mer is lined with WWII photos.

Cost and Hours: €5, June-Aug daily 9:00-19:00, spring and fall Wed-Mon 10:00-12:00 & 14:00-18:00, closed in winter, Le Bray, Colleville-sur-Mer, tel. 02 31 21 53 81.

▲▲▲WWII Normandy American Cemetery and Memorial

The American Cemetery is a pilgrimage site for Americans visiting Normandy. Crowning a bluff just above Omaha Beach, 9,386 brilliant white, marble tombstones honor and remember the Americans who gave their lives on the beaches below to free Europe. France has given the US permanent free use of this 172-acre site, which is immaculately maintained by the American Battle Monuments Commission.

A fine modern visitors center prepares you for your visit. Plan to spend at least 1.5 hours at this stirring site.

Cost and Hours: Free, daily 9:00-18:00, mid-Sept-mid-April until 17:00, tel. 02 31 51 62 00, www.abmc.gov. Guided 45-minute tours are offered a few times a day in high season (usually at 11:00 and 14:00—call ahead to confirm times). The best WC is in the basement of the visitors center.

Getting There: The cemetery is just outside Colleville-sur-Mer, a 30-minute drive northwest of Bayeux. Follow signs on D-514 toward Colleville-sur-Mer; at the big roundabout in town (at the Overlord Museum, described later), follow signs leading to the cemetery (plenty of free parking).

Visiting the Cemetery

From the parking lot, stroll in a counter-clockwise circle through the lovingly tended, park-like grounds, making four stops: at the visitors center, the bluff overlooking Omaha Beach, memorials to the fallen and the missing, and finally the cemetery itself.

Visitors Center: The low-slung, modern building is mostly underground. On the arrival level (after security) are computer terminals providing access to a database containing the Roll of Honor—the names and story of each US serviceman whose remains lie in Europe.

The exhibit downstairs does more than recount the battle. It humanizes the men who fought and died, and are now buried, here. First find a large theater playing the video *Letters,* a touching 16-minute film with excerpts of letters home from the servicemen who now lie at rest here (shown on the half-hour, you can enter late). Next is a more casual theater with a fine 8-minute video, *On Their Shoulders.* Worthwhile exhibits and more videos (including an interview with Dwight Eisenhower) tell the stories of the brave individuals who gave their lives to liberate people they could not know, and shows the few possessions they left behind (about 25,000 Americans died in the battle for Normandy).

Next, a lineup of informational plaques provides a worthwhile and succinct overview of key events from September 1939 to June 5, 1944. Starting with June 6, 1944, the plaques present the progress of the landings in three-hour increments. Omaha Beach was

---

Hitler's Atlantic Wall

Germany defended its empire from Norway to the border of Spain with what Hitler called his "Festung Europa" (Fortress Europe), a supposedly impenetrable military shield, of which the so-called "Atlantic Wall" was a cornerstone.

German-controlled territory was growing from 1941 through 1942. But, after the Battle of Britain defeat, costly campaigns in Russia, the start of the Africa campaign, and the US entry into the war, things stalled for Germany. Rather than expanding, Hitler concentrated on consolidating. In 1942 he embarked on perhaps the greatest engineering project in history—fortifying (where necessary) almost 2,000 miles of European coastline in his Atlantic Wall.

Depending on the geography, Hitler strategically positioned huge gun batteries (to fire at big ships with guns with a 10-mile range) and smaller gun nests (about two per mile were needed—such as along the D-Day beaches).

These bunkers had to evolve quickly as technology and Germany's situation changed. At first, the Germans had air superiority and could leave their guns in the open air. Then, in 1943, the Allies took control of the skies, and the German guns had to be built into heavily fortified bunkers.

A half-million people—mostly forced labor—worked furiously on the Atlantic Wall as D-Day approached, and German commanders wondered exactly where the Allies would strike.

---

secured within 8 hours of the landings; within 24 hours it was safe to jump off your landing vehicle and slog onto the shore.

You'll exit the visitors center through the Sacrifice Gallery, with photos and bios of several individuals buried here, as well as those of some survivors. A voice reads the names of each of the cemetery's permanent residents on a continuous loop.

Bluff Overlooking Omaha Beach: Walk through a park designed to feel like America (with Kentucky bluegrass) to a bluff overlooking the piece of Normandy beach called "that embattled shore, the portal of freedom." Gazing at the quiet and peaceful beach, it's hard to imagine the horrific carnage of June 6, 1944. An orientation table looks over the beach and sea. You can't access the beach directly from here (the path is closed for security)—but those with a car can drive there easily; see Omaha Beach listing, later. A walk on the beach is a powerful experience.

• *With your back to the sea, climb the steps to reach the memorial (on the left).*

Memorial and Garden of the Missing: Overlooking the cemetery, you'll find a striking memorial with a soaring statue representing the spirit of American youth. Around the statue, giant reliefs of the Battle of Normandy and the Battle of Europe are etched on the walls. Behind is the semicircular Garden of the Missing, with the names of 1,557 soldiers who perished but whose remains were never found. A small bronze rosette next to a name indicates one whose body was eventually recovered.

Cemetery: Finally, wander through the peaceful and poignant sea of headstones that surrounds an interfaith chapel in the distance. Names, home states, and dates of death are inscribed on each tombstone, with dog-tag numbers etched into the lower backs. During the campaign, the dead were buried in temporary cemeteries throughout Normandy. After the war, the families of the soldiers could decide whether their loved ones should remain with their comrades or be brought home for burial. (About two-thirds were returned to America.)

Among the notable people buried here are General Theodore Roosevelt Jr., his brother Quentin (who died in World War I but was moved here at the request of the family), and the Niland brothers (of *Saving Private Ryan* fame). There are 33 pairs of brothers lying side by side, 1 father and son, 149 African Americans, 149 Jewish Americans, and 4 women. From the three generals buried here to the youngest casualty (a man of just 17), each grave is of equal worth.

• *To visit Omaha Beach itself, return up the long driveway to the round-about (at the Overlord Museum) and follow signs to* St-Laurent-sur-Mer *(D-514). But first consider popping into the Overlord Museum.*

Near the American Cemetery
Overlord Museum

While there are several museums more worth your sightseeing energy, you'll drive right by this purpose-built warehouse filled with Normandy's most impressive collection of WWII-era vehicles. Offering a good balance of American, British, and German exhibits, the museum's highlights include Germany's 88mm antiaircraft and antitank gun (formidable and feared by the Allies), a strafed German Panther tank (the best tank of the Third Reich), a Sherman tank, and a battlefield crane (recalling the on-the-go construction that took place in the field). You'll also see a horse—a reminder that (contrary to the Hollywood image), much of the German war machine was horse-powered. While there are bullet holes everywhere, this museum offers little in the way of personal accounts.

Cost and Hours: €7.50, daily June-Aug 9:30-19:00, March-

May and Sept 10:00-18:00, shorter hours off-season, closed Jan, tel. 02 31 22 00 55, www.overlordmuseum.com).

• *As you continue west on D-514 toward St-Laurent-sur-Mer, be on the lookout for...*

La Ferme de la Sapinière Calvados Tasting

La Ferme de la Sapinière is a stony apple farm welcoming guests with lots of free tastes along with a few photos of this family's (seven generations on this same farmstead) war experience. Drop-ins are welcome for tastings every day in season, or you can join a one-hour tour that explains the growing, pressing, and fermenting of apples in Normandy (followed by tasting). Try their airy and reasonable café if you're here at lunch.

Cost and Hours: Daily 9:30-19:30 except closed Sun Oct-March; tour/tasting—€3, in English April-mid-Nov Mon-Sat at 14:30, wise to call first; tel. 02 31 22 40 51, www.producteur-cidre.com. The farm is just off D-514 (Route de Port-en-Bessin) between the American Cemetery and St-Laurent-sur-Mer.

• *From the farm, return to westbound D-514. At the next roundabout, follow signs to* Viervilles/Mer par la Côte *to get to Omaha Beach.*

Omaha Beach Sights from St-Laurent to Vierville

Omaha Beach has five ravines (or "draws"), which provided avenues from the beach past the bluff to the interior. These were the goal of the troops that day. You'll drive down one (Avenue de la Libération)—passing the small Omaha Beach Memorial Museum—to reach the beach and two commemorative statues. Then drive west along the beach to the National Guard Memorial before leaving the beach up a second ravine.

Omaha Beach Memorial Museum
(Musée Memorial d'Omaha Beach)

Skip the museum (for most visitors, it's not worth the €7 entry), but WWII junkies should make a quick stop in the parking lot. On display is a rusted metal obstacle called a "Czech hedgehog"—thousands of these were placed on the beaches by the Germans to stop and immobilize landing craft and foil the Allies' advance. Find the American 155mm "Long Tom" gun nearby, and keep it in mind for your stop at Pointe du Hoc (this artillery piece is similar in size to the German guns that US Army Rangers targeted at that site). The Sherman tank here is one of the best examples of the type that landed on the D-Day beaches.

• *You'll hit the beach at a roundabout. Park your car for a look at the two memorials, and to take a little stroll on the beach.*

NORMANDY

On Omaha Beach

Walking on Omaha Beach is a powerful ▲▲▲ experience for history buffs. (While the beach is about 300 yards wide at low tide, it disappears at high tide.) Let the modern world melt away here and try to put yourself in those soldiers' combat boots:

You're wasted from lack of sleep and nervous anticipation. Now you get seasick too, as you're about to land in a small, flat-bottomed boat, cheek-to-jowl with 29 other soldiers. Your water-soaked pack feels like a boulder, and your gun feels even heavier. The boat's front ramp drops open, and you run for your life through water and sand for 500 yards onto this open beach, dodging bullets from above (the landings had to occur at low tide so that mines and obstacles would be visible).

Omaha Beach witnessed by far the most intense battles of any along the D-Day beaches. The hills above were heavily fortified with machine gun and mortar nests. (The aerial, naval, and supporting rocket fire that the Allies poured onto the German defenses failed to put them out of commission.) A single German machine gun could fire 1,200 rounds a minute. That's right—1,200. It's amazing that anyone survived. It's estimated that on the first day of the campaign, the Allies suffered 10,500 casualties (killed, wounded, and missing)—6,000 of whom were Americans. The highest casualty rates occurred here at Omaha Beach. More than 4,000 troops were killed and wounded here that day, many of whom drowned after being hit.

If the tide's out, you may notice remains of rusted metal objects just below the surface. Omaha Beach was littered with obstacles to disrupt the landings. Thousands of metal poles and "Czech hedgehogs," miles of barbed wire, and more than six million mines were scattered along this shore. At least 150,000 tons of metal were taken from the beaches after World War II, and they still didn't get it all. They never will.

▲▲Omaha Beach Viewpoint

Omaha was the most difficult of the D-Day beaches to assault. Nicknamed "Bloody Omaha," nearly half of all D-Day casualties were suffered here.

Two American assault units landed on Omaha Beach—the 1st Infantry Division (the "Big Red One," a veteran formation) and the 29th Infantry Division (a National Guard citizen army unit with little combat experience). For those troops, everything went wrong.

The four-mile-long beach is surrounded on three sides by cliffs—which were all heavily armed by Germans. The Allies pre-invasion bombing was ineffective, and about 500 Germans manning 11 gun nests pummeled the beach all day. Thanks to the concave shape of the beach, German artillery was positioned to hit every landing ship. It was an amphitheater of death.

Those who landed first and survived were pinned down, played dead, and came in with the tide over a period of four hours. Troops huddled against the beachhead for six to eight hours awaiting support—or death. But reinforcements kept coming. By the end of the day, 34,000 Americans had landed on the beach, and the Germans had been pushed back. In the next 34 days, these troops built 34 airfields. The final assault leading to Berlin was underway.

Memorial Statues

You're at the center of Omaha Beach. While only Americans landed on this beach, the flags recognize eight nations that took part

in the invasion. A striking modern metal statue (*The Braves*, 2004) rises from the waves in honor of the liberating forces and symbolizes the rise of freedom on the wings of hope. Next to that is a much older memorial from 1949. Built by thankful French, it was funded by selling scrap metal after the war and honors the two assaulting divisions, the 29th and 1st. You can read the motto of the 1st Division: "No mission too difficult. No sacrifice too great. Duty first."

• *Drive west from here along the beachfront, nicknamed "Golden Beach" before the war for its lovely sand.*

Beachfront Drive

While movie images lead us to believe the D-Day beaches were wild, they were actually lined with humble beach hotels and vacation cottages much like those you see today. After about 200 yards, you'll pass a small memorial at the site of the first temporary American cemetery (which was moved after about three days, as it provided a sad welcome to newly landed troops). If the tide is out, you'll see little skinny lakes between the sandbars. These were blood red on D-Day.

• *Drive until you reach a wharf stretching out from the Hôtel du Casino, at the base of the next ravine, where you'll find a couple of battlements and monuments. Park in one of two free lots.*

National Guard Memorial

The 29th Infantry Division, a National Guard unit, was one of the American assault units that landed on Omaha Beach on D-Day. While well-trained and disciplined, these troops were less experienced than the battle-tested 1st Division, their landing partners. A memorial to their sacrifices is built atop an 88mm German artillery casement.

Stand in front of the casement and look into the gun station. Rather than being aimed out to sea, this gun was aimed at the beach. It could shoot all the way across the beach in two seconds at the rate of two well-aimed shots per minute. Notice the desperate bullet holes all around the gun. Its twin was several miles away at the opposite end of Omaha Beach. In 1944 the Germans built this gun station and hid it inside the facade of a fake beach hotel. A second gun casement with two 50mm guns, a few steps to the west, added to the Omaha Beach carnage.

Another memorial here, with two bronze soldiers, commemorates the so-called Bedford Boys. The little Virginia town of Bedford contributed 35 men to the landing forces—19 were killed.

The nearby pier offers good views—handy if the tide is in. If you'd like to walk out and along the beach, this is the best chance.

Look out to the ocean. It was here that the Americans assembled their own floating bridge and artificial harbor (à la Arromanches; for a description, find the panel near the blue telescope). The harbor was under furious construction for 12 days before being destroyed by an unusually vicious June storm (the artificial port at Arromanches and a makeshift port at Utah Beach survived and were used until November 1944).

• *From here, drive uphill on D-517 to return to coastal road D-514 at Vierville-Sur-Mer (as you head up, immediately look above and to your left to find two small concrete window frames high in the cliff that served as German machine gun nests).*

When you hit D-514, turn right (west) and head toward Pointe du Hoc. Along the way, just past the turn-off for the hamlet of Englesqueville la Percée (D-125), you'll have an opportunity to quench your thirst.

Lebrec Calvados Tasting

A 10th-century fortified farm on the left offers Calvados tastings. To try some, cross the drawbridge and park on the right. Ring the rope bell and meet charming owners Soizic and Bernard Lebrec. They're happy to offer a free three-part tasting: cider, Pommeau (a mix of apple juice and Calvados), and a six-year-old Calvados. Consider their enticing selection of drinkable souvenirs. Bernard likes to share his family's D-Day scrapbook (his farm was requisitioned as a military base in 1944). Ask to see the farm's own D-Day monument. Erected in September 1944—even before the war was over—it's likely one of the earliest in France (farm tel. 09 60 38 60 17).

• *Rejoin D-514, and at next roundabout, follow signs to Pointe du Hoc.*

▲▲▲Pointe du Hoc Ranger Monument

The intense bombing of the beaches by Allied forces is best imagined at this bluff. This point of land was the Germans' most heavily fortified position along the Utah and Omaha beaches. The cliffs are so severe here that the Germans turned their defenses around to face what they assumed would be an attack from inland. Yet US Army Rangers famously scaled the steep cliffs to disable the German gun battery. Pointe du Hoc's bomb-cratered, lunar-like landscape and remaining bunkers make it one of the most evocative of the D-Day sites.

Cost and Hours: Free, daily 9:00-18:00, mid-Sept-mid-April until 17:00, tel. 02 31 51 62 00, www.abmc.gov/cemeteries-memorials. It's off route D-514, 20 minutes west of the American Cemetery, in Cricqueville-en-Bessin.

Crowd Control: The sight is most crowded in the afternoons. Avoid 14:00-16:00 on peak days.

Visiting Pointe du Hoc

Park, get oriented at the visitors center (watch the 8-minute film that explains the daring Ranger mission), and follow the white gravel path (with plenty of info panels) through the cratered landscape, circling counterclockwise with two battlements to climb around before winding your way back to the parking lot.

Lunar Landscape: The craters are the result of 10 kilotons of bombs—nearly the explosive power of the atomic bomb at Hiroshima—but dropped over seven weeks. This was a jumbo German gun battery, with more than a mile of tunnels connecting its battlements. Its six 155mm guns could fire as far as 13 miles—good enough to hit anything on either beach. For the American D-Day landings to succeed, this nest had to be taken out. So the Allies pulverized it with bombs, starting in April 1944 and continuing until June 6—making this the most intensely bombarded of the D-Day targets. Even so, the heavily reinforced bunkers survived.

Walk around. The battle-scarred German bunkers and the cratered landscape remain much as the Rangers left them. You can crawl in and out of the bunkers at your own risk. Upon entering the site, you'll see an opening on your left that's as wide as a manhole cover and about six feet deep. This was a machine-gun nest. Three soldiers would be holed up down there—a commander, a gun loader, and the gunner.

There are three viewing platforms. Work your way to the bunker with the memorial at the edge of the bluff.

Dagger Memorial: The memorial represents the Ranger dagger used to help scale the cliffs. Here, it's thrust into the command center of the battery. Exploring the heavily fortified interior of this observation bunker (officers' quarters, enlisted quarters, and command room) with its charred ceiling and battered hardware, you can imagine the fury of the attack that finally took this station. The slit is only for observing. This bunker was the "eyes" of the guns—from here spotters directed the firing via hard-wired telephone, sending coordinates to the gunners at the six 155mm guns.

Look over the cliff stretching 500 yards to the right, and think about the 225 handpicked Rangers who attempted a castle-style assault on the gun battery. They used rocket-propelled grappling hooks connected to 150-foot ropes, and climbed ladders borrowed from London fire departments.

Timing was critical, though; the Rangers had just 30 minutes to get off the beach before the rising tide would overcome them. After finally reaching the clifftop, the Rangers found that the guns had been moved—the Germans had put telegraph poles in their place as decoys. The Rangers eventually found the operational guns hidden a half-mile inland and destroyed them.

Three American presidents (Eisenhower in 1963, Reagan in 1984, and Clinton in 1994) have stood atop this bunker to honor the heroics of those Rangers.

Viewing Platform: Navigate the craters inland about 100 yards to another bunker capped with a viewing platform. Climb up top to appreciate the intensity of the blasts that made the craters and disabled phone lines—cutting communication between the command bunker and the guns to render them blind.

Following the white gravel lane to circle back to the visitors center, you'll pass a big French 155mm gun barrel from World War I. While state-of-the-art in 1917, 27 years later—in World War II—this gun was still formidable. Six of these were what Pointe du Hoc was all about.

• *Our tour of the American Omaha Beach sights is finished. But to consider the other side of the conflict, it's worth visiting the **German Military Cemetery** at La Cambe. To get there from Pointe du Hoc, follow D-514 west, then turn off in Grandcamp following signs to* La Cambe *and* Bayeux *(D-199). After crossing over the autoroute, turn left at the first country road and follow it around to the cemetery.*

▲German Military Cemetery at La Cambe (Cimetière Militaire Allemand)

To ponder German losses, visit this somber, thought-provoking final resting place of 21,000 German soldiers. Compared to the American Cemetery at St. Laurent, this site is more about humility than hero appreciation. The largest of six German cemeteries in Normandy, it's appropriately bleak, with two graves per simple marker and dark basalt crosses in groups of five scattered about. The circular mound in the middle—with a cross, flanked by a grieving mother and father—covers the remains of about 300 mostly unknown soldiers.

Wandering among the tombstones, notice the ages of the soldiers who gave their lives for a cause some were too young to understand. "Strm" indicates storm trooper—the most ideologically motivated troops which undergirded the German army. About a fifth of the dead are unidentified, listed as "Ein Deutscher Soldat." You'll also notice many who died after the war ended—a reminder that over 5,000 German POWs perished in France clearing the minefields their countrymen had planted.

A field hospital was sited in this area during the war, and originally American troops were buried here. After the war, those remains were moved to the current American Cemetery or returned to the US. A small visitors center, with a focus on building peace, displays the German soldiers' last letters home and a case of German artifacts. Visiting here, you can imagine the complexity of dealing with this for Germans.

Cost and Hours: Free, daily April-Oct 8:00-19:00, off-season generally 9:00-17:00, tel. 02 31 22 70 76.

Getting There: La Cambe is 15 minutes south of Pointe du Hoc and 20 minutes west of Bayeux (from the autoroute, follow signs reading *Cimetière Militaire Allemand*).

Sleeping near Omaha Beach

($$$$ = Splurge, $$$ = Pricier, $$ = Moderate, $ = Budget)
With a car, you can sleep in the countryside, find better deals on accommodations, and wake up a stone's throw from many landing sites. Besides these recommended spots, you'll pass scads of good-value *chambres d'hôtes* as you prowl the D-Day beaches. The last two places are a few minutes toward Bayeux on D-517 in the village of Formigny.

$$ Hôtel la Sapinière** is a find just a few steps from the beach at Vierville-sur-Mer. A grassy, beach-bungalow kind of place, it has 15 sharp, crisp rooms, all with private patios, and a lighthearted, good-value restaurant/bar (family rooms, outside St-Laurent-sur-Mer 10 minutes west of the American Cemetery—take D-517 down to the beach, turn right and keep going to 100 Rue da la 2ème Division D'Infanterie US, tel. 02 31 92 71 72, www.la-sapiniere.fr, sci-thierry@wanadoo.fr).

$$ Hôtel du Casino** is a good place to experience Omaha Beach. This average-looking hotel has surprisingly comfortable and stylish rooms and sits alone, overlooking the beach in Vierville-sur-Mer, between the American Cemetery and Pointe du Hoc. All rooms have views, but the best face the sea: Ask introverted owner Madame Clémençon for *côté mer* (view restaurant with *menus* from

€30, café/bar on the beach below, Rue de la Percée, tel. 02 31 22 41 02, hotel-du-casino@orange.fr, www.logishotels.com). Don't confuse this with Hôtel du Casino in St-Valery-en-Caux.

At **$ Ferme du Mouchel,** animated Odile rents three colorful and good rooms with impeccable gardens in a lovely farm setting in the village of Formigny (cash only, includes breakfast, 3-day minimum in summer, tel. 02 31 22 53 79, mobile 06 15 37 50 20, www.ferme-du-mouchel.com, odile.lenourichel@orange.fr). Follow the sign from the main road (D-517), then turn left down the tree-lined lane when you see the *Le Mouchel* sign.

$ La Ferme aux Chats sits on D-517 across from the church in the center of Formigny and has welcoming owners, a cozy lounge with a library of D-Day information, and four clean, comfortable, modern rooms. Explore the sprawling gardens out back, with chickens, ducks, fish...and nine of those namesake cats (includes breakfast, tel. 02 31 51 00 88, www.lafermeauxchats.fr, info@fermeauxchats.fr).

Utah Beach

Utah Beach, added late in the planning for D-Day, proved critical. This was where two US paratrooper units (the 82nd and the 101st Airborne Divisions) dropped behind enemy lines the night before the invasion, as dramatized in *Band of Brothers* and *The Longest Day.* Many landed off-target. It was essential for the invading forces to succeed here, then push up the peninsula (which had been intentionally flooded by the Nazis) to the port city of Cherbourg.

Utah Beach itself was taken in 45 minutes at the cost of 194 American lives. More paratroopers died (over 1,000) preparing the way for the actual beach landing. Fortunately for the Americans who stormed this beach, it was defended not by Germans but mostly by conscripted Czechs, Poles, and Russians who had little motivation for this fight.

While the brutality on this beach paled in comparison with the carnage on Omaha Beach, many of the paratroopers missed their targets—causing confusion and worse—and the units that landed here faced a three-week battle before finally taking Cherbourg. Ultimately over 800,000 Americans (and 220,000 vehicles) landed on Utah Beach over a five-month period.

• *These sights are listed in order you'll find them coming from Bayeux or Omaha Beach. For the first two, take the Utah Beach exit (D-913) from N-13 and turn right.*

Church at Angoville-au-Plain

At this simple Romanesque church, two American medics—Kenneth Moore and Robert Wright—treated the wounded while battles raged only steps away. On June 6, American paratroopers landed around Angoville-au-Plain, a few miles inland of Utah Beach, and met fierce resistance from German forces. The two medics set up shop in the small church, and treated both American and German soldiers for 72 hours straight, saving many lives. German patrols entered the church on a few occasions. The medics insisted that the soldiers park their guns outside or leave the church—incredibly, they did. In an amazing coincidence, this 12th-century church is dedicated to two martyrs who were doctors.

A faded informational display outside the church recounts the events here; an English handout is available inside. Pass through the small cemetery and enter the church. Inside, several wooden pews toward the rear still have visible bloodstains. Find the new window that honors the American medics and another that honors the paratroopers.

Cost and Hours: €3 requested donation for brochure, daily 9:00-18:00, 2 minutes off D-913 toward Utah Beach.

▲▲▲Utah Beach Landing Museum (Musée du Débarquement)

This is the best museum located on the D-Day beaches, and worth the 45-minute drive from Bayeux. For the Allied landings to succeed, many coordinated tasks had to be accomplished: Paratroopers had to be dropped inland, the resistance had to disable bridges and cut communications, bombers had to soften German defenses by delivering their payloads on target and on time, the infantry had to land safely on the beaches, and supplies had to follow the infantry closely. This thorough yet manageable museum pieces those many parts together in a series of fascinating exhibits and displays.

Cost and Hours: €8, daily June-Sept 9:30-19:00, Oct-Nov and Jan-May 10:00-18:00, closed Dec, last entry one hour before closing, tel. 02 33 71 53 35, off D-913 at Plage de la Madeleine, www.utah-beach.com. Park in the "obligitaire" lot, then walk five minutes to reach the museum.

Film and Tours: Check for the next English video time as you pay. Guided museum tours are offered twice a day: Call ahead for times or ask when you arrive (tours are free, tips appropriate).

Visiting the Museum

Built around the remains of a concrete German bunker, the museum nestles in the sand dunes on Utah Beach with floors above and below beach level. Your visit follows a one-way route past rooms of artifacts. It starts with background about the American landings on Utah Beach (over 20,000 troops landed on the first day alone) and the German defense strategy (Rommel was in charge of maintaining the western end of Hitler's Atlantic Wall—see the sidebar on page 279). See the outstanding 12-minute film, *Victory in the Sand*, which sets the stage.

The highlight of the museum is the display of innovative invasion equipment with videos demonstrating how it all worked: the remote-controlled Goliath mine, the LVT-2 Water Buffalo and Duck amphibious vehicles, the wooden Higgins landing craft, and a fully restored B-26 bomber with its zebra stripes and 11 menacing machine guns, without which the landings would not have been possible (the yellow bomb icons painted onto the cockpit indicate the number of missions a plane had flown).

Upstairs is a large, glassed-in room overlooking the beach. From here, you'll peer over re-created German trenches and feel what it must have felt like to have been defending against such a massive and coordinated onslaught.

Outside the museum, find the beach access where Americans first broke through Hitler's Atlantic Wall. You can hike up to the small bluff, which is lined with monuments to the branches of military service that participated in the fight. A big gun sits atop a buried battlement, part of a vast underground network of German defenses. And all around is the hardware of battle frozen in time.

• *To reach the next several sights, follow the coastal route D-421 and signs to Ste-Mère Eglise.*

▲Ste-Mère Eglise

This celebrated village lies 15 minutes west of Utah Beach and was the first village to be liberated by the Americans. The area around Ste-Mère Eglise was the center of action for American paratroopers, whose objective was to land behind enemy lines before dawn on D-Day and wreak havoc in support of the Americans landing at Utah Beach that day.

For *The Longest Day* movie buffs, Ste-Mère Eglise is a necessary pilgrimage. It was near this village that many paratroopers, facing terrible weather and heavy antiaircraft fire, landed off-target—and many landed in the town. One American paratrooper dangled from the town's church steeple for two hours (a parachute has been reinstalled on the steeple where Private John Steele's became snagged). And though many paratroopers were killed in the first hours of the invasion, the Americans eventually overcame their poor start and managed to take the town. (Steele survived his ordeal and the war.) These troops who dropped (or glided) in behind enemy lines in the dark played a critical role in the success of the Utah Beach landings by securing roads and bridges.

Today, the village greets travelers with flag-draped streets (and plenty of parking). The 700-year-old **medieval church** on the town square now holds two contemporary stained-glass windows. One, in the back, celebrates the heroism of the Allies (made in 1984 for the 40th anniversary of the invasion). The window in the left transept features St. Michael, patron saint of paratroopers (made in 1969 for the 25th anniversary).

The **TI** on the square across from the church has loads of information and rents audiovisual guides with GPS, allowing you to discover the town and D-Day sites in the area on your own (€8, €250 deposit). It's called the **Open Sky Museum**—but actually it's a three-hour driving tour of the region linking all the D-Day sites together (TI open July-Aug Mon-Sat 9:00-18:30, Sun 10:00-16:00; Sept and April-June closes Mon-Sat 13:00-14:00 and Sun at 13:00; shorter hours off-season; 6 Rue Eisenhower, tel. 02 33 21 00 33, www.sainte-mere-eglise.info).

Museums in and near Ste-Mère Eglise
▲Airborne Museum
Housed in three buildings, this collection is dedicated to the daring aerial landings that were essential to the success of D-Day. During the invasion, in the Utah Beach sector alone, 23,000 men were dropped from planes or landed in gliders, along with countless vehicles and tons of supplies.

Cost and Hours: €8, daily May-Aug 9:00-19:00, April and Sept 9:30-18:30, shorter hours off-season and closed Jan, 14 Rue Eisenhower, tel. 02 33 41 41 35, www.airborne-museum.org.

Visiting the Museum: Your visit to the museum unfolds in three parts across three buildings. In the first building, you'll see a **Waco glider,** one of 104 such gliders flown into Normandy at first light on D-Day to land supplies in fields to support the paratroopers. Each glider could be used only once. Feel the canvas fuselage and check out the bare-bones interior. The second, larger building holds a **Douglas C-47** plane that dropped parachutists and supplies. Here you'll find mannequins of soldiers with their uniforms, displays of their personal possessions and weapons, and two movies: One focuses on the airborne invasion (20 minutes), and the other venerates President Ronald Reagan's 1984 trip to Normandy.

A third structure, labeled **Operation Neptune,** puts you into the paratrooper's experience starting with a night flight and jump, then tracks your progress on the ground past enemy fire using elaborate models and sound effects. Don't miss the touching video showing the valor of General Theodore Roosevelt Jr. on D-Day.

• *From Ste-Mère Eglise, head 10 minutes on N-13 (back toward Bayeux) to St-Côme-du-Mont.*

▲D-Day Experience
Just behind the Dead Man's Corner Museum is this new space dedicated to the paratroopers of the 101st Airborne Division. It's a labor of museum love, with lots of artifacts and uniforms capped

by two creative experiences designed to help you feel what it might have been like to be in the 101st. First, enter the briefing room for a 10-minute review of your mission by a hologram commander. Then climb into an authentic Douglas C-47 (built in 1943, it actually flew on D-Day), buckle in, survive a simulated flight through flak across the English Channel, then crash-land before you can parachute out.

Cost and Hours: €12, daily April-Sept 9:30-19:00, Oct-March 10:00-18:00, 2 Vierge de l'Amont (D-913), St-Côme-du-Mont, tel. 02 33 23 61 95, www.paratrooper-museum.org.

Canadian D-Day Sites

The Canadians' assignment for the Normandy invasions was to work with British forces to take the city of Caen. They hoped to make quick work of Caen, then move on. That didn't happen. The Germans poured most of their reserves, including tanks, into the city and fought ferociously for a month. The Allies didn't occupy Caen until August 1944.

Juno Beach Centre

Located on the beachfront in the Canadian sector, this facility is dedicated to teaching travelers about the vital role Canadian forces played in the invasion, and about Canada in general. Canada declared war on Germany two years before the United States, a fact little recognized by most Americans today (after the US and Britain, Canada contributed the largest number of troops—14,000).

Cost and Hours: €7, €11 with guided tour of Juno Beach—highly recommended, daily April-Sept 9:30-19:00, Oct and March 10:00-18:00, Nov-Dec and Feb 10:00-17:00, closed Jan, tel. 02 31 37 32 17, www.junobeach.org.

Tours: The best way to appreciate this sector of the D-Day beaches is to take a tour with one of the Centre's capable Canadian guides, who will take you down into two bunkers and a tunnel of the German defense network (€5.50 for tour alone, €11 with admission, 45 minutes; April-Oct generally at 10:30 and 14:30, July-Aug also at 11:30, 13:30, and 16:30; verify times prior to your visit).

Getting There: It's in Courseulles-sur-Mer, about 15 minutes east of Arromanches off D-514. Approaching from Arromanches, as you enter the village of Grave-sur-Mer, watch for the easy-to-miss *Juno Beach-Mémorial* sign marking the turnoff on the left; you'll drive the length of a sandy spit (passing a marina) to the end of the road at Voie des Français Libres, where you'll find the parking lot.

Visiting Juno Beach: Your visit includes many thoughtful exhibits that bring to life Canada's unique ties with Britain, the US, and France, and explains how the war front affected the home front in Canada. You'll also learn about the heroism of Canadian soldiers and the immense challenges they faced during and after their landings here. A scrolling list honors the 45,000 Canadians who died in World War II; a large hall introduces visitors to the diversity of Canada; and a powerful, 12-minute film captures Canada's D-Day experience. Take advantage of the Centre's eager-to-help, red-shirted "student-guides" (young Canadians working a seven-month stint here).

Nearby: Between the main road and the Juno Beach Centre, you'll spot a huge stainless-steel double cross (by a row of French flags). This is La Croix de Lorraine, marking the site where General de Gaulle returned to France (after four years of exile) on June 14, 1944.

Canadian Cemetery at Bény-sur-Mer

This small, touching cemetery hides a few miles above the Juno Beach Centre. To me, it captures the understated nature of Canadians perfectly. Surrounded by pastoral farmland with distant views to the beaches, you'll find 2,000 graves marked with maple leaves and the soldiers' names and ages. Most fell in the first weeks of the D-Day assault. Like the American Cemetery, this is Canadian territory on French land.

Getting There: From Courseulles-sur-Mer, follow signs to Caen on D-79. After about 2.5 miles, follow signs to the cemetery (and Bayeux) at the roundabout. The cemetery is on Route de Reviers.

Caen Memorial Museum

Caen, the modern capital of lower Normandy, has the most thorough (and by far the priciest) WWII museum in France. Located at the site of an important German headquarters during World War II, its official name is Caen-Normandy Memorial: Center for History and Peace (Mémorial de Caen-Normandie: Cité de l'Histoire pour la Paix). With numerous exhibits on the lead-up to World War II, coverage of the war in both Europe and the Pacific, accounts of the Holocaust and Nazi-occupied France, the Cold War aftermath, and more, it effectively puts the Battle of Normandy into a broader context and is worth ▲▲. But it lacks the sharp focus of some

of the better D-Day museums at the beaches (such as the Utah Beach Landing Museum).

Town of Caen: Though Bayeux or Arromanches—which are smaller—make the best base for most D-Day sights, train travelers with limited time might find urban Caen more practical because of its buses to Honfleur and convenient car-rental offices near the train station.

The **TI** is on Place St. Pierre, 10 long blocks from the train station—take the tram to the St. Pierre stop (Mon-Sat 9:30-18:30, until 19:00 July-Aug, Sun 10:00-13:00 & 14:00-17:00 except closed Sun Oct-March, drivers follow *Parking Château* signs, tel. 02 31 27 14 14, www.tourisme.caen.fr).

A looming château, built by William the Conqueror in 1060, marks the city's center. To the west, modern Rue St. Pierre is a popular shopping area and pedestrian zone. The more historic Vagueux quarter to the east has many restaurants and cafés.

GETTING THERE

By Car: From Bayeux, it's a straight shot on the N-13 to Caen (30 minutes). Finding the Caen Memorial Museum is quick and easy. It's a half-mile off the ring-road expressway (*périphérique nord,* take *sortie* #7, look for white *Le Mémorial* signs). When leaving the museum, follow *Toutes Directions* signs back to the ring road.

By Train or Bus: By train, Caen is two hours from Paris (12/day) and 20 minutes from Bayeux (20/day). The modern train station sits next to the *gare routière,* where buses from Honfleur arrive (2/day express or 4/day via coastal route—see page 247). Car-rental offices are right across the street. There's no baggage storage at the station, though it is available at the museum.

Taxis usually wait in front of the train station and will get you to the museum in 15 minutes (about €15 one-way—more on Sun). A **tram-and-bus** combination takes about 30 minutes (Mon-Sat only): Take the tram right in front of the train station (line A, direction: Campus 2, or line B, direction: St. Clair; buy €1.30 ticket from machine and validate on tram and again on bus, good for entire trip). Get off at the third tram stop (Bernières), then transfer

NORMANDY

to frequent bus #2 (cross the street). For transit maps, see www. twisto.fr.

To return to the station, take bus #2 across from the museum (museum has schedule, buy ticket from driver and validate); transfer to the tram at the Quatrans stop in downtown Caen. Either line A or line B will take you to the station (Gare SNCF stop).

ORIENTATION TO CAEN MEMORIAL MUSEUM

Cost and Hours: €19.50, ticket valid for 24 hours, free for all veterans and kids under 10 (ask about good family rates), €21.50 combo-ticket with Arromanches 360° theater (see page 272). Open March-Oct daily 9:00-19:00; Nov-Dec and Feb Tue-Sun 9:30-18:00, closed Mon; closed most of Jan; last entry one hour before closing; helpful audioguide-€4 (Esplanade Général Eisenhower, tel. 02 31 06 06 44—as in June 6, 1944, www.memorial-caen.fr).

Services: The museum provides free baggage storage and free supervised babysitting for children under 10. There's also a large gift shop with plenty of books in English.

Eating: An all-day sandwich shop/café sits above the entry area, and there's a restaurant with garden-side terrace (lunch only). Picnicking in the gardens is also an option.

Minivan Tours: The museum offers good-value minivan tours covering the key sites along the D-Day beaches. The all-day "D-Day Tour" package (€119) is designed for day-trippers and includes pick-up/drop-off at the Caen train station, a tour of the museum followed by lunch, and a five-hour tour of the American sector. Canadians have a similar tour option to Juno Beach. Full-size bus tours are also available in summer (€45, June-Aug, no tours Tue or Sun, includes museum entry and half-day tour of the beaches).

Planning Your Museum Time: Allow two hours for your visit. The museum is divided into two major wings: one devoted to the years before and during World War II, and the other to the Cold War years and later. Most visitors will want to focus on the World War II wing.

Visiting the Museum

Begin by watching *Jour J (D-Day)*, an old-fashioned 15-minute film that shows the build-up to D-Day (runs every 30 minutes from 10:00 to 18:00, works in any language). Although snippets come from the movie *The Longest Day* and German army training films, some footage is of actual battle scenes.

Opposite from the theater, find *Début de la Visite* signs and begin your museum tour with a downward-spiral stroll, tracing (al-

NORMANDY

most psychoanalyzing) the path Europe followed from the end of World War I to the rise of fascism to World War II.

The **"World Before 1945"** exhibit, on the lower level, gives a thorough look at how World War II was fought—from General Charles de Gaulle's London radio broadcasts to Hitler's early missiles to wartime fashion to the D-Day landings. Videos, maps, and countless displays relate the stories of the Battle of Britain, the French Resistance, Vichy France, German death camps, the Battle of Stalingrad, and the war in the Pacific. Several powerful exhibits summarize the terrible human costs of World War II (Russia alone saw 21 million of its people die during the war; the US lost 300,000). A smaller, separate exhibit (on your way back up to the main hall) covers just D-Day and the Battle of Normandy.

The **"World After 1945"** wing sets the scene for the Cold War with photos of European cities destroyed during World War II. It continues with insights into the psychological battle waged by the Soviet Union and the US for the hearts and minds of their people until the fall of communism. The wing culminates with a major display recounting the division of Berlin and its unification after the fall of the Wall.

Two more worthwhile stops are outside (exit below the cafeteria, then climb down the stairs). First, you can walk through the former **command bunker** of German General Wilhelm Richter, where you'll see exhibits on the Nazi Atlantic Wall defense in Normandy—for which Richter was in charge.

The finale is a walk through the **US Armed Forces Memorial Garden** (Vallée du Mémorial). On a visit here, I was bothered at first by the seemingly unaware laughing of lighthearted children, unable to appreciate the gravity of their surroundings. Then I read this inscription on the pavement: "From the heart of our land flows the blood of our youth, given to you in the name of freedom." And their laughter made me happy.

Mont St-Michel

For more than a thousand years, the distant silhouette of this island abbey has sent pilgrims' spirits soaring. Today, it does the same for tourists. Mont St-Michel, one of the top pilgrimage sites of Christendom through the ages, floats like a mirage on the horizon. For centuries devout Christians endeavored to make a great

pilgrimage once in their lifetimes. If they couldn't afford Rome, Jerusalem, or Santiago de Compostela, they came here, earning the same religious merits. Today, several million visitors—and a steady trickle of pilgrims—flood the single street of the tiny island each year. If this place seems built for tourism, in a sense it was. It's accommodated, fed, watered, and sold trinkets to generations of travelers who visit its towering abbey.

Orientation to Mont St-Michel

Mont St-Michel is surrounded by a vast mudflat and connected to the mainland by a bridge. Think of the island as having three parts: the Benedictine abbey soaring above, the spindly road leading to the abbey, and the medieval fortifications below. The lone main street (Grand Rue), with the island's hotels, restaurants, and trinkets, is mobbed in-season from 11:00 to 16:00. Though several tacky history-in-wax museums tempt visitors with hustlers out front, these are commercial gimmicks with no real artifacts. The only worthwhile sights are the abbey at the summit and a ramble on the ramparts, which offers mudflat views and an escape from the tourist zone.

The "village" on the mainland side of the causeway (called La Caserne) was built to accommodate tour buses. It consists of a lineup of modern hotels, a handful of shops, vast parking lots, and an efficient shuttle bus zipping to and from the island every few minutes.

Remember, the tourist tide comes in each morning and recedes late each afternoon. To avoid crowds, arrive late in the afternoon, sleep on the island or nearby on the mainland, and depart early.

TOURIST INFORMATION

On the mainland, near the parking lot's shuttle stop, look for the excellent **visitors center** (daily April-Sept 9:00-19:00, off-season 10:00-18:00, www.accueilmontsaintmichel.fr). The official **TI** is on the island (just inside the town gate, daily July-Aug 9:15-19:00, March-June and Sept-Oct 9:15-12:30 & 14:00-18:00, shorter hours off-season; tel. 02 33 60 14 30, www.ot-montsaintmichel.com). A post office and ATM are 50 yards beyond the TI.

Either office is a good place to ask about English tour times for the abbey, bus schedules, and the tide table *(horaires des marées)*.

ARRIVAL IN MONT ST-MICHEL

Prepare for lots of walking as the island—a small mountain capped by an abbey—is entirely traffic-free.

By Train: The nearest train station is five miles away in Pontorson (called Pontorson/Mont St-Michel). Be aware that few

An Island Again

In 1878, a causeway was built that allowed Mont St-Michel's pilgrims to come and go regardless of the tide. The causeway increased the flow of visitors, but blocked the flow of water around the island. The result: Much of the bay silted up, and Mont St-Michel was gradually becoming part of the mainland.

An ambitious project to keep it an island was completed in 2015. The first phase was the construction of a dam (barrage) on the Couesnon River, which traps water at high tide and releases it at low tide, flushing the bay and forcing sediment out to the sea. The dam is an attraction in its own right, with informative panels and great views of the abbey from its sleek and picnic-friendly wood benches. Parking lots at the foot of the island were removed and a huge mainland parking lot built, with shuttle buses ferrying visitors to the island.

Finally, workers tore down the old causeway and replaced it with the super-sleek, artistically swooping bridge you see today. The bridge allows water to flow freely around Mont St-Michel, preserving its island character. Those wanting to experience Mont St-Michel at its natural best should plan their trip to coincide with high tide (see www.ot-montsaintmichel.com for tide tables).

trains stop here, and Sunday service is almost nonexistent. Trains are met by buses that take passengers right to Mont St-Michel (€3, 12 buses/day July-Aug, 8/day Sept-June, fewer on Sun, 20 minutes, tel. 02 14 13 20 15, www.accueilmontsaintmichel.com). Taxis between Pontorson and Mont St-Michel get you to the shuttle stop (about €25, €30 after 19:00 and on weekends/holidays; tel. 02 33 60 33 23 or 02 33 60 82 70).

By Bus: Buses from Rennes stop next to the visitor center and shuttle stop in the parking lot. From Bayeux, it's faster by shuttle van (see page 261).

By Car: Day-trippers are directed to a sea of parking (remember your parking area number). To avoid extra walking, take your parking ticket with you and pay at the machines near the visitors center (€11.70/24 hours, no reentry privileges, machines accept cash and US credit cards, parking tel. 02 14 13 20 15). If you arrive after 19:00 and stay only for the evening, parking is free; if you arrive after 19:00 and leave before 11:30 the next morning, the fee is €4.

If you're staying at a hotel on the island or in La Caserne, you'll receive a parking-gate code from your hotel. As you approach the parking areas, follow wheelchair icon signs until you come to a gate. Those staying on the island should turn right here and follow signs for *Parking P3*. Those staying at the foot of the island in La

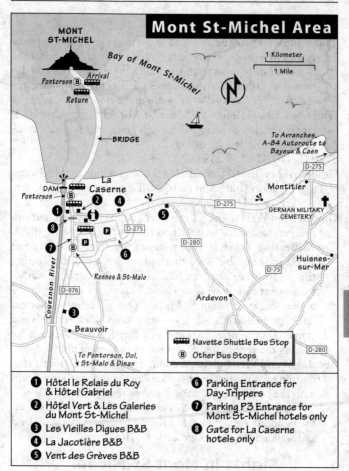

Mont St-Michel Area

MONT
ST-MICHEL

Bay of Mont St-Michel

Pontorson Ⓑ 🚌 *Arrival*

🚌 *Return*

1 Kilometer

1 Mile

◄ BRIDGE

To Avranches,
A-84 Autoroute to
Bayeux & Caen

D-275

DAM
Pontorson Ⓑ

🚌 La
Caserne

❹

D-275

Montitier

GERMAN MILITARY
CEMETERY

❶ 🚌

❷

🚌 ❶

❺

❽ www

P

D-275

D-280

❼

🚌 Ⓑ

P

Huisnes-
sur-Mer

D-75

❻

Rennes & St-Malo

D-976

Ardevon

❸

Beauvoir

Navette Shuttle Bus Stop

Ⓑ Other Bus Stops

D-280

To Pontorson, Dol,
St-Malo & Dinan

❶ Hôtel le Relais du Roy
& Hôtel Gabriel

❷ Hôtel Vert & Les Galeries
du Mont St-Michel

❸ Les Vieilles Digues B&B

❹ La Jacotière B&B

❺ Vent des Grèves B&B

❻ Parking Entrance for
Day-Trippers

❼ Parking P3 Entrance for
Mont St-Michel hotels only

❽ Gate for La Caserne
hotels only

Caserne will continue straight at the first gate (enter your code),
then drive right to their hotel (€4 hotel parking fee added to your
bill; you'll get a ticket to exit the gate).

From the Parking Lot or La Caserne to the Island: You can either **walk** (about 50 level and scenic minutes) or ride the free and
frequent **shuttle bus** (*navette,* 12 minutes). The shuttle makes four
stops: at the parking lot visitors center, in La Caserne village, near
the dam at the start of the bridge, and at the island side of the
bridge, about 200 yards from the island itself. The return shuttle
stop is about a hundred yards farther from the island (where the
benches start). You can also ride either way in the horse-drawn
maringote (double-decker wagon, €5.50).

NORMANDY

HELPFUL HINTS

Tides: The tides here rise above 50 feet—the largest and most dangerous in Europe. High tides *(grandes marées)* lap against the island TI door, where you should find tide tables posted (also posted at mainland visitors center). If you plan to explore the mudflats, it's essential to be aware of the tides.

Groceries: Les Galeries du Mont St-Michel in La Caserne is stocked with souvenirs and enough groceries to make a credible picnic (daily 9:00-20:00).

Taxi: Call 02 33 60 33 23 or 02 33 60 26 89.

Guided Abbey Tours: Considering the information in this chapter and the tours (and audio tours) available at the abbey, a private guide is probably not necessary.

Guided Mud Walks: The TI can refer you to companies that run inexpensive guided walks across the bay (with some English).

Crowd-Beating Tips: If you're staying overnight, arrive after 16:00 and leave by 11:00 to avoid the worst crowds. During the day you can skip the human traffic jam on the island's main street by following this book's suggested walking routes (under "Sights in Mont St-Michel"); the *gendarmerie* shortcut (see page 302) works best if you want to avoid both crowds and stairs. If you're here from mid-July through August, consider touring the abbey after dinner (it's open until midnight).

Best Light and Views: Because Mont St-Michel faces southwest, morning light from the bridge is eye-popping. Early risers win with the best light—and the fewest other tourists.

After dark, the island is magically floodlit. Views from the ramparts are sublime. But for the best view, exit the island and walk out on the bridge a few hundred yards.

Sights in Mont St-Michel

The Bay of Mont St-Michel

Since the 6th century, the vast Bay of Mont St-Michel has attracted hermit-monks in search of solitude. The word "hermit" comes from an ancient Greek word meaning "person of the desert." The next best thing to a desert in this part of Europe was the sea. Imagine the desert this bay provided as the first monk climbed the rock to get close to God. Add to that the mythic tide, which sends the surf speeding eight miles in and out. Long before the original causeway was built, pilgrims would approach the island across the mudflat, aware that the tide swept in "at the speed of a galloping horse" (well, maybe a trotting horse—12 mph, or about 18 feet per second at top speed).

Quicksand was another peril. A short stroll onto the sticky sand helps you imagine how easy it would be to get stuck as the

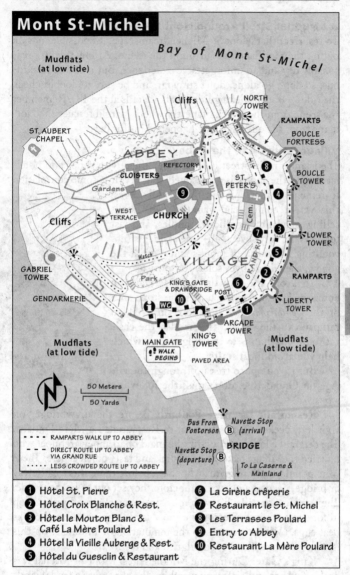

Mont St-Michel

1 Hôtel St. Pierre
2 Hôtel Croix Blanche & Rest.
3 Hôtel le Mouton Blanc & Café La Mère Poulard
4 Hôtel la Vieille Auberge & Rest.
5 Hôtel du Guesclin & Restaurant
6 La Sirène Crêperie
7 Restaurant le St. Michel
8 Les Terrasses Poulard
9 Entry to Abbey
10 Restaurant La Mère Poulard

- - - - RAMPARTS WALK UP TO ABBEY
— — DIRECT ROUTE UP TO ABBEY VIA *GRAND RUE*
• • • • LESS CROWDED ROUTE UP TO ABBEY

NORMANDY

tide rolled in. The greater danger for adventurers today is the thoroughly disorienting fog and the fact that the sea can encircle unwary hikers. (Bring a mobile phone, and if you're stuck, dial 112.) Braving these devilish risks for centuries, pilgrims kept their eyes on the spire crowned by their protector, St. Michael, and eventually reached their spiritual goal.

▲▲Mudflat Stroll Around Mont St-Michel

To resurrect that Mont St-Michel dreamscape, it's possible to walk out on the mudflats that surround the island. At low tide, it's reasonably dry and an unforgettable experience. But it can be hazardous, so don't go alone, don't stray far, and be sure to double-check the tides—or consider a guided walk (details at the TI). Remember the scene from the Bayeux tapestry where Harold rescues the Normans from the quicksand? It happened in this bay.

Village Walk Up to the Abbey

The island's main street (Grand Rue), lined with shops and hotels leading to the abbey, is grotesquely touristy. It is some consolation to remember that, even in the Middle Ages, this was a commercial gauntlet, with stalls selling souvenir medallions, candles, and fast food. With only seven full-time residents (not counting a handful of monks and nuns at the abbey), the village lives solely for tourists.

To avoid the crowds, keep left as you enter the island, passing under the stone arch of the *gendarmerie,* and follow the cobbled ramp up to the abbey. This is also the easiest route up, thanks to the long ramps, which help you avoid most stairs.

But if you opt to trek up through the village on Grand Rue, don't miss the following stops:

Restaurant La Mère Poulard: Before the drawbridge, on your left, peek through the door of Restaurant La Mère Poulard. The original Madame Poulard (the maid of an abbey architect who married the village baker) made quick and tasty omelets here. These were popular with pilgrims who, back before there was a causeway or bridge, needed a quick meal before they set out to beat the tide. The omelets are still a hit with tourists—even at rip-off prices. Pop in for a minute just to enjoy the show as old-time-costumed cooks beat eggs. (When it comes to the temptation of an omelet on this island, I'd make like a good pilgrim and fast.)

King's Gate: During the Middle Ages, Mont St-Michel was both a fortress and a place of worship. The abbot was a feudal landlord with economic, political, and religious power. Mont St-Michel was the abbot's castle as well as a pilgrimage destination. Entering the town, you'll pass two fortified gates before reaching the actual village gate, the King's Gate, with its Hollywood-style drawbridge and portcullis. The old door has a tiny door within it, complete with a guard's barred window (open it). The two lower gates were added for extra defensive credit. Imagine breaching the first gate and being surrounded by defensive troops. The highest tides bring saltwater inside the lowest gate.

Main Street Tourist Gauntlet: Stepping through the King's Gate, you enter the old town commercial center. Look back at the city hall (flying the French flag, directly over the King's Gate). Climb a few steps and notice the fine half-timbered 15th-century house above on the right. (To skirt the main street crowds, stairs lead from here to the ramparts and on to the abbey—see "Ramparts" under the Abbey listing on page 308.) Once upon a time this entire lane was lined with fine half-timbered buildings with a commotion of signs hanging above the cobbles. After many fires, the wooden buildings were replaced by stone. As you climb, you'll see a few stone arches and half-timbered facades that pilgrims also passed by, five centuries ago.

St. Peter's Church (Eglise St-Pierre): At the top of the commercial stretch (on the left) is St. Peter's Church. A statue of Joan of Arc (from 1909, when she became a saint) greets you at the door. She's here because of her association with St. Michael, whose voice inspired her to rally the French against the English. St. Peter's feels alive (giving a sense of what today's barren abbey church might once have felt like). The church is dedicated to St. Peter, patron saint of fishermen, who would have been particularly beloved by the island's parishioners. Just left of the entry is the only surviving 15th-century stained-glass window in town. In the rear (just past the bare rock, granite foundation of the church) find the 1772 painting of pilgrims crossing the mudflat under the protection of St. Michael, who seems to be surfing on a devil's face over a big black cloud. Nearby, the tomb of a 15th-century noblewoman (right of altar) lost its head (notice the empty pillow) during the Revolution—an example of the furious antinobility sentiment expressed by France's 99 percent when they rose up against their 1 percent in 1789. The fine carving you see (altar, lectern, and chairs) is the work of prisoners—the abbey became a prison in 1789 during the Revolution. The church is busy with Masses (daily at 11:00 and special services for pilgrims).

Pilgrims' Stairs to the Abbey: A few steps farther up you'll pass a hostel for pilgrims only (Stella Maris). Reaching the abbey, notice the fortified gate and ramparts necessary to guard the church entry back in the 14th century. Today the abbey, run by just a handful of monks and nuns, welcomes the public.

▲▲▲Abbey of Mont St-Michel

Mont St-Michel has been an important pilgrimage center since A.D. 708, when the bishop of Avranches heard the voice of Archangel Michael saying, "Build here and build high." Michael reassured the bishop, "If you build it...they will come." Today's abbey is

NORMANDY

built on the remains of a Romanesque church, which stands on the remains of a Carolingian church. St. Michael, whose gilded statue decorates the top of the spire, was the patron saint of many French kings, making this a favored site for French royalty through the ages. St. Michael was particularly popular in Counter-Reformation times, as the Church employed his warlike image in the fight against Protestant heresy.

This abbey has 1,200 years of history, though much of its story was lost when its archives were taken to St-Lô for safety during World War II—only to be destroyed during the D-Day fighting. As you climb the stairs, imagine the centuries of pilgrims and monks who have worn down the edges of these same stone steps. Don't expect well-furnished rooms; those monks lived simple lives with few comforts.

Cost and Hours: €9; May-Aug daily 9:00-19:00, until 24:00 Mon-Sat mid-July-Aug; Sept-April daily 9:30-18:00; closed Dec 25, Jan 1, and May 1; last entry one hour before closing; a 15-minute hike above the island TI, www.mont-saint-michel.monuments-nationaux.fr. Mass is held Mon-Sat at 12:00 and Sun at 11:15 (www.abbaye-montsaintmichel.com).

When to Go: To avoid crowds, arrive by 10:00 or after 16:00 (the place gets really busy by 11:00). In summer, consider a **nighttime visit:** You'll enjoy the same access for the same price with romantic lighting and no crowds (mid-July-Aug until 24:00, daytime tickets aren't valid for reentry, but you can visit before 19:00 and stay on).

Tours: The excellent audioguide gives greater detail (€4.50, €6/2 people). You can also take a 1.25-hour English-language guided tour (free but tip requested, 2-4 tours/day, first and last tours usually around 11:00—or 10:45 on Sun—and 15:00, confirm times at TI, meet at top terrace in front of church). These tours can be good, but come with big crowds. You can start a tour, then decide if it works for you—but I'd skip it, instead following my directions, next.

○ Self-Guided Tour: Your visit is a one-way route, so there's no way to get lost—just follow the crowds. You'll climb to the ticket office, then climb some more. Along that final stony staircase, monks and nuns (who live in separate quarters on the left) would draw water from a cistern from big faucets on the right. At the top (just past the WC) is a small view terrace, with a much better one just around the corner.

You've climbed the mount. Stop and look back to the church. Now go through the room marked *Accueil*, with interesting models of the abbey through the ages.

• *Emerging on the other side, find your way to the big terrace, walk to the round lookout at the far end, and face the church.*

West Terrace: In 1776, a fire destroyed the west end of the church, leaving this unplanned grand view terrace. The original extent of the church is outlined with short walls. In the paving stones, notice the stonecutter numbers, which are generally not exposed like this—a reminder that stonecutters were paid by the piece. The buildings of Mont St-Michel are made of granite stones quarried from the Isles of Chausey (visible on a clear day, 20 miles away). Tidal power was ingeniously harnessed to load, unload, and even transport the stones, as barges hitched a ride with each incoming tide.

As you survey the Bay of Mont St-Michel, notice the polder land—farmland reclaimed by Normans in the 19th century with the help of Dutch engineers. The lines of trees mark strips of land regained in the process. Today, the salt-loving plants covering this land are grazed by sheep whose salty meat is considered a local treat. You're standing 240 feet above sea level.

The bay stretches from Normandy (on the right as you look to the sea) to Brittany (on the left). The Couesnon River below marks the historic border between the two lands. Brittany and Normandy have long vied for Mont St-Michel. In fact, the river used to pass Mont St-Michel on the other side, making the abbey part of Brittany. Today, it's just barely—but definitely—on Norman soil. The new dam across this river was built in 2010. Central to the dam is a system of locking gates that retain water upriver during high tide and release it six hours later, in effect flushing the bay and returning sediment to a mudflat at low tide (see "An Island Again" sidebar on page 298).

• *Now enter the...*

Abbey Church: Sit on a pew near the altar, under the little statue of the Archangel Michael (with the spear to defeat dragons and evil, and the scales to evaluate your soul). Monks built the church on the tip of this rock to be as close to heaven as possible. The downside: There wasn't enough level ground to support a sizable abbey and church. The solution: Four immense crypts were built under the church to create a platform to support each of its wings. While most of the church is Romanesque (see the 11th-century round arches behind you), the light-filled apse behind the altar was built later, when Gothic arches were the rage. In 1421, the crypt that supported the apse collapsed, taking that end of the church with it. None of the original windows survive (victims of fires, storms, lightning, and the Revolution).

In the chapel to the right of the altar stands a grim-looking 12th-century statue of St. Aubert, the man with the vision to build the abbey. Directly in front of the altar, look for the glass-covered manhole (you'll see it again later from another angle). Take a spin around the apse and find the suspended pirate-looking ship.

• *Follow* Suite de la Visite *signs to enter the...*

Cloisters: A standard abbey feature, this peaceful zone connected various rooms. Here monks could meditate, read the Bible, and tend their gardens (growing food and herbs for medicine). The great view window is enjoyable today (what's the tide doing?), but was not part of the original design. The more secluded a monk could be, the closer he was to God. (A cloister, by definition, is an enclosed place.) Notice how the columns are staggered. This efficient design allowed the cloisters to be supported with less building material (a top priority, given the difficulty of transporting stone this high up). Carvings above the columns feature various plants and heighten the cloister's Garden-of-Eden ambience. The statues of various saints, carved among some columns, were defaced—literally—by French revolutionaries.

• *Continue on to the...*

Refectory: At its peak, the abbey was home to about 50 monks. This was the dining hall where they consumed both food and the word of God in near silence as one monk read in a monotone from the Bible during meals (pulpit on the right near the far end). The monks gathered as a family here in one undivided space under one big arch (an impressive engineering feat in its day). The abbot ate at the head table; guests sat at the table below the cross. The clever columns are thin but very deep, allowing maximum light and solid support. From 966 until 2001, this was a Benedictine abbey. In 2001, the last three Benedictine monks checked out, and a new order of monks from Paris took over.

• *Stairs lead down one flight to a...*

Stone Relief of St. Michael: This romanticized scene (carved in 1860) depicts the legend of Mont St-Michel: The archangel Michael wanted to commemorate a hard-fought victory over the devil with the construction of a monumental abbey on a nearby island. He sent his message to the bishop of Avranches—St. Aubert—who saw Michael twice in his dreams. But the bishop didn't trust his dreams until the third time, when Michael drove his thumb into the bishop's head, leaving a mark that he could not ignore. Notice the urgent gesture of Michael's hand and arm as the saint points to the uninhabited mount. The bishop finally got the message, and the first chapel was consecrated in 709.

• *Continue down the stairs another flight to the...*

Guests' Hall: St. Benedict wrote that guests should be welcomed according to their status. That meant that when kings (or other VIPs) visited, they were wined and dined without a hint of monastic austerity. This room once exploded in color, with gold stars on a blue sky across the ceiling. (This room's decoration was said to be the model for Sainte-Chapelle in Paris.) The floor was composed of glazed red-and-green tiles. The entire space was bathed in glorious sunlight, made divine as it passed through a filter of stained glass. The big double fireplace, kept out of sight by hanging tapestries, served as a kitchen—walk under it, imagine an entire wild boar on a spit, and see the light.

• *Hike up the stairs through a chapel to the…*

Hall of the Grand Pillars: Perched on a pointy rock, the huge abbey church had four sturdy crypts like this to prop it up. You're standing under the Gothic portion of the abbey church—this was the crypt that collapsed in 1421. Notice the immensity of the columns (15 feet around) in the new crypt, rebuilt with a determination not to let it fall again. Now look up at the round hole in the ceiling and recognize it as the glass "manhole cover" from the church altar above.

• *To see what kind of crypt collapsed, continue on to the…*

Crypt of St. Martin: This simple 11th-century vault, one of the oldest on the mount, is textbook Romanesque. It has minimal openings, since the walls needed to be solid and fat to support the buildings above. As you leave, notice the thickness of the walls.

• *Walking on, study the barnacle-like unplanned stone construction, added haphazardly over the centuries, yet all integrated. Next, you'll find the…*

Ossuary (identifiable by its big treadwheel): The monks celebrated death as well as life. This part of the abbey housed the hospital, morgue, and ossuary. Because the abbey graveyard was small, it was routinely emptied, and the bones were stacked here.

During the Revolution, monasticism was abolished. Church property was taken by the secular government, and from 1793 to 1863, Mont St-Michel was used as an Alcatraz-type prison. Its first inmates were 300 priests who refused to renounce their vows. (Victor Hugo complained that using such a place as a prison was like keeping a toad in a reliquary.) The big treadwheel from 1820—the kind that did heavy lifting for big building projects throughout the Middle Ages—is from the decades when the abbey was a prison. Teams of six prisoners marched two abreast in the wheel, hamster-style, powering two-ton loads of stone and supplies up Mont St-Michel. Spin the rollers of the sled next to the wheel.

From here, you'll pass through a chapel (with a rare fragment of a 13th-century fresco above), walk up the Romanesque-arched North-South Stairs, pass through the Promenade of the Monks (appreciate the fine medieval stonework, built directly into the granite rock of the island), go under more Gothic vaults, and finally descend into the vast…

Scriptorium Hall (a.k.a. Knights Hall): This important room is where monks decorated illuminated manuscripts and transcribed texts. It faces north so its big windows would let in lots of flat, indirect light, the preference of artists throughout time. You'll then spiral down to the gift shop, exiting out the back door (follow signs to the *Jardins*).

• *You'll emerge into the rear garden. From here, look back from where you just came and up at a miracle* (merveille) *of medieval engineering.*

The "Merveille": This was an immense building project—a marvel back in 1220. Three levels of buildings were created: the lower floor for storage, the middle floor for work and study, and the top floor for meditation (in the cloister, open to the heavens). It was a medieval skyscraper. The vision was even grander—the place where you're standing was to be built up in similar fashion to support an expansion of the church. But the money ran out, and the project was abandoned. As you leave the garden, notice the tall narrow windows of the refectory on the top floor.

• *Exiting the abbey, you'll pop out midway up the stairs you climbed to get here. You could descend into tourist Hell. But for a little rampart romance, I'd go up a dozen steps and circle right, following a well-fortified outer rampart with a few awe-inspiring viewpoints before heading back down to the King's Gate and the bridge. (From the high point, look down and right at the former schoolhouse—operational until 1972—with its school bell, small playground, and tree.)*

Ramparts: Mont St-Michel is ringed by a fine example of 15th-century fortifications. They were built to defend against a new weapon: the cannon. They were low, rather than tall—to make a smaller target—and connected by protected passageways, which enabled soldiers to zip quickly to whichever zone was under attack. The five-sided Boucle Tower (1481) was crafted with no blind angles, so defenders could protect it and the nearby walls in all directions. And though the English conquered all of Normandy in the early 15th century, they never took this well-fortified island. Because of its stubborn success against the English in the Hundred Years' War, Mont St-Michel became a symbol of French national identity.

NEAR MONT ST-MICHEL
German Military Cemetery (Cimetière Militaire Allemand)
Located three miles from Mont St-Michel, near tiny Huisnes-sur-Mer, this somber cemetery-mortuary houses the remains of 12,000 German WWII soldiers brought to this location from all over France. The stone blocks on the steps up indicate the regions in France from where they came. A display of letters they sent home offers insights into the soldiers' lives. From the lookout, take in the sensational views over Mont St-Michel. The cemetery is well-signed east of Mont St-Michel (off D-275 at 3 Rue du Mont de Huisnes).

Sleeping in Mont St-Michel

($$$$ = Splurge, $$$ = Pricier, $$ = Moderate, $ = Budget)
Sleep on or near the island so that you can visit Mont St-Michel early and late. What matters is being here before or after the crush of tourists. Sleeping on the island—inside the walls—is a memorable experience for medieval romantics who don't mind small and average rooms, overpriced food, and baggage hassles. To reach a room on the island, you'll need to carry your bags 15 minutes from the *navette* (shuttle) stop. Take only what you need for one night in a smaller bag, but don't leave any luggage visible in your car.

Hotels near the island in La Caserne are a better value (if less romantic). All are a short walk from the free and frequent shuttle to the island.

ON THE ISLAND

Because most visitors day-trip here, finding a room is generally no problem. Though some pad their profits by requesting that guests buy dinner from their restaurant, requiring it is illegal. Higher-priced rooms generally have bay views.

The following hotels, all on Grand Rue, are listed in order of altitude from lowest to highest.

$$$$ Hôtel St. Pierre* and **Hôtel Croix Blanche*** sit side by side and share the same owners and reception desk (at St. Pierre). Each provides comfortable rooms at inflated prices, some with good views (family rooms, lower rates at Hôtel Croix Blanche, tel. 02 33 60 14 03, www.auberge-saint-pierre.fr, contact@auberge-saint-pierre.fr).

$$$ Hôtel le Mouton Blanc* delivers a fair midrange value, with 15 rooms split between two buildings. The pricier main building *(bâtiment principal)* has cozy rooms, wood beams, decent bathrooms (family rooms available); the more modern "annex" has cramped bathrooms but much better rates (tel. 02 33 60 14 08, www.lemoutonblanc.fr, contact@lemoutonblanc.fr).

$$ Hôtel la Vieille Auberge is a small place with sharp rooms at fair prices (pricier but worthwhile view room with deck; check in at their restaurant, but book through Hôtel St. Pierre, listed above).

$$ Hôtel du Guesclin has the cheapest and best-value rooms I list on the island and is the only family-run hotel left there. Rooms have simple decor and provide basic comfort (tel. 02 33 60 14 10, www.hotelduguesclin.com, hotel.duguesclin@wanadoo.fr).

ON THE MAINLAND

Modern hotels with easy parking gather in La Caserne on the mainland (see "Arrival in Mont-St Michel," earlier, for parking details.

$$ Hôtel le Relais du Roy*** houses small but well-configured and plush rooms above appealing public spaces. Most rooms are on the riverside, with countryside views, and many have small balconies allowing "lean-out" views to the abbey (bar, restaurant, 8 Route du Mont Saint-Michel, tel. 02 33 60 14 25, www.le-relais-du-roy.com, reservation@le-relais-du-roy.com).

$$ Hôtel Gabriel*** has 45 modern rooms, both bright and tight, with flashy colors and fair rates (includes breakfast, Route du Mont Saint-Michel, tel. 02 33 60 14 13, www.hotelgabriel-montsaintmichel.com, hotelgabriel@le-mont-saint-michel.com).

$ Hôtel Vert** provides 54 motel-esque rooms at good rates (family rooms, Route du Mont Saint-Michel, tel. 02 33 60 09 33, www.hotelvert-montsaintmichel.com, stmichel@le-mont-saint-michel.com).

CHAMBRES D'HOTES

Simply great values, these converted farmhouses are a few minutes' drive from the island.

$ Les Vieilles Digues, where charming, English-speaking Danielle and Kin will pamper you, is two miles toward Pontorson on the main road (on the left if you're coming from Mont St-Michel). It has a lovely garden and seven homey, borderline-kitschy rooms with subtle Asian touches, all with showers (but no Mont St-Michel views). Ground-floor rooms have patios on the garden (includes good breakfast, easy parking—and you can walk to the free shuttle at the main parking lot, 68 Route du Mont St-Michel, tel. 02 33 58 55 30, search "Les Vieilles Digues" on www.chambres-hotes.fr, les.vieillesdigues@yahoo.fr).

$ La Jacotière is closest to Mont St-Michel and within walking distance of the regional bus stop and the island shuttle (allowing you to avoid all parking fees). Welcoming Véronique offers six immaculate rooms and views of the island from the backyard (studio with great view from private patio, family rooms, includes breakfast, tel. 02 33 60 22 94, www.lajacotiere.fr, la.jacotiere@wanadoo.fr). Drivers coming from Bayeux should turn off the road just prior to the main parking lot. As the road bends to the left away from the bay, look for a regional-products store standing alone on the right. Take the small lane in front of the store signed *sauf véhicule autorisé*—La Jacotière is the next building.

$ Vent des Grèves is about a mile down D-275 from Mont St-Michel (green sign; if arriving from the north, it's just after Auberge de la Baie). Sweet Estelle (who speaks English) offers five bright, big, and modern rooms with good views of Mont St-Michel and a common deck with tables to let you soak it all in (family rooms, includes breakfast, 9 Chemin des Dits, tel. 02 33 48 28 89, www.ventdesgreves.com, ventdesgreves@orange.fr).

Eating in Mont St-Michel

Puffy omelets (*omelette montoise,* or *omelette tradition*) are Mont St-Michel's specialty. Also look for mussels, seafood platters, and locally-raised lamb *pré-salé* (a saltwater-grass diet gives the meat a unique taste, but beware of impostor lamb from New Zealand—ask where your dinner was raised). Muscadet wine (dry, white, and cheap) from the western Loire valley is made nearby and goes well with most regional dishes.

The menus are pretty similar and geared to tourists (with *menus* from €18 to €29, cheap crêpes, and full à la carte choices). Window-shop the places that face the bay from the ramparts walk (several access points—one is across from the post office (La Poste) at the bottom of the village) and arrive early to land a view table. Unless noted, the following restaurants are open daily for lunch and dinner.

$ La Sirène Crêperie offers a good island value and a cozy interior (open daily for lunch, open for dinner in summer only, closed Fri off-season, enter through gift shop across from Hôtel St. Pierre, tel. 02 33 60 08 60).

$$ Hôtel du Guesclin is the top place for a traditional meal, with white tablecloths and beautiful views of the bay from its inside-only tables (closed Thu, book a window table in advance; see details under "Sleeping in Mont St-Michel—On the Island," earlier).

$$ Restaurant le St. Michel is lighthearted, reasonable, family-friendly, and run by helpful Patricia (decent omelets, mussels, salads, and pasta; open daily for lunch, open for dinner July-Aug, closed Thu-Fri off-season, test its toilet in the rock, across from Hôtel le Mouton Blanc, tel. 02 33 60 14 37).

$$ Café La Mère Poulard is a stylish three-story café-*crêperie*-restaurant one door up from Hôtel le Mouton Blanc. (Don't confuse it with the Restaurant La Mère Poulard by the drawbridge.) It's worth considering for its upstairs terrace, which offers the best outside table views up to the abbey (when their umbrellas don't block it). **La Vieille Auberge** has a broad terrace with the next-best views to the abbey. **La Croix Blanche** owns a small deck with partial abbey views and window-front tables with bay views, and **Les Terrasses Poulard** has indoor views to the bay.

Picnics: This is the romantic's choice. The small lanes above the main street hide scenic picnic spots, such as the small park at the base of the ancient treadwheel ramp to the upper abbey. You'll catch late sun by following the ramp that leads you through the *gendarmerie* and down behind the island (on the left as you face the main entry to the island). Sandwiches, pizza by the slice, salads, and drinks are all available to go at shops (open until 19:00) along the main drag. You'll find a better selection at the modest grocery on the mainland (see "Helpful Hints" on page 300).

Mont St-Michel Connections

BY TRAIN, BUS, OR TAXI

Bus and train service to Mont St-Michel is a challenge. Depending on where you're coming from, you may find that you're forced to arrive and depart early or late—leaving you with too much or too little time on the island.

From Mont St-Michel to Paris: There are several ways to get to Paris. Most travelers take the regional bus from Mont St-Michel to Rennes or Dol-de-Bretagne and connect directly to the TGV (4/day via Rennes, 1/day via Dol-de-Bretagne, 4 hours total via either route from Mont St-Michel to Paris' Gare Montparnasse; €15 for bus to Rennes, €8 for bus to Dol-de-Bretagne; not covered by rail pass, buy ticket from driver, all explained in English at www.destination-montstmichel.com). You can also take a short bus ride to Pontorson (see next) and catch one of a very few trains from there (3/day, 5.5 hours, transfer in Caen, St-Malo, or Rennes).

From Mont St-Michel to Pontorson: The nearest train station to Mont St-Michel is five miles away, in Pontorson (called Pontorson/Mont St-Michel). It's connected to Mont St-Michel by bus or by taxi (see details earlier, under "Arrival in Mont St-Michel").

From Pontorson by Train to: Bayeux (2-3/day, 2 hours; faster by shuttle van—see page 261).

From Mont St-Michel by Bus to: Rennes (4/day direct, 2 hours, tel. 02 99 19 70 70, www.keolis-emeraude.com/en).

Taxis are expensive, but are helpful when trains and buses don't cooperate. Figure €90 from Mont St-Michel to St-Malo, and €100 to Dinan (50 percent more on Sun and at night).

BY CAR

From Mont St-Michel to St-Malo, Brittany: The direct (and free) freeway route takes 40 minutes. For a scenic drive into Brittany, take the following route: Head to Pontorson, follow *D-19* signs to St-Malo, then look for *St.*

Malo par la Côte and join D-797, which leads along *La Route de la Baie* to D-155 and on to the oyster capital of Cancale. In Cancale, keep tracking *St. Malo par la Côte* and *Route de la Baie* signs. You'll be routed through the town's port (good lunch stop), then emerge on D-201. Take time to savor Pointe du Grouin, then continue west on D-201 as it hugs the coast to St-Malo (see page 342).

From Mont St-Michel to Bayeux: Take the free and zippy A-84 toward Caen.

NORMANDY

BRITTANY

Dinan • St-Malo • Fougères

The bulky peninsula of Brittany ("Bretagne" in French; "Breizh" in Breton) is windswept and rugged, with a well-discovered coast, a forgotten interior, strong Celtic ties, and a craving for crêpes. This region of independent-minded locals is linguistically, physically, and culturally different from Normandy—and, for that matter, the rest of France. Tradition is everything here, where farmers and fishermen still play a big part in the region's economy.

The Couesnon River skirts the western edge of Mont St-Michel and has long marked the border between Normandy and Brittany. The constant moving of the riverbed made Mont St-Michel at times Norman and at other times Breton. To end the bickering, the border was moved a few miles to the west—making Mont St-Michel a Normandy resident for good.

In 1491, the French King Charles VIII forced Brittany's 14-year-old Duchess Anne to marry him (at Château de Langeais in the Loire Valley). Their union made feisty, independent Brittany a small, unhappy cog in a big country (the Kingdom of France). Brittany lost its freedom but, with Anne as queen, gained certain rights, such as free roads. Even today, more than 500 years later, Brittany's freeways have no tolls, which is unique in France.

Locals take great pride in their distinct Breton culture. In Brittany, music stores sell more Celtic albums than anything else. It's hard to imagine that this music was forbidden as recently as the 1980s. During that repressive time, many of today's Breton pop stars were underground artists. And not long ago, a child would lose French citizenship if christened with a Celtic name.

But *les Bretons* are now free to wave their black-and-white-striped flag, sing their songs, and *parler* their language (there's a Breton TV station and radio station). Look for *Breizh* bumper stickers and flags touting the region's Breton name. Like their Irish counterparts, Bretons are chatty, their music is alive with stories of struggles against an oppressor, and their identities are intrinsically tied to the sea.

PLANNING YOUR TIME

With one full day, spend the morning in Dinan and the afternoon either along the Rance River (walking or biking are best, but driving works) or along Brittany's wild coast, where you can tour Fort la Latte and enjoy the massive views between Sable-d'Or-les-Pins and Cap Fréhel. Try to find a few hours for St-Malo—ideally when connecting Mont St-Michel with Brittany. The coastal route between Mont St-Michel and St-Malo—via the town of Cancale (famous for oysters and a good place for lunch), with a stop at Pointe du Grouin (fabulous ocean views)—gives travelers with limited time a worthwhile glimpse at this photogenic province.

GETTING AROUND BRITTANY

By Car: This is the ideal way to scour the ragged coast and watery towns. Expressways here are free, with a 110 km/hour speed limit. Traffic is generally negligible, except in summer along the coast and around the big city of Rennes.

By Train and Bus: Trains provide barely enough service to Dinan and St-Malo (on Sun, service all but disappears). Key transfer points by train include Rennes and the small town of Dol-de-Bretagne. Some trips are more convenient by bus (including Rennes to Dinan and Dinan to St-Malo).

By Minivan Tour: Westcapades runs daylong minivan tours covering Dinan, St-Malo, and Mont St-Michel. Designed for day-trippers from Paris, the tours leave from St-Malo or Rennes (pickups also possible from Dinan). You can get off at Mont St-Michel (described in the Normandy chapter)—making this tour a convenient way to reach that remote island abbey (€99/day includes abbey entry, tel. 02 23 23 01 96, www.westcapades.com, marc@westcapades.com). A different tour option starts at the Rennes TGV station, includes Mont St-Michel and key D-Day beaches, and ends at the train station in either Bayeux or Caen.

Another small tour company, **Afoot in France,** provides three-day to two-week tours in Brittany and Normandy for small groups or individuals. This service is ideal for people who'd like to have a local tour guide as their personal driver (www.afootinfrance.com, afootinfrance@gmail.com). Both of its guides also lead tours for my company.

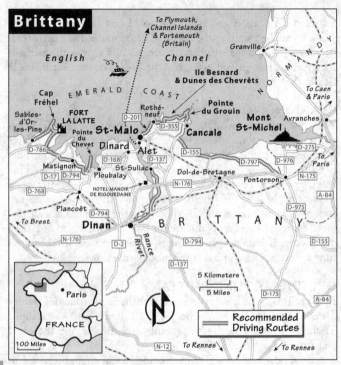

BRITTANY'S CUISINE SCENE

Though the endless coastline suggests otherwise, there is more than seafood in this rugged Celtic land. Crêpes are to Bretons what pasta is to Italians: a basic, reasonably priced, daily necessity. *Galettes* are savory buckwheat crêpes, commonly filled with ham, cheese, eggs, mushrooms, spinach, seafood, or a combination. Purists insist that a *galette* should not have more than three or four fillings—overfilling it masks the flavor (which is the point in certain places).

Oysters *(huitres)*, the second food of Brittany, are available all year. Mussels, clams, and scallops are often served as main courses, and you can also find *galettes* with scallops and *moules marinières* (mussels steamed in white wine, parsley, and shallots). Farmers compete with fishermen for the hearts of locals by growing fresh vegetables, such as peas, beans, and cauliflower.

For dessert, look for *far breton,* a traditional flan-like cake often served with prunes. Dessert crêpes, made with white flour, come with a variety of toppings. Or try *kouign amann,* a puffy, caramelized Breton cake (in Breton, *kouign* means "cake" and *amann* means "butter"). At bakeries, seek out *gâteau breton,* a traditional Breton shortbread cake made with butter, of course.

Cider is the locally produced drink. Order *une bolée de cidre brut, demi-sec* or *doux* (a traditional bowl of hard apple cider, from dry to sweet) with your crêpes. Breton beer is strong and delicious; try anything local (Sant Erwann is my favorite).

Remember, restaurants serve food only during lunch (12:00-14:00) and dinner (19:00-21:00, later in bigger cities); cafés offer food throughout the day.

Dinan

If you have time for only one stop in Brittany, do Dinan. Hefty ramparts corral its half-timbered and cobbled quaintness into

Brittany's best medieval town center. While simply charming today, Dinan was once a formidable city—a residence of the duke of Brittany, a strategic port, and a trading center with powerful guilds and good connections with England and Holland. But in the 13th century, ships outgrew its river port, and the harbor action migrated to nearby St-Malo. This impeccably preserved ancient city escaped the bombs of World War II, and today its stout, mile-long ramparts are like a parkway. Given a chance to replace their venerable walls with a wide, modern boulevard, the people of Dinan chose instead to keep their slice of history—and the traffic congestion that comes with it.

While Dinan has a touristy icing—plenty of *créperies,* shops selling Brittany kitsch, and colorful flags—it's a workaday Breton town filled with about 10,000 people who appreciate the beautiful, peaceful place they call home. It's also conveniently located, about a 45-minute drive from Mont St-Michel. For a memorable day, spend your morning exploring Dinan and your afternoon walking, biking, or boating the Rance River.

BRITTANY

Orientation to Dinan

Dinan's old city, wrapped in medieval ramparts, gathers on a hill well above the Rance River. The vast Place du Guesclin (gek-lahn) welcomes you with acres of parking, Château de Dinan, and the TI. A few blocks from there, Place des Merciers marks the center for shoppers. From the old cobbled core, a steep lane leads down to a sleepy river port—once the reason for the town and now a spring-board for vacation paddles and pedals.

TOURIST INFORMATION

At the TI, pick up a free map and bus schedules and ask about boat trips on the Rance River (July-Aug Mon-Sat 9:30-19:00, Sun 10:00-12:30 & 14:30-18:00; Sept-June Mon-Sat 9:30-12:30 & 14:00-18:00, likely closed Sun; just off Place du Guesclin near Château de Dinan at 9 Rue du Château, tel. 02 96 87 69 76, www. dinan-tourisme.com).

ARRIVAL IN DINAN

By Train: To get to the town center from Dinan's Old World train station (no lockers or baggage storage), hop a taxi (see "Helpful Hints," below) or walk 20 steady minutes (see map on page 320). If walking, veer left out of the train station—passing Hôtel de la Gare—and walk up Rue Carnot. Turn right on Rue Thiers following *Centre Historique/Office de Tourisme* signs, then go left across big Place Duclos-Pinot, passing just left of Café de la Mairie. To reach the TI and Place du Guesclin, go to the right of the café (on Rue du Marchix).

By Bus: Dinan's intercity bus stops are at the station and in front of the post office on Place Duclos-Pinot, minutes below Place du Guesclin. To reach the historic core, cross the square, passing to the left of Café de la Mairie (for more on buses, see "Dinan Connections," later).

By Car: Follow *Centre Historique/Office de Tourisme* signs and park on Place du Guesclin (pay nearby; free overnight from 19:00-9:00 except on Thu market days). If you enter Dinan near the train station, drive the route described above (see "By Train"), and keep to the right of Café de la Mairie to reach Place du Guesclin. Check with your hotelier before leaving your car overnight on Place du Guesclin; it will be towed before 6:00 on market or festival days.

HELPFUL HINTS

Exchange Rate: €1 = about $1.10
Country Calling Code: 33 (see page 1082 for dialing instructions)
Market Days: Every Thursday, a big open-air market is held on

Place du Guesclin (8:00-13:00). On Wednesdays in July and August, there's a flea market on Place St. Sauveur.

Wi-Fi: The TI has free Wi-Fi and computers (small fee).

Laundry: A self-serve launderette is a few blocks from Place Duclos-Pinot at 19 Rue de Brest (Tue-Fri 8:30-12:00 & 13:45-19:00, Sat 8:30-18:00, closed Sun-Mon).

Supermarkets: Groceries are upstairs in the **Monoprix** (Mon-Sat 9:00-19:30, closed Sun, 7 Rue du Marchix). Or try **Carrefour City** on Place Duclos-Pinot (Mon-Sat 7:00-21:00, Sun 8:00-13:00).

Bike Rental: Bords de Rance Café rents standard and electric bikes and is perfectly located on the port to start your ride (standard-€10, electric-€15, these are half-day rates, 18 Rue du Quai Tallard, tel. 02 96 39 34 75).

Kayak Rental: Club Canoë Kayak rents kayaks and canoes; you can go upstream almost to Léhon, and downstream to Taden (€10/1 hour, €20/3 hours, €30/day, cash only, July-Aug daily 10:00-18:00, Sept-June by reservation only, tel. 02 96 39 01 50, www.dinanrancekayak.fr).

Taxi: Call 06 08 00 80 90 (www.taxi-dinan.com). Figure about €60 to St-Malo and €110 to Mont St-Michel.

Tourist Train: This *petit train* runs a circuit connecting the port and upper old town (€7, Easter-Sept 11:00-17:00, runs every 40 minutes, leaves in the old town from in front of Théâtre des Jacobins, a block off Place du Guesclin.

Picnic Park: The small but flowery Jardin Anglais hides behind the Church of St. Sauveur.

BRITTANY

Dinan Walk

Frankly, I wouldn't go through a turnstile in Dinan. The attraction

is the town itself. Enjoy the old town center, ramble around the ramparts, and explore the old riverfront harbor. Here are some ideas, laced together as a relaxed one-hour walk (not including exploring the port). As you wander, notice the pride locals take in their Breton culture.

• *Start in the center of Place du Guesclin (near the TI), and find the statue of the horseback rider.*

Place du Guesclin: This sprawling town square/parking lot is named after Bertrand du Guesclin, a native 14th-century knight and hero (described as small in stature but big-hearted) who became a great French military leader, famous for his daring victories over

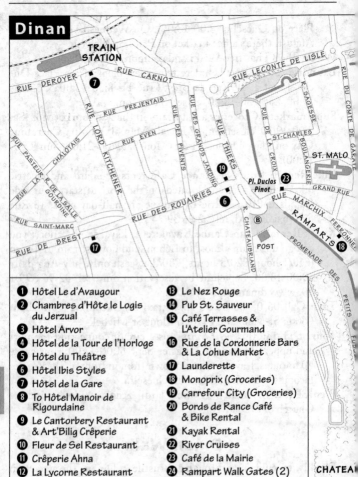

Dinan

- **1** Hôtel Le d'Avaugour
- **2** Chambres d'Hôte le Logis du Jerzual
- **3** Hôtel Arvor
- **4** Hôtel de la Tour de l'Horloge
- **5** Hôtel du Théâtre
- **6** Hôtel Ibis Styles
- **7** Hôtel de la Gare
- **8** To Hôtel Manoir de Rigourdaine
- **9** Le Cantorbery Restaurant & Art'Bilig Crêperie
- **10** Fleur de Sel Restaurant
- **11** Crêperie Ahna
- **12** La Lycorne Restaurant
- **13** Le Nez Rouge
- **14** Pub St. Sauveur
- **15** Café Terrasses & L'Atelier Gourmand
- **16** Rue de la Cordonnerie Bars & La Cohue Market
- **17** Launderette
- **18** Monoprix (Groceries)
- **19** Carrefour City (Groceries)
- **20** Bords de Rance Café & Bike Rental
- **21** Kayak Rental
- **22** River Cruises
- **23** Café de la Mairie
- **24** Rampart Walk Gates (2)

England during the Hundred Years' War (like Joan of Arc, he was a key player in defeating the English). On this very square, he beat Sir Thomas of Canterbury in a nail-biter of a joust that locals talk about to this day. (Bertrand's heart is buried in the church where this walk finishes.) For 700 years, merchants have filled this square to sell their produce and crafts (in modern times, it's Thu 8:00-13:00).

• With the statue of Guesclin behind you, follow Rue Ste. Claire to the right, into the old town and to the...

Théâtre des Jacobins: Fronting a pleasant little square, the theater was once one of the many convents that dominated the town in the 13th century. In fact, in medieval times, a third of Dinan consisted of convents (which, in Europe, are not exclusively for nuns). They're still common in Brittany, which remains the most

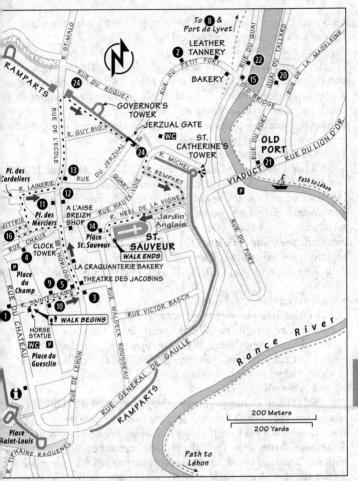

Catholic part of France. The theater today offers a full schedule of events. Across from the theater, the fine building with the colorful half-timbered porch on stone columns is the **Keratry Mansion,** which dates from 1559. It was brought here from a nearby town and reassembled—one of many examples of how Dinan takes pride in its old center. (Posts around town give short descriptions of historic sights like this one.)

• *Walk past the mansion down Rue de l'Horloge ("Clock Street") toward the clock tower. At the first corner, on your left, you'll see...*

Anybody's Tombstone: The tombstone without a head is a town mascot. It's actually a prefab tombstone, mass-produced during the Hundred Years' War, when there was more death than money in France. A portrait bust would be attached to this generic body and they'd chip the deceased's coat of arms onto the blank banner for a proper, yet economical, burial.

• *On your right, 20 yards farther down is...*

La Craquanterie: This shop specializes in Breton cookies and treats. Look for *caramels au beurre salé* (salted butter caramels), *kouign amann* (extremely rich butter cake), *gâteau breton* (traditional cake), *craquants* (crisp cookies with salted butter), and the Breton answer to Nutella—*Craquamel*. There's a good chance your hotel will serve these local treats at breakfast.

• *Continue 20 yards to the...*

Clock Tower: Five hundred years ago, Dinan built this 150-foot tall tower so people would know when to start and stop working. Back when most towns only had church bell towers, this proud and modern civic tower was a symbol of the power of the town's merchants. The tower's 156 steps lead past the clock's original mechanism—from 1498, one of the oldest in Europe—to a sweeping city view. Warning: Plug your ears at the quarter-hour (€4, daily June-Sept 10:00-18:30, April-May 14:00-18:00, closed Oct-March).

• *At the next corner find the store...*

A l'Aise Breizh: This store, with its distinctive name (meaning "take it easy in Brittany"), has been riding the wave of Brittany's cultural renewal since 1996. You may have seen their slogan on bumper stickers throughout the region. Inside, you'll find fun clothing and whimsical souvenirs designed in Brittany.

• *You're in the middle of Dinan's...*

Old Town Center: The arcaded, half-timbered buildings around you are Dinan's oldest. They date from the time when property taxes were based on the square footage of the ground floor. To provide shelter from both the rain and taxes, buildings started with small ground floors, then expanded outward as they got taller. Notice the stone bases supporting the wood columns. Because trees didn't come in standard lengths, builders adjusted the size of the pedestals. Medieval shopkeepers sold goods in front of their homes under the shelter of these traditional porches.

• *Duck for cover at **Le Pole Nord** (a local favorite for ice cream). Then walk to the end of the covered arcade, enjoying the architecture along the way. At the end, angle left and cross to the small well on Place des Merciers.*

Place des Merciers: From this spot spin 360 degrees counterclockwise. Looking back at Le Pole Nord, admire the woody structures. This arcade originally continued left 100 yards past the four modern black lampposts to the next arcade. In the 19th century Dinan had about 1,000 buildings with fine wooden porches, but a 1907 fire destroyed much of the center, and only 17 survive today.

Farther to the left is a shop filled with canned fish from Brittany. Enjoy the swaying, half-timbered facade of Restaurant la Mere Pourcel. On the corner is a colorful carved statue of St. Michael. Below him, a well-beaten corner stone protects the building from carriages careening down Rue de la Cordonnerie. Across the lane is a shop with regional products and a window full of traditional Breton ceramic cups with "ears" as handles and folk paintings inside. The mugs are based on the traditional Breton bowls that every local was raised with—hand-painted with designs of costumed Bretons and each kid's first name.

• *Head up the narrow Rue de la Cordonnerie. (We'll circle from there, around to the right, popping back out into the square at the tinned fish shop.)*

Rue de la Cordonnerie: Many German streets are named for the key commerce that took place there in medieval times. This street, literally "Cobblers' Lane," is now nicknamed "Street of Thirst" for its many pubs. Rue de la Cordonnerie is a good example of a medieval lane, with overhanging buildings whose roofs nearly touch. After a disastrous 18th-century fire, a law required that the traditional thatch be replaced by safer slate. Enjoy the details of the buildings on this characteristic lane.

• *Take your first right (passing a public WC) into a little park where a gate leads to a modern market.*

La Cohue: There's been a market here since the 13th century, but the ambience of La Cohue today is very 21st century. It has a produce stand, wine store, cheese shop, bakery, and more (Tue-Sun 8:00-14:00, Fri-Sat until 19:00, closed Mon).

• *If it's open, explore the market. Then loop back to Place des Merciers, where you reach the shop selling tinned fish.*

La Belle Iloise: For three generations, a fishing family has respected the traditions of canning their fresh catch. Their factory, which is based in southern Brittany and has outlets all over France, produces tasty sardine, mackerel, and tuna spreads.

• *Continue left, past the four modern lampposts, to the end of the square. (The building with the arched stone facade at the end—Les Cordeliers—once a Franciscan monastery, is now a middle school.) Turn right and walk a block down Rue de la Lainerie ("Street of Wool Shops") to the top of a hill. Stop at the top of Rue du Jerzual.*

Rue du Jerzual: Peer down this street that connects the town and its river port. Notice the waist-high stone and wooden shelves that front many of the buildings. Here, medieval merchants could display their products and tempt passersby. These days, the street is lined with welcoming art galleries and inviting craft shops. (From here it's a 10-minute walk down to the port—described later, under "Sights in Dinan.")

• *Head left down Rue de l'Ecole (past the recommended, Cheers-like pub* **Le Nez Rouge***) 200 yards to the medieval gate. Just before the gate, walk right up onto the ramparts (daily 8:00-21:00, until 17:00 off-season). Ahead you see Governor's Tower, and St. Catherine's Tower in the distance next to a big church. First, walk out onto Governor's Tower.*

Governor's Tower and the Ramparts: Although the old port town was repeatedly destroyed, these ramparts were never taken by force. If an attacker got by the *contrescarpe* (second outer wall, now covered in vegetation) and through the (dry) moat, he'd be pummeled by ghastly stuff dropped through the holes lining the ramparts. Today, the ramparts protect the town's residential charm and are lined by private gardens. Cannon slots on the 15th-century Governor's Tower enabled defenders to shoot in all directions.

• *Continue along the ramparts. At the Jerzual Gate look down on Rue du Jerzual, which leads to the port. Continue down the steps onto Rue Michel and turn right. Take the first left, onto Rue du Rempart, which dead-ends at a rampart park. On the far left is a round tower called...*

St. Catherine's Tower: This part of Dinan's medieval defense system allows strategic views of the river valley and over the old port. Below you can see the medieval bridge and the path that leads along the river to the right to Léhon (described later, under "Sights in Dinan"). To the left the Rance River flows toward the sea. The English gardens behind you are much appreciated by locals.

• *Leave the ramparts, walk through the gardens, around the church, and then inside.*

Church of St. Sauveur: When it was built a thousand years ago, this church sat lonely on this hill, as all other activity was focused around the port far below. Step in to see its striking, modern stained-glass windows and beautifully lit nave. Pick up the simple English explanation. The old wood balcony above the entry heaves under the weight of its organ. A capital in the center of the back wall is decorated with camels. According to legend, a local crusader promised to build this church if he survived his crusade. Apparently he was fortunate.

The gangly church is terribly asymmetrical—built in many stages over the centuries. Notice an older section of wall on the right of the nave: The simple, round Romanesque arches bear traces of the original red bull's blood paint, surviving from the 12th century. The fourth chapel on the left has its original 15th-century stained glass (with four Breton saints lined up below the four evangelists). The rest of the church's windows are post-World War II (c. 1950). And in a tomb in the left transept, no longer beats the heart of the Dinan hero, Bertrand du Guesclin.

• *Your tour is over. Good lunch cafés are across the square (see "Eating in Dinan," later), and you are a block below the main Rue de l'Horloge.*

Sights in Dinan

Dinan's Old Port

The port was the birthplace of Dinan a thousand years ago. For centuries, this is where people lived and worked, and today it's a great place for a riverside drink or meal. This once-thriving port is connected to the sea—15 miles away—by the Rance River. The town grew prosperous by taxing river traffic. The tiny medieval bridge dates to the 15th century. Because the port area was so exposed, the townsfolk retreated to the bluff

behind its current fortifications. The viaduct high above was built in 1850 to alleviate congestion and to send traffic around the town. Before then, the main road crossed the little medieval bridge, heading up Rue du Jerzual to Dinan.

Getting There: Walkers following my self-guided walk (described earlier) can reach Dinan's modest little port by continuing steeply down Rue du Jerzual (which becomes Rue du Petit Fort). Just before reaching the port, notice the unusual wood-topped building on the left-hand side. This was the town's **leather tannery**—those wooden shutters could open to dry the freshly tanned hides while the nearby river flushed away the waste (happily, swimming was not in vogue then). The last business on the right before the port is a killer bakery, **La Maison de Tatie Jeanne,** with delicious local specialties, including *far breton* and *kouign amann* (you'll also find good picnic fixings and drinks to go). You deserve a baked break.

Drivers can park at the lot under the viaduct for easy port access.

▲Rance River Valley

The best thing about Dinan's port is the access it provides to lush riverside paths that amble along the gentle Rance River Valley. You can walk, bike, drive, or boat in either interesting direction (perfect for families).

On Foot: For a breath of fresh Brittany air and an easy walk, visit the flower-festooned village of **Léhon.** Cross Dinan's medieval bridge, turn right, and walk 35 minutes.

Arriving in pristine little Léhon—a town of character, as the sign reminds you—visitors are greeted by a beautiful ninth-century abbey that rules the roost (find the cloisters). Explore the village's flowery cobbled lanes, but skip the town-topping castle ruin (free, daily 10:00-19:00 in summer, Sat-Sun only off-season). Enjoy a meal at the adorable **$$ La Marmite de l'Abbaye** restaurant, with seating inside or out. Your hostess, sweet Breton Madame Borgnic, serves wood-fire grilled meats for lunch and dinner (arrive for the 12:00 or 13:30 service, closed Mon-Tue, tel. 02 96 87 39 39). The trail continues on well past Léhon, but you'll need a bike to make a dent in it. The villages of Evran and Treverien are both reachable by bike (allow 45 minutes from Dinan to Evran, and an additional 25 minutes to Treverien).

By Bike: The Rance River Valley could not be more bike-friendly, as there's nary a foot of elevation gain (for bike rentals, ask at the TI). Here's what I'd do with three hours and a bike: Pedal to Léhon (following the "On Foot" route, above—but be aware that rain can make the trail too muddy), then double back to Dinan and follow the bike path along the river downstream to the Port de Lyvet.

To reach the Port de Lyvet, ride through Dinan's port, staying on the old-city side of the river. You'll join a parade of ocean-bound boats as the river opens up, becoming more like an inlet of the sea. It's a breezy, level 30-minute ride past rock faces, cornfields, and slate-roofed farms to the tiny **Port de Lyvet** (cross bridge to reach village, trail ends a short distance beyond). **$ Le Lyvet Gourmand** café/restaurant is well-positioned in the village on the right after the bridge (lunch served Thu-Tue year-round, dinner July-Aug only, closed Wed, tel. 02 96 41 45 48). Serious cyclists should continue on to St-Suliac via La Vicomté (described later, under "By Car").

By Boat: Boats depart from Dinan's port, at the bottom of Rue du Jerzual, 50 feet to the left of the medieval bridge on the Dinan side (schedules depend on tides, get details at TI). The snail-paced, one-hour cruise on the *Jaman V* runs upriver to Léhon (the trip is far better on foot or bike), taking you through a lock and past pretty scenery (€14, April-Oct 4/day except none on Mon, tel. 02 96 39 28 41, www.vedettejamaniv.com). A longer cruise with **Compagnie Corsaire** goes to St-Malo (€33

round-trip—return is by bus, €26 one-way, April-Sept, frequency varies with tide—almost daily July-Aug, slow and scenic 2.5 hours one-way, tel. 08 25 13 81 00, www.compagniecorsaire.com, or ask at TI). Enjoy St-Malo (described later in this chapter), then take the bus back; return by bus takes 30-40 minutes.

By Car: Meandering the Rance River Valley by car requires a good map (orange Michelin #309 worked for me). Drivers connecting Dinan and St-Malo can include this short Rance joyride detour: From Dinan, go down to the port, then follow D-12 with the river to your right toward Taden, then toward Plouër-sur-Rance (Dinan's port-front road is occasionally blocked, in which case you'll join this route beyond the port). Stay straight through La Hisse, then drop down and turn right, following signs to *La Vicomté-sur-Rance.* Cross the Rance on the bridge and find the cute **Port de Lyvet** (lunch café described earlier), then continue to La Vicomté and find D-29 north towards St-Malo.

A little before Pleudihen-sur-Rance, take a 10-minute detour toward **La Cale de Mordreuc** to see "L9," a seal who settled here in 2000 after being rescued and fed for six months in a nearby aquarium. She refused to return to her seal colony near Mont St-Michel and has been the town's top attraction ever since. If she's not around, savor the views from the café on the harbor.

Back on the main road, track your way to **St-Suliac,** a pretty little port town—classified in *les plus beaux villages de France*—with a handful of restaurants, a small grocery store, and a *boulangerie.* Stroll the ancient alleys, find a bench on the grassy waterfront, and contemplate lunch. **$$$ La Ferme du Boucanier** is a good bet (lunch and dinner *menus,* closed Wed off-season and Tue year-round, 10 Rue du Pavé, tel. 02 23 15 06 35). From here, continue on to St-Malo or return to Dinan.

Sleeping in Dinan

Dinan is popular. Weekends and summers are tight; book ahead if you can. Dinan likes its nightlife, so be wary of rooms over loud bars, particularly on lively weekends.

IN THE OLD CENTER

$$ Hôtel Le d'Avaugour**** is Dinan's most central four-star hotel, with an efficient staff, stay-awhile lounge areas, full bar, and backyard garden oasis. It faces busy Place du Guesclin, near the town's medieval wall. The wood-furnished rooms have comfortable queen- or king-sized beds and modern hotel amenities (rooms over garden are best). Likable owner Nicolas strongly encourages two-night stays (bikes available, 1 Place du Champ, tel. 02 96 39 07 49, www.avaugourhotel.com, contact@avaugourhotel.com).

BRITTANY

Sleep Code

Hotels are classified based on the average price of a standard double room without breakfast in high season.

$$$$	**Splurge:** Most rooms over €200
$$$	**Pricier:** €150-200
$$	**Moderate:** €100-150
$	**Budget:** €50-100
¢	**Backpacker:** Under €50
RS%	**Rick Steves discount**
*	**French hotel rating system** (0-5 stars)

Unless otherwise noted, credit cards are accepted, hotel staff speak basic English, and free Wi-Fi is available. Comparison-shop by checking prices at several hotels (on each hotel's own website, on a booking site, or by email). For the best deal, *book directly with the hotel.* Ask for a discount if paying in cash; if the listing includes **RS%,** request a Rick Steves discount.

$$ Chambres d'Hôte le Logis du Jerzual is just about as cozy as it gets, with five warmly decorated rooms and thoughtful touches throughout. Gentle Sylvie Ronserray welcomes guests to her terraced yard in this haven of calm close to the action: It's just up from the port but a long, steep walk below the main town (includes breakfast, no elevator, 25 Rue du Petit Fort, tel. 02 96 85 46 54, www.logis-du-jerzual.com, sylvie.logis@laposte.net). To drop your bags, drive up the steep, narrow, and bumpy Rue du Petit Fort from the port (ignore the pedestrian zone warnings and follow the hotel signs). Parking is nearby.

$ Hôtel Arvor*** is a top-value place with a fine stone facade, ideally located in the old city a block off Place du Guesclin. It's well-run, with 24 comfortable rooms, a cozy lounge, and nine "apartments," all with small kitchens and room to stretch (good breakfast, pay parking, 5 Rue Pavie, tel. 02 96 39 21 22, www.hotelarvordinan.com, contact@hotelarvordinan.com).

$ Hôtel de la Tour de l'Horloge** is a good two-star bet burrowed deep in the town's center, with 12 imaginatively decorated and impeccably maintained rooms fronting the bar-lined Rue de la Chaux (some rooms can be noisy on weekends). Owner Catherine speaks English and gives a warm welcome (no elevator, 5 Rue de la Chaux, tel. 02 96 39 96 92, www.hotel-dinan.com, hotel.pbdelatour@orange.fr).

$ Hôtel du Théâtre is ideal for budget travelers, with four central, surprisingly sharp, clean rooms above a luminous café/bar, across from Hôtel Arvor (no elevator, 2 Rue Ste. Claire, tel. 02 96 39 06 91, theatredinan@free.fr, owner Mickael speaks some English).

CLOSER TO THE TRAIN STATION

$$ Hôtel Ibis Styles,*** with its shiny, predictable comfort, stands tall between Place du Guesclin and the train station. It works especially well for bus and train travelers, as it's central, reasonably priced, and next to the bus stop—convenient for hitting regional destinations such as St-Malo. They may have rooms when others don't (1 Place Duclos-Pinot, tel. 02 96 39 46 15, www.ibishotel.com, h5977@accor.com).

¢ Hôtel de la Gare* faces the station and offers the full Breton Monty, with *charmant* Laurence and Claude (who both love Americans), a local-as-it-gets café hangout, and surprisingly quiet, clean, and comfy rooms for a bargain. The hotel has no email of its own and you won't find it on Booking.com, but it does offer free Wi-Fi—thanks to the owners' teenage son. Call to book (family rooms, Place de la Gare, tel. 02 96 39 04 57).

NEAR DINAN

$$ Hôtel Manoir de Rigourdaine* is *the* place to stay if you have a car and two nights to savor Brittany. Overlooking a splen-

did scene of green meadows and turquoise water, this well-renovated farmhouse comes with wood beams, comfy public spaces, immaculate grounds, and three-star rooms (many with views) for two-star prices (15-minute drive north of Dinan, tel. 02 96 86 89 96, www.hotel-rigourdaine.fr, hotel.rigourdaine@wanadoo.fr). From Dinan, drop down to the port and follow D-12 toward Taden, then follow signs to *Plouër-sur-Rance,* then *Langrolay,* and look for signs to the hotel. If coming from the St-Malo area, take D-137 toward Rennes, then N-176 toward Dinan. Take the Rance Plouër exit, and follow signs to *Langrolay* until you see hotel signs. If coming from Rennes, take D-137 toward St-Malo, then N-176 toward Saint-Brieuc, take the Plouër-sur-Rance exit, and look for signs to *Langrolay* and then the hotel (for location, see the map on page 320).

Eating in Dinan

Dinan has good restaurants for every budget. Since *galettes* (savory crêpes) are the specialty, *crêperies* are a nice, inexpensive choice—and available on every corner. Be daring and try the crêpes with scallops and cream, or go for the egg-and-cheese crêpes. For a good dinner, book Le Cantorbery a day ahead if you can, and think hard

BRITTANY

Restaurant Price Code

I've assigned each eatery a price category, based on the average cost of a typical main course. Drinks, desserts, and splurge items (steak and seafood) can raise the price considerably.

$$$$	**Splurge:** Most main courses over €25
$$$	**Pricier:** €20-25
$$	**Moderate:** €15-20
$	**Budget:** Under €15

In France, a crêpe stand or other takeout spot is **$;** a sit-down brasserie, café, or bistro with affordable *plats du jour* is **$$;** a casual but more upscale restaurant is **$$$;** and a swanky splurge is **$$$$.**

about walking, riding, or driving to nearby Léhon for a charming village experience (see "Rance River Valley," earlier).

$$$ Le Cantorbery is homey yet dressy. It's a warm place (literally), where meats are grilled in the cozy dining-room fireplace *à la tradition* (closed Wed except July-Aug, just off Place du Guesclin at 6 Rue Ste. Claire, indoor dining only, two floors, tel. 02 96 39 02 52, well-run by sincere Madame Touchais).

$$$ Fleur de Sel, run by welcoming Monsieur Guillo, is where locals go for fish (meat dishes also served). The decor is appealing and the choices are varied. You'll find traditional food served with a modern twist (closed Sun eve and all day Mon, 7 Rue Ste. Claire, tel. 02 96 85 15 14).

$$ Crêperie Ahna rocks Dinan. Locals jam the place: The price is right, the dishes are tasty, and owner Gregory sets the tone for a fun experience. His vanilla rum is excellent. The cuisine goes well beyond crêpes; the do-it-yourself *pierrades*—where you cook your meat or fish on a hot stone at your table—are a treat (inside seating only, closed Sun, reservations recommended, 7 Rue de la Poissonnerie, tel. 02 96 39 09 13, http://creperie-ahna.blogspirit.com).

$$ La Lycorne is Dinan's place to go for a healthy serving of mussels prepared 20 different ways and great desserts. The cook-at-your-table *pierrades* are a good deal. The ambience is medieval, especially if you order *Potence Flambée*—meat or fish served on mini gallows. It's situated on a traffic-free street (closed Mon except July-Aug, 6 Rue de la Poissonnerie, tel. 02 96 39 08 13, www.restaurant-lycorne-dinan.com).

$ Art'Bilig is an artsy *crêperie* serving tasty organic crêpes in a convivial setting (closed Sun night and all day Tue-Wed, 8 Rue Sainte Claire, tel. 09 81 00 42 57).

$ Le Nez Rouge ("The Red Nose") is Dinan's down-and-dirty Celtic pub, serving cheap wine, local draft beer, and tasty *tartine* dishes in a raucous but welcoming atmosphere. There's great outdoor seating on a small square, but inside is where the action is. Work your way to the counter, order a glass of wine while you wait for a table, and meet a stranger (closed Mon, reservations help, 4 Rue de l'Ecole, tel. 02 96 85 94 44).

$ Pub St. Sauveur is a local watering hole/café with good prices and a hard-to-beat setting...when it's sunny (closed Sun Oct-March, across from the church at 21 Place St. Sauveur, tel. 02 96 85 30 20). The café next door offers a similar menu and prices.

At the Old Port: Have a before-dinner drink—or a meal if the waterfront setting matters more than the cuisine—at one of the many places on the river. **$$ Café Terrasses** is decent, with nice outdoor seating and moderately priced *menus* (daily March-Oct, tel. 02 96 39 09 60).

$$ L'Atelier Gourmand is loved by locals, who come here to enjoy homemade French fare cooked by Christine and served by her husband Fabrice in a half-covered, riverfront room or at indoor tables. The daily specials have an exotic touch (closed Mon year-round, off-season also closed Sun and Tue evenings, tel. 02 96 85 14 18).

Nightlife: So many lively pub-like bars line the narrow, pedestrian-friendly **Rue de la Cordonnerie** that the street is nicknamed "Rue de la Soif" ("Street of Thirst"). When the weather is good, you can sit outside at a picnic table and strike up a conversation with a friendly, tattooed Breton.

Dinan Connections

Trains from Dinan generally require a change in Dol-de-Bretagne; for some long-distance connections it may be better to take the bus to Rennes, then catch a train from there. For regional destinations the bus is generally better (bus service provided by Tibus for St-Malo and Dinard, www.tibus.fr; by Illenoo for Rennes, www.illenoo-services.fr).

From Dinan by Train to: Dol-de-Bretagne (7/day, 25 minutes), **Paris'** Gare Montparnasse (10/day, 3.5 hours, change in Dol-de-Bretagne, or in Dol and Rennes), **Pontorson/Mont St-Michel** (3/day, 1.5-2.5 hours, change in Dol, then bus or taxi from Pontorson, see "Mont St-Michel Connections" on page 312, **St-Malo** (6/day, 1-2 hours, transfer in Dol, bus is better—see below), **Amboise** (1/day, 6 hours, via Dol, Le Mans, and Tours or via Paris).

By Bus to: Rennes (with good train connections to many destinations, 7/day, 1 hour), **St-Malo** (5/day, none on Sun except in summer, 1 hour; faster, cheaper, and better than train, as bus stops are more central), **Mont St-Michel** (3/day, 3.5 hours, transfer in Rennes), **Dinard** (3/day, fewer on Sun, 45 minutes). All buses de-

BRITTANY

part from Place Duclos-Pinot (near the main post office), and most make a stop at the train station, too.

St-Malo

Come here to experience a true Breton beach resort. The old city (called Intra Muros) is your target, with pretty beaches, powerful ramparts encircling the town, and island fortifications littering the bay. The inner city is eerie, almost claustrophobic, thanks to the concentration of tall stone buildings hemmed in by towering ramparts (though a few pedestrian streets feel more open and lively). The town feels best up top on the walls, which are  *the* sight here. St-Malo is packed in July and August, when the 8,000 people who call the old city home become a minority within their own walls as they host hordes of French holiday-makers.

St-Malo is an easy 45-minute drive—or a manageable bus or train ride—from Mont St-Michel or Dinan. (However, there's no baggage storage anywhere.) If you have a whole day here, stroll St-Malo's ramparts, visit Fort du Petit Bé, cruise to Dinard, and walk to Alet.

Orientation to St-Malo

St-Malo feels simultaneously old and new. Germans occupied the town through much of World War II with almost no damage. But as the Allies pushed into France near after D-Day, Hitler ordered St-Malo's Nazi commander to fight to the end. This led to the near-total destruction of the city in one horrible week in August 1944. The quality of St-Malo's rebuild is a testament to the feisty pride and spirit of its people.

St-Malo is experiencing a spurt of tourism, thanks to the best-selling novel *All the Light We Cannot See* by Anthony Doerr, winner of the 2015 Pulitzer Prize for Fiction. This story, about a young German who joins the Nazis and a blind French girl who flees Paris for St-Malo with her father, brings wartime St-Malo to life and shows the impact of the conflict on average folks on both sides.

BRITTANY

St-Malo's Seafaring Past

St-Malo has been a sailor's town since its origin as an ancient monastic settlement about 1,500 years ago. After the fall of the Roman Empire, Norse and Viking invasions drove people from unfortified settlements to monasteries, which provided security and stability, allowing communities like this one to grow and evolve. By the 1100s, St-Malo was a powerful, fortified island, guarding strategic access to the Rance River Valley from one direction and the English Channel from the other. The town later joined the Hanseatic League (Europe's association of great trading cities), giving it economic power. Its intrepid sailors further enriched the city in the 16th century (and later) by fishing for cod off the distant coast of Newfoundland. Then St-Malo became notorious as the home of the corsairs—French mercenaries working for the king of France, and famous for daring raids on rival countries' ships. Unlike other pirates, these swashbuckling sailors were semi-legal, as they were considered the king's combatants. Until the late 1700s, St-Malo's corsairs enriched themselves—and the king—by wreaking economic havoc on England, Spain, and Holland. You'll see the statue of the last and best-known corsair of St-Malo, Robert Surcouf, as you stroll the rampart walls. The stony fortress city of St-Malo was a haven for these very wealthy, king-endorsed pirates of France.

TOURIST INFORMATION

St-Malo's glassy TI is just outside the walls across from the main city gate (Porte St. Vincent) on Esplanade St. Vincent (Mon-Sat 9:00-19:30, Sun 10:00-18:00; closed at lunchtime April-June and Sept; shorter hours and closed Sun off-season; tel. 08 25 13 52 00, www.saint-malo-tourisme.com). Pick up the helpful city map (€0.30, free at hotels), along with bus, train, and ferry schedules. Downloadable walking tours of the city are available through the TI website.

ARRIVAL IN ST-MALO

By Train: The modern TGV station is a five-minute bus ride on the #1, #2, or #3 lines to Porte St. Vincent (€1.30). If you'd rather walk, go for 15 minutes straight out of the station, then track the pointed spire in the distance for another five minutes.

By Bus: The main bus stops are near Porte St. Vincent and the TI, and at the train station (confirm which stop your bus uses—some stop at both).

By Car: Follow *Intra-Muros/Office de Tourisme* signs to the old center, and park as close as possible to Porte St. Vincent (at the merry-go-round). A big underground parking lot is opposite Porte

St. Vincent (descend near the merry-go-round), and smaller surface lots are scattered around the walls.

HELPFUL HINTS

Audioguides: The **TI** rents €12 audioguide tours for the center of St-Malo.

Wi-Fi: The TI has free Wi-Fi. To get Wi-Fi for the price of a drink, try **Tam's Kaffé** on Place des Frères Lamennais (tel. 02 23 18 24 14, closed Wed off-season). The most central place to get online inside the walls is at **Mokamalo** (closed Sun-Mon, 5 Rue de l'Orme, tel. 02 99 56 60 17).

Services: You'll find pay WCs in some gates *(portes)* leading to the old city.

Laundry: Inside the walls, there's a launderette on the corner of Rue de la Herse and Halle des Grands Degrés (daily 7:00-21:00).

Car Rental: Avis (tel. 02 23 18 07 18) and **Europcar** (tel. 02 99 56 75 17) are both inside the train station.

Bike Rental: You'll find shops willing to rent you a bike, but St-Malo is not bike-friendly. It's better to bike from Dinan, ride here, then explore St-Malo on foot (2-hour ride from Dinan north past Port de Lyvet—see page 326 and get directions at TI).

Minivan Tour: Westcapades guarantees minivan departures at least three times a week from St-Malo. Tours include Dinan and Mont St-Michel, and officially end at the Rennes train station so you can connect to Paris (see page 315).

Sights in St-Malo

The city has no important interiors: The cathedral, rebuilt after 1944, has little touristic interest, and the castle houses the city government. The city itself is the attraction—a stony wonder with some of Europe's finest ramparts in an unforgettable setting, mixing family-friendly beaches and craggy coastline. Simply walking the walls makes a visit here unforgettable.

▲St-Malo's Ramparts

To reach the ramparts, climb the stairs inside Porte St. Thomas. Then tour the walls counterclockwise. It's a rewarding mile-long romp around medieval fortifications with segments dating from the 1100s. (Note that the ramparts described here are the scenic ones: The stretch not described is not worth your time or energy.) Along the way, stairs provide access to the beach and the town. Walk down to the beaches if the tides allow (along with Mont St-Michel, St-Malo has Europe's greatest tidal changes).

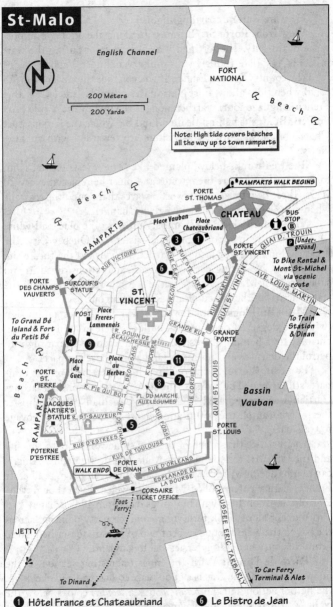

St-Malo

English Channel

FORT NATIONAL

200 Meters
200 Yards

Beach

Note: High tide covers beaches all the way up to town ramparts

RAMPARTS WALK BEGINS

PORTE ST. THOMAS

Place Vauban

Place Chateaubriand

CHATEAU

BUS STOP

QUAI D. TROUIN

PORTE ST. VINCENT

P (Underground)

To Bike Rental & Mont St-Michel via scenic route

RUE VICTOIRE

R. CORNE CERF

RUE STE BARBE

QUAI ST. VINCENT

AVE. LOUIS MARTIN

RAMPARTS

PORTE DES CHAMPS VAUVERTS

SURCOUF'S STATUE

ST. VINCENT

R. PORCON

RUE CARTIER

To Train Station & Dinan

POST

Place Freres-Lammenais

R. GOUIN DE BEAUCHESNE

GRANDE RUE

GRANDE PORTE

To Grand Bé Island & Fort du Petit Bé

Place du Guet

R. BROUSSAIS

R. BOUCHERIE

RUE CORDIERS

QUAI ST. LOUIS

Bassin Vauban

PORTE ST. PIERRE

Place au Herbes

Beach

JACQUES CARTIER'S STATUE

R. PIE QUI BOIT

RUE DE DINAN

RUE FOSSE

PL. DU MARCHE AUX LEGUMES

PORTE ST. LOUIS

RAMPARTS

R. ST-SAUVEUR

RUE D'ESTREES

RUE DE TOULOUSE

POTERNE D'ESTREE

PORTE DE DINAN

RUE D'ORLEANS

WALK ENDS

ESPLANADE DE LA BOURSE

CORSAIRE TICKET OFFICE

Foot Ferry

CHAUSSEE ERIC TABARLY

JETTY

To Dinard

To Car Ferry Terminal & Alet

BRITTANY

❶ Hôtel France et Chateaubriand & Restaurants
❷ Hôtel du Louvre
❸ Hôtel le Nautilus & Hôtel Anne de Bretagne
❹ Le Corps de Garde Crêperie
❺ La Brigantine

❻ Le Bistro de Jean
❼ Coté Sens
❽ Breizh Café & Mokamalo
❾ Brasserie Amoricaine & Tam's Kaffé
❿ La Java Café
⓫ Launderette

Here are your rampart highlights:

View from Porte St. Thomas: Imagine the strategic importance of this city. The fortified islands were built during the wars of Louis XIV (late 1600s) by his military architect, Vauban, to defend the country against England. You can tour the closer forts (€5 each) when tides allow. **Fort National** is nearest (visits only with a French-language tour). Farther along is the more worthwhile **Fort du Petit Bé.** It sits behind Ile du Grand Bé, where the famous poet Chateaubriand is buried and visitors are rewarded with striking views.

The tree trunks below, planted like little forests on the sand, form part of St-Malo's breakwater and must be replaced every 20 years. These help break the powerful waves that pound the seawalls when storms scream in off the English Channel.

View from Porte des Champs Vauverts: The blue-and-white Québec flags fly in honor of St-Malo's sister city, Québec City. The great Breton navigator Jacques Cartier, who visited the future site of Québec City during early Canadian explorations, lived in and sailed from St-Malo. Cartier's statue is further along the wall; the statue here is of the famed pirate, Robert Surcouf.

Mean Bulldogs: Look for the *Chiens du Guet* restaurant sign (with two dogs). At one time, 24 bulldogs were kept in the small, enclosed area behind the restaurant, then let loose late at night to patrol the defenses and no-man's land along these ramparts.

Porte St. Pierre: Next you'll reach a square park on the ramparts still defended by cannon. The statue, commemorating Jacques Cartier, was inaugurated in 1984 by Canadian prime minister Pierre Trudeau on the 450th anniversary of Cartier's first voyage to Canada.

You'll notice that much of the fine stonework of both the city and the ramparts feels rebuilt. St-Malo was decimated by American bombs during World War II as part of the campaign to liberate France. Eighty percent of St-Malo was leveled. Even though they look old, most of the town's buildings date from 1945 or later.

Further along, look for a long, concrete jetty pointing across the bay to the belle époque resort town of Dinard (described later). From this busy harbor big ferries sail to England.

Porte de Dinan: With the most interesting section of the ramparts behind you, this is a good place to descend and check out the harbor action and the *pétanque* (a.k.a. *boules*) courts below the walls (you may see locals playing *boule bretonne*—more like lawn bowling and with bigger balls). The Corsaire ticket kiosk marks the departure point for a foot ferry to Dinard (10 minutes each way with great views, described next).

Strolling the Old Town

After walking the ramparts, see the old town with a stroll through the town center from Porte de Dinan to Porte St. Vincent, eating, browsing, and shopping as you go. The liveliest shopping streets are Rue de Dinan, the delightful Place du Marché aux Légumes (with its medieval timber market hall), Rue de la Vieille Boucherie, and Rue Porcon de la Barbinais.

NEAR ST-MALO
Dinard

This upscale-traditional resort comes with a kid-friendly beach and an old-time, Coney Island-style, beach-promenade feel. A scenic little foot ferry *(Bus de Mer)* shuttles passengers between St-Malo and Dinard in 10 minutes (€8.30 round-trip, worthwhile for the views alone, runs 9:30-18:00, later in summer, none Nov-March). Boats depart from near Porte de Dinan on the south side of the old city—buy tickets from the kiosk labeled *Compagnie Corsaire*. Buses also run from Dinan (see page 331).

Once you're at Dinard beach, there are attractions in several directions. To reach the promenade and pool, face the ferry-ticket office, turn right, and follow the path that leads to a small cove with a couple of restaurants. Continue following the seaside on the circular *Promenade du Moulinet,* where rich Brits settled during the belle époque. When you reach the beachside swimming pool, go under the elevated road and backtrack to the boat terminal.

To get to the family-friendly beach, face the ferry-ticket office and turn left to reach this quieter beach via the yacht club. Along the way you'll see photogenic trees framing views of St-Malo.

Alet

The village of Alet is just a few minutes' drive past St-Malo's port (a 20-minute walk from the ramparts), but it feels a world apart. A splendid walking path leads around this small point with stunning views of crashing waves, the city of Dinard, the open sea, and, finally, St-Malo (allow 30 minutes at a relaxed pace, go in a clockwise direction). WWII bunkers cap the small hill; inside one of the bunkers is the small **Mémorial 39/45** museum, which commemorates the conflict in this region (€6, English leaflet, one-hour guided tours in French only, tel. 02 99 82 41 74, www.ville-saint-malo.fr). Several pleasing cafés face the bay near the Tour Solidor (a 14th-century fortification at the mouth of the Rance River).

Getting There: By **car** from St-Malo's TI or train station, follow *Toutes Directions* signs south until you spot signposts for *Alet*. Follow signs to *Alet*, then *Tour Solidor* to reach parking at the tower

BRITTANY

or nearby on Place St. Pierre. To reach the start of the walking path, walk to the sea, turn right, and climb the stairs at the end of the small bay.

On **foot** from St-Malo, walk from Porte St. Louis along the road and across the drawbridge (note the dry dock on the way to the second roundabout). Pass the *Piscine Olympique* (swimming pool), then cut right through the parking lot to the walking path that leads around the harbor. When you reach the seawall, look left for a set of steps that connects to a path around the point. At the top of the steps, you'll find more steps that lead to the Mémorial 39/45 museum and the bunkers.

Sleeping in St-Malo

($$$$ = Splurge, $$$ = Pricier, $$ = Moderate, $ = Budget)
Spending a night here gives you more time to enjoy the sunset and sea views from the town walls. It is best to park outside the walls and walk in through Porte St. Vincent to reach these hotels.

$$ Hôtel France et Chateaubriand*** is a venerable, Old World establishment near Porte St. Vincent, with fine public spaces and 80 tired rooms at OK rates (secure pay parking, 12 Place Chateaubriand, tel. 02 99 56 66 52, www.hotel-chateaubriand-st-malo. com).

$$ Hôtel du Louvre*** is a modern hotel inside the city walls with comfortable rooms at fair rates (elevator, pay parking, 2 Rue des Marins, tel. 02 99 40 86 62, www.hoteldulouvre-saintmalo. com, contact@hoteldulouvre-saintmalo.com).

$ Hôtel le Nautilus** is a solid, colorful value, run by the affable team of Loïck and Jean-Michel. It's conveniently located inside the walls near Porte St. Vincent (elevator, pay parking, 9 Rue de la Corne de Cerf, tel. 02 99 40 42 27, www.hotel-lenautilus-saint-malo.com, info@lenautilus.com).

$ Hôtel Anne de Bretagne*** offers 34 modern and cheery rooms (behind Hôtel le Nautilus, www.hotel-annedebretagne.com, hotel.annedebretagne@wanadoo.fr, tel. 02 99 56 18 00).

Eating in St-Malo

St-Malo is all about seafood and crêpes. There's no shortage of restaurants, many serving the local specialty of mussels *(moules)* and oysters *(huîtres)*. Look also for bakeries selling *ker-y-pom*, traditional apple-filled shortbread biscuits that are the best-tasting specialty in town, especially when warmed.

$ Le Corps de Garde Crêperie is up on the walls, with St-Malo's cheapest view tables. They serve so-so crêpes at fair prices from 11:30 to 22:00, with a cool ambience indoors or out (daily, 3 Montée Notre Dame, tel. 02 99 40 91 46).

$ La Brigantine offers better crêpes but no view (closed Tue-Wed except July-Aug, 13 Rue de Dinan, tel. 02 99 56 82 82).

$$$ Le Bistro de Jean serves traditional French bistro fare in a cozy, intimate setting (closed Sun, 6 Rue de la Corne de Cerf, tel. 02 99 40 98 68).

$$$ Coté Sens, enthusiastically run by the wife-and-husband team of Sandrine and Olivier, has a small but delightfully fresh selection that Sandrine happily translates for you (*menus* available, daily, 16 Rue de la Herse, tel. 02 99 20 08 12).

$$ Breizh Café has a smart, wood-accented interior and the best gourmet crêpes in St-Malo (closed Mon-Tue, reservations recommended, 6 Rue de l'Orme, tel. 02 99 56 96 08).

$$ Brasserie Amoricaine is a simple and homey spot serving traditional, good-value fare and affordable wine (closed Sun-Mon, 6 Rue du Boyer, tel. 02 99 40 89 13).

$$$ Le Chateaubriand offers two choices. The **ground-floor restaurant** delivers a grand, Old World aura and a full range of choices at decent prices (daily, inside and outdoor dining). At **Le 5,** their gourmet restaurant five floors up, you pay more for the views but the *menu* is a good value (closed Mon-Tue, Place Chateaubriand, tel. 02 99 56 66 52, www.le5-restaurant.com).

Nightlife: The oldest café in St-Malo (open since 1820) also has the longest name (too long to repeat here) and 2,874 dolls along its walls. Locals call it **La Java** and gather here for beer, wine, and *les bons temps.* Even if you won't be staying overnight in St-Malo, it's worth taking a peek at the quirky decor any time of day (near Porte St. Vincent at 3 Rue Ste. Barbe, tel. 02 99 56 41 90, www.lajavacafe.com).

St-Malo Connections

From St-Malo by Train to: Dinan (6/day, 1-2 hours, transfer in Dol-de-Bretagne, bus is better—see below), **Pontorson** (with bus connections to **Mont St-Michel;** 2/day, 2 hours, transfer in Dol), **Rennes** (1 hour, 10/day).

By Bus to: Dinan (5/day, none on Sun except in summer, 1 hour; faster and better than train, as bus stops are more central).

By Train/Bus to Mont St-Michel: (3/day, 1-2.5 hours, train to Pontorson, bus to Mont St-Michel).

Scenic Drives Near St-Malo

▲▲Scenic Drive on the Western Emerald Coast

For drivers, the western Emerald Coast *(Côte d'Emeraude)* between
Cap Fréhel and St-Malo offers the
best look at Brittany's raw beauty.
You'll drive past sweeping views of
sandy beaches with wind-sculpted
rocks and immense cliffs overlooking crashing waves (see map on page
316). The highlight is Fort la Latte, a
medieval castle built on a rocky spur
over the ocean.

Allow a half-day for the entire trip. You'll first drive to the
farthest point of the journey—the resort town of Sables-d'Or-les-
Pins—and then slowly work your way back toward St-Malo. If you
don't have much time and just want to see the fort, it's about an
hour's scenic drive from St-Malo or Dinan. During summer or on
a weekend, do this drive early to avoid crowds. If it's Saturday and
off-season, consider starting at the market in Dinard (described
earlier) and then follow my directions.

Getting to Sables-d'Or-les-Pins from St-Malo: Take D-168
west, which becomes D-786 near Ploubalay. Continue toward
Matignon and Fréhel, then watch for the turnoff to Sables-d'Or-
les-Pins.

Getting to Sables-d'Or-les-Pins from Dinan: Take D-794
to Plancoët. In the town center, follow signs to *St-Brieuc/Toutes directions*. Then follow D-17 to Matignon and D-786 to Fréhel, then
turn off to Sables-d'Or-les-Pins.

Turn left just before entering Sables-d'Or-les-Pins (a little before the Fréhel sign). Look for signs marked *la Fleche Dunaire* and
park along the road under pine trees. Tracking the Flèche Dunaire
trail, walk along the beach. At low tide, you could walk to the small
harbor.

Next, drive 15 lovely minutes on D-34 to Cap Fréhel. Explore
the rugged coast from the parking at Plage de la Fosse. Strong
hikers can park at Fort la Latte instead (see next page) and take a
75-minute walk to visit Cap Fréhel.

Cap Fréhel

This popular destination lies at the tip of a long peninsula and features walking paths over soaring cliffs with views in all directions.
You'll pay €2 to park near Cap Fréhel's stone lighthouse. The place
gets jammed on weekends and summer afternoons (if time is tight,
skip this stop and head directly to Fort la Latte). Views from the

trails are sufficiently expansive, but it is usually possible to climb the lighthouse each afternoon from April to September (€2, Mon-Fri 15:00-17:00, Sat-Sun 14:30-17:30). That's Fort la Latte to the east, your next destination.

▲▲Fort la Latte

This mighty fortress is a five-minute drive east of Cap Fréhel. From the parking lot, it's a 10-minute walk to stunning views of a me-

dieval castle hugging a massive rock above the ocean. Pick up the English flier (€0.20) or learn the historical background of the castle by reading the English info panels.

Cost and Hours: €5.50, daily 10:30-18:00, July-Aug until 19:00, tel. 02 96 41 57 11, www.castlelalatte.com.

Visiting the Fort: The first fort on this site was made from wood and built as a lookout for nasty Normans. What you see today dates from the 14th and 15th centuries, when wars between England and France caught Brittany in the middle for well over a hundred years. While the castle was never successfully attacked from the sea, in 1597 its garrison of 25 men was overwhelmed by a force of 2,000 soldiers coming overland. Later, Louis XIV's military architect Vauban oversaw work shoring up the castle's outer defenses. It was used well into the 18th century.

Touring the site, you'll cross two impressive drawbridges (notice the spiked gates), peer into dungeons (one still holds a prisoner), and wander ramparts towering high above the ocean. The guardroom houses a small gift shop (there's a good book about the castle in English for about €5). The small chapel was added in the 18th century, replacing the original chapel, and is dedicated to St. Michael, protector of warriors. The largest structure inside the fort is the governor's lodge (closed to the public because the owners—from the same family that restored the place in the 1930s—live here).

The highlight of a visit to Fort la Latte is the climb to the top of the castle keep, with a magnificent 360-degree view. You'll pass several beautifully vaulted rooms on the way up. Once on top, as you gaze out from this invincible castle, clinging for its life to a rock, think of Fort la Latte as a symbol of Brittany's determination to remain independent from France. It's no surprise that Hollywood used this castle in the 1958 film *The Vikings* with Kirk Douglas.

BRITTANY

The low-slung *four à boulets* in the western end served as a kiln to heat cannonballs. The defenders aimed hot shots at ships to set them afire. That's cool. One hundred cannon balls could be heated at a time.

If you want to stretch your legs, a trail behind the ticket kiosk links to Cap Fréhel. A 10-minute walk up this path rewards you with sensational views back to the fort; it takes 75 minutes to walk all the way to Cap Fréhel. There's also a short trail down to a rocky beach, giving you a sea-level perspective of the fortress.

Fort la Latte to St-Malo: Go back to D-786 via Plévenon and head east. A worthwhile detour on the way is **Pointe du Chevet.** From D-786, follow D-62 into the sweet little town of St-Jacut-de-la-Mer, then track signs to *Pointe du Chevet*—and don't park until the road ends. Beautiful views (and far fewer people) surround you. If the tide is out, you can hike to an island and study the impressive rows of wooden piers sunk into the bay. These are used to grow mussels, which cling to the wooden poles; farmers eventually harvest them using a machine that pushes a ring around the poles. From here, return to D-786 heading toward Ploubalay and find signs to *St-Malo* or *Dinan.*

▲▲Scenic Drive Between St-Malo and Mont St-Michel

If you have less time, consider this lovely ride—worth ▲▲▲ if it's clear (see route on map on page 316). This quick taste-of-Brittany driving tour samples a bit of the rugged peninsula's coast, with lots of views but no dramatic forts. Allow two hours for the drive between Mont St-Michel and St-Malo, including stops (a more direct route takes 45 minutes). On a weekend or in summer, the drive will take longer—start early. These directions are from St-Malo to Mont St-Michel, but the drive works just as well in reverse order.

St-Malo to Cancale: From St-Malo, take the scenic road hugging the coast east on D-201 to Pointe du Grouin. To find the road, leave St-Malo following *Paramé/Cancale* signs, then look for *Rothéneuf,* where you'll access D-201 which skirts in and out of camera-worthy views. As you drive towards Cancale, you will be surrounded by fields of cauliflowers, potatoes, and onions, reminding you that tourism and agriculture form the economic base of Brittany.

Fans of quirky sights can make a quick stop at **Les Rochers Sculptés** in Rothéneuf. At the end of the 19th century, a Catholic abbot decided to devote his life to sculpture after he became deaf and mute. With a hammer and chisel, he worked for 15 years creating his story out of the rock of a sea cliff (€2.50, daily in summer 9:00-19:00, shorter hours off-season, short introduction provided in English, tel. 02 99 56 23 95). You could make this stop longer by having lunch right here at **$$$$ Le Bénétin,** a mod restaurant serving fresh food with panoramic views (daily April-Sept, tel. 02 99 56 97 64).

Back on the road to Cancale, signs lead to short worthwhile detours to the coast; these are my favorites:

Ile Besnard and Dunes des Chevrêts: A five-minute detour off D-201 leads to this pretty, sandy beach arcing alongside a cres-

cent bay. There are sea-piercing rocks to scramble on, a nature trail above the beach, and a view restaurant (**$$$ La Perle Noire,** tel. 02 99 89 01 60). It's a 10-minute drive from Rothéneuf: Follow signs to *Ile Besnard* and *Dunes des Chevrêts* to the very end (past the campground), and park at the far end of the lot.

Pointe du Grouin: This striking rock outcrop yields views from easy trails in all directions. Park near Hôtel Pointe du Grouin (outdoor café with views), and continue on foot. Pass the *sémaphore du Grouin* (signal station), where paths lead everywhere. Breathe in the sea air. Can you spot Mont St-Michel in the distance? The big rock below is Ile des Landes, an island earmarked for a fort during the French Revolution. The fort was never built, and the island remains home to thousands of birds. What fool would build on an island in this bay?

Cancale: Return to your car and leave Pointe du Grouin, following signs to *Cancale,* Brittany's appealing oyster capital. Follow *le port* signs leading to a quiet harbour and turn left. Slurp oysters at the outdoor stands. There are several types. *Belon* are flat and round—they're finer and pricier than the more common *creuse. Pied de cheval* are older and even more expensive as they are wild, unlike most oysters growing in the seabeds in front of you. Size is rated from #5 (smallest) to #0 (biggest). The port is lined with more than 30 restaurants showing off the label *Site remarquable du goût* (extraordinary place to taste).

My favorite *site remarquable* is **$$$ Le Narval,** named after the fishing boat of Chef Gégé's grandfather. It serves fine seafood and meat dishes (reservations smart, tel. 02 99 89 63 12).

Cancale to Mont St-Michel: Cancale is a 45-minute drive from Mont St-Michel. Head out of Cancale toward Mont St-Michel on D-76/D-155, then D-797, and drive along the *Route de la Baie,* which skirts the bay and passes big-time oyster farming, windmill towers (most lacking their sails), flocks of sheep, and, at low tide, grounded boats waiting for the sea to return. On a clear

BRITTANY

day, look for Mont St-Michel in the distance. On a foggy day, look harder.

Fougères

The very Breton city of Fougères, worth ▲, is a handy stop for drivers traveling between the Loire châteaux and Mont St-Michel.

Fougères has one of Europe's largest medieval castles, a lovely old city center, and a panoramic park viewpoint. Drivers follow *Centre-Ville* signs, then *Château*, and park at the free lot just past the château.

For a memorable loop through new and old Fougères, start at the parking lot near the château. Walk into Fougères with the water-filled moat on your left, then follow the *Château* sign. Stop for a peek in the handsome **Church of St. Sulpice** (English handout inside)—the woodwork is exceptional, especially the choir stalls and altar. Then walk through **Porte Sainte Anne,** the only remaining gate to the walled city. The château is on your left, but there's no reason to visit it unless you need more exercise or want to pick up a town map at the ticket office (€8.50, includes audioguide, June-Sept daily 10:00-19:00, shorter hours and closed Mon off-season, closed Jan, tel. 02 99 99 79 59, www.chateau-fougeres.com).

Next, walk up Rue de la Pinterie (fine views) to the top of the street, then turn right on Rue Nationale at the TI. You are now in the Haute Ville (modern Fougères). Keep walking towards St. Léonard Church, passing the old belfry on a square on your right. At the church, enter the **Jardin Public** and enjoy its floral panorama. From here all paths lead down to the old town. At the bottom of the garden, find various types of *fougères* (ferns). To finish the loop, exit the Jardin Public following signs to the château and cross the little Nançon River. You'll land in the Basse Ville, the old medieval town with lovely half-timbered houses on Place du Marchix. The château is ahead.

Eating in Fougères: You'll find a gaggle of cafés and *crêperies* near the château with good choices and prices. **$$ Le Bonheur Est Dans le Blé** is a notch above the others, serving tasty crêpes on a lovely little terrace overlooking the valley (a block up from the château at 3 Rue Fourchette, tel. 02 99 94 99 72).

THE LOIRE

Amboise • Chinon • Beaucoup de Châteaux

As it glides gently east to west, officially separating northern from southern France, the Loire River has come to define this popular tourist region. The importance of this river and the valley's prime location, in the center of the country just south of Paris, have made the Loire a strategic hot potato for more than a thousand years. The Loire was the high-water mark for the Moors as they pushed into Europe from Morocco. Today, this region is still the dividing line for the country—for example, weather forecasters say, "north of the Loire...and south of the Loire..."

Because of its history, this region is home to more than a thousand castles and palaces of all shapes and sizes. When a "valley address" became a must-have among 16th-century hunting-crazy royalty, rich Renaissance palaces replaced outdated medieval castles. Hundreds of these castles and palaces are open to visitors, and it's castles that you're here to see. Old-time aristocratic château-owners, struggling with the cost of upkeep, enjoy financial assistance from the government if they open their mansions to the public.

Today's Loire Valley is carpeted with fertile fields, crisscrossed by rivers, and laced with rolling hills. It's one of France's most important agricultural regions. It's also under some development pressure, thanks to TGV bullet trains that link it to Paris in well under two hours, and cheap flights to England that make it a prime second-home spot for many Brits, including Sir Mick Jagger.

CHOOSING A HOME BASE

This is a big, unwieldy region, so I've divided it into two halves: east and west of the big city of Tours. Each area is centered around a good, manageable town—**Amboise** (east) or **Chinon** (west)—to

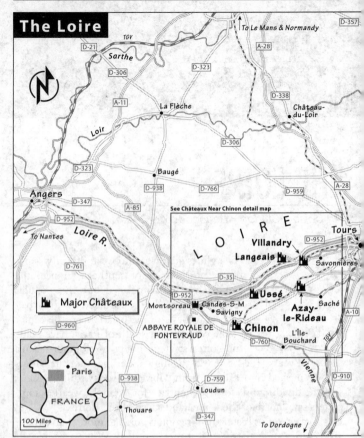

The Loire

To Le Mans & Normandy

TGV — D-21 — Sarthe — D-306 — D-323 — A-28 — D-357 — D-338 — Château-du-Loir

A-11 — La Flèche — D-306 — Loir

D-323 — Baugé — D-938 — D-766 — D-959 — A-28

Angers — D-347 — A-85 — See Châteaux Near Chinon detail map

D-952 — Loire R. — To Nantes — L O I R E — Villandry — Tours — D-952

D-761 — Langeais — Savonnières

🏰 Major Châteaux — D-35 — Ussé — Saché

Montsoreau — Candes-S-M — Azay-le-Rideau — A-10

D-960 — Savigny — Chinon — L'Île-Bouchard

ABBAYE ROYALE DE FONTEVRAUD — D-760

Paris — FRANCE — D-938 — D-759 — Loudun — Vienne — D-910

100 Miles — Thouars — D-347 — To Dordogne ↓

LOIRE

use as a home base for exploring nearby châteaux. Which home base should you choose? That will depend on which châteaux you'd like to visit; for ideas, scan the "Loire Valley Châteaux at a Glance" sidebar on page 350. For many travelers, Amboise is the better choice.

Châteaux-holics and gardeners can stay longer and sleep in both towns. The drive from Amboise to Chinon takes about an hour; if you sleep on one side of Tours and intend to visit castles on the other side, you're looking at a long round-trip drive—certainly doable, but not my idea of good travel. Instead, sleep in or near the town nearest the castles you plan to visit, and avoid crossing traffic-laden Tours. The A-85 autoroute (toll) is the quickest way to link Amboise with châteaux near Chinon. Thanks to this uncrowded freeway, sleepy Azay-le-Rideau is another good base for destinations west of Tours; it also works as a base for sights on both sides of Tours.

East of Tours: Amboise and, to a lesser extent, **Blois** or **Chenonceaux,** make the best home bases for first-timers. Amboise and

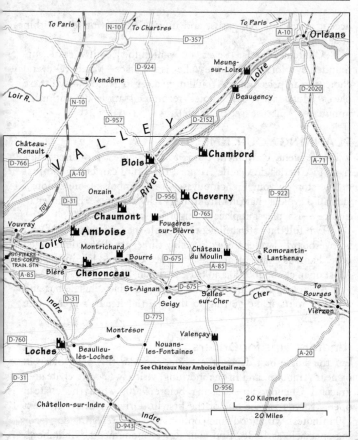

Blois have handy car or bus/minivan access to these important châteaux: elegant Chenonceau, urban Blois, epic Chambord, canine-
crazy Cheverny, royal Amboise, and garden-showy Chaumont-sur-
Loire. Amboise has good minivan service to area sights, and drivers
appreciate its small scale and easy parking; Blois has better train
connections from Paris and better low-cost transportation options
to nearby sights in high season. The serene town of Chenonceaux
works for drivers and hardy bicyclists. Most visitors choose Amboise for its just-right size and more varied tourist appeal.

West of Tours: Chinon, Azay-le-Rideau, and their nearby
châteaux don't feel as touristy; these towns appeal to gardeners and
road-less-traveled types. The key châteaux in this area are historic
Chinon, fairy-tale Azay-le-Rideau, fortress-like Langeais, and
garden-lush Villandry. Lesser sights include the châteaux at Rivau
and Ussé, plus the Abbaye Royale de Fontevraud. Chinon and
Azay-le-Rideau are good for cyclists, with convenient rental shops,

decent access to bike paths, and interesting destinations within pedaling distance.

Château Hotels: If ever you wanted to sleep in a castle surrounded by a forest, the Loire Valley is the place—you have several choices in all price ranges. You'll need a car to get to most of these places. Most of my "castle hotel" recommendations are within 15 minutes of Amboise (see page 372).

PLANNING YOUR TIME

With frequent, convenient trains to Paris and a few direct runs right to Charles de Gaulle Airport, the Loire can be a good first or last stop on your French odyssey (see "Amboise Connections," later). I'd avoid a château blitz strategy; this region—"the garden of France"—is a pleasant place to linger.

Two full days are sufficient to sample the best châteaux. Don't go overboard. Two châteaux, possibly three, are the recommended dose. Famous châteaux are least crowded early and late in the day. Most open at about 9:00 and close between 18:00 and 19:00.

A day trip from Paris to the Loire is doable. Shuttle bus and minivan tours make getting to the main châteaux a breeze (see page 351).

Itinerary Tips for Drivers

For the single best day in the Loire, consider this plan: Sleep in or near Amboise, and in the morning, visit my favorite château—graceful Chenonceau—arriving before 9:00, when the château opens, so you can be one of the first in. Drive to Cheverny next (40 minutes), with good lunch options and an interesting dog feeding spectacle at 11:30. End your day at monumental Chambord, a 15-minute drive from Cheverny. Energetic travelers could visit Chaumont on their way back to Amboise. If you want to see the dog feeding at Cheverny you need to be focused and leave Chenonceau by 10:30—or visit these sights in reverse order, starting with Chambord (arrive close to 9:00 opening), then Cheverny, and ending at Chenonceau (this risks more crowds at Chenonceau).

The next morning, allow time to visit Amboise's sights before heading to your next stop. With a second full day, you could move to Chinon, visiting Villandry and its gardens en route, then devote your afternoon to the château and old town in Chinon.

Try to see one château on your drive in (for example, if arriving from the north, visit Chambord, Chaumont, or Blois; if coming from the west or the south, see Azay-le-Rideau or Villandry). If you're coming from Burgundy, don't miss the one-of-a-kind Château de Guédelon (see page 879 in the Burgundy chapter). If you're driving to the Dordogne from the Loire, the A-20 autoroute via Limoges (near Oradour-sur-Glane) is fastest and toll-free until Brive-la-Gaillarde.

The best map of the area is Michelin #518, covering all the sights described in this chapter (the TI's free map of Touraine—the area surrounding Tours—is also good).

Itinerary Tips for Those Without a Car

Sleep in Amboise and take a minivan excursion (see the next section). This is by far the best plan for most visitors and allows easy access to all châteaux described in this chapter.

Budget travelers with one day can catch the public bus, shuttle van (high season only), or train from Amboise to the town of Chenonceaux, tour Chenonceau (a must-see château), then return to Amboise in the afternoon to enjoy its château and Leonardo's last stand at Clos-Lucé. With a second day, take the short (and cheap) train ride to Blois, and visit massive Chambord (either take a shuttle bus—see page 392—or rent a bike). Try to budget time to also visit Blois itself before returning to Amboise. With more time, those connecting Paris with Amboise or Chinon can lay over in Blois en route (lockers available at Blois château with paid admission).

Budget travelers based in Chinon can bike to Langeais, Ussé, and Villandry, and/or take the train to Azay-le-Rideau and Langeais (but keep in mind that bike and train trips are long and not a good option for most). Minivan excursions from Tours are the best option for most nondrivers staying in Chinon.

GETTING AROUND THE LOIRE VALLEY

Traveling by car is the easiest way to get around, and day rentals are reasonable. Trains, buses, minivan tours, taxis, and bikes allow those without a car to reach the well-known châteaux. But even the less-famous châteaux are accessible: Take a taxi, arrange a custom minivan excursion (affordable for small groups), or ride a bike (great option for those with time and stamina).

By Car

You can rent a car most easily at the St-Pierre-des-Corps TGV station just outside Tours; rentals are also available in Amboise (see page 357). Parking is free at all châteaux except Chambord.

By Train

With easy access from Amboise and Chinon, the big city of Tours is the transport hub for travelers bent on using trains or buses to explore the Loire (but it has little else to offer visitors—I wouldn't sleep there). Tours has two important train stations and a major bus station (with service to several châteaux). The main train station is

Loire Valley Châteaux at a Glance

Which châteaux should you visit—and why? Here's a quick summary. Local TIs sell bundled tickets for several châteaux that save you money and time in ticket lines (see page 357).

Châteaux East of Tours

▲▲▲**Chenonceau** Elegant château arching over the Cher River, with lovely gardens. **Hours:** Daily mid-March-mid-Sept 9:00-19:30, July-Aug until 20:00, closes earlier off-season. See page 379.

▲▲▲**Chambord** Epic grandeur (440 rooms) and fun rooftop views in an evocative setting surrounded by a forest. **Hours:** Daily 9:00-18:00, Oct-March until 17:00. See page 393.

▲▲**Blois** Urban château with a beautiful courtyard and fun sound-and-light show. **Hours:** Daily April-Sept 9:00-18:30 plus July-Aug until 19:00, Oct until 18:00, Nov-March 9:00-12:30 & 14:30-17:30. See page 387.

▲▲**Cheverny** Intimate feeling château with lavish furnishings and daily feeding of the hunting dogs. **Hours:** Daily April-Oct 9:15-18:30, Nov-March 10:00-17:00. See page 397.

▲▲**Chaumont-sur-Loire** Imposing setting over the Loire River, notable for its historic connections to America and impressive Festival of Gardens. **Hours:** Daily 10:00-18:30, Oct until 18:00, Nov-March until 17:00. See page 399.

Chenonceau   *Chambord*

Tours SNCF, and the smaller, suburban TGV station (located between Tours and Amboise) is St-Pierre-des-Corps. Check schedules carefully, as service is sparse on some lines. The châteaux of Amboise, Blois, Chenonceau, Chaumont (via the town of Onzain plus a long walk), Langeais, Chinon, and Azay-le-Rideau all have train and/or bus service from Tours' main SNCF station; Amboise, Blois, Chenonceau, and Chinon are also served from the St-Pierre-des-Corps station. Look under each sight for specifics, and seriously consider a minivan excursion (described next).

▲**Amboise** Supposed burial place of Leonardo da Vinci, with terrific views over Amboise. **Hours:** Daily April-Oct 9:00-18:00, July-Aug until 19:00, shorter hours off-season. See page 355.

▲**Clos-Lucé (in Amboise)** Leonardo da Vinci's final home and gardens, with models of his creations. **Hours:** Daily Feb-Oct 9:00-19:00, July-Aug until 20:00; shorter hours off-season. See page 364.

Châteaux West of Tours
▲▲**Azay-le-Rideau** Set on a romantic reflecting pond, with a fairy-tale facade and beautifully furnished rooms (under renovation until mid-2017). **Hours:** Daily April-Oct 9:30-18:00, July-Aug until 19:00, Nov-March 10:00-17:15. See page 415.

▲▲**Villandry** Average palace boasting the best gardens in the Loire—and possibly all of France. **Hours:** Daily 9:00-19:00, March and Oct until 18:00, Nov-Feb until 17:00. See page 420.

▲**Langeais** Fortress-like setting above an appealing little village with evocative 15th- and 16th-century rooms. **Hours:** Daily July-Aug 9:00-19:00, April-June and Sept-mid-Nov 9:30-18:30, mid-Nov-March 10:00-17:00. See page 418.

Chaumont-sur-Loire   *Azay-le-Rideau*

LOIRE

By Shuttle Bus/Van or Minivan Tour
Shuttle services and minivan tours offer affordable transportation to many of the valley's châteaux. Shuttles connect Amboise, Tours, or Blois with key châteaux in peak season (€6-16), and minivan tours combine several châteaux into a painless day tour (about €35-40/person for scheduled half-day itineraries from Amboise or Tours, €55-60 for all day; figure €230 for custom groups of up to 7 for 4 hours, €400 for 8 hours). Most of these services depart from TIs (who can book them for you) and can save you time (in line)

and money (on admissions) when you purchase your château ticket at a discounted group rate from the driver.

By Shuttle Bus: In high season, a handy excursion bus does a loop route connecting Blois, Chambord, Cheverny, and (skippable) Beauregard, allowing visits to the châteaux with your pick of return times (runs several days per week, daily July-Aug). It departs from the train station in Blois, an easy train ride from Amboise and a good place to bed down (for shuttle details, see "Blois Connections" on page 392). **Public buses** also connect Tours, Amboise, and Chenonceaux (see "Amboise Connections" on page 377).

By Shuttle Van: Touraine Evasion runs a high-season only shuttle linking Amboise with Chenonceau (see "Amboise Connections" on page 377).

By Minivan Tour: Tour operators **Acco-Dispo, Touraine Evasion,** and **Loire Valley Tours** offer half- and full-day itineraries from Amboise and/or Tours that hit all the main châteaux (see "Amboise Connections" on page 377). **Eco Shuttle** runs similar excursions from Blois (see page 393).

Minivan excursions also leave from the Tours TI office (right outside the Tours SNCF train station) to many châteaux; some include wine tasting (book at www.tours-tourisme.fr, tel. 02 47 70 37 37, easy connections from Amboise, Blois, or Chinon; see "By Train," earlier).

By Taxi

Taxi excursions can be affordable when split among several people, especially from the Blois train station to nearby châteaux, or from Amboise to Chenonceau. For details, see "Blois Connections" on page 392, and "Amboise Connections" on page 377.

By Bike

Cycling options are endless in the Loire, where the elevation gain is generally manageable. (However, if you have only a day or two, rent a car or stick to the châteaux easily reached by buses and minivans.) Amboise, Chenonceaux, Blois, Azay-le-Rideau, and Chinon all make good biking bases and have rental options (ask at TIs). A network of nearly 200 miles of bike paths and well-signed country lanes connect many châteaux near Amboise. Pick up the free bike-path map at any TI, buy the more detailed map available at TIs, or study the route options at www.cycling-loire.com.

About five miles from Chinon, a 30-mile bike path runs along the Loire River, passing by Ussé and Langeais. It meets the Cher River at Villandry and continues along the Cher to Tours and beyond. To follow this route, pick up the *La Loire à Vélo* brochure at any area TI.

Hot-Air Balloon Rides

In France's most popular regions, you'll find hot-air balloon companies eager to take you for a ride (Burgundy, the Loire, Dordogne, and Provence are best suited for ballooning). It's not cheap, but it's unforgettable—a once-in-a-lifetime chance to sail serenely over châteaux, canals, vineyards, Romanesque churches, and villages. Balloons don't go above 3,000 feet and usually fly much lower than that, so you get a bird's-eye view of France's sublime landscapes.

Most companies offer similar deals and work this way: Trips range from 45 to 90 minutes of air time, to which you should add two hours for preparation, champagne toast, and transport back to your starting point. Deluxe trips add a gourmet picnic, making it a four-hour event. Allow about €200 for a short tour, and about €300 for longer flights. Departures are, of course, weather-dependent, and are usually scheduled first thing in the morning or in early evening. If you've booked ahead and the weather turns bad, you can reschedule your flight, but you can't get your money back. Most balloon companies charge about €25 more for a bad-weather refund guarantee; unless your itinerary is very loose, it's a good idea.

Flight season is April through October. It's smart to bring a jacket for the breeze, though temperatures in the air won't differ too much from those on the ground. Heat from the propane flames that power the balloon may make your hair stand up—I wear a cap. Airsickness is usually not a problem, as the ride is typically slow and even. Baskets have no seating, so count on standing the entire trip. Group (and basket) size can vary from 4 to 16 passengers. Area TIs have brochures. **France Montgolfières** gets good reviews and offers flights in the areas that I recommend (tel. 02 54 32 20 48, www.france-balloons.com). Others are **Aérocom Montgolfière** (tel. 02 54 33 55 00, www.aerocom.fr) and **Touraine Montgolfière** (tel. 02 47 56 42 05, www.touraine-montgolfiere.fr).

Détours de Loire can help you plan your bike route. They can also deliver rental bikes to most places in the Loire for reasonable rates. They have a full range of bikes—kid-size, tandems, and electric—and will shuttle luggage to your next stop if you reserve ahead. They have shops in Amboise, Blois, and Tours, allowing one-way rentals between these and their partner shops (www.locationdevelos.com).

TOURS IN THE LOIRE VALLEY

Local Guide: Fabrice Maret is an expert in all things Loire and a great teacher. He lives in Blois but can meet you in Amboise to give an excellent walking tour of the city and its sights, or he'll guide you around the area's châteaux using your rental car (€260/day plus transportation from Blois, tel. 02 54 70 19 59, www.chateauxloire. com, info@chateauxloire.com).

Useful Apps: Many major châteaux have free apps that reproduce their rentable audioguides—check château websites for info. The Amboise and Blois TIs also offer free city guide apps. Download these apps before you leave home to save time and money when you get here.

THE LOIRE VALLEY'S CUISINE SCENE

Here in "the garden of France," locally produced food is delicious. Look for seasonal vegetables, such as white and green asparagus, and *champignons de Paris*—mushrooms grown in local caves, not in the capital. Around Chinon, pears and apples are preserved *tapées* (dried and beaten flat for easier storage), rehydrated in alcohol, and served in tasty recipes. Loire Valley rivers yield fresh trout *(truite)*, shad *(alose)*, and smelt *(éperlan)*, which are often served fried *(friture)*. Various dishes highlight *rillons*, big chunks of cooked pork, while *rillettes*, a stringy pile of *rillons*, make for a cheap, mouthwatering sandwich spread (add a baby pickle, called a *cornichon*).

Locally raised pork is a staple, but don't be surprised to see steak, snails, *confit de canard* (a Dordogne duck specialty), and seafood on menus—the Loire borrows much from neighboring regions. The area's wonderful goat cheeses include Crottin de Chavignol (*crottin* means horse dung, which is what this cheese, when aged, resembles), Saint-Maure de Touraine (soft and creamy), and Selles-sur-Cher (mild). For dessert, try a delicious *tarte tatin* (upside-down caramel-apple tart). Regional pastries include *sablés* (shortbread cookies) from Sablé-sur-Sarthe.

Remember, restaurants serve food only during lunch (around 11:30-14:00) and dinner (19:00-21:00, later in bigger cities); bigger cafés offer eats throughout the day.

WINES OF THE LOIRE

Loire wines are overlooked, and that's a shame—there is gold in them thar grapes. The Loire is France's third-largest producer of wine and grows the greatest variety of any region. Four main grapes are grown in the Loire: two reds, gamay and cabernet franc, and two whites, sauvignon blanc and chenin blanc.

The Loire is divided into four subareas, and the name of a wine (its *appellation*) generally refers to where its grapes were grown. The Touraine subarea encompasses the wines of Chinon and Amboise. Using 100 percent cabernet franc grapes, growers in Chinon and Bourgueil are the main (and best) producers of reds. Thanks to soil variation and climate differences year in and out, wines made from a single grape have a remarkable range in taste. The best and most expensive white wines are the Sancerres, made on the less-touristed eastern edge of the Loire. Less expensive, but still tasty, are Touraine Sauvignons and the sweeter Vouvray, whose grapes are grown near Amboise. Vouvray is also famous for its light and refreshing sparkling wines (called *vins pétillants*)—locals will tell you the only proper way to begin any meal in this region is with a glass of it, and I can't disagree (try the *rosé pétillant* for a fresh sensation). A dry rosé is popular in the Loire in the summer and can be made from a variety of grapes.

You'll pass scattered vineyards as you travel between châteaux, though there's no scenic wine road to speak of (the closest thing is around Bourgueil). It's best to call ahead before visiting a winery.

East of Tours

The area east of Tours includes the good home-base towns of Amboise and Blois (each with their own châteaux), and several of the area's top châteaux: popular Chenonceau (in the town of Chenonceaux—another fine home base), massive Chambord, lavish Cheverny, and the strategically-located-up-a-cliff Chaumont.

Amboise

Straddling the widest stretch of the Loire River, Amboise is an inviting town with a pleasing old quarter below its hilltop château. A

castle has overlooked the Loire from Amboise since Roman times. Leonardo da Vinci retired here...just one more of his many brilliant ideas.

As the royal residence of François I (r. 1515-1547), Amboise wielded far more importance than you'd imagine from

a lazy walk through its pleasant, pedestrian-only commercial zone. In fact, its residents are pretty conservative, giving the town an attitude—as if no one told them they're no longer the second capital of France. Locals keep their wealth to themselves; consequently, many grand mansions hide behind nondescript facades.

With or without a car, Amboise is an ideal small-town home base for exploring the best of château country.

LOIRE

Orientation to Amboise

Amboise (pop. 14,000) covers ground on both sides of the Loire, with the "Golden Island" (Ile d'Or) in the middle. The train station is on the north side of the Loire, but nearly everything else is on the south (château) side. Pedestrian-friendly Rue Nationale parallels the river a few blocks inland and leads from the base of Château d'Amboise through the town center and past the clock tower—once part of the town wall—to the Romanesque Church of St-Denis.

TOURIST INFORMATION

The information-packed TI is on Quai du Général de Gaulle (April-Oct Mon-Sat 10:00-18:00 except July-Aug from 9:00, Sun 10:00-12:30; Nov-March Mon-Sat 10:00-12:30 & 14:00-17:00, closed Sun; tel. 02 47 57 09 28, www.amboise-valdeloire.com). Pick up the city map, download their free city guide app, and consider purchasing tickets to key area châteaux (saving money and time in ticket lines—see "Helpful Hints," later). Ask about sound-and-light shows in the region (generally summers only).

The TI stores bags (€2.50 each), books local guides, and can reserve a room for you in a hotel or *chambres d'hôte* (€3 fee). They allow 10 minutes of free Wi-Fi and have a pay public computer. They can also help organize tours to the châteaux with a shuttle bus or minivan service. All minivan tours from Amboise leave from the TI.

ARRIVAL IN AMBOISE

By Train: Amboise's train station is birds-chirping peaceful. You can't store bags here, but you can leave them at the TI or at some châteaux (see "Baggage Storage," later). Allow 20 minutes to walk to the TI from the station: Turn left out of the station (you may have to cross under the tracks first), make a quick right, and walk down Rue Jules Ferry five minutes to the end, then turn right and cross the long bridge leading over the Loire River to the city center. It's an €8 taxi ride from the station to central Amboise, but taxis seldom wait at the station (see "Helpful Hints" for taxi phone numbers).

By Car: Drivers set their sights on the flag-festooned château that caps the hill. Most recommended accommodations and restaurants either have or can help you locate parking (it's free in the big lot along the river across from the TI).

HELPFUL HINTS

Exchange Rate: €1 = about $1.10
Country Calling Code: 33 (see page 1082 for dialing instructions)

Save Time and Money: The TI sells tickets in bundles of two or more to sights and châteaux around Amboise and Chinon, which saves on entry fees—and, more important, time spent in line. You can also get discounted tickets if you take a minivan tour (see "Getting Around the Loire Valley" on page 349).

Market Days: Open-air markets are held on Friday (smaller but more local; food only) and Sunday (the big one) in the parking lot behind the TI on the river (both 8:30-13:00).

Regional Products: Galland, at 29 Rue Nationale, sells fine food and wine products from the Loire (daily 9:30-19:00).

Bookstore: Lu & Approuvé has a small selection of English novels and a big selection of maps and English guidebooks such as Michelin's Green Guide *Châteaux of the Loire;* they also sell English translations of bike-route books (Mon-Sat 8:00-19:00, Sun 9:30-12:30, a block from the TI at 5 Quai du Général de Gaulle).

Baggage Storage: Besides the **Amboise TI,** which stores bags for a fee, most châteaux offer free storage if you've paid admission.

Laundry: The nearest launderette is at **Supermarket LeClerc,** a half-mile from the TI toward Tours on D-751.

Supermarket: Carrefour City is near the TI (Mon-Sat 7:00-22:00, Sun 9:00-13:00, 5 Quai du Général de Gaulle), though the specialty shops on pedestrian-only Rue Nationale are infinitely more pleasing.

Bike Rental: You can rent a bike (leave your passport or a photocopy) at any of these reliable places: **Détours de Loire** (allows one-way trips to any of its partner shops May-Sept, in round building across from TI on Quai du Général de Gaulle, tel. 02 47 30 00 55), **Locacycle** (daily, full-day rentals can be returned the next morning, 2 Rue Jean-Jacques Rousseau, tel. 02 47 57 00 28), or **Cycles le Duc** (good bikes, closed Sun-Mon, 5 Rue Joyeuse, tel. 02 47 57 00 17).

Taxi: There is no taxi station in Amboise, so you must call for one (tel. 02 47 57 13 53, 06 12 92 70 46, 02 47 57 30 39, or 06 88 02 44 10).

Car Rental: It's easiest to rent cars at the St-Pierre-des-Corps train station (TGV service from Paris), a 15-minute drive from Amboise. On the outskirts of Amboise, **Désiré Automobile** rents cars (roughly €58/day for a small car with 100 kilometers/62 miles free, credit card required for €600 deposit; closed Sun, about a mile downriver from the TI at 105 Avenue de Tours, by Renault garage, tel. 02 47 57 17 92, renault-amboise@ orange.fr). Pricier **Europcar** is outside Amboise on Route de Chenonceaux at the Total gas station (about €72/day for a small car, tel. 02 47 57 07 64, reservation tel. 02 47 85 85 85,

LOIRE

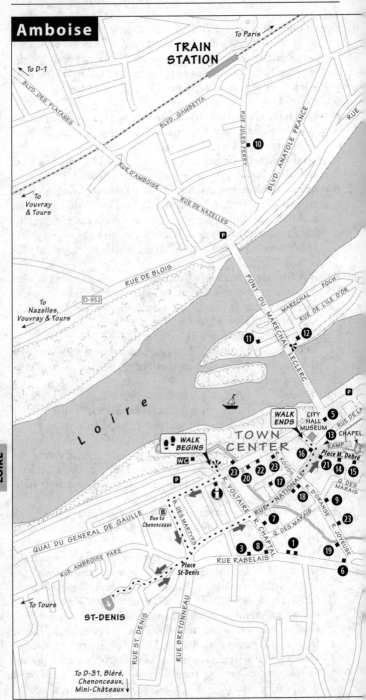

Amboise

To Paris

TRAIN STATION

To D-1

BLVD. DES PLATANES

BLVD. GAMBETTA

RUE JULES FERRY

BLVD. ANATOLE FRANCE

RUE

🔟

RUE D'AMBOISE

To Vouvray & Tours

RUE DE NAZELLES

P

RUE DE BLOIS

D-952

To Nazelles, Vouvray & Tours

PONT DU MARÉCHAL LECLERC

MARÉCHAL FOCH

RUE DE L'ILE D'OR

1️⃣1️⃣

1️⃣2️⃣

L o i r e

P

WALK ENDS

CITY HALL MUSEUM

5️⃣

RUE DE LA

1️⃣3️⃣ CHAPEL

RAMP

TOWN CENTER

1️⃣6️⃣

Place M. Debré

2️⃣1️⃣

1️⃣4️⃣ 1️⃣5️⃣

WALK BEGINS

WC

2️⃣3️⃣ 2️⃣0️⃣ 2️⃣2️⃣ 2️⃣3️⃣

R. ROUSS.

RUE NATIONALE

R. D'ORANGE

Q. DES MARAIS

9️⃣

2️⃣3️⃣

i

R. VOLTAIRE

1️⃣7️⃣

1️⃣8️⃣

R. JOYEUSE

P

A. DES MARTYRS

Bus to Chenonceaux

B

7️⃣

R. CHAPTAL

Q. DES MARAIS

QUAI DU GENERAL DE GAULLE

RUE AMBOISE PARC

3️⃣ 8️⃣

1️⃣

1️⃣9️⃣

RUE RABELAIS

6️⃣

To Tours

Place St-Denis

ST-DENIS

RUE ST. DENIS

RUE BRETONNEAU

To D-31, Bléré, Chenonceaux, Mini-Châteaux

LOIRE

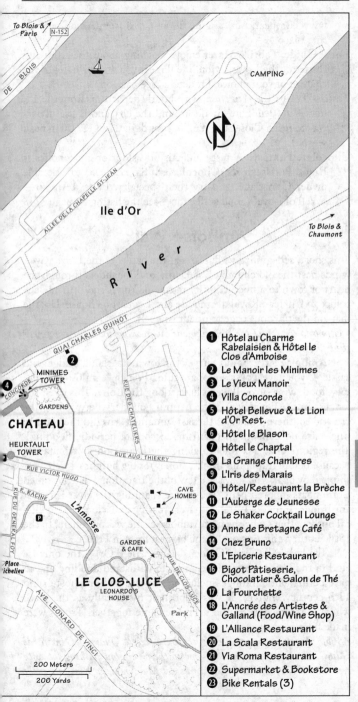

To Blois & Paris — N-152

DE BLOIS

CAMPING

N

ALLEE DE LA CHAPELLE ST-JEAN

Ile d'Or

River

To Blois & Chaumont

QUAI CHARLES GUINOT

MINIMES TOWER

CONCORDE

GARDENS

RUE DES CHATELIERS

CHATEAU

HEURTAULT TOWER

RUE AUG. THIERRY

RUE VICTOR HUGO

R. RACINE

CAVE HOMES

RUE DU GENERAL FOY

L'Amasse

Place Richelieu

GARDEN & CAFE

RUE DE CLOS-LUCE

LE CLOS-LUCE

LEONARDO'S HOUSE

Park

AVE. LEONARD DE VINCI

200 Meters
200 Yards

1 Hôtel au Charme Rabelaisien & Hôtel le Clos d'Amboise
2 Le Manoir les Minimes
3 Le Vieux Manoir
4 Villa Concorde
5 Hôtel Bellevue & Le Lion d'Or Rest.
6 Hôtel le Blason
7 Hôtel le Chaptal
8 La Grange Chambres
9 L'Iris des Marais
10 Hôtel/Restaurant la Brèche
11 L'Auberge de Jeunesse
12 Le Shaker Cocktail Lounge
13 Anne de Bretagne Café
14 Chez Bruno
15 L'Epicerie Restaurant
16 Bigot Pâtisserie, Chocolatier & Salon de Thé
17 La Fourchette
18 L'Ancrée des Artistes & Galland (Food/Wine Shop)
19 L'Alliance Restaurant
20 La Scala Restaurant
21 Via Roma Restaurant
22 Supermarket & Bookstore
23 Bike Rentals (3)

LOIRE

www.europcar.com). Figure €8 for a taxi from Amboise to either place.

Local Guide: Fabrice Maret enjoys teaching about the cities and castles of the Loire region. He'll meet you at your hotel or the château of your choice; for details, see page 353.

Tourist Train: The *petit train,* with hourly departures from the TI, makes a 40-minute circuit around the city and is useful as a way to reach Clos-Lucé (€6.50, runs daily 11:00-17:00 in peak season).

Chocolate Fantasy: A tasty and historic stop for chocoholics is **Bigot Pâtisserie & Chocolatier.** Say *bonjour* to adorable owner Christiane, and try their specialty, Puits d'Amour—"Well of Love" (good coffee too—see the listing on page 374).

Amboise Walk

This short, self-guided walk starts at the banks of the Loire River, winds past the old church of St-Denis, and meanders through the heart of town to a fine little city museum. You'll end near the entrance to Château Royal d'Amboise and Leonardo's house. Use the map on the previous page to orient yourself.

• *Climb to the top of the embankment overlooking the river from near the bridge.*

Amboise Riverbank: Survey the town, its island, bridge, and castle. If you have a passion for anything French—philosophy, history, food, wine—you'll feel it here, along the Loire. This river, the longest in the country and the natural boundary between northern and southern France, is the last "untamed" river in the country (there are no dams or mechanisms to control periodic flooding). The region's châteaux line up along the Loire and its tributaries, because before trains and trucks, stones for big buildings were best shipped by boat. You may see a few of the traditional flat-bottomed Loire boats moored here. The bridge spanning the river isn't just any bridge. It marks a strategic river crossing and a longtime political border. That's why the first Amboise castle was built here. In the 15th century, this was one of the biggest forts in France.

The half-mile-long "Golden Island" (Ile d'Or) is the only island in the Loire substantial enough to withstand flooding and to have permanent buildings (including a soccer stadium, hostel, and 13th-century church). It was important historically as the place where northern and southern France came together. Truces were made here.

• *Walk downstream paralleling the busy street, Quai du Général de Gaulle, and cross it when you come to the riverfront parking lot with trees and a gazebo. Walk up Avenue des Martyrs de la Résistance (the post office—La Poste—is on the corner) and turn right at Place St-Denis to find the old church standing proudly on a bluff to the right.*

Church of St-Denis (Eglise St-Denis): Ever since ancient Romans erected a Temple of Mars here, this has been a place of worship. According to legend, God sent a bolt of lightning that knocked down the statue of Mars, and Christians took over the spot. The current Romanesque church dates from the 12th century. A cute little statue of St. Denis (above the round arch) greets you as you step in. The delightful carvings capping the columns inside date from Romanesque times. The lovely (but poorly lit) pastel-painted *Deposition* to the right of the choir is restored to its 16th-century brilliance. The medieval stained glass in the windows, likely destroyed in the French Revolution, was replaced with 19th-century glass. A plaque in the rear of the church lists Amboise residents who died in the First World War.

From the steps of the church, look out to the hill-capping Amboise château. For a thousand years, it's been God on this hill and the king on that one. It's interesting to ponder how, throughout French history, the king's power generally trumped the Church's, and how the Church and the king worked to keep people down—setting the stage for the French Revolution.

• *Retrace your steps down from the church and across Place St-Denis, go past Amboise's lone cinema, continue walking straight, and follow Rue Nationale through the heart of town toward the castle.*

Rue Nationale: In France, districts around any castle or church officially classified as historic are preserved. The broad, pedestrianized Rue Nationale, with its narrow intersecting lanes, survives from the 15th century. At that time, when the town spread at the foot of the king's castle, this was the "Champs-Elysées" of Amboise. Supporting the king and his huge entourage was a serious industry. The French king spilled money wherever he stayed.

As you walk along this spine of the town, spot surviving bits of rustic medieval oak in the half-timbered buildings. The homes of wealthy merchants rose from the chaos of this street. Side lanes can be more candid—they often show what's hidden behind modern facades.

Stop when you reach the impressive **clock tower** (Tour de l'Horloge), built into part of the 15th-century town wall. This was once a fortified gate, opening onto the road to the city of Tours. Imagine the hefty wood-and-iron portcullis (fortified door) that dropped from above.

• *At the intersection with Rue François I (where you'll be tempted by the Bigot chocolate shop), turn left a couple of steps to the...*

City Hall Museum: This free museum is worth a quick peek for its romantic interior, town paintings, and historic etchings (open Wed-Mon in summer only). In the room dedicated to Leonardo da Vinci are his busts and the gripping deathbed painting of him with caring King François I at his side. In the Salle des Rois (Kings' Room), find portraits of Charles VIII (who coldcocked himself at Amboise's castle; more on this later) and other kings who called Amboise home; I like to admire their distinct noses.

Upstairs, in the still-functioning city assembly hall (last room), notice how the photo of the current president faces the lady of the Republic. (According to locals, her features change with the taste of the generation, and the bust of France's Lady Liberty is often modeled on famous supermodels of the day.)

• *Retrace your steps along Rue François I to Place Michel Debré, at the base of the Château Royal d'Amboise and the end of this walk. Here, at one of the most touristy spots in the Loire, tourism's importance to the local economy is palpable. Notice the fat, round 15th-century fortified tower, whose interior ramp was built for galloping horses to spiral up to castle level (but without a horse, you'll have to walk up the long ramp). Beyond the château is Leonardo's last residence at Clos-Lucé.*

Sights in Amboise

CHATEAUX
▲Château Royal d'Amboise

This historic heap, built mostly in the late 15th century, became the favored royal residence in the Loire under Charles VIII. Charles is famous for accidentally killing himself by walking into a door lintel on his way to a tennis match (seriously). Later, more careful occupants include Louis XII (who moved the royal court to Blois) and François I (who physically brought the Renaissance here in 1516, in the person of Leonardo da Vinci).

Cost and Hours: €12, daily April-Oct 9:00-18:00, July-Aug until 19:00, shorter hours off-season, unnecessary audioguide-€4, Place Michel Debré, tel. 02 47 57 00 98, www.chateau-amboise. com.

Visiting the Château: After climbing the long ramp to the ticket booth and picking up the free and well-done English brochure, your first stop is the petite **chapel** where Leonardo da Vinci is supposedly buried. This flamboyant little Gothic chapel is where the king began and ended each day in prayer. It comes with two fireplaces "to comfort the king" and two plaques "evoking the final resting place" of Leonardo (one in French, the other in Italian). Where he's actually buried, no one seems to know. Look up at the ceiling to appreciate the lacy design.

Enter the **castle rooms** across from Leonardo's chapel. The three-floor route takes you chronologically from Gothic-style rooms to those from the early Renaissance and on to the 19th century. The first room, **Salle des Gardes,** shows the château's origi-

LOIRE

nal, much larger size; drawings in the next room give you a better feel for its original look. Some wings added in the 15th and 16th centuries have disappeared. (The little chapel you just saw was once part of the bigger complex.)

You'll pass the sumptuous **council chambers** (Salle du Conseil) where the king would meet with his key staff (find his throne). King **Henry II's bedroom** is livable. The second son of François I, Henry is remembered as the husband of the ambitious and unscrupulous Catherine de' Medici—and for his tragic death in a jousting tournament.

The rose-colored top-floor rooms are well-furnished from the post-Revolutionary 1800s and demonstrate the continued interest among French nobility in this château. Find the classy portrait of King Louis-Philippe, the last Louis to rule France.

The **Minimes Tower** delivers grand views from its terrace. From here, the strategic value of this site is clear: The visibility is great, and the river below provided a natural defense.

The bulky tower climbs 130 feet in five spirals—designed for a mounted soldier in a hurry. Walk a short distance down the spiral ramp and exit into the **gardens.** Each

summer, bleachers are set up for sound-and-light spectacles—a faint echo of the extravaganzas Leonardo orchestrated for the court. Modern art decorating the garden reminds visitors of the inquisitive and scientific Renaissance spirit that Leonardo brought to town. The flags are those of France and Brittany—a reminder that, in a sense, modern France was created at the nearby château of Langeais when Charles VIII (who was born here) married Anne of Brittany, adding her domain to the French kingdom.

To exit, spiral down the **Heurtault Tower** (through the gift shop). As with the castle's other tower, this was designed to accommodate a soldier on horseback. As you gallop down to the exit, notice the cute little characters and scenes left by 15th-century stone carvers. While they needed to behave when decorating churches and palaces, here they could be a bit racier and more spirited.

Leaving the Château: The turnstile puts you on the road to Château du Clos-Lucé (described next; turn left and hike straight for 10 minutes). Along the way, you'll pass **troglodyte houses**—both new and old—carved into the hillside stone (a type called *tuffeau*, a sedimentary rock). Originally, poor people resided here—the dwellings didn't require expensive slate roofing, came with natural insulation, and could be dug essentially for free, as builders valued the stone quarried in the process. Today wealthy stone lovers are renovating them into stylish digs worthy of *Better Homes and Caves*. You can see chimneys high above. Unfortunately, none are open to the public.

▲Château du Clos-Lucé and Leonardo da Vinci Park

In 1516, Leonardo da Vinci packed his bags (and several of his favorite paintings, including the *Mona Lisa*) and left an imploding Rome for better wine and working conditions in the Loire Valley. He accepted the position of engineer, architect, and painter to France's Renaissance king, François I. This "House of Light" is the plush palace where Leonardo spent his last three years. (He died on May 2, 1519.) François, only 22 years old, installed the 65-year-old Leonardo here just so he could enjoy his intellectual company.

The house is a kind of fort-château of its own, with a fortified rampart walk and a 16th-century chapel. Two floors of finely decorated rooms are open to the public, but none of the furnishings are original, nor are they particularly compelling (though you can stare face-to-face with a copy of Leonardo's *Mona Lisa*). Come to see well-explained models of Leonardo's inventions, displayed inside the house and out in the huge park.

Leonardo came with disciples who stayed active here, using this house as a kind of workshop and laboratory. The place survived the Revolution because the quick-talking noble who owned it was sympathetic to the cause; he convinced the Revolutionaries that, philosophically, Leonardo would have been on their side.

Cost and Hours: The €15 admission (includes house and park) is worth it for Leonardo fans with two hours to fully appreciate this sight. Skip the garden museum and its €5 supplement. Daily Feb-Oct 9:00-19:00, July-Aug until 20:00; shorter hours off-season, last entry one hour before closing, follow the helpful free English handout, tel. 02 47 57 00 73, www.vinci-closluce.com. A free app in English includes background information and audio tours of the château and grounds.

Getting There: It's a 10-minute walk uphill from Château Royal d'Amboise, past troglodyte homes (see end of previous listing). You can also take the *petit train* (listed under "Helpful Hints" on page 360). If you park in the nearby lot, leave nothing of value visible in your car.

Eating: Several garden cafés, including one just behind the house and others in the park, are reasonably priced and appropriately meditative. For a view over Amboise, choose the terrace *crê-perie*.

Visiting the Château and Gardens: Your visit begins with a tour of Leonardo's elegant yet livable Renaissance **home.** This little residence was built in 1450—just within the protective walls of the town—as a guesthouse for the king's château nearby. Today it re-creates (with Renaissance music) the everyday atmosphere Leonardo enjoyed while he lived here, pursuing his passions to the very end. Find the touching sketch in Leonardo's bedroom of François I comforting his genius pal on his deathbed.

The basement level is filled with **sketches** recording the storm patterns of Leonardo's brain and **models** of his remarkable inventions (inspired by nature and built according to his notes). Leonardo was fascinated by water. All he lacked was steam power. It's hard to imagine that this Roman candle of creativity died nearly 500 years ago. Exit into the rose garden, then find another room with 40 small models of his inventions (with handheld English explanations).

Imagine Leonardo's résumé letter to kings of Europe: "I can help your armies by designing tanks, flying machines, wind-up cars, gear systems, extension ladders, and water pumps." The French considered him a futurist who never really implemented his visions.

Your visit finishes with a stroll through the whimsical, expansive and kid-friendly **park grounds,** with life-size models of Leonardo's inventions (including some that kids can operate), "sound stations" (in English), and translucent replicas of some of his paintings. The models make clear that much of what Leonardo observed and created was based on his intense study of nature.

OTHER SIGHTS AND ACTIVITIES
▲Château Royal d'Amboise Sound-and-Light Show
This is considered one of the best shows of its kind in the area. Although it's entirely in French, you can buy the English booklet for €5. Volunteer locals from toddlers to pensioners re-create the life of François I with costumes, juggling, impressive light displays, and fireworks. Dress warmly.

Cost and Hours: Bench—€18, chair—€25, family deals, about 20 performances a year, 1.5-hour show runs several days per week, July 22:30-24:00, Aug 22:00-23:30, tel. 02 47 57 14 47, www.renaissance-amboise.com. Buy tickets online or from the ticket window on the ramp to the château (opens at 20:30).

Mini-Châteaux
This five-acre park on the edge of Amboise (on the route to Chenonceaux) shows the major Loire châteaux in 1:25-scale models,

LOIRE

The Loire and Its Many Châteaux: A Historical Primer

It's hard to overstate the importance of the Loire River to France. Its place in history goes back to the very foundation of the country. As if to proclaim its storied past, the Loire is the last major wild river in France, with no dams and no regulation of its flow.

Traditional flat-bottomed boats romantically moored along embankments are a reminder of the age before trains and trucks, when river traffic safely and efficiently transported heavy loads of stone and timber. With prevailing winds sweeping east from the Atlantic, barge tenders raised their sails and headed upriver; on the way back, boats flowed downstream with the current.

With this transportation infrastructure providing (relatively) quick access to Paris and the region's thick forests—offering plenty of timber, firewood, and hunting terrain—it's no wonder that castles were built here in the Middle Ages. The first stone fortresses went up a thousand years ago, and many of the pleasure palaces you see today rose over the ruins of those original defensive keeps.

The Hundred Years' War—roughly 1336 to 1453—was a desperate time for France. Because of a dynastic dispute, the English had a legitimate claim to the French throne, and by 1415 they controlled much of the country, including Paris. France was at a low ebb, and its king and court retreated to the Loire Valley to rule what remained of their realm. Chinon was the refuge of the dispirited king, Charles VII. He was famously visited there in 1429 by the charismatic Joan of Arc, who inspired the king to get off his duff and send the English packing.

The French kings continued to live in the Loire region for the next two centuries, having grown comfortable with their château culture. The climate was mild, hunting was good, dreamy rivers made nice reflections, wealthy friends lived in similar luxury nearby, and the location was close enough to Paris—but still far enough away. Charles VII ruled from Chinon, Charles VIII preferred Amboise, Louis XII reigned from Blois, and François I held court in Chambord and Blois.

This was a kind of cultural Golden Age. With peace and stability, there was no need for fortifications. The most famous luxury hunting lodges, masquerading as fortresses, were built during this period—including Chenonceau, Chambord, Chaumont, Amboise, and Azay-le-Rideau. Kings (François I), writers (Rabelais), poets (Ronsard), and artists (Leonardo da Vinci) made the Loire a cultural hub. Many years later, these same châteaux attracted other notables, including Voltaire, Molière, and perhaps Benjamin Franklin.

Because French kings ruled effectively only by being constantly on the move among their subjects, many royal châteaux were used infrequently. The entire court—and its trappings—had to be portable. A castle kept empty and cold 11 months of the year would suddenly become the busy center of attention when the king came to town. As you visit the castles, imagine the royal roadies setting up a kingly room—hanging tapestries, unfolding chairs, wrestling big trunks with handles—in the hours just before the arrival of the royal entourage. The French word for furniture, *mobilier,* literally means "mobile."

When touring the châteaux, you'll notice the impact of Italian culture. From the Renaissance onward, Italian ways were fancy ways. French nobles and court ministers who traveled to Italy returned inspired by the art and architecture they saw. Kings imported Italian artists and architects. It's no wonder that the ultimate French Renaissance king, François I, invited the ultimate Italian artist, Leonardo da Vinci, to join his court in Amboise. Tastes in food, gardens, artists, and women were all influenced by Italian culture.

Women had a big impact on Loire château life. Big personalities like kings tickled more than one tiara. Louis XV famously decorated the palace of Chenonceau with a painting of the Three Graces—featuring his three favorite mistresses.

Châteaux were generally owned by kings, their ministers, or their mistresses. A high-maintenance and powerful mistress could get her own place even when a king's romantic interest shifted. In many cases, the king or minister would be away at work or at war for years at a time—leaving home-improvement decisions to the lady of the château, who had unlimited money. That helps explain the emphasis on comfort and the feminine touch you'll enjoy while touring many of the Loire châteaux.

In 1525, François I moved to his newly built super-palace at Fontainebleau, and political power left the Loire. From then on, châteaux were mostly used as vacation and hunting retreats. They became refuges for kings again during the French Wars of Religion (1562-1598)—a sticky set of squabbles over dynastic control that pitted Protestants (Huguenots) against Catholics. Its conclusion marked the end of an active royal presence on the Loire. With the French Revolution in 1789, symbols of the Old Regime, like the fabulous palaces along the Loire, were ransacked. Fast talking saved some châteaux, especially those whose owners had personal relationships with Revolutionary leaders.

Only in the 1840s did the châteaux of the Loire become appreciated for their historic value. The Loire was the first place where treasures of French heritage were officially recognized and protected by the national government. In the 19th century, Romantic Age writers—such as Victor Hugo and Alexander Dumas—visited and celebrated the châteaux. Aristocrats on the Grand Tour stopped here. The Loire Valley and its historic châteaux found a place in our collective hearts and have been treasured to this day.

LOIRE

forested with 2,000 bonsai trees and laced together by a model TGV train and river boats. For children, it's a fun introduction to the real châteaux they'll be visiting (and there's a cool toy store). Essential English information is posted throughout the sight.

You'll find other kid-oriented attractions at Mini-Châteaux; consider playing a round of minigolf and feeding the fish in the moat (a great way to get rid of that old baguette).

Cost and Hours: Adults—€14, kids—€10.50, daily mid-April-June 10:00-18:30, July-Aug 9:30-18:30, Sept-Oct 10:30-18:00, closed Nov-mid-April, last entry one hour before closing, tel. 02 47 23 44 57, www.parcminichateaux.com.

Caveau des Vignerons

This small *cave* offers free tastings of cheeses, pâtés, and regional wines from 10 different vintners (daily mid-March-mid-Nov 10:00-19:00, under Château d'Amboise, across from recommended L'Epicerie restaurant, tel. 02 47 57 23 69).

Biking from Amboise

A signed bike route takes you to Chenonceaux (8 miles one-way) in about an hour. Leading past Leonardo's Clos-Lucé, the first two miles are uphill, and the entire ride is on a road with some traffic. Serious cyclists can continue to Chaumont in 1.5 hours, connecting Amboise, Chenonceaux, and Chaumont in an all-day, 37-mile pedal (see "Bike Route" on the map on page 376). The most appealing pedal from Amboise follows the Loire downstream along a dedicated bike path, though you won't see any great castles. The village of Lussault-sur-Loire makes an easy destination (2.5 miles one-way), or keep on pedaling to Montlouis, two miles past Lussault.

Canoe Trips from Amboise or Chenonceaux

Paddling under the Château de Chenonceau is a memorable experience. **Canoe Company** offers rentals on the Loire and Cher rivers (€12-25/person depending on how far you go, mobile 06 70 13 30 61 or 06 37 01 89 92, www.canoe-company.fr).

NEAR AMBOISE

Wine Tasting in Vouvray

In the nearby town of Vouvray, 10 miles toward Tours from Amboise, you'll find wall-to-wall opportunities for wine tasting (but less impressive vineyards than in other parts of France). From Amboise you can take the speedy D-952 there, or joyride on the more appealing D-1 (see map on page 376). Here are two top choices for testing the local sauce:

The big **Cave des Producteurs** is a smart place to start. It has an English-speaking staff, English-language tours of the winery, and a good selection from the 33 producers they represent, including wines from other Loire areas (free wine tasting, small fee for cellar tour, daily July-Aug 9:00-19:00, Sept-June 9:00-12:30 & 14:00-19:00, cellar tours in English at 11:30 and 16:00—call ahead to confirm, 38 La Vallée Coquette in Vouvray, tel. 02 47 52 75 03, www.cavedevouvray.com). It's just west of Vouvray in Rochecorbon. Go past the smaller Cave des Producteurs outlet you'll see along D-952 in Vouvray, turn when you see the blue signs to *Moncontour,* then follow the small brown signs to *Cave des Producteurs.*

For a more intimate experience, drop by **Marc Brédif,** where you'll find a top-quality selection of Vouvray wines, excellent dessert wines, and red wines from Chinon and Bourgueil. You can also tour their impressive 1.2 miles of 10th-century cellars dug into the hillside (free wine tasting, small fee for cellar tour, Mon-Sat 10:30-12:00 & 14:30-18:00, Sun 10:30-13:00, tel. 02 47 52 50 07, www.deladoucette.fr—select "Domaine Brédif" under "Domaines"). Coming from Amboise, you'll pass it on D-952 after Vouvray; it's on the right, after the Moncontour turnoff.

For tips on wine tasting, see "French Wine-Tasting 101" on page 1078.

Sleeping in Amboise

Amboise is busy in the summer, but there are lots of reasonable hotels and *chambres d'hôtes* in and around the city.

IN THE TOWN CENTER
$$$$ Hôtel au Charme Rabelaisien** is a luxurious 10-room place run by charming Madame Sylvie. Big doors open onto a lovely courtyard with manicured gardens and a heated pool. The beautifully decorated rooms have every comfort conceivable (air-con, private parking, closed Nov-March, 25 Rue Rabelais, tel. 02 47 57 53 84, mobile 06 86 14 10 68, www.hotel-acr.com, info@hotel-acr.com).

$$$ Le Manoir les Minimes** is a good place to experience the refined air of château life in a 17th-century mansion, with antique furniture and precious art objects in the public spaces. Its 15 large, modern rooms work for those seeking luxury digs in Amboise. (Tall folks take note: Top-floor attic rooms have low ceilings.) Several rooms have views of Amboise's château (family rooms, air-con, closed much of winter, three blocks upriver from bridge at 34 Quai Charles Guinot, tel. 02 47 30 40 40, www.manoirlesminimes.com, reservation@manoirlesminimes.com).

$$$ Hôtel le Clos d'Amboise** is a smart urban refuge opening onto beautiful gardens and a small, heated swimming pool. It offers stay-awhile lounges, a lovely rear terrace, and well-

Sleep Code

Hotels are classified based on the average price of a standard double room without breakfast in high season.

$$$$	**Splurge:**	Most rooms over €200
$$$	**Pricier:**	€150-200
$$	**Moderate:**	€100-150
$	**Budget:**	€50-100
¢	**Backpacker:**	Under €50
RS%	**Rick Steves discount**	
*	**French hotel rating system** (0-5 stars)	

Unless otherwise noted, credit cards are accepted, hotel staff speak basic English, and free Wi-Fi is available. Comparison-shop by checking prices at several hotels (on each hotel's own website, on a booking site, or by email). For the best deal, *book directly with the hotel.* Ask for a discount if paying in cash; if the listing includes **RS%,** request a Rick Steves discount.

designed traditional rooms with warm colors and carpets (RS%, family rooms, minifridges, air-con, elevator, sauna, free parking, restaurant and bar, 27 Rue Rabelais, tel. 02 47 30 10 20, www.leclosdamboise.com, infos@leclosamboise.com, helpful Patricia or Pauline are ever-present).

$$$ Le Vieux Manoir*** is an entirely different high-end splurge. American expats Gloria and Bob Belknap have restored this secluded but central one-time convent with an attention to detail that Martha Stewart would envy. Bob and Gloria are slowing down, but they still manage to run a tight ship. The gardens are delightful—as is the atrium-like breakfast room— and its six bedrooms are lovingly decorated. Knowledgeable Gloria is a one-person tourist office (cot-

tages, includes good breakfast, air-con, no room phones or TVs, free parking, 13 Rue Rabelais, tel. 02 47 30 41 27, www.le-vieux-manoir.com, le_vieux_manoir@yahoo.com).

$$$ The **Villa Concorde** hunkers below the castle with four luxurious apartments. Helpful owner Karine will check you in, and then you're on your own (no reception, etc). These well-furnished apartments come with washers/dryers, kitchens, and more (studios, some bigger units can sleep up to 6, free transfer from train station possible if booked ahead, 26 Rue de la Concorde, tel. 02 47 50 64 42, www.villaconcorde.com, info@villaconcorde.com).

$$ Hôtel Bellevue*** is a fair midrange bet with 30

LOIRE

comfortable-enough rooms. Centrally located, it overlooks the river where the bridge hits the town. Its stylish bar/bistro has a good selection of local wines by the glass and filling cheese and charcuterie *planchettes* (family rooms, elevator, 12 Quai Charles Guinot, tel. 02 47 57 02 26, www.hotel-bellevue-amboise.com, contact@hotel-bellevue-amboise.com).

$ **Hôtel le Blason**** is housed in a 15th-century, half-timbered building on a busy street. Run by helpful Damien and Bérengère, it has tight but comfortable and clean rooms with double-paned windows and ceiling fans. Top-floor rooms have air-conditioning, sloped ceilings, and low beams (quieter rooms in back and on top floor, family rooms, secure pay parking, 11 Place Richelieu, tel. 02 47 23 22 41, www.leblason.fr, hotel@leblason.fr).

$ **Hôtel le Chaptal**** is a plain hotel with small but clean and cheap rooms (family rooms, 11 Rue Chaptal, tel. 02 47 57 14 46, www.hotel-chaptal-amboise.fr, infos@hotel-chaptal-amboise.fr).

CHAMBRES D'HOTES

The heart of Amboise offers several solid bed-and-breakfast options.

$ **La Grange Chambres** welcomes with an intimate, flowery courtyard and four comfortable rooms, each tastefully restored with modern conveniences and big beds. There's also a common room with a fridge and tables for do-it-yourself dinners (includes breakfast, reserve with credit card but pay in cash only, where Rues Chaptal and Rabelais meet at 18 Rue Chaptal, tel. 02 47 57 57 22, www.la-grange-amboise.com, lagrange-amboise@orange.fr). Adorable Yveline Savin also rents a small two-room cottage and speaks fluent *franglais*.

$ **L'Iris des Marais** is a budget B&B with three artsy and quaint rooms and a wild garden where you can enjoy a peaceful picnic (family rooms, includes breakfast, 14 Quai des Marais, tel. 02 47 30 46 51, www.irisdesmarais.com).

NEAR THE TRAIN STATION

$ **Hôtel la Brèche**,** a sleepy place near the station, has 14 good-value rooms and a top-notch recommended restaurant. Many rooms overlook the peaceful graveled garden, while those on the street are larger and come with some traffic noise; all are tastefully decorated (family rooms, excellent breakfast, free parking, 15-minute walk from city center and 2-minute walk from station, 26 Rue Jules Ferry, tel. 02 47 57 00 79, www.labreche-amboise.com, info@labreche-amboise.com).

Hostel: ¢ **L'Auberge de Jeunesse** (Centre Charles Péguy) is ideally located on the western tip of the "Golden Island," a 10-minute walk from the train station. This friendly place is open to people

LOIRE

of all ages, and popular with student groups. There are a handful of double rooms—some with partial views to the château—so book ahead (reception open daily 15:00-20:00, no curfew, on Ile d'Or, email is useless—call no more than two weeks ahead to book, tel. 02 47 30 60 90).

NEAR AMBOISE

The area around Amboise is peppered with accommodations of every shape, size, and price range. This region offers drivers the best chance to experience château life at affordable rates—and my recommendations justify the detour. For locations, see the map on page 376. Also consider the recommended accommodations in Chenonceaux.

$$$ **Château de Pray****** allows you to sleep in a 700-year-old fortified castle with hints of its medieval origins. A few minutes from Amboise, the château's 19 rooms aren't big or luxurious, but they come with character and history—and with tubs in most bathrooms. The lounge is small, but the backyard terrace compensates in agreeable weather. A newer annex offers four more-modern rooms (sleeping up to three each) with lofts, terraces, and castle views. A big pool and the restaurant's vegetable garden lie below the château (3-minute drive upriver from Amboise toward Chaumont on D-751 before the village of Chargé, Rue du Cèdre, tel. 02 47 57 23 67, www.chateaudepray.fr, contact@chateaudepray.fr). The $$$$ **dining room,** cut into the hillside rock in the old *orangerie,* is a relaxing place to splurge...and feel good about it. You'll dine outside on a beautiful terrace when the weather agrees (four-course *menus* from €59, reservations required).

$$$ **Château de Perreux***** is a renovated 18th-century castle with a stony, tony feel. Here, upscale bed-and-breakfast service meets château-hotel ambience with 11 plush and tastefully designed rooms just a few minutes from Amboise. A €40 three-course dinner cooked by a respected chef is available for guests who book ahead (family rooms, air-con, elevator, Wi-Fi in library only, parking, on D-1 between Nazelles and Pocé-sur-Cisse; coming from Amboise, turn left at the *Château de Perreux* sign, 36 Rue de Pocé, tel. 02 47 57 27 47, www.chateaudeperreux.fr, info@chateaudeperreux.fr).

$$$ **Château des Arpentis,***** a medieval château-hotel centrally located just minutes from Amboise, makes a fun and classy splurge. Flanked by woods and acres of grass, and fronted by a stream and a moat, you'll come as close as you can to château life during the Loire's Golden Age. Rooms are big with tasteful

decor—and the pool is even bigger. There's no restaurant, but terrace-table picnics are encouraged. Efficient manager Olivier takes good care of his guests (family rooms, air-con, elevator, tel. 02 47 23 00 00, www. chateaudesarpentis.com, contact@chateaudesarpentis.com). It's on D-31 just southeast of Amboise; from the roundabout above the Leclerc Market, follow *Autrèche* signs, then look for small sign on the right next to a tall flagpole.

At **$$ Château de Nazelles Chambres,***** gentle owners Véronique and Olivier Fructus offer six rooms in a 16th-century hillside manor house that comes with a cliff-sculpted pool, manicured gardens, a guest kitchen (picnics are encouraged), views over Amboise, and a classy living room with billiards. The bedrooms in the main building are traditional, while the rooms cut into the hillside come with private terraces and rock-walled bathrooms. They also rent a very comfortable two-room cottage with living area, kitchen, and private garden (RS%, family rooms, includes breakfast, 16 Rue Tue-La-Soif, Nazelles-Négron, tel. 02 47 30 53 79, www.chateau-nazelles.com, info@chateau-nazelles.com). From D-952, take D-5 into Nazelles, then turn left on D-1 and quickly veer right onto the little lane between the town hall and the post office (La Poste)—don't rely on GPS.

$$ Le Moulin du Fief Gentil is a lovely 16th-century mill house set on four acres with a backyard pond (fishing possible in summer, dinner picnics anytime, fridge and microwave at your disposal), and the possibility of home-cooked dinners by English-speaking owner Florence (apartment, includes breakfast, four-course dinner *menu* with wine—must reserve in advance, cash only, Wi-Fi in mechanical mill room, 3 Rue de Culoison, tel. 02 47 30 32 51, mobile 06 64 82 37 18, www.fiefgentil.com, contact@fiefgentil.com). It's located on the edge of Bléré, a 15-minute drive from Amboise and 7 minutes from Chenonceaux—from Bléré, follow signs toward *Luzillé;* it's on the right.

$ L'Auberge de Launay,*** five miles upriver from Amboise, gets positive reviews for its easy driving access to many châteaux, fair prices, and good restaurant (ask for a room on the garden, 4 miles from Amboise, across the river toward Blois, 9 Rue de la Rivière in Limeray, tel. 02 47 30 16 82, www.aubergedelaunay.com, info@aubergedelaunay.com). The star of this place is the country-classy **$$ restaurant** (closed Sun except for hotel guests in season).

$ La Chevalerie owners Ljubisa and Martine Aleksic rent four simple bargain *chambres* that are family-friendly, with a swing set, tiny pond, shared kitchens, and connecting rooms (includes basic breakfast, cash only, in La Croix-en-Touraine, tel. 02 47 57

LOIRE

83 64, lyoubisa.aleksic@orange.fr, owners speak French and German—but not English). From Amboise, take D-31 toward Bléré, look for the *Chambres d'Hôtes* sign on your left at about three miles, and then turn left onto C-105; keep left and continue to the end of the road.

Eating in Amboise

Amboise is filled with inexpensive and forgettable restaurants, but a handful of places are worth your attention. Some offer a good, end-of-meal cheese platter—a rarity in France these days. The epicenter of the city's dining action is on Place Michel Debré, along Rue Victor Hugo, and across from the château entrance. Troll the places here and find a seat if inspired, or consider my suggestions.

For an aperitif or after-dinner drink, cross the bridge for the best castle views, and consider a relaxing sip at **Le Shaker Cocktail Lounge** (daily from 18:00 until later than you're awake, 3 Quai François Tissard).

DINING BELOW THE CHATEAU

$$ Anne de Bretagne serves basic café fare at fair prices with the best view seats over Place Michel Debré (Montée Abdel-Kader, tel. 02 47 57 05 46).

$$ Chez Bruno is a lively and popular place with uneven floors, lowbrow decor, and simple, straightforward food. People come here for classic French dishes at affordable prices (closed Sun-Mon, 38 Place Michel Debré, reservations smart, tel. 02 47 57 73 49, www.bistrotchezbruno.com).

$$$ L'Epicerie, across from the château exit, serves well-presented, traditional cuisine with inconsistent quality at fair prices. Choose a table outdoors facing the château or in the rustically elegant dining room. The snails are scrumptious (July-Sept daily, Oct-June closed Mon-Tue, reserve ahead, 46 Place Michel Debré, tel. 02 47 57 08 94, www.lepicerie-amboise.com).

$$ Bigot Pâtisserie's Salon de Thé serves up tasty quiches and omelets along with delightful homemade ice cream and a terrace view. The €15 Renaissance *menu* includes a savory and a sweet pastry (Mon-Fri 9:00-19:30, Sat-Sun 8:30-20:00, where Place Michel Debré meets Rue Nationale one block off the river, tel. 02 47 57 04 46).

ELSEWHERE IN AMBOISE

$$ La Fourchette is Amboise's tiny family diner, with simple decor and cuisine. Hardworking chef Christine makes everything fresh in her open kitchen, offering just two options for entrée and *plat* at good prices. Book ahead—the morning of the same day is

---

Restaurant Price Code

I've assigned each eatery a price category, based on the average cost of a typical main course. Drinks, desserts, and splurge items (steak and seafood) can raise the price considerably.

$$$$	**Splurge:** Most main courses over €25
$$$	**Pricier:** €20-25
$$	**Moderate:** €15-20
$	**Budget:** Under €15

In France, a crêpe stand or other takeout spot is **$**; a sit-down brasserie, café, or bistro with affordable *plats du jour* is **$$**; a casual but more upscale restaurant is **$$$**; and a swanky splurge is **$$$$**.

fine (closed Sun-Mon and Thu evening, on a quiet corner near Rue Nationale at 9 Rue Malebranche, mobile 06 11 78 16 98).

$ L'Ancrée des Artistes is a reliable, centrally located *crêperie.* This young-at-heart place has music to dine by and easygoing servers (three-course crêpe *menus,* good meat dishes grilled on stones *(pierres)* and casserole-like *cocottes,* daily in July-Aug, off-season closed Sun evening and Mon, 35 Rue Nationale, tel. 02 47 23 18 11).

$$$ L'Alliance, an "alliance" of two chef-brothers and their wives who serve, is a low-key place offering the kind of fresh, delicious French cuisine normally found in more formal restaurants. Here, you'll get quality ingredients prepared with an original twist, not fine decor (children's menu, great but pricey cheese tray, closed Tue and Wed for lunch, reservations recommended, 14 Rue Joyeuse, tel. 02 47 30 52 13, http://restaurantalliance.fr).

At **$$$ Le Lion d'Or,** *le* owner/chef takes his job seriously and serves creative recipes in a *très* contemporary setting (closed Sun evening and Mon, reservations smart, where the bridge meets the town at 7 Quai Charles Guinot, tel. 02 47 57 00 23, www.leliondor-amboise.com).

$$ La Scala is good for inexpensive Italian food with easygoing service and a broad terrace on the noisy main drag (daily, near the TI at 6 Quai du Général de Gaulle, tel. 02 47 23 09 93). They have another location, called **Via Roma,** that's cozier and more central (daily, 10 Place Michel Debré, tel. 02 47 23 08 07).

$$$ Hôtel la Brèche is a deservedly trendy place with excellent service and delicious cuisine at reasonable prices. Dine in a warm, traditional dining room or in the large garden. Stretch your legs and cross the river to the restaurant (daily; for details, see "Sleeping in Amboise," earlier).

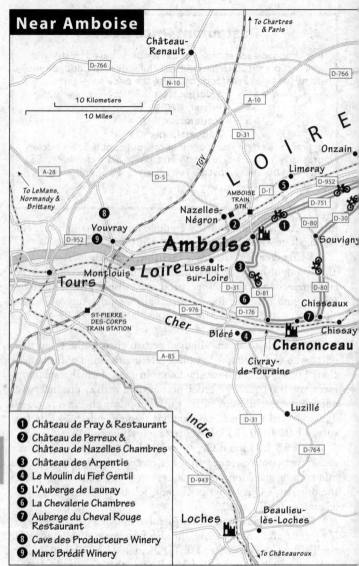

Near Amboise

1. Château de Pray & Restaurant
2. Château de Perreux & Château de Nazelles Chambres
3. Château des Arpentis
4. Le Moulin du Fief Gentil
5. L'Auberge de Launay
6. La Chevalerie Chambres
7. Auberge du Cheval Rouge Restaurant
8. Cave des Producteurs Winery
9. Marc Brédif Winery

NEAR AMBOISE

These options merit the short drive. For an elegant and exquisite castle dining experience (best on a warm evening), consider making the quick drive to **Château de Pray**—call ahead to reserve (for details, see page 372). In summer, head to **Chenonceaux** village for dinner, then enjoy a floodlit walk through the château grounds (see "Eating" under "Town of Chenonceaux" on page 385).

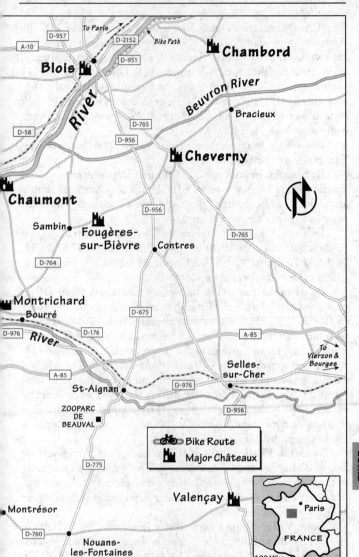

Amboise Connections

By Bus: Buses leave for **Chenonceaux** once or twice daily (Mon-Sat only—none on Sun, 25 minutes, departs Amboise about 9:45, returns from Chenonceaux at about 12:20, allowing you about 1.5 hours at the château during its most crowded time; in summer, there's also an afternoon departure at about 15:00 with a return from Chenonceaux at about 17:50; confirm times with the TI). The Amboise stop—called Théâtre—is between Place St-Denis and the river on the west side of Avenue des Martyrs de la Résistance, across from the Théâtre de Beaumarchais; in Chenonceaux, the bus stops across the street from the TI (a 5-minute walk to the château entrance). For more flexibility, consider taking a train back instead (see page 385; tel. 02 47 05 30 49, www.tourainefilvert. com—search for "line C").

Buses also go regularly to **Tours** (8/day Mon-Sat, none on Sun, buses are cheaper than trains).

By Shuttle: In peak season, **Touraine Evasion** runs minivan shuttle trips to Chenonceau for €16 (2/day but confirm, as shuttle services change frequently; ask at Amboise TI or check with company—see below for contact info).

By Taxi: A taxi from Amboise to Chenonceau costs about €29 (€41 on Sun and after 19:00, €7 pick-up fee, call 02 47 57 13 53, 06 12 92 70 46, 02 47 57 30 39, or 06 88 02 44 10). Most other châteaux are too expensive to visit by cab.

By Minivan Excursion to Nearby Châteaux: Acco-Dispo runs good half- and all-day English tours from Amboise and Tours to all the major châteaux six days a week (Mon-Sat). Costs vary with the itinerary (half day tours-€37/person, full-day-€56/person; meet at the TI, small groups of 2-8 people, mobile 06 82 00 64 51, www.accodispo-tours.com). While on the road, you'll usually get a running commentary—but you're on your own at the sights (discounted tickets available from the driver). Reserve a week ahead by email, or two to three days by phone. (Day-trippers from Paris find this service convenient.) Acco-Dispo also runs multiday tours of the Loire and Brittany.

Touraine Evasion runs half-day tours from Amboise that stop at Chambord and Chenonceau (€37/person) and all-day tours to three châteaux (€57/person). They also have many château options out of Tours (daily in season, none in winter, mobile 06 07 39 13 31, www.tourevasion.com).

Loire Valley Tours offers all-day itineraries from Amboise and Tours. These fully guided, upscale tours include admissions, lunch, and wine tasting (about €145/person, tel. 02 54 33 99 80, www.loire-valley-tours.com, contact@loire-valley-tours.com).

By Train: Amboise provides decent train connections both within the Loire and beyond.

Within the Loire: From Amboise, you can reach **Chenonceaux** (trains are more frequent, but slower and pricier than the bus; 6/day, 1 hour, transfer at St-Pierre-des-Corps—check connections to avoid long waits), **Blois** (14/day, 20 minutes, bus or taxi excursions from there to Chambord and Cheverny—see "Blois Connections" on page 392), **Chaumont** (14/day, 35 minutes, take 10-minute train to Onzain on the Amboise-Blois route, 25-minute walk—you can see château from station), **Tours** (12/day, 25 minutes, allows connections to châteaux west of Tours), **Chinon** (7/day, 1.5-2 hours, transfer in Tours), and **Azay-le-Rideau** (6/day, 1-2 hours, transfer in Tours).

To Destinations Beyond the Loire: Frequent trains link Amboise to the regional train hub of St-Pierre-des-Corps in suburban Tours (20/day, 15 minutes). There you'll find reasonable connections to distant points (including the TGV to Paris' Gare Montparnasse). Transferring in Paris can be the fastest way to reach many French destinations, even in the south.

From Amboise you can catch the train to: **Paris Gare Montparnasse** (8/day, 1.5 hours with change to TGV at St-Pierre-des-Corps, requires TGV reservation), **Paris Gare d'Austerlitz** (3/day direct, 2 hours, no reservation required, more with transfer), **Sarlat-la-Canéda** (3/day, 5-7 hours, change at St-Pierre-des-Corps, then TGV to Libourne, then train through Bordeaux vineyards to Sarlat), **Limoges** (near Oradour-sur-Glane, connection requires both bus and train—see page 485), **Pontorson/Mont St-Michel** (1/day, 5.5 hours with transfers at Nantes and Rennes, longer connections through Paris), **Bayeux** (2/day, 4.5 hours, transfer at St-Pierre-des-Corps and Caen, more with transfer in Paris leaving from Gare St. Lazare), **Beaune** (1/day, 4.5 hours, transfer at St-Pierre-des-Corps, more with additional transfer at Nevers), **Bourges** (roughly hourly—though fewer midday, 2-3 hours, change at St-Pierre-des-Corps).

Chenonceau

Château de Chenonceau is the toast of the Loire and worth ▲▲▲. This 16th-century Renaissance palace arches gracefully over the Cher River and is impeccably maintained, with fresh flower arrangements in the summer and roaring log fires in the winter. The château itself, understandably the most popular in the region, is wonderfully organized for visitors. But it's also one of the most-visited châteaux in France—so carefully follow my crowd-beating tips (see later).

Note that Chenonceau is the name of the château, and Chenonceaux is the name of the town, but they're pronounced the same: shuh-nohn-soh. The town itself—a one-road village with well-priced hotels and some fine eating options—makes a good home base for drivers (see recommendations later, under "Town of Chenonceaux").

Tourist Information: The ignored TI is on the main road from Amboise as you enter the village. It has free Wi-Fi (July-Aug daily 9:00-19:00, closed at lunchtime on Sun; Sept-June Mon-Sat

10:00-12:30 & 14:00-18:30—until 17:30 in winter, closed Sun; tel. 02 47 23 94 45).

GETTING THERE

From Amboise, it's easy to get here by **train** (6/day, 1 hour, transfer at St-Pierre-des-Corps) or even faster, by **bus,** which drops off at the TI (1-2/day, Mon-Sat only, none on Sun, 25 minutes—see page 377 for details on this bus). There are also frequent train connections from Tours (10/day, 30 minutes). The unstaffed train station sits between the village and the château.

Touraine Evasion may run **shuttle trips** from Amboise (€16, high season only). Minivan **excursions** from Amboise and Tours are also available (see "By Minivan Excursion to Nearby Châteaux" under "Amboise Connections" on page 378).

You can also take a **taxi** from Amboise (€29, €41 on Sun and after 19:00, €7 pick-up fee; for contact info, see "Taxi" under "Helpful Hints" for Amboise on page 357).

If **driving,** plan on a 15-minute walk from the parking lot to the château. Don't leave any valuables visible in your car.

ORIENTATION TO CHATEAU DE CHENONCEAU

Cost and Hours: €13, €10 for kids under age 18, daily mid-March-mid-Sept 9:00-19:30, July-Aug until 20:00, closes earlier off-season.

Crowd-Beating Tips: Spaces are tight inside the château, so smart travelers plan around Chenonceau's crowds. This place gets slammed in high season, when you should come early (by 9:00) or late (after 17:00). Avoid slow ticket lines by purchasing your ticket in advance (at area TIs) or from the ticket machines at the main entry (US credit cards work but instructions in English are hit-and-miss—withdraw your card at the prompt *"retirez"*).

Tours and Information: The interior is fascinating—but only if you take advantage of the excellent 20-page **booklet** (included with entry), or rent the wonderful **videoguide** (€4.50). Pay for the guide when buying your ticket (before entering the château grounds), then pick it up just inside the château's door. Tel. 02 47 23 90 07, www.chenonceau.com.

Services: WCs are available by the ticket office and behind the old stables.

Eating: A reasonable **$$** cafeteria is next door to the hospital room. Fancy **$$$** meals are served in the *orangerie* behind the stables (Restaurant l'Orangerie). There's a cheap *crêperie/* sandwich shop at the entrance gate. While picnics are not allowed on the grounds, there are picnic tables in a park near the parking lot.

Chenonceau at Night (Promenade Nocturne): On summer nights, floodlights and period music create a romantic after-dinner cap to your Loire day (gardens only). Just stroll over whenever and for as long as you like (€6, daily July-Aug 21:30-23:30).

Boat Trips: In summer, the château has rental **rowboats**—an idyllic way to savor graceful château views (€7/30 minutes, July-Aug daily 10:00-19:00, 4 people/boat, not available when the river is low).

BACKGROUND

Find a riverside view of the château to get oriented. Although earlier châteaux were built for defensive purposes, Chenonceau was the

first great pleasure palace. Nicknamed the "château of the ladies," it housed many famous women over the centuries. The original owner, Thomas Bohier, was away on the king's business so much that his wife, Katherine Briçonnet, made most of the design decisions during construction of the main château (1513-1521).

In 1547, King Henry II gave the château to his mistress, Diane de Poitiers, who added an arched bridge across the river to access the hunting grounds. She enjoyed her lovely retreat until Henry II died (pierced in a jousting tournament in Paris); his vengeful wife, Catherine de' Medici, unceremoniously kicked Diane out (and into the château of Chaumont, described on page 399). Catherine added the three-story structure on Diane's bridge. She died before completing her vision of a matching château on the far side of the river, but not before turning Chenonceau into *the* place to see and be seen by the local aristocracy. (Whenever you see a split coat of arms, it belongs to a woman—half her husband's and half her father's.)

VISITING THE CHATEAU

Strut like an aristocrat down the tree-canopied path to the château. (There's a fun plant maze partway up on the left.) You'll cross three moats and two bridges, and pass an old round tower, which predates the main building. Notice the tower's fine limestone veneer, added so the top would better fit the new château.

The main château's original **oak door** greets you with the coats of arms of the first owners. The knocker is high enough to be used by visitors on horseback. The smaller door within the large one could be for two purposes: to slip in after curfew, or to enter during winter without letting out all the heat.

Once inside, you'll tour the château in a clockwise direction

LOIRE

(turn left upon entering). Take time to appreciate the beautiful brick floor tiles and lavishly decorated ceilings. As you continue, follow your pamphlet or audioguide, and pay attention to these details:

In the **guard room,** the best-surviving tiles from the original 16th-century floor are near the walls—imagine the entire room covered with these faience tiles. And though the tapestries kept the room cozy, they also functioned to tell news or recent history (to the king's liking, of course). The French-style joist beams feature Catherine de' Medici's monogram. You'll see many more tapestries and monograms in this château.

The superbly detailed **chapel,** with its original 1521 wood gallery above the entry, survived the vandalism of the Revolution because the fast-thinking lady of the palace filled it with firewood. Angry masses were supplied with mallets and instructions to smash everything royal or religious. While this room was both, all they saw was stacked wood. The hatch door provided a quick path to the kitchen and an escape boat downstairs. The windows, blown out during World War II, are replacements from the 1950s. Look for graffiti in English left behind by the guards who protected Mary, Queen of Scots (who stayed here after her marriage to King François II).

The centerpiece of the **bedroom of Diane de Poitiers** is a severe portrait of her rival, Catherine de' Medici, at 40 years old. Take note of the various monograms in the room. You've already seen Catherine's Chanel-like double-C insignia. Henri II flaunts his singular H. And combining the two seems to form mirrored Ds...perhaps showing Henri's preference for his mistress Diane.

The 16th-century tapestries are among the finest in France. Each one took an average of 60 worker-years to make. Study the complex compositions of the *Triumph of Charity* (over the bed) and the violent *Triumph of Force*.

At 200 feet long, the three-story **Grand Gallery** spans the river. The upper stories house double-decker ballrooms and a small museum. Notice how differently the slate and limestone of the checkered floor wear after 500 years. Imagine grand banquets here. Catherine, a contemporary of Queen Elizabeth I of England, wanted to rule with style. She threw wild parties and employed her ladies to circulate and soak up all the political gossip possible from the well-lubricated Kennedys and Rockefellers of her realm. Parties included grand fireworks displays and mock naval battles on the river. The niches once held statues—Louis XIV took a liking to them, and consequently, they now decorate the palace at Versailles.

In summer and during holidays, you can take a quick walk outside for more good palace **views:** Cross the bridge, pick up a re-entry ticket, then stroll the other bank of the Cher (across the river from the château). During World War I, the Grand Gallery served as a military hospital, where more than 2,200 soldiers were cared for—picture hundreds of beds lining the gallery. And in World War II, the river you crossed marked the border between the collaborationist Vichy government and Nazi-controlled France. Back then, Chenonceau witnessed many prisoner swaps, and at night, château staff would help resistance fighters and Jews cross in secret. Because the gallery was considered a river crossing, the Germans had their artillery aimed at Chenonceau, ready to destroy the "bridge" to block any Allied advance.

Double back through the gallery to find the sensational state-of-the-art (in the 16th century) **kitchen** below. It was built near water (to fight the inevitable kitchen fires) and in the basement; because heat rises, it helped heat the palace. Cross the small bridge (watch your head) to find the stove and landing bay for goods to be ferried in and out.

From here, find the **Muse/Three Graces Room** (with a painting featuring King Louis XV's three favorite mistresses), then visit the King Louis XIV Room.

Back on the main floor, the staircase leading **upstairs** wowed royal guests. It was the first nonspiral staircase they'd seen...quite a treat in the 16th century. When open, the balcony provides lovely views of the gardens, which originally supplied vegetables and herbs. (Diane built the one to the right; Catherine, the prettier one to your left.) The estate is still full of wild boar and deer—the primary dishes of past centuries. You'll see more lavish bedrooms on this floor. Small side rooms show fascinating old architectural sketches of the château. The walls, 20 feet thick, were honeycombed with the flues of 224 fireplaces and passages for servants to do their pleasure-providing work unseen. There was no need for plumbing. Servants fetched, carried, and dumped everything pipes do today.

Above the Grand Gallery is the **Medici Gallery,** now a mini-museum for the château. Displays in French and English cover the lives of six women who made their mark on Chenonceau (one of them had a young Jean-Jacques Rousseau, who would later become an influential philosopher, as her personal secretary). There's also a timeline of the top 10 events in the history of the château and a cabinet of curiosities.

Go to the **top floor** to peek inside the somber bedchamber and mourning room of Louise de Lorraine, widow of Henri III. Stabbed by a renegade Dominican monk, the king dictated this message for his wife on his deathbed: "My dear, I hope that I shall bear myself well. Pray to God for me and do not move from there." Louise took him literally and spent the last 11 years of her life in meditation and prayer at Chenonceau. Perpetually dressed in the then-traditional mourning color, she became known as the White

Queen. Take a close look at the silver teardrops that adorn the black walls before paying homage at the 16th-century portrait of Henri III.

To end your visit, escape the hordes by touring the **two gardens** with their postcard-perfect views of the château. The upstream garden hasn't changed since Diane de Poitiers first commissioned it in 1547. Designed in the austere Italian style, the water fountain was revolutionary in its time for its forceful jet. The downstream garden of Catherine de' Medici is more relaxed, with tree roses and lavender gracing its lines in high season.

Military Hospital Room and Traditional Farm: These sights are best seen after you've toured the château and gardens. The military hospital room, located in the château stables, gives an idea of what the Grand Gallery was like when it housed wounded soliders during World War I (effective English explanations). You can taste the owner's wines in the atmospheric **Cave des Dômes** below. Just past the stables you can stroll around a traditional farm. Imagine the production needed to sustain the château while making your way through the vegetable and flower gardens toward the exit.

TOWN OF CHENONCEAUX

This one-road, sleepy village makes a good home base for drivers and a workable base for train travelers who don't mind connections. The château's **gardens** are open on summer evenings with mood lighting and music, making the perfect after-dinner activity for those sleeping here (see "Chenonceau at Night," under "Orientation to Château de Chenonceau," earlier). You can rent **bikes** at the recommended Relais Chenonceaux hotel (May-Sept daily 9:00-19:00).

Sleeping: Hotels are a good value in Chenonceaux, and there's one for every budget. You'll find them *tous ensemble* on Rue du Dr. Bretonneau, all with free and secure parking.

$$$ Auberge du Bon Laboureur** turns heads with its ivied facade, lush terraces, and, inside, cozy lounges and bars. The staff acts a tad stiff, but past the formal pleasantries are lovely four-star rooms with every comfort at three-star prices (family rooms and suites, heated pool, air-con, fine gardens, finer restaurant, 6 Rue du Dr. Bretonneau, tel. 02 47 23 90 02, www. bonlaboureur.com, laboureur@wanadoo.fr).

$$ Hôtel la Roseraie* has a flowery terrace, bar, and 22 warmly decorated rooms. Sabine and Jerome run a good show with good prices for three-star comfort, and their big white Alsatian Achilles watches over it all (queen- or king-size beds, air-con, pool, closed mid-Nov-March, 7 Rue du Dr. Bretonneau, tel. 02 47 23 90 09, www.hotel-chenonceau.com, laroseraie-chenonceaux@orange.fr). The traditional dining room and sweet terrace are ideal for a nice dinner—available for guests and nonguests alike who reserve ahead (daily May-Sept, closed Tue off-season and mid-Nov-mid-March).

$ Relais Chenonceaux** greets guests with a nice patio and a mix of rooms. The best rooms are in the new annex; those in the main building are above a restaurant and plain (family rooms, rental bikes available, tel. 02 47 23 98 11, 10 Rue du Dr. Bretonneau, www.chenonceaux.com, info@chenonceaux.com).

$ Hostel du Roy** offers 30 spartan but well-priced rooms, some around a garden courtyard, and a mediocre but cheap restaurant. Hardworking Nathalie and Edith run the place with papa's help (family rooms, 9 Rue du Dr. Bretonneau, tel. 02 47 23 90 17, www.hostelduroy.com, hostelduroy@wanadoo.fr).

Eating: You'll find eating options for all budgets. All of these are listed above, under "Sleeping": Reserve ahead to dine in formal style at the country-elegant and Michelin-starred **$$$$ Auberge du Bon Laboureur** (€52 and €85 *menus*). **$$$ Hôtel la Roseraie** serves good fixed-price meals in a lovely dining room or on a garden terrace (*menus* for €29 or €37—I'd spring for the more expensive one, May-Sept daily 19:00-21:00, closed Tue off-season and mid-Nov-mid-March). **$$ Relais Chenonceaux** dishes up savory *crêpes*, salads, and *plats* in a pleasant interior or on its terrace (daily). The price is right for the basic cuisine at **$ Hostel du Roy,** with a daily €10 *plat du jour*.

La Maison des Pages has some bakery items, sandwiches, cold drinks to go, and just enough groceries for a modest picnic (closed Wed, on the main drag between Hostel du Roy and Hôtel la Roseraie).

For a French treat, book ahead and drive about a mile to Chisseaux and dine at the *très* traditional **$$$ Auberge du Cheval Rouge.** You'll enjoy some of the region's fine cuisine at affordable prices, either inside or on a verdant patio (closed Mon-Tue, 30 Rue Nationale, Chisseaux, tel. 02 47 23 86 67, www.auberge-duchevalrouge.com).

Connections: From Chenonceaux it's easy to get by train to **Tours** (10/day, 30 minutes), with connections to **Chinon, Azay-le-Rideau,** and **Langeais.** To reach **Amboise,** you can either take the train (6/day, 1 hour, transfer at St-Pierre-des-Corps) or bus (1-2/day, Mon-Sat only, none on Sun, 25 minutes, departs Chenonceaux at about 12:20, in summer also at about 17:50, catch bus across the street from the TI, tel. 02 47 05 30 49, www.tourainefilvert.com).

Blois

Bustling Blois (pronounced "blwah")
feels like the Big Apple after all of
those rural villages and castles—its
urban vibe can be a shock. Blois owns
a rich history, dolled-up pedestrian
areas, and a darn impressive château
smack in its center. With convenient
access to Paris, Blois makes a handy
base for train travelers; Chambord

and Cheverny are within reach by excursion bus (cheap, high season only) or taxi (pricey, any season, also serve Chaumont). Frequent train service to Paris and Amboise enables easy stopovers in
Blois (luggage lockers available at château with paid entry).

If Blois feels more important than other Loire towns, it was.
From this once powerful city, the medieval counts of Blois governed their vast lands and vied with the king of France for dominance. The center of France moved from Amboise to Blois in 1498,
when Louis XII inherited the throne (after Charles VIII had his
unfortunate head-banging incident in Amboise). The château
you see today is living proof of this town's 15 minutes of fame.
But there's more to Blois than just its château. Tour the flying-
buttressed St. Nicholas Church, find the medieval warren of lanes
below St. Louis Cathedral, and relax in a café on Place Louis XII.

Orientation to Blois

Unlike most other Loire châteaux, Blois' Château Royal sits right
in the city center, with no forest, pond, moat, or river to call its own.
It's an easy walk from the train station, near ample underground
parking, and just above the TI. Below the château, Place Louis XII
marks the hub of traffic-free Blois, with cafés and shops lining its
perimeter. Rue du Commerce, leading up from the river, is Blois'
primary shopping street. Atmospheric cafés and restaurants hide in
the medieval tangle of lanes below St. Louis Cathedral and around
St. Nicholas Church. Blois was heavily bombed in World War II,
leaving much of the old town in ruins, but the château survived.
Today, the city largely ignores its river and celebrates Saturdays
with a great market (until about 13:00) centered on Place Louis
XII. Sundays are quiet in Blois.

ARRIVAL IN BLOIS

Train travelers can walk 10 minutes straight out of the station
down Avenue du Dr. Jean Laigret to the TI and château (follow

small brown *Château* signs), or take a two-minute taxi from in front of the station. There's no bag check at the station; see "Helpful Hints," below, for options.

Drivers follow *Centre-Ville* and *Château* signs (metered parking along Avenue du Dr. Jean Laigret or inside at Parking du Château—first 30 minutes free, then about €2/2.5 hours).

TOURIST INFORMATION

The cramped TI is across from the château entrance. They sell discounted tickets when purchased for several châteaux (daily April-Sept 9:00-19:00, Oct-March 10:00-17:00, pay Wi-Fi, pay public computer, 23 Place du Château, tel. 02 54 90 41 41, www. bloischambord.com). To explore the center of Blois, use the TI's handy walking-tour brochure (€2, red and purple routes are best), download their free, well-designed city guide app, or just follow my suggested route on page 390. The TI also has information on bike rentals and routes.

HELPFUL HINTS

Baggage Storage: You can store small and midsize bags in the château's free **lockers** with paid admission—so you can drop off your luggage, tour the château and town, and even take an excursion to Chambord and Cheverny, provided you reclaim your bag before the château closes. **Détours de Loire** is the only place in town to store large suitcases (€2/day per bag, free if you rent bike, see next listing).

Bike Rental: Détours de Loire bike rental is a block below the train station at 39 Avenue du Dr. Jean Laigret (tel. 02 54 56 07 73). As they also have a shop in Amboise, you can rent a bike for a 26-mile one-way ride to Amboise, stopping at garden-rich Chaumont-sur-Loire on the way. See "Biking from Blois," later, for route ideas.

Laundry: A self-service launderette is at 6 Rue St-Lubin (long hours daily).

Local Guide: Fabrice Maret lives in Blois and is a skilled teacher (see page 353 for details).

Sights in Blois

▲▲CHATEAU ROYAL DE BLOIS

A castle has inhabited this site since the 900s. Size up the current one from the big square before entering. Even though parts of the building date from the Middle Ages, notice the complete absence of defensive towers, drawbridges, and other fortifications. Gardens once extended behind the château and up the hill to a forest (where the train station is today). A walk around the building's perimeter (to the right as you face it) reveals more of its beautiful Renaissance facade.

Kings Louis XII and François I built most of the château you see today, each calling it home during their reigns. That's Louis looking good on his horse in the niche. The section on the far right looks like a church but was actually the château's most important meeting room (more on this later).

Cost and Hours: €10, €5 for kids under age 18, €15.50 combo-ticket with House of Magic (described later, under "Other Sights and Activities") or sound-and-light show (see next), €20 covers all three, daily April-Sept 9:00-18:30 plus July-Aug until 19:00, Oct until 18:00, Nov-March 9:00-12:30 & 14:30-17:30.

Sound-and-Light Show: This simple "show" takes place in the center courtyard and features projections with a historical narrative of the "loves, dramas, and mysteries" of French royal life (€8, €15.50 combo-ticket with château, €20 combo-ticket with château and House of Magic, €2 audioguide provides English translation—free with your own headphones; daily April-Sept at about 22:00).

Tours and Information: At the ticket office, pick up the helpful brochure, then read the well-presented displays in each room. The informative audioguide is €4. In July-Aug, 20-minute orientations run at 10:30 and 15:00 and a one-hour guided tour at 13:15 (all in English). Tel. 02 54 90 33 33, www.chateaudeblois.fr.

Visiting the Château: Begin in the **courtyard,** where four wings—ranging from Gothic to Neoclassical—underscore this

château's importance over many centuries. Stand with your back to the entry to get oriented. The medieval parts of the château are the brick-patterned sections (to your left and behind you), both built by Louis XII. While work was underway on Chambord, François I (who apparently was addicted to home renovation) added the elaborate Renaissance wing (to your right; early 16th century), centered on a protruding spiral staircase and slathered with his emblematic salamanders. Gaston d'Orléans inherited the place in the 1600s and wanted to do away with the messy mismatched styles. He demolished a church that stood across from you (the chapel to your left is all that remains) and replaced it with the clean-lined, Neoclassical structure you see today. Luckily, that's as far as he got.

Visit the interior counterclockwise, and focus on the Renaissance wing. Begin in the far-right corner (where you entered the courtyard) and walk under the stone porcupine relief, Louis' symbol, and up the steps into the dazzling **Hall of the Estates-General** (it resembles a church from the outside). This is the oldest surviving part of the château (predating Louis and François), where the Estates-General met twice to deliberate who would inherit the throne from Henry III, who had no male heir. (Keep reading to see how Henry resolved the problem.)

Continue into the small **lapidary museum** (down the steps by the wooden staircase), with an engaging display of statues and architectural fragments from the original château (love the gargoyles).

Stone stairs lead up to the **royal apartments of François I.** Immerse yourself in richly tiled, ornately decorated rooms with some original furnishings (excellent explanations posted). You'll see busts and portraits of some of the château's most famous residents, and near the end, learn about the dastardly 1588 murder of the duke of Guise, which took place in these apartments. In the late 1500s, the devastating Wars of Religion pitted Protestant against Catholic and took a huge toll on this politically and religiously divided city—including the powerful Guise brothers. King Henry III (Catherine de' Medici's son) had the devoutly Catholic duke assassinated to keep him off the throne.

The Neoclassical wing is of less interest; end your visit with a walk through the small **fine-arts museum.** Located just over the château's entry, this 16th-century who's-who portrait gallery lets you put faces to the characters that made this château's history.

OTHER SIGHTS AND ACTIVITIES
House of Magic (Maison de la Magie)

The home of Jean-Eugène Robert-Houdin, the illusionist whose name was adopted by Harry Houdini, offers an interesting but overpriced history of illusion and magic. Kids enjoy the gift shop. Several daily 30-minute shows have no words, so they work in any language.

Cost and Hours: €9, €7 for kids under age 18, €15.50 combo-ticket with château, €20 combo-ticket includes château and sound-and-light show; daily 10:00-12:30 & 14:00-18:30, magic "séance" schedule posted at entry—usually at 11:15, 14:45 or 15:15, and 17:15; at the opposite end of the square from the château, tel. 02 54 90 33 33, www.maisondelamagie.fr.

Wine Cooperative

Sample wines from a variety of local vintners on the château square, next to Le Marignan café (free, daily 11:00-19:00, closed at lunchtime off-season, tel. 02 54 74 76 66).

A Walk Through Blois' Historic Center

There's little to do along the river except to cross Pont Jacques Gabriel for views back to the city. But Blois' old town is well worth a wander. Although much of the historic center was destroyed by WWII bombs, it has been tastefully rebuilt with traffic-free streets and pleasing squares.

For a taste of medieval Blois, drop down the steps below the Maison de la Magie and turn right into Place Louis XII, ground zero in the old city; from here, walk down Rue St-Lubin (after a few blocks it turns into Rue des Trois Marchands). Follow along as the street curves to the left and continue until you see the church of **St. Nicholas.** The towering church, with its flying buttresses, dates from the late 1100s, and is worth a peek inside for its beautifully lit apse and its blend of Gothic and Romanesque styles. Find Rue Anne de Bretagne behind the church and track it back to Place Louis XII. From here, pedestrian-friendly streets like Rue St-Martin lead north to Rue du Commerce, the town's main shopping drag, and to peaceful medieval lanes below Blois' other hill, crowned by **St. Louis Cathedral.** Finish your walk in the lovely rose garden by the cathedral. Nearby Rue de la Foulerie is headquarters for hip Blois.

Biking from Blois

Blois is well-positioned as a starting point for biking forays into the countryside. Cycling from Blois to Chambord is a level, one-hour, one-way ride along a well-marked, 13-mile route, much of it an elaborate bike-only lane that follows the river's left (eastern) bank. You can loop back to Blois without repeating the same route and connect to a good network of other bike paths (the TI's free *Les Châteaux à Vélo* map shows area bike routes). Hardy riders can bike one-way to Amboise via Chaumont by renting at the Détours de Loire bike shop (see "Helpful Hints" for Blois, earlier).

Sleeping in Blois

($$$$ = Splurge, $$$ = Pricier, $$ = Moderate, $ = Budget)
Blois has a scarcity of worthwhile hotels.

$$$ Hôtel Mercure Blois**** is modern, pricey, and made for businesspeople, but it's reliable, with big, superior two-level rooms and a riverfront location a 15-minute walk below the château (aircon, elevator, pay parking, 28 Quai Saint Jean, tel. 02 54 56 66 66, www.mercure.com).

LOIRE

$$ Best Western Blois Château*** has stylish decor, small-but-sharp rooms, and all the comforts you'd expect from this chain. In summer you can have breakfast on their quiet garden terrace (air-con, elevator, across from the train station and behind the château at 8 Avenue du Dr. Jean Laigret, tel. 02 54 56 85 10, www.hotelblois-gare.fr, contact@hotelblois-gare.fr).

$$ La Maison de Thomas is a mod B&B that doubles as a wine-tasting boutique specializing in Loire vintages. It's an old building, but all five rooms have been updated with Euro-chic decor (includes breakfast, cash only, uphill from the château near the pedestrian main drag at 12 Rue Beauvoir, ask for directions to street parking, tel. 09 81 84 44 59, www.lamaisondethomas.fr, resa@lamaisondethomas.fr, Guillaume).

$ Hôtel Anne de Bretagne** offers good value with 29 comfortable, traditional rooms, a central location near the château and train station, and a welcoming terrace. Ask for a room on the quiet side of the building facing the terrace. They also rent bikes—best to book in advance. Say hello to the hotel *chien,* Jappy (family rooms, no elevator or air-con, 150 yards uphill from Parking du Château, 5-minute walk below the train station at 31 Avenue du Dr. Jean Laigret, tel. 02 54 78 05 38, www.hotelannedebretagne.com, contact@hotelannedebretagne.com).

Eating in Blois

Diners can start off their evening with a glass of wine at welcoming **Chez Laurent,** where locals gather to sip and people-watch (5 Rue St-Martin). Another popular watering hole is **Le St. Lubin,** a café-bar (16 Rue St-Lubin).

If you're stopping in Blois around lunchtime, plan on eating at one of the places in the lower part of town. **Le Marignan,** on the square in front of the château, works for a drink to watch the stately mansion opposite the château becoming the "dragon house," as monsters crane their long necks out its many windows at the top of the hour.

BETWEEN THE CHATEAU AND THE RIVER

The traffic-free streets between the château and the river are home to many cafés with standard, easy meals.

$$$ La Banquette Rouge, a block above St. Nicholas Church's left transept, is your best bet for foodie-pleasing pleasures. It features fine regional dishes with creative twists—try the duck or pan-fried veal liver. You'll dine in a long red booth—as the name suggests (closed Sun-Mon, reservations smart, 16 Rue des Trois Marchands, tel. 02 54 78 74 92, www.lesbanquettesrouges.com).

LOIRE

$$ Le Castelet, also near St. Nicholas, is simple and cheap with good vegetarian choices (closed Sun and Wed, 40 Rue St-Lubin, tel. 02 54 74 66 09).

$$ Douce Heure is a modish *salon gourmand* on Place Louis XII's southwest corner. The extensive menu of homemade beverages includes iced teas, traditional hot chocolate, and fruit cocktails—the strawberry, raspberry, and rose are excellent (good quiches, wraps, and salads; great desserts, Tue-Sat 12:00-19:00, closed Sun-Mon, Place Louis XII).

ELSEWHERE IN BLOIS

$$ Poivre et Sel, just a few blocks from the Pont Jacques, is run by Gabriel, who offers new takes on traditional French cuisine in a rustic chic setting. Dine on the ground floor or in the open loft. Weekend reservations are recommended (Mon-Sat 12:00-14:00 & 19:00-22:00, closed Sun, 9 Rue du Chant des Oiseaux, tel. 02 54 78 07 78, www.poivreetsel.fr).

Between the Cathedral and the River: To dine cheaply on an atmospheric square with few tourists in sight, find Place du Grenier à Sel (a block from the river, below St. Louis Cathedral) and consider these places: **$$ La Grolle** specializes in tasty fondues, raclettes, and other melted-cheese dishes, with lighter options available in summer (closed Sun-Mon, 5 Rue Vauvert, tel. 02 36 23 64 65). Next door, **$$ Le Vespa,** does a Franco-Italian mix, including pizzas (pleasant interior seating, closed Sun-Mon except in summer, 11 Rue Vauvert, tel. 02 54 78 44 97).

Save room for dessert and try the crêpes at **$ Les Catalpas** (Sun-Fri 12:00-14:00 & 19:00-23:00, closed Sat, 1 Rue du Grenier à Sel, tel. 02 54 56 86 86).

Blois Connections

From Blois by Train to: Amboise (14/day, 20 minutes), **Tours** (roughly hourly, 40 minutes), **Chinon** (6/day, 2 hours, transfer in Tours and possibly in St-Pierre-des-Corps), **Azay-le-Rideau** (7/day, 1.5 hours, transfer in Tours and possibly in St-Pierre-des-Corps), **Paris** (4/day direct to Gare d'Austerlitz, 1.5 hours, more with transfer in St-Pierre-des-Corps or Orléans).

By Bus to Chambord and Cheverny: In peak season, **Transports du Loir-et-Cher** (TLC) shuttle buses to Chambord, Cheverny, and (less important) Beauregard leave from the Blois train station (daily in July-Aug; Wed, Sat, and Sun only April-June and Sept-Oct). Look for the buses across the parking lot as you leave the station (TLC bus marked *Navette-Châteaux, line #41*). Morning departures from Blois station at 9:30 and 11:30 go to Chambord; from Chambord, departures link Cheverny and

Beauregard with a few return-trip options to Blois. Verify times at a TI or at www.route41.fr (€6 bus fare, discounts offered on château entries including the Château Royal in Blois; buy tickets from TI or bus driver—look for "Navette Châteaux de la Loire"). You can also board these buses at the Blois château (3 minutes later than the train station departure).

By Minivan Tour to Chambord, Cheverny, and Other Châteaux: Eco Shuttle offers several excursions a day to surrounding châteaux leaving from the Blois train station and from Place du Château by the TI. The Chambord-Cheverny trip leaves at 9:15 and returns at 13:30, giving you 1.5 hours at each castle (€39/person, book ahead at TI or online, tel. 06 49 26 34 35, www.ecoshuttle41.com).

By Taxi: Blois taxis wait in front of the station and offer excursion fares to **Chambord, Chaumont,** or **Cheverny** (rates posted in taxi shelter, about €36 one-way from Blois to any of these three châteaux, €110 round-trip to Chambord and Cheverny, €157 for Chambord and Chenonceau, more expensive on Sunday, 8-person minivans available, tel. 02 54 78 07 65). These rates are per cab, making the per-person price downright reasonable for groups of three or four.

Chambord

With its huge scale and prickly silhouette, Château de Chambord, worth ▲▲▲, is the granddaddy of the Loire châteaux. It's surrounded by Europe's largest enclosed forest park, a game preserve defined by a 20-mile-long wall and teeming with wild deer and boar.

Chambord (shahm-bor) began as a simple hunting lodge for bored Blois counts and became a monument to the royal sport and duty of hunting. (Hunting was considered important to keep the animal population under control and the vital forests healthy.)

The château's massive architecture is the star attraction—particularly the mind-boggling double-helix staircase. Six times the size of your average Loire castle, the château has 440 rooms and a fireplace for every day of the year. The château is laid out as a keep in the shape of a Greek cross, with four towers and two wings surrounded by stables. Its four floors are each separated by 46 stairs, creating very high ceilings. The ground floor has reception rooms, the first floor up houses the royal apartments, the second floor up houses temporary exhibits and a hunting museum, and the rooftop offers a hunt-viewing terrace. Special exhibits describing Chambord at key moments in its history help animate the place. Because hunters could see best after autumn leaves fell, Chambord was a winter palace (which helps explain the 365 fireplaces). Only 80 of Chambord's rooms are open to the public—but that's plenty.

If you hate crowds, you'll like Chambord. Because it's so huge, it's relatively easy to escape the hordes. It helps that there's no one-way, mandatory tour route—you're free to roam like a duke surveying his domain.

GETTING THERE

Without a car from Blois, the shuttle bus is best (runs daily in July and August, otherwise only a few days a week); taxis and minivan tours from Blois are also available (see "Blois Connections" on page 392 for details on all of these options). It's a pleasant one-hour bike ride from Blois to Chambord (see page 390). Minivan excursions also run from Amboise (see "Amboise Connections" on page 377).

With a car, allow 45 minutes to drive from Amboise, 55 minutes from Chenonceaux, and 15 minutes from Cheverny. You'll pay €6 to park (pay at machines near the lots, credit cards only). If the machine won't accept your card, pay at the ticket office as you approach the château.

ORIENTATION TO CHATEAU DE CHAMBORD

Cost and Hours: €11, daily 9:00-18:00, Oct-March until 17:00.

Buying Tickets: There are two ticket offices. One is as you approach the château, and another (less crowded) one is in the château entry.

Tours and Information: This château requires helpful information to make it come alive. The free handout is a start, and most rooms have adequate explanations. For more context, rent the €5 audioguide (but skip the useless "Histopad" tablet guide). Tel. 02 54 50 40 00, www.chambord.org.

Services: You'll find a TI by the ticket counter inside the château entry area. The bookshop has a good selection of children's books. Among the collection of services near the château, there's an ATM, souvenir shops, a wine-tasting room, and cafés. There's only one WC at the château itself (in a courtyard corner); otherwise use the pay WC in the village.

Cruising Around the Park: A network of leafy lanes crisscrosses the vast expanse contained within the 20-mile-long wall. Explore the park on a bike (€7/hour) or a golf cart (€28/45 minutes, great value for 2-4 people). Your roaming area is more restricted in the golf cart, but you'll cover lots more ground than on foot.

Horseback and Birds of Prey Show: The 45-minute show is not worth most people's time or money (€14.50, €22 combo-ticket with château, mid-July-Aug daily at 11:45 and 16:00, May-mid-July and Sept-early Oct Tue-Sun at 11:45 only, no show on Mon, reservations recommended, in the stables across the field from the château entry, tel. 02 54 50 50 40).

Views: The best view of the château depends on the light. Walk straight out the main entrance one to two hundred yards for exquisite looks back to the château. On the opposite (parking lot) side, you can cross the small river in front of the château and turn right for terrific frontal views.

BACKGROUND

Starting in 1518, François I created this "weekend retreat," employing 1,800 workmen for 15 years. (You'll see his signature salamander symbol everywhere.) François I was an absolute monarch—with an emphasis on absolute. In 32 years of rule (1515-1547), he never once called the Estates-General to session (a rudimentary parliament in *ancien régime* France). This imposing hunting palace was another way to show off his power. Countless guests, like Charles V—the Holy Roman Emperor and most powerful man of the age—were invited to this pleasure palace of French kings...and were totally wowed.

The grand architectural plan of the château—modeled after an Italian church—feels designed as a place to worship royalty. Each floor of the main structure is essentially the same: four equal arms of a Greek cross branch off of a monumental staircase, which leads up to a cupola. From a practical point of view, the design pushed the usable areas to the four corners. This castle, built while the pope was erecting a new St. Peter's Basilica, is like a secular rival to the Vatican.

Construction started the year Leonardo died, 1519. The architect is unknown, but an eerie Leonardo-esque spirit resides here. The symmetry, balance, and classical proportions combine to reflect a harmonious Renaissance vision that could have been inspired by Leonardo's notebooks.

Typical of royal châteaux, this palace of François I was rarely used. Because any effective king had to be on the road to exercise his power, royal palaces sat empty most of the time. In the 1600s, Louis XIV renovated Chambord, but he visited it only six times (for about two weeks each visit).

VISITING THE CHATEAU

The following information covers the highlights, floor by floor.

Ground Floor: This stark level shows off the general plan—four wings, small doors to help heated rooms stay warm, and a massive staircase. In a room just inside the front door, on the left, you can watch a worthwhile 18-minute video—look for a screen on the side wall for viewing with English subtitles.

The attention-grabbing **double-helix staircase** dominates the open vestibules and invites visitors to climb up. Its two spirals are interwoven, so people can climb up and down and never meet. Find the helpful explanation of the staircase posted on the wall. From the staircase, enjoy fine views of the vestibule action, or just marvel at the playful Renaissance capitals carved into its light tuff stone.

First Floor Up: Here you'll find the most interesting rooms. Starting opposite a big ceramic stove (added in the 18th century), tour this floor basically clockwise. You'll enter the lavish apartments in the **king's wing** and pass through the grand bedrooms of Louis XIV, his wife Maria Theresa, and, at the far end after the queen's boudoir, François I (follow *Logis de François 1er* signs). These theatrical bedrooms place the royal beds on raised platforms—getting them ready for some nighttime drama. The furniture in François' bedroom was designed so it could be easily disassembled and moved with him.

A highlight of the first floor is the seven-room **Museum of the Count of Chambord** (Musée du Comte de Chambord). The last of the French Bourbons, Henri d'Artois (a.k.a. the count of Chambord) was next in line to be king when France decided it didn't need one. He was raring to rule—you'll see his coronation outfits and even souvenirs from the coronation that never happened. Watch the short video about the man who believed he should have become King Henry V but who lived in exile from the age of 10. Although he opened the palace to the public, he actually visited this château only once, in 1871.

The **chapel,** tucked off in a side wing, is interesting only for how unimpressive and remotely located it is. It's dwarfed by the mass of this imposing château—clearly designed to trumpet the glories not of God, but of the king of France.

Second Floor: Beneath beautiful coffered ceilings (notice the "F" for François) is a series of ballrooms that once hosted post-hunt parties. From here, you'll climb up to the rooftop, but first lean to the center of the staircase and look down its spiral.

Rooftop: A pincushion of spires and chimneys decorates the rooftop viewing terrace. From a distance, the roof—with its frilly forest of stone towers—gives the massive château a deceptive lightness. From here, ladies could scan the estate grounds, enjoying the spectacle of their ego-pumping men out hunting. On hunt day, a line of beaters would fan out and work inward from the distant walls, flushing wild game to the center, where the king and his buddies waited. The showy lantern tower of the tallest spire glowed with a nighttime torch when the king was in.

LOIRE

Gaze up at the grandiose tip-top of the tallest tower, capped with the king's fleur-de-lis symbol. It's a royal lily—not a cross—that caps this monument to the power of the French king.

In the Courtyard: In the far corner, next to the summer café, a door leads to the Rolls-Royce of **carriage rooms** and the fascinating **lapidary rooms.** Here you'll come face-to-face with original stonework from the roof, including the graceful lantern cupola, with the original palace-capping fleur-de-lis. Imagine having to hoist that load. The volcanic tuff stone used to build the spires was soft and easy to work, but not very durable—particularly when so exposed to the elements. Several displays explain the ongoing renovations to François' stately pleasure dome. On the opposite side of the courtyard, find the château **kitchen,** with good English explanations.

Cheverny

This stately hunting palace, a ▲▲ sight, is one of the more lavishly furnished Loire châteaux. Because the immaculately preserved Château de Cheverny (shuh-vehr-nee) was built and decorated in a relatively short 30 years, from 1604 to 1634, it has a unique architectural harmony and unity of style. From the start, this château has been in the Hurault family, and Hurault pride shows in its flawless preservation and intimate feel (it was opened to the public in 1922). The charming viscount and his family still live on the third floor (not open to the public, but you'll see some family photos). Cheverny was spared by the French Revolution; the count's relatives were popular then, as today, even among the village farmers.

LOIRE

GETTING THERE

You can reach Cheverny by bus or shuttle excursion from Blois (see "Blois Connections" on page 392), or by minivan excursion from Amboise (see "Amboise Connections" on page 377). If driving, you can park for free at the château.

ORIENTATION TO CHATEAU DE CHEVERNY

Cost and Hours: €11, €15.50 combo-ticket includes Tintin "adventure" rooms (see "Sights near the Château," later), family deals available; daily April-Oct 9:15-18:30, Nov-March 10:00-17:00; tel. 02 54 79 96 29, www.chateau-cheverny.fr.

Eating and Sleeping: The château sits alongside a pleasant village, with a small grocery store and cafés offering good lunch options (the town also has a few hotels).

VISITING THE CHATEAU

As you walk across the manicured grounds toward the gleaming château, the sound of hungry hounds will follow you. Lined up across the facade are sculpted medallions with portraits of Roman emperors, including Julius Caesar (above the others in the center). As you enter the château, pick up the excellent self-guided tour brochure, which describes the interior beautifully.

Your visit starts in the lavish **dining room,** decorated with leather walls and a sumptuous ceiling. Next, as you climb the stairs to the private apartments, look out the window and spot the *orangerie* across the gardens. It was here that the *Mona Lisa* was hidden (along with other treasures from the Louvre) during World War II.

On the first floor, turn right from the stairs and tour the I-could-live-here **family apartments** with silky bedrooms, kids' rooms, and an intimate dining room. On the other side of this floor is the impressive **Arms Room** with weapons, a sedan chair, and a snare drum from the count of Chambord (who would have been king; see page 393). The **King's Bedchamber** is literally fit for a king. Study the fun ceiling art, especially the "boys will be boys" cupids.

On the top floor peek inside the chapel, before backtracking down to the ground floor. Browse the left wing and find a family tree going back to 1490, a grandfather clock with a second hand that's been ticking for 250 years, and a letter of thanks from George Washington to this family for their help in booting out the English.

SIGHTS NEAR THE CHATEAU
Dog Kennel

Barking dogs remind visitors that the viscount still loves to hunt (he goes twice a week year-round). The kennel (200 yards in front of the château, look for *Chenil* signs) is especially interesting when the 70 hounds are fed (daily at 11:30). The dogs—half English foxhound and half French Poitou—are bred to have big feet and bigger stamina. They're given food once a day (two pounds each in winter, half that in summer), and the feeding *(la soupe des chiens)* is a fun spectacle that shows off their strict training. Before chow time, the hungry hounds fill the little kennel rooftop and watch the trainer (who knows every dog's name) bring in troughs stacked with delectable raw meat. He opens the gate, and the dogs gather enthusiastically around the food, yelping hysterically. Only when the trainer says to eat can they dig in. You can see the dogs at any time, but the feeding show is fun to plan for.

Wine Tastings at the Château Gate

Opposite the entry to the château sits a slick wine-tasting room, **La Maison des Vins.** It's run by an association of 32 local vintners. Their mission: to boost the Cheverny reputation for wine (which is fruity, light, dry, and aromatic compared to the heavier, oaky wines made farther downstream). Tasters have two options. You can have four free tastes from featured bottles of the day, offered with helpful guidance (€6-11 bottles). For most, this is the best approach. Wine aficionados can pay to sample among the 96 bottles by using modern automated dispensers (€4 for 3 wines, €6.50 for 7 wines). Even if just enjoying the free tasting, wander among the spouts. Each gives the specs of that wine in English (daily 11:00-13:15 & 14:15-19:00, open during lunch in July-Aug, closed in winter, tel. 02 54 79 25 16, www.maisondesvinsdecheverny.fr).

Other Activities

Tintin comic lovers can enter a series of fun rooms designed to take them into a Tintin adventure (called Les Secrets de Moulinsart, €15.50 combo-ticket with castle); hunters can inspect an antler-filled **trophy room;** and gardeners can prowl the château's fine **kitchen and flower gardens** (free, behind the dog kennel).

Chaumont-sur-Loire

A castle has been located on this spot since the 11th century; the current version is a ▲▲ sight (▲▲▲ for garden or horse lovers). The first priority at Chaumont (show-mon) was defense. You'll appreciate the strategic location on the long climb up from the village below. Gardeners will appreciate the elaborate Festival of Gardens that unfolds next to the château every year, and modern-art lovers will enjoy how works have been incorporated into the gardens, château, and stables. If it's cold, you'll also appreciate that the château is heated in winter (rare in this region).

LOIRE

GETTING THERE

There is no public transport to Chaumont, although the train between Blois and Amboise can drop you (and your bike, if you like) in Onzain, a 25-minute roadside walk across the river to the château (14 trains/day, 10 minutes from Amboise). Other options include biking (Chaumont is about 11 level miles from Amboise or Blois) or a taxi (about €36 from Blois train station; see "Blois Connections" on page 392).

To avoid the hike up, drivers should skip the river-level entrance (closed in winter) and park up top behind the château (open all year). From the river, drive up behind the château (direction: Montrichard); at the first roundabout follow signs to *Château* and *Festival des Jardins*.

ORIENTATION TO DOMAINE DE CHAUMONT-SUR-LOIRE

Cost and Hours: Château and stables-€12; daily 10:00-18:30, Oct until 18:00, Nov-March until 17:00, last entry 45 minutes before closing.

Tours and Information: Audioguide-€4, English handout available, mobile app available in English, tel. 02 54 20 99 22, www.domaine-chaumont.fr.

Festival of Gardens: This annual exhibit, with 25 elaborate gardens arranged around a different theme each year, draws rave reviews from international gardeners. It's as impressive as the Chelsea Flower Show in England, but without the crowds—if you love contemporary garden design, don't miss this (Garden Festival only-€14; €4 more to add château and stables; generally mid-April-mid-Oct daily 10:00-20:00, tel. 02 54 20 99 22, www.domaine-chaumont.fr). When the festival is on, you'll find several little cafés and reasonable lunch options scattered about the hamlet (festival ticket not needed). Chaumont also hosts a winter garden festival inside several greenhouses.

BACKGROUND

The Chaumont château you see today was built mostly in the 15th and 16th centuries. Catherine de' Medici forced Diane de Poitiers to swap Chenonceau for Chaumont; you'll see tidbits about both women inside.

There's a special connection to America here. Jacques-Donatien Le Ray, a rich financier who owned Chaumont in the 18th century, was a champion of the American Revolution. He used his wealth to finance loans in the early days of the new republic (and even let Benjamin Franklin use one of his homes in Paris rent-free for 9 years). Unfortunately, the US never repaid the loans in full and eventually Le Ray went bankrupt.

Ironically, the American connection saved Chaumont during the French Revolution. Le Ray's son emigrated to New York and became an American citizen, but returned to France when his father deeded the castle to him. During the Revolution, he was able to turn back the crowds set on destroying Chaumont by declaring that he was now an American—and that all Americans were believers in *liberté, égalité,* and *fraternité.*

Today's château offers a good look at the best defense design in 1500: on a cliff with a dry moat, big and small drawbridges with classic ramparts, loopholes for archers, and handy holes through which to dump hot oil on attackers.

VISITING THE CHATEAU

Your walk through the palace—restored mostly in the 19th century—is described by the flier you'll pick up when you enter. As the château has more rooms than period furniture, your tour includes a few modern-art exhibits that fill otherwise empty spaces. The rooms you'll visit first (in the east wing) show the château as it appeared in the 15th and 16th centuries. Your visit ends in the west wing, which features furnishings from the 19th-century owners.

The castle's medieval **entry** is littered on the outside with various coats of arms. As you enter, take a close look at the two drawbridges (a new mechanism allows the main bridge to be opened with the touch of a button). Once inside, the heavy defensive feel is replaced with palatial luxury. Peek into the courtyard—during the more stable mid-1700s, the fourth wing, which had enclosed the courtyard, was taken down to give the terrace its river-valley view.

Entering the château rooms, signs direct you along a one-way loop path *(suite de la visite)* through the château's three wings. Catherine de' Medici, who missed her native Florence, brought a touch of Italy to all her châteaux, and her astrologer (Ruggieri) was so important that he had his own (plush) room—next to hers. **Catherine's bedroom** has a 16th-century throne—look for unicorns holding a shield. The Renaissance-style bed is a reproduction from the 19th century.

The exquisitely tiled **Salle de Conseil** has a grand fireplace designed to keep this conference room warm. The treasury box in the **guard room** is a fine example of 1600s-era locksmithing. The lord's wealth could be locked up here as safely as possible in those days, with a false keyhole, no handles, and even an extra-secure box inside for diamonds.

Next comes the **Diane de Poitiers room,** which doesn't have much to do with Diane but does have a fascinating collection of medallions. Look for the case of ceramic portrait busts dating from 1772, when Le Ray invited the Italian sculptor Jean-Baptiste Nini to work for him. In addition to Marie Antoinette, Voltaire, and Catherine the Great, you'll find several medallions depicting Benjamin Franklin.

A big spiral staircase leads up through too many unfurnished rooms and galleries of contemporary art. After the shock of the

LOIRE

21st century, you go back in time about 150 years to rooms decorated in 19th-century style. The **dining room**'s fanciful limestone fireplace is exquisitely carved. Find the food (frog legs, snails, goats for cheese), the maid with the bellows, and even the sculptor with a hammer and chisel at the top (on the left). Your visit ends with a stroll through the 19th-century library, the billiards room, and the living room. The porcupines over the fireplace and elsewhere are thanks to the Duke of Orléans, who adopted the porcupine as his emblem in 1394.

In the **courtyard,** study the entertaining spouts and decor on the walls, and remember that this space was originally enclosed on all sides. Chaumont has one of the best château views of the Loire River—rivaling Amboise for its panoramic tranquility.

The **stables** *(écuries)* were entirely rebuilt in the 1880s. The medallion above the gate reads *pour l'avenir* (for the future), which shows off an impressive commitment to horse technology. Inside, circle clockwise—you can almost hear the clip-clop of horses walking. Notice the deluxe horse stalls, padded with bins and bowls for hay, oats, and water, complete with a strategically placed drainage gutter. The horse kitchen *(cuisine des chevaux)* produced mash twice weekly for the horses, which were named for Greek gods and great châteaux. Beyond the covered alcove where the horse and carriage were prepared for the prince, you'll see four carriages parked and ready to go.

The **estate** is set in a 19th-century landscape, with woodlands and a fine lawn. More English than French, it has rolling open terrain, follies such as a water tower, and a brilliantly designed *potager* (vegetable garden) with an imaginative mix of edible and decorative plants. Its trees were imported from throughout the Mediterranean world to be enjoyed—and to fend off any erosion on this strategic bluff.

West of Tours

You'll find several worthwhile sights in the area west of Tours, including Azay-le-Rideau, Langeais, Villandry, Rivau, Ussé, and the Abbaye Royale de Fontevraud. The town of Chinon makes a fine home base for seeing these sights, as each is no more than a 30-minute drive away. Trains provide access to many châteaux (via Tours) but are time-consuming, so you're better off with your own car or a minivan excursion (see "Chinon Connections," later).

Chinon

This pleasing, sleepy town straddles the Vienne River and hides its ancient streets under a historic royal fortress. Henry II (Henry Plantagenet of England), Eleanor of Aquitaine, Richard the Lionheart, and Joan of Arc all called this town home for a while. Today's Chinon (shee-nohn) is best known for its popular red wines.

Orientation to Chinon

Chinon stretches out along the Vienne River, and everything of interest to travelers lies between it and the hilltop fortress. Charming Place du Général de Gaulle—ideal for café-lingering—is in the center of town. Rue Rabelais is Chinon's traffic-free shopping street, with restaurants, bars, and cafés—as lively as they can be in peaceful Chinon.

TOURIST INFORMATION

The TI is by the river in the town center, a 15-minute walk from the train station. You'll find *chambres d'hôtes* listings, wine-tasting and bike-rental information, and an English-language brochure with a self-guided tour of the town (May-Sept daily 10:00-13:30 & 14:00-19:00; shorter hours and closed Sun off-season; 1 Rue Rabelais, tel. 02 47 93 17 85, www.chinon-loirevalley.com).

HELPFUL HINTS

Market Days: A bustling market takes place all day Thursday (food in the morning only) on Place Jeanne d'Arc (west end of town). There's also a sweet little market on Saturday and Sunday mornings, around Place du Général de Gaulle.

Laundry: Salon Lavoir is near the bridge at 7 Quai Charles VII (daily 7:00-21:00).

Groceries: Carrefour City is across from the Hôtel de Ville, on Place du Général de Gaulle (Mon-Sat 7:00-21:00, Sun 9:00-13:00).

Bike and Canoe Rental: Clan Canoë Kayak & Vélo rents bikes and canoes on the river, next to the campground (bikes-€16/day; canoes-€11/2 hours or €20/half-day, shuttle included; €15-26 to combine bike and canoe in a half/full day; cash only, closed off-season, Quai Danton, mobile 06 23 82 96 33, www.loisirs-nature.fr). For more on biking and canoeing, see page 411.

Taxi: Call 06 83 51 87 88 for taxi service.

Car Rental: It's best to rent one at the St-Pierre-des-Corps train station. Otherwise, ask at the TI.

LOIRE

Parking: You'll find metered but cheap parking in town. Or you can park for free at the fortress (castle) and take the elevator down to the town.

Traditional Riverboat Cruise: One-hour rides on flat-bottom boats are available from April to October at 11:30 and 16:00 (€11, next to bike/canoe rental described above, inquire at the TI).

Best Views: You'll find terrific rooftop views from the fortress and along Rue du Coteau St-Martin (between St. Mexme Church and the fortress—see map on page 406), and rewarding river views to Chinon by crossing the bridge in the center of town and turning right (small riverfront café May-Sept).

Chinon Walk

Chinon offers a peaceful world of quiet cobbled lanes, historic buildings, and few tourists. Follow this self-guided walk (or the TI's self-guided tour brochure) and read plaques at key buildings to gain a good understanding of this city's historic importance.

• *Begin this short walk from the highest point of the bridge that crosses the Vienne River, and enjoy the great view.*

Chinon Riverbank: Chinon is sandwiched between the Vienne River (which flows into the Loire River only a few miles from here) and an abrupt cliff. People have lived along the banks of this river since prehistoric times. The Gallo-Romans built the first defenses in Chinon 1,600 years ago, and there's been a castle up on that hill for more than a thousand years—which pretty much predates every other castle you'll visit in the Loire area. The skinny, rounded clock tower served as the entrance to the middle section of the fortress during the Middle Ages. Starting in 1044, that fortress-castle became an important outpost for the king of France, and by 1150 Henry II Plantagenet (king of England) made this the center of his continental empire. A few hundred years later, Charles VII took refuge behind those walls during the Hundred Years' War, during which Chinon was France's capital city.

Down on the water, you'll see reproductions of the traditional wooden boats once used to shuttle merchandise up and down the river; some boats ventured as far west as the Atlantic. Wow.

• *Walk toward the city, then make a right along the riverbank and find the big statue that honors a famous Renaissance writer and satirist.*

Rabelais Statue: The great French writer François Rabelais was born here in 1494. You'll see many references to him in his proud hometown. His best-known work, *Gargantua and Pantagruel,* describes the amusing adventures of father-and-son giants and was set in Chinon. Rabelais' vivid humor and savage wit are, for many, quintessentially French—there's even a French word for it:

rabelaisien. In his bawdy tales, Rabelais critiqued society in ways that deflected outright censorship—though the Sorbonne called his work obscene. A monk and a doctor, he's considered the first great French novelist, and his farces were a voice against the power of the Church and the king.

• *Turn your back on Rabelais and follow the cobbled sidewalk leading to the center of Chinon's main square.*

Place du Général de Gaulle: The town wall once sat on the wide swath of land running from this square down to the river, effectively walling the city off from the water. This explains why, even now, Chinon seems to turn its back on its river. In medieval times, the market was here, just outside the wall. The town hall building, originally an arcaded market, was renovated only in the 19th century. Today it flies three flags: Europe, France, and Chinon (with its three castles). From here, you can see the handy elevator that connects the town with its castle.

• *Turn left down...*

Rue Voltaire: If the old wall still stood, you'd be entering town through the east gate. (Note the info plaques here and scattered throughout town.) Walk along a fine strip of 16th-, 17th-, and 18th-century houses to find a trio of fun wine-tasting possibilities. A half-block to the right is the charming little **Musée Animé du Vin;** at the next corner is the laid-back **Cave Voltaire wine shop,** and a right turn on the next small lane leads to **Caves Painctes** and the quarry where the stone for the castle originated (all covered later, under "Sights in Chinon").

• *Continue walking a few blocks farther into the historic city center.*

Old Town: In the immediate post-WWII years, there was little money or energy to care for beautiful old towns. But in the 1960s, new laws and sensitivities kicked in, and old quarters like this were fixed up and preserved. Study the local architecture. **La Maison Rouge** (at 38 Rue Voltaire) is a fine example of the town's medieval structures: a stone foundation and timber frame, filled in with whatever was handy. With dense populations crowding within the protective town walls, buildings swelled wider at the top to avoid blocking congested streets. **La Maison Bleue** next door features slate siding and looks like it belongs in Normandy. Notice the plaque that tells us that Joan of Arc dismounted her horse at this spot in 1429.

Pop into the ancient **bookshop** on the corner. I asked the owner where he got his old prints. He responded, "Did you ever enjoy a friend's mushrooms and ask him where he found them? Did he tell you?"

The **town museum** is across the street. Its plaque recalls that this building housed an Estates-General meeting, convened by

LOIRE

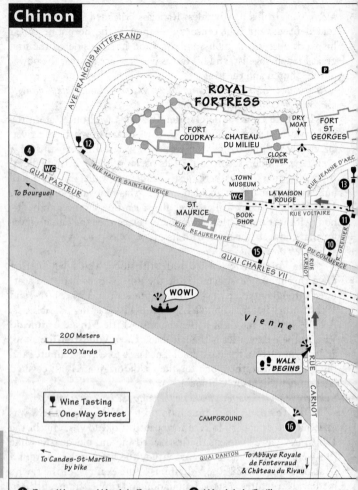

Chinon

ROYAL FORTRESS

FORT COUDRAY

CHATEAU DU MILIEU

DRY MOAT

FORT ST. GEORGES

CLOCK TOWER

AVE FRANÇOIS MITTERRAND

RUE HAUTE SAINT-MAURICE

QUAI PASTEUR

WC

To Bourgueil

TOWN MUSEUM

LA MAISON ROUGE

RUE JEANNE D'ARC

ST. MAURICE

RUE BEAUREPAIRE

BOOK-SHOP

WC

RUE VOLTAIRE

RUE DU COMMERCE

R. GRENIER

RUE CARNOT

QUAI CHARLES VII

WOW!

Vienne

200 Meters

200 Yards

WALK BEGINS

RUE CARNOT

Wine Tasting
One-Way Street

CAMPGROUND

To Candes-St-Martin by bike

QUAI DANTON

To Abbaye Royale de Fontevraud & Château du Rivau

LOIRE

1. Best Western Hôtel de France & Au Chapeau Rouge Rest.
2. Hôtel Diderot
3. Le Plantagenêt Hôtel
4. Hôtel Agnès Sorel
5. Hôtel de la Treille
6. L'Ardoise Restaurant
7. Les Saveurs d'Italie Restaurant
8. Restaurant-Musée Animé du Vin et de la Tonnellerie

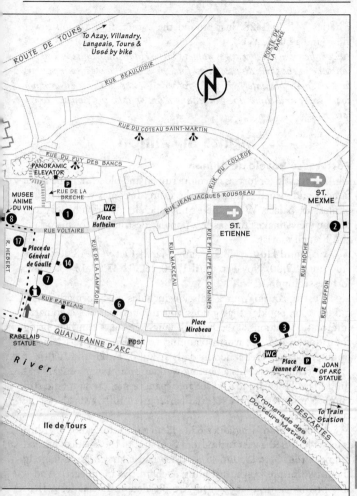

⑨ La Part des Anges Restaurant
⑩ Restaurant Côté Jardin
⑪ La Cave Voltaire Wine Tastings
⑫ Caves Plouzeau Wine Tastings
⑬ Caves Painctes Wine Tastings

⑭ Café Français
⑮ Launderette
⑯ Bike/Canoe Rental
⑰ Grocery Store

Charles VII, in 1428. Just around the corner, find a good tower view (and a public WC).

• From here the street changes names to Rue Haute St-Maurice. You can continue in the same direction and find the Caves Plouzeau wine cellars at #94 (described later). If you'd rather visit the castle, turn around, walk back, and climb up Rue Jeanne d'Arc or take the elevator to the fortress.

Sights in Chinon

Forteresse Royale de Chinon

Chinon's castle (or fortress) is more ruined and older than the more famous and visited châteaux of the Loire. It comes without a hint of pleasure palace. While there's not much left, its rich history and terrific views makes the castle a popular destination for historians and French tourists.

Cost and Hours: €8.50, daily March-Oct 9:30-18:00, May-Aug until 19:00, Nov-Feb until 17:00, tel. 02 47 93 13 45, www.forteressechinon.fr.

Castle Tours: Your admission includes an informative self-guided tour booklet that guides you through various automated information stations. Free English-language tours can help bring the ruins to life. It's worth planning your visit around them (45 minutes, March-Oct generally daily at 11:00, 14:00, and 17:00).

Getting There: It's a bracing walk up from town, or walk behind Place Hofheim to find the free "panoramic" elevator (and still climb 5 minutes). There's a free parking lot 100 yards above the castle entry.

Background: England's King Henry II and Eleanor of Aquitaine, who ruled a vast realm from Scotland to the Spanish border, reigned from here around 1150. They had eight children (among them two future kings, including Richard the Lionheart). And it was in this castle that Joan of Arc pleaded with Charles VII to muster the courage to rally the French and take the throne back from the nasty English. Charles had taken refuge in this well-fortified castle during the Hundred Years' War, making Chinon France's capital city during that low ebb in Gallic history.

Visiting the Castle: The castle has three structures separated by moats. Enter via the oldest part, the 12th-century Fort Saint-Georges. Crossing a dry moat, you'll land in the big courtyard of the Château du Milieu; at the far end is Fort Coudray. The fortress comes

with commanding views of the town, river, and château-studded countryside.

Follow the arrows through eight stark and stony rooms, enjoying the clever teaching videos. There's a small museum devoted to the legendary Joan of Arc and her myth, developed through the centuries to inspire the French to pride and greatness. Chinon—both the city and the castle—developed as its political importance grew. It was the seat of French royalty in the 14th century. Most of the stones were quarried directly below the castle and hauled up through a well. The resulting caverns keep stores of local wine cool to this day.

WINE SIGHTS AND TASTINGS IN AND NEAR CHINON

Chinon reds are among the most respected in the Loire, and there are a variety of ways to sample them. Most of these places are in town and reachable on foot; the last two are outside of town and require a car.

La Cave Voltaire

At the most convenient of Chinon's wine-tasting options, English-speaking sommelier Patrice would love to help you learn about his area's wines. He serves inexpensive cheese, *rillettes,* and sausage appetizers and has wines from all regions of France—the best, of course, are from Chinon. It's a good place to come before dinner. The ambience inside is wine-shop cozy, but the tables outside are hard to resist (April-Oct daily 10:30-23:30, off-season closed Mon, near Place du Général de Gaulle at 13 Rue Voltaire, tel. 02 47 93 37 68).

Caves Plouzeau

This place offers an opportunity to walk through long, atmospheric *caves*—complete with mood lighting—that extend under the château to a (literally) cool tasting room and reasonably priced wines (€7-15/bottle, April-Sept Tue-Sat 11:00-13:00 & 15:00-19:00, closed Sun-Mon; Oct-March Thu-Fri 14:00-18:00, Sat 11:00-13:00, closed Sun-Wed, at the western end of town on 94 Rue Haute St-Maurice, tel. 02 47 93 16 34, www.plouzeau.com).

Caves Painctes

At this *cave,* summer travelers can sample Chinon wines and walk through the cool quarry from which stones for the castle and town's houses were cut. This rock (tuff) is soft and easily quarried, and when exposed to oxygen, it hardens. The *caves,* 300 feet directly below the castle, were dug as the castle was built. Its stones were hauled directly up to the building site with a treadmill-powered hoist. Converted to wine cellars in the 15th century, the former quarry is a pilgrimage site of sorts for admirers of Rabelais, who featured it prominently in his writings. The English tour takes about an hour and includes a 20-minute video and a tasting of three local wines. Designed to promote Chinon wines, it's run by a local winemakers' association (€3, July-Aug Tue-Sun at 11:00, 15:00, 16:30, and 18:00; closed Mon and Sept-June; off Rue Voltaire on Impasse des Caves Painctes, tel. 02 47 93 30 44).

Restaurant-Musée Animé du Vin et de la Tonnellerie (Wine and Barrel Museum/Restaurant)

This combination museum/restaurant is the life's work of a passionate wine lover, the mustachioed Dédé la Boulange. You'll stroll through a few rooms animated by characters re-creating the production of local wines, and smile at the ingenuity of his handiwork (€4.50, €3.50 if you enjoy dinner at his recommended restaurant on the premises, daily mid-March–mid-Oct 10:00-22:00, closed off-season, 12 Rue Voltaire, tel. 02 47 93 25 63).

Château du Petit Thouars

Château du Petit Thouars offers a royal wine-tasting experience just 10 minutes west of Chinon (near Abbaye Royale de Fontevraud), featuring an elegant castle and vineyards that produce fine white, rosé, and red wines. You can drop by for a free tasting or book ahead for a tour (€5 for basic tour and tasting, €15 for more elaborate tasting and tour of cellars, €35 for memorable picnic and tasting package, closed Sun, in St-Germain sur Vienne—see map on page 416, tel. 02 47 95 96 40, www.chateaudptwines.com, contact@chateaudptwines.com).

Domaine de la Chevalerie

For an authentic winery experience in the thick of the vineyards, drive about 25 minutes from Chinon to Domaine de la Chevalerie. This traditional winery has been run by the same family for 14 generations. If you're lucky, fun-loving and English-speaking daughter Stéphanie or brother Olivier will take you through the cavernous hillside cellars crammed with 180,000 bottles, then treat you to a tasting of their 100 percent Cabernet Franc reds from seven different plots of land (€15 includes tastes of several wines, you can drop in and take your chances they'll be there or book an appointment Mon-Sat 10:00-18:30, shorter hours off-season; off the D-35, toward Langeais from Restigné, look for small sign on left, 7 Rue du Peu Muleau, Restigné, for location see map on page 416, tel. 02 47 97 46 32, www.domainedelachevalerie.fr).

OTHER CHINON ACTIVITIES
▲Biking from Chinon
A few good options are available from Chinon (be sure to get maps from the TI or your bike rental shop). The easiest ride—thanks to the level terrain—is to the pretty village of Candes-St-Martin, where the Vienne and Loire rivers meet. Hardy cyclists can manage the longer ride from Chinon to Ussé and back, and some may want to venture even farther to Villandry. To avoid the monumental hill when leaving town, take your bike in the free elevator up to the château level, then follow bike icon signs (get directions from your bike shop). Connecting these château towns is a full-day, 40-mile round-trip ride (see map on page 416 for general route; see "Helpful Hints," earlier, for rental location and costs).

Canoeing/Kayaking from Chinon
From April through September, plastic canoes and kayaks are available to rent next to the campground across the lone bridge in Chinon. The outfitters will shuttle you upriver to tiny Anché for a scenic and fun two-hour, four-mile float back to town—ending with great Chinon fortress views. They also offer a 10-mile, half-day float that starts in Chinon and ends downriver in the sweet little village of Candes-St-Martin. Or do your own biathlon by canoeing one way and biking back (see "Helpful Hints," earlier, for rental location and costs).

Nighttime in Chinon
Café Français, run by Jean François (a.k.a. "Jeff"), is a characteristic local hangout and *the* place for any late-night fun in this sleepy town. It sometimes has live music off-season (open Tue-Sat from 18:00 and Sun from 19:00 until you shut it down, closed Mon year-round and Sun off-season, behind town hall at 37 Rue des Halles, tel. 02 47 93 32 78).

CHATEAUX NEAR CHINON
The best châteaux within day-trip distance of Chinon are Azay-le-Rideau (on an island in a river), Langeais (imposing 15th-century fortress), and Villandry (amazing gardens)—all covered in their own sections later in this chapter. But the following châteaux are closer and worth consideration.

Château du Rivau
Gleaming white and medieval, this château sits wedged between wheat and sunflower fields, and makes for a memorable 15-minute drive from Chinon. Its owners have spared little expense in their decades-long renovation of the 15th-century castle and its extensive gardens. The 14 different flower and vegetable gardens and orchards are kid-friendly (with elf and fairy guides) and lovingly

LOIRE

tended with art installations, topiaries, hammocks, birds, a maze, and more (the medieval castle interior is skippable). The stables near the entry show projections about "Heroic Horses" from history (with English subtitles) and an overview of the gardens across the seasons. A good little café serves reasonable meals in a lovely setting.

Cost and Hours: €10.50, daily 10:00-18:00, May-Sept until 19:00, closed Nov-March, unnecessary audioguide, in Lémeré on D-759—from Chinon follow *Richelieu* signs, then signs to the château; tel. 02 47 95 77 47, www.chateaudurivau.com.

Ussé

This château, famous as an inspiration for Charles Perrault's classic version of the Sleeping Beauty story, is worth a quick photo stop for its fairy-tale turrets and gardens, but don't bother touring the interior of this pricey pearl. The best view, with reflections and a golden-slipper picnic spot, is just across the bridge.

Cost and Hours: €14, daily 10:00-19:00, mid-Feb-March and Sept-mid-Nov until 18:00, closed mid-Nov-mid-Feb, along D-7 20 minutes north of Chinon on the Indre River, tel. 02 47 95 54 05, www.chateaudusse.fr.

Sleeping in Chinon

($$$$ = Splurge, $$$ = Pricier, $$ = Moderate, $ = Budget)
Hotels are a good value in Chinon. If you stay overnight here, walk out to the river and cross the bridge for a floodlit view of the château walls.

$$ Best Western Hôtel de France*** offers good comfort in 28 rooms on Chinon's best square; many have partial views of the fortress (family rooms and suites, several rooms have balconies over the square, some have thin walls, air-con, easy pay parking very near the hotel, 49 Place du Général de Gaulle, tel. 02 47 93 33 91, www.bestwestern-hoteldefrance-chinon.com, elmachinon@aol.com).

$ Hôtel Diderot,** a handsome 18th-century manor house on the eastern edge of town, is the closest hotel I list to the train station. The hotel, run by Floridian Jamie and her French husband Jean-Pierre, surrounds a carefully planted courtyard. Rooms in the main building vary in size and decor, but all are well-maintained, with personal touches. Ground-floor rooms come with private patios. The four good family rooms have connecting rooms,

each with a private bathroom; the breakfast includes a rainbow of homemade jams (limited pay parking, 4 Rue de Buffon, drivers should look for signs from Place Jeanne d'Arc, tel. 02 47 93 18 87, www.hoteldiderot.com, hoteldiderot@wanadoo.fr).

$ Le Plantagenêt*** has 33 comfortable rooms and may have space when others don't. There's a peaceful garden courtyard—picnics encouraged if you buy drinks from hotel—and an onsite washer/dryer. Superior rooms in *Maison Bourgeoise* have a more historic feel (air-con, 12 Place Jeanne d'Arc, tel. 02 47 93 36 92, www.hotel-plantagenet.com, resa@hotel-plantagenet.com).

$ Hôtel Agnès Sorel** is well run by Florent and Daniela. Located at the western end of town, on the river, it's a 30-minute walk from the train station and handy for drivers (but has some traffic noise). Of its 10 sharp rooms, a few have river views, some have balconies, and five surround a small courtyard (family rooms, 4 Quai Pasteur, tel. 02 47 93 04 37, www.hotel-agnes-sorel.com, info@hotel-agnes-sorel.com).

¢ Hôtel de la Treille, run by Stephanie, has five rugged rooms for budget travelers who won't mind the noise from the restaurant below (cheaper rooms with shared bath, 4 Place Jeanne d'Arc, tel. 02 47 93 07 71, resto.latreille@orange.fr).

OUTSIDE CHINON, NEAR LIGRE

$$ Le Clos de Ligré lets you sleep in farmhouse silence, surrounded by vineyards and farmland. A 10-minute drive from Chinon, it has room to roam, a pool overlooking the vines, and a *salon* library room with a baby grand piano. English-speaking Martine offers cavernous and creatively decorated rooms, two of which have low ceiling beams (good family rooms, includes breakfast, €35 dinner serves up the works in a traditional setting, cash only, 37500 Ligré, tel. 02 47 93 95 59, mobile 06 61 12 45 55, www.le-clos-de-ligre.com, descamps.ligre@gmail.com). From Chinon, drive toward Richelieu on D-749, turn right on D-115 at the *Ligré par le vignoble* sign, and continue for about five kilometers. Turn left, following signs to *Ligré;* at the Dozon winery turn left and look for signs to *Le Clos de Ligré* (see map on page 416).

Eating in Chinon

For a low-stress meal with ambience, choose one of the cafés on the photogenic Place du Général de Gaulle.

$$$ Au Chapeau Rouge offers a traditional and elegant *gastronomique* experience. Regional products are used in creative specialties: Try *poires tapées* (dried local pears) or the decadent *déclinaison autour de la fraise* (strawberry dessert medley). There's a large selection of Chinon wines and pleasant outdoor seating (closed

Sun-Mon, reservations recommended, 49 Place du Général de Gaulle, tel. 02 47 98 08 08, www.auchapeaurouge.fr).

$$$ L'Ardoise means "the chalkboard," which is how the menu is presented, reflecting the bistro feel of the place. Dine here to sample carefully prepared, stylishly presented regional cuisine from the owner/chef (closed Sun-Mon, 42 Rue Rabelais, reservations smart, tel. 02 47 58 48 78, www.lardoisechinon.com).

$ Les Saveurs d'Italie, a cheap and cheery deli/diner, comes with a warm greeting from Marion and the town's best Italian cuisine (pizzas and pasta, outside seating, closed Sun-Mon, 19 Place du Général de Gaulle, tel. 09 63 28 42 82).

$$ Restaurant-Musée Animé du Vin et de la Tonnellerie is a simple, one-man show where jolly Dédé dishes up all the wine you can drink and *fouées* you can eat (little pastry shells filled with garlic paste, cheese, or *rillettes*—that's a meat spread), accompanied by *mâche*-and-walnut salad, green beans, dessert *fouées,* and wine—all for €20. It's neither high-class nor high-cuisine (daily for lunch and dinner, closed Nov-mid-March, 12 Rue Voltaire, tel. 02 47 93 25 63).

$$ La Part des Anges is a two-person love affair with food in an intimate setting. Virginie creates contemporary cuisine based on timeless French technique while husband Hervé serves with aplomb (good lunch options, limited outdoor seating, closed Mon-Tue, 5 Rue Rabelais, tel. 02 47 93 99 93).

$$ Restaurant Côté Jardin is a simple place that's all about traditional French cuisine. Along with regional specialties, you'll find French classics such as coq au vin and *coquilles St. Jacques.* Linger in the secluded garden courtyard and order one of the best deals in town—the €15 *menu* that includes a starter, the *plat du jour,* and dessert (closed Sun-Mon, 30 Rue du Commerce, tel. 02 47 93 10 97).

NEAR CHINON

For a memorable countryside meal, drive 25 minutes to **$$$ Etape Gourmande at Domaine de la Giraudière,** in Villandry (see listing on page 422). A trip here combines well with visits to Villandry and Azay-le-Rideau.

Chinon Connections

By Minivan to Loire Châteaux: Acco-Dispo, Loire Valley Tours, and **Touraine Evasion** offer fixed-itinerary minivan excursions from Tours (see "Amboise Connections" on page 377). Take the train to Tours from Chinon (see below), or get several travelers together to book your own van from Chinon.

By Train: Trains and SNCF buses link Chinon daily with

Tours (10/day, 1 hour, connections to other châteaux and minibus excursions from Tours) and to the regional rail hub of St-Pierre-des-Corps in suburban Tours (TGV trains to distant destinations, and the fastest way to Paris). Traveling by train to the nearby châteaux (except for Azay-le-Rideau) requires a transfer in Tours and healthy walks from the stations to the châteaux. Fewer trains run on weekends.

To Loire Châteaux: **Azay-le-Rideau** (7/day, 20 minutes direct, plus long walk to château), **Langeais** (8/day, 2 hours, transfer in Tours), **Amboise** (7/day, 1.5-2 hours, transfer in Tours), **Chenonceau** (4/day, 1.5-2 hours, transfer in Tours), **Blois** (6/day, 2 hours, transfer in Tours and possibly in St-Pierre-des-Corps).

To Destinations Beyond the Loire: **Paris Gare Montparnasse** (8/day, 3-4 hours, transfer in Tours and sometimes also St-Pierre-des-Corps), **Sarlat-la-Canéda** (3/day, 6-7 hours, change at St-Pierre-des-Corps, then TGV to Libourne or Bordeaux-St. Jean, then train through Bordeaux vineyards to Sarlat), **Pontorson/Mont St-Michel** (3/day, 6-8.5 hours with change at Tours main station, Le Mans, and Rennes, then bus from Rennes), **Bayeux** (2/day, 5-6 hours with change in Tours and Caen, more via Tours, St-Pierre-des-Corps, and Paris leaving from Gare St. Lazare).

Azay-le-Rideau

This charming 16th-century château, worth ▲▲, sparkles on an island in the Indre River, its image romantically reflected in the slow-moving waters. The building is a prime example of an early-Renaissance château. With no defensive purpose, it was built simply for luxurious living in a luxurious setting. The ornamental facade is perfectly harmonious, and the interior—with its grand staircases and elegant loggias—is Italian-inspired. But be prepared for scaffolding and some closed rooms as the château is being renovated until mid-2017.

Azay-le-Rideau (ah-zay luh ree-doh) is also the name of the endearing little town, with a small but lively pedestrian zone and a fine boutique hotel for staying the night (described later).

Tourist Information: Azay-le-Rideau's TI is just below Place de la République, a block to the right of the post office (July-Aug daily 9:00-19:00; April-June and Sept daily 9:00-13:00 & 14:00-18:00; shorter hours and closed Sun Oct-March; 4 Rue du Château, tel. 02 47 45 44 40, www.visitazaylerideau.com). The TI sells

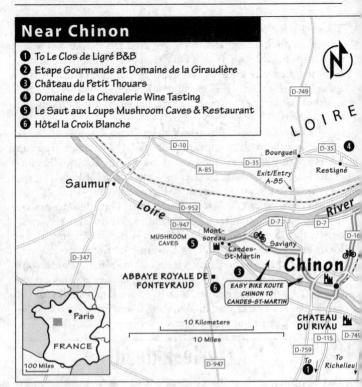

Near Chinon

1. To Le Clos de Ligré B&B
2. Etape Gourmande at Domaine de la Giraudière
3. Château du Petit Thouars
4. Domaine de la Chevalerie Wine Tasting
5. Le Saut aux Loups Mushroom Caves & Restaurant
6. Hôtel la Croix Blanche

reduced-price tickets to all area châteaux, has free Wi-Fi, and offers info for bike rentals.

GETTING THERE

By train, it's easy to connect from Tours (8/day, 30 minutes) and Chinon (7/day, 20 minutes). From Amboise, it's doable but long (6/day, 1-2 hours, transfer in Tours). From the station, it's about a 25-minute walk to the town center (taxi tel. 02 47 45 96 42). Walk down from the station, turn left, and follow *Centre-Ville* signs. Drivers can head for the château and park there.

ORIENTATION TO CHATEAU D'AZAY-LE-RIDEAU

Cost and Hours: €6.50 during renovation, €9 once the work is completed; daily April-Oct 9:30-18:00, July-Aug until 19:00, Nov-March 10:00-17:15, last entry one hour before closing.

Tours and Information: Unnecessary audioguide, storage lockers, tel. 02 47 45 42 04, www.azay-le-rideau.fr.

Renovation: The château is under a massive renovation until mid-2017 but remains open; expect exterior scaffolding and some wings to be closed during this time.

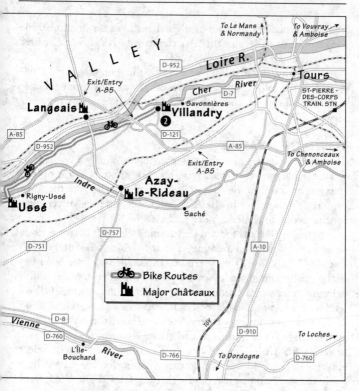

BACKGROUND

The château was built between 1518 and 1527 by a filthy-rich banker —Gilles Berthelot, treasurer to the king of France. The structure has a delightfully feminine touch: Because Gilles was often away for work, his wife, Philippa, supervised the construction. The castle was so lavish that the king, François I, took note, giving it the ultimate compliment: He seized it, causing its owner to flee. Because this château survived the Revolution virtually unscathed, its interior capably demonstrates three centuries of royal styles. The French government purchased it in 1905.

VISITING THE CHATEAU

Rooms are very well described (only serious students should consider the audioguide). Cross the water to the island, enter the château, and climb to the top floor. Your visit starts in the castle attic *(comble)*, where you'll wander under a strikingly beautiful roof support cut from 500-year-old oak trees. Then work your way down through sumptuous Renaissance rooms loaded with elaborate tapestries, colossal fireplaces, and intricately carved wood chests. The room that smells like fresh grass employs a unique reconstruction of Renaissance-era insulation: plaited rush. Pause to admire the king's portrait gallery in the "Apartement du XVII Siècle" (three Louis, three Henrys, and François I).

For many, the highlight of a visit is the romantic garden, designed in the 19th century to show off the already beautiful château. Take a spin on the path around the castle to enjoy romantic views.

TOWN OF AZAY-LE-RIDEAU

The town's appealing center may convince you to set up here. It works well as a base for visiting sights west of Tours by car or bike (but not by train, as the station is a half-mile walk from the town center). It's also close to the A-85 autoroute, offering drivers reasonable access to châteaux near Amboise.

Sleeping: Ideally located on a traffic-free street between Place de la République (easy parking) and the château, **$ Hôtel de Biencourt***** is a find. This sharp yet affordable boutique hotel has thoughtfully appointed rooms, a pleasing garden terrace, and a calming lounge area (family rooms, shared fridge, picnics OK on terrace, closed mid-Nov-late March, 7 Rue de Balzac, tel. 02 47 45 20 75, www.hotelbiencourt.com, contact@hotelbiencourt.fr).

Eating: You'll find fresh and creative cuisine and reasonable prices at **$$ Côté Cour.** Friendly Sandrine offers a few, select choices—local products and mostly organic foods—served in a warm interior or on a great outdoor terrace (closed Tue-Wed, faces the château gate at 19 Rue Balzac, tel. 02 47 45 30 36).

$ L'Epicerie de Julie is a tiny, inexpensive Italian deli-bistro with a limited but cheap menu (closed Sun-Mon, 17 Place Gambetta, tel. 02 47 42 06 45).

If you have a car, seriously consider the 15-minute drive to **$$$ Domaine de la Giraudière** in Villandry (see page 422).

Connections: From Azay-le-Rideau, the **train** runs to **Tours** (8/day, 30 minutes, with connections to Amboise, Langeais, and other châteaux), **Chinon** (7/day, 20 minutes), and **Blois** (7/day, 1.5 hours, transfer in Tours and possibly in St-Pierre-des-Corps). Summertime **buses** run to Villandry and Langeais twice a day (the TI has bus schedules).

Langeais

One of the most imposing-looking fortresses of the Middle Ages, Château de Langeais—rated ▲—was built mostly for show. Towering above its appealing little village, it comes with a moat, a drawbridge, lavish defenses, and turrets.

GETTING THERE
Trains link Langeais with Tours (8/day, 20 minutes), with about 10 connections a day between Tours and Chinon (most by train, some by SNCF bus, 2 hours total, just as fast by bike for experienced riders). In summer, buses run twice a day from Azay-le-Rideau to Langeais.

The A-85 autoroute provides convenient access for drivers coming from points east or west. Drivers should turn right at the foot of the castle, then hug the castle; the parking area is 200 yards in on the right.

ORIENTATION TO CHATEAU DE LANGEAIS
Cost and Hours: €9, daily July-Aug 9:00-19:00, April-June and Sept-mid-Nov 9:30-18:30, mid-Nov-March 10:00-17:00, last entry one hour before closing, tel. 02 47 96 72 60, www. chateau-de-langeais.com.

Eating: The château is within easy walk of several cafés and restaurants.

BACKGROUND
Langeais occupies a key site on the Loire River, 15 miles downstream on the road to Tours (which for a time was the French

capital), and about halfway from Paris along the trading route to Brittany and the Atlantic. This location made Langeais a player in historic events, though the only remaining part of the original castle is the thousand-year-old tower standing across from the castle's garden. (That castle, an English stronghold, was destroyed by the French king in the Hundred Years' War.)

The "new" castle, built in the 15th century, dates from the age of cannons, which would have made quick work of its tough-looking facade. In fact, the imposing walls were mostly for show. This is a transitional piece of architecture: part medieval and part Renaissance. The mullioned windows overlooking the courtyard indicate this was a fancy residence more than a defensive fortress. While Langeais makes a show of its defenses, castles built just 50 years later (such as Azay-le-Rideau) give not a hint of fortification.

VISITING THE CHATEAU
The interior is late Middle-Ages chic. It's the life's work of a 19th-century owner who was a lover of medieval art. He decorated and furnished the rooms with 15th- and 16th-century artifacts or good

LOIRE

facsimiles. Most of what you see is modern-made in 16th-century style.

Langeais tries hard to give visitors a feel for royal life in the 15th century—and it works. The palace is decked out as palaces were—designed to impress, and ready to pack and move. The rooms are well-furnished and well-explained with handy information sheets. The video in the first room sets the stage for your visit. Here's a sampling of what you'll see.

The **banquet room** table would have groaned with food and luxury items—but just one long, communal napkin and no forks. Belgian tapestries on the walls still glimmer with 500-year-old silk thread. In an upstairs **bedroom,** it looks like the master has just left—gloves and other accessories are lying on the bedcovers, and shoes sit below the bed. There were bedrooms for show, and bedrooms for sleeping.

As you wander, notice how the rooms—with hanging tapestries, foldable chairs, and big chests with handles—could have been set up in a matter of hours. Big-time landowners circulated through their domains, moving every month or so. Also notice how each piece of furniture had multiple uses—such as a throne that doubled as a writing desk.

In the so-called **Wedding Hall,** wax figures re-create the historic marriage that gave Langeais its 15 minutes of château fame in 1491. It was here that King Charles VIII secretly wed 14-year-old Anne (duchess of Brittany), a union that brought independent Brittany into France's fold. The gowns are accurate and impressive, and it's interesting to see how short everyone was in the Middle Ages. An eight-minute sound-and-light show explains the event—usually in English at :15 past each hour.

The top-floor museum has a rare series of 16th-century **tapestries** featuring nine heroes—biblical, Roman, and medieval. This is one of just three such sets in existence, with seven of the original nine scenes surviving.

Finish your visit by enjoying commanding **town views** from the ramparts.

Villandry

Château de Villandry (vee-lahn-dree) is famous for its extensive gardens, considered to be the best in the Loire Valley, and possibly all of France. Its château is an average Loire palace, but the grounds—arranged in elaborate geometric patterns and immaculately maintained—make it a ▲▲ sight (worth ▲▲▲ for gardeners). Still, if you're visiting anyway, it's worth the extra euros to tour the château as well.

GETTING THERE

Without a car, your best option is to take a minivan excursion from Amboise or Tours (see "By Minivan Excursion to Nearby Châ-

teaux" under "Amboise Connections" on page 378). Tours is easily accessible by train from Amboise (25 minutes) and Chinon (1 hour). In summer, buses run twice a day from Azay-le-Rideau to Villandry. It's also a popular bike destination (2 hours from Chinon, 1 hour from Azay-le-Rideau).

Drivers will find free parking located across from the entry (hide valuables in your trunk).

ORIENTATION TO CHATEAU DE VILLANDRY

Cost and Hours: €10.50, €6.50 for gardens only, daily 9:00-19:00, March and Oct until 18:00, Nov-Feb until 17:00.

Tours and Information: The excellent handout leads you through the château's 19th-century rooms. Skip the unnecessary audioguide. Tel. 02 47 50 02 09, www.chateauvillandry.fr.

Services: Storage lockers are available.

Gardens: You can stay as late as you like in the gardens, though you must enter before the ticket office closes and exit through the back gate after 19:30.

BACKGROUND

Finished in 1536, Villandry was the last great Renaissance château built on the Loire. It's yet another pet project of a fabulously wealthy finance minister of François I—Jean le Breton. While serving as ambassador to Italy, Jean picked up a love of Italian Renaissance gardens. When he took over this property, he razed the 12th-century castle (keeping only the old tower), put up his own château, and installed a huge Italian-style garden. The château was purchased in 1906 by the present owner's great-grandfather, and the garden—a careful reconstruction of what the original might have been—is the result of three generations of passionate dedication.

VISITING THE CHATEAU AND GARDENS

The **château**'s 19th-century rooms feel so lived-in that you'll wonder if the family just stepped out to get their poodle bathed. Don't miss the 15-minute *Four Seasons of Villandry* slideshow just inside the château. With period music and no narration, it delivers a glimpse at the gardens throughout the year in a relaxing little theater (ask at the ticket window or you may miss it). The literal high point of your château visit is the spiral climb to the top of the keep—the only surviving part of the medieval castle—where you'll find a 360-degree view of the gardens, village, and surrounding countryside. The extra cost for visiting the château seems worth it when you take in the panorama.

The lovingly tended **gardens** are well-described by your handout. Follow its recommended route through the four garden types. The 10-acre Renaissance garden, inspired by the 1530s Italian-style original, is full of symbolism. Even the herb and vegetable sections are put together with artistic flair. The earliest Loire gardens were practical, grown by medieval abbey monks who needed vegetables to feed their community and medicinal herbs to cure their ailments. And those monks liked geometrical patterns. Later Italian influence brought decorative ponds, tunnels, and fountains. Harmonizing the flowers and vegetables was an innovation of 16th-century Loire châteaux. This example is the closest we have to that garden style. Who knew that lentils, chives, and cabbages could look this good?

The 85,000 plants—half of which come from the family greenhouse—are replanted twice a year by 10 full-time gardeners. They use modern organic methods: ladybugs instead of pesticides and a whole lot of hoeing. The place is as manicured as a putting green—just try to find a weed. Stroll under the grapevine trellis, through a good-looking salad zone, and among Anjou pears (from the nearby region of Angers). If all the topiary and straight angles seem too rigid, look for the sun garden in the back of the estate, which has "wilder" perennial borders favored by the Brits. Charts posted throughout identify everything in English.

Bring bread for the piranha-like carp who prowl the fanciful moat. Like the carp swimming around other Loire châteaux, they're so voracious, they'll gather at your feet to frantically eat your spit. Don't miss the fine views from the Belvedere lookout (near the garden exit).

EATING IN AND NEAR VILLANDRY

The pleasant little village of Villandry has several cafés and restaurants, a small grocery store, and a bakery.

$$$ Etape Gourmande at Domaine de la Giraudière offers a wonderfully rustic farmhouse dining experience. Gentle owner Beatrice takes time with every client (ask her how she landed here), and the country-gourmet cuisine is delicious. Choose just a starter and dessert, a starter and main course, or all three if you're starved. The dining room is hunting-lodge cozy, and there's pleasant seating outside (daily 12:00-14:30 & 19:30-21:00, closed mid-Nov-mid-March, reservations smart, a half-mile from Villandry's château toward Druye, for location see map on page 416, tel. 02 47 50 08 60, www.letapegourmande.com). This place works best for lunch, as it's well-signed between Villandry and Azay-le-Rideau on D-121.

Abbaye Royale de Fontevraud

The Royal Abbey of Fontevraud (fohn-tuh-vroh) is a 15-minute journey west from Chinon. This once vast 12th-century abbey provides a good look at medieval monastic life. The "abbey" was actually a 12th-century monastic city, the largest such compound in Europe—with four monastic complexes, all within a fortified wall.

ORIENTATION TO ABBAYE ROYALE DE FONTEVRAUD

Cost and Hours: €11; daily April-Oct 9:30-18:00, June-Aug until 18:30, Nov-Dec and Feb-March 10:00-17:00, closed Jan and on major holidays.

Tours and Information: English translations are posted throughout the abbey, making the well-done, €4.50 audioguide less essential. Kids love the iPad "treasure hunt" (€4.50). Tel. 02 41 51 73 52, www.abbayedefontevraud.com.

Parking: The closest free lot is between the church and the abbey entrance; look for a *P Abbaye* sign.

BACKGROUND

The order of Fontevraud, founded in 1101, was an experiment of rare audacity. This was a double monastery, where both men and women lived under the authority of an abbess while observing the rules of St. Benedict (but influenced by the cult of the Virgin Mary). Men and women lived separately and chastely within the abbey walls. The order thrived, and in the 16th century, this was the administrative head of more than 150 monasteries. Four communities lived within these walls until the Revolution. In 1804, Napoleon made the abbey a prison,

which actually helped preserve the building. It functioned as a prison for 150 years, until 1963, with five wooden floors filled with cells. Designed to house 800 inmates, the prison was notoriously harsh. Life expectancy here was eight months.

VISITING THE ABBEY

Follow *sens de la visite* signs to tour the abbey.

Your visit begins in the bright, 12th-century, Romanesque

LOIRE

abbey church. Sit on the steps, savor the ethereal setting, and feel the weight of this Romanesque structure. Appreciate the finely carved capitals and have fun with the clever touch-screen monitors. At the end of the nave are four painted sarcophagi belonging to Eleanor of Aquitaine; her second husband, Henry II, the first of England's Plantagenet kings; their son Richard the Lionheart; and his sister-in-law. These are the tops of the sarcophagi only. Even though we know these Plantagenets were buried here (because they gave lots of money to the abbey), no one knows the fate of the actual bodies.

You'll leave the church through the right transept into the **cloister.** This was the center of the abbey, where the nuns read, exercised, checked their email, and washed their hands. While visiting the abbey, remember that monastic life was extremely simple: nothing but prayers, readings, and work. Daily rations were a loaf of bread and a half-liter of wine per person, plus soup and smoked fish. You'll learn much about the abbey's time as a prison from the information panels in this section.

Next is the **chapter house,** where the nuns' meetings took place. Renaissance paintings feature portraits of the women who ran this abbey, wearing black habits (look for descriptions on the tables). The **community room/treasury** comes next. The only heated room in the abbey, it's where the nuns embroidered linen and where today you'll see gripping fragments from a 12th-century Last Judgment and other important abbey treasures.

Climb steps up to see the cavernous Grand Dortoir (dormitory), where hundreds of monks could sleep. The nearby **refectory,** built to feed 400 silent monks at a time, was later the prison work yard, where inmates built wooden chairs (exposition rooms above provide insight into this period).

Your abbey visit continues with the unusual, honeycombed, 12th-century **kitchen** (accessed from outside), with five bays covered by 18 chimneys to evacuate smoke. It likely served as a smokehouse for fish farmed in the abbey ponds. Abbeys like this were industrious places, but focused on self-sufficiency rather than trade.

Finish your visit with a refreshment at the **garden café** or in the fancy hotel below and contemplate a wander through the abbey's **medicinal gardens.**

SLEEPING AND EATING AT
ABBAYE ROYALE DE FONTEVRAUD

$$ Hôtel la Croix Blanche*** welcomes travelers with open ter-
races and cushy comfort. This ambitious restaurant-hotel, just
outside the abbey, combines a hunting-lodge feel with polished
service, comfortable public spaces, a pool, and 24 rooms (Place
Plantagenêts—see map on page 416, tel. 02 41 51 71 11, www.
hotel-croixblanche.com, info@hotel-croixblanche.com).

The abbey faces the main square of a cute town with several
handy eateries. The *boulangerie* opposite the entrance to the abbey
serves fine quiche and sandwiches at impossibly good prices.

NEAR FONTEVRAUD: MUSHROOM CAVES

For an unusual fungus find close to the abbey of Fontevraud, visit
the mushroom caves called **Le Saut aux Loups.** France is one of
the world's top mushroom producers, so mushrooms matter. Climb
to a cliff ledge and enter 16 chilly rooms bored into limestone to
discover everything about the care and nurturing of mushrooms.
You'll see them raised in planters, plastic bags, logs, and straw
bales, and you'll learn about their incubation, pasteurization, and
fermentation. Abandoned limestone quarries like this are fertile
homes for mushroom cultivation, and have made the Loire Val-
ley the mushroom capital of France since the 1800s. You'll ogle at
the weird shapes and never take your 'shrooms for granted again.
The growers harvest a ton of mushrooms a month in these caves;
shiitakes are their most important crop. Pick up the English book-
let and follow the fungus. Many visitors come only for the on-site
mushroom restaurant, whose wood-fired *galipettes* (stuffed mush-
rooms with crème fraîche and herbs) are the kitchen's forte (€12 for
three *galipettes*).

Cost and Hours: €6.50, daily 10:00-18:00, closed mid-Nov-
Feb, dress warmly, just north of Fontevraud at Montsoreau's west
end along the river, for location see map on page 416, tel. 02 41 51
70 30, www.troglo-sautauxloups.com.

LOIRE

DORDOGNE

Sarlat-la-Canéda • Dordogne River Valley • Cro-Magnon Caves • Oradour-sur-Glane • St-Emilion • Rocamadour • Lot River Valley

The Dordogne River Valley is a delicious brew, blending natural and man-made beauty. Walnut orchards, tobacco plants, sunflowers, and cornfields carpet the valley, while stone fortresses patrol the cliffs above. During much of the on-again, off-again Hundred Years' War (when this region was called the Périgord), this strategic river—so peaceful today—separated warring Britain and France. Today's Dordogne River carries more travelers than goods, as the region's economy relies heavily on tourism.

The joys of the Dordogne include rock-sculpted villages, fertile farms surrounding I-should-retire-here cottages, magnificent vistas, lazy canoe rides, and a local cuisine worth loosening your belt for. You'll also find an amazing cache of prehistoric artifacts. Limestone caves decorated with prehistoric artwork litter the Dordogne region.

PLANNING YOUR TIME

Although tourists inundate the region in the summer, the Dordogne's charm is protected by its relative inaccessibility. Given the time it takes to get here by car, I'd allow a minimum of two nights (ideally three) and most of two days...or I'd skip it. Whirlwind travelers could consider flying here: Inexpensive flights connect Paris with the region's main city, Brive-la-Gaillarde (where you can rent a car).

Your sightseeing obligations are prehistoric cave art; the Dordogne River Valley, with its villages and castles; the town of Sarlat-la-Canéda (often shortened to "Sarlat," pronounced sar-lah); and, with more time, the less-traveled Lot River Valley.

If you're connecting the Dordogne with the Loire region by

Dordogne at a Glance

▲▲▲**Dordogne River Valley** A lovely brew of natural and man-made beauty, with rock-sculpted villages, fertile farms, and stone fortresses—enjoyable by car or canoe. See page 449.

▲▲▲**Cro-Magnon Caves** Prehistoric caves famous throughout the world—for a rundown of options, see "Prehistoric Sights at a Glance" on page 472.

▲▲▲**Oradour-sur-Glane** Ruined village machine-gunned and burned by Nazi SS troops in 1944 and now preserved as a war memorial. See page 485.

▲▲**Sarlat-la-Canéda** Regional market town with a seductive tangle of cobblestone lanes, peppered with beautiful buildings and stuffed with tourists. See page 434.

▲▲**Eastern Dordogne** Remote and less visited area, highlighted by the rock-cut village of Rocamadour. See page 490.

▲**St-Emilion** Prosperous little town devoted to wine and winemaking, on the western edge of the region. See page 487.

▲**Lot River Valley** Overlooked but beautiful valley, home to dramatically sited villages like St-Cirq Lapopie. See page 500.

car, the fastest path is via the free A-20 autoroute (exit at Souillac for Sarlat-la-Canéda and nearby villages). Break up your trip from the north by stopping in Oradour-sur-Glane. If you're connecting the Dordogne and Carcassonne, explore the Lot River Valley on your way south. If heading west, taste the Bordeaux wine region's prettiest town, St-Emilion.

Those serious about visiting the Dordogne's best caves need to plan carefully and book ahead when possible (explained on page 471).

The following three-day itinerary is designed for drivers, but it's doable—if you're determined—by taxi rides, a canoe trip (the best way to see the Dordogne regardless of whether you've got a car), and a minivan tour.

Day 1—Sarlat-la-Canéda and the Dordogne Valley: Enjoy a morning in Sarlat (best on a market day—Sat or Wed), then spend the afternoon on a canoe trip, with time at the day's end to explore Beynac and Castelnaud. If it's not market day in Sarlat, do the canoe trip, Beynac, and Castel-naud first, and enjoy the late afternoon and evening in Sarlat. (Because the town's essential sights are outdoors, my self-guided Sarlat walk works great after dinner.) The sensational views from Castel-naud's castle and Domme are best in the morning; visit Beynac's castle or viewpoint late in the day for the best light. With a little lead time, some canoe-rental companies can pick up nondrivers in Sarlat. Taxis are reasonable between Sarlat and the river villages.

Day 2—Prehistoric Caves: Start your day in Les Eyzies-de-Tayac at the Prehistory Welcome Center and the National Museum of Prehistory for a solid cave-art introduction. From there your day will depend on the cave(s) you can get an entry for (varies by season, described under each cave later). The Lascaux replica cave delivers an excellent tour and can be reserved, the Grotte de Font-de-Gaume is the best cave with original art (though getting in is a challenge), and the Grotte de Rouffignac makes a good and more reliable substitute. If you visit Lascaux, follow the scenic Vé-zère River, stopping for a coffee or lunch in idyllic little St-Léon.

Without a car, this day's full list of activities is only possible by taxi or excursion tour. By train, you can link Sarlat-la-Canéda and Les Eyzies-de-Tayac, though you have to transfer, and some connections aren't great.

Day 3—Other Sights: Head east and upriver to explore Roca-madour, Gouffre de Padirac, and storybook villages such as Caren-nac, Autoire, and Loubressac. Though Rocamadour is accessible by train and a short taxi ride, the rest of these places are feasible only with your own wheels, by taxi, or on an excursion tour.

CHOOSING A HOME BASE

Sarlat-la-Canéda is the only viable solution for train travelers. Drivers should consider sleeping in a riverside village. For a grand château hotel experience that won't break the bank, sleep near the Lascaux caves at Château de la Fleunie (30 minutes north of Sarlat; see page 481). For the best view hotel I've found in the area, try Hôtel de l'Esplanade in Domme (see page 455).

GETTING AROUND THE DORDOGNE

This region is a joy with a car but tough without one. Consider renting a car for a day, renting a canoe or bike, or taking a minivan excursion. If you're up for a splurge, take a hot-air balloon ride (see page 353).

By Train: Connecting the Dordogne's sights by train is hope-less. The lone helpful train runs from Sarlat-la-Canéda to Les Eyzies-de-Tayac, with the Prehistory Welcome Center and museum and the Grotte de Font-de-Gaume (3-4/day, 1-2.5 hours, transfer in Le Buisson, some long waits, 15-minute walk from sta-

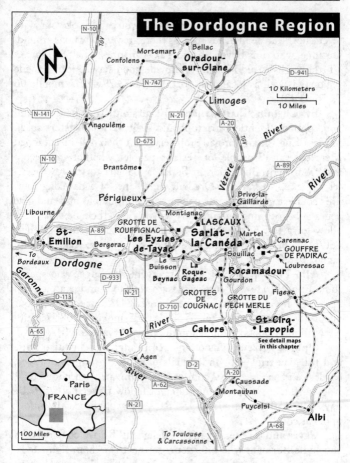

tion to museum, 30-minute walk from station to Font-de-Gaume cave).

By Car: Roads are small, slow, and scenic. There's no autoroute near Sarlat-la-Canéda; count on more travel time than usual. Little Sarlat is routinely snarled with traffic on market days—particularly Saturdays. You can rent a car in Sarlat (see page 438), though bigger cities, such as Libourne, Périgueux, and Brive-la-Gaillarde, offer greater drop-off flexibility. In summer (mid-June–mid-Sept), you'll pay to park in most villages' riverfront lots between 10:00 and 19:00. Leave nothing in your car at night—thieves enjoy the Dordogne, too.

By Taxi: To taxi from Sarlat-la-Canéda to Beynac or La Roque-Gageac, allow €27 (€37 at night and on Sun); from Sarlat to Les Eyzies-de-Tayac, allow €46 one-way (€66 at night and on Sun) or €88 round-trip. Christoph or Philippe (see next) can often pick you up within a few minutes if you call. Book your rides (even short transfers) in advance, as there are very few taxis around. Corinne, who runs Beynac-based **Taxi Corinne,** is helpful, speaks a little English, and is eager to provide good service (can provide regional as well as local transport, tel. 05 53 29 42 07, mobile 06 72 76 03 32).

By Custom Taxi/Minivan Excursion: You have several good options. Gentle **Christoph** and lively **Sarissa Kusters** speak flawless English and provide top service in their Wi-Fi-equipped Mercedes van (7 people) or Tesla (6 people), whether you need a taxi from the train station in Sarlat-la-Canéda to the town center, a pickup in Paris or Oradour-sur-Glane, or a day-long tour. This couple can help organize your trip from soup to nuts and give you a good running commentary as you ride. Their flexible plans allow for a fast or slow pace, based on your interests (€45/hour, €60/hour on Sun, mobile 06 08 70 61 67, www.taxialacarte.com, taxialacarte@gmail.com).

Allô-Philippe Taxi is run by amiable Philippe, who speaks some English. He will custom-design your tour and can pick you up anywhere. For excursions, he charges €43/hour for up to four people (€63/hour on Sun, tel. 05 53 59 39 65, mobile 06 08 57 30 10, www.allophilippetaxi.com, allophilippetaxi@wanadoo.fr).

Ophorus Excursions offers a full range of scheduled half- and full-day trips—for individuals or private groups—to caves, castles, and villages in a comfortable minivan with competent, English-fluent guides and up to eight fellow travelers (€75/half-day, €125-150/day, tel. 05 56 15 26 09, www.ophorus.com, info@ophorus.com).

Caves and Castles is run by a delightful British couple (Steve and Judie Burman) who offer tours to the area's main sights for a day or more. They offer translation services for French-only cave visits, and Steve has plenty of tricks to keep families happy and kids entertained (mobile 0789-972-0482, www.cavesandcastles.com).

Béatrice Mollaret and Bruno Eluere, a fun local guide team headquartered in Sarlat-la-Canéda, create tours tailor-made for travelers wanting to dig into Dordogne culture and get off the beaten track (9 Cours des Fontaines, mobile 06 79 63 28 47, www.dordogne-fellow-traveller.com, contact@dordogne-fellow-traveller.com).

By Boat: Nondrivers should rent a canoe, my favorite way to explore a small but gorgeous slice of this region. A canoe offers easy access to the river's sights and villages at your own pace, and some canoe companies will pick you up in Sarlat-la-Canéda for no extra charge. Because a canoe costs only about €18/person (for the trip I recommend), and you can spend all day on and off the river touring sights I cover, this is a swimmingly good deal. For the same scenery with less work (and no ability to visit villages and castles en route), you can take a boat cruise from Beynac or La Roque-Gageac (€8-9).

By Bike: Cyclists find the Dordogne beautiful but hilly, with lots of traffic on key roads. You can pick up a basic bike for the day in Sarlat-la-Canéda; serious riders will be impressed with **Liberty Bike**'s services and **Aquitaine Bike**'s fleet (see page 437).

By Balloon: The Dordogne is a terrific place to spring for a hot-air balloon trip, taking you high above its gorgeous river and hilly terrain capped with golden stone castles and villages. **Montgolfières du Périgord** is conveniently based in La Roque-Gageac and offers a variety of flights with well-trained pilots (one-hour flight-€200/person, departures in good weather generally just after sunrise and just before sunset, tel. 05 53 28 18 58, www. montgolfiere-du-perigord.com, perigordballoons@wanadoo.fr).

THE DORDOGNE'S CUISINE SCENE

Gourmets flock to this area for its geese, ducks, and wild mushrooms. The geese produce (involuntarily) the region's famous foie gras. (They're force-fed, denied exercise during the last weeks of their lives, and slaughtered for their livers, meat, and fluffy down—see sidebar on page 462.) Foie gras tastes like butter and costs like gold. The main duck specialty is *confit de canard* (duck meat preserved in  its own fat—sounds terrible, but tastes great), but *magret de canard* (sautéed duck breast), smoked duck, and anything fried in duck fat also show up on menus.

Pommes de terre sarladaises are mouthwatering, thinly sliced potatoes fried in duck fat and commonly served with *confit de canard*. Wild truffles are dirty black tubers that grow underground, generally on the roots of oak trees. Farmers traditionally locate them with sniffing pigs and then charge a fortune for their catch (roughly $250 per pound). Native cheeses are Cabécou (a silver-dollar-size, pungent, nutty-flavored goat cheese) and Echourgnac (made by local Trappist monks). You'll find walnuts *(noix)* in salads, cakes, liqueurs, salad dressings, and more.

Wines to sample are Bergerac (red, white, and rosé), Pecharmant (red, must be at least four years old), Cahors (a full-bodied red), and Monbazillac (sweet dessert wine). The *vin de noix* (sweet walnut liqueur) is delightful before dinner.

Remember, restaurants serve only during lunch (11:30-14:00)

DORDOGNE

and dinner (19:00-21:00, later in bigger cities); bigger cafés serve food throughout the day.

DORDOGNE MARKETS

Markets are a big deal in rural France, and nowhere more so than in the Dordogne. I've listed good markets for every day of the week, so there's no excuse for drivers not to experience one. Here's what to look for:

Strawberries *(fraises):* For the French, the Dordogne is the region famous for the very tastiest strawberries. Available from April to November, they're gorgeous, and they smell even better than they look. Buy *une barquette* (small basket), and suddenly your two-star hotel room is a three-star. Look also for *fraises des bois,* the tiny, sweet, and less visually appealing strawberries found in nearby forests.

Fresh Veggies: Outdoor markets allow you to meet the farmer, and give you a chance to buy direct. (See what's fresh, and look for it on your menu this evening.) Subtly check out the hands of the person helping customers—if they're not gnarled and rough from working the fields, move on.

Cheeses *(fromages):* The region is famous for its Cabécou goat cheese (described earlier), though often you'll also find Auvergne cheeses (St. Nectaire and Cantal are the most common) from just east of the Dordogne (usually in big rounds) and Tomme and Brebis (sheep cheeses) from the Pyrenees to the south.

Truffles *(truffes):* Only the bigger markets will have these ugly, jet-black tubers on display. Truffle season is our off-season (Nov-Feb), when you'll find them at every market. During summer, the fresh truffles you might see are *truffes d'été,* a less desirable and cheaper, but still tasty, species. If you see truffles displayed at other times, they've been sterilized (a preservative measure that can reduce flavor). On Sarlat-la-Canéda market days, there's usually a guy in the center of Place de la Liberté with a photo of his grandfather and his truffle-hunting dog. From November to mid-March there's a truffle market on Saturday mornings on Rue Fénelon (details at TI).

Anything with Walnuts *(aux noix): Pain aux noix* is a thick-as-a-brick bread loaf chock-full of walnuts. *Moutarde de noix* is walnut mustard. *Confiture de noix* is a walnut spread for hors d'oeuvres. *Gâteaux de noix* are tasty cakes studded with walnuts. *Liqueur de noix* is a marvelous creamy liqueur, great over ice or blended with a local white wine.

Goose or Duck Livers and Pâté (foie gras): This spread—which you are not supposed to spread but rather to eat in small chunks on toast—is made from geese (better) and ducks (still good) or from a mix of the two. You'll see two basic forms: *entier* and *bloc*. Both are 100 percent foie gras; *entier* is a piece cut right from the product, whereas *bloc* has been blended. Foie gras is best accompanied by a sweet white wine (such as the locally produced Monbazillac or Sauternes from Bordeaux). You can bring the unopened tins back into the US, *pas de problème*. For more on foie gras, see the sidebar on page 462.

Confit de Canard: At butcher stands, look for hunks of duck smothered in white fat, just waiting for someone to take them home and cook them up. If you have kitchen access, try it: Scrape off some of the fat, then sauté the chunks until they're crispy on the outside and heated through. Save some of that fat for roasting potatoes.

Dried Sausages *(saucissons secs):* Long tables piled high with dried sausages covered in herbs or stuffed with local goodies are a common sight in French markets. You'll always be offered a mouthwatering sample. Some of the variations you'll see include *porc, canard* (duck), *fumé* (smoked), *à l'ail* (garlic), *cendré* (rolled in ashes), *aux myrtilles* (with blueberries), *sanglier* (wild boar), and even *âne* (donkey)—and,

but of course, *aux noix* (with walnuts).

Olive Oil *(huile d'olive):* You'll find stylish bottles of various olive oils, as well as vegetable oils flavored with truffles, walnuts, chestnuts *(châtaignes),* and hazelnuts *(noisettes)*—good for cooking, ideal on salads, and great as gifts. Pure walnut oil, pressed at local mills from nuts grown in the region, is a local specialty, best on salads. Don't cook with pure walnut oil, as it will burn quickly.

Olives and Nuts *(olives et noix):* These interlopers from Provence find their way to every market in France.

Brandies and Liqueurs: Although they're not made in this region, Armagnac, Cognac, and other southwestern fruit-flavored liquors are often available from a seller or two. Try the *liqueur de pomme verte,* and sample Armagnac in the tiny plastic cups.

Dordogne Market Days

The best markets are in Sarlat-la-Canéda (Sat and Wed, in that order), followed by the markets in Cahors on Saturday, St-Cyprien on Sunday, and Le Bugue on Tuesday. Markets usually shut down by 13:00.

Sunday: St-Cyprien (lively market, 10 minutes west of Beynac, difficult parking) and St-Geniès (a tiny, intimate market with few tourists; halfway between Sarlat and Montignac)

Monday: Les Eyzies-de-Tayac (April-Oct) and a tiny one in Beynac (mid-June-mid-Sept)

Tuesday: Cénac (you can canoe from here) and Le Bugue (great market 20 minutes west of Beynac)

Wednesday: Sarlat (big market) and Montignac (near Lascaux)

Thursday: Domme

Friday: Souillac (transfer point to Cahors, Carcassonne) and La Roque-Gageac (May-Sept)

Saturday: Sarlat and Cahors (both are excellent), the little *bastide* village of Belvès (small market), and Montignac

Sarlat-la-Canéda

Sarlat–la-Canéda is a pedestrian-filled banquet of a town, serenely set amid forested hills. There are no blockbuster sights. Still, Sarlat delivers a seductive tangle of traffic-free, golden cobblestone

lanes peppered with beautiful buildings, lined with foie gras shops (geese hate Sarlat), and stuffed with tourists. The town is warmly lit at night and ideal for after-dinner strolls. It's just the right size—large enough to have a theater with four screens, but small enough that everything is an easy meander from the town center. And though undeniably popular with tourists, it's the handiest home base for those without a car.

Orientation to Sarlat-la-Canéda

Rue de la République slices like an arrow through the circular old town. The action lies east of Rue de la République. Sarlat's smaller half has few shops and many quiet lanes.

TOURIST INFORMATION

The TI is 50 yards to the right of the Cathedral of St. Sacerdos as you face it (July-Aug Mon-Sat 9:00-19:00, Sun 10:00-13:00 & 14:00-18:00; April-June and Sept closes one hour earlier; Oct Mon-Sat 9:00-12:00 & 14:00-17:00, Sun 10:00-13:00; shorter hours and closed Sun Nov-March; on Rue Tourny, tel. 05 53 31 45 45, www.sarlat-tourisme.com). Ask for information on car, bike, and canoe rental (or see the TI's helpful website).

The TI rents audioguides for self-guided city tours (€5/person, €7 with two sets of earphones). They also offer guided tours of Sarlat in English (€6, Thu at 14:00, mid-May-mid-Oct, no tours off-season).

The TI may sell tickets for the panoramic elevator ride, described on page 440—ask (€5, cash only, handy to buy here because in 2016 you could only pay at the elevator with a chip credit card—though this may change for 2017).

ARRIVAL IN SARLAT-LA-CANEDA

By Train: The sleepy train station keeps a lonely vigil (without a shop, café, or hotel in sight). It's a mostly downhill, 20-minute walk to the town center (taxis are about €8, call ahead). To walk into town, turn left out of the station and follow Avenue de la Gare as it curves downhill, then turn right at the bottom, on Avenue Thiers, to reach the town center. Some trains (such as those from Limoges and Cahors) arrive at nearby Souillac, which is poorly connected to Sarlat's train station by a bus (1-2/day, schedule on www.transperigord.fr).

By Car: The hilly terrain around Sarlat-la-Canéda creates traffic funnels unusual for a town of this size. The closest parking to the center is metered and easy on nonmarket and off-season days (about €6/3 hours, free 19:00-9:00). On market days, avoid the center by parking along Avenue du Général de Gaulle (at the north end of town), or in one of the signed lots on the ring road. You'll also find free parking at Place des Cordeliers, a 5-minute walk north of Place de la Petite Rigaudie.

HELPFUL HINTS

Exchange Rate: €1 = about $1.10
Country Calling Code: 33 (see page 1082 for dialing instructions)
Market Days: Sarlat has been an important market town since

DORDOGNE

Sarlat-la-Canéda

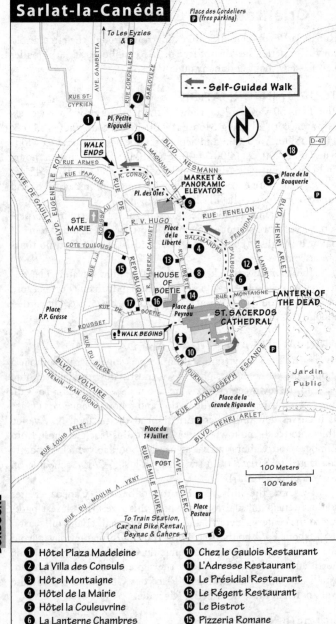

Place des Cordeliers
P (free parking)

To Les Eyzies & P

- - - - Self-Guided Walk

N

D-47

WALK ENDS

MARKET & PANORAMIC ELEVATOR

Place de la Bouquerie

STE. MARIE

Pl. Petite Rigaudie

Pl. des Oies

Place de la Liberté

HOUSE OF BOETIE

Place du Peyrou

LANTERN OF THE DEAD

ST. SACERDOS CATHEDRAL

WALK BEGINS

Place P.P. Grasse

Jardin Public

Place du 14 Juillet

POST

Place Pasteur

To Train Station, Car and Bike Rental, Baynac & Cahors

100 Meters
100 Yards

DORDOGNE

1 Hôtel Plaza Madeleine
2 La Villa des Consuls
3 Hôtel Montaigne
4 Hôtel de la Mairie
5 Hôtel la Couleuvrine
6 La Lanterne Chambres
7 Les Cordeliers Chambres
8 Les Chambres du Glacier & Brasserie
9 La Maison du Notaire Royal

10 Chez le Gaulois Restaurant
11 L'Adresse Restaurant
12 Le Présidial Restaurant
13 Le Régent Restaurant
14 Le Bistrot
15 Pizzeria Romane
16 Mertz Pastry Shop
17 Petit Casino Grocery
18 Launderette

the Middle Ages. Outdoor markets still thrive on Wednesday morning and all day Saturday. Saturday's market swallows the entire town and is best in the morning (produce and food vendors leave around noon). Come before 8:00 to watch them set up; once the market is under way, plant yourself at a well-positioned café to observe the civilized scene. On Thursday evenings (starting at 18:00), a small organic market enlivens the town's lower side (best in summer; just south of the old center at Place du 14 Juillet). From November to March, a truffle market takes place on Saturday mornings on Rue Fénelon. For tips on what to look for at the market, see "Dordogne Markets," earlier.

Supermarket: There's a **Petit Casino** grocery at 32 Rue de la République.

Wi-Fi: Ask the TI where you can get connected. The recommended **Brasserie le Glacier** has free Wi-Fi for customers.

Laundry: Madame Mazzocato, who doesn't speak much English, runs the launderette across from the recommended Hôtel la Couleuvrine (self-serve daily 24 hours, or have your hotel call and ask about full service, 10 Place de la Bouquerie, mobile 06 81 30 57 81). Another **self-serve laundry** is near the hotels north of the center (daily 7:00-21:00, 74 Avenue Gambetta).

Biking: Sarlat-la-Canéda is surrounded by beautiful country lanes that would be ideal for biking were it not for all those hills. Villages along the Dordogne River make good biking destinations, though expect some traffic (bike-rental places can advise quieter routes) and some serious ups and downs between Sarlat and the river. Note that the 16-mile bike-only lane from Sarlat to Souillac doesn't connect the river villages I describe.

Liberty Cycle rents bikes and offers short bike tours from Sarlat (daily, delivery to hotel possible, tel. 07 81 24 78 79, www.liberty-cycle.com, guillaume@liberty-cycle.com). In Castelnaud, **Bike Bus** also offers rentals and tours (daily, €20/day, on the left after the bridge leading to Castelnaud, tel. 05 53 31 10 61, www.bike-bus.com). From Castelnaud, you have access to a bike path that starts along the Dordogne and follows a smaller river for six miles. **Aquitaine Bike,** run by a British-American couple, can deliver top quality hybrid and road bikes to your hotel in and near Sarlat and provides route advice and roadside assistance (4-day minimum for most bikes, tours available, tel. 05 53 30 35 17, mobile 06 32 35 56 50, www.aquitainebike.com, aquitainebike@gmail.com). The TI has info on bike rental outside Sarlat.

Taxi: Call friendly **Christoph Kusters** (mobile 06 08 70 61 67, www.taxialacarte.com, taxialacarte@gmail.com, also offers

DORDOGNE

regional day trips—see page 486) or **Taxi Sarlat** (tel. 05 53 59 02 43).

Car Rental: Try **Europcar** (Le Pontet, at south end of Avenue Leclerc on roundabout, Place du Maréchal de Lattre de Tassigny, 15-minute walk from center—for location, see map on page 445, tel. 05 53 30 30 40).

Sarlat-la-Canéda Walk

This short self-guided walk, rated ▲▲, starts facing the Cathedral of St. Sacerdos (a few steps from the TI). The walk works well in the day—when all the sights are open—but in some ways it's better after dinner, when the gaslit lanes and candlelit restaurants twinkle. (You can always circle back the next day to sights that interest you.) See the map on page 436 to help navigate.

• *Start in front of the Cathedral of St. Sacerdos, on the...*

Place du Peyrou: An eighth-century Benedictine abbey once stood where the Cathedral of St. Sacerdos is today. It provided the stability for Sarlat to develop into an important trading city during the Middle Ages. The old Bishop's Palace, built right into the cathedral (on the right, with its top-floor Florentine-style loggia), recalls Sarlat's Italian connection. The Italian bishop was the boyfriend of Catherine de' Medici (queen of France)—a relationship that got him this fine residence. After a short stint here, he split to Paris with lots of local money. And though his departure scandalized the town, it left Sarlat with a heritage of Italian architecture. (Notice the fine Italianate house of Etienne de la Boëtie on the opposite side of the square and the similar loggia to its right.)

Another reason for Sarlat's Italo-flavored urban design was its loyalty to the king during wartime. Sarlat's glory century was from about 1450 to 1550, after the Hundred Years' War (see sidebar on page 220). Loyal to the French cause—through a century of war—Sarlat was rewarded by the French king, who gave the town lots of money to rebuild itself in stone. Sarlat's new nobility needed fancy houses, complete with ego-boosting features. Many of Sarlat's most impressive buildings date from this prosperous era, when the Renaissance style was in vogue and everyone wanted an architect with an Italian résumé.

• *Take a closer look (opposite the cathedral) at...*

The House of Etienne de la Boëtie: This house was a typical 16th-century merchant's home—family upstairs and open ground floor (its stone arch now filled in) with big, fat sills to display retail goods. Pan up, scanning the crude-but-still-Renaissance carved reliefs. It was a time when anything Italian was trendy (when yokels "stuck a feather in their cap and called it macaroni"). La Boëtie (lah bow-ess-ee), a 16th-century bleeding-heart liberal who spoke and wrote against the rule of tyrannical kings, remains a local favorite.

Notice how the house just to the left arches over the small street. This was a common practice to maximize buildable space in the Middle Ages. Sarlat enjoyed a population boom in the mid-15th century after the Hundred Years' War ended.

• *If you're doing this walk during the day, head into the cathedral now. After hours, skip ahead to the Lantern of the Dead: Face the cathedral, walk around it to the left, up the lane, and through the little door in the wall to the rocket-shaped building on a bluff 30 yards behind the church.*

Cathedral of St. Sacerdos: Though the cathedral's facade has a few well-worn 12th-century carvings, most of it dates from the 18th and 19th centuries. Step inside. The faithful believed that Mary delivered them from the great plague of 1348, so you'll find a full complement of Virgin Marys here and throughout the town. The Gothic interiors in this part of France are simple, with clean lines and nothing extravagant. The first chapel on the left is the baptistery. Locals would come here to give thanks after they made the pilgrimage to Lourdes for healing and returned satisfied. The second column on the right side of the nave shows a long list of hometown boys who gave their lives for France in World War I.

• *Exit the cathedral from the right transept into what was once the abbey's cloisters. Snoop through a maze of quiet, interconnecting courtyards, always bearing left. In the final (deserted) courtyard, cut across diagonally to find the easy-to-miss door in the far corner. You'll wind up at the back of the church, where you'll climb steps (above the monks' graveyard) to a bluff. Here you'll find a bullet-shaped building ready for some kind of medieval takeoff, known as the...*

Lantern of the Dead (Lanterne des Morts): Dating from 1147, this is the oldest monument in town. In four horrible days, a quarter of Sarlat's population (1,000 out of 4,000) died in a plague. People prayed to St. Bernard of Clairvaux for help. He blessed their bread—and instituted hygiene standards while he was at it, stopping the disease. This lantern was built in gratitude.

• *Facing the church, exit downhill and to the right, toward an adorable house with its own tiny tower. Cross one street and keep straight, turn left a block later on Impasse de la Vieille Poste, make a quick right on Rue d'Albusse, and then take a left onto...*

Rue de la Salamandre: The salamander—unfazed by fire or water—was Sarlat's mascot. Befitting its favorite animal, Sarlat was also unfazed by fire (from war) and water (from floods). Walk a few steps down this "Street of the Salamander" and find the Gothic-framed doorway just below on your right. Step back and notice the tower that housed the staircase. Staircase towers like this (Sarlat has about 20) date from about 1600 (after the wars of religion between the Catholics and Protestants), when the new nobility needed to show off.

• *Continue downhill, passing under the salamander-capped arch, and pause near (or better, sit down at) the café on the...*

Place de la Liberté: This has been Sarlat's main market square since the Middle Ages, though it was expanded in the 18th century. Sarlat's patriotic town hall stands behind you (with a café perfectly situated for people-watching). You can't miss the dark **stone roofs** topping the buildings across the square. They're typical of this region: Called *lauzes* in French, the flat limestone rocks were originally gathered by farmers clearing their fields, then made into cheap, durable roofing material (today few people can afford them). The unusually steep pitch of the *lauzes* roofs—which last up to 300 years—helps distribute the weight of the roof (about 160 pounds per square foot) over a greater area. Although most *lauzes* roofs have been replaced by roofs made from more affordable materials, a great number remain. The small window is critical: It provides air circulation, allowing the lichen that coat the porous stone to grow—sealing gaps between the stones and effectively waterproofing the roof. Without that layer, the stone would crumble after repeated freeze-and-thaw cycles.

• *Walk right, to the "upper" end of the square. The bulky Church of Ste. Marie, right across from you, today serves as Sarlat's...*

Covered Market and Panoramic Elevator: Once a parish church dedicated to St. Marie, with a massive *lauzes* roof and a soaring bell tower, this building was converted into a gunpowder factory and then a post office before becoming today's **indoor market** (daily 8:30-13:00). Marvel at its tall, strangely modern, seven-ton doors, and imagine the effort it took to deliver and install them in the center of this tight-laned town.

On the opposite side of this building (walk through if it's open, or around if it's closed), you'll find the entrance to a modern, glass-sided **panoramic elevator,** which whisks tourists up through the center of the ancient church's bell tower for bird's-eye views over the rooftops. Your elevator operator doubles as a guide, who gives a quick history of Sarlat at the top. If they gather enough English-speakers, the spiel is in English; otherwise, it'll be in French and you'll use the good English handout (feel free to ask questions). Because the elevator is open-air, it doesn't run in the rain (€5, buy timed-entry ticket at machines, chip card required, rarely a wait, cash-only tickets may be available

DORDOGNE

at TI; 5/hour, visit lasts 12 minutes, generally open daily in summer 10:00-14:00 & 17:00-21:00, in spring and fall 10:00-13:00 & 14:00-18:00, shorter hours off-season).

• *When you've returned to earth, double back into Place de la Liberté and climb the small lane opposite the market's big doors to meet the "Boy of Sarlat"—a statue marking the best view over Place de la Liberté. Notice the cathedral's tower, with a salamander swinging happily from its spire. Just below you on the stairs are several shops.*

Foie Gras and Beyond: Tourist-pleasing stores like **La Boutique du Badaud** line the streets of Sarlat and are filled with the finest local products. This quiet shop sells it all, from truffles to foie gras to walnut wine to truffle liqueur. They also offer tastings *(dégustations)* of local liquors. To better understand what you're looking at, read the foie gras sidebar on page 462.

• *Turn left behind the boy statue and trickle like medieval rainwater down the ramp into an inviting square. Here you'll find a little gaggle of geese.*

Place des Oies: Feathers fly when geese are traded on this "Square of the Geese" on market days (Nov-March). Birds have been serious business here since the Middle Ages. Even today, a typical Sarlat menu reads, "duck, duck, goose." Trophy homes surround this cute little square on all sides.

Check out the wealthy merchant's home to the right as you enter the square—the **Manoir de Gisson**—with a tower built big enough to match his ego. The owner was the town counsel, a position that arose as cities like Sarlat outgrew the Middle Ages. Town counsels replaced priests in resolving civil conflicts and performing other civic duties. Touring the interior of the manor reveals how the wealthy lived in Sarlat (study the big poster next to the entry). You'll climb up one of those spiral staircase towers, ogle at several rooms carefully decorated with authentic 16th- to 18th-century furniture, and peek inside the impressive *lauzes* roof. It's fun to gaze out the windows and imagine living here, surrounded by 360 degrees of gorgeous cityscape (€7, daily April-Sept 10:00-18:30, until 19:00 July-Aug, closes earlier off-season, borrow English booklet, tel. 05 53 28 70 55, www.manoirdegisson.com).

• *Walk to the right along Rue des Consuls. Just before Le Mirandol restaurant, turn right toward a...*

Fourteenth-Century Vault and Fountain: For generations, this was the town's only source of water, protected by the Virgin Mary (find her at the end of the fountain). Opposite the restaurant and fountain, find the wooden doorway (open late June-Aug only) that houses a massive Renaissance stairway. These showy stairways, which replaced more space-efficient spiral ones, required a big house and a bigger income. Impressive.

• *Follow the curve along Rue des Consuls, and enter the straight-as-an-arrow...*

Rue de la République: This "modern" thoroughfare, known as *La Traverse* to locals, dates from the mid-1800s, when blasting big roads through medieval cities was standard operating procedure. It wasn't until 1963 that Sarlat's other streets would become off-limits to cars, thanks to France's forward-thinking minister of culture, André Malraux. The law that bears his name has served to preserve and restore important monuments and neighborhoods throughout France. Eager to protect the country's architectural heritage, private investors, cities, and regions worked together to create traffic-free zones, rebuild crumbling buildings, and make sure that no cables or ugly wiring marred the ambience of towns like this. Without the Malraux Law, Sarlat might well have more "efficient" roads like Rue de la République slicing through its old town center.

Your tour is over, but make sure you take time for a poetic ramble through the town's quiet side—or, better yet, stroll any of Sarlat's lanes after dark. This is the only town in France illuminated by gas lamps, which cause the warm limestone to glow, turning the romance of Sarlat up even higher. Now may also be a good time to find a café and raise a toast to Monsieur Malraux.

Sleeping in Sarlat-la-Canéda

Even with summer crowds, Sarlat-la-Canéda is the train traveler's best Dordogne home base. Note that in July and August, some hotels require half-pension, and hotels in downtown Sarlat book up first. Parking can be a headache—drivers will find rooms and parking easier just outside of town or in the nearby villages and destinations described later, under "The Best of the Dordogne River Valley" (most are a 15-minute drive away).

HOTELS IN THE TOWN CENTER

$$ Hôtel Plaza Madeleine**** is a central and upscale value with formal service, a handsome pub/wine-bar, stylish public spaces, and 39 very sharp rooms with every comfort. You'll find a pool out back, a sauna, and a whirlpool bath—all free for guests (connecting rooms for families, great breakfast buffet, air-con, elevator, pay garage parking, at north end of ring road at 1 Place de la Petite Rigaudie, tel. 05 53 59 10 41, www.plaza-madeleine.com, contact@plaza-madeleine.com).

$ La Villa des Consuls,*** a cross between a B&B and a hotel, occupies a 17th-century home buried on Sarlat's quiet side with 13 lovely, spacious rooms with microwave ovens and refrigerators; most also have a kitchen and a living room. The rooms surround a small courtyard and come with wood floors, private decks, and high ceilings. English-fluent owner David prices his rooms to encourage longer stays (family rooms, higher prices for 1-night stays, less for 7 or more days, air-con, free use of washers and dryers, pay garage parking, David can organize train station pickup and will help with hauling bags from the street, 3 Rue Jean-Jacques Rousseau, tel. 05 53 31 90 05, www.villaconsuls.fr, villadesconsuls@yahoo.fr).

$ Hôtel Montaigne,*** a good value located a block south of the pedestrian zone, is run by the smiling Martinat family. The 28 rooms are simple, comfortable, and air-conditioned. Of the hotels I list, this is the one nearest to the train station (family rooms, air-con, elevator, easy parking nearby, Place Pasteur, tel. 05 53 31 93 88, www.hotelmontaigne.fr, contact@hotelmontaigne.fr).

$ Hôtel de la Mairie's** rooms are located above its name-sake café, smack dab on the main square (ideal for market days).

The nice but dated, peeling-wallpaper rooms provide basic comfort at OK prices, and most have beamed ceilings; rooms #3 and #6 have the best views. The management is *très* laissez faire (reception in café, lots of stairs, Place de la Liberté, tel. 05 53 59 05 71, www.hotel-mairie-sarlat.com, hoteldelamairie@orange.fr).

$ Hôtel la Couleuvrine** offers 27 simple rooms with character at good rates in a historic building with a handy location—across from the launderette and with easy parking (for Sarlat). Families enjoy *les chambres familles* (several in

DORDOGNE

the tower). Some rooms have tight bathrooms, and a few have private terraces (family rooms, elevator, on ring road at 1 Place de la Bouquerie, tel. 05 53 59 27 80, www.la-couleuvrine.com, contact@la-couleuvrine.com). Half-pension is encouraged during busy periods and in the summer—figure €36 per person beyond the room price for breakfast and a good dinner in the classy restaurant.

HOTELS NORTH OF TOWN

The following hotels are a 10-minute walk north of the old town on Avenue de Selves. All have easy parking. For locations, see the "Greater Sarlat-la-Canéda" map.

$$$ Au Grand Hôtel de Sarlat**** feels *très* American, with a big lobby, professional staff, and 38 way-pricey-for-Sarlat rooms in a modern shell with a year-round swimming pool (RS%, big breakfast, air-con, elevator, pay parking, 93 Avenue de Selves, tel. 05 53 31 50 00, http://au-grand-hotel-de-sarlat.com, augrandhotelsarlat@gmail.com).

$$ Hôtel de Compostelle** features a cheery, spacious lobby and 23 well-maintained, generously sized, and air-conditioned rooms, including several good family rooms (elevator is one floor up, sweet backyard terrace, pay parking, 66 Avenue de Selves, tel. 05 53 59 08 53, www.hotel-compostelle-sarlat.com, info@hotel-compostelle-sarlat.com).

$ Hôtel le Madrigal,** one block past Hôtel de Compostelle, is a charming nine-room hotel with good two-star rooms and rates, all with queen-size beds, air-conditioning, and smallish bathrooms (family rooms, fitness room, pay parking, 50 Avenue de Selves, tel. 05 53 59 21 98, www.hotel-madrigal-sarlat.com, info@hotel-madrigal-sarlat.com).

CHAMBRES D'HOTES

These *chambres d'hôtes* are central and compare well with the hotels listed earlier.

$ La Lanterne, named for the monument it faces, occupies a 500-year-old building that could not be more central nor more welcoming. British Terri Bowen (and dogs Frodo and Fibi) deliver cozy public spaces and four thoughtfully appointed, quiet rooms that surround a sweet little courtyard (cash or PayPal only, 9 bis Rue Montaigne, tel. 05 53 59 17 79, mobile 06 33 38 89 11, www.sarlat.biz, info@sarlat.biz).

$ Les Cordeliers, owned by gentle Brits Chris and Amanda Johnson, offers top comfort at two-star prices. Most of the seven cushy rooms are huge; all are air-conditioned and well-furnished; and a small kitchen is at your disposal with serve-yourself snacks and drinks. The building—a classic old Sarlat address with a mansard roof and sky-blue shutters—overlooks a picturesque square at

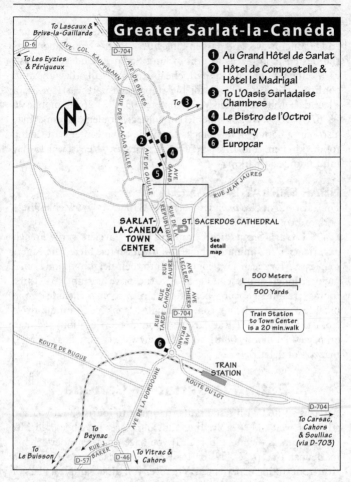

Greater Sarlat-la-Canéda

1. Au Grand Hôtel de Sarlat
2. Hôtel de Compostelle & Hôtel le Madrigal
3. To L'Oasis Sarladaise Chambres
4. Le Bistro de l'Octroi
5. Laundry
6. Europcar

the north end of the old center (big breakfast with fresh fruit and eggs–€8, closed Nov-Feb, 51 Rue des Cordeliers, mobile 06 76 78 04 01, www.hotelsarlat.com, info@hotelsarlat.com).

$ Les Chambres du Glacier, where kind Monsieur Da Costa and son Bruno offer four cavernous, simple, but surprisingly comfortable rooms above an outdoor café, is in the thick of Sarlat's pedestrian zone (perfect for market days). Rooms come with sky-high ceilings, big and soundproof windows over Sarlat's world, polished wood floors, and bathrooms you can get lost in (family rooms, includes breakfast, Place de la Liberté, tel. 05 53 29 99 99, www. chambres-du-glacier-sarlat.com, carlos.da.costa.24@wanadoo.fr).

$ La Maison du Notaire Royal, run by English-speaking Pierre-Henri Toulemon and French-speaking Diane, has four large and simple rooms with a private entry in a 17th-century home

DORDOGNE

located a few steps above the main square. Guests have access to a fridge, microwave, and garden tables. Ask Pierre-Henri about off-the-beaten-path places to visit around Sarlat (includes breakfast, cash only, no deposit required, cheap parking, call a day ahead to confirm arrival time, look for big steps from northeast corner of Place de la Liberté, 4 Rue Magnanat, tel. 05 53 31 26 60, mobile 06 08 67 76 90, www.toulemon.com, contact@toulemon.com). They also rent a cottage a few blocks from the town center with living room, kitchen, and three bedrooms that can sleep seven (3-day minimum, easy parking).

NEAR SARLAT-LA-CANEDA

For a list of good *chambres d'hôtes* near Sarlat, try www.chambres-perigord.com.

$ L'Oasis Sarladaise Chambres gives travelers a true French experience a few minutes above the town center. Here, the eager-to-please Mazzocatos welcome you into their neighborhood home, picnic dinners are encouraged, and the price is right. All three rooms are bird-chirping-peaceful (family rooms, includes good breakfast, cash only, air-con, no English spoken, 5-minute drive from the center at 9 Rue Jacques Monod—for location, see map on page 445; mobile 06 81 30 57 81, www.oasis-sarladaise.fr, fred.mazzo@orange.fr).

Eating in Sarlat-la-Canéda

Sarlat is stuffed with restaurants that cater to tourists, but you can still dine well and cheaply. The following places have been reliable; Le Présidial is the most formal. If you have a car, consider driving to Beynac (see page 459) or La Roque-Gageac (page 456) for a riverfront dining experience. Wherever you dine, sample a glass of sweet Monbazillac wine with your foie gras.

$ Chez le Gaulois is a change from the traditional places that line Sarlat's lanes. Pyrenees-raised Olivier and his wife Nora serve a hearty mountain cuisine featuring fondue, raclette, *tartiflette* (roasted potatoes mixed with ham and cheese—comes with a good salad for €14.50), and thinly sliced ham (Olivier spends all evening slicing away). The €12 *cassolette de légumes* (a ratatouille-like dish) is also tasty. They have a few sidewalk tables, but the fun is inside and the service is English-fluent. The ceiling is cluttered with ham hocks, and the soundtrack is jazz. To eat at prime time (12:00 or 19:00), reservations are smart during the high season (good salads, try *la tarte aux figues*—fig tart—for dessert, closed Sun-Mon except in July-Aug, near the TI at 1 Rue Tourny, tel. 05 53 59 50 64).

$$$ L'Adresse, a sweet little bistro, serves regional specialties with a creative twist—ideal for foodies. It gets rave reviews from

Restaurant Price Code

I've assigned each eatery a price category, based on the average cost of a typical main course. Drinks, desserts, and splurge items (steak and seafood) can raise the price considerably.

$$$$	**Splurge:** Most main courses over €25
$$$	**Pricier:** €20-25
$$	**Moderate:** €15-20
$	**Budget:** Under €15

In France, a crêpe stand or other takeout spot is **$**; a sit-down brasserie, café, or bistro with affordable *plats du jour* is **$$**; a casual but more upscale restaurant is **$$$**; and a swanky splurge is **$$$$**.

locals so try to book ahead, particularly if you want a table on the front terrace, facing a Parisian-style square. There's more space on the terrace out back, in an atmospheric alley (€24-34 *menus* with good choices, closed Sun, 8 Place de la Petite Rigaudie, tel. 05 53 30 56 19).

$$$ Le Présidial is a lovely place for a refined meal in a historic mansion. The setting is exceptional—you're greeted with beautiful gardens (where you can dine in good weather), and the interior comes with high ceilings, stone walls, and rich wood floors (closed Mon all day and Tue for lunch, reservations recommended, 6 Rue Landry, tel. 05 53 28 92 47, www.lepresidial.fr).

$$ Le Régent serves traditional dishes with two terraces on Sarlat's lovely main square; the one above is more intimate. The €25 *menu* gives a good taste of Sarlat's specialties (daily, Place de la Liberté, tel. 05 53 31 06 36).

$$ Le Bistrot has marvelous outside seating across from the cathedral, plus a cozy interior (reserve to land a table outside in high season). The traditional cuisine is served at affordable prices (€18-29 *menus* with good choices, daily, 14 Place du Peyrou, tel. 05 53 28 28 40, www.le-bistrot-sarlat.com).

$ Brasserie le Glacier offers main-square views from its outdoor tables and good, crowd-pleasing café fare nonstop from 11:00-22:00. Come here for good service (Filomena has the big smile); a big salad for €12 (the *salade paysanne*—peasant salad with smoked duck—works for me), pizza, or *un plat*; and a view of the lights warming the town buildings (daily, Place de la Liberté, tel. 05 53 29 99 99, also rents rooms—see "Les Chambres du Glacier," page 445).

$ Pizzeria Romane is a cheap, spacious, and family-friendly eatery where you can watch your pizza bake in the oven and enjoy it in the smoke-free patio (lots of salads, daily July-Aug, otherwise

DORDOGNE

closed Sun-Mon, on the quiet side of Sarlat at 3 Côte de Toulouse, tel. 05 53 59 23 88).

North of the Center: $$$ Le Bistro de l'Octroi, overlooking a busy road a few blocks north of the old town, must provide top cuisine and competitive prices to draw locals—and it does. Quality bistro fare (mostly meat dishes) is served on a generous terrace and within the pleasant interior. The €21-36 three-course *menus* offer many options—order two starters if you prefer (daily, 111 Avenue des Selves—for location see map on page 445, tel. 05 53 30 83 40, www.lebistrodeloctroi.fr).

Pastries: At **$ Mertz,** a classy pastry shop with sidewalk tables along Rue de la République, you can enjoy decadent desserts with a hot drink while people-watching (daily, 33 Rue de la République, tel. 05 53 59 00 85).

Sarlat-la-Canéda Connections

Sarlat's TI has train schedules. Souillac and Périgueux are the train hubs for points within the greater region. For all the following destinations, you could go west on the Libourne/Bordeaux line (transferring in either city, depending on your connection), or east by infrequent bus to Souillac (bus leaves from Sarlat train station). I've listed the fastest path in each case. For any travel to the southeast, it's easier to take a train from Souillac.

From Sarlat-la-Canéda by Train to: Les Eyzies-de-Tayac (3-4/day, 1-2.5 hours, transfer in Le Buisson), **Paris** (4/day, 6-6.5 hours, change in Libourne or Bordeaux-St-Jean; faster to take train in Souillac), **Amboise** (3/day, 5-7 hours, via Libourne, then TGV to Tours' St-Pierre-des-Corps, then local train to Amboise), **Bourges** (4/day, 6-7 hours, 2-4 changes), **Limoges/Oradour-sur-Glane** (4/day, 4 hours, change in Le Buisson and Périgueux—then 15-minute walk to catch bus to Oradour-sur-Glane), **Cahors** (5/day, 3 hours, bus to Souillac or Siorac, then train to Cahors), **Albi** (6/day, 6 hours with 2-3 changes, some require bus from Sarlat to Souillac), **Carcassonne** (5/day, 5.5-7 hours, 1-3 changes, some require bus from Sarlat to Souillac), **St-Emilion** (6/day, 2 hours).

To Beynac, La Roque-Gageac, Castelnaud, and Domme: These are accessible only by taxi or bike (best rented in Sarlat). See Sarlat's "Helpful Hints" on page 435 for specifics.

DORDOGNE

The Best of the Dordogne River Valley

The most striking stretch of the Dordogne lies between Carsac and Beynac. Traveling by canoe is the best way to savor the highlights of the Dordogne River Valley, though several scenic sights lie off the river and require a car or bike. Following my "Dordogne Scenic Loop" (below), you'll easily link Sarlat-la-Canéda with La Roque-Gageac, Beynac and its château, and Castelnaud before returning to Sarlat.

PLANNING YOUR TIME

Drivers should allow a minimum of a half-day to sample the river valley. Drive slowly to savor the scenery and to stay out of trouble (these are narrow, cliff-hanging roads). The area is picnic-perfect, but buy your supplies before leaving Sarlat; pickings are slim in the villages (though view cafés are abundant). Vitrac (near Sarlat) is the best place to park for a canoe ride down the river. La Roque-Gageac, Beynac, and Domme have good restaurants. There are a few good places to witness the *gavage* (feeding of the geese and ducks to make foie gras) between Beynac and Sarlat—their dinnertime is generally about 18:00.

In riverfront villages, you'll pay for parking during the day (about €2-3 for a 3-hour minimum stay, free during midafternoon siesta, pay at meter, then put receipt on your dashboard; cars are checked). Parked cars are catnip to thieves: Take everything out or stow belongings out of sight.

In this section I've given distances in kilometers; drivers can match these with your rental car's odometer.

Self-Guided Tours Along the Dordogne

▲▲DORDOGNE SCENIC LOOP

Following these directions, beginning and ending in Sarlat-la-Canéda, you can see this area by car or bike (27 hilly miles). Cyclists can cut seven miles off this distance and still see most of the highlights by following D-704 from Sarlat toward Cahors, then taking the Montfort turnoff (well-signed after the big Leclerc grocery store at the roundabout with the wooden *séchoir à tabac* sign) and tracking signs to Montfort—see the map on page 452. Once in Montfort, follow the river downstream to La Roque-Gageac.

Key villages along this route are described in detail later in this chapter, under "Dordogne Towns and Sights."

DORDOGNE

The Tour Begins: From Sarlat, follow signs on D-704 toward *Cahors*. Not long after leaving Sarlat, you'll pass the Rougié foie gras outlet store, then the limestone quarry that gives the houses in this area their lemony color.

In about five minutes, be on the lookout for the little signposted turnoff on the right to the *Eglise de Carsac* (Church of Carsac). Set peacefully among cornfields, with its WWI monument, bonsai-like plane trees, and simple, bulky Romanesque exterior, the **Eglise de Carsac** church is part of a vivid rural French scene. Take a break here and enter the church (usually open). The stone capitals behind the altar are exquisitely medieval. Back outside, the small cornfields nearby are busy growing feed for ducks and geese—locals are appalled that humans would eat the stuff.

From here, continue on, following signs to *Montfort*. About a kilometer west of Carsac, pull over to enjoy the scenic viewpoint (overlooking a bend in the river known as Cingle de Montfort). Across the Dordogne River, fields of walnut trees stretch to distant castles, and the nearby hills are covered in oak trees. This area is nicknamed "black Périgord" for its thick blanket of oaks, which stay leafy throughout the winter. The fairy-tale castle you see is **Montfort,** once the medieval home of Simon de Montfort, who led the Cathar Crusades in the early 13th century. Today it's considered mysterious by locals. (It's rumored that the castle is now the home of a brother of the emir of Kuwait.) A plaque on the rock near where you parked honors those who fought Nazi occupiers in this area in 1943.

Pass under Montfort's castle (which you can't tour; its cute little village has a few cafés and restaurants). If you're combining a canoe trip with this drive, cross the river following signs to *Domme*, and find my recommended canoe rental on the right side (see "Dordogne Canoe Trip," next).

The touristy *bastide* (fortified village) of **Domme** is well worth a side-trip from Vitrac or La Roque-Gageac for its sensational views (best early in the day). The driving route continues to the more important riverfront villages of **La Roque-Gageac,** then on to **Castelnaud,** and finally to **Beynac** (all described later in this chapter). From Beynac, it's a quick run back to Sarlat.

▲▲▲DORDOGNE CANOE TRIP

For a refreshing break from the car or train, explore the riverside castles and villages of the Dordogne by canoe.

Renting a Canoe (or Kayak): You can rent plastic boats—

hard, light, and indestructible—from many area outfits. Whether a one-person kayak or a two-person canoe, they're stable enough for beginners. Many rental places will pick you up at an agreed-upon spot (even in Sarlat, provided that your group is big enough, and they aren't too busy). All companies let you put in anytime between 9:30 and 16:00 (start no later than 15:00 to allow time to linger when the mood strikes; they'll pick you up at about 18:00). They all charge about the same and most accept cash only (two-person canoe-€14-18/person, one-person kayak-€16-24). You'll get a life vest and, for about €2 extra, a watertight bucket in which to store your belongings. (The bucket is bigger than you'd need for just a camera, watch, wallet, and phone; if that's all you have bring a resealable plastic baggie or something similar for dry storage.) You must have shoes that stay on your feet; travelers wearing flip-flops will be invited to purchase more appropriate footwear (sold at most boat launches for around €10).

The trip is fun even in light rain—but steady, heavy rains can make the current too fast to handle, so check river levels (ask before you rent).

Beach your boat wherever it works to take a break—it's light enough that you can drag it up high and dry to go explore. (The canoes aren't worth stealing, as they're cheap and clearly color-coded for their parent company.) It's OK if you're a complete novice—the only whitewater you'll encounter will be the rare wake of passing tour boats...and your travel partner frothing at the views.

Périgord-Aventure et Loisirs has a pullout arrangement in Beynac (to get to their Vitrac put-in base, from the main roundabout in the town of Vitrac, cross the Dordogne, and turn right). Readers of this book get a 10 percent discount in 2017, and they'll even pick you up in Sarlat for free (arrange in advance, this allows nondrivers a chance to explore the riverfront villages for the price of a canoe trip—tip the driver a few euros for this helpful service; tel. 05 53 28 23 82, mobile 06 83 27 30 06, www.perigordaventureloisirs. com, info@perigordaventureloisirs.com). Allow time to explore Beynac after your river paddle and before the return shuttle trip. Périgord-Aventure also arranges a longer, 14-mile trip from Carsac to Beynac, adding the gorgeous Montfort loop *(Cingle de Montfort)*. Ask about their canoe-hike-bike options, such as the canoe trip to Beynac, followed with a walk along a riverside trail to Castelnaud, and ending with a bike ride back to your starting point in Vitrac (€30, no discounts, reserve in advance, start or end the loop wherever you like).

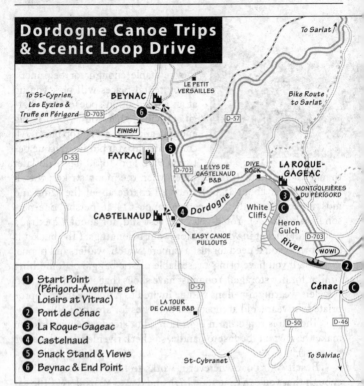

Dordogne Canoe Trips & Scenic Loop Drive

To Sarlat

LE PETIT VERSAILLES

BEYNAC

To St-Cyprien, Les Eyzies & Truffe en Périgord — D-703

Bike Route to Sarlat

FINISH

D-57

⑥

D-53

FAYRAC

⑤

D-703

LE LYS DE CASTELNAUD B&B

DIVE ROCK

LA ROQUE-GAGEAC

MONTGOLFIÈRES DU PÉRIGORD

CASTELNAUD

④ *Dordogne*

③

C

White Cliffs

Heron Gulch

D-703

EASY CANOE PULLOUTS

River

WOW!

②

① Start Point (Périgord-Aventure et Loisirs at Vitrac)
② Pont de Cénac
③ La Roque-Gageac
④ Castelnaud
⑤ Snack Stand & Views
⑥ Beynac & End Point

D-57

LA TOUR DE CAUSE B&B

Cénac C

D-50

D-46

St-Cybranet

To Salviac

The Nine-Mile Paddle from Vitrac to Beynac: This is the most interesting, scenic, and handy trip if you're based in or near Sarlat. Vitrac, on the river close to Sarlat, is a good starting point. And, with its mighty castle and good cafés and restaurants, Beynac delivers the perfect finale to your journey. Allow 2 hours for this paddle at a relaxed pace in spring and fall, and up to 2.5 hours in summer when the river is usually at its lowest flow.

Here's a rundown of the two-hour Vitrac-Beynac adventure: Leave **Vitrac,** paddling at an easy pace through lush, forested land. The fortified hill town of Domme will be dead ahead. Pass through Heron Gulch, and after about an hour you'll come to **La Roque-Gageac** (one of two easy and worthwhile stops before Beynac).

Paddle past La Roque-Gageac's wooden docks (with the tour boats) to the stone ramp leading up to the town. Do a 180-degree turn and beach thyself, dragging the boat high and dry. From there you're in La Roque-Gageac's tiny town center (described on page 456), with a TI and plenty of cafés, snacks, and ice-cream options. Enjoy the town before heading back to your canoe and into the water.

When leaving La Roque-Gageac, float backward to enjoy the village view. About 15 minutes farther downstream, you'll approach views of the feudal village and castle

DORDOGNE

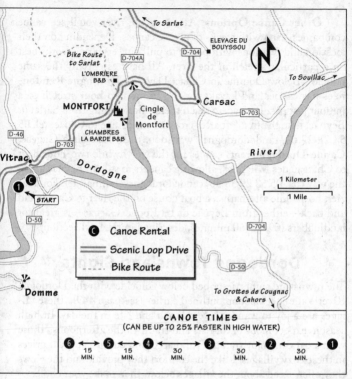

of **Castelnaud.** Look for the castle's huge model of medieval catapults silhouetted menacingly against the sky (it's a steep but worthwhile climb to tour this castle—see page 458). About 15 minutes after you first spot the castle, you'll find two grassy pullouts flanking the bridge below the castle. The bridge arches make terrific frames for castle views. Nearby, there's a small market and charcuterie with all you need for a picnic. La Plage Café serves good café fare with views (near where you pull out).

Another 15 minutes downstream brings views of **Château de Fayrac** on your left. The lords of Castelnaud built this to spy on Beynac during the Hundred Years' War (1336-1453). It's another 15 minutes to your last stop: **Beynac** (described on page 459). The awesome Beynac castle—looming high above the town—gets better and better as you approach. Slow down and enjoy the ride (sometimes there's a snack stand with the same views at the bridge on the right). Keep to the right as you approach the Périgord-Aventure depot. You'll see the ramp just before the parking lot and wooden dock (where the tour boats generally tie up). Do another 180-degree turn, and beach yourself hard. The office is right there. Return your boat, and explore Beynac.

DORDOGNE

Other Canoe Options: All along the river you'll see canoe companies, each with stacks of plastic canoes. Depending on their location and relations with places to pull out, each one works best on a particular stretch of the river. All have essentially the same policies. Below Domme in Cénac, David at **Dordogne Randonnées** has canoes and kayaks for the scenic two-hour stretch to a pullout just past Beynac (to reach their office coming from Sarlat or Beynac, take the first left after crossing the bridge to Cénac, tel. 05 53 28 22 01, randodordogne@wanadoo.fr). In La Roque-Gageac, **Canoe-Dordogne** rents canoes for the worthwhile two-hour float to Château des Milandes, allowing canoers to stop in Beynac along the way (tel. 05 53 29 58 50, canoedordogne@hotmail.fr). For a lazier, no-paddle alternative, a boat cruise on the river to Castelnaud and back—either from Beynac or La Roque-Gageac—is great for landlubbers (€9, 50-60 minutes, described in the next section).

Dordogne Towns and Sights

The towns and sights described below coincide with the Dordogne River Valley scenic loop outlined earlier (see page 449). These villages are a joy to wander before lunch and late in the day. In high season, expect mobs of tourists and traffic in the afternoons. Those with a car can enjoy tranquil rural accommodations at great prices in these cozy villages. I like the comfort they provide and the views they offer. Read about the villages below, then make your choice— you can't go wrong.

SCENIC LOOP: MONTFORT TO BEYNAC
Montfort
There's more to this castle-topped village than meets the eye— leave most tourists behind and find a handful of cafés, restaurants, and *chambres d'hôtes,* including these recommended listings (for locations, see map on page 452).

Sleeping near Montfort: $ Chambres la Barde has five good rooms in a warm, recently built stone home with a swimming pool, cozy lounge, big grass yard, communal kitchen, and views to Montfort castle from most rooms' terraces (family rooms, includes breakfast, cash only, behind Montfort castle—look for green signs, tel. 05 53 28 24 34, mobile 06 86 88 60 93, http://labardemontfort. com, labardemontfort@gmail.com).

$ L'Ombrière, with four elegant rooms and caring Italian hosts Andrea and Barbara, is a calm B&B overlooking a walnut grove with many picnic spaces (includes breakfast, attic rooms have air-con, on east edge of Montfort village—watch for signs, tel. 05 53 28 11 38, www.lombriere.com, info@lombriere.com).

▲▲Domme

This busy little town merits a stop for its stunning view and is ideal early in the day. Otherwise, come late, when crowds recede and the light is best. If you come for lunch or dinner, arrive early enough to savor the cliff-capping setting, and if you come on market day (Thu) expect to hoof it up from a parking lot well below (cars not allowed in old town until the market is over). On other days, follow signs up to *La Bastide de Domme,* and drive right through the narrow gate of the fortified town walls. Park at the pay lot near the view *(Panorama).* You'll find picnic-perfect benches, cafés, and a view you won't soon forget. While the main street is lined with touristy shops that make the town feel greedy, lose yourself in some of the unusually picturesque back lanes, where roses climb over rustic doorways.

Sleeping and Eating in Domme: The town has many forgettable restaurants, but a few places stand out.

$$$ Cabanoix et Châtaigne is a small bistro serving delicious Dordogne fare blended with international flavors. Enjoy the sunset from Domme's viewpoint, then come here to dine in a quaint courtyard with colorful shutters. Book a table ahead—local foodies are all over this place (€31 *menus,* July-Aug open daily for lunch and dinner, Sept-June closed Tue-Wed; from the viewpoint, walk past the church several blocks down Grand Rue and turn left to 3 Rue Geoffroy de Vivans; tel. 05 53 31 07 11, www.restaurantcabanoix.com).

$$ Hôtel de l'Esplanade* delivers the valley's most sensational views from many of its 15 comfortable bedrooms and restaurant tables. If you come for the **$$$** restaurant (€35-65 *menus,* closed Mon lunch), book ahead for view seating. Both the hotel and the restaurant are traditional, formal, and a bit stiff (air-con, tel. 05 53 28 31 41, www.esplanade-perigord. com, esplanade.domme@ wanadoo.fr).

$$ Belvédère Café owns a privileged position at the viewpoint and serves café fare at good prices with million-dollar views from its outside tables. Try to eat here at sunset (daily for lunch and dinner, closed Oct-March, at *Le Panorama,* tel. 05 53 31 12 01).

▲▲▲La Roque-Gageac

Whether you're joyriding, paddling the Dordogne, or taking a hot-air balloon ride, La Roque-Gageac (lah rohk-gah-zhahk) is an essential stop—and a strong contender on all the "cutest towns in France" lists. Called by most simply "La Roque" ("The Rock"), it looks sculpted out of the rock between the river and the cliffs. It also makes a fine base for touring the region.

At the upstream end of town, you'll find plenty of parking and an ATM; the **TI** (daily 10:00-13:00 & 14:00-17:00, July-Aug until 18:00, closed off-season, tel. 05 53 29 17 01); a WC; swings and slides for kids; canoe rental; and *pétanque (boules)* courts, which are lively on summer evenings. A small market brightens La Roque-Gageac on Friday mornings in summer. Though busy with day-trippers, the town is tranquil at night.

Visiting La Roque-Gageac Town: Stand along the river near the TI and survey La Roque-Gageac: It's a one-street town

stretching along the river. The highest stonework (on the far right) was home to the town's earliest inhabitants in the 10th century. High above (about center), 12th-century cave dwellers built a settlement during the era of Norman (Viking) river raids. Long after the Vikings were tamed, French soldiers used this lofty perch as a barracks while fighting against England in the Hundred Years' War. Sturdy concrete supports now reinforce the cave.

Now locate the exotic foliage around the church on the right. Tropical gardens (bamboo, bananas, lemons, cactus, and so on) are a village forte, because limestone absorbs heat.

Those wooden boats on the river are modeled after boats called *gabarres,* originally built here to take prized oak barrels filled with local wine down to Bordeaux. Unable to return against the river current, the boats were routinely taken apart for their lumber. Today, tourists, rather than barrels, fill the boats on river cruises (described later). If you're experiencing a movie-based déjà vu, it's because these actual boats (dolled up, of course) were used by Johnny Depp in the movie *Chocolat,* to the delight of viewers and Juliette Binoche alike.

La Roque-Gageac frequently endures winter floods that would leave you (standing where you are now) underwater. When there's a big rain in central France, La Roque-Gageac floods two days later. The first floors of all the riverfront buildings are vacated off-season. The new riverfront wall, finished in 2014, was pushed out into the river, adding 13 feet of width to the street. Notice the openings at sidewalk level allowing water to flow through in heavy rains. Walk on the main drag to get a closer look. A house about five buildings downriver from Hôtel la Belle Etoile shows various high-water marks (*inondation* means "flood"). Looking farther downstream, notice the fanciful castle built in the 19th century by a British aristocrat (whose family still nurtures Joan of Arc dreams in its turrets). The old building just beyond that (downstream end of town) actually is historic—it's the quarantine house, where lepers and out-of-town visitors who dropped by in times of plague would be kept (after their boats were burned).

Climb into the town by strolling up the cobbled lane to the right of Hôtel la Belle Etoile. Where the stepped path ends, veer right to find the exotic plants and viewpoint (in front of the simple church). From here you can make out Château de Castelnaud downriver, and the village of Domme capping its hill to the left. A left turn at the end of the stepped path takes you to more views and the privately owned Fort Troglodytique (closed to the public). For a terrific medieval fort experience, visit the prehistoric La Roque St-Christophe (described on page 480).

Boat Tours: Tour boats cruise from La Roque-Gageac to Castelnaud and back (one-hour cruise-€9, includes audioguide, 2/hour, April-Nov daily, tel. 05 53 29 40 44).

Hot-Air Balloon Rides: Montgolfières du Périgord, located in La Roque-Gageac, offers a range of flights with well-qualified pilots (one-hour flight-€200/person, tel. 05 53 28 18 58, www.montgolfiere-du-perigord.com).

Sleeping and Eating: Along with Beynac, this is one of the region's most beautiful villages. Park in the lot at the eastern end of town if you're staying in La Roque-Gageac, and take everything of value out of your car.

$$$ Manoir de la Malartrie is a wonderful splurge with five country-classy rooms and one family-ideal apartment with oak-meets-leather public areas, all surrounding a big, heated pool and terraced gardens (begging for a picnic). Your gentle hostess Ouaffa manages her place with elegance (apartment available, cheaper in winter, air-con, free parking, barely downstream from the village—10-minute walk to town on trail above road, mobile 06 18 61 61 18, www.chambresdhotes-lamalartrie.com, lamalartrie@orange.fr).

$ Hôtel la Belle Etoile,* a well-managed hotel-restaurant in the center of La Roque-Gageac, is a terrific value. Hostess Danielle and chef Régis (ray-geez) offer good rooms overlooking the river, a nice terrace, and a fine restaurant (air-con, free parking, closed Nov-March, tel. 05 53 29 51 44, www.belleetoile.fr, hotel.belle-etoile@wanadoo.fr). Régis is the third generation of his family to be chef here and he takes his job seriously. Come to the **$$$** restaurant for a memorable dinner of classic French cuisine with modern accents in a romantic setting. The *oeufs cocottes* are really good (*menus* from €32, closed for lunch Wed and all day Mon; book a few days ahead).

$ L'Auberge des Platanes, across from La Roque-Gageac's TI and parking lot, rents 25 rooms above a sprawling café—guests take a backseat to café clients. Half the rooms are basic and traditional; the other half are modern and pricier (a few rooms have air-con, tel. 05 53 29 51 58, www.aubergedesplatanes.com, contact@ aubergedesplatanes.com).

▲▲Château de Castelnaud

This castle may look a tad less mighty than Château de Beynac (down the river), but it packs a powerful medieval punch.

The concise handout escorts you room by room through the castle-museum. The exhibits—which focus on warfare (armor, crossbows, and catapults) are a bit slicker than Beynac's, but the castle is also more touristy and lacks personality.

Cost and Hours: €9.60, €8.60 before 13:00 in summer; open daily July-Aug 9:00-20:00, April-June and Sept 10:00-19:00, Oct and Feb-March until 18:00, shorter hours Nov-Jan, last entry one hour before closing; daily demonstrations of medieval warfare and guided visits in English mid-July-Aug—call for exact times, tel. 05 53 31 30 00, www.castelnaud.com.

Getting There: From the river, it's a steep 25-minute hike through the village to the castle. Drivers must park in the €4 lot (5-minute walk uphill from there). You can stop at Castelnaud on your canoe trip or hike an hour from Beynac along a riverside path (though it's tricky to follow in parts—it hugs the river as it passes through campgrounds and farms—determined walkers do fine).

Visiting the Castle: After passing the ticket booth, read your essential handout and follow the *suite de la visite* signs. Start by climbing through the tower. Every room has a story to tell, and many have displays of costumed mannequins, suits of armor, weaponry (including the biggest and most artistic crossbows I've ever seen), and artifacts from the Hundred Years' War. Other rooms show informative videos (with English subtitles)—don't miss the catapult video where you'll learn that the big ones could fire only two shots per hour and required up to 250 men to manage. Kids eat it up, in part thanks to the children's guide with fun puzzles. The upper courtyard has a 150-foot-deep well (drop a pebble). On your way back down, you'll see a sparsely furnished medieval kitchen and an iron forge with an interesting video. The rampart views are as unbeatable as the four siege machines are formidable. A few cafés and fun medieval shops await at the foot of the castle.

Sleeping near Castelnaud: This village, ideally situated between La Roque-Gageac and Beynac, has two excellent B&B choices nearby (see map on page 452).

$$ La Tour de Cause is where Belgian owners Igor and Nico have found their heaven, amid their renovated farmhouse with five top-quality rooms. Some have immense walk-in showers, and the upstair rooms have beautiful wood-beam high ceilings. There's also a big pool and, best of all, a *pétanque* court. Your hosts are experienced chefs and happy to prepare a refreshing €35 three-course dinner with wine—if you book ahead (includes breakfast, cash only, 2-night minimum in July-Aug, tel. 05 53 30 30 51, mobile 06 37 32 44 17, www.latourdecause.com, info@latourdecause.com). From the Dordogne River, cross the bridge to Castelnaud, follow signs toward *Daglan*, then make a hard right turn in the hamlet of Pont de Cause and park near their gate.

$ Le Lys de Castelnaud is run by French medieval enthusiasts and travel fanatics Nathalys and Dominique. Nathalys is a Joan of Arc fan who adores her home's namesake castle and loves helping travelers. Public areas are steeped in the Middle Ages, with knights in armor, tapestries, and more. The four lovely rooms are a great value (three have Castelnaud views), and there's a well-designed one-bedroom apartment below with a kitchen (family rooms, cash or PayPal only, French lessons available, tel. 05 53 28 20 27, mobile 06 09 57 21 97, www.chambres-dordogne.com, contact@chambres-dordogne.com). It's well-signed at the foot of the road that leads across the river to Castelnaud.

▲▲▲Beynac

Four miles downstream from La Roque-Gageac, Beynac (bay-nak) is the other must-see Dordogne village. It's also home to one of the most imposing castles in France.

This well-preserved medieval village winds like a sepia-tone film set, from the castle above to the river below (easy parking at the top avoids the steep climb). The stone village—with cobbled lanes that retain their Occitan (old French)

DORDOGNE

names—is just plain pretty, best late in the afternoon and down-right dreamy after dark. For the best light, tour the castle late, or at least walk out to the sensational viewpoint, then have a dinner here.

Drivers can **park** at pay lots located on the river, way up at the castle (follow signs to *Château de Beynac*), or halfway between. The same parking ticket works up at the château if you decide against the climb. The **TI** is near the river, across from Hôtel du Château (daily 10:00-13:00 & 14:00-17:00, July-Aug until 18:00, Oct-March Fri-Sat only, tel. 05 53 29 43 08). Pick up the *Plan du Village* in English for a simple self-guided walking tour, and get information on hiking and canoes. A few steps down from the TI is the post office (ATM outside). If you need a lift, call Beynac-based **Taxi Corinne** (see page 429). From mid-June to mid-September, a cute little market sets up on Monday mornings in the riverfront parking lot.

Château de Beynac: Beynac's brooding, cliff-clinging châ-teau, worth ▲▲, soars 500 feet above the Dordogne River (€8, daily 10:00-18:30, Nov-April until 17:00 or 17:30, last entry 45 minutes before closing, tel. 05 53 29 50 40, www.beynac-en-perigord.com). It's the ultimate for that top-of-the-world, king-of-the-castle feeling. During the Hundred Years' War (see sidebar on page 220), the castle of Beynac housed the French, while the British set up camp across the river at Castelnaud. This sparsely furnished

castle is best for its valley views, but it still manages to evoke a memorable medieval feel. (These castles never had much furniture in any case.) When buying your ticket, notice the list showing the barons of Beynac *(Beynac et Ses Barons)*—Richard the Lionheart *(Coeur de Lion)* spent 10 years here.

You're free to wander on your own, and don't miss the nearby viewpoint (described next). As you tour the castle, swords, spears, and crossbows keep you honest, and the two stone WCs keep kids entertained. I like the soldiers' party room best—park your sword (in the slots at the end of the table) and hang your crossbow (on the hooks above), *s'il vous plaît*. Authentic-looking wooden stockades were installed for the 1998 filming of the movie *The Messenger: The Story of Joan of Arc*. Circling up through the castle, find your way to the highest crenellated terraces for smashing views. Just down the river, mighty Castelnaud—which seems so imposing from up close—looks like a child's playset.

Walks and Viewpoints: A too-busy road separates Beynac

from its river, making walks **along the river** unappealing in the village center. Traffic-free lanes climb steeply uphill from the river to the château—the farther you get from the road, the more medieval the village feels. A riverfront trail begins across from Hôtel Bonnet at the eastern end of town and follows the river toward Castelnaud, with great views back toward Beynac and—for able route-finders—a level one-hour hike to the village of Castelnaud. Make time to walk at least a few hundred yards along this trail to enjoy the view to Beynac.

One of the Dordogne's most commanding views lies a short walk from the castle at the **top of the village** (easy parking). Step just outside the village (on the way between the castle and the upper parking lot) and take the enclosed lane to the right of the little cemetery. Stroll uphill until the view opens up. Castelnaud's castle hangs on the hill in the distance straight ahead. Château de Fayrac (owned by a Texan) is just right of the rail bridge; it was originally constructed by the lords of Castelnaud to keep a closer eye on the castle of Beynac. The Château de Marqueyssac, on a hill to the left, was built by the barons of Beynac to keep a closer eye on the boys at Castelnaud—touché. More than a thousand such castles were erected in the Dordogne alone during the Hundred Years' War. That's right: 1,000 castles in this area alone.

Boat Trips: Boats leave from Beynac's riverside parking lot for relaxing, 50-minute river cruises to Château de Fayrac and back (€8, nearly hourly, departures Easter-Oct daily 10:00-12:30 & 14:00-18:00, more frequent July-Aug, tel. 05 53 28 51 15).

Sleeping in Beynac: $ Hôtel Pontet** is a good budget option in the village, with 10 modern, clean, but *très* gray rooms (air-con, no elevator, Wi-Fi best in lobby, 100 yards from the river on the main street; when reception is closed—11:00-14:00 and after 19:00—check in at the Hostellerie Maleville restaurant on the river, tel. 05 53 29 50 06, www.hostellerie-maleville.com, hostellerie.maleville@orange.fr).

$ Le Petit Versailles does its name justice, with five immaculate rooms that Louis would have appreciated. The place has a quiet terrace and garden, and—best of all—the welcoming Fleurys, Jean-Claude and Françoise (three rooms have fine views, all have big beds, includes large English breakfast, cash only, no smoking anywhere, laundry facilities, Route du Château, mobile 06 71 88 59 72, www.lepetitversailles.fr, info@lepetitversailles.fr). With the river on your right, take the small road—wedged between the hill and Hôtel Bonnet—for a half-mile, turn right when you see the *Résidence de Versailles* sign and continue 100 yards, then take a right down a steep driveway.

Eating in Beynac: Beynac has a few worthwhile places to eat and a bakery with handy picnic-ready lunch items (across from the

Foie Gras and Force-Feeding the Geese and Ducks

Force-feeding geese and ducks has the result of quickly fattening their livers, the principal ingredient of the Dordogne specialty foie gras. Among animal-rights activists, the practice is as controversial as bullfighting (and their case is well-documented). But talking to local farmers, it's fascinating to hear the other side of the story. While awful conditions certainly exist in some places, here in the Dordogne, farmers pride themselves on treating their animals in what they consider a humane manner. Here's their take:

French enthusiasts of *le gavage* (as the force-feeding process is called) say the animals are calm, in no pain, and are designed to take in food in this manner because of their massive gullets and expandable livers (used to store lots of fat for their long migrations). Geese and ducks do not have a gag reflex, and the linings of their throats are tough (they swallow rocks to store in their gizzards for grinding the food they eat). They can eat lots of food easily, without choking. Dordogne ducks and geese live lives at least as comfy as the chickens, cows, and pigs that many people have no problem eating, and they are slaughtered as humanely as any nonhuman can expect in this food-chain existence.

The quality of foie gras depends on a stress-free environment; the birds do best with the same human feeder and a steady flow of good corn. These mostly free-range geese and ducks live six months (most of our factory-farmed chickens in the US live less than two months, and are plumped with hormones). Their "golden weeks" are the last three or four, when they go into the pen to have their livers fattened. With two or three feedings a day, their liver grows from about a quarter-pound to nearly two

TI). Have a drink up high at the café opposite the castle entry, or down below at the **P'tit Malo** café, which hides right on the river (walk down the steps across from Hôtel du Château); stay for dinner if the spirit moves you.

$$ Taverne/Café des Remparts, Beynac's scenic eatery, faces the castle at the top of the town and serves copious salads, good omelets, and *plats.* I can't imagine leaving Beynac without relaxing at their view-perfect café for at least a drink or an ice cream (*glace à la noix*—walnut ice cream—cannot get more local). Sophie promises a free house *apéritif* with this book in 2017 and usually keeps

pounds. A goose with a fattened liver looks like he's waddling around with a full diaper under his feathers. (Signs and placards in the towns of the region show geese with this unique and, for foie-gras lovers, mouthwatering shape.) The same process is applied to ducks to get the marginally less exquisite and less expensive duck-liver foie gras.

The varieties of product you'll be tempted to buy (or order in restaurants) can be confusing. Here's a primer: first, *foie gras* means "fattened liver"; *foie gras d'oie* is from a goose, and *foie gras de canard* is from a duck (you'll also see a blend of the two). *Pâté de foie gras* is a "paste" of foie gras combined with other meats, fats, and seasonings (think of liverwurst). Most American consumers get the chance to eat foie gras only in the form of pâtés—and be careful, because *pâté* in French refers to a pork spread.

The *foie gras d'oie entier* (a solid chunk of pure goose liver) is the most expensive and prized version of canned foie gras, costing about €20 for 130 grams (about a tuna-can-size tin). The *bloc de foie gras d'oie* is made of chunks of pure goose liver that have been pressed together; it's more easily spreadable (figure €14 for 130 grams). The *medaillons de foie gras d'oie* must be at least 50 percent foie gras (the rest will be a pâté filler, about €8 for 130 grams). Stay away from *mousse,* a mixture of several things, with or without wings or liver. When choosing, read the label carefully: *éleveur en Dordogne/Périgord* means that the animal was actually raised locally; *produit en Dordogne/ Périgord/France* means it was processed here, but may have originated elsewhere. It's also trendy to label products *artisan conserveur*—"conserved artisanally"—but again, this promises only that the product was canned locally. Note: Airport security may require you to carry these in your checked baggage, not your carry-on.

After a week in the Dordogne, I leave feeling a strong need for foie gras detox.

DORDOGNE

the place open until at least 20:00—plenty late for most Americans to have dinner. Call ahead to be sure they're open (daily, closed in winter, across from castle, tel. 05 53 29 57 76).

$$$ La Petite Tonnelle, cut into the rock, has a romantic interior and a fine terrace out front. Locals love it for its tasty cuisine served at fair prices, though the service can be slow. It's a block up from Hôtel du Château (€20-42 *menus,* daily, on the road to the castle, tel. 05 53 29 95 18, www.restaurant-petite-tonnelle.fr).

BEYOND THE SCENIC LOOP
Foie Gras Farms

During the evenings, many farms in this area let you witness the force-feeding of geese for the "ultimate pleasure" of foie gras. Look for *Gavage* signs, but beware: It can be hard for the squeamish to watch (read the sidebar for a description before you visit).

Elevage du Bouyssou

This big, homey goose farm, a short drive from Sarlat, is run by a couple who enjoy their work. Denis Mazet (the latest in a long line of goose farmers here) spends five hours a day feeding his gaggle of geese. His wife, Nathalie—clearly in love with country life—speaks wonderful English and enthusiastically shows guests around their idyllic farm. Each evening, she leads a one-hour, kid-friendly tour. You'll meet the goslings, do a little unforced feeding, and hear how every part of the goose (except heads and feet) is used—even feathers (for pillows). Nathalie explains why locals see force-feeding as humane (comparable to raising any other animal for human consumption) before you step into the dark barn where about a hundred geese await another dinner. The tour finishes in the little shop. They raise and slaughter a thousand geese annually, producing about 1,500 pounds of foie gras—most of which is sold directly to visitors at good prices.

Cost and Hours: Free; tours July-Aug daily at 18:30, Sept-June Mon-Sat at 18:30; shop open 9:00-19:30, tel. 05 53 31 12 31, mobile 06 38 95 48 80, www.elevagedubouyssou.com, elevagedubouyssou@gmail.com.

Getting There: Leave Sarlat on the Cahors-bound road (D-704), go about seven kilometers, turn left at the cement plant (where you see the *Camping Aqua-Viva* sign), and follow *Bouyssou* signs until you reach the farm (the last section winds up several curves—keep going—you'll hear the geese).

Truffle Hunting (Truffe en Périgord)

Learn everything there is to know about this dirty delicacy on a two-hour tour with truffle expert Edouard and his adorable dogs (also experts in this field). In sometimes rough but understandable English, you'll hear about the different truffle varieties and techniques for hunting the "black diamond." You'll then head out in the field to accompany the hunt. Carole, Edouard's wife, cooks a divine, truffle-based, €64 four-course lunch, served with wine in their traditional home (must book ahead).

DORDOGNE

Cost and Hours: €10 for tour only, €35 for tour and "grande tasting," daily by appointment only, avoid morning tour groups in July-Aug, tel. 05 53 29 20 44, mobile 06 79 02 48 02, www.truffe-perigord.com, pechalifour@gmail.com.

Getting There: From St. Cyprien (3 kilometers away), follow signs toward *Campagne/Le Bugue,* and then *Péchalifour* and *Truffes du Périgord.*

Cro-Magnon Caves

The area around the town of Les Eyzies-de-Tayac—about a 30-minute drive from Sarlat or the Dordogne Valley—has a rich history of prehistoric cave art. The paintings you'll see in this area's caves are famous throughout the world for their remarkably modern-looking technique, beauty, and mystery. For a rundown of your cave options, see "Prehistoric Sights at a Glance" on page 472. And to fully appreciate the art you'll see, take time to read the following information, written by Gene Openshaw, on the purpose of the art and the Cro-Magnon style of painting.

CAVE ART 101

From 18,000 to 10,000 B.C., long before Stonehenge, before the pyramids, before metalworking, farming, and domesticated dogs,

back when mammoths and saber-toothed cats still roamed the earth, prehistoric people painted deep inside limestone caverns in southern France and northern Spain. These are not crude doodles with a charcoal-tipped stick. They're sophisticated, costly, and time-consuming engineering projects planned and executed by dedicated artists supported by a unified and stable culture—the Magdalenians.

The Magdalenians (c. 18,000-10,000 B.C.): These hunter-gatherers of the Upper Paleolithic period (40,000-10,000 B.C.) were driven south by the Second Ice Age. (Historians named them after the Madeleine archaeological site near Les Eyzies-de-Tayac.) The Magdalenians flourished in southern France and northern Spain for eight millennia—long enough to chronicle the evolution and extinction of several animal species. (Think: Egypt lasted a mere 3,000 years; Rome lasted 1,000; America fewer than 250 so far.)

Physically, the people were Cro-Magnons. Unlike hulking,

DORDOGNE

Cro-Magnon Caves near Sarlat-la-Canéda

To Perigueux &
St-Emilion
via A-89

D-45

D-32

2 Kilometers

2 Miles

GROTTE DE ROUFFIGNAC

St-Léon

D-706

LA ROQUE ST-CHRISTOPHE

D-710

MAISON FORTE DE REIGNAC

D-47

River

D-65

ABRI DU CAP BLANC

D-48

Les Eyzies-de-Tayac

GROTTE DE FONT-DE-GAUME

CHATEAU DE COMMARQUE

D-703

Le Bugue

Vézère

(PREHISTORY WELCOME CENTER & MUSEUM)

D-47

LA TRUFFE EN PERIGORD

D-35

D-48

LE CHEVREFEUILLE CHAMBRES

D O R D O G N E

D-703

St-Cyprien

River

Le Buisson

D-51

D-29

D-25

D-703

D-53

D-25

D-25

Dordogne

D-703

Siorac-en-Périgord

To Bergerac & St-Emilion

CHATEAU DES MILANDES

D-710

D-53

Belvès

D-53

Paris

FRANCE

100 Miles

■ Prehistoric Sites

🦆 Foie Gras Farm

▤ Scenic Loop

DORDOGNE

beetle-browed Neanderthals, Cro-Magnons were fully developed *Homo sapiens* who could blend in to our modern population. We know these people by the possessions found in their settlements: stone axes, flint arrowheads, bone needles for making clothes, musical instruments, grease lamps (without their juniper wicks), and cave paintings and sculptures. Many objects are beautifully decorated.

The Magdalenians did not live in the deep limestone caverns they painted (which are cold and difficult to access). But many did live in the shallow cliffside caves that you'll see throughout your Dordogne travels, which were continuously inhabited from prehistoric times until the Middle Ages.

The Paintings: Though there are dozens of caves painted over a span of more than 8,000 years, they're all surprisingly similar. These Stone Age hunters painted the animals they hunted—bison or bulls (especially at Lascaux and Grotte de Font-de-Gaume), horses, deer, reindeer, ibex (mountain goats), wolves, bears, and cats, plus animals that are now extinct—mammoths (the engravings at Grotte de Rouffignac), woolly rhinoceroses (at Grotte de Font-de-Gaume), and wild oxen.

Besides animals, you'll see geometric and abstract designs, such as circles, squiggles, and hash marks. There's scarcely a *Homo sapiens* in sight (except the famous "fallen hunter" at Lascaux), but there are human handprints traced on the wall by blowing paint through a hollow bone tube around the hand. The hunter-gatherers painted the animals they hunted, but none of the plants they gathered.

Style: The animals stand in profile, with unnaturally big bodies and small limbs and heads. Black, red, and yellow dominate (with some white, brown, and violet). The thick black outlines are often wavy, suggesting the animal in motion. Except for a few friezes showing a conga line of animals running across the cave wall, there is no apparent order or composition. Some paintings are simply superimposed atop others. The artists clearly had mastered the animals' anatomy, but they chose to simplify the outlines and distort the heads and limbs for effect, always painting in the distinct Magdalenian style.

Many of the cave paintings are on a Sistine Chapel-size scale. The "canvas" was huge: Lascaux's main caverns are more than a football field long; Grotte de Font-de-Gaume is 430 feet long; and Grotte de Rouffignac meanders six miles deep. The figures are monumental (one bull at Lascaux is 17 feet long). All are painted high up on walls and ceilings, like the woolly rhinoceros of Grotte de Font-de-Gaume.

Techniques: Besides painting the animals, these early artists also engraved them on the wall by laboriously scratching outlines into the rock with a flint blade, many following the rock's natural contour. A typical animal might be made using several techniques—an engraved outline that follows the natural contour, reinforced with thick outline paint, then colored in.

The paints were mixed from natural pigments dissolved in cave water and oil (animal or vegetable). At Lascaux, archaeologists have found more than 150 different minerals on hand to mix paints. Even basic black might be a mix of manganese dioxide, ground quartz, and a calcium phosphate that had to be made by heating bone to 700 degrees Fahrenheit, then grinding it.

No paintbrushes have been found, so artists probably used a sponge-like material made from animal skin and fat. They may have used moss or hair, or maybe even finger-painted with globs of pure pigment. Once they'd drawn the outlines, they filled everything in with spray paint—either spit out from the mouth or blown through tubes made of hollow bone.

Imagine the engineering problems of painting one of these caves, and you can appreciate how sophisticated these "primitive" people were. First, you'd have to haul all your materials into a cold, pitch-black, hard-to-access place. Assistants erected scaffolding to reach ceilings and high walls, ground up minerals with a mortar and pestle, mixed paints, tended the torches and oil lamps, prepared the "paintbrushes," laid out major outlines with a connect-the-dots series of points...then stepped aside for Magdalenian Michelangelos to ascend the scaffolding and create.

Dating: Determining exactly how old this art is—and whether it's authentic—is tricky. (Because much of the actual paint is mineral-based with no organic material, carbon-dating techniques are often ineffective.) As different caves feature different animals, prehistorians can deduce which caves are relatively older and younger, since climate change caused various animal species to come and go within certain regions. In several cases, experts confirmed the authenticity of a painting because the portrayals of the animals showed anatomical details not previously known—until they were discovered by modern technology. (For instance, in Grotte de Rouffignac, the mammoths are shown with a strange skin flap over their anus, which was only discovered during the 20th century on a preserved mammoth found in Siberian permafrost.) They can also estimate dates by checking the amount of calcium glaze formed over the paint, which can sometimes only be seen by infrared photography.

Why?: No one knows the purpose of the cave paintings. Interestingly, the sites the artists chose were deliberately awe-inspiring, out of the way, and special. They knew their work here would last for untold generations, as had the paintings that came before theirs. Here are some theories of what this first human art might mean.

DORDOGNE

It's no mystery that hunters would paint animals, the source of their existence. The first scholar to study the caves, Abbé Henri Breuil, thought the painted animals were magic symbols made by hunters to increase the supply of game. Or perhaps hunters thought that if you could "master" an animal by painting it, you could later master it in battle. Some scholars think the paintings teach the art of hunting, but there's very little apparent hunting technique shown. Did they worship animals? The paintings definitely depict an animal-centered (rather than a human-centered) universe.

The paintings may have a religious purpose, and some of the caverns are large and special enough that rituals and ceremonies could have been held there. But the paintings show no sacrifices, rituals, or ceremonies. Scholars writing on primitive art in other parts of the world speculate that art was made by shamans in a religious or drug-induced trance, but France's paintings are very methodical.

The order of paintings on the walls seems random. Could it be that the caves are a painted collage of the history of the Magdalenians, with each successive generation adding its distinct animal or symbol to the collage, putting it in just the right spot that established their place in history?

The fact that styles and subject matter changed so little over the millennia might imply that the artists purposely chose timeless images to relate their generation with those before and after. Perhaps they simply lived in a stable culture that did not value innovation. Or were these people too primitive to invent new techniques and topics?

Maybe the paintings are simply the result of the universal human drive to create, and these caverns were Europe's first art galleries, bringing the first tourists.

Very likely there is no single meaning that applies to all the paintings in all the caves. Prehistoric art may be as varied in meaning as current art.

Picture yourself as a Magdalenian viewing these paintings: You'd be guided by someone into a cold, echoing, and otherworldly chamber. In the darkness, someone would light torches and lamps, and suddenly the animals would flicker to life, appearing to run around the cave, like a prehistoric movie. In front of you, a bull would appear, behind you a mammoth (which you'd never seen in the flesh), and overhead a symbol that might have tied the whole experience together. You'd be amazed that an artist could capture the real world and reproduce it on a wall. Whatever the purpose—religious, aesthetic, or just plain fun—there's no doubt the effect was (and is) thrilling.

Today, you can visit the caves and share a common experience with a caveman. Feel a bond with these long-gone people...or stand in awe at how different they were from us. Ultimately, the paintings are as mysterious as the human species.

PLANNING YOUR TIME

While the cave art here is amazing, it can be a headache to strategize. Delicate caves come with strict restrictions on visitors, and

many of them are in out-of-the-way locations—making it time-consuming to fit a cave visit into your vacation (allow three hours for a typical visit, including transit time). Certain caves are so restricted that getting in is nigh impossible (such as Grotte de Font-de-Gaume) and others require long visits, French-only tours, and detours to reach. But some caves are easier to plan for and well-worth a traveler's time, provided you come prepared. Determine which cave(s) best fit into your itinerary.

If seeing the very best matters, plan way ahead and try in January to reserve at the best cave: Grotte de Font-de-Gaume. If you don't score an entry here, good alternatives are Rouffignac and Cougnac (no reservations, but you can generally show up and get in without too much of a wait—call ahead to see how busy they are). Abri du Cap Blanc is bookable at the Font-de-Gaume office—but it only has carvings, not paintings. Grotte du Pech Merle is easy to book ahead and has good English descriptions but requires a considerable detour, making it a good option if you're connecting the Dordogne to Languedoc-Roussillon, Provence, or other points south.

Procrastinators who arrive in the Dordogne without any reservations can show up and take their chances. But if you're dead-set on Font-de-Gaume, you'll have to get up early and wait in line (details in listing).

HELPFUL HINTS

Drivers Fare Best: All the prehistoric caves listed here (except Grotte du Pech Merle) are within an hour of Sarlat-la-Canéda. But public transit is scarce: Without a car you'll be like a caveman without a spear (see page 430 for guided tours that connect some of these sights).

Reserve Ahead or Get Up Early: Be clear on which caves take

Prehistoric Sights at a Glance

You can reserve ahead only for Lascaux IV, Grotte du Pech Merle, Abri du Cap Blanc, and possibly Font-de-Gaume. For the other caves, it's first-come, first-served.

Prehistory Welcome Center at Les Eyzies Free, good intro to region's important prehistoric sites. **Hours:** May-Sept daily 9:30-18:30; Oct-April Sun-Fri 9:30-17:30, closed Sat. **Reservations:** Not necessary. Allow about 30 minutes to visit. See page 474.

▲National Museum of Prehistory at Les Eyzies More than 18,000 well-displayed artifacts—good preparation for your cave visit. **Hours:** July-Aug daily 9:30-18:30; June and Sept Wed-Mon 9:30-18:00, closed Tue; Oct-May Wed-Mon 9:30-12:30 & 14:00-17:30, closed Tue. **Reservations:** Not necessary, but reserve if you want a tour. Allow about one hour. See page 475.

▲▲▲Grotte de Font-de-Gaume Last prehistoric multicolored paintings open to public, with strict limits on the number of daily visitors. **Hours:** Mid-May-mid-Sept Sun-Fri 9:30-17:30, mid-Sept-mid-May Sun-Fri 9:30-12:30 & 14:00-17:30, closed Sat year-round. **Reservations:** Check website in Jan; must book by phone or email. *Sans* reservation, be in line by 7:30 in summer, by 8:30 in spring and fall, and in winter by 9:00. Required 45-minute tour (likely in French). See page 477.

▲Abri du Cap Blanc 14,000-year-old carvings that use natural contours of cave to add dimension, but no cave paintings. **Hours:** Mid-May-mid-Sept Sun-Fri 10:00-18:00, mid-Sept-mid-May Sun-Fri 10:00-12:30 & 14:00-18:00, closed Sat year-round, last entry at about 16:15. **Reservations:** Book a tour time by phone or email, or at the Font-de-Gaume ticket office. Required 45-minute tour (often with some English, usually 6/day); call for times. See page 478.

▲▲International Center for Cave Art at Lascaux Exact replicas of the world's most famous cave paintings, and an interac-

DORDOGNE

reservations (see the "Prehistoric Sights at a Glance" sidebar), and try to reserve your choice; other caves are first-come, first-served. That means it's essential to arrive early to secure a ticket, and then find something to do nearby if you have time to kill. How early you need to arrive varies by cave; I've suggested times for caves where you can't make a reservation. July, August, and holiday weekends are busiest, and rainy weather anytime sends sightseers scurrying for the caves. Nonholiday Saturdays are quieter—but note that Grotte de Font-de-Gau-

tive center on cave art. **Hours:** July-Aug daily 9:00-22:00, night visits possible; April-June and Sept daily 9:30-20:00; Oct-March 10:00-19:00. **Reservations:** Book in advance online, especially in high season. Required 40-minute tour; allow 3 hours total. See page 481.

▲▲**Grotte de Rouffignac** Etchings and paintings of prehistoric creatures, such as mammoths, in a large cave accessed by a little train. **Hours:** Daily July-Aug 9:00-11:30 & 14:00-18:00, April-June and Sept-Nov 10:00-11:30 & 14:00-17:00, closed Dec-March. **Reservations:** Not available or necessary, arrive by 8:30 in mid-July-Aug, otherwise 30 minutes early. Visit lasts one hour. See page 482.

▲**La Roque St-Christophe** Terraced cliff dwellings where prehistoric people lived. **Hours:** Daily April-June and Sept 10:00-18:30, July-Aug until 20:00, shorter hours off-season. **Reservations:** Not available or necessary. Allow 45 minutes to visit on your own. See page 480.

▲▲**Grottes de Cougnac** Oldest paintings (20,000-25,000 years old) open to public, showing rust-and-black ibex, mammoths, giant deer, and a few humans, on a tour more focused on cave geology than art. **Hours:** Mid-July-Aug daily 10:00-17:45; April-mid-July and Sept daily 10:00-11:30 & 14:30-17:00; Oct Mon-Sat 14:00-16:00, closed Sun; closed Nov-March. **Reservations:** Not available. Arrive 10 minutes before it opens in summer. Required 70-minute tour (with minimal English explanation). See page 484.

▲▲**Grotte du Pech Merle** Brilliant cave art of mammoths, bison, and horses, plus Cro-Magnon footprint, about an hour south of the Dordogne in the Lot River Valley. **Hours:** April-Oct daily 9:30-17:00, limited hours off-season. **Reservations:** Book a week ahead in summer (fewer visitors allowed on weekends), or arrive by 9:30. Allow two hours for a complete visit. See page 502.

DORDOGNE

me and Abri du Cap Blanc are closed that day, and from October to April, so is the Prehistory Welcome Center.

Cave Tips: Read "Cave Art 101" (page 465) to gain a better understanding of what you'll see. Dress warmly, even if it's hot outside. Tours can last up to an hour, and the caves are all a steady, chilly 55 degrees Fahrenheit, with 98 or 99 percent humidity. On a tour, lag behind the group to have the paintings to yourself for a few moments. Photos, daypacks, big purses, and strollers are not allowed. (You can take your camera— without using it—and check the rest at the site.)

Local Guide: Angelika Siméon is a passionate guide/lecturer eager to teach you about the caves and well worth spending a day with. She handles cave reservations and makes your cave visit easy and educational (book ahead; €155/half-day, €245/day, prices are for two people, tel. 05 53 35 19 30, mobile 06 24 45 96 28, angelika.simeon@wanadoo.fr).

Les Eyzies-de-Tayac

This single-street town is the touristy hub of a cluster of Cro-Magnon caves, castles, and rivers. It merits a stop for its Prehistory Welcome Center, National Museum of Prehistory, and (if you can get in) the Grotte de Font-de-Gaume cave, a 15-minute walk or two-minute drive outside of town. Les Eyzies-de-Tayac is world-famous because it's where the original Cro-Magnon man was discovered in 1870. That breakthrough set of bones was found just behind the hotel of Monsieur Magnon—Hôtel le Cro-Magnon, which is in business to this day on the western end of the main street. The name "Cro-Magnon" translates as "Mr. Magnon's Hole."

Orientation: Les Eyzies-de-Tayac's **TI** has free Wi-Fi (open July-Aug daily 9:30-18:30; May-June and Sept Mon-Sat 9:30-12:30 & 14:00-18:00, Sun 9:30-12:30; Oct-April same hours except closed Sun; tel. 05 53 06 97 05, www.lascaux-dordogne.com). The train station is a level 500 yards from the town center (turn right from the station to get into town). The street that runs just below the museum is lined with handy lunch eateries.

Sights in Les Eyzies-de-Tayac

Prehistory Welcome Center
(Pôle International de la Préhistoire)

Start your prehistoric explorations at the Pôle International de la Préhistoire (PIP) as you enter town from the east (Sarlat). This glass-and-concrete facility is a helpful resource for planning a visit to the region's important prehistoric sites. The low-slung building houses timelines, slideshows, and exhibits that work together to give visitors a primer on the origins of man. Temporary exhibits are near the entrance, with permanent exhibits farther in. The English-speaking staff is happy to provide maps of the region and give suggestions on places to visit. Park here (for free), then walk out the center's back door 200 yards on a pedestrian-only lane to the National Museum of Prehistory.

Cost and Hours: Free; May-Sept daily 9:30-18:30; Oct-April Sun-Fri 9:30-17:30, closed Sat; free parking across the street, located east of downtown Les Eyzies-de-Tayac at 30 Rue du Moulin—watch for tall silver *PIP* sign, tel. 05 53 06 06 97, www.pole-prehistoire.com.

▲National Museum of Prehistory (Musée National de Préhistoire)

This well-presented, modern museum houses more than 18,000 bones, stones, and crude little doodads that were uncovered locally.

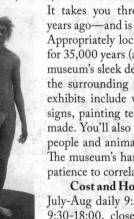

It takes you through prehistory—starting 400,000 years ago—and is good preparation for your cave visits. Appropriately located on a cliff inhabited by humans for 35,000 years (above Les Eyzies-de-Tayac's TI), the museum's sleek design is intended to help it blend into the surrounding rock. Inside, the many worthwhile exhibits include videos demonstrating scratched designs, painting techniques, and how spearheads were made. You'll also see full-size models of Cro-Magnon people and animals that stare at racks of arrowheads. The museum's handheld English explanations require patience to correlate to the exhibits.

Cost and Hours: €6, €8 with temporary exhibits; July-Aug daily 9:30-18:30; June and Sept Wed-Mon 9:30-18:00, closed Tue; Oct-May Wed-Mon 9:30-12:30 & 14:00-17:30, closed Tue; last entry 45 minutes before closing, tel. 05 53 06 45 65, www.musee-prehistoire-eyzies.fr.

Information: For context, read "Cave Art 101," on page 465, before you go.

Tours: To get the most out of your visit, consider a private or semiprivate English-language guided tour; for details, call 05 53 06 45 65 or email reservation.prehistoire@culture.gouv.fr.

Visiting the Museum: Pick up the museum layout with your ticket. Notice the timeline shown on the stone wall starting a mere 7 million years ago. Then enter, walking in the footsteps of your ancestors, and greet the 10-year-old *Turkana Boy,* whose bone fragments were found in Kenya in 1984 by Richard Leakey and date from 1.5 million years ago.

Spiral up the stairs to the first floor, which sets the stage by describing human evolution and the fundamental importance of tools. You'll also see a life-size re-creation of *Megaloceros*—a gigantic deer (with even bigger antlers)—and a skeleton of an oversized steppe bison, both of which appear in some of the area's cave paintings.

The more engaging second floor highlights prehistoric artifacts found in France. Some of the most interesting objects you'll see are displayed in this order: a handheld arrow launcher, a 5,000-year-old flat-bottomed boat (pirogue) made from oak, prehistoric fire pits, amazing cavewoman jewelry (including a necklace labeled *La Parure de St-Germain-la-Rivière*, made of 70 stag teeth—pretty impressive, given that stags only have two teeth each), engravings on stone (find the unflattering yet impressively realistic female figure), a handheld lamp used to light cave interiors *(lampe façonnée)*, and beautiful rock sculptures of horses (much like the sculptures at the cave of Abri du Cap Blanc).

Your visit ends on the cliff edge, with a Fred Flintstone-style photo op on a stone ledge (through the short tunnel) that some of our ancient ancestors once called home.

Sleeping near Les Eyzies-de-Tayac

$ Le Chèvrefeuille, halfway between Les Eyzies-de-Tayac and St-Cyprien, is a family-friendly place offering modern comfort in a farm setting. Ian and Sara Fisk moved to France from England to raise their children. Expert cook Ian prepares scrumptious dinners several nights a week in July and August and offers cooking classes with market visits. Five classy-rustic guest rooms and suites in various configurations handle singles to family groups; common areas include a lounge and kitchen area (family rooms, includes breakfast, pay laundry facilities, cash only, swimming pool and play areas, closed mid-Oct-April, tel. 05 53 59 47 97, www.lechevrefeuille. com, info@lechevrefeuille.com). From near Les Eyzies, head south on D-48 about six kilometers, turn right into the small hamlet of Pechboutier, and look for their sign.

Caves and Other Sights near Les Eyzies-de-Tayac

For convenience, I've arranged these geographically, and included sights that can be handy if you have time to kill while awaiting your cave appointment: the ruined-but-rebuilding Château de Commarque, the stately-for-a-cave Maison Forte de Reignac, and the evocative troglodyte terraces of La Roque St-Christophe. Most of the caves and other sights listed here are within a 20-minute drive of Les Eyzies. Two caves are easier to visit from other bases: the Grottes de Cougnac is south of the river, and Grotte du Pech Merle—listed on page 502—is an hour and a half south, near the Lot River Valley.

JUST EAST OF LES EYZIES-DE-TAYAC

The Grotte de Font-de-Gaume and Abri du Cap Blanc are barely outside of Les Eyzies, and managed by the same office; you can book tickets for either one through the Font-de-Gaume.

▲▲▲Grotte de Font-de-Gaume

Even if you're not a connoisseur of Cro-Magnon art, you'll dig this cave—the last one in France with prehistoric multicolored (poly-chrome) paintings still open to the public. (Lascaux—45 minutes down the road—has replica caves; the other cave paintings open to the public are monochrome.) This cave, made millions of years ago—not by a river, but by the geological activity that created the Pyrenees Mountains—is entirely natural. It contains 15,000-year-old paintings of 230 animals, 82 of which are bison.

On a carefully guided and controlled 100-yard walk, you'll see about 20 red-and-black bison—often in elegant motion—painted with a moving sensitivity. When two animals face each other, one is black, and the other is red. Your guide, with a laser pointer and great reverence, will trace the faded outline of the bison and explain how, 15 millennia in the past, cave dwellers used local minerals and the rock's natural contours to give the paintings dimension. Some locals knew about the cave long ago, when there was little interest in prehistory, but the paintings were officially discovered in 1901 by the village schoolteacher.

Warning: Access to Font-de-Gaume is extremely restricted. The number of available tickets meets only a fraction of the demand. About a third of the slots can be booked ahead by phone or by email (best done in early January). Another option is to get up at the crack of dawn, stand in line, and cross your fingers. Without a ticket, I'd skip this place unless it's off-season. Drivers who can't get a ticket here should try the other interesting caves I recommend. Note that Abri du Cap Blanc can be booked at this same office, and Rouffignac is a safe backup (you're already partway there).

Cost and Hours: €7.50, 17 and under free, includes required 45-minute tour; open mid-May-mid-Sept Sun-Fri 9:30-17:30, mid-Sept-mid-May Sun-Fri 9:30-12:30 & 14:00-17:30, closed Sat year-round; last tour departs 1.5 hours before closing, no photography or large bags, tel. 05 53 06 86 00, www.eyzies.monuments-nationaux.fr, fontdegaume@monuments-nationaux.fr—don't expect a fast reply. Those planning to also visit Abri du Cap Blanc (described next) can reserve and buy tickets here.

Getting a Ticket: To preserve the precious and fragile art, tours are limited to 13 people, and the number of daily visitors allowed is strictly regulated (78/day in 2016). Two tours a day (that's 26 tickets) can be reserved in advance by email or phone; in 2016, these went on sale for the entire year on January 2, and many were sold out by April. Tickets for the remaining four tours are doled out in person each morning starting at 9:30. In summer, plan to be in line by 7:30, in spring and fall no later than 8:30, and in the winter you should be OK if you arrive by 9:00. There are 52 numbered seats outside the entrance, so you'll know where you are in line. (Each person can buy only one ticket, so you can't send one member of your party ahead for the whole group.) You can drop by the sight at any time during opening hours to get the latest on how early you need to show up to get a ticket. You must check in 30 minutes before your tour, or you'll lose your place to sightseeing vultures waiting to snatch up the spots of late arrivals.

Tours: English tours are available but limited; expect to visit with a French guide. Depending on the guide, the actual tour can be either illuminating and enthusiastic, or little more than pointing out legs, eyes, heads, and bellies of the bison. Don't fret if you're not on an English tour—most important is experiencing the art itself. You can buy an informative book afterward.

Getting There: The cave is at the corner of D-47 and D-48, about a two-minute drive (or a 15-minute walk) east of Les Eyzies-de-Tayac (toward Sarlat). There's easy on-site parking. After checking in at the ticket house, walk 400 yards on an uphill path to the cave entrance (where there's a free, safe bag check and a WC).

▲Abri du Cap Blanc

In this prehistoric cave (a 10-minute drive from Grotte de Font-de-Gaume), early artists used the rock's natural contours to add dimension to their sculpture. Your guide spends the tour in a single stone room explaining the 14,000-year-old carvings. The small museum helps prepare you for your visit, and the useful English handout describes what the French-speaking guide is talking about (some guides add English commentary). Look for places where the artists smoothed or roughened the surfaces to add depth. Keep in mind that you'll be seeing carvings, not cave paintings. Impressive as these carvings are, their subtle majesty is lost on some.

Cost and Hours: €7.50, 17 and under free; includes required 45-minute tour, 6 tours/day (35 people each), call for tour times and to reserve. The cave is open mid-May to mid-Sept Sun-Fri 10:00-18:00, mid-Sept-mid-May Sun-Fri 10:00-12:30 & 14:00-18:00, closed Sat year-round, last entry at about 16:15, no photos, tel. 05 53 59 60 30.

Getting a Ticket: Book by phone, by email, or in person through the Font-de-Gaume—see contact information above.

Getting There: Abri du Cap Blanc is well-signed and is located about seven kilometers after Grotte de Font-de-Gaume on the road to Sarlat. From the parking lot, walk 200 yards down to the entry. Views of the Château de Commarque (described next) are terrific as you arrive.

DORDOGNE

▲Château de Commarque

This mystical medieval castle ruin is ripe for hikers wanting to get away from it all. Owner Hubert de Commarque acquired his family's ancestral castle in 1968 and has been digging it out of the forest ever since. (The Commarque clan has the world's only family crest that features the Ark of the Covenant—people call Hubert "Indiana Jones.") While not as striking as other castles in the region, this Back Door alternative offers fewer crowds and a chance to explore a ruined castle that's coming back to life before your eyes. Note that it requires a long hike to visit.

Cost and Hours: €8, daily May-Sept 10:00-19:00, July-Aug until 20:00, April and Oct 11:00-18:00, closed Nov-March, last entry one hour before closing, WCs at parking lot, off D-47 and D-6 between Sarlat and Les Eyzies-de-Tayac—see map on page 466, www.commarque.com.

Getting There: From Sarlat, follow signs to *Les Eyzies*, then follow D-6 to Marquay. As you pass through Marquay, keep right, following *Commarque* signs, then go about two kilometers and turn right. Hearty hikers can walk from Abri du Cap Blanc (see page 478) to the castle in 25 minutes (ask for trail conditions at the site). Signs also direct drivers from here.

Visiting the Castle: From the remote and secluded parking lot, it's a 20-minute walk down through a forest of chestnut trees to a clearing, where the mostly ruined castle appears...like a mirage. Borrow the English binder, and you're free to scour the complex. Near the entrance, peek into the chapel for photos of the overgrown hillside just 50 years ago. Then hike up to the 12th-century keep, which is a work in progress; areas that are completed feature modest exhibits, and the top of the tallest tower provides panoramic views.

Walking out into the field and looking back, you can see that Château de Commarque sits on layers of history: in the river-gouged lower level, troglodyte dwellings (and some 15,000-year-old cave art, not open to the public); just above, fortified early-medieval settlements, where ninth-century residents holed up from Viking attacks; and at the top, a 12th-century castle that is being resurrected in the 21st century.

NORTHEAST OF LES EYZIES-DE-TAYAC

I've listed the following stops—an elegant manor burrowed into the side of a cliff, a medieval cave dwelling, and one of the region's most famous stops for cave art—in the order you reach them traveling northeast from Les Eyzies along the Vézère River on D-706.

DORDOGNE

Maison Forte de Reignac

For over 700 years, a powerful lord ruled from this unusual home carved from a rock face high above the Vézère River. After a short but steep hike to the entry, you'll climb through several floors of well-furnished rooms, some with lit fireplaces. Kids love this tree house of a place. Your tour concludes in a room that houses torture devices and highlights man's creative abilities to inflict unthinkable pain...and a slow death. (This section may be too gruesome for young kids.) The loaner English handout provides good context.

Cost and Hours: €8, April-June and Sept daily 10:00-19:00, July-Aug until 20:00, Oct-Nov and March until 18:00, closed Dec-Feb; just north of the village of Tursac, tel. 05 53 50 69 54, www.maison-forte-reignac.com. From Les Eyzies-de-Tayac, it's a twisty 10-minute drive up D-706 (direction: La Roque St-Christophe).

▲La Roque St-Christophe

Five fascinating terraces carved by the Vézère River have provided shelter to people here for 55,000 years. Although the terraces were

inhabited in prehistoric times, there's no prehistoric art on display—the exhibit (except for one small cave) is entirely medieval.

Cost and Hours: €8.50, daily April-June and Sept 10:00-18:30, July-Aug until 20:00, shorter hours off-season, last entry 45 minutes before closing, lots of steps; eight kilometers north of Les Eyzies-de-Tayac—soon after passing Maison Forte de Reignac—follow signs to *Montignac;* tel. 05 53 50 70 45, www.roque-st-christophe.com.

Background: The official recorded history goes back to A.D. 976, when people settled here to steer clear of the Viking raiders who'd routinely sail up the river. (Back then, in this part of Europe, the standard closing of a prayer wasn't "amen," but "and deliver us from the Norseman, amen.") A clever relay of river watchtowers kept an eye out for raiders. When they came, cave dwellers gathered their kids, hauled up their animals (see the big, re-created winch), and pulled up the ladders. Although there's absolutely nothing old here except for the gouged-out rock (with holes for beams, carved out of the soft limestone), it's easy to imagine the entire village—complete with butcher, baker, and candlestick-maker—in this family-friendly exhibit. This place is a dream for kids of any age who hold fond treehouse memories.

Visiting the Caves: It's simple to visit: There's a free parking lot across the stream, with picnic tables, a WC, and, adjacent to the babbling brook, a pondside café (selling good salads, sandwiches, and drinks—the nearby pretty village of St-Léon provides more lunch choices). Climb through the one-way circuit, which is slippery when damp. Panels show the medieval buildings that once filled this space; don't miss the English translations on the back side. Allow at least 45 minutes for your visit.

▲▲International Center for Cave Art (Lascaux IV Centre International de l'Art Pariétal)

The region's—and the world's—most famous cave paintings are at Lascaux, 14 miles north of Sarlat-la-Canéda and Les Eyzies-

de-Tayac. The Lascaux caves were discovered accidentally in 1940 by four kids and their dog. From 1948 to 1963, more than a million people climbed through the prehistoric wonderland—but the visitors tracked in fungus on their shoes and changed the temperature and humidity with their heavy breathing. In just 15 years, the precious art deteriorated more than during the previous 15,000 years, and the caves were closed.

In 1983, a copy of the cave—accurate to within one centimeter, reproducing the best 40-yard-long stretch, and showing 90 percent of the paintings found in Lascaux—was opened next to the original. Lascaux II—a few hundred yards up the road from the original—can be visited only by small groups. Another replica, Lascaux IV (reproducing 100 percent of the original cave) will open in 2017. Guides assure visitors that the original is every bit as crisp and has just as much contrast as the facsimile you'll see.

The replica cave is a constant 56 degrees year-round, so dress warmly. Pleasant Montignac is worth a wander if you have time to kill.

Cost and Hours: €16, includes required 40-minute tour; July-Aug daily 9:00-22:00, night visits possible; April-June and Sept daily 9:30-20:00; Oct-March 10:00-19:00. Last ticket sold two hours before closing time. Plan to spend three hours here. Tel. 05 53 05 65 60.

Getting Tickets: As this is the first year for Lascaux IV, reservations are strongly suggested in high season. Book online in advance at www.lascaux.fr. Tickets are also sold at the sight itself.

Visiting Lascaux: The International Center for Cave Art is divided into several sections, the most important being the impressive replica cave. Here the reindeer, horses, and bulls of Lascaux I

DORDOGNE

have been painstakingly reproduced by talented artists, using the same dyes, tools, and techniques their predecessors used 15,000 years ago. Seeing the real thing at one of the other caves is thrilling, but coming to Lascaux and taking one of the scheduled tours is a great introduction to the region's cave art. Although it feels a bit rushed—32 people per tour are hustled through the cave reproduction—the paintings are astonishing, and the experience is mystifying. (Forget that these are copies and enjoy being swept away by the prehistoric majesty of it all.)

The center's other sections help visitors understand (through an interactive display and a 3-D film) the role Lascaux played in prehistory, current scientific techniques and research, and the link from cave art to modern art.

Sleeping near Lascaux: $$ Château de la Fleunie* allows you to bed down in a medieval castle at peasant prices (well, almost). Built between the 12th and 16th centuries, this castle shares its land with pastures and mountain goats, a big pool (unheated), worn tennis courts, and play toys. Stay-awhile terraces overlook the scene and its riddled-with-character $$$$ restaurant (€30-70 *menus*). Rooms are located in three buildings: the main château, an attached wing, and the modern pavilion. The château's rooms are old-world-worn with musty and dated bathrooms (many big rooms for families), while the pavilion offers contemporary rooms with private view decks (family rooms, half-pension possible-€40/person, 10-minute drive north of Montignac on D-45 road toward Aubas, near Condat-sur-Vézère, tel. 05 53 51 32 74, www.lafleunie.com, lafleunie@free.fr).

Eating near Lascaux: $$ Aux Berges de la Vézère makes a good stop for lunch or an early dinner with a beautiful view over the river (daily, closed Mon off-season, pizza and other simple dishes, near the river on Place Tourny in Montignac, tel. 05 53 50 56 31).

NORTHWEST OF LES EYZIES
▲▲Grotte de Rouffignac

Rouffignac provides a different experience from other prehistoric caves in this area. Here you'll ride a clunky little train down a giant subterranean riverbed, exploring about half a mile of this six-mile-long gallery. The cave itself was known to locals for decades, but the 15,000-year-old drawings were discovered only in 1956. With a little planning, you'll have no trouble getting a ticket. Dress warmly.

Cost and Hours: €7.50, daily July-Aug 9:00-11:30 & 14:00-18:00, April-June and Sept-Nov 10:00-11:30 & 14:00-17:00, closed Dec-March; essential videoguide-€1.50; one-hour guided tours run 2-3/hour, no reservations; tel. 05 53 05 41 71, www.grottederouffignac.fr.

Getting Tickets: It's really crowded only mid-July-Aug—

during these months the ticket office opens at 9:00 and closes when tickets are sold out for the day—usually by noon. Arrive by 8:30 in summer and 30 minutes early at other times of year, and you'll be fine. Weekends tend to be quietest, particularly Sat.

Getting There: Grotte de Rouffignac is well-signed from the route between Les Eyzies-de-Tayac and Périgueux (don't take the first turnoff, for *Rouffignac;* wait for the *Grotte de Rouffignac* sign); allow 25 minutes from Les Eyzies-de-Tayac.

Visiting the Cave: Your tour will be in French (with high-lights described in caveman English), but the videoguide explains it all. Before the tour begins, read your videoguide's background sections and the informative displays in the cave entry area. Once on the tour it's easy to follow along. Here's the gist of what they're saying on the stops of your train ride:

The cave was created by the underground river. It's entirely natural, but it was much shallower before the train-track bed was excavated. As you travel, imagine the motivation and determina-tion of the artists who crawled more than a half-mile into this dark and mysterious cave. They left behind their art...and the wonder of people who crawled in centuries later to see it all.

You'll ride about five minutes before the first stop. Along the way, you'll see crater-like burrows made by hibernating bears long before the first humans drew here. There are hundreds of them—not because there were so many bears, but because year after year, a few of them would return, preferring to make their own private place to sleep (rather than using some other bear's den). After a long winter nap, bears would have one thing on their mind: Cut those toenails. The walls are scarred with the scratching of bears in need of clippers.

Stop 1: The guide points out bear scratches on the right. On the left, images of woolly mammoths etched into the walls can be seen only when lit from the side (as your guide will demonstrate). As the rock is very soft here, these were simply gouged out by the artists' fingers.

Stop 2: Look for images of finely detailed rhinoceroses out-lined in black. Notice how the thicker coloring under their tum-mies suggests the animals' girth. The rock is harder here, so nothing is engraved. Soon after, your guide will point out graffiti littering the ceiling—made by "modern" visitors who were not aware of the prehistoric drawings around them (with dates going back to the 18th century).

Stop 3: On the left, you'll see woolly mammoths and horses engraved with tools in the harder rock. On the right is the biggest composition of the cave: a herd of 10 peaceful mammoths. A mys-terious calcite problem threatens to cover the art with ugly white splotches.

DORDOGNE

Off the Train: When you get off the train, notice how high the original floor was (today's floor was dug out in the 20th century to allow for visitors). Imagine both the prehistoric makers and viewers of this art crawling all the way back here with pretty lousy flashlight-substitutes. The artists lay on their backs while creating these 60 images (unlike at Lascaux, where they built scaffolds).

The ceiling is covered with a remarkable gathering of animals. You'll see a fine 16-foot-long horse, a group of mountain goats, and a grandpa mammoth. Art even decorates the walls far down the big, scary hole. When the group chuckles, it's because the guide is explaining how the mammoth with the fine detail (showing a flap of skin over its anus) helped authenticate the drawings: These couldn't be fakes, because no one knew about this anatomical detail until the preserved remains of an actual mammoth were found in Siberian permafrost in modern times. (The discovery explained the painted skin flap, which had long puzzled French prehistorians.)

SOUTH OF THE RIVER

Of the caves listed in this section, this is the farthest from Les Eyzies-de-Tayac (about 45 minutes); it's easier to visit from Sarlat or one of the river towns (about 30 minutes from either) and is roughly on the way between the Dordogne Valley and the A-20 autoroute.

▲▲Grottes de Cougnac

Located 23 kilometers south of Sarlat-la-Canéda and three well-signed kilometers north of Gourdon on D-704, this cave holds fascinating rock formations and the oldest (20,000-25,000-year-old) paintings open to the public. Family-run and less touristy than other sites, it provides a more intimate look at cave art, as guides take more time to explain the caves and paintings (your guide should give some explanations in English—ask if he or she doesn't). The art is just one small part of the full tour, which focuses heavily on the cave's geology and unique formations—you'll see spaghetti-style stalactites, curtain stalactites, and much more.

Cost and Hours: €8, includes required 70-minute tour; these hours correspond to first/last tour times: mid-July-Aug daily 10:00-17:45; April-mid-July and Sept daily 10:00-11:30 & 14:30-17:00; Oct Mon-Sat 14:00-16:00, closed Sun; closed Nov-March; free WCs, beverages sold on-site. Tel. 05 65 41 47 54, www.grottesdecougnac.com.

Getting Tickets: Because access is first-come, first-served (and groups are limited to 25), plan your visit carefully. There are no online reservations. You can call right at 10:00 or 14:30 (when the ticket office opens) to check on availability, or just show up and hope for the best. During busy times (in summer and in bad weather), they're most crowded 11:00-12:00 and 15:00-17:00; try to arrive first thing (ideally 10 minutes before opening). At quieter times, you can usually stop by before 11:00 and get in. Outside of July and August, be careful not to arrive too close to the last tour before lunch (11:30)—if that tour is full, you'll have to wait for the 14:30 departure.

Visiting the Cave: The 70-minute tour, likely in French, begins in a cave below the entrance, where the guide explains the geological formations (you'll learn that it takes 70 years for water to make it from the earth's surface into the cave). From this first cave, you'll return to the fresh air and walk eight minutes to a second cave. Inside, you'll twist and twist through forests of stalagmites and stalactites before reaching the grand finale: the paintings you came to see. They are worth the wait. Vivid depictions (about 10) of ibex, mammoths, and giant deer *(Megaloceros),* as well as a few nifty representations of humans, are outlined in rust or black. The rendering of the giant deer's antlers is exquisite, and many paintings use the cave's form to add depth and movement. The art is subtle—small sketches here and there, rather than the grand canvases of some of the more famous caves—but powerful. English-only tours may be possible in peak season, and you can buy a €5 English booklet about the site.

Oradour-sur-Glane

Lost in lush countryside, two hours north of Sarlat-la-Canéda, Oradour-sur-Glane is a powerful experience—worth ▲▲▲.

French children know this town well, as most come here on school trips. **Village des Martyrs,** as it is known, was machine-gunned and burned on June 10, 1944, by Nazi troops. With cool attention to detail, the Nazis methodically rounded up the entire population of 642 townspeople, of whom about 200 were children. The women and children were herded into the town church, where they were tear-gassed and machine-gunned as they tried to escape the burning chapel. Oradour's men were tortured and executed. The town was then set on fire, its victims left under a blanket of ashes.

The reason for the mass killings remains unclear today. Some say the Nazis wanted revenge for the kidnapping of one of their officers, but others believe the Nazis were simply terrorizing the populace in the wake of D-Day. Today, the ghost town, left untouched for more than 70 years (by order of President Charles de Gaulle), greets every pilgrim who enters with only one English word: Remember.

ORIENTATION TO ORADOUR-SUR-GLANE

Cost and Hours: Entering the village is free, but the museum costs €8 (audioguide-€2). Both are open daily mid-May-mid-Sept 9:00-19:00, off-season until 17:00 or 18:00, last visit one hour before closing, tel. 05 55 43 04 30, www.oradour.org. Allow two hours for your visit.

Getting There: For **drivers** coming from the south, Oradour-sur-Glane is well-signed off the (mostly free) A-20. Those driving from the north should take A-10 to Poitiers, then follow signs toward *Limoges* and turn south at Bellac. **Bus** #12 links Oradour-sur-Glane with the train station in Limoges (3/day, 40 minutes, consider taking the bus one way to Oradour and taxi the other; Limoges TI tel. 05 55 34 46 87). Those without a car should consider hiring a **taxi;** Christoph Kusters can pick you up in Limoges and take you to Oradour and other sights on the way to your Dordogne hotel (reverse this plan if leaving the Dordogne; see listing under "Getting Around the Dordogne" on page 428).

VISITING ORADOUR-SUR-GLANE

Follow *Village Martyrs* signs to the parking lot and enter at the rust-colored **underground museum** (Centre de la Mémoire). The pricey-for-what-it-offers museum gives a standard timeline of the rise of Hitler and WWII events, shows haunting footage of everyday life in Oradour before the attack, and offers a day-by-day account of the town's destruction. While thorough explanations are posted, and the 13-minute subtitled movie adds drama, the museum as a whole is skippable for some. At the bookshop, consider picking up a €3 English map to better navigate the site (which has almost no posted information).

From the museum's back door, you pop out at the edge of the ruined village itself. It's shocking just how big and how ruined it is—a harrowing embodiment of the brutality and pointlessness of war.

Join other hushed visitors to walk the length of Oradour's **main street,** past gutted, charred buildings and along lonely streetcar tracks. *Lieu de Supplice* signs show where the townsmen were tormented and murdered. The plaques on the buildings provide the names and occupations of the people who lived there (*laine* means wool, *sabotier* is a maker of wooden shoes, *couturier* is a tailor, *quincaillerie* is a hardware store, *cordonnier* is shoe repair, *menuisier* is a carpenter, and *tissus* are fabrics). You'll pass several cafés and butcher shops and a hôtel-restaurant. This village was not so different from many you have seen on your trip.

At the end of main street, visit the modest **church,** with its bullet-pocked altar. Then double back through the upper part of the village, bearing right at the long, straight street to the **cemetery.** The names of all who died in the massacre on that June day are etched into the rear wall of the cemetery, around an austere pillar. In front of the pillar, glass cases display ashes of some of the victims. Leaving the cemetery, jog right and cut through the hedges to find the entrance to the easy-to-miss, bunker-like **underground memorial,** where you'll see displays of people's possessions found after the attack: eyeglasses, children's toys, sewing machines, cutlery, pocket watches, and so on.

Nearby: The adorable village of **Mortemart** lies 10 minutes south of Bellac with a good café (closed Mon) wedged between its ancient market hall and low-slung château (a block off the main road, to the right; wander behind for a sweet scene).

St-Emilion

Two hours due west of Sarlat-la-Canéda and just 40 minutes from Bordeaux, pretty St-Emilion is carved like an amphitheater into

the bowl of a limestone hill. Its tidy streets connect a few inviting squares with heavy cobbles and scads of well-stocked wine shops. There's little to do in this well-heeled town other than enjoy the setting and sample the local sauce. Sunday is market day.

They've been making wine in St-Emilion for more than 1,800 years—making it the oldest wine producer in the Bordeaux region (though it accounts for barely 5 percent of Bordeaux's famous red wine). Blending cabernet franc and merlot grapes, St-Emilion wines are also the most robust in Bordeaux. About 60 percent of the grapes you see are merlot.

The helpful **TI** is located at the top of the town on Place des Créneaux, across from the town's highest bell tower (open daily year-round, Place Pioceau, tel. 05 57 55 28 28, www.saint-emilion-tourisme.com). The TI rents bikes and has helpful English-language handouts outlining self-guided cycling routes as well as themed, well-marked walking routes through the vineyards. Ask

DORDOGNE

also about their English-language guided tours (see "Tours and Views," below).

Getting There: It's a 20-minute walk from St-Emilion's train station into town. Electric tuk-tuks run between the station and the village (April-Oct, €3/person). Taxis don't wait at the station, but you can call one from there (6 trains/day from Sarlat-la-Canéda, 2 hours; 6/day Mon-Fri from Bordeaux, 4/day Sat-Sun). You can also get off in Libourne (5 miles away), with better train service, easy car rental, taxis, but just one daily bus to St-Emilion.

Drivers will find pay parking in lots at the upper end of the town or along the wall.

Wine Tasting and Wine Shops: Next to the TI, **Maison du Vin** is a fair starting point for an introduction to wine (free, daily, tel. 05 57 55 50 55, www.maisonduvinsaintemilion.com, maisonduvin@vins-saint-emilion.com). They also offer wine-tasting classes (usually daily mid-July-Aug, Sat only April-June and Sept-Oct, register in advance).

Keepers of small shops greet visitors in flawless English, with a free tasting table, maps of the vineyards, and several open bottles. Americans may represent only about 15 percent of the visitors, but we buy 40 percent of their wine. **Cercle des Oenophiles** is an easygoing place where you can taste wines and tour nearby cellars storing more than 400,000 bottles (free, daily except closed 12:30-14:00, 12 Rue Guadet, tel. 05 57 74 45 55).

Château Visits and Excursions: The TI can send you to tastings at selected châteaux (no charge, but a tasting fee may apply). It also offers a variety of tours (some on an open-deck bus, smaller groups in electric tuk-tuks) through the vineyards—in English and French; some include a tasting at one château (€10, 50-60 minutes, usually May-mid-Sept only; verify times on TI website.

Tours and Views: You can climb the bell tower in front of the TI for a good view (ask at TI for key), but the view is best from the Tour du Roy several blocks below.

The TI offers two guided tours in St-Emilion. The interesting 45-minute underground tour makes three stops at sights that otherwise aren't open to visitors: the catacombs (sorry, no bones), monolithic church, and Trinity Chapel (English tour daily, usually at 14:00, more in French, thorough English handout given on French tours). The city walking tour takes 1.5 hours and covers aboveground sights and St-Emilion's back streets.

Quickie Vineyard Loop: This 10-kilometer loop can be done in 20 minutes by car, and in 2 hours by bike. Leave the upper end of St-Emilion on D-243E-1 and head to St-Christophe des Bardes. Pass through the village (direction: St-Genès), then follow signs to the right to *St. Laurent des Combes*. Joyride your way down through hillsides of vines, then find signs looping back to St-Emilion's lower end via D-245, turning right on D-122.

If you need a driver, local guide **Robert Faustin** drives a comfortable station wagon, speaks enough English, and arranges visits to wineries—he knows them all (tel. 05 57 25 17 59, mobile 06 77 75 36 64, www.taxi-lussac-winetour-stemilion.com, robert.faustin@wanadoo.fr).

Sleeping in St-Emilion: There are no cheap hotels in St-Emilion. *Chambres d'hôtes* hidden among the surrounding vineyards offer a better value—ask the TI for a list. Hotel prices skyrocket during the VinExpo festival at the end of June and during harvest time (late Sept).

$$$ Au Logis des Remparts*** offers top comfort, a pool, a tranquil garden with vineyards, and lots of attitude (tel. 05 57 24 70 43, www.logisdesremparts.com, contact@logisdesremparts.com).

At **$$ Logis des Cordeliers Chambres,** gentle Valérie, who speaks just enough English, rents four comfortable rooms in a restored 18th-century mansion. Three rooms offer the best view in town of the Tour du Roy (includes breakfast, 7 Rue Porte Brunet, tel. 07 82 78 01 55, http://logis-des-cordeliers.com, contact@logis-des-cordeliers.com).

$ L'Auberge de la Commanderie** has 17 modern rooms at midrange prices (air-con, elevator, free parking, closed Jan-Feb, tel. 05 57 24 70 19, www.aubergedelacommanderie.com, contact@aubergedelacommanderie.com).

Eating in St-Emilion: Skip most of the cafés lining the street by the TI and instead head to the melt-in-your-chair square, Place du Marché.

$$$ Amelia-Canta Café is *the* happening spot on this popular square, with reasonable *plats du jour,* salads, and veggie options (daily March-Nov, 2 Place de l'Eglise Monolithe, tel. 05 57 74 48 03).

$$$ L'Envers du Décor wine bar-bistro is about fun, wine, and food—in that order. Meat dishes are their forte (daily, a few doors from the TI at 11 Rue du Clocher, tel. 05 57 74 48 31).

$$$$ Logis de la Cadène has street appeal with a pleasing patio terrace, a warm interior, and very pricey fine cuisine (closed Sun-Mon, just above Amelia-Canta Café at 3 Place du Marché du Bois, tel. 05 57 24 71 40, www.logisdelacadene.fr).

At **$$ Les Cordeliers,** enjoy a few bites or a bubbly *apéritif* in the 14th-century cloister (daily May-Sept 11:00-19:00, until 20:00 on weekends and mid-July-mid-Aug, Oct-April 14:00-18:00, 2 bis Rue de la Porte Brunet, tel. 05 57 24 42 13).

DORDOGNE

The Overlooked Eastern Dordogne

This remote, less-visited section of the Dordogne (Quercy *région*) is detour-worthy for those with a full day. Its undisputed highlight is the pilgrimage town of Rocamadour, but there's much more to see. For a good introduction to this area, follow this self-guided driving tour connecting Sarlat and Rocamadour.

Eastern Dordogne Driving Tour

For the most scenic route from Sarlat to Rocamadour, drive about an hour upriver from Souillac, connecting these worthwhile stops: Martel, Carennac, Château de Castelnau-Bretenoux, Loubressac, and Autoire. Rocamadour lies a short hop south of this area, as do the Tom Sawyer-like Gouffre de Padirac caves (both described later in this chapter). Allow 45 minutes from Sarlat to Souillac, then 15 minutes to Martel, and 20 minutes to Carennac (Château de Castelnau-Bretenoux and Loubressac are within 10 minutes of Carennac; Autoire is about 10 minutes beyond Loubressac). From Carennac or Autoire, it's 25 minutes south to Rocamadour. On Mondays, these towns are very quiet, and most shops are closed.

• *From Souillac's center, take D-803 east to...*

Martel: This well-preserved medieval town of 1,500 souls and seven towers offers a good chance to stretch your legs and stock up on picnic items (market days are Wed and Sat on the atmospheric Place des Consuls). Lacking a riverfront or a hilltop setting, Martel is largely overlooked by tourists. Park in the ample lot along the main road, then walk one block behind the buildings to find the market square, with the TI in a smaller, adjoining square. Buy a copy of the TI's well-done walking-tour pamphlet (TI closed 12:30-14:00 and Sun), and enjoy the handsome pedestrian area lined with historic buildings. The walking tour starts at Martel's terrific main square (Place des Consuls)—with a medieval covered market and reasonable lunch cafés—and connects the town's seven towers and the fortress-like church of St. Maur. The town is said to be named for Charles Martel, Charlemagne's grandfather and role model, who stopped the Moors' advance into northern France in 732.

• *From Martel, continue east on D-803 toward Vayrac and Bétaille, then cross the Dordogne on D-20 and turn right to find...*

Carennac: This jumble of peaked roofs and half-timbered walls, lassoed between the river and D-20, begs to be photographed. Park along D-20 and wander the village to the river on

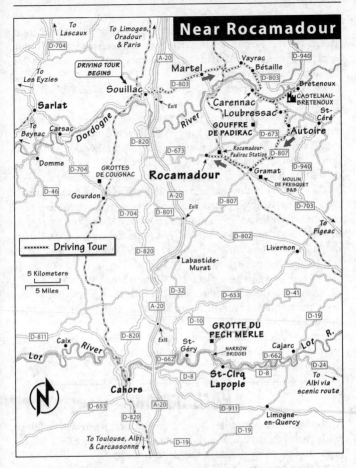

Near Rocamadour

foot. Find the fortified Prieuré St.-Pierre, explore its evocative church, and examine its exquisitely carved tympanum. It was built as an outpost of the Cluny Abbey in the 10th century and then fortified in the 1500s during the French Wars of Religion (a series of civil wars between Catholic and Protestant factions). You can pay €3 (buy token at TI) to enter the tranquil, two-story cloister; in the chapter house, you'll see a life-size statue group surrounding the body of Christ. Cross the small bridge behind the restaurant for more village views.

• *From here, head east on D-30, tracking the Dordogne River. On the left you'll pass the splendidly situated and once-powerful military castle called...*

Château de Castelnau-Bretenoux: This château has views in all directions and a few well-furnished rooms. The reddish-golden stone and massive 12th-century walls make an impression, as does

DORDOGNE

its height—almost 800 feet. Consider detouring for a closer look (watch for the turnoff on the left, over the one-lane bridge), but skip the interior. The village of Bretenoux has good markets on Tuesday and Saturday mornings.

• *From D-30, turn right on D-14 and then left on D-118. You'll come to...*

Loubressac: Mystical Loubressac hangs atop a beefy ridge, with outlandish views and a gaggle of adorable homes at its eastern end. If this is not the most beautiful village in France, I'd like to see the one that is. Park along the central green (with a small grocery store), take a loop stroll through the village, and consider a *café* or meal at the *très* traditional and reasonable **$ Hôtel Lou Cantou****. Or, if you're really on vacation, spend the night, have dinner (restaurant closed Fri and Sun nights and all day Mon), and let owner Marie-Claude take good care of you (half the rooms have valley views, breakfast extra, tel. 05 65 38 20 58, www.loucantou.com, lou_cantou@orange.fr).

• *From here it's a short hop on D-118 to lovely little...*

Autoire: The *other* most beautiful village in France, this one lies a few minutes beyond Loubressac. Visit and decide which village is fairest of them all.

• *From here you can follow signs to Gramat, then on to Rocamadour. The caves of Gouffre de Padirac (described later) are also nearby, and well-signed from this area.*

Rocamadour

An hour east of Sarlat-la-Canéda, this historic town with its dramatic rock-face setting is a ▲▲ sight after dark. Once one of Europe's top pilgrimage sites, today it feels more tacky than spiritual. Still, if you can get into the medieval mindset, its dramatic setting—combined with the memory of the countless thousands of faithful who trekked from all over Europe to worship here—overwhelms the kitschy tourism and makes it a worthwhile (though short) stop.

Those who visit only during the day might wonder why they bothered, as there's little to do here except climb the pilgrims' steps (with scads of people who aren't pilgrims) to a few churches, and then stare at the view. Travelers who arrive late and spend the night enjoy fewer crowds—and a floodlit spectacle. To scenically connect Rocamadour and Sarlat, follow the driving tour outlined in the previous section.

Orientation to Rocamadour

Rocamadour has three basic levels, connected by steps or elevators. The bottom level (La Cité Médiévale, or simply La Cité) is a single, long pedestrian street lined with shops and restaurants. The sanctuary level (Cité Religieuse)—the main attraction—is up 223 holy steps from La Cité. Its centerpiece is a church with seven chapels gathered around a small square. A switchback trail, the Way of the Cross (Chemin de la Croix), leads from the sanctuary to the top level. The top level consists of a cliff-capping château (public access to ramparts only) and—a 15-minute walk away—a small town, called L'Hospitalet. You can drive between the upper town (where you'll approach from the north) and the lower town (where you'll approach from the south), which both have free parking lots.

TOURIST INFORMATION

There are two TIs in Rocamadour: the glassy TI that most drivers come to first, in the village of **L'Hospitalet** above Rocamadour (daily July-Aug 9:30-19:00, April-June and Sept-Oct 10:00-12:30 & 14:00-18:00, closed Nov-March); and another on the level pedestrian street in **La Cité Médiévale** (same hours in summer, off-season 10:00-12:00 & 14:00-17:00, tel. 05 65 33 22 00, www.vallee-dordogne.com).

ARRIVAL IN ROCAMADOUR

By Train: Five daily trains (transfer in Brive-la-Gaillarde) leave you 2.5 miles from the village at an unstaffed station. It's about a €12 taxi ride to Rocamadour (see "Helpful Hints—Taxi," on the next page).

By Car: All of the parking lots around Rocamadour are free. I prefer the **upper lot:** From L'Hospitalet, follow *P Château* signs all the way to the western end of town until you see the *ascenseur incliné* (elevator). From here, it's easy to walk or take the elevator down to the sanctuary.

You can also park in the **lower lot,** but it takes more effort to get up to the sanctuary: Follow signs to *La Cité* and park at *Parking de la Vallée*. Hike 15 minutes up into La Cité Médiévale, or take the little tourist train—called *le petit train* (4/hour, €3.50 round-trip); then either climb the stairs or take the elevator up to the sanctuary.

HELPFUL HINTS

Elevators: This vertical town has two handy elevators. From top to bottom, the *ascenseur incliné* (€2.60 one-way, €4.20 round-trip) connects the sanctuary with the château and parking lot at the top. The *ascenseur cite/sanctuaire* (€2.10 one-way, €3.10 round-trip) links the lower town with the sanctuary. If you buy a round-trip, keep the receipt for your return ride. If no one is staffing the ticket window, press the button to call the elevator, then pay as you exit. Managed by two different companies, the elevators are within 50 yards of one another at the sanctuary level. Note that both elevators stop running at night (after 19:00 in peak season, earlier off-season).

Views After Dark: If you're staying overnight, don't miss the views of a floodlit Rocamadour from the opposite side of the valley (doable by car, on foot, or by tourist train; see next). It's best as a half-hour (round-trip) stroll. From the town's southeast end (Porte du Figuier), follow the quiet road down, cross the bridge, and head up the far side of the gorge opposite the town. Leave before it gets dark, as the floodlighting is best just after twilight. Wear light-colored or reflective clothing, or take a flashlight—it's a dark road with no shoulder. Within the town, climb the steps to just below the sanctuary, and consider a drink with a view at the Hôtel Sainte Marie.

Tourist Train: Most useful for connecting the valley parking lot to the lower town (explained earlier), the *petit train* is an option for enjoying the view after dark—with 50 other travelers, a bad sound system blaring worthless multilingual commentary, a flashing yellow light, and a view-cramping rooftop (€5, 30-minute round-trip, 2 trips/evening April-Sept, departures starting at twilight—the first one is by far the best, check at the TI or call 05 65 33 65 99). Or you can walk the same route in 30 minutes (see above), and take much better photos.

Money: There's an ATM in the upper town (next to the TI) and one in the lower town (near the elevator).

Small Grocery Store: The "Superette" on Place de l'Europe in the upper city is open daily (8:00-20:00).

Taxi: Call 06 86 18 71 55.

Sights in Rocamadour

IN THE UPPER TOWN (L'HOSPITALET)

If you're coming from Sarlat or from the north, your first view of Rocamadour is the same as the one seen by medieval pilgrims—at the top of the gorge from the hamlet of **L'Hospitalet,** named for the hospitality it gave pilgrims. Stop here for the sweeping views, then move along: A right turn takes you to the *Château* parking lot described earlier (for most, this is the best place to park for the sanctuary); a left leads to the glassy TI and—several switchbacks later—La Cité Médiévale and valley parking.

Taking in the view, imagine the impact of this sight in the 13th century, as awestruck pilgrims first gazed on the sanctuary cut from the limestone cliffs. It was through L'Hospitalet's fortified gate that medieval pilgrims gained access to the "Holy Way," the path leading from L'Hospitalet to Rocamadour.

Of the sights below, the cave is right in the town itself, and the château is a two-minute drive (or 15-minute walk from the TI).

Grotte Préhistorique des Merveilles

This cave, located next to the upper TI, has the usual geological formations and a handful of small, blurred cave paintings. It's of no interest if you have seen or will see other prehistoric caves—its sole advantages are that it requires little effort to visit (with only about 10 steps down), and the guide can answer questions in English on the 45-minute tour.

Cost and Hours: €7, daily July-Aug 9:30-19:00, April-June and Sept 10:00-12:00 & 14:00-18:00, Oct until 17:00, closed Nov-March, decent handout available, tel. 05 65 33 67 92, www.grotte-des-merveilles.com.

Château

Dating from the 14th century, the original château fortified a bluff that was an easy base for bandits to attack the wealthy church below. Today's structure is a 19th-century private house that was transformed into a reception spot for pilgrims. It's *privé* unless you are a pilgrim (in which case you can sleep here). All it offers tourists is a short rampart walk for a grand view (not worth the €2 fee; turnstile requires exact change).

The zigzag **Way of the Cross** (Chemin de la Croix—a path marked with 14 Stations of the Cross, with a chapel for each station) gives religious purpose to the 15-minute hike between the château and the sanctuary below.

DORDOGNE

Rocamadour's Religious History

Rocamadour was once one of Europe's top pilgrimage sights. Today tourists replace the pilgrims, enjoying a dramatically situated one-street town under a pretty forgettable church—all because of a crude little thousand-year-old black statue of the Virgin Mary.

Of France's roughly 200 "Black Virgins," this was perhaps the most venerated. Black Virgins date to the end of the pagan era—when black typically symbolized fertility and mother-hood. For newly converted (and still reluctant) pagans, it was easier to embrace the Virgin if she was black.

A thousand years ago, many Europeans expected the world to end, and pilgrimages became immensely popular. About that time, the first pilgrims came here—to a little cave in a cliff—to pray to a crude statue of a Black Virgin. Then, in 1166, a remarkably intact body was found beneath the thresh-old of the troglodyte chapel. People assumed this could only be a hermit (certainly a saintly hermit) who had lived in this cave. He was given the name Amadour (servant of Mary), and the place was named Rocamadour (the rock of the servant of Mary).

Suddenly, this humble site was on the map. Like Mont St-Michel, a single-street town sprouted at its base to handle the needs of its growing pilgrim hordes. During Europe's great age of pilgrimages (12th and 13th centuries), the greatest of pilgrims (St. Louis, St. Dominique, Richard the Lionheart, and so on) all trekked to this spot to pray. Rocamadour became a powerful symbol of faith and hope.

During the 14th century, up to 8,000 people lived in Ro-camadour, earning their living off the pilgrims—who arrived in numbers of up to 20,000 a day. But with the Wars of Religion and the Age of Enlightenment, pilgrimages declined...and so did Rocamadour.

During the Romantic Age of the 19th century, pilgrim-ages were again in vogue, and Rocamadour rebounded. Local bishops rebuilt the château above the sanctuary, making it a pilgrims' reception center, and connecting it to the church with the Way of the Cross. But there hasn't been a bona fide miracle here for eight centuries...and that's not good for the pilgrimage business.

Since the mid-20th century, Rocamadour has become more a tourist attraction, and today, its 650 inhabitants earn a living off its million visitors a year. The vast majority of those who climb the holy steps to the sanctuary are tourists—more interested in burning calories than incense.

BETWEEN THE UPPER AND LOWER TOWNS (LA CITE RELIGIEUSE)

▲▲Sanctuary of Our Lady of Rocamadour

These sights form the heart of your vertical sightseeing. Be sure to read the "Rocamadour's Religious History" sidebar before beginning your visit.

Cost and Hours: Free, open daily generally 8:00-19:00.

Getting There: To reach the sights from the château's parking lot in the upper town, descend the paved Way of the Cross path or take the elevator and walk downhill. If you're coming from the lower town, ride the elevator up or climb the Grand Escalier steps (like a good pilgrim), passing a plaque listing key medieval pilgrims, such as St. Bernard, St. Dominique, and St. Louis (the only French king to become a saint; he brought the Crown of Thorns to Paris and had Sainte-Chapelle constructed to house it). Either way, your destination will be signed *Sanctuaires*.

❍ Self-Guided Tour: Find the concrete bench on the small square facing the cliff. Though the buildings originated much earlier, most of what you see was rebuilt in the 19th century. Crammed onto a ledge on a cliff, the church couldn't follow the standard floor plan, so its seven chapels surround the square (called the *parvis*) rather than the church. The bishop's palace is behind you and to your left, and houses a gift shop selling various pilgrimage mementos, including modern versions of the medallions that pilgrims prized centuries ago as proof of their visit (€13 for a tiny one). The two most historic chapels are straight ahead on either side of the steps.

• *Walk up the flight of steps to the cliff, where a tomb is cut into the rock.*

This is where the miraculously preserved body of **St. Amadour** was found in 1166. Places of pilgrimage do better with multiple miracles, so, along with its Black Virgin and the miracle of St. Amadour's body (see sidebar), Rocamadour has the **Sword of Roland**. The rusty sword of Charlemagne's nephew sticks in the cliffside, above Amadour's tomb (30 feet straight up and a bit to the right, about where the church roof meets the cliff). According to medieval sources, Roland was about to die in battle, but the great warrior didn't want his sword to fall into enemy hands. He hurled it from the far south of France, and it landed here—stuck miraculously into the Rocamadour cliffs just above the Black Virgin. (The sword is clearly from the 18th century, but never mind.)

St. Michael's Chapel is built around the original cave to your left (open only to pilgrims, with little to see inside). A few steps farther along, the tiny **Chapel of St-Louis** is sculpted into the rock with a view terrace just beyond. Since 2011, this chapel has been dedicated to "Notre-Dame du Rugby," honoring a sport that's revered in southwestern France by displaying jerseys on the wall.

Backtrack to the **Chapel of Our Lady** (Chapelle Notre-Dame), the focal point for pilgrims. Step inside. Sitting above the altar is the much-venerated Black Virgin, a 12th-century statue (covered with a thin plating of blackened silver—see sidebar on page 496) that depicts Mary presenting Jesus to the world. The oldest thing in the sanctuary—from the ninth century—is a simple rusted bell hanging from the ceiling. The suspended sailboat models are a reminder that sailors relied on Mary for safe passage.

The adjacent **Church of St. Sauveur** is the sanctuary's main place of worship. You can't miss the dazzling new organ, installed in 2013. The rebuilt wooden balcony overhead was for the monks. Imagine attending a Mass here in centuries past, when pilgrims filled the church and monks lined the balconies. While Rocamadour's church seems more like a tourist attraction, it remains a sacred place of worship. A sign reminds tourists "to admire, to contemplate, to pray. You're welcome to respectfully visit." A bulletin board on the wall usually displays fliers for pilgrimages to Lourdes or Santiago de Compostela. Rocamadour has been both a key destination and staging point for pilgrims for centuries.

• *From here, you can walk down the Grand Escalier to the lower town. Or walk under the Church of St. Sauveur to find the Way of the Cross* (Chemin de la Croix) *and elevators up* (Château par ascenseur) *or down* (La Cité par ascenseur). *The passage under the church is lined with votive plaques, many of them saying* "Merci à Notre-Dame" *(thank you to the Virgin Mary) or* "Reconnaissance" *(in appreciation).*

IN THE LOWER TOWN (LA CITE MEDIEVALE)

Rocamadour's town is basically one long street traversing the cliff below the sanctuary. For eight centuries it has housed, fed, and sold souvenirs to the site's countless visitors. There's precious little here other than tacky trinket shops, but I enjoy popping into the **Galerie le Vieux Pressoir** (named for its 13th-century walnut millstone). It fills a medieval vaulted room with the fine art of a talented couple: Richard Begyn and Veronique Guinard (about 50 yards up from the elevator).

Of Rocamadour's 11 original **gates,** 7 survive (designed to control the pilgrim crowds). In the 14th century, as many as 20,000 people a day from all over Europe would converge on this spot. From the western end of town, 223 steps lead up to the church at the sanctuary level. Traditionally, pilgrims kneel on each and pray an "Ave Maria" to Our Lady.

NEAR ROCAMADOUR
▲Gouffre de Padirac

A 20-minute drive northeast of Rocamadour is the huge sinkhole of Padirac, with its underground river and miles of stalagmites and stalactites (but no cave art). Though it's an impressive cave, if you've seen caves already, it may feel slow in comparison (and there's little English). But the mechanics of the visit are easy, and there's not much to communicate anyway. Here's the drill: After paying, hike the stairs (with big views of the sinkhole—a round shaft about 100 yards wide and deep), or ride the elevator to the river level. Line up and wait for your boat. Pack into the boat with about a dozen others for the slow row past a fantasy world of hanging cave formations. Get out and hike a big circle with your group and guide, enjoying lots of caverns, underground lakes, and mighty stalagmites and stalactites. Get back on the boat and retrace your course. Two elevators zip you back to the sunlight. The visit takes 1.5 hours (crowds make it take longer in summer). Dress warmly. For a knickknack Padirac, don't miss the shop.

Cost and Hours: €12, reserve online at least 48 hours ahead, open daily mid-July-Aug 8:00-21:30, April-mid-July and Sept-early Nov until 18:00, closed mid-Nov-March, tel. 05 65 33 64 56, www.gouffre-de-padirac.com.

Sleeping in and near Rocamadour

($$$$ = Splurge, $$$ = Pricier, $$ = Moderate, $ = Budget)

Hotels are a good deal here. Those in the upper town (L'Hospitalet) have views down to Rocamadour and easier parking, but the spirit of St. Amadour is more present below, in the lower town (La Cité, which I prefer). Every hotel—including the ones I recommend—has a restaurant where they'd like you to dine.

In the Upper Town (L'Hospitalet): **$ Hôtel Belvédère**** has 17 well-maintained, modern, and appealing rooms. Seven rooms have views over Rocamadour, and four have valley views (rooms #14-18 have best views, free parking, tel. 05 65 33 63 25, www.hotel-le-belvedere.fr, lebelvedere-rocamadour@orange.fr).

In the Lower Town (La Cité): **$ Hôtel-Restaurant le Terminus des Pèlerins,**** at the western end of the pedestrian street in La Cité Médiévale, has 12 immaculate, homey rooms with wood furnishings; the best have balconies and face the valley. Reserved, motherly owner Geneviève was born in this hotel (family rooms, tel. 05 65 33 62 14, www.terminus-des-pelerins.com, contact@terminus-des-pelerins.com).

Near Rocamadour: $ Moulin de Fresquet, well worth the 15-minute drive from Rocamadour, is simply idyllic. Here gracious

Gérard and his wife, Claude, have lovingly restored an ancient mill in a lush, park-like setting lined up along a private stretch of river. The five antique-furnished rooms come with wood beams, oodles of character, lovely terraces, chaise lounges, and all the modern comforts. Book well ahead (includes big breakfast, cash only, closed Oct-March, in Gramat, tel. 05 65 38 70 60, mobile 06 08 85 09 21, www.moulindefresquet.com, info@moulindefresquet.com). Go to Gramat, then follow signs toward *Figeac*. The *chambres d'hôte* is well-signed at the east end of Gramat, at a big roundabout.

Eating in Rocamadour

Both of these are in the upper town, L'Hospitalet.

$$ Hôtel Belvédère has the best interior view from its modern dining room. Come early to get a windowside table, ideally for a meal just before sunset (daily, tel. 05 65 33 63 25; also recommended under "Sleeping in and near Rocamadour," earlier).

$ The Bar l'Esplanade hunkers cliffside below Hôtel Belvédère and owns unobstructed views from the tables in its garden café. It's open for lunch, dinner, drinks, and snacks (daily, tel. 05 65 33 18 45).

Lot River Valley

An hour and a half south of the Dordogne, the overlooked Lot River meanders through a strikingly beautiful valley under stubborn cliffs and past tempting villages. If you have a car, the fortified bridge at Cahors, the prehistoric cave paintings at Grotte du Pech Merle, and the breathtaking town of St-Cirq-Lapopie are worthwhile sights in this valley. These sights can be combined to make a terrific day for drivers willing to invest the time (doable as a long day trip from the Sarlat area). They also work well as a day trip from Rocamadour, but are best to visit when connecting the Dordogne with Albi, Puycelsi, or Carcassonne. (If you're going to or coming from the south, you can scenically connect this area with Albi via Villefranche-de-Rouergue and Cordes-sur-Ciel.)

St-Cirq-Lapopie

This spectacularly situated village, clinging to a ledge sailing above the Lot River, knows only two directions—straight up and way down. In St-Cirq-Lapopie, there's little to do but wander the rambling footpaths, inspect the flowers and stones, and thrill over the vistas. You'll find picnic perches, a gaggle of galleries and restaurants, and views from the bottom and top of the village that justify the pain. Leave

no stone unturned in your quest to find the village's best view (the overlook from the rocky monolith across from the TI makes a good start). In this town, every building seems historic. You'll lose most tourists by wandering downhill from the church.

The **TI** is located across from the recommended Auberge du Sombral (May-Sept daily 10:00-13:00 & 14:00-18:00 except July-Aug 10:00-19:00, Oct-April until 17:00 and closed Sun, tel. 05 65 31 31 31). Pick up the visitor's guide in English, with brief descriptions of 22 historic buildings, and ask for information on hikes in the area.

St-Cirq-Lapopie is slammed on weekends and in high season (mid-June–mid-Sept), but is peaceful early and after-hours in any season. Come early and spend a few hours, or arrive late and spend the night—your first views of St-Cirq-Lapopie are eye-popping enough to convince you to stay. The lanes are steep—those with imperfect knees but still wanting a lovely village retreat should sleep an hour south in the level, quiet hilltop village of Puycelsi (see page 520).

Getting There: St-Cirq-Lapopie is well-signed 40 minutes east of Cahors, 75 minutes south of Rocamadour, and just 20 minutes from the cave paintings of Grotte du Pech Merle.

Arriving by car from the west, you'll pass the town across the Lot River, then cross a narrow bridge and climb. There are five parking lots (€3-5) from well below the village to the top; unless it's high season, keep climbing and park at lot closest to the town center near the post office (in high season you'll be directed to lower lots, leaving you a good climb to the center). Pull over for photo stops as you climb.

Sleeping and Eating in St-Cirq-Lapopie: The village has all of 18 rooms, none of which are open off-season (mid-Nov–March).

$ Auberge du Sombral,** run by English-speaking Marion, is a good value in the town center below the TI. She'll welcome you with an oh-so-cozy lobby area and eight comfortable rooms in various sizes above, most with double beds (tel. 05 65 31 26 08, www.lesombral.com, aubergesombral@gmail.com). The good **$$** restaurant serves reliable lunches (every day but Tue) and dinners

(Fri-Sat only) in its lovely dining room or out front on a photogenic terrace (€17 lunch *menus*, €26-30 dinner *menus*).

As restaurants go, **$$ Lou Boulat Brasserie** works for me. It serves low-risk lighter meals (salads, crêpes, pizza, and *plats*) in a low-stress setting, with good views from the pleasant side terrace (daily for lunch and dinner June-Sept, otherwise lunch only, at the upper end of town, off the main road by the post office, tel. 05 65 30 29 04).

$$ L'Oustal is the most traditional restaurant in town, with delicious meals and a handful of cozy tables inside and out on a little terrace (beneath the towering church, tel. 05 65 31 20 17).

Picnicking: This town was made for picnics; consider picking up dinner fixings in the hamlet of La Tour de Faure. There's a small grocery store on the other side of the river just west of the bridge to St-Cirq-Lapopie, and a bakery a short way east of the bridge.

▲▲Grotte du Pech Merle

This cave, about 30 minutes east of Cahors, has prehistoric paintings of mammoths, bison, and horses—rivaling the better-known cave art at Grotte de Font-de-Gaume. With 700 visitors allowed per day, it's a snap to get a reservation compared to other caves, but that also makes it a bit less special. Still, it has brilliant cave art and interesting stalactite and stalagmite formations. I like the mud-preserved Cro-Magnon footprint. Allow a total of two hours for your visit, starting at the small museum, continuing with a 20-minute film subtitled in English, and finishing with the caves. If you can't join an English tour, ask for the English booklet.

Cost and Hours: €11, April-Oct daily 9:30-17:00, limited off-season hours, fewer visitors on weekends, tel. 05 65 31 27 05, www.pechmerle.com. Before you visit, read "Cave Art 101" on page 465.

Getting Tickets: It's smart to reserve your spot in advance (by phone or online), as private groups can fill the cave's quota. Book a week ahead in summer; if you visit without a reservation, arrive by 9:30 and line up.

▲Cahors and the Pont Valentré

Cahors is home to one of Europe's best medieval monuments, the **Pont Valentré**. This massive fortified bridge was built in 1308 to keep the English out of Cahors. It worked. Learn the story of the devil on the center tower, then cross the bridge and have a view drink at the riverside café. Consider walking up the trail across the road away from the city: A short, steep hike leads to terrific views (the rock is dangerous if the trail is wet). This trail was once part of the pilgrimage route to Santiago de Compostela in northwest Spain. Imagine that cars were allowed to cross this bridge until recently.

DORDOGNE

To find the bridge as you're approaching Cahors, follow signs to *Centre-Ville, Gare SNCF*, then *Pont Valentré*. Turn left at the river and find parking lots a few blocks down and a fine riverside promenade to the bridge.

On the city side, Cahors' small **TI** is at the foot of the bridge. Across the street, **Le Cèdre** boutique offers a good selection of Cahors wines at fair prices.

If you need an urban fix, walk for 10 minutes on the street that continues straight from the bridge (Rue de Président Wilson) and find the old city *(Vielle Ville)* after crossing Boulevard Gambetta. Cahors' thriving, pedestrian-friendly center is filled with good lunch options, cafes, cool gardens, and riverside parkways. To find this area by car, follow *Centre-Ville* and *St. Urcisse Eglise* signs, and park where you can.

LANGUEDOC-ROUSSILLON

Albi • Carcassonne • Collioure

From the 10th to the 13th century, this mighty and independent region controlled most of southern France. The ultimate in mean-spirited crusades against the Cathars (or Albigensians) began here in 1208, igniting Languedoc-Roussillon's meltdown and eventual incorporation into the state of France.

The name *languedoc* comes from the *langue* (language) that its people spoke: *Langue d'oc* ("language of Oc," *Oc* for the way they said "yes") was the dialect of southern France; *langue d'oïl* was the dialect of northern France (where *oïl* later became *oui*, or "yes"). Languedoc-Roussillon's language faded with its power.

The Moors, Charlemagne, and the Spanish have all called this area home, with the Roussillon part corresponding closely with its Catalan corner, near the border with Spain. The Spanish influence is still *muy* present, particularly in the south, where restaurants serve paella and the siesta is still respected.

While sharing many of the same attributes as Provence (climate, wind, grapes, and sea), this sunny, intoxicating, south-westernmost region of France is allocated little time by most travelers. Lacking Provence's cachet and sophistication, Languedoc-Roussillon (long-dohk roo-see-yohn) feels more real. Pay homage to Henri de Toulouse-Lautrec in Albi; spend a night in Europe's greatest fortress city, Carcassonne; scamper up to a remote Cathar castle; and sift through sand in Collioure. That wind you feel is called *la tramontane* (trah-mohn-tahn-yuh), this region's version of Provence's mistral wind.

Languedoc-Roussillon

To Clermont-Ferrand
To Cahors & Sarlat-la-Canéda
To Figeac
Rodez
La Malène
A-20
D-820
Gorges de L'Aveyron
St-Antonin
D-922
A-75
Caussade
D-964
N-88
Millau
Penne
Cordes-sur-Ciel
Bruniquel
D-600
Tarn River
Puycelsi
Castelnau
Gaillac
Albi
D-999
A-75
To Bordeaux
A-68
MIDI-PYRENEES
D-607
A-75
A-61
D-612
Toulouse
N-126
See Near Carcassonne Area detail map
D-908
Castres
D-622
Bardou
Mons
To Lourdes & Cirque de Gavarnie
Mazamet
D-907
To Arles & Nice
D-33
D-118
D-612
St-Pons
Castelnaudary
Caunes-Minervois
Minerve
Béziers
D-820
LASTOURS
D-620
Azillanet
Olonzac
Canal du Midi
A-9
D-119
A-61
Carcassonne
Canal du Midi
Narbonne
N-20
D-118
LANGUEDOC-ROUSSILLON
Mediterranean Sea
Foix
Limoux
D-117
Couiza
D-613
PEYREPERTUSE
20 Kilometers
D-14
QUERIBUS
20 Miles
Quillan
Cubières
Maury
D-117
St-Paul
D-2
Ax
N-20
Perpignan
N-116
A-9
D-914
ANDORRA
FRANCE
Collioure
Pyrenees
Céret
D-618
Banyuls
Cerbère
D-618
Portbou
Paris
N-260
FRANCE
C-38
Cadaqués
Figueres (DALI MUSEUM)
100 Miles
Ripoll
SPAIN
To Barcelona
E-15

PLANNING YOUR TIME

Albi or Puycelsi make a good day or overnight stop between the Dordogne region and Carcassonne (figure about two autoroute hours from Albi to either place; Puycelsi is 40 minutes closer to the Dordogne). Plan your arrival in popular Carcassonne carefully: Get there late in the afternoon, spend the night, and leave no later than 11:00 the next morning to miss most day-trippers. Collioure lies a few hours from Carcassonne and is your Mediterranean beach-town vacation from your vacation, where you'll want two nights and a full day. To find the Cathar castle ruins and the village of Minerve, you'll need wheels of your own and a good map. If you're driving, the most exciting Cathar castles—Peyrepertuse and Quéribus—work well as stops between Carcassonne and Collioure on a scenic drive. No matter what kind of transportation you use, Languedoc-Roussillon is a logical stop between the Dordogne and Provence—or on the way to Barcelona, which is just over the border.

GETTING AROUND LANGUEDOC-ROUSSILLON

Albi, Carcassonne, and Collioure are all accessible by train, but a car is essential for seeing the remote sights. Pick up your rental car in Albi or Carcassonne, and buy Michelin Local maps #344 and #338. Roads can be pencil-thin, and traffic slow.

For a scenic one-hour detour route connecting Albi and points north (such as the Dordogne), take D-964 from Gaillac to the villages of Castelnau-de-Montmiral, Puycelsi, and Bruniquel; from there, follow *Caussade* signs to pick up the A-20 autoroute (from here, it's 30 minutes north to Cahors, and another 30 minutes to the exit for Sarlat or Rocamadour). With a bit more time, tie the same towns in with Saint-Antonin-Noble-Val (D-5 and D-926), see "Route of the *Bastides*" on page 519). If you really want to joyride, take a half-day drive through the glorious Lot River Valley via Villefranche-de-Rouergue, Cajarc, and St-Cirq-Lapopie (see the Dordogne chapter).

LANGUEDOC-ROUSSILLON'S CUISINE SCENE

Hearty peasant cooking and full-bodied red wines are Languedoc-Roussillon's tasty trademarks. Be adventurous. Cassoulet, an old Roman concoction of goose, duck, pork, mutton, sausage, and white beans, is the main-course specialty. You'll also see *cargolade,* a satisfying stew of snail, lamb, and sausage. Local cheeses are Roquefort and Pelardon (a nutty-tasting goat cheese). Corbières, Minervois, and Côtes du Roussillon are the area's good-value red wines. The locals distill a fine brandy, Armagnac, which tastes just like cognac and costs less.

Remember, restaurants serve only during lunch (11:30-14:00) and dinner (19:00-21:00, later in bigger cities); some cafés serve food throughout the day.

Albi

Albi, an enjoyable river city of sienna-tone bricks, half-timbered buildings, and a marvelous traffic-free center, is worth a stop for two world-class sights: its towering cathedral and the Toulouse-Lautrec Museum. Lost in the Dordogne-to-Carcassonne shuffle and overshadowed by its big brother Toulouse, unpretentious yet dignified Albi rewards the stray tourist well. For most, Albi works best as a day stop, though some will be smitten by its red-brick charm and lured into spending a night.

Orientation to Albi

Albi's cathedral is home base. For our purposes, this is the city center—all sights, pedestrian streets, and hotels fan out from here and are less than a 10-minute walk away. The Tarn River hides below and behind the cathedral. The best city view is from the 22 Août 1944 bridge. Albi is dead quiet on Sundays and Monday mornings.

TOURIST INFORMATION

The main TI is on the square in front of the **cathedral,** next to the Toulouse-Lautrec Museum (mid-June-Sept Mon-Sat 9:00-18:30, Sun 9:30-17:30; Oct-mid-June Mon-Sat 9:30-12:30 & 13:30-18:00, Sun 9:30-12:30 & 13:30-17:30, shorter hours Nov-Feb; free Wi-Fi, tel. 05 63 36 36 00, www.albi-tourisme.fr).

In summer, a second TI opens in the **Grand Théâtre building** just off Place Lapérouse on Avenue du Général de Gaulle (you can't miss the wild bronze walls and windscreen; July-Aug Mon-Sat 10:30-12:30 & 13:30-17:30, closed Sept-June).

Both sell a combo-ticket that includes the Toulouse-Lautrec museum and the cathedral choir for €12 (saves €2). Ask about concerts, and pick up a map of the city center with walking tours, and the map of *La Route des Bastides Albigeoises* (hill towns near Albi). You can download a free, 19-minute English audio tour of Albi landmarks and the old city from the TI website.

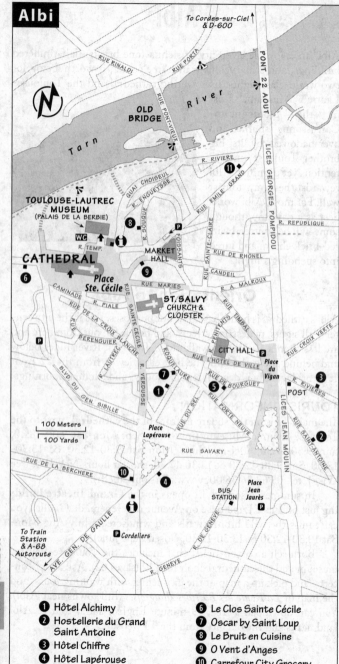

Albi

To Cordes-sur-Ciel
& D-600

RUE RINALDI

RUE PORTA

PONT 22 AOUT

Tarn River

OLD BRIDGE

RUE PONT-VIEUX

R. RIVIERE

LICES GEORGES POMPIDOU

QUAI CHOISEUL

R. ENGUEYSSE

RUE EMILE GRAND

R. REPUBLIQUE

TOULOUSE-LAUTREC MUSEUM
(PALAIS DE LA BERBIE)

RUE DE RHONEL

WC

R. TEMP.

MARKET HALL

RUE SAINTE-CLAIRE

POISSONS

CATHEDRAL

Place Ste. Cécile

RUE MARIES

RUE CANDEIL

R. A. MALROUX

CAMINADE

R. PIALE

ST. SALVY CHURCH & CLOISTER

RUE TIMBAL

RUE DE LA CROIX BLANCHE

RUE SAINTE CÉCILE

PENITENTS

RUE CROIX VERTE

RUE BERENGUIER

R. ROQUELAURE

CITY HALL

RUE DE L'HÔTEL DE VILLE

Place du Vigan

P

RUE LAUTREC

RUE VERDUSSE

RUE DE BOURGUET

R. RIVIERES

BLVD DU GEN. SIBILLE

RUE DU SEL

RUE FORTE NEUVE

POST

LICES JEAN MOULIN

RUE SAINT-ANTOINE

100 Meters

100 Yards

Place Lapérouse

RUE SAVARY

RUE DE LA BERCHERE

BUS STATION

Place Jean Jaurès

To Train Station & A-68 Autoroute

AVE. GEN. DE GAULLE

Cordeliers

R. DE GENEVE

R. GENEVE

LANGUEDOC-ROUSSILLON

1 Hôtel Alchimy
2 Hostellerie du Grand Saint Antoine
3 Hôtel Chiffre
4 Hôtel Lapérouse
5 Le Tournesol Restaurant

6 Le Clos Sainte Cécile
7 Oscar by Saint Loup
8 Le Bruit en Cuisine
9 O Vent d'Anges
10 Carrefour City Grocery
11 Launderette

ARRIVAL IN ALBI

By Train: There are two stations in Albi; you want Albi-Ville. It's a level 15-minute walk to the town center: Exit the station, take the second left onto Avenue Maréchal Joffre, and then take another left on Avenue du Général de Gaulle. Go straight across Place Lapérouse and find the traffic-free street to the left that leads into the city center. This turns into Rue Ste. Cécile, the main shopping street that takes you to my recommended hotels and the cathedral.

By Car: Follow *Centre-Ville* and *Cathédrale* signs (if you lose your way, follow the tall church tower). For a free parking lot close to the old city, follow signs for *Cathédrale* parking along Boulevard Général Sibille. There are also handy pay garages under the market hall *(Marché Couvert)* and Place du Vigan. If you find a spot on the street, note that parking meters are free 12:00-14:00 & 19:00-8:00, and all day Sunday; otherwise pay by the hour with coins.

HELPFUL HINTS

Exchange Rate: €1 = about $1.10

Country Calling Code: 33 (see page 1082 for dialing instructions)

Market Days: The beautiful Art Nouveau market hall, a block past the cathedral square, hosts a market daily except Monday (7:00-14:00). A farmers market is held Saturdays outside the market hall.

Supermarkets: Carrefour City is across from the recommended Hôtel Lapérouse (Mon-Sat 7:00-22:00, Sun 9:00-13:00, 14 Place Lapérouse). There's also a grocery at the market hall (see page 516).

Wi-Fi: The main TI has free Wi-Fi, as do many cafés.

Baggage Storage: The **Toulouse-Lautrec Museum** has large lockers accessible only during the museum's open hours.

Laundry: Do your washing at **Lavomatique,** above the river at 10 Rue Emile Grand (daily 7:00-21:00).

Taxi: Call **Albi Taxi Radio** (mobile 06 12 99 42 46).

Tourist Train: The *petit train* leaves from Place Ste. Cécile in front of the cathedral and makes a 45-minute scenic loop around Albi (€6.50).

Sights in Albi

Everything of sightseeing interest is within a few blocks of the towering cathedral. (I've included walking directions to connect some of the key sights.) Get oriented in the main square (see map; remember that you can download a free audio tour from the TI's website).

Place Ste. Cécile

Grab a bench on the far side of Place Ste. Cécile. With the church directly in front of you, the bishop's palace (along with the Toulouse-Lautrec Museum, river view, and TI) is a bit to the right. The market hall is a block behind you on your right.

Why the big church? At its peak, Albi was the administrative center for 465 churches. Back when tithes were essentially legally required taxes, everyone gave their 10 percent, or *"dime"* (pron. "deem"), to the church. The local bishop was filthy rich, and with all those *dimes,* he had money to build a dandy church. In medieval times, there was no interest in making a space so people could step back and get a perspective on such a beautiful building. A clutter of houses snuggled right up to the church's stout walls, and only in the 19th century were things cleared away. (Just in the past few years the cars were also cleared out—another triumph for pedestrians.)

Why so many bricks? Because there were no stone quarries nearby. Albi is part of a swath of red-brick towns from here to Toulouse (nicknamed "the pink city" for the way its bricks dominate that townscape). Notice on this square the buffed brick addresses next to the sluggish stucco ones. As late as the 1960s, the town's brickwork was considered low-class and was covered by stucco. Today, the stucco is being peeled away, and Albi has that brick pride back.

▲▲Ste. Cécile Cathedral (Cathédrale Ste. Cécile)

When the heretical Cathars were defeated in the 13th century, this massive cathedral was the final nail in their coffin. Big and bold, it made it clear who was in charge. The imposing exterior and the stunning interior drive home the message of the Catholic (read: "universal") Church in a way that would have stuck with any medieval worshipper. This place oozes power—get on board, or get run over.

Cost and Hours: It's free to enter the **church** (daily 9:00-18:30 except Nov-April closed 13:15-14:00). Once inside, you'll pay €5 to visit the **choir** (includes excellent audioguide describing art throughout the church, open daily from 9:30 except Sun when it closes from 10:15 until Mass is over—usually 14:00, last entry one hour before the church closes). The **treasury** (a single room of reliquaries and church art) isn't worth the entry fee or the climb.

Organ Concerts: From mid-July to mid-August, concerts are held at the cathedral at 16:00 on Wed and Sun, and sometimes at St. Salvy Church on Wed (ask TI for schedule).

❷ Self-Guided Tour: Visit the cathedral using the following commentary.

• *Begin facing the...*

Exterior: The cathedral looks less like a church and more like a fortress. That's because it was a central feature of the town's defensive walls. Notice how high the windows are (out of stone-tossing range). The simple Gothic style was typical of this region—designed to be sensitive to the anti-materialistic tastes of the local Cathars.

The top (from the gargoyles and newer, brighter bricks upward) is a fanciful, 19th-century, Romantic-era renovation. The church was originally as plain and austere as the bishop's palace (the similar, bold brick building to the right, now housing the Toulouse-Lautrec Museum). Imagine the church with a rooftop more like that of the bishop's palace.

• *Circle around the left side, and climb up to the extravagant Flamboyant Gothic...*

Entry Porch: The entry was built about two centuries after the original plain church (1494), when concerns about Cathar sensitivities were long passé. Originally colorfully painted, it provided one fancy entry.

• *Head into the cathedral's...*

Interior: The inside of the church—also far from plain—looks essentially as it did in 1500. The highlights are the vast *Last Judgment* painting (west wall, under the organ) and the ornate choir (east end).

• *Walk to the front of the altar and face the...*

Last Judgment: The oldest art in the church (1474), this is also the biggest Last Judgment painting from the Middle Ages. The dead come out of the ground, then line up (above) with a printed accounting of their good and bad deeds displayed in ledgers on their chests. Judgment, here we come. Those on the left (God's right) look confident and comfortable. Those on the right—the hedonists—look edgy. Get closer. Below, on both sides of the arch, are seven frames illustrating a wonderland of gruesome punishments sinners could suffer through while attempting to earn a second chance at salvation. Those who fail to do so end up in the black clouds of Hell (upper right). The assembly above the risen dead (on the left) shows the heavenly hierarchy: The pope and bishops sit closest to the center; then more bishops and priests—before kings—followed by monks; and then, finally, commoners like you and me.

But where's Jesus—the key figure in any Judgment Day painting? The missing arch in the middle (cut out in late-Renaissance times to open the way to a new chapel) once featured Christ overseeing the action. Go back to the last pew and find the black-and-

The Cathars

The Cathars were a heretical group of Christians who grew in numbers from the 11th through the 13th century under tolerant rule in Languedoc-Roussillon. They saw life as a battle between good (the spiritual) and bad (the material), and they considered material things evil and of the devil. Although others called them "Cathars" (from the Greek word for "pure") or "Albigensians" (for their main city, Albi), they called themselves simply "friends of God." Cathars focused on the teachings of St. John, and recognized only baptism as a sacrament. Because they believed in reincarnation, they were vegetarians.

Travelers encounter traces of the Cathars in their Languedoc sightseeing because of the Albigensian Crusades (1209-1240s). The king of France wanted to consolidate his grip on southern France. The pope needed to make a strong point that the only acceptable Christianity was Roman style. They found self-serving reasons to wage a genocidal war together against the Cathars, who never amounted to more than 10 percent of the local population and coexisted happily with their non-Cathar neighbors. After a terrible generation of torture and mass burnings, the Cathars were wiped out. The last Cathar was burned in 1321.

Today, tourists find haunting castle ruins (once Cathar strongholds) high in the Pyrenees, and eat meaty, if misnamed, *salades Cathar*.

white image on a small stand. The picture provides a good guess at how this painting would have looked—though no one knows for sure. To learn more about the *Last Judgment*, tour the choir (described below), which includes an audioguide with commentary on the painting.

The **altar** in front of the *Last Judgment* is the newest art in the church. But this is not the front of the church at all—you're facing west. Turn 180 degrees and head east, for Jerusalem (where most medieval churches point).

• *Stop first in front of the choir—a fancy, more intimate room within the finely carved stone "screen."*

The Choir: In the Middle Ages, nearly all cathedrals had ornate Gothic choir screens like this one. These highly decorated walls divided the church into a private place for clergy and a general zone for the common rabble. The screen enclosed the altar and added mystery to the Mass. In the 16th century, with the success of the Protestant movement and the Catholic Church's Counter-Reformation, choir screens were removed. (In the 20th century, the Church took things one step further, and priests actually turned and faced their parishioners.) Later, French Revolutionary atheists destroyed most of the choir screens that remained—Albi's is a rare survivor.

Pay the entry fee and pick up the audioguide, then follow the English plan as you stroll around the choir. You'll see colorful Old Testament figures along the Dark Ages exterior columns and New Testament figures in the enlightened interior. Stepping inside the choir, marvel at the fine limestone carving. Scan each of the 72 unique little angels just above the wood-paneled choir stalls. Check out the brilliant ceiling, which hasn't been touched or restored in 500 years. A bishop, impressed by the fresco technique of the Italian Renaissance, invited seven Bolognese artists to do the work. Good call.

• *Exit through the side door, next to where you paid for the choir. You'll pass a WC on your way to the...*

▲▲Toulouse-Lautrec Museum (Musée Toulouse-Lautrec)

The Palais de la Berbie (once the fortified home of Albi's archbishop) has the world's largest collection of Henri de Toulouse-Lautrec's paintings, posters, and sketches.

Cost and Hours: €9; July-Sept daily 9:00-18:00; June daily 9:00-12:00 & 14:00-18:00; April-May and Oct daily 10:00-12:00 & 14:00-18:00—but closed Tue in Oct; Nov-March closes at 17:30 and closed Tue; audioguide-€4 (for most, the printed English explanations in every room are sufficient), lockers for day packs-€1; Place Ste. Cécile, tel. 05 63 49 48 70, www.musee-toulouse-lautrec.com.

Background: Henri de Toulouse-Lautrec, born here in 1864, was crippled from youth. After he broke his right leg at age 13 and then his left leg the next year (probably due to a genetic disorder), the lower half of his body stopped growing. His father, once very engaged in parenting, lost interest in his son. Henri moved to the fringes of society, where he gained an affinity for people who didn't quite fit in. He later made his mark painting the dregs of the Parisian underclass with an intimacy only made possible by a man with his life experience.

Visiting the Museum: From the turnstile, walk down a few steps and enter the main floor collection.

The first room is filled with **portraits** of Henri de Toulouse-Lautrec painted by other artists. In the next sections we see his earliest classical paintings, horses, and his **boyhood doodles.** I especially like the dictionary he scribbled all over as a schoolkid. In the 1880s, Henri was stuck in Albi, far from any artistic action. During these years, he found inspiration in nature, in the pages of magazines, and by observing people. This was his Impressionistic stage—find *Cheval de Trait à Céleyran* (in the third section) for a good example.

Next, go down a few more steps to see some of his first portraits of family and friends.

Step into the next room for his most famous stuff: his paintings of the prostitutes and brothels of **Paris.** In 1882, Henri moved to the big city to pursue his passion. In these early Paris works, we see his trademark shocking colors; down-and-dirty street-life scenes emerge. Compare his art-school work and his street work: Henri augmented his classical training with vivid life experience. His subjects were from bars, brothels, and cabarets...Toto, we're not in Albi anymore. In these exploratory years, he dabbled in any style he encountered. The naked body emerged as one of his fascinations. Henri started making money in the 1890s by selling illustrations to magazines and newspapers. Back then, his daily happy hour included brothel visits—1892-1894 was his prostitution period. He respected the ladies, feeling both fascination and empathy toward them. The **prostitutes** accepted him the way he was and let him into their world...which he sketched brilliantly. Notice how he shows the prostitutes as real humans—they are neither glorified nor vulgarized in his works.

At the far end of this room, notice the big *Au Salon de la Rue des Moulins* (1894). There are two versions: the quick sketch, then the finished studio ver-

sion. With this piece, Toulouse-Lautrec arrived—no more sampling. The artist has established his unique style, oblivious to society's norms: colors (strong), subject matter (hidden worlds), and moralism (none). Henri's trademark use of cardboard was simply his quick, snapshot way of working: He'd capture these slice-of-life impressions on the fly on cheap, disposable material, intending to convert them to finer canvas paintings later, in his studio. But the cardboard quickies survive as Toulouse-Lautrec masterpieces.

Spiral up two flights through a room showing off a rare, 13th-century terra-cotta tile floor original to the building. You'll soon come to Toulouse-Lautrec's famous **advertising posters,** which were his bread and butter. He was an innovative advertiser, creating simple, bold, and powerful lithographic images. Look for displays of his original lithograph blocks (simply prepare the stone with a backward image, apply ink—which sticks chemically to the black points—and print posters). Four-color posters meant creating four different blocks. Many of the displayed works show different stages of the printing process—first with black ink, then the red layer, then the finished poster. The **Moulin Rouge** poster established his business reputation in Paris—strong symbols, bold and simple: just what, where, and when. Across the room, cabaret singer and club owner Aristide Bruant (*dans son cabaret*—"in his cabaret") is portrayed as bold and dashing.

Move on to a room with more advertising posters. Henri was fascinated by cancan dancers (whose legs moved with an agility he'd never experience), and he captured them expertly. Then head up a few steps to continue through several more rooms with other portraits of Parisian notables and misfits, and finally the darker works he painted before his death. The exhibit sprawls through several rooms, so make sure you see everything.

One thing you may not see (because it's often away on loan) is Toulouse-Lautrec's **cane,** which offers more insight into this tortured artistic genius. To protect him from his self-destructive lifestyle, loved ones had him locked up in a psychiatric hospital. But, with the help of this clever hollow cane, he still got his booze. Friends would drop by with hallucinogenic absinthe, his drink of choice—also popular among many other artists of the time. With these special deliveries, he'd restock his cane, which even came equipped with a fancy little glass.

In 1901, at age 37, alcoholic, paranoid, depressed, and syphilitic, Henri de Toulouse-Lautrec returned to his mother—the only woman who ever really loved him—and died in her arms. The art world didn't mourn. Obituaries, speaking for the art establishment, basically said good riddance to Toulouse-Lautrec and his ugly art. Although no one in the art world wanted Henri's pieces, his mother and his best friend—a boyhood pal and art dealer named Maurice Joyant—recognized his genius and saved his work. They first offered it to the Louvre, which refused. Finally, in 1922, the mayor of Albi accepted the collection and hung Toulouse-Lautrec's work here in what, for more than a century, had been a boring museum of archaeology.

Your visit ends with a few rooms showing off the one-time grandeur of the Palais de la Berbie and two captivating paintings by 17th-century master Georges de La Tour. And if you still have stamina left, you can climb up to the second floor, with a sprawling exhibit of modern art. You'll see works by Toulouse-Lautrec's classmates and contemporaries (including a fine Matisse).

• *Leaving the museum, curl around to the right of the hulking building to find a gorgeous garden overlooking a fine...*

▲Albi Town View

Albi was situated here because of its river access to Bordeaux (which connected the town to the global market). In medieval times, the fastest, most economical way to transport goods was down rivers like this. The lower, older bridge (Pont Vieux) was first built in 1020. Prior to its construction, the weir (look just beyond this first bridge) provided a series of stepping stones that enabled people to cross the river. The garden of the bishop's palace dates from the 17th century (when the palace at Versailles inspired the French to create fancy gardens). The palace itself grew from the 13th century until 1789, when the French Revolution ended the power of the bishops and the state confiscated the building. Since 1905, it's been a museum.

• *The last two sights are in the town center, roughly behind the cathedral.*

St. Salvy Church and Cloister (Eglise St. Salvi et Cloître)

Although this church (the oldest in town) is nothing special, the cloister creates a delightful space embracing an ancient well and modern garden. Look for the easy-to-miss entrance on main shopping street, just a block from the main square. Delicate arches surround an enclosed courtyard, providing a peaceful interlude from the shoppers that fill the pedestrian streets. Notice the church wall from the courtyard. It was the only stone building in Albi in the 11th century; the taller parts, added later, are made of brick.

This is one of many little hidden courtyards throughout town. In the rough-and-tumble Middle Ages, most buildings faced inward. If doors are open, you're welcome to pop in to courtyards.

• *Leave the cloister, go up the steps, and find a sweet square with quiet cafés.*

Market Hall (Marché Couvert)

Albi's elegant Art Nouveau market is good for picnic-gathering and people-watching—and has a grocery store in its lower level (Tue-Sun 7:00-14:00, closed Mon, 2 blocks from cathedral). On Saturdays, a farmers market sets up outside the market hall.

Sleeping in Albi

$$$ **Hôtel Alchimy****** houses six spacious designer suites and one great-deal standard room in a handsome building on a quiet square (10 Place du Palais, tel. 05 63 76 18 18, http://alchimyalbi. fr, contact@alchimyalbi.fr).

$$ **Hostellerie du Grand Saint Antoine****** is Albi's oldest hotel (established in 1784) and the most traditional place I list. Guests enter an inviting, spacious lobby that opens onto an enclosed garden. Some of the 44 rooms are Old World cozy, while others have a modern flair (private pay parking, a block above big Place

---

Sleep Code

Hotels are classified based on the average price of a standard double room without breakfast in high season.

$$$$	**Splurge:** Most rooms over €200
$$$	**Pricier:** €150-200
$$	**Moderate:** €100-150
$	**Budget:** €50-100
¢	**Backpacker:** Under €50
RS%	**Rick Steves discount**
*	**French hotel rating system** (0-5 stars)

Unless otherwise noted, credit cards are accepted, hotel staff speak basic English, and free Wi-Fi is available. Comparison-shop by checking prices at several hotels (on each hotel's own website, on a booking site, or by email). For the best deal, *book directly with the hotel.* Ask for a discount if paying in cash; if the listing includes **RS%,** request a Rick Steves discount.

---

du Vigan at 17 Rue Saint-Antoine, tel. 05 63 54 04 04, www.hotel-saint-antoine-albi.com, courriel@hotel-saint-antoine-albi.com).

$ Hôtel Chiffre*** is a safe bet, with 38 simple yet comfortable rooms (pay parking garage, traditional restaurant, near Place du Vigan at 50 Rue Séré de Rivières, tel. 05 63 48 58 48, www.hotelchiffre.com, contact@hotelchiffre.com).

$ Hôtel Lapérouse** is a work in progress, one block from the old city and a 10-minute walk to the train station. This family-run hotel offers 24 simple rooms and enthusiastic owners, Quentin and Christèle. Spring for one of the two rooms with a balcony over the big pool and quiet garden where picnics and aperitifs are encouraged (no air-con, no elevator, reception closed 12:00-15:00 and after 20:00, 21 Place Lapérouse, tel. 05 63 54 69 22, www.hotel-laperouse.com, contact@hotel-laperouse.com).

Eating in Albi

Albi is filled with reasonable restaurants that serve a rich local cuisine, including plenty of duck dishes. If you're adventurous, search out these local specialties: tripes (cow intestines), andouillette (sausages made from pig intestines), *foie de veau* (calf liver), and *tête de veau* (calf's head). Choose a restaurant or select one of the many tempting cafés on a traffic-free lane or on a quiet square (the squares behind St. Salvy's cloister and in front of the market hall are two good choices).

$ Le Tournesol is a good lunch option for vegetarians, since that's all they do. The food is delicious, the setting is bright with many windows, and the service is friendly. Try the wonderful

---

Restaurant Price Code

I've assigned each eatery a price category, based on the average cost of a typical main course. Drinks, desserts, and splurge
items (steak and seafood) can raise the price considerably.

$$$$	**Splurge:** Most main courses over €25
$$$	**Pricier:** €20-25
$$	**Moderate:** €15-20
$	**Budget:** Under €15

In France, a crêpe stand or other takeout spot is **$**; a sit-down
brasserie, café, or bistro with affordable *plats du jour* is **$$**;
a casual but more upscale restaurant is **$$$**; and a swanky
splurge is **$$$$**.

---

homemade tarts (open for lunch only, closed Sun, vegan options,
11 Rue de l'Ort en Salvy, tel. 05 63 38 38 14).

$$ Le Clos Sainte Cécile, a short block behind the cathedral,
is an old school transformed into a delightful family-run restau-
rant. Friendly waiters serve delicious dishes in their large, shady
garden—at a French pace (closed Tue-Wed, 3 Rue du Castelviel,
tel. 05 63 38 19 74).

$$$ Oscar by Saint Loup may intimidate some with its fine
stemware and chandeliers, but beyond the formal dining room
lies an inviting courtyard full of happy eaters enjoying well-priced
Mediterranean cuisine (lunch *menus* come with a *plat*, dessert, and
choice of coffee or wine, good-value dinner *menus*, closed Sun-
Mon, 8 Rue Roquelaure, tel. 05 67 67 42 96).

$$ Le Bruit en Cuisine offers refined food with a spectacular
view of the cathedral from its rooftop terrace. Service can be slow,
but the memorable sunset on the cathedral keeps diners happy
(lunch *menu* based on market of the day, evening *menu* with good
choices, reservations recommended, closed Sun-Mon, 22 Rue de la
Souque, tel. 05 63 36 70 31).

$$ O Vent d'Anges, on the market hall square, is a bustling
wine bar good for an evening aperitif or small nibbles. Meals—big
tasty salads and a delicious house burger—are served during lunch
only (Wed-Sat 17:30-2:00 plus Thu-Sat lunch in summer, 9 Place
St-Julien, tel. 05 81 02 62 33).

Albi Connections

You'll connect to just about any destination through Toulouse.

From Albi by Train to: Toulouse (11/day, 70 minutes), **Carcassonne** (12/day, 3 hours, change in Toulouse), **Sarlat-la-Canéda**
(6/day, 6 hours with 2-3 changes, some require bus from Souillac to

Sarlat), **Paris** (6/day, 7-8.5 hours, change in Toulouse; also a night train with change in Toulouse).

Near Albi

ROUTE OF THE BASTIDES

The hilly terrain north of Albi was tailor-made for medieval villages to organize around for defensive purposes. Here, along the Route of the Bastides (La Route des Bastides Albigeoises), scores of fortified villages *(bastides)* spill over hilltops, above rivers, and between wheat fields, creating a ▲ detour for drivers. These planned communities were the medieval product of community efforts organized by local religious or military leaders. Most *bastides* were built during the Hundred Years' War (see sidebar on page 220) to establish a foothold for French or English rule in this hotly contested region, and to provide stability to benefit trade. Unlike other French hill towns, *bastides* were not safe havens provided by a castle. Instead, they were a premeditated effort by a community to collectively construct houses as a planned defensive unit, *sans* castle.

Connect these *bastides* as a day trip from Albi, or as you drive between Albi and the Dordogne. I've described the top *bastides* in the order you'll reach them on these driving routes.

Day Trip from Albi: For a good loop route northwest from Albi, cross the 22 Août 1944 bridge and follow signs to *Cordes-sur-Ciel* (allow 30 minutes). The view of Cordes as you approach is memorable. From Cordes, follow signs to *Saint-Antonin-Noble-Val*, an appealing, flat "hill town" on the river, with few tourists. Then pass vertical little Penne, Bruniquel (signed from Saint-Antonin-Noble-Val), Larroque, Puycelsi (my favorite), and, finally, Castelnau-de-Montmiral (with a lovely main square), before returning to Albi. Each of these places is worth exploring if you have the time.

On the Way to the Dordogne: For a one-way scenic route north to the Dordogne that includes many of the same *bastides,* leave Albi, head toward Toulouse, and make time on the free A-68. Exit at Gaillac, go to its center, and track D-964 to Castelnau-de-Montmiral, Puycelsi, and on to Bruniquel. From here you can head directly to Caussade on D-115 and D-964, then hop on the A-20 northbound (toward *Cahors/Paris*); from here, exits for Cahors, St-Cirque-Lapopie, Rocamadour, and Sarlat-la-Canéda are all well-marked.

Cordes-sur-Ciel

It's hard to resist this brilliantly situated hill town just 15 miles north of Albi, but I would (in high season, at least). Enjoy the fantastic view on the road from Albi, and consider a detour up into town only if the coast looks clear (read: off-season). Cordes, once an important Cathar base, has slipped over the boutique-filled edge to the point where it's hard for me to find the medieval town. But it's a dramatic setting filled with steep streets, beautiful half-timbered buildings, and great views. A rubber-tired train shuttles visitors to the top from near the TI (tel. 05 63 56 00 52, www.cordessurciel.fr).

Bruniquel

This overlooked, *très* photogenic, but less-tended village will test your thighs as you climb the lanes upward to the Châteaux de Bruniquel (€3.50, March-Oct daily 10:00-18:00, July-Aug until 19:00, closed Nov-Feb). Don't miss the dramatic view up to the village from the river below as you drive along D-964.

▲Puycelsi

Forty minutes north of Albi, this town crowns a high bluff overlooking thick forests and sweeping pastures. Drive to the top, where you'll find easy parking and an unspoiled, level village with a couple of cafés, a bistro with a view, a small grocery, a bakery, a few *chambres d'hôtes*, and one sharp little hotel.

Stroll through the village, passing the Puycelsi Roc Café, and make your way through town. Appreciate the fine collection of buildings with lovingly tended flowerbeds. At the opposite side of the village, a rampart walk circles counterclockwise back to the parking lot, reminding us of the village's history as a *bastide*. The park-like ramparts come with picnic benches and grand vistas (ideal at sunset). It's a good place to listen to the birds and feel the wind.

As you wander, consider the recent history of an ancient town like this. In 1900, 2,000 people lived here with neither running water nor electricity. Then things changed. Millions of French men lost their lives in World War I; Puycelsi didn't escape this fate, as the monument (by the parking lot) attests. World War II added to the exodus and by 1968 the village was down to three families. But then running water replaced the venerable cisterns, and things started looking up. Today, there is just enough commercial activity to keep locals happy. The town has a stable population of 110, all marveling at how lucky they are to live here.

Sleeping in Puycelsi: An overnight here is my idea of vacation. Church bells keep a vigil, ringing on the hour throughout the night.

$$ L'Ancienne Auberge is *the* place to sleep, with eight surprisingly smart and comfortable rooms, some with sublime views. Owner/chef Dorothy moved here from New Jersey many moons ago and is eager to share her passion for this region (air-con in some rooms, Place de l'Eglise, tel. 05 63 33 65 90, www.ancienne-auberge.com, contact@ancienne-auberge.com). Ask about their self-catering apartments that can accommodate up to five people, and consider dinner at their view bistro Jardin de Lys (described below).

$ Delphine de Laveleye Chambres is another great choice just behind L'Ancienne Auberge. Warm Delphine and her two dogs fill a cave-like, 17th-century house with a variety of rooms, ranging from a small romantic room for two to a three-bedroom suite with a kitchen, all hovering above a small garden and pool (family rooms, cash only, tel. 05 63 33 13 65, mobile 06 72 92 69 59, www.chezdelphine.com).

Eating in Puycelsi: The **$$ Jardin de Lys** bistro-café clings to the hillside, offering breathtaking views and all-day service. Come for a drink at least, or, better, for a fine dinner based on original recipes and cooked with fresh products (daily, tel. 05 63 33 65 90). **$$ Puycelsi Roc Café**, at the parking lot, has standard café fare, a warm interior, and pleasant outdoor tables (daily for lunch and dinner, shorter hours off-season, tel. 05 63 33 13 67).

Castelnau-de-Montmiral

This overlooked village has quiet lanes leading to a perfectly preserved *bastide* square surrounded by fine arcades and filled with brick half-timbered facades. Ditch your car below and wander up to the square, where a TI, a restaurant, a café, and a small *pâtisserie* await. Have a drink or lunch on the square.

Carcassonne

Medieval Carcassonne is a 13th-century world of towers, turrets, and cobblestones. Europe's ultimate walled fortress city, it's also stuffed with tourists. At 10:00, salespeople stand at the doors of their main-street shops, a gauntlet of tacky temptations poised and ready for their daily ration of customers—consider yourself warned. But early, late, or off-season,

LANGUEDOC-ROUSSILLON

a quieter Carcassonne is an evocative playground for any medievalist. Forget midday—spend the night.

Locals like to believe that Carcassonne got its name this way: 1,200 years ago, Charlemagne and his troops besieged this fortress-town (then called La Cité) for several years. A cunning townsperson named Madame Carcas saved the town. Just as food was running out, she fed the last few bits of grain to the last pig and tossed him over the wall. Splat. Charlemagne's bored and frustrated forces, amazed that the town still had enough food to throw fat party pigs over the wall, decided they would never succeed in starving the people out. They ended the siege, and the city was saved. Madame Carcas *sonne*-d (sounded) the long-awaited victory bells, and La Cité had a new name: Carcas-sonne. It's a cute story... but historians suspect that Carcassonne is a Frenchified version of the town's original name (Carcas).

As a teenager on my first visit to Carcassonne, I wrote this in my journal: "Before me lies Carcassonne, the perfect medieval city. Like a fish that everyone thought was extinct, somehow Europe's greatest Romanesque fortress city has survived the centuries. I was supposed to be gone yesterday, but here I sit imprisoned by choice—curled in a cranny on top of the wall. The wind blows away the sounds of today, and my imagination 'medievals' me. The moat is one foot over and 100 feet down. Small plants and moss upholster my throne."

Avoid the midday mobs and let this place make you a kid on a rampart.

Orientation to Carcassonne

Contemporary Carcassonne is neatly divided into two cities: the magnificent La Cité (the fortified old city, with 200 full-time residents taking care of lots more tourists) and the lively Ville Basse (modern lower city). Two bridges, the busy Pont Neuf and the traffic-free Pont Vieux, both with great views, connect the  two parts. The train station is separated from Ville Basse by the Canal du Midi.

TOURIST INFORMATION
The main TI, in **Ville Basse,** is useful only if you're walking to La Cité (28 Rue de Verdun). A far more convenient branch is in **La Cité,** to your right as you enter the main gate (Narbonne Gate—or Porte Narbonnaise). Both TIs have similar hours (April-Oct daily

9:00-18:00, July-Aug until 19:00; Nov-March daily 9:30-12:30 & 13:30-17:30; tel. 04 68 10 24 30, www.carcassonne-tourisme.com). If you arrive by train, the most convenient TI is the small kiosk across the canal from the **train station** (generally daily April-Sept 9:30-13:00, plus July-Sept 14:00-18:30, closed Oct-May...but you never know).

At any TI, pick up a map of La Cité and the excellent (and free) *Walks* booklet that includes biking ideas. Walking tours in English depart from La Cité TI (€7, April-Oct daily at 10:30, call ahead for departure times). Pass on their City Pass unless you plan to take a guided walking tour. Ask about festivals and guided excursions to sights near Carcassonne (described later, under "Helpful Hints").

ARRIVAL IN CARCASSONNE

By Train: The train station is located in Ville Basse, a 30-minute walk from La Cité. The nearest pay baggage storage is a few blocks away (at the recommended Hôtel Astoria). You have three basic options for reaching La Cité: taxi, bus, or on foot.

Taxis charge €8-10 for the short trip to La Cité but cannot enter the city walls. Taxis wait in front of the train station, or over the canal across from Hôtel Terminus.

Two cheaper options run to La Cité from the Chénier stop (on Boulevard Omer Sarraut, at the far edge of the park a block from the station): **public bus #4** (€1, hourly Mon-Sat, none Sun) and the rubber-tired **train-bus** (€2 one-way, €3 round-trip, hourly 11:00-19:00, July-Aug daily, none Sun June and Sept-mid-Oct, none off-season). Schedules for both bus #4 and the train-bus are posted in the bus shelter.

An **airport bus** departs from in front of the station to Carcassonne's airport, scheduled to coincide with departing flights (€5); most departures also stop at La Cité en route. A taxi to the airport costs around €20.

The 30-minute **walk** through Ville Basse to La Cité ends with a good uphill climb. Walk straight out of the station, cross the canal, then cross the busy ring road, and keep straight on Rue Clemenceau for about seven blocks. After Place Carnot (frequent markets), turn left on Rue de Verdun, walk three blocks, and turn right on the vast Square Gambetta. Angle across the square, turn right after Hôtel Ibis, then cross Pont Vieux (great views). Signs will guide you up Rue Trivalle and Rue Nadaud to La Cité.

By Car: Follow signs to *Centre-Ville*, then *La Cité*. You'll come to a drawbridge at the Narbonne Gate, the walled city's main entrance, where day-trippers will find several huge public pay lots (€10/6 hours, then €1/hour). The underground parking at Square Gambetta in the new town is the cheapest (€6.50/24 hours). Free parking can be found along the river, just north of the Pont Neuf

TRAIN STATION

To Albi via D-118
& Caunes-Minervo

11

12

Canal du Midi

i

PONT MARENGO

R. DE MONTPELLIER

7

RUE

RUE H. BERNARD

10

T

B

6

To Cité

BLVD. OMER SARRAUT

10

ALLEE D'ILENA

RUE CROZALS

RUE DE LA LIBERTE

RUE

RUE DU PALAIS

V I L L E   B A S S E
(NEW CITY)

BLVD. DE VARSOVIE

BLVD. DE VARSOVIE

RUE DU QUATRE SEPTEMBRE

RUE DU DOCTEUR ALBERT

RUE GEORGES

CLEMENCEAU

RUE JEAN-BRINGER

BLVD. JEAN JAURES

RUE MAZAGRA

9

RUE DE LA REPUBLIQUE

RUE DES ETUDES

RUE JULES SAUZEDE

RUE VICTOR HUGO

8

Place Carnot

RUE BARBES

RUE COSTE REBOULH

i

RUE LITTRE

RUE DE VERDUN

RUE

TOMEY

RUE COURTELAIRE

RUE DE VERDUN

Square Gambett

BLVD. MARCOU

BLVD. MARCOU

RUE ARAGO

RUE AIME RAMOND

RUE ANTOINE

RUE VOLTAIRE

R. DU PON

BRASSERS

To Cathar Castles via D-118

BOULEVARD BARBES

Place du Général de Gaulle

BLVD. C. ROUMENS

C. PELLETAN

F. 3 COURONNE

RUE LARAIGNON

RUE DE METZ

R. JOSEPH POUX

CAPITAINE CAZAUX

RUE BASSE

RUE DE LA DIGUE

QUAI BELLEVUE

RUE 24 FEVRIER

RUE DES KAMES

RUE SAINT-MICHEL

RUE OURLIAC

RUE TESSEYRE

RUE ANDRIEU

QUAI DU PAICHEROU

RUE GEN. LAPERRINE

Cimetière Saint-Michel

A u d e   River

CHEMIN DE LA JASSO

Parque Elle

N

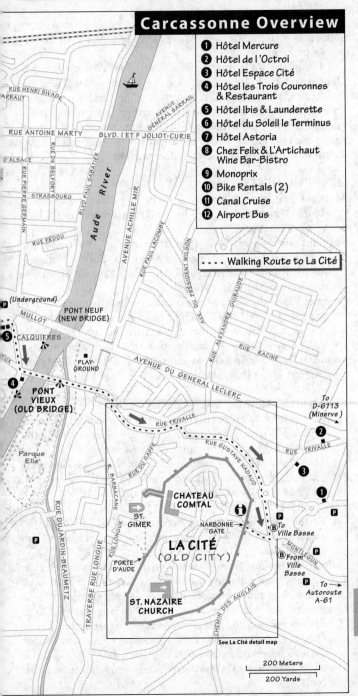

Carcassonne Overview

1. Hôtel Mercure
2. Hôtel de l'Octroi
3. Hôtel Espace Cité
4. Hôtel les Trois Couronnes & Restaurant
5. Hôtel Ibis & Launderette
6. Hôtel du Soleil le Terminus
7. Hôtel Astoria
8. Chez Felix & L'Artichaut Wine Bar-Bistro
9. Monoprix
10. Bike Rentals (2)
11. Canal Cruise
12. Airport Bus

···· Walking Route to La Cité

LANGUEDOC-ROUSSILLON

(follow signs for *CPAM*). Theft is common in public lots—leave nothing in your car at night. Many hotels outside the walls have private parking.

Inside the walls, the recommended Best Western Hôtel le Donjon and Hôtel de la Cité offer pay private parking near the castle moat (pass the small cemetery, heading slightly uphill, and find the attendant; includes bag transfers) or free parking in the main lot below the Narbonne Gate (no bag transfers). You must show your reservation or have the attendant call your hotel. Allow 15 minutes on foot over uneven surfaces to hotels.

HELPFUL HINTS

Market Days: Pleasing Place Carnot in Ville Basse hosts a non-touristy open market (Tue, Thu, and Sat mornings until 13:00; Sat is the biggest).

Supermarkets: There's one in the train station. You'll also find a **Monoprix**—a department store with a grocery section—where Rues Clemenceau and de la République cross, a few blocks from the train station.

Summer Festivals: Carcassonne becomes colorfully medieval during many special events each July and August. Highlights are the *spectacle équestre* (jousting matches) and July 14 (Bastille Day) fireworks. The TI has details on these and other events.

Laundry: Try **Laverie Express** (daily 8:00-22:00, 5 Square Gambetta at Hôtel Ibis; from La Cité, cross Pont Vieux and turn right).

Bike Rental: Bike riding is very popular thanks to the scenic towpath that follows the canal (start at the train station). **Génération VTT** rents bikes (free English map, daily 9:30-18:00, across canal from train station TI kiosk, mobile 07 82 32 67 11, www.generation-vtt.com). **Evasion 2 Roues** also rents bikes, and has tandems (closed Sun-Mon, 85 Allée d'Iéna, tel. 04 68 11 90 40, www.evasion2roues.eu).

Taxi: Call 04 68 71 50 50.

Car Rental: **Avis** is at the train station (tel. 04 68 25 05 84). The airport has all the rental companies, but it's 30 minutes from Carcassonne.

Guided Excursions from Carcassonne: Vin en Vacances runs day-long vineyard tours that mix wine tasting with local food, sightseeing, and cultural experiences. It's run by Wendy Gedney and her team of wine experts. Prices range from €125 to €145 per person and include stops at two wineries, lunch, and visits to key sights such as the Cathar castles. One tour also includes a wine-tasting cruise on the Canal du Midi (mobile 06 42 33 34 09, www.vinenvacances.com, wendy@vinenvacances.com).

Minivan Service: Friendly **Didier** provides comfortable transportation for up to eight passengers to all area châteaux and sights. He's not a guide and speaks just enough English (for 4 passengers plan on about €220/half-day, €400/day; €29/person for the Châteaux of Lastours; mobile 06 03 18 39 95, www.catharexcursions.com, bod.aude11@orange.fr).

Tourist Train or Horse Carriage: You have two options for taking a 20-minute loop around La Cité (both costs €8 and begin at the Narbonne Gate): The tourist train has headphone English commentary and loops outside the wall, while the horse-and-carriage ride is in French and clip-clops between the two walls.

Carcassonne Walk

While the tourists shuffle up the main street, this self-guided walk, rated ▲▲▲, introduces you to the city with history and wonder, rather than tour groups and plastic swords. We'll sneak into the town on the other side of the wall...through the back door (see map on page 529). This walk is wonderfully peaceful and scenic early or late in the day, when the sun is low.

Start on the asphalt outside La Cité's main entrance, the Narbonne Gate (Porte Narbonnaise). On the pillar by the gate, you're welcomed by a contemporary-looking bust of Madame Carcas—which is actually modeled after a 16th-century original of the town's legendary first lady (for her story, see page 521).

• *Cross the bridge toward the...*

Narbonne Gate: Pause at the drawbridge and survey this immense fortification. When forces from northern France finally conquered Carcassonne, it was a strategic prize. Not taking any chances, they evicted the residents, whom they allowed to settle in the lower town (Ville Basse)—as long as they stayed across the river. (Though it's called "new," this lower town actually dates from the 13th century.) La Cité remained a French military garrison until the 18th century.

The drawbridge was made crooked to slow attackers' rush to the main gate and has a similar effect on tourists today.

• *After crossing the drawbridge, lose the crowds and walk left between the walls. At the first short set of stairs, climb to the outer-wall walkway and linger while facing the inner walls.*

Wall View: The Romans built Carcassonne's first wall, upon which the bigger medieval wall was constructed. Identify the ancient Roman bits by looking about one-third of the way up and finding the smaller rocks mixed with narrow stripes of red bricks (and no arrow slits). The outer wall that you're on was not built until the 1300s, more than a thousand years after the Roman walls went up. The massive walls you see today—nearly two miles around, with 52 towers—defended an important site near the intersection of north-south and east-west trade routes.

Look over the wall and down at the moat below (now mostly used for parking). Like most medieval moats, it was never filled with water (or even alligators). A ditch like this—which was originally even deeper—effectively stopped attacking forces from rolling up against the wall in their mobile towers and spilling into the city. Another enemy tactic was to "undermine" (tunnel underneath) the wall, causing a section to cave in. Notice the small, square holes at foot level along the ramparts. Wooden extensions of the rampart walkways (which we'll see later, at the castle) once plugged into these holes so that townsfolk could drop nasty, sticky things on anyone tunneling in. In peacetime this area between the two walls (*les lices*) was used for medieval tournaments, jousting practice, and markets.

During La Cité's Golden Age, the 1100s, independent rulers with open minds allowed Jews and Cathars to live and prosper within the walls, while troubadours wrote poems of ideal love. This liberal attitude made for a rich intellectual life but also led to La Cité's downfall. The Crusades aimed to rid France of the dangerous Cathar movement (and their liberal sympathizers), which led to Carcassonne's defeat and eventual incorporation into the kingdom of France.

The walls of this majestic fortress were partially reconstructed in 1855 as part of a program to restore France's important monuments. The tidy crenellations and the pointy tower roofs are generally from the 19th century (to see authentic towers, find the lightly sloped, red-tiled towers on the opposite side of the fortress).

As you continue your wall walk to higher points, the lack of guardrails is striking. This would never fly in the US, but in France, if you fall, it's your own fault (so be careful). Note the lights embedded in the walls. This fortress, like most important French monuments, is beautifully illuminated every night (for directions to a good nighttime view, see "Night Wall Walk to Pont Vieux" on page 531).

• *You could keep working your way around the walls (though you may be detoured inside the walls for a stretch if special events block your path). If you do the entire walk around the walls, you'll see five authentic Roman towers just before returning to the Narbonne Gate. Walking the entire circle between the inner and outer gate is a terrific 30-minute stroll (and fantastic after dark).*

But for this tour, we'll stop at the first possible entrance into La Cité, the...

Inner Wall Gate: The wall has the same four gates it had in Roman times. Before entering, notice the squat tower on the outer

Carcassonne's La Cité

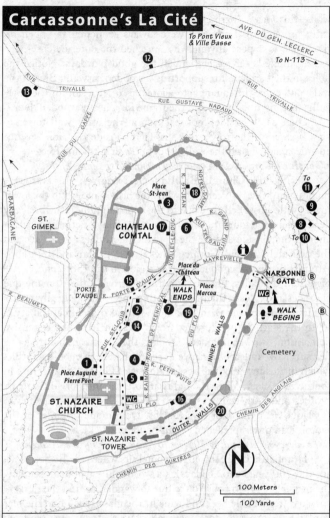

1 Hôtel de la Cité &
   Barbacane Restaurant
2 Best Western Hôtel le Donjon
3 Maison des Remparts, Le St.
   Jean & Restaurant Adelaide
4 Chambres l'Echappée Belle
5 Auberge des Lices Rooms
   & Restaurant
6 Chambres le Grand Puits
7 Hostel Carcassonne
8 Hôtel du Château
9 Hôtel le Montmorency
10 To Hôtel Mercure

11 To Hôtel de l'Octroi &
   Hôtel Espace Cité
12 Chambres les Florentines
13 Hôtel du Pont Vieux
14 Comte Roger Restaurant
15 Le Jardin de la Tour Restaurant
16 Le Bar à Vins Café
17 L'Escargot Restaurant
18 Le Chaudron Restaurant
19 Gérard Sion Galerie (Photos)
20 Parking Entrance for Hôtels
   le Donjon & la Cité

wall—this was a "barbican" (placed opposite each inner gate for extra protection). Barbicans were always semicircular—open on the inside to expose anyone who breached the outer defenses. Invading today is far easier than in the good old days. Notice the holes in the barbican for supporting a wooden catwalk. Breach the walls and enter the square gate—look up to see a slot for the portcullis (the big iron grate) and the frame for a heavy wooden door.

Once safely inside, look back up at the inner wall tower to view *beaucoup de* narrow arrow slits facing inside La Cité—even if enemies made it past the walls, they still weren't home free.

• *Opposite the tower, work your way around to the entry of the...*

St. Nazaire Church (Basilique St. Nazaire): This was a cathedral until the 18th century, when the bishop moved to the lower town (Ville Basse). Today, due to the depopulation of the basically dead-except-for-tourism Cité, it's not even a functioning parish church. Step inside. Notice the Romanesque arches of the nave and the delicately vaulted Gothic arches over the altar and transepts. After its successful conquest of this region in the 13th-century Albigensian Crusades, France set out to destroy all the Romanesque churches and replace them with Gothic ones—symbolically asserting its northern rule with this more northern architectural style. With the start of the Hundred Years' War in 1337, the expensive demolition was abandoned. Today, the Romanesque remainder survives, and the destroyed section has been rebuilt Gothic, which makes it one of the best examples of Gothic architecture in southern France. When the lights are off, the interior—lit only by candles and 14th-century stained glass—is evocatively medieval. A plaque near the door says that St. Dominique (founder of the Dominican order) preached at this church in 1213.

• *The ivy-covered building 50 steps in front of the church entrance is...*

Hôtel de la Cité: This luxury hotel sits where the Bishop's Palace did 700 years ago. Today, it's a worthwhile detour to see how the privileged few travel. You're free to wander, so find the library-cozy bar (reasonable beer and wine by the glass), then find the rear garden and turn right for super wall views that you can't see from anywhere else.

• *From here, take the right fork at the medieval flatiron building, and follow Rue St. Louis for several blocks. Merge right onto Rue Port d'Aude, then look for a small castle-view terrace on your left a block up.*

Château Comtal: Originally built in 1125, Carcassonne's third layer of defense was completely redesigned in later reconstructions. From this impressive viewpoint you can see the wooden rampart extensions that once circled the entire city wall. (Notice the empty peg holes to the left of the bridge.) During sieges, these would be covered with wet animal skins as a fire retardant. When *Robin Hood: Prince of Thieves*, starring Kevin Costner, was filmed here in 1990, the entire city was turned into a film set. Locals enjoyed playing bit parts and seeing their château labeled "Nottingham Castle" in the fanciful film. Château Comtal is a worthwhile visit for those with time and interest (see "Sights in Carcassonne," below). Or just take a stroll through the tranquil garden moat (free), where you'll see people enjoying a very scenic picnic.

• *Fifty yards away, opposite the entrance to the castle, is...*

Place du Château: This busy little square sports a modest statue honoring the man who saved the city from deterioration and neglect in the 19th century. The bronze model circling the base of the statue shows Carcassonne's walls as they looked before the 1855 reconstruction by Eugène Viollet-le-Duc.

• *Backtrack a few steps to face the château entry, then turn right and walk one block to...*

Place du Grand Puits: This huge well is the oldest of Carcassonne's 22 wells. In an age of starve-'em-out sieges, it took more than stout walls to keep a town safe—you also needed a steady supply of water and food.

• *Our walk is finished. You can return to the Château Comtal entrance gate, if you want to tour the castle. Or, if you turn left at the fountain, you'll pop out in the charming, restaurant-lined Place St-Jean; a hard left here takes you down into the château's sweet moat garden.*

Sights in Carcassonne

▲▲▲Night Wall Walk to Pont Vieux

Save some post-dinner energy for a don't-miss walk around the same walls you visited today (great dinner picnic sites as well).

The effect at night is mesmerizing: The embedded lights become torches and unfamiliar voices become the enemy. End at Pont Vieux for a floodlit fantasy. The best route is a partial circumnavigation clockwise between the walls. Start at the Narbonne Gate, and follow my self-guided walk (described earlier) to the Inner Wall Gate. Don't enter La Cité through this gate; instead, continue your walk between the walls (this section is occasionally closed; if so, you'll have to make your way through the village and out the rear along Rue de la Porte d'Aude to meet up with the route described from here).

The path narrows as you walk behind Château Comtal. When you come to a ramp leading down (after about five minutes), make a U-turn to the left, just before the path rises back up. This ramp leads down the hill; make a left when you come to the church (St.

Gimer), then a right on Rue de la Barbacane (follow the *Centre-Ville* sign). Go straight to reach Pont Vieux and exceptional views of floodlit Carcassonne. Return from the bridge the same way you came, and complete your clockwise walk between the walls back to the Narbonne Gate, or take Rue Trivalle to Rue Gustave Nadaud for a quicker return.

▲Château Comtal

Your best look at Carcassonne's medieval architecture is a walk through this castle-within-the-castle. Grab the basic flier in English, cross the drawbridge over the garden moat, and climb to the top of the stairs. A well-done film with booming sound sets the stage for your visit. Next is a room-size model of La Cité—find the black-and-white images of old Carcassonne on the walkway above. From here, a self-guided tour with posted English explanations leads you around the inner ramparts of Carcassonne's castle. You'll see the underpinnings of the towers and of the catwalks that hung from the walls and learn all about medieval defense systems. The views are terrific. Your visit ends with a museum showing bits of St. Nazaire Church and fragments from important homes.

Cost and Hours: €8.50, daily April-Sept 10:00-18:30, shorter hours off-season, last entry 45 minutes before closing, unnecessary audioguide, tel. 04 68 11 70 70, www.remparts-carcassonne.fr.

Riverside Walk

Two scenic paths running southwest along each side of the Aude River below La Cité offer occasional views to the fortress and a verdant escape for runners and walkers. Both paths can be accessed from below the Pont Vieux.

Canal du Midi

Completed in 1681, this sleepy 155-mile canal connects France's Mediterranean and Atlantic coasts and, at about its midpoint, runs directly in front of the train station in Carcassonne. Before railways, Canal du Midi was clogged with commercial traffic; today, it entertains only pleasure craft. Small boats for **canal cruises** leave from in front of the train station. The boats are operated by two companies, on opposite sides of the bridge (about €9/1.5 hours, €11/2.5 hours, April-Oct 2-4/day, closed Tue except July-Aug www.carcassonne-navigation.com or www.bateau-cocagne-canal-carcassonne.fr). The boat company furthest from the train station allows you to take your bike on the boat. (Those with limited time are best off biking along the canal: The path is level, pedaling is a breeze and you can cover far more territory than by boat—for bike rental, see "Helpful Hints," earlier.)

Gérard Sion Galerie

Duck into this impressive photo gallery before selecting which Cathar castles you want to visit (brilliant shots of many monuments in Languedoc-Roussillon, generally daily 10:00-12:30 & 14:00-19:00, just up from Place Marcou at 27 Rue du Plô).

Nightlife in Carcassonne

For relief from all the medieval kitsch, savor a drink in four-star, library-meets-bar ambience at the **Hôtel de la Cité** bar (€7-8 beer and wine, Place de l'Eglise). To taste the liveliest square, with loads of tourists and strolling musicians, sip a drink or nibble a dessert on **Place Marcou.** To be a medieval poet, share a bottle of wine in your own private niche somewhere remote on the ramparts.

Le Bar à Vins (also recommended later, under "Eating in Carcassonne") offers lively music, good €3 wines by the glass, and a young crowd enjoying a garden in the moonshadow of the wall... without any tourists (daily until 2:00 in the morning in high season).

For a fine before- or after-dinner drink and floodlit wall views, pause at the recommended **Hotel du Château**'s broad terrace, below the Narbonne Gate (2 Rue Camille Saint-Saëns).

Sleeping in Carcassonne

($$$$ = Splurge, $$$ = Pricier, $$ = Moderate, $ = Budget)

Sleep within or near the old walls, in La Cité. I've also listed a pair of hotels near the train station. In the summer, when La Cité is jammed with tourists, consider sleeping in quieter Caunes-Minervois. July and August are most expensive, when the town is packed. At other times of the year, prices drop and there are generally plenty of rooms. Hotels have air-conditioning and elevators, unless noted.

IN LA CITE

Pricey hotels, good B&Bs, and an excellent youth hostel offer a full range of rooms inside the walls.

$$$$ Hôtel de la Cité***** offers 59 rooms with deluxe everything in a beautiful building next to St. Nazaire Church. Peaceful gardens, a swimming pool and spa, royal public spaces, the elegant Barbacane restaurant, and reliable luxury are yours—for a price (family rooms, pay parking outside walls, Place Auguste-Pierre Pont, tel. 04 68 71 98 71, www.hoteldelacite.com, h8613@accor.com).

$$$ Best Western Hôtel le Donjon****, big and impersonal, has 61 well-appointed rooms, a polished lobby with a full bar, and a great location inside the walls. Rooms are split between three buildings in La Cité (the main building, a look-alike annex across the street, and the cheaper Maison des Remparts a few blocks away). The main building is most appealing, and the rooms with terraces on the garden are delightful (pay parking, 2 Rue Comte Roger, tel. 04 68 11 23 00, www.hotel-donjon.fr, info@bestwestern-donjon.com).

$$ Chambres l'Echappée Belle, in the center of La Cité, is run by cheery Australian Jacqui. It has four traditional units with wood floors and three with jet showers (includes breakfast, check-in between 16:00 and 18:00, no elevator, near St. Nazaire Church, just off Rue du Plô at 5 Rue Raymond Roger Trencavel, tel. 04 68 25 33 40, mobile 06 40 44 63 18, www.lechappeebelle.co.uk, infolechappeebelle@orange.fr).

$ Auberge des Lices rents two lovely rooms with high ceilings, exposed beams, and stone walls—though the lodgings are an afterthought to the busy restaurant (no elevator, 3 Rue Raymond Roger Trencavel, tel. 04 68 72 34 07, mobile 06 73 69 36 22, aubergedeslices.com, leslices@blasco.fr).

$ Chambres le Grand Puits, across from Maison des Remparts, is a splendid value. It has one cute double room and two cavernous apartment-like rooms that could sleep five, with kitchenette, private terrace, and sweet personal touches. Inquire in the small boutique, and say *bonjour* to happy-go-lucky Nicole (includes self-serve breakfast, cash only, no elevator, no air-con, 8 Place du Grand Puits, tel. 04 68 25 16 67, mobile 06 20 47 02 31, http://legrandpuits.free.fr, nicole.trucco@club-internet.fr).

¢ Hostel Carcassonne is big, clean, and well-run, with an outdoor garden courtyard, a self-service kitchen, a TV room, bar, a washer/dryer, and a welcoming ambience. If you ever wanted to bunk down in a hostel, consider doing it here—all ages are welcome. Reserve ahead for summer (€11/person membership, includes breakfast, rental towels, Rue du Vicomte Trencavel, tel. 04 68 25 23 16, www.hifrance.org or www.hihostels.com, carcassonne@hifrance.org).

JUST OUTSIDE LA CITE

Sleeping just outside La Cité offers the best of both worlds: quick access to the ramparts, less claustrophobic surroundings, and easy parking.

$$$$ Hôtel du Château**** and **$$ Hôtel le Montmorency*****are adjacent hotels that lie barely below La Cité's main gate and are run by the same family. Check-in, parking, and good breakfast with views for both hotels are at Hôtel du Château. Guests enjoy an easy walk to La Cité, a snazzy pool (heated Easter-Nov), a hot tub, view terraces to the walls of Carcassonne, two lazy hounds, and a sweet cat. Hôtel du Château gives four-star comfort with 17 sumptuous rooms (RS%—use code "RICKSTEVES," pay parking, 2 Rue Camille Saint-Saëns, tel. 04 68 11 38 38, www. hotelduchateau.net, contact@hotelduchateau.net). Hôtel Montmorency, a short walk behind Hôtel du Château, has a split personality. Half the rooms are neon-colored-mod, and half are purely *Provençal* and a bit smaller. Several have views to the ramparts, and many come with private decks or terraces (RS%—use code "RICKSTEVES," no elevator but only one floor up, pay parking, 2 Rue Camille Saint-Saëns, tel. 04 68 11 96 70, www.hotelmontmorency. com, contact@hotelmontmorency.com).

$$ Hôtel Mercure**** hides a block behind the Hôtel le Montmorency, a five-minute walk to La Cité. It rents 80 snug-but-comfy, air-conditioned rooms and has a refreshing garden, a good-sized pool, big elevators, and a warm bar-lounge. A few rooms have views of La Cité (many family rooms, free parking, 18 Rue Camille Saint-Saëns, tel. 04 68 11 92 82, www.mercure.com, h1622@accor.com).

CLOSE TO LA CITE ON RUE TRIVALLE

These places are 10 minutes below La Cité and 20 minutes from the train station on foot.

$$ Hôtel de l'Octroi*** delivers colorful, contemporary comfort, efficient service, and a young vibe from its full-service bar to its small, stylish pool and its 21 rooms (RS%—use code "RICKSTEVES," family rooms, no elevator, pay parking, 143 Rue Trivalle, tel. 04 68 25 29 08, www.hoteloctroi.com).

$ Hôtel Espace Cité**, two blocks downhill from Hôtel le Montmorency (described earlier), is a fair value, with 48 small but sharp rooms (family rooms, no elevator, limited free parking—otherwise pay parking in garage, 132 Rue Trivalle, tel. 04 68 25 24 24, www.hotelespacecite.fr, espace-cite@hotelespacecite.fr).

$ Chambres les Florentines is a good-value bed-and-breakfast run by charming Madame Mistler. The five rooms are spacious, traditional, and homey; one room has a big deck and million-dollar views of La Cité (cash only, family rooms, includes breakfast, no air-con, no elevator, pay parking, 71 Rue Trivalle, tel. 04 68 71 51 07, mobile 06 88 89 33 42, www.lesflorentines.net, lesflorentines11@gmail.com).

$ Hôtel du Pont Vieux** offers 19 clean rooms, friendly service, and a peaceful garden. Choose a room with a La Cité view or a more modern room with a garden view (secure parking garage—reserve ahead, no elevator, 32 Rue Trivalle, tel. 04 68 25 24 99, www.hotelpontvieux.com, info@hoteldupontvieux.com).

BETWEEN LA CITÉ AND THE TRAIN STATION

These hotels are close to Pont Vieux, a 15-minute walk below La Cité, and 15 minutes on foot from the train station.

$$ Hôtel les Trois Couronnes*****, a modern hotel in a concrete shell, offers 44 rooms with terrific views up to La Cité—and 26 nonview rooms that you don't want (indoor pool with views, pay parking garage, 2 Rue des Trois Couronnes, tel. 04 68 25 36 10, www.hotel-destroiscouronnes.com, contact@hotel-destroiscouronnes.com). Their reasonably priced restaurant also has a good view (see "Eating in Carcassonne," later).

$ Hôtel Ibis*****, on Square Gambetta, delivers reliable three-star comfort at fair prices in its 48 rooms (request a room off the square, air-con, elevator, 5 Square Gambetta, tel. 04 68 72 37 37, www.ibishotel.com, h1371@accor.com).

NEAR THE TRAIN STATION

$$ Hôtel du Soleil le Terminus*****, across from the train station, is turn-of-the-century faded-grand. The lobby reminds me of a train-station waiting hall. Its 108 rooms are large and have high ceilings (view rooms are pricier and noisier, basement pool, secure pay parking, lots of groups, 2 Avenue Maréchal Joffre, tel. 04 68 25 25 00, www.soleilvacances.com, reservation@soleilvacances.com).

$ Hôtel Astoria*****, run by delightful Marc and Séverine, offers some of the cheapest hotel beds that I list in town, divided between a main hotel and an annex across the street. The 23 colorful rooms are simple and clean. Book ahead—it's popular (cheaper rooms with shared bath, family rooms, fans only in main hotel, no elevator, pay parking—reserve ahead, bike rentals, baggage storage for small fee; from the train station, walk across the canal, turn left, and go two blocks to 18 Rue Tourtel; tel. 04 68 25 31 38, www.astoriacarcassonne.com, hotel-astoria@wanadoo.fr).

IN CAUNES-MINERVOIS

To experience unspoiled, tranquil Languedoc-Roussillon, sleep surrounded by vineyards in the characteristic village of Caunes-Minervois. Comfortably nestled in the foothills of the Montagne Noire, Caunes-Minervois is a 25-minute drive from Carcassonne. Take route D-118 or follow signs toward *Mazamet* to a big roundabout and find D-620. The town offers an eighth-century abbey, two cafés, two good restaurants, a pizzeria, a handful of wineries, and no other tourists. The friendly staff at the town's TI (in the abbey) is eager to help you explore the region. Caunes-Minervois makes an ideal base for exploring area wine roads.

$ Hôtel d'Alibert, in a 15th-century home with ambience galore, sits in the heart of the village. It has a mix of nicely renovated, Old World traditional rooms. It's managed with a relaxed *je* *ne sais quoi* by Frédéric "call me Fredo" Dalibert and his daughter Mathilde (includes breakfast, Place de la Mairie, tel. 04 68 78 00 54, www.hotel-dalibert.com, frederic.dalibert@wanadoo.fr). Eat lunch or dinner in his cozy restaurant with great courtyard tables and let Fredo plan your wine-tasting excursion (closed Sun dinner and Mon).

$ L'Ancienne Boulangerie is a cozy B&B option a few doors down from Hôtel d'Alibert (cash only, tel. 04 68 76 27 17, www. ancienneboulangerie.com, ancienne.boulangerie@orange.fr).

Nearby, in Le Somail: Drivers who want to experience the Canal du Midi boating scene sleep in Le Somail, a picturesque hamlet that has changed little since the construction of the canal in the 1600s. The town has an impressive bookshop, three art galleries, and two restaurants. Sleep at **$ La Maison des Escaliers,** where Tina and Ruud have created a beautiful B&B with a variety of stylish and comfortable rooms in their restored 19th-century house. Breakfast is served by the pool with views of the vineyards (cheaper rooms with shared bath, family rooms, whole house rental available, 6 Rue Paul Riquet, tel. 04 68 48 44 23, mobile 06 79 55 33 37, www.patiasses.com, mail@patiasses.com).

Eating in Carcassonne

($$$$ = Splurge, $$$ = Pricier, $$ = Moderate, $ = Budget)
For a social outing in La Cité, take your pick from a food circus of basic eateries on a leafy courtyard—often with strolling musicians in the summer—on lively Place Marcou. If rubbing elbows with too many tourists gives you hives, go local and dine below in Ville Basse (the new city). Cassoulet (described on page 506) is the traditional must (tip: a dash of vinegar helps the digestion); big salads provide a lighter alternative. For a local before-dinner drink, try a glass of Muscat de Saint-Jean-de-Minervois.

IN LA CITE
On Place St. Jean: My favorite area for dinner in La Cité is on Place St. Jean, where two eateries compete for your business. Both have outside terrace tables with views to the floodlit Château Comtal. **$$ Restaurant Adelaide** is a lively bistro with reasonable prices; they serve a good €16, three-course *menu* with cassoulet, as well as big salads (daily except closed Mon Sept-May, tel. 04 68 47 66 61). **$$ Le St. Jean,** next door, has similar prices and choices (€9 kid *menu*, daily, tel. 04 68 47 42 43).

The recommended Hôtel de la Cité's **$$$$ Barbacane Restaurant** owns La Cité's only Michelin star and prices to go along with it (€85-150 dinner *menus*).

$$$$ Comte Roger's quiet elegance seems out of place in this touristy town. For half the price of the Barbacane, you can celebrate a special occasion with Chef Pierre's fresh Mediterranean cuisine. Ask for a table on the vine-covered patio, or eat inside in their stylish dining room. Book ahead in high season (massive €23 cassoulet, closed Sun-Mon, 14 Rue St. Louis, tel. 04 68 11 93 40, www.comteroger.com).

$$$ Auberge des Lices, a good-value restaurant hidden down a quiet lane, has a courtyard with cathedral views. It manages a delicate balance of price and quality for traditional cuisine with some modern flourishes (daily July-Aug, closed Tue-Wed Sept-June, 3 Rue Raymond Roger Trencavel, tel. 04 68 72 34 07).

$$ Le Jardin de la Tour, run with panache by Elodie for more than 20 years, has cool, windproof seating in the rear parklike garden and a castle-like indoor atmosphere (excellent €17 cassoulet, closed Sun-Mon, lunch served July-Aug only, 11 Rue Porte-d'Aude, tel. 04 68 25 71 24).

$ Le Bar à Vins, popular with the twenty- and thirtysomething set at night, is tucked away in a big garden just inside the wall but away from the crowds. It serves an enticing selection of open wines (€3/glass), appetizers, tapas, and sandwiches (closed Tue except July-Aug, closed Nov-Jan, 6 Rue du Plô, tel. 04 68 47 38 38).

$$ L'Escargot is where locals and tourists alike enjoy tasty tapas with local wine. It's a welcoming place and busy, so reserve ahead for a table outside or in (daily March-Oct, 7 Rue Viollet-Le-Duc, tel 04 68 47 12 55).

$$ Le Chaudron may serve the best cassoulet in town (€15) in a peaceful outdoor setting under the shade of trees or in the simple interior room (daily July-Aug, closed Mon-Tue off-season, 6 Rue St Jean, tel. 04 68 71 09 08).

Picnics: Basic supplies can be gathered at shops along the main drag (generally open until at least 19:30, better to buy outside La Cité). For your beggar's banquet, picnic on the city walls.

IN VILLE BASSE (THE NEW CITY)

$$$ Restaurant les Trois Couronnes, just across the Pont Vieux in the recommended Hôtel les Trois Couronnes, gives you a panorama of Carcassonne from the top floor of a concrete hotel (good €28 *menus,* open daily for dinner only, closed Jan, call ahead, 2 Rue des Trois Couronnes, tel. 04 68 25 36 10).

On Place Carnot: $$ Chez Felix has good seats on the main square, is family-run, and serves traditional cuisine for lunch only (closed Sun, 11 Place Carnot, tel. 04 68 25 17 01). Nearby, snazzy **$$ L'Artichaut Wine Bar-Bistro** serves good-value cuisine and wines (July-Aug open Tue-Sat for lunch and dinner; Sept-June Mon-Wed lunch only, Thu-Sat lunch and dinner; closed Sun year-round; 14 Place Carnot, tel. 09 52 15 65 14).

LANGUEDOC-ROUSSILLON

Carcassonne Connections

From Carcassonne by Train to: Albi (10/day, 3 hours, change in Toulouse), **Collioure** (8/day, 2 hours, most require change in Narbonne), **Sarlat-la-Canéda** (5/day, 5.5-7 hours, 1-3 changes, some require bus from Souillac to Sarlat), **Arles** (4/day direct, 2.5 hours, more with transfer in Narbonne), **Nice** (3/day, 6.5 hours with change in Marseille), **Paris** (Gare de Lyon: 8/day, 5.5 hours, 1 change; Gare d'Austerlitz: 1 direct night train, 8.5 hours), **Toulouse** (nearly hourly, 1 hour), **Barcelona** (1/day direct, 2.5 hours, 4/day with change in Narbonne, 2-3 hours).

Near Carcassonne

The land around Carcassonne is carpeted with vineyards and littered with romantically ruined castles, ancient abbeys, and photogenic villages. The castle remains of Peyrepertuse and Quéribus make terrific stops between Carcassonne and Collioure (allow 2 hours from Carcassonne on narrow, winding roads; from the castles it's another 1.5 hours to Collioure). You can also link them on a fine loop trip from Carcassonne. The gorge-sculpted village of Minerve, 45 minutes northeast of Carcassonne, works well for Provence-bound travelers.

Getting There: Public transportation is hopeless; taxis for up to six people cost €300 for a daylong excursion (taxi tel. 04 68 71 50 50). See page 527 for excursion bus and minivan tours to these places.

▲▲CHATEAUX OF HAUTES CORBIERES

About two hours south of Carcassonne, in the scenic foothills of the Pyrenees, you'll find a series of surreal, mountain-capping castle ruins. Like a Maginot Line of the 13th century, these cloud-piercing castles were strategically located between France and the Spanish kingdom of Roussillon. As you can see by flipping through the picture books in Carcassonne's tourist shops, these castles' crumbled ruins are an impressive contrast to the restored walls of La Cité. If you go, bring a hat (there's no shade) and sturdy walking shoes—and prepare for a vigorous climb.

Connect these castles (ultimately with Collioure if you want) along this incredibly scenic, two-hour drive: From Carcassonne drive to Limoux, then Couiza. At Couiza follow little D-14 to Bugarach (passing through Languedoc's only spa town, Rennes-le-Château). Near Bugarach, views open to rocky ridgelines hovering above dense forests. You'll soon see signs leading the way to Peyrepertuse. At Cubières, canyon lovers can detour to the **Gorges de Galamus,** driving partway into the teeth of white-rock slabs that

Near Carcassonne

seem to get closer the farther in you go (those looping back to Carcassonne can do the whole canyon on their way back). **Peyrepertuse** is a short hop from Cubières; you'll pass snack stands and view cafés on the twisty drive up. After visiting this Cathar castle, your next destination—**Quéribus**—is a well-signed, 15-minute drive away. From Quéribus it's a 1.5-hour drive to the seaside village of Collioure (follow signs in direction: Maury, then direction: Perpignan). If returning to Carcassonne, follow signs for Maury, then

St-Paul-de-Fenouillet, then drive through the Gorges de Galamus and track D-14 to Bugarach, Couiza, Limoux, and Carcassonne.

▲▲Peyrepertuse

The most spectacular Cathar castle is Peyrepertuse (pay-ruh-pair-twos), where the ruins rise from a splinter of cliff: Try to spot it on your drive up from the village. From the parking lot, you'll first hike downhill, curling around the back of the rock wall, then hike steeply up 15 minutes through a scrubby forest to the fortress. The views are sensational in all directions (including to Quéribus, sticking up from an adjacent ridge). But what's most amazing is that they could build this place at all. This was a lookout in the Middle Ages, staffed with 25 very lonely men. Today, it's a scamperer's paradise with weed-infested structures in varying states of ruin. Let your imagination soar, but watch your step as you try to reconstruct this eagle's nest—the footing is tricky. Don't miss the St. Louis stairway to the upper castle ruins—another stiff, 10-minute climb straight up.

Cost and Hours: €6.50, €9 in July-Aug, daily May-Sept 9:00-19:00, until 20:00 July-Aug, shorter hours off-season, theatrical audioguide-€4 (narrated from the perspective of a French captain posted here), free handout gives plenty of background, tel. 04 30 37 00 77, www.chateau-peyrepertuse.com).

▲Quéribus

While Peyrepertuse rides along a high ridge, this bulky castle caps a mountaintop and delivers even more amazing views (find the snow-covered peaks of the Pyrenees). It owns a similar history to Peyrepertuse but has an easier (but still uphill) footpath to access the site and gentler climbing within the ruins. It's famous as the last Cathar castle to fall, and was abandoned after 1659, when the border between France and Spain was moved farther south into the high Pyrenees.

Cost and Hours: €6.50, daily May-Sept 9:30-19:00, until 20:00 July-Aug, shorter hours off-season, same audioguide concept as at Peyrepertuse-€4, good handout, tel. 04 68 45 03 69, www.cucugnan.fr.

Sleeping near Peyrepertuse and Quéribus: To really get away (and I mean really), sleep in the lovely little village of Cucugnan, located between the castles. **$ L'Ecurie de Cucugnan** is a friendly bed-and-breakfast with five comfortable rooms at great rates, a view pool, and a shady garden. Joël, winemaker and owner, doesn't speak English, but his wife—a teacher—does (includes breakfast, full house rental available, 18 Rue Achille Mir, tel. 04 68 33 37 42, mobile 06 76 86 38 52, ecurie.cucugnan@orange.fr).

$$ Bergerie Ferrairolles, about 16 miles northeast of the castle ruins, is a four-room ecological guesthouse run by a Franco-Dutch couple, Rolinka and Antoine (who also work as Rick Steves' Europe tour guides). Located on the scenic route from Carcassonne to Collioure in remote Villeneuve-les-Corbières, it's 30 minutes from the Mediterranean and surrounded by Cathar castles, olive trees, and vineyards (includes breakfast, cash or PayPal only, ask about home-cooked dinners with wine, tel. 09 88 99 34 33, www.ferrairolles.fr, contact@ferrairolles.fr).

CATHAR SIGHTS NEAR CAUNES-MINERVOIS

The next two Cathar sights tie in well with a visit to Caunes-Minervois (where I recommend sleeping—see page 536) and provide an easy excursion from Carcassonne, offering you a taste of this area's appealing countryside.

Châteaux of Lastours

Ten miles north of Carcassonne, four ruined castles cap a barren hilltop and give drivers a handy (if less dramatic) look at the region's Cathar castles. From Carcassonne, follow signs to *Mazamet*, then *Conques-sur-Orbiel*, then *Lastours*. In Lastours you can hike to the castles or drive to a viewpoint.

Hikers park at the lot as they enter the village, walk five minutes upriver to the glass entry, then walk 20 minutes uphill to the castles (allow at least an hour for a reasonable tour and wear sturdy walking shoes). The castles, which once surrounded a fortified village, date from the 11th century. The village welcomed Cathars (becoming a bishop's seat at one point) but paid dearly for this tolerance with destruction by French troops in 1227. Make the short drive to the Belvedere for a smashing panorama over the castles.

Cost and Hours: Castles and belvedere viewpoint—€7, viewpoint only—€2; daily July-Aug 9:00-20:00, April-June and Sept 10:00-18:00, Oct 10:00-17:00; Nov-March weekends only 10:00-17:00, closed Jan-Feb; tel. 04 68 77 56 02.

Eating: An idyllic lunch awaits near the lower entry at **$$ Le Moulin de Lastours,** where a small bakery has a few tables serenely overlooking the river (good quiche, sandwiches, drinks, closed Tue off-season, tel. 04 68 25 23 14).

▲Minerve

A onetime Cathar hideout with Celtic origins, the spectacular vil-

lage of Minerve is sculpted
out of a swirling canyon that
provided a natural defense.
Strong as it was, it couldn't
keep out the pope's armies,
and the village was razed during the vicious Albigensian
Crusades of the early 1200s.

Getting There: Located
between Carcassonne and
Béziers, Minerve is seven miles north of Olonzac and 45 minutes by car from Carcassonne. It makes for a good stop between
Provence and Carcassonne.

Visiting Minerve: As you arrive, follow the *P* signs to the
parking lot above the village (€4). Take in the views from the cliff
at the parking lot, then enter the village and find the **TI** on the
same street (Rue des Martyrs, tel. 04 68 91 81 43, www.minerve-
tourisme.fr). Pick up the brochure with a simple self-guided tour of
the village describing Minerve's history, and ask about hiking into
the canyon below (not difficult).

Minerve has cool cafés (**$$ Café de la Place** is my favorite),
one hotel, a nifty little bookshop, a few wine shops, and a smatter-
ing of art galleries. You'll also find two small museums: a prehis-
tory museum and the compact **Hurepel de Minerve,** with models
from the Cathar era and excellent English descriptions that effec-
tively describe this terrible time (€3, free for children under 14,
interesting for kids, daily April-Oct 10:00-13:00 & 14:00-18:00,
closed Nov-March, Rue des Martyrs, tel. 04 68 91 12 26).

After your village stroll, explore the canyon below by walking
down to the riverbed: Look for a path by the ruined tower near the
parking lot, or follow *Access Remparts* signs from below Café de la
Place. A path across the riverbed leads to a catapult and views back
to Minerve.

Sleeping and Eating in Minerve: Stay here and melt into
southern France (almost literally, if it's summer). **$ Relais Chan-
tovent**'s unpretentious and spotless rooms are designed for those
who come to get away from it all, with no phones or TV...and
ample quiet. All rooms have queen-size beds (tel. 04 68 91 14 18,
www.relaischantovent-minerve.fr, relaischantovent@orange.fr). Its
sharp **$$$$ restaurant** has a marvelous view from its deck and
deserves your business; it's popular, so reserve ahead (closed all day
Wed, Sun, and Tue for dinner year-round).

Collioure

Surrounded by less-appealing resorts, lovely Collioure is blessed
with a privileged climate and a
romantic setting. By Mediterranean standards, this seaside
village should be slammed with
tourists—it has everything. Like
an ice-cream shop, Collioure of-
fers 31 flavors of pastel houses and six petite, scooped-out, pebbled
beaches sprinkled with visitors. The town itself is washed in subtle
earth tones, with a few pops of Crayola color on its sun-dappled,
tree-shaded squares. This sweet scene, capped by a winking lighthouse, sits under a once-mighty castle in the shade of the Pyrenees.

Just 15 miles from the Spanish border, Collioure (Cotlliure
in Catalan) shares a common history and independent attitude
with its Catalan siblings across the border. Undeniably French yet
proudly Catalan, it flies the yellow-and-red flag of Catalunya, displays street names in French and Catalan, and sports a few business
names with *el* and *els,* rather than *le* and *les.* Sixty years ago, most
villagers spoke Catalan; today that language is enjoying a resur-
gence as Collioure rediscovers its roots.

Come here to unwind and regroup. Even with its crowds of
vacationers in peak season (July and August are busy), Collioure is
what many look for when they head to the Riviera—a sunny, relaxing splash in the Mediterranean.

PLANNING YOUR TIME

Check your ambition at the station. Enjoy a slow coffee on *la Med,*
lose yourself in the old town's streets, compare the *gelati* shops on
Rue Vauban, sample the fine local wines, and relax on a pebble-
sand beach (waterproof shoes are helpful). And if you have a car,
don't miss a drive into the hills above Collioure.

Orientation to Collioure

Most of Collioure's shopping, sights, and hotels are in the old town,
near the Château Royal. There are good views of the old town from
across the bay near the recommended Hôtel Boramar and brilliant
views from the hills above. You can walk from one end of Collioure
to the other in 20 minutes.

TOURIST INFORMATION
The TI hides behind the main beachfront cafés at 5 Place du 18 Juin (July-Sept Mon-Sat 9:15-18:45, Sun 10:15-17:45; same hours April-June and Oct except closes Mon-Sat at 17:45; shorter hours and closed Sun Nov-March; tel. 04 68 82 15 47, www.collioure.com).

ARRIVAL IN COLLIOURE
By Train: Walk out of the station (no baggage storage), turn right, and follow Rue Aristide Maillol downhill for about 10 minutes until you see Hôtel Restaurant La Frégate (directions to hotels are listed from this reference point—see "Sleeping in Collioure," later). Before leaving the station, check the schedule for Spanish side-trips or for your next destination (station staffed 9:15-13:00 & 14:30-18:00).

By Car: Collioure is 16 miles south of Perpignan. From the autoroute, take the *Perpignan-Sud Sortie* exit and follow signs to *Argelès-sur-Mer* (also called *Argelès*), then *Collioure par la Corniche*. To reach the center, follow *Collioure Centre-Ville* signs, and turn left onto Rue de la République. Parking is a challenge and almost impossible in summer—arrive early or late. There's a big pay lot (Parking Glacis) accessed from the bottom of Rue de la République, behind the post office (see map on page 548; €12.30/24 hours). I often find a space at Parking Haut Douy, as you drop downhill toward the city center (5-minute walk to the center, 4-hour limit—€5/4 hours). The best deal is Parking du Stade, a 15-minute walk from the center past Fort Miradou (on Route du Pla de las Fourques, €4/6 hours, €8/12 hours). In high season, it's easiest to park at the remote Parking Cap Dourats on the Route de Madeloc (€10/24 hours) and take the free shuttle bus into town (3/hour, daily 10:00-20:00, July-Aug until 24:00). Once parked, take everything of value out of your car.

HELPFUL HINTS
Market Days: Markets are held on Wednesday and Sunday mornings on Place Général Leclerc, across from Hôtel Fregate.

Wi-Fi: The lighthearted **Café Sola,** next to the recommended Hôtel Casa Pairal, has Wi-Fi (daily 7:00-21:00, until much later in-season, 2 Rue de la République, tel. 04 68 82 55 02).

Laundry: A self-serve **launderette** is at 8 Avenue du Général de Gaulle (daily 7:00-20:00, mobile 06 74 57 17 39).

Taxi: Call 04 68 82 27 80 or mobile 07 62 12 68 68.

Tourist Train: Collioure's *petit train* leaves from next to the bridge at the bottom of Rue de la République and toots you to Port Vendres and up to Fort St. Elme for brilliant views, *sans* sweat (€8 round-trip, 45 minutes; €11 one-way with fort entry—return to town on foot).

LANGUEDOC-ROUSSILLON

Sights in Collioure

There's no important sight here except what lies on the beach and the views over Collioure. Indulge in a long seaside lunch, inspect the colorful art galleries, catch up on your postcards, and maybe take a hike. Don't be surprised to see French Marines playing commando in their rafts; Collioure's bay caters to more than just sun-loving tourists. Sightseeing here is best in the evening, when the sky darkens, and yellow lamps reflect warm pastels and deep blues.

▲View from the Beach

Walk out to the jetty's end, past the church and the little chapel, and find a spot along the rail. Collioure has been popular since well before your visit. For more than 2,500 years, people have battled to control its enviable position on the Mediterranean at the foot of the Pyrenees. The mountains rising behind Collioure provide a natural defense, and its port gives it a commercial edge, making Collioure an irresistible target. A string of forts defended Collioure's landlocked side. Panning from left to right, you'll see the low-slung remains of a 17th-century fort, the still-standing Fort St. Elme (built by powerful Spanish king and Holy Roman Emperor Charles V—the same guy who built El Escorial near Madrid) at the top of a hill, and then the 2,100-foot-high observation tower of Madeloc, capping the mountain peak. Topping the village to the far right is the 18th-century *citadelle*, Fort Mirador, now home to a French Marine base. Scattered ruins crown several other hilltops.

Back to the left, that ancient windmill (1344) was originally used for grain; today it grinds out olive oil. The stony soil and dry weather conditions in the hills above Collioure are ideal for growing grapes. Those beautiful terraced vineyards, averaging 250 days of sunshine a year, grow primarily grenache, syrah, and mourvèdre grapes, which make terrific reds and rosés.

Collioure's medieval town hunkers down between its church and royal château, sandwiched defensively and spiritually between the two. The town was batted back and forth between the French and Spanish for centuries. Locals just wanted to be left alone—as Catalans (most still do today—notice the yellow-and-red Catalan flag flying above the château). The town was Spanish for nearly 400 years before becoming definitively French in 1659 (*merci* Louis XIV). After years of neglect, Collioure was rediscovered by artists drawn to its pastel houses and lovely setting. Henri Matisse, André Derain, Pablo Picasso, Georges Braque, Raoul Dufy, and Marc Chagall all dipped their brushes here at one time or another. You're likely to recognize Collioure in paintings in many museums across Europe.

Château Royal (Royal Castle)

The 800-year-old castle, built over Roman ruins, served as home over the years to Majorcan kings, Crusaders, Dominican monks, and Louis XIV (who had the final say on the appearance we see now). Today it serves tourists, offering great rampart walks, views, and mildly interesting local history exhibits.

Cost and Hours: €4, daily June-Sept 10:00-18:00, July-Aug until 19:00, Oct-May 9:00-17:00, tel. 04 68 82 06 43.

Notre-Dame des Anges (Our Lady of the Angels Church)

This waterfront church is worth a gander (daily 8:30-16:30). Find a pew and listen to the waves while searching your soul. Supporting a guiding light (in more than one way), the church's foundations are built into the sea, and its one-of-a-kind lighthouse-bell tower helped sailors return home safely. The highlight is its over-the-top golden altar, unusual in France but typical of Catalan churches across the border. Drop €1 in the box to the left of the altar: lights, cameras, reaction—*oh là là!*

Path of Fauvism (Chemin du Fauvisme)

Art lovers will enjoy meandering along Boulevard Boramar and seeing seven copies of paintings by Derain and Matisse—inspired by the artists' stays in Collioure in 1905—mounted as panels along sidewalk walls. Two additional panels are along Avenue du Mirador on the quieter part of town. The **Maison du Fauvisme** office (behind the TI at 10 Rue de la Prud'homie) sells "Path of Fauvism" fliers and offers a guided town walk (€7, 75 minutes).

If you enjoyed seeing these copies, you can view a good collection of original paintings by Derain and Matisse in the museum in Céret (see page 551) and in the recommended Hôtel les Templiers.

Beaches *(Plages)*

You'll usually find the best sand-to-stone ratio at Plage de Port d'Avall or Plage St. Vincent (chaise lounge rental-€10/day, paddleboat/kayak rentals-€20/hour, summer only). The tiny Plage de la Balette is quietest but rocky, with brilliant views of Collioure.

Wine Tasting

Collioure and the surrounding area produce well-respected wines, and many shops offer informal tastings of the sweet Banyuls and Collioure reds and rosés. Ask at the TI for places to taste. For a

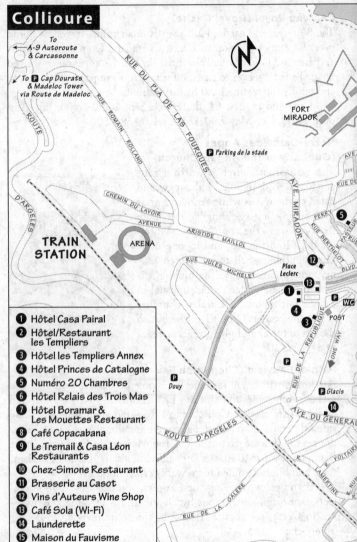

Collioure

To
← A-9 Autoroute
& Carcassonne

To ⓟ Cap Dourats
& Madeloc Tower
via Route de Madeloc

FORT
MIRADOR

ⓟ Parking de la stade

TRAIN STATION

ARENA

RUE DU PLA DE LAS FOURQUES

RUE ROMAIN ROLLAND

ROUTE D'ARGELES

CHEMIN DU LAVOIR

AVENUE ARISTIDE MAILLOL

RUE JULES MICHELET

AVE. MIRADOR

RUE DE

RUE PERTHELOT

FERRY

Place
Leclerc

⓬

⓭

❶

❹

❸

⓯

ⓟ WC

POST

RUE DE LA REPUBLIQUE

ONE WAY

ⓟ

ⓟ Douy

ⓟ Glacis

⓮

AVE. DU GENERAL

ROUTE D'ARGELES

RUE DE LA GALERE

R. VOLTAIRE

R. LAMERTINE

❶ Hôtel Casa Pairal
❷ Hôtel/Restaurant les Templiers
❸ Hôtel les Templiers Annex
❹ Hôtel Princes de Catalogne
❺ Numéro 20 Chambres
❻ Hôtel Relais des Trois Mas
❼ Hôtel Boramar & Les Mouettes Restaurant
❽ Café Copacabana
❾ Le Tremail & Casa Léon Restaurants
❿ Chez-Simone Restaurant
⓫ Brasserie au Casot
⓬ Vins d'Auteurs Wine Shop
⓭ Café Sola (Wi-Fi)
⓮ Launderette
⓯ Maison du Fauvisme

LANGUEDOC-ROUSSILLON

good selection of wines from many wineries and fair prices, try **Vins d'Auteurs** (next to Hôtel Fregate at 6 Place Maréchal Leclerc, daily, tel. 04 68 55 45 22).

WALKS AND HIKES

The four views described here offer different perspectives of this splendid area.

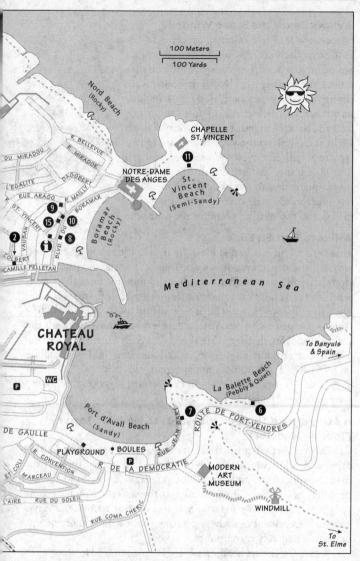

Easy Walk Around the Bay

For a 15-minute postcard stroll, walk all the way around Collioure's bay. Crossing the bridge from the main beach, find the promenade that runs around the base of the château and follow the coastline to the Port d'Avall and La Balette beaches—each with a unique personality. At the end of the line (La Balette), you can go back the way you came, or climb up the stairs to the road, and from there make your way up to the windmill coming back to town via the trail described next.

▲Views Below the Stone Windmill

Stone steps lead five minutes up behind Collioure's modern art museum to fine views that
are positively peachy at sunset. Find the museum's gateway behind Hôtel Triton, and walk
through its stony backyard. Red *le moulin* signs
recommend a clockwise loop up to the windmill and back: Bear left (hugging the museum's
back) and climb up the steps to a small, square
structure with fine views. From here, you can
huff up another five minutes to the windmill
itself (interesting to see, though the views are
less obstructed from lower down). The windmill is also the starting point for the next hike.

▲Hike to Fort St. Elme

This vertical hike is best done early or late (there's no shade) and
is worth the sweat, even if you don't make it to the top (trail starts
from windmill described above, allow 30 minutes from there each
way). You can't miss the square castle lurking high above Collioure.
The privately owned castle has a rich history (built in 1552 by Holy
Roman Emperor Charles V) and medieval exhibits—pick up the
English booklet that explains them (€6, daily April-Sept 10:30-
19:00, shorter hours off-season, closed mid-Nov-mid-Feb, mobile
06 64 61 82 42, www.fortsaintelme.com).

Cheaters can drive there via Port Vendres or take Collioure's
petit train (see "Helpful Hints," earlier).

▲▲Drive/Hike Through Vineyards to Madeloc Tower
(Tour de Madeloc)

Check your vertigo at the hotel, fasten your seatbelt, and take this
drive-and-hike combination high above Collioure. The narrow
road, hairpin turns, and absence of guardrails only add to the experience, as Collioure shrinks to Lego-size and the clouds become
your neighbors. Drive as far as you like on this route—the views
become exceptional quickly and turnouts allow for panorama appreciation and easy turnarounds.

Leave Collioure, heading toward Perpignan, and look for signs
reading *Tour de Madeloc* at the roundabout just above the train station. Climb through steep and rocky terraced vineyards, following
Tour signs and negotiating countless hairpin turns. About eight kilometers past the roundabout, turn right at the intersection toward
Balcon de Madeloc. In three more kilometers (about 20 minutes after
you leave Collioure), you'll come to a fork in the road with a paved
path (marked by a "no entry" symbol that applies to cars) and a road
leading downhill. Park at the fork, and walk up the paved path. The
views everywhere are magnificent—the Pyrenees on one side, and

the beach towns of Port Vendres and Collioure on the other. Allow 40 minutes at a slow-yet-steady pace along the splintered ridgetop to reach the eagle's-nest setting of the ancient tower (La Tour), now fitted with communication devices. Here you can commune with the gods, but beware—there's no shade, so do this hike early or late in the day.

NEAR COLLIOURE
Day Trip to Spain
The 15-mile, 40-minute coastal drive via the Col de Banyuls into Spain is beautiful and well worth the countless curves, even if you don't venture past the border.

To visit the wild **Salvador Dalí Theater-Museum,** take the autoroute to Figueres, which takes about an hour each way (museum: €14; possible to buy timed-entry tickets online in advance; if you miss your time, don't lose your ticket—just wait in the ticket line to exchange it; open July-Sept daily 9:00-20:00; Oct-June Tue-Sun 9:30-18:00—except from 10:30 Nov-Feb, closed Mon; last entry 45 minutes before closing, Spanish tel. 972-677-500, www.salvador-dali.org).

Train travelers can also day-trip to Spain, either to Barcelona (10/day, 3-4 hours, transfer in Perpignan or Portbou) or to the closer Figueres (6/day, 2 hours, transfer in Portbou). Get train schedules at the station.

Céret
To see the art that Collioure inspired, you'll have to drive 25 windy miles inland to this pleasing town, featuring fountains and mountains at its doorstep. Céret's claim to fame is its **modern art museum,** with works by some of Collioure's more famous visitors, including Picasso, Joan Miró, Chagall, and Matisse (€8, July-Sept daily 10:00-19:00, Oct-June until 17:30 and closed Mon, tel. 04 68 87 27 76, www.musee-ceret.com). Allow 40 minutes to Céret by car, or ride the bus—ask at Collioure's TI.

Sleeping in Collioure

($$$$ = Splurge, $$$ = Pricier, $$ = Moderate, $ = Budget)
Collioure has a fair range of hotels at favorable rates. You have two good choices for your hotel's location: central, in the old town (closer to train station); or across the bay, with views of the old town (10-minute walk from the central zone, with easier parking). Unless noted, hotels have air-conditioning and elevators.

IN THE OLD TOWN

Directions to the following places are given from the big Hôtel Fregate, at the edge of the old town, a 10-minute walk down from the train station.

$$ Hôtel Casa Pairal***, opposite Hôtel Fregate and hiding down a short alley (behind Café Sola), is a Mediterranean-elegant oasis. Enter to the sounds of a fountain gurgling in the flowery courtyard. Reclining lounges await in the garden and by the pool. The rooms are quiet and tastefully designed. "Privilege" rooms, on the first floor, have high ceilings and higher prices; some have small balconies over a courtyard (no elevator, pay parking—reserve ahead, good breakfast, Impasse des Palmiers, tel. 04 68 82 05 81, www.hotel-casa-pairal.com, contact@hotel-casa-pairal.com).

$ Hôtel les Templiers**, with three buildings in the heart of the old town, has wall-to-wall paintings in its main building, a perennially popular café-bar, low-key management, and good-value rooms. The paintings are payments in kind and thank-yous from artists who have stayed here: In the bar is a black-and-white photo of the hotel's owner with Picasso. In the main building—where you'll check in—choose between a view to the castle or facing the quieter back lane; many rooms here have traditional Catalan furniture. The annex, a five-minute walk away on Rue de la République, is a notch lower in quality and price. Across the street from the main hotel is a third building with a few cheaper, last-resort rooms (main hotel is a block toward beach from Hôtel Fregate along drainage canal at 12 Quai de l'Amirauté, tel. 04 68 98 31 10, www.hotel-templiers.com, contact@hotel-templiers.com).

$ Hôtel Princes de Catalogne*** offers 30 comfortable, spacious, contemporary rooms. For maximum quiet, get a room on the mountain side, or *côté montagne* (koh-tay mon-tan-yah) (some view rooms, limited free parking, next to Hôtel Casa Pairal, Ruedes Palmiers, tel. 04 68 98 30 00, www.hotel-princescatalogne.com, contact@hotel-princescatalogne.com).

$ Numéro 20 Chambres, with eager-to-help hosts Véronique and Noël, is a good budget value. Their four rooms are simple, clean, spacious, and suitable for families, with small fridges, coffee-makers, and microwaves (family rooms, cash only, air-con, no elevator, on pedestrian street two blocks past Hôtel Fregate at 20 Rue Pasteur, tel. 04 68 82 15 31, mobile 06 17 50 16 89, www.collioure-chambre-peroneille.fr, numero20ruepasteur@gmail.com).

ACROSS THE BAY

$$$ Hôtel Relais des Trois Mas**** clings to the hill above La Balette Beach and delivers 23 modern and comfortable rooms, many with killer views. They have the best view pool and whirlpool in Collioure (no elevator, free valet parking, Michelin-star **$$$$**

restaurant with good-value dinner *menus* from €49 and lunch *menus* from €30, Route de Port Vendres, tel. 04 68 82 05 07, www. relaisdestroismas.com, contact@relaisdes3mas.com).

$ Hôtel Boramar**, across the bay from Collioure's center, is understated and modest (like its owner Thierry), but well-maintained (also like Thierry) and a terrific value. Ten of the 14 rooms face the water, many with balconies, and a fine breakfast terrace faces the beach (family rooms, no air-con, no elevator, Wi-Fi in lobby, Rue Jean Bart, tel. 04 68 82 07 06, www.hotel-boramar.fr, hotelboramar.collioure@orange.fr).

Eating in Collioure

($$$$ = Splurge, $$$ = Pricier, $$ = Moderate, $ = Budget)
Test the local wine and eat anything Catalan, including the fish and anchovies (hand-filleted, as no machine has ever been able to accomplish this precise task). Consistency is elusive with restaurants in Collioure, but those listed below have been reliable. All of my recommended restaurants have indoor and outdoor tables, and most are in the old town. Your task is to decide whether you want to eat well or with a view. Several delicious *gelati* shops and a Grand Marnier crêpe stand next to the Café Copacabana fuel after-dinner strollers with the perfect last course. If you're traveling off-season, call ahead—many restaurants here are closed December through February.

$$ Café Copacabana, on the main beach (Boramar), offers big salads and a few seafood dishes in its sandy café. Skip their sidewalk-bound restaurant (which has a bigger selection but smaller view) and find a chair beachside. The quality is OK, considering the view, and it's family-friendly—kids can play on the beach while you dine or enjoy a sunset drink (closed Tue off-season, Boulevard Boramar, tel. 04 68 82 06 74).

$$$ Le Tremail is an OK choice for contemporary seafood and Catalan specialties served outside or in. With its colorful tile decor, it feels Spanish. It's a small and cozy place one block from the bay, where Rue Arago and Rue Mailly meet (daily year-round, 16 bis Rue Mailly, tel. 04 68 82 16 10).

$$$ Casa Léon, next door, offers similar Mediterranean cuisine but has more outside seating and finer food (daily, closed Sun eve and all day Mon off-season, 2 Rue Rière, tel. 04 68 82 10 74).

The restaurant at the recommended **$$$ Hôtel les Templiers** is popular with locals and dishes up reliable value (daily, 12 Quai de l'Amirauté, tel. 04 68 98 31 10).

$$ Chez-Simone, a lighthearted and *très* popular place, serves cheap tapas, *tartines,* and *plats* with sea views and smiles. Tapas sampler plates are a fun way to enjoy some variety (daily for lunch and dinner June-Sept, open in good weather only in spring and fall, Boulevard Boramar, tel. 04 34 29 93 47).

Around the Bay: $$$ La Plage aux Mouettes, facing Port d'Avall Beach, is a "brasserie on the sea" with reliable seafood-focused cuisine and terrific views (daily, next to the recommended Hôtel Boramar at 17 Rue Jean Bart, tel. 04 68 82 31 85).

$$ Brasserie au Casot owns the best setting away from the crowds, past the church on Plage St. Vincent, and serves salads and *plats* with views for a fair price. Matisse would dig the decor. Ask owner Alix about his homemade sangria (generally June-Sept daily for lunch and dinner, April-May lunch only and closed Wed, closed Oct-March, weather permitting, Plage St. Vincent, tel. 04 68 22 42 46).

Eating Cheaply: Small places sell a variety of meals to go (*à emporter;* ah em-pohr-tay) for budget-minded romantics wanting to dine on the bay.

Collioure Connections

From Collioure by Train to: Carcassonne (8/day, 2 hours, most require change in Narbonne), **Paris** (8/day, 6-7 hours, 1-2 changes, 1 direct night train to Gare d'Austerlitz in 12 hours), **Barcelona,** Spain (8/day, 2-4 hours, most change in Perpignan or Port Bou), **Figueres,** Spain (6/day, 1-2 hours, most change in Perpignan), **Avignon/Arles** (8/day, 3.5-4.5 hours, several transfer points possible).

PROVENCE

Arles • Avignon • Pont du Gard • Les Baux • Orange
• Villages of the Côtes du Rhône • Hill Towns of the Luberon

The magnificent region of Provence is shaped like a giant wedge of quiche. From its sun-burned crust, fanning out along the Mediterranean coast from the Camargue to Marseille, it stretches north along the Rhône Valley to Orange. The Romans were here in force and left many ruins—some of the best anywhere. Seven popes, artists such as Vincent van Gogh and Paul Cézanne, and author Peter Mayle all enjoyed their years in Provence. This destination features a splendid recipe of arid climate, oceans of vineyards, dramatic scenery, lively cities, and adorable hill-capping villages.

Explore the ghost town that is ancient Les Baux, and see France's greatest Roman ruins, the Pont du Gard aqueduct and the theater in Orange. Admire the skill of ball-tossing *boules* players in small squares in every Provençal village and city. Spend a few Van Gogh-inspired starry, starry nights in Arles. Youthful but classy Avignon bustles in the shadow of its brooding Palace of the Popes. It's a short hop from Arles or Avignon into the splendid scenery and villages of the Côtes du Rhône and Luberon regions.

PLANNING YOUR TIME

Make Arles or Avignon your sightseeing base—particularly if you have no car. Italophiles prefer smaller Arles, while poodles pick urban Avignon. **Arles** has a blue-collar quality; the entire city feels like Van Gogh's bedroom. **Avignon**—double the size of Arles—feels sophisticated, with more nightlife and shopping, and makes a good base for nondrivers thanks to its convenient public-transit options. To measure the pulse of rural Provence, spend at least one night in a smaller town (such as Vaison-la-Romaine or Roussillon)

PROVENCE

Provence

To Lyon &
Burgundy
Grignan
Valréas
To
Chamonix
& Alps
Ardèche
Ardèches
Gorges
Bollène
Nyons
Buis-les-
Baronnies
St. Cécile
Vaison-la-Romaine
Rasteau
Rhône
Sablet Séguret Dentelles de
Montmirail
Orange Gigondas
Vacqueyras Suzette Malaucène
Beaumes
de Venise
Châteauneuf-
du-Pape
C
O
T
E
S
D
U
R
H
O
N
E
Mont
Ventoux
Uzès
Gard
To Gorges
du Tarn
PONT DU
GARD
Remoulins
Avignon
Isle-sur-
la-Sorgue
Joucas
Nîmes
Durance
Gordes Roussillon
Beaucaire Tarascon
Oppède Apt
Les Baux St-Rémy
Cavaillon
L U B E R O N
Petit Rhône
Fontvieille
Alpilles
Lourmarin
Arles
Pertuis
CAMARGUE
Aigues-
Mortes
Rhône
To Gorges
du Verdon
Saintes-
Maries-
de-la-Mer
Aix-en-
Provence
Palette
Martigues
To Nice &
Côte d'Azur
FRANCE
Paris
Marseille
Aubagne
Mediterranean Sea
Les Cassis
Calanques
100 Miles
20 Kilometers
20 Miles

or in the countryside. These villages can be terminally quiet from mid-October to Easter.

When budgeting your time, you'll want a full day for sightseeing in Arles and Les Baux (for example, spend most of the day in Arles—best on Wed or Sat, when it's market day—and visit Les Baux in the late afternoon or early evening); a half-day for Avignon; and a day or two for the villages and sights in the countryside.

Pont du Gard is a short hop west of Avignon and on the way to/from Languedoc-Roussillon for drivers. Les Baux works well by car from Avignon and better from Arles, and in high season by bus from Arles. The town of Orange ties in tidily with a trip to the Côtes du Rhône villages. The Côtes du Rhône is ideal for wine connoisseurs and an easy stop for those heading to or from

Provence at a Glance

▲▲▲**Arles** Workaday town of evocative Roman ruins, Van Gogh memories, Provençal "bullgames," and easy pedestrian zones. See page 565.

▲▲▲**Pont du Gard** West of Avignon, a huge stone structure—part bridge and part aqueduct—heralding the greatness of ancient Rome. See page 620.

▲▲▲**Les Baux** Rock-top village sitting in the shadow of its ruined medieval citadel. See page 625.

▲▲**Orange** Leafy café-lined streets and the best-preserved Roman theater in existence. See page 632.

▲▲**Côtes du Rhône Wine Road** A drive through picturesque villages and vineyards, unfurling along a scenic wine-tasting route. See page 647.

▲**Avignon** History-rich city, famous for its medieval bridge and Gothic Palace of the Popes. See page 596.

▲**Vaison-la-Romaine** History-rich town atop a 2,000-year-old Roman site. See page 638.

▲**Hill Towns of the Luberon** Enticing terrain of age-old vineyards, limestone mountains, and sturdy little villages. See page 652.

the north. Vaison-la-Romaine is also ideal for those heading to/from the north, and Isle-sur-la-Sorgue (the most accessible small town by train) is conveniently located between Avignon and the Luberon.

GETTING AROUND PROVENCE

By Bus or Train: Public transit is good between cities and decent to some towns, but marginal at best to the smaller villages. Regular trains link Avignon, Arles, and Nîmes (no more than 30 minutes between each). Avignon has good train connections with Orange and adequate service to Isle-sur-la-Sorgue.

Buses connect many smaller towns, though service can be sporadic. From Arles you can catch a bus to Les Baux (high season only) and Stes-Maries-de-la-Mer (in the Camargue). From Avignon, you can bus to Pont du Gard, Isle-sur-la-Sorgue (also by train), and to some Côtes du Rhône villages.

While a tour of the Côtes du Rhône or Luberon is best on your

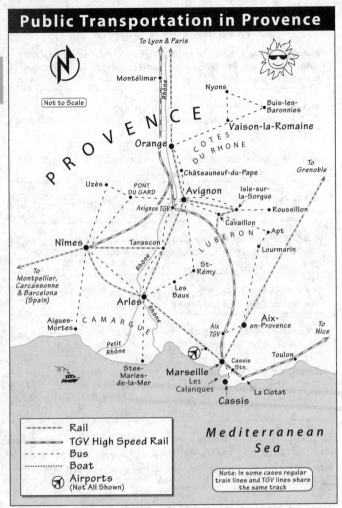

Public Transportation in Provence

To Lyon & Paris

Montélimar

Nyons

Buis-les-Baronnies

Vaison-la-Romaine

P R O V E N C E

Orange

CÔTES DU RHÔNE

Châteauneuf-du-Pape

To Grenoble

Uzès

PONT DU GARD

Avignon

Isle-sur-la-Sorgue

Avignon TGV

Roussillon

Cavaillon

L U B E R O N

Apt

Nîmes

Tarascon

Lourmarin

St-Rémy

To Montpellier, Carcassonne & Barcelona (Spain)

Les Baux

Arles

C A M A R G U E

Aigues-Mortes

Aix-en-Provence

To Nice

Aix TGV

Toulon

Petit Rhône

Cassis Stn.

Stes-Maries-de-la-Mer

Marseille

Les Calanques

La Ciotat

Cassis

Not to Scale

Rhône

Rhône

Rhône

Rail

TGV High Speed Rail

Bus

Boat

Airports (Not All Shown)

Mediterranean Sea

Note: In some cases regular train lines and TGV lines share the same track

own by car, a variety of minivan tours and basic bus excursions are available. (TIs in Arles and Avignon also have information on bus excursions to regional sights that are hard to reach *sans* car; see "Tours in Provence," later.)

By Car: The region is made to order for a car, though travel time between some sights will surprise you—thanks, in part, to narrow roads and endless roundabouts (for example, figure an hour from Les Baux to Pont du Gard, and two hours from Arles to Vaison-la-Romaine). The yellow Michelin maps #332 (Luberon and Côtes du Rhône) and #340 (Arles area) are worth considering; the larger-scale orange Michelin map #527 also includes the Riviera.

Be wary of thieves: Park only in well-monitored spaces and leave nothing valuable in your car. Drivers are smart to offload bags at hotels before sightseeing.

By Bike: Wind, heat, and hilly terrain make this region a challenge to bike. If you're determined, I list bike rental options in most cities (including electric bikes). **Telecycles** in St-Rémy will deliver your bike to your hotel (tel. 04 90 92 83 15 or 06 11 64 04 69, www.telecycles-location.com).

Tours in Provence

Tours with a Wine Focus

Wine Safari

Dutchman Mike Rijken runs a one-man show, taking travelers through the region he adopted more than 20 years ago. His English is fluent, and though his focus is on wine and wine villages, Mike knows the region thoroughly and is a good teacher of its history (€75/half-day, €130/day, priced per person, 2-6-person groups; pickups possible in Arles, Avignon, Lyon, Marseille, or Aix-en-Provence; tel. 04 90 35 59 21, mobile 06 19 29 50 81, www.winesafari.net, mikeswinesafari@orange.fr).

Le Vin à la Bouche

Celine Viany, a wine sommelier and charming tour guide, is an easy-to-be-with expert on her region and its chief product (from €75/half-day per person, from €90/day for up to 6 people, price depends on pickup location and number of clients, tel. 04 90 46 90 80, mobile 06 76 59 56 30, www.levinalabouche.com, contact@degustation-levinalabouche.com).

Avignon Wine Tour

For a playful and distinctly French perspective on wines of the Côtes du Rhône region, contact François Marcou, who runs his tours with passion and energy (€110/person for all-day wine tours that include 4 tastings, €80/person for half-day tours, €350 for private groups, less in winter, mobile 06 28 05 33 84, www.avignon-wine-tour.com, avignon.wine.tour@modulonet.fr).

Wine Uncovered

Passionate Englishman Olivier Hickman takes small groups on focused tours of selected wineries in Châteauneuf-du-Pape and in the villages near Vaison-la-Romaine. Olivier knows his subject matter inside and out. His in-depth tastings include a half-day tour of two or three wineries (€35-70/person for half-day to full-day tours, prices subject to minimum tour fees, mobile 06 75 10 10 01, www.wine-uncovered.com, olivier.hickman@orange.fr).

Tours du Rhône

American Doug Graves, who owns a small wine *domaine* in the Côtes du Rhône, runs custom tours of Châteauneuf-du-Pape, the villages of the Côtes du Rhône, and the Luberon Valley (€125/day per person for up to 4 people, mobile 06 37 16 04 56, www.toursdurhone.com, doug@masdelalionne.com).

Winery Plus Tours

This company offers small group tours centered on wine and food with a good dose of history and local culture. Experienced guide, chef, and wine connoisseur Joe McLean's tours focus on the wines of Uzès, Châteauneuf-du-Pape, and the Côtes du Rhône (ask about his cooking classes). Prices include pickups from Uzès hotels; pickups are possible from Arles and Avignon for a bit more (€60/half-day, €100/day, prices are per person, mobile 06 73 08 23 97, www.promo-vinum.com/gb/winetours, info@promo-vinum.com).

Provence & Wine

Romain Gouvernet is a young and sincere wine guide concentrating on the Côtes du Rhône (€95/half-day, €140/day, prices are per person, mobile 06 86 49 56 76, www.provenceandwine.com, provenceandwine@gmail.com).

Cultural/Historical Tours

Imagine Tours

This organization focuses on cultural excursions, offering personalized tours that allow visitors to discover the "true heart of Provence and Occitania." The itineraries are adapted to your interests, and the guides will meet you at your hotel or the departure point of your choice (€190/half-day, €315/day, prices for up to 4 people starting from near Avignon or Arles, mobile 06 89 22 19 87, www.imagine-tours.net, imagine.tours@gmail.com). They can also help plan your itinerary, book hotel rooms, or address other travel issues.

Local Guides

Catherine d'Antuono is a smart, capable, licensed guide for Aix-en-Provence and the region. She guides tours as far west as Pont du Gard and as far east as St-Tropez (€460/day for 2 people, then €15/person extra up to 8 maximum, mobile 06 17 94 69 61, tour.designer@provence-travel.com, www.provence-travel.com).

Discover Provence was founded by England-born Sarah Pernet, who has lived in Aix-en-Provence since 2001. She and her small team offer a variety of well-organized, easygoing, small-group tours to areas including the Luberon, Cassis, Arles, and St-Rémy (from €130/person for half-day tour, tel. 06 16 86 40 24, sarah@discover-provence.net, www.discover-provence.net).

The Rules of *Boules*

The game of *boules*—also called *pétanque*—is the horseshoes of France. Invented here in the early 1900s, it's a social yet serious sport, and endlessly entertaining to watch—even more so if you understand the rules.

The game is played with heavy metal balls and a small wooden target ball called a *cochonnet* (piglet). Whoever gets his *boule* closest to the *cochonnet* is awarded points. Teams commonly have specialist players: a *pointeur* and a *tireur.* The *pointeur*'s goal is to lob his balls as close to the target as he can. The *tireur*'s job is to blast away opponents' *boules.*

In teams of two, each player gets three *boules.* The starting team traces a small circle in the dirt (in which players must stand when launching their *boules*), and tosses the *cochonnet* about 30 feet to establish the target. The *boule* must be thrown underhand, and can be rolled, launched sky-high, or rocketed at its target. The first *pointeur* shoots, then the opposing *pointeur* shoots until his *boule* gets closer. Once the second team lands a *boule* nearer the *cochonnet,* the first team goes again. If the other team's *boule* is very near the *cochonnet,* the *tireur* will likely attempt to knock it away.

Once all boules have been launched, the tally is taken. The team with a *boule* closest to the *cochonnet* wins the round, and they receive a point for each *boule* closer to the target than their opponents' nearest *boule.* The first team to get to 13 points wins. A regulation *boules* field is 10 feet by 43 feet, but the game is played everywhere—just scratch a throwing circle in the sand, toss the *cochonnet,* and you're off.

Basic Transportation-Only Tours
Visit Provence

This company runs day tours from Avignon, Arles, Marseille, and in Aix-en-Provence. Tours from Avignon run year-round and cover a great variety of destinations; more limited tours from other cities run April through September only. Tours provide introductory commentary, but no guiding at the actual sights. They use eight-seat, air-conditioned minivans (about €60-80/half-day, €100-120/day). Ask about their cheaper big-bus excursions, or consider hiring a van and driver for your private use (plan on €220/half-day, €490/day, tel. 04 90 14 70 00, www.provence-reservation.com).

PROVENCE

HOW ABOUT THEM ROMANS?

Provence is littered with Roman ruins. Many scholars claim the best-preserved ancient Roman buildings are not in Italy, but in France. These ancient stones will be an important part of your sightseeing agenda in this region, so it's worth learning about how they came to be.

Classical Rome endured from about 500 B.C. through A.D. 500—spending about 500 years growing, 200 years peaking, and 300 years declining. Julius Caesar conquered Gaul—which included Provence—during the Gallic Wars (58-51 B.C.), then crossed the Rubicon River in 49 B.C. to incite civil war within the Roman Republic. He erected a temple to Jupiter on the future site of Paris' Notre-Dame Cathedral.

The concept of one-man rule lived on with his grandnephew, Octavian (whom he had also adopted as his son). Octavian killed Brutus, eliminated his rivals (Mark Antony and Cleopatra), and united Rome's warring factions. He took the title "Augustus" and became the first in a line of emperors who would control Rome for the next 500 years—ruling like a king, with the backing of the army and the rubber-stamp approval of the Senate. Rome morphed from a Republic into an Empire: a collection of many diverse territories ruled by a single man.

Augustus' reign marked the start of 200 years of peace, prosperity, and expansion known as the *Pax Romana*. At its peak (c. A.D. 117), the Roman Empire had 54 million people and stretched from Scotland in the north to Egypt in the south, as far west as Spain and as far east as modern-day Iraq. To the northeast, Rome was bounded by the Rhine and Danube rivers. On Roman maps, the Mediterranean was labeled *Mare Nostrum* ("Our Sea"). At its peak, "Rome" didn't just refer to the city, but to the entire civilized Western world.

The Romans were successful not only because they were good soldiers, but also because they were smart administrators and businessmen. People in conquered territories knew they had joined the winning team and that political stability would replace barbarian invasions. Trade thrived. Conquered peoples were welcomed into the fold of prosperity, linked by roads, education, common laws and gods, and the Latin language.

Provence, with its strategic location, benefited greatly from Rome's global economy and grew to become an important part of its worldwide empire. After Julius Caesar conquered Gaul, Emperor Augustus set out to Romanize it, building and renovating cities in the image of Rome. Most cities had a theater (some had several), baths, and aqueducts; the most important cities had sports arenas. The Romans also erected an elaborate infrastructure of roads, post offices, schools (teaching in Latin), police stations, and water-supply systems.

A typical Roman city (such as Nîmes, Arles, Orange, or Vaison-la-Romaine) was a garrison town, laid out on a grid plan with two main roads: one running north-south (the *cardus*), the other east-west (the *decumanus*). Approaching the city on your chariot, you'd pass by the cemetery, which was located outside of town for hygienic reasons. You'd enter the main gate and wheel past warehouses and apartment houses to the town square (forum). Facing the square were the most important temples, dedicated to the patron gods of the city. Nearby, you'd find bathhouses; like today's fitness clubs, these served the almost sacred dedication to personal vigor. Also close by were businesses that catered to the citizens' needs: the marketplace, bakeries, banks, and brothels.

Aqueducts brought fresh water for drinking, filling the baths, and delighting the citizens with bubbling fountains. Men flocked to the stadiums in Arles and Nîmes to bet on gladiator games; eager couples attended elaborate plays at theaters in Orange, Arles, and Vaison-la-Romaine. Marketplaces brimmed with exotic fruits, vegetables, and animals from the far reaches of the empire. Some cities in Provence

were more urban 2,000 years ago than they are today. For instance, Roman Arles had a population of 100,000—double today's size. Think about that when you visit.

When it came to construction, the Romans' magic building ingredient was concrete. A mixture of volcanic ash, lime, water, and small rocks, concrete—easier to work than stone, longer-lasting than wood—served as flooring, roofing, filler, glue, and support. Builders would start with a foundation of brick, then fill it in with poured concrete. They would then cover important structures, such as basilicas, in sheets of expensive marble (held on with nails), or decorate floors and walls with mosaics—proving just how talented the Romans were at turning the functional into art.

PROVENCE'S CUISINE SCENE

The almost extravagant use (by French standards) of garlic, olive oil, herbs, and tomatoes makes Provence's cuisine France's liveliest. To sample it, order anything *à la provençale*. Among the area's spicy specialties are ratatouille (a mixture of vegetables in a thick, herb-flavored tomato sauce), aioli (a rich, garlicky mayonnaise spread

Le Mistral

Provence lives with its vicious mistral winds, which blow 30-60 miles per hour, about 100 days out of the year. Locals say it blows in multiples of threes: three, six, or nine days in a row. The mistral clears people off the streets and turns lively cities into ghost towns. You'll likely spend a few hours or days taking refuge. The winds are strongest between noon and 15:00.

When the mistral blows, it's everywhere, and you can't escape. Author Peter Mayle said it could blow the ears off a donkey (I'd include the tail). According to the natives, it ruins crops, shutters, and roofs (look for stones holding tiles in place on many homes). They'll also tell you that this pernicious wind has driven many people crazy (including young Vincent van Gogh). A weak version of the wind is called a *mistralet*.

The mistral starts above the Alps and Massif Central mountains and gathers steam as it heads south, gaining momentum as it screams over the Rhône Valley (which acts like a funnel between the Alps and the Cévennes mountains) before exhausting itself when it hits the Mediterranean. And though this wind rattles shutters everywhere in the Riviera and Provence, it's strongest over the Rhône Valley...so Avignon, Arles, and the Côtes du Rhône villages bear its brunt. While wiping the dust from your eyes, remember the good news: The mistral brings clear skies.

over vegetables, potatoes, fish, or whatever), tapenade (a paste of pureed olives, capers, anchovies, herbs, and sometimes tuna), *soupe au pistou* (thin yet flavorful vegetable soup with a sauce—called *pistou*—of basil, garlic, and cheese), and *soupe à l'ail* (garlic soup, called *aigo bouido* in the local dialect). Look for *riz de Camargue* (the reddish, chewy, nutty-tasting rice that has taken over the Camargue area) and *taureau* (bull's meat). The native goat cheeses are Banon de Banon or Banon à la Feuille (wrapped in chestnut leaves) and spicy Picodon.

Don't miss the region's prized Cavaillon melons (cantaloupes) or its delicious cherries and apricots, which are often turned into jams and candied fruits.

Wines of Provence: Provence also produces some of France's great wines at relatively reasonable prices (€5-10/bottle on average). Look for wines from Gigondas, Rasteau, Cairanne, Beaumes-de-Venise, Vacqueyras, and Châteauneuf-du-Pape. For the cheapest but still-tasty wines, look for labels showing Côtes du Rhône Villages or Côtes de Provence. If you like rosé, you win. Rosés from Tavel are considered among the best in Provence. For reds, splurge for Châteauneuf-du-Pape or Gigondas, and for a fine aperitif wine or a dessert wine, try the Muscat from Beaumes-de-Venise.

PROVENCE MARKET DAYS

Provençal market days offer France's most colorful and tantalizing outdoor shopping. The best markets are on Monday in Cavaillon, Tuesday in Vaison-la-Romaine, Wednesday in St-Rémy, Thursday in Nyons or Orange, Friday in Lourmarin, Saturday in Arles, Uzès, and Apt, and, best of all, Sunday in Isle-sur-la-Sorgue. Crowds and parking problems abound at these popular events—arrive by 9:00, or, even better, sleep in the town the night before.

Arles

By helping Julius Caesar defeat his archrival Gnaeus Pompey at Marseille, Arles (pronounced "arl") earned the imperial nod and was made an important port city. With the first bridge over the Rhône River, Arles was a key stop on the Roman road from Italy to Spain, the Via Domitia. After reigning as the seat of an important archbishop and a trading center for centuries, the city became a sleepy backwater of little importance in the 1700s. Vincent van Gogh settled here in the late 1800s, but left only a chunk of his ear (now long gone). American bombers destroyed much of Arles in World War II as the townsfolk hid out in its underground Roman galleries. But today Arles thrives again, with its evocative Roman ruins, an eclectic assortment of museums, made-for-ice-cream pedestrian zones, and squares that play hide-and-seek with visitors.

Workaday Arles is a city in search of an economy, and compared to nearby Avignon and Nimes, it feels unpolished and even a little dirty. But to me, that's part of its charm. Locals display a genuine jôie de vivre that's hard to sense in Arles' larger, more cosmopolitan neighbors.

PLANNING YOUR TIME

Start at the Ancient History Museum (at the edge of town, closed Tue; see page 582) for a helpful overview—drivers should try to do this museum on their way into Arles—then dive into the city-center sights, linked by my Arles City Walk. For cost-efficient sightseeing, get the Liberty Passport, which covers the ancient monuments and the Ancient History Museum (see "Helpful Hints").

Orientation to Arles

Arles faces the Mediterranean, turning its back on Paris. And though the town is built along the Rhône, it largely ignores the river. Landmarks hide in Arles' medieval tangle of narrow, winding streets. Hotels have good, free city maps, and helpful street-corner signs point you toward sights and hotels.

TOURIST INFORMATION

The TI is on the ring road Boulevard des Lices, at Esplanade Charles de Gaulle (April-Sept daily 9:00-18:45; Oct-March Mon-Sat 9:00-16:45, Sun 10:00-13:00; tel. 04 90 18 41 20, www.arlestourisme. com). While there, take advantage of free Wi-Fi, pick up the city map and bus schedules, and request English information on nearby destinations such as the Camargue. Ask about walking tours and "bullgames" in Arles and nearby towns (Provence's more humane version of bullfights—see page 587). The TI sells the worthwhile Liberty Passport (see "Helpful Hints," later).

ARRIVAL IN ARLES

By Train or Bus: The train station is on the river, a 10-minute walk from the town center. There's no baggage storage at the station, but you can walk 10 minutes to stow it at Hôtel Régence (see "Helpful Hints," later). The bus station is next to the train station.

To reach the town center or Ancient History Museum from the train station, wait for the free **Navia shuttle** at the glass shelter facing away from the station (cross the street and veer left, 2/hour Mon-Sat 7:00-19:00, none Sun). The bus makes a counterclockwise loop around Arles, stopping near most of my recommended hotels (see map on page 568 for stops). **Taxis** usually wait in front of the station (if there's not a taxi waiting, call 04 90 96 52 76 or the posted telephone numbers, or ask the info desk staff to call for you). Allow about €10-15 to any of my recommended hotels.

By Car: For most hotels, first follow signs to *Centre-Ville*, then *Gare SNCF* (train station). You'll come to a big roundabout (Place Lamartine) with a Monoprix department store to the right. Park along the city wall here (except on Tue night when tow trucks clear things out for the Wed market) and locate your hotel on foot before stashing your car in longer-term parking. The hotels I list are no more than a 15-minute walk from here. All parking is paid except at the train station (10-15-minute walk) and from 19:00-9:00 and all day Sunday (some meters limited to 2.5 hours). Theft is a problem—leave nothing in your car.

Most hotels have garage deals for about €7-12/day. If your hotel doesn't offer parking, Parking des Lices (Arles' only parking garage), near the TI on Boulevard des Lices, is a good fallback (€2.50/hour, €18/24 hours).

PROVENCE

HELPFUL HINTS
Exchange Rate: €1 = about $1.10

Country Calling Code: 33 (see page 1082 for dialing instructions)

Sightseeing Tips: Arles has a smart ticket-and-hours plan for its sightseeing. Ancient monuments, such as the Roman Arena and Classical Theater, all have the **same hours** (daily May-Sept 9:00-19:00, April and Oct 9:00-18:00, Nov-March 10:00-17:00). A good-value €11 combo-ticket—the **Liberty Passport** (Le Passeport Liberté)—covers any four monuments, the Ancient History Museum, and the Réattu Museum (but not the Fondation Van Gogh gallery). Buy the pass at the TI or any included sight.

While only the Ancient History Museum and Roman Arena are essential to enter, the pass makes the city fun to explore, as you can pop into nearly everything, even for just a couple of minutes. The moral: Buy the pass and see more.

Market Days: The big markets are on Wednesdays and Saturdays. For details, see page 587.

Crowds: An international photo event jams hotels the second weekend of July. The let-'er-rip, twice-yearly Féria draws crowds over Easter and in mid-September.

Wi-Fi: The TI has free Wi-Fi.

Baggage Storage and Bike Rental: The recommended **Hôtel Régence** will store your bags for €3 (daily 7:30-22:00 mid-March-mid-Nov, closed in winter, 5 Rue Marius Jouveau). They also rent bikes (€7/half-day, €15/day, reserve ahead for electric bikes, one-way rentals within Provence possible, same hours as baggage storage). From Arles you can ride to Les Baux (25 miles round-trip). It's a darn steep climb going into Les Baux, so rent an electric bike. Those in great shape can consider biking into the level Camargue (40 miles round-trip, forget it in the wind).

Laundry: A launderette is at 41 Rue du 4 Septembre (daily 7:00-21:00).

Car Rental: Europcar and Hertz are downtown (Europcar is at 61 Avenue de Stalingrad, tel. 04 90 93 23 24; Hertz is closer to Place Voltaire at 10 Boulevard Emile Combes, tel. 04 90 96 75 23).

Local Guides: Charming **Agnes Barrier,** who knows Arles and

PROVENCE

Arles

Arles Walk

1. The Yellow House (Easel)
2. Starry Night over the Rhône (Easel)
3. Rue de la Cavalerie
4. Old Town
5. Arena (Easel) & Roman Arena
6. Alpilles Mountains View
7. Jardin d'Eté (Easel)
8. Classical Theater
9. Republic Square
10. Cryptoporticos
11. St. Trophime Church
12. Rue de la République

13. Espace Van Gogh (Easel)
14. Fondation Van Gogh
15. Rue du Docteur Fanton (Daycare, Bar El Paseo)
16. Forum Square & Café at Night (Easel)

Other

17. Hôtel Régence (Baggage Storage & Bike Rental)
18. Launderette
19. To Europcar Car Rental
20. Hertz Car Rental

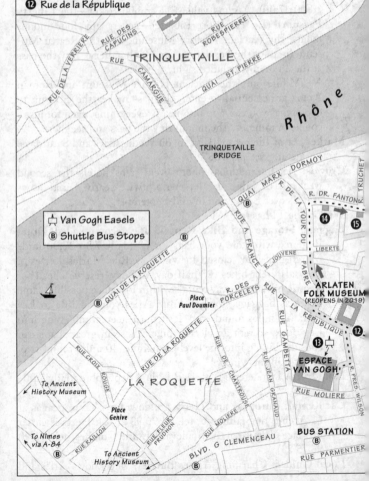

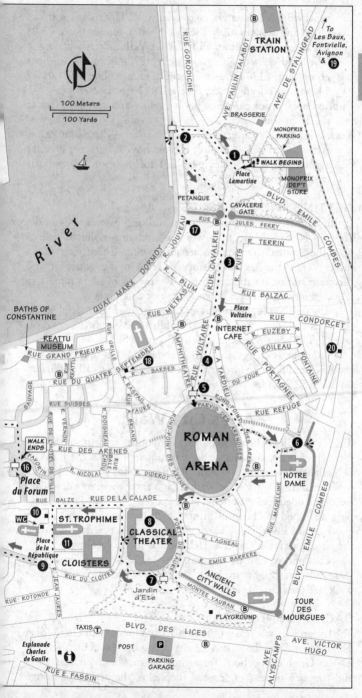

nearby sights intimately, enjoys her work. Her tours cover Van Gogh and Roman history (€130/3 hours, mobile 06 11 23 03 73, agnes.barrier@hotmail.fr). **Alice Vallat** offers a variety of scheduled visits of Arles' key sights (€20/person for 1.5-hour group tour, €130 for 3-hour private tour, mobile 06 74 01 22 54, www.guidearles.com, alice.vallat13@gmail.com.

Public Pools: Arles has three pools (indoor and outdoor). Ask at the TI or your hotel.

Boules: The local "*boul*ing alley" is by the river on Place Lamartine. After their afternoon naps, the old boys congregate here for a game of *pétanque* (see page 561 for more on this popular local pastime).

GETTING AROUND ARLES

In this flat city, everything's within **walking** distance. Only the Ancient History Museum is worth considering a shuttle ride or taxi. The elevated riverside promenade provides Rhône views and a direct route to the Ancient History Museum (to the southwest) and the train station (to the northeast). Keep your head up for *Starry Night* memories, but eyes down for doggie droppings.

The free **Navia shuttle** circles the town, useful for access to the train station, hotels, and the Ancient History Museum (see map on page 568, 2/hour, Mon-Sat 7:00-19:00, none Sun).

Arles' **taxis** charge a set fee of about €11, but nothing except the Ancient History Museum is worth a cab ride. To call a taxi, dial 04 90 96 52 76 or 04 90 96 90 03.

Arles City Walk

The joy of Arles is how its compact core mixes ancient sights, Van Gogh memories, and a raw and real contemporary scene that can be delightfully covered on foot. All dimensions of the city come together in this self-guided walk. If you enter the sights described (recommended, even if briefly; all are covered by the Liberty Passport described in "Helpful Hints," earlier), this walk will take a good part of a day. Think about splitting it over two days or doing the latter half (after the Classical Theater) in the evening.

For context, visit the Ancient History Museum before taking this walk (see "Sights in Arles," later). To trace the route of this walk, see the map on page 568.

BACKGROUND

The life and artistic times of Dutch artist **Vincent van Gogh** form a big part of Arles' draw, and the city does a fine job of highlighting its Van Gogh connection: Throughout town, about a dozen steel-and-concrete panels, or "easels" (depicting the artist's paintings alongside the current view of that painting's subject), provide then-and-now comparisons.

In the dead of winter in 1888, 35-year-old Van Gogh left big-city Paris for Provence, hoping to jump-start his floundering career and social life. He was as inspired as he was lonely. Coming from the gray skies and flat lands of the north, Vincent was bowled over by everything Provençal—the sun, bright colors, rugged landscape, and raw people. For the next two years he painted furiously, cranking out a masterpiece every few days.

Only a few of the 200-plus paintings that Van Gogh did in the south can be found today in the city that so moved him (you can see at least one at the Fondation Van Gogh gallery, which we'll visit on this stroll). But here you can walk the same streets he knew and see the places he painted.

• *Start at the north gate of the city, just outside the medieval wall in Place Lamartine (100 yards in front of the medieval gate, with the big Monoprix store across the street to the right, just beyond the roundabout). A four-foot-tall easel shows Van Gogh's painting.*

❶ *The Yellow House* Easel

Vincent arrived in Arles on February 20, 1888, to a foot of snow. He rented a small house on the north side of Place Lamartine.

The house was destroyed in 1944 by an errant bridge-seeking bomb, but the four-story building behind it—where you see the brasserie—still stands (find it in the painting). The house had four rooms, including a small studio and the cramped trapezoid-shaped bedroom made famous in paintings. It was painted yellow inside and out, and Vincent named it..."The Yellow House." In the distance, the painting shows the same bridges you see today.

In those days, a short walk from Place Lamartine led to open fields. Donning his straw hat, Vincent set up his easel outdoors and painted quickly, capturing what he saw and felt—the blossoming fruit trees, gnarled olive trees, peasants sowing and reaping, jagged peaks, and windblown fields, all lit by a brilliant sun that drove him to use ever-brighter paints.

• *Walk directly to the river. You'll pass a monument in honor of two WWII*

American pilots killed in action during the liberation of Arles (erected in 2002 as a post-9/11 sign of solidarity with Americans), a post celebrating Arles' many sister cities (left), and a big concrete high school (right).

At the river, find the easel in the wall where ramps lead down (often to huge river-cruise boats whose tour groups flood Arles in the morning).

❷ Starry Night over the Rhône Easel

One night, Vincent set up shop along the river and painted the stars boiling above the city skyline. Vincent looked to the night sky for the divine and was the first to paint outside after dark, adapting his straw hat to hold candles (which must have blown the minds of locals back then). As his paintings progressed, the stars became larger and more animated (like Vincent himself). The lone couple in the painting pops up again and again in his work. (Note: This painting is not the *Starry Night* you're thinking of—that one was painted later, in St-Rémy.)

To his sister Wilhelmina, Vincent wrote, "At present I absolutely want to paint a starry sky. It often seems to me that night is still more richly colored than the day; having hues of the most intense violets, blues, and greens. If only you pay attention to it, you will see that certain stars are lemon yellow, others pink or a green, blue, and forget-me-not brilliance." Vincent painted this scene on his last night in Arles.

• *With your back to the river, angle right through the scruffy park of sycamore trees and (if it's afternoon),* pétanque *players. Continue into town through the park and through the stumpy 14th-century stone towers where the city gates once stood.*

❸ Rue de la Cavalerie

Van Gogh walked into town the same way. Arles' 19th-century red light district was just east of Rue de la Cavalerie, and the far-from-home Dutchman spent many lonely nights in its bars and brothels. The street still has a certain edgy local color. Saddle up to the bar in the down-and-dirty café at Hôtel de Paris for a taste. It's a friendly watering hole with fun paintings of football and bull fighting.

• *Continuing along, you'll come to an ornately decorated fountain from 1887: two columns with a mosaic celebrating the high culture of Provence (she's the winged woman who obviously loves music and reading).*

Stay left and keep walking to Place Voltaire, a center of this working-class neighborhood (you'll see the local Communist Party headquarters across on the left).

❹ Old Town

You've left the bombed-out part of town and entered the old town, with buildings predating World War II. The stony white arches of the ancient Roman Arena ahead mark your destination. As you hike up Rue Voltaire, notice the shutters, which contribute to Arles' character. The old town is strictly preserved: These traditional shutters come in a variety of styles but cannot be changed.

• *Keep straight up Rue Voltaire, climb to the Roman Arena, and find the* Arena *easel at the top of the stairs, to the right.*

❺ *Arena* Easel

All summer long, fueled by sun and alcohol, Vincent painted the town. He loved the bullfights in the arena and sketched the colorful surge of the crowds, spending more time studying the people than watching the bullfights (notice how the bull is barely visible). Vincent had little interest in Arles' antiquity—it was people and nature that fascinated him.

• *Now, let's visit the actual...*

Roman Arena (Amphithéâtre)

This well-preserved arena is worth ▲▲ and is still in use today. Nearly 2,000 years ago, gladiators fought wild animals here to the delight of 20,000 scream-  ing fans. Now local daredevils still fight wild animals here— "bullgame" posters around the arena advertise upcoming spectacles (see page 587). Don't miss the tower climb for fantastic views over Arles, the arena, and the Rhône River.

Cost and Hours: €8 combo-ticket with Classical Theater, covered by Liberty Passport; open daily May-Sept 9:00-19:00, April and Oct 9:00-18:00, Nov-March 10:00-17:00, Rond-point des Arènes, tel. 04 90 49 36 86, www.arenes-arles.com.

Visiting the Arena: After passing the ticket kiosk, find the helpful English display under the second arch describing the arena's history and renovation, then take a seat in the theater. Thirty-four rows of stone bleachers extended all the way to the top of those vacant arches that circle the arena. The arches were numbered to help distracted fans find their seats. The many passageways you'll see (called *vomitoires*) allowed for rapid dispersal after the games—fights would break out among frenzied fans if they couldn't leave quickly. The arena is a fine example of Roman engineering...and propaganda. In the spirit of "give them bread and circuses," games were free, sponsored by city bigwigs. The idea was to create a populace that was thoroughly Roman—enjoying the same activities, entertainment, and thoughts (something like how US television contributes to the American psyche).

If you visited Arles' Ancient History Museum, remember the arena model you saw there. An amphitheater is literally a double theater: two theaters facing each other, designed so twice as many people could view a spectacle. The **floor** where the action took place was the *arena* (literally, "sand," which absorbed the blood). The arena's floor, which covered passages and storage areas underneath, came with an elevator for surprise appearances of wild animals. (While Rome could afford exotic beasts, places like Arles made do with snarling local fauna...bulls, wild boars, and lots of bears.) The standard fight was as real as professional wrestling is today—mostly just crowd-pleasing.

After Rome fell and stability was replaced by Dark Ages chaos, this huge structure was put to good use. During medieval times and until the early 1800s, the arches were bricked up and the stadium became a fortified town—with 200 humble homes crammed within its circular defenses. Parts of three of the medieval towers survive. To climb one of those towers and enjoy magnificent **views** over Arles and the arena, find the *Terrasses* sign leading up steps from the outermost, ground-level hall (on the opposite side of the ticket office from which you entered). Next, circumnavigate the stadium following *Covered Walkway* signs and savor the receding views of arches and fine stonework of those Roman masons.

• *Exit the arena to the right. A quarter of the way around, go up the cute stepped lane (Rue Renan, next to Volubilis Restaurant). Take three steps and turn around to study the arena. The big stones are Roman; the little medieval stones—more like rubble—filling the two upper-level archways are a reminder of the arena's time as a fortified town in the Middle Ages. You can even see rooflines and beam holes where the Roman structure provided a solid foundation to lean on.*

Hike up the pretty lane and continue through the parking lot, keeping to the left of the stark and stony church to the highest point in Arles. Take in the view.

❻ Alpilles Mountains View

This view pretty much matches what Vincent Van Gogh, an avid walker, would have seen. Imagine him hauling his easel into those fields under intense sun, leaning against a ferocious wind, struggling to keep his hat on.

Vincent carried his easel as far as the medieval Abbey of Montmajour, that bulky structure three miles straight ahead on the hill. The St. Paul Hospital, where he was eventually treated in St-Rémy, is on the other side of the Alpilles mountains (which look more like hills to me), several miles beyond Montmajour.

• *Now might be a good time to take a break. Several good restaurant options are nearby (see page 594). When you're ready, continue circling the Roman Arena. At the high point, turn left and walk out Rue de Porte de Laure. (You'll pass the Classical Theater on your right, which we'll see later.) After a couple of blocks, just after the street turns left, go right, down the curved staircase into the park. At the bottom of the stairs, take the second right (through the gate and into the park) and find the...*

❼ Jardin d'Eté Easel

Vincent spent many a sunny day painting the leafy Jardin d'Eté. In another letter to his sister, Vincent wrote, "I don't know whether you can understand that one may make a poem by arranging colors...In a similar manner, the bizarre lines, purposely selected and multiplied, meandering all through the picture may not present a literal image of the garden, but they may present it to our minds as if in a dream."

• *Hike uphill through the park toward the three-story surviving tower of the ancient Roman Theater. At the ancient tower, follow the white metal fence to the left along "the garden of stone"—a collection of ancient carved bits of a once grand Roman theater. Go up four steps and around to the right for a fine view of the...*

❽ Classical Theater (Théâtre Antique)

This first-century B.C. Roman theater once seated 10,000...just like the theater in nearby Orange. But unlike Orange, here in Arles there was no hillside to provide structural support. Instead, this elegant, three-level structure had 27 buttress arches radiating out behind the seats. From the outside, it looked much like the adjacent arena.

Cost and Hours: €8 combo-ticket with Roman Arena, covered by Liberty Passport, same hours as Arena.

Visiting the Theater: Start with the 10-minute video outside, which provides helpful background information and images that make it easier to put the scattered stones back in place (crouch in front to make out the small English subtitles).

Then walk into the theater and pull up a stone seat in a center aisle. (For more context, read the description of Orange's Roman theater on page 634 while you rest.) Imagine that for 500 years, ancient Romans gathered here for entertainment. The original structure was much higher, with 33 rows of seats covering three levels to accommodate demand. During the Middle Ages, the old theater became a convenient town quarry—much of St. Trophime Church was built from theater rubble. Precious little of the original theater survives—though it still is used for events, with seating for 2,000 spectators.

Two lonely Corinthian columns are all that remain of a three-story stage wall that once featured more than 100 columns and statues painted in vibrant colors (a model in the Ancient History Museum shows the complete theater). Principal actors entered through the central arch, over which a grandiose statue of Caesar Augustus stood (it's now on display at the Ancient History Museum). Bit players entered through side arches. The orchestra section is defined by a semicircular pattern in the stone in front of you. Stepping up onto the left side of the stage, look down to the slender channel that allowed the brilliant-red curtain to disappear below, like magic. The stage, which was built of wood, was about 160 feet across and 20 feet deep. The actors' changing rooms are backstage, down the steps.

• *From the theater, walk downhill on Rue de la Calade. Take the first left into a big square.*

❾ Republic Square (Place de la République)

This square used to be called "Place Royale"...until the French Revolution. The obelisk was the former centerpiece of Arles' Roman Circus (outside of town). The lions at its base are the symbol of the city, whose slogan is (roughly) "the gentle lion." Observe the age-old scene: tourists, peasants, shoppers, pilgrims, children, and street musicians. The City Hall (Hôtel de Ville) has a French Baroque facade, built in the same generation as Versailles. Where there's a city hall, there's always a free WC (if you win the Revolution, you can pee for free at the mayor's home). Notice the flags: The yellow-and-red of Provence is the same as the yellow-and-red of Catalunya, its linguistic cousin in Spain.

• *Today's City Hall sits upon an ancient city center. Inside you'll find the entrance to an ancient* cryptoportico *(foundation).*

❿ Cryptoporticos (Cryptoportiques)

This dark, drippy underworld of Roman arches was constructed to support the upper half of Forum Square. Two thousand years ago, most of this gallery of arches was at or above street level; modern Arles has buried about 20 feet of its history over the millennia. Through the tiny windows high up you would have seen the sandals of Romans on their way to the forum. Other than dark arches and broken bits of forum littering the dirt floor, there's not much down here beyond ancient memories (€3.50, covered by Liberty Passport, same hours as Arena).

• *The highlight of Place de la République is...*

⓫ St. Trophime Church

Named after a third-century bishop of Arles, this church, worth ▲▲, sports the finest Romanesque main entrance I've seen anywhere. The Romanesque and Gothic interior—with tapestries, relics, and a rare painting from the French Revolution when this was a "Temple of Reason"—is worth a visit.

Cost and Hours: Free, daily 9:00-12:00 & 14:00-18:30, until 17:00 Oct-March.

Exterior: Like a Roman triumphal arch, the church **facade** trumpets the promise of Judgment Day. The tympanum (the semi-

circular area above the door) is filled with Christian symbolism. Christ sits in majesty, surrounded by symbols of the four evangelists: Matthew (the winged man), Mark (the winged lion), Luke (the ox), and John (the eagle). The 12 apostles are lined up below Jesus. It's Judgment Day...some are saved and others aren't. No-

tice the condemned (on the right)—a chain gang doing a sad bunny-hop over the fires of hell. For them, the tune trumpeted by the three angels above Christ is not a happy one. Below the chain gang, St. Stephen is being stoned to death, with his soul leaving through his mouth and instantly being welcomed by angels. Study the exquisite detail. In an illiterate world, long before the vivid images of our Technicolor time, this was colorfully painted, like a neon billboard over the town square. It's full of meaning, and a medieval pilgrim understood it all.

Interior: Just inside the door on the right, a yellow chart locates the interior highlights and helps explain the carvings you just saw on the tympanum. The tall 12th-century Romanesque nave is decorated by a set of tapestries (typical in the Middle Ages) showing scenes from the life of Mary (17th century, from the French town of Aubusson). Circle the church counterclockwise.

Stop into the first open chapel, the **Chapel of Baptism,** to view a statue of St. John Paul II under the window. Facing the window, look to the right wall where you'll see a faded painting of a triangle with a sunburst from 1789. The French Revolution secularized the country and made churches "Temples of Reason." This painting is the only example I've seen of church decor from this age.

Amble around the ambulatory toward the **Gothic apse.** Choose which chapel you need or want: If you have the plague or cholera, visit the chapel devoted to St. Roch—notice the testimonial plaques of gratitude on the wall. Some spaces are still available...if you hurry.

Two-thirds of the way around, find the **relic chapel** behind the ornate wrought iron gate, with its fine golden boxes that hold long-venerated bones of obscure saints. These relics generated lots of money for the church from pilgrims through the ages. Pop in a coin to share some light. The next chapel houses the skull of St. Anthony of the Desert.

Nearing the exit, look for two black columns and the early-Christian **sarcophagi** from Roman Arles (dated about A.D. 300). One sarcophagus shows Moses and the Israelites crossing the Red Sea. You'll see Christians wearing togas and praying like evangelicals do today—hands raised. The heads were likely lopped off during the French Revolution.

This church is a stop on the ancient pilgrimage route to Santiago de Compostela in northwest Spain. For 800 years pilgrims on their way to Santiago have paused here...and they still do today. Notice the modern-day pilgrimages advertised on the far right near the church's entry.

• *To reach the adjacent peaceful cloister, leave the church, turn left, then left again through a courtyard.*

St. Trophime Cloisters

Worth seeing if you have the Liberty Passport (otherwise €4, same hours as Arena), the cloisters' many small columns were scavenged from the ancient Roman theater and used to create an oasis of peace in Arles' center. Enjoy the delicate, sculpted capitals, the rounded Romanesque arches (12th century), and the pointed Gothic ones (14th century). The pretty vaulted hall exhibits 17th-century tapestries showing scenes from the First Crusade to the Holy Land. Up one floor, there's an instructive video and a chance to walk outside along an angled rooftop designed to catch rainwater: Notice the slanted gutter that channeled the water into a cistern and the heavy roof slabs covering the tapestry hall below.

• *From Place de la République, exit on the far corner (opposite the church and kitty-corner from where you entered, to stroll a delightful pedestrian street.*

⑫ Rue de la République

Rue da la République is Arles' primary shopping street. Walk downhill, enjoying the scene and popping into shops that catch your interest.

Near the start is **Maison Soulier Bakery**. Inside you'll be tempted by *fougasse* (bread studded with herbs, olives, and bacon bits), *sablés Provençal* (cookies made with honey and almonds), *tarte lavande* (a sweet almond lavender tart), and big crispy meringues (the egg-white-and-sugary answer to cotton candy—a cheap favorite of local kids). A few doors down is **Restaurant L'Atelier** (with two prized Michelin stars), **L'Occitane en Provence** (local perfumes), and **Puyricard Chocolate** (with enticing €1 treats and *calisson,* a sweet/bitter almond delight), as well as local design and antique shops. The fragile spiral columns on the right (just before the tourist-pleasing Lavender Boutique on the corner) show what 400 years of weather can do to decorative stonework.

• *Take the first left onto Rue Président Wilson. Just after the butcher shop (Chez Mère Grand, with local pork-and-bull sausages hanging above a counter filled with precooked dishes to take home and heat up), turn right to find the* **Hôtel Dieu,** *a hospital made famous by one of its patients: Vincent van Gogh.*

⑬ *Espace* Van Gogh Easel

In December 1888, shortly after his famous ear-cutting incident (see *Café at Night* easel, described later), Vincent was admitted into the local hospital—today's Espace

Van Gogh cultural center (the Espace is free, but only the courtyard is open to the public). It surrounds a flowery courtyard that the artist loved and painted when he was being treated for blood loss, hallucinations, and severe depression that left him bedridden for a month. The citizens of Arles circulated a petition demanding that the mad Dutchman be kept under medical supervision. Félix Rey, Vincent's kind doctor, worked out a compromise: The artist could leave during the day so that he could continue painting, but he had to sleep at the hospital at night. Look through the postcards sold in the courtyard and find a painting of Vincent's ward showing nuns attending to patients in a gray hall *(Ward of Arles Hospital).*

• *Return to Rue de la République. Take a left and continue two blocks downhill. Take the second right on Rue Tour de Fabre and follow signs to* Fondation Van Gogh. *After a few steps, you'll pass* **La Main Qui Pense** *(The Hand That Thinks) pottery shop and workshop, where Cécile Cayrol is busy creating and teaching. A couple blocks farther down, turn right onto Rue du Docteur Fanton (where you see "Vincent"). On your immediate right is the...*

⑭ Fondation Van Gogh

This art foundation, worth ▲, delivers a refreshing stop for modern-art lovers and Van Gogh fans, with two temporary exhibits per year in which contemporary artists pay homage to Vincent through thought-provoking interpretations of his works. You'll also see at least one original work by Van Gogh (painted during his time in the region). The gift shop has a variety of souvenirs, prints, and postcards.

Cost and Hours: €9, daily 11:00-19:00 except closed be-

PROVENCE

tween exhibits and likely Mon off-season—check website for current hours, audioguide-€3, Hôtel Leautaud de Donines, 35 Rue du Docteur Fanton, tel. 04 90 49 94 04, www.fondation-vincentvangogh-arles.org.

• *Continue down Rue du Docteur Fanton toward the river.*

⓰ Rue du Docteur Fanton

A string of recommended restaurants is on the left. On the right is the **Crèche Municipale.** Open workdays, this is a free government-funded daycare where parents can drop off their infants up to two years old. The notion: No worker should face financial hardship in order to receive quality childcare. At the next corner is the recommended **Soleileis,** Arles' top ice cream shop.

At the strawberry-and-vanilla ice cream cone, turn right and step into **Bar El Paseo** at 4 Rue des Thermes. The main museum-like room is absolutely full of bull—including the mounted heads of three big ones who died in the local arena and a big black-and-white photo of Arles' arena packed to capacity. Senora Leal—whose family is famous for its bullfighters—has wallpapered the place with photos and bullfighting memorabilia, and serves good Spanish Rioja wine and sangria.

• *A few steps farther is...*

⓰ Forum Square (Place du Forum)

Named for the Roman forum that once stood here, Forum Square, worth ▲, was the political and religious center of Roman Arles.

Still lively, this café-crammed square is a local watering hole and popular for a *pastis* (anise-based aperitif). The bistros on the square can put together a passable salad or *plat du jour*—and when you sprinkle on the ambience, that's €14 well spent.

At the corner of Grand Hôtel Nord-Pinus (a favorite of Pablo Picasso), a plaque shows how the Romans built a foundation of galleries to make the main square level in order to compensate for Arles' slope down to the river. The two columns are all that survive from the upper story of the entry to the forum. Steps leading to the entrance are buried—the Roman street level was about 20 feet below you.

The statue on the square is of **Frédéric Mistral** (1830-1914). This popular poet—who wrote in the local dialect rather than in French—was a champion of Provençal culture. After receiving the Nobel Prize in Literature in 1904, Mistral used his prize money to preserve and display the folk identity of Provence. He founded a regional folk museum (the Arlaten Folk Museum, closed until 2019) at a time when France was rapidly centralizing and regions like Provence were losing their unique identities. (The local mistral wind—literally "master"—has nothing to do with his name.)

• *Facing the brightly painted yellow café from its lower end, find your final Van Gogh easel.*

Café at Night Easel

In October 1888, lonely Vincent—who dreamed of making Arles a magnet for fellow artists—persuaded his friend Paul Gauguin to come. He decorated Gauguin's room with several humble canvases of sunflowers (now some of the world's priciest paintings), knowing that Gauguin had admired a similar painting he'd done in Paris. Their plan was for Gauguin to be the "dean" of a new art school in Arles, and Vincent its instructor-in-chief. At first, the two got along well. They spent days side by side, rendering the same subject in their two distinct styles. At night they hit the bars and brothels. Van Gogh's well-known *Café at Night* captures the glow of an absinthe buzz at Café la Nuit on Place du Forum.

After two months together, the two artists clashed over art and personality differences (Vincent was a slob around the house, whereas Gauguin was meticulous). The night of December 23, they were drinking absinthe at the café when Vincent suddenly went ballistic. He threw his glass at Gauguin. Gauguin left. Walking through Place Victor Hugo, Gauguin heard footsteps behind him and turned to see Vincent coming at him, brandishing a razor. Gauguin quickly fled town. The local paper reported what happened next: "At 11:30 p.m., Vincent van Gogh, painter from Holland, appeared at the brothel at no. 1, asked for Rachel, and gave her his cut-off earlobe, saying, 'Treasure this precious object.' Then he vanished." He woke up the next morning at home with his head wrapped in a bloody towel and his earlobe missing. Was Vincent emulating a successful matador, whose prize is cutting off the bull's ear?

The **bright-yellow café**—called Café la Nuit—was the subject of one of Vincent van Gogh's most famous works in Arles. Although his painting showed the café in a brilliant yellow from the glow of gas lamps, the facade was bare limestone, just like the other cafés on this square. The café is now a tourist trap painted by its current owners to match Van Gogh's version...and to cash in on the Vincent-crazed hordes who pay too much to eat or drink here.

In spring 1889, the bipolar genius (a modern diagnosis) checked himself into the St. Paul Monastery and Hospital in St-Rémy-de-Provence. He spent a year there, thriving in the care of nurturing doctors and nuns. Painting was part of his therapy, so they gave him a studio to work in, and he produced more than 100 paintings. Alcohol-free and institutionalized, he did some of his wildest work. With thick, swirling brushstrokes and surreal colors, he made his placid surroundings throb with restless energy.

Eventually, Vincent's torment became unbearable. In the spring of 1890, he left Provence to be cared for by a sympathetic doctor in Auvers-sur-Oise, just north of Paris. On July 27, he wandered into a field and shot himself. He died two days later.

• *With this walk, you have seen the best of Arles. The colorful Roquette District and the charming Réattu Museum are each a short walk away (both described later). But I'd rather enjoy a drink on the Place du Forum and savor the joy of experiencing the essence of Provence.*

Sights in Arles

The Ancient History Museum provides valuable background on Arles' Roman history: Visit it first, before delving into the rest of the city's sights (drivers should stop on the way into town). For a deeper understanding, read "How About Them Romans?" on page 562. Many of Arles' city-center sights are covered on my self-guided walk, earlier.

ON THE OUTSKIRTS
▲▲Ancient History Museum
(Musée Départemental Arles Antiques)

Begin your town visit here, for Roman Arles 101. Located on the site of the Roman chariot racecourse (the arc of which is followed

by today's parking lot), this air-conditioned, all-on-one-floor museum is just west of central Arles along the river. Models and original sculptures re-create the Roman city, making workaday life and culture easier to imagine. While this excellent museum describes most of its treasures only in French, the English brochure gives general descriptions and an English audioguide may be available (ask).

Cost and Hours: €8, free first Sunday of month, covered by Liberty Passport; open Wed-Mon 10:00-18:00, closed Tue; Presqu'île du Cirque Romain, tel. 04 13 31 51 03, www.arles-antique.cg13.fr.

Getting There: Drivers will see signs for the museum as you enter the city. Without a car, to reach the museum from the city center, take the free **Navia shuttle** (stops at the train station and along Rue du 4 Septembre, then along the river—see map on page 568; 2/hour Mon-Sat, none Sun). **On foot** from the city center it's about a 20-minute walk: Turn left at the river and take the scruffy riverside path under two bridges to the big, modern blue building (or better, stroll through Arles' enjoyable La Roquette neighborhood, described on page 584). As you approach the museum, you'll pass the verdant Hortus Garden—designed to recall the Roman circus and chariot racecourse that were located here. A **taxi** ride costs €11 (museum can call a taxi for your return).

Visiting the Museum: The permanent collection is housed in a large hall flooded with natural light. Highlights include models of the ancient city and its major landmarks, a 2,000-year-old Roman boat, statues, mosaics, and sarcophagi. Here's a rundown of what you'll see:

A wall **map** of the region during the Roman era greets visitors and shows the geographic importance of Arles: Three important Roman trade routes—via Domitia, Grippa, and Aurelia—all converged on or near Arles.

After a small exhibit on pre-Roman Arles, you'll come to fascinating **models** of the Roman city and the impressive Roman structures in (and near) Arles. These breathe life into the buildings as they looked 2,000 years ago. Start with the model of Roman Arles and ponder the city's splendor when Arles' population was double that of today. Find the forum—still the center of town, though only two columns survive (the smaller section of the forum is where today's Place du Forum is built).

At the museum's center stands the original **statue** of Julius Caesar that once graced Arles' ancient theater stage wall. From there find individual **models** of the major buildings shown in the city model: the elaborately elegant forum; the theater (with its magnificent stage wall), and 20 steps behind it, the floating wooden bridge that gave Arles a strategic advantage (over the widest, and therefore slowest, part of the river); the arena (with its movable cover to shelter spectators from sun or rain); and the hydraulic mill of Barbegal (with its 16 waterwheels powered by water cascading down a hillside).

Don't miss the large model of the **chariot racecourse.** Part of the original racecourse was just outside the windows, and though long gone, it likely resembled Rome's Circus Maximus.

Next, step into the hall dedicated to the museum's newest and most exciting exhibit: a **Gallo-Roman vessel** and much of its cargo (English translations on panels). This almost-100-foot-long Roman barge was hauled out of the Rhône in 2010, along with some 280 amphorae and 3,000 ceramic artifacts. It was typical of flat-bottomed barges used to shuttle goods between Arles and ports along the Mediterranean (vessels were manually towed upriver). This one hauled limestone slabs and rocks—no wonder it sank. A worthwhile 20-minute video about the barge (with English subtitles) plays continuously in a tiny theater at the end of the hall.

Elsewhere in the museum, you'll see displays of pottery, jewelry, metal, and glass artifacts, as well as well-crafted mosaic floors that illustrate how Roman Arles was a city of art and culture. The many **statues** are all original, except for the greatest—the *Venus of Arles,* which Louis XIV took a liking to and had moved to Versailles.

MORE SIGHTS IN ARLES
La Roquette District
To escape the tourist beat, take a detour into Arles' little-visited western fringe. Find Rue des Porcelets near the Trinquetaille Bridge and stroll several blocks into pleasing Place Paul Doumier, where you'll find a lively assortment of cafés, bakeries, and inexpensive bistros with nary a tourist in sight (see map on page 568 and "Eating in Arles," later, for recommendations). Continue along Rue de la Roquette and turn right on charming Rue Croix Rouge to reach the river. Those walking to or from the Ancient History Museum can use this appealing stroll as a shortcut.

Baths of Constantine (Thermes de Constantin)
These partly intact Roman baths were built in the early fourth century when Emperor Constantine declared Arles an imperial residence. Roman cities such as Arles had several public baths like this, fed by aqueducts and used as much for exercising, networking, and chatting with friends as for bathing. These baths were located near the Rhône River for easy water disposal. You can get a pretty good look at the baths through the fence. If you enter, you'll walk elevated metal corridors at the original floor level. Imagine the elaborate engineering: the hypocaust system for heating the floor and big tubs with various temperatures—hot, tepid, and cold—next to a sauna and steam room heated by slave-stoked, wood-burning ovens.

Cost and Hours: €3, covered by Liberty Passport, same hours as Roman Arena—daily May-Sept 9:00-19:00, April and Oct 9:00-18:00, Nov-March 10:00-17:00.

▲Réattu Museum (Musée Réattu)
Housed in the former Grand Priory of the Knights of Malta, this modern-art collection, while always changing, is a stimulating and well-lit mix of new and old. Picasso loved Arles and came here regularly for the bullfights. At the end of his life in 1973, he gave the city a series of his paintings, some of which are always on display

here. The permanent collection usually includes a series of works by homegrown Neoclassical artist Jacques Réattu.

Cost and Hours: €8, covered by Liberty Passport, March-Oct Tue-Sun 10:00-18:00, Nov-Feb until 17:00, closed Mon year-round, 10 Rue du Grand Prieuré, tel. 04 90 49 37 58, www. museereattu.arles.fr.

NEAR ARLES
The Camargue

Knocking on Arles' doorstep, the Camargue region, occupying the vast delta of the Rhône River, is one of Europe's most important wetlands. This marshy area exists where the Rhône splits into two branches (big and little), just before it flows into the Mediterranean. Over the millennia, a steady flow of sediment has been deposited at the mouth of the rivers—thoroughly land-locking villages that once faced the sea.

Today the Camargue Regional Nature Park is a protected "wild" area, where pink flamingos, wild bulls, nasty boars, nastier mosquitoes (in every season but winter—come prepared), and the famous white horses wander freely through lagoons and tall grass. The dark bulls are harder to spot (white horses and flamingos are easier), so go slow and make use of the viewing platforms. The best time to visit is in spring, when the flamingos are out in full force; the worst time to visit is summer, when birds are fewest and the mosquitoes are greatest. For helpful information on the Camargue, check www.kustgids.nl/camargue-en.

Camargue Scenic Drive: My favorite route from Arles through the Camargue is toward **Salin de Giraud** (see map on page 586): Leave Arles driving clockwise on its ring road, then find signs to *Stes-Maries-de-la-Mer* and join D-570. Skip the D-36 turnoff to Salin de Giraud (you'll return along this route). After about 3.5 miles (6 kilometers), enthusiasts can consider a stop at the **Camarguais Museum** (folk museum with a 2-mile nature trail, €5, closed Tue, English handout, www.parc-camargue.fr). Next, continue along D-570 past swampy rice fields, then turn left on D-37 and follow it as it skirts the Etang de Vaccarès lagoon. The lagoon is off-limits, but this area has opportunities to get out of the car for views and to smell the marshes (look for viewing stands, but any dirt turnoff works). Turn right off D-37 onto the tiny road at Villeneuve, following signs for C-134 to *La Capelière* and *La Fiélouse* (poorly marked—it's where D-36b leads back to Arles).

Make time for a stop at **La Capelière** (headquarters for Camargue sightseers), where you can pick up a good map, ask the staff questions, and enjoy a small exhibit (€3, handheld English explanations) and one-mile walking trail with some English information on the Camargue (daily 9:00-13:00 & 14:00-18:00). Birders

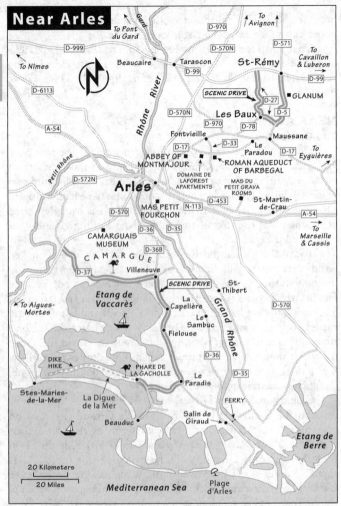

can check the register to see what birds have been spotted recently (observations in English are in red), and can buy the €5 Camargue booklet, *Fiches Camargue*, in English.

The next stretch to and around **La Digue de la Mer,** about six scenic miles past La Capelière, is where you're most likely to witness the memorable sight of platoons of flamingos in flight. At La Digue de la Mer, park near where the pavement ends, then walk a few hundred yards to where the dirt road curves left to reach a good spot. This is a critical reproduction area for flamingos (about 13,000 couples produce 5,000 offspring annually). If you rented a mountain bike, now would be the right time to use it: It's about eight bumpy but engaging miles between water and sand dunes to Stes-Maries-de-la-Mer.

Retrace your route back to Villeneuve, then continue straight onto D-36b, leading back to Arles.

Experiences in Arles

▲▲Markets

On Wednesday and Saturday mornings, Arles' ring road erupts into an open-air festival of fish, flowers, produce...and everything Provençal. The main event is on Saturday, with vendors jamming the ring road from Boulevard Emile Combes to the east, along Boulevard des Lices near the TI (the heart of the market), and continuing down Boulevard Georges Clemenceau to the west. Wednesday's market runs only along Boulevard Emile Combes, between Place Lamartine and Avenue Victor Hugo; the segment nearest Place Lamartine is all about food, and the upper half features clothing, tablecloths, purses, and so on. On the first Wednesday of the month, a flea market doubles the size of the usual Wednesday market along Boulevard des Lices near the main TI. Both markets are open until about 12:30.

▲▲Bullgames (Courses Camarguaises)

Provençal "bullgames" are held in Arles and in neighboring towns. Those in Arles occupy the same seats that fans have used for nearly 2,000 years, and deliver the city's most memorable experience—the *courses camarguaises* in the ancient arena. The nonviolent "bullgames" are more sporting than bloody bullfights (though traditional Spanish-style bullfights still take place on occasion). The bulls of Arles (who, locals insist, "die of old age") are promoted in posters even more boldly than their human foes. In the bullgame, a ribbon *(cocarde)* is laced between the bull's horns.

The *razeteur*, with a special hook, has 15 minutes to snare the ribbon. Local businessmen encourage a *razeteur* (dressed in white) by shouting out how much money they'll pay for the *cocarde*. If the bull pulls a good stunt, the band plays the famous "Toreador" song from *Carmen*. The following day, newspapers report on the games, including how many *Carmens* the bull earned.

Three classes of bullgames—determined by the experience of the *razeteurs*—are advertised in posters: The *course de protection* is for rookies. The *trophée de l'Avenir* comes with more experience. And the *trophée des As* features top professionals. During Easter

(Féria du Pâques) and the fall rice-harvest festival *(Féria du Riz)*, the arena hosts traditional Spanish bullfights (look for *corrida*) with outfits, swords, spikes, and the whole gory shebang. (Nearby villages stage *courses camarguaises* in small wooden bullrings nearly every weekend; TIs have the latest schedule.)

Bullgame tickets usually run €14-20; bullfights are pricier (€36-100). Schedules for bullgames vary (usually July-Aug on Wed and Fri)—ask at the TI or check www.arenes-arles.com.

Sleeping in Arles

Hotels are a great value here—many are air-conditioned, though few have elevators. The Calendal, Musée, and Régence hotels offer exceptional value.

$$ Hôtel le Calendal*** is a service-with-a-smile place ideally located between the Roman Arena and Classical Theater. The hotel opens to the street with airy lounges and a lovely palm-shaded courtyard, providing an enjoyable refuge. They offer snacks and drinks at their café/sandwich bar (daily 8:00-19:00). The rooms sport Provençal decor and come in random shapes and sizes (some rooms with balcony, family rooms, air-con, good-value parking, just above arena at 5 Rue Porte de Laure, tel. 04 90 96 11 89, www.lecalendal.com, contact@lecalendal.com). They also run the nearby budget Hostel La Maison du Pelerin, described later.

$ Hôtel du Musée** is a quiet, affordable manor-home hideaway tucked deep in Arles (if driving, ask for access code to street barrier so you can drop off your bags). This delightful place comes with 28 wood-floored rooms, a flowery courtyard, and comfortable lounges. Lighthearted Claude and English-speaking Laurence are good hosts (family rooms, no elevator, pay parking garage, follow *Réattu Museum* signs to 11 Rue du Grand Prieuré, tel. 04 90 93 88 88, www.hoteldumusee.com, contact@hoteldumusee.com).

$ Hôtel de la Muette** is a small, good-value hotel located in a quiet corner of Arles, with hardworking owners Brigitte and Alain. Its tasteful rooms come with tiled floors and stone walls and bathrooms (RS%, family rooms, no elevator, pay parking garage, 15 Rue des Suisses, tel. 04 90 96 15 39, www.hotel-muette.com, hotel.muette@wanadoo.fr).

$ Hôtel Régence,** a top budget deal, has a riverfront location near the train station, comfortable Provençal rooms, and safe parking (family rooms, choose river-view or quieter courtyard rooms, good buffet breakfast extra, no elevator but only two floors, pay parking garage; from Place Lamartine, turn right after passing between towers to reach 5 Rue Marius Jouveau; tel. 04 90 96 39

Sleep Code

Hotels are classified based on the average price of a standard double room without breakfast in high season.

$$$$	**Splurge:** Most rooms over €200
$$$	**Pricier:** €150-200
$$	**Moderate:** €100-150
$	**Budget:** €50-100
¢	**Backpacker:** Under €50
RS%	**Rick Steves discount**
*	**French hotel rating system** (0-5 stars)

Unless otherwise noted, credit cards are accepted, hotel staff speak basic English, and free Wi-Fi is available. Comparison-shop by checking prices at several hotels (on each hotel's own website, on a booking site, or by email). For the best deal, *book directly with the hotel.* Ask for a discount if paying in cash; if the listing includes **RS%,** request a Rick Steves discount.

85, www.hotel-regence.com, contact@hotel-regence.com). Gentle Valérie and Eric speak English.

$ **Hôtel Acacias,**** just off Place Lamartine and inside the old city walls, is a modern hotel with small yet inviting and comfortable rooms (family rooms, air-con, pay parking garage, 2 Rue de la Cavalerie, tel. 04 90 96 37 88, www.hotel-acacias.com, contact@hotel-acacias.com).

¢ **Hôtel Voltaire** rents 12 small, spartan rooms with ceiling fans and nifty balconies overlooking a colorful, working-class square a block below the arena. Rooms have some rough edges but are cheap. "Mr." Ferran loves the States, and hopes you'll add to his license plate or postcard collection (cheaper rooms with shared bath, no air-con, no elevator, Wi-Fi in restaurant only, 1 Place Voltaire, tel. 04 90 96 49 18, www.hotel-voltaire-arles.com, levoltaire13@orange.fr).

¢ **Hostel La Maison du Pelerin** offers good dorm rooms with a shared kitchen and homey living area. It's a great value for pilgrims, backpackers, and those on a shoestring. Check in next door at the recommended Hôtel le Calendal (just above the Roman Arena at 26 Place Pomme, tel. 06 99 71 11 89, www.arles-pelerins.fr).

NEAR ARLES

Many drivers, particularly those with families, prefer staying outside Arles in the peaceful countryside, with easy access to the area's sights. (See also "Sleeping in and near Les Baux," on page 630.)

$$ **Mas du Petit Grava** is a vintage Provençal farmhouse 15

PROVENCE

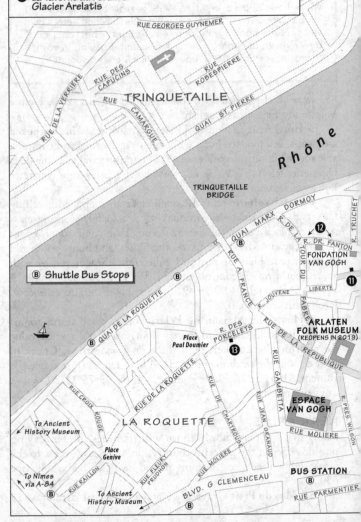

Arles Hotels & Restaurants

1. Hôtel/Rest. le Calendal & Hostel La Maison du Pelerin
2. Hôtel du Musée
3. Hôtel de la Muette
4. Hôtel Régence
5. Hôtel Acacias
6. Hôtel/Rest. Voltaire
7. To Mas du Petit Grava & Mas Petit Fourchon
8. To Domaine de Laforest
9. La Taverne du Forum & Glacier Arelatis
10. Cafés de la Major
11. La Cuisine de Comptoir
12. Rue du Dr. Fanton Eateries
13. La Chistera Restaurant
14. Le Criquet Restaurant
15. Delicate and Saine Wine Bar
16. L'Atelier & A Côté Restaurants
17. Soleileis Ice Cream

RUE GEORGES GUYNEMER

RUE DES CAPUCINS

RUE ROBESPIERRE

RUE DE LA VERRIERE

RUE CAMARGUE

TRINQUETAILLE

QUAI ST. PIERRE

Rhône

TRINQUETAILLE BRIDGE

QUAI MARX DORMOY

R. DE LA FANTON

R. TRUCHET

R. DR. FANTON

FONDATION VAN GOGH

RUE A. FRANCE

R. DE LA TOUR DU FABRE

LIBERTE

Ⓑ Shuttle Bus Stops

R. JOUVENE

ARLATEN FOLK MUSEUM (REOPENS IN 2019)

QUAI DE LA ROQUETTE

R. DES PORCELETS

RUE DE LA REPUBLIQUE

Place Paul Doumier

RUE DE LA ROQUETTE

RUE DE CHARTROUSE

RUE GAMBETTA

ESPACE VAN GOGH

To Ancient History Museum

RUE CROIX ROUGE

LA ROQUETTE

RUE JEAN GRANAUD

R. PRES. WILSON

RUE MOLIERE

To Nîmes via A-84

Place Genive

RUE KAILLON

RUE FLEURY PRUDHON

RUE MOLIERE

BUS STATION

BLVD. G. CLEMENCEAU

RUE PARMENTIER

To Ancient History Museum

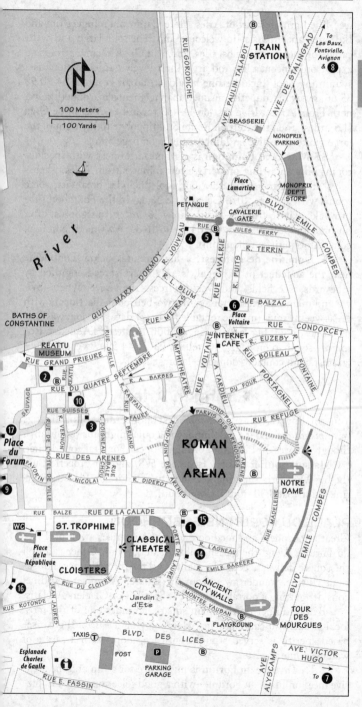

tree-lined minutes east of Arles. Here California refugees Jim and Ike offer an enthusiastic welcome and rent four large and well-cared-for rooms with tubs, tiles, and Van Gogh themes (Jim is an expert on Vincent's life and art). Their lovely garden surrounds a swimming pool (includes fine breakfast, no air-con, tel. 04 90 98 35 66, www.masdupetitgrava.net, management@masdupetitgrava.net). From Arles, drive east on D-453 toward St-Martin de Crau (1.5 miles), then turn left on Route St. Hippolyte to the right of the large white-and-blue building (see map on page 586).

$$ Mas Petit Fourchon is a grand farmhouse with spacious rooms on a sprawling property a few minutes from Arles. There's acres of room to roam and a big pool (includes breakfast, some rooms with air-con, 1070 Chemin de Nadal in the Fourchon suburb; take exit #6 from N-113 toward *l'hopital,* turn right just after hospital and follow signs; tel. 04 90 96 16 35, www.petitfourchon.com, info@petitfourchon.com).

$ Domaine de Laforest, a few minutes below Fontvieille near the aqueduct of Barbegal, is a 320-acre spread engulfed by vineyards, rice fields, and swaying trees. The sweet owners (Sylvie and mama Mariette) rent eight two-bedroom apartments with great weekly rates (may be rentable for fewer days, air-con, washing machines, pool, big lawn, swings, 1000 Route de l'Aqueduc Romain—see map on page 586, tel. 06 23 73 44 59, www.domaine-laforest.com, contact@domaine-laforest.com).

Eating in Arles

You can dine well in Arles on a modest budget (most of my listings have *menus* for under €25). Sunday is a quiet night for restaurants, though eateries on Place du Forum are open. For a takeout dinner, try **Maison Soulier Bakery** (see page 578) and for groceries, use the big Monoprix supermarket/department store on Place Lamartine (Mon-Sat 8:30-20:00, closed Sun).

PLACE DU FORUM NEIGHBORHOOD

Great atmosphere and mediocre food at fair prices await on Place du Forum. Avoid the garish yellow Café la Nuit. Other cafés on the square deliver acceptable quality and terrific ambience. For serious cuisine, wander away from the square. Wherever you dine, consider getting a portable dessert at Soleileis or Glaciers Arelatis.

Before dinner on the main square, consider one of the most local rituals you can enjoy in Arles: enjoying a *pastis.* This anise-based aperitif is served straight with ice, along with a carafe of water—dilute to taste.

$ La Taverne du Forum is my choice for a fun and inexpensive meal on Place du Forum—with a good selection of salads, piz-

Restaurant Price Code

I've assigned each eatery a price category, based on the average cost of a typical main course. Drinks, desserts, and splurge items (steak and seafood) can raise the price considerably.

$$$$	**Splurge:** Most main courses over €25
$$$	**Pricier:** €20-25
$$	**Moderate:** €15-20
$	**Budget:** Under €15

In France, a crêpe stand or other takeout spot is **$**; a sit-down brasserie, café, or bistro with affordable *plats du jour* is **$$**; a casual but more upscale restaurant is **$$$**; and a swanky splurge is **$$$$**.

zas, and *plats*. Their tables are the best on the square, it's family friendly, and the servers are fun to clown around with (13 Place du Forum, no indoor seating, tel. 04 90 96 08 80).

$ Cafés de la Major is *the* place to go to recharge with some serious coffee or tea (Tue-Sat 8:30-19:00, closed Sun-Mon, 7 bis Rue Réattu, tel. 04 90 96 14 15).

$ La Cuisine de Comptoir offers light and cheap dinners of *tartine*—a cross between pizza and bruschetta, served with soup or salad for €11—and offers a fun array of pizza-style tartine toppings. This Provençal answer to a pizzeria—run by Vincent—has indoor seating only (closed Sun, just off the lower end of Place du Forum at 10 Rue de la Liberté, tel. 04 90 96 86 28).

On Rue du Docteur Fanton

This pedestrian-friendly street—with a pleasing lineup of restaurants, all with good outside and inside dining—is my favorite place to comparison-shop for dinner.

$$$$ Le Galoubet is a trendy local spot, blending a warm interior, traditional French cuisine, and friendly service, thanks to owner Frank. It's the most expensive of the places I list on this street and the least flexible, serving only a €32 *menu*. If it's cold, a roaring fire keeps you toasty (closed Sun-Mon, great fries and desserts, 18 Rue du Docteur Fanton, tel. 04 90 93 18 11).

$$ Les Filles du 16 is a warm, affordable place to enjoy a fresh salad, or a fine two- or three-course dinner inside or out. The choices, while tasty, are limited, so check the selection before sitting down (closed Sat-Sun, 16 Rue du Docteur Fanton, tel. 04 90 93 77 36).

$$$ Le Plaza la Paillotte buzzes with happy diners enjoying delicious, well-presented Provençal cuisine at good prices. Attentive owners Stéphane and Graziela (he cooks, she serves) welcome diners with a comfortable terrace and a smart interior (closed Wed Oct-March, 28 Rue du Docteur Fanton, tel. 04 90 96 33 15).

Nearby: For a less-touristy-feeling dining experience, wander into the La Roquette neighborhood (see page 584). Have a drink on Place Paul Doumier and consider staying for dinner. **$$$ La Chistera,** an intimate local spot, dishes up classic dishes with Provençal accents at good prices and fine quality (closed Tue, 16 Rue des Porcelets, tel. 04 90 96 86 13).

NEAR THE ROMAN ARENA

$$ Le Criquet, possibly the best value in Arles, is a sweet little place two blocks above the arena, serving well-presented and delicious Provençal classics with joy at good prices. Sisters Lili and Charlotte serve while mama and papa run the kitchen. If you're really hungry, try the mouthwatering €26 *bourride*—a creamy fish soup thickened with aioli and garlic and stuffed with mussels, clams, calamari, and more. Book ahead for an outdoor table (21 Rue Porte de Laure, tel. 04 90 96 80 51).

$ Delicate and Saine Wine Bar has no real kitchen and only a handful of outdoor tables, but Julie Moreau manages to dish up enticing €5-10 gourmet dishes, matched with a nice list of wine by the glass and huge arena views (closed Sun, 30 Rond-Point des Arènes, tel. 06 82 44 88 74).

$ Hôtel le Calendal, just around the corner from the arena without the view, serves light seasonal food in its lovely courtyard or at the café (delicious and cheap little sandwiches, daily 8:00-19:00, see hotel listing, earlier, for location).

$ Hôtel Voltaire, on a low-key square away from most tourists, serves simple three-course lunches and dinners at honest prices, including hearty *plats* and filling salads for €11—try the *salade Latine,* or, if tapenade is your thing, the filling *assiette Provençale* (closed Sun evening, on Place Voltaire below the arena, tel. 04 90 96 49 18).

A GASTRONOMIC DINING EXPERIENCE

One of France's most recognized chefs, Jean-Luc Rabanel, runs two very different places 50 yards from Place de la République (at 7 Rue des Carmes). They sit side by side, both offering indoor and terrace seating.

$$$$ L'Atelier, a destination restaurant with two Michelin stars (notice the red plaque), attracts people from great distances to happily pay €150 or more for dinner with wine (about half that for lunch). There is no menu, just a parade of delicious taste sensations served in artsy dishes (called *"touches de gout"*—taste touches). Don't plan on a quick dinner, and don't come for a traditional setting: Everything is enthusiastically contemporary. You'll probably see or hear the famous chef with his long salt-and-pepper hair and deep voice (closed Mon-Tue, book ahead, friendly servers will hold your hand through this palate-widening experience, tel. 04 90 91 07 69, www.rabanel.com).

$$$$ A Côté, next door, offers a smart wine bar/bistro ambience and top-quality cuisine for much less money. Here you can sample the famous chef's talents with the €32 three-course *menu* (limited selection of wines by the glass, open daily, tel. 04 90 47 61 13, www.bistro-acote.com).

AND FOR DESSERT...

Soleileis scoops up fine ice cream, made with organic milk, fresh fruit, all-natural ingredients, and creative flavors that fit the season. There's also a shelf of English books for exchange (daily 14:00-18:30, later on weekends, closed in winter, a block off the Forum at 9 Rue du Docteur Fanton, run by Marijtje). **Glacier Arelatis** advertises "gourmet ice cream," which looks more like tasty gelato to me (9 Place du Forum, daily until late).

Arles Connections

BY TRAIN

Note that some trains in and out of Arles require a reservation. These include connections with Nice to the east and Bordeaux to the west (including intermediary stops). Ask at the station.

Compare train and bus schedules: For some nearby destinations the bus may be the better choice, and it's usually cheaper.

From Arles by Train to: Paris (11/day, 2 direct TGVs—4 hours, 9 more with transfer in Avignon—5 hours), **Avignon Centre-Ville** (roughly hourly, 20 minutes), **Nîmes** (9/day, 30 minutes), **Orange** (4/day direct, 35 minutes, more with transfer in Avignon), **Aix-en-Provence Centre-Ville** (10/day, 2 hours, transfer in Marseille, train may separate midway—be sure your section is going to Aix-en-Provence), **Marseille** (11/day, 1 hour), **Cassis** (7/day, 2 hours), **Carcassonne** (4/day direct, 2.5 hours, more with transfer in Narbonne, direct trains may require reservations), **Beaune** (10/day, 5 hours), **Nice** (11/day, 4 hours, most require transfer in Marseille), **Barcelona** (3/day, 4.5 hours, transfer in Nîmes), **Italy** (3/day, transfer in Marseille and Nice; from Arles, it's 5 hours to Ventimiglia on the border, 8 hours to Milan, 9 hours to Cinque Terre, 11 hours to Florence, and 13 hours to Venice or Rome).

BY BUS

Arles' bus station is next to its train station. All buses to regional destinations depart from here and most cost under €2. Get schedules at the TI or from the bus company (tel. 08 10 00 13 26, www. lepilote.com).

From Arles Train Station to Avignon TGV Station: The direct SNCF bus is easier than the train (€7.10, 9/day, 1 hour, included with rail pass). You can also take the train from Arles to Avignon's Centre-Ville Station, then a shuttle train to the TGV station (see page 597).

From Arles by Bus to Les Baux and St-Rémy: Bus #57 connects Arles to St-Rémy-de-Provence via Les Baux (6/day daily July-Aug, Sat-Sun only in May-June and Sept, none Oct-April; 35 minutes to Les Baux, 50 minutes to St-Rémy, then runs to Avignon). Bus #54 also goes to St-Rémy but not via Les Baux (5/day Mon-Fri, 3/day Sat, none on Sun, 1 hour). For other ways to reach Les Baux and St-Rémy, see page 625.

By Bus to Other Destinations: Nîmes (8/day Mon-Sat, 3/day Sun, 1 hour), **Aix-en-Provence** (faster than trains, 5/day Mon-Sat, 2/day Sun, 1.5 hours), **Fontvieille** (6/day, 10 minutes), **Camargue/Stes-Maries-de-la-Mer** (bus #20, 6/day Mon-Sat, 3/day Sun, 1 hour).

Avignon

Famous for its nursery rhyme, medieval bridge, and brooding Palace of the Popes, contemporary Avignon (ah-veen-yohn) bustles and prospers behind its mighty walls. For nearly 100 years (1309-1403) Avignon was the capital of Christendom, home to seven popes. (And, for a difficult period after that—during the Great Schism when there were two competing popes—Avignon was "the other Rome.") During this time, it grew from a quiet village into a thriving city. Today, with its large student population and fashionable shops, Avignon is an intriguing blend of medieval history, youthful energy, and urban sophistication. Street performers entertain the international throngs who fill Avignon's ubiquitous cafés and trendy boutiques. And each July the city goes crazy during its huge theater festival (with about 2,000 performances, big crowds, higher prices, and hotels booked up long in advance). Clean, lively, and popular with tourists, Avignon is more impressive for its outdoor ambience than for its museums and monuments.

PROVENCE

Orientation to Avignon

Cours Jean Jaurès, which turns into Rue de la République, runs straight from the Centre-Ville train station to Place de l'Horloge and the Palace of the Popes, splitting Avignon in two. The larger eastern half is where the action is. Climb to the Jardin du Rochers des Doms for the town's best view, tour the pope's immense palace, lose yourself in Avignon's back streets (following my "Discovering Avignon's Back Streets" self-guided walk), and find a shady square to call home.

TOURIST INFORMATION

The TI is located on the main street linking the Centre-Ville train station to the old town. It offers lots of information about the city and the region (April-Oct Mon-Sat 9:00-18:00, Sun 10:00-17:00, daily until 19:00 in July; Nov-March Mon-Fri 9:00-18:00, Sat 9:00-17:00, Sun 10:00-12:00; free Wi-Fi, at 41 Cours Jean Jaurès, tel. 04 32 74 32 74, www.avignon-tourisme.com).

At the TI, pick up the free **Avignon Passion Pass** (for up to 5 family members, includes map and short guidebook). Get it stamped at your first sight to receive discounts at the others (e.g., €2 off at the Palace of the Popes and €3 off at the Petit Palais). The TI also has several good (but tricky-to-follow) walking tours and bike maps for the area, including the Ile de la Barthelasse.

ARRIVAL IN AVIGNON
By Train

Avignon has two train stations: Centre-Ville and TGV (linked to downtown by shuttle trains). Some TGV trains stop at Centre-Ville—verify your station in advance.

The **Centre-Ville station** *(Gare Avignon Centre-Ville)* gets all non-TGV trains (and a few TGV trains). To reach the town center, cross the busy street in front of the station and walk through the city walls onto Cours Jean Jaurès. The TI is three blocks down, at #41; bag storage is close by (see "Helpful Hints," later).

The **TGV station** *(Gare TGV)*, on the outskirts of town, has a summer-only TI (short hours), but no baggage storage (see "Help-

ful Hints," later, for bag storage). Car rental, buses, and taxis are outside the north exit *(sortie nord)*. To reach the city center, take the **shuttle train** from platform A or B to Centre-Ville station (€1.60, 2/hour, 5 minutes, buy ticket from machine on platform or at *billeterie* in main hall). A **taxi** ride between the TGV station and downtown Avignon costs about €16.

If you're connecting from the Avignon TGV station to other points, you'll find **buses** to Arles' Centre-Ville train station at the second bus shelter (€7.20, 9/day, 1 hour, included with rail pass, schedule posted on shelter and available at info booths inside TGV station).

If you're **driving** a rental car directly to St-Rémy-de-Provence, Les Baux, or the Luberon, leave the station following signs to *Avignon Sud,* then *La Rocade.* You'll soon see exits to *St-Rémy* (follow this for Les Baux) and *Cavaillon* (for Luberon villages). Arles is well-signed from the station for drivers.

By Bus

The efficient bus station *(gare routière)* is 100 yards to the right as you leave the Centre-Ville train station, beyond and below Hôtel Ibis (info desk open Mon-Sat 7:00-19:30, closed Sun, tel. 04 90 82 07 35).

By Car

Drivers entering Avignon follow *Centre-Ville* and *Gare SNCF* (train station) signs. You'll find central pay lots (about €12/half-day, €20/24 hours) in the garage next to the Centre-Ville train station and at the Parking Jean Jaurès under the ramparts across from the station (enter the old city through the Porte St-Michel gate). Hotels have advice for overnight parking, and some offer parking deals.

Two free parking lots have complimentary shuttle buses to the center except on Sunday (follow *P Gratuit* signs): **Parking de l'Ile Piot** is across Daladier Bridge (Pont Daladier) on Ile de la Barthelasse, with shuttles to Place Crillon; **Parking des Italiens** is along the river east of the Palace of the Popes, with shuttles to Place Carnot (allow 30 minutes to walk from either to the center). Street parking is free in *bleu* zones 12:00-14:00 and 19:00-9:00. It's €2 for about three hours 9:00-12:00 and 14:00-19:00. (Hint: If you put €2 in the meter anytime between 19:00 and 9:00, you're good until 14:00.)

No matter where you park, leave nothing of value in your car.

HELPFUL HINTS

Book Ahead for July: During the July theater festival, rooms are sparse—reserve very early, or stay in Arles.

Local Help: David at **Imagine Tours,** a nonprofit group whose goal is to promote this region, can help with hotel emergencies and special event tickets (mobile 06 89 22 19 87, www.

imagine-tours.net, imagine.tours@gmail.com). If you don't get an answer, leave a message.

Wi-Fi: The TI has free Wi-Fi, as does the park next door (one hour/day only). Many bigger cafés provide free Wi-Fi with purchase.

English Bookstore: Try **Camili Books & Tea,** a secondhand bookshop with a refreshing courtyard and hot drinks (Tue-Sat 12:00-19:00, closed Sun-Mon, free Wi-Fi, 155 Rue Carreterie, in Avignon's northeast corner).

Baggage Storage: **La Consigne** is near the TI (€9/day, June-Sept daily 8:00-21:00; Oct-May Mon-Sat 9:00-19:00, closed Sun; 1 Avenue Marechal de Lattre de Tassigny, tel. 09 82 45 20 24, www.consigne-avignon.fr).

Laundry: At **La Blanchisseuse,** you can drop off your laundry and pick it up the same day for about €14 a load (daily 7:00-21:00, a few blocks west of main TI at 24 Rue Lanterne, tel. 04 90 85 58 80). The **launderette** at 66 Place des Corps-Saints, where Rue Agricol Perdiguier ends, is handy to most hotels (daily 7:00-20:00).

Grocery Store: Carrefour City is central and has long hours (Mon-Sat 7:00-22:00, Sun 9:00-12:00, until 20:00 in high season, 2 blocks from TI toward Place de l'Horloge on Rue de la République). There is a second Carrefour City near Les Halles at 19 Rue Florence (same hours).

Bike Rental: Rent pedal and electric bikes and scooters near the train station at **Provence Bike** (April-Oct 9:00-18:30, 7 Avenue St. Ruf, tel. 04 90 27 92 61, www.provence-bike.com). You'll enjoy riding on the Ile de la Barthelasse (the TI has bike maps), but biking is better in and around Isle-sur-la-Sorgue and Vaison-la-Romaine.

Car Rental: The TGV station has counters for all the big companies; only Avis is at the Centre-Ville station.

Shuttle Boat: A free shuttle boat, the *Navette Fluviale,* plies back and forth across the river (as it did in the days when the town had no functioning bridge) from near St. Bénezet Bridge (3/ hour, daily April-June and Sept 10:00-12:15 & 14:00-18:00, July-Aug 11:00-20:45; Oct-March weekends and Wed afternoons only). It drops you on the peaceful Ile de la Barthelasse, with its recommended riverside restaurant, grassy walks, and bike rides with terrific city views. If you stay on the island for dinner, check the schedule for the last return boat—or be prepared for a taxi ride or a pleasant 25-minute walk back to town.

Private Guide: Isabelle Magny is a good local guide for the city and region (€160/half-day, €330/full-day, no car, mobile 06 11 82 17 92, magnyisab@numericable.fr).

PROVENCE

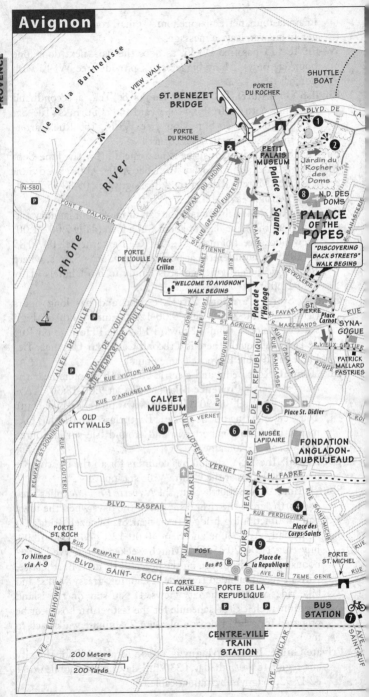

Avignon

Ile de la Barthelasse

VIEW WALK

Rhône River

N-580

FONT E. DALADIER

ST. BENEZET BRIDGE

PORTE DU ROCHER

SHUTTLE BOAT

BLVD. DE LA

❶

❷

PORTE DU RHONE

PETIT PALAIS MUSEUM

Jardin du Rocher des Doms

❽ N.D. DES DOMS

PALACE OF THE POPES

"DISCOVERING BACK STREETS" WALK BEGINS

R. RAMPART DU RHONE

R. RUE GRANDE FUSTERIE

Palace "Square"

RUE BALANCE

PORTE DE L'OULLE

Place Crillon

RUE ETIENNE VERNET

PEYROLERIE

R. FAVART

ST. PIERRE

Place Carnot

SYNA-GOGUE

R. VIEUX SEXTIER

PATRICK MALLARD PASTRIES

"WELCOME TO AVIGNON" WALK BEGINS

Place de l'Horloge

RUE JOSEPH VERNET

RUE PETITE FUST.

R. ST AGRICOL

LA BOUQUERIE

RACINE

RUE RACHE

R. MARCHANDS

RUE GALANTE

RUE DANCASSE

RUE ROUGE

ALLÉE DE L'OULLE

BLVD. DE L'OULLE

RUE REMPART DE L'OULLE

RUE VICTOR HUGO

RUE D'ANNANELLE

OLD CITY WALLS

CALVET MUSEUM

R. VERNET

❹

❻

RUE DE LA REPUBLIQUE

❺ Place St. Didier

MUSÉE LAPIDAIRE

R. ROI

FONDATION ANGLADON-DUBRUJEAUD

R. REMPART ST-DOMINIQUE

RUE VELOUTERIE

RUE JOSEPH VERNET

JEAN JAURES

R. H. FABRE

❶

←

RUE SAINT-MICHEL

BLVD. RASPAIL

RUE SAINT-CHARLES

❹ RUE PERDIGUIER

Place des Corps-Saints

PORTE ST. ROCH

To Nimes via A-9

RUE REMPART SAINT-ROCH

BLVD. SAINT-ROCH

POST

Bus #5 Ⓑ

COURS JEAN JAURES

❾ Place de la Republique

AVE. DE 7EME GENIE

PORTE ST. MICHEL

AVE. EISENHOWER

PORTE ST. CHARLES

PORTE DE LA REPUBLIQUE

P P

CENTRE-VILLE TRAIN STATION

AVE. MONCLAR

BUS STATION 🚲

❼

AVE. ST-RUF

200 Meters

200 Yards

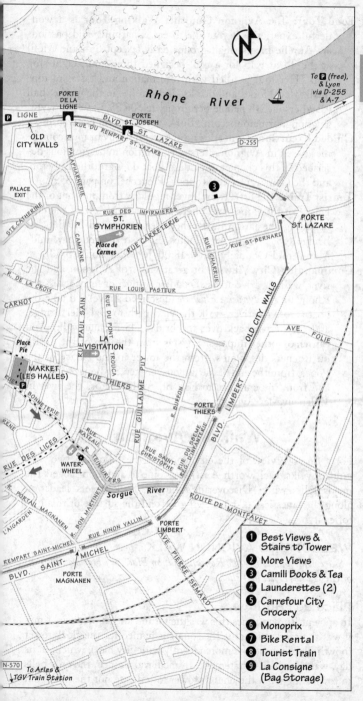

PROVENCE

Rhône River

To **P** (free),
& Lyon
via D-255
& A-7

P LIGNE

PORTE
DE LA
LIGNE

OLD
CITY WALLS

BLVD ST. JOSEPH

RUE DU REMPART ST. LAZARE

PORTE
ST. LAZARE

ST. LAZARE

D-255

PALACE
EXIT

STE. CATHERINE

R. PALAPHARNERIE

PORTE
ST. LAZARE

RUE DES INFIRMIERES

ST.
SYMPHORIEN

Place de
Carmes

RUE CARRETERIE

R. CAMPANE

RUE CHARRUE

RUE ST-BERNARD

OLD CITY WALLS

R. DE LA CROIX

CARNOT

RUE LOUIS PASTEUR

AVE. FOLIE

RUE PAUL SAIN

RUE DU PONT TROUCA

LA
VISITATION

Place
Pie

MARKET
(LES HALLES)

P

RUE THIERS

RUE GUILLAUME PUY

R. BUFFON

PORTE
THIERS

BLVD. LIMBERT

BONNETERIE

RENE

RUE DES LICES

WATER-
WHEEL

RUE
RATEAU

R. TEINTURIERS

RUE SAINT-
CHRISTOPHE

RUE DU 58EME
REG. D'INFANTERIE

Sorgue River

ROUTE DE MONTFAVET

R. PORTAIL MAGNANEN

R. BON MARTINET

RUE NINON VALLIN

PORTE
LIMBERT

L'AIGARDEN

REMPART SAINT-MICHEL

SAINT-
MICHEL

BLVD. SAINT-

PORTE
MAGNANEN

AVE. PIERRE SEMARD

N-570

To Arles &
TGV Train Station

1 Best Views &
Stairs to Tower

2 More Views

3 Camili Books & Tea

4 Launderettes (2)

5 Carrefour City
Grocery

6 Monoprix

7 Bike Rental

8 Tourist Train

9 La Consigne
(Bag Storage)

Food Tour: The **Avignon Gourmet Walking Tour** is a wonderful experience if you like to eat. Charming and passionate Aurélie meets small groups daily (except Sun and Mon) at the TI at 9:15 for a well-designed three-hour, eight-stop walk. Her tour is filled with information and tastes of top-quality local foods and drinks, and finishes in the market hall (€59/person, 2-8 people per group, tel. 06 35 32 08 96, www. avignongourmetours.com). Book in advance on her website.

Guided Excursions from Avignon: Several minivan tour companies based in Avignon offer transportation to destinations described in this chapter, including Pont du Gard, the Luberon, and the Camargue (see "Tours in Provence" on page 559).

Tourist Train: The little train leaves regularly from in front of the Palace of the Popes and offers a decent overview of the city, including the Jardin du Rochers des Doms and St. Bénezet Bridge (€8, 2/hour, 40 minutes, English commentary, mid-March-mid-Oct daily 10:00-18:00, July-Aug until 20:00).

Commanding City Views: For great views of Avignon and the river, walk or drive across Daladier Bridge, or ferry across the Rhône on the *Navette Fluviale* (described above). I'd take the boat across the river, walk the view path to Daladier Bridge, and then cross back over the bridge (45-minute walk). You can enjoy other impressive vistas from the top of the Jardin du Rochers des Doms, from the tower in the Palace of the Popes, from the end of the famous, broken St. Bénezet Bridge, and from the entrance to Fort St. André, across the river in Villeneuve-lès-Avignon.

Walks in Avignon

For a fine overview of the city, combine the following two self-guided walks, each worth ▲▲. "Welcome to Avignon" covers the major sights, while "Discovering Avignon's Back Streets" leads you along the lanes less taken, delving beyond the surface of this historic city.

WELCOME TO AVIGNON WALK

• *Start your tour where the Romans did, on Place de l'Horloge, in front of City Hall (Hôtel de Ville).*

Place de l'Horloge

In ancient Roman times this was the forum, and in medieval times it was the market square. The square is named for the clock tower (now hiding behind the more recently built city hall), which, in its day, was a humanist statement. In medieval France, the only bells in town rang from the church tower to indicate not the hours but the calls to prayer. With the dawn of the modern age, secular clock towers like this rang out the hours as people organized their lives.

Taking humanism a step further, the City Hall (Hôtel de Ville), built after the French Revolution, obstructed the view of the old clock tower while celebrating a new era. The slogan "liberty, equality, and brotherhood" is a reminder that the people supersede the king and the church. And today, judging from the square's jammed cafés and restaurants, it is indeed the people who rule.

The square's present popularity arrived with the trains in 1854. Facing City Hall, look left down the main drag, Rue de la République. When the trains came to Avignon, proud city fathers wanted a direct, impressive way to link the new station to the heart of the city—so they plowed over homes to create Rue de la République and widened Place de l'Horloge. This main drag's Parisian feel is intentional—it was built not in the Provençal manner, but in the Haussmann style that is so dominant in Paris (characterized by broad, straight boulevards lined with stately buildings). Today, this Champs-Elysées of Avignon is lined with department stores and banks.

• *Walk slightly uphill past the Neo-Renaissance facade of the theater and the carousel (public WCs behind). Look back to see the late Gothic bell tower. Then veer right at the Palace of the Popes and continue into...*

Palace Square (Place du Palais)

Pull up a concrete stump just past the café. Nicknamed *bites* (slang for penis), these effectively keep cars from double-parking in areas designed for people. Many of the metal ones slide up and down by remote control to let privileged cars come and go.

Now take in the scene. This grand square is lined with the Palace of the Popes, the Petit Palais, and the cathedral. In the 1300s the entire headquarters of the Roman Catholic Church was moved to Avignon. The Church bought Avignon and gave it a complete makeover. Along with clearing out vast spaces like this square and building a three-acre palace, the Church erected more than three miles of protective wall (with 39 towers), "appropriate" housing for cardinals (read: mansions), and residences for its entire bureaucracy. The city was Europe's largest construction zone. Avignon's population grew from 6,000 to 25,000 in short order. (Today, 13,000 people live within the walls.) The limits of prepapal Avignon are outlined on your city map: Rues Joseph Vernet, Henri Fabre, des Lices, and Philonarde all follow the route of the city's earlier defensive wall (about half the diameter of today's wall).

The imposing facade behind you, across the square from the Palace of the Popes' main entry, was "the papal mint," which served as the finance department for the Holy See. The Petit Palais (Little

Palace) seals the uphill end of the square and was built for a cardinal; today it houses medieval paintings (museum described later).

Avignon's 12th-century Romanesque cathedral, just to the left of the Palace of the Popes, has been the seat of the local bishop for more than a thousand years. Predating the Church's purchase of Avignon by 200 years, its simplicity reflects Avignon's modest, pre-papal population. The gilded Mary was added in 1854, when the Vatican established the doctrine of her Immaculate Conception.

• *You can visit the massive **Palace of the Popes** (described on page 606) now, but it works better to visit that palace at the end of this walk, then continue directly to the "Discovering Avignon's Back Streets" walk, described later.*

Now is a good time to take in the...

Petit Palais Museum (Musée du Petit Palais)

This former cardinal's palace now displays the Church's collection of mostly art. You'll find some English information but not a lot of detail. Still, a visit here before going to the Palace of the Popes helps furnish and populate that otherwise barren building. You'll see bits of statues and tombs—an inventory of the destruction of exquisite Church art wrought by the French Revolution (which tackled established French society with Taliban-esque fervor). Next come many rooms filled with religious Italian paintings, organized in chronological order from early Gothic to late Renaissance.

Cost and Hours: €6, discount with Avignon Passion Pass, Wed-Mon 10:00-13:00 & 14:00-18:00, closed Tue, at north end of Palace Square, tel. 04 90 86 44 58.

• *From Palace Square, head up to the cathedral (enjoy the viewpoint overlooking the square), and fill your water bottle just outside the gate. Now zigzag up the ramps to the top of a rocky hill where Avignon was first settled. Atop the hill is an inviting café and pond in a park—the Jardin du Rocher des Doms. At the far side is a viewpoint high above the river from where you can see Avignon's beloved broken bridge.*

▲Jardin du Rocher des Doms

Enjoy the view from this bluff. On a clear day, the tallest peak you see, with its white limestone cap, is Mont Ventoux ("Windy Mountain"). Below and just to the right, you'll spot free passenger ferries shuttling across the river, and—tucked amidst the trees on the far side of the river—a fun, recommended restaurant, Le Bercail, a local favorite. The island in the river is the Ile de la Barthelasse,

PROVENCE

a lush nature preserve where Avignon can breathe. To the left in the distance is the TGV rail bridge.

The Rhône River marked the border of Vatican territory in medieval times. Fort St. André (across the river on the hill) was across the border, in the kingdom of France. The fort was built in 1360, shortly after the pope moved to Avignon, to counter the papal incursion into this part of Europe. Avignon's famous bridge was a key border crossing, with towers on either end—one was French, and the other was the pope's. The French one, across the river, is the Tower of Philip the Fair (described later, under "More Sights in Avignon").

Cost and Hours: Free, park gates open daily April-May and Sept 7:30-20:00, June-Aug until 21:00, Oct-March until 18:00.
· *Take the walkway down to the left and find the stairs (closed at dusk) leading down to the tower. You'll catch glimpses of the...*

Ramparts

The only bit of the rampart you can walk on is accessed from St. Bénezet Bridge (pay to enter—see next). Just after the papacy took control of Avignon, the walls were extended to take in the convents and monasteries that had been outside the city. What you see today was partially restored in the 19th century.
· *When you come out of the tower on street level, exit out of the walls, then turn left along the wall to the old bridge. Pass under the bridge to find its entrance shortly after.*

▲St. Bénezet Bridge (Pont St. Bénezet)

This bridge, whose construction and location were inspired by a shepherd's religious vision, is the "Pont d'Avignon" of nursery-rhyme fame. The ditty (which you've probably been humming all day) dates back to the 15th century: *Sur le Pont d'Avignon, on y danse, on y danse, sur le Pont d'Avignon, on y danse tous en rond* ("On the bridge of Avignon, we will dance, we will dance, on the bridge of Avignon, we will dance all in a circle").

And the bridge was a big deal even outside of its kiddie-tune fame. Built between 1171 and 1185, it was strategic—one of only three bridges crossing the mighty Rhône in the Middle Ages, important to pilgrims, merchants, and armies. It was damaged several times by floods and subsequently rebuilt. In 1668 most of it was knocked out for the last time by a disastrous icy flood. The townsfolk decided not to rebuild this time, and for more than a century, Avignon had no bridge across the Rhône. While only four arches survive today, the original bridge was huge: Imagine a 22-arch, 3,000-foot-long bridge extending from Vatican territory across the island to the lonely Tower of Philip the Fair, which marked the beginning of France (see displays of the bridge's original length).

Cost and Hours: €5, includes audioguide, €13.50 combo-ticket includes Palace of the Popes, same hours as Palace of the Popes—see next listing, tel. 04 90 27 51 16. Download the free "Avignon 3D" app before your visit to see what the bridge looked like in the 14th and 17th centuries (the bright Provençal sun makes it difficult to use the app on the bridge, so skip the €2 tablet).

• *To get to the Palace of the Popes from here, leave via the riverfront exit, turn left, then turn left again back into the walls. Walk to the end of the short street, then turn right following signs to* Palais des Papes. *Next, look for brown signs leading left under the passageway, then stay the course up the narrow steps to Palace Square.*

▲▲Palace of the Popes (Palais des Papes)

In 1309 a French pope was elected (Pope Clément V). His Holiness decided that dangerous Italy was no place for a pope, so he

moved the whole operation to Avignon for a secure rule under a supportive French king. The Catholic Church literally bought Avignon (then a two-bit town), and popes resided here until 1403. Meanwhile, Italians demanded a Roman pope, so from 1378 on, there were twin popes—one in Rome and one in Avignon—causing a schism in the Catholic Church that wasn't fully resolved until 1417.

Cost and Hours: €11, €13.50 combo-ticket includes St. Bénezet Bridge, discount with Avignon Passion Pass, daily March-Oct 9:00-19:00, July-Aug until 20:00, Nov-Feb 9:30-17:45, last entry one hour before closing; thorough and essential audioguide-€2; tel. 04 90 27 50 00, www.palais-des-papes.com.

Visiting the Palace: Visitors follow a one-way route. A big room near the start functions as "the museum," with artifacts (such as cool 14th-century arrowheads) and a good intro video.

The palace was built stark and strong, before the popes knew how long they'd be staying (and before the affluence and fanciness of the Renaissance and Baroque ages). This was the most fortified palace of the time (remember, the pope left Rome to be more secure). With 10-foot-thick walls, it was a symbol of power. There are huge ceremonial rooms (rarely used) and more intimate living quarters. The bedroom comes with the original wall paintings, a decorated wooden ceiling, and fine tiled floor. And there's one big "chapel" (twice the size of the adjacent cathedral) that, while simple, is majestic in its pure French Gothic lines.

This largest surviving Gothic palace in Europe was built to accommodate 500 people as the administrative center of the Holy See and home of the pope. Seven popes ruled from here, making this the center of Christianity for nearly 100 years. The last pope checked out in 1403, but the Church owned Avignon until the French Revolution in 1791. During this interim period, the palace still housed Church authorities. Avignon residents, many of whom had come from Rome, spoke Italian for a century after the pope left, making the town a cultural oddity within France.

The palace is pretty empty today—nothing portable survived both the pope's return to Rome and the French Revolution. You can climb the tower (Tour de la Gâche) for grand views. The artillery room is now a gift shop channeling all visitors on a full tour of knickknacks for sale.

• *You'll exit at the rear of the palace, where my "Discovering Avignon's Back Streets" walk begins. Or, to return to Palace Square, make two rights after exiting the palace.*

DISCOVERING AVIGNON'S BACK STREETS

Use the map in this section or the TI map to navigate this easy, level, 30-minute walk. We'll begin in the small square (Place de la Mirande) behind the Palace of the Popes. If you've toured the palace, this is where you exit. Otherwise, from the front of the palace, follow the narrow, cobbled Rue de la Peyrolerie—carved out of the rock—around the palace on the right side as you face it.

• *Our walk begins at the...*

Hôtel La Mirande: Located on the square, Avignon's finest hotel welcomes visitors. Find the atrium lounge and consider a coffee break amid the understated luxury (€15 afternoon tea served daily 15:00-18:00, includes a generous selection of pastries).

• *Turn left out of the hotel and left again on Rue de la Peyrolerie ("Coppersmiths Street"), then take your first right on Rue des Ciseaux d'Or ("Street of the Golden Scissors"). On the small square ahead you'll find the...*

Church of St. Pierre: The original walnut doors were carved in 1551, when tales of New World discoveries raced across Europe. (Notice the Indian headdress, top center of left-side door.) The fine Annunciation (eye level on right-side door) shows Gabriel giving Mary the exciting news in impressive Renaissance 3-D. The five niches are empty except for one mismatched Mary and Child filling the center niche. (The original was ransacked by the Revolution.) Now take 10 steps back from the door and look way up. The tiny statue breaking the skyline of the church is the pagan god Bacchus, with oodles of grapes. What's he doing sitting atop a Christian church? No one knows. The church's interior holds a beautiful Baroque altar.

• *Facing the church door, turn left and pass the recommended L'Epicerie restaurant, then follow the alley, which was covered and turned into a tunnel during the town's population boom. It leads into...*

Place des Châtaignes: The cloister of St. Pierre is named for the chestnut *(châtaigne)* trees that once stood here (now replaced by plane trees). The practical atheists of the French Revolution destroyed the cloister, leaving only faint traces of the arches along the church side of the square.

• *Continue around the church and cross the busy street. At the start of little Rue des Fourbisseurs find the classy...*

15th-Century Building: With its original beamed eaves showing, this is a rare vestige from the Middle Ages. Notice how this building widens the higher it gets. A medieval loophole based taxes on ground-floor square footage—everything above was tax-free. Walking down Rue des Fourbisseurs ("Street of the Animal Furriers"), notice how the top floors almost touch. Fire was a constant danger in the Middle Ages, as flames leapt easily from one home to the next. In fact, the lookout guard's primary responsibility was watching for fires, not the enemy.

• *Walk down Rue des Fourbisseurs past lots of shops and turn left onto the traffic-free Rue du Vieux Sextier ("Street of the Old Balance," for weighing items); another left under the first arch leads in 10 yards to one of France's oldest synagogues.*

Synagogue: Jews first arrived in Avignon with the Diaspora (exile after the Romans destroyed their great temple) in the first century. Avignon's Jews were nicknamed "the Pope's Jews" because of the protection that the Church offered to Jews expelled from France. Although the original synagogue dates from the 1220s, in the mid-19th century it was completely rebuilt in a Neoclassical Greek-temple style by a non-Jewish architect. This is the only synagogue under a rotunda. It's an intimate, classy place—where a community of 200 local Jews worships—dressed with white colonnades and walnut furnishings. It's best to email before you visit if you want to enter (free, visits possible Mon-Fri 9:00-11:00 only, ring doorbell on gray door, 2 Place Jerusalem, tel. 04 90 85 21 24, rabinacia@hotmail.fr).

• *Retrace your steps to Rue du Vieux Sextier and turn left. A few steps down the street (on the right) is Patrick Mallard—the most venerable pastry shop in town. It's one of two shops authorized to sell Avignon's one-of-a-kind, thistle-shaped candy called* papalines d'Avignon *(dark chocolate wrapped in pink-hued chocolate and filled with a liquor made from local plants).*

Continue down Rue du Vieux Sextier to the big square (across the busy street) and find the big, boxy market building with the hydroponic garden growing out its front wall.

Market (Les Halles): In 1970, the town's open-air market was replaced by this modern one. The market's jungle-like hydroponic

green wall reflects the changes of seasons and helps mitigate its otherwise stark exterior (Tue-Sun until 13:00, closed Mon). Step inside for a sensual experience of organic breads, olives, and festival-of-mold cheeses. Cheap cafés, bars, and good cheese shops are mostly on the right—the stinky fish stalls are on the left. This is a wonderful place for lunch (doors close weekdays at 13:30, Sat-Sun at 14:00)—

especially if you'd fancy a big plate of mixed seafood with a glass of white wine (see "Eating in Avignon," later).

• *Walk through the market and exit out the back door, turn left on Rue de la Bonneterie ("Street of Hosiery"), and track the street for five minutes to the plane trees, where it becomes...*

Rue des Teinturiers: This "Street of the Dyers" is a tie-dyed, tree- and stream-lined lane, home to earthy cafés and galleries. This was the cloth industry's dyeing and textile center in the 1800s. The stream is a branch of the Sorgue River. Those stylish Provençal fabrics and patterns you see for sale everywhere were first made here, after a pattern imported from India.

About three small bridges down, you'll pass the Grey Penitents chapel on the right. The upper facade shows the GPs, who dressed up in robes and pointy hoods to do their anonymous good deeds back in the 13th century. (While the American KKK dresses in hoods to hide their hateful racism, these hoods symbolized how all are equal in God's eyes.) As you stroll on, you'll see the work of amateur sculptors, who have carved whimsical car barriers out of limestone. Fun restaurants on this atmospheric street are recommended later, under "Eating in Avignon."

• *Farther down Rue des Teinturiers, you'll come to the...*

Waterwheel: Standing here, imagine the Sorgue River—which hits the mighty Rhône in Avignon—being broken into several canals in order to turn 23 such wheels. Starting in about

1800, waterwheels powered the town's industries. The little cog-wheel above the big one could be shoved into place, kicking another machine into gear behind the wall.

• *To return to the center of town, double back on Rue des Teinturiers and turn left on Rue des Lices, which traces the first medieval wall. ("Lice" is the no-man's-land along a protective wall.) After a long block you'll pass a striking four-story building that was a home for the poor in the 1600s, an army barracks in the 1800s, a fine-arts school in the 1900s, and is a deluxe condominium today (much of this neighborhood is going high-class residential). Eventually you'll return to Rue de la République, Avignon's main drag.*

More Sights in Avignon

Most of Avignon's top sights are covered earlier by my self-guided walks. With more time, consider these options.

Musée Angladon

Visiting this museum is like being invited into the elegant home of a rich and passionate art collector. It mixes a small but enjoyable collection of art from Post-Impressionists to Cubists (including Paul Cézanne, Vincent van Gogh, Edgar Degas, and Pablo Picasso), with re-created art studios and furnishings from many periods. It's a quiet place with a few superb paintings.

Cost and Hours: €8, Tue-Sun 13:00-18:00, closed Mon, 5 Rue Laboureur, tel. 04 90 82 29 03, www.angladon.com.

Calvet Museum (Musée Calvet)

This fine-arts museum, ignored by most, impressively displays a collection highlighting French Baroque works and Northern masters such as Hieronymus Bosch and Pieter Bruegel. You'll find a few gems upstairs: a painting each by Manet, Sisley, Géricault, and David. On the ground floor is a room dedicated to more modern artists, with works by Soutine, Bonnard, and Vlamnick.

Cost and Hours: €6, includes audioguide, Wed-Mon 10:00-13:00 & 14:00-18:00, closed Tue, in the western half of town at 65 Rue Joseph Vernet, tel. 04 90 86 33 84, www.musee-calvet-avignon.com.

Nearby: The museum's antiquities collection, **Le Musée Lapidaire,** is hosted in a church a few blocks away at 27 Rue de la République. If you plan to visit this small museum, get your Avignon Passion Pass stamped here first for the best discount (€2 without pass, €7 combo-ticket with Calvet Museum; same hours except open Tue and closed Mon, tel. 04 90 85 75 38, www.musee-calvet-avignon.com).

Collection Lambert

This new modern art museum housed in a grand 18th-century mansion is the talk of Avignon. The collection, with works from the 1960s to the present, comes from the famous art dealer Yvon Lambert, whose goal was to make well-known contemporary art accessible outside of Paris. The recommended Le Violette restaurant in the courtyard is worth the visit alone.

Cost and Hours: €10, Tue-Sun 11:00-18:00, closed Mon except July-Aug when it's open until 19:00, 5 Rue Violette, tel. 04 90 16 56 20, www.collectionlambert.fr.

NEAR AVIGNON, IN VILLENEUVE-LES-AVIGNON
▲Tower of Philip the Fair (Tour Philippe-le-Bel)

Built to protect access to St. Bénezet Bridge in 1307, this hulking tower, located in nearby Villeneuve-lès-Avignon, offers a terrific view over Avignon and the Rhône basin. It's best late in the day.

Cost and Hours: €2.50; Tue-Sun May-Oct 10:00-12:30 & 14:00-18:00, Feb-April 14:00-17:00, closed Nov-Jan and Mon year-round.

Getting There: To reach the tower from Avignon, drive five minutes (cross Daladier Bridge, follow signs to *Villeneuve-lès-Avignon*), or take bus #5 (2/hour, catch bus in front of post office on Cours Président Kennedy across from train station).

Sleeping in Avignon

($$$$ = Splurge, $$$ = Pricier, $$ = Moderate, $ = Budget)

Hotel values are better in Arles, though I've found some pretty good deals in Avignon. Avignon is crazy during its July festival, when you must book long ahead and pay inflated prices. Drivers should ask about parking discounts through hotels.

NEAR CENTRE-VILLE STATION

These listings are a five- to ten-minute walk from the Centre-Ville train station.

$$ Hôtel Bristol* is a big, professionally run place on the main drag, offering predictable "American" comforts at fair rates. Enjoy spacious public spaces, large rooms with neutral tones, and a generous buffet breakfast (family rooms, pay parking—reserve ahead, 44 Cours Jean Jaurès, tel. 04 90 16 48 48, www.bristol-hotel-avignon.com, contact@bristol-avignon.com).

$$ Hôtel Ibis Centre Gare* offers predictable comfort and generous public spaces near the central train and bus stations (42 Boulevard St. Roch, tel. 04 90 85 38 38, www.ibishotel.com, h0944@accor.com).

$ Hôtel Colbert is on a quiet lane, with a dozen spacious

PROVENCE

Avignon Hotels & Restaurants

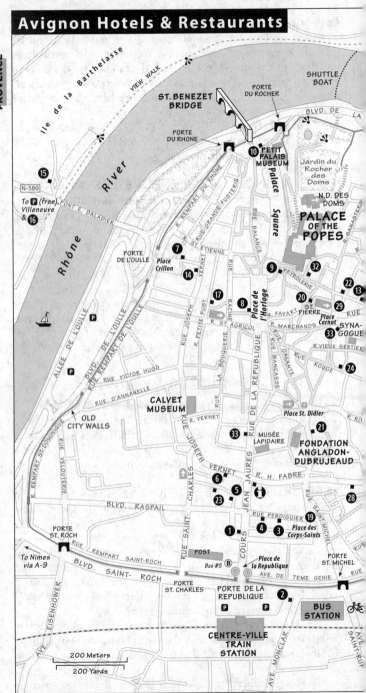

Ile de la Barthelasse

VIEW WALK

ST. BENEZET BRIDGE

PORTE DU ROCHER

SHUTTLE BOAT

BLVD. DE LA

PORTE DU RHONE

10

PETIT PALAIS MUSEUM

Palace Square

Jardin du Rocher des Doms

N.D. DES DOMS

PALACE OF THE POPES

N-580

15

To P (free) Villeneuve & **16**

PONT E. DALADIER

R. REMPART DU RHONE

R. GRANDE FUSTERIE

RUE ETIENNE

RUE BALANCE

RUE BANASTERIE

PORTE DE L'OULLE

Place Crillon

7

14

RUE JOSEPH VERNET

R. PETITE FUSTE

R. ST. AGRICOL

17

8

Place de l'Horloge

RUE RACINE

9

PEYROLERIE

32

22

13

ALLÉE DE L'OULLE

BLVD. DE L'OULLE

RUE DE L'OULLE

RUE VICTOR HUGO

RUE RACINE

R. FAVART

RUE MARCHANDS

ST. PIERRE

20

Place Carnot

29

33

SYNA-GOGUE

Rhône River

P

P

RUE D'ANNANELLE

RUE LA BOUQUERIE

RUE GALANTE

RUE VIEUX SEXTIER

RUE ROUGE

24

OLD CITY WALLS

CALVET MUSEUM

R. VERNET

RUE DE LA REPUBLIQUE

RUE BANCASSE

Place St. Didier

R. RO

R. REMPART ST-DOMINIQUE

RUE VELOUTERIE

RUE JOSEPH VERNET

RUE CHARLES

33

MUSÉE LAPIDAIRE

21

FONDATION ANGLADON-DUBRUJEAUD

RUE SAINT-MICHEL

To Nimes via A-9

R. REMPART SAINT-ROCH

BLVD. RASPAIL

RUE CHARLES

JEAN JAURES

R. H. FABRE

6

5

i

23

28

PORTE ST. ROCH

POST

COURS

Place de la Republique

1

Bus #5 **B**

RUE PERDIGUIER

4

3

Place des Corps-Saints

19

PORTE ST. MICHEL

RUE

AVE. EISENHOWER

BLVD. SAINT-ROCH

PORTE ST. CHARLES

PORTE DE LA REPUBLIQUE

AVE. DE

7EME GENIE

2

BUS STATION

P

P

CENTRE-VILLE TRAIN STATION

AVE. MONCLAR

AVE. SAINT-RU

200 Meters

200 Yards

1. Hôtel Bristol
2. Hôtel Ibis Centre Gare
3. Hôtel Colbert
4. Hôtel les Corps Saints
5. Hôtel Boquier
6. Hôtel Innova/Cardabella
7. Hôtel d'Europe & La Vieille Fontaine Restaurant
8. Hôtel de l'Horloge
9. Hôtel Mercure Palais des Papes
10. Hôtel Pont d'Avignon
11. Autour du Petit Paradis Apts.
12. Aux Augustins Apartments
13. Hôtel Médiéval
14. Hôtel Mignon
15. Auberge Bagatelle (Hostel)
16. To Jardin de Bacchus B&B
17. L'Essentiel Restaurant
18. Restaurant Numéro 75
19. L'Agape & Place des Corps-Saints Eateries
20. L'Epicerie Restaurant
21. Le Fou de Fafa Restaurant
22. La Vache à Carreaux Rest.
23. Le Violette Restaurant
24. L'Amista Restaurant
25. Le Zinzolin Restaurant
26. La Cave des Pas Sages Wine Bar & Restaurant des Teinturiers
27. Le Bercail Restaurant
28. L'Epice and Love Restaurant
29. Place des Châtaignes Eateries
30. Restaurant Françoise
31. Les Halles Market
32. Hôtel La Mirande (Aft. Tea)
33. Groceries (2)

rooms gathered on four floors around a skinny spiral staircase (no elevator). Patrice decorates each room as if it were his own with a colorful (occasionally erotic) flair. There are warm public spaces and a sweet little patio (some tight bathrooms, rooms off the patio can be musty, closed Nov-March, 7 Rue Agricol Perdiguier, tel. 04 90 86 20 20, www.lecolbert-hotel.com, contact@avignon-hotel-colbert.com).

$ Hôtel les Corps Saints,** run by young and eager Agnes and Fabrice, rents 16 bright rooms with tight baths at fair rates (no elevator, 17 Rue Agricol Perdiguier, tel. 04 90 86 14 46, www.avignon-splendid-hotel.com, splendidavignon@gmail.com).

$ Hôtel Boquier,** run by engaging managers Madame Sylvie and husband Pascal, has 12 quiet, good-value, and homey rooms under wood beams in a central location (family rooms, steep and narrow stairways to some rooms, no elevator, pay parking nearby, near the TI at 6 Rue du Portail Boquier, tel. 04 90 82 34 43, www.hotel-boquier.com, contact@hotel-boquier.com).

$ Hôtel Innova/Cardabella* is a shy little place with 11 modest rooms at good rates (cheaper rooms with shared bath, no aircon, no elevator, 100 Rue Joseph Vernet, tel. 04 90 82 54 10, www.hotel-cardabella.fr, hotel.cardabella@orange.fr).

IN THE CENTER, NEAR PLACE DE L'HORLOGE

$$$$ Hôtel d'Europe,***** with Avignon's most prestigious address, lets peasants sleep royally without losing their shirts—but only if they land one of the 13 reasonable "classique" rooms. Enter through a shady courtyard, linger in the lounges, and savor every comfort. The hotel is located on the handsome Place Crillon, near the river (pay garage parking, near Daladier Bridge at 12 Place Crillon, tel. 04 90 14 76 76, www.heurope.com, reservations@heurope.com). The hotel's fine restaurant is described in "Eating in Avignon," later.

$$$ Hôtel de l'Horloge**** is as central as it gets—on Place de l'Horloge. It offers 66 unimaginative but comfortable rooms at fair rates, some with terraces and views of the city and the Palace of the Popes (elaborate €18 buffet breakfast/brunch served until 11:00, 1 Rue Félicien David, tel. 04 90 16 42 00, www.hotel-avignon-horloge.com, hotel.horloge@hotels-ocre-azur.com).

$$$ Hôtel Mercure Palais des Papes,**** about a block from the Palace of the Popes, has an ugly exterior but 86 big, smartly designed rooms, many with small balconies (about half the rooms have views over Place de l'Horloge, 1 Rue Jean Vilar, tel. 04 90 80 93 00, www.mercure.com, h1952@accor.com).

$$$ Hôtel Pont d'Avignon,**** just inside the walls near St. Bénezet Bridge, is part of the same chain as Hôtel Mercure Palais des Papes, with the same prices for its 87 rooms. There's an airy atrium breakfast room and small garden terrace (direct access to a garage makes parking easier than at the other Mercure hotel, parking deals, on Rue Ferruce, tel. 04 90 80 93 93, www.mercure.com, h0549@accor.com).

$$ Autour du Petit Paradis Apartments and **Aux Augustins,** run by Sabine and Patrick, offer 22 contemporary, well-furnished apartments spread over two locations. **Petit Paradis,** in a restored 17th-century mansion, is a bit more centrally located; **Augustins** has bigger rooms, all on a shaded courtyard, and lovely stone from its period as a 14th-century monastery (2-night minimum, no elevator, 5 Rue Noël Biret and 16 Rue Carreterie, tel. 04 90 81 00 42, www.autourdupetitparadis.com, contact@autourdupetitparadis.com).

$ Hôtel Médiéval,** burrowed deep a few blocks from the Church of St. Pierre, was built as a cardinal's home. This stone mansion's grand staircase leads to 35 comfortable, pastel rooms (no elevator, kitchenettes, 5 blocks east of Place de l'Horloge, behind Church of St. Pierre at 15 Rue Petite Saunerie, tel. 04 90 86 11 06, www.hotelmedieval.com, hotel.medieval@wanadoo.fr, run by helpful Régis).

$ Hôtel Mignon* is a good-enough, one-star place with fair comfort, air-conditioning, no elevator, worn-out wallpaper, and tiny bathrooms (family rooms, 12 Rue Joseph Vernet, tel. 09 70 35 37 67, www.hotel-mignon.com, reservation@hotel-mignon.fr).

ON THE OUTSKIRTS

Auberge Bagatelle offers dirt-cheap beds in two buildings—a **$** budget hotel and a **¢** youth hostel—and has a young and lively vibe, café, grocery store, launderette, great views of Avignon, and campers for neighbors (cheaper rooms with shared bath, family rooms, across Daladier Bridge on Ile de la Barthelasse, bus #5 from main post office, tel. 04 90 86 30 39, http://campingbagatelle.com, auberge.bagatelle@wanadoo.fr).

NEAR AVIGNON

At **$$ Jardin de Bacchus,** a 15-minute drive northwest of Avignon by car and convenient to Pont du Gard, enthusiastic and English-speaking Christine and Erik offer two double rooms in their village home overlooking the famous rosé vineyards of Tavel (includes breakfast, fine €30 dinner if arranged in advance, swimming pool, great patio, possible bike rentals). They also offer apartments for two or four people (4-night minimum in off-season, one-week minimum in summer, tel. 04 66 90 28 62 or 06 74 41 77 94, www.jardindebacchus.fr, jardindebacchus@gmail.com). By car, it's just off the A-9 autoroute (exit 22); by bus, it's a 30-minute ride from Avignon (www.edgard-transport.fr).

PROVENCE

Eating in Avignon

($$$$ = Splurge, $$$ = Pricier, $$ = Moderate, $ = Budget)

Avignon offers a good range of restaurants and settings, from lively squares to atmospheric streets. Skip the overpriced, underwhelming restaurants on Place de l'Horloge and find a more intimate location for your dinner. Avignon is brimming with delightful squares and back streets lined with little restaurants eager to feed you. If you need to dine before 19:00, find **Restaurant Françoise** on Place Pie (described later). At the finer places, reservations are generally smart (especially on weekends); your hotel can call for you, www.melido.fr.

FINE DINING WORTH THE SPLURGE

$$$$ L'Essentiel is where in-the-know locals go for a fine meal at reasonable prices. The setting is classy-contemporary inside, the back terrace is romantic, the wine list is extensive, the cuisine is classic French, and gentle owner Dominique makes timid diners feel at ease (inside and outdoor seating, closed Sun-Mon, 2 Rue Petite Fusterie, tel. 04 90 85 87 12, www.restaurantlessentiel.com).

$$$$ La Vieille Fontaine, just inside the gates of Hôtel d'Europe, serves gourmet traditional cuisine in an elegant dining room and on a spacious courtyard terrace. Do your best to dress up for this place, and plan to spend about €60 for the dinner *menu* (€50 for lunch, near Daladier Bridge at 12 Place Crillon, tel. 04 90 14 76 76, www.heurope.com).

$$$$ Restaurant Numéro 75 is worth the walk. It fills the Pernod mansion (of *pastis* liquor fame) with a romantic, chandeliered, Old World dining hall that extends to a leafy, gravelly courtyard. They serve delightful lunch salads, fish is a forte, and the French cuisine is beautifully presented (Mon-Sat 12:00-14:00 & 19:30-22:00, closed Sun, 75 Rue Guillaume Puy, tel. 04 90 27 16 00, www.numero75.com).

$$$$ L'Agape shares an atmospheric square with cafés and cheaper places. Here, discerning diners can eat well while enjoying great outdoor ambience (closed Sun-Mon, 21 Place des Corps-Saints, tel. 04 90 85 04 06).

PROVENCE

DINING WELL IN THE OLD CENTER

$$$$ L'Epicerie sits alone under green awnings on the romantic Place St-Pierre square and is ideal for dinner outside (or in the small but cozy interior). The cuisine is as delicious as the setting (daily, 10 Place St-Pierre, tel. 04 90 82 74 22).

$$$ Le Fou de Fafa is a warm place with ample space between its 12 tables and a menu of delicious cuisine at good prices. Delightful Antonia serves while her husband cooks (inside dining only, book ahead or arrive early, Tue-Sat from 18:30, closed Sun-Mon, 17 Rue des Trois Faucons, tel. 04 32 76 35 13).

$$ La Vache à Carreaux venerates cheese and wine while offering a range of choices from its big chalkboard. It's a young, lively place, with colorful decor, easygoing service (thanks to owner Jean-Charles) and a reasonable wine list featuring €5 wines by the glass (daily, evening only, just off atmospheric Place des Châtaignes at 14 Rue de la Peyrolerie, tel. 04 90 80 09 05).

$$$ Le Violette, in the peaceful courtyard of the Collection Lambert modern art museum, serves fresh modern cuisine and is gorgeous when lit by the museum rooms at night (daily July-Aug, Sept-June closed Sun afternoons and all day Mon, 5 Rue Violette, tel. 04 90 85 36 42).

$$ L'Amista ("the spot to meet friends"), a cozy, welcoming place run by Delphine, offers a Provençal-Spanish-inspired menu that always includes vegetarian options. Tapas-style snacks are great for sharing and daily specials are a tasty value. Desserts are homemade and you can even have a crêpe to go (Tue-Sat 12:00-22:00, closed Sun-Mon, 23 Rue Bonneterie, tel. 09 86 19 36 86).

BOHEMIAN CHIC, CANALSIDE ON RUE DES TEINTURIERS

Rue des Teinturiers' fun concentration of midrange, popular-with-the-locals eateries justifies the long walk. It's a trendy, youthful area, spiffed up but with little hint of tourism. You'll find wine bars, vegetarian options, and live music at rickety metal tables under shady trees along the canal. I'd walk the street's entire length to find the best ambience before making a choice. (Note that the finer Restaurant Numéro 75, listed earlier, is just around the corner.)

$$ Le Zinzolin is a bohemian bistro serving international cuisine at fair prices with a few vegetarian options. The atmosphere is good inside and out—check out the €15 meal-size salads (daily, 22 Rue des Teinturiers, tel. 04 90 82 41 55).

$$ La Cave des Pas Sages, a characteristic wine bar, is a fun place to start your evening (even if you're not eating in the area). Linger with the locals over a cheap glass of regional wine or beer. Choose from the blackboard by the bar that lists all the open bottles, then join the gang outside by the canal (Mon-Sat 10:00-24:00, closed Sun, across from waterwheel at 41 Rue des Teinturiers).

$$$ Restaurant des Teinturiers, run by Chef Guillaume and his mom, combines a casual setting with upscale nouvelle French cuisine and presentation. Guests leave comments on the chalkboard about their "semi-gastronomic meals" (daily 12:00-14:30 & 19:00-22:00, reservations smart, near the waterwheel at 5 Rue des Teinturiers; tel. 04 90 33 43 83, http://restaurantdesteinturiers. com).

LOCAL FAVORITE ACROSS THE RHONE

$$$$ Le Bercail offers a fun opportunity to get out of town (barely) and take in *le fresh air* with a terrific riverfront view of Avignon, all while enjoying big portions of Provençal cooking (daily April-Oct, serves late, reservations recommended, tel. 04 90 82 20 22, www.restaurant-lebercail.fr). Take the free shuttle boat (located near St. Bénezet Bridge) to the Ile de la Barthelasse, turn right, and walk five minutes. As the boat usually stops running at about 18:00 (except in July-Aug, when it runs until 21:00), you can either taxi back or walk 25 minutes along the pleasant riverside path and over Daladier Bridge.

GOOD BUDGET PLACES IN THE CENTER

$$ L'Epice and Love (pronounced "lay peace and love") is a tiny, flower-child-like restaurant with a few colorfully decorated tables (inside only). Friendly, English-speaking owner Marie stokes the conviviality and changes her selections weekly: tasty meat, fish, and vegetarian/vegan dishes with a Provençal flavor, all served at good prices (Tue-Sat 15:00-21:00, closed Sun-Mon, 30 Rue des Lices, tel. 04 90 82 45 96).

Place des Châtaignes: This square offers cheap meals and a fun commotion of tables. The **$ Crêperie du Cloître** makes OK dinner crêpes and salads but has the best seating on the square (daily). **$ La Pause Gourmande** bakery/deli is tops on the square for lunch (great *fougasse,* quiche with salad, or *plats;* lunch only, closed Sun).

Place des Corps-Saints: This welcoming square offers the best feeling of a neighborhood dining, drinking, and simply living outdoors together. It's my choice for outdoor dining in Avignon, with several eateries in all price ranges sharing the same great setting under big plane trees. Survey the square before deciding. With tables crammed into every nook and cranny, there's standard café fare, Italian options, and finer dining choices. **$ Ginette & Marcel: Bistrot à Tartines** serves salads, big slices of toast smothered in a variety of toppings, and has tasty desserts (daily, tel. 04 90 85 58 70).

Place Pie: Avignon's youth make their home on this big square filled with cafés. Just off the square, **$ Restaurant Françoise** is a fine deli-café, where fresh-baked tarts—savory and sweet—and a variety of salads and soups make a healthful meal, and vegetarian options are plentiful. Order at the counter and eat inside or out (Wi-Fi, Mon-Sat 8:00-19:00, closed Sun, a block off Place Pie at 6 Rue Général Leclerc, tel. 04 32 76 24 77).

Farmers Market: Les Halles (described in the "Discovering Avignon's Back Streets" walk) has a handful of wonderfully characteristic and cheap places serving locals the freshest of food surrounded by all that market fun. You'll need to be done by 13:30 (14:00 on weekends), as that's when they lock the place up (closed Mon).

Avignon Connections

BY TRAIN

Remember, there are two train stations in Avignon: the suburban TGV station and the Centre-Ville station in the city center (€1.60 shuttle trains connect the stations, buy ticket from machine on platforms or at a counter, 2/hour, 5 minutes). TGV trains usually serve the TGV station only, though a few depart from Centre-Ville station (check your ticket). The TGV station has almost all the car rental agencies; only Avis is at Centre-Ville station. Some cities are served by slower local trains from Centre-Ville station as well as by faster TGV trains from the TGV station; I've listed the most convenient stations for each trip.

From Avignon's Centre-Ville Station to: Arles (roughly hourly, 20 minutes, less frequent in the afternoon), **Orange** (15/day, 20 minutes), **Nîmes** (12/day, 60 minutes), **Isle-sur-la-Sorgue** (10/day on weekdays, 5/day on weekends, 30 minutes), **Carcassonne** (8/day, 7 with transfer in Narbonne or Nîmes, 3 hours), **Barcelona** (5/day, 5 hours, change in Nîmes, faster from Avignon TGV).

From Avignon's TGV Station to: Nice (10/day, most by TGV, 4 hours, many require transfer in Marseille), **Marseille** (10/day, 35 minutes), **Cassis** (7/day, transfer in Marseille, 1.5 hours), **Aix-en-Provence TGV** (12/day, 25 minutes), **Lyon** (12/day, 70 minutes), **Paris'** Gare de Lyon (10/day direct, 2.5 hours; more connections with transfer, 3-4 hours), **Paris' Charles de Gaulle airport** (7/day, 3.25 hours), **Barcelona** (1/day, 4 hours).

BY BUS

The bus station *(gare routière)* is just past and below Hôtel Ibis, to the right as you exit the train station. Nearly all buses leave from this station (a few leave from the ring road outside the station—ask, buy tickets on bus, small bills only). Service is reduced or nonexistent on Sundays and holidays. Check your departure time before-hand, and make sure to verify your destination with the driver.

From Avignon to Pont du Gard: Take bus #15 to this famous Roman aqueduct (5/day, 50 minutes).

By Bus to Other Regional Destinations: Arles (9/day, 1 hour, leaves from TGV station); **Nîmes** (10/day, 1 hour), **Aix-en-Provence** (6/day Mon-Sat, 3/day Sun, 75 minutes, faster and easier than train), **Uzès** (5/day, 60-80 minutes, stops at Pont du Gard); **St-Rémy-de-Provence** (Cartreize #57 bus, 10/day Mon-Sat, 6/day Sun, 45 minutes); **Orange** (Mon-Sat hourly, 5/day Sun, 1 hour—take the train instead); **Isle-sur-la-Sorgue** (bus #6, 6-8/day Mon-Sat, 3-4/day Sun, 45 minutes); For the **Côtes du Rhône** area, the bus runs to **Vaison-la-Romaine, Nyons, Sablet,** and **Sé-guret** (3-6/day during the school year—*période scolaire,* 3/day oth-erwise; 1/day from TGV station; 1.5 hours, all buses pass through Orange—faster to take train to Orange, and transfer to bus there, express bus runs to Vaison-la-Romaine from Avignon, 1/day, 1 hour). For the **Luberon** area—including **Lourmarin, Roussillon,** and **Gordes**—take the bus to Cavaillon, then take bus #8 toward Pertuis for Lourmarin (3/day) or bus #15.3 for Gordes/Roussillon (only 1/day); you must reserve a day ahead for buses from Cavaillon (tel. 04 90 74 20 21).

Pont du Gard

Throughout the ancient world, aqueducts were like flags of stone that heralded the greatness of Rome. A visit to this sight still works to proclaim the wonders of that age. This impressively preserved Roman aqueduct was built in about 1 A.D., and while most of it is on or below the ground, at Pont du Gard it spans a canyon on a massive bridge over the Gardon River—one of the most remarkable surviving Roman ruins anywhere. The 30-mile aqueduct supported a small canal that, by dropping one inch for every 350 feet, supplied nine million gallons of water per day (about 100 gallons per second) to Nîmes—one of ancient Europe's largest cities. Allow about four or five hours for visiting Pont du Gard (including transportation time from Avignon).

GETTING TO PONT DU GARD

The famous aqueduct is between Remoulins and Vers-Pont du Gard on D-981, 17 miles from Nîmes and 13 miles from Avignon.

By Car: Pont du Gard is a 30-minute drive due west of Avi-gnon (follow N-100 from Avignon, tracking signs to *Nîmes* and *Remoulins,* then *Pont du Gard* and *Rive Gauche*), and 45 minutes

northwest of Arles (via Tarascon on D-6113). If going to Arles from Pont du Gard, follow signs to *Nimes* (not *Avignon*), then D-6113, or A-54 (autoroute) to Arles.

By Bus: Buses run to Pont du Gard (on the Rive Gauche side) from Avignon (3/day, 50 minutes), Nîmes, and Uzès. If there's not a convenient return trip, consider busing to Nîmes and taking the train back to Avignon from there. Buses stop at the traffic roundabout 400 yards from the museum (stop name: Rond Point Pont du Gard; see Pont du Gard map for stop locations). In July and August, however, buses usually drive into the Pont du Gard site and stop at the parking lot's ticket booth. If leaving by bus, make sure you're waiting on the correct side of the traffic circle (stops have schedules posted), and wave your hand to signal the bus to stop for you—otherwise, it may drive on by. Buy your ticket when you get on and verify your destination with the driver.

By Taxi: From Avignon, it's about €60 for a taxi to Pont du Gard (tel. 04 90 82 20 20). Consider splurging on a taxi to the aqueduct in the morning, then take the early-afternoon bus back.

PROVENCE

ORIENTATION TO PONT DU GARD

There are two riversides to Pont du Gard: the Left Bank (Rive Gauche) and Right Bank (Rive Droite). Park on the Rive Gauche, where you'll find the museums, ticket booth, TI, ATM, cafeteria, WCs, and shops—all built into a modern plaza. A restaurant and ice-cream kiosk are on the Rive Droite. You'll see the aqueduct in two parts: first the fine museum complex, then the actual river gorge spanned by the ancient bridge.

Cost: €18 per car (regardless of number of passengers). (The €23 annual pass lets your carload come back for the evening lights without paying double.) Those arriving on foot, by bus, or by bike pay €7 per person. This gives you access to the aqueduct, museum, film, and outdoor *garrigue* nature area.

Hours: Museum—daily March-May and Oct 9:00-18:00, until 19:00 in June and Sept, until 20:00 in July and Aug, until 17:00 Nov-Feb, closed two weeks in Jan; aqueduct and parking lot—daily until 24:00.

Information: Tel. 04 66 37 50 99, www.pontdugard.fr.

Pont du Gard After Hours: During summer months, the site is open until midnight so people can hike, enjoy a picnic or the riverside restaurant, and watch the music-and-light show projected on the monument. The parking lot is staffed and guarded until 24:00, and after the museum closes you'll pay only €10 per carload to enter. If you don't care to see the museum, seeing Pont du Gard in the evening is dramatic (and cheap). The aqueduct is illuminated on summer evenings (June-Aug 22:00-24:00). The music-and-light show is projected from the north, so those in the picnic area and at the restaurant enjoy a good view.

Hiking Tour Across Pont Du Gard: In July and August, several tours per day go through the water channel at the top of the aqueduct (€4, pay guide directly, includes 10-minute intro and 20-minute hike, commentary in French and English, generally starting at the bottom of the hour from 10:30—check times posted at the museum and entry). No reservations are taken; you just wait at the metal gate on top of the bridge on the side opposite the museum. The first 33 people get in. If you do this tour, notice the massive calcium buildup lining the channel from more than 400 years of flowing water.

Canoe Rental: Floating under Pont du Gard by canoe is an unforgettable experience. Collias Canoes will pick you up at Pont du Gard (or elsewhere, if prearranged) and shuttle you to the town of Collias. You'll float down the river to the nearby town of Remoulins, where they'll pick you up and take you back to Pont du Gard (€23/person, €12/child under 12, usually 2 hours, though you can take as long as you like, reserve the day before in July-Aug, tel. 04 66 22 87 20).

Plan Ahead for Swimming and Hiking: Pont du Gard is perhaps best enjoyed on your back and in the water—bring along a swimsuit and flip-flops for the rocks. (Note that local guides warn that the bridge can create whirlpools and be dangerous to swim under.) The best Pont du Gard viewpoints are up steep hills with uneven footing—bring good shoes, too.

SIGHTS AT PONT DU GARD
▲▲▲Viewing the Aqueduct

A park-like path leads to the aqueduct. Until a few years ago, this was an actual road—adjacent to the aqueduct—that had spanned

the river since 1743. Before you cross the bridge, walk to the riverside viewpoint: Pass under the bridge and aqueduct and hike about 300 feet along the riverbank to the concrete steps leading down to a grand view of the world's second-highest standing Roman structure. (Rome's Colosseum is only 6 feet taller.)

This was the biggest bridge in the whole 30-mile-long aqueduct. The arches are twice the width of standard aqueducts, and the main arch is the largest the Romans ever built—80 feet across (the width of the river). The bridge is about 160 feet high and was originally about 1,200 feet long.

Though the distance from the source (in Uzès, on the museum side of the site) to Nîmes was only 12 miles as the eagle flew, engineers chose the most economical route, winding and zigzagging 30 miles. The water made the trip in 24 hours with a drop of only 40 feet. Ninety percent of the aqueduct is on or under the ground, but a few river canyons like this required bridges. A stone lid hides a four-foot-wide, six-foot-tall chamber lined with waterproof mortar that carried the stream for more than 400 years. For 150 years, this system provided Nîmes with good drinking water. Expert as the Romans were, they miscalculated the backup caused by a downstream corner, and had to add the thin extra layer you can see just under the lid to make the channel deeper.

The stones that jut out—giving the aqueduct a rough, unfinished appearance—supported the original scaffolding. The protuberances were left, rather than cut off, in anticipation of future repair needs. The lips under the arches supported wooden templates that allowed the stones in the round arches to rest on something until the all-important keystone was dropped into place. Each stone weighs from two to six tons. The structure stands with no mortar (except at the very top, where the water flowed)—taking full advantage of the innovative Roman arch, made strong by gravity.

Hike over the bridge for a closer look and the best views. Steps lead up a high trail (marked *view point/panorama*) to a superb vista

(go right at the top; best views are soon after the trail starts descending).

Back on the museum side, steps lead up to the Rive Gauche side of the aqueduct, where you can follow the canal path along a trail (marked with red-and-white horizontal lines) to find some remains of the Roman canal. You'll soon reach another *panorama* with more great views of the aqueduct. Hikers can continue along the path, following the red-and-white mark-ings that lead through a forest, after which you'll come across more remains of the canal (much of which are covered by vegetation). There's not much left to see because of medieval cannibalization—frugal builders couldn't resist the precut stones as they constructed area churches. The path continues for about 15 miles, but there's little reason to go farther.

▲Museum

In this state-of-the-art museum (well-presented in English), you'll enter to the sound of water and understand the critical role fresh water played in the Roman "art of living." You'll see copies of lead pipes, faucets, and siphons; walk through a mock rock quarry; and learn how they moved those huge rocks into place and how those massive arches were made. A wooden model shows how Roman engineers determined the proper slope. While actual artifacts from the aqueduct are few, the exhibit shows the immensity of the un-dertaking as well as the payoff. Imagine the jubilation when this extravagant supply of water finally tumbled into Nîmes. A relaxing highlight is the scenic video of a helicopter ride along the entire 30-mile course of the structure, from its start at Uzès all the way to the Castellum in Nîmes.

Other Activities

Several additional attractions are designed to give the sight more meaning (but for most visitors, the museum is sufficient). A 15-min-ute film plays in the same building as the museum on a loop. The nearby kids' museum, called *Ludo*, offers a scratch-and-sniff teach-ing experience (in English) of various aspects of Roman life and the importance of water. The extensive outdoor *garrigue* natural area, closer to the aqueduct, features historic crops and landscapes of the Mediterranean.

Les Baux

The hilltop town of Les Baux crowns the rugged Alpilles (ahl-pee) mountains, evoking a tumultuous medieval history. Here, you can imagine the struggles of a strong community that lived a rough-and-tumble life—thankful more for their top-notch fortifications than for their dramatic views. It's mobbed with tourists most of the day, but Les Baux rewards those who arrive by 9:00 or after 17:30. (Although the hilltop citadel's entry closes at the end of the day, once you're inside, you're welcome to live out your medieval fantasies all night long, even with a picnic.) Sunsets are dramatic, the castle is brilliantly illuminated after dark, and nights in Les Baux are pin-drop peaceful.

GETTING TO LES BAUX

By Car: Les Baux is a 20-minute drive from Arles: Follow signs for *Avignon*, then *Les Baux*.

By Bus: From Arles, Cartreize **bus #57** runs to Les Baux (daily July-Aug, in May-June and Sept Sat-Sun only, none Oct-April, 6/day, 35 minutes; via Abbey of Montmajour, Fontvieille, and Le Paradou; destination: St-Rémy/Avignon, timetables at www.lepilote.com).

St-Rémy, about seven miles north of Les Baux, is a workable transit point for those home-basing in Avignon: Ride Cartreize bus #57 from Avignon to St-Rémy (6/day, 45 minutes); you can continue to Les Baux on the same bus daily in July-August and on weekends in May-June and September (none Oct-April, timetables at www.lepilote.com). Otherwise, continue to Les Baux by taxi (next).

By Taxi: If buses aren't running to Les Baux, you can taxi there from St-Rémy, then take another taxi to return to St-Rémy or to your home base. Figure €35 for a taxi one-way to Les Baux from Arles, €65 from Avignon, and €25 from St-Rémy (mobile 06 80 27 60 92).

By Minivan Tour: The best option for many is a minivan tour, which can be both efficient and economical (easiest from Avignon; see page 561).

PROVENCE

Orientation to Les Baux

Les Baux is actually two visits in one: castle ruins perched on an almost lunar landscape, and a medieval town below. Savor the castle, then tour—or blitz—the lower streets on your way out. While the town, which lives entirely off tourism, is packed with shops, cafés, and tourist knickknacks, the castle above stays manageable because crowds are dispersed over a big area. The lower town's polished-stone gauntlet of boutiques is a Provençal dream come true for shoppers.

TOURIST INFORMATION

The TI is immediately on the left as you enter the village (April-Sept Mon-Fri 9:00-18:00, Sat-Sun 10:00-17:30; off-season daily 10:00-17:30). The TI has free Wi-Fi and can call a cab for you.

ARRIVAL IN LES BAUX

Drivers pay €5 to park near the village. Pay at the machines (some accept exact coins only). You can park for free at the small parking at the **Carrières de Lumières** (described later) and walk along the road to Les Baux (be careful—the road is narrow, with blind curves).

After parking, walk up the cobbled street into town, where you're greeted first by the TI. From here the main drag leads directly to the castle—just keep going uphill (a 10-minute walk).

Sights in Les Baux

▲▲▲THE CASTLE RUINS (CHATEAU DES BAUX)

The sun-bleached ruins of the stone fortress of Les Baux are carved into, out of, and on top of a rock 650 feet above the valley floor.

Many of the ancient walls of this striking castle still stand as a testament to the proud past of this once-feisty village.

Cost and Hours: €8, €10 if there's "entertainment" (see next), €16 or €18 combo-ticket with Carrières de Lumières (described later), daily Easter-June and Sept 9:00-19:00, July-Aug 9:00-20:00, March and Oct 9:30-18:30, Nov-Feb 10:00-17:00, includes excellent audioguide available up to one hour before closing, tel. 04 90 54 55 56, www. chateau-baux-provence.com. If you're inside the castle when the entry closes, you can stay as long as you like.

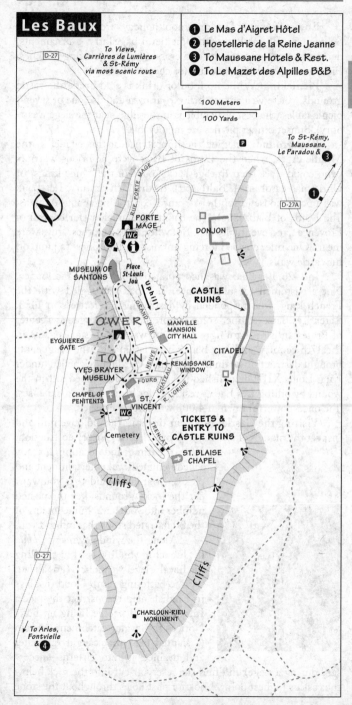

Les Baux

PROVENCE

1 Le Mas d'Aigret Hôtel
2 Hostellerie de la Reine Jeanne
3 To Maussane Hotels & Rest.
4 To Le Mazet des Alpilles B&B

100 Meters
100 Yards

To Views,
Carrières de Lumières
& St-Rémy
via most scenic route

D-27

To St-Rémy,
Maussane,
Le Paradou & 3

D-27A

1

RUE PORTE MAGE

PORTE
MAGE

WC

2

MUSEUM OF
SANTONS

Place
St-Louis
Jou

DONJON

CASTLE
RUINS

CITADEL

LOWER

GRAND RUE

Uphill!

MANVILLE
MANSION
CITY HALL

EYGUIERES
GATE

TOWN

YVES BRAYER
MUSEUM

NEUVE

FOURS

CHATEAU

RENAISSANCE
WINDOW

R. L'ORINE

CHAPEL OF
PENITENTS

ST.
VINCENT

WC

TICKETS &
ENTRY TO
CASTLE RUINS

Cemetery

TRENCAT

ST. BLAISE
CHAPEL

Cliffs

D-27

Cliffs

CHARLOUN-RIEU
MONUMENT

To Arles,
Fontvielle
& 4

Entertainment: During school holidays from April through September, the castle presents medieval pageantry, tournaments, demonstrations of catapults and crossbows, and jousting matches. Pick up a schedule as you enter (or check online).

Picnicking: While no food or drink is sold inside the castle grounds, you're welcome to bring your own and use one of several picnic tables (the best view table is at the edge near the siege weaponry). Sunset dinner picnics are memorable.

Background: Imagine the importance of this citadel in the Middle Ages, when the Lords of Baux were notorious warriors (who could trace their lineage back to one of the "three kings" of Christmas-carol fame, Balthazar). In the 11th century, Les Baux was a powerhouse in southern France, controlling about 80 towns. The Lords of Baux fought the counts of Barcelona for control of Provence...and eventually lost. But while in power, these guys were mean. One ruler enjoyed forcing unransomed prisoners to jump off his castle walls.

In 1426, Les Baux was incorporated into Provence and France. Not accustomed to subservience, Les Baux struggled with the French king, who responded by destroying the fortress in 1483. Later, Les Baux regained some importance and emerged as a center of Protestantism. Arguing with Rome was a high-stakes game in the 17th century, and Les Baux's association with the Huguenots brought destruction again in 1632 when Cardinal Richelieu (under King Louis XIII) demolished the castle. Louis rubbed salt in the wound by billing Les Baux's residents for his demolition expenses. The once-powerful town of 4,000 was forever crushed.

Visiting the Castle: Buy your ticket in the old olive mill and inspect the models of Les Baux before its 17th-century destruction.

Note the time and location for any scheduled medieval entertainment and pick up your audioguide. As you wander the rocky grounds, key the posted number into your audioguide for any of the 30 narrated stops that interest you.

Along the windblown spur (*baux* in French), you'll pass kid-thrilling medieval siege weaponry (go ahead, try the battering ram). Good displays in English help reconstruct the place. Imagine 4,000 people living up here. Notice the water-catchment system (a slanted field that caught rainwater and drained it into cisterns—necessary during a siege) and find the reservoir cut into the rock below the castle's highest point. Look for post holes throughout the stone walls that reveal where beams once supported floors. For the most sensational views, climb to the blustery top of the citadel. Hang on. The mistral wind just might blow you away.

▲LOWER TOWN

After your castle visit, you can shop and eat your way back through the lower town. Or, escape some of the crowds by visiting these minor but worthwhile sights as you descend. I've linked the sights with walking directions.

• *Follow the main drag about 100 yards through the town and look for the flags marking...*

Manville Mansion City Hall

The 15th-century City Hall offers art exhibits under its cool vaults. It occasionally flies the red-and-white flag of Monaco amid several others, a reminder that the Grimaldi family (longtime rulers of the tiny principality of Monaco) owned Les Baux until the French Revolution (1789). In fact, in 1982, Princess Grace Kelly and her royal husband, Prince Rainier Grimaldi, came to Les Baux to receive the key to the city.

Exit left and walk uphill 20 steps to the empty 1571 **Renaissance window frame.** This beautiful stone frame stands as a reminder of this town's Protestant history. This was probably a place of Huguenot worship—the words carved into the lintel, *Post tenebras lux,* were a popular Calvinist slogan: "After the shadow comes the light."

• *Continue walking uphill, and turn right on Rue des Fours to find the...*

Yves Brayer Museum (Musée Yves Brayer)

This enjoyable museum lets you peruse three floors of paintings (Van Gogh-like Expressionism) by Yves Brayer (1907-1990), who spent his final years in Les Baux. Like Van Gogh, Brayer was inspired by all that surrounded him, and by his travels through Morocco, Spain, and the rest of the Mediterranean world. Pick up the descriptive English sheet at the entry.

Cost and Hours: €5, daily April-Sept 10:00-12:30 & 14:00-18:30, shorter hours and closed Tue Oct-Dec and March, closed Jan-Feb, tel. 04 90 54 36 99, www.yvesbrayer.com.

• *Next door is...*

St. Vincent Church

This 12th-century Romanesque church was built short and wide to fit the terrain. The center chapel on the right (partially carved out of the rock) houses the town's traditional Provençal processional chariot. Each Christmas Eve, a ram pulled this cart—holding a lamb, symbolizing Jesus, and surrounded by candles—through town to the church.

• *As you leave the church, WCs (dug into the stone wall) are to the left and up the stairs. Directly in front of the church is a vast view, making clear the strategic value of this rocky bluff's natural fortifications. A few steps away is the...*

Chapel of Penitents

Inside, notice the nativity scene painted by Yves Brayer, illustrating the local legend that says Jesus was born in Les Baux.

• *As you leave the church, turn left and find the old town "laundry"— with a pig-snout faucet and 14th-century stone washing surface designed for short women.*

  Continue past the Yves Brayer Museum again, branch off to the left, and walk 100 yards down steep Rue de la Calade, passing a café with wonderful views, the town's fortified wall, and one of its two gates. Before long, you'll run into the...

Museum of Santons

This free and fun "museum" displays a collection of *santons* ("little saints"), popular folk figurines that decorate local Christmas mangers. Notice how the nativity scene "proves" once again that Jesus was born in Les Baux. These painted clay dolls show off local dress and traditions (with good English descriptions).

NEAR LES BAUX

▲Carrières de Lumières (Quarries of Light)

A 10-minute walk from Les Baux, this colossal quarry-cave with immense vertical walls offers a mesmerizing sound-and-slide experience. Enter a darkened world filled with floor-to-ceiling images and booming music. Wander through a complex of cathedral-like aisles, transepts, and choirs (no seating provided) as you experience the spectacle. There's no storyline to follow, but information panels by the café give some background. The show lasts 40 minutes and runs continuously. If you'd like an intermission, you can exit the "show" into a part of the quarry that opens to the sky and take a break at the café before reentering. Dress warmly, as the cave is cool.

Cost and Hours: €12, €16-18 combo-ticket with Les Baux castle ruins, daily April-Oct 9:30-19:00, July-Aug until 19:30, March and Nov-Dec 10:00-18:00, closed Jan-Feb, tel. 04 90 54 47 37, www.carrieres-lumieres.com.

Sleeping in and near Les Baux

In Les Baux: **$$ Le Mas d'Aigret*** is a 10-minute walk east of Les Baux on the road to St-Rémy (D-27). From this refuge, you can stare up at the castle walls rising beyond the heated swimming pool, or enjoy valley views from the groomed terraces while

playing *pétanque*. The rooms are simple but tastefully arranged, and Dutch Marieke and French Eric are wonderful hosts (family rooms, some view rooms, two cool troglodyte rooms, convenient half-pension dinner and breakfast option, air-con, rooms have some daytime road noise, free parking, tel. 04 90 54 20 00, www.masdaigret.com, contact@masdaigret.com).

$ Hostellerie de la Reine Jeanne** is just inside the gate to Les Baux, across from the TI. It's warmly run by Marc and English-speaking Gaelle, who rent a handful of good-value, tastefully decorated rooms above their busy restaurant (family room, air-con in some rooms, for view deck ask for *chambre avec terrasse,* tel. 04 90 54 32 06, www.la-reinejeanne.com, marc.braglia@wanadoo.fr).

In Maussane: The untouristed village of Maussane lies a few minutes' drive south of Les Baux (15 minutes from Arles). It has a few hotels, a handful of restaurants, and a smattering of shops that revolve around its inviting café-lined square. There's also a small TI (tel. 04 90 54 33 60, www.maussane.com). These two accommodations are worth considering.

$ Hôtel les Magnanarelles,** in the center of Maussane, gives solid two-star value in its 18 tastefully-designed rooms above a handsome restaurant and swimming pool (ask for room off the street, no air-con, 104 Avenue de la Vallée des Baux, tel. 04 90 54 30 25, www.logishotels.com, hotel.magnanarelles@wanadoo.fr).

$ Le Mas de l'Esparou *chambres d'hôte* is welcoming and kid-friendly, with four simple-yet-spacious rooms, a big swimming pool, table tennis, swings, and distant views of Les Baux. Jacqueline loves her job, and her lack of English only makes her more animated. She dislikes email though, so you'll have to call (family rooms, includes breakfast, cash only, no air-con, between Les Baux and Maussane on D-5, look for white sign with green lettering, close to the *gendarmerie,* tel. 04 90 54 41 32).

In Le Paradou: $ Le Mazet des Alpilles is a small home with three tidy, air-conditioned rooms around a lovely garden, located just outside the sleepy village of Le Paradou, five minutes south of Les Baux (ask for largest room, includes breakfast, cash only, child's bed available, drive into Le Paradou and look for signs, Route de Brunelly, GPS coordinates: latitude 43 42' 50", longitude 4 46' 45", tel. 04 90 54 45 89, or 06 12 14 93 06, www.lemazetdesalpilles.com, lemazet@wanadoo.fr).

Eating in and near Les Baux

You'll find quiet cafés with views as you follow my walking directions through the **lower town.** The recommended **$$$ Hostellerie de la Reine Jeanne** offers friendly service and good-value meals indoors or out (open daily).

You'll also find several worthwhile places in Maussane, a short hop south of Les Baux. **$$ Place de la Fontaine,** the town's central square, makes a good stop for café fare (several good choices). **$$ Pizza Brun** has tasty wood-fired pizza to take out or eat in, with fun seating indoors and out (closed Mon-Tue, 1 Rue Edouard Foscalina; with your back to Place de la Fontaine, walk to the right for about 10 minutes and look for colored tables in an alleyway; tel. 04 90 54 40 73).

Orange

Orange, called *Arausio* in Roman times, is notable for its Roman arch and grand Roman Theater. Orange was a thriving city in ancient times—strategically situated on the Via Agrippa, connecting the important Roman cities of Lyon and Arles. It was initially founded as a comfortable place for Roman army officers to enjoy their retirement. Even in Roman times, professional military men retired with time for a second career. Did the emperor want thousands of well-trained, relatively young guys hanging around Rome? No way. What to do? "How about a nice place in the south of France...?"

Today's Orange (oh-rahnzh) is a busy, workaday city with a gritty charm that reminds me of Arles. Leafy café-lined squares, a handful of traffic-free streets, a gorgeous Hôtel de Ville (City Hall), and that theater all give the town some serious street appeal. For some, Orange works well as a base, with its quick access to the Côtes du Rhône wine villages by car (slower but OK by bus) and quick rail access to Avignon (that even drivers should consider).

Orientation to Orange

TOURIST INFORMATION
The unnecessary TI is located next to the fountain and parking area at 5 Cours Aristide Briand (April-Sept Mon-Sat 9:00-18:30, Sun 9:00-13:00 & 14:00-18:30; shorter hours and closed Sun off-season; tel. 04 90 34 70 88, www.otorange.fr).

Market Day: Thursday is market day, and it's a big deal here, with all the town's streets and squares crammed with produce and

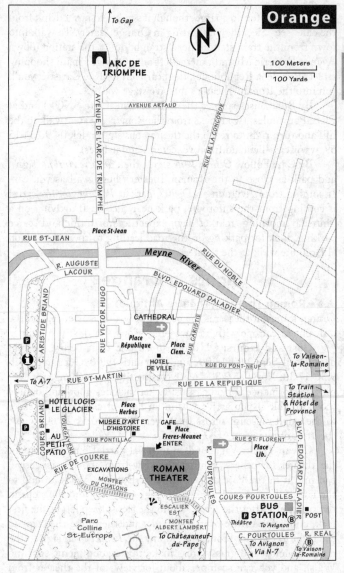

local goods for sale until 12:30. I like this market because it focuses on locals' needs and not touristy kitsch.

ARRIVAL IN ORANGE

By Train: Orange's train station is a level 15-minute walk from the Roman Theater (or an €8 taxi ride, mobile 06 66 71 58 02). The recommended Hôtel de Provence, across from the station, will keep your bags for no charge, though it's polite to buy a drink from the café (see "Sleeping and Eating in Orange," later). To walk into town from the train station, head straight out of the station (down Avenue Frédéric Mistral), merge left onto Orange's main shopping street (Rue de la République), then turn left on Rue Caristie; you'll run into the Roman Theater's massive stage wall.

By Bus: Buses stop at the train station (Gare SNCF) and at Place Pourtoules, two blocks from the Roman Theater (walk to the hill and turn right to reach the theater, bus station tel. 04 90 34 15 59, www.cars-lieutaud.fr/provence/en/regular-lines).

By Car: Follow *Centre-Ville* signs, then *Théâtre Antique* signs, and park as close to the Roman Theater's huge wall as you can. If coming from Avignon on D-907, park at *Parking Théâtre* signs; if coming from the autoroute, park near the TI. If arriving on a Thursday morning (market day), expect lots of traffic and scarce parking; look for parking on the road leading to the train station (15-minute walk to the theater).

Sights in Orange

▲▲▲Roman Theater (Théâtre Antique)

Orange's ancient theater is the best-preserved in existence, and the only one in Europe with its (awesome) acoustic wall still standing.

Cost and Hours: €9, drops to €8 one hour before closing; daily April-Sept 9:00-18:00, June-Aug until 19:00; Oct and March 9:30-17:30; Nov-Feb 9:30-16:30; closing times can change for evening performances or rehearsals; ticket includes good audioguide (not available if you arrive within an hour of closing), and entry to the small museum across the street; tel. 04 90 51 17 60, www.theatre-antique.com.

Cheap Trick: Vagabonds wanting a partial-but-free view of the theater (or others wanting the view-from-above perspective) can find it in the Parc de la Colline St-Eutrope. Walk around to the left of the theater (see map on page 633) and find the steps to the right, just after the *tabac*. Climb the steps, keep left at the first fork, climb for a little over 100 yards, and then take the steps to the right to the top. From here, follow the *Point de Vue* sign to the right. Benches and grassy areas make this a good picnic spot (no WCs), and you can scamper about for views of the theater from different angles.

Visiting the Theater: If you pay to enter, after you go in (to the right of the actual theater), you'll see a huge dig—the site of the Temple to the Cult of the Emperor (English explanations posted). *Arausio* is the Roman name for the town.

Duck into the worthwhile 15-minute **film** across from the

entry for a good historical account of the theater and its uses since the Romans packed up and left (English subtitles).

Now enter the theater, then climb the steep stairs to find a seat high up to appreciate the acoustics (eavesdrop on people by the stage). Contemplate the idea that 2,000 years ago, Orange residents enjoyed grand spectacles here, with high-tech sound and lighting effects—such as simulated thunder, lightning, and rain. If you've been to Arles' Ancient History Museum, conjure up the theater model and imagine this place covered with brilliant white marble.

A grandiose **Caesar** overlooks everything, reminding attendees of who's in charge. If it seems like you've seen this statue before, you probably have. Countless identical sculptures were mass-produced in Rome and shipped throughout the empire to grace buildings like this theater for propaganda purposes. To save money on shipping and handling, only the heads of these statues were changed with each new ruler. The permanent body wears a breastplate emblazoned with the imperial griffon (body of a lion, head and wings of an eagle) that only the emperor could wear. When a new emperor came to power, new

heads were made in Rome and shipped off throughout the empire to replace the pop-off heads on all these statues. (Imagine Barack Obama's head on George W. Bush's body—on second thought...)

The horn has blown. It's time to find your **seat:** row 2, number 30. Sitting down, you're comforted by the "EQ GIII" carved into the seat (*Equitas Gradus* #3...three rows for the Equestrian order). You're not comforted by the hard limestone bench (thinking it'll probably last 2,000 years). The theater is filled with 10,000 people. Thankfully, you mix only with your class, the nouveau riche—merchants, tradesmen, and city big shots. The people seated above you are the working class, and way up in the "chicken roost" section is the scum of the earth—slaves, beggars, prostitutes, and youth hostellers. Scanning the orchestra section (where the super-rich sit on real chairs), you notice the town dignitaries hosting some visiting VIPs.

OK, time to worship. They're parading a bust of the emperor from its sacred home in the adjacent temple around the **stage.** Next is the ritual animal sacrifice called *la pompa* (so fancy, future generations will use that word for anything full of such...pomp). Finally, you settle in for an all-day series of spectacles and dramatic entertainment. All eyes are on the big stage door in the middle—where the Angelina Jolies and Brad Pitts of the day will appear. (Lesser actors come out of the side doors.)

With an audience of 10,000 and no amplification, **acoustics** were critical. A roof made of linen (called the velarium) originally covered the stage, somewhat like the glass-and-iron roof you see today (installed to protect the stage wall). The original was designed not to protect the stage from the weather, but to project the voices of the actors into the crowd. For further help, actors wore masks with leather caricature mouths that functioned as megaphones. The theater's side walls originally rose as high as the stage wall and supported a retractable roof that gave the audience some protection from the sun or rain. After leaving the theater, look up to the stage wall from the outside and notice the supports for poles that held the velarium in place, like the masts and sails of a ship.

The Roman Theater was all part of the "give them bread and circuses" approach to winning the support of the masses. The spectacle grew from 65 days of games per year when the theater was first built (and when Rome was at its height) to about 180 days each year by the time Rome finally fell.

One floor up (to the left with your back to the stage), you'll find the amusing Ghosts of the Theater **multimedia show,** which covers four periods of performance history (including rock concerts).

Nearby: Pop into the **Musée d'Art et d'Histoire** across the street (included with ticket, free audioguide) to see a few theater details and a rare marble grid, ordered by Emperor Vespasian in 79 A.D. This was to be used as the official property-ownership registry—each square represented a 120-acre plot of land.

▲Roman "Arc de Triomphe"

This 60-foot-tall arch is in the center of a big traffic circle, a level 15-minute walk from the theater heading due north. Technically the only real Roman arches of triumph are in Rome's Forum, built to commemorate various emperors' victories. But this arch was the model for those in Rome, preceding both the famous arches of Septimius Severus and Constantine. This municipal arch was erected in about A.D. 19 to commemorate a general named Germanicus, who protected the town. The facade is covered with reliefs of military exploits, including naval battles and Romans beating up on barbarians and those rude, nasty Gauls.

Hôtel de Ville

Orange owns Provence's most beautiful city hall, worth the short detour to appreciate it (in the heart of the old town on Place Georges Clemenceau).

Sleeping and Eating in Orange

Sleeping: $ Hôtel de Provence,** at the train station, is air-conditioned, quiet, comfortable, and affordable. This traditional place is run with grace (family rooms, small rooftop pool, café, pay parking, 60 Avenue Frédéric Mistral, tel. 04 90 34 00 23, www.hotelprovence-orange.com, hoteldeprovence84@orange.fr).

$$ Hôtel Logis le Glacier,*** across from the TI, is run by English-speaking and affable Philippe. It's a solid value, with easy parking, a small bar in a comfortable lobby, and well-designed rooms (elevator, air-con, a few parking spaces, 46 Cours Aristide Briand, tel. 04 90 34 02 01, www.logishotels.com, info@le-glacier.com).

Eating: Orange has several inviting squares with ample choices in all price ranges. Across from the theater, **$$ V Café** works well, with a large terrace and reasonable *tartines* and €10 *plats du jour* (daily, 2 Place des Frères Mounet, tel. 04 90 66 32 14). You'll find more choices and appealing squares by wandering the lanes behind V Café. For a more refined meal, **$$$$ Au Petit Patio** delivers elegant dining and fine cuisine (closed Wed-Thu and Sun, 58 Cours Aristide Briand, tel. 04 90 29 69 27).

Orange Connections

From Orange by Train to: Avignon (15/day, 20 minutes), **Arles** (4/day direct, 35 minutes, more frequent with transfer in Avignon), **Lyon** (16/day, 2 hours).

By Bus to: Vaison-la-Romaine (3-6/day, 45 minutes), **Avignon** (Mon-Sat hourly, 5/day Sun, 1 hour—take the train instead). Buses to **Vaison-la-Romaine** and other **wine villages** depart from the train station and from Place Pourtoules (see map on page 633). Bus #4 to Vaison-la-Romaine leaves from across the street and to the right of the main shelter/stop (look for blue bus icon in front of mansion).

Villages of the Côtes du Rhône

The sunny Côtes du Rhône wine road—one of France's most engaging—starts at Avignon's doorstep and winds north along a mountainous landscape carpeted with vines, studded with warm stone villages, and presided over by the Vesuvius-like Mont Ventoux. The wines of the Côtes du Rhône (grown on the *côtes,* or hillsides, of the Rhône River Valley) are easy on the palate and on your budget. But this hospitable place offers more than wine—its

PROVENCE

hill-capping villages inspire travel posters, its Roman ruins add a historical perspective, and the locals are often as excited about their region as you are.

PLANNING YOUR TIME

Vaison-la-Romaine is the handy small-town hub of this region, offering limited bus connections with Avignon and Orange, bike rental, and a mini Pompeii in the town center. Nearby, you can follow my self-guided driving tour of Côtes du Rhône villages and wineries, or pedal along peaceful roads to nearby towns. The vineyards' centerpiece, the Dentelles de Montmirail mountains, are laced with hiking trails.

To explore this area, allow two nights for a decent dabble. Drivers should head for the hills (read this section's self-guided driving tour before deciding where to stay). Those without wheels find that Vaison-la-Romaine or Orange make the only practical home bases (or, maybe better, consider a minivan tour for this area).

GETTING AROUND THE COTES DU RHONE

By Car: Pick up Michelin maps #332 or #527. Landmarks like the Dentelles de Montmirail and Mont Ventoux make it easy to get your bearings. I've described my favorite driving route on page 647.

By Bus: Buses run to Vaison-la-Romaine from Orange and Avignon (3-6/day, 45 minutes from Orange, 1.5 hours from Avignon) and connect several wine villages with Vaison-la-Romaine and Nyons to the north. Scant buses also run from Vaison-la-Romaine to Carpentras, serving Crestet, Malaucène, and Le Barroux (3/day Mon-Sat, none on Sun, tel. 04 90 36 05 22, www.cars-lieutaud.fr). All routes provide scenic rides through this area.

By Train: Trains get you as far as Orange (from Avignon: 15/day, 20 minutes).

By Minivan Tour: There's no shortage of people willing to take you for a ride through this marvelous region—so buyer beware. For my recommendations on wine-focused tours, more general tours, and private guides, see "Tours in Provence" on page 559.

Vaison-la-Romaine

With quick access to vineyards, villages, and Mont Ventoux, this lively little town of 6,000 makes a good base for exploring the Côtes du Rhône region. You get two villages for the price of one: Vaison-la-Romaine's "modern" lower city has Roman ruins, a lone pedestrian street, and a lively main square—café-lined

Place Montfort. The car-free medieval hill town looms above, with meandering cobbled lanes, art galleries and cafés, and a ruined castle with a fine view from its base.

Orientation to Vaison-la-Romaine

The city is split in two by the Ouvèze River. The Roman Bridge connects the lower town (Ville-Basse) with the hill-capping medieval upper town (Ville-Haute).

TOURIST INFORMATION

The TI is in the lower city, between the two Roman ruin sites, at Place du Chanoine Sautel (June-Aug Mon-Fri 9:00-18:45, Sat-Sun

9:00-12:30 & 14:00-18:45; Sept-May Mon-Sat 9:30-12:00 & 14:00-17:45, Sun 9:30-12:00—except closed Sun mid-Oct-March; tel. 04 90 36 02 11, www.vaison-ventoux-tourisme.com). Say *bonjour* to *charmante* and ever-so-patient Valerie and Agnes, use the free Wi-Fi, ask about festivals and other events, and pick up information on walks and bike rides. The big wall map shows area hiking trails.

ARRIVAL IN VAISON-LA-ROMAINE

By Bus: Bus stops are in front of the Cave la Romaine winery. Tell the driver you want the stop for the *Office de Tourisme.* When you get off the bus, walk five minutes down Avenue Général de Gaulle to reach the TI and recommended hotels.

By Car: Follow signs to *Centre-Ville,* then *Office de Tourisme;* and park in or near the big lot across from the TI. Parking is free in Vaison-la-Romaine.

HELPFUL HINTS

Market Day: Sleep in Vaison-la-Romaine on Monday night, and you'll wake to an amazing ▲▲ Tuesday market, one of France's best. If you spend a Monday night, avoid parking at market sites and where signs indicate *Stationnement Interdit le Mardi,* or you won't find your car where you left it—ask your hotelier where you can park.

Supermarket: A handy **Casino** is on Place Montfort in the thick of the cafés (Mon-Sat 7:30-13:00 & 15:30-19:30, Sun 9:00-13:00).

Wi-Fi: The **TI** and **Café Universal,** on atmospheric Place Montfort, offer free Wi-Fi.

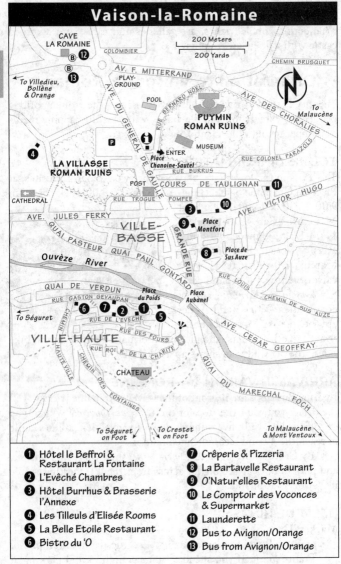

Vaison-la-Romaine

1. Hôtel le Beffroi & Restaurant La Fontaine
2. L'Evêché Chambres
3. Hôtel Burrhus & Brasserie l'Annexe
4. Les Tilleuls d'Elisée Rooms
5. La Belle Etoile Restaurant
6. Bistro du 'O
7. Crêperie & Pizzeria
8. La Bartavelle Restaurant
9. O'Natur'elles Restaurant
10. Le Comptoir des Voconces & Supermarket
11. Launderette
12. Bus to Avignon/Orange
13. Bus from Avignon/Orange

Laundry: The self-service **Laverie la Lavandière** is on Cours Taulignan, near Avenue Victor Hugo (figure about €10, daily 8:00-22:00, English instructions).

Bike Rental: The TI has a list. For help with bike rental and biking plans, contact John and Monique at the recommended **L'Ecole Buissonnière Chambres** (see listing later, under "Sleeping in Vaison-la-Romaine").

Taxi: Call 04 90 36 00 04 or 04 90 46 89 42.

Car Rental: You can rent cars by the day, though they must be returned to Vaison-la-Romaine; ask at the TI for locations.

Local Guide: Let sincere and knowledgeable **Melanie Melard** bring the Roman ruins to life for you (tel. 04 90 36 50 48). Scottish by birth and an attorney by profession, **Janet Henderson** offers in-depth historic walks of Vaison-la-Romaine (€30/person, minimum 3 people or €80, allow 2 hours, janet. henderson@wandoo.fr, www.provencehistorytours.com).

Tourist Train: The *petit train* stops in front of the TI and does a loop around the town.

Cooking Classes: Charming **Barbara Schuerenberg** offers reasonably priced cooking classes from her view home in Vaison-la-Romaine, where you'll pick herbs from the garden to use in the recipes (€90, cash only, includes lunch, 4-person maximum, tel. 04 90 35 68 43, www.cuisinedeprovence.com, cuisinedeprovence@gmail.com).

Sights in Vaison-la-Romaine

Roman Ruins

Ancient Vaison-la-Romaine had a treaty that gave it a preferred "federated" relationship with Rome (rather than simply being a colony). This, along with a healthy farming economy (olives and vineyards), made it a most prosperous place...as a close look at its sprawling ruins demonstrates. About 6,000 people called Vaison-la-Romaine home 2,000 years ago. When the barbarians arrived, the Romans were forced

out, and the townspeople fled into the hills. The town population has only recently recovered from those barbaric times, with the number of residents again reaching Roman-era number.

Cost and Hours: €8; daily April-May 9:30-18:00, June-Sept until 18:30, shorter hours off-season, closed Jan-Feb; video-guide-€3 or download free app, tel. 04 90 36 50 48, www.vaison-la-romaine.com.

Visiting the Ruins: Vaison-la-Romaine's Roman ruins are split by a modern road into two sites: Puymin and La Villasse. Each is well-presented, thanks to the videoguide and occasional English information panels, offering a good look at life during the Roman Empire. The Roman town extended all the way from here to the river, and its main square (forum) still lies under today's main square, Place Montfort. What you can see is only a small fraction of the Roman town's extent—most is still buried under today's city. For helpful background about Roman civilization, read "How About Them Romans" on page 562.

Visit **Puymin** first. Nearest the entry are the scant but impressive ruins of a sprawling mansion. Find the faint remains of a colorful frescoed wall. Climb the hill to the good little **museum** (pick up your videoguide here; exhibits also explained in English loaner booklet). Be sure to see the **film** that takes you inside the home of a wealthy Vaison resident and explores daily life some 2,000 years ago. Behind the museum is a still well-used, 6,000-seat theater, with just enough seats for the whole town (of yesterday and today).

Back across the modern road in **La Villasse,** you'll explore a "street of shops" and the foundations of more houses. You'll also see a few wells, used before Vaison's two aqueducts were built. (You can also see the sight perfectly well without entering by following the path immediately to its left with your back to the TI.)

Lower Town (Ville Basse)

Vaison-la-Romaine's lower town centers on café-friendly Place Montfort. Tables grab the north side of the square, conveniently sheltered from the prevailing mistral wind while enjoying the generous shade of the ubiquitous plane trees. The trees are cut way back each year to form a leafy canopy. Nearby, the pedestrian-only Grand Rue is a lively shopping street leading to the small river gorge and the Roman Bridge.

Roman Bridge

The Romans cut this sturdy, no-nonsense vault into the canyon rock 2,000 years ago, and it has survived ever since. Approaching from the lower-town end of the bridge, find the information panel on the left of the bridge. Until the 20th century, this was the only way to cross the Ouvèze River. See also the stone plaque *(Septembre 22-92...)* on the wall to the right showing the high-water mark of the record flood that killed 30 people. The flood swept the modern top of this bridge—and several other modern bridges—downstream, but couldn't budge the 55-foot Roman arch.

Upper Town (Ville Haute)

Although there's nothing of particular importance to see in the fortified medieval old town atop the hill, the cobbled lanes and enchanting fountains make you want to break out a sketchpad. Vaison-la-Romaine was ruled by a prince-bishop starting in the fourth century. He came under attack by the Count of Toulouse in the 12th century. Anticipating a struggle, the prince-bishop abandoned the lower town and built a castle on this rocky outcrop (about 1195). Over time, the townspeople followed, vacating the lower town and building their homes at the base of the château behind the upper town's fortified wall.

To reach the upper town, hike up from the Roman Bridge (passing memorials for both world wars) through the medieval gate, under the lone tower crowned by an 18th-century wrought-iron bell cage. Look for occasional English information plaques as you meander. The château itself is closed, but a steep, uneven trail to its base rewards hikers with a sweeping view.

Wine Tasting

Cave la Romaine, a five-minute walk up Avenue Général de Gaulle from the TI, offers a big variety of good-value wines from nearby villages in a pleasant, well-organized tasting room (free tastes, Mon-Sat 9:00-18:30 but closes for lunch, Sun 9:00-12:00, Avenue St-Quenin, tel. 04 90 36 55 90, www.cave-la-romaine.com).

▲Hiking

The TI has information on hikes into the hills above Vaison-la-Romaine, and sells a printed hiking guide.

It's about 1.25 hours to the quiet hill town of Crestet, though views begin immediately. To find the trail, drive or walk on the road past the upper town (with the rock base and castle on your left), continue on Chemin des Fontaines (blue signs), and stay the course as far as you like (follow yellow *Crestet* signs). Cars are not allowed on the road after about a mile.

To find the five-mile trail to Séguret (allow 2 hours), take the same road above Vaison-la-Romaine and look for a yellow sign to the right. For either hike, consider hiking one way and taking a taxi back.

Biking

The TI has details on several manageable biking routes, with directions in English, as well as infomation on mountain-biking trails (also available at bike shops). If the air's calm, the five-mile ride to cute little Villedieu (with the recommended La Maison Bleue restaurant) is a delight. Renting an electric bike makes this an easier outing (see "Helpful Hints," earlier). The bike route is signed along small roads; from Vaison-la-Romaine find the road to Villedieu at the roundabout by Cave la Romaine (see map on page 640). With a bit more energy, you can pedal beyond Villedieu on the lovely road to Mirabel (from Villedieu, follow signs to *Nyons*). Make a detour to Pigeon (to avoid that busy section of road between Mirabel and Vaison), then rejoin the busy D-938 to reach Vaison (figure about 18 miles total). Alternatively, get a good map and connect the following villages for an enjoyable 11-mile loop ride: Vaison-la-Romaine, St-Romain-en-Viennois, Puyméras (with the recommended La Girocedre restaurant), Faucon, and St-Marcellin-lès-Vaison.

Sleeping in Vaison-la-Romaine

($$$$ = Splurge, $$$ = Pricier, $$ = Moderate, $ = Budget)

Hotels in Vaison-la-Romaine are a good value and are split between the upper medieval village (with all the steps) and the lower main town (with all the services). Those in the upper town (Ville-Haute) are quieter, cozier, cooler, and give you the feeling of sleeping in a hill town (some come with views), with all the services of a real town steps away. But they require a 10-minute walk down then up to the town center and Roman ruins. If staying at one of the first three places, follow signs to *Cité Médiévale* and park just outside the upper village entry (driving into the Cité Médiévale itself is a challenge—tiny lanes and nearly impossible parking).

If you have a car, consider staying in one of the Côtes du Rhône villages near Vaison-la-Romaine. I've listed a few nearby places here; for more suggestions see the "Côtes du Rhône Wine Road," later.

In the Upper Town: $$ Hôtel le Beffroi*** hides deep in the upper town, just above a demonstrative bell tower (you'll hear what I mean). It offers 16th-century red-tile-and-wood-beamed-cozy lodgings with nary a level surface. The rooms—split between two buildings a few doors apart—are Old World comfy, and some have views. You'll enjoy antique-filled public spaces, a garden with view tables (meals available in good weather), a small pool with more views, and animated Nathalie at the reception (several good family rooms, Rue de l'Evêché, tel. 04 90 36 04 71, www.le-beffroi.com, lebeffroi@wanadoo.fr). The hotel's **$$$ restaurant** offers *menus* from €29 (see "Eating in Vaison-la-Romaine," later).

$ L'Evêché Chambres, a few doors away from Hôtel le Beffroi, is a five-room melt-in-your-chair B&B. The owners (the Verdiers) have an exquisite sense of interior design and are passionate about books, making this place feel like a cross between a library and an art gallery (the *solanum* suite is worth every euro, Rue de l'Evêché, tel. 04 90 36 13 46, http://eveche.free.fr, eveche@aol.com).

In the Lower Town: $ Hôtel Burrhus** is equal parts art gallery and ramshackle hotel—but a good value. It's a central, laid-back place, with a terrific terrace over Place Montfort and surprisingly good rooms (for maximum quiet, request a back room). Its floor plan will confound even the ablest navigator, but the jukebox works in the lobby (family rooms, air-con, 1 Place Montfort, tel. 04 90 36 00 11, www.burrhus.com, info@burrhus.com).

$ Les Tilleuls d'Elisée is a terrific *chambres d'hôte* in a stone, blue-shuttered home near the Notre-Dame de Nazareth Cathedral, a few minutes' walk below the TI. Anne and Laurent Viau run this comfortable five-room place with grace and great rates. Relax in the garden with views to the upper town and ask about €7 wine tastings in their small wine cellar (includes breakfast, air-con, 1 Avenue Jules Mazen, tel. 04 90 35 63 04, www.vaisonchambres. info, anne.viau@vaisonchambres.info).

Near Vaison-la-Romaine: $ L'Ecole Buissonnière Chambres is run by an engaging Anglo-French team, John and Monique, who share their peace and quiet 10 minutes north of Vaison-la-Romaine. This creatively restored farmhouse has three character-filled, half-timbered rooms and comfy public spaces. Getting to know John, who has lived all over the south of France, is worth the price of the room. The outdoor kitchen allows guests to picnic in high fashion in the tranquil garden (family rooms, includes breakfast, cash only; between Villedieu and Buisson on D-75—leave Vaison following signs to *Villedieu*, then follow D-51 toward Buisson and turn left onto D-75; tel. 04 90 28 95 19, www.buissonniere-provence.com, ecole.buissonniere@wanadoo.fr).

Eating in Vaison-la-Romaine

Vaison-la-Romaine offers a handful of good dining experiences—arrive by 19:30 in summer or reserve ahead, particularly on weekends. And while you can eat very well on a moderate budget in Vaison, it's well worth venturing to nearby Côtes du Rhône villages to eat. I've listed three nearby places; for recommendations farther afield see the "Côtes du Rhône Wine Road," later. Wherever you dine, begin with a fresh glass of Muscat from the nearby village of Beaumes-de-Venise.

In the Upper Town: $$$$ Restaurant La Fontaine, located at the recommended **Hotel le Beffroi,** serves traditional cuisine in the lovely hotel gardens when the weather agrees, and in the pleasant dining room when it doesn't. If they're serving in the garden, you won't find a better setting in Vaison (daily, tel. 04 90 36 04 71).

$$$ La Belle Etoile is a special place. Locals come here for simple, fresh, and good-value meals in a fun, eclectic setting. It's a little like eating in your hip grandma's living room. The cuisine is inspired by owner Jerome's travels, and there's no menu as the selection varies daily (based in his inspiration). Outside tables come with views over the lower town (daily April-Oct, closes when they run out of food or inspiration; it's the first place you pass when coming from the lower town, 1 Rue du Pont, tel. 04 90 37 31 45).

$$$ Bistro du'O dishes up fine, creative, and well-presented

PROVENCE

cuisine in a stone Provençal setting in the lower part of Ville Haute (closed Sun-Mon, Rue Gaston Gevaudan, tel. 04 90 41 72 90).

$ You'll also find a simple *crêperie* with a view deck and a **pizzeria** on the main street leading up to the old town. Both have indoor and outdoor seating, some views over the river, and cheap, basic food (good for families).

In the Lower Town: $$$ La Bartavelle, run by friendly Berenger, is a good place to savor traditional French cuisine, with a tourist-friendly mix-and-match choice of local options. Her €30 *menu* gets you four courses; the €23 *menu* gives you top-end main-course selections and dessert (closed Mon, Fri lunch, and off-season Sun; small terrace outside, air-con, 12 Place de Sus Auze, tel. 04 90 36 02 16).

$$$ O'Natur'elles is a sweet little place. It's ideal for vegetarians, but good for all persuasions as the all-organic dishes can be served with or without meat. The cuisine is delicious but the place is small (closed Tue evening, reservations smart, 38 Place Montfort, tel. 04 90 65 81 67).

Cafés on Place Monfort: Come here for lighter café fare and to observe the daily flow of life in Vaison-la-Romaine. It's best to dine outside. **$$ Brasserie l'Annexe** serves good café fare and has a loyal following (open daily), while **$$ Le Comptoir des Voconces** is the happening hangout with a pub-like ambience.

Near Vaison-la-Romaine: $ La Maison Bleue, about four miles north of Vaison-la-Romaine on Villedieu's delightful little square, serves good pizzas and salads with great outdoor ambience. Skip it if the weather forces you inside (March-Oct Thu-Sun open for lunch and dinner, closed Mon-Wed except July-Aug closed Mon only, tel. 04 90 28 97 02).

$$ Auberge d'Anaïs, at the end of a dirt road 10 minutes from Vaison-la-Romaine, is a fun Provençal experience. Outdoor tables gather under cheery lights with views and good cuisine. Ask for a table *sur la terrasse* (closed Sun evening and Mon, tel. 04 90 36 20 06). Heading east of Vaison-la-Romaine, follow signs to *Carpentras,* then *St. Marcellin.* Signs will guide you from there.

Vaison-la-Romaine Connections

The most central **bus stop** is a few blocks up Avenue Général de Gaulle from the TI at the main winery, Cave la Romaine. Buses to Orange and Avignon stop on the winery side; buses to Nyons, Crestet, and Carpentras stop opposite the winery.

From Vaison-la-Romaine by Bus to: Avignon (3-6/day, local buses pass through Orange, 1.5 hours) **Orange** (3-6/day, 45 minutes), **Nyons** (3-5/day, 45 minutes), **Crestet** (lower village below Crestet, 2/day, 5 minutes), **Carpentras** (2/day, 45 minutes).

Côtes du Rhône Wine Road

To experience the best of the Côtes du Rhône vineyards and villages, take this ▲▲▲ loop around the rugged Dentelles de Montmirail mountain peaks (allow a half-day). You'll experience the finest this region has to offer: natural beauty, glowing limestone villages, inviting wineries, and rolling hills of vineyards (see the map on page 649).

You can start anywhere along this circular route. See below for a description of each stop, along with good restaurant and hotel options. It's a picnic-friendly route; buy groceries in Vaison-la-Romaine.

Séguret: Start just south of Vaison-la-Romaine in little Séguret. This town is best for a visit early or late, when it's quieter. The village is ideal for a morning coffee break (the lone café opens at 10:00), then drive up and up to the Domaine de Mourchon winery.

Crestet: From Séguret, drive to Vaison-la-Romaine then follow signs toward Carpentras/Malaucène. Pass through lower Crestet, then follow signs leading up to Le Village on D-76.

Dentelles de Montmirail: From Crestet, follow signs back down to Malaucène. Turn right on D-90 (direction: Suzette) just before the gas station. The D-90 route is the scenic highlight of this loop, which follows the back side of the Dentelles de Montmirail past mountain views, remote villages, and beautifully situated wineries (Domaine de Coyeux is best). Take your time for this drive: You'll pass trailheads, scenic pullouts, and good picnic spots.

Gigondas: D-90 ends in Beaumes de Venise. Follow signs toward Vacqueyras then Vaison-la-Romaine to find the village of Gigondas.

VILLAGES AND WINERIES ALONG THE COTES DU RHONE WINE ROAD
❶ Séguret

Séguret's name comes from the Latin word *securitas* (meaning "security"). The bulky entry arch came with a massive gate, which drilled in the message of the village's name. In the Middle Ages, Séguret was patrolled 24/7—they never took their *securitas* for granted. Walk through the arch. To appreciate how the homes' outer walls provided security in those days, drop down the first passage on your right (near the fountain). These tunnel-like exit passages, or *poternes*, were needed in periods of peace to allow the town to expand below. Wander deep. Rue Calade leads up to the unusual 12th-century St. Denis church for views (the circular village you see below is Sablet). Côté Terrasse makes a great place for a drink, lunch, or dinner (see next).

Sleeping and Eating in Séguret: $$ Restaurant/Café Côte Terrasse delivers big portions, good prices, top quality, and cheerful service (daily from 10:00, Rue des Poternes, tel. 04 90 28 03 48). **$$ Domaine de Cabasse***** is a lovely spread flanked by vineyards at the foot of Séguret (with a walking path to the village). Winemaking is their primary business—free tastings are offered every evening from April through September. Each of the 23 rooms has tasteful decor, air-conditioning, and views over vines; all the first-floor rooms have balconies or decks (elevator, big heated pool, on D-23 between Sablet and Séguret, entry gate opens automatically... and slowly, tel. 04 90 46 91 12, www.cabasse.fr, hotel@cabasse. fr). The **$$$$** classy country **restaurant** offers fine cuisine and is worth booking ahead.

❷ Domaine de Mourchon Winery

This high-flying winery blends state-of-the-art technology with traditional winemaking methods (a shiny ring of stainless-steel

vats holds grapes grown on land plowed by horses). The wines are winning the respect of international critics. Free and informative English tours of the vineyards are usually offered (wines—€9-33/bottle; winery open Mon-Sat 9:00-18:00, Sun by appointment only; from Easter-Sept, call to verify; tel. 04 90 46 70 30, info@domainedemourchon.com).

❸ Crestet

This quiet village—founded after the fall of the Roman Empire, when people banded together in high places like this for protection from marauding barbarians—followed the usual hill-town evolution. The outer walls of the village did double duty as ramparts and house walls. The castle above (from about A.D. 850) provided a final safe haven when the village was attacked.

Wander the peaceful lanes and appreciate the amount of work it took to put these stones in place. Notice the elaborate water channels. Crestet was served by 18 cisterns in the Middle Ages. Imagine hundreds of people living here and animals roaming everywhere. The bulky Romanesque church (unpredictable hours) is built into the hillside and has an unusual stained-glass window behind the altar.

Drivers should pass by the first parking lot and keep climbing to park at Place du Château to the top of town. Signs from the top of the village lead to the footpath to Vaison-la-Romaine.

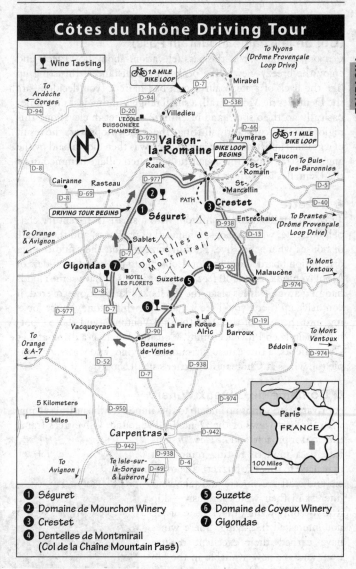

PROVENCE

Côtes du Rhône Driving Tour

🍷 Wine Tasting

🚲 18 MILE BIKE LOOP

To Nyons
(Drôme Provençale
Loop Drive)

To
Ardèche
Gorges

D-94

D-7

Mirabel

D-538

L'ÉCOLE
BUISSONIÈRE
CHAMBRES

D-20

D-975

D-94

Villedieu

D-46

🚲 11 MILE BIKE LOOP

Vaison-
la-Romaine

Puyméras

BIKE LOOP
BEGINS

Faucon

To Buis-
les-Baronnies

Roaix

D-8

Cairanne

Rasteau

D-8

D-69

D-977

PATH

St-
Romain

St-
Marcellin

D-5

D-40

DRIVING TOUR BEGINS

Séguret

Crestet

Entrechaux

D-938

To Brantes
(Drôme Provençale
Loop Drive)

Sablet

D-7

D-13

Dentelles de
Montmirail

To Mont
Ventoux

Gigondas

HOTEL
LES FLORETS

Suzette

Malaucène

D-90

D-974

D-8

D-977

D-7

La Fare

La
Roque
Alric

D-19

Le
Barroux

To Mont
Ventoux

Vacqueyras

Beaumes-
de-Venise

Bédoin

D-974

To Orange
& A-7

D-52

D-7

D-938

5 Kilometers

5 Miles

D-950

D-974

To
Avignon

To Isle-sur-
la-Sorgue
& Luberon

D-942

D-942

D-938

D-4

D-49

Carpentras

Paris
FRANCE

100 Miles

❶ Séguret
❷ Domaine de Mourchon Winery
❸ Crestet
❹ Dentelles de Montmirail
    (Col de la Chaîne Mountain Pass)

❺ Suzette
❻ Domaine de Coyeux Winery
❼ Gigondas

Eating in Crestet: The village's only business, the recommended café-restaurant **$$$ Le Panoramic,** is well-signed at the top of town. It serves good-enough omelets, salads, crêpes, and *plats* for too much—until you consider the vista, from what must be Provence's greatest view tables. Stop for a coffee or drink and enjoy the top deck (April-Nov daily 10:30-22:00, closed in bad weather and Dec-March, tel. 04 90 28 76 42).

❹ Dentelles de Montmirail (Col de la Chaîne Mountain Pass)

Get out of your car at the pass (elevation: about 1,500 feet) and enjoy the breezy views. The peaks in the distance—thrusting up like the back of a stegosaurus or a bad haircut (you decide)—are the Dentelles de Montmirail, a small range running just nine miles basically north to south and reaching 2,400 feet in elevation. This region's land is constantly shifting. Those rocky tops were the result of a gradual uplifting of the land, which was then blown bald by the angry mistral wind. That beautifully situated village hemmed in by the Dentelles is our next stop...

❺ Suzette

Tiny Suzette floats on its hilltop, with a small 12th-century chapel, one café, wine tastings, a handful of residents, and the gaggle of houses where they live. Park in Suzette's lot, then find the big orientation board above the lot. Look out to the broad shoulders of Mont Ventoux. At 6,000 feet, it always seems to have some clouds hanging around. If it's clear, the top looks like it's snow-covered; if you drive up there, you'll see it's actually white stone. You're looking into the eyes of the Alps (behind Ventoux), and those "foothills" help keep Provence sunny. Consider lunch or a drink at **Les Coquelicots,** a tiny eatery surrounded by vines and views, or sample the wines at **Château Redortier**'s small shop.

❻ Domaine de Coyeux Winery

A private road winds up and up to this impossibly beautiful setting, with the best views of the Dentelles I've found. Olive trees frame the final approach, and *Le Caveau* signs lead to a modern tasting room (you may need to ring the buzzer). The owners and staff are sincere and take your interest in their wines seriously—skip it if you only want a quick taste or are not interested in buying. These wines have earned their excellent reputation, and are now available in the US (wines–€9-16/bottle; winery generally  open daily 10:00-12:00 & 14:00-18:00, except closed Sun off-season and no midday closure July-Aug; tel. 04 90 12 42 42, http:// domainedecoyeux.com/en, contact@domainedecoyeux.com, some English spoken).

❼ Gigondas

This upscale village produces some of the region's best reds and is ideally situated for hiking, mountain biking, and driving into the mountains. The **TI** has Wi-Fi, lists of wineries and *chambres d'hôte*, rental bikes, and tips for good hikes or drives (Mon-Sat 10:00-12:30 & 14:00-18:00, closed Sun, Place du Portail, tel. 04 90 65 85 46, www.gigondas-dm.fr).

Take a short walk through the village lanes, climbing from the recommended Du Verre à l'Assiette restaurant and find a good viewing area over the heart of the Côtes du Rhône vineyards; you'll find even better views a little higher at the church.

Several good tasting opportunities lie on the main square. **Le Caveau de Gigondas** is the best, where Sandra and Barbara await your visit in a handsome tasting room with a large and free selection of tiny bottles for sampling, filled directly from the barrel (daily 10:00-12:00 & 14:00-18:30, close to the TI on the main town square, tel. 04 90 65 82 29, www.caveaudugigondas.com). Here you can compare wines from 75 private producers in an intimate, low-key surrounding.

Sleeping and Eating in and near Gigondas: The shaded red tables of **$$ Du Verre à l'Assiette** ("From Glass to Plate") entice lunchtime eaters (also good interior ambience, open for lunch daily except Wed, open for dinner Fri-Sat nights, located diagonally across from TI, Place du Village, tel. 04 90 12 36 64).

$$ Hôtel les Florets,** with tastefully designed rooms, is a half-mile above Gigondas, buried in the foothills of the Dentelles de Montmirail. It comes with an excellent restaurant, a vast terrace with views, and hiking trails into the mountains (several good family rooms, annex rooms by pool have front patios, tel. 04 90 65 85 01, www.hotel-lesflorets.com, accueil@hotel-lesflorets.com).

The **$$$$ restaurant** at Hôtel les Florets is a traditional, family-run place that's well worth the cost—particularly if you dine on the magnificent terrace. Dinners blend classic French cuisine with Provençal accents, served with class by English-speaking Thierry. The weighty wine list is literally encyclopedic (closed Wed except to hotel guests, service can be slow).

Hill Towns of the Luberon

Just 30 miles east of Avignon, the Luberon region hides some of France's most captivating hill towns and sensuous landscapes. Those

intrigued by Peter Mayle's best-selling *A Year in Provence* love joyriding through the region, connecting I-could-live-here villages, crumbled castles, and meditative abbeys. Mayle's book, which marked its 25th anniversary in 2015, describes the ruddy local culture from an Englishman's perspective as he buys a stone farmhouse, fixes it up, and adopts the region as his new home. *A Year in Provence* is a great read while you're here—or, better, get it as an audiobook and listen while you drive.

The Luberon terrain in general (much of which is a French regional natural park) is as enticing as its villages. Gnarled vineyards and wind-sculpted trees separate tidy stone structures from abandoned buildings—little more than rock piles—that challenge city slickers to fix them up. Mountains of limestone bend along vast ridges, while colorful hot-air balloons survey the scene from above.

There are no obligatory museums, monuments, or vineyards in the Luberon. Treat this area like a vacation from your vacation. Downshift your engine. Brake for views, and lose your car to a walk. Get on a first-name basis with a village.

What follows is a rundown of my favorite villages and stops in this beautiful area. The D-900 highway cuts the Luberon in half like an arrow. The villages I describe sit just north and south of it (see map on page 654).

GETTING AROUND THE LUBERON

By Car: Luberon roads are scenic and narrow. With no major landmarks, it's easy to get lost—and you will get lost—but that's the point. Consider buying Michelin map #332 or #527 to navigate, and look for a copy of the free *Carte Touristique du Pays d'Apt* at local TIs. Popular towns charge a small fee to park. Expect headaches parking in Isle-sur-la-Sorgue during its market days.

By Bus: Isle-sur-la-Sorgue is connected with Avignon's town center by the Raoux-TransVaucluse bus line #6 (€2 one-way, 6-8/day Mon-Sat, 3-4/day Sun, 45 minutes, central stop—called Robert Vasse—is near post office in Isle-sur-la-Sorgue, ask for schedule at TI or download French-only schedule from www.voyages-raoux.fr/lignes/index.php). Without a car or minivan tour, skip the more famous hill towns of the Luberon.

By Train: Trains get you to Isle-sur-la-Sorgue (station called "L'Isle-Fontaine de Vaucluse") from Avignon (10/day on weekdays, 5/day on weekends, 30 minutes) or from Marseille (8/day, 1.5 hours). If you're day-tripping by train, check return times before leaving the station.

By Minivan Tour: I list several minivan tour companies and private guides who can guide you through this marvelous region (see "Tours in Provence" on page 559).

By Taxi: Contact **Luberon Taxi** (based in Maubec off D-3, mobile 06 08 49 40 57, www.luberontaxi.com, contact@luberontaxi.com).

By Bike: Isle-sur-la-Sorgue makes a good base for biking, with level terrain and good rental options. Hardy bikers can ride from Isle-sur-la-Sorgue to Gordes, then to Roussillon, connecting other villages in a full-day loop ride (30 miles round-trip to Roussillon and back, with lots of hills). Several appealing villages are closer to Isle-sur-la-Sorgue and offer easier biking options. **Sun-e-Bike,** based in Bonnieux and St-Rémy-de-Provence, rents electric bikes and has a network of partners with spare batteries scattered across the Luberon, extending the range of your e-bike trip. They can also arrange bike tours and shuttle your bags between hotels (1 Avenue Clovis Hugues in Bonnieux, tel. 04 90 74 09 96, www.sun-e-bike.com).

Isle-sur-la-Sorgue

This sturdy market town—literally, "Island on the Sorgue River"—sits within a split in its crisp, happy little river at the foot of the Luberon. It's a workaday town that feels refreshingly real after so many adorable villages. It's also one of the only smaller towns in this region easily accessible by train and bus (see "Getting Around the Luberon," earlier).

Although Isle-sur-la-Sorgue is renowned for its market days (Sun and Thu), it's an otherwise pleasantly average town with no important sights and a steady trickle of tourism. It's lively on weekends, calm most weeknights, and calmer on Mondays. The town revolves around its river, the church square, and two pedestrian-only streets, Rue de la République and Rue Carnot.

The **TI** has an essential town map, Wi-Fi, hiking information, biking itineraries, and a line on rooms in private homes, all of which are outside town (April-Sept Mon-Sat 9:00-12:30 & 14:30-

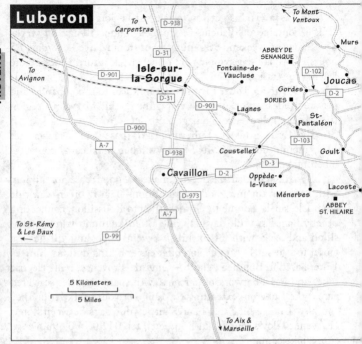

Luberon

To Carpentras — D-938
To Mont Ventoux
Murs
ABBEY DE SENANQUE
D-31
Fontaine-de-Vaucluse — D-102
Joucas
To Avignon — D-901
Isle-sur-la-Sorgue
Gordes
BORIES
D-2
D-31
D-901
Lagnes
St-Pantaléon
D-900
D-103
A-7
D-938
Coustellet
Goult
Cavaillon — D-2
D-3
Oppède-le-Vieux
Lacoste
D-973
Ménerbes
ABBEY ST. HILAIRE
A-7
To St-Rémy & Les Baux
D-99

5 Kilometers
5 Miles

To Aix & Marseille

18:00—14:00-17:30 Oct-March, Sun 9:00-12:30; in town center next to church, tel. 04 90 38 04 78, www.oti-delasorgue.fr).

Visiting Isle-sur-la-Sorgue: In Isle-sur-la-Sorgue—called the "Venice of Provence"—the Sorgue River's extraordinarily clear and shallow flow divides like cells, producing water, water everywhere. The river has long nourished the region's economy. Today, antique shops power the town's economy. Navigate by the town's splintered streams and nine mossy **waterwheels,** which, while still turning, power only memories of the town's wool and silk industries. At its peak, Isle-sur-la-Sorgue had 70 waterwheels; in the 1800s, the town competed with Avignon as Provence's cloth-dyeing and textile center.

Find **Le Bassin,** where the Sorgue River crashes into the town and separates into many branches (carefully placed lights make this a beautiful sight after dark). With its source (a spring) a mere five miles away, the Sorgue River never floods and has a constant flow and temperature in all seasons. Despite its exposed (flat) location, Isle-sur-la-Sorgue prospered in the Middle Ages, thanks to the natural protection this river provided.

Peek into **Notre-Dame des Anges** church with its festive Baroque interior and colorful walls (closed 12:00-15:15). The town erupts into a carnival-like **market** frenzy each Sunday and Thursday, with hardy crafts and local produce. The Sunday market is as-

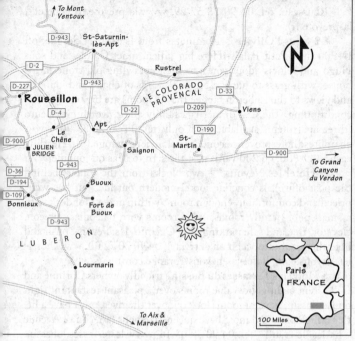

tounding and famous for its antiques; the Thursday market is more intimate and focused more on produce than antiques. Find a table across from the church at **Café de France** and enjoy the scene.

Biking: Isle-sur-la-Sorgue is ideally situated for short biking forays into the mostly level terrain. Pick up a biking itinerary at the TI, or consult with David at **Vélo Services** (3 Rue Docteur Tallet, mobile 06 38 14 49 50, http://veloservices.jimdo.com).

Sleeping in and near Isle-sur-la-Sorgue

($$$$ = Splurge, $$$ = Pricier, $$ = Moderate, $ = Budget)
Pickings are slim for good sleeps in Isle-sur-la-Sorgue, though the few I've listed provide solid values. A *laverie automatique* (self-service launderette) is in the town center, just off Rue de la République on Impasse de l'Hôtel de Palerme (open daily 24 hours).

$$$ La Prévôté*** has the town's highest-priced digs. Its five meticulously decorated rooms—located above a classy restaurant—are adorned in earth tones, with high ceilings, a few exposed beams, and carefully selected furnishings. Séverine manages the hotel while chef-hubby Jean-Marie controls the kitchen (includes breakfast, limited check-in/check-out times, no elevator, rooftop deck with hot tub, no parking, one block from the church at 4 Rue

J. J. Rousseau, tel. 04 90 38 57 29, www.la-prevote.fr, contact@la-prevote.fr).

$$ Sous l'Olivier is 10 minutes from Isle-sur-la-Sorgue, off D-900 near Petit Palais. Here big Julien, quiet Carole, and sons Hugo and Clovis adopt you into their sprawling old stone farmhouse, with grass to burn, a big pool, yards of chairs and lounges, and views to the Luberon range. The six rooms are big but lack air-conditioning. The €34 dinner is a family affair, worth every euro (three apartments available, cash only, tel. 04 90 20 33 90, www.chambresdhotesprovence.com, souslolivier@orange.fr). Heading east on D-900, go 200 yards past the sign to Mas du Jonquier.

$ Hôtel les Névons,*** two blocks from the center (behind the post office), is concrete motel-modern outside, but has well-priced and comfortable-enough rooms within and a roof deck with a small pool (family rooms, some rooms with balconies, air-con, elevator, free and safe parking, 205 Chemin des Névons, push and hold the gate button a bit on entry, tel. 04 90 20 72 00, www.hotel-les-nevons.com, hotel-les-nevons@orange.com).

$ Hôtel les Terrasses du Bassin's friendly owners Corinne and Gilles rent eight good-value rooms over a pleasant restaurant right on Le Bassin. Several rooms look out over the river, most have a little traffic noise, and most have queen-size beds (air-con, 2 Avenue Charles de Gaulle, tel. 04 90 38 03 16, www.lesterrassesdubassin.com, corinne@lesterrassesdubassin.com).

Eating in and near Isle-sur-la-Sorgue

Cheap and mediocre restaurants are a dime a dozen in Isle-sur-la-Sorgue. You'll see several brasseries on the river, good for views and basic café fare. The three restaurants I list offer good values, but none of them is really "cheap."

$$ Les Terrasses du Bassin is a sure riverside option with a brasserie-like feel, reasonable prices, and tasty choices. Come for a full meal or just a *plat*, or a salad and eat on the river if you can (closed Wed year-round and Tue off-season, 2 Avenue Charles de Gaulle, tel. 04 90 38 03 16).

$$$ La Balade des Saveurs' Sophie and Benjamin deliver fresh, Provençal cuisine at riverside tables or in their elegantly sky-lit interior at fair prices. The asparagus soup with egg is a winning twist on a French classic (daily, 3 Quai Jean Juarès, tel. 04 90 95 27 85, www.balade-des-saveurs.com).

$$$$ La Prévôté is the place in town to do it up. Its lovely dining room is country-classy but not stuffy. A stream runs under the restaurant, visible through glass windows (closed Mon-Wed, on narrow street that runs along left side of church as you face it, 4 Rue J. J. Rousseau, tel. 04 90 38 57 29, www.la-prevote.fr).

Roussillon

With all the trendy charm of Santa Fe on a hilltop, photogenic Roussillon requires serious camera and café time. An enormous deposit of ochre gives the earth and the buildings that distinctive reddish color.

The little **TI** is in the center, across from the Chez David restaurant (usually Mon-Sat April-Oct 9:30-12:30 & 14:00-18:00, Nov-March 14:00-17:30, closed Sun year-round, Place de la Poste, tel. 04 90 05 60 25, www.luberon-apt.fr). There are several options for **parking:** Parking des Ocres ("P2") is the large lot on the hill toward the ochre cliffs with the best capacity—day-trippers should head straight here. Parking Sablons is next to the recommended Maison des Ocres hotel. Parking Pasquier is closest to the village center, but has only 16 spots and a three-hour limit.

Visiting Roussillon: Climb from any parking lot (small fee) to the village center, cross the cute square, and then climb under the bell tower and past the church to find the orientation table and the **viewpoint** at the top of the village. Roussillon sits atop appropriately named Mont Rouge ("Red Mountain") at about 1,000 feet above sea level. During the Middle Ages, a castle occupied this space. On your way down, duck into the pretty 11th-century Church of St. Michel (originally within the castle walls), then linger over *un café,* or—if it's later in the day—*un pastis,* in the picturesque **village square** (Place de la Mairie). While Roussillon receives scads of day-trippers, mornings and evenings are romantically peaceful on this square.

Roussillon was Europe's capital for ochre production until World War II. A stroll to the south end of town, beyond the upper parking lot, shows you why: Roussillon sits on the world's largest known ochre deposit. A radiant orange path—the ▲▲ **Ochre Cliffs Trail** (Le Sentier des Ocres)—leads around the richly colored, Bryce Canyon-like cliffs. Allow a minimum of 30 easy minutes of walking for a quick loop through the cliffs; a longer loop takes an hour (€2.50, €7.50 combo-ticket with Ochre Conservatory—described next; March-April and Oct 10:00-17:00, May-June and Sept 9:30-18:30, July-Aug 9:00-19:30, shorter hours off-season, closed Jan).

For a good introduction to the history and uses of ochre, visit the **Ochre Conservatory** (Conservatoire des Ocres et de la Couleur), an intriguing reconstructed ochre factory. You'll take a self-guided tour with lots of English information showing how ochre has been used since prehistoric times and how it is converted from an ore to a pigment—allow 40 minutes (€6.50, €7.50 combo-ticket with ochre cliffs, daily 9:00-18:00 but closed for lunch, July-Aug until 19:00, about a half-mile below Roussillon toward Apt on D-104, tel. 04 90 05 66 69, www.okhra.com.

Sleeping in and near Roussillon

($$$$ = Splurge, $$$ = Pricier, $$ = Moderate, $ = Budget)
The TI posts a list of hotels and *chambres d'hôte*.

$$$ Le Clos de la Glycine* delivers Roussillon's plushest accommodations with nine lovely rooms located dead-center in the village (some view rooms, off-season deals, air-con, ask about parking, located at the recommended refined restaurant Chez David—they prefer you pay for half-pension, across from the TI on Place de la Poste, tel. 04 90 05 60 13, www.luberon-hotel.com, contact@luberon-hotel.fr).

$$ At Le Mas d'Estonge, charming Christiane and Robert ("call me Bob") welcome you into their little Provençal paradise in a small neighborhood 10 minutes from Roussillon. Their four well-furnished and comfy rooms share a sweet patio, a common kitchen, and a pool (dinner possible—€31 for the works if you book ahead, 10 minutes from Roussillon on D-227, tel. 04 90 05 63 13, www.destonge.com, destonge@gmail.com).

$$ Maison des Ocres,* well-located on the edge of the village center at the Sablons parking area, provides comfortable, tastefully decorated rooms and a small pool (some rooms with balconies, family rooms, air-con, Route de Gordes, tel. 04 90 05 60 50, www.lamaisondesocres-hotel.com, contact@lamaisondesocres-hotel.com Coming from Gordes and Joucas, it's the first building you pass in Roussillon.

$ Le Clos des Cigales is a good refuge run by friendly Philippe and his wife, Brigitte. Of their five blue-shuttered, stylish bungalows, two are doubles and three are two-room suites with tiny kitchenettes; all have private patios facing a big pool. When you arrive, you'll understand the name—the cacophony from the *cigales* (cicadas) is deafening (family rooms, includes breakfast, table tennis, hammock, 5 minutes from Roussillon toward Goult on D-104, tel. 04 90 05 73 72, www.leclosdescigales.com, philippe.lherbeil@wanadoo.fr).

$ Hostellerie des Commandeurs has simple, good-value rooms in the center of lovely little Joucas. It's kid-friendly, with a big pool and a sports field/play area next door. Ask for a south-facing room *(côté sud)* for the best views. All rooms have showers and air-conditioning (minifridges, above park at village entrance, hotel open March-Oct, tel. 04 90 05 78 01, www.lescommandeurs.com,

PROVENCE

hostellerie@lescommandeurs.com). The traditional **$$ restaurant** offers Provençal cuisine at fair prices (succulent lamb, memorable crème brûlée with lavender, restaurant closed Wed). Village kids like to hang out around the bar's pool table.

Eating in and near Roussillon

Restaurants change with the mistral here—what's good one year disappoints the next. Consider my suggestions, then go with what looks best.

On Place de la Poste: $$$$ Chez David, at the recommended hotel Le Clos de la Glycine (described earlier), is a good place to splurge. You can enjoy a fine meal on the terrace or from an elegant interior window table with point-blank views over the ochre cliffs. The Provençal cuisine is as fabulous as the scenery (daily, Place de la Poste, tel. 04 90 05 60 13).

$$ Le Comptoir des Arts is the only "normal" restaurant at moderate prices in Roussillon. The view terrace is a fine place to appreciate your surroundings, while the interior has a red-leather-seat, bistro feel (Place du Pasquier, tel. 04 90 74 11 92).

On Place de la Mairie: The places on this atmospheric square offer similar ambience and value—but may be closed for dinner due to the difficulty of finding workers for evening shifts. **$$ Le Bistrot de Roussillon** is best, with decent salads and *plats* for the right price. There's a breezy terrace in back and a comfy interior (daily, tel. 04 90 05 74 45).

More Luberon Hill Towns and Sights

I'd make a loop out of these villages and sights, doing them in the order described below. If you're sleeping in or near Roussillon, start there (mornings are peaceful), then follow signs to Gordes, then Oppède-Le-Vieux, and so on (making a counterclockwise loop through the Luberon). If you're staying elsewhere (like Isle-sur-la-Sorge), start with Gordes, then Oppède-le-Vieux (ending with Roussillon). Each town is about a 10-minute drive from the last and the route is well-signed.  Bonnieux looks better from a distance, and its center has no pedestrian focus—skip it.

Gordes

The Luberon's most impressively situated hill town is

worth a quick stop to admire its setting. As you approach Gordes, veer right when you see the viewpoint icon. Get out, stroll along the road and admire the sensational view. Now consider this: In the 1960s Gordes was a ghost town of derelict buildings with no economy. Today it has been renovated from top to bottom (notice how every stone seems perfectly placed), and is filled with people who live in a world without calluses. Many Parisian big shots and mon-eyed foreigners invested heavily, restoring dream homes and putting property values and café prices out of sight for locals. Beyond its stunning views, the village has little of interest. Move along.

Abbey Notre-Dame de Sénanque

This still-functioning and beautifully situated Cistercian abbey was built in 1148 as a back-to-basics reaction to the excesses of

Benedictine abbeys. The abbey is worth the trip for its splendid and remote setting alone. Come first thing, or linger later and stop at a pullout for a bird's-eye view as you descend, then wander the abbey's perimeter. The abbey church is al-ways open (except during Mass, but you're welcome to attend) and high-lights the utter simplicity sought by these monks. In late June through much of July, the five hectares of lavender fields that surround the abbey make for breathtaking pic-tures and draw loads of visitors. Those arriving as the abbey opens find a peaceful place they can tour on their own (good English handout). Those arriving after 11:00 must visit the abbey on a 50-minute, French-only tour (English booklet with translations available). The interior, which doesn't measure up to the abbey's spectacular setting, is a letdown—skip the tour and just wander the grounds.

Cost and Hours: €7.50, with or without the French-only tour (mandatory Feb-Oct after 11:00), no individual visits on Sun or holidays, reservations strongly recommended, call or check website for tour times (tel. 04 90 72 05 72, www.senanque. fr). You can attend Mass (Mon-Sat at 11:45, Sun at 10:00, check website or call to confirm). Modest dress is required for entry—shoulders and knees must be covered.

▲Oppède-le-Vieux

This off-the-beaten-path fixer-upper of a village was completely abandoned in 1910, and today feels like the ideal place to escape the law. Climb the path 20 minutes up to the small church and castle ruins for territorial views. Back down in town, reward yourself with a drink and views of the ruins at the little **$$ Petit Café** (closed Wed and mid-Dec-Feb). Petit Café also offers simple but comfy **$** rooms, all with nice views (closed to check in Tue-Wed, includes breakfast, air-con, indoor hot tub and sauna, rooftop terrace, tel. 04 90 76 74 01, www.lepetitcafe.fr, info@lepetitcafe.fr).

Ménerbes

Ménerbes, (in)famous as the village that drew author Peter Mayle's attention to this region, has an upscale but welcoming feel in its small center (€3 parking). Wine bars, cafés, and a smattering of galleries gather where key lanes intersect. To explore the linear rocktop-village, follow *Eglise* signs. Find **Maison de la Truffe et du Vin,** which offers "truffle discovery workshops," fine meals, and wine tastings (Place de l'Horloge, tel. 04 90 72 38 37, www.vin-truffe-luberon.com). Pass the Hotel de Ville for more views (the church is closed but the views aren't) then double back and find Rue Corneille, which leads to the town's cute château (closed to public). Find the even cuter prison room outside the château and walk back along the path.

A fine lunch or snack awaits at the **$$ Auzet Salon de Thé,** with a cozy interior or view tables from the small terrace. You'll find cheap quiche and savory pies with salad, delicious baked goods, and more (52 Rue du Portail Neuf, tel. 04 90 72 37 53).

Lacoste

This town is worth a stop to wander its steep pretty lanes to the base of the castle for views and to stop for a meal at the **$$ Bar/Restaurant de France**'s outdoor tables overlooking Bonnieux (reasonably priced omelets and *plats,* daily, lunch-only off-season, tel. 04 90 75 82 25). A small *épicerie* near the church has just enough fixings to make a picnic.

Julien Bridge (Pont Julien)

Due south of Roussillon, just below D-900 (see map on page 654), this delicate, three-arched bridge survives as a testimony to Roman engineers—and to the importance of this rural area 2,000 years ago. It's the only surviving bridge on what was the main road from northern Italy to Provence—the primary route used by Roman armies. The 215-foot-long Roman bridge was under

construction from 27 B.C. to A.D. 14. Mortar had not yet been invented, so (as with Pont du Gard) the stones were carefully set in place. Amazingly, the bridge survives today, having outlived Roman marches, hundreds of floods, and decades of automobile traffic. A modern bridge finally rerouted traffic from this beautiful structure in 2005.

THE FRENCH RIVIERA

La Côte d'Azur: Nice • Villefranche-sur-Mer
• The Three Corniches • Monaco • Antibes • Inland Riviera

A hundred years ago, celebrities from London to Moscow flocked to the French Riviera to socialize, gamble, and escape the dreary weather at home. Today, budget vacationers and heat-seeking Europeans fill belle époque resorts at France's most sought-after fun-in-the-sun destination.

Some of the Continent's most stunning scenery and intriguing museums lie along this strip of land—as do millions of sun-worshipping tourists. Nice has world-class museums, a splendid beachfront promenade, a seductive old town, and all the drawbacks of a major city (traffic, crime, pollution, and so on). The day-trip possibilities are easy and exciting: Fifteen minutes east of Nice, little Villefranche-sur-Mer stares across the bay to woodsy and exclusive Cap Ferrat; the eagle's-nest Eze-le-Village surveys the scene from high above; Monaco offers a royal welcome and a fairytale past; Antibes has a thriving port and silky sand beaches; and the inland hill towns present a rocky and photogenic alternative to the beach scene. Evenings on the Riviera, a.k.a. la Côte d'Azur, were made for a promenade and outdoor dining.

CHOOSING A HOME BASE

My favorite home bases are Nice, Antibes, and Villefranche-sur-Mer.

Nice is the region's capital and France's fifth-largest city. With convenient train and bus connections to most regional sights, this is the most practical base for train travelers. Urban Nice also has museums, a beach scene that rocks, the best selection of hotels in all price ranges, and good nightlife options. A car is a headache in Nice.

The French Riviera

To Digne • Entrevaux

Alpes • Maritimes

To Grand Canyon du Verdon, Digne & Chamonix

ROUTE NAPOLÉON

D-6085

D-6202

ITALY To Genoa

A-8

Venti-miglia

Menton

Gorges du Loup

Gourdon

Tourrettes

Le Bar

St-Paul

Vence

La Turbie

MONACO

Eze-le-Village

Villefranche-sur-Mer

Nice

Grasse

Biot

Cap Ferrat

Vallauris

Antibes

A-8

Juan-les-Pins

Cannes

Mediterranean Sea

To Arles & Avignon

A-8

D-6098

Massif de l'Estérel

D-559

SCENIC DRIVE

Fréjus

St-Raphaël

D-559

St-Tropez

10 Kilometers

10 Miles

Paris

FRANCE

100 Miles

Nearby **Antibes** is smaller, with a bustling center, a lively night scene, great sandy beaches, grand vistas, good walking trails, and a Picasso museum. Antibes has frequent train service to Nice and Monaco. It's the most convenient overnight stop for drivers, with light traffic and easy hotel parking.

Villefranche-sur-Mer is the romantic's choice, with a serene setting and small-town warmth. It has sand-pebble beaches; quick public transportation to Nice, Monaco, and Cap Ferrat; and a small selection of hotels in most price ranges.

PLANNING YOUR TIME

Ideally, allow a full day for Nice, a day for Monaco and the Corniche route that connects it with Nice, and a half-day for Antibes, Villefranche-sur-Mer, or Cap Ferrat (or better, a full day combining Villefranche and Cap Ferrat). Monaco and Villefranche-sur-Mer are radiant at night, and Antibes works well day (good beaches and hiking) and night (fine choice of restaurants and a lively after-hours scene). Hill-town-loving naturalists should add a day to explore the charming hill-capping hamlets near Vence.

RIVIERA

French Riviera at a Glance

▲▲▲**Nice** Classy resort town with beaches, seafront promenade, a fine palette of museums, and a ramble-worthy old town. See page 672.

▲▲▲**Villefranche-sur-Mer** Romantic pastel-orange beach village with a yacht-filled harbor and small-town ambience. See page 711.

▲▲▲**Monaco** Tiny independent municipality known for its classy casino and Grand Prix car race. See page 732.

▲▲**Along the Three Corniches** Scenic coastal roads highlighted by the exclusive woodsy Cap Ferrat peninsula, flowery hill-capping Eze-le-Village, and the Roman monument of Trophée des Alpes. See page 721.

▲▲**Antibes** Laid-back beach town with a medieval center, worthwhile Picasso museum, sandy beaches, and view hikes. See page 743.

▲▲**Inland Riviera** Up and away from the beaches, postcard-perfect St-Paul-de-Vence, crammed with boutiques and tourists, and appealing little Vence, host to a Matisse chapel. See page 757.

HELPFUL HINTS

Exchange Rate: €1 = about $1.10

Country Calling Code: 33 (see page 1082 for dialing instructions)

Medical Help: Riviera Medical Services has a list of English-speaking physicians all along the Riviera. They can help you make an appointment or call an ambulance (tel. 04 93 26 12 70, www.rivieramedical.com).

Closed Days: Mondays and Tuesdays can frustrate market lovers and museumgoers. Closed on Monday: Nice's Modern and Contemporary Art Museum, Fine Arts Museum, and Cours Saleya produce and flower market; Antibes' Picasso Museum and market hall (Sept-May). Closed on Tuesday: the Chagall, Matisse, Masséna, and Archaeological museums in Nice. On Fridays Matisse's Chapel of the Rosary in Vence is closed.

Sightseeing Pass: The **French Riviera Pass** includes entry to many museums and sights, including Monaco's Oceanography Museum, Villa Ephrussi de Rothschild on Cap Ferrat, and Nice's Chagall Museum (which is not included in the €10 combo-ticket that covers most Nice museums). This pass is likely worthwile only if you intend to do the included Trans Côte d'Azur cruise (see "Tours in Nice") or have an aggressive sight-seeing plan (€26/24 hours, €38/28 hours, €56/72 hours, tel. 04 92 14 46 14, http://en.frenchrivierapass.com).

Events: The Riviera is famous for staging major events. Unless you're taking part in the festivities, these occasions give you only room shortages and traffic jams. Here are the three biggies: **Nice Carnival** (two weeks in mid-late-Feb, www.nicecarnaval.com), **Cannes Film Festival** (12 days in mid-May, www.festival-cannes.com), and the **Grand Prix of Monaco** (4 days in late May, www.acm.mc). To accommodate the busy schedules of the rich and famous (and really mess up a lot of normal people), the film festival and car race often overlap.

Local Guides with Cars: These two energetic and delightful women have comfortable minibuses and enjoy taking couples and small groups anywhere in the region: **Sylvie Di Cristo** (€600/day, €350/half-day for up to 8 people, mobile 06 09 88 83 83, www.frenchrivieraguides.net, dicristosylvie@gmail.com) and **Ingrid Schmucker** (€490/day for 4 people or €550/day for 5-7 people, €180/half-day or €285/day if you don't need transportation, tel. 06 14 83 03 33, www.kultours.fr, info@kultours.fr). Their websites explain their programs well. The TI and most hotels have information on more economic shared minivan excursions from Nice (roughly €50-70/person per half-day, €80-120/person per day).

Local Guides Without Cars: For a guided tour of Nice or the region using public transit or your own car, consider **Pascale Rucker,** an art-loving guide with 25 years of experience who teaches with the joy and wonder of a flower child (€160/half-day, €260/day, tel. 06 16 24 29 52, pascalerucker@gmail.com), or **Agnès Dumartin**, a good teacher who understands Nice particularly well and loves all forms of art. Agnès doesn't drive, but she's ideal for walks in Nice and can join you in your car for regional sights (€210/half-day, €295/day, mobile 06 81 82 17 67, agnes.dumartin@orange.fr).

Foodie Tours: For food and wine walking tours and cooking classes offered in Nice, see page 679.

Longer-Stay Rentals: Riviera Pebbles offers a wide range of apartments throughout the Riviera and gets good reviews from happy clients (www.rivierapebbles.com).

Connecting to the Alps: If driving from the Riviera north to the Alps (see next chapter), consider taking **La Route Napoléon.** After getting bored in his toy Elba empire, Napoléon gathered his entourage, landed on the Riviera, bared his breast, and told his fellow Frenchmen, "Strike me down or follow me." France followed. But just in case, he took the high road, returning to Paris along the

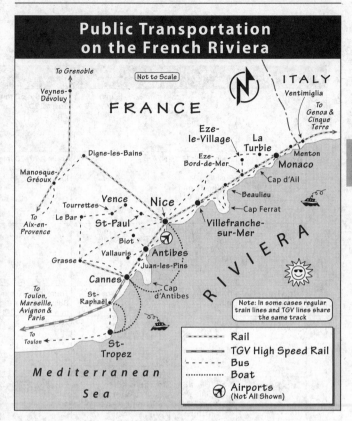

route known today as La Route Napoléon. (Waterloo followed shortly afterward.) The route is beautiful (from south to north, follow signs: *Digne, Sisteron,* and *Grenoble*). Little Entrevaux is worth a quick leg-stretch. Climb high to the citadel for great views and appreciate the unspoiled character of the town. Several pleasant villages with inexpensive hotels lie along this route, making an overnight easy. You can also foray into the Alps via the narrow-gauge train from Nice (see page 697).

GETTING AROUND THE RIVIERA

If taking the train or bus, have coins handy. Ticket machines don't take US credit cards or euro bills, smaller train stations may be unstaffed, and bus drivers can't make change for large bills.

By Public Transportation: Trains and buses do a good job of connecting places along the coast, with bonus views along many routes. Buses also provide reasonable service to some inland hill

RIVIERA

Public Transportation on the French Riviera

		To		
		Cannes	Antibes	Nice
From	**Cannes**	N/A	Train: 2/hr, 15 min Bus: #200, 2-4/hr, 35 min	Train: 2/hr, 30 min Bus: #200, 2-4/hr, 2 hrs
	Antibes	Train: 2/hr, 15 min Bus: #200, 2-4/hr, 35 min	N/A	Train: 2/hr, 20 min Bus: #200, 2-4/hr, 1.5 hrs
	Nice	Train: 2/hr, 30 min Bus: #200, 2-4/hr, 2 hrs	Train: 2/hr, 20 min Bus: #200, 2-4/hr, 1.5 hrs	N/A
	Villefranche-sur-Mer	Train: 2/hr, 50 min	Train: 2/hr, 40 min	Train: 2/hr, 10 min Bus: #100, 3-4/hr, 2 min; also #81, 2-3/hr, 20 min
	Cap Ferrat	Train: Bus #81 to Beaulieu-sur-Mer (2-3/hr, 10 min), then train to Cannes (2/hr, 1 hr)	Train: Bus #81 to Beaulieu-sur-Mer (2-3/hr, 10 min), then train (2/hr, 40 min) Bus: #81 to Nice (2-3/hr, 30 min), then #200 (2-4/hr, 1.5 hrs)	Bus: #81, 2-3/hr, 30 min
	Eze-le-Village	Bus/Train: Bus #83 to Eze-Bord-de-Mer (8/day, 15 min), then train (2/hr, 1 hr)	Bus/Train: Bus #83 to Eze-Bord-de-Mer (8/day, 15 min), then train (2/hr, 45 min)	Bus/Train: Bus #83 to Eze-Bord-de-Mer (8/day, 15 min), then train (2/hr, 15 min) Bus: #82/#112, 8-16/day, 40 min
	Monaco	Train: 2/hr, 70 min	Train: 2/hr, 50 min	Train: 2/hr, 20 min Bus: #100, 3-4/hr, 45 min

Note: Bus frequencies are given for Monday-Saturday (Sunday often has limited or no bus service).

...lefranche-sur-Mer	Cap Ferrat	Eze-le-Village	Monaco
...in: 2/hr, 50 min	Train: 2/hr, 1 hr to Beaulieu-sur-Mer, then bus #81 (2-3/hr, 10 min)	Train: 2/hr, 1 hr to Eze-Bord-de-Mer, then bus #83 (8/day, 15 min)	Train: 2/hr, 70 min
...in: 2/hr, 40 min	Train: 2/hr, 40 min to Beaulieu-sur-Mer, then bus #81 (2-3/hr, 10 min) Bus: #200 to Nice (2-4/hr, 1.5 hrs), then #81 (2-3/hr, 30 min)	Train: 2/hr, 45 min to Eze-Bord-de-Mer, then bus #83 (8/day, 15 min)	Train: 2/hr, 50 min
...in: 2/hr, 10 min s: #100, 3-4/hr, 20 n; also #81, 2-3/hr, min	Bus: #81, 2-3/hr, 30 min	Train: 2/hr, 15 min to Eze-Bord-de-Mer, then bus #83 (8/day, 15 min) Bus: #82/#112, 8-16/day, 40 min	Train: 2/hr, 20 min Bus: #100, 3-4/hr, 45 min
...A	Bus: #81, 2-3/hr, 20 min	Train: 2/hr, 5 min to Eze-Bord-de-Mer, then bus #83 (8/day, 15 min) Bus: #100 to Eze-Bord-de-Mer, then transfer to #83; also #82/#112 from upper Villefranche	Train: 2/hr, 10 min Bus: #100, 3-4/hr, 25 min
s: #81, 2-3/hr, 20 n	N/A	Bus: #100 to Eze-Bord-de-Mer (3-4/hr, 30 min), then bus #83 (8/day, 15 min)	Bus: #100, 3-4/hr, 20 min
s/Train: Bus #83 to e-Bord-de-Mer (8/ y, 15 min), then train /hr, 5 min) s: #83 to Eze-Bord--Mer, then transfer #100; also #82/#112 upper Villefranche	Bus: #83 to Eze-Bord-de-Mer (8/day, 15 min), then bus #100 (3-4/hr, 30 min)	N/A	Bus: #112, 6/day, 20 min
...in: 2/hr, 10 min s: #100, 3-4/hr, min	Bus: #100, 3-4/hr, 20 min	Bus: #112, 6/day, 20 min	N/A

towns, and are typically less expensive and more convenient. Trains are generally faster and more expensive.

Buses are an amazing deal in the Riviera. Any one-way bus or tram ride costs €1.50 (€10 for 10 tickets) whether you're riding just within Nice or to Villefranche-sur-Mer, Monaco, or Antibes. The €1.50 ticket is good for 74 minutes of travel in one direction anywhere within the bus system except for airport buses. Buy your bus ticket from the driver or from machines at stops, and validate your ticket in the machine on board. Your ticket allows transfers between the buses of the Lignes d'Azur (the region's main bus company, www.lignesdazur.com) and the TAM (Transports Alpes-Maritimes); if you board a TAM bus and need a transfer, ask for *un ticket correspondance*. A €5 all-day ticket is good on Nice's city buses, tramway, and selected buses serving nearby destinations (such as Villefranche, Cap Ferrat, and Eze-le-Village). The general rule of thumb: If the bus number has one or two digits, it's covered with the all-day ticket; with three digits it's not.

The **train** is more expensive but much faster (Nice to Monaco by train is about €4, versus €1.50 by bus), and there's no quicker way to move about the Riviera (http://en.voyages-sncf.com). Speedy trains link the Riviera's beachfront destinations. Never board a train without a ticket or valid pass—fare inspectors accept no excuses. The minimum fine: €70. (See page 677 for a tip on avoiding lines when buying regional train tickets in Nice.)

Nice makes the most convenient base for day trips, though public transport also works well from Riviera towns such as Antibes and Villefranche-sur-Mer. Details are provided under each destination's "Connections" section. For a scenic inland train ride, take the narrow-gauge train into the Alps (see page 697).

For an overview of the most useful Riviera train and bus connections, see the "Public Transportation in the French Riviera" chart on page 668.

By Car: This is France's most challenging region to drive in. Beautifully distracting vistas (natural and human), loads of Sunday-driver tourists, and every hour being lush-hour in the summer make for a dangerous combination. Parking can be exasperating. Bring lots of coins and patience.

The Riviera is awash with scenic roads. To sample some of the Riviera's best scenery, connect Provence and the Riviera by driving the splendid coastal road between Cannes and Fréjus (D-6098 from Cannes/D-559 from Fréjus). Once in the Riviera, the most

scenic and thrilling road trip is along the three coastal roads—
called "corniches"—between Nice and Monaco (see page 721).

By Boat: Trans Côte d'Azur offers seasonal boat service
from Nice to Monaco (tel. 04 92 98 71 30, www.trans-cote-azur.
com). For details, see "Getting Around the Riviera from Nice" on
page 678.

THE RIVIERA'S ART SCENE

The list of artists who have painted the Riviera reads like a Who's
Who of 20th-century art. Pierre-Auguste Renoir, Henri Matisse,
Marc Chagall, Georges Braque, Raoul
Dufy, Fernand Léger, and Pablo Picasso all lived and worked here—and
raved about the region's wonderful light.
Their simple, semi-abstract, and—most
importantly—colorful works reflect the
pleasurable atmosphere of the Riviera.
You'll experience the same landscapes
they painted in this bright, sun-drenched
region, punctuated with views of the
"azure sea." Try to imagine the Riviera
with a fraction of the people and development you see today.

But the artists were mostly drawn to
the uncomplicated lifestyle of fishermen
and farmers that has reigned here since
time began. As the artists grew older,
they retired in the sun, turned their backs on modern art's "isms,"
and painted with the wide-eyed wonder of children, using bright
primary colors, basic outlines, and simple subjects.

A collection of modern- and contemporary-art museums
(many described in this book) dot the Riviera, allowing art lovers to appreciate these masters' works while immersed in the same
sun and culture that inspired them. Many of the museums were
designed to blend pieces with the surrounding views, gardens, and
fountains, thus highlighting that modern art is not only stimulating, but sometimes simply beautiful.

THE RIVIERA'S CUISINE SCENE

While many of the same dishes served in Provence are available in
the Riviera (see "Provence's Cuisine Scene" on page 563), there
are differences, especially if you look for anything Italian or from
the sea. When dining on the Riviera, I expect views and ambience
more than top-quality cuisine.

La salade niçoise is where most Riviera meals start. A true specialty from Nice, the classic version is a base of green salad with

boiled potatoes, tomatoes, anchovies, olives, hard-boiled eggs, and lots of tuna. This is my go-to salad for a tasty, healthy, cheap (€13), and fast lunch. I like to spend a couple of extra euros and eat it in a place with a nice ambience and view.

For lunch on the go, look for a *pan bagnat* (like a *salade niçoise* stuffed into a hollowed-out soft roll). Other tasty bread treats include *pissaladière* (bread dough topped with onions, olives, and anchovies), *fougasse* (a spindly, lace-like bread sometimes flavored with nuts, herbs, olives, or ham), and *socca* (a thin chickpea crêpe, seasoned with pepper and olive oil and often served in a paper cone by street vendors).

Bouillabaisse is the Riviera's most famous dish; you'll find it in seafront villages and cities. It's a spicy fish stew based on recipes handed down from sailors in Marseille. This dish often requires a minimum order of two and can cost up to €40-60 per person.

Those on a budget can enjoy other seafood soups and stews. Far less pricey than bouillabaisse and worth trying is the local *soupe de poisson* (fish soup). It's a creamy soup flavored like bouillabaisse, with anise and orange, and served with croutons and *rouille* sauce (but has no chunks of fish).

The Riviera specializes in all sorts of fish and shellfish. Options include *fruits de mer*, or platters of seafood (including tiny shellfish, from which you get the edible part only by sucking really hard), herb-infused mussels, stuffed sardines, squid (slowly simmered with tomatoes and herbs), and tuna *(thon)*. The popular *loup flambé au fenouil* is grilled sea bass, flavored with fennel and torched with *pastis* prior to serving.

For details on dining in France's restaurants, cafés, and brasseries, getting takeout, and assembling a picnic—as well as a rundown of French cuisine—see the "Eating" section in the Practicalities chapter (page 1062).

Wines of the Riviera: Do as everyone else does, and drink wines from Provence. Bandol (red) and Cassis (white) are popular and from a region nearly on the Riviera. The only wines made in the Riviera are Bellet rosé and white, the latter often found in fish-shaped bottles.

Nice

Nice (sounds like "niece"), with its spectacular Alps-to-Mediterranean surroundings, is the big-city highlight of the Riviera. Its traffic-free old town mixes Italian and French fla-

vors to create a spicy Mediterranean dressing, while its big squares, broad seaside walkways, and long beaches invite lounging and people-watching. Nice may be nice, but it's hot and jammed in July and August—reserve ahead and get a room with air-conditioning. Everything you'll want to see in Nice is either within walking distance, or a short bike, bus, or tram ride away.

Orientation to Nice

Focus your time on the area between the beach and the train tracks (about 15 blocks apart). The city revolves around its grand Place Masséna, where pedestrian-friendly Avenue Jean Médecin meets Vieux (Old) Nice and the Promenade du Paillon parkway (with quick access to the beaches). It's a 20-minute walk (or about €14 by taxi) from the train station to the beach, and a 20-minute stroll along the promenade from the fancy Hôtel Negresco to the heart of Vieux Nice.

A 10-minute ride on the smooth-as-silk tram through the center of the city connects the train station, Place Masséna, Vieux Nice, and the port (from nearby Place Garibaldi). Work is underway on a new tram line (much of it underground) that will parallel the Promenade des Anglais (scheduled for completion in 2019).

TOURIST INFORMATION

Nice has several helpful TIs (tel. 08 92 70 74 07, www.nicetourisme. com), including branches at the **airport** (daily 9:00-18:00), the **train station** (summer daily 9:00-19:00, rest of year Mon-Sat 9:00-18:00, Sun 10:00-17:00), at 5 **Promenade des Anglais** (daily 9:00-18:00, July-Aug until 19:00), and on the north side of **Place Masséna,** called "Pavillon" (May-mid-Sept only, daily 10:00-18:00). Pick up a free Nice map, and ask for day-trip information (including maps of Monaco or Antibes, details on boat excursions, and bus stop locations and schedules).

ARRIVAL IN NICE

By Train: All trains stop at Nice's main station, called Nice-Ville (you don't want the suburban Nice Riquier Station). With your back to the tracks, car rentals are to the right, and airport bus #99 stops in front. The TI is straight out the main doors. There's no baggage storage at the station, but you can stash your bags a short block away at the recommended Hôtel Belle Meunière.

Nice's single **tram line** zips you to the center in a few minutes

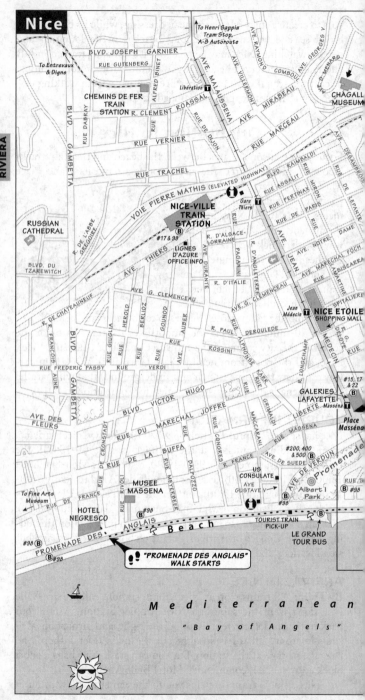

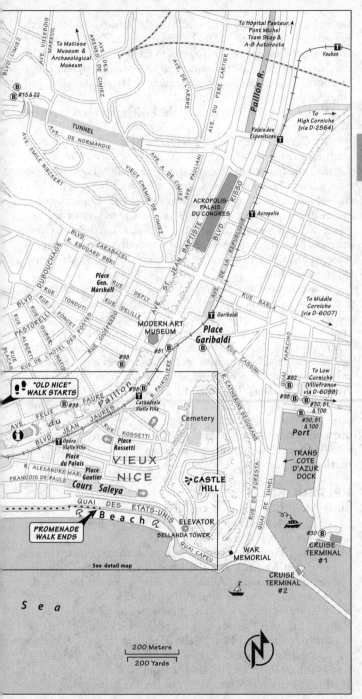

(several blocks to the left as you leave the station, departs every few minutes, direction: Hôpital Pasteur; for details, see "Getting Around Nice" on page 677). To walk to the beach, Promenade des Anglais, or many of my recommended hotels, cross Avenue Thiers in front of the station, go down the steps by Hôtel Interlaken, and continue down Avenue Durante.

By Bus: See "Getting Around the Riviera from Nice" on page 678 for stop information.

By Car: To reach the city center on the autoroute from the west, take the first Nice exit (for the airport—called *Côte d'Azur, Central*) and follow signs for *Nice Centre*. Hoteliers know where to park (allow €18-30/day; many hotels offer deals but space is limited—book ahead). The parking garage at the Nice Etoile shopping center on Avenue Jean Médecin is near many recommended hotels (ticket booth on third floor, about €28/day, 18:00-8:00). Other centrally located garages have similar rates. All on-street parking is metered (usually with a 2-hour limit) every day but Sunday, when it is typically free.

You can avoid driving in the center—and park for free during the day (no overnight parking)—by stashing your car at a parking lot at a remote tram or bus stop. Look for blue-on-white *Parcazur* signs (find locations at www.lignesdazur.com), and ride the bus or tram into town (10/hour, 15 minutes, must buy round-trip tram or bus ticket and keep it with you because you'll need it later to exit the parking lot; for details on riding the tram, see "Getting Around Nice," later). The easiest lot to use is Parcazur Henri Sappia, right off the Nice Nord autoroute exit—it always has room and saves you from navigating city streets (daily until 2:30). As lots are unguarded, don't leave anything of value in your car.

By Plane: For information on Nice's airport, see "Nice Connections" on page 708.

HELPFUL HINTS

Theft Alert: Nice has its share of pickpockets (especially at the train station, on the tram, and trolling the beach). Stick to main streets in Vieux Nice after dark.

Sightseeing Tips: The Cours Saleya produce and flower market is closed Monday, and the Chagall and Matisse Museums are closed Tuesday. All Nice museums—except the Chagall Museum—share the same €10 combo-ticket (valid 48 hours, €20/7 days, buy at any participating museum).

Baggage Storage: You can store your bags near the train station at the recommended **Hôtel Belle Meunière** (€5/bag per day) or at the **Bag Guys** in Vieux Nice (€8/bag per day, daily 10:00-19:00, 22 Rue Centrale, info@bagguys.fr).

Wi-Fi: The city offers free Wi-Fi in the Promenade du Paillon,

Place Masséna, Place Garibaldi, and along the Cours Saleya in Vieux Nice (network: Spot Wifi Nice).

Grocery Store: Small grocery shops are easy to find. The big **Monoprix** on Avenue Jean Médecin and Rue Biscarra has it all (open daily, see map on page 706).

Boutique Shopping: The chic streets where Rue Alphonse Karr meets Rue de la Liberté and then Rue de Paradis are known as the "Golden Square." If you need pricey stuff, shop here.

Regional Train Tickets: If station ticket lines are long, you can buy tickets for Riviera destinations at the desk called **Guichet Zou Billeterie,** near the car rental offices (Mon-Fri 7:30-17:30).

Lignes d'Azur Bus Tickets: The office is located kitty-corner from the train station, where Rue Auber crosses Rue Thiers (closed Sun, 53 Rue Berlioz).

Renting a Bike (and Other Wheels): Bike-rental shops are a breeze to find in Nice, and several companies offer bike tours of the city. Bikes *(vélos)* can be taken on trains. **Holiday Bikes** has multiple locations, including one across from the train station, and they have electric bikes (www.loca-bike.fr). **Roller Station** is well-situated near the sea and rents bikes, roller-blades, skateboards, and Razor-style scooters (bikes-€5/hour, €10/half-day, €15/day, leave ID as deposit, open daily, 49 Quai des Etats-Unis—see map on page 686, tel. 04 93 62 99 05).

Car Rental: Renting a car is easiest at Nice's airport, which has offices for all the major companies. Most companies are also represented at Nice's train station and near the southwest side of Albert I Park.

Views: For panoramic views, climb Castle Hill (see page 696), or take a one-hour boat trip (page 680).

Beach Tips: To make life tolerable on the rocks, swimmers should buy a pair of the cheap, plastic beach shoes sold at many shops. **Go Sport** at #13 on Place Masséna is a good bet (open daily, see map on page 686). Locals don't swim in July and August, as the warming sea brings swarms of stinging jellyfish. Ask before you dip.

GETTING AROUND NICE
By Public Transportation

Although you can walk to most attractions, smart travelers make good use of the buses and tram.

Tickets: Both buses and trams are covered by the same €1.50 single-ride ticket, or you can pay €10 for a 10-ride ticket that can be shared (each use good for 74 minutes in one direction, including transfers between bus and tram). The €5 all-day pass is valid on city buses and trams, as well as buses to some nearby destinations (but not airport buses). You must validate your ticket on every trip. Buy single tickets from the bus driver or from the ticket machines on tram platforms (coins only—press the green button once to validate choice and twice at the end to get your ticket). Passes and 10-ride tickets are also available from machines at tram stops and from the Lignes d'Azur office (see above, under "Helpful Hints"). Info: www.lignesdazur.com.

Buses: The bus is handy for reaching the Chagall and Matisse museums (for specifics, see museum listings under "Sights in Nice"), and the Russian Cathedral. Validate your ticket in the machine—watch locals to learn how. Route diagrams in the buses identify each stop.

Trams: Nice has a single modern and efficient L-shaped tram line. Trams run every few minutes along Avenue Jean Médecin and Boulevard Jean Jaurès, and connect the main train station with Place Masséna and Vieux Nice (Opéra stop), the port (Place Garibaldi stop), and buses east along the coast (Vauban stop). Trams also stop near the Chemins de Fer de Provence train station (Libération stop)—the departure point for the scenic narrow-gauge rail journey (see page 697).

Boarding the tram in the direction of Hôpital Pasteur takes you toward the beach and Vieux Nice (direction: Henri Sappia goes the other way). Validate your ticket on the tram (http://tramway.nice.fr).

By Taxi or Uber
While pricey, cabs can be useful for getting to Nice's less-central sights (figure €8 for shortest ride, €15 from Promenade des Anglais to the Chagall Museum). Cabbies normally pick up only at taxi stands *(tête de station)*, or you can call 04 93 13 78 78.

Uber works here like it does at home (including your US app and account), and is generally a better bet than taking taxis. Drivers are nicer and more flexible, it's cheaper, and you can generally get a car within five minutes. Uber drivers find you and pick you up anywhere, so you don't have to track down a taxi stand.

GETTING AROUND THE RIVIERA FROM NICE
By Train and Bus
Nice is perfectly situated for exploring the Riviera by public transport. Monaco, Eze-le-Village, Villefranche-sur-Mer, Antibes, Vence, and St-Paul-de-Vence are all within about a one-hour bus or train ride. With a little planning, you can

link key destinations in an all-day circuit. For example: Nice, Monaco, and Eze-le-Village or La Turbie, then loop back to Nice (see page 742 for details). For a summary of train and bus connections, see the "Public Transportation in the French Riviera" sidebar on page 668; see also "Nice Connections" on page 708.

Trains serving Nice arrive at and depart from Nice-Ville Station. To connect to regional destinations, use the following east- and westbound bus stops (see maps on pages 674 and 686 for stop locations; www.lignesdazur.com).

Eastbound Buses: Due to tram line construction, expect some changes to bus stops. The closest stop for eastbound buses is at the Garibaldi tram stop, near Place Garibaldi (see map on page 674). Bus #81 to Villefranche-sur-Mer and Cap Ferrat likely stops only at the Promenade des Arts stop by the Modern Art Museum and at the port. Bus #100 to Monaco likely stops only at the port. Ask at the TI if a closer bus stop is available. Buses to Eze-le-Village and La Turbie leave from the Vauban tram stop. Use the tram to reach any of these eastbound buses (free transfer to all of these destinations, except Monaco).

Westbound Buses: To St-Paul-de-Vence, Vence, Cannes, and Antibes, use the Albert I/Verdun stop on Avenue de Verdun, a 10-minute walk along the parkway west of Place Masséna. See map on page 674.

By Boat

In summer, Trans Côte d'Azur offers scenic trips several days a week from Nice to Monaco. Boats to **Monaco** depart at 9:30 and 16:00, and return at 11:00 and 18:00 (€39 round-trip, €32 if you don't get off in Monaco, 45 minutes each way, June-Sept Tue, Thu, and Sat only). Drinks and WCs are available on board.

Reservations are required (tel. 04 92 00 42 30, www.transcote-azur.com). Boats leave from Nice's port, Bassin des Amiraux, just below Castle Hill—look for the ticket booth *(billeterie)* on Quai de Lunel (see map on page 674). The same company also runs one-hour round-trip cruises along the coast to Cap Ferrat (see listing under "Tours in Nice," next).

Tours in Nice

ON WHEELS
Hop-On, Hop-Off Bus

Le Grand Tour Bus provides a 14-stop, hop-on, hop-off service on an open-deck bus with headphone commentary. The route includes the Promenade des Anglais, the old port, Cap de Nice, and the Chagall and Matisse museums (1-day pass-€23, 2-day pass-€26, night tour—€15, buy tickets on bus, 2/hour, daily 10:00-19:00, 1.5-hour loop, main stop near where Promenade des Anglais and Quai des Etats-Unis meet—across from the Plage Beau Rivage lounge, tel. 04 92 29 17 00, www.nicelegrandtour.com). While neither an economical nor efficient way to get to the Chagall and Matisse museums, it works if you're looking for a city overview.

Tourist Train

For €10, you can spend 45 minutes on the tourist train tooting along the promenade, through the old city, and up to Castle Hill (2/hour, daily 10:00-18:00 or 19:00, recorded English commentary, meet train near Le Grand Tour Bus stop on Quai des Etats-Unis, tel. 02 99 88 47 07).

BY BOAT

▲Trans Côte d'Azur Cruise

To see Nice from the water, hop on this one-hour tour run by Trans Côte d'Azur. You'll cruise in a comfortable yacht-size vessel to Cap Ferrat and past Villefranche-sur-Mer, then return to Nice with a final lap along Promenade des Anglais.

Guides play Robin Leach (in French and English), pointing out mansions owned by famous people, including Elton John, Sean Connery, and Microsoft co-founder Paul Allen (€19, covered by French Riviera Pass—see page 665; April-Oct Tue-Sun 2/day, usually at 11:00 and 15:00, no boats Mon or in off-season; verify schedule, arrive 30 minutes early to get best seats; for directions to the dock and contact information, see "Getting Around the Riviera from Nice—By Boat," earlier).

ON FOOT

Local Guides and Walking Tours

If interested in hiring a local guide for Nice and other regional destinations, see page 666 for suggestions.

The TI on Promenade des Anglais organizes weekly walking tours of Vieux Nice in French and English (€12, May-Oct only, usually Sat morning at 9:30, 2.5 hours, reservations necessary, depart from TI, tel. 08 92 70 74 07). They also have evening art walks on Fridays at 19:00.

Food Tours and Cooking Classes

Charming Canadian Francophile Rosa Jackson—a food journalist, Cordon Bleu-trained cook, and longtime resident of France—runs a cooking school, **Les Petits Farcis,** and offers a good food-market tour in Vieux Nice (€75/person). She also teaches a variety of cooking classes that include a morning shopping trip to the market on Cours Saleya and an afternoon cooking session (€195/person, 12 Rue Saint Joseph, tel. 06 81 67 41 22, www.petitsfarcis.com).

Walks in Nice

PROMENADE DES ANGLAIS WALK

This leisurely, level self-guided walk, worth ▲▲▲, is a straight line along this much-strolled beachfront. It begins near the landmark Hôtel Negresco and ends just before Castle Hill. While this one-mile section is enjoyable at any time, the first half makes a great stroll before or after breakfast or dinner (meals served at some beach cafés). If extending this stroll to Castle Hill, it's ideal to time things so you wind up on top of the hill at sunset. Allow one hour at a promenade pace to reach the elevator up to Castle Hill. To trace the route of this walk, see the map on page 674.

Biking the Promenade: To rev up the pace of your promenade saunter, rent a bike and glide along the coast in either or both directions (about 30 minutes each way; for rental info see page 677). The path to the **west** stops just before the airport at perhaps the most scenic *boules* courts in France (for more on this game, see page 561). If you take the path heading **east,** you'll round Castle Hill to the harbor of Nice, with a chance to survey some fancy yachts.
• *Start your walk at the pink-domed...*

Hôtel Negresco

Nice's finest hotel is also a historic monument, offering up the city's most expensive beds and a museum-like interior. If you wonder why such a grand hotel has such an understated entry, it's because today's front door was originally the back door. In the 19th century, elegant people stayed out of the sun, and any posh hotel that cared about its clientele would design its entry on the shady north side. If you walk around to the back you'll see a grand but unused front door.

The hotel is technically off-limits to non-guests, but if you explain to the doorman that you'd like to shop at their store or get a drink at Negresco's Bar (opens 11:30 in high season, 14:30 in off-season), you may be allowed past the registration desk.

If you do get in, walk straight until you reach a huge ballroom, the **Salon Royal.** The chandelier hanging from its Eiffel-built dome is made of 16,000 pieces of crystal. It was built in France for the Russian czar's Moscow palace...but thanks to the Bolshevik Revolution in 1917, he couldn't take delivery. Bronze portrait busts of Czar Alexander III and his wife, Maria Feodorovna—who returned to her native Denmark after the revolution—are to the right, facing the shops. Circle the interior and then the perimeter to enjoy both historic and modern art. Fine portraits include Emperor Napoleon III and wife Empress Eugénie (who acquired Nice for France from Italy in 1860), and Jeanne Augier (who owns the hotel).
• *Across the street from the Hôtel Negresco to the east is...*

Nice at a Glance

▲▲▲Promenade des Anglais Nice's sun-struck seafront promenade. **Hours:** Always open. See page 681.

▲▲▲Chagall Museum The world's largest collection of Marc Chagall's work, popular even with people who don't like modern art. **Hours:** May-Oct Wed-Mon 10:00-18:00, Nov-April Wed-Mon 10:00-17:00, closed Tue year-round. See page 692.

▲▲Vieux Nice Charming old city offering enjoyable atmosphere and a look at Nice's French-Italian cultural blend. **Hours:** Always open. See page 685.

▲Matisse Museum Modest collection of Henri Matisse's paintings, sketches, and paper cutouts. **Hours:** Wed-Mon 10:00-18:00, closed Tue. See page 694.

▲Russian Cathedral Finest Orthodox church outside Russia. **Hours:** Tue-Sat 9:00-12:00 & 14:00-19:00, Sun 9:00-12:00, closed Mon. See page 696.

▲Castle Hill Site of an ancient fort boasting great views. **Hours:** Park closes at 20:00 in summer, earlier off-season. See page 696.

Modern and Contemporary Art Museum Ultramodern museum with enjoyable collection from the 1960s and '70s, including Warhol and Lichtenstein. **Hours:** Tue-Sun 10:00-18:00, closed Mon. See page 695.

Fine Arts Museum Lush villa shows off impressive paintings by Monet, Sisley, Bonnard, and Raoul Dufy. **Hours:** Tue-Sun 10:00-18:00, closed Mon. See page 695.

Masséna Museum Lavish beachfront mansion houses museum of city history, including exhibits of Napoleonic paraphernalia and images of Nice over the years. **Hours:** Wed-Mon 10:00-18:00, closed Tue. See page 695.

Villa Masséna

When Nice became part of France, France invested heavily in what it expected to be the country's new high-society retreat—an elite resort akin to Russia's Sochi. The government built this fine palace for the military hero of the Napoleonic age, Jean-Andre Masséna, and his family. Take a moment to stroll around the lovely garden (free, open daily 10:00-18:00).

The Masséna Museum inside (described on page 695) offers an interesting look at belle-époque Nice.

• *From Villa Masséna, head for the beach and begin your Promenade des Anglais stroll. But first, grab a blue chair and gaze out to the...*

Bay of Angels (Baie des Anges)

Face the water. The body of Nice's patron saint, Réparate, was supposedly escorted into this bay by angels in the fourth century. To your right is where you might have been escorted into France—Nice's airport, built on a massive landfill. The tip of land beyond the runway is Cap d'Antibes. Until 1860, Antibes and Nice were in different countries—Antibes was French, but Nice was a protectorate of the Italian kingdom of Savoy-Piedmont, a.k.a. the Kingdom of Sardinia. During that period, the Var River—just west of Nice—was the geographic border between these two peoples (and to this day the river functions as a kind of cultural border). In 1850 the people here spoke Italian and ate pasta. As Italy was uniting, the region was given a choice: Join the new country of Italy or join France (which was enjoying prosperous times under the rule of Napoleon III). The vast majority voted in 1860 to go French...and *voilà!* (While that was the official story, in reality the Italian king needed France's support in helping Italian regions controlled by Austria break away to join the emerging union of Italian states. Italy's price for France's support against Austria: the city and region of Nice.)

The lower green hill to your left is Castle Hill (the end of this walk). Farther left lie Villefranche-sur-Mer and Cap Ferrat (marked by the tower at land's end, and home to lots of millionaires), then Monaco (which you can't see, with more millionaires), then Italy. Behind you are the foothills of the Alps, which trap threatening clouds, ensuring that the Côte d'Azur enjoys sunshine more than 300 days each year. While half a million people live here, pollution is carefully treated—the water is routinely tested and is very clean. But with climate change, the warmer water is attracting jellyfish in the summer, making swimming a stinging memory.

• *With the sea on your right, begin strolling.*

The Promenade

Nearby sit two fine belle-époque establishments: the West End and Westminster hotels, both boasting English names to help those original guests feel at home (the West End is now part of the Best Western group...to help American guests feel at home). These hotels symbolize Nice's arrival as a tourist mecca in the 19th century, when the combination of leisure time and a stable economy allowed visitors to find the sun even in winter.

Along the first portion of this promenade, you may notice memorials commemorating those who died in the July 2016 terror attack here. As you walk, be careful to avoid the green bike lane. The promenade you're walking on was originally much narrower. It's been widened over the years to keep up with tourist demand, including increased bicycle use.

You'll pass a number of separate rocky beaches. You can go local and rent gear—about €16 for a *chaise longue* (long chair) and a *transat* (mattress), €6 for an umbrella, and €6 for a towel. You'll also pass several beach restaurants. Some of these eateries serve breakfast, all serve lunch, some do dinner, and a few have beachy bars...tailor-made for a break from this walk.

Find the easel showing a painting of La Jetée Promenade. Even a hundred years ago, there was sufficient tourism in Nice to justify building its first casino (a leisure activity imported from Venice). Part of an elegant casino, La Jetée Promenade stood on those white-covered pilings (with flags flapping) just offshore, until the Germans destroyed it during World War II. When La Jetée was thriving, it took gamblers two full days to get to the Riviera by train from Paris. The painting shows how much of an event strolling the Promenade was—like going to the Opera, it was all about dressing up, being seen, and looking good.

Although La Jetée Promenade is gone, you can still see the striking 1927 Art Nouveau facade of the **Palais de la Méditerranée,** a grand casino, hotel, and theater. It became one of the grandest casinos in Europe, and today is one of France's most exclusive hotels, though the casino feels cheap and cheesy, and the architecture overbearing.

The unappealing Casino Ruhl (with the most detested facade on the strip) disfigures the next block. Anyone can drop in for some one-armed-bandit fun, but to play the tables at night you'll need to dress up and bring your passport.

Albert I Park is named for the Belgian king who enjoyed wintering here—these were his private gardens. While the English came first, the Belgians and Russians were also big fans of 19th-century Nice. That tall statue at the edge of the park commemorates the 100-year anniversary of Nice's union with France. The happy statue features two beloved women embracing the idea of union (Marianne—Ms. Liberty, Equality, and Brotherhood, and the symbol of the Republic of France—and Catherine Ségurane, a 16th-century heroine who helped Nice against the Saracen pirates).

The park is a long, winding greenbelt called the Promenade du Paillon. The Paillon River flows under the park on its way to the sea. This is the historical divide between Vieux Nice and the new town. Continue along, past the vintage belle-époque carousel. You're now on Quai des Etats-Unis ("Quay of the United States").

This name was given as a tip-of-the-cap to the Americans for finally entering World War I in 1917. The big, blue chair statue celebrates the inviting symbol of this venerable walk and kicks off the best stretch of beach—quieter and with less traffic. Check out the laid-back couches at the Plage Beau Rivage lounge and consider a beachfront drink.

Those tall, rusted **steel girders** reaching for the sky were erected in 2010 to celebrate the 150th anniversary of Nice's union with France. (The seven beams represent the seven valleys of the Nice region.) Done by the same artist who created the popular Arc of the Riviera sculpture in the parkway near Place Masséna, this "art" justifiably infuriates many locals as an ugly waste of money.

A block ahead, on the left, the elegant back side of Nice's opera house faces the sea. In front of it, a tiny bronze Statue of Liberty reminds all that this stretch of seafront promenade is named for the USA. The long, low building lining the walk on the left once served the city's fishermen. Behind its gates bustles the Cours Saleya Market—long the heart and soul of Vieux Nice, with handy WCs under its arches.

Farther along, on the far right side of the Quai des Etats-Unis, find the three-foot-tall white **metal winch.** It's a reminder that long before tourism and long before Nice dredged its harbor, hardworking fishing boats, rather than vacationing tourists, lined the beach. The boats were hauled in through the surf by winches like this and tied to the iron rings on either side.

• *Your walk is over. From here you have several great options: Continue 10 minutes along the coast to the* ***port***, *around the foot of Castle Hill (fine views of the entire promenade and a monumental war memorial carved into the hillside); hike or ride the elevator up to* ***Castle Hill*** *(catch the elevator next to Hôtel Suisse, see listing for Castle Hill on page 696); head into the* ***old town*** *(you can follow my "Old Nice Walk," next); or grab a blue chair or piece of* ***beach*** *and just be on vacation—Riviera style.*

OLD NICE WALK

This self-guided walk through Nice's old town, known as **Vieux Nice,** gives you a helpful introduction to the city's bicultural heritage and its most interesting neighborhoods. Allow about an hour at a leisurely pace for this level walk from Place Masséna to Place Rossetti (rated ▲▲). It's best done in the morning (while the outdoor market thrives), and preferably not on a Sunday, when things are quiet. This ramble is also a joy at night, when fountains glow and pedestrians control the streets.

• *Start where Avenue Jean Médecin hits the people-friendly Place Masséna—the successful result of a long, expensive city upgrade and the new center of Nice.*

Vieux Nice Hotels & Restaurants

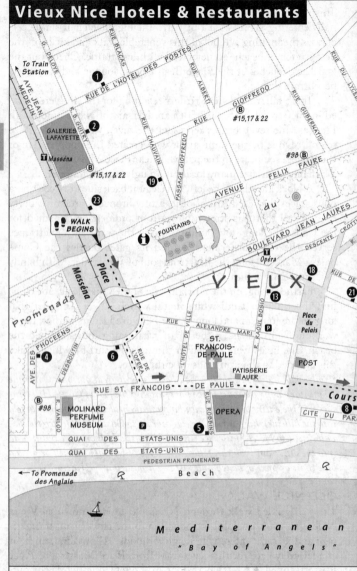

1. Hôtel Lafayette
2. Villa Saint Exupéry Beach Hostel
3. Hôtel la Perouse & Hôtel Suisse
4. Hôtel Albert 1er
5. Hôtel Mercure Marché aux Fleurs
6. Hôtel de la Mer & Suites Masséna
7. Le Safari Restaurant
8. Pizzeria Rossopomodoro
9. L'Acchiardo Restaurant
10. Chez Palmyre Restaurant
11. Bistrot du Fromager
12. Bistrot D'Antoine
13. La Merenda Restaurant
14. Lou Pilha Leva Restaurant
15. Oliviera Shop/Restaurant
16. Restaurant Castel

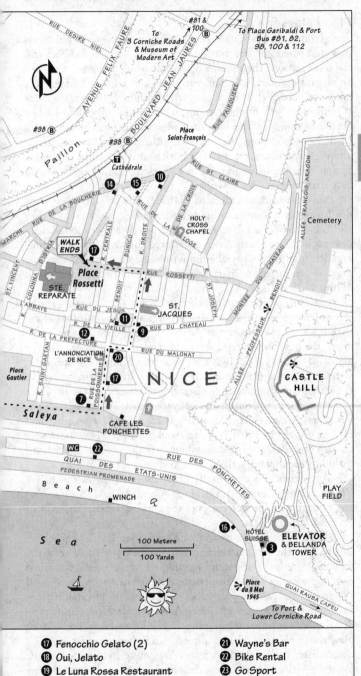

RIVIERA

⑰ Fenocchio Gelato (2)
⑱ Oui, Jelato
⑲ Le Luna Rossa Restaurant
⑳ Distilleries Ideales

㉑ Wayne's Bar
㉒ Bike Rental
㉓ Go Sport

Place Masséna

The grand Place Masséna is Nice's drawing room, where old meets new, and where the tramway bends between Vieux (Old) Nice and the train station. The square's black-and-white pavement feels like an elegant outdoor ballroom, with the sleek tram waltzing across its dance floor. While once congested with cars, the square today is frequented only by these trams, which swoosh silently by every couple of minutes. The men on pedestals sitting high above are modern-art additions that arrived with the tram. For a mood-altering experience, return after dark and watch the illuminated figures float yoga-like above. Place Masséna is at its sophisticated best after the sun goes down.

This vast square dates from 1848 and pays tribute to Jean-André Masséna, a French military leader during the Revolutionary and Napoleonic wars. Not just another pretty face in a long lineup of French military heroes, he's considered among the greatest commanders in history—anywhere, anytime. Napoleon called him "the greatest name of my military Empire." No wonder this city is proud of him.

Standing on the square with your back to the fountains, start a clockwise spin tour: The towering **modern swoosh sculpture** in the park is meant to represent the "curve of the French Riviera"—the arc of the bay. To the right stretches modern Nice, born with the arrival of tourism in the 1800s. **Avenue Jean Médecin,** Nice's main street, cuts from here through the new town to the train station. In the distance are the tracks, the freeway, and the Alps beyond. Once crammed with cars, buses, and delivery vehicles tangling with pedestrians, Avenue Jean Médecin was turned into a walking and cycling nirvana in 2007. I used to avoid this street. Now I can't get enough of it. Businesses along it flourish in the welcoming environment of generous sidewalks and no traffic.

Appreciate the city's Italian heritage—it feels as much like Venice as Paris. The portico flanking Avenue Jean Médecin is Italian, not French. The rich colors of the buildings reflect the taste of previous Italian rulers.

Turn to the fountains and look east to see Nice's ongoing effort to "put the human element into the heart of the town." An ugly concrete bus station and parking structure were demolished not long ago, and the **Promenade du Paillon** was created to fill the space. Today, this pedestrian-friendly parkway extends from the sea to the Museum of Modern Art—a modern-day Promenade des Anglais. Forming a key spine for biking, walking, and kids at play, this ambitious 30-acre project is another example of Nice's determination to make its urban center more livable. Notice the fountain—its surprise geysers delight children by day and its fine lighting enhances romance at night. Beyond the fountain stands a bronze statue of the square's namesake, Masséna. The hills beyond separate Nice from Villefranche-sur-Mer. A stroll down the Promenade du Paillon is a delight any time of day.

Turn farther to the right to see the old town, with its jumbled and colorful facades below Castle Hill. The **statue of Apollo** has horsy hair and holds a beach towel, as if to say, "It's beer o'clock, let's go."

• *Walk past Apollo into the old town. A block down Rue de l'Opéra, you'll see a grouping of rusted beams (described on page 685). Turn left onto Rue St. François de Paule.*

(described on page 685)

RIVIERA

Rue St. François de Paule

This colorful street leads into the heart of Vieux Nice. On the left is the Hôtel de Ville (City Hall). Peer into the **Alziari olive oil shop** (at #14 on the right). Dating from 1868, the shop produces top-quality stone-ground olive oil. The proud and charming owner, Gilles Piot, claims that stone wheels create less acidity, since metal grinding builds up heat (see photo in back over the door). Locals fill their own containers from the huge vats.

La Couqueto is a colorful shop filled with Provençal handicrafts, including lovely folk characters *(santons)*. Walk in for a lavender smell sensation—is madame working the sewing machine upstairs?

Next door is Nice's grand **opera house.** Imagine this opulent jewel back in the 19th century, buried deep in the old town of Nice. With all the fancy big-city folks wintering here, this rough-edged town needed some high-class entertainment. And Victorians needed an alternative to those "devilish" gambling houses. (Queen Victoria, so disgusted at casinos, would actually close the drapes on her train window when passing Monte Carlo.) The four statues on top represent theater, dance, music, and party poopers.

Across the street, **Pâtisserie Auer**'s grand old storefront would love to tempt you with chocolates and candied fruits. It's changed little over the centuries. The writing on the window says, "Since 1820 from father to son." The gold royal shields on the back wall remind shoppers that Queen Victoria indulged her sweet tooth here.

• *Continue on, sifting your way through a cluttered block of tacky souvenir shops to the big market square.*

Cours Saleya

Named for its broad exposure to the sun *(soleil)*, Cours Saleya (koor sah-lay-yuh)—a commotion of color, sights, smells, and people—has been Nice's main market square since the Middle Ages (flower market all day Tue-Sun, produce market Tue-Sun until 13:00, antiques on Mon). While you're greeted by the ugly mouth of an underground parking lot, much of this square itself was a parking lot until 1980, when the mayor of Nice had this solution dug.

The first section is devoted to the Riviera's largest flower market. In operation since the 19th century, this market offers plants and flowers that grow effortlessly and ubiquitously in this climate, including the local favorites: carnations, roses, and jasmine. Locals know the season by what's on sale (mimosas in February, violets in March, and so on). Until the recent rise in imported flowers, this region supplied all of France with flow-

ers. Still, fresh flowers are cheap here, the best value in this notoriously expensive city. The Riviera's three big industries are tourism, flowers, and perfume (made from these flowers...take a whiff).

The boisterous produce section trumpets the season with mushrooms, strawberries, white asparagus, zucchini flowers, and more—whatever's fresh gets top billing. What's in season today?

The market opens up at Place Pierre Gautier. It's also called Plassa dou Gouvernou—you'll see bilingual street signs here that include the old Niçois language, an Italian dialect. This is where farmers set up stalls to sell their produce and herbs directly.

Look up to the **hill** that dominates to the east. In the Middle Ages, a massive castle stood there with soldiers at the ready. Over time, the city grew down to where you are now. With the river guarding one side (running under today's Promenade du Paillon parkway) and the sea the other, this mountain fortress seemed strong—until Louis XIV leveled it in 1706. Nice's medieval seawall ran along the line of two-story buildings where you're standing.

Now, look across Place Pierre Gautier to the large "palace." The **Ducal Palace** was where the kings of Sardinia, the city's Italian rulers until 1860, resided when in Nice. (For centuries, Nice was under the rule of the Italian capital of Torino.) Today, the palace is the local police headquarters. The land upon which the Cours Saleya sits was once the duke's gardens and didn't become a market until Nice's union with France.

• *Continue down Cours Saleya. The faded golden building that seals the end of the square is where Henri Matisse spent 17 years. I imagine he was inspired by his view. The* **Café les Ponchettes** *is perfectly positioned for you to enjoy the view too if you want a coffee break. At the café, turn onto...*

Rue de la Poissonnerie

Look up at the first floor of the first building on your right. **Adam and Eve** are squaring off, each holding a zucchini-like gourd. This scene represents the annual rapprochement in Nice to make up for the sins of a too-much-fun Carnival (Mardi Gras, the pre-Lenten festival). Residents of Nice have partied hard during Carnival for more than 700 years.

Next, check out the small **Baroque church** (Notre-Dame de l'Annonciation) dedicated to Ste. Rita, the patron saint of desperate causes and desperate people (see display in window). She holds a special place in locals' hearts, making this the most popular church in Nice. Drop in for a peek at the dazzling Baroque. Inside, the first chapel on the right is dedicated to St. Erasmus, protector of mariners.

• *Turn right on the next street, where you'll pass Vieux Nice's most happening bar (Distilleries Ideales), with a Pirates of the Caribbean-style interior. Pause at the next corner and simply study the classic Vieux Nice scene. Now turn left on Rue Droite and enter an area that feels like Little Naples.*

Rue Droite

In the Middle Ages, this straight, skinny street provided the most direct route from river to sea within the old walled town. Pass the recommended restaurant L'Acchiardo. Notice stepped lanes leading uphill to the castle. Stop at **Espuno's bakery** (at Place du Jésus) and say "*Bonjour,* what's cooking?" to Natalie from England and her husband, Fabrice, who's from here. Notice the firewood stacked behind the oven. Try the house specialty, *tourte aux blettes* (sweet or savory)—a tart stuffed with Swiss chard, apples, pine nuts, and raisins. Ask if Fabrice is making scones.

Pop into the Jesuit **Eglise St-Jacques** (also called Eglise du Gésu) for an explosion of Baroque exuberance hidden behind that plain facade.

We're turning left onto Rue Rosetti...but if you continued another block along Rue Droite you'd find the **Palais Lascaris** (c. 1647), home of one of Nice's most prestigious families. Today it's a museum (covered by Nice museum combo-ticket and worth a quick look). Inside you'll find a collection of antique musical instruments—harps, guitars, violins, and violas (good English explanations) along with elaborate tapestries and a few well-furnished rooms. The palace has four levels: The ground floor was used for storage, the first floor was devoted to reception rooms (and musical events), the owners lived a floor above that, and the servants lived at the top. Look up and make faces back at the guys under the balconies.

• *You'll cross Rue Benoît shortly after making a left on Rue Rosetti.*

In the 18th century, Rue Benoît served as a **ghetto** for Nice's Jews. At sunset, gates would seal the street at either end, locking people in until daylight. To identify Jews as non-Christians, the men were forced to wear yellow stars and the women wore yellow scarves. The white columns across from #19 mark what was the synagogue until 1848, when revolution ended the notion of ghettos in France.

• *Continue down Rue Rosetti to...*

Place Rossetti

The most Italian of Nice's piazzas, Place Rossetti comes alive after dark—in part because of the **Fenocchio gelato shop,** popular for its many innovative flavors.

Check out the **Cathedral of St. Réparate**—an unassuming building for a big city cathedral. It was relocated here in the 1500s, when Castle Hill was temporarily converted to military use only. The name comes from Nice's patron saint, a teenage virgin named Réparate, whose martyred body, accompanied by angels, floated to Nice in the fourth century. The beautiful interior is worth a wander.

• *This is the end of our walk. From here you can hike up **Castle Hill** (from Place Rossetti, take Rue Rossetti uphill; see Castle Hill listing on page 696). Or you can have an ice cream and browse the colorful lanes of Vieux Nice. Or you can grab Apollo and hit the beach.*

Sights in Nice

Some of Nice's top attractions—the Promenade des Anglais, the beach, and the old town—are covered earlier in my self-guided walks. But Nice offers some worthwhile sights as well.

MUSEUMS

All of Nice's museums (except the Chagall Museum) share the same €10 **combo-ticket** (valid 48 hours, €20/7 days, buy at any participating museum). The Chagall Museum is a separate €8 admission (and well worth it).

The first two museums (Chagall and Matisse) are a long walk northeast of Nice's city center. Because they're in the same direction and served by the same bus line (see below), try to visit them on the same trip. From Place Masséna, the Chagall Museum is a 10-minute bus ride, and the Matisse Museum is a few stops beyond that.

▲▲▲Chagall Museum (Musée National Marc Chagall)

Even if you don't get modern art, this museum—with the world's largest collection of Marc Chagall's work in captivity—is a delight. After World War II, Chagall returned from the United States to settle in Vence, not far from Nice. Between 1954 and 1967 he painted a cycle of 17 large murals designed for, and donated to, this museum. These paintings, inspired by the biblical books of Genesis, Exodus, and the Song of Songs, make up the "nave," or core, of what Chagall called the "House of Brotherhood."

Cost and Hours: €8, €1-2 more with special exhibits, includes audioguide, Wed-Mon 10:00-18:00, Nov-April until 17:00, closed Tue year-round, Avenue Docteur Ménard, tel. 04 93 53 87 20, http://en.musees-nationaux-alpesmaritimes.fr. An idyllic **$** café awaits in the corner of the garden.

Getting There: Taxis to and from the city center cost about €12. Buses connect the museum with downtown Nice and the train station. From downtown, catch bus #15 (Mon-Sat 6/hour, 10 minutes; on Sun take bus #22). Catch either bus from the east end of the Galeries Lafayette department store, near the Masséna tram stop, on Rue Sacha Guitry (see map on page 674). Watch for a *Musée Chagall* sign on the bus shelter where you'll get off (on Boulevard de Cimiez).

Visiting the Museum: This small museum consists of six rooms: two rooms (the main hall and Song of Songs room) with

the 17 murals, two rooms for special exhibits, an auditorium with stained-glass windows, and a mosaic-lined pond (viewed from inside).

In the **main hall** you'll find the core of the collection (Genesis and Exodus scenes). Each painting is a lighter-than-air collage of images that draws from Chagall's Russian folk-village youth, his Jewish heritage, biblical themes, and his feeling that he existed somewhere between heaven and earth. He believed that the Bible was a synonym for nature, and that color and biblical themes were key to understanding God's love for his creation. Chagall's brilliant blues and reds celebrate nature, as do his spiritual and folk themes. Notice the focus on couples. To Chagall, humans loving each other mirrored God's love of creation. The painted harpsichord is the latest addition to the museum.

The adjacent **octagonal room** houses five more paintings. The paintings in this room were inspired by the Old Testament Song of Songs. Chagall was one of the few "serious" 20th-century artists to portray unabashed love. Where the Bible uses the metaphor of earthly, physical, sexual love to describe God's love for humans, Chagall uses unearthly colors and a mystical ambience to celebrate human love. These red-toned canvases are hard to interpret literally, but they capture the rosy spirit of a man in love with life.

Back near the entry, the wall **mosaic** reflected in the pond evokes the prophet Elijah in his chariot of fire (from the Second Book of Kings)—with Chagall's own addition of the 12 signs of the zodiac, which he used to symbolize time.

The **auditorium** is worth a peaceful moment to enjoy three Chagall stained-glass windows depicting the seven days of creation. This is also where you'll find a wonderful film (52 minutes) on Chagall, which plays at the top of each hour (not available during special exhibits).

Leaving the Museum: From here, you can return to downtown Nice or the train station area, or go to the Matisse Museum. Taxis usually wait in front of the museum. For the bus back to downtown Nice, turn right out of the museum, then make another right down Boulevard de Cimiez, and ride bus #15 or #22 heading downhill. To continue on to the Matisse Museum, catch #15 or #22 using the uphill stop located across the street. To walk to the train station area from the museum takes about 20 minutes (turn left out of the museum, take your first left, and then go left down the path at the green wall then cross under the highway).

▲Matisse Museum (Musée Matisse)

This small and neglected little museum, which fills an old mansion in a park surrounded by scant Roman ruins, contains a sampling of works from the various periods of Henri Matisse's artistic career. The museum offers an introduction to the artist's many styles and materials, both shaped by Mediterranean light and by fellow Côte d'Azur artists Picasso and Renoir.

Matisse, the master of leaving things out, could suggest a woman's body with a single curvy line—letting the viewer's mind fill in the rest. Ignoring traditional 3-D perspective, he expressed his passion for life through simplified but recognizable scenes in which dark outlines and saturated, bright blocks of color create an overall decorative pattern. As you tour the museum, look for Matisse's favorite motifs—including fruit, flowers, wallpaper, and sunny rooms—often with a window opening onto a sunny landscape. Another favorite subject is the *odalisque* (harem concubine), usually shown sprawled in a seductive pose and with a simplified, masklike face. You'll also see a few souvenirs from his travels, which influenced much of his work.

Cost and Hours: Covered by €10 Nice combo-ticket—described earlier, Wed-Mon 10:00-18:00, closed Tue, 164 Avenue des Arènes de Cimiez, tel. 04 93 81 08 08, www.musee-matisse-nice.org.

Getting There: Take a cab (€15 from Promenade des Anglais). Alternately, hop bus #15 Mon-Sat or #22 on Sun (see getting to Chagall Museum above; from train station catch #17). Get off at the Arènes-Matisse bus stop (look for the crumbling Roman arena), then walk 50 yards into the park to find the pink villa.

Leaving the Museum: Turn left from the museum into the park, exiting at the Archaeological Museum, and turn right at the street. The bus stop across the street is for bus #17, which goes to the train station, and #20, which heads to the port. For buses #15 and #22 (frequent service to downtown and the Chagall Museum), continue to walk—with the Roman ruins on your right—to the small roundabout, and find the shelter (facing downhill).

Modern and Contemporary Art Museum (Musée d'Art Moderne et d'Art Contemporain)

This ultramodern museum features an explosively colorful, far-out, yet manageable collection focused on American and European-American artists from the 1960s and 1970s (Pop Art and New Realism are highlighted). The exhibits cover three floors and include a few works by Andy Warhol, Roy Lichtenstein, and Jean Tinguely, and images of Christo's famous wrappings. You'll find rooms dedicated to Robert Indiana, Yves Klein, and Niki de Saint Phalle. Don't leave without exploring the views from the rooftop terrace.

Cost and Hours: Covered by €10 Nice combo-ticket, Tue-Sun 10:00-18:00, closed Mon, near Vieux Nice on Promenade des Arts, tel. 04 93 62 61 62, www.mamac-nice.org.

Fine Arts Museum (Musée des Beaux-Arts)

Housed in a sumptuous Riviera villa with lovely gardens, this museum holds 6,000 artworks from the 17th to 20th centuries. Start on the first floor and work your way up to enjoy paintings by Monet, Sisley, Bonnard, and Raoul Dufy, as well as a few sculptures by Rodin and Carpeaux.

Cost and Hours: Covered by €10 Nice combo-ticket, Tue-Sun 10:00-18:00, closed Mon; inconveniently located at the western end of Nice, take bus #12 from train station to Rosa Bonheur stop and walk to 3 Avenue des Baumettes; tel. 04 92 15 28 28, www.musee-beaux-arts-nice.org.

Archaeological Museum (Musée Archéologique)

This museum displays various objects from the Romans' occupation of this region. It's convenient—just below the Matisse Museum—but has little of interest to anyone but ancient Rome aficionados.

Cost and Hours: Covered by €10 Nice combo-ticket, Wed-Mon 10:00-18:00, closed Tue, near Matisse Museum at 160 Avenue des Arènes de Cimiez, tel. 04 93 81 59 57.

Masséna Museum (Musée Masséna)

Like Nice's main square, this museum was named in honor of Jean-André Masséna (born in Antibes), a highly regarded commander during France's Revolutionary and Napoleonic wars. The beachfront mansion is worth a look for its lavish decor and lovely gardens alone (no English labels in museum, but a €3 booklet in English is available).

Cost and Hours: Covered by €10 Nice combo-ticket, always free to enter gardens, Wed-Mon 10:00-18:00, closed Tue, 35 Promenade des Anglais, tel. 04 93 91 19 10.

OTHER SIGHTS IN NICE
▲Russian Cathedral (Cathédrale Russe)

Nice's Russian Orthodox church—claimed by some to be the finest outside Russia—is worth a visit. Five hundred rich Russian families wintered in Nice in the late 19th century, and they needed a worthy Orthodox house of worship. Czar Nicholas I's widow provided the land and Czar Nicholas II gave this church to the Russian community in 1912. (A few years later, Russian comrades who *didn't* winter on the Riviera assassinated him.) Here in the land of olives and anchovies, these proud onion domes seem odd. But, I imagine, so did those old Russians.

Pick up an English info sheet on your way in. The one-room interior is filled with icons and candles, and traditional Russian music adds to the ambience. The park around the church makes a fine setting for picnics.

Cost and Hours: Free; Tue-Sun 9:00-12:00 & 14:00-18:00, Mon 9:00-12:00; chanted services Sat at 17:30 or 18:00, Sun at 10:00; no tourist visits during services, no shorts, 17 Boulevard du Tzarewitch, tel. 04 93 96 88 02, www.cathedrale-russe-nice.ru/fr.

▲Castle Hill (Colline du Château)

This hill—in an otherwise flat city center—offers sensational views over Nice, the port (to the east, created for trade and military use in the 15th century), the foothills of the Alps, and the Mediterranean. The views are best early, at sunset, or whenever the weather's clear.

Nice was founded on this hill. Its residents were crammed onto the hilltop until the 12th century, as it was too risky to live in the flatlands below. Today you'll find a playground, a café, and a cemetery—but no castle—on Castle Hill.

Cost and Hours: Park is free and closes at 20:00 in summer, earlier off-season.

Getting There: You can get to the top by foot, by elevator (free, daily 10:00-19:00, until 20:00 in summer, next to beachfront Hôtel Suisse), or by pricey tourist train (see page 680).

See the "Promenade des Anglais Walk" on page 681 for a pleasant stroll that ends near Castle Hill.

Leaving Castle Hill: After enjoying the views and hilltop fun, you can walk via the cemetery directly down into Vieux Nice (just follow the signs), descend to the beach (via the elevator or a stepped lane next to it), or hike down the back side to Nice's port (departure point for boat trips and buses to Monaco and Ville-franche-sur-Mer).

EXCURSION FROM NICE
Narrow-Gauge Train into the Alps
(Chemins de Fer de Provence)

Leave the tourists behind and take the scenic train-bus-train combination that runs between Nice and Digne through canyons, along whitewater rivers, and through tempting villages (5/day, departs Nice from Chemins de Fer de Provence Station, two blocks from the Libération tram stop, 4 Rue Alfred Binet, tel. 04 97 03 80 80, www.trainprovence.com).

An appealing stop on the scenic railway is little **Entrevaux,** a good destination that feels forgotten and still stuck in its medieval shell (about €25 round-trip, 1.5 scenic hours from Nice). Cross the bridge, meet someone friendly, and consider the steep hike up to the citadel (€3, TI tel. 04 93 05 46 73). Sisteron's Romanesque church and the view from the citadel above make this town worth a stop.

Nightlife in Nice

The city is a walker's delight after dark. Promenade des Anglais, Cours Saleya, Vieux Nice, Promenade du Paillon, and Place Masséna are all worth an evening wander. I can't get enough of the night scene on Place Masséna and around the adjacent fountains.

Nice's bars play host to a happening late-night scene, filled with jazz, rock, and trolling singles. Most activity focuses on Vieux Nice. Rue de la Préfecture and Place du Palais are ground zero for bar life, though Place Rossetti and Rue Droite are also good targets. **Distilleries Ideales** is a good place to start or end your evening, with a lively international crowd, a *Pirates of the Caribbean* interior, and a *Cheers* vibe (15 beers on tap, where Rue de la Poissonnerie and Rue Barillerie meet, happy hour 18:00-21:00). **Wayne's Bar** is a happening spot for the younger, English-speaking backpacker crowd (15 Rue Préfecture; see map on page 686 for both bar locations). Along the Promenade des Anglais, the plush bar at **Hôtel Negresco** is fancy-cigar old English.

Sleeping in Nice

Don't look for charm in Nice. I prefer to stay in the new town—a 10-minute walk from the old town—for modern, clean, and air-conditioned rooms. The rates listed here are for April through

Sleep Code

Hotels are classified based on the average price of a standard double room without breakfast in high season.

$$$$	**Splurge:** Most rooms over €200
$$$	**Pricier:** €150-200
$$	**Moderate:** €100-150
$	**Budget:** €50-100
¢	**Backpacker:** Under €50
RS%	**Rick Steves discount**
*	**French hotel rating system** (0-5 stars)

Unless otherwise noted, credit cards are accepted, hotel staff speak basic English, and free Wi-Fi is available. Comparison-shop by checking prices at several hotels (on each hotel's own website, on a booking site, or by email). For the best deal, *book directly with the hotel.* Ask for a discount if paying in cash; if the listing includes **RS%,** request a Rick Steves discount.

October. Prices generally drop considerably November through March, but go sky-high during the Nice Carnival (two weeks in mid-late-Feb, www.nicecarnaval.com), the Cannes Film Festival (12 days in mid-May, www.festival-cannes.com), and Monaco's Grand Prix (late May, www.acm.mc). Between the film festival and the Grand Prix, the second half of May is slammed. Nice is also one of Europe's top convention cities, and June is convention month here. For parking, ask your hotelier, or see "Arrival in Nice—By Car" on page 676.

IN THE CITY CENTER

The train station area offers Nice's cheapest sleeps, but the neighborhood can feel seedy after dark. The cheapest places are older, well-worn, and come with some street noise. Places closer to Avenue Jean Médecin are more expensive and in a more comfortable area.

$$ Hôtel Durante*** feels Mediterranean—a happy, orange building with rooms wrapped around a flowery courtyard. All but two of its quiet rooms overlook the well-maintained patio. The rooms are good enough (mostly modern decor), the price is right enough, and the parking is free on a first-come, first-served basis (family rooms, 16 Avenue Durante, tel. 04 93 88 84 40, www.hotel-durante.com, info@hotel-durante.com).

$$ Hôtel Lafayette,*** located a block behind the Galeries Lafayette department store, is a modest, homey place with 17 mostly spacious and good-value rooms (some with thin walls, some traffic noise, all one floor up from the street). It's family-run by Kiril and George (RS%, no elevator, 32 Rue de l'Hôtel des Postes—see

RIVIERA

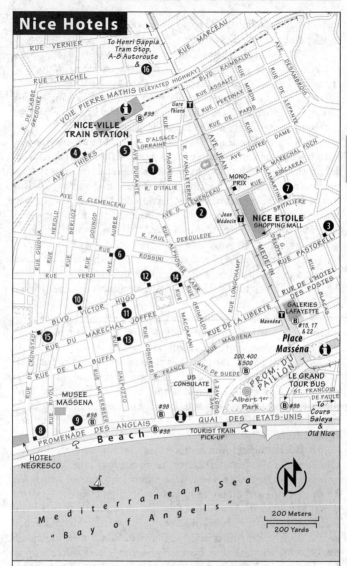

Nice Hotels

To Henri Sappia Tram Stop, A-8 Autoroute & ⑯

NICE-VILLE TRAIN STATION

Gare Thiers

NICE ETOILE SHOPPING MALL

MONO-PRIX

Jean Médecin

GALERIES LAFAYETTE

Masséna

Place Masséna

#15, 17 & 22

200, 400 & 500

US CONSULATE

#98

#98

Albert 1er Park

LE GRAND TOUR BUS
ST. FRANCOIS

#98

To Cours Saleya & Old Nice

MUSEE MASSENA

QUAI DES ETATS-UNIS

TOURIST TRAIN PICK-UP

Beach

HOTEL NEGRESCO

PROMENADE DES ANGLAIS

Mediterranean Sea
"Bay of Angels"

200 Meters
200 Yards

❶ Hôtel Durante
❷ Hôtel St. Georges
❸ Hôtel Vendôme
❹ Hôtel Ibis Nice Centre Gare
❺ Hôtel Belle Meunière
❻ B&B Nice Home Sweet Home
❼ Auberge de Jeunesse les Camélias
❽ Hôtel Negresco
❾ Hôtel West End
❿ Hôtels Splendid & Gounod
⓫ Hôtel Villa Victoria
⓬ Hôtel Carlton
⓭ Hôtel les Cigales
⓮ Hôtel Le Grimaldi
⓯ Hôtel Victor Hugo
⓰ To Chemins de Fer Station

map on page 686, tel. 04 93 85 17 84, www.hotellafayettenice.com, info@hotellafayettenice.com).

$$ Hôtel St. Georges,** five blocks from the station toward the sea, offers a good location, a pleasant backyard patio, and friendly Houssein at the reception. Rooms are dark and basic but adequate and fairly priced (family rooms, limited parking—book ahead, 7 Avenue Georges Clemenceau, tel. 04 93 88 79 21, www. hotelsaintgeorges.fr, contact@hotelsaintgeorges.fr).

$$$ Hôtel Vendôme*** gives you a whiff of the belle époque, with pink pastels, high ceilings, and grand staircases in a mansion set off the street. The modern rooms come in all sizes; many have balconies (limited pay parking—first-come, first-served; 26 Rue Pastorelli at the corner of Rue Alberti, tel. 04 93 62 00 77, www. hotel-vendome-nice.com, contact@vendome-hotel-nice.com).

$$ Hôtel Ibis Nice Centre Gare,*** 100 yards to the right as you leave the station, provides a secure refuge in this seedy area. It's big (200 rooms), modern, and a decent value with well-configured rooms, a refreshing pool, and cheap overnight parking (bar, café, 14 Avenue Thiers, tel. 04 93 88 85 85, www.ibishotel.com, h1396@ accor.com).

$ Hôtel Belle Meunière,* in an old mansion built for Napoleon III's mistress, attracts budget-minded travelers of all ages with cheap beds and private rooms a block below the train station. Creaky but well-kept, the place has adequate rooms, thin mattresses, and charismatic Mademoiselle Marie-Pierre presiding with her perfect English (family rooms, dorms, breakfast free if you book directly, no air-con, no elevator, laundry service, limited pay parking, 21 Avenue Durante, tel. 04 93 88 66 15, www.bellemeuniere. com, hotel.belle.meuniere@cegetel.net).

$ B&B Nice Home Sweet Home is a good-budget value. Genevieve (a.k.a. Jennifer) Levert rents out four large rooms and one small single in her home. Her rooms (only one of which has a private bath) are simply decorated, with high ceilings, big windows, and space to spread out (cheaper rooms with shared bath, includes breakfast, elevator, one floor up, pay washer/dryer, kitchen access, 35 Rue Rossini at intersection with Rue Auber, mobile 06 50 83 25 85, www.nicehomesweethome.com, glevert@free.fr).

Hostels: ¢ Auberge de Jeunesse les Camélias is a fun, good-value, and laid-back hostel with a handy location, modern facilities, and lively evening atmosphere (includes breakfast, rooms closed 11:00-15:00 but can leave bags, laundry, kitchen, safes, bar, 3 Rue Spitalieri, tel. 04 93 62 15 54, www.hihostels.com, accueil.nice@ hifrance.org).

¢ Villa Saint Exupéry Beach is a hostel-hotel in the center of Nice with a young and friendly vibe, fun bar, cheap restaurant, and *beaucoup* services including laundry, yoga classes, and scuba diving (no curfew, 6 Rue Sacha Guitry—see map on page 686, tel. 04 93 16 13 45, www.villahostels.com, beach@villahostels.com).

IN OR NEAR VIEUX NICE

These Vieux Nice hotels are either on the sea or within an easy walk of it. For locations, see the map on page 686.

$$$$ Hôtel la Perouse,** built into the rock of Castle Hill at the east end of the bay, is a fine splurge. This refuge-hotel is top-to-bottom flawless in every detail—from its elegant rooms (satin curtains, velour headboards) and attentive staff to its rooftop terrace with hot tub, sleek pool, and lovely **$$$$** garden restaurant. Sleep here to be spoiled and escape the big city (good family options, 11 Quai Rauba Capeu, tel. 04 93 62 34 63, www.hotel-la-perouse.com, lp@hotel-la-perouse.com).

$$$$ Hôtel Suisse,** below Castle Hill, has Nice's best sea and city views for the money, and is surprisingly quiet given the busy street below. Rooms are comfortable and the decor is tasteful, but the service feels impersonal. Sleep elsewhere if you don't land a view (most view rooms have balconies, 15 Quai Rauba Capeu, tel. 04 92 17 39 00, www.hotels-ocre-azur.com, hotel.suisse@hotels-ocre-azur.com).

$$$ Hôtel Albert 1er* is a fair deal in a great location on Albert I Park, two blocks from the beach and Place Masséna. The staff is formal and the rooms are well-appointed, with heavy brown tones. Some have views of the bay, others overlook the park, and some have small decks (4 Avenue des Phocéens, tel. 04 93 85 74 01, www.hotelalbert-1er.com, info@hotel-albert1er.com).

$$$ Hôtel Mercure Marché aux Fleurs** is ideally situated near the sea and Cours Saleya. Rooms are sharp, and prices can be either reasonable or exorbitant (superior rooms worth the extra euros, especially those with views; 91 Quai des Etats-Unis, tel. 04 93 85 74 19, www.hotelmercure.com, h0962@accor.com).

$$ Hôtel de la Mer is an intimate, 12-room place with an enviable position overlooking Place Masséna, just steps from Vieux Nice. Rooms are modern, comfortable, and well-priced (4 Place Masséna, tel. 04 93 92 09 10, www.hoteldelamernice.com, hotel.mer@wanadoo.fr). They also run the **$$$$ Suites Masséna** in the same building, with huge, modern, high-ceilinged rooms—designed for two but with room for three (tel. 04 93 13 48 11, www.lessuitesmassena.com).

NEAR THE PROMENADE DES ANGLAIS

These hotels are close to the beach. The Negresco and West End are big, vintage Nice hotels that open onto the sea from the heart of the Promenade des Anglais. For locations, see the map on page 699.

$$$$ Hôtel Negresco*** owns Nice's most prestigious address on the Promenade des Anglais and knows it. Still, it's the kind of place that if you were to splurge just once in your life... Rooms are opulent, tips are expected, and it seems the women staying here have cosmetically augmented lips (some view rooms, Old World bar, 37 Promenade des Anglais, tel. 04 93 16 64 00, www. hotel-negresco-nice.com, reservations@hotel-negresco.com).

$$$$ Hôtel West End**** opens onto the Promenade des Anglais with formal service and decor, classy public spaces, and high prices (some view rooms, 31 Promenade des Anglais, tel. 04 92 14 44 00, www.hotel-westend.com, reservation@westsendnice. com).

$$$$ Hôtel Splendid**** is a worthwhile splurge if you miss your Marriott. The panoramic rooftop pool, bar/restaurant, and breakfast room almost justify the cost...but throw in plush rooms, a free gym, and spa services, and you're as good as at home (pricey pay parking, 50 Boulevard Victor Hugo, tel. 04 93 16 41 00, www. splendid-nice.com, info@splendid-nice.com).

$$$$ Hôtel Villa Victoria**** is a fine place managed by cheery and efficient Marlena, who welcomes travelers into her spotless, classy old building with a spacious, attractive lobby overlooking a sprawling garden-courtyard. Rooms are plush and well-kept (pay parking, 33 Boulevard Victor Hugo, tel. 04 93 88 39 60, www.villa-victoria.com, contact@villa-victoria.com).

$$ Hôtel Carlton*** is well-run, unpretentious, and comfortable (26 Boulevard Victor Hugo, tel. 04 93 88 87 83, www.hotel-carlton-nice.com, info@hotel-carlton-nice.com).

$$ Hôtel les Cigales,*** a few blocks from the Promenade des Anglais, is a sweet little pastel place with 19 sharp rooms and a nifty upstairs terrace, all well-managed by friendly Stephane, Veronique, and Elaine (RS%, 16 Rue Dalpozzo, tel. 04 97 03 10 70, www.hotel-lescigales.com, info@hotel-lescigales.com).

$$$$ Le Grimaldi,**** a traditional place with an appealing lobby, rents 48 spacious rooms with high ceilings and tasteful decor (big breakfast extra, a few suites and connecting rooms ideal for families, 15 Rue Grimaldi, tel. 04 93 16 00 24, www.le-grimaldi. com, info@le-grimaldi.com).

$$$ Hôtel Gounod*** is behind Hôtel Splendid. Because the two share the same owners, Gounod's guests are allowed free access to Splendid's pool, hot tub, and other amenities. Most rooms are quiet, with high ceilings but tired bathrooms (family rooms, pay parking, 3 Rue Gounod, tel. 04 93 16 42 00, www.gounod-nice.com, info@gounod-nice.com).

$$ Hôtel Victor Hugo, a traditional and spotless seven-room hotel, is an adorable time-warp place where Gilles warmly welcomes guests. It's a short walk from the Promenade des Anglais but a long walk from Vieux Nice. All rooms come with mini kitchen-

Restaurant Price Code

I've assigned each eatery a price category, based on the average cost of a typical main course. Drinks, desserts, and splurge items (steak and seafood) can raise the price considerably.

$$$$ **Splurge:** Most main courses over €25
$$$ **Pricier:** €20-25
$$ **Moderate:** €15-20
$ **Budget:** Under €15

In France, a crêpe stand or other takeout spot is **$**; a sit-down brasserie, café, or bistro with affordable *plats du jour* is **$$**; a casual but more upscale restaurant is **$$$**; and a swanky splurge is **$$$$**.

ettes (RS%, includes breakfast, 59 Boulevard Victor Hugo, tel. 04 93 88 12 39, www.hotel-victor-hugo-nice.com).

NEAR THE AIRPORT

Several airport hotels offer a handy and cheap port-in-the-storm for those with early flights or who are just stopping in for a single night: **$$$ Hôtels Campanile** (www.campanile.fr) and **$$$ Nouvel** (www.novotel.com) are closest; **$$ Hôtel Ibis Budget Nice Aéroport** (www.ibis.com) is a few minutes away. Free shuttles connect these hotels with both airport terminals.

Eating in Nice

My favorite places to eat out are in Vieux Nice. It's well worth booking ahead for these spots—even just a day or two does it. If Vieux Nice is too far, I've listed some great places handier to your hotel. Promenade des Anglais is ideal for picnic dinners on warm, languid evenings or a meal at a beachside restaurant. For a more romantic (and expensive) meal, head for nearby Villefranche-sur-Mer (see page 719). Avoid the fun-to-peruse but terribly touristy eateries lining Rue Masséna.

IN VIEUX NICE

Nice's dinner scene converges on Cours Saleya, which is entertaining enough in itself to make the generally mediocre food a good deal. It's a fun, festive spot to compare tans and mussels. Most of my recommendations are on side lanes inland from here. Even if you're eating elsewhere, wander through here in the evening. For locations, see the map on page 686.

On Cours Saleya

While local foodies would avoid Cours Saleya like a McDonalds, the energy of wall-to-wall restaurants taking over the old town's market square each evening is enticing. Here are two good bets—one for local cuisine and the other for pizza.

$$$ Le Safari is a fair option for Niçois cuisine and outdoor dining. This venerable place, convivial and rustic with the coolest interior on the Cours, is packed with locals and tourists, and staffed with hurried waiters (open daily, 1 Cours Saleya, tel. 04 93 80 18 44, www.restaurantsafari.fr).

$ Pizzeria Rossopomodoro is a fun little place serving excellent, wood-fired Naples-style pizzas either inside or on the square (closed Wed and Sun, 26 Cours Saleya, tel. 04 93 80 02 99).

Characteristic Places in the Old Town

$$ L'Acchiardo is a homey eatery that mixes loyal clientele with hungry tourists. As soon as you sit down you know this is a treat. Its simple, hearty Niçois cuisine is served by Monsieur Acchiardo and his good-looking sons Jean-François and Raphael. The small plaque under the menu outside says the restaurant has been run by father and son since 1927 (closed Sat-Sun and Aug, indoor seating only, 38 Rue Droite, tel. 04 93 85 51 16).

$ Chez Palmyre, your best budget bet in the old town, is tiny and popular, so book ahead (two weeks is advised). The ambience is rustic and fun, with people squeezed onto shared tables to enjoy the home-style cooking. Philippe serves everyone his three-course, €17 *menu*, which changes every two weeks (closed Sat-Sun, 5 Rue Droite, tel. 04 93 85 72 32).

$$$ Bistrot du Fromager, run by brothers crazy about cheese and wine, is a find. Come here to escape the heat and dine in cozy, cool, vaulted cellars surrounded by shelves of wine. Hugo cooks while gregarious Gregoire serves delicious dishes featuring fresh fish, pasta, and ham—most with cheese as a key ingredient. This is a good choice for vegetarians, and for singles who enjoy eating at the counter and watching the chef work (book ahead, closed Sun for dinner, just off Place du Jésus at 29 Rue Benoît Bunico, tel. 04 93 13 07 83).

$$$ Bistrot D'Antoine has street appeal. It's a warm, popular, vine-draped option whose menu emphasizes Niçois cuisine and good grilled selections. The food is delicious and the prices are reasonable. Call several days ahead to reserve a table—the upstairs room is quieter (closed Sun-Mon, 27 Rue de la Préfecture, tel. 04 93 85 29 57).

$$ La Merenda is a shoebox where you'll sit on small stools and dine on simple, home-style dishes in a communal environment. The menu changes with the season, but the hardworking owner, Dominique, does not. This place fills fast, so arrive early, or better yet, drop by during lunch to reserve for dinner—there are two seatings at 19:00 and 21:00 (closed Sat-Sun, cash only, 4 Rue Raoul Bosio, no telephone).

$ Lou Pilha Leva delivers fun and cheap lunch or dinner options with Niçois specialties and always-busy, outdoor-only, picnic-table dining (daily, located where Rue de la Loge and Rue Centrale meet).

$$$ Oliviera venerates the French olive. This shop/restaurant serves both oil tastings and a menu of dishes paired with specific oils (like a wine pairing). Owner Nadim speaks excellent English, knows all his producers, and provides "Olive Oil 101" explanations with his tastings (best if you buy something afterward or have a meal). You'll learn how passionate he is about his products, and once you've had a taste, you'll want to stay and eat—allow €40 with wine (Tue-Sat 10:00-22:00, closed Sun-Mon, indoor seating only, 8 bis Rue du Collet, tel. 04 93 13 06 45).

Dining on the Beach

$$$$ Restaurant Castel is a fine eat-on-the-beach option, thanks to its location at the very east end of Nice, under Castle Hill. The city vanishes as you step down to the beach. The food is creative and nicely presented, and the tables feel elegant, even at the edge of the sand. Arrive for the sunset and you'll have an unforgettable meal (open for dinner mid-May-Aug, lunch April-Sept, 8 Quai des Etats-Unis, tel. 04 93 85 22 66, www.castelplage.com). Sunbathers can rent beach chairs and have drinks and meals served literally on the beach (lounge chairs €16/half-day, €19/day).

And for Dessert...

Gelato lovers should save room for the tempting ice-cream stands in Vieux Nice (open daily until late). **Fenocchio** is the city's favorite, with mouthwatering displays of dozens of flavors ranging from lavender to avocado (two locations: 2 Place Rossetti and 6 Rue de la Poissonnerie). Gelato connoisseurs should head for **Oui, Jelato,** where the quality is the priority rather than the selection (5 Rue de la Préfecture, on the Place du Palais).

IN THE CITY CENTER
Near Nice Etoile, on Rue Biscarra

An appealing lineup of bistros overflowing with outdoor tables stretches along the broad sidewalk on Rue Biscarra (just east of Avenue Jean Médecin behind Nice Etoile, all closed Sun). Come here to dine with area residents away from the tourists. **$$ Le 20 sur Vin** is a neighborhood favorite with a cozy, wine-bar-meets-café ambience (tel. 04 93 92 93 20).

RIVIERA

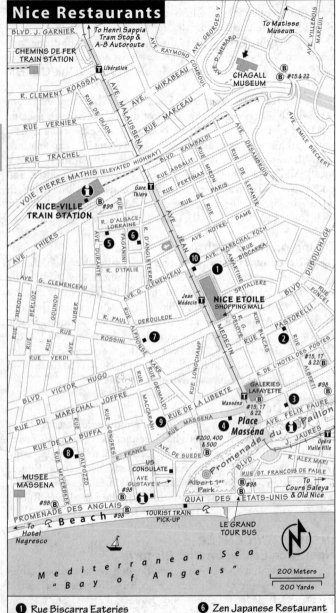

Nice Restaurants

1. Rue Biscarra Eateries
2. L'Ovale & Les 5 Sens Restaurants
3. Le Luna Rossa Restaurant
4. La Maison de Marie Rest.
5. Voyageur Nissart Rest.
6. Zen Japanese Restaurant
7. Rolancy's Restaurant & Bistrot des Viviers
8. Coco & Rico Restaurant
9. Crêperie Bretonne
10. Monoprix Grocery Store

Near Place Masséna

$$ Le Luna Rossa is a small neighborhood place serving delicious French-Italian dishes. Owner Christine welcomes diners with attentive service and reasonable prices. Dine inside (classy tables) or outside on a sidewalk terrace (closed Sun-Mon, just north of parkway at 3 Rue Chauvain—see map on page 686, tel. 04 93 85 55 66).

$$ L'Ovale takes its name from the shape of a rugby ball. Come here for an unpretentious and local café-bistro experience. Young Matthieu serves while David cooks traditional dishes from southwestern France (rich and meaty). Dining is inside only. Consider the *cassoulet,* the hearty *salade de manchons* with duck and walnuts, or the €18-23 three-course *menus* (daily, 29 Rue Pastorelli, tel. 04 93 80 31 65).

$$$ Les 5 Sens (The Five Senses) is a lively, smart, and welcoming bistro serving classic French fare at reasonable prices (daily, 37 Rue Pastorelli, tel. 09 81 06 57 00).

$$$ La Maison de Marie is a surprisingly high-quality refuge off Nice's touristy restaurant row—Rue Masséna. The interior tables are candlelit, white-tablecloth classy, while the tables in the courtyard are relaxed with a bistro feel. Expect some smokers outside. The *menu* is a good value (daily, 5 Rue Masséna, tel. 04 93 82 15 93).

Near the Train Station

Both of these restaurants, a block below the train station, provide good indoor and outdoor seating as well as excellent value.

$ Voyageur Nissart has blended good-value cuisine with friendly service since 1908. Kind owner Max and his able assistant Cédric make great hosts, and the quality of their food makes this place both very popular and a good choice for travelers on a budget (book ahead, leave a message in English). Try anything *à la niçoise,* including the fine *salade niçoise* (good €18 three-course *menus,* inexpensive wines, closed Mon, 19 Rue d'Alsace-Lorraine, tel. 04 93 82 19 60).

$ Zen Japanese Restaurant provides a break from French cuisine. Interior seating is arranged around the chef's stove, and the tasty specialties draw a strong following (open daily, 27 Rue d'Angleterre, tel. 04 93 82 41 20).

Near Boulevard Victor Hugo

$$$$ Rolancy's Restaurant & Bistrot des Viviers attract those looking for formal service and authentic Niçois cuisine with a big emphasis on fish. This classy splurge offers two intimate settings: a soft, formal restaurant (*menus* from €52), and a cozy bistro (€38 *menus*) with some outdoor seating (closed Sun, 5-minute walk west of Avenue Jean Médecin at 22 Rue Alphonse Karr, tel. 04 93 16 00 48).

$$$ Coco & Rico is a find away from the tourist fray. Kind Isabelle welcomes you to her cozy bistro with homemade dishes. The cuisine and wine list represent many regions of France, with a focus on fish and fresh ingredients (bistro closed Sun-Mon, indoor seating only; wine shop open Tue-Sat 10:00-20:00, closed Sun-Mon; 3 Rue Dalpozzo, tel. 04 83 50 09 60).

$ Crêperie Bretonne is the only *crêperie* I list in Nice. Dine on the broad terrace or inside with relaxed service and jukebox-meets-gramophone ambience. Their top-end, house-special crêpes are creative and enticing. Split a salad to start—try the goat cheese salad with honey (closed Sun, on Place Grimaldi, tel. 04 93 82 28 47).

Nice Connections

BY TRAIN

For a comparison of train and bus connections from Nice to nearby coastal towns, see the "Public Transportation in the French Riviera" sidebar on page 668.

Most long-distance train connections to other French cities require a change in Marseille. The Grande Ligne train to Bordeaux (serving Antibes, Cannes, Toulon, and Marseille—and connecting from there to Arles, Nîmes, and Carcassonne) requires a reservation.

From Nice by Train to: Cannes (2/hour, 30 minutes), **Antibes** (2/hour, 20 minutes), **Villefranche-sur-Mer** (2/hour, 10 minutes), **Eze-le-Village** (2/hour, 15 minutes to Eze-Bord-de-Mer, then bus #83 to Eze, 8/day, 15 minutes), **Monaco** (2/hour, 20 minutes), **Menton** (2/hour, 25 minutes), **Grasse** (15/day, 1 hour, better by bus), **Marseille** (18/day, 2.5 hours), **Cassis** (hourly, 3 hours, transfer in Toulon or Marseille), **Arles** (11/day, 4 hours, most require transfer in Marseille or Avignon), **Avignon** (10/day, most by TGV, 4 hours, many require transfer in Marseille), **Paris'** Gare de Lyon (hourly, 6 hours, may require change; 11-hour night train goes to Paris' Gare d'Austerlitz), **Aix-en-Provence** TGV Station (10/day, 2-3 hours, usually changes in Marseille), **Chamonix** (4/day, 10 hours, many change in St-Gervais and Lyon), **Beaune** (7/day, 7 hours, 1-2 transfers), **Florence** (6/day, 8 hours, 1-3 transfers), **Milan** (3 Thello trains/day, 4 hours, www.thello.com), **Venice** (5/day, 9 hours, all with transfers), **Barcelona** (1/day via Montpellier, 10 hours, more with multiple changes).

BY BUS

Regardless of length, most one-way rides on regional buses (except express airport buses) cost €1.50. Tickets are good for up to 74 minutes of travel in one direction, including transfers.

From Nice by Bus to: Cannes (#200, 4/hour Mon-Sat, 2/hour Sun, 2 hours), **Antibes** (#200, 4/hour Mon-Sat, 2/hour Sun, 1.5 hours), **Villefranche-sur-Mer** (#100, 3-4/hour, 20 minutes; or #81, 2-3/hour, 20 minutes), **St-Jean-Cap-Ferrat** (#81, 2-3/hour, 30 minutes), **Eze-le-Village** (#82 or #112, 16/day Mon-Sat, 8/day Sun, 40 minutes), **La Turbie** (6/day, 45 minutes, Mon-Sat #116 from Vauban tram stop, Sun #T-66 from Pont St. Michel tram stop), **Monaco** (#100, 3-4/hour, 45 minutes), **Menton** (#100, 3-4/hour, 1.5 hours), **St-Paul-de-Vence** (#400, 2/hour, 45 minutes), **Vence** (#400, 2/hour, 50 minutes), **Grasse** (#500, 2/hour, 1 hour).

BY PLANE

Nice's easy-to-navigate airport (Aéroport de Nice Côte d'Azur, airport code: NCE) is literally on the Mediterranean—with landfill runways—a 30-minute drive west of the city center. Planes leave roughly hourly for Paris (one-hour flight, about the same price as a train ticket, check www.easyjet.com for the cheapest flights to Paris' Orly airport). The two terminals are connected by shuttle buses *(navettes)*. Both terminals have TIs, banks, ATMs, and buses to Nice (tel. 04 89 88 98 28, www.nice.aeroport.fr).

Getting from the Airport to the City Center

By Taxi: A taxi into the center is expensive considering the short distance (figure €35 to Nice hotels, €60 to Villefranche-sur-Mer, €70 to Antibes, small fee for bags). Nice's airport taxis are notorious for overcharging. Before riding, confirm that your fare into town is roughly €35 (or €40 at night or on Sun). Don't pay much more. It's always a good idea to ask for a receipt *(reçu)*.

By Airport Shuttle: These work better for trips from your hotel to the airport, since they require you to book a precise pickup time in advance—even though you can't ever know exactly when your flight will actually arrive. Shuttle vans offer a fixed price (about €30 for one person, a little more for additional people or to Villefranche-sur-Mer). Your hotel can arrange this. Try **Nice Airport Shuttle** (1-2 people-€32, additional person-€14, mobile 06 60 33 20 54, www.nice-airport-shuttle.com) or **Med-Tour** (tel. 04 93 82 92 58, mobile 06 73 82 04 10, www.med-tour.com). Several other shuttle options exist.

By Bus: Two bus lines connect the airport with the city center, offering good alternatives to high-priced taxis. **Bus #99** (airport express) runs to Nice's main train station (€6, 2/hour, 8:00-21:00, 30 minutes, drops you within a 10-minute walk of many recom-

RIVIERA

mended hotels). To take this bus *to* the airport, catch it right in front of the train station (departs on the half-hour). If your hotel is within walking distance of the station, #99 is your best budget bet.

Bus #98 runs along Promenade des Anglais and along the edge of Vieux Nice (€6, 3/hour, from the airport 6:00-23:00, to the airport until 21:00, 30 minutes, see map on page 674 for stops).

For all buses, buy tickets from the driver. To reach the bus information office and stops at Terminal 1, turn left after passing customs and exit the doors at the far end. Buses serving Terminal 2 stop across the street from the airport exit (information kiosk and ticket sales to the right as you exit).

Getting from the Airport to Nearby Destinations

To get to **Villefranche-sur-Mer** from the airport, take bus #98 (described above) to Place Garibaldi. From there, use the same ticket to transfer to bus #81 or #100 (see "Nice Connections—By Bus," earlier, for bus frequencies and the map on page 674 for stop locations; note that in 2017 you'll likely need to walk to the Promenade des Arts stop by the Modern Art Museum or to the port to catch eastbound buses due to work on the tram system). Consider an airport shuttle van.

To reach **Antibes,** take bus #250 from either terminal (about 2/hour, 40 minutes, €10). For **Cannes,** take bus #210 from either terminal (1-2/hour, 50 minutes on freeway, €20). Express bus #110 runs from the airport directly to **Monaco** (2/hour, 50 minutes, €20).

BY CRUISE SHIP

Nice's port is at the eastern edge of the town center, below Castle Hill; the main promenade and old town are on the other side of the hill. Cruise ships dock at either side of the mouth of this port: Terminal 1 to the east, or Terminal 2 to the west.

Getting into the City Center: To reach Vieux Nice or the tram, head to Place Garibaldi by walking or riding the shuttle bus to the top of the port, then angling up Rue Cassini to the square (20-minute walk from either cruise terminal). From here it's a short **walk** to Vieux Nice or to the tram stop. You can ride the **tram** to Place Masséna for the start of my "Old Nice Walk" or to catch a bus to the Chagall or Matisse museums (#15 or #22).

If arriving at Terminal 2 and heading to Vieux Nice, you can skip the walk to Place Garibaldi and stroll directly there by heading around the base of the castle-topped hill, with the sea on your left (10-15 minutes).

Other options to get into town include a **taxi** from the terminals (about €20 to points within Nice) or the **hop-on, hop-off bus,** which has a stop at the top of the port (see page 679).

Getting to Nearby Destinations: To visit Villefranche-sur-Mer or Monaco, it's best to take **bus #100** (the train is faster, but the bus stop is much closer to Nice's port). The bus stops along the top of the port, near the right end of Place de l'Ile de Beauté (see map on page 684).

To take the **train** to Villefranche-sur-Mer, Monaco, Antibes, Cannes, or elsewhere, hop on the tram (stop near Place Garibaldi, described earlier), then ride to the Gare Thiers stop and walk one long block to the main train station. For bus and train connections to nearby destinations, see page 708.

Taxis at the terminals charge about €40 one-way to Villefranche-sur-Mer, or €95 one-way to Monaco.

Villefranche-sur-Mer

In the glitzy world of the Riviera, Villefranche-sur-Mer offers travelers an easygoing slice of small-town Mediterranean life. From here convenient day trips allow you to gamble in Monaco, saunter the Promenade des Anglais in Nice, or enjoy views from Eze-le-Village and the Grande Corniche.

Villefranche-sur-Mer feels more Italian than French, with pastel-orange buildings; steep, narrow lanes spilling into the sea; and pasta on menus. Luxury yachts glisten in the bay. Cruise ships make regular calls to Villefranche-sur-Mer's deep harbor, creating periodic rush hours of frenetic shoppers and bucket-listers. Sand-pebble beaches, a handful of interesting sights, and quick access to Cap Ferrat keep other visitors just busy enough.

Orientation to Villefranche-sur-Mer

TOURIST INFORMATION

The TI is off the road that runs between Nice and Monaco, located in a park (Jardin François Binon) below the Nice/Monaco bus stop, labeled *Octroi* (mid-June-mid-Sept daily 9:00-18:00; mid-Sept-mid-June Mon-Sat 9:00-12:00 & 14:00-17:00, closed Sun; tel. 04

93 01 73 68, www.villefranche-sur-mer.com). Pick up regional bus schedules and information on seasonal sightseeing boat rides. The TI has an excellent brochure-map showing seaside walks around neighboring Cap Ferrat and information on the Villa Ephrussi de Rothschild's gardens.

ARRIVAL IN VILLEFRANCHE-SUR-MER

By Bus: Get off at the Octroi stop. To reach the old town, walk downhill past the TI along Avenue Général de Gaulle, take the first stairway on the left, then make a right at the street's end.

By Train: Not all trains stop in Villefranche-sur-Mer (you may need to transfer to a local train in Nice or Monaco). Villefranche-sur-Mer's train station is just above the beach, a short stroll from the old town and most of my recommended hotels (or take a taxi for about €15).

By Car: From Nice's port, follow signs for *Menton, Monaco*, and *Basse Corniche*. In Villefranche-sur-Mer, turn right at the TI (first signal after Hôtel la Flore) for parking and hotels. For a quick visit to the TI, park at the pay lot just below the TI (first 20 minutes free; enter license plate number). Some hotels have their own parking. You'll pay to park in all public parking except during 19:00-9:00 (€15 weekly pass available). The waterfront Wilson parking lot costs €2/hour.

By Plane: Allow an hour from Nice's airport to Villefranche-sur-Mer (for details on this connection, see page 710).

HELPFUL HINTS

Market Day: A fun bric-a-brac market enlivens Villefranche-sur-Mer on Sundays (on Place Amélie Pollonnais by Hôtel Welcome, and in Jardin François Binon by the TI). On Saturday and Wednesday mornings, a small food market sets up in Jardin François Binon. A small trinket market springs to action on Place Amélie Pollonnais whenever cruise ships grace the harbor.

Wi-Fi: There's free city Wi-Fi at the port. On Place du Marché, both **Chez Net** and **L'X Café** have Wi-Fi.

Laundry: A self-serve launderette is just below the main road on Avenue Sadi Carnot (daily 7:00-20:00, opposite #6).

Electric Bike Rental: The adventurous can try **Eco-Loc** electric bikes as an alternative to taking the bus to Cap Ferrat, Eze-le-Village, or even Nice. You get about 25 miles on a fully charged battery (after that you're pedaling; €20/half-day, €30/day, mid-April-Sept daily 9:00-17:00, deposit and ID required, best to reserve 24 hours in advance; helmets, locks, and baskets available; pick up bike by cruise terminal entry at the port, mobile 06 66 92 72 41, www.ecoloc06.fr).

Spectator Sports: Lively *boules* action takes place each evening just below the TI and the huge soccer field (for more on this sport, see page 561).

GETTING AROUND VILLEFRANCHE-SUR-MER

By Bus: Little **minibus #80** saves you the sweat of walking uphill, but it runs only about once per hour from the old port to the top of the hill, stopping at Place Amélie Pollonnais, Hôtel la Fiancée du Pirate, and the Col de Villefranche stop (for buses to Eze-le-Village), before going to the outlying suburban Nice Riquier train station (€1.50, runs daily 7:00-19:00, see map on page 714 for stop locations, schedule posted at stops and available at TI). Many buses serve Villefranche from other Riviera towns (see page 720).

By Taxi: General taxi tel. 04 93 55 55 55. Beware of taxi drivers who overcharge. The five-minute trip from the waterfront up to the main street level (to bus stops on the Low Corniche or to the train station) should be about €10. Normal weekday, daytime rates to outside destinations should be about €25 to Cap Ferrat, €40 to central Nice or Eze-le-Village, and €60 to the airport or Monaco. For a reliable taxi in Villefranche-sur-Mer, call or email **Didier** (mobile 06 15 15 39 15, taxididier.villefranchesurmer@orange.fr).

Villefranche-sur-Mer Town Walk

For tourists, Villefranche is a tiny, easy-to-cover town that snuggles around its harbor under its citadel. This quick self-guided walk

laces together everything of importance, starting at the waterfront near where cruise-ship tenders land and finishing at the citadel.

• *If arriving by bus or train, you'll walk five minutes to the starting point. Go to the end of the little pier directly in front of Hôtel Welcome, where we'll start with a spin tour (spin to the right) to get oriented.*

The Harbor: Look out to sea. Cap Ferrat, across the bay, is a landscaped paradise where the 1 percent of the 1 percent compete for the best view. The Rothschilds' pink mansion, Villa Ephrussi (slightly left of center, hugging the top), is the most worthwhile sight to visit in the area. To its right, in the saddle of the hill, the next home, with the big red-tiled roof, belongs to Paul Allen. Geologically, Cap Ferrat is the southern tip of the Alps. The range emerges from the sea here and arcs all across Europe, over 700 miles, to Vienna.

At 2,000 feet, this is the deepest natural harbor on the Riviera and was the region's most important port until Nice built its

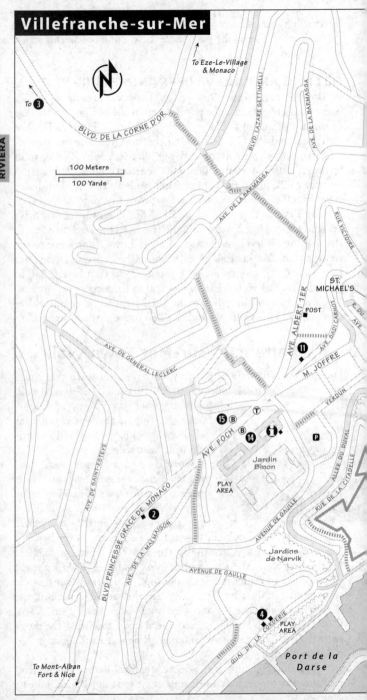

Villefranche-sur-Mer

RIVIERA

To Eze-Le-Village & Monaco

To 3

BLVD. DE LA CORNE D'OR

BLVD. LAZARE SETTIMELLI

AVE. DE LA BARMASSA

RUE VICTORIE

100 Meters
100 Yards

AVE. DE LA BARMASSA

AVE. DE GENERAL LECLERC

ST. MICHAEL'S

AVE. ALBERT 1ER

POST

AVE. SADI CARNOT

R. DU

AVE.

11

M. JOFFRE

VERDUN

AVE. DE SAINT-ESTEVE

AVE. FOCH

15 B

T

B

14

i

P

ALLEE DU DUVAL

Jardin
Binon

PLAY
AREA

RUE DE LA CITADELLE

2

BLVD. PRINCESSE GRACE DE MONACO

AVE. DE LA MALMAISON

AVENUE DE GAULLE

Jardins
de Narvik

AVENUE DE GAULLE

4

PLAY
AREA

QUAI DE LA CORDERIE

Port de la
Darse

To Mont-Alban
Fort & Nice

❶ Hôtel Welcome
❷ Hôtel La Flore
❸ To Hôtel la Fiancée du Pirate
❹ Hôtel de la Darse &
   La Trinquette Restaurant
❺ La Grignotière Restaurant
❻ L'Aparté & Casino Grocery
❼ Le Serre Restaurant
❽ La Mère Germaine Restaurant
❾ Les Palmiers & Cosmo Brasserie
❿ Wi-Fi
⓫ Launderette
⓬ Boat Rides &
   Electric Bike Rental
⓭ Dark Pelican Motor
   Boat Rental
⓮ Octroi Bus Stop (from Nice;
   to Monaco & Cap Ferrat)
⓯ Octroi Bus Stop (to Nice;
   from Monaco & Cap Ferrat)

own in the 18th century. Today, ships bring not pirates but tourists. The bay here is generally filled with beautiful yachts. (In the evenings, you might see well-coiffed captains being ferried in by dutiful mates to pick up statuesque call girls.)

Up on the hill, the 16th-century citadel (where this walk ends) is marked by flags. The yellow fisherman's chapel (with the little-toe bell tower) has an interior painted by Jean Cocteau. Hôtel Welcome offers the balconies of dreams. Up the lane is the baroque facade of St. Michael's Church. The promenade, lined by fancy fish restaurants, leads to the town beach. Fifty yards above the beach stands the train station, and above that, supported by arches, is the Low Corniche road, which leads to Monaco. Until that road was built in the 1860s, those hills were free of any development all the way to Monaco. The big, yellow building beyond is rentable for €300,000 a month (as Madonna did for a recent birthday).

• *Walk left 30 yards past the last couple of fishing boats surviving from the town's once-important fishing community to a small bronze bust of Jean Cocteau, the artist who said, "When I look at Villefranche, I see my youth." Step up to the little chapel he painted.*

Chapel of St. Pierre (Chapelle Cocteau): This chapel is the town's cultural highlight. Cocteau, who decorated the place, was a Parisian transplant who adored little Villefranche-sur-Mer and whose career was distinguished by his work as an artist, poet, novelist, playwright, and filmmaker. Influenced by his pals Marcel Proust, André Gide, Edith Piaf, and Pablo Picasso, Cocteau was a leader among 20th-century avant-garde intellectuals. At the door, Marie-France—who is passionate about Cocteau's art—collects a €3 donation for a fishermen's charity. She then sets you free to enjoy the chapel's small but intriguing interior. She's happy to give explanations if you ask (open Wed-Mon 10:00-12:00 & 15:00-19:00, usually closed Tue, hours vary with cruise-ship traffic and season).

• *From the chapel, stroll the harbor promenade 100 yards past romantic harborside tables. **Restaurant La Mère Germaine** is named for Mother Germaine, who famously took care of US Navy troops in World War II (step inside to see sketches and old photos on the wall). Just past the restaurant, a lane (signed* Vieille Ville*) leads up into the old town. Walk a few steps until you reach a long tunnel-like street.*

Rue Obscure, the Old Town, and St. Michael's Church: Here, under these 13th-century vaults, you're in another age. Before the long stepped lane (which we'll climb later), turn right and walk to the end of Rue Obscure (which means "dark street"). At the end, wind up to the sunlight past a tiny fountain at Place du Conseil, and a few steps beyond that to a viewpoint overlooking the beach. Then stroll back past the fountain and gently downhill. At Place des Deux Canons, turn right and climb the stepped lanes, and then take your first left at Le Serre restaurant to St. Michael's

Church, facing a delightful square (Place de l'Eglise) with a single magnolia tree. The church features an 18th-century organ, a particularly engaging crucifix at the high altar, and (to the left) a fine statue of a recumbent Christ—carved, they say, from a fig tree by a galley slave in the 1600s.

• *Leaving St. Michael's, go downhill halfway to the water, where you hit the main commercial street. Go right on Rue du Poilu to Place de la République. (Browse real-estate windows if you'd like to move here.) Head through the square and angle left, up the hill to the...*

Citadel: The town's mammoth castle was built in the 1500s by the Duke of Savoy to defend against the French. When the region joined France in 1860, the castle became just a barracks. Since the 20th century, it's housed the police station, city hall, a summer outdoor theater, and art galleries. The single fortified entry—originally a drawbridge over a dry moat (a.k.a. kill zone)—still leads into this huge complex. The exterior walls slope thickly at the base, indicating that they were built in the "Age of Black Powder"—the 16th century—when the advent of gunpowder made thicker, cannonball-deflecting walls a necessity for any effective fortification. The bastions are designed for smarter crossfire during an attack.

• *And that concludes our introductory walk.*

Activities in Villefranche-sur-Mer

Boat Rides *(Promenades en Mer)*

To view this beautiful coastline from the sea, consider taking a quick **sightseeing cruise** with AMV (€11-21 cruises, some as far as Monaco, select days June-Sept, departs across from Hôtel Welcome, tel. 04 93 76 65 65, www.amv-sirenes.com). You can also rent your own **motor boat** through Dark Pelican (€100/half-day, €170/day, deposit required, on the harbor at the Gare Maritime, tel. 04 93 01 76 54, www.darkpelican.com).

Seafront Walks

A seaside walkway originally used by customs agents to patrol the harbor leads under the citadel and connects the old town with the workaday harbor (Port de la Darse). At the port you'll find a few cafés, France's Institute of Oceanography (an outpost for the University of Paris oceanographic studies), and an 18th-century dry dock. This scenic walk turns downright romantic after dark. You can also wander the other direction along Villefranche-sur-Mer's waterfront and continue beyond the train station for postcard-perfect views back to Villefranche-sur-Mer (ideal in the morning—go before breakfast).

Hike to Mont-Alban Fort

This fort, with a remarkable setting on the high ridge that separates Nice and Villefranche-sur-Mer, is a good destination for hikers (also accessible by car; info at TI). From the TI, walk on the main road toward Nice about 500 yards past Hôtel La Flore. Look for wooden trail signs labeled *Escalier de Verre* and climb about 45 minutes as the trail makes long switchbacks through the woods up to the ridge. Find your way to Mont-Alban Fort (interior closed to tourists) and its view terrace. (To visit with a much shorter hike, bus #14 from Nice drops you five minutes away.)

RIVIERA

Sleeping in Villefranche-sur-Mer

($$$$ = Splurge, $$$ = Pricier, $$ = Moderate, $ = Budget)

You have a handful of good hotels to choose from in Villefranche-sur-Mer. The ones I list have sea views from at least half of their rooms—well worth paying extra for.

$$$$ Hôtel Welcome**** has the best location in Villefranche-sur-Mer, and charges for it. Anchored seaside in the old town, with all of its 35 comfortable, balconied rooms overlooking the harbor and a lounge/wine bar that opens to the water, this place lowers my pulse (pricey parking garage—must reserve, 3 Quai Amiral Courbet, tel. 04 93 76 27 62, www.welcomehotel. com, resa@welcomehotel.com).

$$$ Hôtel La Flore***is a fine value if your idea of sightseeing is to enjoy the view from your spacious bedroom deck. It's a 15-minute uphill hike from the old town, but the parking is free, and the bus stops for Nice and Monaco are close by (on main road at 5 Boulevard Princesse Grace de Monaco; tel. 04 93 76 30 30, www.hotel-la-flore.fr, infos@hotel-la-flore.fr).

$$$ Hôtel la Fiancée du Pirate***is a family-friendly refuge high above Villefranche-sur-Mer on the Middle Corniche with no street appeal (best for drivers, although it is on bus lines #80, #82, and #112 to Eze-le-Village and Nice). Inside, Eric and Laurence offer 15 bright, tasteful, and comfortable rooms, a large pool, a nice garden, and a view lounge area. The big breakfast features homemade crêpes (RS%, laundry service, free parking, 8 Boulevard de la Corne d'Or, Moyenne Corniche/N-7, tel. 04 93 76 67 40, www. fianceedupirate.com, info@fianceedupirate.com).

$ Hôtel de la Darse***is a shy little hotel burrowed in the shadow of its highbrow neighbors and the only budget option in Villefranche. It's less central—figure 10 scenic minutes of level walking to the harbor and a steep 15-minute walk up to the main road (hourly minibus #80 stops in front). Seaview rooms are easily worth the extra euros (no elevator, tel. 04 93 01 72 54, www. hoteldeladarse.com, info@hoteldeladarse.com). From the TI, walk or drive down Avenue Général de Gaulle (walkers should turn left on Allée du Colonel Duval into the Jardins de Narvik and follow steps to the bottom; for drivers, free parking is usually available nearby).

Eating in Villefranche-sur-Mer

Comparison-shopping is half the fun of dining in Villefranche-sur-Mer. Make an event out of a predinner stroll through the old

city. Check what looks good on the lively Place Amélie Pollonnais (next to Hôtel Welcome), where the whole village seems to converge at night; saunter the string of pricey candlelit places lining the waterfront; and consider the smaller, less expensive eateries embedded in the old town.

$$$ La Grignotière, hiding in the back lanes, serves generous and tasty *plats*. The mixed-seafood grill is a smart order, as are the spaghetti and *gambas* (shrimp), and the chef's personal-recipe bouillabaisse. Dining is inside, making this a good choice for cooler days (daily except closed Wed Nov-April, 3 Rue du Poilu, tel. 04 93 76 79 83).

$$$ L'Aparté is where locals go for fresh cuisine and a special experience. Book ahead, then order from the chalkboard. The focus is seafood, servings are generous, and the presentation is tops (closed Mon, a few steps up from the port at 1 Rue Obscure, tel. 04 93 01 84 88).

$ Le Serre, nestled in the old town below St. Michael's Church, is a simple place with a hardworking owner. Sylvie serves well-priced dinners to a loyal local clientele. Choose from the many pizzas (named after US states), salads, and meats; or try the three-course *menu* (open evenings only, cheap house wine, 16 Rue de May, tel. 04 93 76 79 91).

$$$$ La Mère Germaine, right on the harbor, is the only place in town classy enough to lure a yachter ashore. It's dressy, with formal service and high prices. The name commemorates the current owner's grandmother, who fed hungry GIs during World War II. Try the bouillabaisse, served with panache (daily, reserve for harborfront table, 9 Quai de l'Amiral Courbet, tel. 04 93 01 71 39, www.meregermaine.com).

$$ La Trinquette is a relaxed, low-key place away from the fray on the "other port," next to the recommended Hôtel de la Darse (a lovely 10-minute walk from the other recommended restaurants). Jean-Charles runs the place with charm. The cuisine is good, and weekends bring a cool live-music scene (daily in summer, closed Wed off-season, 30 Avenue Général de Gaulle, tel. 04 93 16 92 48).

On Place Amélie Pollonnais: $$ Les Palmiers and **$$ Le Cosmo** each serves average brasserie fare on the town's appealing main square (daily).

Grocery Store: A handy **Casino** is a few blocks above Hôtel Welcome at 12 Rue du Poilu (Thu-Tue 8:00-12:30 & 15:30-19:30 except closed Sun afternoon and all day Wed).

Dinner Options for Drivers: If you have a car and are staying a few nights, take the short drive up to Eze-le-Village or, better still, La Turbie (dining suggestions for each later in this chapter). If it's summer (June-Sept), the best option of all is to go across to one of Cap Ferrat's beach restaurants for a before-dinner drink or a dinner you won't soon forget.

Villefranche-sur-Mer Connections

For a comparison of connections by train and bus, see the "Public Transportation in the French Riviera" sidebar on page 668. If you're going to Nice's airport, take a cab or an airport shuttle van (see "Nice Connections" on page 708).

BY TRAIN

Trains are faster and run later than buses (until 24:00). It's a level, 10-minute walk from the port to the train station.

From Villefranche-sur-Mer by Train to: Monaco (2/hour, 10 minutes), **Nice** (2/hour, 10 minutes), **Antibes** (2/hour, 40 minutes), and **Eze-Bord-de-Mer** (2/hour, 5 minutes)—transfer to bus #83 for Eze-le-Village (see page 728).

BY BUS

All buses in this area cost €1.50 per ride (buy ticket from driver). Tickets are good for 74 minutes in one direction and for transfers. In Villefranche-sur-Mer, the most convenient stop is Octroi, just above the TI.

These are the key routes: **Bus #81** follows a circular route from Nice through Villefranche-sur-Mer, Beaulieu-sur-Mer, then to all Cap Ferrat stops, ending at the port in the village of St-Jean (2-3/hour, daily 6:35-20:15 from Nice, last return trip from St-Jean at 20:50). **Bus #100** runs along the coastal road between Nice, Monaco, and Menton (3-4/hour). The last bus leaves Nice for Villefranche-sur-Mer at about 19:45; the last bus from Villefranche-sur-Mer to Nice departs at about 20:30.

From Villefranche-sur-Mer by Bus to: St-Jean-Cap-Ferrat (#81, 20 minutes; for other transportation options, see "Getting to Cap Ferrat," later), **Beaulieu-sur-Mer** (#81 or #100, 10 minutes),

Monaco (#100, 35 minutes), **Nice** (#81 or #100, 20 minutes), and **Eze-le-Village** (#100 to Eze-Bord-de-Mer and transfer to #83; also #82 or #112 from Col de Villefranche stop).

BY CRUISE SHIP

Tenders deposit passengers at a slick terminal building (Gare Maritime) at the Port de la Santé, right in front of Villefranche-sur-Mer's old town.

Getting into Town: It's easy to **walk** to various points in Villefranche-sur-Mer. The town's charming, restaurant-lined square is a straight walk ahead from the terminal, the main road (with the TI and bus stop) is a steep hike above, and the train station is a short stroll along the beach. **Minibus #80,** which departs from in front of the cruise terminal, saves you some hiking up to the main road and bus stop (see page 713).

Getting to Nearby Towns: To connect to other towns, choose between the **bus** or **train.** Leaving the terminal, you'll see directional sights pointing left, to *Town center/bus* (a 10- to 15-minute, steeply uphill walk to the Octroi bus stop with connections west to Nice or east to Monaco); and right, to *Gare SNCF/train station* (a 10-minute, level stroll with some stairs at the end). See train and bus connections above.

Taxis wait in front of the cruise terminal and charge exorbitant rates (minimum €15 charge to train station, though many will refuse such a short ride). For farther-flung trips, see the price estimates on page 713. For an all-day trip, you can try negotiating a flat fee (e.g., €300 for a 4-hour tour).

Along the Three Corniches

Nice, Villefranche-sur-Mer, and Monaco are linked by three coastal routes: the Low, Middle, and High Corniches. The roads are nicknamed after the decorative frieze that runs along the top of a building (cornice). Each Corniche (kor-neesh) offers sensational views and a different perspective. You can find the three routes from Nice by driving up Boulevard Jean Jaurès past Vieux Nice. For the Low Corniche, follow signs to N-98 *(Monaco par la Basse Corniche),* which leads past Nice's port. Shortly after the turnoff to the Low Corniche, you'll see signs for N-7 *(Moyenne Corniche)* leading to the Middle Corniche. Signs for the High *(Grande)* Corniche appear a bit after that; follow D-2564 to *Col des 4 Chemins* and the *Grande Corniche.*

Low Corniche: The Basse Corniche (also called "Corniche Inférieure") strings ports, beaches, and seaside villages together for

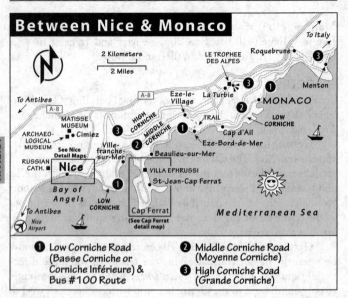

Between Nice & Monaco

2 Kilometers
2 Miles

To Italy

Roquebrune

LE TROPHEE
DES ALPES

Menton

To Antibes

A-8

Eze-le-
Village

La Turbie

MONACO

HIGH
CORNICHE

TRAIL

LOW
CORNICHE

MATISSE
MUSEUM

Cimiez

MIDDLE
CORNICHE

Cap d'Ail

ARCHAEO-
LOGICAL
MUSEUM

See Nice
Detail Maps

Ville-
franche-
sur-Mer

Eze-Bord-de-Mer

RUSSIAN
CATH.

Nice

Beaulieu-sur-Mer

Bay of
Angels

VILLA EPHRUSSI

St-Jean-Cap Ferrat

LOW
CORNICHE

Mediterranean Sea

To Antibes

Nice
Airport

Cap Ferrat

(See Cap Ferrat
detail map)

❶ Low Corniche Road
(Basse Corniche or
Corniche Inférieure) &
Bus #100 Route

❷ Middle Corniche Road
(Moyenne Corniche)

❸ High Corniche Road
(Grande Corniche)

RIVIERA

a traffic-filled ground-floor view. It was built in the 1860s (along with the train line) to bring people to the casino in Monte Carlo. When this Low Corniche was finished, many hill-town villagers descended to the shore and started the communities that now line the sea. Before 1860, the population of the coast between Ville-franche-sur-Mer and Monte Carlo was zero. Think about that as you make the congested trip today.

Middle Corniche: The Moyenne Corniche is higher, quieter, and far more impressive. It runs through Eze-le-Village and provides breathtaking views over the Mediterranean, with several scenic pullouts.

High Corniche: Napoleon's crowning road-construction achievement, the Grande Corniche caps the cliffs with staggering views from almost 1,600 feet above the sea. Two thousand years ago, this was called the Via Aurelia, used by the Romans to conquer the West.

Villas: Driving from Villefranche-sur-Mer to Monaco, you'll come upon impressive villas. A particularly grand entry leads to "La Leopolda," the sprawling estate named for a previous owner, King Leopold II of Belgium in the 1930s (who owned the entire peninsula of Cap Ferrat in addition to this estate). Those driving up to the Middle Corniche from Villefranche-sur-Mer can look down on this yellow mansion and its lush garden, which fill an entire hilltop. The property was later owned by the Agnelli family (of Fiat fame and fortune), and then by the Safra family (Brazilian bankers). Its current value is a half-billion dollars.

The Best Route: For a ▲▲▲ route, **drivers** should take the Middle Corniche from Nice or Villefranche-sur-Mer to Eze-le-Village; from there, follow signs to the *Grande Corniche* and *La Turbie*, keeping an eye out for brilliant views back over Eze-le-Village, then finish by dropping down into Monaco. **Buses** travel each route; the higher the Corniche, the less frequent the buses.

Cap Ferrat

This exclusive peninsula, rated ▲▲, decorates Villefranche-sur-Mer's views. Cap Ferrat is a peaceful eddy off the busy Nice-Monaco route (Low Corniche). You could spend a leisurely day on this peninsula, wandering the sleepy port village of St-Jean-Cap-Ferrat (usually called "St-Jean"), touring the Villa Ephrussi de Rothschild mansion and gardens, and walking on sections of the beautiful trails that follow the coast. If you owned a house here, some of the richest people on the planet would be your neighbors.

Tourist Information: The main TI is near the harbor in St-Jean (May-Sept Mon-Sat 9:30-18:30, Sun 10:00-17:30; Oct-April Mon-Sat 9:00-17:00, closed Sun; 5 Avenue Denis Séméria, bus #81 stops here at the *office du tourisme*). A smaller TI is near the Villa Ephrussi (closed Sun and Sat off-season, 59 Avenue Denis Séméria, tel. 04 93 76 08 90, office-tourisme@saintjeancapferrat.fr).

PLANNING YOUR TIME
Here's how I'd spend a day on the Cap: From Nice or Villefranche-sur-Mer, take the bus (#81) to the Villa Ephrussi de Rothschild stop (called Passable), then visit the villa. Walk 30 minutes, mostly downhill, to St-Jean for lunch (many options, including grocery shops for picnic supplies) and poke around the village. Consider the 45-minute walk on the Plage de la Paloma trail (ideal for picnics). After lunch, follow a beautiful 30-minute trail to the Villa Kérylos in Beaulieu-sur-Mer and tour that villa (see "Walks around Cap Ferrat," later). Return to Villefranche-sur-Mer, Nice, or points beyond by train or bus.

Here's an **alternative plan** for the star-gazing, nature-loving beach bum: Visit Villa Ephrussi first thing, walk to St-Jean for lunch, hike six miles around the entirety of Cap Ferrat (2-3 hours), and enjoy the late afternoon on the beach at Plage de Passable. At sunset, have dinner at the recommended Restaurant de la Plage de Passable, then walk or catch a taxi back.

GETTING TO CAP FERRAT
From Nice or Villefranche-sur-Mer: Bus #81 (direction: *Port de St-Jean*) runs to all Cap Ferrat stops (see "Villefranche-sur-Mer

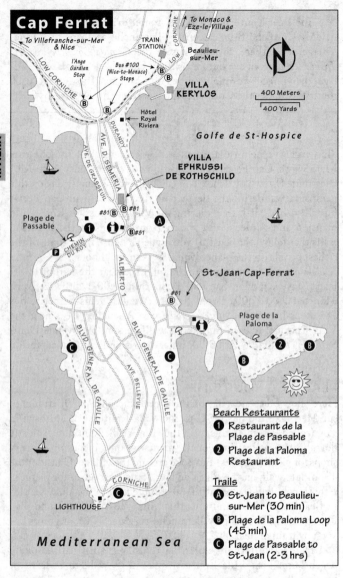

Cap Ferrat

To Villefranche-sur-Mer & Nice

To Monaco & Eze-le-Village

TRAIN STATION

l'Ange Gardien Stop

Bus #100 (Nice-to-Monaco) Stops

LOW CORNICHE

Beaulieu-sur-Mer

VILLA KERYLOS

Hôtel Royal Riviera

AVE. DURANDY

AVE. D. SEMERIA

AVE. DE GRASSEUIL

Golfe de St-Hospice

VILLA EPHRUSSI DE ROTHSCHILD

400 Meters
400 Yards

Plage de Passable

CHEMIN DU ROY

#81

#81

St-Jean-Cap-Ferrat

ALBERTO 1

BLVD. GENERAL DE GAULLE

AVE. BELLEVUE

Plage de la Paloma

CORNICHE

LIGHTHOUSE

Mediterranean Sea

Beach Restaurants
1. Restaurant de la Plage de Passable
2. Plage de la Paloma Restaurant

Trails
Ⓐ St-Jean to Beaulieu-sur-Mer (30 min)
Ⓑ Plage de la Paloma Loop (45 min)
Ⓒ Plage de Passable to St-Jean (2-3 hrs)

Connections," earlier). For the Villa Ephrussi de Rothschild, get off at the Passable stop (allow 30 minutes from Nice and 10 minutes from Villefranche-sur-Mer's Octroi stop). The return bus (direction: *Nice*) begins in St-Jean. **Warning:** Late-afternoon buses back to Villefranche-sur-Mer or Nice along the Low Corniche can be jammed (worse on weekends), potentially leaving passengers stranded at stops for long periods. To avoid this, either take the train or board bus #81 on the Cap itself (before it gets crowded).

Cap Ferrat is quick by **car** (take the Low Corniche) or **taxi** (allow €26 one-way from Villefranche-sur-Mer, €55 from Nice).

Sights on Cap Ferrat

▲Villa Ephrussi de Rothschild

In what seems like the ultimate in Riviera extravagance, Venice, Versailles, and the Côte d'Azur come together in the pastel-pink Villa Ephrussi. Rising above Cap Ferrat, this 1905 mansion has views west to Villefranche-sur-Mer and east to Beaulieu-sur-Mer.

Cost and Hours: Palace and gardens-€13.50, includes audioguide; mid-Feb-Oct daily 10:00-18:00, July-Aug until 19:00; Nov-mid-Feb Mon-Fri 14:00-18:00, Sat-Sun 10:00-18:00; tel. 04 93 01 33 09, www.villa-ephrussi.com.

Getting There: With luck, drivers can find a free spot to park along the entry road just inside the gate. There's a small turnaround at the top. The nearest bus stop is Passable, just a few minutes after the bus turns onto Cap Ferrat (bus #81, 10-minute walk uphill to the villa). If returning to Nice or Villefranche-sur-Mer by bus, check the posted schedule, and keep in mind that you're only a minute from the time-point listed for Port de St-Jean.

Visiting the Villa: Pick up the audioguide and garden map as you enter, then start with the well-furnished belle époque **interior** (well-described by the audioguide). Upstairs, an 18-minute film (with English subtitles) explains the gardens and villa and gives you good background on the life of rich and eccentric Béatrice, Baroness de Rothschild, the French banking heiress who built and furnished the place. Don't miss the view over the gardens from the terrace.

As you stroll through the rooms, you'll pass royal furnishings and personal possessions, including the baroness's porcelain collection and her bathroom case for cruises. Her bedroom, sensibly, has views to the sea on both the port and starboard sides, and toward the bow, stretching like the prow of a vast cruise ship, is her garden. An appropriately classy **$$ garden-tearoom** serves drinks and lunches with a view (12:00-17:30).

The gorgeous gardens are why most come here (pick up the garden map when you get your audioguide). The literally shipshape gardens were inspired by Béatrice's many ocean-liner trips. She even dressed her small army of gardeners like sailors. Behind the mansion, stroll through the seven lush gardens re-created from locations all over the world and with maximum sea views. Don't miss the Jardin Exotique's wild cactus, the rose garden at the far end, and the view back to the house from the "Temple of Love" gazebo.

Plage de Passable

This pebbly little beach, located below the Villa Ephrussi, comes with great views of Villefranche-sur-Mer. It's a peaceful place, popular with families. One half is public (free, with snack bar, shower, and WC), and the other is run by a small restaurant (€25-35 includes changing locker, lounge chair, and shower; they have 260 "beds," but still reserve ahead in summer or on weekends as this is a prime spot, tel. 04 93 76 06 17). If you were ever to do the French Riviera rent-a-beach ritual, this would be the place.

To park near the beach (curbside or in a nearby lot), figure about €8/day. Bus #81 stops just above the beach.

For me, the best reason to come here is for dinner. Arrive before sunset, then watch as darkness descends and lights flicker over Villefranche-sur-Mer's heavenly setting. **$$$ Restaurant de la Plage de Passable** is your chance to dine on the beach with romance and class while enjoying terrific views and the sounds of children still at play (daily late May-early Sept, always make a reservation, tel. 04 93 76 06 17, www.plage-de-passable.com).

Plage de la Paloma

This half-private, half-public beach is a 10-minute walk from St-Jean-Cap-Ferrat. For €25 you get a lounge chair and the freedom to relax on the elegant side. Or enjoy the pebbly free beach (with shower and WC).

$$$ Plage de la Paloma Restaurant is inviting for dining on the beach, with salads for lunch and elegant dinners (daily from 12:00 and from 20:00, closed late Sept-mid-April, tel. 04 93 01 64 71, www.paloma-beach.com).

St-Jean-Cap-Ferrat

This quiet harbor town lies in Cap Ferrat's center, yet is off most tourist itineraries and feels overlooked. St-Jean houses yachts, boardwalks, views, and boutiques packaged in a "take your time, darling" atmosphere. It's a few miles off the busy Nice-to-Monaco road—convenient for drivers. A string of restaurants line the port, with just enough visitors to keep them in business. St-Jean is especially peaceful at night.

For picnics, the short pedestrian street in St-Jean has all you need (grocery store, bakery, charcuterie, and pizza to go), and you'll have no trouble finding portside or seaside seating. Plage de la Paloma, described earlier, is a 10-minute walk away.

WALKS AROUND CAP FERRAT

The Cap is perfect for a ▲▲ walk; you'll find well-maintained foot trails covering most of its length. You have three easy, mostly level options of varying lengths. The TIs in Villefranche-sur-Mer and St-Jean have maps of Cap Ferrat with walking paths marked.

Between St-Jean and Beaulieu-sur-Mer

A level 30-minute walk takes you past sumptuous villas, great views, and fun swimming opportunities. From St-Jean's port, walk along the harbor and past the beach with the water on your right. Head up the steps to Promenade Maurice Rouvier and continue. Before long you'll see smashing views of the whitewashed **Villa Kérylos**—in 1902, an eccentric millionaire modeled this mansion after a Greek villa (€11.50, audioguide included; June-Sept daily 10:00-19:00, shorter hours off-season; tel. 04 93 01 47 29, www.villakerylos.fr).

To get from Beaulieu-sur-Mer to St-Jean or the Villa Ephrussi, start at the Villa Kérylos (with the sea on your left), walk toward the Hôtel Royal Riviera, and find the trail. If going to St-Jean, stay left at the Villa Sonja Rello (about halfway down); if going to the Villa Ephrussi, look for signs leading uphill before Villa Aurora (walk up the path to Avenue Henri Honoré Sauvan, then keep going). If you're walking from St-Jean to the Villa Ephrussi, turn left off the trail about 50 yards after passing Villa Aurora.

Plage de la Paloma Loop Trail

Just east of St-Jean's port, a scenic 45-minute trail offers an easy sampling of Cap Ferrat's beauty. From the port, walk or drive about a quarter-mile east (with the port on your left, passing Hôtel La Voile d'Or); parking is available at the port or on streets near Plage de la Paloma. You'll find the trailhead where the road comes to a T—look for a *Plage Paloma* sign pointing left, but don't walk left. Cross the small gravel park marked *Jardin de la Paix* to start the trail, and do the walk counterclockwise. The trail is level and paved, yet uneven enough that good shoes are helpful. Plunk your picnic on one of the benches along the trail, or eat at the restaurant on Plage de la Paloma at the end of the walk (described earlier).

Plage de Passable Around the Cape to St-Jean

For a longer 2-3 hour hike that circles the cape, follow the signs below the Villa Ephrussi marked *Plage Passable* (10 minutes downhill on foot from the villa, parking available near the trailhead). Walk down to the beach (you'll find a good café that's ideal for lunch), turn left, and cross the beach. Go along a paved road behind the apartment building, and after about 60 yards, take the steps down to the trail *(Sentier Littoral)*. It's about six miles (10 kilometers) around the cape. Near the end of the trail, you'll pass by the port of St-Jean, from where you can take bus #81 back to Villefranche-sur-Mer, walk back to the Villa Ephrussi and Plage de Passable via the shorter inland route, or continue on to Beaulieu-sur-Mer and take a bus to Monaco or Nice.

Eze-le-Village

Capping a peak high above the sea, flowery and flawless Eze-le-Village (don't confuse it with the seafront town of Eze-Bord-de-Mer) is entirely consumed by tourism. This *village d'art et de gastronomie* (as it calls itself) is home to perfume outlets, stylish boutiques, steep cobbled lanes, and magnificent views. Touristy as it is, its stony state of preservation and magnificent hilltop setting over the Mediterranean affords a fine memory. Day-tripping by bus to Eze-le-Village

from Nice, Monaco, or Villefranche-sur-Mer works well. While Eze-le-Village can be tranquil early and late, during the day it is mobbed by cruise-ship and tour-bus groups.

GETTING TO EZE-LE-VILLAGE

There are two Ezes: Eze-le-Village (the spectacular hill town on the Middle Corniche) and Eze-Bord-de-Mer (a modern beach resort far below the "village" of Eze).

From Nice and upper Villefranche-sur-Mer, buses #82 and #112 provide 16 buses per day to Eze-le-Village (8 on Sun, 30 minutes from Villefranche). From Nice, Villefranche-sur-Mer, or Monaco, you can also take the train or the Nice-Monaco bus to Eze-Bord-de-Mer, getting off at the Gare d'Eze stop. From there, take the infrequent #83 shuttle bus straight up to Eze-le-Village (8/day, daily about 9:00-18:00, schedule posted at stop, 15 minutes).

To connect Eze-le-Village directly with Monte Carlo in Monaco, take bus #112 (6/day Mon-Sat, none on Sun, 20 minutes). A taxi between the two Ezes or from Eze-le-Village to La Turbie will run you about €27 (tel. 06 09 84 17 84).

Orientation to Eze-le-Village

The helpful **TI** is adjacent to Eze-le-Village's main parking lot, just below the town's entry. Ask here for bus schedules. Call a week in advance to arrange a €10, one-hour English-language tour of the village that includes its (€6) gardens (TI open April-Oct daily

9:00-18:00, July-Aug until 19:00; Nov-March Mon-Sat 9:00-17:00, closed Sun; Place de Gaulle, tel. 04 93 41 26 00, www.eze-tourisme.com).

The stop for **buses** to Nice is across the road by the Avia gas station, and the stops for buses to Eze-Bord-de-Mer and Monaco are on the village side of the main road, near the Casino grocery. Public **WCs** are just behind the TI and in the village behind the church. For **food,** there's a handy Casino grocery at the foot of the village by the bus stop (daily 8:00-19:30) and a sensational picnic spot at the beginning of the trail to Eze-Bord-de-Mer. Or try Le Cactus, near the entry to the old town (daily, tel. 04 93 41 19 02). For a splurge, dine at Château Eza (described next, on my "Eze-le-Village Walk").

Eze-le-Village Walk

This self-guided walk gives you a quick orientation to the village.
• *From the TI and parking lot, hike uphill into the town. You'll come to an exclusive hotel gate and the start of a steep trail down to the beach, marked Eze/Mer. For a panoramic view and an ideal picnic perch, side-trip 80 steps down this path (for details, see "Hike to Eze-Bord-de-Mer," later). Continuing up into the village, find the steps immediately after the ritzy hotel gate and climb to...*

Place du Centenaire: In this square, a stone plaque in the flower bed (behind the candy stand) celebrates the 100th anniversary of the 1860 plebiscite, the time when all 133 Eze residents voted to leave the Italian Duchy of Savoy and join France. A town map here helps you get oriented.
• *Now pass through the once-formidable town gate and climb into the 14th-century village.*

As you walk, stop to read the information plaques (in English) and contemplate the change this village has witnessed in the last 90 years. Eze-le-Village was off any traveler's radar until well after World War II (running water was made available only in the 1930s), yet today hotel rooms outnumber local residents two to one (66 to 33).
• *Wandering the narrow lanes, follow signs to the...*

Château Eza: This was the winter getaway of the Swedish royal family from 1923 until 1953; today it's a hotel. The château's tearoom (Salon de Thé), on a cliff overlooking the jagged Riviera and sea, offers you the most scenic coffee or beer break you'll ever enjoy—for a price. The sensational view terrace is also home to an expensive-but-excellent **$$$$** restaurant (open daily, tel. 04 93 41 12 24).
• *Backtrack a bit and continue uphill (follow signs: Jardin Exotique). The lane ends at the hilltop castle ruins—now blanketed by the...*

Jardin d'Eze: You'll find this prickly festival of cactus and exotic plants suspended between the sea and sky at the top of Eze-le-Village. Since 1949, the ruins of an old château have been home to 400 different plants 1,400 feet above the sea (€6, daily, hours usually June-Sept 9:00-19:00, Oct-May until dusk, well-described in English, tel. 04 93 41 10 30). At the top, you'll be treated to a commanding 360-degree view, with a helpful *table d'orientation*. On a clear day (they say...) you can see Corsica. The castle was demolished by Louis XIV in 1706. Louis destroyed castles like this all over Europe (most notably along the Rhine), because he didn't want to risk having to do battle with their owners at some future date.

• *As you descend, drop by the...*

Eze Church: Though built during Napoleonic times, this church has an uncharacteristic Baroque fanciness—a reminder that 300 years of Savoy rule left the townsfolk with an Italian savoir faire and a sensibility for decor.

Sights in Eze-le-Village

Fragonard Perfume Factory

This factory, with its huge tour-bus parking lot, lies on the Middle Corniche, 100 yards below Eze-le-Village. Designed for tour groups, it cranks them through all day long. If you've never seen mass tourism in action, this place will open your eyes. (The gravel is littered with the color-coded stickers each tourist wears so that salespeople know which guide gets the kickback.) Drop in for an informative and free tour (2/hour, 15 minutes). You'll see how the perfume and scented soaps are made before being herded into the gift shop.

Cost and Hours: Daily 8:30-18:30; best Mon-Fri 9:00-11:00 & 14:00-15:30, when the "factory" actually has people working; tel. 04 93 41 05 05.

Hike to Eze-Bord-de-Mer

A steep trail leaves Eze-le-Village from the foot of the hill-town entry, near the fancy hotel gate (60 yards up from the main road), and descends 1,300 feet to the sea along a no-shade, all-view trail. The trail is easy to follow but uneven—allow 45 minutes (good walking shoes are essential; expect to be on all fours in certain sections). Once in Eze-Bord-de-Mer, you can catch a bus or train to all destinations between Nice and Monaco. While walking this trail in the late 1800s, Friedrich Nietzsche was moved to write his unconventionally spiritual novel, *Thus Spoke Zarathustra*.

Le Trophée des Alpes

High above Monaco, on the Grande Corniche in the overlooked village of La Turbie, lies the ancient Roman "Trophy of the Alps," one of this region's most evocative historical sights (with dramatic views over the entire country of Monaco as a bonus). Rising well above all other buildings, this massive monument, worth ▲, commemorates Augustus Caesar's conquest of the Alps and its 44 hostile tribes. It's exciting to think that, in a way, Le Trophée des Alpes (also called "Le Trophée d'Auguste" for the emperor who built it) celebrates a victory that kicked off the Pax Romana—joining Gaul and Germania, freeing up the main artery of the Roman Empire, and linking Spain and Italy.

Walk around and notice how the Romans built a fine stone exterior, filled in with rubble and coarse concrete. Flanked by the vanquished in chains, the towering inscription (the longest such inscription surviving from ancient times) tells the story: It was erected "by the senate and the people to honor the emperor." The good little one-room **museum** shows a reconstruction and translation of the dramatic inscription, which lists all the feisty alpine tribes that put up such a fight.

Cost and Hours: €6, Tue-Sun mid-May-mid-Sept 9:30-13:00 & 14:30-18:30, off-season 10:00-13:30 & 14:30-17:00, closed Mon year-round; audioguide-€3; tel. 04 93 41 20 84, www.la-turbie. monuments-nationaux.fr.

Getting There: By **car,** take the High Corniche to La Turbie, ideally from Eze-le-Village (La Turbie is 10 minutes east of, and above, Eze-le-Village), then look for signs to *Le Trophée d'Auguste.* Once in La Turbie, park in the lot in the center of town (Place Neuve, follow *Monaco* signs for a short block) and walk from there (go five minutes around the old village, with the village on your right); or drive to the site by turning right in front of La Régence Café. Those coming from farther afield can take the efficient A-8 to the La Turbie exit. To reach Eze-le-Village from La Turbie, follow signs to *Nice,* and then look for signs to *Eze-le-Village.*

From Nice, you can get here weekdays and Saturday on **bus** #116 (from the Vauban tram stop); on Sunday take bus #T-66 (from the Pont St. Michel tram stop). Both buses run about 6 times day and take 45 minutes. From Monaco, bus #11 connects to La Turbie (8/day Mon-Sat, 5/day Sun, 30 minutes). La Turbie's bus stop is near the post office (PTT), on Place Neuve.

Eating in La Turbie: The sweet old village of La Turbie sees almost no tourists, but it has plenty of cafés and restaurants. **$$ Restaurant La Terrasse** is your best bet, with tables under umbrellas and big views (daily for lunch and dinner, near the post office at the main parking lot, 17 Place Neuve, tel. 04 93 41 21 84).

Monaco

Despite high prices, wall-to-wall day-time tourists, and a Disney-esque atmosphere, Monaco is a Riviera must. Monaco is on the go. Since 1929, cars have raced around the port and in front of the casino in one of the world's most famous auto races, the Grand Prix de Monaco. The modern  breakwater—constructed elsewhere and towed in by sea—enables big cruise ships to dock here, and the district of Fontvieille, reclaimed from the sea, bristles with luxury high-rise condos. But don't look for anything too deep in this glittering tax haven. Many of its 36,000 residents live here because there's no income tax—there are only about 6,000 true Monegasques.

This minuscule principality (0.75 square mile) borders only France and the Mediterranean. The country has always been tiny, but it used to be...less tiny. In an 1860 plebiscite, Monaco lost two-thirds of its territory when the region of Menton voted to join France. To compensate, France suggested that Monaco build a fancy casino and promised to connect it to the world with a road (the Low Corniche) and a train line. This started a high-class tourist boom that has yet to let up.

Although "independent," Monaco is run as a piece of France. A French civil servant appointed by the French president—with the blessing of Monaco's prince—serves as state minister and manages the place. Monaco's phone system, electricity, water, and so on, are all French.

The glamorous romance and marriage of the American actress Grace Kelly to Prince Rainier added to Monaco's fairy-tale mystique. Princess Grace first came to Monaco to star in the 1955 Alfred Hitchcock movie *To Catch a Thief*, in which she was filmed racing along the Corniches. She married the prince in 1956 and adopted the country, but tragically, the much-loved princess died in 1982 after suffering a stroke while driving on one of those same scenic roads. She was just 52 years old. The death of Prince Rainier in 2005 ended his 56-year-long enlightened reign. Today Monaco is ruled by Prince Albert Alexandre Louis Pierre, Marquis of Baux—son of Prince Rainier and Princess Grace.

Monaco is a special place: There are more people in Monaco's

RIVIERA

philharmonic orchestra (about 100) than in its army (about 80 guards). Yet the princedom is well-guarded, with police and cameras on every corner. (They say you could win a million dollars at the casino and walk to the train station in the wee hours without a worry.) Stamps are printed in small quantities and increase in value almost as soon as they're available. And collectors snapped up the rare Monaco versions of euro coins (with Prince Rainier's portrait) so quickly that many Monegasques have never even seen one.

Orientation to Monaco

The principality of Monaco has three tourist areas: Monaco-Ville, Monte Carlo, and La Condamine. Monaco-Ville fills the rock high

above everything else and is referred to by locals as Le Rocher ("The Rock"). This is the oldest part of Monaco, home to the Prince's Palace and all the sights except the casino. Monte Carlo is the area around the casino. La Condamine is the port, which lies between Monaco-Ville and Monte Carlo. From here it's a 25-minute walk up to the

Prince's Palace or to the casino, or three minutes by bus to either (see "Getting Around Monaco," later).

TOURIST INFORMATION

The main TI is at the top of the park above the casino (Mon-Sat 9:00-19:00, Sun 11:00-13:00, 2 Boulevard des Moulins, tel. 00-377/92 16 61 16 or 00-377/92 16 61 66, www.visitmonaco.com). The TI may move locations in 2017, though it will remain near the casino. Another TI is at the train station (Tue-Sat 9:00-18:00, also open Sun-Mon in July-Aug, closed 12:00-14:00 off-season).

ARRIVAL IN MONACO

By Bus from Nice and Villefranche-sur-Mer: Bus riders need to pay attention, as stops are not always announced. Cap d'Ail is the town before Monaco, so be on the lookout after that (the last stop before Monaco is called "Cimetière"). You'll enter Monaco through the modern cityscape of high-rises in the Fontvieille district. When you see the rocky outcrop of old Monaco, be ready to get off.

There are three stops in Monaco. Listed in order from Nice, they are *Place d'Armes* (at the base of Monaco-Ville), *Princesse Antoinette* (on the port), and *Monte Carlo-Casino* (near the casino and the TI on Boulevard des Moulins).

By Train from Nice: You know your train is in Monaco when you're in a long, modern underground station. The station is in the

Monaco

T ACCESS TO TRAIN STATION
B BUS STOP

To Menton

MIDDLE CORNICHE

To Nice

FRANCE

MONEGHETTI

BLVD. PRINCESSE

TRAIN STATION (UNDERGROUND)

MONA

B #100 to Nice

B # 1 & 2 and #100 from Nice

BLVD. DU JARDIN EXOTIQUE

RUE GRIMALDI

R. PRIN. ANT.

BLVD. ALBERT 1

LA CONDAMINE

R. SUFFREN-REYMOND

BLVD. RAINIER III

RUE DE LA TURBIE

Jardin Exotique

T

1

2

R. PRINCESSE CAROLINE

T

B Place d'Armes (Local Buses)

#100 to Nice
B

LOW CORNICHE

B #1 & #2

B #1 & #2

B #100 from Nice

AVE. DE FONTVIELLE

RAMPE MAJOR

PRINCE'S PALACE

AVE. DE LA

RUE DES REMPARTS

RUE BASSE

3

R. COMTE GASTARDI

R. EMILE DE LOTH

POST

To Nice

AVE. ALBERT II

Place du Palais

WALK BEGINS

R. COL. BELL. DE CASTRO

4

CATHEDRAL

AVE. SAINT

LOUIS II SOCCER STADIUM

Port du Fontvielle

Jardin Botanique

FONTVIEILLE

BEAUSOLEIL

To Villa
Sauber &
Menton

BLVD. DES MOULINS

#112 to Eze-le-Village

#100 from Nice &
#11 to La Turbie

Casino
Gardens

AVE. SPEL

#1 & 2
and #100 to Nice

#1 & 2

CHARLOTTE

AMERICAN-
STYLE
CASINO

BLVD. LARVOTTO

Place du
Casino

CASINO

C O

MONTE CARLO

AVE. DE LA COSTA

AVE. D'OSTENDE

PALAIS DES
CONGRES &
P "Le Casino"

SHUTTLE
BOAT

Port

LOTSA
YACHTS!

CRUISE
TENDER
DOCK

MONACO-
VILLE

AVE. QUARANTINE

PORTE NEUVE

FORT
ANTOINE

Place de la
Visitation

P

Mediterranean
Sea

RUE EMILE DE LOTH

#1 & 2

Petit Train
Stop

MARTIN

P "Le Palais"

WALK
ENDS

OCEANOGRAPHY
MUSEUM

300 Meters

300 Yards

1 Hôtel de France
2 Huit et Demi Rest.
3 Boulangerie
4 U Cavagnetu Rest.

center of Monaco, a 15-minute walk to the casino or to the port, and about 25 minutes to the palace. The station has no baggage storage.

The TI, train-ticket windows, and WCs are up the escalator at the Italy end of the station. There are three exits from the train platform level (one at each end and one in the middle).

To reach Monaco-Ville and the palace, take the exit at the Nice end of the tracks (signed *Sortie Fontvieille/Le Rocher*), which leads through a long tunnel to the base of Monaco-Ville at Place d'Armes. From here, it's about a 15-minute hike up to the palace, or take the bus (#1 or #2).

To reach Monaco's port and the casino, take the middle exit, following *Sortie Port* signs down the steps and escalators, and then *Accès Port* signs until you pop out at the port, where you'll see the stop for buses #1 and #2 across the busy street. From here it's a 20-minute walk to the casino (up Avenue d'Ostende to your left), or a short trip via buses #1 or #2.

To return to Nice by train after 20:30, when ticket windows close, buy your return tickets now or be sure to have about €4 in coins for the ticket machines.

By Car: Follow *Centre-Ville* signs into Monaco (warning: traffic can be heavy), then watch for the red-letter signs to parking garages at *Le Casino* (for Monte Carlo) or *Le Palais* (for Monaco-Ville). You'll pay about €10 for four hours.

HELPFUL HINTS

Combo-Ticket: If you plan to see both of Monaco's big sights (Prince's Palace and Oceanography Museum), buy the €20.50 combo-ticket.

Changing of the Guard: This popular event takes place daily in good weather at 11:55 at the Prince's Palace. Arrive by 11:30 to get a good viewing spot.

Loop Trip from Nice to Monaco: From Nice you can get to Monaco by bus or train, then take a bus from Monaco to Eze-le-Village or La Turbie, and return to Nice from there by bus. For bus numbers, frequencies, and stop locations, see "Monaco Connections" on page 742.

Evening Events: Monaco's Philharmonic Orchestra (tel. 00-377/98 06 28 28, www.opmc.mc) and Monte Carlo Ballet (tel. 00-377/99 99 30 00, www.balletsdemontecarlo.com) offer performances at reasonable prices.

Passport Stamp: For an official memento of your visit, get your passport stamped at the TI (listed earlier).

GETTING AROUND MONACO

By Local Bus: Buses #1 and #2 link all areas with frequent service (single ticket–€2, 6 tickets–€11, day pass–€5.50, pay driver or save a little and buy from curbside machines, 10/hour, fewer on Sun, buses run until 21:00). You can split a six-ride ticket with your travel partners. Bus tickets are good for a free transfer if used within 30 minutes.

For a **cheap and scenic loop ride** through Monaco, ride bus #2 from one end to the other and back (25 minutes each way). You need two tickets and must get off the bus at the last stop and then get on again.

By Open Bus Tour: You could pay €22 for a hop-on, hop-off open-deck bus tour that makes 12 stops in Monaco, but I wouldn't. If you want a scenic tour of the principality that includes its best views, take local bus #2 (see above).

By Tourist Train: "Monaco Tour" tourist trains are an efficient way to enjoy a blitz tour of Monaco. They begin at the Oceanography Museum and pass by the port, casino, and palace (€9, 2/hour, 40 minutes, recorded English commentary).

By Taxi: If you've lost all track of time at the casino, you can call the 24-hour taxi service (tel. 00-377/93 15 01 01)...provided you still have enough money to pay for the cab home.

Monaco-Ville Walk

All of Monaco's major sights (except the casino) are in Monaco-Ville, packed within a few cheerfully tidy blocks. This self-guided walk connects these sights with a tight little loop, starting from the palace square.

• *To get from anywhere in Monaco to the palace square (Monaco-Ville's sightseeing center and home of the palace), take bus #1 or #2 to the end of the line at Place de la Visitation. Turn right as you step off the bus and walk five minutes down Rue Emile de Loth. You'll pass the post office, a worthwhile stop for its collection of valuable Monegasque stamps.*

If you're walking up from the port or the Place d'Armes stop for bus #100, a well-marked lane leads directly to the palace.

Palace Square (Place du Palais)

This square is the best place to get oriented to Monaco. Facing the palace, go to the right and look out over the city (er...principality). This rock gave birth to the little pastel Hong Kong look-alike in 1215, and it's managed to remain an independent country for most of its 800 years. Looking beyond the glitzy port, notice the faded green roof above and to the right: It belongs to the casino that put Monaco on the map in the 1800s. It was located away from Monaco-Ville because Prince Charles III (r. 1856-1889) wanted to shield his people from low-life gamblers.

The modern buildings just past the casino mark the eastern limit of Monaco. The famous Grand Prix runs along the port and then up the ramp to the casino (at top speeds of 180 mph). Italy is so close, you can almost smell the pesto. Just beyond the casino is France again (which flanks Monaco on both sides)—you could walk one-way from France to France, passing through Monaco in about 60 minutes.

The odd statue of a woman with a fishing net is dedicated to the glorious reign of **Prince Albert I** (1889-1922). The son of Charles III (who built the casino), Albert I was a true Renaissance Man. He had a Jacques Cousteau-like fascination with the sea (and built Monaco's famous aquarium, the Oceanography Museum) and was a determined pacifist who made many attempts to dissuade Germany's Kaiser Wilhelm II from becoming involved in World War I.

• *As you head toward the palace, you'll find a statue of a monk grasping a sword nearby.*

Meet **François Grimaldi,** a renegade Italian dressed as a monk, who captured Monaco in 1297 and began the dynasty that still rules the principality. Prince Albert is his great-great-great... grandson, which gives Monaco's royal family the distinction of being the longest-lasting dynasty in Europe.

• *Now walk to the...*

Prince's Palace (Palais Princier)

A medieval castle sat where the palace is today. Its strategic setting has had a lot to do with Monaco's ability to resist attackers. Today, Prince Albert and his wife live in the palace, while poor Princesses Stephanie and Caroline live down the street. The palace guards protect the prince 24/7 and still stage a **Changing of the Guard** ceremony with all the pageantry of an important nation (daily at 11:55, fun to watch but jam-packed, arrive by 11:30). Audioguide tours take you through part of the prince's lavish palace in 30 minutes. The rooms are well-furnished and impressive, but interesting only if you haven't seen a château lately.

Cost and Hours: €8, includes audioguide, €20.50 combo-ticket also covers Oceanography Museum; hours vary but generally April-Oct daily 10:00-18:00, July-Aug until 19:00, closed Nov-March; tel. 00-377/93 25 18 31, www.palais.mc.

• *Head to the west end of the palace square. Below the cannonballs is the district known as...*

Fontvieille

Monaco's newest, reclaimed-from-the-sea area has seen much of Monaco's post-WWII growth (residential and commercial—notice the lushly planted building tops). Prince Rainier continued—some say, was obsessed with—Monaco's economic growth, creating landfills (topped with apartments, such as in Fontvieille), flashy ports, more beaches, a big sports stadium marked by tall arches, and a rail station. (An ambitious new landfill project is in the works and would add still more prime real estate to Monaco's portfolio.) Today, thanks to Prince Rainier's past efforts, tiny Monaco is a member of the United Nations. (If you have kids with you, check out the nifty play area just below.)

• *With your back to the palace, leave the square through the arch on the right (Rue Colonel Bellando de Castro) and find the...*

Cathedral of Monaco (Cathédrale de Monaco)

The somber but beautifully lit cathedral, rebuilt in 1878, shows that Monaco cared for more than just its new casino. It's where centuries of Grimaldis are buried, and where Princess Grace and Prince Rainier were married. Inside, circle slowly behind the altar (counterclockwise). The second tomb is that of Albert I, who did much to put Monaco on the world stage. The second-to-last tomb—inscribed *"Gratia Patricia, MCMLXXXII"* and displaying the 1956 wedding photo of Princess Grace and Prince Rainier—is where Princess Grace was buried in 1982. Prince Rainier's tomb lies next to Princess Grace's (daily 8:30-19:15).

• *Leave the cathedral and dip into the immaculately maintained **Jardin Botanique**, with more fine views. In the gardens, turn left. Eventually you'll find the impressive building housing the...*

Oceanography Museum (Musée Océanographique)

Prince Albert I built this cliff-hanging aquarium in 1910 as a monument to his enthusiasm for things from the sea. The museum's aquarium, which Jacques Cousteau captained for 32 years, has 2,000 different specimens, representing 250 species. You'll find Mediterranean fish and colorful tropical species (all well described in English). Rotating exhibits occupy the entry floor. Upstairs, the fancy Albert I Hall is filled with ship models, whale skeletons, oceanographic instruments and tools, and scenes of Albert and his beachcombers hard at work—but sadly, only scant English information is provided here. Don't miss the elevator to the rooftop terrace view café.

Cost and Hours: €11-16, kids-€7-12, €20.50 combo-ticket includes Prince's Palace; daily April-Sept 10:00-19:00, July-Aug 9:30-20:00, Oct-March 10:00-18:00; down the steps from Monaco-Ville bus stop, at the opposite end of Monaco-Ville from the palace; tel. 00-377/93 15 36 00, www.oceano.mc.

• *The red-brick steps across from the Oceanography Museum lead up to stops for buses #1 and #2, both of which run to the port, the casino, and the train station. To walk back to the palace and through the old city, turn left at the top of the brick steps. If you're into stamps, walk down Rue Emile de Loth to find the* **post office,** *where philatelists and postcard writers with panache can buy—or just gaze in awe at—the impressive collection of Monegasque stamps (Mon–Fri 8:00–19:00, Sat 8:00–13:00, closed Sun).*

Sights in Monaco

Jardin Exotique

This cliffside municipal garden, located above Monaco-Ville, has eye-popping views from France to Italy. It's home to more than a thousand species of cacti (some giant) and other succulent plants, but worth the entry only for view-loving botanists (some posted English explanations provided). Your ticket includes entry to a skippable natural cave, an anthropological museum, and a view snack bar/café. You can get similar views over Monaco for free from behind the souvenir stand at the Jardin's bus stop; or, for even grander vistas, cross the street and hike toward La Turbie.

Cost and Hours: €7.20, daily 9:00–19:00, Oct–April until about dusk, take bus #2 from any stop in Monaco, tel. 00-377/93 15 29 80, www.jardin-exotique.com.

▲Monte Carlo Casino (Casino de Monte-Carlo)

Monte Carlo, which means "Charles' Hill" in Spanish, is named for the prince who presided over Monaco's 19th-century makeover.

In the mid-1800s, olive groves stood here. Then, with the construction of casino and spas, and easy road and train access, one of Europe's poorest countries was on the Grand Tour map—*the* place for the vacationing aristocracy to play. Today, Monaco has the world's highest per-capita income.

The Monte Carlo casino is intended to make you feel comfortable while losing your retirement nest egg. Charles Garnier designed the place (with an opera house inside) in 1878, in part to thank the prince for his financial help in completing Paris' Opéra Garnier (which the architect also designed). The central doors provide access to slot machines, gaming rooms, and the opera house. The gaming rooms occupy the left wing of the building.

Cost and Hours: Hours and entry fees are shuffled regularly. Plan on €10 to enter at any hour, whether you gamble or not. Public areas are open daily 9:00-12:00 (no gambling). Take an English brochure and tour on your own. From 14:00 to very late the gaming rooms are open to appropriately attired humans over 18 (bring your passport as proof). Tel. 00-377/92 16 20 00, www. montecarlocasinos.com.

Dress Code: Before 19:00, shorts are allowed in the atrium area, though you'll need decent attire to go any farther. After 19:00, shorts are off-limits everywhere, and tennis shoes are not permitted. Men should wear a jacket and slacks, and women should dress appropriately.

Eating: The casino has two dining options. The **$$$$ Train Bleu** restaurant is for James Bond types for whom price is no object and elegance is everything. **$$$ Le Salon Rose** offers brasserie food—big salads and pasta dishes. Show your casino ticket to be reimbursed for the entrance fee before asking for the bill.

Visiting the Casino: Count the counts and Rolls-Royces in front of Hôtel de Paris (built at the same time, visitors allowed in the hotel, no shorts, www.montecarloresort.com), then strut inside the casino to the sumptuous **atrium.** This is the lobby for the 520-seat opera house (open Nov-April only for performances). A model of the opera house is at the far right side of the room, near the marble WCs.

The **first rooms** (Salle Renaissance, Salon de l'Europe, and Salle des Amériques) have European and English roulette, plus Trente et Quarante, Punto Banco—a version of baccarat—and slot machines. The more glamorous **game rooms** (Salons Touzet, Salle Medecin, and Terrasse Salle Blanche) have those same games and Ultimate Texas Hold 'Em poker, but you play against the cashier with higher stakes.

The **park** behind the casino offers a peaceful **café** with a good view of the building's rear facade and of Monaco-Ville.

Take the Money and Run: The stop for buses returning to Nice and Villefranche-sur-Mer and for local buses #1 and #2 is on Avenue de la Costa, at the top of the park above the casino (at the small shopping mall). To reach the train station from the casino, take bus #1 or #2 from this stop, or walk about 15 minutes down Avenue d'Ostende toward the port, and follow signs to *Gare SNCF*.

Sleeping and Eating in Monaco

($$$$ = Splurge, $$$ = Pricier, $$ = Moderate, $ = Budget)
Sleeping in Monaco-Ville: $$ Hôtel de France** is centrally located, comfortable, well run by friendly Sylvie, and reasonably priced—for Monaco (air-con, no elevator, includes breakfast, near

RIVIERA

west exit from train station at 6 Rue de la Turbie, tel. 00-377/93 30 24 64, www.hoteldefrance.mc, hoteldefrance@monaco.mc).

Eating on the Port: Several cafés serve basic, inexpensive fare (day and night) on the port. Troll the places that line the flowery and traffic-free Rue de la Princesse Caroline between Rue Grimaldi and the port. **$$$ Huit et Demi** is a reliable choice, with a white-tablecloth-meets-director's-chair ambience and good outdoor seating (closed Sun, 7 Rue de la Princesse Caroline, tel. 00-377/93 50 97 02).

Eating in Monaco-Ville: You'll find massive *pan bagnat,* quiche, and sandwiches at the yellow-bannered **$ Boulangerie,** a block off Place du Palais (open daily until 19:00, 8 Rue Basse). At **$$ U Cavagnetu,** just a block from Albert's palace, you'll dine cheaply on specialties from Monaco (daily, 14 Rue Comte Félix Gastaldi, tel. 00-377/97 98 20 40). Monaco-Ville has other pizzerias, *crêperies,* and sandwich stands, but the neighborhood is dead at night.

Monaco Connections

BY TRAIN
For a comparison of train and bus connections, see the "Public Transportation in the French Riviera" sidebar on pages 668. Most trains heading west will stop in Villefranche-sur-Mer and Nice (ask). Note that the last train leaves Monaco for Villefranche-sur-Mer and Nice at about 23:30. If you plan to leave Monaco by a late train (after 20:30, when ticket windows close), buy your tickets in advance or bring enough coins for the machines.

From Monaco by Train to: Villefranche-sur-Mer, Nice, Antibes, or **Cannes** (2/hour).

BY BUS
Bus #100, which runs along the Low Corniche back to **Nice** (3-4/hour, 45 minutes), is often crowded. To have a better chance of securing a seat, board it at the stop near the TI on Avenue de la Costa (see map on page 734) rather than the stop near Place d'Armes. Bus #100 also stops near **Cap Ferrat** (20 minutes plus 20-minute walk or transfer to bus #81) and in **Villefranche-sur-Mer** (35 minutes). The last bus leaves Monaco for Nice at about 20:00. In the other direction, bus #100 goes to **Menton** (40 minutes).

Bus #112, which goes along the scenic Middle Corniche to **Eze-le-Village** (6/day Mon-Sat, none on Sun, 20 minutes), departs Monaco from Place de la Crémaillère, one block above the main TI and casino park. Walk up Rue Iris with Barclays Bank to your left, curve right, and find the bus shelter across the street at the green Costa à la Crémaillère café (bus number not posted).

RIVIERA

Bus #11 to **La Turbie** (8/day Mon-Sat, 5/day Sun, 30 minutes) stops just past the TI (same side of street).

Bus #110 express takes the freeway to **Nice Airport** (2/hour, 50 minutes, €22).

BY CRUISE SHIP

Cruise ships tender passengers to the end of Monaco's yacht harbor, a short walk from downtown. It's a long walk or a short bus ride to most sights in town. To reach other towns, such as Villefrance-sur-Mer or Nice, you can take public transportation. To summon a taxi (assuming none are waiting when you disembark), look for the gray taxi call box near the tender dock—just press the button and wait for your cab to arrive.

Getting into Town: To reach **Monaco-Ville,** which towers high over the cruise terminal, you can either hike steeply and scenically up to the top of the hill, or walk to Place d'Armes and hop on bus #1 or #2, which will take you up top sweat-free. It's a 15-minute, level walk to the bus stop from the port: Cross Boulevard Albert I, follow green *Gare S.N.C.F./Ferroviare* signs, and take the public elevator to Place d'Armes.

The ritzy skyscraper zone of **Monte Carlo** is across the harbor from the tender dock, about a 25-minute walk. You can also ride the little electric "bateau bus" shuttle boat across the mouth of the harbor (works with a bus ticket). To reach the upper part of Monte Carlo—with the TI and handy bus stops (including for Eze-le-Village and La Turbie)—catch bus #1 or #2 at the top of the yacht harbor, along Boulevard Albert I.

Getting to Sights Beyond Monaco: Monaco is connected to most nearby sights by both train and bus. **Trains** run about twice hourly to Villefranche-sur-Mer (10 minutes), then on to Nice (20 minutes). The train station is about a 20-minute walk from the tender harbor—first walk to Place d'Armes (directions above), then follow Rue Grimaldi to find stairs and an elevator to the station.

Buses run regularly to nearby towns (see "By Bus," earlier, for bus stop locations and frequencies). If taking bus #112 to Eze-le-Village or bus #11 to La Turbie, first ride bus #1 or #2 to the TI and casino, then follow the directions above.

Antibes

Antibes has a down-to-earth, easygoing ambience. Its old town is a warren of narrow streets and red-tile roofs rising above the blue Med, protected by twin medieval towers and wrapped in extensive ramparts. Visitors making the short trip from Nice can browse Europe's biggest yacht harbor, snooze on a sandy beach, loiter through an enjoyable old town, and hike along a sea-swept trail. The town's cultural claim to fame, the Picasso Museum (closed on Mondays), shows off its appealing collection in a fine, old building.

Though much smaller than Nice, Antibes has a history that dates back just as far. Both towns were founded by Greek traders in the fifth century B.C. To the Greeks, Antibes was "Antipolis"— the town *(polis)* opposite *(anti)* Nice. For the next several centuries, Antibes remained in the shadow of its neighbor. By the turn of the 20th century, the town was a military base—so the rich and famous partied elsewhere. But when the army checked out after World War I, Antibes was "discovered" and enjoyed a particularly roaring '20s—with the help of party animals like Rudolph Valentino and the rowdy (yet silent) Charlie Chaplin. Fun seekers even invented water-skiing right here in the 1920s.

Orientation to Antibes

Antibes' old town lies between the port and Boulevard Albert I and Avenue Robert Soleau. Place Nationale is the old town's hub of activity. Stroll above the sea between the old port and Place Albert I (where Boulevard Albert I meets the water). The best beaches lie just beyond Place Albert I, and the walk is beautiful. Good play areas for children are along this path and on Place des Martyrs de la Résistance (close to recommended Hôtel Relais du Postillon).

TOURIST INFORMATION
The TI is a few blocks from the train station at 42 Avenue Robert Soleau (July-Aug daily 9:00-19:00; Sept-June Mon-Fri 9:00-12:30 & 13:30-18:00, Sat 9:00-12:00 & 14:00-18:00, Sun 9:00-13:00; free Wi-Fi, tel. 04 22 10 60 10, www.antibesjuanlespins.com).

ARRIVAL IN ANTIBES
By Train: Bus #14 runs frequently from the train station to the *gare routière* (bus station; near several recommended hotels and the old town), and continues to the fine Plage de la Salis, with quick access to the Phare de la Garoupe trail (2/hour, none on Sun, bus stop 100 yards to right as you exit train station). **Taxis** usually wait in front of the station.

To **walk** to the port, the old town, and the Picasso Museum (15 minutes), cross the street in front of the station, skirting left of the café, and follow Avenue de la Libération downhill as it bends left. At the end of the street, head right along the port. If you walk on the water's edge, you'll see the yachts get bigger as you go. To walk directly to the TI and recommended hotels in the old town, turn right out of the station and walk down Avenue Robert Soleau.

There's no baggage check at the station. The last train back to Nice leaves at about midnight.

By Bus: Regional buses (including airport bus #250) stop at the long bus platform behind the train station (called the *Pôle d'Echange,* bus info office). Take the pedestrian overpass from behind the train station. City buses use the bus station at the edge of the old town on Place Guynemer, a block below Place Général de Gaulle (info desk open Mon-Fri 7:30-19:00, Sat 8:30-12:00 & 14:30-17:30, closed Sun, www.envibus.fr).

By Car: Day-trippers follow signs to *Centre-Ville,* then *Port Vauban.* The easiest place to park is a convenient but pricey underground parking lot located outside the ramparts near the archway leading into the old town (€9/4 hours, €20/12 hours, see map on page 746). A free lot is available opposite Fort Carré (north of the port). It's a 15-minute walk to the old town from here; you can also catch bus #14. Street parking is free Monday through Friday (12:00-14:00 & 19:00-8:00), and all day Saturday and Sunday.

If you're sleeping here, follow *Centre-Ville* signs, then signs to your hotel. The most appealing hotels in Antibes are best by car, and Antibes works well for drivers—compared with Nice, parking is easy, traffic is minimal, and it's a convenient springboard for the Inland Riviera. Pay parking is available at Antibes' train station, so drivers can ditch their cars here and day-trip from Antibes by train.

HELPFUL HINTS

Markets: Antibes' old-time market hall (Marché Provençal) hosts a vibrant produce market (daily until 13:00, closed Mon Sept-May), and a lively antiques/flea market fills Place Nationale and Place Audiberti, next to the port (Thu and Sat 7:00-18:00). A clothing market winds through the streets around the post office on Rue Lacan (Thu 9:00-18:00).

English Bookstore: Antibes Books has a welcoming vibe and a good selection of new and used books, with many guidebooks—including mine (Tue-Sat 10:00-19:00, Sun-Mon 11:00-18:00, 13 Rue Georges Clemenceau, tel. 04 93 61 96 47, www.antibesbooks.com).

Laundry: There's a launderette at 19 Avenue du Grand Cavalier (daily 8:00-20:45).

Taxi: For a taxi, call 04 93 67 67 67.

Car Rental: The big-name agencies have offices in Antibes (all close Mon-Sat 12:00-14:00 and all day Sun). The most central are **Avis** (at the train station, tel. 04 93 34 65 15) and **Hertz**

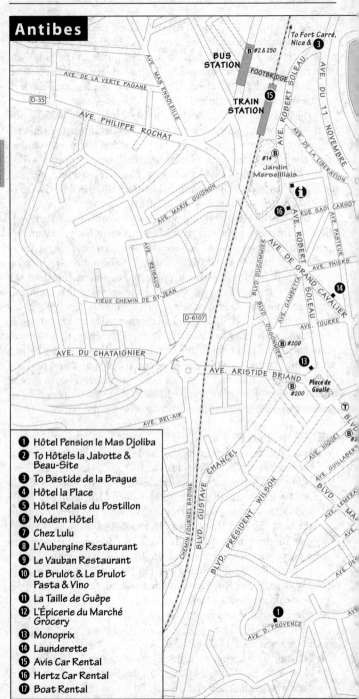

Antibes

RIVIERA

1 Hôtel Pension le Mas Djoliba
2 To Hôtels la Jabotte &
   Beau-Site
3 To Bastide de la Brague
4 Hôtel la Place
5 Hôtel Relais du Postillon
6 Modern Hôtel
7 Chez Lulu
8 L'Aubergine Restaurant
9 Le Vauban Restaurant
10 Le Brulot & Le Brulot
   Pasta & Vino
11 La Taille de Guêpe
12 L'Épicerie du Marché
   Grocery
13 Monoprix
14 Launderette
15 Avis Car Rental
16 Hertz Car Rental
17 Boat Rental

RIVIERA

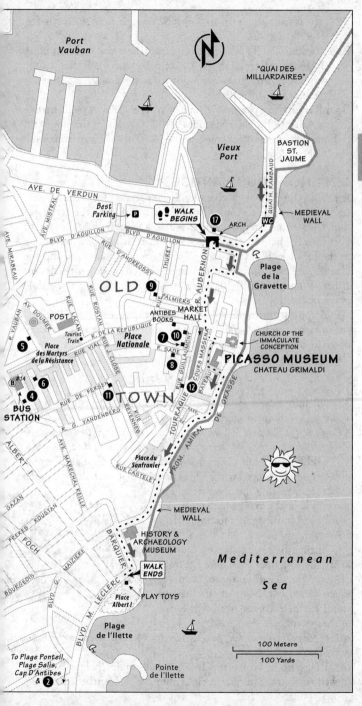

(across from the train station at 52 Avenue Robert Soleau, tel. 04 92 91 28 00).

Bike Rental: The TI has a list of places where you can rent bikes (including electric bikes). A bike path leads along the sea toward Nice, and bikes are a good way for nondrivers to reach the hikes described later.

Boat Rental: You can motor your own seven-person yacht thanks to **Antibes Bateaux Services** (€100/half-day, at the small fish market on the port, mobile 06 15 75 44 36, www.antibes-bateaux.com).

GETTING AROUND ANTIBES

Antibes' buses (Envibus) cost €1 and are handiest for carless travelers wanting access to Cap d'Antibes. **Bus #14** links the train station, bus station, old town, and Plage de la Salis. It also takes you to Fort Carré, where free parking is available. **Bus #2** provides access to the best beaches, the path to La Phare de la Garoupe, and the Cap d'Antibes trail. It runs from the bus station down Boulevard Albert I (daily 7:00-19:00, every 40 minutes). Pick up a schedule at the bus station.

A **tourist train** offers 40-minute circuits around old Antibes, the port, the ramparts, and to Juan-les-Pins (€8, departs from pedestrian-only Rue de la République).

Antibes Walk

This 40-minute self-guided walk will help you get your bearings, and works well day or night.

• *Begin at the old port (Vieux Port) at the southern end of Avenue de Verdun. Stand at the port, across from the archway with the clock.*

Old Port: Locals claim that this is Europe's first and biggest pleasure-boat harbor, with 1,600 stalls. That star-shaped stone structure crowning the opposite end of the port is **Fort Carré,** which protected Antibes from foreigners for more than 500 years.

The pathetic remains of a once-hearty **fishing fleet** are moored in front of you. The Mediterranean is pretty much fished out. Most of the seafood you'll eat here comes from fish farms or the Atlantic.

• *With the port on your left, pass the sorry fleet and duck under the arches to the shell-shaped...*

Plage de la Gravette: This normally quiet public beach is tucked right in the middle of old Antibes. Consider the scale of the ramparts that protected this town. Because Antibes was the last fort before the Italian border, the French king made sure the ramparts were top-notch. The twin towers crowning the old town are the church's bell tower and the tower topping Château Grimaldi (today's Picasso Museum). As you face the old town, forested Cap d'Antibes is the point of land in the distance to the left. Is anyone swimming? Locals don't swim much in July and August because of jellyfish—common now in warmer water. Throughout the Mediterranean, you'll see red flags warning of dangerous storms or tides. Many beaches now also have white flags with jellyfish symbols warning that swimming might be a stinging experience.

• For a close-up look at the megayachts and a walk along the ramparts, follow this fun detour. Otherwise, skip ahead to the "Market Hall" stop.

Antibes' Megayacht Harbor: For a glimpse at the epitome of conspicuous consumption, take a three-block detour to the right as you leave Plage de la Gravette. You'll walk along the harbor under the ramparts; enjoy the historic drawings and photos of the port along the wall.

You'll eventually reach a restricted area harboring massive yachts. Walk in and browse the line of huge pleasure craft sterntied to the pier (which was built in the 1970s with financial aid from mostly Saudi Arabian yacht owners, who wanted a decent place to tie up). Locals call this the *Quai des Milliardaires* ("billionaire's dock").

Just outside the restricted area, climb up the rampart and make your way to the **modern white sculpture.** *Nomade*—a man of letters looking pensively out to sea—was created in 2010 by the Spaniard Jaume Plensa. You can sit in it and ponder how communication forms who we are and links all people.

• Now let's backtrack to where we started and enter Antibes' old town through the arch under the clock. You can walk directly up the main street to get to our next stop, but here's a more scenic option: Passing through the gate, turn immediately left, walk along the wall, and then up the stairs. At the terrace corner is another fine viewpoint. Turn right and walk straight through the arch at #14 and into Place du Revely, the most picturesque corner of the old town. On Place du Revely, turn right, and go downhill under three arches. Continue down the ramp and uphill straight into the old town and Antibes' market hall, Le Marché Provençal.

Market Hall: Antibes' market hall bustles under a 19th-century canopy, with flowers, produce, Provençal products, and beach accessories. The market wears many hats: produce until 13:30 (daily except closed Mon Sept-May), handicrafts most afternoons

(Thu-Sun), and fun outdoor dining in the evenings, on Cours Masséna.

On the right (at the corner of Rue Sade), a pretty shop hides an atmospheric **absinthe bar** in its ninth-century vaulted cellar. You're welcome to go through the shop (or enter on Rue Sade) and descend to find an amazing collection of absinthe fountains, the oldest dating from the 1860s. Frédéric will gladly show you his memorabilia. You can even taste the now-legal drink to better understand Picasso.

• *Facing the front of the market, go left uphill on Rue Christian Chessel and find the pretty pastel...*

Church of the Immaculate Conception: Built on the site of a Greek temple, this is worth a peek inside. A church has stood on this site since the 12th century. This one served as the area's cathedral until the mid-1200s. The stone bell tower standing in front of the church predates it by 600 years, when it was part of the city's defenses. Many of those heavy stones were pillaged from Antibes' Roman monuments.

• *Looming above the church on prime real estate is the white-stone...*

Château Grimaldi: This site was home to the acropolis of the Greek city of Antipolis and later a Roman fort. Later still, the château was the residence of the Grimaldi family (a branch of which still rules Monaco). Today it houses Antibes' Picasso Museum. Its proximity to the cathedral symbolized the sometimes too-cozy relationship between society's two dominant landowning classes: the Church and the nobility. (In 1789, the French Revolution changed all that.)

• *After visiting the **Picasso Museum** (described below), exit to the left. Work your way through the warren of pretty lanes, then head out to the water, turn right along the ramparts, and find a sweeping sea view. As you walk, you'll pass a charming neighborhood (La Commune Libre du Safranier) on your right. The rampart walk leads to a viewpoint atop the History and Archaeology Museum.*

Viewpoint: From this perch you can enjoy a clear view of **Cap d'Antibes** (to the south), crowned by its lighthouse and studded with mansions (a proposed hike here is described later). The Cap was long the refuge of Antibes' rich and famous, and a favorite haunt of F. Scott Fitzgerald and Ernest Hemingway.

• *After taking a quick spin through the **History and Archaeology Museum** (see page 752), continue hugging the shore past Place Albert I until you see the views back to old Antibes. Benches and soft sand await. Energetic walkers can continue on the trail, which leads all the way to Cap d'Antibes (see page 753); others can return to old Antibes and wander around in its peaceful back lanes.*

Sights in Antibes

▲▲Picasso Museum (Musée Picasso)

Sitting serenely where the old town meets the sea, this compact three-floor museum offers a manageable collection of Picasso's paintings, sketches, and ceram-

ics. Picasso lived in this castle for four months in 1946, when he cranked out an amazing amount of art (most of the paintings you'll see are from this short but prolific stretch of his long and varied career). He was elated by the end of World War II, and his

works show a celebration of color and a rediscovery of light after France's long nightmare of war. Picasso was also re-energized by his young and lovely companion, Françoise Gilot (with whom he would father two children). The resulting collection (donated by Picasso) put Antibes on the tourist map.

Cost and Hours: €6; mid-June-mid-Sept Tue-Sun 10:00-18:00 plus July-Aug Wed and Fri until 20:00, mid-Sept-mid-June Tue-Sun 10:00-12:00 & 14:00-18:00, closed Mon year-round; tel. 04 92 90 54 20, www.antibes-juanlespins.com.

Visiting the Museum: The museum's highlight is on the top floor, where you'll find the permanent collection of Picasso's works. Visitors are greeted by a large image of Picasso and a display of photographs of the artist at work and play during his time in Antibes. The first gallery room (up the small staircase to your left) houses several famous works, including the lively, frolicking, and big-breasted *La Joie de Vivre* painting (from 1946). This Greek bacchanal sums up the newfound freedom of a just-liberated France and sets the tone for the rest of the collection. You'll also see the colorless, three-paneled *Satyr, Faun, and Centaur with Trident* and several ceramic creations. Tour the rest of the floor clockwise, noticing the focus on sea creatures, tridents, and other marine themes (*oursin* is a sea urchin, *poulpe* is an octopus, and *poisson* is, well, fishy). *Nature morte* means still life, and you'll see many of these in this collection.

As you tour the museum, you'll see both black-and-white and colorful ink sketches that challenge the imagination—these show off Picasso's skill as a cartoonist and caricaturist. Look also for the Basque fishermen and several Cubist-style nudes *(nus couchés)*, one painted on plywood.

Near the end, don't miss the wall devoted to Picasso's ceramic plates. In 1947, inspired by a visit to a ceramics factory in nearby Vallauris, Picasso discovered the joy of this medium. He was smitten by the texture of soft clay and devoted a great deal of time to exploring how to work with it—producing over 2,000 pieces in one year. In the same room, the wall-sized painting *Ulysses and the Sirens* screams action and anxiety. Lashed to the ship mast, Ulysses survives the temptation of the sirens.

History and Archaeology Museum (Musée d'Histoire et d'Archéologie)

More than 2,000 years ago, Antibes was the center of a thriving maritime culture. It was an important Roman city with aqueducts, theaters, baths, and so on. This museum—the only place to get a sense of the city's ancient roots—displays Greek, Roman, and Etruscan odds and ends in two simple halls (no English descriptions). Your visit starts at an 1894 model of Antibes and continues past displays of Roman coins, cups, plates, and scads of amphorae. The lanky lead pipe connected to a center box was used as a bilge pump; nearby is a good display of Roman anchors made of lead.

Cost and Hours: €3; mid-June-mid-Sept Tue-Sun 10:00-12:00 & 14:00-18:00, mid-Sept-mid-June Tue-Sun 10:00-13:00 & 14:00-17:00, closed Mon year-round; on the water between Picasso Museum and Place Albert I, tel. 04 92 95 85 98, www.antibes-juanlespins.com.

Fort Carré

This impressively situated, mid-16th-century citadel, on the headland overlooking the harbor, protected Antibes from Nice (which until 1860 wasn't part of France). You can tour this unusual star-shaped fort (€3) for the fantastic views over Antibes, but there's little to see inside.

▲Beaches *(Plages)*

Good beaches stretch from the south end of Antibes toward Cap d'Antibes. They're busy but manageable in summer and on weekends, with cheap snack stands and good views of the old town. The closest beach to the old town is at the port (Plage de la Gravette), which seems calm in any season.

HIKES

I list two good hikes below. Where Boulevard Albert I meets the beach (at Place Albert I), you get a good view of Plage de la Salis and Cap d'Antibes. That tower on the hill is your destination for the first hike. The longer Cap d'Antibes hike begins on the next beach, just over that hill. The two hikes are easy to combine by bus, bike, or car.

▲▲Chapelle et Phare de la Garoupe Hike

The territorial views—best in the morning, skippable if hazy—from this viewpoint more than merit the 20-minute uphill climb from Plage de la Salis (a few blocks after Maupassant Apartments, where the road curves left, follow signs and the rough, cobbled Chemin du Calvaire up to lighthouse tower). An orientation table explains that you can see from Nice to Cannes and up to the Alps.

Getting There: Take bus #2 or bus #14 to the Plage de la Salis stop and find the trail a block ahead. By car or bike, follow signs for *Cap d'Antibes*, then look for *Chapelle et Phare de la Garoupe* signs.

▲▲Cap d'Antibes Hike (Sentier Touristique de Tirepoil)

Cap d'Antibes itself is filled with exclusive villas and mansions protected by high walls. Roads are just lanes, bounded on both sides by the high and greedy walls in this home of some of the most expensive real estate in France (and where "public" seems like a necessary evil). But all the money in the world can't buy you the beach in France, so a thin strip of rocky coastline  forms a two-mile long, park-like zone with an extremely scenic, mostly paved, but often rocky, trail (Sentier Touristique de Tirepoil).

As you walk, you'll have fancy fences with security cameras on one side and dramatic sea views on the other. The public space is rarely more than 50 yards wide and often extremely rocky—impassible if not for the paved trail carved out of it for the delight of hikers.

At a fast clip you can walk the entire circle in just over an hour. Don't do the hike without the tourist map (available at hotels or the TI). While you can do it in either direction (or in partial segments), I'd do the entire loop counterclockwise like this:

From the La Fontaine bus stop (see "Getting There," later), walk five minutes down Avenue Mrs. L. D. Beaumont to the gate of the Villa Eilenroc. From here leave the road and enter a trail, skirting the villa on your left, and walk five more minutes to the rocky coastal trail. Now turn left and follow the trail for nearly an hour around Cap Gros. There's no way to get lost without jumping into the sea or scaling villa security walls. You return to civilization at a tiny resort (Plage de la Garoupe), with an expensive restaurant, a fine beach (both public and private), and a fun and inexpensive beachside bar/restaurant. From here it's a 10-minute walk uphill to your starting point and the bus stop. With a car (or bike), you could start and end at Plage de la Garoupe. For a shorter version, walk from Plage de la Garoupe to Cap Gros and back.

Getting There: Ride bus #2 from Antibes for about 15 minutes to the La Fontaine stop at Rond-Point A. Meiland (next to the recommended Hôtel Beau-Site). By car or bike, follow signs to *Cap d'Antibes,* then to *Plage de la Garoupe,* and park there. The trail begins at the far-right end of Plage de la Garoupe.

NEAR ANTIBES

Juan-les-Pins Town

The low-rise town of Juan-les-Pins, sprawling across the Cap d'Antibes isthmus from Antibes, is where the action is...after hours. It's a modern waterfront resort with good beaches, plenty of lively bars and restaurants, and a popular jazz festival in July. The town is also known for its clothing boutiques that stay open until midnight (people are too busy getting tanned to shop at normal hours). As locals say, "Party, sleep in, shop late, party more."

Getting There: Buses, trains, and even a tourist train (see "Getting Around Antibes" on page 748) make the 10-minute trip to and from Antibes constantly.

Sleeping in Antibes

($$$$ = Splurge, $$$ = Pricier, $$ = Moderate, $ = Budget)

Several sleepable options are available in the town center, but my favorite Antibes hotels are farther out and most convenient for drivers.

OUTSIDE THE TOWN CENTER

$$$ Hôtel Pension le Mas Djoliba*** is a traditional manor house with chirping birds and a flower-filled moat. While convenient for drivers, it's workable for walkers (10-minute walk to Plage de la Salis, 15 minutes to old Antibes). Bigger rooms are worth the additional cost, and several rooms come with small decks (several good family rooms, no elevator but just three floors, *boules* court and loaner balls; 29 Avenue de Provence—from Boulevard Albert I, look for gray signs two blocks before the sea, turn right onto Boulevard Général Maizière, and follow signs; tel. 04 93 34 02 48, www.hotel-djoliba.com, contact@hotel-djoliba.com, Delphine).

$$$ Hôtel la Jabotte** is a cozy boutique hotel hidden along an ignored alley a block from the famous beaches and a 15-minute walk from the old town. Run with panache by Nathalie, the hotel's rich colors and decor show a personal touch. The cozy rooms have tight bathrooms and individual terraces facing a small, central garden where you'll get to know your neighbor (free breakfast for Rick Steves readers, free parking for Rick Steves readers if available, 13 Avenue Max Maurey, take the third right after passing Hôtel Josse, tel. 04 93 61 45 89, www.jabotte.com, info@jabotte.com).

$$$ Hôtel Beau-Site,*** my only listing on Cap d'Antibes, is a 10-minute drive from town. It's a terrific value if you want to get away...but not *too* far away. (Without a car, you'll feel isolated.) Helpful Nathalie and Francine welcome you with a pool, a comfy patio garden, and free, secure parking. Rooms are spacious and comfortable, and several have balconies (electric bikes available, 141 Boulevard Kennedy, tel. 04 93 61 53 43, www.hotelbeausite. net, contact@hotelbeausite.net). The hotel is a 10-minute walk from Plage de la Garoupe on the Cap d'Antibes loop hike (described earlier).

$$ Bastide de la Brague is an easygoing bed-and-breakfast hacienda up a dirt road a 10-minute drive east of Antibes. The fun-loving family (wife Isabelle, who speaks English, and hubby Franck) rent seven comfy rooms; several are ideal for families. For a down-home experience, consider staying here (RS%, family rooms, includes breakfast, 55 Avenue No. 6, tel. 04 93 65 73 78, www. labastidedelabrague.com, bastidebb06@gmail.com). From Antibes, follow *Nice par Bord de la Mer* signs, turn left toward Marineland, then right at the roundabout (toward Groules), then follow the green signs. Antibes bus #10 drops you five minutes away, and if arranged in advance, they can pick you up at the Biot or Antibes train station.

IN THE TOWN CENTER

$$$ Hôtel la Place*** is central, pricey, and cozy. It overlooks the ugly bus station with tastefully designed rooms and a comfy lounge (no elevator, 1 Avenue 24 Août, tel. 04 97 21 03 11, www.la-place-hotel.com, contact@la-place-hotel.com).

$$ Hôtel Relais du Postillon,** with cute rooms at good rates, is a mellow place above a peaceful café on a central square. There are a few cheap true singles and 16 tastefully decorated doubles, some with small balconies, and others with good terraces (tiny elevator, pay parking, 8 Rue Championnet, tel. 04 93 34 20 77, www. relaisdupostillon.com, relais@relaisdupostillon.com).

$ Modern Hôtel,** in the pedestrian zone behind the bus station, is suitable for budget-conscious travelers. The 17 standard-size rooms are simple and spick-and-span (no elevator, 1 Rue Fourmillière, tel. 04 92 90 59 05, www.modernhotel06.com, modern-hotel@wanadoo.fr).

Eating in Antibes

($$$$ = Splurge, $$$ = Pricier, $$ = Moderate, $ = Budget)
Antibes is a fun place to dine out. With so many good options, all within a few blocks of each other, I'd take a walk and survey these places for yourself.

Antibes' market hall (Marché Provençal) is chockablock with diners each evening after the market stalls close. The food can be good, prices are usually reasonable, and sucking snails under a classic 19th-century canopy can make for a great memory. If considering dinner here, remember that tourists generally eat early while the locals dine late.

$$ Chez Lulu is a fun family dining adventure that seems out of place on the Riviera. Diners fork over €25, and owner Greg (who speaks good English) does the rest, dishing out charcuterie, salads, a main course, and desserts to be shared family-style. Tables seat 6-10, and the setting is warm. It's a great way to meet others (book a day ahead or arrive early, opens at 19:00, closed Sun-Mon, tel. 04 89 89 08 92, 5 Rue Frédéric Isnard).

$$ L'Aubergine's is an intimate and feminine-feeling little place where Jenny delivers fine cuisine at fair prices, including good vegetarian options (from 18:30, closed Wed, 7 Rue Sade, tel. 04 93 34 55 93).

$$$$ Le Vauban is a dressy place, popular with locals for a special event and its seafood (closed for lunch Mon and Wed and all day Tue, opposite 4 Rue Thuret, tel. 04 93 34 33 05, www.levauban.fr).

$$$ Le Brulot, an institution in Antibes, is known for its Provençal cuisine and meats cooked on an open fire. It's a small place, overflowing onto the street, with a few outside tables and a dining room below (big, splittable portions, closed Sun, 2 Rue Frédéric Isnard, tel. 04 93 34 17 76).

$$ Le Brulot Pasta & Vino serves hearty pizza and big portions of pasta. This family-friendly place has indoors-only seating in a noisy and fun, air-conditioned cellar under stone arches (daily, dinners only, 3 Rue Frédéric Isnard, tel. 04 93 34 19 19).

$$$ La Taille de Guêpe is a local favorite with fresh, colorful, and light cuisine. The interior blends stone walls with feminine decor and modern touches. The well-presented and health-conscious cuisine is delicious, and the *moëlleux au chocolat* is a perfect way to end your meal (reservations recommended, closed Sun-Mon, 24 Rue de Fersen, tel. 04 93 74 03 58).

Picnic on the Beach or Ramparts: Romantics on a shoestring can drop by the handy **L'Épicerie du Marché** (a little grocery store open daily until 23:00, up the hill from the market hall at 3 Cours Masséna) and assemble their own picnic dinner to enjoy on the beach or ramparts. There's also a **Monoprix,** located on Place Général de Gaulle (Mon-Sat 8:30-20:30, Sun 9:00-12:30).

Antibes Connections

For a comparison of train and bus connections, see the "Public Transportation in the French Riviera" sidebar on page 668.

From Antibes by Train: TGV and local trains serve Antibes' little station. Trains go to **Cannes** (2/hour, 15 minutes), **Nice** (2/hour, 20 minutes), **Grasse** (1/hour, 40 minutes), **Villefranche-sur-Mer** (2/hour, 40 minutes), **Monaco** (2/hour, 50 minutes), and **Marseille** (16/day, 2.5 hours).

By Bus: All the buses listed below serve the Pôle d'Echange bus stops behind the train station. Handy **bus #200** ties everything together, but runs at a snail's pace when traffic is bad (4/hour Mon-Sat, 2/hour Sun, any ride costs €1.50). This bus goes west to **Cannes** (35 minutes) and east to **Nice** (1.5 hours).

Bus #250 runs from behind Antibes' train station to **Nice Airport** (2/hour, 40 minutes, €11; cross over the tracks on the pedestrian bridge—it's the last shelter to the right).

Inland Riviera

For a verdant, rocky, fresh escape from the beaches, head inland and upward. Some of France's most perfectly perched hill towns and splendid scenery hang overlooked in this region that's more famous for beaches and bikinis. Driving is the easiest way to get around, though the bus gets you to many of the places described. Vence and St-Paul-de-Vence are well served by bus from Nice (see "Nice Connections" on page 708). For a scenic inland train ride, take the narrow-gauge train from Nice into the Alps (see page 697).

St-Paul-de-Vence

This most famous Riviera hill town is also the most-visited village in France. And it feels that way—like an overrun and over-restored artist shopping mall. Its attraction is understandable, as every cobble and flower seems just so, and the setting is postcard-perfect. Avoid visiting between 11:00 and 18:00, particularly on weekends. Beat the crowds by skipping breakfast at your hotel and eating it in St-Paul-de-Vence, or come for dinner and experience the village at its tranquil best.

Orientation to St-Paul-de-Vence

The helpful **TI**, just through the gate into the old city on Rue Grande, has maps with minimal explanations of key buildings (daily 10:00-18:00, June-Sept until 19:00, closed for lunch on weekends). The TI offers walking tours with English translations, including tours focused on history, art, and *pétanque (boules)*. Call or email in advance to reserve (€7, tel. 04 93 32 86 95, www.saint-pauldevence.com, serviceguide@saint-pauldevence.com).

Arrive early to park near the village (cars are not allowed inside St-Paul). Bus #400 (connects with Nice and Vence) stops on the main road, a short walk from the village. If the traffic-free lane leading to the old city is jammed, walk along the road that veers up and left just after Café de la Place, and enter the town through its side door.

Sights in St-Paul-de-Vence

The Old Town

St-Paul's old city has no essential sights, though its lovely cobbled lanes and peekaboo views delight most who come. You'll pass the vintage **Café de la Place** on entering the village—a classic place to have a coffee and croissant and watch as waves of tourists crash into the town (daily from 7:00, tel. 04 93 32 80 03). On the square, serious *boules* competitions take place all day long. Meander deep into St-Paul-de-Vence's quieter streets to find panoramic views. Visit Marc Chagall's grave in the cemetery at the opposite end of town (from the cemetery entrance, turn right, then left; it's the third gravestone). Walk up the stairs to the view platform and try to locate the hill town of Vence at the foot of an impressive mountain. Is the sea out there—somewhere?

▲Fondation Maeght

This inviting, pricey, and far-out private museum is situated a steep walk or short drive above St-Paul-de-Vence. Fondation Maeght (fohn-dah-shown mahg) offers an excellent introduction to modern Mediterranean art by gathering many of the Riviera's most famous artists under one roof. Sadly, there are no English explanations anywhere.

Cost and Hours: €15, €5 to take photos, daily July-Sept 10:00-19:00, Oct-June 10:00-18:00, tel. 04 93 32 81 63, www.fondation-maeght.com.

Getting There: The museum is a steep uphill-but-doable 20-minute walk from St-Paul-de-Vence and the bus stop. Signs indicate the way (parking is usually available at the upper lot). From the lower lot, signed *Parking Conseille,* a shortcut on a steep, dirt path through the trees leads directly to the green gate in front of the ticket booth.

Visiting the Museum: The founder, Aimé Maeght, long envisioned the perfect exhibition space for the artists he supported and befriended as an art dealer. He purchased this arid hilltop, planted 35,000 plants, and hired an architect (José Luis Sert) with the same vision.

A sweeping lawn laced with amusing sculptures and bending pine trees greets visitors. On the right, a chapel designed by Georges Braque—in memory of the Maeghts' young son, who died of leukemia—features a moving purple stained-glass work over the altar. The unusual museum building is purposely low profile, to let its world-class modern-art collection take center stage. Works by Fernand Léger, Joan Miró, Alexander Calder, Georges Braque, and Marc Chagall are thoughtfully arranged in well-lit rooms. The backyard of

the museum has views, a Gaudí-esque sculpture labyrinth by Miró, and a courtyard filled with the wispy works of Alberto Giacometti. The only permanent collection in the museum consists of the sculptures, though the museum keeps a good selection of paintings by the famous artists here year-round. There's also a great gift shop and cafeteria.

Eating in St-Paul-de-Vence

$$$ Le Tilleul is the place to dine well in St-Paul, with inviting tables on a broad terrace or in the cozy interior (à la carte only, open daily, tel. 04 93 32 80 36, www.restaurant-letilleul.com).

Book well ahead at **$$$$ La Colombe d'Or,** a historic place where the menu hasn't changed in 50 years. Back when the town was teeming with artists, this restaurant served as their clubhouse. Walls are covered with paintings by Picasso, Miró, Braque, Chagall, and others, who were given free meals in exchange for their art. Dine on good-enough cuisine inside by the fire to best feel its pulse; figure €60/person with wine (across from Café de la Place, closed Nov-Dec, tel. 04 93 32 80 02, www.la-colombe-dor.com; for reservations, email contact@la-colombe-dor.com).

Vence

Vence is a well-discovered yet appealing town set high above the Riviera. While growth has sprawled beyond Vence's old walls, and cars jam its roundabouts, the mountains are front and center, and the breeze is fresh. Vence bubbles with workaday life and ample tourist activity in the day but is quiet at night, with fewer visitors and cooler temperatures than along the coast. Vence makes a handy base for travelers wanting the best of both worlds: a hill-town refuge near the sea.

Orientation to Vence

Vence's fully loaded **TI** faces the main square at 8 Place du Grand Jardin, across from the merry-go-round. It offers free Wi-Fi, bus schedules, and a city map with a well-devised self-guided walking tour that incorporates informative wall plaques. Pick up the list of art galleries with helpful descriptions of the collections. Ask about their *pétanque* instructions with *boules* to rent and about guided walking tours in English (April-Oct Mon-Sat 9:00-19:00, Sun 10:00-18:00; Nov-March Mon-Sat 10:00-17:00, closed Sun; tel. 04 93 58 06 38, www.ville-vence.fr).

Bus #94 or **#400** (from Nice, Cagnes-sur-Mer, and St-Paul-de-Vence) drops you at the bus stop labeled *Halte Routière de l'Ara*, which is on a roundabout at Place Maréchal Juin. It's a 10-minute walk to the town center along Avenue Henri Isnard or Avenue de la Résistance. If arriving by **car**, follow signs to *cité historique* and park in the underground Parking Grand Jardin, across from the TI. Some hotels offer discounted rates for parking.

Market day in the *cité historique* (old town) is on Friday mornings on Place Clemenceau. A big all-day antiques market is on Place du Grand Jardin every Wednesday. If you miss market day, a Monoprix **supermarket** is on Avenue de la Résistance, across from the entrance to the Marie Antoinette parking lot (grocery store upstairs, Mon-Sat 8:30-20:00, Sun 9:00-13:00). For a **taxi,** call 04 93 58 11 14.

Sights in Vence

Château de Villeneuve

This 17th-century mansion, adjoining an imposing 12th-century watchtower, bills itself as "one of the Riviera's high temples of modern art," with a rotating collection. Check with the TI to see what's playing in the temple.

Cost and Hours: €6, Tue-Sun 11:00-18:00, closed Mon, tel. 04 93 58 15 78.

RIVIERA

▲Chapel of the Rosary (Chapelle du Rosaire)

The chapel, a short drive or 20-minute walk from town, was designed by an elderly and ailing Henri Matisse as thanks to the Dominican sister who had taken care of him (he was 81 when the chapel was completed). While the chapel is the ultimate pilgrimage for his fans, the experience may underwhelm others. (Picasso thought it looked like a bathroom.)

Cost and Hours: €5; Mon, Wed, and Sat 14:00-17:30, Tue and Thu 10:00-11:30 & 14:00-17:30, Sun only open for Mass at 10:00 followed by tour of chapel, closed Fri and mid-Nov-mid-Dec; 466 Avenue Henri Matisse, tel. 04 93 58 03 26.

Getting There: It's a 20-minute walk from the TI. Turn right out of the TI and take your first right and then a quick left onto Avenue Henri Isnard, then continue all the way to the traffic circle. Turn right across the one-lane bridge on Avenue Henri Matisse, following signs to *St-Jeannet*.

Visiting the Chapel: The modest chapel holds a simple series of charcoal black-on-white tile sketches and uses three symbolic colors as accents: yellow (sunlight and the light of God), green (nature), and blue (the Mediterranean sky). Bright sunlight filters through the stained-glass windows and does a cheery dance across the sketches.

Your entry ticket includes a 20-minute tour from one of the kind nuns who speaks English. Photography is not allowed. Downstairs you'll find displays of the vestments Matisse designed for the priests, his models of the chapel, and sketches.

Matisse was the master of leaving things out. Decide for yourself whether Matisse met the goal he set himself: "Creating a religious space in an enclosed area of reduced proportions and to give it, solely by the play of colors and lines, the dimension of infinity."

Sleeping in Vence

($$$$ = Splurge, $$$ = Pricier, $$ = Moderate, $ = Budget)
These places tend to close their reception desks between 12:00 and 16:00. Make arrangements in advance if you plan to arrive during this time.

$$$ La Maison du Frêne is a modern, art-packed B&B with four sumptuous suites centrally located behind the TI. Energetic and art-crazy Thierry and Guy make fine hosts (includes good breakfast, kids sleep free; next to the Château de Villeneuve at 1 Place du Frêne—turn right out of the TI, then right again, then left; tel. 04 93 24 37 83, www.lamaisondufrene.com, contact@lamaisondufrene.com).

$ Auberge des Seigneurs feels medieval. It's a central, funky, dark-wooded place in a 17th-century building with six simple but spacious rooms over a restaurant. Ring the bell if no one is present (Wi-Fi in lobby, includes parking voucher, 1 Rue du Docteur Binet, tel. 04 93 58 04 24, www.auberge-seigneurs.com, sandrine.rodi@wanadoo.fr).

NEAR VENCE IN ST-JEANNET

To melt into the Inland Riviera's quiet side, drive 15 minutes from Vence to the remarkably situated, no-tourist-in-sight hill town of St-Jeannet. Views are endless and everywhere. It's so quiet, it's hard to believe that the beach is only 10 miles away.

At **$$ The Frogs' House,** Benôit and Corinne welcome travelers with a full menu of good rooms, cooking lessons, hikes in the area, and day trips. If you don't have wheels, they'll pick you up at the train station or airport. Rooms are small but sharp (some rooms with balconies, family rooms, includes hearty breakfast, full-house rentals available in winter, tel. 04 93 58 98 05, mobile 06 28 06 80 28, www.thefrogshouse.fr, info@thefrogshouse.fr). A parking lot is at the bottom of St-Jeannet, a few blocks from this small hotel.

Eating in Vence

Tempting outdoor eateries litter the old town. Lights embedded in the cobbles illuminate the way after dark.

$$$ La Cassolette is an intimate place with reasonable prices and a romantic terrace across from the floodlit church (closed Tue-Wed except July-Aug, 10 Place Clemenceau, tel. 04 93 58 84 15, www.restaurant-lacassolette-vence.com).

At **$$$ Les Agapes,** Chef Jean-Philippe goes beyond the standard fare with lavish presentations, creative food combinations, and moderate (for the Riviera) prices. Try the *sphere chocolat* dessert to round out your meal (closed Mon and also Sun in off-season, 4 Place Clemenceau, tel. 04 93 58 50 64, www.les-agapes.net).

Nearby, **$$$ La Litote** is lauded by locals as a good value, with outdoor tables on a quiet, hidden square, and a cozy interior (closed Sun, 7 Rue de l'Evêché, tel. 04 93 24 27 82).

For less expensive, casual dining, head to Place du Peyra, where you'll find ample outdoor seating and early dinner service. At **$$ Bistro du Peyra,** enjoy a relaxed dinner salad or pasta dish outdoors to the sound of the town's main fountain (daily April-Oct, off-season closed Wed-Thu at lunch, closed Jan-Feb, 13 Place du Peyra, tel. 04 93 58 67 63).

THE FRENCH ALPS

Annecy • Chamonix

The Savoie region grows Europe's highest mountains and is the penthouse of the French Alps (the lower Alpes-Dauphiné lie to the south). More than just a pretty-peaked face, stubborn Savoie maintained its independence from France until 1860, when mountains became targets, rather than obstacles, for travelers. Savoie's borders once stretched south to the Riviera and far west across the Rhône River Valley. Home to the very first winter Olympics (1924, in Chamonix), today's Savoie is France's mountain-sports capital, showcasing 15,780-foot Mont Blanc as its centerpiece. Boasting wooden chalets overflowing with geraniums and cheese fondue in every restaurant, Savoie feels more Swiss than French.

The scenery is drop-dead spectacular. Serenely self-confident Annecy is a postcard-perfect blend of natural and man-made beauty. In Chamonix, it's just you and Madame Nature—there's not a museum or important building in sight. Take Europe's ultimate cable-car ride to the 12,602-foot Aiguille du Midi in Chamonix.

PLANNING YOUR TIME

Lakefront Annecy has boats, bikes, and hikes with mountain views for all tastes and abilities. Its arcaded walking streets and good transportation connections (most trains to Chamonix pass through Annecy) make it a convenient stopover, but if you're pressed for time and antsy for Alps, slide your sled to Chamo-

nix. There you can skip along alpine ridges, glide over mountain meadows, zip down the mountain on a luge (wheeled bobsled), or meander riverside paths on a mountain bike. Plan a minimum of two nights and one day in Chamonix, and try to work in an additional night and a day in Annecy. Weather is everything in this area: Check the forecast. If it looks good, make haste to Chamonix; if it's gloomy, Annecy offers more distraction.

The Alps have twin peaks: the summer and winter seasons, when hotels and trails or slopes are slammed. June and November are dead quiet in Chamonix (many hotels and restaurants close) as locals recover from one high season and prepare for the next.

GETTING AROUND THE ALPS

Annecy and Chamonix are well-connected by trains. Buses run from Chamonix to nearby villages, and the Aiguille du Midi lift takes travelers from Chamonix to Italy over Europe's most scenic border crossing. If you have a car, autoroutes make the going easy, and scenic drives near Annecy allow you to savor remarkable views.

Entering Switzerland by Car: Drivers passing through Switzerland need a "vignette" decal to use Swiss autoroutes (about €37, valid one calendar year)—even if only to reach Geneva's airport from bordering France (though locals suggest this section is not heavily patrolled, and skipping the autoroute via local roads through Geneva is possible but a headache). You can buy Swiss vignettes at Annecy's Automobile Club (15 Rue de la Préfecture) or on the autoroute at the border crossing.

SAVOIE'S CUISINE SCENE

Savoie cuisine is mountain-hearty. Its Swiss-similar specialties include *fondue savoyarde* (melted Beaufort and Comté cheeses and local white wine, sometimes with a dash of Cognac), raclette (chunks of semi-melted cheese served with potatoes, pickles, sausage, and bread), *tartiflettes* (hearty scalloped potatoes with melted cheese), *poulet de Bresse* (the best chicken in France), Morteau (smoked pork sausage), *gratin savoyard* (a potato dish with cream, cheese, and garlic), and fresh fish. Local cheeses are Morbier (look for a charcoal streak down the middle), Comté (like Gruyère), Beaufort (aged for two years, hard and strong), Reblochon (mild and creamy), and Tomme de Savoie (mild and semi-hard). Evian water comes from Savoie, as does Chartreuse liqueur. Apremont and Crépy are two of the area's surprisingly good white wines. The local beer, Baton de Feu, is more robust than other French beers.

Restaurants serve only during lunch (11:30-14:00) and dinner (19:00-21:00, later in bigger cities and resorts like Chamonix); some cafés serve food throughout the day.

Annecy

There's something for everyone in this lakefront city that knows how to entertain: mountain views, romantic canals, a hovering

château, and swimming in—or boating on, or biking around—the translucent lake. Sophisticated yet outdoors-oriented and bike-crazy, Annecy (ahn-see) is France's answer to Switzerland's Luzern, and, though you may not have glaciers knocking at your door as in nearby Chamonix, the distant peaks frame a darn pretty picture with Annecy's lakefront setting. Don't bother with museums in Annecy: You're here for the vistas and outdoor activities. During the winter holidays, Christmas markets and festive decorations animate the city. Annecy is a joy before noon in any season, but high-season weekend afternoons will try your patience. Spend your mornings in the old city and afternoons around the lake.

Orientation to Annecy

Modern Annecy (pop. 50,000) sprawls for miles, but we're interested only in its compact old town, on the northwest corner of the lake (known as Lac d'Annecy, or Lake Annecy). The old town is split by the Thiou River (which looks more like a canal) and bounded by the château to the south, and the TI and Rue Royale to the north.

TOURIST INFORMATION

The TI is a few blocks from the old town, across from the big grass field, inside the Bonlieu shopping center (June-mid-Sept daily 9:00-18:30 except closed Sun 12:00-13:45; mid-Sept-June Mon-Sat 9:00-12:30 & 13:45-18:00, Sun 10:00-13:00 except closed Sun mid-Nov-March; 1 Rue Jean Jaurès, tel. 04 50 45 00 33, www.lac-annecy.com). Use the free Wi-Fi, get a city map, the *Town Walks* walking-tour brochure (describes several themed walks and has basic historical information), the map of the lake showing the bike trail, and, if you're staying awhile, the helpful *Annecy Guide*. Ask about walking tours in English (€6.50, July-Aug only, normally Tue and Fri at 16:00). You'll also find TIs in most villages on the lake (many open weekends and summers only).

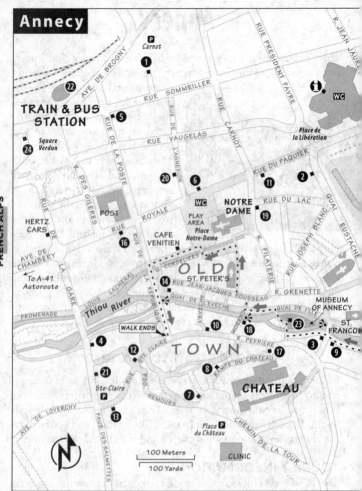

Annecy

TRAIN & BUS STATION

Square Verdun

HERTZ CARS

To A-41 Autoroute

POST

PLAY AREA
Place Notre-Dame

CAFE VENITIEN

NOTRE DAME

OLD ST. PETER'S

Thiou River

WALK ENDS

MUSEUM OF ANNECY

ST. FRANCO

TOWN

Ste-Claire

CHATEAU

Place du Château

CLINIC

100 Meters
100 Yards

ARRIVAL IN ANNECY

By Train and Bus: The stations sit side by side. To reach the old town and TI, cross the street in front of the stations, turn left, and walk to the Hôtel des Alpes. Turn right on Rue de la Poste, then left on Rue Royale to reach the TI and some hotels, or continue straight to more recommended hotels. Baggage storage is available nearby (see "Helpful Hints," later).

By Car: Annecy can be a traffic mess in high season and on weekends. Smart drivers plan to arrive early, during lunch, or late. Avoid most of the snarls by taking exit #16 from the autoroute (headed north, it's signed *Annecy-Centre;* headed south, the sign reads *Albertville*). Avoid exit #17, the other Annecy option. From

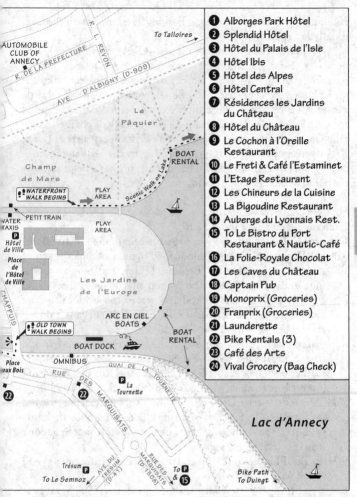

1. Alborges Park Hôtel
2. Splendid Hôtel
3. Hôtel du Palais de l'Isle
4. Hôtel Ibis
5. Hôtel des Alpes
6. Hôtel Central
7. Résidences les Jardins du Château
8. Hôtel du Château
9. Le Cochon à l'Oreille Restaurant
10. Le Freti & Café l'Estaminet
11. L'Etage Restaurant
12. Les Chineurs de la Cuisine
13. La Bigoudine Restaurant
14. Auberge du Lyonnais Rest.
15. To Le Bistro du Port Restaurant & Nautic-Café
16. La Folie-Royale Chocolat
17. Les Caves du Château
18. Captain Pub
19. Monoprix (Groceries)
20. Franprix (Groceries)
21. Launderette
22. Bike Rentals (3)
23. Café des Arts
24. Vival Grocery (Bag Check)

FRENCH ALPS

exit #16, follow *Annecy/Albertville* signs. Upon entering Annecy, follow signs to *Le Lac* or *Le Château* depending on the location of your hotel. (Don't follow signs for *Annecy-le-Vieux*.)

Refer to the map of Annecy for parking lots. The first 30 minutes are free; after that figure €1.30 per hour (about €16/24 hours). Ask your hotel for a free overnight parking pass for the Hôtel de Ville or Bonlieu parking lots. Upon arrival, ditch your car at the first lot you come to, then get advice from your hotel for more convenient parking. Parking Ste. Claire and Parking du Château work for the hotels I list away from the lake. On the lake, you can park near the big boat docks at the underground Hôtel de Ville lot or at Parking La Tournette, or a block farther along at Parking Stade

Nautique. If all else fails, the big Parking Trésum, just off the lake, usually has spaces.

By Plane: From Geneva's airport (GVA, www.gva.ch), Annecy is a 45-minute autoroute drive (Swiss vignette required; see page 766). To get from the airport to Annecy sans car, take the direct bus (6/day Mon-Sat, 2/day Sun, www.gva.ch), book a shuttle van in advance (www.genevashuttle.com), or make the cheap but scenic 2.5-hour slog by bus and train (10/day). Taxis charge an outrageous 200 Swiss francs. From Lyon's St-Exupéry airport (LYS, www.lyonaeroports.com), allow 1.5 hours by car—all autoroute—or 2.5 hours by train (10/day). Geneva's airport has a helpful transportation desk at baggage claim.

HELPFUL HINTS

Exchange Rate: €1 = about $1.10

Country Calling Code: 33 (see page 1082 for dialing instructions)

Market Days: A thriving outdoor food market occupies much of the old town center on Tuesday, Friday, and Sunday mornings until about 12:30. The biggest market in Annecy is on Saturday, but it's less central and geared toward locals (more clothes, fewer crafts; until 12:30, around Boulevard Taine—several blocks behind the TI).

Supermarkets: The **Monoprix** is at the corner of Rue du Lac and Rue Notre-Dame (Mon-Sat 8:30-19:50, closed Sun, supermarket upstairs). A smaller **Franprix** is on Rue de l'Annexion just off Rue Royale (Mon-Sat 8:00-20:30, Sun 9:00-19:00).

Bike Alert: Pedestrians do well to be aware of bike riders and avoid walking in bike lanes. If you ride a bike here, obey the same rules you would when driving a car (look before merging, don't stop in a travel lane, etc.).

Wi-Fi: The **TI** has free Wi-Fi, and many Annecy cafés offer Wi-Fi access with a purchase.

Baggage Storage: Store your bags for a small fee at the Vival grocery across from the train station (1 Rue de l'Industrie, Mon 13:00-21:00, Tue-Sun 9:00-21:00, see map on page 768). Bike renters can leave their bags at all bike-rental shops (except Véloncey).

Laundry: Lav' Confort Express launderette is at the western edge of the old town near where Rue de la Gare meets Rue Ste. Claire (6 Rue de la Gare).

Bike and Paddleboard Rental: Several places rent bikes for about €20/day (leave ID as deposit, includes helmet and basket, half-day rentals; electric, tandem, and kids' bikes/carriers available; hours generally daily 9:00-12:30 & 14:00-18:30). All but Véloncey can keep your bags while you ride.

Roul' ma Poule, near the lakefront bike path across from

Brief History of Annecy

People have called Annecy home for more than 5,000 years. The city has had its ups and downs over the millennia (more ups than downs) and has thrived thanks to its proximity to Geneva's powerful counts and its easy access to routes over the Alps to Italy. In Roman times, Annecy was an important city of about 2,000 people, complete with a forum, temples, and thermal baths. After the Roman Empire fell, locals headed for the hills and occupied the area around the château. A few centuries later, they moved down to the banks of the Thiou River at the lake's mouth. The medieval town then spread to both sides of the river and was protected by the castle you see today. In 1401, Annecy became part of the Savoie region, eventually serving as capital of a large slice of the House of Savoie. The 1800s saw the rise of hydroelectric power in Annecy and the establishment of a reliable industrial base. The 1900s brought tourism to the lake, and today, tourism still drives the economy.

the lake steamers, rents rollerblades, bikes, paddleboards (about €25/half-day), and more (open March-Oct, 4 Rue Marquisats, tel. 04 50 27 86 83, www.roulemapoule.com). **Cyclable** is also near the lake on Place aux Bois (more choices, open daily 9:00-19:00, tel. 04 50 51 51 50, www.cyclable.com). **Véloncey Bikes** is at the train station and requires a €250 deposit (closed Sun, tel. 04 50 51 38 90).

Car Rental: Avis is at the train station (tel. 08 20 61 16 68). **Hertz** is a block from the station (15 bis Avenue de la Gare, tel. 04 50 51 19 89).

Taxi: Call 04 50 45 05 67.

Bad Weather: If it's raining, consider a day trip to Lyon (10 trains/day, 2 hours, some by bus). The last train back to Annecy usually leaves Lyon at about 21:00, allowing a full day in the big city.

Sights in Annecy

▲▲Old Town Walk

Most of the old city is wonderfully traffic-free. The river, canals, and arcaded streets are made for ambling, as described in the TI's *Town Walks* brochure (see "Tourist Information," earlier). This 45-minute walking tour includes aspects of the TI's walks and will get you familiar with Annecy *toute de suite*. Do it early to allow time for *un pause café* at a canalfront café, or later so you can enjoy the old town's soft lighting. No sight in Annecy merits an entry fee. Slow your pace—as you wander Annecy's lovely lanes you'll be following in the footsteps of Jean-Jacques Rousseau, who adored strolling here (see sidebar).

Start in the center of the **bridge** on Quai Eustache Chappuis (it's the bridge closest to the lake). With your back to the lake, take in the iconic view of the old town. You're looking down the Thiou River, which starts its puny 2.2-mile trek here (running from the lake into tributaries of the Rhône River). It splits the old town in two and has provided power and resources for Annecy's economy since the Middle Ages. The Museum of Annecy (Palais de l'Isle) covers the tiny island in the river straight ahead, the St. François de Sales Church (1610) sits to your right, and the château (built in 1219, described later) looms above to the left.

Stroll down the left side of the river toward the island. In about 50 yards you'll spot twin metal gates allowing overflow from the Thiou to pass under the **St. François de Sales Church** and into the St. Dominique Canal. The pretty church was converted into a textile factory after the Revolution (and became a church again in 1923). Keep straight along the river at the first bridge, skirting past the **Museum of Annecy,** and then cross onto the minuscule island at the next bridge. You'll pass the artsy Café des Arts (opens at 10:00) and the entrance to the museum (described later).

Resume your walk by crossing to the other side of the Thiou and turn left on Quai de I'Ile. Notice the homes with doors right at river level. The river is carefully controlled with overflow gates and locks to maintain its level, allowing it to run safely through the heart of the city. At the next **bridge** (Pont Morens), look for the small attached outhouse on the third floor of the building across the canal. This bridge was smothered with houses in the Middle Ages, when a central address was all-important.

Turn your back to the canal and walk under those heavy arches, then make a left onto Rue J. Jacques Rousseau. You'll come to Annecy's plain **St. Peter's Cathedral** (built in 1535, and used by the Counts of Geneva during the Reformation). Turn right just before the cathedral on Passage de la Cathédrale, then make a left at the next canal. Notice the merging of two canals and wooden walkways. The canal running under the building is the Notre Dame Canal; the other is the Vassé Canal (both were instrumental in Annecy's economic development). Cross the wooden bridge, take a short detour into the big square, **Place Notre-Dame,** to admire the flowers, then double back and continue along the canal. Consider a canalfront pause at the peaceful Café Vénitien (open daily at 8:00).

Continue on and turn left when you reach **Rue de la République.** When you get back to the Thiou River, stop on the bridge to take in the view over Quai de l'Evêché. Those metal gates (on either side of the bridge) once fed water to a turbine that powered a cotton factory in the late 1800s. Continue along Rue de la Répub

Jean-Jacques Rousseau (1712-1778)

"Man is born free, and everywhere he is in chains. Those who think themselves the masters of others are indeed greater slaves than they." (*The Social Contract,* 1762)

Though born in Geneva, Jean-Jacques Rousseau was shaped in Annecy. He arrived here a 16-year-old runaway. He was taken in by a wealthy 29-year-old baroness, who lived on the street known today as Rue Jean-Jacque Rousseau. For the next 14 years, he lived in Annecy as a student, music teacher, flute player, and boyfriend of the baroness. Under the spell of the awesome beauty of the Alps and the free spirit of his mistress, Rousseau's basic philosophy was formed—that man in his pure natural state is good, but becomes corrupted by the artificial institutions of modern society.

At age 30, Rousseau moved to Paris, where he wrote a mildly successful opera and a wildly successful novel. Next came works on political philosophy that would literally "Revolution"-ize France.

Rousseau questioned the legitimacy of the authority of the state over the individual, who, he said, was "born free." He saw the state as little more than powerful people manipulating the weak to take more than their fair share. He examined the "social contract"—the unspoken agreement between rulers and ruled—in which citizens give up their rights in exchange for protection. Rousseau argued that a better social contract would be between the individual and the collective body of citizens. This contract would benefit everyone equally, respect the individual's inalienable rights, and give everyone a voice—i.e., democracy. His controversial writings threw gas on the already-simmering concept of revolution. When Rousseau went so far as to say that men (like animals) were born pure in nature, not tainted by the Christian idea of original sin, his books were banned, and he was exiled.

In 1767, on the lam and in disguise, Rousseau returned to Annecy. He lived there several years until the storm passed and he could return to Paris.

Rousseau's words encouraged people to rethink their roles as citizens and as human beings. His *Discourse on the Origin and Basis of Inequality Among Men* and *The Social Contract* are considered the foundation of modern political and social thought. His personal passions and love of nature inspired the 19th-century movement known as Romanticism. And much of that legacy can be traced to his formative years in a small town in the foothills of the awe-inspiring Alps.

FRENCH ALPS

lique, returning to the lake by taking a left along the arcaded and pedestrian-popular Rue Ste. Claire. Any lanes to the right lead up to the **Château Museum** (described below).

Museum of Annecy (Palais de l'Isle)

This serenely situated 13th-century building cuts like the prow of a ship through the heart of the Thiou River. Once a prison, it held captured French Resistance fighters during World War II. Today, you can still see several of the prison cells, but most of the museum is taken up with exhibits on local architecture since the war and is skippable.

Cost and Hours: €3.80, €7.20 combo-ticket includes Château Museum, Wed-Mon June-Sept 10:30-18:00, Oct-May 10:00-12:00 & 14:00-17:00, closed Tue year-round, free English leaflet.

Château Museum (Musée-Château d'Annecy)

The castle, built in 1219 by aristocrats from nearby Geneva, reminds us of the historic and important ties Annecy had with its big sister city. The castle itself cuts an impressive figure as it hangs above the lake in the old city. But there's little to see inside: a few rooms devoted to local folklore, anthropology, and natural history, and a modern-art collection that rotates regularly. Skip it.

Cost and Hours: €5.50, €7.20 combo-ticket with Museum of Annecy, same hours as Museum of Annecy.

▲Annecy's Waterfront

Stroll the bike/walking path in either direction for lake and mountain views. The best views are found walking east with the lake on your right. The peaks of Mont Veyrier and La Tournette dominate the left (east) side of the lake while Le Semnoz and the tallest viewable peak—La Sambuy at 7,200 feet—control the west and south views. A *petit* tourist train runs along the lake from near the small Pont des Amours to the Imperial Palace Hotel and beach (in good weather only, 2/hour, €4 one way, €6 round-trip, see map on page 768 for departure point).

Beaches in and Around Annecy

Annecy's lake is ringed with good beaches offering great swimming and views. Some are private and charge a small fee, others are free. In Annecy, **Plage d'Albigny** is a good, sandy public beach but also draws lots of people in summer (free). **Plage d'Imperial** offers the most kid fun, with water slides and more (small fee, www.plage-imperial.com). **Plage Municipal de Sevrier,** 10 minutes from Annecy, is a sandy beach with great views on the lake's bike path (entry fee).

SCENIC RIDES, STROLLS, AND HIKES

Lakeside paths and short, steep hikes up hillsides offer rewarding views, even with clouds. Boats, bikes, and cars make this lake's villages, hikes, and views accessible. Here are a few suggestions for where to go around the lake.

▲▲Boating

This is one of Europe's cleanest, clearest lakes, and the water is warmer than you'd think (average summer water temperature is 72 degrees Fahrenheit).

On Your Own: To tool around the lake, rent a **paddleboat** (*pédalos*, some equipped with a slide, about €20/hour for 2 people;

some boats can handle 6 passengers) or a **motorboat** (*hors-bord*, no license needed; about €60/hour for 2 people, up to 7 people, several companies all have the same rates). **Water taxis** will take you for a personal cruise or to destinations along the lake such as Talloires or Duingt (figure €140/hour for up to 5 passengers for a cruise, mobile 06 28 06 74 87, info@water-taxi.fr).

Organized Cruises: Compagnie des Bateaux du Lac d'Annecy runs several worthwhile lake cruises. The **one-hour cruise** makes no stops but has frequent departures (€14.30, 8-10/day May-Aug, 6-8/day April and Sept-mid-Oct, generally 1/day off-season, no cruises in Jan). The **two-hour cruises,** called Circuit Omnibus, stops at several villages on a clockwise loop around the lake (about €19 for entire loop, 3-5/day late April-Sept); these are ideal for hikers and cyclists (see below). Another boat offers 2.5-hour **lunch cruises** for about €60 and elaborate **dinner and dancing** cruises (€56-90). Get schedules and prices for all boat trips at the TI or on the lake behind Hôtel de Ville (tel. 04 50 51 08 40, www.annecy-croisieres.com). Yet another company, **L'Arc en Ciel,** runs lake cruises in smaller boats at prices similar to what the big boats charge (www.arcenciel-annecy.com).

▲▲Biking Annecy's Lake Path

Annecy was made for biking. It's an ain't-it-great-to-be-alive way to poke around the lake (sun or clouds) and test waterfront cafés and grassy parks and beaches. An elaborate lakefront bike trail runs along the entire west side of the lake. Even a short ride on the path is worth the effort, as there are no hills, you're separated from car traffic, and the lake and mountain views make you forget the hard seat. Expect big crowds on weekends. Wear sunglasses and bring water and a bathing suit.

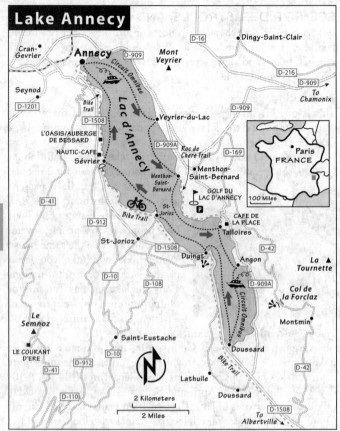

Leave Annecy passing right by the big boats with the lake on your left, pedal as far as your legs take you, break for a lakefront café, and consider a swim at one of the many grassy beaches. You'll pass wheat fields, farms, towns, and lots of other riders (treat the trail like a highway—merge carefully, don't stop in your lane, etc.). My favorite easy ride is the seven-mile stretch from Annecy to the village of **Duingt** (described below)—steady pedalers make it in 45 minutes; smell-the-roses types need an hour. You can ride to Duingt and take your bike on the Circuit Omnibus boat back to Annecy, or vice versa (about €10, 3/day from Duingt, 45 minutes; generally at 11:45, 15:30, and 18:00; more departures in summer, verify at boat dock or TI). Riding 20 minutes past Duingt to the lake's southern end at Doussard brings some of the best lake views (Circuit Omnibus boat stops here, one-hour trip back to Annecy). Serious cyclists can make it all the way around the lake in about 3-4 hours (be prepared for narrow roads, limited stretches of bike path, and a few steep hills).

Brake for a Break: About 15 minutes after leaving Annecy you'll pass **L'Oasis/Auberge de Bessard** chalet/café, a Shangri-la kind of place that only fools would pass up (serves smoothies, coffee, beer, salads, and complete meals; daily March-Oct from about 9:00). In another 10 minutes you'll pass the peaceful, low-key **Nautic-Café,** with a few tables at the water's edge (cheap coffee and beer, daily from 9:00). It's in Sevrier's marina: Turn left when you see the wood slat building on your left marked *Cercle de Voile/Club Kayak.*

▲Duingt

The quiet village of Duingt is a good destination by boat (see "Lake Cruises," earlier) or bike from Annecy. Here you'll find a café, bakery, tiny boat dock, and a good hike (see below). Bike riders exit the trail just before the rail tunnel, cross under the trail, and turn right (for the village center and the hike). If you arrive by boat, walk through the park with the lake on your right, and cross into the village. By car it's a 20-minute drive from Annecy. Park behind Duingt's church and walk along the asphalt lane past the little TI (open summers only) and the old rail tunnel (now the bike path).

Duingt's boulangerie sells good sandwiches, quiches, and drinks and is on the lakefront road, 50 yards toward Annecy from the Hotel du Roselet. The small park between the castle and the boat dock has picnic tables and views.

Hike: A short, steep, and beautiful trail leading up to glorious lake views starts from the rear of the village (100 yards from the old rail tunnel toward the town center). Find signs to *Grotte N-D du Lac Belvedere,* and walk up the trail passing the Stations of the Cross. In another 20 minutes, great views and benches await at the end of the paved walkway. From here, a steep dirt trail continues up for even better vistas (some rocky, uneven sections).

▲▲Talloires

From this upscale and charming village you can hike (and I mean hike) along the Roc de Chère trail up to jaw-dropping views over the village and Lake Annecy. To reach Talloires from Annecy, allow 30 minutes by car, 45 minutes by Circuit Omnibus boat (and 90 scenic minutes back as the boat does a one-way loop around the lake). The lack of bike paths makes Talloires an unappealing bike trip.

Those arriving by car can avoid the steep climb on the Roc

de Chère trail by turning at signs for the Golf du Lac d'Annecy golf course between Menthon-St-Bernard and Talloires—you'll soon find hiking signs by the wood shelter (parking available). It's a 20-minute walk from there to the lake views.

If coming by boat, plan on about two hours for the hike. Walk from the Talloires dock, veering left up and up through the quaint village to the main road (D-909). Turn left on the road and follow the narrow sidewalk. A few minutes after passing Chalet Christine, find the short staircase leading left into the trees (after the hairpin curve). The trail climbs for 20 extremely steep minutes up a rocky path with some very uneven footing. You'll pass a map of the trails that crisscross the Roc de Chère and come to benches with glorious views. Follow *Liaison Menthon-St-Bernard* signs to continue to that village (and catch the Circuit Omnibus boat there).

You could hike the Roc de Chère trail from Menthon-St-Bernard's boat dock, but finding the trail takes patience: Turn right off the boat, walk to the big hotel/palace, turn left and walk 200 yards up the road, then take a right on a path marked *Roc de Chère*. This leads to a small road (turn right again), taking you up to the trail. If you need lunch in Talloires, find **$$ Café de la Place** (daily, tel. 04 50 64 40 74).

Driving Around the Lake

The busy roads that link villages along the lake (D-1508 on the west side and D-909 on the east) deliver mostly modest, though occasionally spectacular, lake views (better from D-909). They eventually lead to a scenic route to Chamonix and access to fantastic view drives (described next). Read the bike route description earlier for suggested stops along the lake's west side. Be prepared for afternoon traffic on weekends and on any day in summer.

Several roads off D-1508 and D-909 lead to remarkable views of this gorgeous area. Go early for clearest skies, go late for sunsets, and skip it if it's hazy. Both of the views below are worth ▲▲ in clear weather.

Le Semnoz: For majestic mountain panoramas near Annecy that include Mont Blanc, drive or take the summer-only bus up... and up...and up to Le Semnoz (about 5,000 feet). To **drive,** follow D-41 from near the lake (see map on page 776). Allow about 30 minutes one-way and expect lots of bicycles on weekends. After leaving the city, you'll pass through Annecy's forest and climb past tree level to grandiose views over the high Alps, featuring Monsieur Blanc. Just before the top, you'll pass a great summer luge (Luge d'Eté, about €4/ride in summer, July-Aug daily, May-June and Sept-Oct Wed, Sat-Sun, and holidays). Carry on, climbing above the luge area, pass the hotel, and park when you see the chalet-café **Le Courant d'Ere** (fun for a drink, snacks, or meal; open daily for lunch, tel. 04 50 01 23 17). Climb to the chairlift station above the café for a magnificent panorama in all directions. Ligne d'Eté **buses** to Le Semnoz (and this viewpoint) leave from the Annecy train station (€6 round-trip, 6/day, daily July-Aug, Sat-Sun only in June, none Sept-May, 40 minutes, stops at the luge, details at TI and www.sibra.fr).

Col de la Forclaz: For drop-dead gorgeous views that take in the entire lake, drive 18 miles from Annecy (allow 45 minutes one-way) to Col de la Forclaz. Start by taking D-1508 south toward Albertville. Three kilometers (about one mile) after leaving the lake at Doussard, turn left on D-42 (signed *Col de la Forclaz*), then wind your way up a narrow lane for five miles past lovely scenery to the Col de la Forclaz (3,600 feet). Look out for cyclists on this climb. At the top, you'll find a sensational viewpoint, cafés and restaurants, and paragliders galore. Several outfits offer a chance to jump off a cliff and sail over the lake, including the appropriately named Adrenaline Parapente (www.annecy-parapente.fr). This trip ties in well with the scenic route to Chamonix via D-1508; it also works as a loop back to Annecy (follow D-42 down to Menthon-St-Bernard from the Col de la Forclaz).

FRENCH ALPS

Sleeping in Annecy

Annecy is popular, particularly on weekends and during the summer. Hotel rates drop from about mid-October through late April and increase in summer. Most hotels can help you find free overnight parking (in lots, usually after 19:00 until 9:00 in the morning). Unless otherwise noted, these hotels do not have elevators. For more hotel listings, try Annecy's TI website: www.lac-annecy.com.

IN THE TOWN CENTER

This part of town is pedestrian-friendly and comes with some noise.

$$$ Alborges Park Hôtel rents designer rooms in a handsome mansion in a quiet location near the station, with nice lounge spaces and an outdoor terrace (11 Rue Sommeiller, tel. 04 50 45 03 11, www.allobroges.com, info@allobroges.com).

$$ Splendid Hôtel*** decorates Annecy's busy, parkfront street and makes an impression with its grand, American-style facade. Inside, standard rooms are tight but quiet and well-appointed, and public spaces are comfortable (larger rooms available, aircon, elevator, big beds, bar, terrace, 4 Quai Eustache Chappuis, tel. 04 50 45 20 00, www.splendidhotel.fr, info@splendidhotel.fr).

$$ Hôtel du Palais de l'Isle*** offers a romantic canal-side location in the thick of the old town and 34 contemporary rooms—several with canal or rooftop views and little fridges. The

Sleep Code

Hotels are classified based on the average price of a standard double room without breakfast in high season.

$$$$	**Splurge:** Most rooms over €200
$$$	**Pricier:** €150-200
$$	**Moderate:** €100-150
$	**Budget:** €50-100
¢	**Backpacker:** Under €50
RS%	**Rick Steves discount**
*	**French hotel rating system** (0-5 stars)

Unless otherwise noted, credit cards are accepted, hotel staff speak basic English, and free Wi-Fi is available. Comparison-shop by checking prices at several hotels (on each hotel's own website, on a booking site, or by email). For the best deal, *book directly with the hotel.* Ask for a discount if paying in cash; if the listing includes **RS%,** request a Rick Steves discount.

wine bar/TV room doubles as a comfy lounge (family rooms available, air-con, elevator, 13 Rue Perrière, tel. 04 50 45 86 87, www.palaisannecy.com, palisle@wanadoo.fr).

$$ Hôtel Ibis*** is a good choice, with updated, well-configured rooms (all with queen-size beds), a canalside lounge, and easy underground parking. It's well-situated on the edge of the old town, a few blocks from the train station (air-con, elevator, 12 Rue de la Gare, tel. 04 50 45 43 21, www.ibishotel.com, h0538@accor.com).

$ Hôtel des Alpes,** a fine value, has 32 pleasant rooms at a busy intersection a block from the train station. Rooms on the courtyard are quieter, but those on the street have effective double-pane windows (family rooms, 12 Rue de la Poste, tel. 04 50 45 04 56, www.hotelannecy.com, info@hotelannecy.com).

$ Hôtel Central is just that and more. Run by your Annecy mother, Corinne, this modest, homey, and hyper-decorated place makes a fun stay. Every well-maintained room has a different theme, from Seville to India. It's located in the rear of a modest, ivy-covered courtyard (family rooms, 6 bis Rue Royale, tel. 04 50 45 05 37, www.hotelcentralannecy.com, hotelcentralannecy@orange.fr).

AT THE FOOT OF THE CHATEAU

These places are in a quiet area, a steep five-minute walk up from the old town on Rampe du Château.

$ Résidences les Jardins du Château, run by Denis *(duh-knee),* is an urban refuge above the fray near the château entry. It has a small garden and a picnic-perfect upstairs terrace, along with eight simple but comfy rooms. There are no phones or TVs, but most rooms come with kitchenettes (good family rooms, cash only, 1 Place du Château, mobile 06 67 91 94 23, www.jardinduchateau. sitew.com, rent74@free.fr).

$ Hôtel du Château,** an unpretentious place run by unpretentious Romain and Amélie, sits barely below the château. It comes with a view terrace and 16 simple, deep yellow, spotless rooms—about half have views. It's first-come, first-get for the few free parking spots (family rooms, rental bikes available, 16 Rampe du Château, tel. 04 50 45 27 66, www.annecy-hotel.com, hotelduchateauannecy@gmail.com).

Eating in Annecy

Although the touristy old city is well-stocked with forgettable restaurants, I've found a few worthy places. And though you'll pay more to eat with views of the river or canal, the experience is uniquely Annecy. The ubiquitous and sumptuous *gelati* shops remind me how close Italy is. If it's sunny, assemble a gourmet picnic at the arcaded stores and dine lakeside.

$$$ Le Cochon à l'Oreille ("The Pig's Ear") is a meat lover's nirvana. Just off the Thiou River, it welcomes diners with a leafy courtyard and a raucous, higgledy-piggledy interior. Amicable owners "Fred" and Jean speak enough English (and fluent pig) and are serious about their cooking (ask to see their pig collection). The accent is on fresh products and meat dishes (particularly ham and pork), though fish options are available. Melted cheese is not their thing (huge salads, closed Mon, Quai du Perrière, tel. 04 50 45 92 51).

$ Le Freti is a reliable restaurant for local cuisine at fair prices. It's *the* place to go for good fondue, raclette, or anything with cheese. There's good outside seating under the arcade, and inside upstairs, where each booth comes with its own outlet for melting raclette (arrive early in summer or expect a long wait, fondue, cheap wine, air-con, open daily for dinner, open for lunch on weekends only, walk through door at 12 Rue Ste. Claire and go upstairs, tel. 04 50 51 29 52).

$$ Café l'Estaminet, a pub-like place with a cozy interior and a few waterside tables on the back terrace, dishes out salads, omelets, pasta, mussels, fries, and more for fair prices (daily in summer, closed Sun evening and Mon, 8 Rue Ste. Claire, tel. 04 50 45 88 83).

$$ L'Etage is a good choice if you can't decide what you want. Regional specialties and a good range of standard brasserie fare are served at respectable prices. Dine along the pedestrian street terrace or upstairs under wood beams around a big fireplace (fondue and raclette, daily, 13 Rue du Paquier, tel. 04 50 51 03 28).

FRENCH ALPS

Restaurant Price Code

I've assigned each eatery a price category, based on the average cost of a typical main course. Drinks, desserts, and splurge items (steak and seafood) can raise the price considerably.

$$$$	**Splurge:** Most main courses over €25
$$$	**Pricier:** €20-25
$$	**Moderate:** €15-20
$	**Budget:** Under €15

In France, a crêpe stand or other takeout spot is **$**; a sit-down brasserie, café, or bistro with affordable *plats du jour* is **$$**; a casual but more upscale restaurant is **$$$**; and a swanky splurge is **$$$$**.

$$$ Les Chineurs de la Cuisine is a cozy place for a refined meal in the thick of the old town. Locals come here for French and regional classics. The interior mixes nostalgic knickknacks and fine dining ambience; outdoor tables are few and need to be booked ahead (daily, 26 Rue Ste. Claire, tel. 04 50 10 02 18).

$ La Bigoudine has been serving simple and cheap *savoyard* specialties for more than 20 years. It's a great value, with tables inside a modest-but-cheery interior and good outside tables (closed Wed, 15 Faubourg Ste. Claire, tel. 04 50 51 31 22).

$$$ Auberge du Lyonnais is a classy, well-respected river-front eatery that specializes in seafood (indoor and outdoor seating). The outgoing owners love Americans; ask Dominique about his many trips to the States, and about his Ford pickup (daily except closed Wed off-season, 9 Rue de la République, tel. 04 50 51 26 10).

Lakefront Dining: Many cafés and restaurants ring Annecy's postcard-perfect lake. If you have a car and want views, prowl the many waterfront villages. **$$$$ Le Bistro du Port,** a nautical place five minutes from Annecy by car, is beautifully situated on the boat dock at the southern end of Sévrier-Centre (daily, Port de Sévrier, turn off D-1508 at the McDonald's, tel. 04 50 52 45 00).

Dessert: Wherever you eat, don't miss an ice-cream-licking stroll along the lake after dark. But if it's chocolate you crave, head for **La Folie-Royale** (closed all day Sun and Mon morning, 13 Rue Royale, tel. 04 50 52 28 58).

Drinks: Start or end your evening at one of these local and different-as-night-and-day places. At the cozy wine bar, **Les Caves du Château,** you'll escape the crowds by heading just 20 steps up the Rampe du Château from busy Rue Ste. Claire. They offer a good choice of wines by the glass from throughout France and tasty appetizers (daily except closed Mon Sept-June, 6 Rampe du Château, tel. 09 51 17 29 98). **Café des Arts** is Annecy's most atmospheric café, marooned on the island at the Palais de l'Ile. With good prices, it attracts a mix of local hipsters and the odd tourist (daily from early to late, 4 Passage de l'Isle, tel. 04 50 51 56 40).

At the **Captain Pub** (arrr, matey!) you'll step down into a venerable pirate's pub deep in Annecy's old town. Half the place works as a **$$ restaurant** with nice seating inside and out, the other half is the pirate's den pub (open 11:00—late, 10 beers on tap, 50 more in bottles, 11 Rue du Pont Morens, tel. 04 50 45 79 80).

Annecy Connections

From Annecy by Train to: Chamonix (11/day, 2.5 hours, change in St-Gervais), **Lyon** (10/day, 2 hours, some by bus), **Beaune** (7/day, 4-6 hours, change in Lyon), **Nice** (4/day, 7 hours, start with bus or train to Lyon, more with 2-3 changes), **Paris'** Gare de Lyon (hourly, 4 hours, many with change in Lyon), **Geneva** (about hourly, 2 hours; bus-and-train options available from Geneva's airport in 2.5 hours).

FRENCH ALPS

Chamonix

Surrounded by snow-capped peaks, powerful—if receding—glaciers, and richly rewarding hiking trails, Chamonix (shah-moh-

nee) is France's favorite alpine resort. Officially called Chamonix-Mont Blanc, it's the largest of five villages lining the valley at the base of Mont Blanc. Ever since tourists eclipsed cows as the basis of the town's economy a couple of hundred years ago, Chamonix's purpose has been to dazzle visitors with some of Europe's top alpine thrills. But you'll also learn a thing or two about glaciers and get a look into the wild world of mountain climbing. Chamonix is a busy place from early July through late August and during winter holidays, but it's plenty

peaceful at other times. Chamonix's sister city is, logically, Aspen, Colorado.

PLANNING YOUR TIME

Summers—or any time a sunny day follows a rainy stretch—bring crowds and long lift lines. Ride the lifts early (crowds and clouds roll in later in the morning).

If you're a good hiker and have one sunny day, spend it this way: Start with the Aiguille du Midi lift (go early, reservations possible and recommended July-Aug), take it all the way to Pointe Helbronner, double back to Plan de l'Aiguille, hike to Montenvers and its Mer de Glace (with good shoes and snow level permitting), explore there, then take the train down to Chamonix. End your day with a well-deserved drink at a view café in town.

Orientation to Chamonix

The frothy Arve River splits Chamonix in two—with mountains (Mont Blanc and the Aiguilles Rouges peaks) towering on either side. The thriving pedestrian zone forms Chamonix's core. The TI is just above the pedestrian zone, and the train station is two long blocks across the river. To get your mountain bearings, head to the TI and find the big photo in front. And to see the town, follow my self-guided Chamonix Walk (described later) from that point.

Located where Switzerland, Italy, and France come together, this town has always drawn an international crowd. Today about half of its foreign visitors are British—many have stayed and found jobs in hotels and restaurants.

TOURIST INFORMATION

Visit the TI to make plans. Get the weather forecast, pick up the free town and valley map and the "panorama" map of all the valley lifts, and maybe the €5 *Carte des Sentiers* hiking map (see "Chamonix-Area Hikes" on page 802). Ask about snow levels, hours of lifts and trains, and consider buying the Multipass lift ticket (described later). The TI's helpful website and free app have updated sightseeing info, weather forecasts, and more (daily July-Aug and mid-Dec-mid-April 9:00-19:00, off-season generally 9:00-12:30 & 14:00-18:00; tel. 04 50 53 00 24, www.chamonix.com, info@chamonix.com).

Pull up a beachy sling chair outside the TI and plan your hike, or go online using their free Wi-Fi.

ARRIVAL IN CHAMONIX

By Train: Walk straight out of the station and up Avenue Michel Croz. In three blocks, you'll reach the town center; turn left at the big clock, then right for the TI. While the train station has no baggage storage, you can leave bags at the Absolute Café/Tabac shop (a block in front of the station on the right at 223 Avenue Michel Croz, €5/day).

By Bus: The long-distance bus station is south of the town center (234 Avenue de Courmayeur, behind the bowling alley). It's a 10-minute walk to the town center (see map on page 786). Or take the free shuttle bus called Le Mulet, see page 790.

By Car: For many of my recommended hotels and the TI, take

Chamonix: A Quick History

1091 Chamonix is first mentioned in local documents.

1786 Jacques Balmat and Michel-Gabriel Paccard are the first to climb Mont Blanc.

1818 First ascent of Aiguille du Midi.

1860 The Savoie region (including Chamonix) becomes part of France. After a visit by Napoleon III, alpine tourism begins to boom.

1901 Train service reaches Chamonix, making it accessible to the masses.

1908 The cogwheel train to Montenvers is completed.

1924 The first Winter Olympics are held in Chamonix.

1930 Le Brévent *téléphérique* (gondola lift) opens to tourists.

1955 Aiguille du Midi *téléphérique* opens to tourists.

1965 The Mont Blanc tunnel is built.

2017 You visit Chamonix.

FRENCH ALPS

the Chamonix Nord turnoff—coming from Annecy and Geneva, it's the second exit after you pass under the Aiguille du Midi cable car—and follow signs to *Centre-Ville*. Take the exit before the Aiguille du Midi lift station for hotels south of the TI. Most parking is metered and well-signed; your hotel can direct you to free parking. From mid-July to late August, traffic and parking are a mess in Chamonix—plan ahead or arrive before 10:00 to get a spot.

The Mont Blanc tunnel (7.2 miles long, about a 15-minute drive) allows quick access between Chamonix and Italy (one-way-€44, round-trip-€55 with return valid for 1 week, www.tunnelmb.com).

By Plane: The nearest international airport is in Geneva, Switzerland (Genève airport, airport code: GVA, www.gva.ch; hourly trains, 4 hours with two changes; 2 hours by car, airport shuttle van or bus—see "Chamonix Connections" on page 819). Also nearby is Lyon (St-Exupéry airport, airport code: LYS, www.lyonaeroports.com; linked by 6 trains/day, 4 hours; 3 hours by car).

HELPFUL HINTS

Crowd-Beating Tips: The only lift with serious crowd challenges is the big one: Aiguille du Midi. In high season (especially on a good day after a stretch of bad weather), take the first lift to beat the crowds and afternoon clouds. Have a view breakfast on top. Regardless of the weather, good restaurants can be

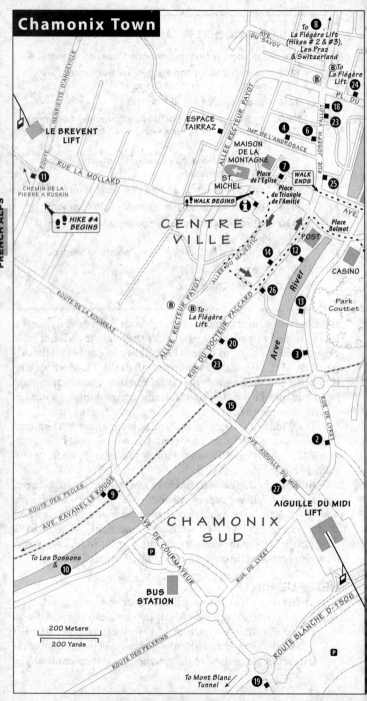

Chamonix Town

FRENCH ALPS

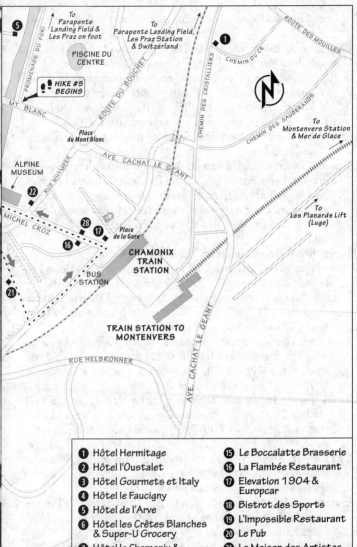

1. Hôtel Hermitage
2. Hôtel l'Oustalet
3. Hôtel Gourmets et Italy
4. Hôtel le Faucigny
5. Hôtel de l'Arve
6. Hôtel les Crêtes Blanches & Super-U Grocery
7. Hôtel le Chamonix & Le Chamonix Bar & Café
8. To Hôtel Aiguille Verte
9. Le Vagabond Gîtes
10. To Hôtels l'Aiguille du Midi & Slalom
11. Chalet Ski Station
12. Atmosphère Restaurant
13. Restaurant Bizes
14. La Calèche & La Maison du Burger
15. Le Boccalatte Brasserie
16. La Flambée Restaurant
17. Elevation 1904 & Europcar
18. Bistrot des Sports
19. L'Impossible Restaurant
20. Le Pub
21. La Maison des Artistes
22. Galerie Mario Colonel
23. Le Refuge Payot (2)
24. Casino Grocery
25. Librarie Landru
26. Maison de la Presse
27. Launderette & Technique Extrême
28. Absolute Café/Taba (Baggage Storage)

booked solid for summer evenings. It's smart to make reservations.

Plan Ahead: Bright snow abounds up high, so bring sunglasses and dress for the cold. For Chamonix's weather, check at your hotel, the TI, or online at www.chamonix.com or www.chamonix-meteo.com. For current lift information and to book the Aiguille du Midi lift, use the Compagnie du Mont Blanc website (www.compagniedumontblanc.fr).

Open-Air Market: Chamonix's Saturday-morning market fills big Place Mont Blanc.

Supermarkets: Little **Casino** markets are plentiful. The **Super-U** is central and big (next to Hôtel les Crêtes Blanches on Rue Joseph Vallot). Supplement your run-of-the-mill groceries with gourmet local specialties from **Le Refuge Payot** (two locations: 166 Rue Joseph Vallot and 255 Rue du Docteur Paccard).

Inexpensive Mountain Gear: The best deals on sunglasses, light-weight gloves, daypacks, and the like are at **Technique Extrême** (daily 9:00-19:00, 200 Avenue de l'Aiguille du Midi).

English Books: Small collections are kept at **Librarie Landru** (open daily, 74 Rue Joseph Vallot) and at **Maison de la Presse** (daily, 93 Rue du Docteur Paccard).

Laundry: Two self-service *laverie* are handy: One is a block up from the Aiguille du Midi lift at 174 Avenue de l'Aiguille du Midi (daily 8:00-22:00); the other is near the train station (8:00-22:00 daily, 120 Passage du Grepon).

Taxis: There's usually one at the train station. If not, try **Alp Taxi** (mobile 06 81 78 79 51, www.alp-taxi.com) or **Taxi Michel Buton** (mobile 06 07 19 70 36, www.taxi-buton-chamonix.com).

Car Rental: **Europcar** is across from the train station (Mon-Sat 8:30-12:00 & 14:00-18:00, closed Sun, 36 Place de la Gare, tel. 04 50 53 63 40, mobile 06 85 40 07 72).

Private Guides: Local guides can be hired through the TI or the local guides bureau (half-day in English-€200, full day-€270, visitechamonix@hotmail.fr).

Local Firewater: Pick up a little (5 cl) bottle of **génépi** liqueur, the local herb schnapps, and nip on it throughout your high-altitude adventures. It'll warm you and make you feel like a local.

GETTING AROUND (AND UP AND DOWN) THE VALLEY

Lifts and cogwheel trains are named for their highest destination (e.g. Aiguille du Midi, Montenvers, and Le Brévent). More details on individual lifts are given under "Sights in Chamonix," later. You can find current lift information and book the big Aiguille du

Midi lift on the clunky Compagnie du Mont Blanc website (www.compagniedumontblanc.fr). You can also buy tickets (and reserve the Aiguille du Midi lift) at any of valley lift stations.

By Lift: Gondolas *(téléphériques)* climb mountains all along the valley. The mightiest one—Aiguille du Midi—leaves from Chamonix. Though sightseeing is optimal from the Aiguille du Midi gondola, there are more hiking options from the Le Brévent and La Flégère gondolas.

The lift to Aiguille du Midi is open summer and winter (usually closed Nov-mid-Dec). The *télécabines* on the Panoramic Mont Blanc lift to Helbronner (atop the Italian border) run only from late June to early September, and even then only in good weather. The lift called Skyway Monte Bianco (on the Italian side of the mountain) runs from Helbronner down to Pontal d'Entrèves and rotates 360 degrees for panoramic views en route.

Other area lifts are generally open from January to mid-April and from mid-June to late September. Because maintenance closures can occur anytime, verify schedules for all lifts at the TI.

The **Multipass lift ticket** saves time and money for most, particularly if you're spending two or more days in the Chamonix valley. It allows unlimited access to all the lifts and trains (except the Helbronner gondola to Italy). Reservations cost €2 extra (for both Aiguille du Midi and Montenvers). You also get discounts for activities in Chamonix, such as the Parc de Loisirs des Planards.

Your pass is a smart card, valid for the day (not 24 hours). With it you can scan your way to the top and to ride lifts you'd otherwise skip. You could hop on a lift just to have a drink from a view café at the top (€61/1 day, €75/2 days, €86/3 days, €100/4 days, €113/5 days; kids ages 4-15—and kids over 64—pay about 15 percent less for two-day and longer passes, kids under 4 may not be allowed). The one-day pass is a good value if you plan to do the round-trip lift from Chamonix to Aiguille du Midi plus the round-trip train from Chamonix to Montenvers (and not hike between the two). Families benefit from reduced fares. The pass is sold online (www.compagniedumontblanc.fr), at participating lift stations, and at some hotels.

By Foot: See "Chamonix-Area Hikes" on page 802.

By Bike: The peaceful river valley trail is ideal for bikes (and pedestrians). The TI has a brochure showing bike-rental shops and the best mountain-biking routes.

By Bus or Train: One road and one scenic rail line lace together the valley's towns and lifts. To help reduce traffic and pollution, your hotel offers a free **Chamonix Guest Card** good for free travel during your stay (non-hotel guests can buy it at the TI for €10). The cards are valid on all Chamonix-area buses (includ-

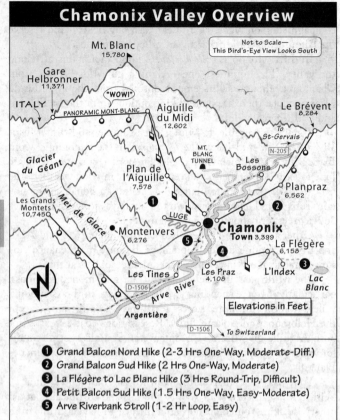

Chamonix Valley Overview

Not to Scale—
This Bird's-Eye View Looks South

Mt. Blanc
15,780

Gare
Helbronner
11,371

ITALY

"WOW!"

PANORAMIC MONT-BLANC

Aiguille
du Midi
12,602

Le Brévent
8,284

To
St-Gervais

N-205

Glacier
du Géant

Plan de
l'Aiguille
7,578

MT.
BLANC
TUNNEL

Les
Bossons

Les Grands
Montets
10,745

Mer de Glace

LUGE

Montenvers
6,276

Planpraz
6,562

Chamonix
Town 3,399

La Flégère
6,158

Les Tines

Les Praz
4,108

L'Index

Lac
Blanc

D-1506

Arve River

Elevations in Feet

Argentière

D-1506   To Switzerland

1 Grand Balcon Nord Hike (2-3 Hrs One-Way, Moderate-Diff.)
2 Grand Balcon Sud Hike (2 Hrs One-Way, Moderate)
3 La Flégère to Lac Blanc Hike (3 Hrs Round-Trip, Difficult)
4 Petit Balcon Sud Hike (1.5 Hrs One-Way, Easy-Moderate)
5 Arve Riverbank Stroll (1-2 Hr Loop, Easy)

ing in-town Le Mulet minibuses) and the scenic valley train (from Servoz to Vallorcine). This is a great value for those with time to explore the valley.

Local buses #1 and #2 run to valley villages (2/hour, details in English at www.chamonix.montblancbus.com/en). The three main Chamonix stops are: Chamonix Sud (near the base of the Aiguille du Midi lift); town center, 200 yards to the right when you leave the TI (past Hôtel Mont Blanc—look for the bus shelters); and east side (on Rue Joseph Vallot where it crosses Avenue du Mont Blanc). Direction "Le Tour" on bus #1 and "Les Praz/Flégère" on bus #2 will take you toward Les Praz (for Hikes #2 and #3) and Switzerland (see map on page 806).

Le Mulet minibuses circulate around Chamonix village. They're especially handy to or from the Aiguille du Midi lift, which is a 15-minute walk from many hotels (free with Chamonix Guest

Chamonix Activities at a Glance

▲▲▲**Aiguille du Midi Gondola** The valley's most spectacular and popular lift, taking you to magnificent views at 12,602 feet. From here you can ride cute *télécabines* over the Alps to the Italian border and back, take Chamonix's greatest hike to the Mer de Glace (from the halfway-up stop at Plan de l'Aiguille), or just enjoy the views. Whether hiking or just changing gondolas, be sure to enjoy some nature-loving time at Plan de l'Aiguille.

▲▲▲**Train to Montenvers** Cogwheel train to the eight-mile-long Mer de Glace, where you can walk inside the glacier, admire jagged mountain peaks, and have lunch with a view at the Montenvers hotel. Many people hike to Montenvers from halfway down the Aiguille du Midi lift.

▲▲▲**Le Brévent Gondola** Second-most-spectacular lift from Chamonix, allowing access to the mountain range on the opposite side of the valley from Mont Blanc (closed late April–mid-June and mid-Sept). Get off halfway at the Planpraz station for the Grand Balcon Sud hike to the La Flégère lift (although the hike is best in the other direction), or go all the way to Le Brévent for sky-high views and a restaurant.

▲▲▲**La Flégère Lift** Starting point for hikes to Lac Blanc and to the Grand Balcon Sud trail back to Planpraz (on the Le Brévent gondola). Refuge-Hôtel La Flégère, at the station, offers drinks, snacks, and accommodations, all with a view.

Arve Riverbank Stroll Several trails allow a level walk or bike ride in the woods between Chamonix and Les Praz. See paragliders make dramatic landings and enjoy mountain views outside Chamonix to the sound of the Arve River.

Card, every 10 minutes, mid-June–early-Sept and mid-Dec–mid-April daily 7:45-19:00).

The train ride toward **Martigny** in Switzerland is gorgeous, and villages such as Les Praz and Tines (10 minutes by bus) offer quiet escapes from busy Chamonix.

Chamonix Walk

Cut in half by a raging little river and with lifts reaching to staggering mountain peaks on either side of its valley, Chamonix really feels like a mountain resort. Yet hiding in its pedestrian-mall town center, among all the outdoor shops and restaurants, is a little history. This quick self-guided walk will help you understand the town that for a thousand years had more cows than people. Then, with the 19th century, came the realization that mountains can be great vacation destinations. Chamonix became the springboard to Europe's tallest peak and was transformed into an alpine resort.

• *Start at the map in front of the tourist office.*

Triangle of Friendship and TI: The pictorial map of the surrounding peaks offers a fun review of the reasons you're here. From this point you can see the Aiguille du Midi lift on one side of the valley and, opposite it, the similarly staggering Le Brévent lift. The town square is actually a triangle. Known as the Triangle of Friendship, it celebrates the peaceful and productive collaboration of France, Switzerland, and Italy (whose borders come together near here). Facing the TI is the Hôtel de Ville, which has been the city hall since 1910. There is almost always some kind of cultural exhibition on the square.

• *Look for the church bell tower.*

St. Michael's Church and Maison de la Montagne: Facing the square is Chamonix's historic St. Michael's Catholic Church. The church is made from granite just like the surrounding mountains. Inside are circa-1925 stained-glass windows celebrating winter sports, with saints looking down over the participants enjoying the local nature.

While most of the building is relatively new, its stone tower dates from Romanesque times (800 years ago), and there was a church on this spot centuries before that. In 1091 the owner of the valley had no use for this remote land and gave it to an Italian monastery. The monks built the first church and a priory next door, today's **Maison de la Montagne,** which houses the guide and mountaineering headquarters (see page 802). Behind the church, a stony overpass leads to the Crystal Museum (see page 812).

• *From this triangular square, stroll past the TI and right, down Allée du Majestic. Go straight through an ugly parking lot. On the right is a public WC and behind that is the handy **local bus stop.** (This is the best town center stop for bus #1 or #2 to Flégère, and the departure point for the Ouibus—formerly Starshipper—shuttle bus to Geneva airport.) At the WC, turn left and walk down a lane to the busy pedestrian street, Rue du Docteur Paccard. Then head left a few steps to the next square.*

Mountain Guides Fresco: Ahead is the eye-catching *Mountain Guides* fresco, built in 2010, with impressive 3-D effects and featuring a cast of 20 leading characters from Chamonix history. An info board in the square explains the story in English.

• *Continuing on beyond the fresco, you'll pass the **cinema** on the left (movies listed as v.o.—version originale—are shown in their original languages) and the **post office** on the right (a rare place that actually changes cash). Hook right to the statue (immediately over the river) of two men looking up at the mountains, which marks...*

Place Balmat and the Arve River: The centerpiece of Place Balmat is the statue erected here in 1886—100 years after Jacques Balmat, a mountaineer, and Michel-Gabriel Paccard, a doctor, made the first ascent of 15,780-foot Mont Blanc. Shown in this statue is Balmat, pointing excitedly up to the summit, along with scientist Horace de Saussure (the smart-looking guy), whom Balmat led to the top a year later. The statue was erected with funds donated by alpine clubs from as far afield as Boston (see the granite engraving). If you look up the river about a block there's another statue, this one of Paccard, erected in 1986 to honor the 200th anniversary of the first ascent. Both Paccard and Balmat forever enjoy a fine view of the mountain they were the first to conquer.

Raging underneath is the **Arve River.** Born near the Swiss border, it flows to Geneva where it joins the Rhône River. Sediment from glacial melt makes the water milky. (In winter, when little is melting, the river is smaller and much clearer.) In medieval times the first bridge here was made of wood and used mostly by cows. Today's stone bridge dates from 1880. Historically, whenever there's a big melt and a heavy rain, the Arve would flood the town. But in the 1960s the river was channeled into a canal, and since then it's been regularly dredged to help prevent flooding.

• *Look across the street to the...*

Casino: This was once one of Chamonix's oldest hotels—built for Romantic Age travelers back when local guides carried aristocrats in sedan chairs up to see a glacier. The building has a northern Italian design—a reminder that this town (like Nice) was once part of the northern Italian kingdom of Savoy. Napoleon III came here in 1860, and from this building's balcony he welcomed the citizens of Chamonix after they had voted to join France. The hotel later became a casino, part of Chamonix's drive to be considered a real tourist resort.

• *Walk to the left of the casino and into a grassy park, created in 2014, when its original huge trees were cut down (you'll see the stumps and the massive timbers used for benches).*

Park Couttet: The grassy expanse covers a hill, or moraine (rocky debris left by a receding glacier)—a reminder that a glacier once filled this valley. Informative panels tell about the geology. Walk to the back of the park to find **La Maison des Artists,** an eclectic granite mansion that dates from the 1920s. Today it's a popular jazz bar mixing great mountain views with booze and live music almost nightly in high season.

• *When you reach the big street, walk left 200 yards to the train station.*

Protestant Church: Across the street from the train station, hiding in a woodsy lot, is a Protestant church—built in the 1860s for the many English visitors who traveled here on their Grand Tours. From here, with your back to the station, a walk straight down the main drag (Avenue Michel Croz) takes you back to the river, the statue of Paccard, and the center of Chamonix.

Sights in Chamonix

MOUNTAIN LIFTS, GONDOLAS, AND TRAINS
▲▲▲Aiguille du Midi

The Aiguille du Midi (ay-gwee doo mee-dee) is the most spectacular mountain lift in Europe—and the most popular ride in the valley. If the weather's clear, the price doesn't matter. Take an early lift and have breakfast above 12,000 feet. Remember, it's freezing cold up there and you'll need sunglasses.

Cost: From Chamonix to Plan de l'Aiguille—round-trip-€31 (one-way-€16); Aiguille du Midi—round-trip-€59 (one-way-€49, not including parachute). Tickets for the Panoramic Mont Blanc *télécabines* from Aiguille du Midi to Pointe Helbronner (Italy) are sold at both base and summit lift stations with no difference in price (round-trip-€28). As conditions can change, I wouldn't buy the Helbronner ticket until I'm at the top of Aiguille du Midi, where it's easy to purchase. If dropping into Italy on the Skyway Monte Bianco, buy that ticket at Helbronner (€48, baggage allowed).

Discounts: The prices listed above are for ages 16 and over; kids ages 4-15 cost about 15 percent less (family rates for 2 adults and 2 children ages 15 and under are also available). While going all the way up and only halfway down (and hiking from Plan de l'Aiguille) costs the same as a round-trip ticket, those with a round-trip ticket who hike over to Montenvers can use it to ride the train back into Chamonix.

Hours: Lifts generally run daily July-Aug 6:30-17:00, late May-June and Sept 7:30-17:00, and Oct-late May 8:00-15:30, closed Nov-mid-Dec. Be warned: Hours can change with the weather among other reasons. Always confirm plans locally. Gondolas run every 10 minutes during busy times; the last return from Aiguille du Midi is generally one hour after the last ascent. The last *télécabine* departure to Pointe Helbronner is about 14:30, and the last train down from Montenvers (for hikers) is about 17:30.

Crowd-Beating Strategies: To beat the hordes and clouds, ride the Aiguille du Midi lift (up and down) as early as you can. To beat major delays in summer, leave no later than 7:00 or reserve ahead (first lift departs at 6:30 or 7:00, verify in advance). Crowds are worst on a sunny day after a string of bad days. If you arrive

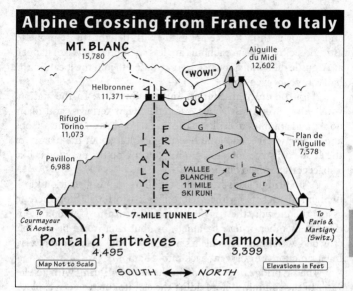

Alpine Crossing from France to Italy

MT. BLANC
15,780

Aiguille
du Midi
12,602

"WOW!"

Helbronner
11,371

Rifugio
Torino
11,073

Plan de
l'Aiguille
7,578

Pavillon
6,988

ITALY / FRANCE

G
l
a
c
i
e
r

VALLEE
BLANCHE
11 MILE
SKI RUN!

To
Courmayeur
& Aosta

7-MILE TUNNEL

To
Paris &
Martigny
(Switz.)

Pontal d' Entrèves
4,495

Chamonix
3,399

Map Not to Scale

SOUTH ← → NORTH

Elevations in Feet

later in the day, you'll likely be assigned a lift time and will have to come back.

From July to August, smart travelers reserve the Aiguille du Midi lift in advance (€2 fee). You can reserve at the information booth next to the lift, online at www.compagniedumontblanc.fr, by phone (year-round, tel. 04 50 53 22 75, automated reservations in English), or in person at this or other lifts. Reservations are taken from one to seven days in advance (not same day); pick tickets up at the lift station 20 minutes before departure (the information booth at the Aiguille du Midi lift tells you which window to use for priority access). Reservations are not possible for the *télécabines* to Helbronner.

Time to Allow: Chamonix to Aiguille du Midi—20 minutes one-way, 2 hours round-trip, 3 hours in peak season; Chamonix to Helbronner—about 45 minutes one-way, 3 hours round-trip. (In peak season, you can get hung up by crowds at Helbronner.) On busy days, minimize delays returning to Chamonix by making a reservation for your return lift time upon arrival at the top of Aiguille du Midi. (When crowded, attendants hand out return-time cards as you arrive—ask for advice when you get to the top.)

Visiting the Aiguille du Midi

Pile into the *téléphérique* (gondola), try to grab a window spot, and soar to the tip of a rock needle 12,602 feet above sea level (you'll be packed into the gondola like sardines; take off your daypack to allow more room). Chamonix shrinks as trees fly by, soon replaced by whizzing rocks, ice, and snow. Change gondolas at Plan de l'Aiguille to reach the top. No matter how sunny it is, it's cold and the air is thin. People are giddy with delight (those prone to altitude sickness or agoraphobia are less so). Fun things can happen at Aiguille du Midi if you're not too winded to join the locals in the halfway-to-heaven tango.

Aiguille du Midi Station and the Summit: In the station, you'll find several gift shops, cafeterias, view terraces, and many nooks and crannies to explore. The actual gondola station has shops and a view terrace, and an interesting exhibit about the history of the 1950s construction. The summit tower atop the peak looks like a spacecraft perched on an alp.

A **skybridge** leads from the station past an information kiosk (which sells tickets for the Helbronner lift to Italy). Stop there to assess the crowds, the trip to Italy, and return-to-Chamonix options (remember, it may be quiet now, but later it can be horribly crowded with hours-long delays if you're sloppy). Ask about reserving a time for your descent back into Chamonix.

The skybridge deposits you in the **main building** with an elevator to the summit. Before riding the elevator up, you can explore. An exhibit called "Vertical Space Extreme" thrills with amazing photos of daredevil mountaineers. A tubular walkway called "The Tube" lets you circle the summit.

Follow *Vallée Blanche* signs to a drippy **"ice tunnel"** where skiers and mountain climbers make their exit. The views are sensational; merely observing is exhilarating. Peek down the icy cliff and ponder the value of an ice ax. Skiers make the 11-mile run to the Mer de Glace from here. Next to that is the gondola station for the Panoramic Mont Blanc lift to Helbronner (Italy).

By far the highlight of your ascent is riding the **elevator to the summit**—12,602 feet above sea level (you'll want to pose with the much-photographed altitude sign). From this ultimate platform, the Alps spread out before you. Use the orientation posters to identify key peaks: You can see the main Swiss and Italian summits rising above 13,000 feet. If it's really clear, you can see the bent little Matterhorn—the tall, shady pyramid listed in French on the observation table as "Cervin—4,505 meters" (14,775 feet). And looming on the other side is Mont Blanc, the Alps' highest point, at 4,810 meters (15,780 feet).

Use the telescopes to spot mountaineers (roped up and following guides); more than 2,000 people scale Mont Blanc each year. A long but not technically challenging climb, the summit was first conquered in 1786, more than 170 years before this lift was built. Find the giant's tooth, spot the *télécabines* to Italy, and identify lift stations of the Aiguilles Rouges mountain range across the valley, on the other side of Chamonix. That rusty tin-can needle above you serves as a communications tower. Check the temperature next to the elevator.

At the summit, the "Step Into the Void" glass box offers a chance to stand in what feels like midair. (They'll take your photo for a fee.) But, it can be a long wait for a small payoff.

Taking the Gondola to Italy: For your private glacial dream world, embark on the little red Panoramic Mont Blanc *télécabine* and sail south to Pointe Helbronner, the mountaintop Italian border station (typically open late June-early Sept). This line stretches three miles over ice, snow, and rocks. In a gondola for four (if it's not too crowded, you can usually get a private one for two if you ask), you'll dangle silently for 40 minutes as you glide over glaciers and past a forest of peaks to Italy. Hang your head out the window. Enjoy the silence. Explore every corner of your view. From Helbronner, you can turn around and return to Aiguille du Midi, or descend into Italy on the Skyway Monte Bianco lift (described later, under "Day Trips near Chamonix")—but for most there's really no point unless you're traveling on into Italy.

Helbronner station, at over 11,000 feet, has a whole different crowd (people coming up from Italy with no intention of going to Aiguille du Midi). There's a cafeteria, a crystal hall, an elevator down to a passage that leads to the Torino Refugio climber's refuge (with view terrace and restaurant), and, most importantly, spiraling stairs leading to a 360-degree viewing platform for killer views from the Matterhorn to Mont Blanc (called Monte Bianco here in Italy). Unfortunately, you need to keep an eye on the crowds and the slow line to assure your timely return to Aiguille du Midi.

Returning to Chamonix via Plan de l'Aiguille: To get from Aiguille du Midi to Chamonix, you'll need to change gondolas at **Plan de l'Aiguille.** Take some time here on your way down. Gondolas depart every few minutes, and those boarding here never have to wait. At Plan de l'Aiguille you'll find a scenic café with sandwiches, drinks, cheap sunglasses, outdoor tables, paragliders jumping off cliffs (except in July-Aug), and rocky perches for private sunbathing. It's a great place to just relax. But the best reason to get off here is to follow the wonderful **trail** to the Mer de Glace, then catch the train back into Chamonix (for details, see "Chamonix-Area-Hikes—Hike #1" on page 803).

For a shorter alternative hike, take a 35-minute round-trip walk below the lift station to the ignored and peaceful **$ Refuge-Plan de l'Aiguille** for reasonable meals (good omelets, pastas, salads, and mouthwatering tarts, made by welcoming manager

Claude—no English, no problem) and drinks inside or out (open daily May-late Oct, tel. 06 65 64 27 53). This makes an easy mini-hike for hurried travelers (or a great overnight for a steal—see "Sleeping in Chamonix," later).

Don't hike all the way down to Chamonix from Plan de l'Aiguille or Montenvers-Mer de Glace; it's a long, steep walk through thick forests with few views. Ride the gondola down, and notice as you're finally dropping back into Chamonix the highway disappearing into the mountain—that's the Mont Blanc Tunnel.

▲▲▲Mer de Glace (Montenvers)

From Gare de Montenvers (the little station over the tracks from Chamonix's main train station), the cute cogwheel Train du Mon-

tenvers toots you up to tiny Montenvers (mohn-tuh-vehr). Sit on the left-hand side as you go up for good views among pine trees over the valley. There you'll see a dirty, rapidly receding glacier called the Mer de Glace (mayr duh glahs, "Sea of Ice") and fantastic views up the white valley (Vallée Blanche) of splintered, snow-capped peaks. (As the glacier recedes, it is literally pulling away from the train station; in coming years you'll see construction as the train tracks are extended to catch up with the ice.)

Cost and Hours: Round-trip-€31, one-way-€25, family rates available, prices include gondola and ice caves entry, daily 8:30-17:00, July-Aug 8:00-18:00, last trip down at 16:30, 2/hour, 20 minutes, confirm times with TI or call 04 50 53 12 54.

Visiting the Glacier: Find the **view deck** across from the train station. France's largest glacier, at eight miles long, is impressive from above and below. The swirling glacier extends under the dirt about a half-mile downhill to the left. Imagine that it recently reached as high as the vegetation below (see the dirt cliffs—called moraines—left behind in its retreat). In 1860, this glacier stretched all the way down to the valley floor (see the "Understanding the Alps" sidebar on page 800).

Use an **orientation table** as you look up to the peaks. **Aiguille du Dru**'s powerful spire, at about 11,700 feet, makes an irresistible target for climbers. It was first scaled in 1860 (long before the train you took here was built) and was recently free-climbed (no ropes, belays, etc.); the colored lines indicate different routes taken. The smooth snow field to the left of Dru's spire (Les Grands Montets) is the top of Chamonix's most challenging ski run, with a vertical drop of about 6,500 feet (down the opposite side). The path to the right (as you face the glacier) leads to a fine view café and a reconstruction of a crystal cave.

The glacier's **ice caves** are beneath you. Take the free, small gondola down and prepare to walk about 460 steps each way. (Several years ago, it was 280 steps.) This glacier is beating a hasty retreat—as you walk down you'll pass signs that bring this point home by showing the extent of the glacier over the years. The ice cave, a hypnotizing shade of blue-green, is actually a long tunnel dug about 75 yards into the glacier. Informative panels describe the digging of the cave.

The **Refuge-Grand Hôtel du Montenvers,** a few minutes' walk toward Chamonix from the viewing platform outside the station, offers a full-service restaurant, view tables (fair prices, limited selection), and a warm interior (you can even bunk here—see "Sleeping in Chamonix," later). The hotel was built in 1880, when tourists arrived on foot or by mule. (It's likely closed in 2017 for a big remodeling project.)

The three-hour trail to **Plan de l'Aiguille** (see page 803 for a description) begins across from the hotel. Walk above the two stone buildings and follow the trail as it rises just above the Mer de Glace valley (follow *itinéraire conseillé* signs toward *Signal Plan de l'Aiguille*). For terrific views, hike toward Plan de l'Aiguille—even just a short distance. The views get better fast, and the higher you climb, the better they get as the peaks of the Aiguilles Rouges come into sight behind you. Bring a picnic.

A **Glaciorium** lies 50 yards behind the hotel along the main walkway. It houses a small but worthwhile exhibit on glaciers of the world with dioramas, interactive displays, and terrific images that explain the life of a glacier (free, daily 9:30-18:00 in summer, 10:00-16:00 in winter).

▲▲▲Gondola Lifts to Le Brévent and La Flégère

Though Aiguille du Midi gives a more spectacular ride, the Le Brévent and La Flégère lifts *(téléphériques)* offer worthwhile hiking and viewing options, with unobstructed panoramas across to the Mont Blanc range and fewer crowds. The Le Brévent (luh bray-vahn) lift is in Chamonix; the La Flégère (lah flay-zhair) lift is in nearby Les Praz (lay prah). The lifts are connected by a scenic hike or by bus along the valley floor (free with Chamonix Guest Card, see Hike #2 in the next section); both have sensational view cafés. Both lifts are closed from late April to mid-June and again by mid-September (reopening when ski season starts, usually in Dec).

FRENCH ALPS

Understanding the Alps

The Alps were formed about 100 million years ago by the collision of two continents: the African plate pushing north against the stable plates of Europe and Asia. In the process, the sediments of the ancient Tethys Ocean (which occupied the general real estate of the modern Mediterranean) became smooshed between the landmasses. Shoving all this material together made the rocks and sediments fold, shatter, and pile on top of each other; over millennia, this growing jumble built itself up into today's Alps. Up in the mountains, look for folds and faults in the rocks that hint at this immense compression, which is still happening today: The Alps continue to rise by at least a millimeter each year (while erosion wears them down at about the same rate).

The current shape of the mountains and valleys is the handiwork of at least five ice ages over the last two million years. Glaciers flowed down the mountain valleys, scooped out beautiful alpine lakes, and carried rocks far away from where they formed. The Alps were the first mountains extensively studied by geologists, and many of the geological terms that describe mountains originated here. Once you learn how to recognize a few of the landforms shaped by glaciers, you can easily spot these features when you visit other alpine areas. Study glacier exhibits to train your eye to recognize what you're seeing.

Glaciers are big and blunt, so they make simple, large-scale marks on the landscape. If a valley is U-shaped, like Chamonix's (with steep sides and a rounded base), it's probably been scoured out by a glacier. (California's Yosemite Valley is another classic example.)

A **cirque** (French for "circus")
is the amphitheater-like depression carved out at the upper part of a valley by a glacier. If two adjacent cirques erode back close to each other, a sharp, steep-sided ridge forms, called an **arête** (French for "fishbone"). Cirques and arêtes are common in moun-

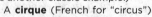

Le Brévent and Planpraz

This lift is a steep 10-minute walk up the road above Chamonix's TI. It takes two lifts to reach Le Brévent's top. The first lift to Planpraz, with automated eight-person *télécabines*, runs every minute. Sit backward and watch Chamonix shrink below (round-trip to Planpraz-€17, one-way-€14, pleasant restaurant, great views and good hiking options, see Hike #2 in the next section).

The second gondola to Le Brévent station leaves from Planpraz and runs every 15 minutes. At the top, you get 360-degree

tains that have had glaciers. More rarely, when three or more cirques erode toward one another, a pyramidal peak is created—called a **horn.** Switzerland's Matterhorn (visible—barely—from the

Aiguille du Midi) is the world's most famous example. Glaciers flowed down all sides of this mountain, scooping material away as they went to leave its distinctive sharp peak.

A common feature left behind by retreating glaciers is a **moraine,** a pile of dirt and rocks that was carried along on the glacier as it advanced, then was dumped as the glacier melted (plainly visible around the Mer de Glace).

Alpine glaciers can only originate above the snowline, so if you see any of these landforms (U-shaped valleys, cirques, horns, or moraines) in lower elevations, you know that the climate there used to be colder. The effects of a warming climate have profoundly hit the glaciers of the Alps, which have lost at least a third of their volume since the 1950s. At that rate, some studies project that most here could virtually disappear by the end of the 21st century, affecting water storage and hydroelectric power generation, and making mountainsides less stable.

Another consequence of the warming climate is that winter weather no longer reliably produces snow at altitudes that it did in the past—which is bad news for Europe's huge ski industry. Seeing a future of ever-warmer winters, alpine resorts are putting their ingenuity to the test. This goes beyond snow machines: Many resorts are investing hugely in new spas, convention centers, and other attractions that don't require snow. Meanwhile, European governments strive to invest in environmentally friendly technologies in hopes of keeping their mountains white and their valleys green.

FRENCH ALPS

views, more hikes, and a view restaurant. For most, Planpraz is plenty high (round-trip from Chamonix to Le Brévent–€31, one-way–€23; daily 8:45-17:00, July-Aug 8:15-18:00, last return from Planpraz one hour after last ascent, closed late April-mid-June and Oct, tel. 04 50 53 13 18).

La Flégère and L'Index

This lift runs from the neighboring village of Les Praz to La Flégère station every 15 minutes; to go higher, take the chairlift to

Kids' Activities

Chamonix provides a wealth of fun opportunities for kids; ask the TI to suggest family-friendly activities. Here are a few options:

Parc de Loisirs des Planards: Chamonix's fun park for kids of all ages. It includes a luge (summer only) and a Parc d'Aventure with tree courses, Tarzan swings, trampolines, electric motorbikes, Jet Skis, and more (for details, see "Luge" listing on page 809).

Piscine du Centre Sportif Richard Bozon: A large pool complex with a big waterslide, water garden, Jacuzzi, and more (€5.50 for those 17 and under, €7 for adults, open June-early-Sept Mon-Sat in the afternoon and all day Sun, closed early Sept-May).

Parc de Merlet: Animal sanctuary with trails that let you discover mountain animals (marmots, mountain goats, llamas, deer, and more). It's located in Coupeau above Les Houches, and comes with exceptional views (so parents get some scenery while kids get to see animals). You can get there by car (20-minute drive) or hike for two beautiful hours from Chamonix. If you drive, head to the very top parking lot, as you'll be hiking uphill for 20-30 minutes just to reach the entry. There's a lot more walking inside the park to find the animals—bring good shoes and water (€4 for kids ages 4-14, free for kids 3 and under, €7 for adults, view café with salads and regional dishes, no picnics allowed; July-Aug daily 9:30-19:30; May-June and Sept Tue-Sun 10:00-18:00, closed Mon; tel. 04 50 53 47 89, www.parcdemerlet.com).

L'Index (La Flégère round-trip-€17, one-way-€14; L'Index round-trip-€28, one-way-€23; daily 8:15-16:45, summer 8:00-17:30, last return from La Flégère 15 minutes after last ascent, closed late April-mid-June and mid-Sept, tel. 04 50 53 18 58). Hikes to Planpraz and Lac Blanc leave from the top of this station (see Hikes #2 and #3 in the next section). Les Praz is easy to reach from Chamonix by local bus (10 minutes—it's the first stop after Chamonix).

CHAMONIX-AREA HIKES

The **Maison de la Montagne** service center is a good first stop for serious hikers (located across from the TI, first-floor WC). On the second floor, the **Office de Haute-Montagne** (High Mountain Office) can help you plan your hikes and tell you about trail and snow conditions (daily 9:00-12:00 & 15:00-18:00, tel. 04 50 53 22 08, www.chamoniarde.com). The staff speaks enough English and has vital weather reports and maps, as well as some English hiking guidebooks to consult. Ask to look at the trail guidebook (sold in many stores and at the TI, includes the helpful *Carte des*

Sentiers, the region's hiking map). Across the hall is a scale model of the valley and its mountains, and a vivid "risks of the mountain" exhibit in French.

At **Compagnie des Guides de Chamonix** on the ground floor, you can hire a hiking or climbing guide (about €200/half-day, €320/day, less per person for groups) to help you scale Mont Blanc, or hike to the Matterhorn and Zermatt (open daily 9:00-12:00 & 14:30-19:00, closed Sun-Mon off-season, tel. 04 50 53 00 88, www.chamonix-guides.com). Up a few steps is an adventure-sports office.

In this section, I describe three fairly strenuous hikes and three easier walks (see the map on page 806). Start early, when the weather's generally best. This is most important in summer as trails become more crowded as the day goes on. If hiking late in the day, confirm lift closing hours to avoid a long, steep hike down.

For your hike, bring sunglasses, sunscreen, rain gear, water, snacks, and maybe light gloves. Pack warm layers (mountain weather can change in a moment) and wear good shoes (trails are rocky and uneven). Take your time, watch your footing, don't take shortcuts, and say *"Bonjour!"* to your fellow hikers. Note that there's no shade on Hikes #1, #2, and #3.

▲▲Hike #1
Plan de l'Aiguille to Montenvers-Mer de Glace
(Le Grand Balcon Nord)

This 2.5-hour hike is the most efficient way to incorporate a high-country adventure into your ride down from the valley's greatest lift,

and check out a world-class glacier to boot. The well-used trail rises but mostly falls (dropping 1,500 feet from Plan de l'Aiguille to Montenvers and the Mer de Glace) and is moderately difficult, provided the snow is melted (generally covered by snow until June; get trail details at the Office de Haute-Montagne, listed earlier). Some stretches are steep and strenuous, with uneven footing and slippery rocks. Note the last train time from Montenvers-Mer de Glace back to Chamonix, or you'll be hiking another hour and a half straight down.

Here's an overview: From the Aiguille du Midi lift, get off halfway down at Plan de l'Aiguille, *sortie* to the café/bar, then find signs leading down to *Montenvers-Mer de Glace.* Follow the main trail that is parallel to the gondola cables. You'll drop steadily for 15 minutes down to a small refuge (good prices for meals and drinks), then go right, hiking the spectacularly scenic, undulating, and (for short periods) strenuous trail to Montenvers (overlooking the Mer de Glace glacier). Plan on lots of boulder-stepping and occasional stream crossings.

After about an hour at a steady pace, the trail splits. Follow signs up the steep trail to *Le Signal* (more scenic and easier), rather than to the left toward *Montenvers* (looks easier, but becomes very difficult). At this point, you'll grind it out up switchbacks for about 30 minutes to the best views of the trail at Le Signal. Savor the views you worked so hard to reach. From here, it's a long, sometimes steep, but always memorable drop to Montenvers and the Mer de Glace (where you can visit

the ice cave). In Montenvers, take the train back to Chamonix. Don't walk the rest of the trail down from Montenvers (long, steep, disappointing views).

▲▲Hike #2
La Flégère to Planpraz (Le Grand Balcon Sud)

This lovely hike traverses for 2.5 hours above Chamonix Valley, with staggering views of Mont Blanc, countless other peaks, glaciers, wildflowers, and a fraction of the crowds that the Aiguille du Midi lift draws. While you'll start at 1,900 meters (6,230 feet) and end at 2,000 meters (6,560 feet), there's more than just 100 meters (330 feet) of climbing between the La Flégère and Planpraz lift stations. While it's possible to hike the trail in either direction, it's better to start in La Flégère. (I won't even describe the other direction.)

This hike is relatively easy (but still requires stamina and appropriate shoes). The trail is a mix of dirt paths, ankle-twisting rocky sections, and short stretches of service roads. You'll pass by winter lifts and walk through meadows and along small sections of forest. Keep your eyes out for signs to *Planpraz;* red-and-white markers also help identify the trail.

The round-trip rate saves about €3 over two one-way tickets and lets you go up the La Flégère lift and down at Planpraz. To reach La Flégère, take free bus #1 or #2 from Chamonix, or walk 40 minutes along the Arve River to Les Praz (see Hike #5, described later). Take the lift up to La Flégère, then walk out the back to near the snack stand, La Chalet de la Flégère (reasonable and hearty sandwiches, crêpes, drinks) to get your bearings. Before setting out, stop by the lift ticket booth to confirm your hike plan, the trail, and the time of the last descent from Planpraz (if you're there by that time, you won't be stuck). Enjoy views of the receding Mer de Glace glacier and the cliff-hanging Hôtel du Montenvers on the opposite side of Chamonix's valley. Walk down to the refuge just below the lift station and turn right, crossing under the gondola cables to *Planpraz*. (You don't want *Les Praz-Chamonix*—that's straight down.)

Signage is inconsistent, so expect to do some route-finding along the way. There are two points where you could miss the trail, each when you reach a small road. At the first road, cross and follow the *Croisement du Sentier a 100 m* sign, and later a sign to *Planpraz*. At a second road, above a ski lift, cross the road and take the rocky trail steeply uphill, following the *Le Brévent par Planpraz* sign. At the end, there's a steep climb to the (Planpraz) gondola station (great view cafés and a fascinating history exhibit). Descend to Chamonix from here or take the gondola up to Le Brévent for more views.

▲▲Hike #3
La Flégère to Lac Blanc

This is the most demanding hiking trail of those I list; it climbs steeply and steadily over a rough, boulder-strewn trail for 1.5 hours to snowy Lac Blanc (pronounced "lock blah"). Some footing is tricky, and good shoes or boots are a must. I like this trail, as it gets you away from the valley edge and opens views to peaks you don't see from other hikes.

The destination is a snow-white lake framed by peaks and the nifty Refuge-Hôtel du Lac Blanc, which offers good lunches (and dinners, if you stay the night, summers only). The views on the return trip are breathtaking. Check for snow conditions on the trail (often a problem until July) and go early (particularly in summer), as there is no shade and this trail is popular.

Follow the directions for Hike #2 to La Flégère station, then walk out the station's rear door past the snack stand to get oriented. Track the trail as it drops way down to that winter chairlift station, then hooks hard left back up a steep hill. You can avoid this considerable down-and-up by taking the L'Index chairlift behind you (about €9 one-way, €11 round-trip, €27 from the base). Confirm that the trail from L'Index is free of snow, as this shortcut can be dicey, especially for kids. However you start, the trail is well-signed to Lac Blanc, and its surface improves as you climb.

▲Hike #4
Petit Balcon Sud to Chalet de la Floria and Les Praz

This trail runs above the valley on the Brévent side from the village of Les Houches to Argentière, passing Chamonix about halfway, and is handy when snow or poor weather make other hikes problematic. No lifts are required—just firm thighs to climb up and down. Access paths link the trail to villages below. Once you're up, the trail rises and falls with some steep segments and uneven foot-

Chamonix-Area Hikes

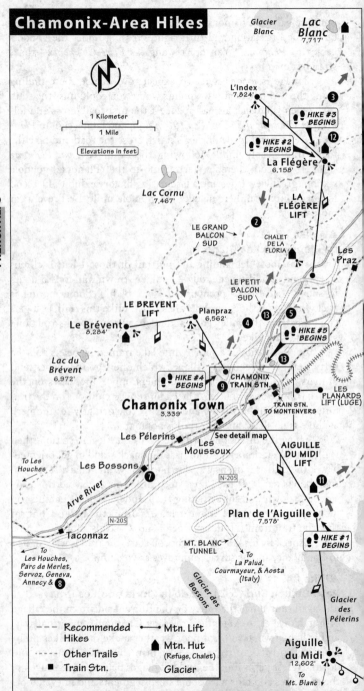

FRENCH ALPS

1 Kilometer
1 Mile
Elevations in feet

Glacier Blanc

Lac Blanc 7,717'

L'Index 7,824'

HIKE #3 BEGINS

3

12

HIKE #2 BEGINS

La Flégère 6,158'

Lac Cornu 7,467'

LA FLÉGÈRE LIFT

LE GRAND BALCON SUD

2

CHALET DE LA FLORIA

Les Praz

LE PETIT BALCON SUD

13

LE BRÉVENT LIFT

Planpraz 6,562'

Le Brévent 8,284'

4

5

HIKE #5 BEGINS

13

Lac du Brévent 6,972'

HIKE #4 BEGINS

9

CHAMONIX TRAIN STN.

Chamonix Town 3,339'

TRAIN STN. TO MONTENVERS

LES PLANARDS LIFT (LUGE)

Les Pélerins

See detail map

Les Moussoux

AIGUILLE DU MIDI LIFT

To Les Houches

Les Bossons

7

Arve River

N-205

N-205

11

Plan de l'Aiguille 7,578'

HIKE #1 BEGINS

Taconnaz

To Les Houches, Parc de Merlet, Servoz, Geneva, Annecy &

8

MT. BLANC TUNNEL

To La Palud, Courmayeur, & Aosta (Italy)

Glacier des Bossons

Glacier des Pélerins

Aiguille du Midi 12,602'

To Mt. Blanc

--- Recommended Hikes
····· Other Trails
■ Train Stn.
●— Mtn. Lift
▲ Mtn. Hut (Refuge, Chalet)
Glacier

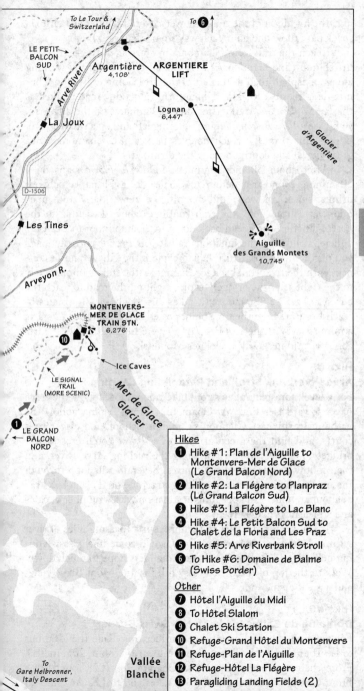

FRENCH ALPS

To Le Tour & Switzerland

To **6**

LE PETIT BALCON SUD

Arve River

Argentière 4,108'

ARGENTIÈRE LIFT

La Joux

Lognan 6,447'

Glacier d'Argentière

D-1506

Les Tines

Arveyon R.

Aiguille des Grands Montets 10,745'

MONTENVERS-MER DE GLACE TRAIN STN. 6,276'

10

Ice Caves

LE SIGNAL TRAIL (MORE SCENIC)

Mer de Glace Glacier

1

LE GRAND BALCON NORD

Hikes

1 Hike #1: Plan de l'Aiguille to Montenvers-Mer de Glace (Le Grand Balcon Nord)

2 Hike #2: La Flégère to Planpraz (Le Grand Balcon Sud)

3 Hike #3: La Flégère to Lac Blanc

4 Hike #4: Le Petit Balcon Sud to Chalet de la Floria and Les Praz

5 Hike #5: Arve Riverbank Stroll

6 To Hike #6: Domaine de Balme (Swiss Border)

Other

7 Hôtel l'Aiguille du Midi

8 To Hôtel Slalom

9 Chalet Ski Station

10 Refuge-Grand Hôtel du Montenvers

11 Refuge-Plan de l'Aiguille

12 Refuge-Hôtel La Flégère

13 Paragliding Landing Fields (2)

To Gare Helbronner, Italy Descent

Vallée Blanche

ing. The highlight of the trail is flower-covered **Chalet de la Floria** snack bar (allow one hour each way from Chamonix).

Reach the trail from Chamonix by starting at the Le Brévent lift station (find signs to *Le Petit Balcon Sud*). Begin by walking along an asphalt road to the left of the lift leading uphill (on Chemin de la Pierre à Ruskin), which turns into a dirt road marked as the *Petit Balcon Sud* trail. After about 20 minutes on the dirt road, you'll see a *Petit Balcon Sud* sign pointing left and up a smaller trail. Bypass this turnoff (which doubles back above Chamonix with great views) and continue along the dirt road.

After about 30 more minutes, follow *la Floria* signs on a 20-minute round-trip detour to Chalet de la Floria, which has drinks, snacks, flowers, and magnificent views (daily mid-June–mid-Oct). From here, the trail continues above Les Praz to the north; junction trails lead back down to Chamonix or to Les Praz village. Following the junction trail to *Les Praz* eventually lands you on the main road; turn left to explore the village and to connect with the river trail back to Chamonix (the trail is immediately to the right after the bridge), or turn right on the road to reach the bus stop back to Chamonix (it takes bus #1 about 20 minutes to reach Les Praz from the time point posted in Le Tour; bus #2 starts a minute away at the Les Praz/La Flégère lift, and bus #21 starts about 17 minutes away at Col des Montets).

Hike #5
Arve Riverbank Stroll and Paragliding Landing Field

For a level, forested-valley stroll, bike ride, or jog, follow the Arve River toward Les Praz. At Chamonix's Hôtel Alpina, follow the path upstream past Chamonix's middle school, red-clay tennis courts, and find the green arrow to *Les Praz*. You'll cross a few bridges to the left, turn right along the rushing Arve River, and then follow Promenade des Econtres. Several trails loop through these woods; if you continue walking straight, you'll reach Les Praz in about an hour—an appealing destination with a number of cafés and a pleasing village green.

If you keep right after the tennis courts (passing piles of river sediment dredged to deter flooding), you'll come to a grassy landing field, signed *Parapente,* where paragliders hope to touch down. Walk to the top of the little grassy hill for fine Mont Blanc views and a great picnic spot.

Hike #6
Domaine de Balme—Hike to the Swiss Border

For a memorable and easy hike, consider this: Ride the local bus to Le Tour (free with Chamonix Guest Card, 2/hour, 20 minutes). From there, catch the gondola to Charamillon (€28 round-trip). From Charamillon a chairlift (€17) takes you to Les Autannes at over 7,200 feet. At the top it's an easy 20-minute walk in an alpine wonderland through meadows and past cows to the Swiss border at Col de Balme. There you'll find a stone marked with France on one side and Switzerland on the other and, nearby, a mountain hut. When you're ready to head back, backtrack the way you came and find the trail near the top of the chairlift. It's a one-hour hike down to the top of the gondola for the ride back down to Le Tour.

OTHER ACTIVITIES

▲Luge (Luge d'Eté)

Here's something for fun-seekers: Ride a plastic sled on rails up the hill, and then scream down a twisty, banked, slalom course. Young or old, hare or tortoise, any fit person can manage a luge. *Freinez* signs tell you when to brake. The luge course is set in a grassy park with kids' play areas.

Cost and Hours: One ride-€5.50, €7.50 for double sled; six rides-€31, €40 for double sled; kids under age 8 must ride with adult, entry includes all activities in Parc de Loisirs des Planards—see "Kids' Activities" on page 802; generally July-Aug daily 10:00-18:30, mid-April-June and Sept-Oct Sat-Sun and select weekdays 13:30-18:00, check website for hours; 15-minute walk from town center, over the tracks from train station and past Montenvers train station; tel. 04 50 53 08 97, www.chamonixparc.com.

▲▲▲Paragliding (Parapente)

When it's sunny and clear, the skies above Chamonix sparkle with colorful parachute-like sails that circle the valley like birds of prey. For €100-110 plus the cost of the lift up to Planpraz (Le Brévent ski area) or Plan de l'Aiguille, you can launch yourself off a mountain in a tandem paraglider with a trained, experienced pilot and fly like a bird for about 20 minutes (true thrill-seekers can launch from Aiguille du Midi, €240, 40-minute ride). Most pilots will meet you at the lift station in Chamonix (usually from Le Brévent side, as it has the most reliable conditions, though you can ask them to fly you from Plan de l'Aiguille if you'll be there anyway and are pressed for time—not possible July-Aug). **Sean Potts** is English (no language barrier) and easy to work with (info@fly-chamonix.com). You can also try **Summits Parapente** (smart to reserve a day ahead, open year-round, tel. 04 50 53 50 14, mobile 06 84 01 26 00, www.summits.fr).

For a sneak preview, walk to one of the two main landing areas and watch paragliders perfect their landings (see "Chamonix-Area Hikes—Hike #5," earlier).

Winter Sports in Chamonix

Chamonix offers some of the best expert-level skiing in the world, a huge choice of terrain at reasonable prices (cheaper than Switzerland), access to lots of high-elevation runs (which means good snow and views), and great nightlife. Ski here for jaw-dropping views and a good balance between true mountaineer culture and touristy glitz.

The slopes are strung out along the valley for about 10 miles, so you must drive or catch the often-crowded shuttle buses to ski more than one area. There's also limitless *off-piste* (ungroomed) skiing, best explored with an experienced guide.

Nonskiers won't be bored. The lifts described in this chapter lead to top-notch views. Swimming, saunas, tennis, skating, and climbing are available at Chamonix's Centre Sportif. You can also relax in a spa, go bowling or dog-sledding, and hike along groomed winter footpaths.

When to Go

High season is usually from December to April. Chamonix is packed from Christmas through New Year's Day and busy February through April (during European winter and spring breaks). It's quieter in early December, in January after New Year's, and in May (Easter can be very busy). Thanks to easy access to high-elevation runs, you'll usually find good powder in late April and May, when it's less crowded. Chamonix is one of the great resorts for spring skiing, and you can usually find special spring package deals.

Tickets

Adult lift tickets covering Chamonix's three main areas, including the lower-elevation beginner areas, are €48/1 day, €94/2 days, €133/3 days, €176/4 days, €220/5 days (about 15 percent less for skiers older than 64 or younger than 16). Or consider the Mont Blanc Unlimited pass—covering all the areas in the Chamonix Valley (details on the websites listed later, under "Information").

Ski Rentals

Prices don't vary much, so go with something convenient to where you're staying and ask your hotel for deals with nearby shops. You'll pay about €14-24/day for skis and about €8-12/day for boots. **Technique Extrême** has the best deals on rentals and gear (tel. 04 50 53 38 25, 200 Avenue de l'Aiguille du Midi, www.technique-extreme.com). **Snell Sports** is a respected shop that's been around for many years (tel. 04 50 53 02 17, 104 Rue du Docteur Paccard, www.cham3s.com). **Sports Alpins** provides great service (tel. 04 50 53 13 60, 7 Place Edmond Désailloud, Chamonix Sud).

Where to Go

It's tough to find one area in Chamonix that offers a perfect mix of terrain for every level of skier, but here's a rundown of Chamonix's key ski areas:

Le Brévent/La Flégère: A 10-minute walk from Chamonix's center, this area has one of the valley's better mixes of terrain. If you're staying in Chamonix and have just a day, ski Le Brévent/La Flégère. Runs are good for intermediates, with some expert options, but not great for beginners. You'll enjoy fantastic views of Mont Blanc.

Les Grands Montets: Above the village of Argentière (about 10 minutes from Chamonix by bus), this area is internationally renowned for its expert terrain (and killer views from the observation deck). Part of Les Grands Montets lies on the Argentière glacier, and there's plenty of vertical. Hire a local guide to explore the *off-piste* options.

Les Houches: A five-minute bus or train ride from Chamonix, Les Houches covers a large area with a variety of runs for most skill levels (good for families), but it has fewer expert options. This area is less crowded than other Chamonix Valley areas, and the tree skiing is good.

Domaine de Balme: The area above the nearby town of Le Tour offers good options for beginners, intermediates, and those looking for mellow cruising runs.

Lower Areas Good for Beginners: Le Savoy is at the bottom of Le Brévent, near Chamonix's center, with scads of kids and a few rope-tows. Les Planards is a short walk from the town center and the largest area for kids and beginners. These areas depend on good snow conditions.

The Vallée Blanche: This unique-to-Chamonix run starts on the sky-high Aiguille du Midi lift and takes you 13 miles down a glacier past astounding views and terrain to Montenvers (easy train back to Chamonix). It requires a lift ticket and hiring a guide or joining a group tour (figure about €320 for a private tour of up to 4 people, €25/additional person, maximum 6 people).

Ski Guides
You can hire a private guide for about €335 for your group or join another group. The Compagnie des Guides de Chamonix (CGC) puts together small groups for about €80/person (tel. 04 50 53 00 88, www.chamonix-guides.com, info@chamonix-guides.com). Groups can accommodate strong intermediate through advanced skiers. Guides also give experts the option to ski even more difficult terrain.

Information
For general information about Chamonix and lift rates, check www.chamonix.com, www.leshouches.com, and www.compagniedumontblanc.fr, or contact the Chamonix TI.

FRENCH ALPS

RAINY-DAY OPTIONS

If the weather disagrees with your plans, stay cool and check out the following options.

Alpine Museum (Musée Alpin)

Situated in one of Chamonix's oldest "palaces," this place has good exhibits about Chamonix's evolution from a farming area to one focused on skiing. The museum shows off Chamonix's mountaineering, skiing, and mineralogical history (explanations in French only) and has exhibits on the first Winter Olympics, held right here.

Cost and Hours: €6, July-Aug daily 10:00-12:00 & 14:00-19:00, otherwise 10:00-14:00 and closed on Tue, 89 Avenue Michel Croz, tel. 04 50 53 25 93.

Espace Tairraz: Crystal Museum and Mountaineering Center (Musée des Cristaux and Espace Alpinisme)

The Espace Tairraz has two parts: a fascinating collection of crystals (with samples from all over the world in every color, shape, and size), and a fascinating mountaineering museum covering the sport from 1786 to the present day. You'll learn of the great climbers through the ages, trace the evolution of mountain huts, and experience some of the best local ascents on video footage. The interactive climbing simulator is a hit with children and adults alike.

Cost and Hours: €6, daily 14:00-18:00, from 10:00 July-Aug, 615 Allée Recteur Payot, tel. 04 50 55 53 93, www.cc-valleedechamonixmontblanc.fr—choose "Culture" and "Musées."

Galerie Mario Colonel

One of Chamonix's most celebrated nature photographers displays his mesmerizing photographs of the scenery high above you. Don't miss the photos upstairs. These are so good you may not miss seeing the real thing.

Cost and Hours: Free, daily 10:00-12:30 & 15:00-19:30, no midday closure July-Aug, a block from the train station at 19 Rue Whymper, tel. 04 50 91 40 20, www.mario-colonel.com.

Day Trips near Chamonix

A Day in French-Speaking Switzerland

Plenty of tempting alpine and cultural thrills await just an hour or two away in Switzerland. A scenic road and rail route sneaks you from Chamonix to the Swiss town of Martigny. Train travelers cross without formalities, but drivers are charged a one-time fee of 40 Swiss francs (roughly €37) for a permit, known as a vignette, to use Swiss autobahns.

A Little Italy

The remote Valle d'Aosta and its historic capital city of Aosta offer a serious change of culture. The side-trip is worthwhile if you'd like to taste Italy (spaghetti, gelato, and cappuccino), enjoy the town's great evening ambience, or view the ancient ruins in Aosta (often called the "Rome of the North").

Getting There: Take the spectacular lift (Aiguille du Midi–Helbronner—described on page 791) to Italy. From Helbronner, ride the Skyway Monte Bianco lift, which stops at Pavillon du Mont Fréty on its way down to Pontal d'Entrèves (www.montebianco.com). It's an amazing ride—the gondola rotates 360 degrees as you sail along. From Pontal d'Entrèves, you can take the bus to Aosta (hourly, change in Courmayeur). Aosta's train station has connections to anywhere in Italy (about every 2 hours, usually on slow trains via Turin).

For a more down-to-earth experience, you can take the bus from Chamonix to Aosta via the Mont Blanc Tunnel (about €19 one-way, €30 round-trip, reservation required in summer, 5/day July-mid-Sept, 3/day mid-Sept-June, 2 hours). Get schedules at the SAT ticket office at 13 Avenue Michel Croz, near the Alpine Museum (tel. 04 50 53 01 15, www.sat-montblanc.com), or in summer at Chamonix's bus station, 234 Avenue de Courmayeur, close to the bowling alley. Drivers can travel straight through the Mont Blanc toll tunnel (one-way-€44, round-trip-€55 with return valid for 1 week, www.tunnelmb.com).

Sleeping in Chamonix

($$$$ = Splurge, $$$ = Pricier, $$ = Moderate, $ = Budget, ¢ = backpacker)

Reasonable hotels and dorm-like chalets abound in Chamonix, with easy parking and quick access from the train station. The TI can help you find budget accommodations anytime—either in person or by email (reservation@chamonix.com). Outside of winter, mid-July to mid-August is most difficult, when some hotels have five-day minimum-stay requirements. Very few hotels offer air-conditioning, but most have elevators. Prices tumble off-season (outside July-Aug and Dec-Jan). Many hotels and restaurants are closed in May, June, and November, but you'll still find a room and a meal. If you want a view of Mont Blanc, ask for *côté Mont Blanc* (coat-ay mohn blah). Travelers who visit June through September should contemplate a night high above in a refuge-hotel.

Ask at your hotel about the free Chamonix Guest Card, which provides complimentary use of most buses and trains during your stay (described on page 789).

IN THE CITY CENTER

$$$ Hôtel Hermitage, **** a 10-minute walk from the town center, is a gorgeous chalet hotel with the coziest lounges in Chamonix and a lovely garden with good kids' areas (swings, slides, ping-pong). It has a small bar (great stools), a small sauna, and 28 alpine-elegant rooms, all with balconies and reasonable prices considering the quality (big family rooms and suites, easy parking, closed mid-Sept-mid-Dec and mid-April-mid-June, near train station at 63 Chemin du Cé, tel. 04 50 53 13 87, www.hermitage-paccard.com, info@hermitage-paccard.com).

$$ Hôtel l'Oustalet*** is a chalet hotel warmly run by two sisters (Véronique and Agnès) who understand the importance of good service. The place is family-friendly, with lots of grass, a big pool, and six family suites. All rooms are wood-paneled, with views and balconies (family rooms, terrific breakfast-€14, try the *teurgoule* rice pudding, sauna and hot tub, free and secure parking, near Aiguille du Midi lift at 330 Rue du Lyret, tel. 04 50 55 54 99, www.hotel-oustalet.com, infos@hotel-oustalet.com).

$$ Hôtel Gourmets et Italy*** is a 36-room place with comfy public spaces, a cool riverfront terrace, balcony views from many of its appealing rooms, and a small pool (some rooms with Mont Blanc view, a few good family rooms, closed late April-early June and Nov, 2 blocks from casino on Mont Blanc side of river, 96 Rue du Lyret, tel. 04 50 53 01 38, www.hotelgourmets-chamonix.com, info@hotelgourmets-chamonix.com).

$$ Hôtel le Faucigny*** is a peaceful, polished place with a Scandinavian feel and a welcoming vibe. This full-service hotel includes free loaner bikes, sauna and Jacuzzi, and afternoon tea and treats in the linger-longer lounge. The front terrace provides a tranquil retreat with mountain views, and its 27 rooms are bright and tight but comfortable (family rooms, great breakfast extra, no elevator, 118 Place de l'Eglise, tel. 04 50 53 01 17, www.hotelfaucigny-chamonix.com, reservation@hotelfaucigny-chamonix.com).

$ Hôtel de l'Arve*** offers midrange comfort with a contemporary alpine feel in its 37 rooms, some right on the Arve River looking up at Mont Blanc. This hotel comes with a fireplace lounge, a pool table, a pleasant garden, a sauna, a climbing wall, and easy parking. Check their website for deals like a cheaper breakfast (family rooms, several "apartments" ideal for families, 60 Impasse des Anémones, tel. 04 50 53 02 31, www.hotelarve-chamonix.com, reservation@hotelarve-chamonix.com).

$ Hôtel les Crêtes Blanches*** is a central and sweet little place wrapped around a peaceful courtyard (with outdoor tables) just off Rue Joseph Vallot. Rooms are smallish and well-designed, with appealing wood paneling; all come with views of Mont Blanc and most have small balconies (family rooms, adorable dollhouse-sized chalet with kitchen, 16 Impasse du Génépy, tel. 04 50 53 05 62, www.cretes-blanches.com, cretes-blanches-chamonix@ wanadoo.fr).

$ Hôtel le Chamonix,** across from the TI and above a café, has simple alpine charm, with 16 paneled rooms at fair rates and no elevator. The rooms facing Mont Blanc have great views, are larger and brighter, and have little balconies...but also attract noise from *le café* below, which closes late on weekends (breakfast extra, 11 Rue de l'Hôtel de Ville, tel. 04 50 53 11 07, www.hotel-le-chamonix. com, hotel-le-chamonix@wanadoo.fr).

$ Hôtel Aiguille Verte* provides simple one-star comfort at appropriate prices in a creaky 12-room chalet a 10-minute walk from the center of town, toward the village of Les Praz. Rooms are clean, but may need a bit of refreshing, and many have small balconies (633 Rue Joseph Vallot, tel. 04 50 53 01 73, mobile 06 33 04 12 76, hotel-aiguilleverte@orange.fr).

¢ Le Vagabond Gîtes offers the best cheap digs in Chamonix in a fun chalet just south of the town center. Dorm rooms have bunks, with basic showers and toilets down the hall; all rooms have sinks. The top floor has one family room. The owner is Welsh, the staff is a mix of other British expats, and the feel is relaxed, with a bar and outside terrace (private rooms available, includes breakfast, linen charge, reception closed 10:00-16:30, 305 Avenue Ravanel le Rouge, tel. 04 50 53 15 43, www.gitevagabond.com, info@vaga. eu).

NEAR CHAMONIX

If Chamonix overwhelms you, spend the night in one of the valley's often-overlooked, lower-profile villages.

$$ Hôtel l'Aiguille du Midi,*** a mountain retreat, lies in the village of Les Bossons, about two miles from Chamonix toward Annecy. It's run by the English-speaking Farini family in a park-like setting with point-blank views of Mont Blanc and the Bossons Glacier. This family-friendly place has a swimming pool, a clay tennis court, table tennis, a massage room, and a laundry room to boot. Half of the alpine-comfortable rooms come with modern bathrooms, many have decks with views, and several are good for families. The classy restaurant offers à la carte and *menu* options, with *menus* from €25 (RS%, family rooms, elevator, easy by train, get off at Les Bossons, tel. 04 50 53 00 65, www.hotel-aiguilledumidi.com, info@hotel-aiguilledumidi.com).

$$ Hôtel Slalom in nearby little Les Houches makes a lovely, contemporary mountain base for hikers looking for more tranquility. The town has all amenities and is served by train. The rooms and public spaces are stylish, and the owners are welcoming (44 Rue de

FRENCH ALPS

Bellevue, closed mid-April-mid-June and mid-Oct-early-Dec, tel. 04 50 54 40 60, www.hotelslalom.net, info@hotelslalom.net).

REFUGES AND REFUGE-HOTELS NEAR CHAMONIX

Chamonix has the answer for hikers who want to sleep high above, but aren't into packing it in: refuge-hotels (generally open mid-June to mid- or late September, depending on snow levels). Refuge-hotels usually have some private rooms (but mostly dorm rooms), hot showers down the hall, and restaurants. Most expect you to take dinner and breakfast there (a great value). Reserve in advance (a few days is generally enough), then pack a small bag for a memorable night among new international friends. The **Office de Haute-Montagne** in Chamonix can explain your options (see page 802).

¢ **Chalet Ski Station**, filling a 300-year-old building, is spartan but clean, well-run, cheap, and bustles with youthful energy. Gentle Veronique rents 44 beds to a mostly young and sporty crowd. Unfortunately, it's located a steep 10-minute climb above town at the base of the Le Brévent lift (self-serve kitchen, 6 Route des Moussoux, tel. 04 50 53 20 25, www.hostel-skistation-chamonix.com, chaletskistation@wanadoo.fr).

¢ **Refuge-Grand Hôtel du Montenvers,** Chamonix's oldest refuge, delivers an Old World experience at the Montenvers train stop. It was built in 1880 as a climbing base for mountain guides before the train went there, so materials had to be gathered from nearby. The 12 simple wood-cozy rooms, top-floor dorm room, and dining room feel as though they haven't been modified since then (open July-Aug only, reserve online, good showers down the hall for all, tel. 04 50 53 14 14, www.compagniedumontblanc.fr). For directions, see "Hike #1" on page 803.

¢ **Refuge-Plan de l'Aiguille** is my favorite refuge experience near Chamonix. It's a small, welcoming, easy-to-reach refuge a 15-minute walk below the Plan de l'Aiguille lift, right on the trail between the Aiguille du Midi and Montenvers-Mer de Glace. It has a warm interior and a killer view café. The friendly cook and guardian Claude is a retired pastry chef, so the meals are good and the desserts heavenly (open May-Oct only, mobile 06 65 64 27 53, http://refuge-plan-aiguille.com, claudius74@hotmail.com).

¢ **Refuge-Hôtel La Flégère** hangs on the edge right at the La Flégère lift station. It's simple and big, but ideally located for hiking to Lac Blanc or Planpraz (open mid-June-mid-Sept only, fireplace, cool bar-café, mobile 06 03 58 28 14, bellay.catherine@wanadoo.fr). For directions, see "Hike #2" on page 804.

FRENCH ALPS

Eating in Chamonix

($$$$ = Splurge, $$$ = Pricier, $$ = Moderate, $ = Budget)

You have plenty of dining options in Chamonix: cozy, traditional *savoyard* restaurants serving classic local dishes; rustic sports bars with typical brasserie fare; big, kitschy family-friendly eateries that smell like cheese from all the fondue and raclette they serve; and trendy, modern foodie haunts. You can sit on a terrace overlooking the rushing river or on the main square watching the steady stream of outdoor enthusiasts. Restaurants seek to satisfy ravenous hikers with the hearty and filling regional cuisine. The most popular beer is the local Mont Blanc brew (including a prize-winning amber), and water is free for the asking. Menus are often similar—it's the atmosphere that varies.

IN THE TOWN CENTER

$$$$ Atmosphère Restaurant is a serious restaurant, pricey but a good value. Dressy and jazzy with a white-tablecloth ambience, they serve a mix of *savoyard* and French cuisine from an elegant menu. In high season they offer two dinner seatings on their long, skinny riverfront terrace: 19:15 and 21:15. To get a table literally over the torrent, make a reservation (daily, 123 Place Balmat, tel. 04 50 55 97 97, info@restaurant-atmos.fr, www.restaurant-atmosphere.com).

$$$$ Restaurant Bizes (Little Kisses) is a hip little place foodies like, offering fine dining (inside and out) in a small modern spot right on the rushing river. While they are enthusiastic about vegetarian and gluten-free dishes, they also do lots of grilling in their charcoal oven. With modern international dishes (ranging from smoked prawns to chicken curry), this place offers a fun break from heavy traditional fare (daily, 64 Rue des Lyret, tel. 09 51 92 25 03).

$$$ La Calèche is a kitschy, touristy, and traditional place with a fun, family-friendly energy, reasonable prices, and wild boars and stuffed birds on the walls. If you want to eat fondue or raclette (served in the traditional way) and feel like you're in an alpine museum (find the luge from the Chamonix 1924 Olympic Games), this is it. It's often still hopping when other places have closed for the night (daily, centrally located just off Place Balmat at 18 Rue du Docteur Paccard, tel. 04 50 55 94 68).

$$ Le Boccalatte Brasserie is more about good, basic food than decoration. Hardworking Thierry (from Alsace) serves good-value meals in a casual interior and on a big, easygoing terrace. The *tartiflette* with salad will fill you up, or choose from a large selection of salads, pizzas, and Alsatian dishes. They have 20 kinds of beer, including Mont Blanc amber, on tap (daily 12:00-22:00, 59 Avenue de l'Aiguille du Midi, tel. 04 50 53 52 14).

$$$ La Flambée serves traditional dishes at reasonable prices in what feels like an alpine flea market. They dish out everything from burgers and pizza to fondue and steaks as diners chat under a backdrop of old skis, sleds, and historical photos (closed Mon, a block from the train station at 232 Avenue Michel Croz, tel. 04 50 54 12 96).

$$ Elevation 1904 is a down-and-dirty climbers' haunt across from the train station, serving cheap and tasty sandwiches, burgers, pasta, and salads (daily until about 22:00, 263 Avenue Michel Croz, tel. 04 50 53 00 52).

$$ Bistrot des Sports is where you'll feel like you're hanging out with the locals. The lively bar has a fun energy, and the big back room is a casual, family-friendly restaurant with a French brasserie menu featuring big salads, regional specialties and fondue, pastas, and vegetarian dishes. Local craft beers on tap, an enticing wine list, and plenty of wines by the glass adds to the conviviality of the place. While you can sit outside, I'd come here to eat in (daily, kitchen closes at 21:30, 176 Rue Joseph Vallot, tel. 04 50 53 00 46).

$$ Le Chamonix Bar-Café is a classic bar with a fun, cheap, and accessible menu. Sitting below Chamonix's pretty little church (facing the TI) with terrific mountain views, they serve simple, tasty light meals. Their hot open-faced sandwiches *(tartine)* and *café gourmande* (coffee with a selection of desserts) are a hit (daily until 21:00, Place de l'Eglise, tel. 04 50 53 32 14).

$ La Maison du Burger is a simple takeout joint with a few plastic tables on the pedestrian street right downtown. They serve a fun array of burgers, toasted sandwiches, and crêpes—both sweet and savory (daily until 24:00, across from the recommended La Calèche restaurant).

Mountain-View Cafés and Eateries on Place Balmat: The main square in Chamonix, where the statue of early mountaineers directs everyone's attention to the highest mountain in Europe, and where it seems all pedestrian lanes in town converge, is ringed by small cafés and eateries serving mediocre food at inflated prices. Each has its own style and twist, and after a quick survey, you'll pick whichever one speaks to you. Behind it all is the white noise of the rushing Arve River, plus great views both of the mountains and the people.

Away from the Pedestrian Center: $$$$ L'Impossible, housed in a beautiful farmhouse a 10-20-minute walk from most recommended hotels, is *the* place to go for refined organic cuisine with an Italian bias. Bring your food allergies: This place offers gluten-free, lactose-free, and fat-free (well, maybe not) dishes without sacrificing flavor. Even if eating healthfully doesn't boost your boots, you'll appreciate the exquisite meals and attention to detail. Papa (who hails from Tuscany) cooks, while Mama serves (closed Tue except in Aug, 5-minute walk from Aiguille du Midi lift on Route des Pélerins, tel. 04 50 53 20 36).

Après Hike: **Bistrot des Sports** is where locals hang their ice axes after a hard day in the mountains. Drinks are cheap, local beers are on tap, the crowd is loud, and the ambience works (see listing above for food).

Le Pub is aptly named and a good spot to raise a glass with the British crowd (225 Rue du Docteur Paccard, tel. 04 50 55 92 88).

La Maison des Artistes, in the park behind the casino, is the latest addition to the music scene in Chamonix. Started by popular French musician André Manoukian, it has a recording room and offers free concerts, mainly jazz (daily in summer, 84 Chemin de la Tournette, www.lamaisondesartistes.fr).

Chamonix Connections

Bus and train service to Chamonix is surprisingly good. Some train routes pass through Switzerland to reach Chamonix (such as from Paris and Colmar) and require supplements if you have a France-only rail pass. You can avoid passing through Switzerland if you plan ahead, but it usually takes longer, and you miss some great scenery. The **route to Colmar** (via Bern and Basel) is beautiful and costs roughly €60 for the Swiss segment. You'll get a fun taste of Switzerland's charms, and, though you'll make many transfers en route, they all work like a Swiss clock.

Chamonix's **bus station** is in a parking lot near the Aiguille du Midi lift station at 234 Avenue de Courmayeur. However, the ticket office at the bus station is only open in July and August (daily 8:15-12:15 & 13:15-18:15). From September to June, buy tickets at the SAT office at 13 Avenue Michel Croz, near the Alpine Museum (daily 8:00-12:00 & 14:30-18:30 except Sat until 18:00 with midday break 10:00-15:00, tel. 04 50 53 01 15, www.sat-montblanc.com).

From Chamonix by Train to: Annecy (11/day, 2.5 hours, change in St-Gervais), **Beaune** and **Dijon** (7/day, 7 hours, change in St-Gervais and Lyon, some require additional changes), **Nice** (4/day, 10 hours, change in St-Gervais and Lyon), **Arles** (5/day, 7-8 hours, change in St-Gervais and Lyon), **Paris'** Gare de Lyon (7/day, more in summer and winter, 5.5-7 hours, some change in Switzerland), **Colmar** (hourly, 6 hours via Switzerland with 3-6 changes), **Martigny,** Switzerland (nearly hourly, 2 hours, scenic trip), **Geneva,** Switzerland, and its airport (roughly hourly, 3.5-5 hours, 2 changes).

From Chamonix by Bus to: Geneva Airport, Switzerland

FRENCH ALPS

(4/day, about 2 hours, on Ouibus—formerly Starshipper, https://booking.ouibus.com), **Courmayeur,** Italy (3-5/day, 45 minutes, reservation required in summer), **Aosta,** Italy (3-5/day, 2 hours, reservation required in summer). For more on buses to Italy, see "Day Trips near Chamonix" on page 812.

Airport shuttles also provide service between Chamonix's city center and the airport in **Geneva,** Switzerland (2 hours). **Chamexpress** is British-run and easy to work with (€35/person, €22 if booked in advance online, desk near arrival gate, www.chamexpress.com). You can also try **Chamonix Taxis** (www.chamonix-transfer.com).

BURGUNDY

Beaune • Burgundy Wine Villages • Abbey of Fontenay •
Vézelay • Château de Guédelon • Bourges • Cluny • Taizé

The rolling hills of Burgundy gave birth to superior wine, fine cuisine, spicy mustard, and sleepy villages smothered in luscious landscapes. This deceptively peaceful region witnessed Julius Caesar's defeat of the Gauls, then saw the Abbey of Cluny rise from the ashes of the Roman Empire to vie with Rome for religious influence in the 12th century. Burgundy's last hurrah came in the 15th century, when its powerful dukes controlled an immense area stretching north to Holland.

Today, bucolic Burgundy (roughly the size of Belgium) runs from about Auxerre in the north to near Lyon in the south. Crisscrossed with canals and dotted with quiet farming villages, it's also the transportation funnel for eastern France and makes a convenient stopover for travelers (car or train), with easy access north to Paris or Alsace, east to the Alps, and south to Provence.

Traditions are strong. In Burgundy, both the soil and the farmers who work it are venerated. Although many of the farms you see are growing grapes, only a small part of Burgundy is actually covered by vineyards.

This is a calm, cultivated, and serene region, where nature is as sophisticated as the people. If you're looking for quintessential French culture, you'll find it in Burgundy.

PLANNING YOUR TIME

With limited time, stay in or near Beaune. If you only have one day, spend the morning in Beaune and the afternoon exploring the surrounding vineyards and wine villages (good by bike, car, or minibus tour). If you have a car (cheap rentals are available), or

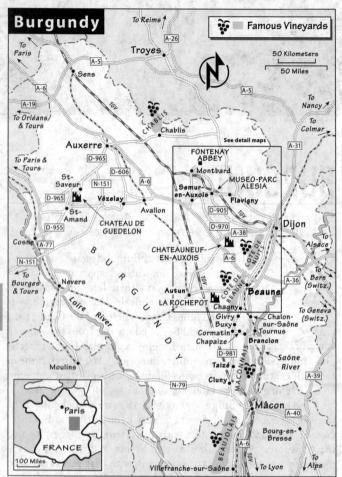

Burgundy

Famous Vineyards

To Reims
To Paris
Troyes
A-26
A-5
Sens
A-6
A-19
To Orléans
& Tours
50 Kilometers
50 Miles

N

CHABLIS
Chablis
See detail maps

Auxerre
D-965
To Paris &
Tours
D-606
A-6
FONTENAY
ABBEY
Montbard
MUSEO-PARC
ALESIA
A-31
To
Nancy
To
Colmar

St-
Saveur
N-151
Semur-
en-Auxois
Flavigny
St-
Amand
Vézelay
D-965
D-955
Avallon
D-905
D-970
TGV
Dijon
To
Alsace

Cosne
A-77
CHATEAU DE
GUEDELON
CHATEAUNEUF-
EN-AUXOIS
A-38
CÔTE DE
NUITS
N-151
To
Bourges
& Tours
Nevers
Loire River
A-6
TGV
CÔTE DE
BEAUNE
Autun
LA ROCHEPOT
Beaune
A-36
To
Bern
(Switz.)
To Geneva
(Switz.)

B
U
R
G
U
N
D
Y
Chagny
Givry
Buxy
Cormatin
Chapaize
D-981
Talzé
Cluny
N-79
Chalon-
sur-Saône
Tournus
Branclon
Saône
River
A-39

Moulins

Mâcon
A-40
Bourg-en-
Bresse

MÂCONNAIS

Paris
FRANCE
100 Miles

BEAUJOLAIS
A-6
Villefranche-sur-Saône
To Lyon
To
Alps

good legs and a bike, the best way to spend your afternoon is by following my scenic vineyard drive to Château de la Rochepot.

With more time, visit unspoiled Semur-en-Auxois or Flavigny-sur-Ozerain, the museum dedicated to the historic victory that won Gaul for Julius Caesar (in Alise-Ste-Reine), and France's best-preserved medieval abbey complex at Fontenay. These are all close to each other and on the way to Paris, or doable as a long day trip from Beaune. The soul-stirring church at Vézelay is more famous but harder to reach, and is best done as an overnight trip, or

---

Burgundy at a Glance

▲▲**Beaune** Prosperous little wine capital and home to a landmark medieval hospital that's now a fine museum. See page 826.

▲▲**Wine Villages and Vineyard Loops** Beautiful routes connecting wine villages, with plenty of tasting opportunities, pleasantly reachable by car or bike. See page 849.

▲▲**Between Burgundy and the Loire** Route linking the Romanesque hilltop church at Vézelay, the stained-glass wonders of Bourges Cathedral, and a medieval castle being built today—with 13th-century technology. See page 875.

▲**Between Beaune and Paris** Route linking Châteauneuf-en-Auxois (castle town), Alise-Ste-Reine (Roman battle site), and Fontenay (medieval abbey). See page 864.

---

en route to Paris or the Loire Valley. If you're connecting Burgundy with the Loire, don't miss the medieval castle construction at Guédelon and the fine "High" Gothic cathedral in Bourges (either of these pairs well with Vézelay). And if you're driving between Beaune and Lyon, take the detour to adorable Brancion and once-powerful Cluny, then head south along the Beaujolais wine route.

For up-to-date information on accommodations, restaurants, events, and shopping, see www.burgundyeye.com.

GETTING AROUND BURGUNDY

Trains link Beaune with Dijon to the north and Lyon to the south; some stop in the wine villages of Meursault, Nuits-St-Georges, Gevrey-Chambertin, and Santenay. Several buses per day cruise between vineyards north of Beaune on D-974, though precious few buses connect Beaune with villages to its south (see "Beaune Connections" on page 847). Bikes, minibus tours, and short taxi rides get non-drivers from Beaune into the countryside. Buses connect Semur-en-Auxois with the Dijon and Montbard train stations. Drivers enjoy motoring on Burgundy's lovely roads; you'll cruise along canals, past manicured vineyards, and on tree-lined lanes. Navigate using the excellent (and free) map of the region available at all TIs.

BURGUNDY'S CUISINE SCENE

Arrive hungry. Considered by many to be France's best, Burgundian cuisine is peasant cooking elevated to an art. Entire lives are spent debating the best restaurants and bistros.

Several classic dishes were born in Burgundy: *escargots de Bourgogne* (snails served sizzling hot in garlic butter), *bœuf bourguignon* (beef simmered for hours in red wine with onions and mushrooms), coq au vin (rooster stewed in red wine), and

œufs en meurette (poached eggs in a red wine sauce, often served on a large crouton), as well as the famous Dijon mustards. Look also for delicious *jambon persillé* (cold ham layered in a garlic-parsley gelatin), *pain d'épices* (spice bread), and *gougères* (light, puffy cheese pastries). Those white cows (called Charolais) dotting the green pastures are Burgundian and make France's best steak and *bœuf bourguignon*.

Native cheeses are Époisses and Langres (both mushy and great), and my favorite, Montrachet (a tasty goat cheese). Crème de cassis (black currant liqueur) is another Burgundian specialty; look for it in desserts and snazzy drinks (try a *kir*).

Remember, restaurants serve only during lunch (11:30-14:00) and dinner (19:00-21:00, later in bigger cities); some cafés serve food throughout the day.

BURGUNDY'S WINES

Along with Bordeaux, Burgundy is why France is famous for wine. From Chablis to Beaujolais, you'll find great fruity reds, dry whites, and crisp rosés. The three key grapes are chardonnay (dry white wines), pinot noir (medium-bodied red wines), and gamay (light, fruity red wines, such as Beaujolais). Sixty percent of the wines are white, thanks to the white-only impact of the Chablis and Mâcon regions.

The Romans brought wine-making knowledge with them to Burgundy more than 2,000 years ago, but medieval monks perfected the art a thousand years later, establishing the foundations for Burgundy's famous wines. Those monks determined that pinot noir and chardonnay grapes grew best with the soil and climate in this region, a lesson that is followed to the letter by winemakers today. The French Revolution put capitalists in charge of the vineyards (no longer a monkish labor of love), which led to quantity over quality and a loss of Burgundy's esteemed status. Phylloxera insects destroyed most of Burgundy's vines in the late 1800s, and forced growers to rethink how and where to best cultivate grapes in Burgundy. This led to a return of the monks' approach, with the veneration of pinot noir and chardonnay grapes, a focus on quality over quantity, and a big reduction in the land area devoted to vines.

Today the government controls how much farmers can produce (to sustain high quality). This has a huge effect—in Burgundy, the average yield is only about 40 hectoliters per hectare (about 1,000 gallons), whereas in California it's more than double that. There are about 4,200 wineries in 44 villages in Burgundy. (I describe about a third of them in this chapter—it's a dirty job...) The wineries are tiny here (12-15 acres on average) thanks to Napoleon, who decided that land should be equally divided among a family's children when parents died. In many cases a farmer owns just a few rows in a vineyard and pieces together enough parcels to make a go of it.

In Burgundy, location is everything, and winery names take a back seat to the place where the grape is grown. Every village produces its own distinctive wine, from Chablis to Meursault to Chassagne-Montrachet. Road maps read like fine-wine lists. If the wine village has a hyphenated name, the second half usually comes from the town's most important vineyard (such as Gevrey-Chambertin, Aloxe-Corton, and Vosne-Romanée).

Burgundy wines are divided into four classifications: From top to bottom you'll find *grand cru, premier cru* (or *1er cru*), *village*, and *Bourgogne*. Each level allows buyers to better pinpoint the quality and origin of the grapes in their wine. With *Bourgogne* wines, the grapes can come from anywhere in Burgundy; *village* identifies the exact village where they were grown; and *grand cru* and *premier cru* locate the actual plots of land. As you drop from top to bottom, production increases—there is far more *Bourgogne* made than *grand cru*. In general, the less wine a vine produces, the higher the quality.

Look for *Dégustation Gratuite* (free tasting) signs, and prepare for serious wine tasting—and steep prices, if you're not careful. For a more easygoing tasting experience, head for the hills: The less prestigious Hautes-Côtes (upper slopes) produce some terrific, inexpensive, and overlooked wines. The least expensive wines are Bourgogne and Passetoutgrain (both red) and whites from the Mâcon and Chalon areas (St-Véran whites are also a good value). If you like rosé, try Marsannay, considered one of France's best. And *les famous* Pouilly-Fuissé grapes are grown near the city of Mâcon. For tips on tasting, see the sidebar on page 840.

Beaune

You'll feel comfortable right away in this prosperous, popular, and perfectly French little wine capital, where life centers on the production and consumption of the prestigious Côte d'Or wines. *Côte d'Or* means "Gold Coast" (from when the sea covered the valley in the Jurassic era). Today, Burgundy's "gold coast" is a spectacle to enjoy in late October as the leaves turn around Beaune.

Medieval monks and powerful dukes of Burgundy laid the groundwork that established this town's prosperity. The monks cultivated wine and cheese, and the dukes cultivated power. A ring road (with a bike path) follows the foundations of the medieval walls, and parking lots just outside keep most traffic from seeping into the historic center. One of the world's most important wine auctions takes place here every year during the third weekend of November.

Orientation to Beaune

Beaune is compact (pop. 25,000), with a handful of interesting monuments and vineyards knocking at its door. Limit your Beaune ramblings to the town center, lassoed within its medieval walls and circled by a one-way ring road, and leave time to stroll into the vineyards. All roads and activities converge on the town's two squares, Place Carnot and Place de la Halle. Beaune is quiet on Sundays and Monday mornings. The city's monuments are beautifully lit at night, making Beaune ideal for a post-dinner stroll. The lighting gets downright dazzling from June to September, when a glimmering light show called "Les Chemins de Lumières" plays on seven important buildings (ask at TI or hotel for map).

TOURIST INFORMATION

The **main TI** is located across from the post office on the ring road's southeastern corner (look for the *Porte Marie de Bourgogne* sign above the doorway; daily June-Sept 9:00-19:00, April-May and Oct until 18:30, Nov-March 9:00-12:30 & 13:30-18:00, closes earlier Sun year-round; tel. 03 80 26 21 30, www.beaune-tourisme.fr). A small **TI annex** (called "Point-I") is in the market hall, across from Hôtel Dieu (daily 9:30-13:00 & 14:00-18:00).

The main TI offers free Wi-Fi and rents audioguides (€5, 1.5 hours); both TIs have extensive information on wine tasting in the area, a room-finding service, a list of *chambres d'hôtes*, bus schedules, and an excellent, free regional road map. They can also arrange a local guide (figure €200/4 hours, €350/all day, reserve ahead, guides@beaune-toursime.fr). Skip the TI's €3 bike map; you'll get what you need for free from your bike rental shop.

The TI offers discounts on some key sights in Burgundy (including Abbey of Fontenay and the Château of Clos Vougeot) and some wine cellars (including the recommended Patriarche Père et Fils). Buy tickets at the TI or online.

For a shortcut into Beaune's center from the main TI, walk out the back door, cross a small street, continue straight through a long courtyard, and land on Place Carnot.

ARRIVAL IN BEAUNE

By Train: To reach the city center from the train station (no baggage storage), walk straight out of the station up Avenue du 8 Septembre, cross the busy ring road, and continue up Rue du Château. Follow it as it angles left and pass to the left of the mural, veering right onto Rue des Tonneliers. A left on Rue de l'Enfant leads to Beaune's pedestrian zone, Place Carnot, and the TI annex.

By Bus: Beaune has no bus station—only several stops along the ring road (see map on page 830 for stop locations). Ask the driver for *le Centre-Ville*. The Jules Ferry (zhul fair-ee) stop is central and closest to the train station. (For details on bus service, see "Getting Around the Beaune Region" on page 848.)

By Car: Follow *Centre-Ville/Place de la Madeleine* signs and park for free in Place Madeleine. If the lot is full—which it often is—spaces usually open up before long. The free Parking du Jardin Anglais at the north end of the ring road (see map on page 830) usually has spaces, and there are free parking spots all along the ring road. Parking inside Beaune's ring road is metered from 9:00 to 12:30 and 14:00 to 19:00; there's a convenient parking garage next to the main TI on the ring road.

HELPFUL HINTS

Exchange Rate: €1 = about $1.10

Country Calling Code: 33 (see page 1082 for dialing instructions)

Market Days: Beaune hosts a smashing Saturday market and a smaller Wednesday market. Both are on Place de la Halle and run until 12:30. The Saturday market fires up much of the old town and is worth planning ahead for. For either market, watch the action from the **Baltard Café** on Place de la Halle, then do as the locals do and have lunch at an outdoor café (see "Eating in Beaune," later, for ideas; sit down by 12:30 or forget it).

Supermarkets: Supermarché Casino has several small shops in Beaune, a store in the town center on Rue Carnot, and a mothership store through the arch off Place Madeleine (daily 8:30-19:30 except closed Sun afternoon).

Beaune's Best Wine and Food Stores

Beaune overflows with wine boutiques eager to convince you that their food products or wines are best. Here are a few to look for (to locate these, see the map on page 830).

The wine shop **Denis Perret,** with helpful English-speaking staff, offers a good selection in all price ranges, though most are from large merchants *(négociants).* They can chill a white for your picnic and offer informal tastings by the glass, with some *grands crus* (€1.50-3/taste, Mon-Sat 9:00-12:00 & 14:00-19:00, Sun 14:00-19:00 except Oct-mid-April closed Sun, on Place Carnot, tel. 03 80 22 35 47, www.denisperret.fr).

For an exquisite selection of fruit liqueurs (such as crème de cassis—a Burgundian treat), fruit syrups, and Burgundian brandy, find **Védrenne** at 28 Rue Carnot (closed Sun afternoon).

For food, **Alain Hess** offers an elegant display of local cheeses, mustards, and other gourmet products (7 Place Carnot). At the corner, **Mulot-Petitjean Pain d'Epices** shows off exquisite packages of this tasty local spice bread, also handy as gifts (1 Place Carnot).

BURGUNDY

Wi-Fi: The main TI offers free Wi-Fi, as does **Dix Carnot Café**—provided you consume (daily 8:00-19:00, on Place Carnot next to the Athenaeum's back-door entrance, great outside terrace, good €9.50 breakfast). The recommended **Bistrot Bourguignon** offers Wi-Fi with wine.

Post Office: The main post office is across from the main TI at 7 Boulevard St. Jacques. A handy Poste annex sells stamps and Colissimo boxes for international shipping (see page 1085), as well as mobile phone credit (Tue-Fri 13:00-17:00, closed Sat-Mon, 37 Rue Carnot).

Laundry: Beaune's lone launderette is open daily 7:00-21:00 (65 Rue Lorraine).

Bike Rental: See "Getting Around the Beaune Region—By Bike" on page 848.

Taxi: Call 06 11 83 06 10 or 06 09 35 63 12.

Car Rental: ADA is cheap and close to the train station (allow €60/day for a small car that includes 100 kilometers—about 60 miles, Mon-Sat 8:00-12:00 & 14:00-18:00, closed Sun, 26 Avenue du 8 Septembre, tel. 03 80 22 72 90). **Hertz** is at the BP gas station a few blocks toward the autoroute from the ring road (10 Avenue Charles de Gaulle, tel. 03 55 87 05 50). **Europcar** is less centrally located (53 Route de Pommard, tel. 03 80 22 32 24).

Cooking and Wine: For a one-stop Burgundy experience combining your stay with cooking classes and wine tastings, consider the **Domaine de Cromey** (see listing on page 851).

Best Souvenir Shopping: The **Athenaeum** has a great variety of souvenirs, including wine and cookbooks in English, with a good children's section. They also offer wine tastings (three tastes-€5-15, daily 10:00-19:00, across from Hôtel Dieu at 7 Rue de l'Hôtel Dieu).

Tours in and Around Beaune

Tourist Train
A TGV-esque little "Visiotrain" putts around Beaune and nearby vineyards (€7.50, runs April-Oct 11:00-17:30, almost hourly departures from Hôtel Dieu, no morning trips on Wed and Sat market days, 45 minutes, it waits for 10 people before it starts).

Private Guides
You have several great choices for walking or driving tours.

Kelly Kamborian is an effective teacher who trained as an archaeologist in the US. She has 20 years of experience guiding walking tours of Beaune and driving tours of the region (€220/ half-day, €380/day, mobile 06 63 41 21 10, kellykamborian@gmail. com).

For tours that focus on vineyards and Burgundian history, **Colette Barbier** is an engaging guide who is fluent in English and passionate about her region. Recently retired from the University of Burgundy, where she taught the history of gastronomy and wines for more than 25 years, she knows Burgundy as only a local can (her family has lived in the region for 250 years). Book well in advance, though last-minute requests sometimes work (€290/half-day, €460/day, tel. 03 80 23 94 34, mobile 06 80 57 47 40, www. burgundy-guide.com, cobatour@sfr.fr).

Delightful and wine-smart **Stephanie Jones** came from her native Britain to Burgundy to get a degree in oenology while working in Burgundian wine cellars. Today she leads informative, enjoyable, private tours of the vineyards (discounted for Rick Steves readers: €110/half-day, €210/day; prices are per person, 2-person minimum; tel. 03 80 61 29 61, mobile 06 10 18 04 12, www.burgundywinetours.fr, stephnwine@aol.com).

Robert Pygott, British by birth but Burgundian by choice, offers relaxed and informative tours exploring Burgundy wines (€230-300/day, mobile 06 38 53 15 27, www.burgundydiscovery. com, robert@burgundydiscovery.com).

BURGUNDY

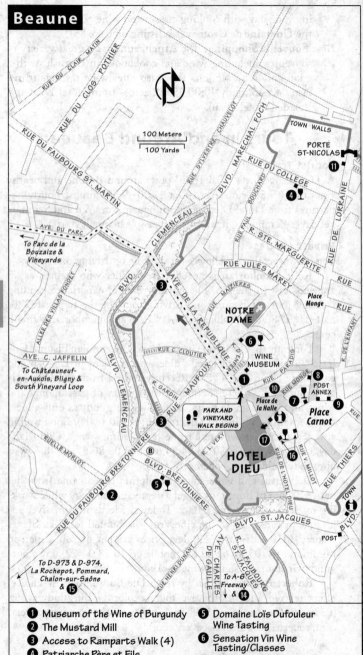

Beaune

TOWN WALLS

PORTE ST-NICOLAS

❶ Museum of the Wine of Burgundy
❷ The Mustard Mill
❸ Access to Ramparts Walk (4)
❹ Patriarche Père et Fils Wine Tasting
❺ Domaine Loïs Dufouleur Wine Tasting
❻ Sensation Vin Wine Tasting/Classes
❼ Denis Perret Wine Shop
❽ Védrenne Liqueurs

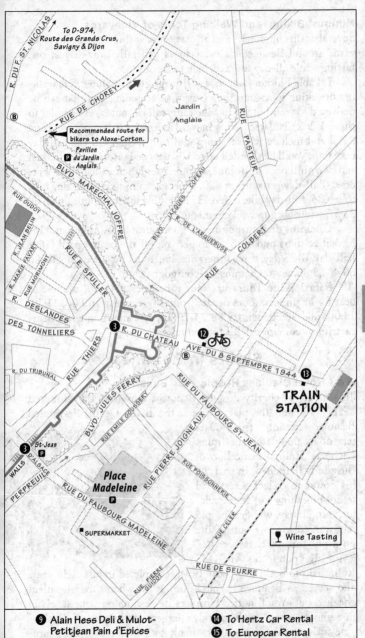

To D-974, Route des Grands Crus, Savigny & Dijon

Jardin Anglais

Recommended route for bikers to Aloxe-Corton.

Pavillon du Jardin Anglais

BLVD. MARECHAL JOFFRE

RUE DE CHOREY

R. DU F. ST. NICOLAS

RUE PASTEUR

RUE COLBERT

BLVD. JACQUES COPEAU

BLVD. DE L'ARQUEBUSE

RUE OUDOT

RUE JEAN BELIN

RUE MARIE FAVART

RUE MORIMONT

RUE E. SPULLER

R. DESLANDES

DES TONNELIERS

RUE THIERS

R. DU TRIBUNAL

❸ R. DU CHATEAU

⑫ 🚲

AVE. DU 8 SEPTEMBRE 1944

⑬

TRAIN STATION

BLVD. JULES FERRY

RUE DU FAUBOURG ST. JEAN

RUE EMILE GOUSSERY

❸ St-Jean

WALLS

D'ALSACE

PERPREUILLE

RUE DU FAUBOURG MADELEINE

Place Madeleine

RUE PIERRE JOIGNEAUX

RUE POISSONNERIE

RUE CELER

SUPERMARKET

RUE DE SEURRE

RUE PIERRE GUIDOT

🍷 Wine Tasting

BURGUNDY

❾ Alain Hess Deli & Mulot-Petitjean Pain d'Epices
❿ Baltard Café
⓫ Launderette
⑫ Bike Rental
⑬ ADA Car Rental

⑭ To Hertz Car Rental
⑮ To Europcar Rental
⑯ Athenaeum Bookstore & Dix Carnot Café (Wi-Fi)
⑰ Tourist Train Departures

Minibus, Biking, and Walking Tours of Vineyards

Several outfits offer half- and all-day tours of the villages and vineyards around Beaune. Half-day tours generally provide just one tasting while all-day tours include three or more.

Likable Florian Garcenot at **Bourgogne Evasion** offers walking or biking tours into the vineyards and rents bikes that can be delivered to your hotel. His bike tours follow routes very similar to those I describe later (see "Vineyard Loops near Beaune" on page 855), and include wine tastings and sightseeing. On the full-day bike tour, you'll be shuttled up to Château de la Rochepot and then sail downhill back to Beaune, stopping for lunch and at a few wineries (half-day walks from €20, 6-person minimum; half-day bike tour-€36, full-day bike tour-€135 including lunch; mobile 06 64 68 83 57, www.burgundybiketour.com).

Chemins de Bourgogne is a good outfit running fun and informative tours and an SUV to get you off the beaten path (€60/ half-day, €125/day, three itineraries, lunch not included, mobile 06 60 43 68 86, www.chemins-de-bourgogne.com).

Safari Wine Tours has four itineraries (€45-60, tour #2 is best for beginners; tours depart from TI generally at 9:00, 11:30, 14:00, and 16:30; tel. 03 80 24 79 12, www.burgundy-tourism-safaritours.com, or call TI to reserve).

Sights in Beaune

▲▲▲Hôtel Dieu des Hospices de Beaune

This medieval charity hospital is now a museum. The Hundred Years' War and the plague (a.k.a. the Black Death) devastated Beaune, leaving three-quarters of its population destitute. Nicholas Rolin, chancellor of Burgundy (enriched, in part, by his power to collect taxes), had to do something for "his people" (or, more likely, was getting old and wanted to close out his life on a philanthropic, rather than a greedy, note). So, in 1443  Rolin paid to build this place. It was completed in just eight years and served as Beaune's hospital until 1971, when the last patient checked out. You'll notice Hospices de Beaune on wine labels in fine shops—they are Burgundy's largest landowner of precious vineyards, thanks to donations made by patients over the centuries (and still happening today). Besides its magnificently decorated courtyard, Hôtel Dieu is famous for Rogier van der Weyden's superb *Last Judgment* altarpiece, which Rolin commissioned. It's also wonderfully animated from the outside during Beaune's summer light show (see page 826).

Cost and Hours: €7.50, €14 combo-ticket with Museum of the Wine of Burgundy, includes audioguide, daily April-mid-Nov 9:00-18:30, mid-Nov-March 9:00-11:30 & 14:00-17:30, last entry one hour before closing; it's dead center in Beaune, dominating Place de la Halle; tel. 03 80 24 45 00, www.hospices-de-beaune. com. River-cruise tour groups crowd the place from 9:30 to 11:00 in high season.

❍ Self-Guided Tour: While the included audioguide delivers key facts and good information, this self-guided tour gives your visit more meaning (posted information is in French only). Tour the rooms, which circle the courtyard, in a clockwise direction (following *Sens de la Visite* signs). Allow an hour for this tour.

• *To start your visit, enter the courtyard and find the stone bench.*

Courtyard of Honor: Honor meant power, and this was all about showing off. The exterior of the hospital and the town side of the courtyard are intentionally solemn, so as not to attract pesky 15th-century brigands and looters. The dazzling inner courtyard features a colorful glazed tile roof, establishing what became a style recognized in France as typically "Burgundian." The sturdy tiles, which last 300 years, are fired three times: once to harden, again to burn in the color, and finally for the glaze. They were last redone in 1902. The building is lacy Flamboyant Gothic with lots of decor— and boasts more weathervanes than any other building in France.

• *Now enter the hospice from the courtyard on the left side (follow* Salle des Pôvres *signs).*

Paupers' Ward: This grandest room of the hospital was the ward for the poorest patients. The vault, typical of big medieval rooms, was constructed like the hull of a ship. The screen separates the ward from the chapel at the front. Every three hours, the door was opened, and patients could experience Mass from their beds. Study the ceiling. Crossbeams are held by the mouths of creatively carved monsters—each mouth is stretched realistically, and each face has individual characteristics. Between the crossbars are busts of real 15th-century townsfolk—leading citizens, with animals humorously indicating their foibles (for example, a round-faced glutton next to a pig).

The carved wooden statue over the door you just entered shows a bound Christ—demonstrating graphically to patients that their Savior suffered and was able to empathize with their ordeal. Its realism shows that Gothic art had moved beyond the stiff formality of Romanesque carving. Behind the little window next to the statue was the nuns' dorm. The sisters (who were the first nurses) would check on patients from here. Notice the scrawny candleholder; if a patient died in the night, the candle was extinguished.

Find the small tables near the beds on the right. Rolin, who believed every patient deserved dignity, provided each patient with a pewter jug, mug, bowl, and plate. A painting on an easel at the left shows patients being treated in this room in 1949, 500 years after the hospital's founding. During epidemics, there were two to a bed. The ward didn't get heat until the 19th century (notice the heating grates on the floor), and the staff didn't get the concept of infection (and the basic practices of hand-washing) until the late 19th century (thanks to Louis Pasteur). Before then, most patients would have been better off left in a ditch outside.

• *Enter the chapel.*

Chapel: The hospice was not a place of hope. People came here to die. Care was more for the soul than the body. (Local guides are routinely instructed in writing by American tour companies not to use the word "hospice," because it turns off their clients. But this was a hospice, plain and simple, and back then, death was apparently less disturbing.) The stained glass shows Nicolas Rolin (lower left) and his wife, Guigone (lower right), dressed as a nun to show her devotion. Nicolas' feudal superior, the Duke of Burgundy, is portrayed above him; St. Nicholas is shown in green and St Anthony in yellow (the saints you want on your side if death looks imminent).

Notice the action on Golgotha. As Jesus is crucified, the souls of the two criminals crucified with him (portrayed as miniature naked humans) are being snatched up—one by an angel and the other by a red devil. At the bottom, Mary cradles the dead body of Christ. You're standing on tiles with the love symbol (or "gallant device") designed by Nicolas and Guigone to celebrate their love (as noble couples often did). The letters *N* and *G* are entwined in an oak branch, meaning that their love was strong. The word *seule* ("only one") and the lone star declare that Guigone is the only star in Nicolas' cosmos.

• *As you enter the St. Hugue ward, you'll pass a display of photos of the hospice as a hospital in the 1960s. Notice that nuns were still providing care for the patients.*

St. Hugue Ward: In the 17th century, this smaller ward was established for wealthy patients (who could afford Cadillac insurance plans). They were more likely to survive, and the decor displays themes of hope, rather than resignation: The series of Baroque paintings lining the walls shows the biblical miracles that Jesus performed. As the wealthy would lie in their beds, they'd stare at the ceiling—a painting with the bottom of an angel's foot, surrounded by the sick waiting to be healed by Jesus in his scarlet robe.

St. Nicolas Room: Originally divided into smaller rooms—one used for "surgery" (a.k.a. bloodletting and amputation), the other as an extension of the kitchen that you'll see next—this room now holds a model of the steep roof support and tools of the doctoring trade (amputation saws, caulking gun-size syringes, pans for bloodletting, and so on). The glass panel in the floor's center shows the stream running below; the hole provided a primitive but convenient disposal system after dinner or surgery. Living downstream from the hospital was a bad idea. Notice the display case showing the *Vente aux Enchères des Hospices de Beaune*. Operation of the hospice was primarily funded through auctions of its great wines (made from land donated by grateful patients over the years). Today, the auction of Hospices de Beaune wines is an internationally followed event, and gives the first indication of prices for the previous year's wines. Proceeds from the auction still support the "modern" hospital in Beaune.

• *Continue to the kitchen.*

Kitchen: Five nuns manned the kitchen at all times, preparing mostly soups and some meat dishes for their patients. Notice the 16th-century rotisserie. When fully wound, the cute robot would crank away, and the spit would spin slowly for 45 minutes. The 19th-century stove provided running hot water, which spewed from the beaks of swans. This kitchen dished food until 1985 (serving its retirement home residents). A five-minute, French-only sound-and-light show runs every 15 minutes.

• *Before entering the pharmacy, peek out back to the garden and outbuildings. Before those buildings were added, this was a huge garden growing herbs and other plants used for medications. The buildings were added in the early 1900s to serve as a retirement home.*

Pharmacy: Inside the pharmacy, strange and wondrous concoctions were mixed, cooked, distilled, and then stored in pottery jars. In the first room, the big bow over the mortar (large container) allowed the weighty pestle to be worked more easily for hours on end, grinding ingredients into fine pastes and powders. A painting on the back wall shows the gardens before the retirement home addition. The second room displays jars whose shapes corresponded to the types of medications they contained—the biggest jar (by the window) was for *theriaca* ("panacea," or cure-all). The most commonly used medicine back then, it was a syrup of herbs, wine, and opium.

• *Continue to the St. Louis Ward, which provides access to the room with the* Last Judgement.

St. Louis Ward: A maternity ward until 1969, this room is lined with fine 16th- and 17th-century tapestries illustrating mostly Old Testament stories. Dukes traveled with tapestries to cozy up the humble places they stayed in while on the road. The 16th-century pieces have better colors but inferior perspective. (The most precious 15th-century tapestries are displayed in the next room,

BURGUNDY

where everyone is enthralled by the great Van der Weyden painting.)

Rogier van der Weyden's *Last Judgment:* This exquisite painting, the treasure of Hôtel Dieu, was commissioned by Rolin in 1450 for the altar of the Paupers' Ward. He spared no cost, hiring the leading Flemish artist of his time. The entire altarpiece survives. The back side (on right wall) was sliced off so everything could be viewed at the same time. The painting is full of symbolism. Christ presides over Judgment Day. The lily is mercy, the sword is judgment, the rainbow promises salvation, and the jeweled globe at Jesus' feet symbolizes the universality of Christianity's message. As four angels blow their trumpets, St. Michael the archangel—very much in control—determines which souls are heavy with sin. Mary and the apostles pray for the souls of the dead as they emerge from their graves. But notice how both Michael and Jesus are expressionless—at this point, the cries of the damned and their loved ones are useless. In the back row are real people of the day.

The intricate detail, painted with a three-haired brush, is typical of Flemish art from this period. While Renaissance artists employed mathematical tricks of perspective, these artists captured a sense of reality by painting minute detail upon detail. (The attendant is dying to be asked to move the magnifying glass—*le loup*—into position to help you appreciate the exquisite detail in the painting.) Stare at Michael's robe and wings. Check out John's delicate feet and hands. Study the faces of the damned; you can almost hear the gnashing of teeth. The feet of the damned show the pull of a terrible force. On the far left, notice those happily entering the pearly gates. On the far right, it's the flames of hell (no, this has nothing to do with politics).

Except for Sundays and holidays, the painting was kept closed and people saw only the panels that now hang on the right wall: on top, the Annunciation—the beginning of man's salvation; and at the bottom, Nicolas and Guigone piously at the feet of St. Sebastian, invoked to fight the plague, and St. Anthony, whom patients called upon for help in combating burning skin diseases.

The unusual 15th-century tapestry *A Thousand Flowers*, hanging on the left wall, tells the medieval story of St. Eligius.

Collégiale Notre-Dame

Built in the 12th and 13th centuries, during the transition from Romanesque to Gothic architecture, Beaune's cathedral was a "daughter of Cluny" (built in the style of the Cluny Abbey, described on page 889). The church features a mix of both styles: Its foundation is decidedly Romanesque while much of the rest is Gothic. View it from the square before entering. That porch was added in the 16th century and (sadly) masks the original facade. Enter the second chapel on the left to see the faint remains of frescoes depicting the life of Lazarus, and then, behind the altar, find five vibrant, 15th-century tapestries illustrating the life of the Virgin Mary (English explanations available for frame-by-frame descriptions).

Cost and Hours: Free to enter cathedral, €3 to see tapestries; tapestries on view June-Sept Wed-Mon 10:00-13:00 & 14:00-18:00, closed Tue; April-May and Oct-Nov on view Fri-Sun only. Tapestries are removed Dec-March.

Museum of the Wine of Burgundy
(Musée du Vin de Bourgogne)

From this well-organized folk-wine museum, which fills the old residence of the Dukes of Burgundy, it's clear that the history and culture of Burgundy and its wine were fermented in the same bottle. Wander into the free courtyard (beautifully illuminated during summer light shows—see next listing) for a look at the striking palace, antique wine presses, and a concrete model of Beaune's 15th-century street plan (a good chance to appreciate the town's once-impressive fortified wall). Inside the museum, you'll find rooms with helpful English descriptions devoted to the region's topography, wine tools of the trade, barrel making, traditional wine festivals and my favorite—the Art of Drinking. Unfortunately, there's no tasting.

Cost and Hours: €7.80, €14 combo-ticket with Hôtel Dieu, April-Sept Wed-Mon 10:00-13:00 & 14:00-18:00, Oct-Nov and March 11:00-18:00, closed Dec-Feb and Tue year-round; in the Hôtel des Ducs on Rue d'Enfer, tel. 03 80 22 08 19, www.musees-bourgogne.org.

Getting There: With your back to the cathedral, turn left down the cobbled alley called Rue d'Enfer ("Hell Street," named for the fires of the Duke's kitchens once located on this street), keep left, and enter the courtyard of Hôtel des Ducs. There's also an entrance off Rue Paradis, opposite Le Petit Paradis restaurant.

Les Chemins de Lumières Light Show (Pathway of Lights)

Nightly from June through September, and off-season on holiday weekends, Beaune puts on an entertaining light show accenting the exteriors of many buildings in the town center and along its ramparts walk. The main attractions are seven razzle-dazzle light shows (lasting about five minutes each) highlighting Beaune's most historic buildings. The most centrally located are Hôtel Dieu, Collégiale Notre-Dame church, the Museum of the Wine of Burgundy courtyard, and the bell tower at Place Monge (behind the Notre-Dame church). The lights start when daylight ends, making this ideal for an after-dinner event (TIs have maps with all the details).

The Mustard Mill (La Moutarderie Fallot)

The last of the independent mustard mills in Burgundy opens its doors for guided tours in French (with a little English). They offer two tours: one with a focus on production and another that highlights the history of mustard. The tours are long yet informative—you'll learn why Burgundy was the birthplace of mustard (it's about wine juice), and where they get their grains today (Canada). It takes over an hour to explain what could be explained in half that time—you'll see a short film, learn about the key machines used in processing mustard, and finish with a tasting.

Cost and Hours: €10, daily at 10:00 and 11:30, also on summer afternoons, call to reserve or book online—space is limited; free mustard tasting—daily 9:30-18:00, except closed at lunch in winter and Sun afternoon year-round; across ring road in the appropriately yellow building at 31 Rue du Faubourg Bretonnière, tel. 03 80 22 10 10, www.fallot.com.

Park and Vineyard Walk

Stroll across the ring road, through a pleasant Impressionist-like park, and into Beaune's beautiful vineyards. This walk is ideal for those lacking a car, families (good play toys in park), and vine enthusiasts. The vine-covered landscape is crisscrossed with narrow lanes and stubby stone walls and provides memorable early morning and sunset views.

Follow Avenue de la République west from the center, cross the ring road, and parallel the stream along a few grassy blocks for about five minutes, then turn right into the serene park (Parc de la Bouzaize, opens at 8:00 and closes a bit before sunset). Walk through the park on either side of the pond and pop out at the right rear (northwest) corner (find the small opening in the iron fence by veering right at the end of the pond). Turn left on the small road, and enter the Côte de Beaune vineyards. Find the big poster showing how the land is sliced and diced among different plots (called *clos*, for "enclosure"). Each *clos* is named; look for the stone marker identifying the area behind the poster as Clos Les Teurons *(1er cru).* See "Burgundy's Wines," earlier, for more about the wines produced here.

Poke about Clos Les Teurons, noticing the rocky soil (wine grapes need to struggle). As you wander, keep in mind that subtle differences of soil and drainage between adjacent plots of land can be enough to create very different-tasting wines—from grapes grown only feet apart. *Vive la différence.* (Read "Wine Tasting in Burgundy" on page 840 to learn more.) A perfectly situated picnic table awaits under that lone tree up Chemin des Tilleuls.

Ramparts Walk

You can wander along sections of the medieval walls that protected Beaune from les bad guys. Much of the way is a paved lane used for parking, storage, and access to homes built into the wall, but you'll still get a feel for the ramparts' size and see vestiges of defensive towers. Find the path just inside the ring road that stretches counterclockwise from Avenue de la République to Rue de Lorraine (see map on page 842). The section near Avenue de la République is ideal for picnics, with shade, benches, and views to vineyards. You can enter or exit the ramparts at any cross street (free, always open).

WINE TASTING IN BEAUNE

Here are two good places to learn about Burgundy wines without leaving Beaune. For tastings in nearby wine villages, see page 849.

Patriarche Père et Fils

Home to Burgundy's largest and most impressive wine cellar, this is the best of the big wineries to visit in the city. With helpful video presentations at key points, you'll tour some of their three miles of underground passages and finish in the atmospheric tasting room, where you'll try several Burgundian classics (3 whites and 5-10 reds, depending on the visit you choose); each bottle sits on top of its own wine barrel. The long walk back to *la sortie* helps sober you up.

Cost and Hours: €12 for 8 tastes, €17 for 13 tastes, daily 9:30-11:30 & 14:00-17:30, 5 Rue du Collège, tel. 03 80 24 53 78, www.patriarche.com.

Sensation Vin

For a good introduction to Burgundy wines, try the informative wine classes given by Céline or Damien. You'll gather around a small counter in the comfortable wine bar/classroom and learn while you taste. Since the young owners do not make wine, you'll get an objective education (with blind tastings) and sample from a variety of producers. Call, email, or book online to arrange a class/tasting.

Cost and Hours: Class length and wines tasted vary by season (€35 for 1.5-hour class with 8 wines—4 whites, 4 reds; €90 for half-day tastings covering 10 wines, 2-person minimum—aspirin and pillow provided). Ask about their intimate tastings-in-the-vineyards class for two people (3-4 hours, €250/person; open daily, near Collégiale Notre-Dame at 1 Rue d'Enfer, tel. 03 80 22 17 57, www.sensation-vin.com, contact@sensation-vin.com).

Wine Tasting in Burgundy

Countless opportunities exist for you to learn the finer points of Burgundy's wines. Many shops and wineries in the region offer informal and informative tastings (with the expectation that you'll buy something or pay a tasting fee). You can taste directly at the *domaine* (winery) or at a *caveau* representing a variety of wineries (I list several options for both). To sample older vintages you'll have to visit a winery because *caveaux* usually stock only younger wines. When visiting a cellar, don't mind the mossy ceilings. Many cellars have spent centuries growing this "angel's hair"—the result of humidity created by the evaporation of the wines stored there. For tips on wine tasting, see the sidebar on page 1078.

The limits on our ability to bring wines back to North America can lead to tricky dynamics, particularly at smaller places. Busy winemakers naturally prefer to spend their time with folks who can buy enough wine to make it worth their while—and in most cases, that's not you (as nice as you are). They hope you'll like their wines, buy several bottles or a dozen, and ask for them at your shop back home. Most places now charge an entry fee, allowing you to taste a variety of wines (with less expectation that you'll buy). If you're not serious about buying at least a few bottles, look for places that charge for tastings.

Taking Wine Home: Some shops and wineries can arrange ship-

Sleeping in Beaune

Beaune has accommodations with all levels of comfort in all price ranges. To sleep peacefully (and usually for less), choose one of the nearby wine villages (see page 849).

IN THE CENTER

$$$$ Hôtel le Cep**** is *the* venerable place to stay in Beaune, if you have the means. Buried in the town center, this historic building comes with fine public spaces inside and out, and 65 gorgeous wood-beamed, traditionally decorated rooms in all sizes (family rooms, air-con, fitness center, spa, pricey pay parking, 27 Rue Maufoux, tel. 03 80 22 35 48, www.hotel-cep-beaune.com, resa@hotel-cep-beaune.com).

$$$ Les Jardins de Loïs**** is a four-star B&B run by welcoming winemakers Philippe and Anne-Marie. The five big rooms all overlook large gardens and show a no-expense-spared attention to comfort (also huge all-equipped apartment, includes custom-order breakfast; elevator, parking, on the ring road a block after Hôtel de la Poste at 8 Boulevard Bretonnière, tel. 03 80 22 41 97, mobile 06 73 85 11 06, www.jardinsdelois.com, contact@jardinsdelois.

ping (about €15 per bottle to ship a case, though you save about 20 percent on the VAT tax when shipping—so expensive wines are worth the shipping cost). To learn more about shipping wine, **Côte d'Or Imports** works with many sellers in Burgundy and has earned a reputation for safe and reliable shipping (www.cotedor-pdx.com). The simplest solution for bringing six or so bottles back is to pack them well and check the box on the plane with you. Good packing boxes are usually available where you taste, or you can wrap them well and put them in a hard-sided suitcase. US customs allows one bottle duty-free; the duty on additional bottles is 10 percent.

Tasting in Beaune: Visit the cellars listed under "Wine Tasting in Beaune" on page 839.

Visiting Vineyards by Car: Follow one of my two self-guided routes (starting on page 855), which can work well for bikers, too.

Visiting Vineyards Without Your Own Wheels: Rent a bike, take a taxi, or ride a train (long walks to villages from most stations) to nearby villages (see "Wine Villages and Sights near Beaune," later), or take Transco bus #44 to wine villages on La Route des Grand Crus (see page 848). You can also book a minibus tour or hire a recommended local guide (see page 829).

BURGUNDY

com). Their atmospheric wine cellar, **Domaine Loïs Dufouleur,** offers free tastings for guests (arrange ahead).

$$$ Hôtel Athanor*** has a privileged location—a block from the cathedral—and offers a mix of modern comfort with a touch of old Beaune. The atmospheric lounge sports a pool table and a full-service bar. The hallways are faded and rooms are a tad pricey; some have a little street noise (most rooms with air-con, family rooms, elevator, 9 Avenue de la République, tel. 03 80 24 09 20, www.hotel-athanor.com, reservation@hotel-athanor.com).

$$ Hôtel des Remparts*** is a peaceful oasis in a rustic manor house built around a soothing courtyard. It features attentive service, Old World comfort, many rooms with beamed ceilings, big beds, and a few good family suites (RS%, air-con, laundry service, bike rental, pay garage parking, just inside ring road between train station and main square at 48 Rue Thiers, tel. 03 80 24 94 94, www.hotel-remparts-beaune.com, hotel.des.remparts@wanadoo.fr, run by the formal Epaillys).

OUTSIDE THE WALLS

The first three hotels are a few blocks from the city center and train station, with easy parking.

Beaune Hotels & Restaurants

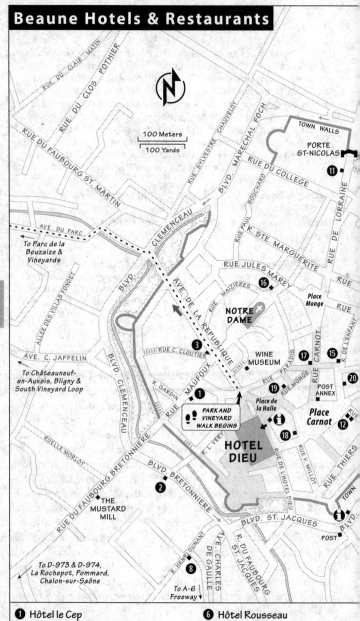

BURGUNDY

1 Hôtel le Cep

2 Les Jardins de Loïs B&B

3 Hôtel Athanor &
Maison du Colombier

4 Hôtel des Remparts

5 Hôtel de la Paix

6 Hôtel Rousseau

7 Hôtel de France &
Le Tast'Vin Restaurant

8 Hôtel Ibis

9 Hôtel La Villa Fleurie

10 Caveau des Arches Restaurant

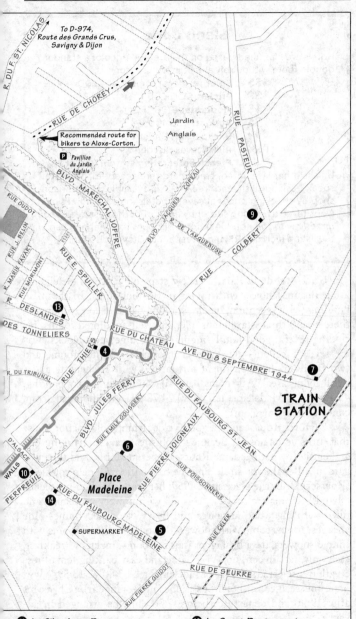

11 La Ciboulette Restaurant
12 Les Pôpiettes; F and B Restaurants
13 La Table de Guigone
14 Les Caves Madeleine Rest.
15 Le Conty Restaurant
16 Le Goret Restaurant
17 Brasserie le Carnot
18 Le Vintage
19 Le Bistrot Bourguignon
20 Bistrot du Coin

> # Sleep Code
>
> Hotels are classified based on the average price of a standard double room without breakfast in high season.
>
> | | |
> |---|---|
> | **$$$$** | **Splurge:** Most rooms over €200 |
> | **$$$** | **Pricier:** €150-200 |
> | **$$** | **Moderate:** €100-150 |
> | **$** | **Budget:** €50-100 |
> | **¢** | **Backpacker:** Under €50 |
> | **RS%** | **Rick Steves discount** |
> | ***** | **French hotel rating system** (0-5 stars) |
>
> Unless otherwise noted, credit cards are accepted, hotel staff speak basic English, and free Wi-Fi is available. Comparison-shop by checking prices at several hotels (on each hotel's own website, on a booking site, or by email). For the best deal, *book directly with the hotel.* Ask for a discount if paying in cash; if the listing includes **RS%**, request a Rick Steves discount.

$$ Hôtel de la Paix,*** a few steps off Place Madeleine, is a top Beaune choice, with rooms in two buildings. In the main building (with reception, breakfast room, bar, and comfy lounges), there are 30 three-star, handsome, and well-appointed rooms, including several good family rooms. In an annex two blocks away are seven excellent-value, very comfortable two-star rooms and two family rooms (apartment for up to 6 with kitchenette and a small living area). All rooms have air-conditioning (pay parking, 45 Faubourg Madeleine, tel. 03 80 24 78 08, www.hotelpaix.com, contact@hotelpaix.com).

$ Hôtel Rousseau is a good-value, frumpy old manor house that turns up its nose at Beaune's sophistication. Cheerful, quirky, and elusive owner Madame Rousseau, her pet birds, and the quiet garden will make you smile, and the tranquility will help you sleep. (Rousseau's run the place since 1959; her granddaughter now lends a hand). Rooms are spotless, covered with flowery wallpaper, and filled with big wood armoires and heavy wood bed frames. The cheapest rooms come with showers down the hall; the rooms with simple showers are a bit bigger (family rooms, includes breakfast, cash only, no air-con, no Wi-Fi, free and easy parking, email reservations preferred, 11 Place Madeleine, tel. 03 80 22 13 59, www.hotel-rousseau.com, hotelrousseaubeaune@orange.fr). Check-ins after 19:00 and departures before 7:30 must be arranged in advance.

$ Hôtel de France*** is a good place that's easy for train travelers and drivers. It has standard rooms with air-conditioning and is run by fun, English-speaking owners Nicolas and Virginie (family rooms, bar, good bistro, pay garage parking, 35 Avenue du 8

Septembre, tel. 03 80 24 10 34, www.hoteldefrance-beaune.com, contact@hoteldefrance-beaune.com).

$ Hôtel Ibis,*** with free and easy parking a few blocks south of Hôtel Dieu, has 73 efficient if unimaginative rooms. It's a good value—better if you have kids and want a pool. The bigger-and-better appointed "Club" rooms are worth the extra euros (air-con, 1 smoking floor, free parking, 5-minute walk to town center, 7 Rue Henri Dunant, tel. 03 80 22 75 67, www.hotelibis.com, h1363@accor.com). There are two other Ibis hotels in Beaune and a gaggle of Motel 6-type places closer to the autoroute.

$ Hôtel La Villa Fleurie, an adorable 10-room refuge, is a great value and run well by affable Madame Chartier (a 15-minute walk from the center). First-floor-up rooms are wood-floored, plush, and *très* traditional; second-floor rooms are carpeted and cozy. Most rooms have queen-size beds, and all rooms have big bathrooms (family rooms, community fridge, easy and free parking, 19 Place Colbert, tel. 03 80 22 66 00, www.lavillafleurie.fr, contact@lavillafleurie.fr). From Beaune's ring road, turn right in front of the Bichot winery.

BURGUNDY

Eating in Beaune

For a small town, Beaune offers a wide range of reasonably priced restaurants. Review my suggestions before setting out, and reserve at least a day ahead to avoid frustration (especially on weekends). Many places are closed Sunday and Monday. This region offers a bounty of worthwhile upscale dining options (I've listed several), but before you book, check their wine lists (easiest to do online)—the prices may double your total dinner cost. For eating recommendations in the wine villages near Beaune, see page 849.

$$$ Caveau des Arches is a reliable choice if you want to dine on Burgundian specialties in romantic stone cellars. It has a €25 *menu* with the classics, a €33 *menu* with greater choices, and a €52 gourmand *menu*, but portions can be small (closed Sun-Mon and Aug, great wine list, where the ring road crosses Rue d'Alsace—which leads to Place Madeleine—at 10 Boulevard Perpreuil, tel. 03 80 22 10 37, www.caveau-des-arches.com).

$$$ La Ciboulette, intimate and family-run with petite Hélèna as your hostess, offers reliable cuisine that mixes traditional Burgundian flavors with creative dishes and lovely presentation. It's worth the longer walk—and you can do your laundry next door while you dine (indoor seating only, closed Mon-Tue; from Place Carnot, walk out Rue Carnot to 69 Rue Lorraine; tel. 03 80 24 70 72).

$$$ Les Pôpiettes is a lively place and popular with locals and foodies, with a communal table on one side, booths on the other,

Restaurant Price Code

I've assigned each eatery a price category, based on the average cost of a typical main course. Drinks, desserts, and splurge
items (steak and seafood) can raise the price considerably.

$$$$ **Splurge:** Most main courses over €25
$$$ **Pricier:** €20-25
$$ **Moderate:** €15-20
$ **Budget:** Under €15

In France, a crêpe stand or other takeout spot is **$**; a sit-down
brasserie, café, or bistro with affordable *plats du jour* is **$$**;
a casual but more upscale restaurant is **$$$**; and a swanky
splurge is **$$$$**.

and a cheery ambience. The chef-owner produces an eclectic blend
of delicious and inventive—though limited in choice—cuisine,
such as risotto and snails (inside dining only, closed Tue-Wed, 10
Rue d'Alsace, tel. 03 80 21 91 81).

$$$ F and B sits next door, with a sleek bistro interior, terrific
outside seating, and helpful owner Jerome at the helm. The cuisine
is bistro-classic with an accent on Burgundian dishes (closed Sun,
8 Rue d'Alsace, tel. 03 80 21 04 19).

$$ La Table de Guigone is away from the fray and a good
place for Burgundy specialties—such as a €26 *menu* featuring
snails, *bœuf bourguignon*, and a cheese course. It welcomes diners with a cozy interior and outside seating on a quiet corner near
Hôtel des Remparts (other *menus* available, tel. 03 80 21 16 04, 1
Place du Docteur Jorrot).

$$ Le Tast'Vin, across from the train station at the recom-
mended Hôtel de France, has a good-value €26 *menu* and fun
cheeseburgers with Burgundian cheese (closed Sat and Mon for
lunch and all day Sun, 35 Avenue du 8 Septembre, tel. 03 80 24 10
34, www.hoteldefrance-beaune.com).

At **$$$ Les Caves Madeleine,** step down into the warm little
dining room and choose a private table—or better, join the com-
munal table, where good food and wine kindle conversation and
new friendships (making the place noisy for some). Owner/chef
Martial's recipes are inspired by his grandmother's favorites but
service can be slow and wine by the glass or half-bottle is scarce
(closed Wed and Sun, near Place Madeleine at 8 Rue du Faubourg
Madeleine, tel. 03 80 22 93 30).

$$$ Le Conty has a prized position at the junction of two
pedestrian lanes, with great outdoor and indoor seating and re-
fined cuisine with Burgundy and French classics (closed Sun-Mon,
5 Rue Ziem, tel. 03 80 22 63 94, www.leconty.fr).

$$$ Le Goret (slang for pig) turns its back on Beaune's sophistication, serving farmer-sized portions of regional dishes prepared by a jolly chef. Pork is their thing, and dietary concerns are not. This is the place to experience down-and-dirty Burgundy. There are no fixed *menus* (order from the pig chalkboards), and the selection is limited. You won't find first courses here, only big servings of well-garnished main courses and killer desserts (closed Sun-Mon and Thu evening, inside tables only, reserve ahead, behind Collégiale Notre-Dame at 10 Place Notre-Dame, tel. 03 80 22 05 94).

$$ Brasserie le Carnot is a perennially popular café with good inside seating and better exterior tables in the thick of the pedestrian zone. It serves pizza, salads, and pasta dishes as well as the usual café offerings (open daily, where Rue Carnot and Rue Monge meet, tel. 03 80 22 32 93).

Wine Bars: Le Vintage is ideal in good weather, with tables on Place Carnot (inside seating is less appealing) and a service-oriented owner. Cheese and charcuterie plates are served inside and out (daily, 14 Place Carnot, tel. 03 80 22 13 39).

$$ Maison du Colombier operates as a wine bar and bistro. The picturesque outside terrace has views of the church; inside, stone walls meet wood beams, creating a cozy ambience with counter-height tables and stools (entrées, tapas, tartines, and *plats,* 1 Rue Charles Cloutier, tel. 03 80 26 16 26).

$$$ Le Bistrot Bourguignon is a laid-back wine bar/bistro with 15 types of *vin* available by the glass (order by number from display behind the bar). Come for a glass of wine and to use their Wi-Fi, or for a light dinner. Dine at the counter, the sidewalk tables, or in the casually comfortable interior (closed Sun-Mon, on pedestrian street at 8 Rue Monge, tel. 03 80 22 23 24).

$$ Bistrot du Coin is a warm and welcoming shoebox-size place whose fun owner Alex clearly loves his work as much as he does making clients feel at ease. Prices are reasonable, though seating is limited to a few bar stools (kitty-corner from Le Conty at 2 Place Ziem, Tue-Fri 17:00-24:00, Sat 10:00-24:00, closed Sun-Mon).

Beaune Connections

From Beaune by Train to: Meursault (hourly, 5-30 minutes, 15-minute walk into town), **Gevrey-Chambertin** (hourly, 20 minutes, 15-minute walk into town), **Dijon** (15/day, 20 minutes), **Paris** Gare de Lyon (nearly hourly, 2.5 hours, most require reservation and easy change in Dijon; more via Dijon to Paris' Gare de Bercy, no reservation required, 3.5 hours), **Bourges** (1/day direct, 2.5 hours, more with transfer in Nevers), **Colmar** (10/day, 2.5-4 hours via TGV between Dijon and Mulhouse, reserve well ahead, changes in Dijon and Mulhouse or Belfort), **Arles** (10/day, 4.5-5 hours, 9 with transfer in Lyon and Nîmes or Avignon), **Chamonix** (7/day, 7 hours, change in Lyon and St-Gervais, some require additional changes), **Annecy** (7/day, 4-6 hours, change in Lyon), **Amboise** (1/day, 4.5 hours, transfer at St-Pierre-des-Corps; more with additional transfer at Nevers).

Touring Burgundy's Wine Villages

Exploring the villages and vineyards in the region near Beaune, by car or by bike, is a delight.

GETTING AROUND THE BEAUNE REGION

By Car: Driving provides the ultimate flexibility for touring the vineyards, though drivers should prepare for narrow lanes and use the handy buckets to spit back after tasting.

By Bike: Pedaling on a bike from Beaune takes you into the world-famous vineyards of the Côte d'Or within minutes. The many quiet service roads and bike-only lanes make this area wonderful for biking. (Beware of loose gravel on shoulders and along small roads.) A signed bike route, *La Voie Verte*, runs south from Beaune all the way to Cluny, and a new route from Beaune north to Dijon may be in place by your visit. My favorite rides are described in detail in "Vineyard Loops near Beaune" (see page 855).

Well-organized, helpful, and English-speaking Florian and Cédric at **Bourgogne Randonnées** rent excellent bikes of all types, bike racks, kid bikes, and trailers, and offer maps and detailed itineraries. Ask about their favorite routes that follow only small roads and dedicated bike paths, and soak up their trustworthy wine-tasting tips. They can deliver a bike to your hotel anywhere in France if booked well ahead (bikes-€6/hour, €19/day, electric bikes-€35/day, includes helmet, daily 9:00-12:00 & 13:30-18:00, near Beaune train station at 7 Avenue du 8 Septembre, tel. 03 80 22 06 03, www.bourgogne-randonnees.fr, helloinfobr@aol.com).

By Bus: Transco bus #44 links Beaune with all the important wine villages to the north along the famous Route des Grands Crus, and runs to Dijon's train station (7/day; www.mobigo-bourgogne.eu—click on English flag, then find "Transco" under "Transport networks"). Three #44 bus stops are along Beaune's ring road (see map on page 830 and look for Transco decals in shelters). Bus service south of Beaune to villages like Meursault and Puligny-Montrachet is hopeless—take a taxi, hop a train (limited options), or rent a bike.

By Train: Hourly trains stop in the wine villages of Meursault and Santenay to the south of Beaune, and Nuits-St-Georges, Vougeot (10-minute walk to Château de Clos Vougeot), and Gevrey-Chambertin to the north. Most of these stations require a 15-minute walk to the town center. In 2016 bikes were still allowed on local trains—great for bikers, though the service may be discontinued due to overuse. Check with your bike shop if you plan to take your bike on a train.

By Minibus Tour: Try **Chemins de Bourgogne** or **Safari Wine Tours** (see page 832).

By Taxi: Call **Julien Dupont** (mobile 06 11 83 06 10); for another taxi, see page 827.

Wine Villages and Sights near Beaune

You'll find exceptional tasting, eating, and sleeping values in the workaday villages and towns within a 10- to 15-minute drive of Beaune. The Côte d'Or has scads of *chambres d'hôtes*; get a list at the TI and reserve ahead in summer. See also the suggestions along the Route des Grands Crus (page 861).

For driving/biking loops that tie these villages together, see page 855; for the Route des Grands Crus, see page 861.

SOUTH OF BEAUNE
Pommard

The small village of Pommard lies on the bike path just two miles south of Beaune. Walkers can follow the bike path and make it here in 45 minutes. Pommard has cafés, restaurants, and many tasting opportunities.

Domaine Lejeune is a small family winery with an unusual twist—it has been handed from mother to daughter for seven generations, a rare occurrence in this traditionally male-dominated business. During the hour-long tour you will see old-style wooden vats and the cellar before sampling three wines for free, including a Pommard (Mon-Sat 9:00-12:00 & 14:00-18:00, OK to stop by but better to call ahead; by appointment only Jan-March, behind the church, tel. 03 80 22 90 88, www.domaine-lejeune.fr, aubert-lefas@domaine-lejeune.fr).

Eating in Pommard: You'll find several good lunch options just off the main road. Facing Pommard's big church, **$$$$ Auprès du Clocher** has stylish, contemporary decor one floor up with windows on the village, a formal atmosphere, and a focus on *la cuisine gastronomique* (closed Tue-Wed, 1 Rue Nackenheim, tel. 03 80 22 21 79, www.aupresduclocher.com).

Meursault

This appealing town 10 minutes south of Beaune is like a mini-Beaune, with a vast main square ringed with cafés, wine shops, and a small grocery market. A good selection of hotels and restaurants is available in its compact center. Eat or sleep here for that small-town feel and quick access to Beaune, vineyards, and villages. The train station is a 15-minute walk from the town center.

Sleeping and Eating in Meursault: $$ Hôtel les Charmes,*** in the heart of town, is a sweet place with fine, traditional rooms and a homey Old World feel, thanks to the easygoing owners (les Grimprets). There's a veritable park in the back and a big pool (10 Place du Murger, tel. 03 80 21 63 53, www.hotellescharmes.com, contact@hotellescharmes.com).

These two good places feature Burgundian cuisine at fair prices and offer rooms at reasonable rates: **$$ Hotel/Restaurant le Chevreuil** attracts foodies and locals wanting a fine meal served in a country-elegant setting with a pleasant terrace overlooking the château. This place merits a detour from Beaune (book ahead, closed Wed and Sun for dinner, 9 Place de la République, tel. 03 80 21 23 25, reception@lechevreuil.fr).

$ Hôtel du Centre offers an unpretentious menu for lunch or dinner, a sweet courtyard, and simple, cheap rooms (open daily, 4 Rue de Lattre de Tassigny, tel. 03 80 21 20 75, contact@hotel-du-centre-meursault.com).

Puligny-Montrachet

This village of around 400 people is situated about a 15-minute drive (or 60 minutes by bike) south of Beaune, on the scenic route to Château de la Rochepot (see page 856). It has just enough commercial activity to keep travelers well fed and housed.

Located on the village's central roundabout, the user-friendly **Caveau de Puligny-Montrachet** has a convivial wine-bar-like tasting room, a smart outdoor terrace, and no pressure to buy. Knowledgeable owner Julien is happy to answer your every question. He has wines from 200 Burgundian vintners, from Chablis to Pouilly-Fuissé, but his forte is Puligny-Montrachet and Meursault whites, which is why I taste here. His reds are young and less ready to drink (€20 for 6 wines, can ship to the US; March-Oct daily 9:30-19:00, sometimes closes at lunch; Nov-Feb Tue-Sun 10:00-12:00 & 15:00-18:00, closed Mon; tel. 03 80 21 96 78, www.caveau-puligny.com, wallerand.julien@wanadoo.fr).

If you're looking for an upscale wine château experience, visit **Château de Chassagne-Montrachet** (just a few minutes south of town). In this elegant mansion, an informative 45-minute tour takes you through gorgeous cellars—some dating to the 11th century. You'll taste five of the family Picard's impressive wines from throughout Burgundy, with an emphasis on whites. You'll learn about their clever wine barrel color-coding system and appreciate how Monsieur Picard grew his 2 hectares of vines to 135 hectares in 30 years (€17 includes tour and tasting, daily 10:00-18:00, best to call ahead but drop-ins OK, tel. 03 80 21 98 57, www. chateaudechassagnemontrachet.com).

Sleeping in Puligny-Montrachet: $$ Domaine des Anges is a lovely place run by a British couple (John and Celine) who pamper their guests with the Queen's English, lovely rooms, linger-longer lounges inside and out, laundry service, and afternoon tea every day. It's also ideally located in the center of Puligny-Montrachet (includes a smashing breakfast, no children under 16, Place des Marronniers, tel. 03 80 21 38 28, mobile 06 23 86 63 91, www. domainedesangespuligny.com, domainedesanges@yahoo.fr).

$ Chambres les Gagères is a swinging deal with four cozy and spotless rooms—some with vineyard views, and all with a common kitchen and view terraces overlooking vineyards. Adorable Maria speaks little English but manages to get her point across (includes breakfast, 17 Rue Drouhin, tel. 03 80 21 97 46, mobile 06 15 97 64 71, maria.adao2@orange.fr).

Eating in Puligny-Montrachet: At **$$$$ Le Montrachet,** settle in for a truly traditional Burgundian experience—a justifiable splurge if you want a refined and classy dining experience without stuffiness. This is a good choice for a gourmet lunch on a lovely terrace at somewhat affordable prices—€32 lunch *menu*, €65-97 dinner *menus,* and pricey wine list (open daily, on Puligny-Montrachet's main square at 10 Place des Marronniers, tel. 03 80 21 30 06, www.le-montrachet.com, info@le-montrachet.com). Come early for a glass of wine before dinner with Julien at the Caveau de Puligny-Montrachet (described earlier).

$$$ L'Estaminet des Meix, a contemporary wine bar/café in the heart of the village, serves good brasserie fare at reasonable prices and has fun outdoor seating (€19 dinner *menu* includes snails, *bœuf bourguignon,* and dessert; closed Mon evening and all day Tue, Place des Marronniers, tel. 03 80 21 33 01).

Sleeping and Eating near Puligny-Montrachet: $$$$ Domaine de Cromey offers foodies and wine lovers the complete Burgundy experience with three-night packages combining cooking workshops, wine tastings, and accommodations in a sublime setting 15 minutes from Puligny-Montrachet. Wine expert/exporter Dennis Sherman and chef/cookbook author Eleanor Garvin (both American expats) have fused their passions and 30 years of experience in Burgundy into a gorgeous six-room manor house with exquisite public spaces and a view pool (includes breakfast, tel. 03 85 93 52 83, https://heartofburgundy.com, eldenwine@gmail.com).

BURGUNDY

▲Château de la Rochepot

Splendid both inside and out, this pint-size, very Burgundian castle rises above its village, eight miles from Beaune. Tour half on your own and the other half with a French guide (get the English handout; most guides speak some English and can answer questions).

Cost and Hours: €8 on your own, €11 includes 25-minute guided tour, usually on the hour 10:00-17:00 but no tour at 13:00; open May-Sept Wed-Sun 10:00-17:30, until 18:30 July-Aug, closed off-season and Mon-Tue year-round, tel. 03 80 20 04 00, www.larochepot.com, office@larochepot.com.

Getting There: The highly recommended scenic route from Beaune to the château is described in the "South Vineyard Loop" (see page 856). Or, to reach the château more directly from Beaune, follow signs for *Chalon-sur-Saône* from Beaune's ring road, then follow signs to *Autun* for 15 lovely minutes.

Visiting the Castle: Cross the drawbridge under the Pot family coat of arms and (as instructed) knock three times with the ancient knocker to enter. If no one comes, knock harder, or find a log and ram the gate.

Construction began during the end of the Middle Ages (when castles were built to defend) and was completed during the Renaissance (when castles became luxury homes). So it's neither a purely defensive structure (as in the Dordogne) nor a palace (as in the Loire)—it's a bit of both. The castle was never attacked by foreigners, though the French Revolution laid waste to a good part of it. After being used as a quarry, it was purchased by a local family and rebuilt. The same family owns it today.

The furnishings are surprisingly cushy given the military look of the exterior. Enter through the guard's room, and appreciate the weight of a good suit of armor. I could sleep like a baby in the Captain's Room, surrounded by nine-foot-thick walls. Don't miss the 15th-century alarmed safe. Notice the colorful doorjamb. These same colors were used to paint many buildings (including castles and churches) and remind us that medieval life was not monochromatic. The kitchen will bowl you over; the dining room sports a 15th-century walnut high chair. Look for paintings of the pre-Revolution castle to get a feel for its original appearance.

Climb the tower (fine views) and see the out-of-place Chinese room, sing chants in the resonant chapel, and make ripples in the 240-foot-deep well. (Can you spit a bull's-eye?) Paths outside lead you on a worthwhile walk around the castle. Don't leave without driving, walking, or pedaling up D-33 a few hundred yards toward St-Aubin (behind Hôtel Relais du Château) for a romantic view.

Chagny

The only reason to come to this unexceptional town 20 minutes south of Beaune is to eat very well (trains allow easy access for non-drivers).

Eating in Chagny: Well known as one of France's finest restaurants, **$$$$ Maison Lameloise** has Michelin's top rating (three stars). The setting is elegant (as you'd expect), the service is relaxed and patient (which you might not expect), the cuisine is Burgundy's best, and the overall experience is memorable. If you're tempted to dive into the top of the top of French cuisine, book this place well ahead (*menus* from about €150 at diner and €80 at lunch, very pricey wines, open daily, 36 Place d'Armes, tel. 03 85 87 65 65, www.lameloise.fr). Or consider their nearby contemporary bistro **$$$ Pierre et Jean,** where you get the same quality with a simpler menu for less money (*menus* from €34, around the corner at 2 Rue de la Poste, tel. 03 85 87 08 67, www.pierrejean-restaurant.fr).

NORTH OF BEAUNE
Aloxe-Corton

This small, prestigious village has good tasting rooms (and not much more); it's just a 10-minute drive north of Beaune.

At the **Domaines d'Aloxe-Corton** *caveau,* you can sample four makers of the famous Aloxe-Corton wines in a comfortable and relaxed setting. Prices are affordable, and the easygoing staff speaks enough English (small fee for tasting, free if you buy two bottles, Thu-Mon 10:00-13:00 & 15:00-19:00, no midday break on high-season weekends, closed Tue-Wed, tel. 03 80 26 49 85, http://aloxe.corton.free.fr). You'll find the *caveau* a few steps from the little square in Aloxe-Corton.

Mischief and Mayhem is a dream come true for Anglophones serious about Burgundian wine. British-born-and-raised Fiona and Michael make fine wines and sell them at fair prices (€13-60, but little middle ground). They are thoroughly immersed in Burgundian culture and can help you make sense of this region's wine culture. It's a small operation and, considering that the owners work the vineyards, tasting is by appointment only—call ahead (a few blocks below the church on D-115d to Ladoix-Serrigny at 10 Impasse du Puits, mobile 06 30 01 23 76, www.mischiefandmayhem. com).

Domaine Comte Senard is famous for its prestigious wines and *table d'hôte,* where you get a full lunch with matching wines and thorough explanations from the wine steward as you go (lunch served Tue-Sat 11:30-13:30, €49 with 3 wines, €69 with 6 wines, €95 with 6 *grands crus*). It's best to book ahead for this fun, convivial way to spend two hours learning about the local product. Another option is a free tasting of two basic wines—or guided tastings with a sommelier (€24 for 4 fine wines for the first person, €5/person after that, 5-person maximum, Tue-Sat 10:00-11:30 & 14:00-17:30, closed Sun-Mon, reserve ahead by phone, 1 Rue des Chaumes, tel. 03 80 26 41 65, www.domainesenard.com, table@domainesenard.com).

Sleeping in Aloxe-Corton: $$$ Hôtel Villa Louise*** is a romantic place burrowed deep in this wine hamlet. Many of its 14 spacious and tastefully decorated rooms overlook the backyard vineyards (book ahead), and a large, grassy garden made for sipping the owner's wine—but, sadly, no picnics are allowed. There's a small covered pool, a cozy lounge, and tastings of the owner's wines (suites available, sauna, near the château at 9 Rue Franche, tel. 03 80 26 46 70, www.hotel-villa-louise.fr, contact@hotel-villa-louise.fr).

BURGUNDY

Magny-les-Villers

This Hautes-Côtes village is located 15 minutes north of Beaune via one of Burgundy's most scenic wine roads (drive up into Pernand Vergeles to find this road signed on the right).

Domaine Naudin-Ferrand is overlooked by most, but makes fine reds and whites at excellent prices, and offers an authentic, small-producer experience (simple tasting room with helpful Claire who speaks enough English). Its best values are wines from the Hautes-Côtes vineyards. Tasting is by appointment only—call or email (Mon-Fri 9:00-12:00 & 13:30-17:30, Sat 14:00-18:00, closed Sun, Rue du Meix-Grenot, carefully track the faded signs, tel. 03 80 62 91 50, www.naudin-ferrand.com, info@naudin-ferrand.com).

Savigny-lès-Beaune

About five minutes from Beaune, Savigny-lès-Beaune is a thriving village with all the services travelers need, but no central square or focal point to make me want to sleep here.

Savigny-lès-Beaune is home to **Henri de Villamont,** a bigtime enterprise with a huge range of wines and a modern, welcoming tasting room. They grow their own grapes and also buy grapes from other vineyards, but make all the wines themselves. This allows them to create a vast selection of wines featuring grapes from virtually all of the famous wine villages, from Pouilly-Fuissé to Chablis (free tasting, hours vary but generally Mon-Fri 10:00-12:30 & 13:30-18:00, call for weekend hours or to book a cellar visit, Rue du Dr. Guyot, tel. 03 80 21 52 13, www.hdv.fr).

Sights in Savigny-lès-Beaune: The medieval castle **Château de Savigny** comes with a moat and an eclectic collection that includes 100 fighter jets, Abarth antique racing cars, tractors and fire-engines, 300 motorcycles, 6,000 airplane models, vineyards—and no furnishings (castle—€10, daily mid-April-mid-Oct 9:00-18:30, shorter hours off-season, last entry 1.5 hours before closing, English handout; wine tasting—€4 for 7 of the owner's wines, €3 for 5 wines; tel. 03 80 21 55 03, www.chateau-savigny.com).

Eating in Savigny-lès-Beaune: Beyond the château in the village, the **$$ R. De Famille** café-pizzeria faces a little square and has good outdoor seating (closed Mon). A grocery shop and a bakery are a few blocks past the café (grocery usually closed 12:30-15:00).

Vineyard Loops near Beaune

In this section, you'll find two vineyard loops near Beaune and recommendations for touring the Route des Grands Crus between Beaune and Dijon. These

drives combine great scenery with some of my favorite wine destinations (for more on these towns, see "Wine Villages and Sights near Beaune," earlier). Certain sections are doable by bike depending on your bike fitness and determination. Before planning to take your bike on the train, check with the bike shop to be sure it's allowed on board.

If time is tight and you have a car, drive the beautiful **"South Vineyard Loop"** to Château de la Rochepot (with off-the-beaten-path villages and ample tasting opportunities). The last part is a tough ride on a bike (unless it's electric), so most bikers will prefer doing just the first section of this route (ideally to Puligny-Montrachet and back—an easy, level ride).

My **"North Vineyard Loop"** takes you to Savigny-lès-Beaune and is good by car or by bike (manageable hills and distances). I also list good stops on the famous **"Route des Grands Crus,"** connecting Burgundy's most prestigious wine villages farther north of Beaune.

Along these routes, I avoid famous wine châteaux (such as those in Pommard and Meursault) and look for smaller, more personal places. Although you can drop in unannounced at a wine château or a *caveau* that represents multiple wineries (*comme un cheveu sur la soupe*—"like a hair on the soup"), at private wineries it's best to call ahead and arrange an appointment (ask your hotelier for help). At free tastings, you're expected to buy at least a bottle or two unless you're on a group tour.

Before heading out, read the section on Burgundian wines (page 824). You'll almost certainly see workers tending the vines. In winter, plants are pruned way back (determining the yield during grape harvest in the fall). Starting in spring, plants are trimmed to get rid of extraneous growth, allowing just the right amount of sun to reach the grapes. The arrival date of good weather in spring determines the date of harvest (100 days later).

South Vineyard Loop

Beaune to Château de la Rochepot

Take this pretty, peaceful route, worth ▲▲, for the best approach to La Rochepot's romantic castle, and to glide through several of Burgundy's most reputed vineyards. Read ahead and note the open hours of wineries and sights along the route (you can also do this loop in reverse). There are wonderful picnic spots along the way; my favorite is just before entering Puligny-Montrachet from the north (turn right, pass the first picnic spot, and continue 100 yards farther to one closer to the hills).

Bikers can follow the first part of this route to Puligny-Montrachet, along Burgundy's best bike path (connects the wine villages of Pommard, Volnay, Meursault, and Puligny-Montrachet for a level, 18-mile loop; allow two hours round trip). All but power riders should avoid the hills to La Rochepot.

● **Self-Guided Tour:** Drivers leave Beaune's ring road, following signs for *Chalon-sur-Saône* (often abbreviated "Chalon-s/S.," first turnoff after Auxerre exit), then follow signs to *Pommard/Autun.* Cyclists take the vineyard bike path by leaving the ring road toward Auxerre, and turning left at the signal after Lycée Viticole de Beaune (look for bike-route icons).

Whether on a bike or in car, when you come to Pommard, you'll pass several lunch and wine-tasting opportunities, including **Domaine Lejeune** (see page 849).

South of Pommard, the road gradually climbs past Volnay and terrific views (bikers take their own parallel path, following bike icons). From here, follow signs into **Meursault** (fine square, bakeries, grocery shops, and good restaurants; see page 850).

Follow *Toutes Directions* (and D-974) to the lower end of the village, turn right on D-113b, and follow signs for *Puligny-Montrachet.* You'll pass through low-slung vineyards south of Meursault, then enter **Puligny-Montrachet** (town and wineries described on page 850)—with good picnic spots on the right as you enter. At the big roundabout with a bronze sculpture of vineyard workers, find the **Caveau de Puligny-Montrachet** and a chance to sample

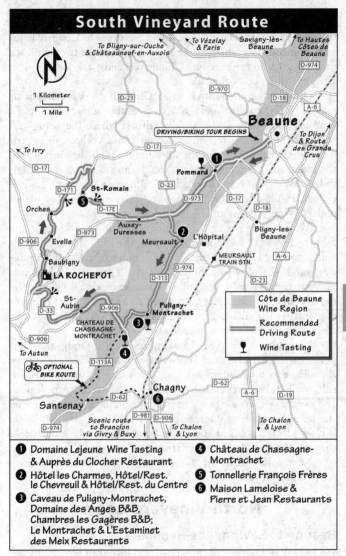

South Vineyard Route

To Bligny-sur-Ouche & Châteauneuf-en-Auxois

To Vézelay & Paris

Savigny-lès-Beaune

To Hautes Côtes de Beaune

D-974

1 Kilometer
1 Mile

D-23

D-970

D-18

A-6

Beaune

To Dijon & Route des Grands Crus

To Ivry

D-17

DRIVING/BIKING TOUR BEGINS

D-17

Pommard ❶

D-171

St-Romain ❺

D-23

D-973

D-17

D-18

Orches

D-17E

Auxey-Duresses

D-973

Meursault

L'Hôpital

Bligny-les-Beaune

Evelle

D-906

A-6

Baubigny

D-974

MEURSAULT TRAIN STN.

LA ROCHEPOT

D-113

D-23

St-Aubin

D-906

Puligny-Montrachet ❷

Côte de Beaune Wine Region

Recommended Driving Route

Wine Tasting

D-33

CHATEAU DE CHASSAGNE-MONTRACHET ❸

D-906

To Autun

D-113A ❹

To Chalon & Lyon

🚲 OPTIONAL BIKE ROUTE

Chagny

D-62

D-19

Santenay

D-62

D-981

D-906

❻

D-974

Scenic route to Brancion via Givry & Buxy

To Chalon & Lyon

❶ Domaine Lejeune Wine Tasting & Auprès du Clocher Restaurant

❷ Hôtel les Charmes, Hôtel/Rest. le Chevreuil & Hôtel/Rest. du Centre

❸ Caveau de Puligny-Montrachet, Domaine des Anges B&B, Chambres les Gagères B&B; Le Montrachet & L'Estaminet des Meix Restaurants

❹ Château de Chassagne-Montrachet

❺ Tonnellerie François Frères

❻ Maison Lameloise & Pierre et Jean Restaurants

BURGUNDY

from vines that produce "the world's best whites." A block straight out the door of the *caveau* leads to a small grocery and the town's big square (Place des Marronniers), with **Hôtel-Restaurant Le Montrachet** and **Café de l'Estaminet des Meix**.

Go back to the roundabout and follow signs to *Chassagne-Montrachet* and *St. Aubin* (D-113a), leading through more manicured vineyards. To tour **Château de Chassagne-Montrachet** turn left on D-906, and in 150 yards you'll see it to the right.

From here, cyclists can double back to Beaune or continue on the bike path to Santenay, then along the canal to **Chagny** (with a recommended restaurant—see page 853) and take the train back to Beaune (2/hour weekdays, 1/hour weekends, ask for *la gare* in Chagny—it is poorly signed).

Drivers should continue on to **Château de la Rochepot** by making a hard right on D-906 to St-Aubin and following *La Rochepot* signs onto D-33. (Bikers, this is where the going gets very difficult and not recommended on a bike without an electric motor.) After heading over the hills and through the vineyards of the Hautes-Côtes (upper slopes), you'll come to a drop-dead view of the castle (stop mandatory). Turn right when you reach La Rochepot, and follow *Le Château* signs to the castle (described earlier under "Wine Villages and Sights near Beaune").

After visiting the castle, turn right out of its parking lot and take the first left into Baubigny, tracking the D-17 through Evelles and rock-solid Orches. After Orches, climb to the top of Burgundy's world—keeping straight on D-17, you'll pass several **lookouts** on your right (simple dirt pullouts with exceptional views). Get out of your car and wander cliffside for a postcard-perfect Burgundian image. The village of St-Romain swirls below, and if it's really clear, look for Mont Blanc on the eastern horizon.

Next drive down to **St-Romain,** passing Burgundy's most important wine-barrel maker, **Tonnellerie Francois Frères** (it's above the village in the modern building, www.francoisfreres.com). Inside, well-stoked fires heat the oak staves to make them flexible, and sweaty workers use heavy hammers to pound iron rings around the barrels as they've done since medieval times. The workshop is closed to the public, but discreet travelers can take quick peeks through the glass doors to the far left.

Next, follow signs for *Auxey-Duresses,* and then *Beaune* for a scenic finale to your journey.

North Vineyard Loop

Beaune to Savigny-lès-Beaune

For an easy and rewarding spin by car—or ideally by bike—through waves of vineyards that smother traditional villages, follow this relatively level 10-mile loop from Beaune, worth ▲ (with stops, allow a half-day by bike or 1.5 hours by car). It laces together three renowned wine villages—Aloxe-Corton, Pernand-Vergelesses, and Savigny-lès-Beaune—connecting you with Burgundian nature and village wine culture. Those wanting a little more should take the beautiful and short extension from Pernand-Vergelesses to Magny-les-Villers (described on page 860). Bring water and snacks, as there is precious little available until the end of this route. There's a

North Vineyard Loop & Route des Grands Crus

Route des Grands Crus

5 Ferme Fruirouge

6 Romanée-Conti Vineyards

7 Château du Clos de Vougeot

8 Le Caveau des Musignys & Le Millésime Restaurant

9 Caveau des Vignerons, Chambres d'Hôtes Le Saint Nicolas & Le Castel des Très Girard Hôtel/Rest.

10 Philippe LeClerc Winery, Hôtel les Grands Crus, Le Bar à Vins, Bistrot Lucien & Chez Guy

D-10   D-905   **Dijon**

D-108

Marsannay-la-Côte

A-311

D-122

Fixin   D-974

2 Kilometers

2 Miles

Quemigny-Poisot   D-35

D-31

Gevrey-Chambertin   TRAIN STN.   **10**

To Nancy & Metz and Colmar via A-36

A-31

D-122

Paris

FRANCE

100 Miles

Ternant

9 Morey-St-Denis   Broindon

D-25

Chambolle-Musigny   **8**   TRAIN STN.   A-31

D-35   **7**   D-25

Concoeur   **6**   **Vougeot**

ROUTE DES GRANDS CRUS

D-25   **5**   Vosne-Romanée

D-25   **Nuits-St-Georges**

Arcenant   D-115   D-8

D-8

TRAIN STN.   D-8

BURGUNDY

HAUTE CÔTE DE NUITS

Echevronne   Villers-la-Faye   D-974

HAUTE CÔTE DE BEAUNE

D-2   D-18   **3**

Magny-les-Villers

D-974

Pernand-Vergelesses   **2**   D-20F   A-31

4   **1** Aloxe-Corton   D-2

Savigny-lès-Beaune

To Paris   A-6   Ladoix-Serrigny

NORTH VINEYARD LOOP   CÔTE DE BEAUNE   Chorey   D-20

DRIVING/BIKING TOUR BEGINS

Beaune   TRAIN STN.

To La Rochepot   CÔTE DE BEAUNE   D-974   D-973

D-2   A-6

D-17   To Chalon & Lyon

Legend

Famous Wine Regions

Recommended Driving Route

Wine Tasting

North Vineyard Loop

1 Aloxe-Corton Wine Tastings & Hotels

2 La Grappe de Pernand Café

3 Domaine Naudin-Ferrand

4 Henri de Villamont Wine Tasting, Château de Savigny & R. De Famille Café-Pizzeria

dreamy picnic spot with shade on the small road halfway between Aloxe-Corton and Pernand-Vergelesses. Your tour concludes in Savigny-lès-Beaune, where you'll find a café-pizzeria, wine tastings, a small grocery, and a unique château.

❍ Self-Guided Tour: This loop drive/pedal starts in Beaune. Drivers can also combine this loop with the "Route des Grands Crus," described later.

• *From Beaune's ring road, drivers take D-974 north toward Dijon. Soon, follow signs for* Savigny-lès-Beaune, *leading left at the signal and then quickly right. On the outskirts of town you'll cross over the autoroute, then veer right, following the second signs you see to* Pernand-Vergelesses *(D-18). Turn right at the first sign to* Aloxe-Corton, *and glide into the town. Make a hard left at the stop sign and climb uphill to find a small parking area with several recommended wine-tastings close by.*

Bikers follow a different route leaving Beaune. From Beaune's ring road, turn right on Rue de Chorey after passing the public pool, following signs for Gigny *(just before D-974 to Dijon). Continue following signs toward* Gigny *into Chorey-les-Beaune. In Chorey-les Beaune, veer left onto Rue Pavelot, pass through two stop signs, then follow the lane as it enters the vineyards and eventually turns left. Cross busy D-974, go straight up the tree-lined road, then make a hard left at the stop sign and climb uphill into...*

Aloxe-Corton: This tiny town, with a world-class reputation among wine enthusiasts, is packed with top tasting opportunities (but no cafés). The easygoing **Domaines d'Aloxe-Corton,** English-owned **Mischief and Mayhem,** and more upscale **Domaine de Senard** all offer different kinds of tastings (see page 853).

• *Leave Aloxe-Corton and head up the hill on Rue des Chaumes, following signs for* Pernand-Vergelesses *(you'll pass an idyllic picnic spot on the left just after the last building in Aloxe-Corton). At the T-intersection with D-18, most bikers will want to turn left and pick up the directions for leaving Pernand-Vergelesses (below). Otherwise, turn right and head into...*

Pernand-Vergelesses: As you enter the village, look for a cute little café called **$$ La Grappe de Pernand** (follow the umbrellas down to the right and find reasonably priced food and drink, closed Mon in off-season and Tue year-round, tel. 03 80 21 59 46).

Drivers and strong bikers should consider two worthwhile detours from Pernand-Vergelesses: Climbing well above the village leads to one of the best vineyard panoramas in Burgundy. To get there, enter Pernand-Vergelesses, look for a small roundabout and head up, turning right on Rue du Creux St. Germain, and then continue straight and up along Rue Copeau. Curve up past the church until you see small *Panorama* signs. Drivers and bikers wanting to extend their ride can also follow signs (just after passing the church, en route to the panorama) to **Magny-les-Villers** and track a gorgeous and hilly wine lane for about two miles to one of my favorite wineries, **Domaine Naudin-Ferrand** (see page 854). Just a short distance down this lane brings rewards; the views are best on your return to Pernand-Vergelesses.

• *Leaving Pernand-Vergelesses, bikers and drivers both follow the main road (D-18) back toward Beaune, and turn right into the vineyards on the first lane (at the* Vignobles Pernand-Vergelesses *sign, about 400 yards from Pernand-Vergelesses). Keep left at the first fork and rise gently to lovely views. Drop down and turn right when you come to a T, then joyride along the vine service lanes (bikers should watch for loose gravel). To reach Savigny-lès-Beaune, keep going until you see a 5T sign. Turn left just before the sign, then take the first right, and right again when you reach the T-intersection at the bottom. Merge onto the larger road; you'll soon come to a three-way intersection in...*

Savigny-lès-Beaune: The left fork leads back to Beaune, the middle fork leads to *Centre-Ville,* and the road to the right leads to a good wine tasting at **Henri de Villamont.** Follow the middle fork to find the four-towered **Château de Savigny** and the **R. De Famille** café-pizzeria (all described on 854).

• *From Savigny-lès-Beaune, drive or pedal following signs back into Beaune. To avoid busy D-18 into Beaune, bikers can take a slightly longer route following D-2a from Savigny, crossing D-974 and taking the first right in Chorey-les-Beaune (along the stone wall), and then following* Route de Beaune *signs. Those with a car can continue along the "Route des Grands Crus," next.*

Route des Grands Crus

While I prefer the areas south and west of Beaune, a more northern stretch of the Route des Grands Crus is a ▲ must for wine connoisseurs with a car, as it passes through Burgundy's most fabled vineyards.

The first part, between Aloxe-Corton and Nuits-St-Georges, forces you onto the busy highway (D-974). But from Vougeot north, the route improves noticeably if you stick to D-122. Locals call this section the "Champs-Elysées of Burgundy." Between Vosne-Romanée and Gevrey-Chambertin, the road runs past 24 *grand cru* wineries of the Côte de Nuits—Pinot Noir paradise, where 95 percent of the wines are red. The path of today's busy D-974 road was established by monks in the 12th century to delineate the easternmost limit of land on which good wine grapes could be grown. (Land to the east of this road is good for other crops but not for wine.) For lunch fixings, you'll find grocery stores in Nuits-St-Georges and in Gevrey-Chambertin.

Here's a rundown of my favorite places on the northern Route

BURGUNDY

des Grands Crus, listed from Beaune toward Dijon (for locations, see the map on page 859).

Concoeur

Come to this little village high above the wine route (northwest of Nuits-St-Georges) for a Back Door stop at the shop called **Ferme Fruirouge.** Adorable owners Sylvain and Isabelle grow cherries, raspberries, and black currants, and make crème de cassis, vinegars, mustards, and jams with passion. They (or their equally adorable staff) will explain their time-honored process for crafting these products. You can sample everything—including their one-of-a-kind cassis-ketchup—and get free recipe cards in French (Thu-Mon 9:00-12:00 & 14:00-19:00, closed Tue-Wed, 2 Place de l'Eglise, tel. 03 80 62 36 25, www.fruirouge.fr, call ahead to arrange for a good explanation of their operation).

Vosne-Romanée

The fabled Romanée-Conti vineyards of this tiny hamlet produce the priciest wines in Burgundy (figure $6,000 per bottle minimum; sorry, all bottles are presold).

Vougeot

In many ways, this is the birthplace of great Burgundian wines. In the 12th century, monks from the abbey of Cîteaux (8 miles southeast from here) built the magnificent stone **Château du Clos de Vougeot** to store equipment and make their wines. Their careful study of winemaking was the foundation for the world-famous reputation of Burgundian wines. It was here that monks discovered that pinot noir and chardonnay grapes were best suited to the local soil and climate. There's little to see inside except for the fine stone construction, four ancient and massive wine presses, and the room where the Confrérie des Chevaliers Tastevin (a Burgundian brotherhood of wine tasters) meets to celebrate their legacy—and to apply their label of quality to area wines, called *le Tastevinage.* You can see the historic courtyard and cellar where bottles of each *Tastevinage* are stored and enter the classy gift shop before having to pay admission (which is enough for many). The château has a good English handout and posted information, but no tastings (€7.50, daily April-Oct 9:00-18:30 except Sat until 17:00, Nov-March 10:00-17:00, tel. 03 80 62 86 09, well-signed just outside town, www.closdevougeot.fr).

Chambolle-Musigny

Le Caveau des Musignys is a fine place to sample Burgundy's rich variety of wines. Say bonjour to sweet Annie, who will introduce you to the region's wines in a cool, vaulted tasting room. Representing 45 producers (recent vintages only for tasting), she has wines in all price ranges from throughout Burgundy. The whites and reds from the Hautes-Côtes are a good value, as are the mid-range reds from Chambolle-Musigny and Vosne-Romanée (free tasting, shipping available, Wed-Sun 9:00-18:00, closed Mon-Tue, a block north of the church at 1 Rue Traversière, tel. 03 80 62 84 01). You can eat upstairs in an elegant setting, where modern blends with tradition, at the lovely **$$$ Le Millésime** (€20 lunch *menus* except Sat, €32-55 dinner *menus*, indoor seating only, dazzling wine shelves, closed Sun-Mon, tel. 03 80 62 80 37).

Morey-St-Denis

This village houses more vineyards, a café, a bakery, and another worthwhile tasting stop at the **Caveau des Vignerons,** with reasonably priced wines from 13 small producers (each too small to have its own tasting room). Gentle Catherine speaks enough English to welcome you to her free tasting room, where you can sample wines from the Côtes de Nuits (good selection of wines from Gevrey-Chambertin, though I prefer those from Morey-St-Denis, Wed-Mon 10:00-13:00 & 14:00-18:30, closed Tue, next to the church, tel. 03 80 51 86 79).

Sleeping and Eating in Morey-St-Denis: Sleep very well for cheap nearby at **$ Chambres d'Hôte Le Saint Nicolas,** buried in the village but well-signed, where Madame Beaumont rents four traditional rooms and a spacious apartment at the vineyard's edge for a steal (family rooms, includes breakfast, wine tastings available, tel. 03 80 58 51 83, www.le-saint-nicolas.com, contact@le-saint-nicolas.com).

At the bottom end of the village lies an intimate, upscale hotel-restaurant, **$$$ Le Castel des Très Girard****.** This eight-room hotel delivers top service and classy comfort, including cozy lounges, a pool, and a restaurant that locals go out of their way for (air-con, poolside tables, tel. 03 80 34 33 09, www.castel-tres-girard.com, info@castel-tres-girard.com).

Gevrey-Chambertin

For many pinot noir lovers, a visit to this flowery village is the pinnacle of their Burgundian pilgrimage. The appealing village has a TI (daily, 1 Rue Gaston Roupnel, tel. 03 80 34 38 40), a small grocery, a café, a pizzeria, two restaurants, and a good-value hotel.

Gevrey-Chambertin produces nine of the 32 *grand cru* wines from Burgundy. All are pinot noirs (no whites in sight), and all use the suffix "Chambertin" ("Gevrey" is the historic name of the village; "Chambertin" is its most important vineyard). As you drive through the countryside south of the village, look for signs identifying the famous vineyards. **Philippe LeClerc**'s winery, nestled in the town center, gets positive reviews for its atmospheric wine cellar, good tastings, and intriguing wine museum (€10 for museum and 6 tastes, free if you buy, daily 9:30-19:00, Rue des Halles, tel. 03 80 34 30 72).

Sleeping in Gevrey-Chambertin: You can sleep well at $ **Hôtel les Grands Crus,***** with simple, spotless, and traditional rooms overlooking vineyards, plus a pleasant patio and free, secure parking. And it's an easy walk to the village center (air-con, at the northwest edge of town on Rue de Lavaux, tel. 03 80 34 34 15, www.hoteldesgrandscrus.com, hotel.lesgrandscrus@nerim.net).

Eating in Gevrey-Chambertin: Hang out at the local watering hole, $$ **Le Bar à Vins** café (closed Tue), and have a Burgundian dinner experience at the Rotisserie du Chambertin's $$$$ **Bistrot Lucien,** where stone walls meet stone floors, and the dining is classy inside and out (closed Sun-Mon, in the Rotisserie building at 6 Rue du Chambertin, tel. 03 80 34 33 20). You can also dine at $$$ **Chez Guy,** with snazzy outdoor seating and modern, stylish decor (in the village center, open daily, 3 Place de la Mairie, tel. 03 80 58 51 51).

Between Beaune and Paris

North of Beaune, you'll find a handful of worthwhile places that string together well for a full-day excursion: towering Châteauneuf-en-Auxois, sleepy Semur-en-Auxois, remote Fontenay's abbey, pretty little Flavigny-sur-Ozerain, and Julius Caesar's victorious battlefield at Alise-Ste-Reine (with its good museum, MuséoParc Alésia).

As a bonus, following my driving tour of this area takes you along several stretches of the **Burgundy Canal** (Canal de Bourgogne). As in much of France, Burgundy's canals were dug 200 years ago, in the early Industrial Age, as an affordable way to transport heavy materials. The Burgundy canal was among the most important, linking Paris with the Mediterranean Sea. The canal is 145 miles long, with 209 locks, and rises over France's continental divide in Pouilly-en-Auxois, just below Châteauneuf-en-Auxois (where the canal runs underground for about two miles). Digging began in 1727 and the canal was completed in 1832—ironically, just in time for the invention of steam engines on rails, which soon eliminated the need for waterway transport.

Back-Door Burgundy Towns and Sights

The towns and sights described below can be connected with my "Back-Door Burgundy Driving Tour" outlined on page 872.

Châteauneuf-en-Auxois

This living hill town hunkers in the shadow of its castle and merits exploring. The perfectly medieval castle once monitored passage between Burgundy and Paris, with hawk-eye views from its 2,000-foot-high setting. *Châteauneuf* means "new castle," so you'll see many in France. This one is in the Auxois area, so it's Châteauneuf-en-Auxois. Park at the lot in the very upper end of the village (where the road ends), and don't miss the **panoramic viewpoint** nearby. The military value of this site is powerfully clear from here. Find the Burgundy Canal and the three reservoirs that have maintained the canal's flow for more than 200 years. The small village below is Châteauneuf's port, Vandenesse-en-Auxois—you'll be there shortly. If not for phylloxera—the vine-loving insect that ravaged France in the late 1800s, killing all of its vineyards—you'd see more vineyards than wheat fields.

Saunter into the village, where every building feels historic and stocky farmers live side by side with tattooed artists. Walk into the courtyard, but skip the **château**'s interior (€5, Tue-Sun 10:00-12:00 & 14:00-18:00, closed Mon, English handout). You'll get better moat views and see the more important castle entry by walking beneath the Hôstellerie du Château, and then turning right, following *Eglise* signs.

Sleeping in Châteauneuf-en-Auxois: You won't break the bank sleeping at the **$ Hôstellerie du Château,**** a simple place housing an enticing budget-vacation ensemble: nine homey, inexpensive rooms with a rear garden overlooking the brooding floodlit castle at night (tel. 03 80 49 22 00, www.hostellerie-de-chateauneuf. com, contact@hostellerie-de-chateauneuf.com). Their **$$$** restaurant offers regional cuisine, good salads and grilled meats, and a great-value €25 three-course *menu* (closed Wed off-season).

Eating in Châteauneuf-en-Auxois: Châteauneuf has several affordable cafés and restaurants along its main drag. **$$ Orée du Bois** is cozy inside and out, and makes good crêpes, including one stuffed with snails.

Alise-Ste-Reine

A united Gaul forming a single nation animated by the same spirit could defy the universe.
—Julius Caesar, *The Gallic Wars*

Historians are convinced that Julius Caesar defeated the Gallic leader Vercingétorix on these lands surrounding the vertical village of Alise-Ste-Reine in 52 B.C., thus winning Gaul for the Roman Empire and forever changing France's destiny. Visit the impressive museum-park and stand where Caesar did, and drive above the village to see things from the Gauls' perspective.

▲MuséoParc Alésia

This circular museum, looking like a modern sports arena, does this important site justice with easy-to-follow exhibits and well-delivered information. The circular structure symbolizes how, more than 2,000 years ago, Cae-sar ordered his outnumbered forces to surround the Gauls' *oppidum* (hilltop village), starving them out and winning a decisive victory (see sidebar).

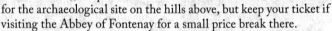

Cost: €10, includes essential audioguide (there's also a fun chil-dren's version), skip the €2 extra for the archaeological site on the hills above, but keep your ticket if visiting the Abbey of Fontenay for a small price break there.

Hours: Daily April-Sept 10:00-18:00, until 19:00 July-Aug, shorter hours off-season, closed Feb, tel. 03 80 96 96 23, www.alesia.com.

Visiting the Museum: With the help of the audioguide, touchscreens, and posted information, you'll gain a keen under-standing of the events that led up to this battle, why it happened here, and how it unfolded. You'll learn much about the two pro-tagonists, Caesar and Vercingétorix, their armies, and their mo-tivations, and be drawn into the conflict with an 18-minute film.

Allow an hour for the museum's single floor of exhibits, then climb to the top floor for views from a Roman perspective. Finally, walk out back to inspect the full-scale reconstruction of a section of the Roman wall and lookouts that pinned the Gauls to that hilltop.

Friendly staff dressed as Romans or Gauls are often present in-side or out back to answer your questions and give demonstrations (some English spoken). Pick up the chain-mail suit (30 pounds), and learn that it took more than half a mile of metal line to make one. To add more meaning to this sight, read "How About Them Romans" (see page 562).

Nearby: Drive through the village of Alise-Ste-Reine and follow the *Statue de Vercingétorix* signs leading to the park with the huge **statue** of the Gallic warrior overlooking his Waterloo (skip the archaeological site). Stand as he did—imagining yourself

The Dying Gauls

In 52 B.C., General Julius Caesar and his 60,000 soldiers surrounded Alésia (today's Alise-Ste-Reine), hoping to finally end the uprising of free Gaul and establish Roman civilization in central and northern France (they had long controlled southern France). Holed up inside the hilltop fortress were 80,000 die-hard (long-haired, tattooed) Gauls under their rebel chief, Vercingétorix (pronounced something like "verse-an-zhet-or-eex"). Having harassed Caesar for months with guerrilla-war attacks, they now called on their fellow Gauls to converge on Alésia to wipe out the Romans.

Rather than attack the fierce-fighting Gauls, Caesar's soldiers patiently camped at the base of the hill and began building a wall. In six weeks, they completed a 12-foot-tall, stone-and-earth wall all the way around Alésia (11 miles around—blue line on the orientation table at the hilltop site), and then a second, larger one (13 miles around—red line on the orientation table), trapping the rebel leaders with the intention of starving them out. If the Gauls tried to escape, not only would they have to breach the two walls, they'd first have to cross a steep no-man's-land dotted with a ditch, a moat, and booby traps (including sharp stakes in pits and buried iron spikes).

The starving Gauls inside Alésia sent their women and children out to beg for mercy from the Romans. The Romans (with little food themselves) refused. For days, the women and children wandered the unoccupied land, in full view of both armies, until they starved to death.

After months of siege, Vercingétorix's reinforcements finally came riding to save him. With 90,000 screaming Gallic warriors (Caesar says 250,000) converging on Alésia, and 80,000 more atop the hill, Caesar ordered his men to move between the two walls to fight a two-front battle. The Battle of Alésia raged for five days—a classic struggle between the methodical Romans and the impetuous "barbarians." When it became clear the Romans would not budge, the Gauls retreated.

Vercingétorix surrendered, and Gallic culture was finished in France. During the three-year rebellion, one in five Gauls had been killed, enslaved, or driven out. Roman rule was established for the next 500 years, strangling the Gallic/Celtic heritage. Vercingétorix spent his last years as a prisoner, paraded around as a war trophy. In 46 B.C., he was brought to Rome for Caesar's triumphal ascension to power, where he was strangled to death in a public ritual.

trapped on this hilltop—then find the orientation table under the gazebo and appreciate the peekaboo views through the trees.

Flavigny-sur-Ozerain

A few minutes from Alise-Ste-Reine, little Flavigny-sur-Ozerain's (flah-veen-yee sur oh-zuh-rain) red-tile roofs cover its hilltop with a movie-set panorama. The town had its 15 minutes of fame in 2000, when the movie *Chocolat* was filmed here, but otherwise this unassuming and serenely situated village feels permanently stuck in the past. Flavigny makes a good coffee or lunch stop, as there's little to do here but appreciate the setting, admire its beautiful church, and sample the local *anis* (anise) candies.

Flavigny has been home to an abbey since 719, when the first (Benedictine) abbey of St. Pierre was built. The town thrived during the Middle Ages thanks to its proximity to Vézelay (with its relics of Mary Magdalene) and the flood of pilgrims coming through en route to Santiago de Compostela in northwest Spain. The little town was occupied by the Brits during the Hundred Years' War (15th century), then ever-so-gradually slid into irrelevance. By the time the French Revolution rolled around, it had no religious or defensive importance. The movie *Chocolat* put the town back on the map—at least for a while. The TI and *anis* shop have booklets of photos taken during the filming and can locate key buildings featured in the movie for you. Today, Flavigny has been reinvigorated by the return of 50 Benedictine monks to the Abbey of St. Joseph.

Park in the designated lot and enter the village, passing the café-restaurant along the Rue de l'Abbaye. You'll soon come to the charming **Anis de Flavigny shop** and factory at the former Abbaye de St-Pierre. The shop has a cool café, information about the village, and tours of its candy production. The candies are sold in pretty tins for €2.50 and make great souvenirs—try the coffee-flavored ones (open daily 9:00-19:00). Pick up a village map here or from the **TI** (limited hours, a block down from the church on Rue de l'Eglise). Take a peek into the evocative ninth-century Carolingian crypt next door.

The town revolves around its medieval **Church of St. Genest,** with its mesmerizing interior (closed 12:30-14:30). Climb to the balcony for fine views (*Chocolat* movie fans can relive the young priest's nervous sermons). Outside the church, just below the recommended Grange restaurant, spot the location for the movie's chocolate shop (behind the rounded brown window sills).

Eating in Flavigny-sur-Ozerain: You'll eat for a steal at **$$ La Grange** ("The Barn") on cheap, farm-fresh fare, including luscious quiche, salads, *plats du jour,* fresh cheeses, pâtés, and delicious fruit pies (April-mid-Oct daily 12:30-18:00; open Sun only in off-season and closed Dec-Jan; across from church, look for brown doors and listen for lunchtime dining, tel. 03 80 35 81 78).

▲▲Abbey of Fontenay

The entire ensemble of buildings composing this isolated Cistercian abbey has survived, giving visitors perhaps the best picture

of medieval abbey life in France. In the Middle Ages, it was written, "To fully grasp the meaning of Fontenay and the power of its beauty, you must approach it trudging through the forest footpaths...through the brambles and bogs...in an October rain." Those arriving by car will still find Fontenay's secluded setting—blanketed in birdsong and with a garden lovingly used "as a stage set"—truly magical.

Cost and Hours: €10, daily April-mid-Nov 10:00-19:00, mid-Nov-March 10:00-12:00 & 14:00-17:00, tel. 03 80 92 15 00, www.abbayedefontenay.com. Tours of the abbey in English can be booked by calling ahead (€100/group).

Getting There: The abbey is a 10-minute drive (4 miles) north of Montbard. There's no bus service—allow about €28 round-trip for a taxi from Montbard's train station (taxi mobile 06 08 26 61 55 or 06 08 82 20 61), or rent a bike at Montbard's TI and ride 30 minutes each way (TI tel. 03 80 92 53 81).

Background: This abbey—one of the oldest Cistercian abbeys in France—was founded in 1118 by St. Bernard as a back-to-basics reaction to the excesses of Benedictine abbeys like Cluny. The Cistercians worked to recapture the simplicity, solitude, and poverty of the early Church. Bernard created "a horrible vast solitude" in the forest, where his monks could live like the desert fathers of the Old Testament. They chose marshland ("Cistercian" is derived from "marshy bogs") and strove to be separate from the world (which required the industrious self-sufficiency these abbeys were so adept at). The movement spread, essentially colonizing Europe religiously. In 1200, there were more than 500 such monasteries and abbeys in Europe.

Like the Cistercian movement in general, Fontenay flourished from the 13th to 15th century. A 14th-century proverb said, "Wherever the wind blows, to Fontenay money flows." Fontenay thrived as a prosperous "mini-city" for nearly 700 years, until the French Revolution, when it became the property of the nation and was eventually sold.

Visiting the Abbey: Like visitors centuries ago, you'll enter through the abbey's **gatehouse.** The main difference: Anyone with a ticket gets in, and there's no watchdog barking angrily at you (through the small hole on the right). Pick up the excellent English self-guided tour flier with your ticket. Your visit follows the route described here (generally clockwise). Arrows keep you on course, and signs tell you which sections of the abbey are private (as its owners still live here).

Start at the stone bench 75 yards from the **abbey church.** Read the abbey flier for background. Enter the **church.** Inside it's pure Romanesque and built to St. Bernard's specs: Latin cross plan, no fancy stained glass, unadorned columns, earthen floors—nothing to distract from prayer. The lone statue is the 13th-century *Virgin of Fontenay,* a reminder that the church was dedicated to Mary. Enjoy the ethereal light. Quiet your mind and listen carefully to hear the brothers chanting.

Stairs lead from the end of the church to a vast 16th-century, oak-beamed **dormitory** where the monks slept—together, fully dressed, on thin mats. Monastic life was pretty simple: prayer, reading, work, seven services a day, one meal in the winter, two in the summer. Daily rations: a loaf of bread and a quarter-liter of wine.

Back down the stairs, enter the **cloister.** Stand in the center surrounded by a platoon of unadorned, rounded arches—so beautiful in their simplicity. This was the heart of the community, where monks read, exercised, washed, did small projects—and, I imagine, gave each other those silly haircuts.

The shallow alcove (next to the church door) once stored prayer books; notice the slots for shelves. Next to that, the vaulted **chapter room** was where the abbot led discussions and community business was discussed. The adjacent **monks' hall** was a general-purpose room, likely busy with monks hunched over tables copying sacred texts (a major work of abbeys). The dining hall, or refectory, also faced the cloister (closed to the public).

Across the garden stands the huge abbey **forge.** In the 13th century, the monks at Fontenay ran what many consider Europe's first metalworking plant. Iron ore was melted down in ovens with big bellows. Tools were made and sold for a profit. The hydraulic hammer, which became the basis of industrial manufacturing of iron throughout Europe, was first used here. Leaving the building, walk left around the back to see the stream, which was diverted to power the wheels that operated the forge. Water was vital to abbey life. The **pond**—originally practical, rather than decorative—was a fish farm (some whopper descendants still swim here).

Leave through the small museum and gift shop, which was the public **chapel** in the days when visitors were not allowed inside the abbey grounds. Upstairs you'll see a **model** of the abbey complex and appreciate the isolation these monks found here. Next to it a sign displays a quote from St. Bernard: *"We learn more from the woods than from books; the trees and rocks teach us things we could not learn elsewhere."*

Semur-en-Auxois

This sleepy town feels real. There are 4,500 residents, few tourists, and no important sights to digest—just a pleasing jumble of Burgundian alleys perched above the meandering Armançon River and behind the town's four massive towers, all beautifully illuminated after dark.

Locals like to believe that Hercules built Semur-en-Auxois (suh-moor-ahn-ohx-wah) on his return from Spain. But Semur's ancient origins date back to Neolithic times, long before Hercules' visit. Today the town works as a handy leg-stretching stop or photo op—don't miss the smashing panorama of Semur from the viewpoint across from the Citroën shop, where D-980 and D-954 intersect (parking close by). Find the orientation table and take in the memorable view of the red roofs, spires, and towers—especially striking at night.

The **TI** is across from Hôtel Côte d'Or, at Semur's medieval entry (2 Place Gaveau, tel. 03 80 97 05 96). Pick up a city-walking brochure and tour the town. Enter through the Sauvigny and Guiller gates, then saunter along the Hollywood set-like Rue Buffon, Semur's oldest commercial street. You'll come to the 13th-century **Church of Notre-Dame,** the town's main sight, which dominates its small square and is worth a quick look (closed 12:00-14:00, decent English handout). As you leave the church, glance at the second-to-last chapel on your right, with a large plaque honoring American soldiers who died in World War I.

For **postcard-perfect views,** stroll several blocks down from the church along Rue Févret, turn left where it ends (at Rue du Rempart), then turn left again down Rue du Fourneau and amble along the Armançon River (if you cross the medieval Pont Pinard you'll find a riverside path to the right that is open to the public). In the Middle Ages, 18 towers connected by defensive ramparts protected the center city. Caught in the crossfire between the powerful Dukes of Burgundy and the king of France, Semur's defenses were heavily damaged by Louis XI in 1478 and finished off during the Wars of Religion in 1602.

BURGUNDY

Sleeping in Semur-en-Auxois: If this quiet town seduces you into spending a night, try the well-run **$$ Hôtel de la Côte d'Or,** across from the TI (1 Rue de la Liberté, tel. 03 80 97 24 54, http://auxois.fr, info@auxois.fr), or stay for less at the frumpy and faded **$ Hôtel les Cymaises,**** offering comfortable rooms in a manor house with a quiet courtyard (family rooms, private parking, good deals with the restaurants listed below, 7 Rue du Renaudot, tel. 03 80 97 21 44, www.hotelcymaises.com, contact@hotelcymaises.com).

Eating in Semur-en-Auxois: Cafés along Rue du Buffon offer ambience and average quality. **$$ L'Entract** is where everybody goes for pizza, pasta, salads, and more in a relaxed atmosphere (daily, below the church on 4 Rue Févret, tel. 03 80 96 60 10). **$$$ La Parenthèse** is the place to be for fine Burgundian cuisine at reasonable prices served in a contemporary interior or on a terrific terrace in front (€35 Burgundian *menu,* closed all day Mon and for lunch on Tue, 12 Place Notre-Dame, tel. 03 80 92 06 11, www.parenthese-semur.com).

Back-Door Burgundy Driving Tour

This all-day loop links Châteauneuf-en-Auxois, Alise-Ste-Reine, and Fontenay, with short stops suggested in Flavigny-sur-Ozerain and Semur-en-Auxois. The trip trades vineyards for wheat fields, canals, and pastoral landscapes. You'll drive along the Burgundy canal and visit a Cistercian abbey, medieval villages, and the site of Gaul's last stand against the Romans. It requires a car and a good map (Michelin maps #320 or #519 work well). If you're heading to/from Paris, this tour works well en route or as an overnight stop; I've listed accommodations and described sights along the way in greater detail under "Back-Door Burgundy Towns and Sights," earlier.

Here's how I'd spend this day: Get out early and joyride to MuséoParc Alésia in Alise-Ste-Reine (with at least a photo stop for Châteauneuf-en-Auxois), tour the museum and battle site, have lunch a few minutes away in Flavigny, drive to Fontenay and tour the abbey, then consider a stop in Semur-en-Auxois for a stroll on your way home (this plan also works for those continuing to Paris). Energetic sightseers could add Vézelay to this plan by getting on the road no later than 8:00 and focusing on Alise-Ste-Reine and Fontenay, then darting over to Vézelay on the way back.

The museum and battlefield at Alise-Ste-Reine and the Abbey of Fontenay are your primary goals; allow an hour to tour each. With no stops, this one-way drive from Beaune to Fontenay should take about an hour and a half. But you should be stopping—a lot. (Those in a hurry can get from Beaune to Fontenay in about an

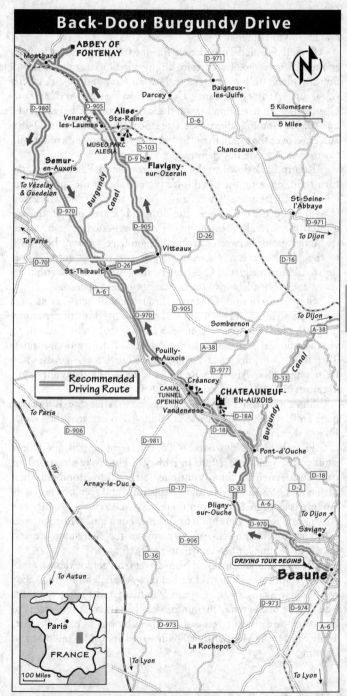

Back-Door Burgundy Drive

hour via the autoroute: take exit #21 to Semur en Auxois, then follow D-980 to Fontenay.)

❯ **Self-Guided Tour:** Leave Beaune following signs for *Auxerre* and *Bligny-sur-Ouche;* from Bligny-sur-Ouche, take D-33 to Pont d'Ouche (following signs to *Pont du Pany* and *Dijon*), where you'll turn left along the canal (D-18), following signs to *Château de Châteauneuf.* In five minutes, you'll see the castle at **Châteauneuf-en-Auxois** looming above (see page 865). Turn right on D-18a and cross over the canal, then the freeway, for great views of the hill town, even if you're not visiting it.

Return back down to the canal, press on to Vandenesse, and turn right, crossing the canal (nice picnic spot on the "port," with views of Châteauneuf-en-Auxois). Next, turn left to Créancey (D-18) and pause once there. The Burgundy Canal tunnels underground for several miles through Pouilly-en-Auxois, as it passes its highest point between Paris and Dijon (rivers east of here flow to the Mediterranean, those to the west to the Atlantic). Look for small brown signs in Créancey reading *Entrée de Souterrain du Canal* for a short detour to see the canal tunnel's opening.

Stay on D-18 from Créancey through Pouilly-en-Auxois, and then follow signs (on D-970) to Vitteaux. In St-Thibault turn right on D-26 toward Vitteaux. Consider a quick stop in St-Thibault to view its unusual 13th-century church (English descriptions inside). Turn left in Vitteaux on D-905 and drive north toward Alise-Ste-Reine. Just before Alise-Ste-Reine, look for signs to **Flavigny-sur-Ozerain** (5 scenic minutes away on D-9).

Signs lead from Flavigny's parking lot to **Alise-Ste-Reine** (see page 868), where Julius Caesar is said to have defeated the Gauls. Follow signs to *Alésia* and *MuséoParc.*

From here drop down to D-905, turn right (north), and follow signs to the secluded Cistercian **Abbey of Fontenay** (described on page 869). After the abbey, continue up D-905 to Montbard, then turn onto D-980 and drive south to peaceful and scenic **Semur-en-Auxois** (see page 871). From there, take D-970 via Pouilly-en-Auxois and retrace your route to Beaune. For a quicker option, you can dart from Semur-en-Auxois across to the A-6 autoroute and take it to Beaune (or head north to Paris).

Public Transit Options: Non-drivers can get to Alésia by taking the train from Dijon to Les Laumes-Alésia, and to the Abbey of Fontenay by taking the train to Montbard and a taxi from there (see Abbey of Fontenay listing for details). There are no trains to Semur-en-Auxois, but you can get there by bus (3/day Mon-Sat, 1/day Sun, from Montbard or Dijon—runs morning, midday, and evening).

Between Burgundy and the Loire

These three sights—Vézelay and its Romanesque Basilica of Ste. Madeleine; the under-construction Château de Guédelon; and the underrated, overlooked city of Bourges, with its grand "High" Gothic cathedral—make good stops for drivers connecting Burgundy and the Loire Valley. Visiting all three in one day is impossible, so pick two and get an early start (allow 6 hours of driving from Beaune to the Loire, plus time to stop and visit the sights). The first two sights also work if you're linking Burgundy and Paris (skip Bourges, which requires a long detour).

Vézelay

For more than eight centuries, travelers have hoofed it up through this pretty little town to get to the famous hilltop church, the Basilica of Ste. Madeleine. In its 12th-century prime, Vézelay welcomed the medieval masses. Cultists of Mary Magdalene came to file past her (supposed) body. Pilgrims rendezvoused here to march to Spain to venerate St. James' (supposed) relics in Santiago de Compostela. Three Crusades were launched from this hill: the Second Crusade (1146), announced by Bernard of Clairveaux; the Third Crusade (1190), under Richard the Lionheart and King Philippe Auguste; and the Seventh Crusade (1248), by King (and Saint) Louis IX. Today, tourists flock to Vézelay's basilica, famous for its place in history, its soul-stirring Romanesque architecture—reproduced in countless art books—and for the relics of Mary Magdalene.

Tourist Information: Vézelay's TI is a block uphill as you climb through the village (12 Rue St. Etienne, daily 10:00-13:00 & 14:00-18:00, until 19:00 July-Aug, closed Thu Oct-April and Sun Nov-March; free Wi-Fi, tel. 03 86 33 23 69, http://en.vezelaytourisme.com, vezelay.otsi@wanadoo.fr).

Getting There: Vézelay is about 45 minutes northwest of **Semur-en-Auxois.** Drivers take the Avallon exit from A-6 and follow *Vézelay* signs for about 20 minutes. Parking is available at the lower end of the village (about €4/day). Train travelers go to **Sermizelles** and take the SNCF shuttle bus (2/day, free with rail pass; allows you about 4 hours in Vézelay or an easy overnight) or a taxi (6 miles, allow €20 one-way, mobile 06 74 53 45 76, www.cathytaxi-vezelay.fr). From Paris, Gare de Bercy trains run directly to Sermizelles (6/day, 2.5 hours); from other places, you'll transfer in Auxerre or Avallon.

BURGUNDY

Sights in Vézelay

▲▲Basilica of Ste. Madeleine

To accommodate the growing crowds of medieval pilgrims, the abbots of Vézelay enlarged their original church (1104), then rebuilt it after a disastrous 1120 fire. The building we see today—one of the largest and best-preserved Romanesque churches anywhere—was built in stages: nave (1120-1140), narthex (1132-1145), and choir (1215). The construction spanned the century-long transition from the Romanesque style (round barrel arches like the ancient Romans', thick walls, small windows) to Gothic (pointed arches, flying buttresses, high nave, lots of stained glass). Vézelay blends elements of both styles.

Cost and Hours: Free, daily 7:00-20:00; Mass Mon-Fri at 18:30, Sat at 12:30 and 18:30, Sun at 11:00.

Getting There: Allow 20 minutes to walk uphill from the parking lots and bus stop at the bottom of the village to the basilica. A free shuttle van runs continuously along this climb (July-Oct 11:00-18:00, details at TI). You'll be tempted by shops, galleries, and cafés as you ascend—just as pilgrims have for 800 years.

Tours: At the **Maison du Visiteur** center (on the main drag a few blocks below the basilica), exhibits, a film, and short lecture in English will prep you for your visit to the basilica—with a focus on light and mysticism (€8; Mon-Sat at 10:30, 11:00, 14:30, and 15:00 plus July-Aug at 16:30 and 17:00; private church tours-€120, tel. 03 86 32 35 65, www.vezelay-visiteur.com, maisonduvisiteur@orange.fr). Monk- or nun-guided basilica tours are possible (€50/up to 10 people, tel. 03 86 33 39 50, www.basiliquedevezelay.org). Or be your own guide, either by following the route I describe next or buying the €8 guidebook as you enter.

Visiting the Basilica: The **facade**—with one tower missing its original steeple, another that's unfinished, and an inauthentic tympanum—isn't why you came. Step inside.

The **narthex,** or entrance hall, served several functions. Religiously, it was a place to cross from the profane to the sacred. Practically, it gave shelter to overflow pilgrim crowds (even overnight, if necessary) as they shuffled through one of the three doorways. And aesthetically, the dark narthex prepares the visitor for the radiant nave.

The **tympanum** (carved relief) over the central, interior doorway is one of Romanesque's signature pieces. It shows the risen Christ standing on a tomb with welcoming arms wide open, ascending to heaven in an almond-shaped cloud, shooting Holy Ghost rays at his apostles and telling them to preach the Good News to the ends of the earth. The whole diversity of humanity (appropriate, considering Vézelay's function as a gathering place)

Mary Magdalene

France has a special affection for Mary Magdalene (La Madeleine), and Vézelay is one of several churches dedicated to her—a rarity in Europe, where most churches honor Jesus' mother, the Virgin Mary.

The Bible says that Mary Magdalene, one of Jesus' followers, was exorcised of seven demons (Luke 8:2), witnessed the Crucifixion (Matthew 27:56), and was the first mortal to see the resurrected Jesus (Mark 16:9-11)—the other disciples didn't believe her.

Some theologians have fleshed out Mary's reputation by associating her with biblical passages that don't specifically name her—e.g., the sinner who washed Jesus' feet with her hair (Luke 7:36-50), the forgiven adulteress (John 8), or the woman with the alabaster jar who anointed Jesus (Matthew 26:7-13).

In medieval times, legends appeared (especially in France) that, after the Crucifixion, Mary Magdalene fled to southern France, lived in a cave, converted locals, performed miracles, and died in Provence. Renaissance artists portrayed her as a fanciful blend of Bible and legend: a red-headed, long-haired prostitute who was rescued by Jesus, symbolizing the sin of those who love too much.

In recent times, feminists have claimed Mary Magdalene was a victim of male-dominated Catholic suppression. Bible scholars cite passages in two ancient (but noncanonical) gospels that cryptically allude to Mary as Jesus' special "companion." The Da Vinci Code—a popular if unhistorical novel—seized on this, slathering it with medieval legend and asserting that Mary Magdalene was actually Jesus' wife who bore him descendants, and that her relics lie not in Vézelay but in a shopping mall in Paris.

appears beneath: hunters, fishermen, farmers, pygmies, and men with long ears, feathers, and dog heads—the grotesque figures depicting those not touched by God's word. The signs of the zodiac arch over the scene.

Gaze through the central doorway into the **nave** at the rows and rows of arches that seem to recede into a luminous infinity. The nave is long, high, and narrow (200 feet by 60 feet by 35 feet), creating a tunnel effect formed by 10 columns and arches on each side. Overhead is the church's most famous feature—barrel vaults (wide arches) built of stones alternating between creamy-white and light-brown. The nave rises up between the low-ceilinged side aisles, lined with slender floor-to-ceiling columns that unite both stories. The interior glows with an even light from the unstained glass of the clerestory windows. The absence of distractions or bright colors makes this simple church perfect for meditation.

The capitals of the nave's **columns** are masterpieces carved by several sculptors of saints and Bible scenes. All are worth studying (the guidebook sold at the entry identifies each scene). Here are some you might recognize. Start on the right aisle and locate the Conversion of St. Eustace (third column up), depicting the Christian conversion of Roman general Placidus and the ensuing challenges to his faith. On the next (fourth) column find the well-known "Mystical Mill," showing Old Testament Moses and New Testament Paul working together to fill sacks with grain (and, metaphorically, the Bible with words). Cross to the left aisle and find David and Goliath (fourth column), Adam and Eve (ninth column), and Peter Freed from Prison (10th and final column).

The light at the end of the tunnel-like nave is the **choir,** radiating a brighter, blue-gray light. Constructed when Gothic was the rage, the choir has pointed arches and improved engineering, but for me it feels cold and sterile.

In the right transept stands a **statue** of the woman this church was dedicated to—not the Virgin Mary (Jesus' mother) but one of Jesus' disciples, Mary Magdalene. She cradles an alabaster jar of ointment she used (according to some Bible interpretations) to anoint Jesus.

Go down into the **crypt** for the ultimate medieval experience in one of Europe's greatest medieval churches. You're entering the foundations of the earlier ninth-century church that monks built here on the hilltop after Vikings had twice pillaged their church at the base of the hill. Step carefully across the crude floor, and pause on a pew to reflect on the pure, timeless scene. Notice the utter simplicity of these capitals compared to those you saw earlier. File past the small container with the **relics of Mary Magdalene.** In medieval times, Vézelay claimed to possess Mary's entire body, but the relics were later damaged and scattered by anti-Catholic Huguenots (16th century) and Revolutionaries (18th century), leaving only a few pieces.

Are they really her mortal remains? We only have legends—many different versions—that first appeared in the historical record around A.D. 1000. The most popular says that Mary Magdalene traveled to Provence, where she died, and that her bones were brought here by a monk to save them from Muslim pirates. In the 11th century, the abbots of Vézelay heavily marketed the notion that these were Mary's relics, and when the pope authenticated them in 1058, tourism boomed.

Vézelay prospered until the mid-13th century, when King Charles of Anjou announced that Mary's body was not in Vézelay, but had been found in another town. Vézelay's relics suddenly looked bogus, and pilgrims stopped coming. For the next five centuries, the church fell into disrepair and then was vandalized by secularists in the Revolution. The church was restored (1840-1860) by a young architect named Eugène Viollet-le-Duc, who would later revamp Notre-Dame in Paris and build the base of the Statue of Liberty.

A **glorious view** over the Burgundian countryside hides in a park behind the basilica's cloisters (out the right transept).

Sleeping and Eating in Vézelay

Sleeping in Vézelay: Hotels are gathered at the base of the village on Place du Champ-de-Foire, near parking and the bus stop.

$$ Hôtel de la Poste et du Lion d'Or*** has 39 pricey but comfortable, country-classy rooms (pay parking, air-con, at the foot of the village, Place du Champ-de-Foire, www.hplv-vezelay. com, reservation@hplv-vezelay.com, tel. 07 61 25 48 41).

$ Hôtel le Compostelle** offers a solid value with 18 spotless rooms and a view breakfast room (Place du Champ-de-Foire, www.lecompostellevezelay.com, le.compostelle@wanadoo.fr, tel. 03 86 33 28 63).

Eating in Vézelay: You'll find pleasant cafés with reasonable food all along the street leading to the church.

$$ Le Cheval Blanc serves tasty Burgundian cuisine at pleasant outside tables or in their cozy dining room (closed Tue-Wed, Place du Champ-de-Foire, tel. 03 86 33 22 12).

$$ La Dent Creuse has the best terrace tables at the lower end of the village (left side), with salads, pizza, and such (daily until 22:00, Place du Champ-de-Foire, tel. 03 86 33 36 33).

$ Le Vézelien bar/café, halfway up to the basilica, features cheap and tasty omelets and a small selection of salads and *plats* with appealing seating outside or in (closed Tue-Wed, 1 Place du Grand Puits, tel. 03 86 33 25 09).

Café Calabus offers tea, coffee, and other drinks in an atmospheric setting just below the basilica (Rue St. Pierre).

Château de Guédelon

A historian's dream (worth ▲▲, or ▲▲▲ for kids), this castle

is being built by 35 enthusiasts using only the tools, techniques, and materials available in the 13th century.

Cost and Hours: €14 for adults, €12 for kids ages 5-17, cheaper if bought online, free for kids 4 and under, picnic area and good-value lunch café with many options inside; castle open mid-March-early Nov 10:00-17:30, July-Aug until 19:00; closed early Nov-mid-March, Wed and weekends in March, the first two Wed in April, and every Wed in Sept (tel. 03 86 45 66 66, www.guedelon.fr).

Tours: There's a good English handout, some posted information, and a downloadable audio tour on the castle website, but this medieval construction site cries out for a live guide to answer the questions it inspires. Expertly guided **tours** in English are available most days in July and August for an additional €3/person; check online for updated times. Guided private tours can be arranged at other times of year and are well worth the investment (1.5-hour tour-€160, contact sarah.preston@guedelon.fr).

Getting There: Guédelon lies an hour west of Vézelay on D-955, between St-Amand-en-Puisaye and St-Saveur-en-Puisaye. Finding it requires patient route-finding skills and time. Allow 2.5 hours from Paris or Beaune at a steady pace. Coming from Paris, take exit #18 off the A-6 autoroute (well before Auxerre) and follow D-3 to Toucy; then join D-955 south. Coming from Beaune, exit A-6 at Avallon, then carefully track signs to Vézelay (take a break to visit its basilica), Clamecy, Entrains-sur-Nohain, St-Amand-en-Puisaye, and finally Guédelon. The castle is inaccessible by public transport.

Visiting the Castle: The project is the dream of two individuals who wanted to build a medieval castle (this one is based on plans drafted in 1228). Started in 1997, it will ultimately include four towers surrounding a central courtyard with a bridge and a moat (images of the finished castle are on postcards and in books in the gift shop). The goal of this exciting project is to give visitors a better appreciation of medieval construction, and for the builders to learn about medieval techniques while they work. The castle won't be complete for another 12 years or so, so you still have time to watch the process.

Enter the project to the sound of chisels chipping rock and the sight of people dressed as if it were 800 years ago. Human-powered hamster wheels carefully hoist 440 pounds of stone up tower walls (the largest tower will reach six stories when completed). Carpenters whack away at massive beams, creating supports for stone arches, while weavers demonstrate how clothing was made (a sheep's pen provides raw materials). Thirteen workstations help visitors learn about castle construction, from medieval rope-making to blacksmithing. Ask the workers questions—some speak English, and their job is to answer your questions as best they can. If it's been raining, be prepared for mud—you are, after all, on a construction site.

You can also visit the working reconstruction of a medieval

flour mill, a quarter-mile walk from the construction site along a woodland path—wear good walking shoes.

Kids can't get enough of Guédelon. It's a favorite for local school field trips, so expect lots of children. And if you can't get enough, there's a program for those wanting to join the workers and help (one-week minimum, check the website).

Sleeping near Guédelon: Guédelon is remote. To sleep nearby, try **$ Hôtel Les Grands Chênes,** where British Rachael and French Alain have restored a pretty manor home with a nice pool among trees, lakes, and waves of grass (family rooms, on D-18 between St-Fargeau and St-Amand-en-Puisaye, tel. 03 86 74 04 05, www.hotellesgrandschenes.com, contact@hotellesgrandschenes.com).

Bourges

Nestled between rolling vineyards and thick forests in the geographical center of France, unpretentious Bourges (pronounced "boorzh") is among France's most overlooked and authentic cities. Here you'll uncover a wonderful collection of medieval houses, a Gothic cathedral to rival any you've seen, and a down-to-earth, Midwest-like friendliness. Situated three hours due south of Paris, two hours west of Beaune, and 1.5 hours east of Amboise, Bourges is a handy stopover on the drive through the French heartland between Burgundy and the Loire.

Little-known Bourges has a big story to tell, thanks largely to its strategic location between two once-powerful regions, Burgundy and the Loire. It began as a Celtic city, became one of the first Christian towns in Gaul, and later served as the northern boundary of the sophisticated Kingdom of Aquitaine. Bourges reached its peak in the Middle Ages, when its great cathedral was built. It was home to future King Charles VII (r. 1422-1461), the man who, at Joan of Arc's insistence, rallied the French and drove out the English. During that Hundred Years' War, Bourges was a provisional capital of France, which explains its impressive legacy of medieval architecture.

TOURIST INFORMATION

If the cathedral had a transept, the TI would lie outside the south portal (may be closed in 2017; in general Mon-Sat 9:00-19:00 except Oct-March until 18:00; Sun 10:00-18:00 except Oct-March 14:00-17:00; free Wi-Fi, 21 Rue Victor Hugo, tel. 02 48 23 02 60, www.bourges-tourisme.com). Pick up one of their excellent English walking guides—wine lovers should ask for the *Route des Vignobles* map, and historians the *Route Jacques Cœur* map.

BURGUNDY

ARRIVAL IN BOURGES

By Train: From the station, it's about a half-mile walk south to the town center and cathedral. Head straight out onto Avenue Henri Laudier and turn left onto Rue du Commerce to find the TI.

By Car: Parking Mairie-Cathédrale is on the south side of the cathedral (€3/3 hours, free on Sun). The stairs up to the street land you in front of the TI. Parking Séraucourt/Centre Historique on Rue de Séraucourt, several blocks south of the cathedral, is free.

HELPFUL HINTS

Street Markets: Bourges is known for its good morning markets (all close by 13:00). The biggest is held on Saturdays on Place de la Nation. A smaller Thursday market takes place near the cathedral on Place des Maronniers, and Place St-Bonnet has a good market on Sundays.

Sound-and-Light Show: Bourges' **Nuits Lumière** starts at sundown every night in July and August, and every Thursday, Friday, and Saturday in June and September. The town's facades, courtyards, and monuments are lit up, accompanied by medieval and Renaissance music.

Music Festival: Every April, Bourges hosts **Printemps de Bourges,** a huge music festival (www.printemps-bourges.com).

Laundry: Try **Laverie Excelclean** (1 Rue Wittelsheim, daily 7:00-21:00, mobile 06 80 24 64 41), or ask at the TI.

Sights in Bourges

The city's medieval lanes, dotted with half-timbered buildings, are best appreciated on foot. The only sights in Bourges that charge admission are the Palais Jacques Cœur and the cathedral tower/crypt (both worth paying for). The handful of municipal museums are all free.

▲▲Cathedral of St. Etienne

One of Europe's great Gothic churches, Bourges' Cathedral of St. Etienne is known for its simple but harmonious design, flying buttresses, stained glass, and mammoth size. A Christian church has stood on this spot since the third century, including a Romanesque cathedral where Eleanor of Aquitaine received her crown in 1137. The present church was started in 1195, and finished just 55 years later—an astonishingly short amount of time for such a large structure. The design was inspired by Paris' Notre-Dame Cathedral, and it was built at the same time as the cathedral in Chartres. These three churches sum up the "High" Gothic style in France, and Bourges is one of the best-preserved, having been spared the ravages of the French Revolution and both world wars.

Cost and Hours: Church interior—free and open daily April-Sept 8:30-19:15, Oct-March 9:00-17:45; tower and crypt—€7.50 for both, €5.50 for tower only, €11 combo-ticket with Palais Jacques Cœur; open Mon-Sat 9:45-11:30 & 14:00-17:30, Sun 14:00-17:30, tel. 02 48 65 49 44, www.bourges-cathedrale.fr.

Visiting the Cathedral: Use this commentary to get oriented, starting with the exterior. The magnificent **west facade** is exceptionally wide (135 feet), dominated by five elaborately carved portals. The five doors reflect the church's unique interior—a central nave, flanked on each side by not one but two aisles. The frightening Last Judgment over the central doorway shows a seated Christ presiding over Judgment Day and deserves your attention.

The church's mismatched **towers** were a problem from the start. In an age of build-'em-high-and-fast, Bourges competed with Chartres to erect the ultimate Gothic cathedral. Bourges arguably won, but at a cost. The hastily built south tower had to be shored up several times—hence the squat tower that sits alongside it. Since the south tower was never strong enough to house any bells, locals call it "The Deaf Tower." The north tower collapsed altogether on New Year's Eve 1506 and had to be rebuilt, financed by donors who were granted an indulgence to eat butter during Lent—hence its nickname, the "Tour de Beurre."

The elegant **flying buttresses** form two rows, supporting both the lower and upper walls. The buttresses slope upward, enfolding the church in a pyramid shape as it rises to the peaked roofline.

Head inside. The view down the **nave** is overwhelming—at 300 feet, this is one of the longest naves in France. It seems even longer because the church has no transept to interrupt the tunnel effect. Notice elements of the "High" Gothic style of the 1200s: The church is tall, filled with light from many windows, and built with slender columns and thin walls (thanks to efficient flying buttresses). It rises up like a three-tiered step-pyramid—the outermost aisles are 30 feet high, the inner aisles are 70 feet, and the central nave is a soaring 120 feet from floor to rib-arched ceiling.

The best **stained glass** (c. 1215) is at the far end of the church, in the apse. Also, the Jacques Cœur Chapel (on the north side near the ambulatory) has a colorful Annunciation in stained glass.

The towering **astronomical clock,** on the south side of the nave, celebrates the most famous wedding the cathedral witnessed: that of hometown boy (and future king) Charles VII and Marie d'Anjou. The old clock, from 1424, still works.

Climbing the Tower: Don't leave the cathedral without climbing the 396 steps up the north tower for terrific views.

Crypt: To see the crypt, you need to join a tour in French... but you don't have to pay attention. Once inside, find the tomb statue of Duke Jean de Berry (1340-1416), the great collector of illuminated manuscripts and patron of this church. He lies on his back atop a black marble slab, dressed in ermine. At his feet sleeps a muzzled bear, representing the duke's quiet ferocity. Nearby, the colorfully painted Holy Sepulchre statues (c. 1530) enact the story of Christ's body being prepared for burial. See how realistic the marble looks as the mourners tug the ends of Christ's shroud—remarkably supple.

Nearby: The Archbishop's Garden (Jardin de l'Archevêché), just behind the cathedral, has a fine classical design and point-blank views of the flying buttresses. On Sundays when the weather agrees, old-school *guinguette* balls (picture a Renoir scene) are held here.

▲Medieval Quarter Stroll

Bourges' old city (Vieille Ville) is lassoed within Rues Bourbon-noux, Mirebeau, Coursarlon, Edouard Branly, and des Arènes. Richly decorated Renaissance mansions, many of which house small museums (worth entering), mix it up with France's greatest concentration of half-timbered homes (more than 500), most of them connected below street level by a labyrinth of underground passages. Look for Hôtel Lallemant (home to the Musée des Arts Décoratifs), Hôtel des Echevins (Musée Estève, with contemporary paintings by Maurice Estève), and Hôtel Cujas (Musée du Berry, with Roman tombstones and the famously expressive mourner statues from the Duke of Berry's elaborate tomb). For a historic stroll by the Gallo-Roman walls, take the steps up on the narrow lane between #44 and #50 on Rue Bourbonnoux and immediately turn left. Joan of Arc stayed in one of these fourth-century towers.

▲Palais Jacques Cœur

Bourges matters to travelers because of Jacques Cœur (c. 1395-1456), financier and minister to King Charles VII, who was born in Bourges. Monsieur Cœur helped establish Bourges as a capital for luxury goods and arms manufacturing. He also bankrolled Joan of Arc's call to save France from the English. His extravagant home is an impressive example of a Gothic civil palace, combining all the best elements of a château in an urban mansion. To visit the palace, join a French-only tour or pick up the English handout and go on your own.

Cost and Hours: €7.50, €11 combo-ticket with cathedral crypt and tower, daily 9:45-12:00 & 14:00-17:15, May-Aug until 18:15 or 18:30, 10 bis Rue Jacques-Cœur, tel. 02 48 24 79 42, www. palais-jacques-coeur.fr.

Sleeping and Eating in Bourges

Hotels and restaurants are a good value here. Ground zero for dining in Bourges is Place Gordaine and the nearby streets, where you'll find easygoing cafés and *bistrots*.

Sleeping: $$ Best Western Hôtel d'Angleterre Bourges**** is a fine place and as central as it gets (includes buffet breakfast, air-con, lounge bar, 1 Place des Quatre-Piliers, tel. 02 48 24 68 51, www.bestwestern-angleterre-bourges.com, hotel@bestwestern-angleterre-bourges.com).

$ Hôtel le Christina* is a good hotel 10 blocks from the cathedral (air-con, 5 Rue de la Halle, tel. 02 48 70 56 50, www.le-christina.com, info@le-christina.com).

Eating: $ La Crêperie des Remparts offers a great range of inexpensive crêpes and salads (closed Sun-Mon, 59 Rue Bourbonnoux, tel. 02 48 24 55 44).

$$ Au Sénat is a local favorite for good-value traditional cuisine (closed Wed year-round and Thu in winter, on Place Gordaine at 8 Rue de la Poissonnerie, tel. 02 48 24 02 56).

$$$ La Suite in the old city is a fine place to do it up right (closed Sun-Mon, 50 Rue Bourbonnoux, tel. 02 48 65 96 26).

$$$ Le Bourbonnoux offers good *menus,* fair prices, and copious servings (closed Fri, Sat for lunch, and Sun evening; 44 Rue Bourbonnoux, tel. 02 48 24 14 76).

$ Cake Thé is run by friendly Aude, who makes everything in this grand 14th-century vaulted cellar—her lemon meringue tart is a delight. Peaceful seating inside and out (Tue-Sat 12:00-14:00 & 15:00-19:00, Sun afternoon only, closed Mon, 74 bis Rue Bourbonnoux, parallel to the street by the ramparts, 02 48 24 94 60).

Bourges Connections

From Bourges by Train to: Paris (15/day, 2-3 hours, most with 1 change), **Amboise** (roughly hourly—though fewer midday, 2-3 hours, 1 change), **Beaune** (2/day, 4 hours, transfer in Nevers or Moulins-sur-Allier), **Sarlat-la-Canéda** (4/day, 9 hours, 2 changes).

Between Burgundy and Lyon

Drivers traveling south from Beaune should think about detouring into the lovely, unspoiled Mâconnais countryside. Brancion, Chapaize, Cluny, and Taizé gather a few minutes from one another, about 30 minutes west of the autoroute between Mâcon and Tournus (see map on page 822). Drivers day-tripping to this area from

Beaune should take the autoroute south to Tournus (then D-14 to Brancion), and take D-981 back to Beaune (described next). Route D-14 from Brancion meets D-981 at Cormatin.

For a romp through vineyards and unspoiled villages, connect Cluny and Beaune along D-981 (via Cormatin, Buxy, and Givry). Notice how many villages have signs to their *Eglise Romaine* (Romanesque churches are a dime a dozen here). Be on the lookout for bikers and a surprising château on the west side of the road in cute little Sercy (just south of Buxy).

Non-drivers can reach Cluny and Taizé by bus (see info under each listing for details).

Brancion and Chapaize

An hour south of Beaune by car (12 miles west of Tournus on D-14) are two tiny villages, each with "daughters of Cluny"—churches that owe their existence and architectural design to the nearby and once-powerful Cluny Abbey. Between the villages you'll pass a Stonehenge-era menhir (standing stone) with a cross added on top at a later point—evidence that this was sacred ground long before Christianity (from Brancion, it's on the right just after passing the bulky Château de Nobles).

Brancion

This is a classic feudal village. Back when there were no nations in Europe, control of land was delegated from lord to vassal. The

Duke of Burgundy ruled here through his vassal, the Lord of Brancion. His vast domain—much of south Burgundy—was administered from this tiny fortified town.

Within the town's walls, the feudal lord had a castle, a church, and all the necessary administrative buildings to deliver justice, collect taxes, and so on. Strategically perched on a hill between two river valleys, he enjoyed a complete view of his domain. Brancion's population peaked centuries ago at 60. Today, it's home to a handful of full-time residents.

The **castle,** part of a network of 17 castles in the region, was destroyed in 1576 by Protestant Huguenots. After the French Revolution, it was sold to be used as a quarry and spent most of the 19th century being picked apart. Though the flier gives a brief tour and the audioguide a longer one, the small castle is most enjoyable for its evocative angles and the lush views from the top of its keep (€6, daily April-Sept 10:00-12:30 & 13:00-18:30, until 17:00 Oct-mid-Nov, closed mid-Nov-March, audioguide-€1).

Wandering from the castle to the church, you'll pass L'Auberge du Vieux Brancion, a 15th-century market hall that was used by farmers from the surrounding countryside until 1900, a handful of other buildings from that period and a few cafés.

The 12th-century warm-stone **church** is the town's highlight. Circumnavigate the small building—this is Romanesque at its pure, unadulterated, fortress-of-God best (thick walls, small windows, once colorfully painted interior, no-frills exterior). Notice the stone roof (made using a flat flagstone called *lauze*) and the orange-tinted stone of the church walls. Inside, you'll see faint paintings surviving from 1330, some moved to canvas in the early 1900s and displayed today (look for English explanations). From its front door, enjoy a lord's view over one glorious Burgundian estate.

Sleeping and Eating in Brancion: $ L'Auberge du Vieux Brancion serves traditional Burgundian fare and also offers a perfectly tranquil place to spend the night. Say *bonjour* to François (very simple and frumpy rooms, family rooms, cheaper rooms with shared bath, tel. 03 85 51 03 83, mobile 06 83 50 92 91, www.brancion.fr, fdemurard@gmail.com).

Chapaize

This hamlet, a few miles west of Brancion on D-14, grew up around its Benedictine monastery—only its 11th-century church survives. It's a pristine place (cars park in a lot at the edge of town) peppered with flowers, appealing cafés, and rustic decay. The classic Romanesque church gets all the attention. Enter through its cemetery: The WWI monument near the entry, with so many names from such a tiny hamlet, is a reminder of the 5.6 million young French men who were wounded or died in the war that *didn't* end all wars. Inside the church, study the fine stonework by Lombard masons and appreciate how it contrasts with the church in Brancion (different rock, higher nave, funky pillars). The leaning structure seems determined to challenge the faith of parishioners (the nave collapsed once already—900 years ago). Wander around the back for a view of the belfry, and then ponder Chapaize across the street while sipping a café au lait.

Cluny

People come from great distances to admire Cluny's great abbey that is no more. This mother of all abbeys once vied with the Vatican as the most important power center in Christendom (Cluny's abbot often served as mediator between Europe's kings and the pope). The building was destroyed during the French Revolution, and, frankly, there's not a lot to see today. Still, the abbey makes a worthwhile visit for history buffs and pilgrims looking to get some idea of the scale of this vast complex.

The pleasant little town that grew up around the abbey maintains its medieval street plan, with plenty of original buildings and even the same population it had in its 12th-century heyday (4,500). That's stability. As you wander the town, which claims to be the finest surviving Romanesque town in France, enjoy the architectural details on everyday buildings. Many of the town's fortified walls, gates, and towers survive.

Getting There: Drivers park at designated lots (best is Parking le Rochefort, the first lot you see coming from the north) and follow *Centre-Ville* signs on foot. Bus Céphale makes several trips to Cluny from Mâcon and Chalon-sur-Saône on the same line (7/day, 30 minutes from Mâcon, 1.5 hours from Chalon-sur-Saône; toll-free tel. 08 00 07 17 10, www.cg71.fr, French only, click *"se déplacer,"* then *"Horaires Buscéphale"*). There is no train station in Cluny.

Orientation to Cluny

Everything of interest is within a few minutes' walk of the **TI,** 100 yards to the right as you face the abbey entrance (daily April-Sept 9:30-18:30, except closed for lunch in April; Oct-March Mon-Sat 9:30-12:30 & 14:30-17:00, closed Sun except in Oct; 6 Rue Mercière, tel. 03 85 59 05 34, www.cluny-tourisme.com).

The TI is at the base of the **Tour des Fromages**—"Cheese Tower"—so named because it was used to age cheese (or perhaps for the way tourists smell after climbing to the top). The tower offers a sweeping city view (€2, same hours as TI).

A **farmers market** animates the old town each Saturday morning.

History of Cluny and Its (Scant) Abbey

In 1964, St. Benedict (480-547), founder of the first monastery (at Montecassino, south of Rome) from which a great monastic movement sprang, was named the patron saint of Europe. Christians and non-Christians alike recognize the impact that monasteries had in establishing a European civilization out of the dark chaos that followed the fall of Rome.

The Abbey of Cluny was the ruling center of the first great international chain of monasteries in Europe. It was the heart of an upsurge in monasticism, of church reform, and an evangelical revival that spread throughout Europe—a phenomenon that historians call the Age of Faith (11th and 12th centuries). From this springboard came a vast network of abbeys, priories, and other monastic orders that kindled the establishment of modern Europe.

In 910, 12 monks founded a house of prayer at Cluny, vowing to follow the rules of St. Benedict. The cult of saints and relics was enthusiastically promoted, and the order was independent and powerful. From the start, the Abbot of Cluny answered only to the pope (not to their local bishop or secular leader). The abbots of the other Cluniac monasteries were answerable only to the Abbot of Cluny (not to their local bishop or prince). This made the Abbot of Cluny arguably the most powerful person in Europe.

The abbey's success has been attributed to a series of wise leaders. In fact, four of the first six abbots actually became saints. They preached principles of piety (they got people to stop looting the monasteries) and practiced shrewd fundraising (convincing wealthy landowners to will their estates to the monasteries in return for perpetual prayers for the benefit of their needy and frightened souls).

From all this grew the greatest monastic movement of the High Middle Ages. A huge church was built at Cluny, and by 1100 it was the headquarters of 10,000 monks who ran nearly a thousand monasteries and priories across Europe. Cluny peaked in the 12th century, then faded in influence (though monasteries continued to increase in numbers and remain a force until 1789).

Sights in Cluny

Site of Cluny Abbey

It's free to view the site of the former abbey. The best point from which to appreciate the abbey's awesome dimensions is from just below the Museum of Art and Archaeology (100 yards up from the Hôtel de Bourgogne). Find the marble table that shows the original floor plan (*vous êtes ici* means "you are here"). Look out to the remaining tower (there used to be three). You're standing above the front of the central nave, the largest of five naves that stretched all the way to those towers.

Some of today's old town stands on the site of what was the largest church in Christendom. It was almost two football fields long (555 feet) and crowned with five soaring towers. The whole complex (church plus monastery) covered 25 acres. Revolutionaries destroyed it in 1790, and today the National Stud Farm and a big school obliterate much of the floor plan of the abbey. Only one tower and part of the transept still stand (5 percent of its original size). The visitor's challenge: Visualize it. Get a sense of its grandeur.

Walk downhill past the nubs that remain of the once-massive columns, work your way down the nave and around the right at the bottom, and climb a stairway to find today's abbey entry.

Abbey Interior

Once inside the one-time abbey complex (now a mishmash of bits of the original church and other, more recent buildings), follow *Suite de la Visite* signs. Information displays (in English) designed to introduce the abbey and provide historical context help put the pieces of the ruined building back together. You'll see a 12-minute 3-D film giving a virtual tour of the 1,100-year-old church that helps you grasp the tragedy of its destruction (use headset for translation and pick up your 3-D glasses). Consult the English flier to tour what little of the abbey still stands. You'll gaze up to the tallest Romanesque vault in the world (100 feet tall) in the lone remaining bell tower (awesome) and see parts of an adjacent transept. Your visit ends at the flour mill *(Tour du Moulin);* make sure to go upstairs to see the intricate wood roof supports. (A left turn out of the abbey exit leads quickly to the old town and TI.)

Cost and Hours: €9.50 ticket covers abbey interior and Museum of Art and Archaeology; both sights open daily April-Sept 9:30-18:00, until 19:00 July-Aug, until 17:00 Oct-March; audioguide-€4.50 for abbey only, €6 includes museum; tel. 03 85 59 15 93, www.cluny-abbaye.fr. Historians should invest in *The Abbey of Cluny* guidebook (€7), sold at the abbey only, or take a free 90-minute tour (in English) when available.

Museum of Art and Archaeology (Palais Jean de Bourbon)

The small abbey museum fills the Palace of the Abbot, 100 yards straight out from the entrance to the abbey interior. The modest collection features artifacts from the medieval town of Cluny and provides context for your visit to the abbey site. There's a terrific model of the village and abbey complex. You'll also see a beautifully carved stone frieze from a mansion in Cluny (first floor up) and fragments of the main entry (Grand Portail) to the abbey church set within a model of the doorway (near the ticket counter).

Cost and Hours: Same ticket and hours as the abbey interior—see previous listing.

National Stud Farm (Les Haras Nationaux)

Napoleon (who needed *beaucoup de* horses for his army of 600,000) established this farm in 1806. Today, 50 thoroughbred stallions kill time in their stables. If the stalls are empty, they're out doing their current studly duty...creating strapping racehorses. Since 2010, the complex has been home to the National School of Equestrian Activities. French-only tours are offered from the entry gate next to Hôtel de Bourgogne (tours-€6.50, 75 minutes, 4/day in summer, 1/day April-Sept, 2/week March and Oct, no tours in winter).

Sleeping and Eating in Cluny

If you're spending the night, bed down at the homey, traditional, and spotless **$ Hôtel de Bourgogne,***** built into the wall of the abbey's right transept and central for enjoying the town. All rooms have queen- or king-size beds (pay parking garage, Place de l'Abbaye, tel. 03 85 59 00 58, www.hotel-cluny.com, contact@hotel-cluny.com).

$ Brasserie du Nord owns the best abbey view from its outdoor tables (skip the mod interior) and serves standard café fare at fair prices (daily, tel. 03 85 59 09 96, 1 Place du Marché).

BURGUNDY

Taizé

To experience the latest in European monasticism, drop by the booming Christian community of Taizé (teh-zay), a few miles

north of Cluny on the road to Brancion. The normal, uncultlike ambience of this place—with thousands of mostly young, European pilgrims asking each other, "How's your soul today?"—is remarkable. Even if this sounds a little airy, you might find the 30 minutes it takes to stroll from one end of the compound to the other a worthwhile detour.

Notice how everyone of any age seems to be in a good mood. A visit to Taizé can be a thought-provoking experience, particularly after a visit to Cluny. A thousand years ago, Cluny had a similar power to draw the faithful in search of direction and meaning in life.

Getting There: Drivers follow *La Communauté* signs in Taizé and park in a dirt lot. SNCF buses (free with rail pass) serve Taizé from Chalon-sur-Saône to the north (4/day, 1 hour) and from Mâcon to the south (6/day, 1 hour).

Tourist Information: At the southern (Cluny) end, the Welcome Office provides an orientation and daily schedule, and makes a good first stop (daily 9:30-12:20 & 14:30-20:20). Ask to see the short film about Taizé.

Visiting Taizé: Taizé is an ecumenical movement—prayer, silence, simplicity—welcoming Protestant as well as Catholic Christians. Though it feels Catholic, it isn't. (But, as some of the brothers are actually Catholic priests, Catholics may take the Eucharist here.) The Taizé style of worship is well known among American Christians for its hauntingly beautiful chants—songbooks and CDs are the most popular souvenirs from here. The Exposition (next to the church) is the thriving community shop, with books, CDs, handicrafts, and other souvenirs.

The community welcomes visitors who'd like to spend a few days getting close to God through meditation, singing, and simple living. Although designed primarily for youthful pilgrims in meditative retreat (there are about 5,000 here in a typical week), people of any age are welcome to pop in for a meal or church service. Time your visit for one of the services (Mon-Sat at 8:15, 12:20, and 20:30; Sun at 10:00 and 20:20; Catholic and Protestant communion available daily).

During services, the bells ring and worshippers file into the long, low, simple, and modern Church of Reconciliation. It's dim—candlelit with glowing icons—as the white-robed brothers enter. The service features responsive singing of chants (from well-worn songbooks that list lyrics in 19 languages), reading of biblical passages, and silence, as worshippers on crude kneelers stare into icons. The aim: "Entering together into the  mystery of God's presence." (Secondary aim: Helping Lutherans get over their fear of icons.)

Sleeping and Eating in Taizé: Those on retreat fill their days with worship services; workshops; simple, relaxed meals; and hanging out in an international festival of people searching for meaning in their lives. Visitors are welcome for free. The cost for a real stay is about €20-35 per day (based on a sliding scale; those under 18 stay for less) for monastic-style room and board. Adults (over age 30) are accommodated in a more comfortable zone, but count on ¢ simple dorms. Call or email first if you plan to stay overnight (reception open Mon-Fri 10:00-12:00 & 18:00-19:00, tel. 03 85 50 30 02). The Taizé community website explains everything—in 29 languages (www.taize.fr).

The **$$ Oyak** (near the parking lot) is where those in a less monastic mood can get a beer or burger.

LYON

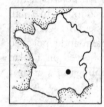

Straddling the mighty Rhône and Saône rivers between Burgundy and Provence, Lyon has been among France's leading cities since Roman times. In spite of its workaday, business-first facade, Lyon is France's most historic and culturally important city after Paris. You'll experience two different-as-night-and-day cities: the Old World cobbled alleys, pastel Renaissance mansions, and colorful shops of Vieux Lyon; and the more staid but classy, Paris-like buildings and shopping streets of the Presqu'île. Once you're settled, this big city feels relaxed, welcoming, and surprisingly untouristy. It seems everyone's enjoying the place—and they're all French.

PLANNING YOUR TIME

Just 70 minutes south of Beaune and two hours north of Avignon, Lyon is France's best-kept urban secret. Lyon deserves at least one night and a full day. With frequent and fast service to Paris, Provence, Burgundy, and the Alps, the city makes a handy overnight stop for train travelers. Those who spend the night can experience the most renowned cuisine in France at appetizing prices and enjoy one of Europe's most beautifully floodlit cities.

For a full day of sightseeing, take a funicular up to Fourvière Hill, visit the Notre-Dame Basilica, and tour the Roman Theaters and Gallo-Roman Museum. Ride the other funicular back down to Vieux Lyon and have a French (read: slow) lunch, then explore the old town and its hidden passageways. Finish your day touring the Museum of Fine Arts, Resistance Center, or Lumière Museum (covering the history of early filmmaking). Most of Lyon's important sights are closed on Mondays or Tuesdays, or both. Dine well in the evening (book ahead if possible; your hotelier can help) and cap your day enjoying a stroll through the best-lit city in France.

LYON'S CUISINE SCENE

In Lyon, how well you eat determines how well you live. The best restaurants are all the buzz—a favorite conversation topic likely to generate heated debate. Here, great chefs are more famous than professional soccer players. (Paul Bocuse is the chef MVP.) Restaurants seem to outnumber cars, and all seem busy. With an abundance of cozy, excellent restaurants in every price range, it's hard to go wrong—unless you order tripe (cow intestines, also known

as *tablier de sapeur*), *foie de veau* (calf's liver), or *tête de veau* (calf's head). Beware: These questionable dishes are common in small bistros *(bouchons)*. Look instead for these classics: St. Marcellin cheese, *salade lyonnaise* (croutons, fried bits of ham, and a poached egg on a bed of lettuce), green lentils *(lentilles)* served on a salad or with sausages, *quenelles de brochet* (fish dumplings in a creamy sauce), and *filet de sandre* (local whitefish).

LYON AREA WINES

Fruity and fresh Gamay Beaujolais grapes, which grow in vineyards just north of Lyon, produce a light, fruity, easy-to-drink red wine. Beaujolais vines are grown on granite rock slopes, yielding wines with a distinct flavor. While there are several premier *crus* producing lovely wines, the area is most famous for its simple Beaujolais Nouveau wines, opened just six weeks after bottling. The arrival of the new Beaujolais is cause for lighthearted celebration and mischief in this otherwise hard-to-impress country. At midnight on the third Thursday of November, the first bottles are opened to great fanfare, road rallies carry the new wine to destinations throughout France, and cafés everywhere post signs announcing its arrival.

Big, luscious reds made from mostly syrah grapes grow on impossibly steep slopes to the city's south. Look for Saint-Joseph and (my favorite) Crozes-Hermitage wines. In the village of Condrieu, only viognier grapes are allowed to grow; they produce a rich and perfumy white wine.

Orientation to Lyon

Despite being France's third-largest city (after Paris and Marseille), with about 1.5 million inhabitants in its metropolitan area, the traveler's Lyon (home to 485,000 people) is peaceful and manageable. Traffic noise is replaced by pedestrian friendliness in the old center—listen to how quiet this big city is. Notice the emphasis on environmentally friendly transport: Electric buses have replaced

diesel buses in the historic core, bike lanes run everywhere, and pedal taxis (called *cyclopolitains,* seek-loh-poh-lee-tan) are used instead of traditional taxis for short trips (about €1/kilometer). Lyon's network of more than 5,000 city-owned rental bikes was in place years before Paris started its program.

Lyon provides the organized traveler with a full day of activities. Sightseeing can be enjoyed on foot from any of my recommended hotels, though it's smart to make use of trams, funiculars, and the Métro. Lyon's sights are concentrated in three areas: **Fourvière Hill,** with its white Notre-Dame Basilica glimmering over the city; historic **Vieux Lyon,** which hunkers below on the bank of the Saône River; and the **Presqu'île** (home to my recommended hotels), lassoed by the Saône and Rhône rivers. Huge and curiously empty Place Bellecour, which lies in the middle of the Presqu'île, always seems to be hosting an event.

TOURIST INFORMATION

The well-equipped TI can reserve a hotel for you at no charge (daily 9:00-18:00, tel. 04 72 77 69 69, www.lyon-france.com, corner of Place Bellecour, free public WCs behind the TI building). Pick up the city map (with good enlargements of central Lyon and Vieux Lyon; hotels have similar maps) and an event schedule (ask about concerts in the Roman Theaters during Les Nuits de Fourvière— early June to early Aug—and events at the Opera House). They also have a brochure on the Beaujolais wine road north of Lyon. Ask about a pocket Wi-Fi device that gives you service all over town;

you can leave it in any mailbox before departing Lyon (€8/day, €4 with Lyon City Card).

Walking Tours: The TI's **audioguide** (€10/day) offers good, self-guided walking tours of Vieux Lyon. Live **guided walks** of Vieux Lyon are usually offered at 14:30 on weekends and on most days July through early September (€10-15, 2 hours, several in English, some starting near Vieux Lyon Métro station—verify days and times with TI or sign up online, www.visiterlyon.com). Other, less-frequent English-language walks include tours of the La Croix-Rousse district and the silk workshops.

Sightseeing Pass: The TI sells a good-value **Lyon City Card** for serious sightseers (€24/1 day, €33/2 consecutive days, €42/3 consecutive days, under age 16 half-price, https://lyoncitycard. com). This pass includes all Lyon museums plus free use of buses, funiculars, the Métro, and the river shuttle boat *Le Vaporetto*. It also covers a river cruise (April-Oct), a tram tour of the hilly La Croix-Rousse neighborhood, and a walking tour of Vieux Lyon with a live guide or use of the TI's audioguide. The one-day pass pays for itself if you visit the Gallo-Roman Museum and the Resistance and Deportation History Center, plus take a guided walking tour and use public transit.

Helpful Website: For useful information in English about visiting Lyon, check out www.angloinfo.com/lyon.

ARRIVAL IN LYON

By Train: Lyon has two train stations—Part-Dieu and Lyon-Per-rache. Many trains stop at both, and some through trains connect the two stations. Both stations are well-served by Métro, bus, tram, and taxi (figure €15 for a taxi from either station to my recommended hotels near Place Bellecour), and both have the standard car-rental companies. Only Part-Dieu has baggage storage (daily 6:15-23:00), along with free Wi-Fi in the waiting area. The all-day transit ticket is a great value—buy it upon arrival at the station if you plan to do much sightseeing that day (coin machines only), or wait to pick up a Lyon City Card—which covers transit—at the TI (for more on public transportation and tickets, see "Getting Around Lyon," later).

Arriving at Part-Dieu Station: This is where most visitors arrive. There are two exits from the station: *Porte du Rhône* and *Porte des Alpes*. Bag check is near the *Porte des Alpes* exit. To reach Place Bellecour in the **city center** (close to most hotels and the TI), exit by following *Sortie Porte du Rhône* signs, then enter the Métro station and buy your ticket from the machine. Take the blue Métro line B toward Gare d'Oulins, transfer at Saxe-Gambetta to the line D/Gare de Vaise route, and get off at Bellecour. At Bellecour, follow *Sortie Rue République* signs.

The other main exit, *Sortie Porte des Alpes*, offers access to the handy **airport** train (called Rhône Express, described later under "By Plane"). Also out this exit are SNCF buses to Annecy and Grenoble (but train connections are more frequent). Taxis wait outside either exit, though they seem more plentiful at the *Sortie Porte des Alpes*.

Arriving at Perrache Station: This station is within a 20-minute walk of Place Bellecour (no baggage storage). Follow green *Place Carnot* signs out of the station, then cross Place Carnot and walk up pedestrian Rue Victor Hugo to reach the TI and most of my recommended hotels. Or take the Métro (direction: Vaulx-en-Velin) two stops to Bellecour and follow *Sortie Rue République* signs.

By Car: The city center has good signage and is manageable to navigate, though you'll hit traffic on surrounding freeways. If autoroute A-6 is jammed (not unusual), you'll be directed to bypass freeways (such as A-46). Either way, follow *Centre-Ville* and *Presqu'île* signs, and then follow *Office de Tourisme* and *Place Bellecour* signs. Park in the lots under Place Bellecour or Place des Célestins (yellow *P* means "parking lot") or get advice from your hotel. The TI's map identifies all public parking lots. Overnight parking (generally 19:00-8:00) is only €4.50, but day rates are €2 per hour (figure about €30/24 hours). Garages near Perrache station are cheaper than those near Bellecour.

By Plane: Lyon's sleek little airport (and TGV station), St-Exupéry, is 15 miles from the city center, and is a breeze to navigate (ATMs, English information booths, airport code: LYS, tel. 08 26 80 08 26, www.lyonaeroports.com). It has air and rail connections to major European cities, including two flights per hour to Paris' Charles de Gaulle Airport and direct TGV service to many French cities. Car rental is a snap. Four **Rhône Express** shuttles per hour make the 30-minute trip from the airport (follow red tram car icons) to Part-Dieu Station, described earlier (€16 one-way, €28 round-trip, buy ticket from machine with bills, coins, or chip-and-PIN credit card—conductors can help). Allow €50 for a taxi if you have baggage.

HELPFUL HINTS

Exchange Rate: €1 = about $1.10

Country Calling Code: 33 (see page 1082 for dialing instructions)

Market Days: A small market stretches along the Saône River near the Passerelle du Palais de Justice bridge (daily until 12:30). Tuesday through Sunday, it's produce; Monday, it's textiles. On Sunday morning, a crafts and contemporary art market is on the other side of the bridge near the Court of Justice. Another bustling morning produce market takes place on Boule-

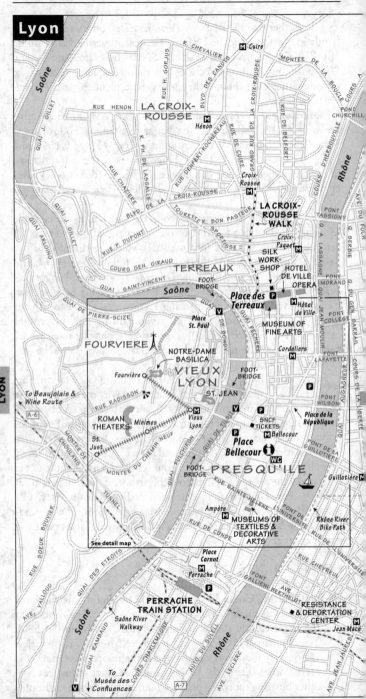

Lyon

LYON

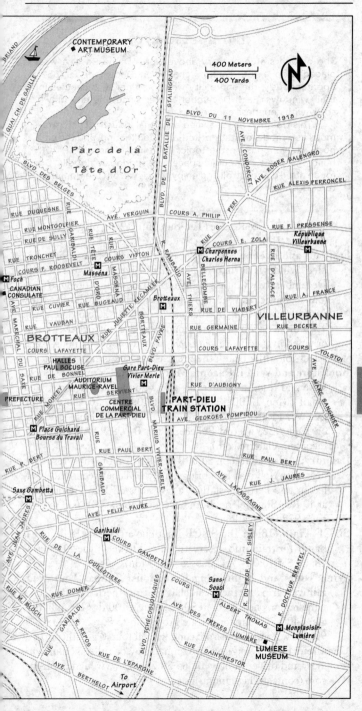

Illuminated Lyon

The golden statue of Mary above Notre-Dame Basilica was placed atop a 16th-century chapel on December 8, 1852. Spontaneously, the entire city welcomed her with candles in their windows. Each December 8 ever since, the city glows softly with countless candles.

This tradition has spawned an actual industry. Lyon is famous as a model of state-of-the-art floodlighting, and the city hosts conventions on the topic. Each night, more than 200 buildings, sites, and public spaces are gloriously floodlit. Go for an after-dinner stroll and enjoy the view from the Bonaparte Bridge after dark.

vard de la Croix-Rousse (Tue-Sun until 12:30, biggest on Sun, see page 914).

Festivals and Events: Lyon celebrates the Virgin Mary with candlelit windows during the Festival of Lights each year in early December (www.lumieres.lyon.fr). Les Nuits de Fourvière (dance, music, and theater) takes place from early June to early August in the Roman Theaters (www.nuitsdefourviere.com). To browse upcoming performances and events, check youth-oriented magazine *A Nous Lyon*'s website at www.anous.fr and select "Save the Date"; the French-only site is easy to use.

Bookstore and Wi-Fi: Raconte Moi La Terre is a traveler's bookstore and resource center; it's also a good place to check your email (Mon 12:00-19:30, Tue-Sat 10:00-19:30, closed Sun, free Wi-Fi at their café, air-con, 14 Rue du Plat—see map on page 922, Métro: Bellecour, tel. 04 78 92 60 22, www.racontemoilaterre.com).

Laundry: A launderette is at 7 Rue Mercière on the Presqu'île, near the Alphonse Juin bridge; another is between Place Bellecour and Perrache station, a few steps off Rue Victor Hugo at 19 Rue Ste. Hélène. Both have long hours daily (see map on page 922 for locations).

SNCF Train Office: The SNCF Boutique at 2 Place Bellecour is handy for train info, reservations, and tickets (Tue-Fri 10:00-18:45, Sat 10:00-17:45, closed Sun-Mon).

Wine Tours and Sightseeing Excursions: Kanpai Tours runs minivan trips to the Beaujolais and northern Rhône Valley wine regions near Lyon (€80/half-day, €100/day for individuals, €400-750/day for private groups up to 8, tel. 06 84 52 14 99, www.kanpai-tourisme.com, kanpai.tours@gmail.com).

Chauffeur Hire: Design your own half-day or full-day tour with a car and driver (mobile 06 65 38 75 08, www.lugdunum-ips.com, contact@lugdunum-ips.com).

LYON

Local Guide: Virginie Moré, a talented guide and former language teacher in Montana, offers private tours to discover Lyon, including city walks, food-tasting tours, and museum visits. She also leads tours for my company (virginiemore@yahoo.fr, mobile 06 52 90 88 61).

Riverside Bike Path and Promenade: A bike path/walkway along the east side of the Rhône River is ideal for adults and children (see map on page 922). For more information on the path and bike rentals, ask at the TI or check www.angloinfo.com/lyon. A walkway along the Saône's eastern bank brings beautiful views of the old town and is great for picnicking (see map on page 922). The walkway goes as far south as the futuristic-looking Musée des Confluences science museum.

Children's Activities: The Parc de la Tête d'Or is vast, with rowboat rentals, a miniature golf course, pony rides, a free zoo and botanical gardens, and easy access to the riverside bike path described earlier (across Rhône River from La Croix-Rousse neighborhood, Métro: Masséna, www.loisirs-parcdelatetedor. com).

GETTING AROUND LYON

Lyon has a user-friendly public transit system, with five modern tram lines (T1-T4 and the Rhône Express line to the airport), four underground Métro lines (A-D), an extensive bus system, and two funiculars to get you up that hill. The subway is similar to Paris' Métro in many ways (e.g., routes are signed by *direction* for the last stop on the line) but is more automated (buy tickets at coin-op machines), cleaner, less crowded, and less rushed (drivers linger longer at stops). Study the wall maps to find your direction; ask a local if you're not certain. Yellow signs lead to transfers, and green signs lead to exits *(Sortie).*

Tickets: You can transfer between Métro, tram, and bus lines with the same ticket (valid one hour) and can do round-trips, but you must revalidate your ticket whenever boarding (€1.80/1 hour, €3/2 hours, €5.50/1 day, €16.20/10 rides, all tickets cover funicular). The **one-day ticket** is a great deal (even if you only use the funicular and visit one of the outlying museums—Resistance Center or Lumière Museum) and a great time-saver, as you only have to buy a ticket once. Also remember that the Lyon City Card (described earlier, under "Tourist Information") covers transit.

To use the ticket machines, change the display language to English. Then use the black roller to *selectionner* your ticket, firmly push the top button twice to *confirmer* your request, and then insert coins (no bills, US credit cards won't work). In the Métro, insert your ticket in the turnstile, then reclaim it.

For a short cruise on the Saône River with nice views of Vieux

Lyon at a Glance

▲▲**Roman Theaters and Gallo-Roman Museum** Fine museum covering Roman Lyon. **Hours:** Museum—Tue-Sun 10:00-18:00, closed Mon; theaters—daily until 19:00, May-Sept until 21:00 except during Les Nuits de Fourvière festival in early June-early Aug, when they can close as early as 17:00. See page 906.

▲▲**Vieux Lyon** The city's fascinating traffic-free historic core, with intriguing covered *traboules* (passageways). **Hours:** Passageways usually open daily 8:00-19:30. See page 908.

▲**Notre-Dame Basilica** Lyon's ornate version of Paris' Sacré-Cœur. **Hours:** Daily 7:00-19:00; Mass usually at 7:30, 9:30, 11:00, and 17:00. See page 904.

▲**Museum of Fine Arts** One of France's most important fine-arts museums. **Hours:** Wed-Mon 10:00-18:00, Fri from 10:30, closed Tue. See page 913.

▲**Resistance and Deportation History Center** Displays and videos telling the inspirational story of the French Resistance. **Hours:** Wed-Sun 10:00-18:00, closed Mon-Tue. See page 915.

▲**Lumière Museum** A museum of film, dedicated to the Lumière brothers' pivotal contribution. **Hours:** Tue-Sun 10:00-18:30, closed Mon. See page 916.

Lyon, hop aboard *Le Vaporetto*. This shuttle boat makes a 30-minute trip between Vieux Lyon and the Confluence shopping mall, with a stop at Pont Bonaparte bridge along the way (€2 one-way, daily 10:00-21:00 except no service mid-Dec-Feb, leaves from the Pont de la Feuillée bridge in Vieux Lyon on the hour and departs from the Confluence mall on the half-hour (last departure 20:30). For stops, see map on page 898.

You can also use handy, city-owned **Vélo'v Bikes** for transportation. Buy a day ticket (€1.50, from machine using only a true chip-and-PIN credit card or online with any credit card; see www.velov.grandlyon.com), pick the bike up at one location, and leave it at another. The first 30 minutes are free, then the cost rises quickly to encourage short-term use. There are discounted rates with a Lyon City Card.

St. Jean Cathedral Gothic church with 700-year-old astronomical clock and lovely stained-glass windows. **Hours:** Mon-Fri 8:15-19:45, Sat-Sun until 19:00. See page 908.

Gadagne Museums Two museums bringing to life Lyon's glory days and the tradition of Guignol puppets, housed in gorgeous Renaissance building. **Hours:** Wed-Sun 11:00-18:30, closed Mon-Tue. See page 911.

Atelier de la Soierie Workshop demonstrating handmade silk printing and screen painting. **Hours:** Mon-Fri 9:30-13:00 & 14:00-18:30, Sat 9:00-13:00 & 14:00-18:00, closed Sun. See page 912.

La Croix-Rousse Fun, avant-garde, historic neighborhood with great morning produce market and vertical pedestrian lanes. **Hours:** Market open Tue-Sun until 12:30; lanes always strollable. See page 914.

Museums of Textiles and Decorative Arts Pair of museums, one tracing the development of textile weaving over 2,000 years, the other featuring 18th-century decor in a mansion. **Hours:** Tue-Sun 10:00-17:30, closed Mon. See page 913.

The Confluence Neighborhood Cutting-edge, modern urban development featuring dazzling architecture, cafés, bars, shopping, a museum, and public spaces. **Hours:** Best visited from midday to early evening. See page 917.

Bonaparte Bridge Spin-Tour

This central bridge (Pont Bonaparte), just a block from Place Bellecour, is made to order for a day-or-night self-guided spin-tour.

• *Stand on the bridge and face the golden statue of the Virgin Mary marking the Notre-Dame Basilica on Fourvière Hill. (It's actually capping the smaller chapel, which predates the church by 500 years.) The basilica is named for the Roman Forum (fourvière) upon which it sits. Now begin to look clockwise.*

The Metallic Tower (called La Tour Métallique—not La Tour Eiffel), like the basilica, was finished just before World War I. It was originally an observation tower but today functions only as a TV tower. The husky, twin-towered church on the riverbank below (St. Jean Cathedral) marks the center of the old town. A block upstream, the Neoclassical columns are part of the Court of Justice (where Klaus Barbie, head of the local Gestapo—a.k.a. "the Butcher of Lyon"—was sentenced to life in prison). Way upstream, the hill covered with tall, pastel-colored houses is the La Croix-Rousse district, former home of the city's huge silk industry. With the invention of the Jacquard looms, which required 12-foot-tall ceilings, new factory buildings were needed and the new weaving center grew up on this hill. In 1850, it was churning with 30,000 looms.

You are standing over the Saône River, which, along with the Rhône, makes up Lyon's duo of power rivers. The Saône drains the southern area of the Vosges Mountains in Alsace and runs for about 300 miles before joining the Rhône (barely south of here), which flows to the Mediterranean. The Place Bellecour side of the river (behind you) is the district of Presqu'île. This strip of land is sandwiched by the two rivers and is home to Lyon's Opera House, City Hall, theater, top-end shopping, banks, and all of my recommended hotels. A morning market sets up daily under the trees (upriver, just beyond the red bridge). The simple riverfront cafés *(buvettes)* are ideal for a drink with a view (best at night).

Speaking of bridges, all of Lyon's bridges—including the one you're standing on—were destroyed by the Nazis as they checked out in 1944. Looking downstream, the stately mansions of Lyon's well-established families line the left side of the river. Across the river, still downstream, the Neo-Gothic St. Georges Church marks the neighborhood of the first silk weavers. The ridge behind St. Georges is dominated by a big building—once a seminary for priests, now a state high school—and leads us back to Mary.

• *Walk across the bridge and continue two blocks to find the funicular station and ride up Fourvière Hill to the basilica (catch the train marked* Fourvière, *not* St. Just*). Sit up front and admire the funicular's funky old technology (€2.80 round-trip, Métro/tram tickets valid). Or you can skip Fourvière Hill and go directly into the old town* (Vieux Lyon) *by turning right at* **St. Jean Cathedral.**

Sights in Lyon

FOURVIERE HILL

On Fourvière Hill, you can tour the basilica, enjoy a panoramic city view, and visit the Roman Theaters and Gallo-Roman Museum, then catch another funicular back down and explore the old town. I've listed key sights below according to this route.

▲Notre-Dame Basilica
(Basilique Notre-Dame de Fourvière)

This ornate, gleaming church fills your view as you exit the funicular. In about the year 1870, the bishop of Lyon vowed to build a worthy tribute to the Virgin Mary if the Prussians spared his city. They did, so construction started in earnest, with more than 2,000

workers on site (similar deal-making led to the construction of the basilica of Sacré-Cœur in Paris). Building began in 1872, and the church was ready for worship by World War I.

Cost and Hours: Free, daily 7:00-19:00; Mass usually at 7:30, 9:30, 11:00, and 17:00.

Visiting the Basilica: Before entering, view the fancy facade, the older chapel on the right (supporting the statue of Mary), and the top of the Eiffel-like TV tower on the left.

Climb the steps and enter. You won't find a more Mary-centered church. Everything—floor, walls, ceiling—is covered with elaborate mosaics. Scenes glittering on the walls tell stories of the Virgin (in Church history on the left, and in French history on the right). Amble down the center aisle at an escargot's pace and examine some of these scenes:

First scene on the left: In 431, the Council of Ephesus declared Mary to be the "Mother of God."

Across the nave, first on the right: The artist imagines Lugdunum (Lyon)—the biggest city in Roman Gaul, with 50,000 inhabitants—as the first Christian missionaries arrive. The first Christian martyrs in France (killed in A.D. 177) dance across heaven with palm branches.

Next left: In 1571, at the pivotal sea battle of Lepanto, Mary provides the necessary miracle as the outnumbered Christian forces beat the Ottomans.

Next right (view from right to left): Joan of Arc hears messages from Mary, rallies the French against the English at the Siege of Orléans in 1429 (find the Orléans coat of arms above and the timid French King Charles VII—whom Joan inspired to take a stand and fight the English—on his horse in the center), and is ultimately burned at the stake in Rouen at age 19 (1431).

Back across the nave on the left: In 1854, Pope Pius I proclaims the dogma of the Immaculate Conception in St. Peter's Square (establishing the belief among Catholics that Mary was conceived without the "Original Sin" of apple-eating Adam and Eve). To the left of the Pope, angels carry the tower of Fourvière Church; to the right is the image of the Virgin of Lourdes (who miraculously appeared in 1858).

Finally, on the right: Dashing Louis XIII offers the crown of France to the Virgin Mary. (The empty cradle hints that while he had her on the line, he asked, "Could I please have a son?" Louis

LYON

XIV was born shortly thereafter.) Above marches a parade of pious French kings and emperors, from Clovis and Charlemagne to Napoleon (on the far right—with the white cross and red coat). Below are the great Marian churches of France (left to right)—Chartres, Paris' Sacré-Cœur and Notre-Dame, Reims (where most royalty was crowned), and this church. These six scenes in mosaic all lead to the altar where Mary reigns as Queen of Heaven.

Lower Church and Adjacent Chapel: Exit under Joan of Arc and descend to the lower church, dedicated to Mary's earthly husband, Joseph. Priorities here are painfully clear, as money ran out for Joseph's church. Today, it's used as a concert venue (notice the spongy-yellow acoustic material covering the vaulting). Return on the same stairs to the humble 16th-century chapel to the Virgin (push the door); outside, glance up to see the glorious statue of Mary that overlooks Lyon.

Nearby: Just around this chapel (past the church museum and the recommended Restaurant Panoramique) is a commanding **view** of Lyon. You can see parts of both rivers and north from the La Croix-Rousse district south to the Bonaparte Bridge, with greater Lyon spread out before you in the distance. The black barrel-vaulted structure to the left is the Opera House, and the rose-colored skyscraper in the distance is called, appropriately, "Le Crayon" (The Pencil). The skyline's latest addition and tallest building is the tower nicknamed "La Gomme" (The Eraser). The "pencil sharpener" is just down the Saône River in the new Confluence neighborhood (described later). The big green space along the river to the left, across from the La Croix-Rousse hill, is Lyon's massive park (La Tête d'Or). On a clear afternoon, you'll get a glimpse of Mont Blanc (the highest point in Europe, just left of the pencil-shaped skyscraper).

• *To get to the Roman Theaters and Gallo-Roman Museum, walk back to the funicular station and turn left down Rue Roger Radisson. The museum hides in the concrete bunker down the steps, where Rue Roger Radisson meets Rue Cléberg. Before entering, get the best overview of the site by taking a few steps left down Rue Cléberg and finding the ramp that leads to the museum's rooftop (open the gate).*

▲▲Roman Theaters and Gallo-Roman Museum (Musée Gallo-Romain)

Founded as Lugdunum in A.D. 43, Lyon was a critical transportation hub for the administration of Roman Gaul (and much of modern-day France—much like today). The city became the central metropolis of the Three Gauls—the integrated Roman provinces of Aquitania (Aquitaine), Belgica (Belgium), and Lugdunensis (Lyon region)—and Emperors Claudius and Caracalla were both born here (for more on the Romans, see "How About Them Romans?" on page 562).

This worthwhile museum—constructed in the hillside with views of the two Roman Theaters—makes clear Lyon's importance in Roman times. Visit the museum first, then tour the theaters.

Cost and Hours: Museum—€4 (includes good audioguide), €7.50 if special exhibits are on, free on Thu, open Tue-Sun 10:00-18:00, closed Mon; theaters—free, daily until 19:00, May-Sept until 21:00 except during Les Nuits de Fourvière festival early June-early Aug, when they can close as early as 17:00; 17 Rue Cléberg, tel. 04 72 38 49 30, www.museegalloromain.grandlyon.com.

➋ **Self-Guided Tour:** The route described below gives an overview of the museum's highlights, while the well-done audioguide, excellent posted English explanations, and helpful staff add as much substance to this museum as you can stomach.

The collection takes you on a chronological stroll down several floors through ancient Lyon. After a brief glimpse at prehistoric objects, dive into the Gallo-Roman rooms. The artifacts you'll see were found locally. The unusual remains of a bronze chariot date from the seventh century B.C.

Next, sit close to the interactive **model** of Lyon with its hills and rivers and listen on your audioguide to the history of Lugdunum while following its evolution on the model. It was a city of 50,000 in its second-century A.D. glory days. Gauls and Romans lived and worked side by side in Roman Lyon. Notice that an arena stood where the basilica does today, hanging on the cliff edge. You'll see the arena's ruins if you follow my walking route of today's La Croix-Rousse neighborhood.

Those curved stones you pass next were actual arena seats—inscribed with the names of big shots who sat there. Soon after, look for a big, black-bronze **tablet** placed up high. Carved into it is the transcription of a speech given by Emperor Claudius in A.D. 48—his (long-winded) account of how he integrated the Gauls into the empire by declaring them eligible to sit in the Roman Senate (also recorded: the interjections of senators begging him to get to the point already—see the English translation on the wall). A few steps farther is a stone Roman pump that looks like an engine block (read the explanation or follow on the TV screen to find out how it worked).

You'll soon come upon displays of Roman **coins and tools,** and models of a few key Roman buildings in Lyon. Past those you can see fragments of a second-century A.D. calendar. A bit farther along, behind the model of the big and small theaters (the originals are out the window), check out the mechanics of a Roman theater stage curtain, which was raised instead of lowered. Go ahead... push the button. The last section of the museum shows how Lyon's

LYON

wealthy merchants built large homes with interior courtyards often tiled with mosaics. Your visit ends with displays on Roman religious life and the onset of Christianity.

· *Exit the museum through the elevator and into the **Roman Theaters**.*

The closer **big theater** was built under the reign of Emperor Augustus and expanded by Hadrian—at its zenith, it held 10,000 spectators. Today it seats 3,000 for concerts. The **small theater,** an "odeon" (from the Greek "ode" for song), was acoustically designed for speeches and songs. The grounds are peppered with gravestones and sarcophagi. Find a seat in the big theater and read up on Roman theaters (see page 575).

From early June through early August, the theaters host **Les Nuits de Fourvière,** an open-air festival of concerts, theater, dance, and film. Check programs at the TI and purchase tickets here at the theaters (box office at gate exit toward the Minimes funicular station, Mon-Sat 11:00-18:00, closed Sun), or online at www. nuitsdefourviere.com.

· *The ancient road between the Roman Theaters leads down and out, where you'll find the Minimes funicular station (to the right as you leave). Take the funicular to Vieux Lyon (not St. Just), where it deposits you only a few steps from St. Jean Cathedral. Take some time to explore Vieux Lyon. Or, from the Vieux Lyon funicular stop, you can take Métro line D directly to the Lumière Museum or (with an easy transfer) to the Resistance and Deportation History Center (both described later).*

VIEUX LYON (OLD LYON)
St. Jean Cathedral

Stand back in the square for the best view of the cathedral (brilliant at night and worth returning for). This mostly Gothic cathedral took 200 years to build. It doesn't soar as high as its northern French counterparts; influenced by their Italian neighbors, churches in southern France aren't nearly as vertical as their sisters to the north. This cathedral, the seat of the "primate of the Gauls" (as Lyon's bishop is officially titled), serves what's considered the oldest Christian city in France. Its interior houses some beautiful 13th- and 14th-

century stained glass above the altar and adorning each transept (look for descriptions of the windows in English, near the altar).

Under the north transept is a medieval astronomical clock (1383); it has survived wars of all kinds, including the French Revolution. Amazingly, its 700-year-old mechanism can compute Catholic holidays, including those that change each year, such as Easter, until 2019 (demonstrations at 12:00, 14:00, 15:00, and 16:00).

Cost and Hours: Free, Mon-Fri 8:15-19:45, Sat-Sun until 19:00.

Nearby: Outside (make two right turns as you leave) are the ruins of a mostly 11th-century church, destroyed during the French Revolution (the cathedral was turned into a "temple of reason"). What's left of a baptistery from an early Christian church (c. A.D. 400) is under glass.

▲▲The Heart of Vieux Lyon

Vieux ("Old") Lyon offers the best concentration of well-preserved Renaissance buildings in the country. The city grew rich from its trade fairs and banking, and was the center of Europe's silk industry from the 16th to 19th centuries. The most prominent vestiges of Lyon's Golden Age are the elegant pastel buildings of the old center, which were inspired by Italy and financed by the silk industry. Busy Rue St. Jean, leading north from the cathedral to Place du Change, is the main drag. It's flanked by parallel pedestrian streets (Rue Juiverie and Rue du Bœuf are quieter and more appealing) and punctuated with picturesque squares and courtyards—the best example of an Italian courtyard can be found north of Place du Change at 8 Rue Juiverie. The pedestrian-friendly lanes of Vieux Lyon were made for ambling, window-shopping, and café lingering.

• Stroll along Rue St. Jean and take a short detour by making a left up Rue de la Bombarde to the colorful courtyard of...

La Basoche: This beautifully restored Renaissance building gives you a good idea of what hides behind many facades in Vieux Lyon—and a whiff of Lyon's Golden Age. (At the time, the building served as a kind of legal center.) Check out the black-and-white photos that show this structure before its 1968 renovation, and imagine most of Vieux Lyon in this state.

• Back on Rue St. Jean, *A La Marquise* pastry shop sells Lyon's dessert specialty: la tarte à la praline, *an almond and cream treat that's as sweet as it is pink. This is my favorite place to sample it (closed Mon). You are now filled with energy to push open the heavy doors leading to Lyon's...*

Traboules: The old city's serpentine *traboules* (passageways) worked as shortcuts, linking the old town's three main north-south streets and providing important shelter from the elements when

Vieux Lyon

1. Daniel et Denise Rest.
2. Café Restaurant du Soleil
3. Les Lyonnais Rest.
4. Les Retrouvailles Restaurant
5. Les Adrets Rest.
6. Bistrot de St. Jean
7. Nardone René Glacier
8. James Joyce Pub
9. La Basoche Renaissance Building
10. A La Marquise Pastries
11. Courtyard Entrance at #8 Rue Juiverie
12. Courtyard Entrance at #28 Rue St. Jean
13. Traboule Entrance at #54 Rue St. Jean
14. Traboule Entrance at #27 Rue St. Jean
15. Walking Tour Meeting Point

LYON

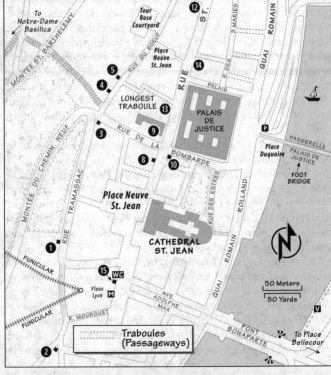

unfinished silk goods were being moved from one stage of production to the next. These hidden paths give visitors a hide-and-seek opportunity to discover pastel courtyards, lovely loggias, and delicate arches. Spiral staircases were often shared by several houses.

Several short *traboules* leading to courtyards are accessible (if a doorway is open, you can wander in—#28 Rue St. Jean is a good example). Just a few of Vieux Lyon's many *traboules* that connect different streets are open to the public. The longest *traboule* links #54 Rue St. Jean with #27 Rue du Bœuf; another, with gorgeous loggias, leads from #27 Rue St. Jean to #6 Rue de Trois Maries.

Traboules are generally accessible from 8:00 until 19:30. Press the button next to the street-front door to release the door when entering, push the lit buttons to illuminate dark walkways, and slide the door-handle levers when leaving. You're welcome to explore—but please be respectful of the residents, and don't go up any stairs.

While you wander Vieux Lyon, look for door plaques giving a history of each building and *traboule*. After walking through a *traboule*, you'll understand why Lyon's old town was an ideal center for the Resistance fighters to slip in and out of as they confounded the Nazis.

• *At the north end of Rue St. Jean is...*

Place du Change: This was the banking center of medieval Lyon. Its money scene developed after the city was allowed to host trade fairs in 1420. Its centerpiece is France's first stock exchange, La Loge (now a Reformed Church), which was completely renovated in the 18th century (creating a stark contrast to the Renaissance architecture around it).

• *From Place du Change, with your back to the river, head up Rue de la Loge and turn left on Rue de Gadagne to nearby Place du Petit Collège, where you can peek (for free) into the wonderfully restored courtyard of the...*

Gadagne Museums (Musées Gadagne)

This pair of museums covers two topics (both nicely described in English). The **Lyon History Museum** is overkill for most, taking you from the city's Roman period to the present day—and every era in between (the rooms devoted to its silk industry are interesting, showing looms and sample fabrics). The **Puppets of the World Museum** celebrates Guignol puppetry, the still-vibrant tradition first created in Lyon by an unemployed silk worker. Here you'll see examples of beautifully crafted Guignol puppets from around the world; the fun audioguide narrative may keep some kids engaged for a while. Don't leave the museum without enjoying *une pause* on the rooftop terrace café.

Cost and Hours: €6 for one museum, €9 for both, includes audioguide and English brochure, Wed-Sun 11:00-18:30, closed Mon-Tue, 1 Place du Petit Collège, tel. 04 78 42 03 61, www. gadagne.musees.lyon.fr.

• *A short block down Rue de la Fronde leads to a fun shop selling puppets (and housing its own puppet museum). A little north of here, ice-cream connoisseurs must stop at the recommended* **Nardone René Glacier** *(on river near Place du Change). From here it's a short walk to Place des Terreaux and the Museum of Fine Arts (cross Pont de la Feuillée and continue straight four blocks).*

PRESQU'ILE

This bit of land (French for "peninsula," and literally meaning "almost-an-island") between the two rivers is Lyon's shopping spine,

with thriving pedestrian streets (see map on page 922). The neighborhood's northern focal point is the...

Place des Terreaux

This grand square (undergoing some serious renovation) hosts the City Hall (Hôtel de Ville), the Museum of Fine Arts, and an action-packed fountain by Frédéric-Auguste Bartholdi (the French sculptor who designed the Statue of Liberty). The fountain features Marianne (the Lady of the Republic) riding a four-horse-powered chariot, symbolically leading Lyon's two great rivers to the sea. It was originally destined for the city of Bordeaux, which (ultimately) realized that it could not afford the price tag, so the sculptor shopped it at the 1889 World Expo in Paris. There, Lyon's mayor fell in love and had to have it. After Bartholdi modified it to fit Lyon's needs, the massive fountain was installed in 1891—and relocated in 1992 to its current location to accommodate access to a parking garage below the square (imagine moving this thing).

Atelier de Soierie

This silk workshop, just off Place des Terreaux on Rue Romarin (behind Café le Moulin Joli, a Resistance hangout during World War II), welcomes the public to drop in to see silk printing and screen painting by hand. Keep in mind that this is a lost art that today has mostly been replaced by machines. Within the shop, you'll see stretched silk canvases, buckets of dye, and artists in action. Friendly staff members speak some English and are happy to field questions while they work. Climb the staircase to visit a boutique selling handmade silk creations. Prices range from €25 to €250.

Cost and Hours: Free entry, Mon-Fri 9:30-13:00 & 14:00-

18:30, Sat 9:00-13:00 & 14:00-18:00, closed Sun, tel. 04 72 07 97 83.

▲Museum of Fine Arts (Musée des Beaux-Arts)

Located in a former abbey, which was secularized by Napoleon in 1803 and made into a public museum, this fine-arts museum has an impressive collection, ranging from Egyptian antiquities to Impressionist paintings. The inner courtyard is a pleasant place to take a peaceful break from city streets. The helpful museum map and free audioguide make touring it a pleasure. Plan your arrival carefully, as several key sections close for lunch. A bar/café with calming terrace seating is on the first floor, next to the bookstore.

Cost and Hours: €9, includes audioguide, Wed-Mon 10:00-18:00 except Fri, when it opens at 10:30, closed Tue, pick up museum map when you enter, picnic-perfect courtyard, 20 Place des Terreaux, Métro: Hôtel de Ville, tel. 04 72 10 17 40, www.mba-lyon.fr.

Visiting the Museum: After passing the ticket taker, walk up a short flight of stairs to the Chapel, a dreamy Orsay-like display of 19th- and 20th-century statues, including works by Auguste Rodin and Bartholdi. The next flight of steps leads to *Les Antiquités* (first floor on map), a fine collection of ancient (especially Egyptian) art, medieval art, and Art Nouveau (furniture). Be aware that the first floor is closed 12:00-14:00.

The second floor up displays a pretty selection of paintings from the last six centuries (no famous works, but a good Impressionist collection). You'll see Renaissance and Baroque paintings by Veronese, Cranach, Rubens, and Rembrandt, and "modern" works by Monet, Matisse, Pissarro, Gaugin, and Picasso. The highlight is a series of Pre-Raphaelite-type works called *Le Poème de l'Âme* ("The Poem of the Soul"), by Louis Janmot. This cycle of 18 paintings and 16 charcoal drawings traces the story of the souls of a boy and a girl as they journey through childhood, adolescence, and into adulthood. They struggle with fears and secular temptations before gaining spiritual enlightenment on the way to heaven. The boy loses his faith and enjoys a short but delicious hedonistic fling that leads to misery in hell. But a mother's prayers intercede, and he reunites with the girl to enjoy heavenly redemption.

Museums of Textiles and Decorative Arts (Musées des Tissus et des Arts Décoratifs)

These museums, between Place Bellecour and Perrache station, fill two buildings (sharing a courtyard and connected with an interior hallway). The **Museum of Textiles** was founded in the mid-1800s to "maintain the commercial advantage of Lyon's silk manufacturers by showing their discerning taste for the arrangements and color settings of original motifs." It holds the world's most valuable

LYON

collection of textiles, going back over 4,000 years and touching all corners of the world. The museum shows off some breathtaking silk work—you'll see tunics, shawls, dresses, coats, capes, and more from around the world and made from a variety of fabrics. There is zero, zilch, nada English information in this museum, nor is there any in the other one.

The **Museum of Decorative Arts** fills a luxurious mansion and is decorated to the hilt with 18th-century furniture, textiles, and tapestries in a plush domestic setting. Entire rooms from aristocratic Lyonnaise homes have been re-created, including an 18th-century kitchen. There's plenty of china and a dazzling display of designer teakettles and coffee servers.

Cost and Hours: €10, €8 after 16:00, covers both museums, Tue-Sun 10:00-17:30, closed Mon, 34 Rue de la Charité, Métro: Bellecour, tel. 04 78 38 42 00, www.mtmad.fr.

Shopping and Eating on the Presqu'île

There's more to this "almost-an-island" than the sights listed here. Join the river of shoppers on sprawling Rue de la République (north of Place Bellecour) and the teeming and less fancy Rue Victor Hugo pedestrian mall (south of Place Bellecour). Smart clothing boutiques line Rue Président Edouard Herriot. Peruse the *bouchons* (characteristic bistros—especially characteristic in the evening) of Rue Mercière.

Passage de l'Argue is an Old World, covered shopping passage from the 1800s that predates shopping malls (78 Rue Président Edouard Herriot).

Grand Café des Négociants is ideal for an indoor break. This *grand café,* which has been in business since 1864, feels like it hasn't changed since then, with its soft leather chairs, painted ceilings, and glass chandeliers (daily, 2 Place Francisque Régaud, near Cordeliers Métro stop, tel. 04 78 42 50 05).

La Croix-Rousse

Hilly, untouristy, and SoHo-esque, this neighborhood to the north of Presqu'île hummed with some 30,000 silk looms in the 1800s. Today this part of town is popular with Lyon's tie-dye types, drawn here by abandoned, airy apartment spaces (built in the age of the Jacquard loom, which required exceptionally high ceilings).

The smartest way to visit the district is to take the Métro to the top, then follow a series of scenic slopes and stairs back down (see map on page 898). On the 20-minute stroll from top to bottom, you'll pass bohemian cafés, art galleries, creative graffiti, and used-clothing shops on your way to the Presqu'île. (Or—to burn off last night's *Lyonnaise* feast—follow this suggested route in reverse.)

Begin by exiting Métro line C at the La Croix-Rousse stop. Every day except Monday, until about 12:30, a local produce market stretches across the square and down Boulevard de la Croix-Rousse (best on Sun). The statue at the center of the square is Monsieur Jacquard, inventor of the loom that powered Lyon's economy in the mid-1800s.

Start your downhill stroll from behind the Métro stop along Rue des Pierres Plantées. Pause to appreciate the views from the top of the Montée de la Grande Côte, and notice how the small concrete square may be used as a soccer field, a tricycle track, an outdoor café, and any other purpose the neighbors can find for it. Continue down the stairs, through the gardens along the Montée de la Grande Côte. Detour a block to the right on Rue des Tables Claudiennes for a view over the Roman Amphitheater of the Three Gauls. It's hard to imagine that this ruined arena was once the same size as the one in Arles, holding 20,000 spectators. Parts of the arena were destroyed in the 1800s for city development; serious excavation did not begin until the 1960s. Backpedal to the hill climb and continue your descent, working your way down to Place des Terreaux via Place des Capucins.

AWAY FROM THE CENTER
▲Resistance and Deportation History Center
(Centre d'Histoire de la Résistance et de la Déportation)
Located near Vichy (capital of the French puppet state) and neutral Switzerland, Lyon was the center of the French Resistance from 1942 to 1945. These "underground" Resistance heroes fought the Nazis tooth and nail. Bakers hid radios inside loaves of bread to secretly contact London. Barmaids passed along tips from tipsy Nazis. Communists in black berets cut telephone lines while printers countered Nazi propaganda with anonymous pamphlets. Farmers hid downed airmen in haystacks and housewives spread news from the front with their gossip. Without their bravery, the liberation of France would not have been possible.

Cost and Hours: €6, Wed-Sun 10:00-18:00, closed Mon-Tue, 14 Avenue Berthelot, tel. 04 78 72 23 11, www.chrd.lyon.fr.

Tours: Free tablets deliver a grand, short, or themed multimedia tour (numbers indicate rooms, letters indicate specific objects). For the best experience, use your own earbuds rather than the headset provided. Printed explanations are also available.

Getting There: The easiest way to reach the museum is to ride the Métro to Perrache station and transfer to the T2 tram (cross the tram tracks after exiting the Métro and board the T2 tram). You can also take Métro line B to Jean Macé, exit toward the elevated train line, and transfer to the T2 tram (going right). Get off the tram at Centre Berthelot.

Visiting the Museum: Though these days it's dedicated to the history of the Resistance, the center actually served as a Nazi tor-

LYON

ture chamber and Gestapo headquarters under Klaus Barbie (who was finally tried and convicted in 1987 here in Lyon after extradition from Bolivia). More than 11,000 people were killed or deported to concentration camps during his reign.

The museum gives visitors a thorough understanding of how Lyon became an important city in the Resistance, what life was like for its members, and the clever strategies they employed to fight the Germans. You'll also learn about the fate of the Jews in Lyon during the war. The museum uses interviews with people involved in the fight, reconstructed rooms, and numerous photos and exhibits to tell the inspiring story of the French Resistance.

▲Lumière Museum (Musée Lumière)

Antoine Lumière and his two sons, Louis and Auguste—the George Eastmans of France—ran a huge factory with 260 workers in the 1880s, producing four million glass photographic plates a day. Then, in 1895, they made the first *cinématographe,* or movie. In 1903, they pioneered the "autochrome" process of painting frames to make "color photos." This museum tells their story.

Cost and Hours: €6.50, Tue-Sun 10:00-18:30, closed Mon, essential audioguide-€3, tel. 04 78 78 18 95, www.institut-lumiere.org.

Getting There: Take Métro line D to the Monplaisir-Lumière stop. The museum is in the large mansion with the tiled roof on the square, kitty-corner from the Métro stop at 25 Rue du Premier-Film.

Visiting the Museum: The museum fills Villa Lumière, the family's belle époque mansion, built in 1902. Many interesting displays and the essential audioguide do a great job of explaining the history of filmmaking. After leaving this place, where the laborious yet fascinating process of creating moving images is driven home, you'll never again take the quality of today's movies for granted.

Before your visit, pick up the informative museum plan. The museum's highlights are the many antique cameras (ground floor) and the screens playing the earliest "movies." The first film reels held about 950 frames, which played at 19 per second, so these first movies were only 50 seconds long. About 1,500 Lumière films are catalogued between 1895 and 1907. The very first movie ever made features workers piling out of the Lumière factory at the end of a workday. People attended movies at first not for the plot or the action, but rather to be mesmerized by the technology that allowed them to see moving images. After their initial success, the Lumières sent cameramen to capture scenes from around the world, connecting diverse cultures and people in a way that had never been done before.

Upstairs, the museum features exhibits on still photography

and the Lumière living quarters (furnished c. 1900). One room has tablets where you can select movies to watch (notice that each movie is tagged with its "Catalog Lumière" number). The cinema features an hour-long selection of short movies with commentaries (English subtitles). Across the park from the mansion is a shrine of what's left of the warehouse where the first movie was actually shot. In a wonderful coincidence, *lumière* is the French word for "light."

The Confluence Neighborhood

At the southern tip of the Presqu'île, where the Rhône and Saône rivers converge, you'll experience France's cutting-edge, urban-design energy. Called **La Confluence,** this expansive urban renewal project (one of Europe's most ambitious) features futuristic offices, sustainable residential buildings, shopping, and vast public spaces in an area that only recently was a vast wasteland. When completed, the Confluence project will double the size of Lyon's historic center—that's right, double.

To get here, cruise down the Saône River on the shuttle boat *Le Vaporetto*, from either the northern end of Vieux Lyon or near Pont Bonaparte, to the Confluence shopping mall dock. Here you'll see the Confluence project's latest eye-catching showpiece, the **Place Nautique**—a snazzy pleasure-boat marina lined with restaurants, cafés, shops, and dazzling architecture.

From here it's a 15-minute walk along the river (not along the tram route) to the Presqu'île's southern end and the **Musée des Confluences** (a science and anthropology museum). As you follow the pedestrian walkway you'll pass revamped dock warehouses, wild-and-crazy office buildings, and restaurant barges. The Musée des Confluences is worth a gander—at least from the outside—for its daring design. Inside, the permanent collection recounts the great story of human existence from our origins to the present day (€9, Tue-Fri 11:00-19:00, Thu until 22:00, Sat-Sun 10:00-19:00, closed Mon, 86 Quai Perrache, tel. 04 28 38 11 90, www.museedesconfluences.fr).

To return, catch the T1 tram (in front of museum, direction: Feyssine) back to the Confluence mall and board *Le Vaporetto* to Vieux Lyon, or continue on T1 to the Perrache stop where you can connect to the Métro and other tram lines (see map on page 898).

Nightlife in Lyon

Lyon has France's second-largest cultural budget after Paris, so there are always plenty of theatrical productions and concerts to attend (in French, of course). The TI has the latest information and schedules. From mid-June through mid-September, the terrace-café at the Opera House hosts an outdoor jazz café with free concerts (usually Mon-Sat, www.opera-lyon.com).

After dinner, stroll through Lyon to savor the city's famous illuminations (see sidebar on page 900).

For lively bar and people-watching scenes in Presqu'île, prowl Rue de la Monnaie (angles off "restaurant row" Rue Mercière to the south) and the streets between Place des Terreaux and the Opera House. The **James Joyce** Irish pub, in the heart of Vieux Lyon, is a cozy English-speaking place (daily, 68 Rue St. Jean, tel. 04 78 37 84 28).

Sleeping in Lyon

Hotels in Lyon are a steal compared with those in Paris. Weekends are generally discounted (Sundays in particular) in this city that lives off business travelers. Prices rise and rooms disappear when trade fairs are in town, so it's smart to reserve your room in advance. If you have trouble, the TI can help for free in person or by email (resa@lyon-france.com). All of my listings are on the Presqu'île except for the youth hostel. Hotels have air-conditioning—a godsend when it's hot (hottest June-mid-Sept)—and elevators unless otherwise noted. Expect to push buttons to gain access to many hotels.

ON OR NEAR PLACE DES CELESTINS

Book ahead to sleep in this classy yet unpretentious neighborhood (Métro: Bellecour). Just a block off the central Place Bellecour and a block to the Saône River, this area gives travelers easy access to Lyon's sights. Join shoppers perusing the upscale boutiques, or watch children playing in the small square fronting the Théâtre des Célestins. Warning: Weekend nights can be noisy if you score a room facing Place des Célestins.

$$$$ Hôtel Globe et Cecil** is the most professional and elegant of my listings, with refined comfort on a refined street and a service-oriented staff. Its rooms are tastefully decorated and mostly spacious (good breakfast, 21 Rue Gasparin, tel. 04 78 42 58 95, www.globeetcecilhotel.com, accueil@globeetcecilhotel.com).

$$ Hôtel des Artistes,** ideally located on Place des Célestins, is a comfortable, business-class hotel that offers a fair value on weekdays and a good value on weekends (standard rooms are comfortable but tight, 8 Rue Gaspard-André, tel. 04 78 42 04 88, www.hotel-des-artistes.fr, reservation@hotel-des-artistes.fr).

$$ Hôtel des Célestins**,** just off Place des Célestins, is warmly run by Cornell-grad Laurent. Its cheery rooms aren't cheap but are filled with thoughtful touches. Streetside rooms have more light and are bigger (beautiful suites ideal for families or those in need of room to roam, completely non-smoking, laundry service,

Sleep Code

Hotels are classified based on the average price of a standard double room without breakfast in high season.

$$$$	**Splurge:** Most rooms over €200
$$$	**Pricier:** €150-200
$$	**Moderate:** €100-150
$	**Budget:** €50-100
¢	**Backpacker:** Under €50
RS%	**Rick Steves discount**
*	**French hotel rating system** (0-5 stars)

Unless otherwise noted, credit cards are accepted, hotel staff speak basic English, and free Wi-Fi is available. Comparison-shop by checking prices at several hotels (on each hotel's own website, on a booking site, or by email). For the best deal, *book directly with the hotel.* Ask for a discount if paying in cash; if the listing includes **RS%**, request a Rick Steves discount.

4 Rue des Archers, tel. 04 72 56 08 98, www.hotelcelestins.com, info@hotelcelestins.com).

$ Elysée Hôtel,** a few blocks off Place des Célestins, is a simple little hotel with excellent rates and two-star comfort. Gentle Monsieur Larrive is your host (elevator from first floor up, 92 Rue Président Edouard Herriot, tel. 04 78 42 03 15, www.hotel-elysee.fr, accueil@hotel-elysee.fr).

$ Hôtel du Théâtre** has no air-conditioning and requires stamina to reach the lobby, as it's 40 steps from street level. But the hotel is well-located on Place des Célestins and offers a solid deal. Owners Monsieur and Madame Kuhn run a tight ship, most of the rooms and bathrooms are spacious, and the beds are firm (no elevator, 10 Rue de Savoie, enter from hotel's rear, tel. 04 78 42 33 32, www.hotel-du-theatre.fr, contact@hotel-du-theatre.fr).

OTHER PLACES ON THE PRESQU'ILE

$ Le Boulevardier,** a great budget option located a few blocks south of Place des Terreaux, has 14 rooms situated above a jazz café. The well-priced rooms are full of charm, some with stone walls, antique furniture, and toys; others have sweet church views (larger rooms worth the extra euros, no air-con but fans, 5 Rue de la Fromagerie, tel. 04 78 28 48 22, www.leboulevardier.fr, hotelboulevardier@gmail.com).

$ Hôtel la Résidence,*** south of Place Bellecour and my closest listing to Perrache station, has 67 plain but good-value rooms. Most are spacious and have high ceilings and bathtub-showers (family rooms, reserve ahead for nearby pay parking, 18

Victor Hugo, tel. 04 78 42 63 28, www.hotel-la-residence.com, hotel-la-residence@wanadoo.fr).

ELSEWHERE IN LYON

Hostel: ¢ **Vieux Lyon Youth Hostel** is impressively situated—it's only a 10-minute walk above Vieux Lyon. Open daily (except 13:00-14:00 & 20:00-21:00), it has a lively common area with kitchen access and a snack bar (includes breakfast, small safes available, 45 Montée du Chemin Neuf, Métro: Vieux Lyon, tel. 04 78 15 05 50, www.hihostels.com, lyon@hifrance.org). Book only through website. Take the funicular to Minimes, exit the station and make a left U-turn, and follow the station wall downhill to Montée du Chemin Neuf.

Eating in Lyon

Dining is a ▲▲▲ attraction in Lyon and comes at a bearable price. Half the fun is joining the procession of window shoppers mulling over where they'll *dîner ce soir.* In the evening, the city's population seems to double as locals emerge to stretch their stomachs. The tried-and-true *salade lyonnaise* (usually filling) followed by *quenelles* is one of my favorite one-two punches in France. You won't want dessert.

Lyon's characteristic *bouchons* are small bistros that evolved from the days when Mama would feed the silk workers after a long day. True *bouchons* are simple places with limited selection and seating (just like Mama's), serving only traditional fare and special 46-centiliter *pot* (pronounced "poh") wine pitchers. The lively pedestrian streets of Vieux Lyon and Rue Mercière on the Presqu'île are *bouchon* bazaars, worth strolling even if you dine elsewhere. Though food quality may be better away from these popular restaurant rows, you can't beat the atmosphere. Many of Lyon's restaurants close on Sunday and Monday and during August, except along Rue Mercière. If you plan to dine somewhere special, reserve ahead (ask your hotelier for help), and if you do reserve, don't expect to be asked for an arrival time—the table is yours all evening.

IN OR NEAR VIEUX LYON

Come to Vieux Lyon for an ideal blend of ambience and quality (if you choose carefully). For the epicenter of restaurant activity, go to Place Neuve St. Jean, and survey the scene and menus before sitting down. All of these places are located on the map on page 910.

Restaurant Price Code

I've assigned each eatery a price category, based on the average cost of a typical main course. Drinks, desserts, and splurge items (steak and seafood) can raise the price considerably.

$$$$	**Splurge:** Most main courses over €25
$$$	**Pricier:** €20-25
$$	**Moderate:** €15-20
$	**Budget:** Under €15

In France, a crêpe stand or other takeout spot is **$**; a sit-down brasserie, café, or bistro with affordable *plats du jour* is **$$**; a casual but more upscale restaurant is **$$$**; and a swanky splurge is **$$$$**.

$$$ Daniel et Denise is worth booking ahead. Reputed chef Joseph Viola has created a buzz by providing wonderful cuisine at affordable prices in a classic *bouchon* setting (*menus* from €33, indoor seating only, closed Sun-Mon, 36 Rue Tramassac, tel. 04 78 42 24 62, www.danieletdenise.fr).

$$ Café Restaurant du Soleil serves Lyon's tastiest *quenelles*, offering five different types, including the traditional *brochet* (pike), scallops (my favorite), and original varieties made with wild garlic (indoor and good outdoor seating, no lunch/Sun-Mon, 2 Rue Saint Georges, tel. 04 78 37 60 02).

$$ Les Lyonnais is barely a block off the Rue du Bœuf action, making it a bit quieter. Its lighthearted interior has rich colors, wood tables, and a photo gallery of loyal customers. Sincere Stéphane runs the place with grace, offering a good €25 *menu* with *salade lyonnaise* and *quenelles*, or fine and filling €14 salads (closed Mon, small terrace, 1 Rue Tramassac, tel. 04 78 37 64 82, http://restaurant-lyonnais.com).

$$$ Les Retrouvailles serves tasty, less traditional Lyonnaise cuisine in a charming setting under wood-beam ceilings with an open kitchen. Tables are grouped around a central buffet displaying delectable desserts that inspire diners to eat their vegetables. Here your dining experience is carefully managed by adorable owners Pierre *(le chef)* and Odile (*menus* from €27, indoor dining only, dinner only, closed Sun evening, 38 Rue du Bœuf, tel. 04 78 42 68 84).

$$$ Les Adrets is where *bouchon* meets beer hall. This linear, heavy-beamed place, lined with velvet booths and cheery lights, is crammed with a lively crowd enjoying good-value Lyonnaise cuisine (*menus* from €27, indoor dining only, closed Sat-Sun and Aug, reservations recommended, 30 Rue du Bœuf, tel. 04 78 38 24 30).

$$$ Restaurant Panoramique de Fourvière, atop Fourvière Hill with a spectacular view overlooking Lyon, serves fine traditional cuisine in a superb setting. Choose from the modern interior

Vieux Lyon & Presqu'île

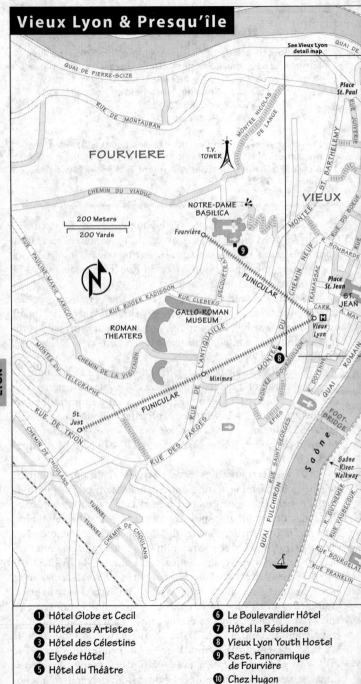

See Vieux Lyon detail map

QUAI DE PIERRE-SCIZE

RUE DE MONTAUBAN

FOURVIERE

MONTÉE NICOLAS DE LANGE

T.V. TOWER

CHEMIN DU VIADUC

200 Meters
200 Yards

NOTRE-DAME BASILICA

Fourvière

Place St. Paul

VIEUX

RUE DU BOEUF

RUE BOMBARDE

CHEMIN NEUF

FUNICULAR

Place St. Jean

ST. JEAN
A. MAX

RUE PAULINE-MARIE JARICOT

RUE ROGER RADISSON

RUE CLEBERG

GALLO-ROMAN MUSEUM

ROMAN THEATERS

CHEMIN DE LA VISTATION

MONTÉE DU TELEGRAPHE

FUNICULAR

Minimes

Vieux Lyon

MONTÉE DE L'ANTIQUAILLE

MONTÉE DU CHOULANS

St. Just

RUE DE TRION

RUE DES FARGES

RUE SAINT-GEORGES

RUE DOYENNE

QUAI ROMAIN

FOOT-BRIDGE

Saône

Saône River Walkway

CHEMIN DE CHOULANS

TUNNEL

TUNNEL

CHEMIN DE CHOULANS

QUAI FULCHRON

R. GUYNEMER

R. VAUBECOUR

RUE BOURGELAT

RUE FRANKLIN

- ❶ Hôtel Globe et Cecil
- ❷ Hôtel des Artistes
- ❸ Hôtel des Célestins
- ❹ Elysée Hôtel
- ❺ Hôtel du Théâtre
- ❻ Le Boulevardier Hôtel
- ❼ Hôtel la Résidence
- ❽ Vieux Lyon Youth Hostel
- ❾ Rest. Panoramique de Fourvière
- ❿ Chez Hugon

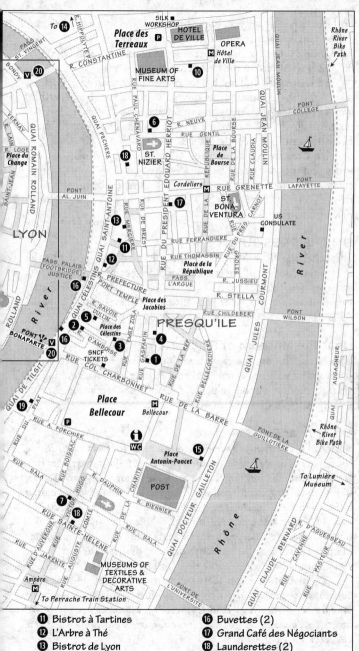

11	Bistrot à Tartines	**16**	Buvettes (2)
12	L'Arbre à Thé	**17**	Grand Café des Négociants
13	Bistrot de Lyon	**18**	Launderettes (2)
14	To Archange Restaurant	**19**	Bookstore & Wi-Fi
15	Brasserie le Sud	**20**	Le Vaporetto Boat Stop (2)

or the better, leafy terrace, both with views. Reserve well ahead for a view table (*menus* from €30, daily until 22:00, 9 Place de Fourvière, near Notre-Dame Basilica—see map on page 922, tel. 04 78 25 21 15, www.restaurant-fourviere.fr).

$$ Bistrot de St. Jean is a time-warp place with an old-school owner and cheap lunch prices serving basic cuisine. It's cheerfully located on a leafy square with fun seating outside. Bring Gérald a pin to add to his collection (closed Sun evening and all day Mon, 3 Place du Petit Collège, tel. 04 78 37 15 81).

Ice Cream: Nardone René Glacier, with pleasant outdoor seating on the river near Place du Change, serves up Lyon's best ice cream, made fresh daily next door. Ask Armelle about her peanut ice cream (May-Sept daily 8:30-24:00, off-season 9:00-20:00, 3 Place Ennemond Fousseret).

ON THE PRESQU'ILE

The pedestrian Rue Mercière is the epicenter of *bouchons* on the Presqu'île. Along this street, an entertaining cancan of restaurants stretches four blocks from Place des Jacobins to Rue Grenette. Enjoy surveying the scene and choose whichever eatery appeals. All of these restaurants appear on the map on page 922.

Near the Museum of Fine Arts

$$$ Chez Hugon is a cozy, traditional *bouchon* tucked in a tiny street where well-respected local chef Arlette has been cooking for years. She offers a good-value €27 *menu* (closed weekends, 12 Rue Pizay, tel. 04 78 28 10 94).

On or near Rue Mercière

$ Bistrot à Tartines is a young and fun place for tasty *tartines* (big slice of bread topped with goodies) offered at unbeatable prices by a friendly staff. The interior, which feels like an antique general store, has good seating inside and out. Food is served all day, including killer €4 desserts (daily, 2 Rue de la Monnaie, tel. 04 78 37 70 85).

$ L'Arbre à Thé provides a break in this meat-loving city, with light quiches, salads, and great desserts. This cute and quaint tea salon is convenient for an early lunch or dinner (Tue-Sat 11:30-19:00, closed Sun-Mon, 4 Rue du Petit David, tel. 04 72 40 06 68).

$$ Bistrot de Lyon feels *très* touristy but still bustles with authentic Lyonnaise atmosphere and reliable cuisine. It must be famed chef-owner Jean-Paul Lacombe's least expensive establishment (€22 *quenelles*, €13 *salade lyonnaise*, open daily, 64 Rue Mercière, tel. 04 78 38 47 47).

Refined Dining

$$$ Archange is a softly lit, white-tablecloth place accommodating 26 happy diners, all eager to sample the popular chef's creations that infuse a hint of Asian influence with refined French cuisine. Ask your hotelier to book your table ahead (dinner only, closed Mon, near Place des Terreaux at 6 Rue Hippolyte Flandrin, tel. 04 78 28 32 26, www.archangecafe.com).

$$$$ Brasserie le Sud is one of four places in Lyon where you can sample legendary chef Paul Bocuse's cuisine at affordable prices. His brasseries feature international cuisine from different corners of the world (each named for the corner it represents—north, south, east, and west). Le Sud is the most accessible, with a Mediterranean feel inside and out, but less easygoing service than you'll find at my other recommended restaurants (higher prices on Sun, reasonably priced *plats*, daily, reservations recommended, 11 Place Antonin-Poncet, a few blocks off Place Bellecour, tel. 04 72 77 80 00, www.nordsudbrasseries.com).

Lyon Connections

After Paris, Lyon is France's most important rail hub. Train travelers find this gateway to the Alps, Provence, the Riviera, and Burgundy an easy stopover. And now the Eurostar connects Lyon with London in a little over five hours.

Two main train stations serve Lyon: Part-Dieu and Perrache. Most trains officially depart from Part-Dieu, though many also stop at Perrache, and trains run between the stations (service can be infrequent). Double-check which station your train departs from.

From Lyon by Train to: Paris (at least hourly, 2 hours), **Annecy** (10/day, 2 hours, some by bus), **Chamonix** (6/day, 4 hours, most change at St-Gervais), **Strasbourg** (7/day, 4 hours), **Dijon** (hourly, 2 hours), **Beaune** (at least hourly, 2 hours), **Avignon** (22/day; 12 to TGV Station in 70 minutes, 10 to center station in 2 hours), **Arles** (14/day, 2.5-3.5 hours, most change in Avignon, Marseille, or Nîmes), **Nice** (6/day, 4.5 hours), **Carcassonne** (4/day, 4 hours), **Venice** (2/day, 9 hours, change in Turin), **Rome** (3/day, 9.5 hours, change in Milan or Turin), **Florence** (4/day, 8-12 hours), **Geneva** (8/day, 2 hours), **Barcelona** (1/day direct, 5 hours, more with change in Perpignan, Narbonne, or Valence), **London** (1/day "direct" but border check at Lille, 5.5 hours on Eurostar, more with easy change in Lille).

Near Lyon: The Rhône Valley

The Rhône Valley is the narrow part of the hourglass that links the areas of Provence and Burgundy. The region is bordered to the west by the soft hills of the Massif Central, and with the rolling foothills of the Alps just to the east, it's the gateway to the high Alps (the region is called Rhône-Alpes). The mighty Rhône River rumbles through the valley from its origin in the Swiss Alps to its outlet 500 miles away in the Mediterranean near Arles.

Vineyards blanket the western side of the Rhône Valley, from those of the Beaujolais just north of Lyon to the steep slopes of Tain-Hermitage below Lyon. On the eastern side of the river and closer to Avignon are the vineyards of the famous Côtes du Rhône.

The Rhône Valley has always provided the path of least resistance for access from the Mediterranean to northern Europe, and today, Roman ruins litter the valley between Lyon and Orange.

BEAUJOLAIS WINE ROUTE

Between Mâcon (near Cluny) and Lyon, the Beaujolais region makes for an appealing detour, thanks to its beautiful vineyards and villages and easygoing wine tasting (for more on Beaujolais wines, see page 894).

The Beaujolais wine road starts 45 minutes north of Lyon and runs from Villefranche-sur-Saône to Mâcon. The *Route du Beaujolais* winds up, down, and around the hills just west of the A-6 autoroute and passes through Beaujolais' most important villages: Chiroubles, Fleurie, Chénas, and Juliénas. Look for *Route du Beaujolais* signs, and expect to get lost more than a few times (Lyon's TI has a route map, and you can check there for more information).

Along the wine route, you'll pass Moulin à Vent's famous vineyards and see its trademark windmill. You'll enter the Mâconnais wine region and pass signs to the famous villages of Pouilly and Fuissé as you near Mâcon. Trains running between Lyon and Mâcon stop at several wine villages, including Romanèche-Thorins (described next; 6 trains/day from Lyon). While Villefranche-sur-Saône may be the Beaujolais capital, it's a big, unappealing city that's best avoided. Focus your time on the small villages, and look for *dégustation* (tasting) signs.

For a high-priced but thorough introduction to this region's wines, visit **Le Hameau Dubœuf** in Romanèche-Thorins. The king of Beaujolais, Georges Dubœuf, has constructed a Disney-esque introduction to wine at his museum, which immerses you in the life of a winemaker and features impressive models, exhibits, films, and videos. You'll be escorted from the beginning of the vine to present-day winemaking, with a focus on Beaujolais wines. It also has a lovely garden with fragrant flowers, fruits, herbs, and spices that represent the rich aromas present in wine (€19, keep receipt for discount if you intend to visit the Abbey of Cluny—see page 888, includes a small tasting, free English headphones and a *petit train* ride, plan to spend half a day, daily 10:00-18:00; in Romanèche-Thorins, follow signs labeled *Le Hameau Dubœuf* from D-306, then *La Gare* signs, and look for the old train-station-turned-winery; tel. 03 85 35 22 22, www.hameauduboeuf.com).

ALSACE

Colmar • Route du Vin • Strasbourg

The province of Alsace stands like a flower-child referee between Germany and France. Bounded by the Rhine River on the east and the Vosges Mountains on the west, this is a green region of Hansel-and-Gretel villages, ambitious vineyards, and vibrant cities. Food and wine are the primary industry, topic of conversation, and perfect excuse for countless festivals.

Alsace has changed hands between Germany and France several times because of its location, natural wealth, naked vulnerability—and the fact that Germany considered the mountains the natural border, while the French saw the Rhine as the dividing line.

On a grander scale, Alsace is Europe's cultural divide, with Germanic nations to the north and Romantic ones to the south. The region is a fault line marking the place where cultural tectonic plates collide—it's no wonder the region has been scarred by a history of war.

Through the Middle Ages, Alsace was part of the Holy Roman Empire when German culture and language ruled. After the devastation of the Thirty Years' War (1618-1648), Alsace started to become integrated into France—revolutionaries took full control in 1792. But in 1871, after France's defeat in the Franco-Prussian War, Alsace "returned" to Germany. Almost five decades later, Germany lost World War I—and Alsace "returned" to France. Except for a miserable stint as part of the Nazi realm from 1940 to 1945, Alsace has been French ever since.

Having been a political pawn for 1,000 years, Alsace has a hybrid culture: Natives who curse do so bilingually, and the local cuisine features sauerkraut with fine wine sauces. In recent years,

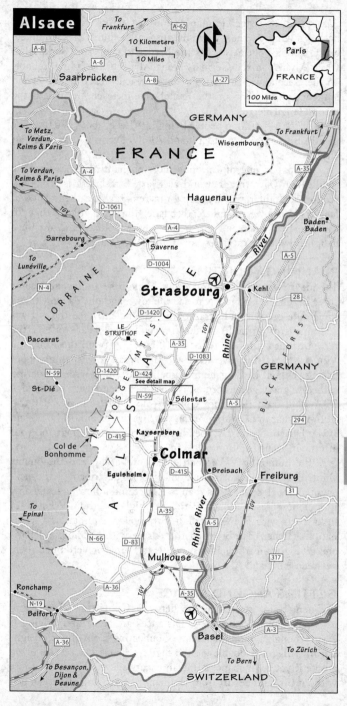

Alsace and its sister German region just across the border have been growing further apart linguistically—but closer commercially. People routinely cross the border to shop and work. And, while Alsace's mixed German/French dialects are fading, schools on the German side are encouraged to teach French as the second language and schools on the French side to teach German as the second language.

Of the 1.8 million people living in Alsace, about 270,000 live in Strasbourg (its biggest city) and 70,000 live in Colmar (its best city).

Colmar is one of Europe's most enchanting cities—with a small-town warmth and world-class art. Strasbourg is a big-city version of Colmar, worth a stop for its remarkable cathedral and to feel its high-powered and trendy bustle. The small villages that dot the wine road between them are like petite Colmars and provide a delightful and charming escape from the two cities.

PLANNING YOUR TIME

The ideal plan: Make Colmar your home base and spend two or three nights. Take one day to see the town and one day to explore the Route du Vin and Strasbourg. To efficiently see the villages and vineyards of the Route du Vin, you'll need a car—or take the recommended minivan tour (see "Getting Around the Route du Vin," later). If you have a car and like small towns, think about basing yourself in Eguisheim. Urban Strasbourg, with its soaring cathedral and vigorous center, is a headache for drivers but a quick 35-minute train ride from Colmar—do it by train as a day trip from Colmar or as a stopover on your way in or out of the region. If you have only one day, spend your morning in Colmar and your afternoon along the Route du Vin.

The humbling WWI battlefields of Verdun and the bubbly vigor of Reims in northern France (both described in the next chapter) are closer to Paris than to Alsace and follow logically only if your next destination is Paris. The high-speed TGV-Est train links Paris with Reims, Verdun, Strasbourg, Colmar, and destinations farther east, bringing the Alsace within 2 hours of Paris and giving train travelers easy access to Reims or Verdun en route between Paris and Alsace.

GETTING AROUND ALSACE

Frequent trains make the trip between Colmar and Strasbourg a snap (2/hour, 35 minutes). Distances are short and driving is easy—though a good map helps. Connecting Colmar with neighboring villages is doable via the region's sparse bus service or on a bike if you're in shape. Minivan excursions are handy for those without cars and depart from Colmar or Strasbourg. Taking a taxi

Early Crockpots

For old-school Alsatian comfort food, order the ubiquitous *Baeckeoffe,* which is still served at your table in traditional pottery. The dish gets its name from where it was cooked—in the "baker's oven." For centuries Alsatian women combined the week's leftover pork, beef, and veal with potatoes, onions, and leeks in a covered clay pot, then added white wine. Carrying the pot on their way to church on Sunday, the women would pass by the bakery and put their pot in one of the large stone ovens, still warm from baking the morning bread. During the three-hour Mass, the meat would simmer and be perfectly stewed in time for lunch. The pottery, which is still produced and sold locally, remains an integral part of every Alsatian household.

between towns is another worthwhile option. Once in the Route du Vin villages, you can hike or rent bikes to explore further (for details on all of these options, see "Alsace's Route du Vin," later).

ALSACE'S CUISINE SCENE

Alsatian cuisine is a major tourist attraction in itself. You can't mistake the German influence: sausages, potatoes, onions, and sauerkraut. Look for *chou-croute garnie* (sauerkraut and sausage—although it seems a shame to eat it in a fancy restaurant), the more traditionally Alsatian *Baeckeoffe* (see sidebar), *Rösti* (an oven-baked potato-and-cheese dish), *Spätzle* (soft egg noodles), *quenelles*  (dumplings made of pork, beef, or fish), fresh trout, and foie gras. For lighter fare, try the *poulet au Riesling,* chicken cooked ever-so-slowly in Riesling wine (*coq au Riesling* is the same dish done with rooster). At lunch, or for a lighter dinner, try a *tarte à l'oignon* (like an onion quiche, but better) or *tarte flambée* (like a thin-crust pizza with onion and bacon bits). If you're picnicking, buy some stinky Munster cheese. Dessert specialties are *tarte alsacienne* (fruit tart) and *Kugelhopf glacé* (a light cake mixed with raisins, almonds, dried fruit, and cherry liqueur).

Remember, restaurants serve only during lunch (11:30-14:00) and dinner (18:00 or 19:00-21:00, later in bigger cities), but some cafés serve food throughout the day. Many Alsatian restaurants open at 18:00, reflecting the region's Germanic heritage.

ALSATIAN WINES

Thanks to Alsace's Franco-Germanic culture, its wines are a kind of hybrid. The bottle shape, grapes, and much of the wine terminology are inherited from its German past, though wines made today are distinctly French in style (and generally drier than their German sisters). Alsatian wines are named for their grapes—unlike in Burgundy or Provence, where wines are commonly named after villages, or in Bordeaux, where wines are often named after châteaux. White wines rule in Alsace. Try one of the four "noble grapes" of the Alsace: riesling, gewürztraminer, pinot gris, or muscat. You'll also come across a local version of Champagne, called Crémant d'Alsace, and several varieties of *eaux-de-vie* (strong fruit-flavored brandy). For a helpful rundown of the regional wines, see "Route du Vin Wines" on page 960.

Colmar

Colmar feels made for wonderstruck tourists—its essentially traffic-free city center is a fantasy of steeply pitched roofs, pastel stucco, and aged timbers. Plus, it offers a few heavyweight sights in a comfortable, midsize-town package. Historic beauty was usually a poor excuse for being spared the ravages of World War II, but it worked for Colmar. The American and British military were careful not to bomb the half-timbered old burghers'

houses, characteristic red- and green-tiled roofs, and cobbled lanes of Alsace's most beautiful city. The town's distinctly French shutters combined with the ye-olde German half-timbering give Colmar an intriguing ambience.

Today, Colmar is alive with colorful buildings, impressive art treasures, and German tourists. Antiques shops welcome browsers, homeowners fuss over their geraniums, and hoteliers hurry down the sleepy streets to pick up fresh croissants in time for breakfast.

Orientation to Colmar

There isn't a straight street in Colmar—count on getting lost. Thankfully, most streets are pedestrian-only, and it's a lovely town to be lost in. Navigate by church steeples and the helpful signs that seem to pop up whenever you need them (directing visitors to the various sights). For tourists, the town center is Place Unterlinden (a 20-minute walk from the train station), where you'll find Colmar's most important museum, the TI (close by), and a big Monoprix supermarket/department store. City bus routes as well as the touristic mini trains start near Place Unterlinden.

Colmar is busiest from May through September and during its festive Christmas season (www.noel-colmar.com). Weekends draw crowds all year (best to book lodging far ahead). The impressive music festival fills hotels the first two weeks of July (www.festival-colmar.com), and the local wine festival rages in July and August. An open-air market bustles next to the Church of St. Martin on Saturdays.

TOURIST INFORMATION

The well-organized TI is next to the Unterlinden Museum on Rue Unterlinden (Mon-Sat 9:00-18:00, Sun 10:00-13:00, Nov-March Mon-Sat closed 12:00-14:00, tel. 03 89 20 68 92, www.tourisme-colmar.com). The TI can reserve hotel rooms for Colmar and the region. Get information about concerts and festivals in Colmar and in nearby villages, and ask about Colmar's Folklore Evenings held on summer Tuesdays (described later under "Nightlife in Colmar"). The TI has free Wi-Fi, bike maps, and a list of launderettes. Pick up the free Route du Vin map and get information on bike rental and bus schedules for touring the wine villages.

ARRIVAL IN COLMAR

By Train and Bus: The old and new (TGV) parts of Colmar's train station are connected by an underground passageway. For the old station and town center, exit the tunnel following signs toward *Avenue de la République.* Day-trippers can check their bags at **Colmar Vélo** to the left as you leave the old station (€2, see "Helpful Hints," next page).

The old train station was built during Prussian rule using the same plans as the station in Danzig (now Gdańsk, Poland). Check out the charming 1991 window that shows two local maidens about to be run over by a train and rescued by an artist. Opposite, he's shown painting their portraits.

Buses to Route du Vin villages arrive and depart from stops to the left and right as you leave the old station (stop locations can change—ask a driver on any bus), as well as from stops closer to the city center (ask at the TI and see "Alsace's Route du Vin," later).

To reach the town center, **walk** straight out past Hôtel Bristol, turn left on Avenue de la République, and keep walking (15 minutes total). For a faster trip, take any **Trace bus** from the station (to the left as you leave the old station) to the Champ de Mars stop (Place Rapp) or the Théâtre stop, next to the Unterlinden Museum

ALSACE

(€1.30, pay driver, infrequent service on Sun, see map on page 938, tel. 03 89 20 80 80, www.trace-colmar.fr). Allow €12 for a **taxi** to any hotel in central Colmar (taxi stand 50 yards on the left as you leave station).

By Car: Follow signs for *Centre-Ville*, then Place Rapp. Parking is available at a huge pay-parking garage under Place Rapp. Hotels can advise you where to park (many get deals at pay lots for their guests—ask). There's metered parking along streets in the city center. Half the spots at Parking de la Montagne Verte near Hôtel St. Martin are free (follow signs from the ring road; during the evening, spaces open up even if full during the day). Drivers can also find free street parking on residential streets just outside the city center (off Boulevard St-Pierre near the recommended Le Maréchal and Turenne hotels).

When entering or leaving on the Strasbourg side of town (north, near the Colmar airport), look for the big Statue of Liberty replica erected on July 4, 2004, to commemorate the 100th anniversary of the death of sculptor Frédéric-Auguste Bartholdi. At two traffic circles closer to Colmar (look for a red devil sculpture in the middle) are the imposing army barracks built by the Germans after annexing the region in 1871.

HELPFUL HINTS

Exchange Rate: €1 = about $1.10

Country Calling Code: 33 (see page 1082 for dialing instructions)

Market Days: Markets take place inside the vintage market hall (*marché couvert;* Tue-Sat generally 8:00-18:00, Sun 10:00-14:00, no market on Mon). The Saturday morning market on Place St. Joseph is where locals go for fresh produce and cheese (over the train tracks, 15 minutes on foot from the center, no tourists). Textiles are on sale Thursdays on Place de la Cathédrale (all day) and Saturdays on Place des Dominicains (afternoons only). A flea market happens every Friday from June to August on Place des Dominicains.

Department/Grocery Store: The big **Monoprix,** with a supermarket, is across from the Unterlinden Museum (Mon-Sat 8:00-20:00, closed Sun). A small **Petit Casino** supermarket stands across from the recommended Hôtel St. Martin (Mon-Sat 8:30-19:00, closed Sun).

Wine Tasting in Colmar: Maison Jund is a fun in-town tasting opportunity. Winemakers André and Myriam Jund, with their 3 children, own 44 acres of vineyards and grow all 7 of the Alsatian grapes. Son Sébastien hosts the tastings in excellent English. Plan one hour for the full experience (€6, call for appointment, 12 Rue de l'Ange, tel. 03 89 41 58 72, www.

ALSACE

martinjund.com, martinjund@hotmail.com). Also see my listing for their guesthouse under "Sleeping in Colmar," later.

Laundry: 5àsec, across the street from the Champ de Mars park, offers €20 wash, dry, and fold service (32 Avenue de la République, Mon 13:30-19:00, Tue-Fri 8:30-12:30 & 13:30-19:00, Sat 9:00-18:00, closed Sun, tel. 03 89 41 75 73). For more recommendations, ask your hotelier or the TI.

Bike Rental: Colmar Vélo rents bikes at the train station (€8-12/day, €20/day for electric bike, €150 deposit and ID required, behind bike racks on the left as you leave the old station, Mon-Fri 8:00-12:00 & 14:00-19:00, Sat-Sun 9:00-19:00, shorter weekend hours off-season, tel. 03 89 41 37 90). I prefer renting a bike along the Route du Vin in Eguisheim or Ribeauvillé (suggestions given later in this chapter; tours also available). If you plan to do much biking, buy a bike map either at the TI or a *librairie* (bookstore).

Taxis: You can find one at the train station (to your left as you walk out), or call 06 79 50 99 96. You can also try William (03 89 23 10 33, mobile 06 14 47 21 80) or Michele (mobile 06 72 94 65 55).

Car Rental: Avis is the only rental office at the train station (tel. 03 89 23 16 89). The TI has a list of other options. Warning: Some offices are located well outside the city center; verify location before booking.

Poodle Care: To give your poodle a shampoo and a haircut (or just watch the action), drop by **Quatt' Pattes** (near Hôtel-Restaurant le Rapp at 8 Rue Berthe Molly).

Guided Tours: There are no scheduled city tours in English, but private English-speaking **guides** are available through the TI if you book in advance (€170/3 hours, tel. 03 89 20 68 95, guide@tourisme-colmar.com). **Muriel Brun** works independently and is a good choice and speaks English well (tel. 03 89 79 70 92, muriel.h.brun@calixo.net).

TOURS IN COLMAR
Tourist Train

Colmar has two competing choo-choo trains (green and white) that jostle along the cobbles of the old part of town offering visitors a relaxing, narrated tour (but with scant recorded commentary in English) under a glass roof (departures daily 9:00-18:30). Both trains leave across from the Unterlinden Museum. The green train is a little shorter (30 minutes, €6.50, kids under 12-€3.50). The white train ranges a little farther (40 minutes, €7—small discount with ticket to Unterlinden Museum or Bartholdi Museum, kids 6-14-€5). In the summer, **horse-drawn carriages** do a similar route.

ALSACE

Canal Cruise

Little flat-bottomed boats glide silently on a straight stretch of the city's canal, making a simple 30-minute lap back and forth with little or no narration (€6, departures every 10 minutes, daily 10:00-12:00 & 13:30-18:30). With eight others, you'll pack onto the boat, gliding peacefully—powered by a silent electric motor—through a lush garden world under willows. While the route is kind of pathetic, the tranquility is enjoyable. Try to sit in front for an unobstructed view. Boats depart from docks near the bridges on Rue de Turenne and Boulevard St. Pierre, both in Petite Venise (those leaving from the bridge at St. Pierre offer a better tour, tel. 03 89 41 01 94, info@barques-colmar.fr).

Colmar Old Town Walk

This self-guided walk—good by day, romantic by night—is a handy way to link the city's three worthwhile sights (see this chapter's Colmar map to help navigate). Supplement my commentary by reading the sidewalk information plaques that describe points of interest in the old town. Allow an hour for this walk at a peaceful pace (longer if you enter sights). Colmar is wonderfully floodlit after dark on Fridays and Saturdays and during various festivals, when the lighting is changed to give different intensities and colors—and to welcome visiting VIPs.

• *Start in front of the Customs House (where Rue des Marchands hits Grand Rue). Face the old...*

Customs House (Koïfhus): Colmar is so attractive today because of its trading wealth. And that's what its Customs House is all about. The city was an economic powerhouse in the 15th, 16th, and 17th centuries because of its privileged trading status.

In the Middle Ages, most of Europe was fragmented into chaotic little princedoms and dukedoms. Merchant-dominated cities were natural proponents of the formation of large nation-states (proto-globalization). That's why they banded together to form "trading leagues" (the World Trade Organizations of their day). Rather than being ruled by some duke or prince, they worked directly with the emperor.

The Hanseatic League was the superleague of northern Europe. Prosperous Colmar was the leading member of a smaller league of 10 Alsatian cities, called the Decapolis (founded 1354).

This "Alsatian Big Ten" enjoyed special tax and trade privileges, including the right to build fortified walls and run their internal affairs. As "Imperial" cities they were ruled directly by the Holy Roman Emperor rather than by one of his lesser princes. This was preferable and, by banding together, they negotiated to protect this special status and won the Holy Roman Emperor's promise not to sell them to some other, likely more aggressive, prince. The 10 mostly Alsatian towns of the Decapolis enjoyed this status until the 17th century.

This street—Rue des Marchands—is literally "Merchants Street" and throughout the town you'll notice how street names bear witness to the historic importance of merchants in Colmar. They controlled the power. In front of the Customs House, find the carved plaque in the wall at #23. This is a "stone of banishment," declaring that the town's merchants kicked a noble family out of Colmar, and that family could never live here again.

Get closer to the Customs House. Delegates of the Decapolis would meet here to sort out trade issues, much like the European Union does in nearby Strasbourg today. In Colmar's heyday, this was where the action was. Notice the fancy green roof tiles and the intricate railing at the base of the roof. Note also the plaque above the door with the double eagle of the Holy Roman Emperor—a sign that this was an Imperial city.

By the way, the Dutch-looking gabled building on the left was the birthplace of Colmar's most famous son, General Jean Rapp, who distinguished himself during France's Revolutionary Wars to become one of Napoleon's most trusted generals.

Walk under the archway to Place de l'Ancienne Douane and face the Frédéric-Auguste Bartholdi statue of General Lazarus von Schwendi—arm raised (Statue of Liberty-style) and clutching a bundle of pinot gris grapes. He's the man who brought the grape from Hungary to Alsace.

From here, do a 360-degree spin to appreciate a gaggle of gables. This was the center of business activity in Colmar, with trade routes radiating to several major European cities. All goods that entered the city were taxed here. Today, it's the festive site of outdoor cafés and, on many summer evenings, fun wine tastings (open to everyone). Local vintners each get 10 days to share their wine here at the site of the town's medieval wine fair.

• *Follow the statue's left elbow and walk down Petite Rue des Tanneurs (not the larger "Rue des Tanneurs"). The half-timbered commotion of higgledy-piggledy rooftops on the downhill side of the fountain marks the...*

Tanners' Quarter: These vertical 17th- and 18th-century rooftops competed for space in the sun to dry their freshly tanned hides, while the nearby river channel flushed the waste products. Notice the openings just below the roofs where hides would be hung out to dry. When the industry moved out of town, the neighborhood became a slum. It was restored in the 1970s—a trendsetter in the government-funded renovation of old quarters. Residents had to play along or move out. At the street's end, carry on a few steps, and then turn back. Stinky tanners' quarters were always at

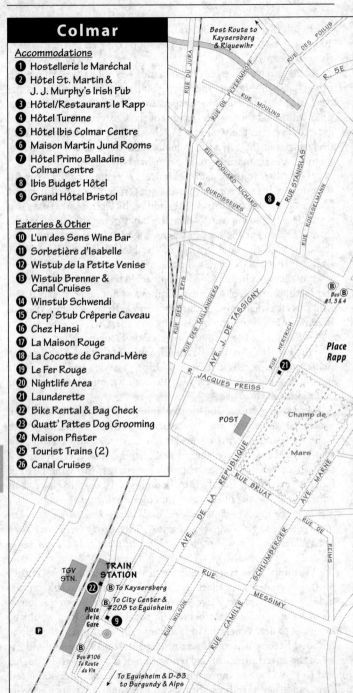

Colmar

Accommodations

1 Hostellerie le Maréchal
2 Hôtel St. Martin & J. J. Murphy's Irish Pub
3 Hôtel/Restaurant le Rapp
4 Hôtel Turenne
5 Hôtel Ibis Colmar Centre
6 Maison Martin Jund Rooms
7 Hôtel Primo Balladins Colmar Centre
8 Ibis Budget Hôtel
9 Grand Hôtel Bristol

Eateries & Other

10 L'un des Sens Wine Bar
11 Sorbetière d'Isabelle
12 Wistub de la Petite Venise
13 Wistub Brenner & Canal Cruises
14 Winstub Schwendi
15 Crep' Stub Crêperie Caveau
16 Chez Hansi
17 La Maison Rouge
18 La Cocotte de Grand-Mère
19 Le Fer Rouge
20 Nightlife Area
21 Launderette
22 Bike Rental & Bag Check
23 Quatt' Pattes Dog Grooming
24 Maison Pfister
25 Tourist Trains (2)
26 Canal Cruises

ALSACE

Best Route to Kaysersberg & Riquewihr

RUE DES POILUS
RUE DU JURA
R. 5 E
RUE DE PEYERIMHOF
RUE MOULINS
RUE EDOUARD RICHARD
RUE STANISLAS
R. OURDISSEURS
RUE ROESSELMANN
RUE DES 3 EPIS
RUE DES TAILLANDIERS
AVE. J. DE TASSIGNY
RUE HERTRICH
R. AVE. J. DE TASSIGNY
R. JACQUES PREISS

Bus #1, 3 & 4

Place Rapp

POST

Champ de

Mars

AVE. DE LA REPUBLIQUE
RUE BRUAT
AVE. MARNE
RUE DE REIMS
SCHLUMBERGER
RUE MESSIMY
RUE WILSON
RUE CAMILLE

TGV STN.

TRAIN STATION

To Kaysersberg
To City Center & #208 to Eguisheim

Place de la Gare

P

Bus #106 To Route du Vin

To Eguisheim & D-83 to Burgundy & Alps

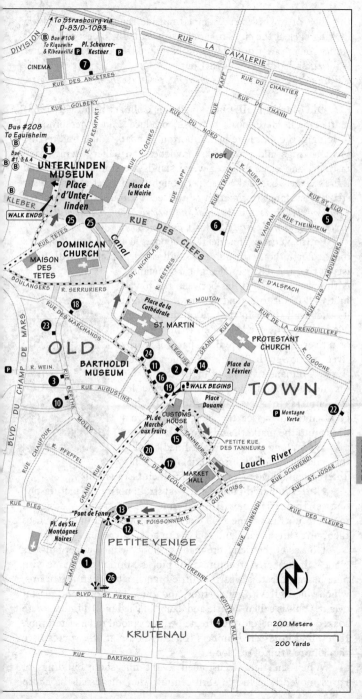

To Strasbourg via
D-83/D-1083

DIVISION

RUE LA CAVALERIE

B Bus #106
To Riquewihr
& Ribeauvillé

Pl. Scheurer-
Kestner P

CINEMA

7

RUE DES ANCETRES

RUE RAPP

RUE DU CHANTIER

RUE DU THANN

RUE GOLBERY

RUE DU REMPART

RUE CLOCHES

RUE DU NORD

Bus #208
To Eguisheim
B

Bus
#1, 3 & 4
B

i

B

UNTERLINDEN
MUSEUM

Place
d'Unterlinden

RUE RAPP

POST

R. RUEST

RUE ST ELOI

KLEBER

WALK ENDS

25

25

Place de
la Mairie

RUE ETROITE

RUE VAUBAN

RUE THEINHEIM

5

RUE DES CLEFS

6

RUE DES LABOUREURS

RUE TETES

DOMINICAN
CHURCH

Canal

ST. NICHOLAS

ST. PRETRES

R. D'ALSPACH

MAISON
DES
TETES

BOULANGERS

R. SERRURIERS

Place de la
Cathédrale

R. MOUTON

RUE DE LA GRENOUILLERE

RUE DES MARCHANDS

18

ST. MARTIN

R. L'EGLISE

GRAND RUE

PROTESTANT
CHURCH

R. CIGOGNE

23

OLD

BARTHOLDI
MUSEUM

24

11

2

14

Place du
2 Février

P

R. WEIN

16

TOWN

RUE BETTE

MOLLY

RUE AUGUSTINS

19

WALK BEGINS

3

Place
Douane

22

10

P Montagne
Verte

BLVD. DU CHAMP DE MARS

RUE CHAUFFOUR

GRAND RUE

Pl. de
Marché
aux Fruits

CUSTOMS
HOUSE

15

TANNEURS

PETITE RUE
DES TANNEURS

Lauch River

R. PFEFFEL

20

17

RUE DES ECOLES

MARKET
HALL

QUAI POISS.

RUE SCHWENDI

RUE ST. JOSSE

RUE BLES

GRAND RUE

"Pont de Fanny"

13

R. POISSONNERIE

RUE SCHWENDI

RUE DES FLEURS

Pl. des Six
Montagnes
Noires

12

PETITE VENISE

RUE TURENNE

RUE SCHWENDI

1

R. MANEGE

26

LE
KRUTENAU

BLVD. ST. PIERRE

4

ROUTE DE BALE

N

200 Meters

200 Yards

RUE BARTHOLDI

ALSACE

the edge of town. You've stepped outside the old center and are looking back at the city's first defensive wall. The oldest and lowest stones you see are from 1230, now built into the row of houses; later walls encircled the city farther out.

• *Walk with the old walls on your right, then take the first left along the stream.*

Old Market Hall: On your right is Colmar's historic (c. 1865) market hall. Here locals buy fish, produce, and other products (originally brought here by flat-bottomed boat). You'll find terrific picnic fixings and produce, sandwiches and bakery items, wine tastings, and clean WCs. Several stands are run like cafés, and there's even a bar. Take a spin through the market and see what strikes your fancy (for market hours, see "Helpful Hints," earlier).

• *Back on the street, cross the canal and turn right on Quai de la Poissonnerie ("Wharf of the Fish Market"), and you'll enter...*

Petite Venise: This neighborhood, a collection of Colmar's most colorful houses lining the small canal, is popular with tourists during the day. But at night it's romantic, with fewer crowds. It lies between the town's first wall (built to defend against arrows) and its later wall (built in the age of gunpowder). Medieval towns needed water. If they weren't on a river, they'd often redirect parts of nearby rivers to power their mills and quench their thirst. Colmar's river was canalized this way for medieval industry—to provide water for the tanners, to allow farmers to barge their goods into town (see the steps leading from docks into the market), and so on.

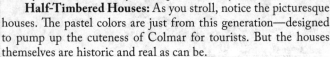

Walk along the flower-box-lined canal to the end of Rue de la Poissonnerie. At #3, Chez Thierry would love to let you sample their tasty *saucisson*.

Half-Timbered Houses: As you stroll, notice the picturesque houses. The pastel colors are just from this generation—designed to pump up the cuteness of Colmar for tourists. But the houses themselves are historic and real as can be.

Houses of the rich were made of stone, while budget builders made half-timbered structures. The process: Build your frame with pine beams; create a weave of little branches between the beams, which you'd fill with mud, straw, and gunk; let it dry; and plaster over it. (This is called "wattle and daub" in England.) Timbers were soaked in vinegar and then treated with ox blood to be waterproof. If you find unrestored timbers (like the house at #8), you can see the faint red tint of ox blood.

When the rich (accustomed to the fine stone buildings of Paris) moved here in the 18th century, they disguised the cheap wattle and daub with a thick layer of plaster. To them, the half-timbers looked cheap...and German. To be French was *à la mode* and that meant no half-timbers. Today, in the 21st century, half-timbered has become charming, so the current owners have peeled away the plaster to reveal the old beams.

Rich or poor, all homes sat on a stone base. There are several explanations: to prevent them from sinking into the marshy ground; to prevent the moist ground from rotting the timbers; and/or to preserve the ground floor in case of a fire—commonplace back then. You can identify true stone homes by their windowsills: Wooden sills mean they're half-timbered,; stone sills indicate the entire building is built of stone.

As you explore the town, notice how upper floors are cantilevered out. This was a structural support trick and a tax dodge, as real-estate taxes were based on the square footage of the ground floor.

Enjoy the old timbered houses toward the end of Rue de la Poissonnerie, as the lane narrows into a sort of alleyway. When you emerge, on your right is "Pont de Fanny," a bridge so popular with tourists for its fine views that you see lots of fannies lined up along the railing. Walk to the center of the bridge, and enjoy the scene. To the right you'll see examples of the flat-bottomed gondolas used to transport goods on the small river. Today, they give tourists sleepy, scenic, 30-minute canal tours (described earlier).

• *Cross the bridge to find a fountain in the square to your left. Another Bartholdi work, this one was commissioned to honor Jean Roesselmann, a 13th-century town provost who died defending his beloved city when the bishop of Strasbourg tried unsuccessfully to seize it. Take the second right on Grande Rue. Walk for several blocks to the Customs House (green-tiled roof) and land back where you started. With your back to the Customs House, look uphill along Rue des Marchands ("Merchants' Street")—one of the most scenic intersections in town. (The ruler of Malaysia was so charmed by this street that he had it re-created in Kuala Lumpur.)*

Walk up Rue des Marchands, and you'll soon come face-to-face with the...

Maison Pfister (Pfister House): This richly decorated merchant's house dates from 1537. Here the owner displayed his wealth for all to enjoy (and to envy). The external spiral-staircase turret, a fine loggia on the top floor, and the bay windows (called oriels) were pricey add-ons. The painted walls illustrate the city elites' taste for Renaissance humanism.

The cozy wine shop, Vinum, on the ground floor sells fine wines, but they are most proud of their locally-made whisky. David enjoys offering tastings, so go ahead, take a hit and see what you think—ask *"Déguster un whisky Alsatian?"*

ALSACE

Now that you're in a happy mood, stand outside facing the Pfister House for a little review. Find the four main styles of Colmar architecture: the Gothic church (right), local medieval half-timbered structures, Renaissance (that's Mr. Pfister's place), and (behind you) the urbane and elegant shutters and ironwork of Paris from the 19th century.

• *As you stagger on, check out the next building (at #9).*

Meter Man: The man carved into the side of this building was a drapemaker; he's shown holding a bar, Colmar's local measure of about one meter (almost equal to a yard). In the Middle Ages, it was common for cities to have their own units of length; it's one reason that merchants supported the "globalization" efforts of their time to standardize measuring systems.

The building shows off the classic half-timbered design—the beams (upright, cross, angular supports) are grouped in what's called (and looks like) "a man." Typical houses are built with a man in the middle flanked by two "half men." A short block farther up the street on the left is the **Bartholdi Museum** (described later, under "Sights in Colmar"), located in the home where the famous sculptor Frédéric-Auguste Bartholdi lived. Next door (at #28) is Au Croissant Doré, with its charming Art Nouveau facade and interior.

• *A passage opposite (on the right) leads you through the old guards' house to...*

Church of St. Martin: The city's cathedral-like church replaced a smaller Romanesque church that stood here earlier. It was erected in 1235 after Colmar became an Imperial city and needed a bigger place of worship. Colmar's ruler at the time was Burgundian, so the church has a Burgundian-style tiled roof.

The side door (facing the old guard's house) still has the round Romanesque tympanum, starring St. Martin, from the earlier church. Notice how it fits into the pointed Gothic arch. This was the lepers' door—marked by the four totem-like rows of grotesque faces and bodies representing lepers. They could "go to church" but had to stay outside, away from the other people.

On your right, the pharmacy at #16 is in Maison Adolf, one of Colmar's oldest buildings, dating from 1350 (find the plaque). Stand in front of this building for a view of the stork nest atop the church's apse. Two storks have made this nest their home, and locals have named the pair Martin and Martine.

Walk left, under expressive gargoyles, to the west portal. Facing the front of the church, notice that the relief over the main door depicts not your typical Last Judgment scene but the Three Kings who visited Baby Jesus. The Magi, whose remains are nearby in the Rhine city of Cologne, Germany, are popular in this region. The interior is dark, but it holds a few finely carved and beautifully painted altarpieces. The church's beautiful Vosges-stone exterior radiates color in the late afternoon.

• *Walk past the church, go left around Café Jupiler, and wander up the pedestrian-only Rue des Serruriers ("Locksmiths Street") to the...*

Dominican Church: Compare the Church of St. Martin's ornate exterior with this simple Dominican structure. While both churches were built at the same time, each makes different statements. The "High Church" of the 13th century was fancy and corrupt. The Dominican order was all about austerity. It was a time of crisis in the Roman Catholic Church. Monastic orders (as well as heretical movements like the Cathars in southern France) preached a simpler faith and way of life. In the style of St. Dominic and St. Francis, they tried to get Rome back on a Christ-like track. This church houses the exquisite *Virgin in the Rose Bush* by Martin Schongauer (described later).

• *Continuing past the Dominican Church, Rue des Serruriers becomes Rue des Boulangers—"Bakers Street." Stop at #16.*

Skyscrapers and Biscuits: The towering six-story house at #16, dating from the 16th century, was one of Colmar's tallest buildings from that age. Notice how it contrasts with the string of buildings to the right, which are lower, French-style structures— likely built after a fire cleared out older, higher buildings.

As this is Bakers Street, check out the one right here at #16. Maison Alsacienne de Biscuiterie sells traditional, home-baked *biscuits* (cookies), including Christmas delights year-round. *Macarons* and *biscuits* are sold by weight.

• *Turn right on Rue des Têtes (notice the beautiful swan sign over the* pharmacie *at the corner). Walk a block to the fancy old house festooned with heads (on the right) and stand in front of the Esprit boutique for the best view.*

Maison des Têtes ("House of Heads"): Colmar's other famous merchant's house, built in 1609 by a big-shot winemaker (see the grapes hanging from the wrought-iron sign and the happy man at the tip-top), is playfully decorated with about 100 faces and masks. On the ground floor, the guy in the window's center has pig's feet.

Look four doors to the right to see a 1947 bakery sign (above the big pretzel), which shows the *boulangerie* basics in Alsace: croissant, *Kugelhopf,* and baguette. Notice the colors of the French flag indicating that this house supported French rule.

Across from the Maison des Têtes, study the early 20th-century store sign trumpeting the tasty wonders of a butcher who once occupied these premises (with the traditional maiden with her goose about to be force-fed, all hanging shaped like the beak of a chicken).

• *Angle down Rue de l'Eau ("Water Street") for a shortcut to the TI and the Unterlinden Museum, with its namesake linden trees lining the front yard (popular locally for making the calming "Tilleul" tea). Your walk is over here, at the doorstep of Colmar's top museum.*

Sights in Colmar

▲▲▲Unterlinden Museum

This museum is Colmar's touristic claim to fame. Its extensive yet manageable collection ranges from Roman Colmar to medieval winemaking exhibits to Monet and Renoir, and from traditional wedding dresses to paintings that give vivid insight into the High Middle Ages.

Cost and Hours: €13, includes good tour app (you can also download it from the museum website); Wed-Mon 10:00-18:00, Thu until 20:00, closed Tue; 1 Rue d'Unterlinden, tel. 03 89 20 15 50, www.musee-unterlinden.com.

Visiting the Museum: The newly designed museum has three parts: the 13th-century convent cloisters and chapel (where you will spend most of your time), the underground gallery, and the new Ackerhof wing (modern art and temporary exhibits). The first room you enter (after showing your ticket) includes a model and wall map of the museum.

Cloister: Step into the soothing cloister (the largest 13th-century cloister in Alsace). This was a Dominican convent founded by (and for) noblewomen in 1230. It functioned until the French Revolution, when the building became a garrison.

Rooms with museum exhibits branch off from here. You'll find several worthwhile works by **Martin Schongauer** (who painted the *Virgin in the Rose Bush* displayed in the Dominican Church) and a few paintings by Lucas Cranach. As you enjoy the medieval and Renaissance art, remember that Alsace was historically German and part of the upper Rhine River Valley. The Three Kings (of Bethlehem fame) are prominently featured throughout this region because their remains ended up in Cologne's cathedral (nearby, on the Rhine).

Throughout the museum you'll see small photos of engravings, illustrating how painters were influenced by other artists' engravings. Most German painters of the time were also engravers (that's how they made money—making lots of copies to sell).

In the last room on the first floor, find a small alcove with **15th-century stained glass.** Note the fine details painted into the glass, originally intended for "God's eyes only"—they were too tiny for worshippers to see from the floor below. The glass is essentially a jigsaw puzzle connected by lead. Around here, glass this old is rare—most of it was destroyed by rampaging Protestants in the Reformation wars.

Isenheim Altarpiece: Located in the chapel, the museum's highlight is Matthias Grünewald's gripping *Isenheim Altarpiece* (c. 1515). It's actually a series of three paintings on hinges that pivot like shutters (you'll find several models in the cloisters). As the church calendar changed, priests would change the painting by opening or closing these panels. Designed to help people in a medieval hospital endure horrible skin diseases (such as St. Anthony's Fire, later called rye ergotism)—long before the age of painkillers—it's one of the most powerful paintings ever produced. Germans know this painting like Americans know the *Mona Lisa*.

Stand in front of the altarpiece as if you were a medieval peasant, and feel the agony and suffering of the Crucifixion. It's an intimate drama. The point—Jesus' suffering—is drilled home: The weight of his body bends the crossbar (unrealistically, creating an almost crossbow effect). His elbows are pulled from their sockets by the weight of his dead body. People who are crucified die of asphyxiation,  as Jesus' chest illustrates. His mangled feet are swollen with blood. The intended viewers—the hospital's patients—may have felt that Jesus understood their suffering, because he looks like he had a skin disease (though the marks on his skin represent lash marks from whipping). Study the faces and the Christian symbolism. The grief on Mary's face is agonizing. She is wrapped in the white shroud that will cover Jesus' body in the tomb. The sorrowful composition on the left is powerful. On the far left stands St. Sebastian (called upon by those with the plague) and on the right is St. Anthony (called upon by those with ergot poisoning from rotten rye).

The predella (the horizontal painting below) shows a hyper-realistic Entombment of Jesus. Jesus' fingernails are black—as is the case with any corpse, and Mary Magdalene's face is red with anguish.

Walk around to the other side of this panel. The Resurrec-

ALSACE

tion scene is unique in art history. (Grünewald was a mysterious artistic genius who had no master and no students.) Jesus rockets out of the tomb as man is transformed into God. As if proclaiming once again, "I am the Light," he is radiant. His shroud is the color of light: Roy G. Biv. Around the rainbow is the "resurrection of the flesh." Jesus' perfect pink flesh would appeal to the patients who meditated on the scene.

The right half of this panel depicts the Annunciation—the angel (accompanied by a translucent dove representing the Holy Spirit) telling Mary she'll give birth to the Messiah. The normally sanguine Mary looks unsettled, as if she's been hit by some unexpected news. She's shown reading the Bible passage that tells of this event.

In the nativity scene on the next panel—set in the Rhineland—the much-adored Mary is tender and loving, true to the Dominican belief that she was the intercessor for all in heaven. The happy ending is a psychedelic explosion of Resurrection joy. The scene on the left is the Concert of Angels. Looking at the last panel, zoom in on the agonizing Temptation of St. Anthony. The other panel shows Anthony's visit to St. Paul, the hermit. The final scene (behind you), carved in wood by Nikolaus Hagenauer, is St. Anthony on his throne.

Patients who meditated on this painting were reminded that they didn't have it so bad. They were also reminded to stay the course (religiously) and to not stray from the path of salvation.

Alsatian Folklore: Upstairs (level 1) are rooms displaying local and folk history. The works here are well worth a look. You'll see wrought-iron signs, cast-iron ovens, massive church bells, and chests with intricate locking systems. There are also ornate armoires, medieval armor, muskets, pottery, kitchen tools, and antique jewelry boxes.

A new exhibit on the history of the *Isenheim Altarpiece* is promised on this floor for 2017.

Gallo-Roman Archeology and Gothic Statues: Downstairs in the basement, be sure to find the *Mosaic of Bergheim*, dating from the third century. Discovered and moved here in 1848, it was the floor decoration in a villa in the town of Bergheim.

On this level you'll also find 14th-century Gothic statues from the facade of the nearby Church of St. Martin and other area churches. Study the Romanesque detail of the capitals and the faces of the statues. Even though they endured the elements outdoors for more than 500 years, it's still clear that they were sculpted with loving attention to detail. The masons knew their fine stone-work would not be seen from below—it was "for God's eyes only." The reddish stone is quarried from the Vosges Mountains, giving these works their unusual coloring. Notice the faint remnants of paint still visible on some statues—then imagine all of these works brightly painted.

Alsatian Cellar (Cave Alsacienne): This wine room contains 17th-century oak presses and finely decorated casks. Those huge presses were turned by animals. Wine revenue was used to care for Colmar's poor. Nuns owned many of the best vineyards around, and production was excellent. So was consumption. Find the cask with Bacchus and his big tummy straddling a keg. The quote from 1781 reads: "My belly's full of juice. It makes me strong. But drink too much and you lose dignity and health."

Rest of the Museum: Modern-art fans will want to save time for the **underground gallery** showcasing 19th- and 20th-century paintings, including works by Monet, Renoir, Picasso, Leger, Bonnard, and Dubuffet. The adjacent **Ackerhof** houses more modern art and temporary exhibits.

▲▲▲Dominican Church (Eglise des Dominicains)

This beautiful Gothic church is simple—in keeping with the austerity integral to the Dominican style of Christianity. It's plain on the outside and stripped-down on the inside. Instead of gazing at art, worshippers would just listen to the word of God being preached from the pulpit.

Cost and Hours: €2, April-December daily 10:00-13:00 & 15:00-18:00, June-Oct Fri-Sat no midday closure, closed Jan-March, tel. 03 89 41 27 20.

Visiting the Church: This church houses a mesmerizing medieval masterpiece—Martin Schongauer's angelically beautiful *Virgin in the Rosebush* (1473), which looks as if it were painted yesterday. Here, graceful Mary is shown as a welcoming mother. Jesus clings to her, reminding the viewer of the warmth of his relationship with Mary. The Latin on her halo reads, "Pick me also for your child, O very Holy Virgin." Rather than telling a particular Bible story, this is a general scene, designed to meet the personal devotional needs of any worshipper.

Nature is not a backdrop; Mary and Jesus are encircled by it. Schongauer's robins, sparrows, and goldfinches bring extra life to an already impressively natural rosebush. The white rose (over Mary's right shoulder) anticipates Jesus' crucifixion. The frame, with its angelic orchestra, dates only from 1900 and feels to me a bit over-the-top.

The painting was located in the Church of St. Martin until 1972, when it was stolen. After being recovered, it was moved to the better-protected Dominican Church. Detailed English explanations are in the nave to the right of the painting as you face it. The contrast provided by the simple Dominican setting heightens the elegance of this Gothic masterpiece.

As for the rest of the church, the columns are thin to allow worshippers to see the speaker, even if the place is packed. The windows are precious 14th-century originals depicting black-clad Dominican monks busy preaching. Notice how windows face the sun on the south side while the north side is walled against the cloister. If you look at the columns in the rear of the nave, you can see how 14th-century Colmar's street level was about two feet below today's.

▲Bartholdi Museum

This little museum recalls the life and work of the local boy who gained fame by sculpting America's much-loved Statue of Liberty. Frédéric-Auguste Bartholdi (1834-1904) was a dynamic painter/photographer/sculptor with a passion for the defense of liberty and freedom. Although Colmar was his home, he spent most of his career in Paris, refusing to move back here while Alsace was German.

Bartholdi devoted years of his life to realizing the vision of a statue of liberty for America that would stand in New York City's harbor. While Lady Liberty is his most famous work, you'll see several Bartholdi statues gracing Colmar's squares.

Cost and Hours: €6, free on July 4, open March-Dec Wed-Mon 10:00-12:00 & 14:00-18:00, closed Tue and Jan-Feb, €2 audioguide, in heart of old town at 30 Rue des Marchands, tel. 03 89 41 90 60, www.musee-bartholdi.fr. Curiously, even though entry is free on the Fourth of July, there is no English posted in this museum, but ask for the English handout at the ticket desk.

Visiting the Museum: The **courtyard** is dominated by a bronze statue, *Les Grands Soutiens du Monde*. It was cast in 1902—two years before Bartholdi died—and shares his personal philosophy. The world is supported by three figures representing patriotism, hard work, and justice. Mr. Hard Work holds a book, symbolizing intellectual endeavors, and a hammer, a sign for physical labor. Ms. Justice has her scales. And Mr. Patriotism holds a flag and a sword—sheathed but ready to be used. All have one foot stepping forward: ahead for progress, the spirit of the Industrial Age.

On the **ground floor,** the room to the right of the ticket desk houses temporary exhibits. To the left are exhibits covering Bartholdi's works commissioned in Alsatian cities, commonly dedicated to military heroes.

Climbing the stairs to the middle floor, you pass a portrait of the artist. Rooms re-create Bartholdi's high-society flat in Paris. At the end of the hallway on the left, the dining room is lined with portraits of his aristocratic family.

In the next room hangs a beautiful portrait of the sculptor (by Jean Benner), facing his mother (on a red chair). Bartholdi was very close to his mom, writing her daily letters when he was working in New York. Many see his mother's face in the Statue of Liberty. Scenes on the ceilings represent aspects of Bartholdi's Freemason philosophy.

In the hallway leading right, a room dedicated to Bartholdi's most famous French work, the *Lion of Belfort,* celebrates the Alsatian town that fought so fiercely in 1871 that it was never annexed into Germany. Photos show the red sandstone lion sitting regally below the mighty Vauban fortress of Belfort—a symbol of French spirit standing strong against Germany. Small models give a sense of its gargantuan scale. (If you're linking Burgundy with Alsace by car, you'll pass the city of Belfort and see signs directing you to the *Lion.*)

The rest of the floor shows off Bartholdi's French work. Small wax models let you trace his creative process. A glass case is filled with the tools of his trade. Notice how his patriotic pieces tend to have one arm raised—*Vive la France*...God bless America...Freedom!

The top floor is dedicated to Bartholdi's American works—the paintings, photos, and statues that Bartholdi made during his many travels to the States. You'll see statues of Columbus pointing as if he knew where he was going, and Lafayette (who was only 19 years old when he came to America's aid) with George Washington.

Two rooms are dedicated to the evolution and completion of Bartholdi's dream of a Statue of Liberty. Fascinating photos show the Eiffel-designed core, the frame being covered with plaster, and then the hand-hammered copper plating, which was ultimately riveted to the frame. The statue was assembled in Paris, then dismantled and shipped to New York, in 1886...10 years late. The big ear in the exhibit is half-size.

Though the statue was a gift from France, the US had to come up with the cash to build a pedestal. This was a tough sell, but Bartholdi was determined to see his statue erected. On 10 trips to the US, he worked to raise funds and lobbied for construction, bringing with him this painting and a full-size model of the torch—which the statue would ultimately hold. (Lucky for Bartholdi and his cause, his cousin was the French ambassador to the US.)

Eventually, the project came together—the pedestal was built, and the Statue of Liberty has welcomed waves of immigrants into New York ever since. Thank you, Frédéric-Auguste Bartholdi.

Nightlife in Colmar

No one would come to Colmar solely for its nightlife. But if you're out after dinner, you'll see that Colmar puts lots of creative energy into its floodlit cityscapes, making evening strolls memorable.

Every July and August, five local vintners take 10 days each to show off local wines at a small **wine festival.** It's held under the historic arches of the Customs House (daily 12:00-24:00). It's self-service, there's no food, and glasses are cheap (€1-3). And if you're here on a Tuesday in May to September, there's likely Alsatian folk dancing at the town's **Folklore Evening** (Soirée Folklorique, starts at 20:30) to give your wine tasting a little color.

Rue du Conseil Souverain (stretching from the Customs House to the "Pont de Fanny") has a fun line of watering holes—three bars and a cocktail lounge—where you can enjoy mellow outdoor seating with the locals on balmy evenings or characteristic interiors of your choice when it's cold.

Les Incorruptibles attracts younger locals, with some Alsatian edginess and great beers on tap, including Chimay, the milkshake of gourmet Belgian monk-made beers (1 Rue des Ecoles).

Pub James'On (at #2) has a big, pubby interior and draws a more mature crowd.

Sport's Café is a big-screen, Red Bull-and-foosball place. This is *the* place to be if there's a big sporting event on TV and you want to share it with a gang of French enthusiasts. They have Pelforth Blonde, the best French lager, on tap (3 Rue du Conseil Souverain).

J. J. Murphy's Irish Pub invites you to share a picnic table on the street or take a trip to Ireland at the bar, where you can enjoy a classic pub vibe and Murphy's Irish Stout on tap (48 Grand Rue).

Sleeping in Colmar

Hotels are a reasonable value in Colmar. They're busiest on weekends in May, June, September, and October, and every day in July and August. If you have trouble finding a bed, ask the TI for help or look in a nearby village, where small hotels and bed-and-breakfasts are plentiful (see my recommendations in nearby Eguisheim, later).

IN THE CENTER

$$$ At **Hostellerie le Maréchal,****** in the heart of La Petite Venise, Colmar's most characteristic digs are surprisingly affordable. Though the rooms are on the small side (three-star quality and prices), the setting is romantic, the decor is cozy, and the service is

Sleep Code

Hotels are classified based on the average price of a standard double room without breakfast in high season.

$$$$	**Splurge:** Most rooms over €200
$$$	**Pricier:** €150-200
$$	**Moderate:** €100-150
$	**Budget:** €50-100
¢	**Backpacker:** Under €50
RS%	**Rick Steves discount**
*	**French hotel rating system** (0-5 stars)

Unless otherwise noted, credit cards are accepted, hotel staff speak basic English, and free Wi-Fi is available. Comparison-shop by checking prices at several hotels (on each hotel's own website, on a booking site, or by email). For the best deal, *book directly with the hotel.* Ask for a discount if paying in cash; if the listing includes **RS%**, request a Rick Steves discount.

professional (some rooms have whirlpool tubs, pay garage parking, 4 Place des Six Montagnes Noires, tel. 03 89 41 60 32, www.le-marechal.com, info@le-marechal.com). The hotel is more famous for the quality of its well-respected **$$$$ restaurant;** many French clients travel to dine here (€35-85 *menus*, reserve ahead).

$$ Hôtel St. Martin,*** ideally situated near the old Customs House, is a family-run place that began as a coaching inn (since 1361). It has 40 mostly traditional, fairly priced, well-equipped rooms with air-conditioning and big beds. The rooms are woven into its antique frame and joined together by a peaceful courtyard. The 12 units in the back have charming chalet-style decor, but they don't have elevator access (family rooms, good breakfast-€12, air-con, free public parking nearby at Parking de la Vieille Ville, 38 Grand Rue, tel. 03 89 24 11 51, www.hotel-saint-martin.com, colmar@hotel-saint-martin.com).

$$ Hôtel le Rapp,*** conveniently located off Place Rapp and near a big park, holds rooms for many budgets, a full-service bar, a café, and a good restaurant. The cheapest rooms are tight but smartly configured; the bigger rooms are tastefully designed, usually with queen-size beds. There's also a small basement pool, a sauna, and a Turkish bath. It's well-run and family-friendly (family rooms, good buffet breakfast-€13, air-con, elevator, 1 Rue Weinemer, tel. 03 89 41 62 10, www.rapp-hotel.com, rapp-hotel@calixo.net).

$$ Hôtel Turenne*** is less central (a 10-minute walk from the city center) with a *winstub* ambience in its reception area and a welcoming vibe. Its 54 rooms vary in size (some are tiny), though all are air-conditioned and well-appointed (family rooms, park for free on the street or book ahead to park in one of their three pay spaces, elevator for most rooms, 10 Route de Bâle, tel. 03 89 21 58 58, www.turenne.com, infos@turenne.com).

$ Hôtel Ibis Colmar Centre,*** on the ring road, rents tight rooms with small bathrooms at acceptable rates (air-con, 10 Rue St. Eloi, tel. 03 89 41 30 14, www.ibishotel.com, h1377@accor.com).

$ Maison Martin Jund holds my favorite budget beds in Colmar. This ramshackle yet historic half-timbered house—the home of likeable winemakers André and Myriam—feels like a medieval tree house soaked in wine and filled with flowers. The rooms are modest but spacious and comfortable enough. Some have air-conditioning and many are equipped with kitchenettes (big family apartments, fun tasting room—see "Helpful Hints" earlier, no elevator, 12 Rue de l'Ange, tel. 03 89 41 58 72, www.martinjund.com, martinjund@hotmail.com). Leave your car at Parking de la Vieille Ville. Train travelers can take any Trace bus from the station to the Unterlinden Museum and walk from there. There is no real reception—though good-natured Myriam or her daughter Cécile seems to be around, somewhere, most of the time (call if you'll arrive after 20:00).

$ Hôtel Primo Balladins Colmar Centre,** near the ring road, is a characterless, efficient, clean, and cheap place to sleep. They'll hold a room for you until 18:00 if you call ahead. Rooms facing the big square *(grand place)* are quieter (family rooms, elevator, free parking in big square in front, 5 Rue des Ancêtres, tel. 03 89 24 22 24, www.hotel-primo.fr, colmar.centre@balladins.com).

$ Ibis Budget Hôtel offers bright, efficient, all-the-same rooms with three beds—one bed is a bunk—and ship-cabin bathrooms (secure pay parking or park for free on Place Scheurer-Kestner, 10-minute walk from city center at 15 Rue Stanislas, tel. 08 92 68 09 31, www.ibisbudget.com, h5079@accor.com).

NEAR THE TRAIN STATION

$$$ Grand Hôtel Bristol**** has little personality but works if you want overpriced, four-star comfort at the train station (air-con, 7 Place de la Gare, tel. 03 89 23 59 59, www.grand-hotel-bristol.com, reservation@grand-hotel-bristol.com).

Eating in Colmar

Colmar is full of good restaurants offering traditional Alsatian *menus* for €20-30. (To dine in a smaller town nearby, see "Eating in Eguisheim," later.)

Before Dinner: L'un des Sens is a cool little wine bar, good for a glass of wine and an appetizer (long list of wines from many countries) and a short list of foods (meat plates, fancy foie gras,

Restaurant Price Code

I've assigned each eatery a price category, based on the average cost of a typical main course. Drinks, desserts, and splurge items (steak and seafood) can raise the price considerably.

$$$$	**Splurge:** Most main courses over €25
$$$	**Pricier:** €20-25
$$	**Moderate:** €15-20
$	**Budget:** Under €15

In France, a crêpe stand or other takeout spot is **$**; a sit-down brasserie, café, or bistro with affordable *plats du jour* is **$$**; a casual but more upscale restaurant is **$$$**; and a swanky splurge is **$$$$**.

cheese plates, Tue-Thu 16:00-22:00, Fri-Sat 10:00-22:30, closed Sun-Mon, ask about blind tastings—offered only in French, 18 Rue Berthe Molly, tel. 03 89 24 04 37, www.lun-des-sens.alsace).

After Dinner: Sorbetière d'Isabelle sells Colmar's best sorbet; you can eat at an outdoor table or to go. Ask about her syrup toppings (Mon 14:00-19:00, Tue-Sun 11:00-19:00, until 22:30 July-Aug and busy weekends, near Maison Pfister at 13 Rue des Marchands, tel. 03 89 41 67 17). If you want lively café and bar action, find **Rue du Conseil Souverain** (described earlier).

IN PETITE VENISE

To dine in Colmar's coziest neighborhood, head into Petite Venise and make your way to the photo-perfect "Pont de Fanny" on Rue Turenne, where you'll find several picturesque places within a couple of blocks.

$$$ Wistub de la Petite Venise bucks the touristy trend in this area with caring owners Virginie and Julien. It combines a wood-warm, chalet ambience (no outside seating) with the energy of an open kitchen. The menu is limited in selection—heavy on the meats—but generous in quality. Chef Julien is proud of his *jambonneau*, though his *choucroute* and foie gras are tasty, too (closed at lunch Thu and Sun, closed all day Wed, 4 Rue de la Poissonnerie, tel. 03 89 41 72 59).

$$$ Wistub Brenner is perhaps your best mix of economy, quality cooking, accessible selections, and characteristic ambience. The outside seating is better than inside, but either way you'll enjoy attentive service and seasonal specialties. Their formula is freedom: You can choose any first course to go along with any main course on their €26 *menu* deal (1 Rue Turenne, tel. 03 89 41 42 33).

IN THE OLD CITY CENTER

$$ Winstub Schwendi has fun, German pub energy inside with seven beers on tap, a lively vibe, and hustling waiters. The big terrace outside is more sedate, but it's ideal for a warm evening. Choose from a dozen filling, robust Swiss *Rösti* plates (that arrive at your table still sizzling in their Staub Dutch ovens) or *tarte flambée*—I like the *strasbourgeoise flambée* (also good salad and main dish options, local wines, daily 12:00-22:30, facing the Customs House at 3 Grand Rue, tel. 03 89 23 66 26). If the Winstub is full, you'll find several similar places with good outdoor seating around Place de l'Ancienne Douane.

$ Crep' Stub Crêperie Caveau is a good place for crêpes in the old center. Sébastien serves with smiles while Dominique cooks with vigor; there's great outside seating on Place de l'Ancienne Douane or inside in a cute little back room (€10 dinner crêpes, closed Mon, 10 Rue des Tanneurs, tel. 03 89 24 51 88).

$$$ Chez Hansi, a half-block up from the Customs House, is where Colmarians go for a traditional meal (served by women in Alsatian dresses). This place feels real, even though it's in the thick of the touristic center. Attentive Annie manages your dining experience; ask her what's good today, or try local specialties such as *poulet* or *saumon au Riesling* (chicken or salmon in Riesling sauce) with *Spätzle* (soft egg noodles), or medieval "pub grub" like *choucroute garnie* (*menus* from €22, indoor seating only, closed Wed-Thu, 23 Rue des Marchands, tel. 03 89 41 37 84).

$$$ La Maison Rouge, with a folk-museum interior and sidewalk seating, has tasty, reasonably priced, beautifully presented Alsatian cuisine and an understandably loyal following. You'll be greeted by manager Cécile and *jambon à l'os*—ham cooking on the bone—but they take their vegetarian plate seriously (*menus* from €26, try the veal cordon bleu with Munster or the *tarte flambée au chèvre-basilic,* closed Sun-Mon, 9 Rue des Ecoles, tel. 03 89 23 53 22).

$$$ Hôtel-Restaurant le Rapp is a traditional place to savor a slow, elegant meal served with grace and fine Alsatian wine. While busy with locals during the day, it may be quiet at dinner. If you want to order high on the menu, this is the perfect place to do it. They have great *Baeckeoffe* or *choucroute* for €19 that makes a whole meal—or order a three-course *menu* from €30, adding €10 for a glass of wine to match each course (good vegetarian options, closed Mon-Tue, air-con, 1 Rue Berthe Molly, tel. 03 89 41 62 10).

$$ La Cocotte de Grand-Mère offers a break from Alsatian food and decor, with traditional French cuisine fresh from the market. Their €15 "surprise" lunch *menu* is unveiled online every morning. This spot gets busy with locals, so reservations are recommended (*menus* from €18, closed Sat-Sun, 14 Place de l'Ecole, tel. 03 89 23 32 49, www.lacocottedegrandmere.com).

$$$ Le Fer Rouge, across from the Customs House in a recently restored historic building, is a good place for traditional Alsatian specialties. Try the *jambonneau* in honey and thyme sauce *(Fondant de Jambonneau braisé au miel et au thym)* or *tarte flambée* by the whole or half order (daily, 52 Grand Rue, tel. 03 89 20 80 69).

Colmar Connections

From Colmar by Train to: Strasbourg (about 2/hour, 35 minutes), **Reims** (TGV: 7/day, 2.5 hours, most change in Strasbourg), **Verdun** (7/day, 4-5.5 hours, 2-3 changes, many with 30-minute bus ride from Gare de Meuse), **Beaune** (10/day, 2.5-4 hours, fastest by TGV via Mulhouse, reserve well ahead, possible changes in Mulhouse or Belfort and Dijon), **Paris'** Gare de l'Est (3 direct, 2.5 hours, more with change in Strasbourg), **Amboise** (13/day, 5-6 hours, most with transfer in Strasbourg and Paris), **Basel,** Switzerland (hourly, 45 minutes), **Karlsruhe,** Germany (TGV: 7/day, 1.5-2.5 hours, best with change in Strasbourg; non-TGV: hourly, 2-3.5 hours, change in Strasbourg and Appenweier or Offenburg; from Karlsruhe, it's 1.5 hours to Frankfurt, 3 hours to Munich).

Alsace's Route du Vin

Alsace's Route du Vin (Wine Road) is an asphalt ribbon that ties 90 miles of vineyards, villages, and medieval fortress ruins into an understandably popular tourist package. With France's driest

climate, this stretch of vine-covered land has made for good wine and happy tourists since Roman days.

This is France's smallest wine region. It's long (75 miles) and skinny (just over a mile wide on average), with vineyards strategically planted to be above the floodline of the marshy plains yet below the frostline of the higher ground. Everyone scrambles for the finest land. The region's 50 *grand cru* vineyards (the highest quality) get the privilege of putting up their names on big signs along the hillsides.

Peppering the landscape are Route du Vin villages, full of quaint half-timbered architecture corralled within medieval walls (for a refresher course, see page 940). The towns with evocative castle ruins are often strategically located at the end of valleys.

ALSACE

Their names can reveal their histories—towns ending with "heim" and "wihr" were born as farmsteads (Eguisheim was Egui's farm, Riquewihr was Rick's farm).

Colmar and Eguisheim are well-located for exploring the 30,000 acres of vineyards blanketing the hills from Marlenheim to Thann.

As you tour the Route du Vin, you'll see stork nests on church spires and city halls, thanks to a campaign to reintroduce the birds to this area. (Those nests can weigh over 1,000 pounds, posing a danger if they fall and forcing villagers to shore them up.) Look also for crucifixion monuments scattered about the vineyards—intended to get a little divine intervention for a good harvest.

PLANNING YOUR TIME

If you have only a day, focus on towns within easy striking range of Colmar. World War II hit many Route du Vin villages hard. While some of the towns are amazingly preserved from centuries past, several were entirely rebuilt after the war. It all depended on where the war went in 1944. Villages that emerged from World War II unscathed include Eguisheim, Kaysersberg, Hunawihr, Turckheim, Ribeauvillé, and the *très* popular Riquewihr.

A sampling of two villages works well for most. If driving, distances are short, and you can lace together what you like. If taking a minibus tour, you can see a representative sampling in a half-day or cover the highlights of the entire region in a full day. Those without wheels need to be more selective and deal with the meager-but-workable bus schedules.

Towns are most alive during their weekly morning (until noon) farmers markets (Mon—Kaysersberg; Tue—Munster; Fri—Turckheim; Sat—Ribeauvillé and Colmar). Riquewihr and Eguisheim have no market days.

GETTING AROUND THE ROUTE DU VIN
By Car

Drivers can pick up a detailed map of the Route du Vin at any area TI. To reach the Route du Vin north of Colmar, leave Colmar following signs to Ingersheim. From here roads fan out northeast to Kaysersberg; north through Sigolsheim to Riquewihr, Hunawihr, Ribeauvillé, and Château du Haut-Kœnigsbourg; or south to Eguisheim. Look for *Route du Vin* signs. For the quickest way to Eguisheim from Colmar, head for the train station and take D-30 and then D-83 south toward Belfort.

Drivers can use some of the scenic wine service lanes known as *sentiers viticoles*—provided they drive at a snail's pace. I've recommended my favorite segments.

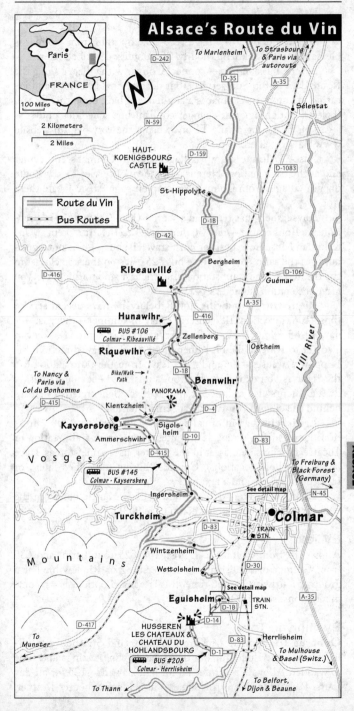

By Train or Bus

The only Route du Vin village accessible by train from Colmar is pleasant little Turckheim (hourly, 20 minutes, described later).

Several bus companies connect Colmar with villages along the Route du Vin (no Sun service), but deciphering schedules and locating bus stops in Colmar is a challenge. I have done this for you (below), but things can change; confirm bus schedules and stop locations by asking at any TI or by using the very helpful website www.vialsace.eu/en.

Buses to Route du Vin villages stop in Colmar's city center and at the train station. Here is a rundown of service to key Route du Vin villages from Colmar (see map on page 957 to locate these stops).

Kaysersberg has reasonable service (Kunegel bus #145, direction: Le Bonhomme, 7/day, 30 minutes). The Théâtre stop near Unterlinden Museum is best for most travelers; bus #145 is not signed but uses the same stop as Trace bus #25—it's on the side closest to the theater. At the train station, find the last stop to the left as you leave the station (signed as *145*).

Riquewihr, Hunawihr, and **Ribeauvillé** have decent service (bus #106, direction: Illhaeusern, 6/day in summer, otherwise 10/day, 30-45 minutes, big midday service gaps in summer). You can also get to Ribeauvillé on Kunegel bus #109 (4/day, direction: St-Hippolyte). Buses #106 and #109 leave from the train station (on the right as you exit), but the stop is unsigned—it's best to ask a driver. There's also a signed stop near Place Scheurer-Kestner; it's behind the cinemas on Rue de la 5ème Division.

Eguisheim has minimal service—look for bus #208 (direction: Herrlisheim, 4/day, 15 minutes, leaves from train station or Théâtre stop on side closest to the theater, uses same stop as Trace bus #26 at both locations). Consider biking (described later), or take the bus there and a taxi back.

Château du Haut-Kœnigsbourg has a shuttle bus from the Séléstat train station (explained on page 963).

By Taxi

Allow €15 from Colmar to Eguisheim (€25 round-trip) and €35 from Colmar or Eguisheim to Kaysersberg or Riquewihr. For a group of four with limited time, this is a smart option. For recommendations, see page 934.

By Minivan Tour

Ophorus Tours offers trips from Colmar and Strasbourg to villages along the Route du Vin that include wine tastings and time to wander. Allow €75 per person for half-day and €125 for all-day tours. Pick up location in Colmar is at 1 Place Scheurer-Kestner, in front of the cinema (tel. 05 56 15 26 09, mobile 06 63 04 91 11, www.ophorus.com, info@ophorus.com). They offer private tours as well.

Alsascope also offers tours departing from Colmar and Strasbourg (€110/day, €75/half-day, tel. 03 89 44 38 21, mobile 06 82 87 50 73, www.alsascope.fr, info@alsascope.fr).

Vinotours is yet another option, this one with a wine focus (€120/person for all-day shared tours; €490/day or €290/half-day for private tours of up to seven passengers, mobile 06 51 94 05 17, www.vinotours-alsace.fr, contact@vinoroute.fr).

By Bike

With over 2,500 miles of bike-friendly lanes, Alsace is among France's best biking regions. The Route du Vin has an abundance of well-marked trails and *sentier viticole* service roads that run up and down the slopes, offering memorable views and the fewest cars but tough pedaling. Start by getting advice and a good map from a TI or bike shop. Bikers can rent in Colmar, Kaysersberg, Eguisheim, or Ribeauvillé (I've listed rental options for each; Kaysersberg and Eguisheim have electric bikes for rent and make great starting points).

Riding round-trip between Ribeauvillé and Kaysersberg via Hunawihr and Riquewihr along the upper *sentier viticole* yields sensational views but very hilly terrain (you can reduce some of the climbing by following lower wine-service lanes; details provided later).

From Colmar to Eguisheim, it's a level, five-mile ride on a bike lane through Wintzenheim and Wettolsheim to Eguisheim. Leaving Colmar, go to the far side of the train station on Avenue Général de Gaulle, which becomes Route de Wintzenheim. Keep straight on the bike lane uphill until you find bike signs for *V-11*, leading left toward Wettolsheim and then Eguisheim. Though just the last stretch through vines and towns is scenic, it's a handy option to reach the village. You can loop back to Colmar via Turckheim for a longer but still-level ride.

Bike tours work well too (about €35-60 for 2-4 hours with a guide). **Alsa Cyclo** in Eguisheim runs tours using electric bikes; for details, see "Orientation to Eguisheim," later.

On Foot

Hikers can stroll along *sentier viticole* service roads and paths (explained earlier) into vineyards from each town on short loop trails (each TI has brochures), or connect the villages on longer walks. Consider taking a bus or taxi from Colmar to one village and hiking to another, then taking a bus or taxi back to Colmar (Ribeauvillé and Riquewihr, or Kaysersberg and Riquewihr make good combinations—see details later in this chapter). Hikers can also climb high to the ruined castles of the Vosges Mountains (Eguisheim and Ribeauvillé are good bases).

ROUTE DU VIN WINES

Romans planted the first grapevines in Alsace over 2,000 years ago. Wine and Rhine worked together to form the backbone of the region's medieval economy. Barrels of wine were shipped along the nearby Rhine to international destinations (Scandinavia, the Low Countries, and Britain were big buyers). This created enormous wealth for Alsatians; their investments financed many of the beautiful buildings and villages we see today. Until the 17th century, Alsace produced more (and better) wine than any other region in the Holy Roman Empire. The Thirty Years' War, French Revolution, and Franco-Prussian War buried Alsace's wine dominance. Two world wars didn't help. Today Alsace is struggling to get its foot back in the door of international wine markets—where the big money is.

To help earn this recognition, they eagerly welcome visitors. Most Route du Vin towns have wineries that give tours (some charge a fee), and scores of small producers open their courtyards with free and fun tastings (remember, it's polite to buy a bottle or two if you like the wines). The cooperatives at Eguisheim, Bennwihr, Hunawihr, and Ribeauvillé, created after the destruction of World War II, provide a good look at modern and efficient methods of production. Before you set off, review "French Wine-Tasting 101" on page 1078.

Learn to recognize the basic grapes and wines of this region. The simplest wines are blended from several grapes and usually called **Edelzwicker.** Despite being cheapest, these wines can be delicious and offer very good value.

Here are the key grapes to look for; the first four are the "noble grapes" of the Alsace:

Riesling is the king of Alsatian grapes. It's more robust than sylvaner, but drier than the German style you're probably used to. The name comes from the German word that describes its slightly smoky smell, with a note of *goût petrol* ("gasoline taste").

Pinot gris was called Tokay d'Alsace until about 10 years ago, when the term was banned to avoid confusion with Tokaji wines in Hungary (where these grapes originated). These are more full-bodied, spicier, and distinctly different from other pinot gris wines you may have tried.

Muscat is best as a before-dinner wine. Compared with other French muscat wines, the Alsatian version is very dry, usually with a strong floral taste.

Gewürztraminer is "the lady's wine"—its bouquet is like a rosebush, its taste is fruity, and its aftertaste is spicy—as its name implies (*gewürtz* means "spice" in German). Drink this with pâtés and local cheeses.

Pinot noir, the local red wine, is very light and fruity—if you want a red wine with body, look beyond Alsace. Pinot noir is generally served chilled.

Sylvaner—fresh and light, fruity and cheap—is a good wine for a hot day.

Pinot blanc is easy to drink as it's a middle-of-the-road but refreshing wine. It's neither too fruity or sweet nor too strong or dry—it's also not too memorable.

Crémant d'Alsace, the Alsatian sparkling wine, is very good—and much cheaper than Champagne.

You'll also see *eaux-de-vie,* powerful fruit-flavored brandies—try the *framboise* (raspberry) flavor.

In case you really get "Alsauced," the French term for headache is *mal à la tête.*

Towns and Sights Along the Route du Vin

These sights are listed in the order you'll encounter them if you're heading out from Colmar.

SOUTH OF COLMAR
Eguisheim
This is the most charming village of the region (described on page 964).

Vieil-Armand WWI Memorial (Hartmannswillerkopf)
This powerful memorial evokes the slaughter of the Western Front in World War I, when Germany and France bashed heads for years in a war of attrition. It's up a windy road above Cernay (20 miles south of Colmar). From the parking lot, walk 10 minutes to the vast cemetery, and walk 30 more minutes through trenches to a hilltop with a grand Alsatian view. Here you'll find a stirring memorial statue of French soldiers storming the trenches in 1915-1916—facing near-certain death—and rows of simple crosses marking the graves of those who lost their lives here.

ALSACE

NORTHWEST OF COLMAR
Turckheim
With a picturesque square and a garden-filled moat, this quiet town is refreshingly untouristy, just enough off the beaten path to be overlooked. Its 13th-century walls are some of the oldest in the region. Once upon a time, all foreign commerce entered Turckheim through its France Gate, which faces the train station. Today "foreign commerce" entering the gate includes tourists. Just inside the wall you'll see the **TI**, offering a helpful town map with a suggested stroll (Rue Wickram, tel. 03 89 27 38 44, www.turckheim. com).

Turckheim has a rich history and has long been famous for its wines. It gained town status in 1312, became a member of the Decapolis league of cities in 1354, and was devastated in the Thirty Years' War. In the 18th century it was rebuilt, thanks to the energy of Swiss immigrants. Reviving an old tradition, from May to October there's a town crier's tour each evening at 22:00 (in Alsatian and French).

Turckheim's **"Colmar Pocket" museum** (Musée Mémorial des Combats de la Poche de Colmar), chronicling the American push to take Alsace from the Nazis, is a hit with WWII buffs (€4, minimal English information; Wed-Sat 14:00-18:00, Sun 10:00-12:00 & 14:00-18:00, closed Mon-Tue except July-Sept 14:00-18:00, closed mid-Oct-mid-April, tel. 03 89 80 86 66, www. musee.turckheim-alsace.com).

Kaysersberg
This is the most historic town outside Colmar in the region. It has a fascinating medieval old center, Dr. Albert Schweitzer's house, and plenty of hiking opportunities (described on page 970).

Bennwihr
After this town was completely destroyed during World War II, the only object left standing was the compelling statue of two girls depicting Alsace and Lorraine (outside its modern church). The war memorials next to the statue list the names of those who died in both world wars. During World War II, 130,000 Alsatian men aged 17-37 were forced into military service under the German army (after fighting against them); most were sent to the deadly Russian front.

Riquewihr
This adorable town is the most touristed on the Route du Vin—and understandably so. If you find crowds tiresome, this town is exhausting (described on page 976).

ALSACE

Zellenberg
This place has an impressive setting and is worth a quick stop for the views from either side of its narrow perch.

Hunawihr
This bit of wine-soaked Alsatian cuteness is far less visited than its more famous neighbors, and features a 16th-century fortified church that today is shared by both Catholics and Protestants (the Catholics are buried next to the church; the Protestants are buried outside the church wall). Park at the village washbasin *(lavoir)* and follow the trail up to the church, then loop back through the village. Kids enjoy Hunawihr's small nature-conservation park, **Centre de Réintroduction,** where they'll spot otters *(loutre),* over 150 storks *(cigogne),* and more (€10, kids-€7-9, May-Sept daily 10:00-18:00, ticket booth closed for lunch in May and Sept, shorter hours in April and Oct, closed Nov-March, other animals take part in the afternoon shows—times listed on website, tel. 03 89 73 72 62, www.centredereintroduction.fr). A nearby **butterfly exhibit** (Le Jardin des Papillons) houses thousands of the delicate insects from around the world (€8, kids-€5.50, includes audioguide, Easter-Sept daily 10:00-18:00, until 17:00 in March-April and Oct, closed Nov-Easter, tel. 03 89 73 33 33, www.jardinsdespapillons.fr).

Ribeauvillé
This appealing town, less visited by Americans, is well situated for hiking and biking. It's a linear place with a long pedestrian street (Grande Rue) and feels less tourist-dependent than other towns. A steep but manageable trail leads from the top of the town into the Vosges Mountains to three castle ruins and is ideal for hikers wanting a walk in the woods to sweeping views. Follow Grand Rue uphill to the Hôtel aux Trois Châteaux and find the cobbled lane leading up from there. St. Ulrich is the most interesting of the three ruins (allow 2 hours round-trip, or 3 hours to see all 3 castles, or just climb 10 minutes for a view over the town—get info at TI at 1 Grand Rue, tel. 03 89 73 23 23, www.ribeauville-riquewihr. com). It's a short, sweet, and really hilly bike loop from Ribeauvillé to Hunawihr and Riquewihr (can be extended to Kaysersberg). You can rent a **bike** at Cycles Binder (Tue-Sat 8:30-12:00 & 14:30-19:00 or by appointment, closed Sun-Mon, 82 Grand Rue, tel. 03 89 73 65 87) or at Ribo' Cycles (Tue-Sat 9:00-12:00 & 14:00-18:00, Sat until 17:00, closed Sun-Mon, 17 Rue de Landau, tel. 03 89 73 72 94, www.ribocycles.fr).

▲Château du Haut-Kœnigsbourg
This granddaddy of Alsatian castles tiptoes along on a rocky spur of the Vosges Mountains, 2,500 feet above the flat Rhine plain. Here

ALSACE

you'll get an eagle's-nest perspective over the Vosges and villages below.

Cost and Hours: €9, kids 6-17-€5, ticket booth open daily April-Sept 9:15-17:15, June-Aug until 18:00; March and Oct 9:30-17:00; Nov-Feb 9:30-12:00 & 13:00-16:30; castle closes 45 minutes after ticket booth, audioguide-€4.50, about 15 minutes north of Ribeauvillé above St-Hippolyte, tel. 03 69 33 25 00, www.haut-koenigsbourg.fr.

Tours: An English leaflet and posted descriptions give a reasonable overview of key rooms and history, but the one-hour audioguide is a good investment for serious students. There's also an English-language guided tour offered daily at 11:45 in summer (call to confirm).

Getting There: A €4 shuttle bus runs to the castle from the Sélestat train station (8/day mid-April-mid-May and mid-June-mid-Sept, weekends only off-season, none Jan-mid-March, 30 minutes, timed with trains, call château for schedule or check website). Your shuttle ticket saves you €2 on the château entry fee. If driving in high season, expect to park along the road well below the castle (unless you come early). Parking can be a zoo in the summer—it's limited to roadside spaces.

Visiting the Castle: While the elaborate castle was rebuilt barely 100 years ago, it's a romantic's dream, sprawling along its sky-high ridge and providing helpful insight into this 15th-century mountain fortress.

Started in 1147 as an Imperial castle in the extensive network that served the Holy Roman Empire, Haut-Kœnigsbourg was designed to protect valuable trade routes. It was constantly under siege and eventually destroyed by rampaging Swedes in the 17th century. The castle sat in ruins until the early 1900s, when an ambitious restoration campaign began (which you'll learn much about—a model in the castle storeroom shows the castle before its renovation).

Today's castle—well-furnished by medieval standards—highlights Germanic influence in Alsatian history with decorations and weapons from the 15th through 17th centuries. Don't miss the top-floor Grand Bastion with its elaborate wooden roof structure and models showing its construction. There are cannons and magnificent views in all directions.

Eguisheim

Just a few miles south of Colmar's suburbs, this circular, flower-festooned little wine town (pop. 1,600), often mobbed by tourists, is a delight. In 2013 it was named France's favorite town.

Eguisheim ("ay-gush-I'm") is ideal for a relaxing lunch and vineyard walks—and the town is all about welcoming guests. If you have a car, it can make a good small-town base for exploring Alsace. It's a cinch by car (easy parking) and manageable by bike (see "Getting Around the Route du Vin—By Bike," earlier), but barely accessible by bus (except during the Christmas season, when special shuttles run). Consider taking the bus one way and taxi the other to Colmar or other villages (bus schedules available at TIs and posted at key stops).

Orientation to Eguisheim

The **TI** has free Wi-Fi and information on bus schedules, festivals, vineyard walks, and Vosges Mountain hikes (May-Oct Mon-Sat 9:30-12:30 & 13:30-18:00—but closes Sat at 17:00, Sun 10:30-12:30 & 13:30-16:30; shorter hours and closed Sun off-season, 22 Grand Rue, tel. 03 89 23 40 33, www.ot-eguisheim.fr). They're happy to call a taxi for you (about €15 to Colmar).

Eguisheim's **bus stop** is at the top end of the village, close to Place Charles de Gaulle (see map, same stop for both directions).

Alsa Cyclo Tours has rental bikes with GPS and recorded directions in English (electric bike-€25/half-day, €35/day; regular bike-€15/half-day, €25/day; GPS-€3; May-Oct daily 9:00-18:00, 6 Rue Rempart Sud, mobile 06 19 23 53 62, www.alsacyclotours.alsace). They also offer bike tours from Colmar (€35, 2.5 hours, includes electric bike).

Public **WC**s are located in the lower pay parking lot, and automatic WC cabins are a few steps from the fountain on Place du Château Saint-Léon, in a courtyard off Cours Unterlinden (hidden on the right).

Eguisheim Walk

Draw a circle and then cut a line straight through it. That's your plan with this inviting little town. The main drag (Grand Rue) cuts through the middle, with gates at either end and a stately town square in the center. And, while Eguisheim's town wall is long gone, it left a circular lane (Rue du Rempart—Nord and Sud) lined with gingerbread-cute houses.

Start your self-guided walk at the bottom of town (near the TI) and circle the former ramparts clockwise, walking left up Rue du Rempart Sud (just after the Auberge du Rempart hotel). The most enchanting and higgledy-piggledy view in town is right at the

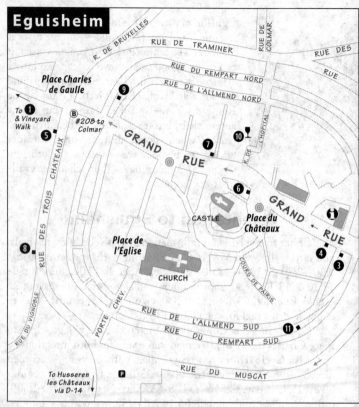

Eguisheim

ALSACE

start of the loop (at the tight Y in the road; go left and uphill). Rue du Rempart Sud is more picturesque than Rue du Rempart Nord, but I'd walk the entire circle. You'll see that what was once the wall is now lined with 13th- to 17th-century houses—a cancan of half-timbered charm. You're actually walking a lane between the back of fine homes (on the left) and their barns (on the right). Look for emblems of daily life: religious and magical symbols, dates on lintel stones, little hatch doors leading to wine or coal cellars, and so on. (Everything looks sharp because the government subsidizes the work locals do on their exteriors.) Along the way, you may bump into Chez Thierry's *saucisson* stand (plenty of tasty samples) and Frederic Hertzog's farmhouse cheese shop (try the Munster cheese—made in the town of Munster just up the valley). The loop takes a decidedly hip turn along its northern half, as you pass an art gallery, a cool coffee shop, and a trendy bar.

When exploring the town, you may come upon some of its 20 "tithe courtyards." Farmers who worked on land owned by the Church came to these courtyards to pay their tithes (10 percent of

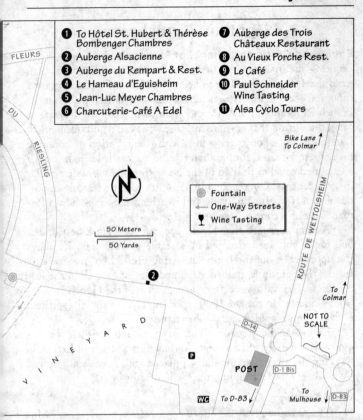

- **1** To Hôtel St. Hubert & Thérèse Bombenger Chambres
- **2** Auberge Alsacienne
- **3** Auberge du Rempart & Rest.
- **4** Le Hameau d'Eguisheim
- **5** Jean-Luc Meyer Chambres
- **6** Charcuterie-Café A Edel
- **7** Auberge des Trois Châteaux Restaurant
- **8** Au Vieux Porche Rest.
- **9** Le Café
- **10** Paul Schneider Wine Tasting
- **11** Alsa Cyclo Tours

their production). With so many of these courtyards, it's safe to conclude that the farming around here was *formidable*.

When you've finished the loop, walk up Grand Rue to Eguisheim's main square—Place du Château Saint-Léon. It's lined with fine Renaissance houses; many were mansions for the managers of wealthy estates and vineyards owned by absentee landowners. The mini castle is privately owned and closed to the public—its chapel (described below) was built into it more than 100 years ago.

The 19th-century fountain sports a statue of St. Leo IX—the only Alsatian pope. Leo was born, likely in this castle, in 1002. A bishop at 24, he was famed for his pastoral qualities, tending the sick and poor, and working to reform the Church (which had grown corrupt). Made pope in 1048, Leo's pontificate lasted just five years.

Your walk is over. Enjoy sampling the shops, cafés, and fruits of the local vine.

ALSACE

Sights in Eguisheim

Eguisheim Castle and Chapel of St. Leo IX

Fronting the main square, the town castle has an octagonal plan from the 13th century. There's been some kind of castle here for a thousand years—the first was the fortress of a local duke. After the French Revolution, the castle was state-owned and, as the state so often did during that no-nonsense age, it was sold and dismantled. Later, a local bishop purchased it with the intention of honoring his hometown saint. Rather than rebuild the castle keep, he built a chapel dedicated to St. Leo in the Neo-Romanesque style popular in 19th century. Consecrated in 1894, it's of little historic importance. But it's beautiful inside and worth a peek to see how a Romanesque church may have been painted.

As you approach the church, you can see a stork nest on the bell tower and are welcomed by a statue of Pope Leo IX above the doorway—note the lions supporting him ("Leo" means lion). Inside, the paintings, stained glass, and carvings are all in the Romanesque Revival style. After the paganism of the French Revolution, romantics in the late 1800s used this style to signal a spiritual revival—a new golden age of Christianity.

Linger awhile to soak it all in. To the right of the altar is a reliquary with a piece of Leo's jaw. To the left is a statue of Leo. And flanking the altar, two fine stained-glass angels majestically spread their wings (drop a coin into the €0.50 box for light).

Wine Tasting

Don't leave without visiting one of Eguisheim's countless cozy wineries. And please, if you taste for free, purchase at least one bottle.

Paul Schneider's independent winery is located in a one-time hospice, now run by a third-generation family winemaker. They are licensed as a bar, so enjoy a glass (€3-7), or try a few wines in the traditionally furnished tasting room before buying a bottle. Ask Claire to explain the abstract paintings on the walls (also found on the labels of their Grands Crus)—they give a modern twist to some old Alsatian traditions. Call ahead for a short but worthwhile tour of the two cellars (daily 9:00-12:00 & 14:00-18:30, 1 Rue de l'Hôpital, tel. 03 89 41 50 07, www.vins-paul-schneider.fr, vins.paul.schneider@wanadoo.fr).

Views over Eguisheim

If you have a car, follow signs up to *Husseren Les Cinq Châteaux*, then walk 20 minutes to the ruined castle towers for a good view of the Vosges Mountains above and vineyards below (road closed mid-Nov to mid-March). For even better views, drive to Château du Hohlandsbourg and scamper on its ramparts (www.chateau-hohlandsbourg.com).

ALSACE

By mountain bike or on foot, find any path through the vineyards above Eguisheim for great views (the TI has a free map). Here's the most direct route: Walk uphill on Grand Rue, cross the ring road, follow *Camping* signs, and enter the vineyards past the campground. Orient yourself using the big vineyard-display panel and wander the lanes as high as you like. It's OK to walk on dirt paths between the vines. You'll find occasional vineyard information posted in English and see the five châteaux of Husseren floating above. The TI's map shows a longer walk through the vineyards from the same starting point.

Sleeping in Eguisheim

($$$$ = Splurge, $$$ = Pricier, $$ = Moderate, $ = Budget)

$$ Hôtel St. Hubert* offers 15 spotless rooms with modern, German-hotelesque comfort (and strict management to match), and an indoor pool and sauna. The 10-minute walk from the town center is rewarded with vineyards out your window (family rooms, 4 rooms have patios, reception open 8:00-12:00 & 15:00-21:00, 6 Rue des Trois Pierres, tel. 03 89 41 40 50, www.hotel-st-hubert. com, reservation@hotel-st-hubert.com).

$ Auberge Alsacienne* is conveniently located near the lower parking area with reasonably priced, sharp rooms in a picturesque building (12 Grand Rue, tel. 03 89 41 50 20, www.auberge-alsacienne.net, auberge-alsacienne@wanadoo.fr).

$ Auberge du Rempart is a rockin' deal. It's atmospheric, with bright, airy rooms with big beds and surprisingly elaborate decor above a lively café/restaurant deep inside the town. Rooms get some noise from the restaurant on warm nights (rooms with air-con cost more, great family suite, near TI at 3 Rue du Rempart Sud, tel. 03 89 41 16 87, www.auberge-du-rempart.com, auberge-du-rempart@wanadoo.fr). The reception desk is in the restaurant and is usually open only during lunch and after 18:00.

CHAMBRES D'HOTES

$ Le Hameau d'Eguisheim, on the grounds of the Pierre Henri Ginglinger organic winery, has five big, bright, tastefully decorated rooms. Stéphanie has transformed the 17th-century place into a cozy cocoon (family rooms and apartments from €170, includes breakfast in the old cellar). She also rents two triple-bed studios for up to six people (3-night minimum, fully equipped kitchen, no breakfast, across from TI at 33 Grand Rue, tel. 03 89 24 18 66, www.hameau-eguisheim.com, contact@hameau-eguisheim.com).

$ Winemaker Jean-Luc Meyer rents modern rooms, some with balcony, and apartments for 2 to 12 people at good rates (includes breakfast in their tasting room, kitchenettes, good family

ALSACE

options, Wi-Fi at reception only, 4 Rue des Trois Châteaux, tel. 03 89 24 53 66, www.vins-meyer-eguisheim.com, info@vins-meyer-eguisheim.com).

$ Thérèse Bombenger is sweet, speaks some English, and has a contemporary French home just above Eguisheim with three rooms and nice views into the vineyards and over town (includes breakfast, communal fridge and microwave, across from Hôtel St. Hubert at 3 Rue des Trois Pierres, tel. 03 89 23 71 19, mobile 06 61 94 31 09, bombenger.marie-therese@wanadoo.fr). She'll pick you up at the station in Colmar if scheduled in advance, and she'll do your laundry if you ask nicely.

Eating in Eguisheim

$ Charcuterie-Café A Edel, on Place du Château St. Léon IX, has killer quiche "to go" and everything you need for a fun picnic, including small tubs of chopped veggies (daily until 19:00). You can picnic by the fountain or eat at their adjacent restaurant while listening to the trickling of the square's fountain (restaurant open Thu-Mon until 18:00, closed Tue-Wed, *tartes flambées* and quiche served with small salads, 2 Place du Château St. Léon IX, tel. 03 89 41 22 40).

$$ Auberge des Trois Châteaux is straight out of *Hansel and Gretel,* with cozy ambience and traditional cuisine (affordable *plats du jour,* closed Tue evening and all day Wed, 26 Grand Rue, tel. 03 89 23 70 61).

$$ Auberge du Rempart is best for outdoor dining in a pleasant courtyard around a big fountain. Come here for less expensive and lighter meals (closed Mon, Thu, and Sun evenings Sept-June; near TI at 3 Rue du Rempart Sud, tel. 03 89 41 16 87).

$$$ Au Vieux Porche is a wood-beamed, white-tablecloth affair serving a blend of regional favorites and cuisine from other areas. It's ideal for a leisurely meal or a special occasion (closed Tue, upper end of town at 16 Rue des Trois Châteaux, tel. 03 89 24 01 90, www.auvieuxporche.fr).

$$ Le Café, a cool hangout morning and night, is run by English-speaking Reiner (drinks and light snacks only, cozy outdoor seating, on Rue Allmend Nord near the top of the village, daily 10:00-22:00).

Kaysersberg

The domain of Germanic princes for much of its history, Kaysersberg ("Emperor's Mountain") was of strategic importance, thanks to its location guarding the important route over the Vosges Mountains that links Colmar with the big city of Nancy. Today,

philosopher-physician Albert Schweitzer's hometown offers a cute jumble
of 15th-century homes under a romantically ruined castle with easy vineyard
trails at its doorstep, and plenty of tourists. Reasonable bus service from Colmar
makes Kaysersberg a convenient day trip
(bus #145, direction: Le Bonhomme, 7/
day, 30 minutes, check schedule at www.
vialsace.eu).

Orientation to Kaysersberg

The **TI** is two blocks from the town's main entry, inside Hôtel de
Ville at 39 Rue du Général de Gaulle (mid-June-Sept Mon-Sat
9:00-12:30 & 14:00-18:00, Sun 9:30-12:30; mid-Sept-mid-June
Mon-Sat 9:30-12:00 & 14:00-17:30, closed Sun; tel. 03 89 78 22
78, www.kaysersberg.com). The TI has a free guest computer, rents
audioguides for touring Kaysersberg (€5, €150 deposit, allow 1.5
hours, includes castle ruins), and rents electric bikes (€13/half-
day, €20/day, April-Oct only, reserve in advance). Pick up town
and valley maps, bus schedules, and detailed descriptions of hiking trails between wine villages (€0.50 each; see "Walking/Biking
Trails from Kaysersberg," later).

All buses from Colmar serve the Rocade Verte stop at a parking lot on the village's south side, just outside the town walls (best
stop for return trip). Drivers will find pay lots (€2/day) along the
town's ring road. Porte Basse Parking works best, but all lots offer
easy walking access to the center.

Find **WC**s next to the TI and across from the Schweitzer Museum. There's a fun **Monday-morning market** at the top of town,
across from the Schweitzer Museum, and a smaller food-and-drink
market at the Porte Basse parking lot on Friday evenings (16:30-
19:00).

Kaysersberg Walk

Start your self-guided town stroll in the center of Kaysersberg at
the main square, Place de la Mairie. Face Hôtel de Ville and walk
along the main drag to its left.

After a few steps, you'll find a round arch from 1604 on the
right. Walking through the arch, you'll go past a former gunpowder
storehouse (now a hall used for free art exhibits) and a well. Walk
into a typical Alsatian courtyard with a wooden gallery and cas-
cades of geraniums. The painting from 1993 celebrates the 700th
anniversary of Kaysersberg's status as an Imperial city. In 1293, a

Albert Schweitzer
(1875-1965)

I don't know what your destiny will be, but one thing I do know: The only ones among you who will be really happy are those who have sought and found how to serve.

—Albert Schweitzer

Albert Schweitzer—theologian, musician, philosopher, and physician—was an unusually gifted individual who never hesitated to question accepted beliefs and practices. He is probably most famous for his work with sufferers of leprosy and tuberculosis in Africa.

Born to German parents in 1875 in Kaysersberg, he studied philosophy and theology at the University of Strasbourg, eventually becoming a pastor at his church. Not satisfied with that, Schweitzer studied music and soon gained fame as a musical scholar and organist. After trying his hand at writing with *The Quest of the Historical Jesus,* which challenged contemporary secular views of Jesus, he shifted his attention to medicine. He married Helene Bresslau, and the couple left for Africa and founded a missionary hospital in Gabon (then called Lambaréné). During World War I, Schweitzer and his wife were forced out of Africa by the French.

After the war, Schweitzer returned to Gabon on his own, where he remained for most of the rest of his life. He received the 1952 Nobel Peace Prize for his service to humanity, particularly for founding the Albert Schweitzer Hospital in Gabon, where he died in 1965. He was 90 years old.

ALSACE

local prince gave Kaysersberg trade and tax status and the right to build strong city walls. Later, in 1354, the town was a founding member of the Decapolis.

Go back through the arch, turn right, and continue up the main street, Rue de Général de Gaulle. Kaysersberg is known for its handmade glass, and at **Verrerie d'Art de Kaysersberg** (across from the Church of the Holy Cross), you can see glassblowers at work and browse their showroom (workshop generally open Tue-Sat 10:00-12:30 & 14:00-18:00). While the craft almost died out here in the 18th century, it's alive and well now.

Opposite the glassworks (on the side of the church), read some of the names on the **war memorial**—that's a lot of war dead for a small town. We're in France now, but all of this fighting was done for Germany. In World War I they fought on the Western Front. After Hitler annexed Alsace in World War II, local boys were sent to Russia and Poland (far from home, so they couldn't desert). Notice also the noncombatant victims: Some were sent to death camps and others died in bombing raids. In 1944 Allied bombers destroyed 45 percent of Kaysersberg—and that included many of its citizens.

In front of the **Church of the Holy Cross** stands a fountain featuring the Roman Emperor Constantine—holding a cross and honored here because he was the first Christian emperor. Up on the simple Romanesque facade of the church is his mom, Helen. She converted her son to Christianity and, according to Church lore, brought pieces of the True Cross to Rome from Jerusalem.

Before stepping into the church, take a moment to enjoy the architecture surrounding this square. The church dates from the 13th and 14th centuries (free, daily 9:00-18:00). I know, Gothic was in high gear elsewhere, but back then Alsace was about a hundred years behind the artistic curve. Look at the tympanum (carved relief over the door) and notice how crude and naive it is. The carved red sandstone figures remind me of Archaic Greek statues.

Step inside. The nave is Romanesque, but the side aisles, dating from the 15th century when the church was expanded, are more Gothic. The medieval stained glass was destroyed in 1944; what you see is modern. The impressive statue of a crucified Christ is carved out of linden wood and painted. Notice the attempt to manage the perspective by making Jesus' legs shorter than they actually would have been.

Walk up close to the altarpiece (from 1518) and study the finely carved Passion of Christ. These scenes show the events of Jesus' last week—from entering Jerusalem (on the left) to the Resurrection (on the right). The carvings—which are high relief in the center but low relief in the wings so it will all fit when closed—were inspired by 15th-century engravings by Martin Schongauer.

On the right side of the nave (as you leave), check out the statue of the Deposition, showing Christ after his death by crucifixion. A metal hatch on his chest shows where the communion bread was kept back in the 16th century.

Continue walking along this busy street. At #62, the **Kaysersberg History Museum** has a forgettable exhibit of religious and domestic artifacts filling three rooms—without a word of English (€2; July-Aug Wed-Mon 10:00-12:00 & 14:00-18:00, closed Tue; closed off-season; enter from the courtyard between the twin gables). The **Biscuiterie La Table Alsacienne,** tempting visitors with all the traditional baked goods at #70, is more interesting. Next door, you can pop inside the Moulin des Arts to see what's left of an old town mill.

Follow the main drag to the top of the town. Just before the bridge, check out a huge house standing at the top of the road—this was an old inn and bathhouse (handy WCs behind). To its right, a quieter lane leads past a fountain with drinking water, a charming pottery shop, and on to the castle (with a loop path back to the TI).

Maison Herzer, on the right at #101, dates from 1592. Its finely restored ornamentation includes fun faces (could be the owners) and a gargoyle-supported pulley high above to lift hay up to the attic. Look around. Notice how some buildings lining the main drag have settled in the soft ground.

Just before the bridge, walk a few steps up the riverside lane to see where the town's canal starts—an example of the importance of water power in the Middle Ages.

Kaysersberg's bridge was fortified on the upstream side to stop enemy boats from entering town. Look downstream; the helter-skelter roofs were for drying the leather and hides of a tannery.

On this 16th-century bridge, find the emblems of the Holy Roman Empire (double eagle) and of Kaysersberg (two bags with a belt to tie goods to the trader's horse). These signs—plus the nearby saint-in-a-cage emblem (Constantine with the Holy Cross and Christ)—meant this bridge offered both political and religious protection for people coming and going.

At the end of World War II, as the Nazis were preparing to retreat, they planned to destroy the bridge. Locals reasoned with the commander, agreeing to dig an anti-tank ditch just beyond the bridge—and the symbol of the town was saved.

Cross the bridge and look back above the bathhouse with its stork nest. (Storks are choosy and often don't like man-made nest cages like this one.) High on the ridge is the town's 12th-century castle and city wall.

Your walk is finished. The castle is an easy climb, and the Albert Schweitzer Museum is a block beyond the bridge.

SIGHTS IN KAYSERSBERG
Wine Tasting

The Cave des Vignerons de Kaysersberg represents 150 winemakers from around Kaysersberg, including several Grands Crus, and offers free and easy wine tastings with experts who speak "a leetl" English (Wed-Sun 10:30-13:00 & 14:00-18:30, closed Mon-Tue except July-Aug, near TI at 20 Rue du Général de Gaulle, tel. 03 89 47 18 43).

Albert Schweitzer Museum

The home of Dr. Albert Schweitzer is a small museum offering two rooms of scattered photos and artifacts from his time in Africa. Schweitzer was a Renaissance man who opened people's eyes to conditions in the Third

World (€2, Easter-Oct Thu-Tue 9:00-12:00 & 14:00-18:00, closed Wed and Nov-Easter, 126 Rue du Général de Gaulle, tel. 03 89 47 36 55).

Walking/Biking Trails from Kaysersberg

Trails start just outside the TI (get details at the TI). To find the main trail, turn left as you walk out of the TI and walk under the arch. Signs lead hikers up through the vineyards to grand views over the town. It's a worthwhile 10-minute climb to the ruined **castle** (free, always open, more great views and benches, 113 steps up a dark stairway to the top of the tower—worth the climb). Loop back down behind the castle and enter the town near its 16th-century bridge. Or hikers can continue past the castle for more views and trails (TI has detailed map for €0.50). For great views of Kaysersberg sans the climb, follow the trail described next (toward Kientzheim) for about 10 minutes.

For a scenic 2-hour hike—or 40-minute bike ride—along a paved lane over vine-covered hills to **Riquewihr,** turn right on the main trail near the TI. You'll start on a bike path *(piste cyclable)* to **Kientzheim** (well-marked with green crosses and bike icons). In Kientzheim, follow the *sentier viticole* uphill through vineyards to wonderful views and on to Riquewihr. If you get turned around, stop any biker or vineyard worker and ask, *"À Riquewihr?"* (ah reek-veer). Drivers can follow the same signs from Kientzheim to Riquewihr.

NEAR KAYSERSBERG
World War II Sights

The Second World War rolled wildly back and forth through this region. Some towns were entirely destroyed. Others made it through unscathed. Towns with gray rather than red-tiled roofs were rebuilt after 1945. Kientzheim has an American-made tank parked in its front yard (and a wine museum in its castle grounds) and a network of tiny streams trickling down its streets (as was commonplace around here before World War II). The towns of Sigolsheim (which was the scene of fierce fighting—note its sterile, rebuilt Romanesque church) and nearby Bennwihr are modern, as they were taken and lost a dozen times by the Allies and Nazis and completely ruined.

The hill just north of Kaysersberg is soaked in soldiers' blood. It houses a **World War II Memorial** and is still called "Bloody Hill" by locals (as it was nicknamed by German troops). The spectacular setting, best at sunset, houses a monument to the American divisions that helped liberate Alsace in World War II (find the American flag). Up the lane, a beautiful cemetery is the final resting place of 1,600 men who fought in the French army (many gravestones are Muslim, for soldiers from France's North African colonies—Morocco, Algeria, and Tunisia). From this brilliant viewpoint you can survey the entire southern section of the Route du Vin and into Germany. The castle hanging high to the north is the Château du Haut-Kœnigsbourg (described earlier).

Riquewihr

This little village, wrapped in vineyards, is so picturesque today because it was so rich centuries ago, thanks to wine exports. You can recognize its old wealth because it has the most stone houses of any place in Alsace. The village is crammed with shops, cafés, galleries, cobblestones, flowers, and German tourists. Arrive early or visit late if you can, as midday crowds can trample its ample charms.

Orientation to Riquewihr

Buses drop you off at the lower end of the village, opposite the post office; drivers can park in spaces along the ring road or at the lots on either end of town (€3/2 hours). Walk into town under Hôtel de Ville's archway; the main drag runs uphill from here. The **TI** is halfway up at 2 Rue de la 1ère Armée (Mon-Sat 9:30-12:00 & 14:00-18:00, Sun 10:30-13:30, shorter hours off-season and closed Sun; tel. 03 89 73 23 23, www.ribeauville-riquewihr.com). A good WC is behind the TI. Quieter lanes lead off the main drag. For a taxi, call 03 89 73 73 71 or mobile 06 46 84 40 05.

Riquewihr Walk

Start your self-guided walk at the bottom of town. At the **archway** going through Hôtel de Ville, notice the three flags: Europe, France, and Alsace. Notice also the clever bench just outside designed for ladies with loads on their heads (perhaps baskets of grapes) to sit and take a load off their head. Entering the sleepy (except for tourism) town of 1,300 people, you realize that sans wine and tourism, this place would have no economy. Find the historic map designed to help you imagine Riquewihr in 1644 and appreciate its double wall and moat.

Strolling up Riquewihr's **main street,** Rue de Général de Gaulle, which cuts straight through town, enjoy the architecture. It's fun to remember that before street numbers, each house had a name—often related to an animal—which made it a kind of landmark. Because villages often had only two or three family names, you couldn't say "the Jones house." You'd say, rather, "the Unicorn House."

The vineyards surrounding town belonged to absentee princes.

The impressive **mansions** all around were the domains of men who managed the estate of a feudal lord and, in return, got a cut of the production. At #14 you can see what would have been considered a skyscraper in the 16th century—the highest Renaissance building in Alsace. At #18, notice the broad arches for wagons of grapes. Venture into the courtyard (filled with restaurant tables; lookie-lous are welcome) with its traditional Alsatian galleries and evocative old well. At the entry is a collection of 200-year-old iron stove plates. Decorated with old German texts, these were placed behind the fire to both protect the back wall and reflect heat out. All the way in the back, you'll find the mammoth 1817 wine press that drained juice directly into the cellar.

At the town's main intersection is a street leading to two churches (Protestant to the right, Catholic to the left and neither of sightseeing interest). Before the age of private plumbing, public fountains were scattered through town.

Find the sign for the **town gourmet** at #42. The word "gourmet" originated here in France, where each town in winemaking regions had an official wine judge, appraiser, and middleman. The gourmet was instrumental in effectively connecting the vintner with the thirsty market. He facilitated sales and set prices. To judge the wine, he needed to have a little fine food to complement the tasting. The town appointed the gourmet, and the position—quite lucrative as you can see by this fine house—was then handed down from father to son. While the traditional function of the gourmet died out in the 1930s, the concept of the person with the best food in town—the gourmet—survives to this day.

Wander through the gourmet's courtyards. Notice the nails on timbers designed to hold stucco. In the 18th and 19th centuries, half-timbered houses were considered "low class," so owners stuccoed over the wood to make it look like a stone home. Follow the gangly wooden structures to the roofline in back to see a stone wall protruding above the roof tiles—built to stop fires. Back when roofs were made with wood shingles (rather than today's safer terra-cotta), fire was a serious problem.

At the top of town stands one of the most impressive **guard towers** in Alsace (Le Dolder, from 1291). The Dolder Museum, inside the tower, has small rooms covering its history—but doesn't merit the climb or €4 entry fee. Look for the engraving of 13th-century Riquewihr by the fountain opposite the tower's entry.

Older towns were fortified with **walls** built to withstand arrows. When they grew bigger—and war technology advanced to include gunpowder and cannons—the townspeople built a stouter wall outside the original wall. In this case, it left an area in the middle for "newer" 18th-century houses. Notice how homes were built right into the defensive walls.

ALSACE

From the top of town, it's rewarding to turn left and explore the quiet lanes and their picturesque houses. Pass under the bell tower, take a left on Rue des Remparts, and explore. Turn right when you see steps down to the moat (and the big wine press), and double back to the top of the town along the moat.

Sights in Riquewihr

Tourist Train
Within a few yards of the town entry, you'll see the *petit train* (€7, next departure time posted, 30 minutes). For those without a car, it's handy as it choo-choos into the vineyards, offering terrific views over the village.

Wine Tasting
The vines surrounding Riquewihr produce some of Alsace's most prestigious wines—and the village is lined with good places to sample them. **Caves Dopff et Irion** sits just above Hôtel de Ville and provides a handsome wine-tasting experience with an English-speaking staff (€7-20 bottles, most about €10, special counter for *eau-de-vie* tastings, daily 10:00-18:00, shorter hours in winter, tel. 03 89 49 08 92, www.dopff-irion.com). **Caves Hugel,** another well-respected producer, has an intimate tasting room on the main drag a bit past the TI (daily 9:00-12:00 & 13:00-18:00, tel. 03 89 47 92 15, www.hugel.com).

Musée de la Communication
This museum, located near the bottom of town (at its château), takes you through the evolution of man's ability to send messages, from mail delivery to mobile phones. The fascinating and substantial museum, with lots of historic artifacts, is by far the most important sight to see in town (€5, some English descriptions, April-Oct and Dec daily 10:00-17:30, closed Nov and Jan-March, tel. 03 89 47 93 80, www.shpta.com).

Scenic Routes from Riquewihr
A path with sensational views leads from the north edge of town. Find the *sentier viticole* at the lower end of town (a few blocks to the right as you face Hôtel de Ville) and climb into the vineyards as high as your legs allow. With a car, as you leave town at the main roundabout, take D-311 toward Ribeauvillé and find the signs *(sentier viticole des grands crus)* on the left leading up toward Hunawihr.

On the town's south side, another *sentier viticole* leads to Kientzheim (then Kaysersberg), starting from the TI and heading out Rue de la 1ère Armée. Follow blue signs to *Kientzheim* on this beautiful walk or bike ride. The lane rises, then drops into the village—revealing spectacular views all the way (allow 1.75 hours to hike at a steady pace to Kaysersberg, 40 minutes by bike). Drivers can follow the same route and get the same great views, but must go slowly and watch out for bikers.

Strasbourg

Strasbourg is urban Alsace at its best—it feels like a giant Colmar with rivers and streetcars. It's a progressive, livable city, with generous space devoted to pedestrians, scads of bikes, mod trams, meandering waterways,  and a young, lively mix of university students, Eurocrats, and street people. This city of about 275,000 residents has an Amsterdam-like feel. Bordering the west bank of the Rhine River, Strasbourg provides the ultimate blend of Franco-Germanic culture, architecture, and ambience. A living symbol of the hope for perpetual peace between France and Germany, Strasbourg was selected as home to the European Parliament, the European Council (sharing administrative responsibilities for the European Union with Brussels, Belgium), and the European Court of Human Rights.

PLANNING YOUR TIME

Strasbourg makes a good day trip from Colmar. And, thanks to high-speed TGV-train service, it also makes a handy stop for train travelers en route to or from Paris (baggage storage available). The Alsatian Museum is the only museum worth the admission—you're here to see the cathedral, wander the waterways, and take a bite out of the big city. Plan on three hours to hit the highlights, starting at Strasbourg's dazzling cathedral (arrive in Strasbourg by 10:30 if you want to see the noon cathedral clock performance—popular but skippable) and ending with the district called La Petite France (ideally for lunch).

Orientation to Strasbourg

TOURIST INFORMATION

Strasbourg's main TI faces the cathedral (daily 9:00-19:00, 17 Place de la Cathédrale, tel. 03 88 52 28 28, www.otstrasbourg.fr, info@otstrasbourg.fr). Learn about special events (like the summer sound-and-light show at the cathedral, mentioned in "Sights in Strasbourg," later) and buy the €1.50 city map, which describes a

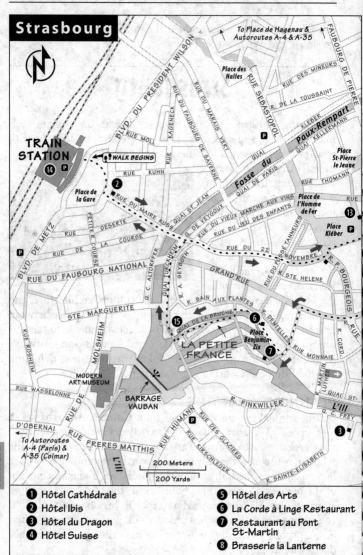

Strasbourg

- ① Hôtel Cathédrale
- ② Hôtel Ibis
- ③ Hôtel du Dragon
- ④ Hôtel Suisse
- ⑤ Hôtel des Arts
- ⑥ La Corde à Linge Restaurant
- ⑦ Restaurant au Pont St-Martin
- ⑧ Brasserie la Lanterne

decent walking tour in English, or pay €5.50 to rent an audioguide that covers the cathedral and old city in more detail than most need (includes a cute little map of the route, allow 1.5 hours). The TI also has bike maps for the city (€1 with English explanations) and surrounding areas.

The **Strasbourg Pass** (€19, kids-€10-13), valid three days, is a great value for travelers wanting to do it all. It includes one free museum entry and a half-off coupon for another museum, a discount on the town audioguide, free half-day bike rental, free boat

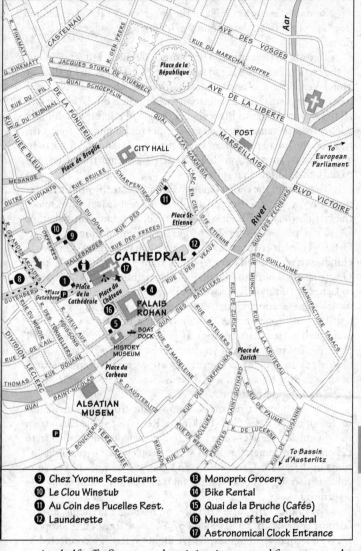

9	Chez Yvonne Restaurant	**13**	Monoprix Grocery
10	Le Clou Winstub	**14**	Bike Rental
11	Au Coin des Pucelles Rest.	**15**	Quai de la Bruche (Cafés)
12	Launderette	**16**	Museum of the Cathedral
		17	Astronomical Clock Entrance

cruise, half-off a Segway and a mini train tour, and free entry to the cathedral narthex view and the astrological clock tour.

ARRIVAL IN STRASBOURG

By Train: TGV trains serve Strasbourg's gleaming train station (free Wi-Fi). Limited baggage storage is available at platform 1 (daily 6:15-21:15, allow time for its airport-type security screening, cash only). WCs are in the station's south *(sud)* hall, across from the stairs to platform 2. Ticket counters are on the north *(nord)* side.

Rental bikes are available in the lower level of the glass atrium (see "Helpful Hints," later), and you'll find many budget eating options.

To **walk** to the cathedral in 15 urban minutes, exit straight out of the station, cross the big square (Place de la Gare), and walk past Hôtel Vendôme and up Rue du Maire Kuss. Cross the river, and continue up serpentine, pedestrian-friendly Rue du 22 Novembre all the way to the grand Place Kléber. Angle a bit left through Place Kléber (whose namesake graces the center of the square), then turn right on the broad pedestrian street (Rue des Grandes Arcades). In a few blocks, turn left on Rue Mercière (just after the merry-go-round), then follow that spire.

To get from the train station to the city center by **public transportation,** catch the caterpillar-like tram that leaves from under the station (buy €1.70 one-way ticket, €3.30 round-trip ticket, or €4.30 day pass, deals for 2-3 people, buy from machines on platforms—coins or credit card with a chip, then validate in skinny machines, www.cts-strasbourg.fr). Take tram #A (direction: Illkirch Graffenstaden) or tram #D (direction: Aristide Briand) three stops to Langross-Grande Rue, two blocks from the cathedral. (You can return to the station, Gare Centrale, from the same stop.)

By Car: You're better off day-tripping in by train (it's faster and much easier than driving). If you must drive, take sortie #4 from A-35. From this exit you can follow *Centre-Ville* and *Cathédrale* signs to the city center, then park at metered street spaces or in a central lot signed as *La Petite France, Gare Centrale,* or *la Cathédrale* (figure €3/hour).

For less money and stress, follow signs from the same autoroute exit to the *Elsau P+R* (Parking & Relais) lot at the Elsau tram station outside the city center (€4.10/day includes round-trip tram tickets to the center for up to seven people; take green-line "F" tram in direction: Centre-Ville and exit at Homme de Fer stop, validate parking ticket at scanner on tram platform both going and returning).

By Plane: The user-friendly Strasbourg-Entzheim airport (airport code: SXB, tel. 03 88 64 67 67, www.strasbourg.aeroport. fr), with frequent, often inexpensive flights to Paris, is connected by train to the main rail station (€2.60, 10-minute trip).

HELPFUL HINTS

Quiet Transportation: Beware of quiet trams and bicycles—look both ways before crossing streets.

Post Office: It's at the cathedral (Mon-Fri 9:00-18:00, Sat 9:00-17:00, closed Sun).

Laundry: You'll find a handy launderette at 15 Rue des Veaux, near my recommended hotels (daily 7:00-21:00).

ALSACE

Bike Rental: You can rent bikes at **Vélhop,** one level below street level at the train station (€5/day, €150 deposit, Mon-Fri 8:00-19:00, Sat-Sun 9:30-19:00, shorter hours off-season, follow bike signs, Place de la Gare, tel. 09 60 17 74 63, www.velhop. strasbourg.eu).

Taxi: Call 03 88 36 13 13 or mobile 06 80 43 22 25.

Car Rental: All major companies are at or near the train station.

Route du Vin Tour: See page 958 for recommended minivan tours of the Route du Vin.

Sights in Strasbourg

▲▲Strasbourg Cathedral
(Cathédrale de Notre-Dame)

Stand in front of Hôtel de la Cathédrale and crane your neck way back. If this church, with its cloud-piercing spire and pink sand-

stone color, drops your jaw today, imagine its impact on medieval tourists. At 466 feet, that spire was the world's tallest until the mid-1800s. A matching second tower was planned but never built. The delicate Gothic style of the cathedral (begun in 1176, not finished until 1429) is another Franco-German concoction that somehow survived the French Revolution, the Franco-Prussian War, World War I, and World War II (though it was damaged by British and American WWII bombing raids).

    Cost and Hours: Free, daily 7:00-11:15 & 12:45-19:00. The midday closing is for a special €2 viewing of the astronomical clock (described later).

    Visiting the Cathedral: Before entering the cathedral, survey the scene. The **square** in front of the cathedral makes the ideal stage for street performers—it's a medieval fair. This stage was Roman 2,000 years ago and then, as now, it was the center of activity. The dark half-timbered building to your left, next to the TI, was the home of a wealthy merchant in the 16th century and symbolizes the virtues of capitalism that Strasbourg has long revered (today it's a restaurant). Goods were sold under the ground-floor arches; owners lived above.

    Strasbourg made its medieval mark as a trading center, milking its position at the crossroads of Europe and its access to the important Rhine River to charge tolls for the movement of goods. Its robust economy allowed for the construction of this glorious cathedral. Strasbourg's location drew all kinds of people to the city (just like today), making it susceptible to new ideas. As at Wittenberg, Martin Luther's theses were posted on the cathedral's main

ALSACE

doors, and after the wars of religion, this cathedral was Protestant for more than 100 years. (Louis XIV returned it to Catholicism in 1621.) Strasbourg remains a tolerant city today.

The dark-red **stone** that differentiates this cathedral from other great Gothic churches in France is quarried from the northern part of the Vosges Mountains (compare it to the yellow stone of St. Martin's in Colmar). You'll see this stone on display in many other buildings as you tour Strasbourg.

A Romanesque cathedral on this site burned down in 1176, allowing Strasbourg's bishop to rebuild it bigger and better—which he did. Construction began in the same Romanesque style as before. But after learning from the architects of Chartres' cathedral, the work was stopped and much of the structure was torn down to start over with the new Gothic style.

Study the intricate decorations on the facade. Notice the sculpture over the left portal (complacent, spear-toting Virtues getting revenge on those nasty Vices). Enter the cathedral and walk down the center (English displays are scattered about the interior). The stained glass on the lower left windows shows various rulers of Strasbourg; the stained glass on your right depicts Bible stories. An exquisite, gold-leafed organ hangs above the second pillars. Admire the elaborately carved stone pulpit. Walk to the choir and find a seat. Gaze into the Byzantine-like scene and find the stained-glass image of Mary with the European Union flag at the top.

Inside the right transept is a high-tech, 15th-century **astronomical clock** (restored in 1883) that gives a ho-hum performance every 15 minutes (keep your eye on the little angel about 15 feet up, slightly left of center). The show is better on the half-hour (angel on the right) and best at 12:30 (everybody gets in the act, including a rooster and 12 apostles—for the 12 hours; this performance is viewable only with a special ticket, described next).

The church is cleared out every day but Sunday between 11:15 and 12:45 for a boring presentation of the clock. Visitors pay €2 to enter through the right transept and see a sad 20-minute movie (with English) that explains the clock's workings, then witness the real event. All in all, this is too crowded and not worth the time.

For €5 you can climb 330 steps to the **top of the narthex** for an amazing view over Strasbourg, the Alsace, the Rhine, and the Black Forest (free first Sun of the month, access on right side of cathedral, daily April-Sept 9:30-20:00, Oct-March 10:00-17:15).

Nearby: Find flying buttress views outside the cathedral's right transept near **Palais Rohan** (described later). Before leaving the cathedral area, investigate the network of tidy pedestrian streets that connect the cathedral with the huge Place Kléber. Each street is named for the primary trade that took place there.

▲Alsatian Museum

One of Strasbourg's oldest and most characteristic homes hosts this extensive and well-presented collection of Alsatian folk art. Thanks to its thorough audioguide and printed English explanations, you'll learn much about Alsatian life and traditions from birth to death. Rooms you'd find in traditional homes are beautifully re-created here (including an impressive kitchen), and models explain the ins and outs of half-timbered construction. The tools, pottery, toys, and costumes cover Alsatian culture over the centuries, including a good overview of the life of a winemaker.

Cost and Hours: €6.50, free first Sunday of the month, Wed-Mon 10:00-18:00, closed Tue, across the river and down a block to the right from the boat dock, at 23 Quai St. Nicholas—see map on page 980, tel. 03 88 52 50 01, www.musees.strasbourg.eu.

Other Strasbourg Museums

These four museums lie outside the cathedral's right transept and are interesting only for aficionados with particular interests or who have a full day in Strasbourg. The first three are in **Palais Rohan,** a stately former palace. The **Archaeological Museum,** the best one, has a stellar presentation of Alsatian civilization through the millennia (includes free audioguide). The **Museum of Decorative Arts** feels like the Versailles of Strasbourg, with grand reception rooms, a king's bedroom (where Louis XV and Marie-Antoinette both slept), a big library, and rooms displaying ceramic dishes, ancient clocks, and more—borrow the English booklet. The **Museum of Fine Arts** holds a small, well-displayed collection of paintings from the Middle Ages to the Baroque period, some by artists you'll recognize. The **Museum of the Cathedral** (Musée de l'Œuvre Notre-Dame) is a well-organized museum near Palais Rohan that has plenty of church artifacts.

Cost and Hours: €6.50 for each museum, €12 day pass covers all four, free for those under 18 and on the first Sun of the month; open Wed-Mon 10:00-18:00, closed Tue—except for Museum of the Cathedral, which is closed Mon but open Tue 10:00-18:00; Palais Rohan—2 Place du Château, Museum of the Cathedral—3 Place du Château; tel. 03 88 52 50 00, www.musees.strasbourg.eu.

▲La Petite France

The historic home to Strasbourg's tanners, millers, and fishermen, this charming area is laced with canals, crowned with magnificent half-timbered homes, carpeted with cobblestones, and filled with tourists. As quaint as it looks, keep in mind that this neighborhood was leveled in World War II.

From the cathedral, walk down to Place Gutenberg and continue straight, following Rue Gutenberg (on the square's right side). Cross big Rue des Francs-Bourgeois and keep straight (now

ALSACE

on Grande Rue). Turn left on the third little street (Rue du Bou-clier, street signs are posted behind you), and make your way to the middle of the bridge (Pont St. Martin) for a good view. Step back off the bridge, and continue down Rue des Dentelles deep into La Petite France. Make friends with a leafy café table on **Place Benjamin Zix,** or find the siesta-friendly parks between the canals across the bridge at Rue des Moulins. Notice the sloping roofs with openings where leather hides were dried. Climb the once-fortified grassy wall (Barrage Vauban) for a decent view—the glass structure behind you is the splashy modern-art museum (interesting more for its architecture than its collection).

La Petite France's coziest café tables line the canal on **Quai de la Bruche.** From here it's a 10-minute walk back to the station: With the river on your left, walk along Quai de Turckheim, cross the third bridge, and find Rue du Maire Kuss.

STRASBOURG ACTIVITIES
Boat Ride on the Ill River
To see the cityscape from the water, take a loop cruise around Strasbourg on the Ill River. The glass-topped boats are air-con-

ditioned and sufficiently comfortable—both sides have fine views. You'll pass through two locks as you circle the old city clock-wise. The highlight for me was cruising by the Euro-pean Parliament buildings and the European Court of Human Rights.

Cost and Hours: Adults-€12.50, 70 minutes, good English commentary with live guide or audioguide; April-Oct daily 9:45-19:30, runs later in high season, shorter hours off-season, dock is 2 blocks outside cathe-dral's right transept, where Rue Rohan meets the river, tel. 03 88 84 13 13, www.batorama.fr.

Traditional Music and Dancing
On Sunday mornings from late July to late August, look for Alsa-tian folk dancing on Place Gutenberg (starts at about 10:45). Dur-ing the same season on Mondays, Tuesdays, and Wednesdays from 20:30 to 22:00, listen to traditional music on these squares (Mon—Place des Tripiers, Tue—in La Petite France on Place Benjamin Zix, and Wed—Place du Marché aux Cochons de Lait).

Summer Outdoor Shows

Strasbourg keeps its visitors entertained until the wee hours in summer. Every day, from about mid-July to mid-September, the soaring cathedral is bathed in colorful lights that allow visitors to "contemplate the cathedral and its architecture from a new, contemporary perspective." The **sound-and-light show** is free and runs every 30 minutes until 24:30 (starts at 22:30 in July, 22:15 in Aug, and 21:15 in Sept). The city offers other nighttime events every summer; ask at the TI or check www.ete.strasbourg.eu.

Christmas Market

From the last Saturday of November until December 31, the city bustles and sparkles with its delightful Christkindelsmärik, held on several squares in the old town (hotel rates climb, and rooms book up well in advance).

Sleeping in Strasbourg

($$$$ = Splurge, $$$ = Pricier, $$ = Moderate, $ = Budget)
Strasbourg is quiet in the summer (July-Aug), when 4,000 Eurocrats leave town and hotel prices fall—and slammed when the parliament is in session, throughout December (thanks to the Christmas market), and during major conferences.

$$$ Hôtel Cathédrale*** is comfortable, contemporary, but a little tired, with a Jack-and-the-beanstalk spiral stairway (elevator begins one floor up) and a hopelessly confusing floor plan. This modern-yet-atmospheric place lets you stare at the cathedral point-blank from your room (air-con, laundry service, free bicycles for up to 2 hours, book ahead for one of 5 pay parking spaces, 12 Place de la Cathédrale, tel. 03 88 22 12 12, toll-free in France 08 00 00 00 84, www.hotel-cathedrale.fr, booking@hotel-cathedrale.fr).

$$ Hôtel Ibis*** faces the train station (you can't miss it) and delivers its usual comfort and amenities at fair rates (10 Place de la Gare, tel. 03 88 23 98 98, www.ibishotel.com, h3018@accor.com).

$$ Hôtel du Dragon*** is a tasteful, well-run, and spotless business-class place that's handy for drivers, as they'll park your car for free overnight (12 Rue du Dragon, tel. 03 88 35 79 80, www.dragon.fr, hotel@dragon.fr).

$ Hôtel Suisse,** across from the cathedral's right transept and off Place du Château, is a welcoming, central, and solid two-star value (elevator, no air-con, cozy lounge-café, 2 Rue de la Râpe, tel. 03 88 35 22 11, www.hotel-suisse.com, info@hotel-suisse.com, engaging owner Edith).

$ Hôtel des Arts,** located in the thick of things above a busy café, is a simple, sparse budget option. It has tight bathrooms but is comfortable enough and offers good value. Rooms in front are fun but noisy (air-con, 10 Place du Marché aux Cochons de Lait, tel. 03 88 37 98 37, www.hotel-arts.com, reservation@hotel-arts.com).

Eating in Strasbourg

($$$$ = Splurge, $$$ = Pricier, $$ = Moderate, $ = Budget)
Atmospheric *winstubs* (wine bars) serving affordable salads and *tarte flambée* are a snap to find. If the weather is nice, head for La Petite France and choose ambience over cuisine—dine outside at any café/*winstub* that appeals to you. Stock up on picnic supplies at the Monoprix (Mon-Sat 8:30-20:30) on Place Kléber or at gourmet Alsatian specialty shops on Rue des Orfèvres and take them to the park near Barrage Vauban.

IN AND NEAR LA PETITE FRANCE

I like the cool location, vibe, and prices at **$$ La Corde à Linge** (The Clothesline) on 2 Place Benjamin Zix (big salads, burgers, and several intriguing *Spätzle plats,* tel. 03 88 22 15 17).

The touristy **$$ Restaurant au Pont St-Martin** owns a postcard-perfect facade and a fine position on the river, with the best seating on the riverside balcony. It serves good-enough meals at reasonable prices (15 Rue des Moulins, tel. 03 88 32 45 13).

$ Brasserie la Lanterne, between La Petite France and the cathedral, is a down-and-dirty, Alsatian microbrewery filled with students and young, hip locals. This place is known for its home brews and cheap cuisine (€6-7 *tarte flambée*) and makes me want to plot a revolution (daily 16:00-very late, near Place Kléber at 5 Rue de la Lanterne, tel. 03 88 32 10 10).

NEAR THE CATHEDRAL

For a real meal, skip the touristy restaurants on the cathedral square and along Rue du Maroquin. Consider these nearby places instead; the first two are one block behind the TI (go left out of the TI, then take the first left through the passageway and keep walking).

$$ Chez Yvonne (marked *S'Burjerstuewel* above windows), right out of a Bruegel painting, has a tradition of good food at fair prices. Try the *coq au Riesling* or *choucroute garnie* or the *salade alsacienne* (reservations smart on weekends and holidays, dinner served from 18:00, open late daily, 10 Rue du Sanglier, tel. 03 88 32 84 15, www.restaurant-chez-yvonne.net).

$$ The very cozy **Le Clou Winstub** is half a block left down Rue du Chaudron at #3. This place often looks closed from the outside, but don't be shy. It offers a few tables outside in good weather (closed Sun, dinner served from 18:00, tel. 03 88 32 11 67).

$$$$ Au Coin des Pucelles is an institution in the gourmet world of Strasbourg. Roland Rohfritsch and his sister Myriam welcome diners at shared tables in a warm atmosphere and serve generous portions of Alsatian dishes—try the duck *choucroute* (dinner only from 19:00, closed Sun and sometimes Mon, reservations recommended, 12 Rue des Pucelles, tel. 03 88 35 35 14).

Strasbourg Connections

Strasbourg makes a good side-trip from Colmar or a stop on the way to or from Paris.

From Strasbourg by Train to: Colmar (2/hour, 35 minutes), **Reims** (10/day, 2 hours, change at Gare Champagne-Ardennes), **Paris'** Gare de l'Est (hourly, 2 hours), **Lyon** (4/day direct, 4-5 hours), **Baden-Baden,** Germany (TGV: 1/day direct, 30 minutes; non-TGV train: roughly hourly, 70 minutes, change in Appenweier or Offenburg), **Karlsruhe,** Germany (TGV: 4/day direct, 40 minutes; non-TGV train: hourly, 1-1.5 hours, most with change in Appenweier or Offenburg), **Munich,** Germany (TGV; 5/day, 4 hours, most with 1 change; non-TGV train: 5/day, 5 hours, 2 changes), **Basel,** Switzerland (regional train: about 2/hour, 1.5 hours).

ALSACE

REIMS & VERDUN

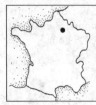

Different as night and day, bubbly Reims and brooding Verdun offer worthwhile stops between Paris and Alsace. The administrative capital of the Champagne region, bustling, modern Reims greets travelers with cellar doors wide open. It features a lively center, a historic cathedral, and, of course, Champagne tasting. Often overlooked, quiet Verdun is famous for the brutal World War I battles that surrounded the city and pummeled the countryside, and offers an exceptional opportunity to learn about the Great War. High-speed TGV trains make both of these destinations easily accessible to travelers (particularly if coming from Paris).

PLANNING YOUR TIME

Organized travelers can see Reims and Verdun in a day and a half as they travel between Paris and the Alsace (with an overnight in Reims). Plan on most of a day for Reims and a half-day for Verdun. It's about 70 miles between the two towns, making a day trip from Reims to Verdun worth considering if you have a car—but it's too difficult by train. Day-tripping by train from Paris to Reims is a breeze, but day-tripping to Verdun from Paris requires careful planning.

GETTING AROUND REIMS AND VERDUN

A car is *sans* doubt the most efficient way to tour this region. You can do without one in Reims: The town is easily walkable and offers excellent public transportation, with trams, an electric shuttle, and handy buses linking its major sights. But for touring Verdun battlefield sights, it's close to essential to rent a car—whether you choose to drive yourself or arrange at the TI for a private guide to accompany you. Your no-wheels options are riding a hop-on, hop-off bus or taking a taxi (see "Getting Around the Battlefields," later). Many find Reims a good place to pick up a rental car for a longer trip after leaving Paris (rental agencies are closed 12:00-14:00). Train travelers from Paris will reach Reims before drivers get out of the city.

Frequent high-speed TGV trains link central Paris and Reims in 50 minutes, and a few TGV trains link Paris and Verdun in 1.5 hours. Four trains per day connect Charles de Gaulle Airport to Reims (via its Champagne-Ardennes train station) in about one hour. (Book TGV trains online in advance for best rates.) Most train connections between Reims and Verdun are slow, due to transfers.

CHAMPAGNE'S CUISINE SCENE

Contrary to popular belief, Champagne is wine that can easily accompany an entire meal. Locals drink Champagne with everything here. And just as the Burgundians cook many of their meat and poultry dishes with their local red wine, the Champenois cook with bubbly (on menus you'll see *à la champenoise*).

This is a "meaty" region: Most menus will offer foie gras, raw *tartares,* lots of beef, and some dishes you may choose to avoid, such as *rognons, ris de veau, tête de veau, pieds de porc, andouillette,* and *boudin noir* (kidneys, sweetbreads, calf's head, pig's feet, tripe sausage, and blood sausage, respectively). Despite its reputation, I find *boudin noir* delicious. *La potée champenoise* (also called *la Joute*) is like a *pot-au-feu* stew, made of smoked ham, chicken, sausage, and vegetables with lots of cabbage. *Boudin blanc* is a moist, white sausage made from pork or chicken, eggs, cream, and spices. Many salads and starters include *jambon de Reims,* the local smoked ham. *Andouillette de Troyes* is a tripe sausage that you can smell from across the room. Ample rivers make for flavorful trout *(truite)* dishes. You may also find rooster cooked in the rare local red wine known as Bouzy Rouge *(coq au vin de Bouzy).*

Brie de Meaux cheese, made on Champagne's border, is the most flavorful Brie as it's unpasteurized. Other local cheeses include Cendré de Champagne (similar to Brie but the size of a large Camembert, with a thin ash covering), Chaource (a young, creamy, and mild cheese in a cylindrical shape), and Langres (orange-colored rind, creamy and pungent, usually aged). All of these listed cheeses have edible rinds.

Biscuits roses de Reims (pink cookies) are on every bakery shelf in town. Traditionally dunked in Champagne, this ladyfinger-style treat also goes well with afternoon coffee or tea and is often used

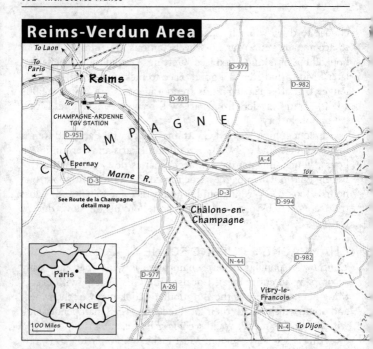

Reims-Verdun Area

in local desserts, such as *charlotte aux biscuits roses* (trifle). Fruit-flavored brandies are a common way to end an evening.

Reims

With its Roman gate, Gothic cathedral, Champagne *caves,* and vibrant pedestrian zone, Reims feels both historic and youthful. And thanks to the TGV bullet train, it's less than an hour's ride from Paris.

Reims (pronounced like "rance") has a turbulent history: This is where 25 French kings were crowned, where Champagne first bubbled, where WWI devastation met miraculous reconstruction during the Art Deco age, and where the Germans officially surrendered in 1945, bringing World War II to a close in Europe. The town's sights give you an entertaining peek at the entire story.

PLANNING YOUR TIME

You can see Reims' essential sights in an easy day, either as a day trip from Paris or as a stop en route to or from Paris. Frequent TGV trains make the trip from Paris a breeze. Trains also connect Charles de Gaulle Airport directly with Reims, making this a handy first-night or last-night stop. If using a rail pass, book your

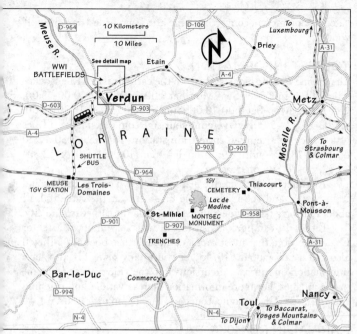

TGV reservations as soon as possible. Take a morning train from Paris and explore the cathedral and city center before lunch, then spend your afternoon below ground, in a cool, chalky Champagne cellar or *cave* (pronounced "kahv"). You can be back at your Parisian hotel by dinner. Those continuing to destinations farther east find Reims a convenient place to rent a car. With a car, it's worth taking a few hours to joyride the Champagne road that leaves from Reims' back step (described later).

To best experience contemporary Reims, explore the busy shopping streets between the cathedral and the Reims-Centre train station. Rue de Vesle, Rue Condorcet, and Place Drouet d'Erlon are most interesting. Try to visit Reims on a Saturday, when the market erupts inside the dazzling Halles Boulingrin, and surrounding streets are lively. Sundays are *très* quiet and worth avoiding—handy buses don't run, and so much is closed that it's hard to get a feel for the town.

Orientation to Reims

Reims' hard-to-miss cathedral marks the city center and makes an easy orientation landmark. Most sights of interest are within a 15-minute walk from the Reims-Centre train station. City buses and taxis connect the harder-to-reach Champagne *caves* with the central train station and cathedral. The city has ambitiously renovated its downtown, converting large areas into pedestrian-friendly zones.

TOURIST INFORMATION

The main TI is one block away from the **cathedral** at 6 Rue Rockefeller (TI open Easter-Sept Mon-Sat 9:00-19:00, Sun 10:00-18:00, Oct-Easter Mon-Sat 9:00-18:00, Sun 10:00-12:30 & 13:30-17:00; tel. 03 26 77 45 00, www.reims-tourisme.com). A smaller TI lies just outside the Reims-Centre **train station** (Mon-Sat 8:30-12:30 & 13:30-18:00—until 19:00 on Fri, Sun 10:00-11:30 & 12:30-16:00, closed Sun off-season).

At either TI, pick up free maps of the town center, the bus and tram routes, and the Champagne *caves*. Ask at the cathedral TI about renting a tablet videoguide for visiting the cathedral and city.

Either TI can book a visit to the *caves* at Mumm, Martel, or Cazanove (note that most *caves* require advance booking). They'll also call a taxi (about €10) to get you to any *cave*. TIs also have information on minivan excursions into the vineyards and Champagne villages. For more information on reservations and reaching the *caves*, see "Champagne Tours and Sights" on page 1007.

ARRIVAL IN REIMS

By Train: From Paris' Gare de l'Est station, take the direct TGV to the **Reims-Centre Station** (12/day, 50 minutes, no baggage check). In Reims, the small TI is to your right as you exit; a taxi office is to your left (taxis wait in front of the station at busy times).

Trains run directly from Charles de Gaulle Airport to the **Champagne-Ardennes TGV Station** five miles away (4/day, 45 minutes). Other TGV trains from Paris destined for Germany or Alsace also stop at the Champagne-Ardenne Station (4/day, 40 minutes). From there, you can take a local "milk-run" (TER) train to Reims-Centre Station (TER usually leaves 15 minutes after TGV arrival, 15 minutes to Reims-Centre Station), or ride tram #B into town (3/hour, 20 minutes, direction: Neufchâtel; walk downhill from the station to find the stop; see "Getting Around Reims" for ticket information).

There are also two daily local TER trains that go from Paris through Epernay to Reims (2 hours).

By Car: Day-trippers should follow *Cathédrale* signs, and park in metered spots on or near the street approaching the cathedral (Rue Libergier) or in the well-signed Parking Cathédrale structure. If you'll be staying the night, take the *Reims-Centre* exit from the autoroute for most of my recommended hotels, and park in the Erlon parking garage—enter from Boulevard du Général Leclerc.

HELPFUL HINTS

Exchange Rate: €1 = about $1.10

Country Calling Code: 33 (see page 1082 for dialing instructions)

Department Store: Monoprix, inside the Espace Drouet d'Erlon shopping center, provides one-stop shopping for toiletries, cheap clothing, and groceries (Mon-Sat 9:00-20:00, Sun until 13:00, basement level, 53 Place Drouet d'Erlon, follow *FNAC* signs).

Laundry: A convenient launderette is just south of the cathedral (daily 8:00-20:00, doors lock automatically at 20:00, 59 Rue Chanzy).

Bike Rental: Manu Loca Vélo delivers bikes within about 10 miles of Reims (€15/day, €10/half-day, reservations required, manulocavelo@hotmail.fr, mobile 06 51 27 24 10).

Taxi: Taxi offices are at the train station and at 40 Rue Carnot, next to the Opéra. Or you can call 03 26 03 03 00.

Car Rental: Single-day or longer car rental in Reims is usually reasonable even when booked late. **Avis** is just outside the central train station at 20 Rue Pingat (tel. 03 26 47 10 08, use the *Clairmarais* exit from the station, turn right, and walk 200 yards); another office is in front of the Champagne-Ardenne TGV station (03 61 58 82 71). **Europcar** is at 76 Boulevard Lundy (tel. 03 26 88 59 40); **Hertz** is at 26 Boulevard Joffre (tel. 03 26 47 98 78). Rental agencies are usually open Mon-Sat 8:00-12:00 & 14:00-18:00; most are closed Sun and some close early Sat afternoon.

City Bus Tours: "Reims Open Tour" offers two routes: a one-hour circuit of the city (€12, 3-5 trips/day in summer, fewer in winter, recorded commentary), or an afternoon excursion to nearby vineyards with a tasting at the Moulin de Verzenay winery, owned by Mumm (€35/person, Fri-Sun only, departs 14:15, 3 hours, commentary by a live guide). Both tours have the top open in good weather (tickets and departure from TI at the cathedral, save 10 percent by booking online at www.reims-tourisme.com).

Champagne Tours: See page 1007.

GETTING AROUND REIMS

By Bus or Tram: Reims has an integrated network of colorful buses, trams, and an electric shuttle bus (www.citura.fr, French only, but excellent maps). You can purchase tickets on the bus and shuttle from the driver but not on trams; better to use ticket machines at

Reims

MUSEUM OF
THE SURRENDER

RUE DES ROMAINS

RUE DU MONT D'ARENE

RUE EDOUARD MIGNOT

REIMS-
CENTRE
TRAIN
STATION

AVE. DE LAON

WWI
MEMORIAL

Place de la
République

CHARLES DE
CAZANOVE

Boulingrin

RUE DU CHAMP DE MARS

Cemetery

#7

RUE DE L...

PORTE DE
MARS

HALLES
BOULINGRIN

RUE DU TEMPLE

BLVD. JOFFRE

Grande Allée
des Promenades

Gare Centre

RUE DE MARS

RUE LINGUET

R. ROUSSEAU

RUE VERNOUILLET

RUE DE SAINT-BRICE

RUE ANDRE PINGAT

RUE DE COURCELLES

BLVD. FOCH

BLVD. THIERS

COURS JEAN BAPTISTE LANGLET

TOWN
HALL

Place de
l'Hôtel
de Ville

CRYPTO-
PORTIQUE

STATUE

Square
Colbert

#2, 6, 7
& 11

Place Drouet d'Erlon

Erlon

Langlet

Place du
Forum

Place
Royale

POST

BLVD. LOUIS ROEDERER

BLVD. DU GENERAL LECLERC

R. DE CHATIVESTE

R. DE L'ETAPE

CIRQUE

RUE BUIRETTE

RUE JEANNE D'ARC

RUE GONDREAU

Opéra

OPERA

AVE. BREBANT

To
Paris
A-4

Reims
Centre
Exit

La Vesle

Comédie

CHAUSSEE BOCQUAINE

ST.
JACQUES

Vesle

RUE DE VESLE

Cathédrale

CATHEDRAL

#2, 4, 5
6 & 9

Pl. du Luçon

PALAIS DU TAU
& CARNEGIE
LIBRARY

RUE LIBERGIER

RUE PAYEN

RUE CHABAUD

RUE CLOVIS

HINCMAR

RUE DES CAPUCINS

RUE BRULEE

CHANZY

Delaune

Parc
Léo Lagrange

STADE

BLVD. PAUL DOUMER

Canal de l'Aisne à la Marne

SYNAGOGUE

RUE DE VENISE

R. FOLLE PEINE

STADE
NAUTIQUE

Cathedral
Exit

AVE. DU GENERAL DE GAULLE

RUE DEMOISELLES

RUE DE COURLANCY

AVE. PAUL MARCHANDEAU

CHAUSSEE BOCQUAINE

CHAUSSEE SAINT-MARTIN

A-4

Courlancy

Tram #B to Gare
Champagne TGV
Station

200 Meters
200 Yards

BLVD. PRESIDENT WILSON

To Verdun
& Strasbourg

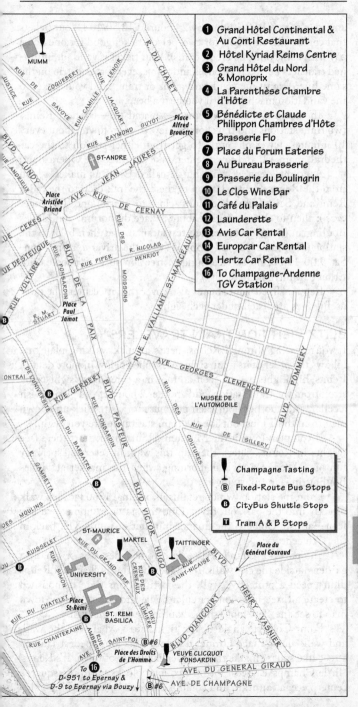

1. Grand Hôtel Continental & Au Conti Restaurant
2. Hôtel Kyriad Reims Centre
3. Grand Hôtel du Nord & Monoprix
4. La Parenthèse Chambre d'Hôte
5. Bénédicte et Claude Philippon Chambres d'Hôte
6. Brasserie Flo
7. Place du Forum Eateries
8. Au Bureau Brasserie
9. Brasserie du Boulingrin
10. Le Clos Wine Bar
11. Café du Palais
12. Launderette
13. Avis Car Rental
14. Europcar Car Rental
15. Hertz Car Rental
16. To Champagne-Ardenne TGV Station

Champagne Tasting
B Fixed-Route Bus Stops
B CityBus Shuttle Stops
T Tram A & B Stops

REIMS & VERDUN

any tram stop (€1.60/1 hour, €4/24 hours, €12.50/10 1-hour tickets that can be shared, €2.70 for two-person ticket good for one hour; pay with coins only, no credit cards). Your ticket is valid for unlimited transfers between all buses and trams, even a round-trip on the same line. Each time you board a bus or tram, hold your ticket to the validation machine until you hear a beep.

The **tram** system's two lines—#A and #B—connect Reims' two train stations and travel on to a few stops in town (about every 10 minutes, fewer on Sun). To get from either station to the cathedral, main TI, and town center, take a tram to the Opéra stop.

A bright-green electric shuttle called **CityBus** makes a loop from the Reims-Centre station to the cathedral; then to the Saint Remi and Saint Timothée stops (close to Martel and Taittinger *caves*); then to the Carnegie Library, Place du Forum, and Halles Boulingrin (near recommended restaurants); and then back to the station (30 minutes for full loop). Wave at the driver to stop (Mon-Sat 9:00-19:00, no service Sunday, free for up to 5 people with Erlon parking garage receipt).

Regular **fixed-route buses** also cover the city center; the most useful ones are listed under each sight.

BLITZ VISIT FOR TRAIN TRAVELERS

If you're racing through Reims, here's a quick walking plan that follows the order of its main sights (described below in more detail). Reims' highlights can be seen on foot in a three-hour sightseeing stroll from the train station (add another 2 hours if you plan to visit a cellar, and another hour each per museum visit). Pick up a town map from the TI just outside the train station before you begin.

If you plan to visit the Museum of Surrender, start there (see "Sights in Reims," later), then do this walk in reverse (especially fun on a Wed, Fri, or Sat morning, when the market at Halles Boulingrin is in full swing).

From the station (which retains its original 1860 facade), walk directly into the park out front. Find the statue of hometown boy Jean-Baptiste Colbert, the finance minister of Louis XIV back in the 17th century.

The **park,** or Grande Allée des Promenades, was originally a garden outside the city walls. In 1848, when it was clear that Reims didn't need a protective wall, the fortifications were demolished to create a three-mile-long circular boulevard. Look at your town map to see the "left-foot"-shaped outline left by the wall.

From Colbert, angle to the right, cross what was the wall, and walk along **Place Drouet d'Erlon.** This long, pedestrianized street-like square marks the commercial center of town. It's Reims' "little Champs-Elysées." Stroll two long blocks up to the square's centerpiece: a **fountain** and column crowned by a glistening gold-winged figure of Victory. (The original Victory, from 1906, was melted down by the Nazis—the current one is a recent replacement.) The fountain—with four voluptuous women—celebrates the four major rivers of this district. Years ago, after one too many pranks in which local students (this is a big university town) put soap in the fountain, the mayor turned off the water. But after some serious restoration, the fountain will function again in 2017.

While World War II left the city unscathed, World War I devastated Reims. It was the biggest city on France's Western Front, and it was hammered. Sixty-five percent of Reims was destroyed by shelling, and in 1918 only 70 buildings remained undamaged. The area around you was entirely rebuilt in the 1920s. If it looks eclectic, that's because the mayor at the time said to build any way you like—just build. Make a little spin tour to survey the facades.

All around you'll see the stylized features—geometric reliefs, motifs in ironwork, rounded corners, and simple concrete elegance—of **Art Deco.** The only hints that this was once a medieval town are the narrow lots that struggle to accommodate today's buildings. Continue along the square to check out the building at #15, which is fake half-timbered (in concrete), and the three Art Deco facades at #19-21. Where Place Drouet d'Erlon ends (at a small fountain), pop into the **Waida Pâtisserie** at #5 for a pure, typical Art Deco interior.

While at Waida, consider picking up a quiche and some pastries to enjoy on the cathedral square. They also sell *Biscuits roses de Reims*—light, rose-colored egg-and-sugar cookies that have been made since 1756. They're the locals' favorite munchie to accompany a glass of Champagne—you're supposed to dunk them, but I like them dry (many places that sell these treats offer free samples).

From here, cut over to the left (Rue Condorcet works), then take a right on Rue de Talleyrand; you can't miss **Reims Cathedral.**

The **cathedral museum** (Palais du Tau) and **Carnegie Library** are next to the church. From the Cathédrale stop near the TI, you can catch the electric CityBus to Taittinger and Martel Champagne *caves* (see "Champagne Tours and Sights," later), or continue your walk via **Place du Forum** (the former Roman forum) to **Porte de Mars** (the old Roman gate). Near Porte de Mars you can't miss the restored 1927 **Art Deco covered market hall** (Halles Boulingrin). From here, the **Museum of the Surrender** is a short walk across the intersection, behind the train station. Just like that, you've seen the highlights of the city. Now it's time for a nice glass of Champagne.

Sights in Reims

▲▲▲REIMS CATHEDRAL

The cathedral of Reims is a glorious example of Gothic architecture, and one of Europe's greatest churches. (Expect to see scaffolding on the central portal while they restore the rose window.) It celebrated its 800th birthday in 2011. Clovis, the first Christian king of the Franks, was baptized at a church on this site in A.D. 496, establishing France's Christian roots, which still hold firm today. Since Clovis' baptism, Reims Cathedral has served as *the* place for the coronation of 26 French kings, giving it a more important role in France's political history than Notre-Dame Cathedral in Paris. This cathedral is to France what Westminster Abbey is to England.

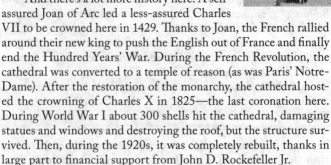

And there's a lot more history here. A self-assured Joan of Arc led a less-assured Charles VII to be crowned here in 1429. Thanks to Joan, the French rallied around their new king to push the English out of France and finally end the Hundred Years' War. During the French Revolution, the cathedral was converted to a temple of reason (as was Paris' Notre-Dame). After the restoration of the monarchy, the cathedral hosted the crowning of Charles X in 1825—the last coronation here. During World War I about 300 shells hit the cathedral, damaging statues and windows and destroying the roof, but the structure survived. Then, during the 1920s, it was completely rebuilt, thanks in large part to financial support from John D. Rockefeller Jr.

Luckily, World War II spared the church, and since then it has come to symbolize reconciliation. A French plaque set in the pavement just in front recalls the 1962 Mass of Reconciliation between France and Germany. A German version of the marker was added in 2012, commemorating 50 years of friendship and celebrating the belief that another war today between these two nations would be unthinkable.

Cost and Hours: Free, daily 7:30-19:15, helpful information boards in English throughout the church (www.reims-cathedral.culture.fr). You could rent tablet-based videoguides at the cathedral TI, but my self-guided tour below works well for most.

Getting There: The cathedral is a 15-minute walk from the Reims-Centre station. Follow *sortie* signs for Place de la Gare, then walk to the TI on the right. Cross the tree-lined parkway and enter the pedestrianized Place Drouet d'Erlon. Turn left on Rue Condorcet, then right on Rue de Talleyrand. You can also catch the green electric CityBus from in front of the station (5-minute ride to the cathedral).

Cathedral Tower: An escorted one-hour tour climbs the 250 steps of the tower to explore the rooftop and get a close-up look at the Gallery of Kings statuary (€7.50, €11 combo-ticket with Palais du Tau; tours depart hourly May-Aug Tue-Sat 10:00-11:00 & 14:00-17:00, Sun 14:00-17:00, closed Mon; off-season Sat-Sun only; closed Nov-mid-March; get tickets and meet escort in the Palais du Tau). Smart to reserve tickets by phone—up to one week ahead (tel. 03 26 47 84 74 or palaisdutau@monuments-nationaux.fr).

Cathedral Sound-and-Light Show (Rêve de Couleurs): For a memorable experience, join the crowd in front of the cathedral for a free, 25-minute sound-and-light show on most summer evenings. The colorful lights and booming sound take you through the ages, evoking the building's design and construction, the original appearance of the statuary, the coronations that occurred here, the faith of the community, and—during the centennial of the Great War—the shelling it absorbed during World War I. Sit directly in front of the cathedral or settle more comfortably into a seat at a café with a clear view through the trees. The show generally starts when it's dark—between 21:30 and 23:00 (TI has the schedule, nightly except Mon July-Aug, Fri-Sun only in May-June and Sept). Sometimes a second show commences 10 minutes after the first show ends.

⊙ Self-Guided Tour: Begin your visit by admiring the cathedral's **West Portal.** It's perhaps the best west portal anywhere. Built under the direction of four different architects, it is remarkable for its unity and harmony. The church was started in about 1211 and mostly finished just 60 years later. The 260-foot-tall towers were added in the 1400s; the spires intended to top them were never installed for lack of money.

Like the cathedrals in Paris and Chartres, this church is dedicated to **"Our Lady"** (Notre Dame). Statues depicting the crowning of the Virgin take center stage on the facade. For eight centuries Catholics have prayed to the Mother of God, kneeling here to ask her to intervene with God on their behalf. In 1429, Joan of Arc received messages here from Mary encouraging her to rally French troops against the English at the Siege of Orléans (a statue of Joan from 1896 is over your left shoulder as you face the church).

An ornate facade like this comes with a cohesive and carefully designed message. Study the carving. A good percentage of the statues are original and date from around 1250. There are **three main doors,** each with a theme carved into the limestone.

On the left is the **Passion** (the events leading up to and including the Crucifixion). Among the local saints shown below is the famous Smiling Angel, whose jovial expression has served the city well as its marketing icon. The central portal is dedicated to the **Virgin Mary,** featuring the Coronation of Mary with scenes from her life below. And on the right is the **Last Judgment,** with scenes from the apocalypse. Above the great rose window are reliefs of David (with his dog) and Goliath. Notice the fire damage, from 1914, around the rose window (fire melts limestone). Across the top is the **Gallery of Kings,** depicting 56 of France's kings. They flank the country's first Christian king, Clovis, who appears to be wearing a barrel—he's actually kneeling prayerfully at a baptismal font. These anonymous statues, without egos, are unnamed kings whose spiritual mission is to lead their people to God.

Before going inside, step around to the right side and study the exoskeletal nature of the church's structure. Braces on the outside—**flying buttresses**—soar up the sides of the church. These massive "beams" are critical to supporting the building, redirecting the weight of the roof outward (and into the ground), rather than downward on the supporting walls. With the support provided by the columns, arches, and buttresses, the walls—which no longer needed to be so solid and thick—became window holders.

The architects of Reims Cathedral were confident in their building practices. Gothic architects had learned by trial and error—many church roofs caved in as they tested their theories and strove to build ever higher. Work on Reims Cathedral began decades after the Notre-Dame cathedrals in Paris and Chartres, allowing architects to take advantage of what they'd learned from those magnificent earlier structures.

Contemplate the lives of the people in Reims who built this huge building in the 13th century. Construction on a scale like this required a wholesale community effort—all hands on deck. The builders of the Reims Cathedral gave it their all, in part because this was the church of France—where its kings were crowned. Most townsfolk who participated donated their money or their labor knowing that neither they, nor their children, would likely ever see it completed—such was their pride, dedication, and faith. Imagine the effort it took to raise the funds and manage the workforce. Master masons supervised, while the average Jean did much of the sweat work.

Now, step inside and stand at the back of the nearly 500-foot-long **nave.** The weight of the roof is supported by a few towering columns that seem to sprout crisscrossing pointed arches. This load-bearing skeleton of columns, arches, and buttresses allowed the church to grow higher, and liberated the walls to become window frames. Sun pours through the **stained glass,** bathing visitors and worshippers in divine light.

Take a look at the wall of **52 statues** stacked in rectangular blocks inside the door. (Cover the light from the door with this book to see better.) Imagine the 13th-century technology employed to carve each of these blocks in the nearby workshop and then install them so seamlessly here. These blocks continue the stories told by the statues on the outside.

Walk up the central aisle until you find a **plaque in the floor** marking the site of Clovis' baptism in 496. Back then, a much smaller, early-Christian Roman church stood here. And back then you couldn't enter a church until you were baptized. Baptisteries stood outside churches, like the one that welcomed Clovis into the Christian faith.

Walk ahead to the **choir.** The set of candlesticks and crucifix at the high altar were given to the church by Charles X on the occasion of his coronation in 1825. Look back at the west wall. The original windows were lost in World War I; these, rebuilt from photographs, date from the 1930s.

Walk into the **south transept.** The WWI-destroyed windows here were replaced in 1954 by the local Champagne makers. The windows' scenes portray the tending of vines (left), the harvest (center), and the time-honored double-fermentation process (right). Notice, around the edges, the churches representing all the grape-producing villages in the area.

Looking high above at the ceiling, you'll see evidence of **bomb damage** from 1917, when the roof took direct hits and collapsed. (The lighter bricks are from the repair job in the 1920s.) The gray/white "grisaille" windows in this transept were installed in the 1970s. Many of the darker, more richly colored medieval glass windows were replaced by clear glass in the 18th and 19th centuries (when tastes called for more light).

The **apse** (east end, behind the altar) holds a luminous set of **Marc Chagall stained-glass windows** from 1974. Chagall's in-

imitable style lends itself to stained glass, and he enjoyed opportunities to adorn great churches with his windows. The left window illustrates scenes from the Old Testament, with the Tree of Jesse (with Jesse himself sleeping at the bottom) reaching up to Mary with the Christ Child. In the central panels, the cohesion of the Old and New Testament scenes is emphasized by the ladder that connects one to the other. On the right the Tree of Jesse—which is essentially a genealogical diagram of Christ's lineage—is extended to symbolically include the royalty of France, thus affirming the divine power of the monarchs and stressing their responsibility to rule with wisdom and justice. Featured are Clovis (at the bottom, with his bishop); St. Louis XIII (seen at the cathedral; and then dispensing justice); Charles VII (on the right in green), and Joan of Arc, in blue, holding her sword (on the far right).

For the cathedral's 800th anniversary, in 2011, six modern, **abstract windows** were installed on either side of the Chagall windows. Just to the left is a 1901 statue of Joan of Arc, her face carved from ivory.

From here, behind the high altar, enjoy the best view of the entire nave. Seen from this distance, the west wall is an ensemble seemingly made entirely of glass. Look at the confidence of the design. Even the corners outside the rose window were glass, made without stone. The architects pulled out all the stops in this triumph of Gothic.

OTHER REIMS SIGHTS
Palais du Tau
This former Archbishop's Palace, named after the Greek letter *T (tau)* for its shape, houses artifacts from the cathedral next door and a pile of royal goodies. You'll look into the weathered eyes of original statues from the cathedral's facade, see precious tapestries, coronation jewels, and more.

Cost and Hours: €7.50, €11 combo-ticket includes cathedral tower tour, May-Aug Tue-Sun 9:30-18:30, Sept-April Tue-Sun 9:30-12:30 & 14:00-17:30, closed Mon year-round, scant English information though an audioguide is available at TI for €6, good bookshop, tel. 03 26 47 81 79, www.palais-du-tau.fr.

Visiting the Palace: The collections are in two distinct parts—the royal chapel and treasury with jewels and artifacts, and the cathedral museum with statues and tapestries. Most of the exhibits are on the upper level. Use these descriptions along with the museum's English handout and map.

On the **ground floor** (Room 1), you'll start in the hall dedicated to the rebuilding of the cathedral after WWI bombings and the enlightened philanthropy of John D. Rockefeller Jr. When the roofs of Gothic churches burned, the lead that covered them melted and cascaded down like flowing rivers. Here, the gargoyles with once-molten lead spewing out of their storm-drain mouths make that much easier to envision.

Upstairs, the **royal chapel** (Room 5) was where the king would spend the night before his coronation, secluded in prayer. Inlaid in the floor are fleurs-de-lis, symbol of the French monarchy. At the altar are six candlesticks used at Napoleon's wedding in 1810.

Flanking the entry to the chapel are **treasury rooms** (Rooms 6 and 7) filled with royal valuables. On the left are examples that survived the melt-it-down mania of the French Revolution. Imagine the fury of the revolutionaries, who would melt down precious crowns and chalices to satisfy their practical need for gold and silver. Very little survived that wasn't buried away—these varied treasures were excavated from royal tombs in the 1920s (and survive in perfect condition). Don't miss the ninth-century talisman worn by Charlemagne and the exquisite chalice used by French royalty in the 12th century.

Room 8 is filled with gold-plated silver regalia made for the coronation of Charles X in 1825. The new pieces were necessary because the historic regalia had been melted down.

In the next room (9) ponder the royal portraits and the 60-pound mantle of the divine king. Think of the dramatic swings in France's history: A generation after you cut off a king's head, you welcome a new king as if he were divine.

Turning right into Room 10, where the **cathedral museum** section begins, let your gaze soar high. An original 13th-century statue of Goliath measures a whopping 17.7 feet. In the next rooms, find cases with tiny statues with traces of original paint. Admire the amazing detail of the carving.

The highlight and grand finale (Room 15) is the original centerpiece of the cathedral's west facade: the fire-damaged Coronation of Mary group, carved in the 12th century. In the same room, six figures from the Gallery of Kings stand as if guarding 16th-century tapestries. Originally hung around the choir in the center of the cathedral, the themes of these tapestries illustrating the Virgin's life supported the prayers and preaching of the faithful.

▲Carnegie Library (Bibliothèque Carnegie)

The legacy of the Carnegie Library network, funded generously by the 19th-century American millionaire Andrew Carnegie and his

steel fortune (notice the American flag above the main entrance on the left), extends even to Reims. Carnegie believed knowledge could put an end to war, and he built several thousand such libraries around the world (he dedicated $200,000 for the one in Reims). Built in 1921 in the flurry of interwar reconstruction, this beautiful Art Deco building still houses the city's public library. Considering that admission is free and it's just behind the cathedral, it's worth a quick look.

Visitors are welcome to poke around but are asked not to enter the reading room. In the onyx-laden entry hall, small marble mosaics celebrate different fields of knowledge, and a chandelier hangs down like the sleek dress of a circa-1920s flapper. Peek through the reading room door to admire the stained-glass windows of this temple of thought. The gorgeous wood-paneled card-catalogue room takes older visitors back to their childhoods. Go ahead, finger the laboriously created typewritten files, and imagine the technology available back in 1928, the year the library was inaugurated.

Cost and Hours: Free; Tue-Wed and Fri-Sat 10:00-13:00 & 14:00-18:00, Thu 14:00-18:00, closed Sun-Mon; Place Carnegie, tel. 03 26 77 81 41.

Getting There: From the station, walk 15 minutes or take the electric CityBus shuttle to the Carnegie stop.

Place du Forum

Reims' main square recalls the forum, or market, that marked the center of the ancient city. Legend has it that Reims was founded by Remus (brother of Romulus), and so the tribe that lived here came to be called "Remes." This old town of 50,000 people was the capital of the Roman province of Gaullia-Belgica. From Place du Forum, you can climb down steps into the **Cryptoportique,** a first-century A.D. Roman gallery. About 10 feet below today's street level, this cool retreat was once the cloister that defined a sacred temple zone in the middle of the Roman Forum (free, daily June-Sept 14:00-18:00 only, closed Oct-May). This is also a pleasant place to dine *al fresco* on warm summer evenings (see "Eating in Reims," later).

Porte de Mars

The only above-ground monument surviving from ancient Reims is this entry gate to the city (free, always open, at Place du Boulingrin). The Porte de Mars, built in the second century A.D., was one of four principal entrances into the ancient Gallo-Roman town. Inspired by triumphal arches that Rome built to herald war victories, this one was constructed to celebrate the Pax Romana (the period of peace and stability after Rome had vanquished all its foes). Unlike most structures in the rest of town, the gate was undamaged in World War I, but it bears the marks of other eras, such as its integration into the medieval ramparts.

Near the Porte de Mars (on Place de la République) stands a huge **WWI memorial.** Reims, the biggest city on the Western Front during the Great War, endured 1,051 days of shelling during those four years.

Covered Market Hall (Halles Boulingrin)

Built in 1927, this jewel of Art Deco architecture was reopened in 2012 for this first time in 20 years after an estimated €31 million renovation. The vaulted roof consists of a mere 2.75 inches of reinforced concrete and rises 65 feet. Its splendid, bustling morning market spills over to include surrounding streets (open Sat 6:00-14:00, also Wed and Fri 7:00-13:00; tiny organic market Fri 16:00-20:00, closed other days, 50 Rue de Mars).

▲Museum of the Surrender (Musée de la Reddition)

Anyone interested in World War II will enjoy visiting the place where US General Dwight Eisenhower and the Allies received the

unconditional surrender of all German forces on May 7, 1945. The news was announced the next day, turning May 8 into Victory in Europe (V-E) Day. The extensive collection of artifacts is fascinating, and it's thrilling to see the war room (or Signing Room), where Allied operations were managed.

Start with the 10-minute video (next to the entry). Then climb upstairs to the museum and Signing Room. Imagine running the European Theater of Operation from here, as General Eisenhower did from February to May 1945 (after the Allies gained control of the airspace). The walls are covered with floor-to-ceiling maps showing troop positions, fuel supplies, where train lines were functioning, and so on. Progress was painstakingly marked and updated daily. The chairs around the table, with name tags each in its original spot, show where the signatories sat.

Cost and Hours: €4, Wed-Mon 10:00-12:00 & 14:00-18:00, closed Tue, 12 Rue Franklin Roosevelt, tel. 03 26 47 84 19.

Getting There: It's a 10-minute walk from the Reims-Centre train station.

▲▲CHAMPAGNE TOURS AND SIGHTS

Reims, the capital of the Champagne region, offers many opportunities to visit its world-famous cellars. All charge entry fees, most have several daily English tours, and most require a reservation (only Taittinger allows drop-in visits). Call, email, or visit the website for the schedule and to secure a spot on a tour. The TI can make reservations for the Mumm and Martel cellars, and they offer minivan excursions into the nearby vineyards. **Champagne Tours by Cris** is one you can book directly (€62/person, €8 more on Sun mornings; tours daily 9:00-13:00 and 14:00-18:00, tel. 09 86 18 56 67, www.cris-event.fr). **France Bubble Tours** is another option (tel. 02 54 33 99 79, www.france-bubbles-tours.com).

Which *cave* should you visit? Martel offers the most personal and best-value tour. Taittinger and Mumm have the most impressive cellars. Veuve Clicquot is popular with Americans and fills up

REIMS & VERDUN

weeks in advance. Cazanove is closest to the train station and the cheapest, but you get what you pay for.

All told, Mumm is close to the city center and train station, and offers one of the best tours in Reims. Without a car, the others—except for Cazanove—involve a long **walk** (40 minutes) or a 15-minute **shuttle bus** (except on Sun) or **taxi** ride (for more, see "Getting There," under "*Caves* Southeast of the Cathedral," later). A **taxi** from either train station to the farthest Champagne *cave* will cost about €10 each way. To return, ask the staff at the *caves* to call a taxi for you. Warning: The meter starts running once they are called, so count on €5 extra for the return trip. Wherever you go, bring a sweater, even in summer, as the *caves* are cool and clammy.

Champagne in the City Center
Mumm

Mumm ("moome") is one of the easiest *caves* to visit, as it's a short walk from the central train station. Reservations are essential, especially on weekends (book in advance online at www.mumm.com). You must choose which tasting you want when getting your ticket (the cheapest Cordon Rouge tasting is fine for most, though you can pay more for the same tour with extra "guided" tastings). The tour starts with a quick promotional video explaining the Champagne-making process. Then a guided walk takes you through the industrial-size chalk cellars, where 25 million bottles are stored (Mumm is Champagne's largest producer), and a museum of old Champagne-making tools and traditions. The tour ends with your tasting choice.

Cost and Hours: €20-39 depending on tasting level, includes one-hour tour; tours March-Oct daily 9:30-11:30 & 14:00-16:30, Nov-Feb Mon-Sat 9:30-10:50 & 14:00-16:00, closed Sun; 34 Rue du Champ de Mars—go to the end of the courtyard and follow *Visites des Caves* signs; tel. 03 26 49 59 70, www.mumm.com, guides@mumm.com.

Getting There: It's a 15-minute walk from the Reims-Centre train station or from the cathedral. From the station, turn left on Boulevard Joffre and walk to Place de la République; pass through the square, and continue along on Rue du Champ de Mars (to the left of the Europcar office). You can also take bus #7 from the station (direction: Béthany) to the Justice stop, turn right (south) onto Rue de la Justice, and then left onto Rue du Champ de Mars. To return to the station on bus #7, turn left from Mumm and walk a block down Rue du Champ de Mars to the bus shelter (direction: Apollinaire).

Charles de Cazanove

If you're in a rush and not too concerned about quality, Cazanove is closest to the train station and has a cheap and basic tasting. (Martel's tasting for same price is far superior; see "Martel," later.) There are no chalk *caves* and no Champagne is made on-site, but it's a short walk from the station (€13, includes "tour" with 3 tastings; daily 10:00-13:00 & 14:00-19:00, 5-minute walk from the station up Boulevard Joffre to 8 Place de la République, tel. 03 26 88 53 86, www.champagnedecazanove.com).

Caves Southeast of the Cathedral

Taittinger and Martel, offering contrasting looks at two very different *caves*, are a few blocks apart, and can easily be combined in one visit. Veuve Clicquot Ponsardin is a bit farther out and pricey—but it has impressive cellars and that memorable name. It's also a big draw for American travelers and must be booked well in advance.

Getting There from the Town Center: It's a 30-minute **walk** to Taittinger and Martel—starting from behind the cathedral's south transept, it's a straight stroll down Rue de l'Université, then Rue du Barbâtre. Veuve Clicquot is another 15 minutes farther on foot (see map on 996). There's a handy **taxi stand** at 40 Rue Carnot, next to the Opéra (about €10).

To reach Martel and Taittinger by **bus,** take the small green **CityBus** from the train station or from the Cathédrale stop (near TI one block in front of the cathedral)—and ride 10 minutes to the St. Timothée stop (ask the driver to point you in the right direction). Use the same stop to return to the cathedral or station.

To get near Veuve Clicquot, take bus #6 from the train station (to the Droits de l'Homme stop, 4/hour, direction: ZI Farman, return stop is on opposite side of the big roundabout on Boulevard Dieu Lumière, bus stop Cimitière du Sud, direction: Gare Centre).

Taittinger

One of the biggest, slickest, and most renowned of Reims' *caves,* Taittinger (tay-tan-zhay) runs morning and afternoon tours in English through their vast and historic cellars (call for times, best to show up early, no reservation necessary, about 25 people per tour). After seeing their 10-minute promo-movie (hooray for Taittinger!), descend with your guide for 60 chilly minutes in a chalky underworld of *caves,* the deepest of which were dug by ancient Romans. You'll tour part of the three miles of *caves,* see ruins of an abbey and a Roman chalk quarry, pass some of the three million bottles stored here, and learn all you need to know about the Champagne-making process from your well-informed guide. Popping corks signal that the tour's done and the tasting's begun.

Cost and Hours: €17-45 depending on tasting level, includes one-hour tour, April-mid-Nov daily 9:30-17:30; mid-Nov-March Mon-Fri 9:30-13:00 & 13:45-17:30, closed Sat-Sun; 9 Place St. Niçaise, tel. 03 26 85 84 33, www.taittinger.fr, visites@taittinger.fr.

Martel

This small operation with less extensive *caves* offers a homey contrast to Taittinger's big-business style, and it's a great deal. Call to set up a visit and expect a small group that might be yours alone. Friendly Emmanuel and Christine run the place with a relaxed manner. Only 20 percent of their product is exported, so you won't find much of their Champagne in the US. Their visit includes an informative 10-minute film, a tour of their small cellars (which are peppered with rusted old winemaking tools), and a tasting of three different Champagnes in a casual living-room atmosphere.

Cost and Hours: €13, includes one-hour tour and tasting, daily 10:00-11:30 & 14:00-17:30, reservations not required but advised, TI can call ahead for you, 17 Rue des Créneaux, tel. 03 26 82 70 67, www.champagnemartel.com, boutique@champagnemartel.com.

Veuve Clicquot Ponsardin

Because it's widely exported in the US, Veuve Clicquot is inundated with American travelers. Reservations are required and fill up three weeks in advance, so book early (easy by email or the website) before you start your trip.

Cost and Hours: €25 for one-hour tour and flute of non-vintage Champagne, €50 for the same tour and tasting, plus a second flute of "La Grande Dame," €120 for 2.5-hour visit that includes cheese pairing and 4 different tastings; mid-March-mid-Nov Tue-Sat 9:30-12:30 & 13:30-17:30, closed Sun-Mon and rest of year; 1 Place des Droits de l'Homme, tel. 03 26 89 53 90, www.veuve-clicquot.com, visitscenter@veuve-clicquot.fr.

Route de la Champagne

Drivers can joyride through the pretty Montagne de Reims area just south of Reims and experience the chalky soil and rolling hills of vines that produce Champagne's prestigious sparkling wines. At the Reims TI, ask for maps of the Route de la Champagne and *The Discovery Guide* for the Marne region. Roads are well-marked: brown *Route Touristique de la Champagne* signs lead along much of our route and take you to some great viewpoints. The only rail-accessible destination along this route is Epernay.

There are thousands of small-scale producers of Champagne in these villages—unknown outside France and producing fine-quality Champagne without the high costs associated with big brand-name houses in Reims and Epernay. These less famous producers

Pop Pop, Fizz Fizz

Like perfume and Cognac, Champagne is synonymous with good living and good form in France. When invited to a French home for dinner, your aperitif choice always includes Champagne, as it is the proper way to start an evening with friends. Though many wine-growing regions in France produce sparkling wines (called Crémant, Mousseux, or Blanquette), only grapes from this region can be called Champagne. The beverage produced here is commonly regarded as the finest sparkling wine in the world.

Given the notoriety of the Champagne region, surprisingly little of its land is planted in vines (about 60,000 acres), and sparkling wines have little history compared to France's famous wines. While the Romans planted the first grapes here, Champagne was not "invented" until the late 17th century, and then it was by virtue of necessity—the local climate and chalky soil did not produce competitive still wines.

Champagne is made from three grapes: the red pinot noir and pinot meunier, and the white chardonnay. Most Champagne is roughly an equal blend of these grapes, though some smaller producers will make Champagne from 100 percent of any one of the three grapes. Then it's called *blanc de blancs* ("white from white," from chardonnay) or *blanc de noirs* ("white from black"—in France red grapes are considered black grapes—from pinot noir and pinot meunier).

To guarantee quality, the rules governing Champagne production are the strictest in France. The *méthode champenoise* involves two fermentations, the first in casks to make a still wine and the second in bottles (after more sugar and yeast are added) to trap the bubbles. As wine turns bubbly, sediment forms in the bottle and must be removed. In the traditional manner, it's done by hand in a painstaking process of turning and tilting each bottle slightly each day. Nowadays this is mostly done by machines. Once inverted, and the sediment collected in the neck of the bottle, the bottle is opened and the solids are ejected or "disgorged." The Champagne is then topped up, corked, and cellared for additional aging. Most bottles are aged for two to five years, then sold, as Champagne does not improve with age. Champagne is usually blended from several vintages to maintain consistency in taste.

Champagnes are classified by their level of sweetness: *brut* and *extra-brut* are dry (and very dry); *demi-sec* is sweeter; and *doux,* the sweetest, is intended for dessert courses. Bottles labeled *tête de cuvée* are as good as it gets; from there, the ranking proceeds to *grand cru* (from top vines), *premier cru* (next best), and *cru* (table Champagne). The smaller the bubbles, the better the Champagne. The signature aromas of Champagne include brioche, toast, and baked bread, due to the yeast cells present during the second fermentation.

harvest the grapes themselves and make wine only from their own grapes (identified as *"récoltant manipulant"* or just *"RM"* on bottles and elsewhere). It takes a little work to find them, and you must call ahead if you want to tour a cellar rather than just taste, but this usually pays off with a more intimate, rewarding cultural experience. Ask your hotelier or a TI for help, or check in with Les Vignerons Indépendents de Champagne (Independent Winemakers of Champagne, open-house events and tastings Sat-Sun only April-Oct, usually 3-4 different wineries a day, tel. 03 26 59 55 22, www.vignerons-independants-champagne.com).

If you're doing this drive without reservations, it's easier on a weekend, when more places are open and likely to welcome drop-in tasters. If you plan to picnic, you'll find all you need in the sweet little town of Aÿ. There's also a bakery and a small grocery in Bouzy (unpredictable hours).

⊙ **Self-Guided Driving Tour:** For an afternoon ramble over the hills (the Montagne de Reims) and through the vineyards from Reims, try this leisurely loop drive (allow three hours, including stops). If you're pressed for time, you can still sample the vineyard scenery by driving just a few minutes outside Reims, or by working parts of this route into your drive to or from Reims (the best stop is Hautvillers).

• *Leave Reims on A-4 (direction: Châlons-en-Champagne), then exit south to Cormontreuil on D-9, following signs to Louvois (first tasting opportunity). You'll pass through the usual commercial fringe before popping out into lovely scenery just 15 minutes after leaving Reims. Brake for photographs. If you toured Mumm's cellars, you'll notice their hilltop property with a windmill well off in the distance (on the left) as you climb the Montagne de Reims. Remember that the best grapes are grown along the slopes of the Montagne de Reims.*

Louvois: Consider a stop at **Guy de Chassey,** where drop-ins are welcome to enjoy a tasting (assuming the place isn't busy). Call ahead, though, if you want to tour their property (Mon-Sat 10:00-12:00 & 14:00-17:30, Sun 10:00-13:00, closed Aug and mid-Dec-mid-March, bottles €15-20, on the roundabout as you enter town at 1 Place de la Demi-Lune, tel. 03 26 57 04 45, www.champagne-guy-de-chassey.com).

• *Take D-34 out of town. A little after leaving Louvois, look for* Route de la Champagne *signs leading left along a vineyard lane into the appropriately named village of Bouzy. Take the short detour off to the* point de vue *for a fine view over the village and vines.*

Bouzy: There are 30 producers of Champagne in little Bouzy alone, some of whom are famous for their Bouzy Rouge (a still red wine made only from pinot noir grapes, and not made every year). Most places require reservations to visit, but drop-ins are welcome for the fun tasting at **Champagne Herbert Beaufort.**

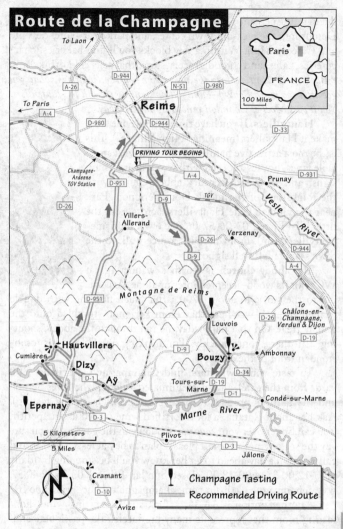

Route de la Champagne

You'll likely be served by Monsieur Beaufort or his English-speaking son, Ludovic. Arrive at 10:30 or 15:30 for visits to their cellars (free tastings, €17-23 bottles, Mon-Fri 9:30-11:30 & 14:00-17:30, Sat 9:30-11:30 & 14:30-17:00, Sun 10:00-12:00 in summer, closed Sun Sept-Easter, first *domaine* on your left coming from Louvois on D-34 at 32 Rue de Tours, tel. 03 26 57 01 34, www. champagnebeaufort.fr).

• *From Bouzy, leave the vineyards following D-19 to Tours-sur-Marne, then turn right onto D-1 and carefully track signs to Aÿ.*

Aÿ: This lively little town (pronounced "eye") boasts of producing 100 percent *grand cru* Champagne from all its vineyards. Detour into the pleasant town center, and park near Hôtel de Ville and Café du Midi. Within a few blocks you'll find bakeries, charcuteries, cafés, and a good grocery store (that sells cold drinks).

• *Back on D-1, drive into the next town—Dizy (which is what you get after too much Bouzy)—and follow signs up the hill to Hautvillers. You'll pass Moët et Chandon vineyards on your way.*

Hautvillers: If you have time for only one stop, make it Hautvillers (meaning "High Village"). This is the most attractive hamlet in the area, with strollable lanes, houses adorned with wrought-iron shop signs, and a seventh-century abbey church with the tombstone of the monk Dom Pérignon. Park near the vintage Café Hautvillers, across from the little TI (TI tel. 03 26 57 06 35, www.tourisme-hautvillers.com). From here it's a nice walk to the town's sights (all well signed).

The **abbey church** is worth a wander (great WCs) for its wood-accented interior alone. According to the story, in about 1700, after much fiddling with double fermentation, it was here that Dom Pérignon stumbled onto the bubbly treat. On that happy day, he ran through the abbey, shouting, "Brothers, come quickly...I'm drinking stars!" Find his tombstone in front of the altar.

To taste your own stars, find **Champagne G. Tribaut** (300 yards from the café), and meet animated Valerie, who loves her job and the family's product (€16-24 bottles, €2/glass for a tasting). Ask her about Ratafia, a local fortified wine served as an aperitif. You can linger over your *coupette* of bubbly in the garden as you survey the sea of vineyards, but please, plan to buy at least a bottle, and call or email a day ahead to let her know you'll be stopping by (daily 9:00-12:00 & 14:00-18:00, closed Sun Jan-Feb, tel. 03 26 59 40 57, www.champagne.g.tribaut.com, champagne.tribaut@wanadoo.fr).

Another option is **Au 36,** a slick and interesting wine shop/tasting room that represents many producers. The passionate staff will help you understand the differences among grape varieties (€10-15 tastings with 3 contrasting Champagnes, good prices for purchase, Tue-Sun 10:30-18:00, closed Mon, a block from Café Hautvillers at 36 Rue Dom Pérignon, tel. 02 26 51 58 37).

For a simply spectacular picnic spot (with tables and benches, but no WCs) and **sweeping views** over vineyards and the Marne River, drive to the abbey church and follow Rue de l'Eglise past it for three minutes. Get out of the car and wander among the vineyards. That picture-perfect village down below is Cumières.

• *Exit the town or picnic site downhill, toward the river to Cumières, then turn left on D-1 and follow signs home to Reims (about 20 minutes back on the speedy D-951). You could also pass through Cumières and drive two miles into* **Epernay,** *home to Moët et Chandon (see below). True connoisseurs can continue along the Route Touristique de Champagne south of Epernay toward Vertus, along the chardonnay grape-filled* **Côte des Blancs.**

Champagne in Epernay

Champagne purists may want to visit Epernay, about 16 miles from Reims (and also well connected to Paris). Epernay is most famously home to Moët et Chandon, which sits along Avenue de Champagne, the Rodeo Drive of grand Champagne houses.

Arrival in Epernay: Trains run frequently between Reims-Centre Station and Epernay (12/day, 30 minutes). From the Epernay station, walk five minutes straight up Rue Gambetta to Place de la République, and take a left to find Avenue de Champagne. Moët et Chandon (described below) is at #20, and the TI is at #7 (mid-April-mid-Oct Mon-Sat 9:30-12:30 & 13:30-19:00, Sun 10:30-13:00 & 14:00-16:30; in off-season closes at 17:30 and on Sun; tel. 03 26 53 33 00, www.ot-epernay.fr).

Tasting in Epernay: The granddaddy of Champagne companies, **Moët et Chandon** offers one-hour tours with pricey tasting possibilities (€22-35 for one or two tastes, no reservation needed, kids 10-18 can join the tour for €10—but no tasting, under 10 free, April-Sept daily 9:30-11:30 & 14:00-16:30, closed weekends off-season, closed Jan, 20 Avenue de Champagne, tel. 03 26 51 20 20, www.moet.com).

To sip a variety of different Champagnes from smaller producers, stop by the wine bar **C Comme Champagne** (meaning "C like Champagne"). Start with a peek in the wine cellar, then snuggle into an armchair and order by the taste, glass, or bottle. Ask about the ever-changing flight selections—but don't expect great deals (daily 10:00-24:00, except Wed open at 15:00, 8 Rue Gambetta, tel. 03 26 32 09 55).

Sleeping in Reims

$$ Grand Hôtel Continental*** is a fine, creaky old hotel on lively Place d'Erlon with rooms in every size, shape, and price. Those in the main building come with traditional decor, high ceilings, and big old-style bathrooms; those in the new wing are plush and *très* modern (RS%, good family options; air-con, elevator, pay parking, 5-minute walk from central train station at 93 Place Drouet d'Erlon, tel. 03 26 40 39 35, www.grandhotelcontinental.com, reservation@grandhotelcontinental.com).

$$ Hôtel Kyriad Reims Centre*** is a good three-star hotel that underwent a major renovation in 2016; expect rates to rise (air-

Sleep Code

Hotels are classified based on the average price of a standard double room without breakfast in high season.

$$$$	**Splurge:**	Most rooms over €200
$$$	**Pricier:**	€150-200
$$	**Moderate:**	€100-150
$	**Budget:**	€50-100
¢	**Backpacker:**	Under €50
RS%	**Rick Steves discount**	
*	**French hotel rating system** (0-5 stars)	

Unless otherwise noted, credit cards are accepted, hotel staff speak basic English, and free Wi-Fi is available. Comparison-shop by checking prices at several hotels (on each hotel's own website, on a booking site, or by email). For the best deal, *book directly with the hotel.* Ask for a discount if paying in cash; if the listing includes **RS%,** request a Rick Steves discount.

con, 29 Rue Buirette, tel. 03 26 47 39 39, www.kyriad.com/en/hotels/kyriad-reims-centre, reims.centre@kyriad.fr).

$ Grand Hôtel du Nord** is a decent two-star value with clean and modern comfort at fair rates in surprisingly quiet rooms, despite being right on the lively square. Each wing is named after a stage in the Champagne-making process. Top-floor rooms have lowest ceilings (family rooms, elevator, no air-con, 2 bikes for rent, 75 Place Drouet d'Erlon, tel. 03 26 47 39 03, www.hotel-nord-reims.com, contact@grandhoteldunord.fr).

$ La Parenthèse has five well-equipped rooms (some have cathedral views) with kitchenettes and is situated closer to the river with easy car access and pay parking. A pleasant garden and public spaces are available. The owners live off-site, so check-in must be arranged in advance (2-night minimum, make deposit through PayPal and pay balance in cash only, no air-con, 83 Rue Clovis, tel. 03 26 40 39 57, www.laparenthese.fr, contact@laparenthese.fr).

$ Bénédicte et Claude Philippon Chambres d'Hôte is a fine value and a lovely experience. This friendly couple offer two comfortable, homey, and centrally located rooms on Place du Chapitre (#21), 100 yards from the cathedral's north (left) transept. Look for the yellow *Chambres d'Hôte* sign (all rooms share bathroom, cash only, includes French breakfast, third floor with elevator, no air-con, parking on square, tel. 03 26 91 06 22, mobile 06 77 76 20 13, claude.philippon@sfr.fr).

Restaurant Price Code

I've assigned each eatery a price category, based on the average cost of a typical main course. Drinks, desserts, and splurge items (steak and seafood) can raise the price considerably.

$$$$	**Splurge:** Most main courses over €25
$$$	**Pricier:** €20-25
$$	**Moderate:** €15-20
$	**Budget:** Under €15

In France, a crêpe stand or other takeout spot is **$;** a sit-down brasserie, café, or bistro with affordable *plats du jour* is **$$;** a casual but more upscale restaurant is **$$$;** and a swanky splurge is **$$$$.**

Eating in Reims

Dining in Reims is as much about the area you eat in as the restaurant you choose. I've described areas to troll for dinner as well as a few specific restaurants. If you're just looking for cheap picnic fixings, head to the grocery store at Monoprix (see "Helpful Hints" on page 995).

ON PLACE DROUET D'ERLON

This bustling line of cafés and restaurants serves mostly cheap and mediocre meals but has the city's best people-watching and café action. Linger over a drink at one of the cafés on the square, then eat elsewhere. You'll find exceptions to the forgettable offerings at the recommended Grand Hôtel Continental's **$$ Au Conti,** with quiet, inside-only dining, classy decor, and top service thanks to maître d' Frédéric (good three-course *menu* includes a drink or half-bottle of wine, closed Sun evenings, 93 Place Drouet d'Erlon, tel. 03 26 40 39 35), and across the square at **$$$ Brasserie Flo,** with an established clientele, a woody brasserie interior, and fine terrace tables outside (open daily, 96 Place Drouet d'Erlon, tel. 03 26 91 40 50).

ON OR NEAR PLACE DU FORUM

This quieter but popular spot serves a young professional crowd at several bistros that spill onto the square. Come here for a more wine-focused, intimate meal with more locals. Among several appealing options, consider **$$ Bistrot du Forum,** an informal place with small wooden tables, a cool zinc bar, and good terrace seating. They serve hearty salads (try the *salade au boudin blanc*), bruschetta, and burgers, as well as traditional meat and fish dishes. You'll also find a good selection of wines (and Champagne, *bien sûr*) by the glass (daily, 6 Place Forum, tel. 03 26 47 56 58).

Just off the square, on Rue Courmeaux, you'll find **$$$ L'Epicerie au Bon Manger,** a foodie refuge whose mantra is "In Good We Trust." They have a handful of tables, stacks of organic local wines (by smaller, hard-to-find producers), smelly cheese, and charcuterie to go or to enjoy sitting down. It's a handy place if you're eating outside the rigid French lunch hours, because they serve nibbles all day (Tue-Sat 10:00-20:00, closed Sun-Mon, 7 Rue Courmeaux, tel. 03 26 03 45 29).

ON THE CATHEDRAL SQUARE

The attraction here is to eat outdoors under the towering west fa-cade of the cathedral, where you'll find ample low stone walls—ideal for picnicking while you admire the impressive church. This spot is sensational after dark, when the floodlighting and sound-and-light show make the view a performance. **$$ Au Bureau,** one of a handful of eateries on the square, is worth it only if you grab a table outside and are OK with average café fare and indifferent service—but it's a good place to linger over coffee (daily until late, at the cathedral at 9 Place du Cardinal Luçon, tel. 03 26 35 84 83).

DINING ELSEWHERE IN REIMS

$$$ Brasserie du Boulingrin is a grand old brasserie. This Reims institution serves traditional French cuisine (including fresh oysters and a seafood platter) at reasonable prices (closed Sun; 10-minute walk from the Reims-Centre train station at 31 Rue de Mars, not far from Porte de Mars and next to the renovated Covered Market Hall, tel. 03 26 40 96 22).

Near the Covered Market Hall (Halles Boulingrin): The pe-destrian street Rue du Temple, along the south side of the mar-ket hall, is filled with cafés and brasseries—all with inviting out-door terraces and a pleasant atmosphere. It's especially lively on Saturday mornings during the weekly market. Consider a glass of Champagne in the cozy courtyard of the **Le Clos** wine bar at #25 (Tue-Thu 18:00-24:00, Fri 18:00 until late, Sat 11:00 until late, closed Sun-Mon, live music some evenings, tel. 03 26 07 74 69).

$$$$ Café du Palais is appreciated by older locals who don't mind paying a premium to eat a meal or sip coffee wrapped in 1930s ambience. Reims' most venerable café-bistro stands across from the Opéra and is good even just for a glass of wine (serves hot food during lunch hours and snacks the rest of the day, Mon-Sat 9:00-20:30, open later for dinner on Sat, closed Sun, 14 Place Myron Herrick, tel. 03 26 47 52 54, www.cafedupalais.fr).

Reims Connections

Reims has two train stations—Reims-Centre and Champagne-Ardennes. Most trains to or from Paris use Reims-Centre, while TGV trains traveling to or from points east (such as Strasbourg or Colmar) use Champagne-Ardennes (5 miles from the center of Reims; frequent connection by local TER train or by tram to Reims-Centre station). Trains that stop at Reims-Centre don't stop at Champagne-Ardennes. For more on Reims' train stations, see "Arrival in Reims" on page 994.

From Reims-Centre Station by Train to: Paris Gare de l'Est (via TGV: 12/day, 50 minutes; by local train: 2/day, 2 hours), **Epernay** (12/day, 30 minutes), **Verdun** (8/day, 2-5 hours, most with change in Châlons or Metz).

From Reims Champagne-Ardennes Station by Train to: Paris Gare de l'Est (via TGV: 4/day, 40 minutes), **Strasbourg** (via TGV: 10/day, 2 hours), **Colmar** (via TGV: 10/day, 3 hours, most change in Strasbourg).

Verdun

While World War I was fought a hundred years ago, and there are no more survivors to tell its story, the WWI sights and memorials scattered around Europe do their best to keep the devastation from fading from memory.

Perhaps the most powerful WWI sightseeing experience a traveler can have is at the battlefields of Verdun, where, in 1916, roughly 300,000 lives were lost in what is called the "Battle of 300 Days and Nights."

Today, the lunar landscape left by WWI battles is buried under thick forests—all new growth. But there are plenty of rusty remnants of the battle and memorials to the carnage left to be experienced.

A string of Verdun battlefields lines an eight-mile stretch of road outside the town of Verdun. From here (with a tour, rental car, or taxi) you can ride through the eerie moguls left by the incessant shelling, pause at melted-sugar-cube forts, ponder plaques marking spots where towns once existed, and visit a vast cemetery. In as little as three hours you can see the most important sights and appreciate the horrific scale of the battles. While 2014 marked the centennial of the start of World War I, 2016 marked the centennial of the "Hell of Verdun."

TOURIST INFORMATION

Verdun's TI is east of Verdun's city center (just across the river—cross at Pont Chausée, on Avenue du Général Mangin; May-Sept Mon-Sat 9:00-12:30 & 13:30-18:30, Sun 9:00-13:00; Oct-April Mon-Sat 9:00-12:00 & 13:30-17:30, Sun 9:00-12:00, Nov-Feb often closed Sat-Sun; tel. 03 29 86 14 18, www.tourisme-verdun.fr, contact@tourisme-verdun.fr). Ask for the free Pass Lorraine, which is good for discounts at many sights in the region. The TI also has free Wi-Fi. The pleasant park nearby provides a good picnic setting.

Open-roof hop-on, hop-off buses get you to the battlefield sights when you don't have wheels (depart from the TI, run by Open Tours, tickets sold on bus, see "Getting Around the Verdun Battlefields," later). The TI can also arrange private guides, but you'll need your own car (about €130/2 hours, promotion@tourisme-verdun.fr).

ARRIVAL IN VERDUN

By Train: Verdun is served by two train stations: the Meuse TGV station (18 miles from Verdun) and the Central train station (within walking distance of town).

Three daily TGV trains from Paris' Gare de l'Est serve the **Meuse TGV station;** a 30-minute shuttle bus connects the TGV station with Verdun's Central station (free with ticket to Verdun or a rail pass, leaves shortly after train arrives). This high-speed service puts Verdun within 1.5 hours of Paris (compared with 3.5 hours by local train—see "Verdun Connections," later in this section).

Verdun's lonely **Central** train station, also called Verdun SNCF, is 15 minutes by foot from the TI. Shuttle buses to the TGV station leave from the building next door. To reach the town center and TI, walk straight out of the station (no baggage check), cross the parking lot and the roundabout, and keep straight down Avenue Garibaldi, then follow *Centre-Ville* signs on Rue St. Paul. Turn left on the first traffic-free street in the old center and walk past the towers and across the river to the TI.

By Car: Drivers can bypass the town center and head straight for the TI or the battlefields. To find the TI, follow signs to *Centre-Ville,* then *Office de Tourisme.* To reach the battlefields, follow signs reading *Verdun Centre-Ville,* then signs toward *Longwy,* then find signs to *Douaumont* and *Champs de Bataille* (battlefields) on D-112, then D-913. Follow signs to *Fort de Douaumont* and *Ossuaire.* The map in this book is adequate for drivers visiting all the basic sights I describe.

Orientation to Verdun Town

While the Battle of Verdun took place in the hills outside town, the town of Verdun itself is worth a look if time allows—except on Sundays and Mondays, when most shops and businesses are closed. It's a handy base for exploring the battlefield sights.

With a history going back to Roman times, Verdun's strategic location has left it with a hard-fought history. Locals call it "the most decorated town in France," and war memorials seem to be everywhere. It's a monochrome place, with bullet holes still pocking its stony buildings. And it's small, with only 16,000 people—4,000 fewer than at the start of World War I. Most of the action seems to be along the Meuse River on the Quai de Londres, where you'll find cafés and restaurants, as well as recreational boats from all over this part of Europe.

Along the river, you'll also find the town's mighty 14th-century gate, which still offers visitors a wary greeting and whose state-of-the-art (in the 17th century) fortifications still seem poised to repel foreign armies. Just across the river, a thicker wall—built in 1871 in anticipation of a German attack—supports a mammoth monument to the victims of German invaders in both world wars.

Verdun is crowned by its **Victory Monument,** high above the river, with a cascading fountain connecting it to the pedestrian heart of town. The fountain's centerpiece, a towering warrior, plants his sword in the ground in a declaration of peace. He's flanked by twin cannons—made by the French for the Russians but ultimately used by the Germans against the French at Verdun. While the monument originally honored French and Allied troops, today it honors Germans, too. Now that a century has passed, the varied sights of the Verdun battlefields have risen above national bias and memorialize all victims of that senseless war.

Today the city is a springboard for visitors to the battlefield sights, but in 1916 Verdun was the departure point for the battlefront. The **Citadelle Souterraine** was where French soldiers assembled and had their last good bed, meal, and shower before heading into the shelling zone. The citadel, with 2.5 miles of tunnels cut into a rock, was a teeming military city. How big? Its bakery cranked out 23,000 rations of bread every day. Today, it tries to give the public a glimpse at life on the front with a childish 30-minute ride on a Disneyesque wagon that comes with a recorded narration (€9, open daily). Your Verdun time is better spent at other battlefield sights.

Eating in Verdun: You'll find several inexpensive restaurants in the pedestrian zone and along the river. **$ Bolzon Charcuterie** on the pedestrian-only Rue Chaussée (#21, tel. 02 29 86 02 62) has good salads, quiche, and dishes to go. While the town of Verdun has lots of eateries, there's only one café near the battlefields (near the Ossuary, described under "L'Ossuaire de Douaumont" sight listing). If you're short on time, consider assembling a picnic from shops in Verdun or at an autoroute minimart.

Verdun Connections

High-speed TGV trains serve the Verdun area from the Meuse TGV Station, 30 minutes south of Verdun. Regular trains run to Verdun's Central station. For TGV connections listed below, allow an additional 30 minutes to reach Verdun's Central station by shuttle bus (included with ticket to Verdun or rail pass).

From Verdun by Train to: Strasbourg (6/day, 3-4 hours, most change in Metz), **Colmar** (7/day, 4-5.5 hours, 2-3 changes), **Reims** (8/day, 2-5 hours, most with a change), **Paris** Gare de l'Est (3/day direct via shuttle bus and TGV, 1.5 hours; by regional train 3.5 hours with transfer in Chalôns-en-Champagne).

The Battlefields of Verdun

Verdun's battlefields are littered with monuments and ruined forts. For most travelers, a half-day is enough, though historians could spend days here. We'll concentrate on the two most important sights, the Ossuaire de Douaumont and Fort de Douaumont, and a smattering of smaller nearby sights. If you want to see where American forces fought in World War I under General John Pershing, head to the St-Mihiel area, south of Verdun (for details, see "Other Battlefields Near Verdun" at the end of this chapter).

Information: Sights are adequately described in English (some provide audioguides). If you want more, the TI and all sights sell helpful books in English describing the Battle of Verdun. The simple but adequate booklet *Verdun du Ciel* provides helpful details (in three languages) and black-and-white photos for about €5. More readable is *The Battle of Verdun* by Yves Buffetaut. The best is Alistair Horne's *The Price of Glory,* which sorts through the complex issues surrounding Verdun and offers perspectives from both sides of the conflict—if you can, read it ahead of your visit (available at the Verdun tourist office).

GETTING AROUND THE BATTLEFIELDS

The most interesting battlefield sights all lie along an easy eight-mile stretch of road from the town of Verdun. To lace these sights together, you have four choices:

By Car: Cheap car rental is available a block straight out of

Verdun's Central Train Station at **AS Location** (about €44/day with 100 km/60 miles included—that's plenty, Mon-Fri 8:30-12:00 & 14:00-18:00, no office hours Sat-Sun but prebooked rentals possible, 22 Rue Louis Maury, tel. 03 29 86 58 58, www.location-vehicule-verdun55.fr, fg.location@sfr.fr). I've included basic route tips in my "Verdun Battlefield Driving Tour," later.

By Hop-On, Hop-Off Bus: Two handy hop-on, hop-off open-roof buses circulate around the battlefields. One route, called Line 14-18, gets you from the TI to the Mémorial de Verdun museum and the Ossuary. A second route, called Line Champs de Bataille (Battlefield), runs from the Ossuary or the museum to sights described in the "Verdun Battlefield Driving Tour," later. The buses allow you 1-2 hours at each monument before the next bus arrives. Sparse commentary is provided. Buses run daily June-Sept, Sat-Sun only Oct-mid-Nov and April-May, no service in winter (Line 14-18, 4/day, €3; Line Champs de Bataille, 7/day, €5; €7 ticket covers both lines). Confirm times with TI or on their website, www.tourisme-verdun.fr; select "Guided tour by bus."

By Taxi: For about €50 round-trip, taxis can drop a carload at one sight and pick up at another (walk between sights). Ask to be dropped at Fort de Douaumont and picked up three or so hours later at the Ossuaire de Douaumont; it's 1.3 level miles from the one sight to the other (figure 40 minutes on foot). Taxis normally meet trains at the station; otherwise they park at the TI (taxi mobile 06 07 02 24 16 or 06 80 08 10 09). It's easiest to arrange a taxi with the help of the TI, though you can save the walk from the train station to the TI if you arrange to be picked up at the station in advance.

By Private Guide: It's possible to hire a private guide to join you in your car for a tour. Try **Ingrid Ferrand** (mobile 06 79 45 30 98, ingrid.ferrand@nordnet.fr) or **Florence Lamousse** (tel. 03 29 85 21 83, florence.lamousse@aliceadsl.fr, www.lorrainetouristique.com), who are good English-speaking guides (€200/half-day, €350/day). **Sonia Boudrot** is another English-speaking guide (mobile 06 45 65 34 70, boudrot.sonia@gmail.com, www.visites-guidees-verdun.fr).

BATTLEFIELD BACKGROUND

After the annexation of Alsace and Lorraine following the German victory in the Franco-Prussian War in 1871, Verdun found itself just 25 miles from the German border. This was too close for comfort for the French, who invested mightily in new fortifications ringing Verdun, hoping to discourage German thoughts of in-

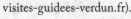

REIMS & VERDUN

vasion. It was as if the French knew they'd be seeing German soldiers again before too long.

The plan failed. World War I erupted in August 1914, and after a lengthy stalemate, in 1916 the Germans elected to strike a powerful knockout punch at the heart of the French defense, to demoralize them and force a quick surrender. They chose Verdun as their target. By defeating the best of the French defenses, the Germans would cripple the French military and morale. The French chose to fight to the bitter end. Three hundred days of nonstop trench warfare ensued. France eventually prevailed, but at a terrible cost. Historically, this is as far as Germany ever got.

World War I introduced modern technology to the age-old business of war. Tanks, chemical weapons, monstrous cannons, rapid communication, and airplanes made their debut, conspiring to kill nearly 10 million people in just four years. In addition, the war ultimately seemed senseless: It started with little provocation, raged on with few decisive battles, and ended with nothing resolved, a situation that sowed the seeds of World War II.

The Battle of Verdun was fought from February through December of 1916. This was one chapter in a horrific "battle of attrition" in which the leaders of Germany and France decided to wage a fierce fight, knowing that they would suffer unprecedented losses. Each side calculated that the other would bleed white and drop first.

During the "Hell of Verdun" (hell for troops and hell for locals), Germany and France dropped 60 million artillery shells on each other. While we have an image of rifle fire and hand-to-hand combat, most of the casualties were caused by shells bursting into lethal fragments. An estimated 95 percent of the deaths at Verdun were from artillery shrapnel. Shells were fired from as far away as nine miles, with poor accuracy. Death by enemy fire was commonplace...as was death by friendly fire.

Today, soft, forested lands hide the memories of World War I's longest battle. Millions of live munitions are still scattered in vast cordoned-off areas. It's not unusual for French farmers or hikers to be injured by until-now unexploded mines. It's difficult to imagine today's lush terrain as it was just a few generations ago...a gray, treeless, crater-filled landscape, smothered in mud and littered with shattered weaponry and body parts as far as the eye could see. But as you visit, it's good to try.

Verdun Battlefield Driving Tour

Take D-603 from Verdun (direction: Longwy), and then take a left on D-112. As all but a couple of the sights described here are along the same road, and Fort de Douaumont is the most distant

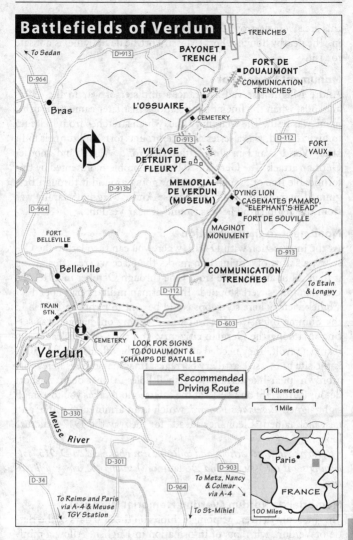

Battlefields of Verdun

TRENCHES

To Sedan

D-913

BAYONET TRENCH

FORT DE DOUAUMONT

D-964

CAFÉ

COMMUNICATION TRENCHES

Bras

L'OSSUAIRE

CEMETERY

D-913

D-112

FORT VAUX

VILLAGE DETRUIT DE FLEURY

Trail

D-913b

MEMORIAL DE VERDUN (MUSEUM)

DYING LION

D-964

CASEMATES PAMARD, "ELEPHANT'S HEAD"

FORT DE SOUVILLE

FORT BELLEVILLE

MAGINOT MONUMENT

D-913

Belleville

COMMUNICATION TRENCHES

To Etain & Longwy

D-112

TRAIN STN.

D-603

CEMETERY

Verdun

LOOK FOR SIGNS TO DOUAUMONT & "CHAMPS DE BATAILLE"

Recommended Driving Route

1 Kilometer

1 Mile

Meuse

D-330

River

D-301

Paris

D-903

FRANCE

D-34

To Metz, Nancy & Colmar via A-4

D-964

100 Miles

To Reims and Paris via A-4 & Meuse TGV Station

To St-Mihiel

REIMS & VERDUN

stop, simply follow signs for *Douaumont*. With the simple map in this book, you should have no problem. Along the way (within easy view of the road), you'll see the sights described below.

Communication Trenches near the Massif Fortifié de Souville

At this parking and picnic area, find a curving trench and craters, similar to those that mark so much of the land here. A few communication trenches like this remain—they protected reinforcements and supplies being shuttled to the front, and sheltered the wounded being brought back. But the actual trenches defining the front in this area were destroyed during the battles or have since been filled in. The nearby Souville Fort (Massif Fortifié de Souville) is not safe to visit.

Monument to Maginot

André Maginot served as France's minister of war in the 1920s and '30s, when the line of fortifications that later came to bear his name was built. The Maginot Line, which stretches from Belgium to Switzerland, was a series of underground forts and tunnels built after World War I in anticipation of World War II and another German attack. The Germans solved the problem presented by this formidable line of French defense by going around it through Belgium. The monument is here because André Maginot's family was from this region, and he was wounded near Verdun.

Monument to the Dying Lion

At the intersection with D-913, where you can turn left to the Ossuary, a statue of a dying lion marks the place where, after giving it their all in an offensive from June through October in 1916, the German forces were stopped. The German military had hoped for a quick victory here so troops could be sent to fight the British in the Somme offensive. The war was dragging on, hunger was setting in among the German citizenry, and the German leadership feared a revolt. They needed a boost—but the offensive failed. This is the site of massive artillery barrages: Imagine no trees here, only a brown lunar-like terrain with shell holes 20 feet deep. A short detour (turn right on D-913 at the intersection) takes you to a small sight signed *Casemates Pamard*, which is an armored machine gun nest nicknamed "Elephant's Head" for the way the 1917 structure looks.

• *Return to the intersection, and continue straight ahead on D-913 (following signs to* Ossuaire *and* Douaumont*). Along the way you'll pass the...*

Mémorial de Verdun (Verdun Memorial Museum)

This museum delivers gripping exhibits on the 300 days of the Battle of Verdun, with lots of information in English. Allow a minimum of one hour to visit.

The ground floor sets the scene with videos and exhibits that take you into the battle. You'll pass displays that help you imagine the experiences of men on the front line. You'll see soldiers' personal effects (pull open the drawers to see what a typical soldier took to the battlefield), uniforms, guns, trucks, and more. A battlefield replica lies below you, visible through the glass floor, complete with mud, shells, trenches, and WWI military equipment.

The upper floor continues with exhibits providing a broader context for the Battle of Verdun and WWI. Your visit finishes on the top floor with a terrace overlooking the actual battlefields (small snack bar).

Cost and Hours: €11, €3 off with the free Pass Lorraine—get at TI, Feb-Dec daily 9:30-19:00, closes 17:00 in winter, closed Jan; last entry one hour before closing; tel. 03 29 84 35 34 or 03 29 88 19 16, http://memorial-verdun.fr.

Village Détruit (Destroyed Village) de Fleury

Thirty villages caught in the hell of Verdun were destroyed. Six—like this one—were never rebuilt. Though gone, these villages (signposted as *Villages Détruites*) have not been forgotten: One mayor and two adjunct mayors represent the villages and work on preserving their memory.

Park on the roadside and stroll through the cratered former townscape. The rebuilt church stands where the village church once did. Plaques locate the butcher, the baker, and so on. There's also a memorial to two French officers who were executed by the French military because, by leaving the battlefield briefly to take a wounded soldier to safety, they disobeyed the order to "stand your ground until the last drop of blood." Ponder the land around you. Not one square meter was left flat or unbombed.

• *Drive on, following signs to the tall, missile-like building surrounded by a sea of small white crosses.*

L'Ossuaire de Douaumont (Douaumont Ossuary)

This is the tomb of countless French and German soldiers whose last homes were the muddy trenches of Verdun. In the years after

the war, a local bishop wandered through the fields of bones—the bones of an estimated 100,000 French soldiers and even more German soldiers. Concluding there needed to be a decent final resting place, he began the project in 1920. It was finished in 1932. The unusual artillery shell-shaped **tower** and cross design of this building symbolizes war...and peace (imagine a sword plunged into the ground up to its hilt). Over time, fewer visitors come as pilgrims and more as tourists. Yet even someone who's given little thought to the human cost of this battle of attrition will be deeply moved by a thoughtful visit to this somber place.

Cost and Hours: Free entry, €6 for film and tower; April-Sept Mon-Fri 9:00-18:00, Sat-Sun 10:00-18:00, July-Aug until 18:30; shorter hours off-season, closed Jan; tel. 03 29 84 54 81, www.verdun-douaumont.com.

Eating: The nearby **$$ Café Abri des Pelerins** is the only place to eat among all these Verdun monuments (closed Mon off-season, just beyond the Ossuary on the road to Douaumont, 1 Place Monseigneur Ginisty, tel. 03 29 85 50 58).

Visiting the Ossuary: Park behind the **theater/shop/tower.** In the back, look through the low windows at the bones of countless unidentified soldiers—probably more German bones than French ones. From there, steps lead down to the shop and theater where you can see the excellent 20-minute film (English-speakers get headphones with adjustable volume) and hike 200 steps up the tower (skippable). While you can visit the interior of the memorial for free, the film and access to the tower require a €6 ticket. The little picture boxes in the gift shop adjacent to the theater are worth a look and worthy of a museum in themselves. Appropriate attire is required, and men are asked to remove their hats.

The **Mémorial Ossuaire** is a humbling, moving tribute to the soldiers who believed the propaganda that this, The Great War, would be "the war to end all wars" and that their children would grow up in a world at peace. The building has 22 sections with 46 granite graves, each holding remains from different sectors of the battlefields. The red lettering on the walls lists a soldier's name, rank ("Lt" is lieutenant, "Cal" is corporal, "St" is sergeant), regiment, and dates of birth and death.

Walk through the **cemetery** and reflect on a war that ruined an entire generation, leaving half of all Frenchmen ages 15 to 30 dead or wounded. Rows of 15,000 Christian crosses and Muslim headstones (oriented toward Mecca), all with roses, decorate the cemetery.

Just beyond the main cemetery you'll find memorials to the Muslim and Jewish victims of Verdun. The Muslim memorial (built in 2006, just across the street from the cemetery) recalls the 600,000 "colonial soldiers" who fought for France, most of whom were Muslims from North Africa. These men were often thrown into the most suicidal missions and were considered instrumental in France's ultimate victory at Verdun (a fact often overlooked by anti-immigration, right-wing politicians in France today).

Jews (who were offered French citizenship if they enlisted) also fought and died in great numbers. The Jewish memorial (which you'll pass as you drive out of the Ossuary) survived World War II. That's because the Nazi governor of this part of France, who had fought at Verdun and respected soldiers of any faith, covered it up.

• *Leaving the Ossuary parking lot, follow signs to the...*

Tranchée des Baïonnettes ("Bayonet Trench")

There is a legend that an entire company of French troops was buried in their trench by an artillery bombardment—leaving only their bayonets sticking above the ground to mark their standing graves. The memorial to this "bayonet trench" is a few minutes' drive beyond the Ossuary. The bulky concrete monument, donated by the US and free to enter (notice the inscription reading *"Leurs frères d'Amérique,"* meaning "Brothers from America"), opened in 1920, and was the first such monument at Verdun.

In fact, most of the Third Company of the 137th Infantry Regiment was likely wiped out here because they had no artillery support and died in battle—still tragic, just not quite as vivid as the myth. The notion of the "bayonet trench" could have come from the German habit of making "gun graves"—burying dead French soldiers with their guns sticking up so that their bodies could be found later and given a proper burial. Walking around this monument provides a thought-provoking opportunity to wander into the silent and crater-filled second-growth forest that now blankets the battlefields of Verdun.

• *Backtrack toward the Ossuary, and follow signs to* Fort de Douaumont. *Between the Ossuary and the fort, on either side of the road, you'll pass what remains of the London Communication Trench. This served as a means of communication and resupply for the Fort de Douaumont. Notice the concrete-reinforced sides. You'll see the ruins of several* abris *(shelters) on the hillside above the trench—these provided a safe haven for the trench's soldiers.*

Fort de Douaumont

This was the most important stronghold among 38 hilltop fortifications built to protect Verdun after Germany's 1871 annexation of Alsace and the Moselle region of Lorraine. First constructed in 1882, it was built atop and into the hillside and ultimately served as a strategic command center for both sides at various times. Soldiers were protected by a thick layer of sand (to muffle explosions) and a wall of concrete five to seven feet thick. Inside, there are two miles of cold, damp hallways—enlivened by the included audioguide.

Experiencing these corridors will add to your sympathy for the soldiers who were forced to live here like moles. Climb to the bombed-out top of the fort and check out the round, iron-gun emplacements that could rise and revolve. The massive central gun turret was state-of-the-art in 1905, antiquated in 1915, and essentially useless when the war arrived in 1916.

Cost and Hours: €4, includes excellent 45-minute audioguide, daily May-June 10:00-18:30, July-Aug until 19:00, April and Sept until 18:00, Oct until 17:30, Nov-Dec and Feb-March until 17:00, closed Jan; tel. 03 29 84 41 91.

OTHER BATTLEFIELDS NEAR VERDUN
St-Mihiel

For a better understanding of the American role in WWI battles and to see real battle trenches, detour south of Verdun (on D-34 or D-964) to the area known as the St-Mihiel salient (a salient is a territory surrounded on three sides by the enemy). Here, American and French forces joined in 1918 under the command of General John Pershing, in hopes of breaking the Germans' will by gaining the important city of Metz. The joint attack on the St-Mihiel salient caught the Germans by surprise and was initially successful, but later became bogged down by poor roads and related supply problems. The Americans didn't make it to Metz, and the Germans were able to regroup and hunker down.

Today, you can see good examples of WWI trenches (many are reconstructions) and appreciate how close the opposing sides were. German trenches are generally still in good condition since they were built with concrete. The French built trenches mostly with sandbags (perhaps assuming, or hoping for, a short-lived war) that have not held up as well. Start with the trenches (maps available at Verdun's TI show their locations), then visit the cemetery.

To see the best **trenches,** take D-907 east from St-Mihiel, following signs for *Apremont le Forêt* and *Pont à Mousson,* and drive about five kilometers out of the city. You'll see signs to the right to several trenches (first, *Bois d'Ailly/Tranchées de la Soif,* then *Tranchées des Bavarois et de Roffignac*). Both are interesting and worth a stop. The third set of trenches (to the right) are signed as *Bois Brûlé/Croix des Redoutes.* Here you'll find original German trenches—still in good condition—and French trenches made from sandbags. The French trenches have been rebuilt in their original locations.

The somber **St-Mihiel American Cemetery and Memorial** at Thiaucourt has 4,153 graves (daily 9:00-17:00, 30 kilometers east of St-Mihiel—follow signs to *Pont à Mousson*).

About 19 kilometers farther south, the **Montsec Monument** (Butte de Montsec) marks the conquest of the St-Mihiel salient by the American First Army. From the monument, which offers a fine tribute to American soldiers, you can appreciate views over the battlefields and see the ruins of several forts.

Skip the town of St-Mihiel, which is far from these places of interest.

FRANCE: PAST & PRESENT

FRENCH HISTORY IN AN ESCARGOT SHELL

About the time of Christ, Romans "Latinized" the land of the Gauls. With the fifth-century fall of Rome, the barbarian Franks and Burgundians invaded. Today's France evolved from this unique mix of Latin and Celtic cultures.

While France wallowed with the rest of Europe in medieval darkness, it got a head start in its development as a nation-state. In 507, Clovis, the king of the Franks, established Paris as the capital of his Christian Merovingian dynasty. Clovis and the Franks would eventually become Louis and the French. The Frankish military leader Charles Martel stopped the spread of Islam by beating the North African Moors at the Battle of Tours (a.k.a. the Battle of Poitiers). And Charlemagne ("Charles the Great"), the most important of the "Dark Age" Frankish kings, was crowned Holy Roman Emperor by the pope in 800. Charlemagne presided over the "Carolingian Renaissance" and effectively ruled an empire that was vast for its time.

The Treaty of Verdun (843), which divided Charlemagne's empire among his grandsons, marks what could be considered the birth of Europe. For the first time, a treaty was signed in vernacular languages (French and German), rather than in Latin. This split established a Franco-Germanic divide, and heralded an age of fragmentation. While petty princes took the reigns, the Frankish king ruled only Ile de France, a small region around Paris.

Vikings, or Norsemen, settled in what became Normandy. Later, in 1066, these "Normans" invaded England. The Norman king, William the Conqueror, consolidated his English domain, accelerating the formation of modern England. But his rule also muddied the political waters between England and France, kicking off a centuries-long struggle between the two nations.

Typical Church Architecture

History comes to life when you visit a centuries-old church. Even if you wouldn't know your apse from a hole in the ground, learning a few simple terms will enrich your experience. Note that not every church has every feature, and a "cathedral" isn't a type of church architecture, but rather a designation for a church that's a governing center for a local bishop.

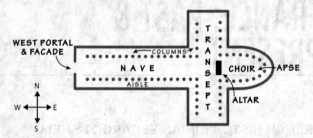

Aisles: The long, generally low-ceilinged arcades that flank the nave.

Altar: The raised area with a ceremonial table (often adorned with candles or a crucifix), where the priest prepares and serves the bread and wine for Communion.

Apse: The space beyond the altar, often bordered with small chapels.

Barrel Vault: A continuous round-arched ceiling that resembles an extended upside-down U.

Choir: A cozy area, often screened off, located within the church nave and near the high altar where services are sung in a more intimate setting.

Cloister: Covered hallways bordering a square or rectangular open-air courtyard, traditionally where monks and nuns got fresh air.

Facade: The front exterior of the church's main (west) entrance, usually highly decorated.

Groin Vault: An arched ceiling formed where two equal barrel vaults meet at right angles. Less common usage: term for a medieval jock strap.

Narthex: The area (portico or foyer) between the main entry and the nave.

Nave: The long, central section of the church (running west to east, from the entrance to the altar) where the congregation sits or stands through the service.

Transept: In a traditional cross-shaped floor plan, the transept is one of the two parts forming the "arms" of the cross. The transepts run north-south, perpendicularly crossing the east-west nave.

West Portal: The main entry to the church (on the west end, opposite the main altar).

Typical Castle Architecture

Castles were fortified residences for medieval nobles. Castles come in all shapes and sizes, but knowing a few general terms will help you understand them.

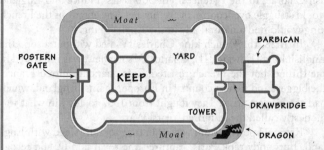

Barbican: A fortified gatehouse, sometimes a stand-alone building located outside the main walls.

Crenellation: A gap-toothed pattern of stones atop the parapet.

Drawbridge: A bridge that could be raised or lowered, using counterweights or a chain-and-winch.

Great Hall: The largest room in the castle, serving as throne room, conference center, and dining hall.

Hoardings (or Gallery or Brattice): Wooden huts built onto the upper parts of the stone walls. They served as watch towers, living quarters, and fighting platforms.

Keep (or Donjon): A high, strong stone tower in the center of the complex; the lord's home and refuge of last resort.

Loopholes (or Embrasures): Narrow wall slits through which soldiers could shoot arrows.

Machicolation: A stone ledge jutting out from the wall, with holes through which soldiers could drop rocks or boiling oil onto wall-scaling enemies below.

Moat: A ditch encircling the wall, sometimes filled with water.

Parapet: Outer railing of the wall walk.

Portcullis: An iron grille that could be lowered across the entrance.

Postern Gate: A small, unfortified side or rear entrance. In wartime, it became a "sally-port" used to launch surprise attacks, or as an escape route.

Towers: Square or round structures with crenellated tops or conical roofs serving as lookouts, chapels, living quarters, or the dungeon.

Turret: A small lookout tower rising from the top of the wall.

Wall Walk (or Allure): A pathway atop the wall where guards could patrol and where soldiers stood to fire at the enemy.

Yard (or Bailey): An open courtyard inside the castle walls.

In the 12th century, Eleanor of Aquitaine (a separate country in southwest France) married Louis VII, king of France, bringing Aquitaine under French rule. They divorced, and she married Henry of Normandy (soon to be Henry II of England). This marital union gave England control of a huge swath of land from the English Channel to the Pyrenees. For 300 years, France and England would struggle over control of Aquitaine. Any enemy of the French king would find a natural ally in the English king.

In 1328, the French king Charles IV died without a son. The English king (Edward III), Charles IV's nephew, was interested in the throne, but the French resisted. This quandary pitted France, the biggest and richest country in Europe, against England, which had the biggest army. They fought from 1337 to 1453 in what was modestly called the Hundred Years' War.

Regional powers from within France actually sided with England. Burgundy took Paris, captured the royal family, and recognized the English king as heir to the French throne. England controlled France from the Loire north, and things looked bleak for the French king.

Enter Joan of Arc, a 16-year-old peasant girl driven by religious voices. France's national heroine left home to support Charles VII, the dauphin (boy prince, heir to the throne but too young to rule). Joan rallied the French, ultimately inspiring them to throw out the English. In 1430, Joan was captured by the Burgundians, who sold her to the English, who convicted her of heresy and burned her at the stake in Rouen. But the inspiration of Joan of Arc lived on, and by 1453 English holdings on the Continent had dwindled to the port of Calais. (For more on Joan of Arc, see page 218.)

By 1500, a strong, centralized France had emerged, with borders similar to today's. Its kings (from the Renaissance François I through the Henrys and all those Louises) were model divine monarchs, setting the standards for absolute rule in Europe.

Outrage over the power plays and spending sprees of the kings—coupled with the modern thinking of the Enlightenment (whose leaders were the French *philosophes*)—led to the French Revolution (1789). In France, it was the end of the *ancien régime*, as well as its notion that some are born to rule, while others are born to be ruled.

The excesses of the Revolution in turn led to the rise of Napoleon, who ruled the French empire as a dictator. Eventually, *his* excesses ushered him into a South Atlantic exile, and after another half-century of monarchy and empire, the French settled on a compromise role for their leader. The modern French "king" is ruled by a constitution. Rather than dress in leotards and powdered wigs, France's president goes to work in a suit and carries a briefcase.

The 20th century spelled the end of France's reign as a military and political superpower. Devastating wars with Germany in 1870, 1914, and 1940—and the loss of her colonial holdings—left France with not quite enough land, people, or production to be a top player on a global scale. But the 21st century may see France rise again: Paris is a cultural capital of Europe, and France—under the EU banner—is a key player in integrating Europe as a single, unified economic power.

FRANCE TODAY

In 2015 and 2016, France was hit with a series of Islamist terrorist attacks—at the Paris offices of the satirical magazine *Charlie Hebdo*, at Paris' Bataclan theater and environs, and then at a Bastille Day celebration in Nice. The French are still reeling from the realization that many of the attackers were French citizens. The attacks raised serious questions about immigration, policing, class divisions, and what it means to be French.

In addition to terrorism, the other main political issue in France is the economy. France weathered the 2008 downturn better than the US, because it was less invested in risky home loans and the volatile stock market. But now France, along with the rest of Europe, is struggling. Growth has flatlined. Unemployment remains high: The overall rate is around 10 percent, but it's a staggering 25 percent for those under 30. France hasn't balanced its books since 1974, and public spending, at over half of GDP, chews up a bigger chunk of output than in any other eurozone country. The challenge for French leadership is to address its economic problems while maintaining the high level of social services that the French people expect from their government.

France has its economic strengths: a well-educated workforce, an especially robust services sector and high-end manufacturing industry, and more firms big enough to rank in the global Fortune 500 than any other European country. Ironically, while France's economy may be one of the world's largest, the French remain skeptical about the virtues of capitalism and the work ethic. Globalization conflicts in a fundamental way with French virtues—many fear losing what makes their society unique in the quest for a bland, globalized world. Business conversation is generally avoided, as it implies a fascination with money that the French find vulgar. (It's considered gauche even to ask what someone does for a living.) In France, CEOs are not glorified as celebrities—chefs are.

The French believe that the economy should support social good, not vice versa, and that people are entitled to secure jobs from which they cannot be fired easily. This has produced a cradle-to-grave social security system of which the French are proud. France's poverty rate is half of that in the US, proof to the French that they are on the right track. On the other hand, if you're considering starting a business in France, think again—taxes are *formidable* (figure a total small-business tax rate of around 66 percent—and likely to increase). French voters are notorious for their belief in the free market's heartless cruelty, and they tend to see globalization as a threat. France is routinely plagued with strikes, demonstrations, and slowdowns as workers try to preserve their rights. During a strike in 2016, oil refineries were blocked—making gas scarce for cars, trucks, and buses—and train workers and air traffic controllers staged walkouts. But strikes usually only last a few days in France, and soon life returned to normal.

France is part of the European Union, a kind of "United States of Europe" that has dissolved borders and implemented a common currency, the euro. France's governments have been decidedly pro-EU. But many French are Euro-skeptics, afraid that EU meddling threatens their job security and social benefits. With the recent vote in Britain to leave the EU, this view could become even more widespread.

The French political scene is complex and fascinating. France is governed by a president (currently François Hollande), elected by popular vote every five years (2017 is a presidential election year). The president then selects the prime minister, who in turn chooses the cabinet ministers. Collectively, this executive branch is known as the *gouvernement*. The parliament consists of a Senate (348 seats) and the 577-seat Assemblée Nationale.

In France, compromise and coalition-building are essential to keeping power. Unlike America's two-party system, France has a half-dozen major political parties, plus more on the fringes. A simple majority is rare. Even the biggest parties rarely get more than a third of the votes. Since the parliament can force the *gouvernement* to resign at any time, it's essential that the *gouvernement* work with them.

For a snapshot of the current political landscape, look no further than the 2012 elections that brought François Hollande to power. He faced incumbent President Nicolas Sarkozy of the center-right party—the man who had cut taxes, reduced the size of government, limited the power of unions, cut workers' benefits, and (most controversially) raised the retirement age from 60 to 62.

Hollande's Socialist Party (PS) was just one of Sarkozy's challengers. There was the radical Left Front Party (which includes the once-powerful Communists) and the environmental Green Party (Les Verts). On the far-right was the National Front (FN), led by Marine Le Pen. She called for expulsion of ethnic minorities, restoration of the French franc as the standard currency, secession from the EU, and broader police powers.

After several months and one TV debate (yes, the French election season is that short), Hollande emerged victorious. And just one month later, his Socialist Party captured more than half of the 577 seats of the Assemblée Nationale. Nevertheless, Hollande has to work closely with legislators, including a strong minority from opposing parties. Though Hollande is a "Socialist" (a word that spooks Rush Limbaugh), he's in the mainstream of the European political spectrum.

But today Hollande faces many challenges. On the sluggish economy, he favors government expansion and stimulus rather than austerity: hiring thousands of teachers, building hundreds of thousands of homes, and launching countless public works projects (you'll likely experience road work in every region). He favors relaxing hiring and firing rules to spur employment (not popular with the masses). And he's had to abandon his promise to return the retirement age—at least for some workers—to 60. Thanks to the economic mess, Hollande has become the most unpopular French president since World War II: Liberals and conservatives alike are furious over his policies. In the spring of 2016 his approval rating was below 15 percent.

In recent years the French political scene has become as polarized as it is in the United States, although the recent terrorist attacks brought some unity, if only for a short period. The government's challenge: to respond with sufficient intensity to deter would-be terrorists without infringing on the rights of its Muslim population. You'll notice tight security at tourist sights and a visible police presence in urban areas.

Another ongoing issue that French leaders must work together to address is immigration, which is shifting the country's ethnic and cultural makeup in ways that challenge French society. Ten percent of France's population is of North African descent, mainly immigrants from former colonies. The increased number of Muslims raises cultural issues in this heavily Catholic society that institutes official state secularism. The French have (quite controversially) made it illegal for women to wear a full, face-covering veil *(niqāb)* in public. They continue to debate whether banning the veil enforces democracy—or squelches diversity.

With a presidential election in May, 2017 will be a fascinating year in French politics. Many seem tired of mainstream parties (sound familiar?) and at this point, there's no clear favorite. The incumbent Hollande and his Socialist Party are suffering from low public approval numbers. The far-right National Front led by Marine le Pen has proven strong, given worries over the economy and immigration, and the general frustration with mainstream parties.

Then there are the personalities. Sarkozy is constantly rumored to be preparing a comeback. Former Prime Minister Alain Juppé is Sarkozy's strongest challenger as leader of the center-right party—which recently changed its name to "The Republicans."

Top French Notables in History

Madame and Monsieur Cro-Magnon: Prehistoric hunter-gatherers who moved to France (c. 30,000 B.C.), painted cave walls at Lascaux and Font-de-Gaume, and eventually settled down as farmers (c. 10,000 B.C.).

Vercingétorix (72 B.C.-46 B.C.): This long-haired warrior rallied the Gauls against Julius Caesar's invading Roman legions (52 B.C.). Defeated by Caesar, France fell under Roman domination, resulting in 500 years of peace and prosperity. During that time, the Romans established cities, built roads, taught in Latin, and converted people to Christianity.

Charlemagne (742-814): For Christmas in 800, the pope gave King Charlemagne the title of Emperor, thus uniting much of Europe under the leadership of the Franks ("France"). Charlemagne stabilized France amid centuries of barbarian invasions. After his death, the empire was split, carving the outlines of modern France and Germany.

Eleanor of Aquitaine (c. 1122-1204): The beautiful, sophisticated ex-wife of the King of France married the King of England, creating an uneasy union between the two countries. During her lifetime, French culture was spread across Europe by roving troubadours, theological scholars, and skilled architects pioneering "the French style"—a.k.a. Gothic.

Joan of Arc (1412-1431): When France and England fought the Hundred Years' War to settle who would rule (1337-1453), teenager Joan of Arc—guided by voices in her head—rallied the French troops. Though Joan was captured and burned as a heretic, the French eventually drove England out of their country for good, establishing the current borders. Over the centuries, the church upgraded Joan's status from heretic to saint (canonized in 1920).

François I (1494-1547): This Renaissance king ruled a united, modern nation, making it a cultural center that hosted the Italian Leonardo da Vinci. François set the tone for future absolute monarchs, punctuating his commands with the phrase, "For such is our pleasure."

Louis XIV (1638-1715): Charismatic and cunning, the "Sun King" ruled Europe's richest, most populous, most powerful nation-state. Every educated European spoke French, dressed in Louis-style leotards and powdered wigs, and built Versailles-like palaces. Though Louis ruled as an absolute monarch (distracting the nobility with courtly games), his reign also fostered the arts and philosophy, sowing the seeds of democracy and revolution.

Marie-Antoinette (1755-1793): As the wife of Louis XVI, she came to symbolize (probably unfairly) the decadence of France's ruling class. When Revolution broke out (1789), she was arrested, imprisoned, and executed—one of thousands who were guillotined on Paris' Place de la Concorde as an enemy of the people.

Napoleon Bonaparte (1769-1821): This daring young military man became a hero during the Revolution, fighting Europe's royalty.

He went on to conquer much of the Continent, become leader of France, and eventually rule as a dictator with the title of emperor. In 1815, an allied Europe defeated and exiled Napoleon, reinstating the French monarchy—though future kings and emperors (including Napoleon's nephew, who ruled as Napoleon III) were somewhat subject to democratic constraints.

Claude Monet (1840-1926): Monet's Impressionist paintings captured the soft-focus beauty of the belle époque—middle-class men and women enjoying drinks in cafés, walks in gardens, and picnics along the Seine. At the turn of the 20th century, French culture reigned supreme while its economic and political clout was fading, soon to be shattered by the violence of World War I.

Charles de Gaulle (1890-1970): A career military man, de Gaulle helped France survive occupation by Nazi Germany during World War II with his rousing radio broadcasts and unbending faith in his countrymen. He left politics in the postwar period, but after France's divisive wars in Vietnam and Algeria, he came to the rescue, becoming president of the Fifth Republic in 1959. De Gaulle shocked supporters and allies by granting Algeria its independence, blocking Britain's entry into the Common Market, and withdrawing from the military wing of NATO. The turbulent student riots in the late 1960s eventually led to his resignation in 1969.

Contemporary French: Which recent French people will history remember? President François Mitterrand (1916-1996), the driving force behind La Grande Arche and Opéra Bastille? Marcel Marceau (1923-2007), white-faced mime? Chef Paul Bocuse (b. 1926), inventor of nouvelle cuisine? Brigitte Bardot (b. 1934), film actress, crusader for animal rights, and popularizer of the bikini? Yves Saint Laurent (1936-2008), one of the world's greatest fashion designers? Marine Le Pen (b. 1968), leader of the far-right National Front party, with staunch antiimmigration policies? Bernard Kouchner (b. 1939), cofounder of Doctors Without Borders and minister of foreign affairs under President Nicolas Sarkozy? Zinédine Zidane (b. 1972), France's greatest soccer player, whose Algerian roots helped raise the status of Arabs in France? Or Dominique Strauss-Kahn (b. 1949), disgraced International Monetary Fund chief? (I hope not.)

And for the Socialists? Manuel Valls, the Socialist prime minister since 2014, is young, dashing, and ambitious. There's also Ségolène Royal, a leader in the party who lost to Sarkozy in 2007 (and to Hollande in the run-up to the 2012 presidential elections). In 2014, she was appointed France's minister of ecology. As it happens, Royal and Hollande know each other well: They met in college, lived together for 30 years, and raised four children before splitting up in 2007. They never married—French politics makes strange bedfellows. But that's personal...

For more about French history, consider Europe 101: History and Art for the Traveler *by Rick Steves and Gene Openshaw, available at www.ricksteves.com.*

PRACTICALITIES

Tourist Information 1041
Travel Tips 1042
Money 1043
Sightseeing. 1049
Sleeping. 1051
Eating. 1062
Staying Connected 1080
Transportation 1086
Resources from Rick Steves 1110

This chapter covers the practical skills of European travel: how to get tourist information, pay for things, sightsee efficiently, find good-value accommodations, eat affordably but well, use technology wisely, and get between destinations smoothly. To study ahead and round out your knowledge and skills, check out "Resources from Rick Steves."

Tourist Information

The French national tourist office is a wealth of information. **Before your trip,** scan their website—http://us.france.fr. It has particularly good resources for special-interest travel and plenty of free-to-download brochures. Paris' official TI website, www.parisinfo.com, offers practical information on hotels, special events, museums, children's activities, fashion, nightlife, and more.

In France, a good first stop is generally the tourist information office (abbreviated **TI** in this book)—except in Paris, where they aren't very necessary. You can get plenty of information online—but I still make a point to swing by the local TI to confirm sightseeing plans, pick up a city map, and get information on public transit (including bus and train schedules), walking tours, special events, and nightlife. Prepare a list of questions and a proposed plan to double-check. Some TIs have information on the entire country or at least the region, so try to pick up maps and printed information for destinations you'll be visiting later in your trip. Towns with a lot of tourism generally have English-speaking guides available for private hire through the TI (about €100 for a two-hour guided town walk, double that for Paris).

The French call TIs by different names: *Office de Tourisme* and *Bureau de Tourisme* are used in cities; *Syndicat d'Initiative* and *Information Touristique* are used in small towns. Also look for *Accueil* signs in airports and at popular sights. These information booths are staffed with seasonal helpers who provide tourists with limited, though generally sufficient, information. Smaller TIs are often closed from 12:00 to 14:00 and on Sundays.

Other Helpful Services: Several private companies offer trip-planning services for a fee. **Detours in France** offers self-drive itinerary packages, hotel bookings, and guided tours of any region in France—ask for helpful Sarah (tel. 09 83 20 71 56, www.detours-in-france.com, sarah@detours-in-france.com). **Paris Webservices** focuses on Paris-specific assistance (tel. 01 45 56 91 67 or 09 52 06 02 59, www.pariswebservices.com, contactpws@pariswebservices.com).

Travel Tips

Emergency and Medical Help: In France, dial 112 for any emergency. For English-speaking police, call 17. To summon an ambulance (SAMU in French), call 15. If you get sick, do as the locals do and go to a pharmacist for advice. Or ask at your hotel for help—they'll know the nearest medical and emergency services.

Theft or Loss: To replace a passport, you'll need to go in person to an embassy or consulate (see page 1114). If your credit and debit cards disappear, cancel and replace them (see "Damage Control for Lost Cards" on page 1046). File a police report, either on the spot or within a day or two; you'll need it to submit an insurance claim for lost or stolen rail passes or travel gear, and it can help with replacing your passport or credit and debit cards. For more information, see www.ricksteves.com/help.

Time Zones: France, like most of continental Europe, is generally six/nine hours ahead of the East/West Coasts of the US. The exceptions are the beginning and end of Daylight Saving Time: Europe "springs forward" the last Sunday in March (two weeks after most of North America), and "falls back" the last Sunday in

October (one week before North America). For a handy online time converter, see www.timeanddate.com/worldclock.

Business Hours: You'll find much of France closed weekdays from 12:00 to 14:00 (lunch is sacred). On Sunday, most businesses are closed (family is sacred), though some small shops such as *boulangeries* (bakeries) are open until noon; special events and weekly markets pop up; and museums are open all day (but public transportation options are scant). On Mondays, some businesses are closed until 14:00 and possibly all day. Smaller towns are often quiet and downright boring on Sundays and Mondays, unless it's market day. Saturdays are virtually weekdays, with earlier closing hours at some shops. Banks are generally open on Saturday and closed on Sunday and possibly Monday. Friday and Saturday evenings are lively; Sunday evenings are quiet.

Watt's Up? Europe's electrical system is 220 volts, instead of North America's 110 volts. Most newer electronics (such as laptops, battery chargers, and hair dryers) convert automatically, so you won't need a converter, but you will need an adapter plug with two round prongs, sold inexpensively at travel stores in the US. Avoid bringing older appliances that don't automatically convert voltage; instead, buy a cheap one in Europe. You can buy low-cost hair dryers and other small appliances at Darty and Monoprix stores, which you'll find in major cities (ask your hotelier for the closest branch).

Discounts: Discounts for sights are generally not listed in this book. However, many sights offer discounts for youths (usually up to age 18), students (with proper identification cards, www.isic. org), families, and groups of 10 or more. Always ask, and have your passport available at sights for proof. Seniors (age 60 and over) may get the odd discount, though these are often limited to citizens of the European Union (EU). To inquire about a senior discount, ask, *"Réduction troisième âge?"* (ray-dewk-see-ohn trwah-zee-ehm ahzh).

Online Translation Tips: Google's Chrome browser instantly translates websites. You can also paste text or the URL of a foreign website into the translation window at http://translate.google. com. The Google Translate app converts spoken English into most European languages (and vice versa) and can also translate text it "reads" with your mobile device's camera.

Money

This section offers advice on how to pay for purchases on your trip (including getting cash from ATMs and paying with plastic), dealing with lost or stolen cards, VAT (sales tax) refunds, and tipping.

WHAT TO BRING

Bring both a credit card and a debit card. You'll use the debit card at cash machines (ATMs) to withdraw local cash for most purchases, and the credit card to pay for larger items. Some travelers carry a third card, in case one gets demagnetized or eaten by a temperamental machine. For an emergency reserve, consider bringing €200 in hard cash in €20 bills (bring euros, as dollars can be hard to change in France).

CASH

Although credit cards are widely accepted in Europe, day-to-day spending is generally more cash-based. I find cash is the easiest—and sometimes only—way to pay for cheap food, bus fare, taxis, and local guides. Having cash on hand can help you avoid a stressful predicament if you find yourself in a place that won't accept your card.

Throughout Europe, ATMs are the easiest and smartest way for travelers to get cash. They work just like they do at home. To withdraw money from an ATM (known as a *distributeur* in France; dee-stree-bew-tur), you'll need a debit card (ideally with a Visa or MasterCard logo), plus a PIN code (numeric and four digits). For increased security, shield the keypad when entering your PIN code, and don't use an ATM if anything on the front of the machine looks loose or damaged (a sign that someone may have attached a "skimming" device to capture account information). Try to withdraw large sums of money to reduce the number of per-transaction bank fees you'll pay.

When possible, use ATMs located outside banks—a thief is less likely to target a cash machine near surveillance cameras, and if your card is munched by a machine during banking hours, you can go inside for help. Stay away from "independent" ATMs such as Travelex, Euronet, YourCash, Cardpoint, and Cashzone, which charge huge commissions, have terrible exchange rates, and may try to trick users with "dynamic currency conversion" (described at the end of "Credit and Debit Cards," next). Although you can use a credit card to withdraw cash at an ATM, this comes with high bank fees and only makes sense in an emergency.

While traveling, if you want to access your accounts online, be sure to use a secure connection (see page 1085).

Pickpockets target tourists. To safeguard your cash, wear a money belt—a pouch with a strap that you buckle around your waist like a belt and tuck under your clothes. Keep your cash, credit cards, and passport secure in your money belt, and carry only a day's spending money in your front pocket or wallet.

Exchange Rate

1 euro (€) = about $1.10

To convert prices in euros to dollars, add about 10 percent: €20 = about $22, €50 = about $55. (Check www.oanda.com for the latest exchange rates.) Just like the dollar, one euro (€) is broken down into 100 cents. You'll find coins ranging from €0.01 to €2, and bills from €5 to €500 (bills over €50 are rarely used).

CREDIT AND DEBIT CARDS

For purchases, Visa and MasterCard are more commonly accepted than American Express. Just like at home, credit or debit cards work easily at larger hotels, restaurants, and shops. I typically use my debit card to withdraw cash to pay for daily purchases. I use my credit card sparingly: to book and pay for hotel rooms, to buy advance tickets for events or sights, to cover major expenses (such as car rentals or plane tickets), and to pay for things online or near the end of my trip (to avoid another visit to the ATM). While you could instead use a debit card for these purchases, a credit card offers a greater degree of fraud protection.

Ask Your Credit- or Debit-Card Company: Before your trip, contact the company that issued your debit or credit cards.

Confirm that your **card will work overseas,** and alert them that you'll be using it in Europe; otherwise, they may deny transactions if they perceive unusual spending patterns.

Ask for the specifics on transaction **fees.** When you use your credit or debit card—either for purchases or ATM withdrawals—you'll typically be charged additional "international transaction" fees of up to 3 percent (1 percent is normal). Some banks have agreements with European partners that help save on fees (for example, Bank of America customers don't have to pay the transaction fee when using French Paribas-BNP ATMs). If your card's fees seem high, consider getting a different card just for your trip: Capital One (www.capitalone.com) and most credit unions have low-to-no international fees.

Verify your daily ATM **withdrawal limit,** and if necessary, ask your bank to adjust it. I prefer a high limit that allows me to take out more cash at each ATM stop and save on bank fees; some travelers prefer to set a lower limit in case their card is stolen. Note that foreign banks also set maximum withdrawal amounts for their ATMs.

Get your bank's emergency **phone number** in the US (but not its 800 number, which isn't accessible from overseas) to call collect if you have a problem.

Ask for your credit card's **PIN** in case you need to make an emergency cash withdrawal or you encounter payment machines using the chip-and-PIN system; the bank won't tell you your PIN over the phone, so allow time for it to be mailed to you.

Chip-and-PIN Credit Cards: Europeans use chip-and-PIN credit cards (embedded with an electronic security chip and requiring a four-digit PIN). Major US banks are beginning to offer similar credit cards. Most of these are not true chip-and-PIN cards, but instead are chip-and-signature cards, for which your signature verifies your identity. These cards work in Europe for live transactions and at most payment machines, but won't work for offline transactions such as at self-serve gas pumps.

Older American cards with just a magnetic stripe may not work at unattended payment machines, such as those at train and subway stations, toll plazas, parking garages, bike-rental kiosks, and gas pumps. If you have problems with either type of American card, try entering your card's PIN, look for a machine that takes cash, or find a clerk who can process the transaction manually.

If you're concerned, ask if your bank offers a true chip-and-PIN card. Andrews Federal Credit Union (www.andrewsfcu.org) and the State Department Federal Credit Union (www.sdfcu.org) offer these cards and are open to all US residents.

No matter what kind of card you have, it pays to carry euros; remember, you can always use an ATM to withdraw cash with your magnetic-stripe debit card.

Dynamic Currency Conversion: If merchants, hoteliers, or ATMs offer to convert your purchase price into dollars (called dynamic currency conversion, or DCC), refuse this "service." You'll pay even more in fees for the expensive convenience of seeing your charge in dollars. Always choose the local currency.

Damage Control for Lost Cards

If you lose your credit or debit card, you can stop people from using your card by reporting the loss immediately to the respective global customer-assistance centers. Call these 24-hour US numbers collect: Visa (tel. 303/967-1096), MasterCard (tel. 636/722-7111), and American Express (tel. 336/393-1111). In France, to make a collect call to the US, dial 08 00 90 06 24, then say "operator" for an English-speaking operator. European toll-free numbers (listed by country) can be found at the websites for Visa and MasterCard. For another option (with the same results), you can call these toll-free numbers in France: Visa (tel. 08 00 90 11 79) and MasterCard (tel. 08 00 90 13 87). American Express has a Paris office, but the call isn't free (tel. 01 47 77 70 00, greeting is in French, dial 1 to speak with someone in English).

If you are the secondary cardholder, you'll need to provide

the primary cardholder's identification-verification details (such as birth date, mother's maiden name, or Social Security number). You can generally receive a temporary card within two or three business days in Europe (see www.ricksteves.com/help for more).

If you report your loss within two days, you typically won't be responsible for any unauthorized transactions on your account, although many banks charge a liability fee of $50.

TIPPING

Tipping *(donner un pourboire)* in France isn't as automatic and generous as it is in the US. For special service, tips are appreciated, but not expected. As in the US, the proper amount depends on your resources, tipping philosophy, and the circumstances, but some general guidelines apply.

Restaurants: At cafés and restaurants, a service charge is included in the price of what you order, and it's unnecessary to tip extra, though you can for superb service. For details on tipping in restaurants, see page 1069.

Taxis: For a typical ride, round up your fare a bit (for instance, if the fare is €13, pay €14). If the cabbie hauls your bags and zips you to the airport to help you catch your flight, you might want to toss in a little more. But if you feel like you're being driven in circles or otherwise ripped off, skip the tip.

Services: In general, if someone in the tourism or service industry does a super job for you, a small tip of a euro or two is appropriate...but not required. If you're not sure whether (or how much) to tip, ask a local for advice.

GETTING A VAT REFUND

Wrapped into the purchase price of your French souvenirs is a Value-Added Tax (VAT) of about 20 percent. You're entitled to get most of that tax back if you purchase more than €175 (about $195) worth of goods at a store that participates in the VAT-refund scheme. Typically, you must ring up the minimum at a single retailer—you can't add up your purchases from various shops to reach the required amount.

Getting your refund is straightforward and, if you buy a substantial amount of souvenirs, well worth the hassle. If you're lucky, the merchant will subtract the tax when you make your purchase. (This is more likely to occur if the store ships the goods to your home.) Otherwise, you'll need to:

Get the paperwork. Have the merchant completely fill out the necessary refund document, called a *bordereau de détaxe*. You'll have to present your passport. Get the paperwork done before you leave the store to ensure you'll have everything you need (including your original sales receipt).

Get your stamp at the border or airport. Process your VAT document at your last stop in the European Union (such as at the airport) with the customs agent who deals with VAT refunds. Arrive an additional hour before you need to check in for your flight to allow time to find the local customs office—and to stand in line. It's best to keep your purchases in your carry-on. If they're too large or dangerous to carry on (such as knives), pack them in your checked bags and alert the check-in agent. You'll be sent (with your tagged bag) to a customs desk outside security; someone will examine your bag, stamp your paperwork, and put your bag on the belt. You're not supposed to use your purchased goods before you leave. If you show up at customs wearing your chic new shoes, officials might look the other way—or deny you a refund.

Collect your refund. You'll need to return your stamped document to the retailer or its representative. Many merchants work with services, such as Global Blue or Premier Tax Free, that have offices at major airports, ports, or border crossings (either before or after security, probably strategically located near a duty-free shop). At Charles de Gaulle, you'll find them at the check-in area (or ask for help at an orange ADP info desk). These services, which extract a 4 percent fee, can refund your money immediately in cash or credit your card (within two billing cycles). Other refund services may require you to mail the documents from home, or more quickly, from your point of departure (using an envelope you've prepared in advance or one that's been provided by the merchant). You'll then have to wait—it can take months.

CUSTOMS FOR AMERICAN SHOPPERS

You are allowed to take home $800 worth of items per person duty-free, once every 31 days. You can take home many processed and packaged foods: vacuum-packed cheeses, dried herbs, jams, baked goods, candy, chocolate, oil, vinegar, mustard, and honey. Fresh fruits and vegetables and most meats are not allowed, with exceptions for some canned items. As for alcohol, you can bring in one liter duty-free (it can be packed securely in your checked luggage, along with any other liquid-containing items).

To bring alcohol (or liquid-packed foods) in your carry-on bag on your flight home, buy it at a duty-free shop at the airport. You'll increase your odds of getting it onto a connecting flight if it's packaged in a "STEB"—a secure, tamper-evident bag. But stay away from liquids in opaque, ceramic, or metallic containers, which usually cannot be successfully screened (STEB or no STEB).

For details on allowable goods, customs rules, and duty rates, visit http://help.cbp.gov.

Sightseeing

Sightseeing can be hard work. Use these tips to make your visits to France's finest sights meaningful, fun, efficient, and painless.

MAPS AND NAVIGATION TOOLS

A good map is essential for efficient navigation while sightseeing. The black-and-white maps in this book are concise and simple, designed to help you locate recommended destinations, sights, and local TIs, where you can pick up more in-depth maps. More detailed maps are sold at newsstands and bookstores.

You can also use a mapping app on your mobile device. Be aware that pulling up maps on the fly or looking up turn-by-turn walking directions usually requires an Internet connection—to use this feature, it's smart to get an international data plan (see page 1080) or only connect using Wi-Fi. With Google Maps or Apple Maps, it's possible to download a map while online, then go offline and navigate without incurring data-roaming charges—though you can't search for an address or get real-time walking directions. A handful of other apps, including City Maps 2Go, OffMaps, and Navfree, also allow you to use maps offline.

PLAN AHEAD

Set up an itinerary that allows you to fit in all your must-see sights. For a one-stop look at opening hours, see the "At a Glance" sidebars for Paris, Nice, Lyon, the Loire Valley châteaux, and the Dordogne's prehistoric sights. Most sights keep stable hours, but you can easily confirm the latest by checking with the TI or visiting museum websites.

Don't put off visiting a must-see sight—you never know when a place will close unexpectedly for a holiday, strike, or restoration. Many museums are closed or have reduced hours at least a few days a year, especially on holidays such as Christmas, New Year's, and Labor Day (May 1). A list of holidays is on page 1114; check online for possible museum closures during your trip. In summer, some sights may stay open late; in the off-season, hours may be shorter.

Going at the right time helps avoid crowds. This book offers tips on the best times to see specific sights. Try visiting popular sights very early (arrive at least 15 minutes before opening time) or very late. Evening visits are usually peaceful, with fewer crowds. For example, Paris' Louvre and Orsay museums are open selected evenings, and the abbey at Mont St-Michel is open on summer evenings.

Many French monuments and cities (and some villages) are beautifully lit at night, making evening walks a joy. Sound-and-light shows *(son et lumière)* are outdoor events held at major buildings after dark; you'll take a seat and watch an array of colored lights illuminate the facade (e.g., of the town's cathedral) while a narrator or audioguide melodramatically tells the story of the place. These spectacles, which usually require a fee, can be a fun experience (though once is usually enough for most).

At Mont St-Michel and Carcassonne, it's best to arrive at about 17:00, spend the night, and explore in the evening and the next morning before the crowds descend. Visit these places first thing or late in the day: Versailles, Château de Chenonceau, Les Baux, Roussillon, St-Paul-de-Vence, the Dordogne's riverfront villages, St-Cirq-Lapopie, and Pont du Gard.

Most travelers should buy a Paris Museum Pass, which can speed you through lines and save you money. It's also smart to book advance tickets for popular sights (for details, see page 46). For more money-saving tips in pricey Paris, see "Affording Paris' Sights" on page 56.

Study up. To get the most out of the self-guided tours and sight descriptions in this book, read them before you visit. The Louvre is more interesting if you understand why the *Venus de Milo* is so disarming.

AT SIGHTS

Here's what you can typically expect:

Entering: Several cities offer sightseeing passes that can be worthwhile values. You may not be allowed to enter if you arrive less than 30 to 60 minutes before closing time. And guards start ushering people out well before the actual closing time, so don't save the best for last.

Many sights have a security check, where you must open your bag or send it through a metal detector. Allow extra time for these lines in your planning. Some sights require you to check daypacks and coats. (If you'd rather not check your daypack, try carrying it tucked under your arm like a purse as you enter.)

At churches—which often offer interesting art (usually free) and a cool, welcome seat—a modest dress code (no bare shoulders or shorts) is encouraged though rarely enforced.

Photography: If the museum's photo policy isn't clearly posted, ask a guard. Generally, taking photos without a flash or tripod is allowed. Some sights ban selfie sticks; others ban photos altogether.

Temporary Exhibits: Museums may show special exhibits in addition to their permanent collection, which can elevate the entry price.

Expect Changes: Artwork can be on tour, on loan, out sick, or shifted at the whim of the curator. Pick up a floor plan as you enter, and ask museum staff if you can't find a particular item. Say the title or artist's name, or point to the photograph in this book and ask for its location by saying, *"Où est?"* (oo ay).

Audioguides and Apps: Many sights rent audioguides, which generally offer worthwhile recorded descriptions in English. If you bring your own earbuds, you can enjoy better sound and avoid holding the device to your ear. To save money, bring a Y-jack and share one audioguide with your travel partner. Increasingly, museums and sights offer apps—often free—that you can download to your mobile device (check their websites). I've produced free, downloadable audio tours for my Historic Paris Walk and self-guided tours of the Louvre, Orsay Museum, and Versailles; look for the Ω in this book. For more on my audio tours, see page 14.

Services: Important sights may have a reasonably priced onsite café or cafeteria (handy places to rejuvenate during a long visit). The WCs at sights are free and generally clean.

Before Leaving: At the gift shop, scan the postcard rack or thumb through a guidebook to be sure that you haven't overlooked something that you'd like to see.

Every sight or museum offers more than what is covered in this book. Use the information in this book as an introduction—not the final word.

Sleeping

Good-value accommodations in France are generally easy to find. Choose from one- to five-star hotels (two and three stars are my

mainstays), bed-and-breakfasts (*chambres d' hôtes*, usually cheaper than hotels), hostels, campgrounds, and even homes (*gîtes*, rented by the week).

I favor hotels and restaurants that are handy to your sightseeing activities. Rather than list hotels scattered throughout a

city, I choose hotels in my favorite neighborhoods. My recommendations run the gamut, from dorm beds to fancy rooms with all of the comforts.

Extensive and opinionated listings of good-value rooms are a major feature of this book's Sleeping sections. I like places that are clean, central, relatively quiet at night, reasonably priced, friendly, small enough to have a hands-on owner or manager and stable staff, and run with a respect for French traditions. I'm more impressed by a convenient location and a fun-loving philosophy than flat-screen TVs and a fancy gym. Most places I recommend fall

PRACTICALITIES

Sleep Code

Hotels are classified based on the average price of a standard double room without breakfast in high season.

$$$$	**Splurge:** Most rooms over €200
$$$	**Pricier:** €150-200
$$	**Moderate:** €100-150
$	**Budget:** €50-100
¢	**Backpacker:** Under €50
RS%	**Rick Steves discount**
*	**French hotel rating system** (0-5 stars)

Unless otherwise noted, credit cards are accepted, hotel staff speak basic English, and free Wi-Fi is available. Comparison-shop by checking prices at several hotels (on each hotel's own website, on a booking site, or by email). For the best deal, *book directly with the hotel.* Ask for a discount if paying in cash; if the listing includes **RS%,** request a Rick Steves discount.

---

short of perfection. But if I can find a place with most of these features, it's a keeper.

Book your accommodations well in advance, especially if you want to stay at one of my top listings or if you'll be traveling during busy times. Reserving ahead is particularly important for Paris—the sooner, the better. Wherever you're staying, be ready for crowds during these holiday periods: Easter weekend; Labor Day; Ascension weekend; Pentecost weekend; Bastille Day and the week during which it falls; and the winter holidays (mid-Dec-early Jan). In August and at other times when business is slower, some Paris hotels offer lower rates to fill their rooms. Check hotel websites for the best deals.

See page 1114 for a list of major holidays and festivals in France; for tips on making reservations, see page 1058.

Some people make reservations as they travel, calling hotels and *chambres d'hôtes* a few days to a week before their arrival. If you anticipate crowds (weekends are worst) on the day you want to check in, call hotels at about 9:00 or 10:00, when the receptionist knows who'll be checking out and which rooms will be available. Some apps—such as HotelTonight.com—specialize in last-minute rooms, often at business-class hotels in big cities. If you encounter a language barrier, ask the fluent receptionist at your current hotel to call for you.

RATES AND DEALS

I've categorized my recommended accommodations based on price, indicated with a dollar-sign rating (see sidebar). The price ranges suggest an estimated cost for a one-night stay in a standard double room with a private toilet and shower in high season, don't include breakfast, and assume you're booking directly with the hotel (not through a booking site, which extracts a commission and logically closes the door on special deals). Room prices can fluctuate significantly with demand and amenities (size, views, room class, and so on), but these relative price categories remain constant.

Room rates are especially volatile at larger hotels that use "dynamic pricing" to predict demand. Rates can skyrocket during festivals and conventions, while business hotels can have deep discounts on weekends when demand plummets. For this reason, of the many hotels I recommend, it's difficult to say which will be the best value on a given day—until you do your homework.

Once your dates are set, check the specific price for your preferred stay at several hotels. You can do this either by comparing prices online on the hotels' own websites, or by emailing several hotels directly and asking for their best rate. Even if you start your search on a booking site such as TripAdvisor or Booking.com, you'll usually find the lowest rates through a hotel's own website. Some hotels offer a discount to those who stay longer than three nights. To cut costs further, try asking for a cheaper room (for example, with a shared bathroom or no window).

Additionally, some accommodations offer a special discount for Rick Steves readers, indicated in this guidebook by the abbreviation "RS%." Discounts vary: Ask for details when you book. Generally, to qualify you must book directly (that is, not through a booking site), mention this book when you reserve, show the book upon arrival, and sometimes stay a certain number of nights. In some cases, you may need to enter a discount code (which I've provided in the listing) in the booking form on the hotel's website. Rick Steves discounts apply to readers with ebooks as well as printed books. Understandably, discounts do not apply to promotional rates.

Hotels in France must charge a daily tax *(taxe du séjour)* of about €1-2 per person per day. Some hotels include it in their prices, but most add it to your bill.

TYPES OF ACCOMMODATIONS
Hotels

In this book, the price for a double room ranges from €40 (very simple; toilet and shower down the hall) to €400-plus (grand lobbies, maximum plumbing, and the works), with most clustering around €80-120 (with private bathrooms; more for hotels in Paris).

H

★ ★ ★ ★

2019 CLASSEMENT VALABLE 5 ANS
MINISTÈRE CHARGE DU TOURISME

france

The French have a simple hotel rating system based on amenities and rated by stars (indicated in this book by asterisks, from * through *****). One star is modest, two has most of the comforts, and three is generally a two-star with a fancier lobby and more elaborately designed rooms. Four-star places give marginally more comfort than those with three. Five stars probably offer more luxury than you'll have time to appreciate. Two-star and above hotels are required to have an English-speaking staff, though nearly all hotels I recommend have someone who speaks English.

The number of stars does not always reflect room size or guarantee quality. One- and two-star hotels are less expensive, but some three-star (and even a few four-star hotels) offer good value, justifying the extra cost. Unclassified hotels (no stars) can be bargains...or depressing dumps.

Within each hotel, prices vary depending on the size of room, whether it has a tub or shower, and the bed type (tubs and twins cost more than showers and double beds). If you have a preference, ask for it. Hotels often have more rooms with tubs (which the French prefer) and are inclined to give you one by default. You can save lots by finding the rare room without a private shower or toilet.

Most French hotels now have queen-size beds—to confirm, ask, *"Avez-vous des lits queen-size?"* (ah-vay-voo day lee queen-size). Some hotels push two twins together under king-size sheets and blankets to make *le king-size*. If you'll take either twins or a double, ask for a generic *une chambre pour deux* (room for two) to avoid being needlessly turned away. Many hotels have a few family-friendly rooms that open up to each other *(chambres communiquantes)*.

Extra pillows and blankets are often in the closet or available on request. To get a pillow, ask for *"Un oreiller, s'il vous plaît"* (uhn oh-ray-yay, see voo play). Hotel elevators, while becoming more common, can be tiny—pack light. You may need to send your bags up one at a time.

Hotel lobbies, halls, and breakfast rooms are off-limits to smokers, though they can light up in their rooms. Still, I seldom smell any smoke in my rooms. Some hotels have nonsmoking rooms or floors—ask.

Most hotels offer some kind of breakfast (see page 1063), but it's rarely included in the room rates—pay attention when comparing rates between hotels. The price of breakfast correlates with the price of the room: The more expensive the room, the more expensive the breakfast. This per-person charge rises with the number of stars the hotel has and can add up, particularly for families. While hotels hope you'll buy their breakfast, it's optional unless otherwise noted; to save money, head to a bakery or café instead.

Some hoteliers, especially in resort towns, strongly encourage their peak-season guests to take *demi-pension* (half-pension)—that

French Hotel-Room Lingo

Study the price list on the hotel's website or posted at the desk, so you know your options. Receptionists often don't mention the cheaper rooms—they assume you want a private bathroom or a bigger room. Here are the types of rooms and beds:

French	English
une chambre avec douche et WC (ewn shahm-bruh ah-vehk doosh ay vay-say)	room with private shower and toilet
une chambre avec bain et WC (ewn shahm-bruh ah-vehk ban ay vay-say)	room with private bathtub and toilet
une chambre avec cabinet de toilette (ewn shahm-bruh ah-vehk kah-bee-nay duh twah-leht)	room with a toilet (shower down the hall)
une chambre sans douche ni WC (ewn shahm-bruh sahn doosh nee vay-say)	room without a private shower or toilet
chambres communiquantes (shahm-bruh koh-mew-nee-kahnt)	connecting rooms (ideal for families)
une chambre simple, un single (ewn shahm-bruh san-pluh, uhn san-guhl)	a true single room
un grand lit (uhn grahn lee)	double bed (55 in. wide)
deux petits lits (duh puh-tee lee)	twin beds (30-36 in. wide)
un lit queen-size (uhn lee "queen size")	queen-size bed (63 in. wide)
un king size (uhn "king size")	king-size bed (usually two twins pushed together)
un lit pliant (uhn lee plee-ahn)	folding bed
un bérceau (uhn behr-soh)	baby crib
un lit d'enfant (uhn lee dahn-fahn)	child's bed

is, breakfast and either lunch or dinner. By law, they can't require you to take half-pension unless you are staying three or more nights, but, in practice, some do during summer. And though the food is usually good, it limits your ability to shop around. I've indicated where I think *demi–pension* is a good value.

Hoteliers uniformly detest it when people bring food into bedrooms. Dinner picnics are particularly frowned upon: Hoteliers

Keep Cool

If you're visiting France in the summer, booking an air-conditioned room is the way to go. Most French air conditioners are operated with a control stick (like a TV remote; the hotel may require a deposit). You'll likely see these symbols and features: fan icon (click to toggle through wind power, from light to gale); louver icon (steady airflow or waves); snowflake and sunshine icons (cold air or heat); clock ("O" setting: run X hours before turning off; "I" setting (wait X hours to start); and the temperature control (20 degrees Celsius is comfortable; also see the thermometer diagram on page 1122). When you leave your room for the day, turning off the air-conditioning is good form.

worry about cleanliness, smells, and attracting insects. Be tidy and considerate.

If you're arriving in the morning, your room probably won't be ready. Check your bag safely at the hotel and dive right into sightseeing.

Hoteliers can be a good source of advice. Most know their city well, and can assist you with everything from public transit and airport connections to calling an English-speaking doctor, or finding a good restaurant, Wi-Fi hotspot (*point Wi-Fi*, pwan wee-fee), a late-night pharmacy, or a self-service launderette (*laverie automatique*, lah-vay-ree oh-to-mah-teek).

Even at the best places, mechanical breakdowns occur: sinks leak, hot water turns cold, toilets may gurgle or smell, the Wi-Fi goes out, or the air-conditioning dies when you need it most. Report your concerns clearly and calmly at the front desk. For more complicated problems, don't expect instant results.

To guard against theft in your room, keep valuables out of sight. Some rooms come with a safe, and other hotels have safes at the front desk. I've never bothered using one.

While it's customary to pay for your room upon departure, think about settling your bill the day before, when you're not in a hurry and while the manager's in. Some hoteliers will ask you to sign their *Livre d'Or* (literally "Golden Book," for client comments). They take this seriously and enjoy reading your remarks.

Above all, keep a positive attitude. Remember, you're on vacation. If your hotel is a disappointment, spend more time out enjoying the place you came to see.

Modern Hotel Chains: France is littered with ultramodern hotels, providing drivers with low-stress accommodations and often located on cheap land just outside town. You'll find some in city centers as well. The clean and inexpensive Ibis Budget chain (about €55/room for up to three people), the more attractive and spacious standard Ibis hotels (€80-110 for a double), and the cushier Mercure and Novotel hotels (€130-250 for a double) are all run by the same company, Accor (www.accorhotels.com). Though hardly quaint, these can be a good value (look for deals on their websites), particularly when they're centrally located; I list several in this book. Other chains to consider are Kyriad, with moderate prices and good quality (www.kyriad.com) and the familiar-to-Americans Best Western (www.bestwestern.com). Château and Hotels Collection has more cushy digs (www.chateauxhotels.com).

Bed & Breakfasts

B&Bs (*chambres d'hôte,* abbreviated "CH") generally are found in smaller towns and rural areas. They're usually family-run and a great deal, offering double the cultural intimacy for less than most hotel rooms. While you may lose some hotel conveniences— such as lounges, TVs, daily bed-sheet changes, and credit-card payments—I happily make the trade-off for the personal touch and lower rates. It's always OK to ask to see the room before you commit. And though some CHs post small *Chambres* or *Chambres d'hôte* signs in their front windows, many are found only through the local tourist office.

I recommend reliable CHs that offer a good value and/or unique experience (such as CHs in renovated mills, châteaux, and wine *domaines*). While *chambres d'hôte* have their own star-rating system, it doesn't correspond to the hotels' rating system. To avoid confusion, I haven't listed these stars for CHs. But virtually all of my recommended CHs have private in-room bathrooms and Wi-Fi, and some have common rooms with refrigerators. Doubles generally cost €60-80; fancier places are about €100-120. Breakfast is usually included—ask. *Tables d'hôte* are CHs that offer an optional, reasonably priced, home-cooked dinner (usually a fine value, must be requested in advance). And though your hosts may not speak English, they will almost always be enthusiastic and pleasant.

Gîtes

These countryside homes (pronounced "zheet") are usually urbanites' second homes, rentable by the week, from Saturday to Saturday. The objective of the *gîte* program was to save characteristic rural homes from abandonment and to make it easy and affordable for families to enjoy the French countryside. The government offers subsidies to renovate such homes, then coordinates rentals to make it financially feasible for the owner. Today, France has more than 9,000 *gîtes*. One of your co-authors restored a farmhouse in Burgundy, and even though he and his wife are American, they received the same assistance that French owners get.

Making Hotel Reservations

Reserve your rooms several weeks (or even months) in advance at popular destinations or for popular hotels. Note that some national holidays merit your making reservations far in advance (see page 1114).

Requesting a Reservation: It's easiest to book your room through the hotel's website. (For the best rates, use the hotel's official site and not a booking agency's site.) If there's no reservation form, or for complicated requests, send an email (see below for a sample). Most recommended hotels take reservations in English.

The hotelier wants to know:
- the size of your party and type of rooms you need
- your arrival and departure dates, written European-style—day followed by month and year (for example, 18/06/17 or 18 June 2017); include the total number of nights
- special requests (such as en suite bathroom vs. down the hall, cheapest room, twin beds vs. double bed, quiet room)
- applicable discounts (such as a Rick Steves reader discount, cash discount, or promotional rate)

Confirming a Reservation: Most places will request a credit-card number to hold your room. If they don't have a secure online reservation form—look for the *https*—you can email it (I do), but it's safer to share that confidential info via a phone call or fax.

Canceling a Reservation: If you must cancel, it's courteous—and smart—to do so with as much notice as possible, especially for smaller family-run places (which describes most of the hotels

Gîtes are best for drivers (they're usually rural, with little public-transport access) and ideal for families and small groups (since they can sleep many for the same price). Homes range in comfort from simple cottages and farmhouses to restored châteaux. Most have at least two bedrooms, a kitchen, a living room, and a bathroom or two (BYO soap, shampoo, etc.). Sheets or linens may be included or provided for a bit extra. Like hotels, all *gîtes* are rated for comfort from one to four *épis* (ears of corn). Two or three *épis* generally indicate sufficient quality, but I'd lean toward three for more comfort. Prices generally range from €500 to €1,500 per week, depending on house size and amenities such as pools. Some owners may not speak English, so be prepared for doing business in French. For more information on *gîtes*, visit www.gites-de-france.com (with the most rentals), www.gite.com, or www.provence-guide.com.

Short-Term Rentals

A short-term rental—whether an apartment, house, or room in

From: rick@ricksteves.com
Sent: Today
To: info@hotelcentral.com
Subject: Reservation request for 19-22 July

Dear Hotel Central,

I would like to stay at your hotel. Please let me know if you have a room available and the price for:
• 2 people
• Double bed and en suite bathroom in a quiet room
• Arriving 19 July, departing 22 July (3 nights)

Thank you!
Rick Steves

I list). Cancellation policies can be strict; read the fine print or ask about these before you book. Many discount deals require pre-payment, with no refunds for cancellations.

Reconfirming a Reservation: Always call or email to reconfirm your room reservation a few days in advance. For B&Bs or very small hotels, I call again on my day of arrival to tell my host what time I expect to get there (especially important if arriving late—after 17:00).

Phoning: For tips on calling hotels overseas, see page 1082.

a local's home—is an increasingly popular alternative to a guesthouse or hotel, especially if you plan to settle in one location for several nights. For stays longer than a few days, you can usually find a rental that's comparable to—or even cheaper than—a hotel room with similar amenities.

The rental route isn't for everyone. Many places require a minimum night stay, and compared to hotels, rentals usually have less-flexible cancellation policies. Also you're generally on your own: There's no hotel reception desk, breakfast, or daily cleaning service.

Finding Accommodations: Websites such as www.airbnb. com, www.roomorama.com, and www.vrbo.com let you browse properties and correspond directly with European property owners or managers. Or, for more guidance, consider using a rental agency such as www.interhomeusa.com or www.rentavilla.com. Agency-represented apartments may cost more, but this route often offers more help and safeguards than booking directly.

To find a place, try the resources listed above, or one of these: **France Homestyle,** run by Claudette, a service-oriented French

The Good and Bad of Online Reviews

User-generated review sites and apps such as Yelp, Booking. com, and TripAdvisor are changing the travel industry. These sites can give you a consensus of opinions about everything from hotels and restaurants to sights and nightlife. If you scan reviews of a hotel and see several complaints about noise or a rotten location, it tells you something important that you'd never learn from the hotel's own website.

But review sites are only as good as the judgment of their reviewers. And while these sites work hard to weed out bogus users, my hunch is that a significant percentage of user reviews are posted by friends or enemies of the business being reviewed.

As a guidebook writer, my sense is that there is a big difference between this uncurated information and a guidebook. A user-generated review is based on the experience of one person, who likely stayed at one hotel and ate at a few restaurants, and doesn't have much of a basis for comparison. A guidebook is the work of a trained researcher who visited many alternatives to assess their relative value. I recently checked out some top-rated user-reviewed hotel and restaurant listings in various towns; when stacked up against their competitors, some were gems, while just as many were duds.

Both types of information have their place, and in many ways, they're complementary: If something is well-reviewed in a guidebook, and also gets good ratings on one of these sites, it's likely a winner.

woman from Seattle who handpicks every home and apartment she lists (US tel. 206/325-0132, www.francehomestyle.com, info@francehomestyle.com), or **Ville et Village,** which has a bigger selection of higher-end places (US tel. 510/559-8080, www. villeetvillage.com). For a list of rental agencies in Paris, see page 132.

Before you commit to a rental, be clear on the details, location, and amenities. I like to virtually "explore" the neighborhood using the Street View feature on Google Maps. Also consider the proximity to public transportation, and how well-connected it is with the rest of the city. Ask about amenities that are important to you (elevator, laundry, coffee maker, Wi-Fi, parking, etc.). Reading reviews from previous guests can help identify trouble spots that are glossed over in the official description.

Apartments and Rental Houses: If you're staying somewhere for four nights or longer, it's worth considering an apartment or house (anything less than that isn't worth the extra effort involved, such as arranging key pickup, buying groceries, etc.). Apartment and house rentals can be especially cost-effective for groups and families. European apartments, like hotel rooms, tend to be small by US standards. But they often come with laundry machines and small, equipped kitchens, making it easier and cheaper to dine in. If you make good use of the kitchen (and Europe's great produce markets), you'll save on your meal budget.

Private and Shared Rooms: Renting a room in someone's home is a good option for those traveling alone, as you're more likely to find true single rooms—with just one single bed, and a price to match. Beds range from air-mattress-in-living-room basic to plush-B&B-suite posh. Some places allow you to book for a single night; if staying for several nights, you can buy groceries just as you would in a rental house. While you can't expect your host to also be your tour guide—or even to provide you with much info— some may be interested in getting to know the travelers who come through their home.

Other Options: Swapping homes with a local works for people with an appealing place to offer, and who can live with the idea of having strangers in their home (don't assume where you live is not interesting to Europeans). A good place to start is HomeExchange (www.homeexchange.com).

To sleep for free, Couchsurfing.com is a vagabond's alternative to Airbnb. It lists millions of outgoing members, who host fellow "surfers" in their homes.

Hotel Barges

These are a fun option in canalside towns; I've listed a few in this book. If you're interested in renting one for more than a night or two, try **Papillon Barge** (mobile 06 86 28 11 55, www.burgundycanalvacations.com) or the cheaper bed-and-breakfast **Barge Nilaya** (May-Sept mobile 06 89 18 80 67, Oct-April UK mobile—from the US dial 011-44-7909-151-611, www.bargenilaya.com). For a comprehensive source on enjoying the rivers and canals of France, check www.french-waterways.com.

Hostels

A hostel *(auberge de jeunesse)* provides cheap beds in dorms where you sleep alongside strangers for about €23-35 per night. Travelers of any age are welcome if they don't mind dorm-style accommodations and meeting other travelers. Most hostels offer kitchen facilities, guest computers, Wi-Fi, and a self-service laundry. Hostels almost always provide bedding, but the towel's up to you (though you can usually rent one for a small fee). Family and private rooms are often available.

Independent hostels tend to be easygoing, colorful, and informal (no membership required; www.hostelworld.com). You may pay slightly less by booking directly with the hostel. **Official**

hostels are part of Hostelling International (HI) and share an online booking site (www.hihostels.com). HI hostels typically require that you either have a membership card or pay extra per night.

Hip Hop Hostels is a clearinghouse for budget hotels and hostels in Paris. It's worth a look for its good selection of cheap accommodations (tel. 01 48 78 10 00, www.hiphophostels.com).

Camping

In Europe, camping is more of a social than an environmental experience. It's a great way for American travelers to make European friends. Camping sites average about €24 per night, and almost every destination recommended in this book has a campground within a reasonable walk or bus ride from the town center and train station. A tent, pillow, and sleeping bag are all you need. Many campgrounds have small grocery stores and washing machines, and some even come with cafés and miniature golf. Local TIs have camping information. You'll find more detailed information in the annually updated *Michelin Camping France*, available in the United States and at most French bookstores.

Eating

The French eat long and well. Relaxed and tree-shaded lunches with a chilled rosé, three-hour dinners, and endless hours of sitting in outdoor cafés are the norm. Here, celebrated restaurateurs are as famous as great athletes, and mamas hope their babies will grow up to be great chefs. Cafés, cuisine, and wines should become a highlight of any French adventure: It's sightseeing for your palate. Even if the rest of you is sleeping in a cheap hotel, let your taste buds travel first-class in France. (They can go coach in Britain.)

You can eat well without going broke—but choose carefully: You're just as likely to blow a small fortune on a mediocre meal as you are to dine wonderfully for €20. Read the information that follows, consider my restaurant suggestions in this book, and you'll do fine. When restaurant-hunting, choose a spot filled with locals, not the place with the big neon signs boasting, "We Speak English and Accept Credit Cards." Venturing even a block or two off the main drag can lead to higher-quality food for less than half the price of the tourist-oriented places.

In Paris, lunches are a particularly good value, as most places offer the same quality and similar selections for far less than at dinner. If you're on a budget or just like going local, try making lunch your main meal, then have a lighter evening meal at a café.

Restaurant Price Code

I've assigned each eatery a price category, based on the average cost of a typical main course. Drinks, desserts, and splurge items (steak and seafood) can raise the price considerably.

$$$$	**Splurge:** Most main courses over €25
$$$	**Pricier:** €20-25
$$	**Moderate:** €15-20
$	**Budget:** Under €15

In France, a crêpe stand or other takeout spot is **$;** a sit-down brasserie, café, or bistro with affordable *plats du jour* is **$$;** a casual but more upscale restaurant is **$$$;** and a swanky splurge is **$$$$.**

RESTAURANT PRICING

I've categorized my recommended eateries based on price, indicated with a dollar-sign rating (see sidebar). The price ranges suggest the average price of a typical main course—but not necessarily a complete meal. Obviously, expensive items (steak, seafood, truffles), fine wine, appetizers, and dessert can significantly increase your final bill.

The dollar-sign categories also indicate the overall personality and "feel" of a place:

$ Budget eateries include street food, takeaway, order-at-the-counter shops, basic cafeterias, bakeries selling sandwiches, and so on.

$$ Moderate eateries are typically nice (but not fancy) sit-down restaurants, ideal for a straightforward, fill-the-tank meal. Most of my listings fall in this category—great for getting a good taste of the local cuisine on a budget.

$$$ Pricier eateries are a notch up, with more attention paid to the setting, presentation, and cuisine. These are ideal for a memorable meal that's still relatively casual and doesn't break the bank. This category often includes affordable "destination" or "foodie" restaurants.

$$$$ Splurge eateries are dress-up-for-a-special-occasion-swanky—Michelin star-type restaurants, typically with an elegant setting, polished service, pricey and intricate cuisine, and an expansive (and expensive) wine list.

I haven't categorized places where you might assemble a picnic, snack, or graze: supermarkets, delis, ice-cream stands, cafés or bars specializing in drinks, chocolate shops, and so on.

BREAKFAST

Most hotels offer an optional breakfast, which is usually pleasant and convenient (generally €10-20). They almost all offer a buffet breakfast (cereal, yogurt, fruit, cheese, ham, croissants, juice, and hard-boiled eggs). Some add scrambled eggs and sausage. Before committing to breakfast, scan the offerings to be sure it's to your liking. Once committed, it's self-service and as much as you want. Coffee is often self-serve from a machine or a thermos. If there's no coffee machine and you want to make your own *café au lait*, find the hot milk and mix it with your coffee. If your hotelier serves your coffee, ask for *café avec du lait*.

If all you want is coffee or tea and a croissant, the corner café offers more atmosphere and is less expensive (though you get more coffee at your hotel). Go local at the café and ask for *une tartine* (ewn tart-een), a baguette slathered with butter or jam. If you crave eggs for breakfast, drop into a café and order *une omelette* or *œufs sur le plat* (fried eggs). Some cafés and bakeries offer worthwhile breakfast deals with juice, croissant, and coffee or tea for about €7 (for more on coffee and tea drinks, see page 1077).

To keep it cheap, pick up some fruit at a grocery store and pastries at your favorite *boulangerie* and have a picnic breakfast, then savor your coffee at a café bar *(comptoir)* while standing, like the French do.

PICNIC DINING AND FOOD TO GO

Whether going all out on a perfect French picnic or simply grabbing a sandwich to eat on an atmospheric square, dining with the city as your backdrop can be one of your most memorable meals.

Picnics

Great for lunch or dinner, French picnics can be first-class affairs and adventures in high cuisine. Be daring. Try the smelly cheeses, ugly pâtés, sissy quiches, and minuscule yogurts. Shopkeepers are accustomed to selling small quantities of produce. Get a succulent salad-to-go, and ask for a plastic fork. If you need a knife or corkscrew, borrow one from your hotelier (but don't picnic in your room, as French hoteliers uniformly detest this). Though drinking wine in public places is taboo in the US, it's *pas de problème* in France.

Assembling a Picnic: Visit several small stores to put together a complete meal. Shop early, as many shops close from 12:00 or 13:00 to 15:00 for their lunch break. Say *"Bonjour madame/monsieur"* as you enter, then point to what you want and say, *"S'il vous plaît."* For other terminology you might need while shopping, see the sidebar on page 1065.

At the **boulangerie** (bakery), buy some bread. A baguette usually does the trick, or choose from the many loaves of bread on display: *pain aux céréales* (whole grain with seeds), *pain de campagne* (country bread, made with unbleached bread flour), *pain complet*

Picnic Vocabulary

English	French
please	*s'il vous plaît* (see voo play)
a plastic fork	*une fourchette en plastique* (ewn foor-sheht ahn plah-steek)
a plastic cup	*un goblet en plastique* (uhn goh-blay ahn plah-steek)
a paper plate	*une assiette en papier* (ewn ah-see-eht ahn pahp-yay)
napkins	*les serviettes* (lay sehr-vee-eht)
a small box	*une barquette* (ewn bar-keht)
a knife	*un couteau* (uhn koo-toh)
corkscrew	*tire-bouchon* (teer-boo-shohn)
sliced	*tranché* (trahn-shay)
a slice	*une tranche* (ewn trahnsh)
a small slice	*une petite tranche* (ewn puh-teet trahnsh)
more	*plus* (plew)
less	*moins* (mwan)
It's just right.	*C'est bon.* (say bohn)
That'll be all.	*C'est tout.* (say too)
Thank you.	*Merci.* (mehr-see)

(wheat bread), or *pain de seigle* (rye bread). To ask for it sliced, say "*Tranché, s'il vous plaît.*"

At the *pâtisserie* (pastry shop, which is often the same place you bought the bread), choose a dessert that's easy to eat with your hands. My favorites are *éclairs* (*chocolat* or *café* flavored), individual fruit *tartes* (*framboise* is raspberry, *fraise* is strawberry, *citron* is lemon), and *macarons* (made of flavored cream sandwiched between two meringues, not coconut cookies like in the US).

At the *crémerie* or *fromagerie* (cheese shop), choose a sampling of cheeses *(un assortiment)*. I usually get one hard cheese (like Comté, Cantal, or Beaufort), one soft cow's milk cheese (like Brie or Camembert), one goat's milk cheese (anything that says chèvre), and one blue cheese (Roquefort or Bleu d'Auvergne). Goat cheese usually comes in individual portions. For all other large cheeses, point to the cheese you want and ask for *une petite tranche* (a small slice). The shopkeeper will place a knife on the cheese indicating the size of the slice they are about to cut, then look at you for approval. If you'd like more, say, "*Plus.*" If you'd like less, say "*Moins.*" If it's just right, say "*C'est bon!*"

At the **charcuterie** or **traiteur** (for deli items, prepared salads, meats, and pâtés), I like a slice of *pâté de campagne* (country pâté

Market Day *(Jour du Marché)*

Market days are a big deal throughout France. They have been a central feature of life in rural areas since the Middle Ages. No single event better symbolizes the French preoccupation with fresh products, and their strong ties to the soil, than the weekly market. Many locals mark their calendars with the arrival of fresh produce.

Markets *(marchés)* combine products from area farmers and artisans, and offer a mind-boggling array of choices, from the perishable (produce, meats, cheeses, breads, and pastries) to the nonperishable (kitchen wares, inexpensive clothing, brightly colored linens, and pottery). *Les marchés brocantes* specialize in quasi-antiques and flea-market bric-a-brac. Many *marchés* have good selections of produce and some *brocantes.*

Notice the signs as you enter towns indicating the *jours du marché* (essential information to any civilized soul, and a reminder not to park on the streets the night before—be on the lookout for *stationnement interdit* signs that mark "no parking" areas). Most *marchés* take place once a week in the town's main square; larger *marchés* spill into nearby streets.

---

made of pork) and *saucissons sec* (dried sausages, some with pepper crust or garlic—you can ask to have it sliced thin like salami). I get a fresh salad, too. Typical options are *carottes râpées* (shredded carrots in a tangy vinaigrette), *salade de betteraves* (beets in vinaigrette), and *céleri rémoulade* (celery root with a mayonnaise sauce). The food comes in takeout boxes, and they may supply a plastic fork.

At a **cave à vin** you can buy chilled wines that the merchant is usually happy to open and re-cork for you.

At a **supermarché, épicerie,** or **magasin d'alimentation** (small grocery store or minimart), you'll find plastic cutlery and glasses, paper plates, napkins, drinks, chips, and a display of produce. Local *supermarchés* are less colorful than smaller stores, but cheaper, more efficient, and offer adequate quality. Department stores often have supermarkets in the basement. On the outskirts of cities, you'll find the monster *hypermarchés.* Drop in for a glimpse of hyper-France in action.

Another option is to visit open-air markets *(marchés),* which are fun and photogenic, but shut down around 13:00

Usually, the bigger the market, the greater the overall selection—particularly of nonperishable goods. Bigger towns (such as Beaune and Arles) may have two weekly markets. The biggest market days are usually on weekends, so that everyone can go.

Market day is as important socially as it is commercially—it's a weekly chance for locals to resume friendships and get the current gossip. Here neighbors can catch up on Henri's barn renovation, see photos of Jacqueline's new grandchild, and relax over *un café*. Dogs are tethered to café tables while friends exchange kisses. Tether yourself to a table and observe: three cheek-kisses for good friends (left-right-left), a fourth for friends you haven't seen in a while. (The appropriate number of kisses varies by region—Paris, Lyon, and Provence have different standards.) It's bad form to be in a hurry on market day. Allow the crowd to set your pace.

It's a joy to assemble picnics at an open-air market. Most perishable items are sold directly from the producers—no middlemen, no credit cards, just really fresh produce (*du pays* means "grown locally"). Sometimes you'll meet a widow selling a dozen eggs, two rabbits, and a wad of herbs tied with string. But most vendors follow a weekly circuit of markets they feel works best for them, showing up in the same spot every week, year in and year out. Notice how much fun they have chatting up their customers and one another. Many vendors speak enough English to assist you in your selection. Markets usually end by 13:00—in time for lunch, allowing the town to reclaim its streets and squares.

(many are listed in this book; local TIs have complete lists). For more information, see the sidebar.

To-Go Food

You'll find plenty of to-go options at *crêperie*s, bakeries, and small stands. Baguette sandwiches, quiches, and pizza-like items are tasty, filling, and budget-friendly (about €5).

Sandwiches: Anything served *à la provençale* has marinated peppers, tomatoes, and eggplant. A sandwich *à la italienne* is a grilled *panini*. Here are some common sandwiches:

Fromage (froh-mahzh): Cheese (white on beige)

Jambon beurre (zhahn-bohn bur): Ham and butter (boring for most but a French classic)

Jambon crudités (zhahn-bohn krew-dee-tay): Ham with tomatoes, lettuce, cucumbers, and mayonnaise

Pain salé (pan sah-lay) or *fougasse* (foo-gahs): Bread rolled up with salty bits of bacon, cheese, or olives

Poulet crudités (poo-lay krew-dee-tay): Chicken with tomatoes, lettuce, maybe cucumbers, and always mayonnaise

Saucisson beurre (saw-see-sohn bur): Thinly sliced sausage and butter

Thon crudités (tohn krew-dee-tay): Tuna with tomatoes, lettuce, and maybe cucumbers, but definitely mayonnaise

Quiche: Typical quiches you'll see at shops and bakeries are *lorraine* (ham and cheese), *fromage* (cheese only), *aux oignons* (with onions), *aux poireaux* (with leeks—my favorite), *aux champignons* (with mushrooms), *au saumon* (salmon), or *au thon* (tuna).

Crêpes: The quintessentially French thin pancake called a crêpe (rhymes with "step," not "grape") is filling, usually inexpensive, and generally quick. Place your order at the *crêperie* window or kiosk, and watch the chef in action. But don't be surprised if they don't make the crêpe for you from scratch; at some *crêperie*s, they might premake a stack of crêpes and reheat them when they fill your order.

Crêpes generally are *sucrée* (sweet) or *salée* (savory). Technically, a savory crêpe should be made with a heartier buckwheat batter, and is called a *galette*. However, many cheap and lazy *crêperies* use the same sweet batter *(de froment)* for both their sweet-topped and savory-topped crêpes. A *socca* is a chickpea crêpe.

Standard crêpe toppings include cheese (*fromage;* usually Swiss-style Gruyère or Emmental), ham *(jambon),* egg *(œuf),* mushrooms *(champignons),* chocolate, Nutella, jam *(confiture),* whipped cream *(chantilly),* apple jam *(compote de pommes),* chestnut cream *(crème de marrons),* and Grand Marnier.

RESTAURANT AND CAFE DINING

To get the most out of dining out in France, slow down. Allow enough time, engage the waiter, show you care about food, and enjoy the experience as much as the food itself.

French waiters probably won't overwhelm you with friendliness. As their tip is already included in the bill (see "Tipping," below), there's less schmoozing than we're used to at home. Notice how hard they work. They almost never stop. Cozying up to clients (French or foreign) is probably the last thing on their minds. They're often stuck with client overload, too, because the French rarely hire part-time employees, even to help with peak times. To get a waiter's attention, try to make meaningful eye contact, which is a signal that you need something. If this doesn't work, raise your hand and simply say, *"S'il vous plaît"* (see voo play)—"please."

This phrase should also work when you want to ask for the check. In French eateries, a waiter will rarely bring you the check unless you request it. For a French person, having the bill dropped off before asking for it is *très gauche*. But busy travelers are often

PRACTICALITIES

ready for the check sooner rather than later. If you're in a hurry, ask for the bill when your server comes to clear your plates or checks in to see if you want dessert or coffee. To request your bill, say, *"L'addition, s'il vous plaît."* If you don't ask now, the wait staff may become scarce as they leave you to digest in peace. (For a list of other restaurant survival phrases, see page 1130.)

Note that all café and restaurant interiors are smoke-free. Today the only smokers you'll find are at outside tables, which—unfortunately—may be exactly where you want to sit.

For a list of common French dishes that you'll see on menus, see page 1073. For details on ordering drinks, see page 1076.

Tipping: At cafés and restaurants, a 12-15 percent service charge is always included in the price of what you order (*service compris* or *prix net*), but you won't see it listed on your bill. Unlike in the US, France pays servers a decent wage. Because of this, most locals only tip a little, or not at all. If you feel the service was good, tip a little—up to 5 percent. If you want the waiter to keep the change when you pay, say *"C'est bon"* (say bohn), meaning "It's good." If you are using a credit card, leave your tip in cash—credit-card receipts don't even have space to add a tip. Never feel guilty if you don't leave a tip.

Cafés and Brasseries

French cafés and brasseries provide user-friendly meals and a relief from sightseeing overload. They're not necessarily cheaper than many restaurants and bistros, and famous cafés on popular squares can be pricey affairs. Their key advantage is flexibility: They offer long serving hours, and you're welcome to order just a salad, a sandwich, or a bowl of soup, even for dinner. It's also OK to share starters and desserts, though not main courses.

Cafés and brasseries usually open by 7:00, but closing hours vary. Unlike restaurants, which open only for dinner and sometimes for lunch, some cafés and all brasseries serve food throughout the day (usually with a limited menu during off hours), making them the best option for a late lunch or an early dinner. *Service Continu* or *Service Non-Stop* signs indicate continued service throughout the day. Cafés in smaller towns often close their kitchens from about 14:00 until 18:00.

Check the price list first, which by law must be posted prominently (if you don't see one, go elsewhere). There are two sets of prices: You'll pay more for the same drink if you're seated at a table *(salle)* than if you're seated or standing at the bar or counter *(comptoir)*. (For tips on ordering coffee and tea, see page 1077.)

At a café or a brasserie, if the table is not set, it's fine to seat yourself and just have a drink. However, if it's set with a placemat

Vegetarians, Allergies, and Other Dietary Restrictions

Many French people think "vegetarian" means "no red meat" or "not much meat." If you're a strict vegetarian, be specific: Tell your server what you don't eat—and it can be helpful to clarify what you do eat. Write it out on a card and keep it handy.

But be reasonable. Think of your meal (as the French do) as if it's a finely crafted creation by a trained artist. The chef knows what goes well together, and substitutions are considered an insult to his training. Picky eaters should try their best to just take it or leave it.

However, French restaurants are willing to accommodate genuine dietary restrictions and other special concerns, or at least point you to an appropriate choice on the menu. These phrases might help:

French	English
Je suis végétarien/végétarienne. (zhuh swee vay-zhay-tah-ree-an/vay-zhay-tah-ree-ehn)	I am vegetarian.
Je ne peux pas manger de _____. (zhuh nuh puh pah mahn-zhay duh _____)	I cannot eat _____.
Je suis allergique à _____. (zhuh sweez ah-lehr-zheek ah _____)	I am allergic to _____.
Pas de _____. (pah duh _____).	No _____.

and cutlery, you should ask to be seated and plan to order a meal. If you're unsure, ask the server before sitting down.

Ordering: A salad, crêpe, quiche, or omelet is a fairly cheap way to fill up. Each can be made with various extras such as ham, cheese, mushrooms, and so on. Omelets come lonely on a plate with a basket of bread.

Sandwiches, generally served day and night, are inexpensive, but most are very plain (*boulangeries* serve better ones). To get more than a piece of ham *(jambon)* on a baguette, order a *sandwich jambon crudités* (garnished with veggies). Popular sandwiches are the *croque monsieur* (grilled ham-and-cheese) and *croque madame* (*monsieur* with a fried egg on top).

Salads are typically large and often can be ordered with warm ingredients mixed in, such as melted goat cheese, fried gizzards, or roasted potatoes. One salad is perfect for lunch or a light dinner. See page 1073 for a list of classic salads.

The daily special—*plat du jour* (plah dew zhoor), or just *plat*—is your fast, hearty, and garnished hot plate for about €12-20. At most cafés, feel free to order only *entrées* (which in French means the starter course); many people find these lighter and more interesting than a main course. A vegetarian can enjoy a tasty, filling meal by ordering two *entrées*.

Regardless of what you order, bread is free but almost never comes with butter; to get more bread, just hold up your basket and ask, *"Encore, s'il vous plaît?"*

Restaurants

Choose restaurants filled with locals. Consider my suggestions and your hotelier's opinion, but trust your instincts. If a restaurant doesn't post its prices outside, move along. Refer to my restaurant recommendations to get a sense of what a reasonable meal should cost.

Restaurants open for dinner around 19:00 and are most crowded about 20:00 (21:00 in cities). The early bird gets the table. Last seating is usually about 21:00 (22:00 in cities and on the French Riviera; possibly later in Paris).

Tune into the quiet, relaxed pace of French dining. The French don't do dinner and a movie on date nights; they just do dinner. The table is yours for the night. Notice how quietly French diners speak in restaurants and how this improves your overall experience. Learn from this.

Ordering: In French restaurants, you can choose something off the menu (called the *carte*), or you can order a multicourse, fixed-price meal (confusingly, called a *menu*). Or, if offered, you can get one of the special dishes of the day *(plat du jour)*. If you ask for *un menu* (instead of *la carte*), you'll get a fixed-price meal.

Ordering **à la carte** gives you the best selection. I enjoy going à la carte especially when traveling with others and eating family style (waiters are happy to accommodate this approach and will bring small extra plates). It's traditional to order an *entrée* (a starter—not a main dish) and a *plat principal* (main course), though it's becoming common to order only a *plat principal*. *Plats* are generally more meat-based, while *entrées* usually include veggies. Multiple-course meals, while time-consuming (a positive thing in France), create the appropriate balance of veggies to meat. Elaborate meals may also have *entremets*—tiny dishes served between courses. Wherever you dine, consider the waiter's recommendations and anything *de la maison* (of the house), as long as it's not an organ meat (tripe, *rognons*, or andouillette).

Two people can split an *entrée* or a big salad (small-size dinner salads are usually not offered á la carte) and then each get a *plat principal*. At restaurants, it's seen as inappropriate for two diners to share one main course. If all you want is a salad or soup, go to a café or brasserie.

Fixed-price *menus*—which usually include two, three, or four courses—are generally a better deal than eating à la carte, and help you pace your meal like the locals. At most restaurants offering fixed-price *menus*, the price for a two- or three-course *menu* is only slightly higher than a single main course from the à la carte list. With a three-course *menu* you'll choose a starter of soup, appetizer, or salad; select from three or four main courses with vegetables; and finish up with a cheese course and/or a choice of desserts. It sounds like a lot of food, but portions are smaller in France, and what we cram onto one large plate they spread out over several courses. Wine and other drinks are extra, and certain premium items add a few euros to the price, clearly noted on the menu (*supplément* or *sup.*). Most restaurants offer less expensive and less filling two-course *menus*, sometimes called *formules*, featuring an *entrée et plat*, or *plat et dessert*. Many restaurants have a reasonable *menu-enfant* (kid's meal).

Lunch: If a restaurant serves lunch, it generally begins at 12:00 and goes until around 14:00, with last orders taken at about 13:30. If you're hungry when restaurants are closed (late afternoon), go to a *boulangerie*, brasserie, or café (see previous section). Even fancy places usually have affordable lunch *menus* (often called *formules* or *plat de midi*), allowing you to sample the same gourmet cooking for generally about half the cost of dinner.

Rural Dining: Restaurants are almost always a better value in the countryside than in Paris. If you're driving, look for red-and-blue *Relais Routier* decals on main roads outside cities, indicating that the place is recommended by the truckers' union. These truck-stop cafés offer inexpensive and hearty fare.

FRENCH CUISINE

General styles of French cooking include **haute cuisine** (classic, elaborately prepared, multicourse meals); **cuisine bourgeoise** (the finest-quality home cooking); **cuisine des provinces** (traditional dishes of specific regions); and **nouvelle cuisine** (a focus on smaller portions and closer attention to the texture and color of the ingredients). Sauces are a huge part of French cooking. In the early 20th century, the legendary French chef Auguste Escoffier identified five French "mother sauces" from which all others are derived: *béchamel* (milk-based white sauce), *espagnole* (veal-based brown sauce), *velouté* (stock-based white sauce), *hollandaise* (egg yolk-based white sauce), and *tomate* (tomato-based red sauce).

The following list of items should help you navigate a typical French menu. Galloping gourmets should bring a menu translator. The most complete (and priciest) menu reader around is *A to Z of French Food* by G. de Temmerman. The *Marling Menu-Master* is also good. The *Rick Steves French Phrase Book & Dictionary*, with a menu decoder, works well for most travelers. For dishes specific to each region, see the "Cuisine Scene" sections throughout this book.

If you're interested in learning to cook French cuisine (not just eat it), look for my listings of food tours and cooking classes or check out L'Atelier des Chefs, a network of cooking schools located in many cities throughout France, with top classes at good rates (half-hour course-€15, 1 hour-€36, 2 hours-€72, www.atelierdeschefs.fr).

First Course (Entrée)

Crudités: A mix of raw and lightly cooked fresh vegetables, usually including grated carrots, celery root, tomatoes, and beets, often with a hefty dose of vinaigrette dressing. If you want the dressing on the side, say, *"La sauce à côté, s'il vous plaît"* (lah sohs ah koh-tay, see voo play).

Escargots: Snails cooked in parsley-garlic butter. You don't even have to like the snail itself. Just dipping your bread in garlic butter is more than satisfying. Prepared a variety of ways, the classic is *à la bourguignonne* (served in their shells).

Foie gras: Rich and buttery in consistency—and hefty in price— this pâté is made from the swollen livers of force-fed geese (or ducks, in *foie gras de canard*). Spread it on bread, and never add mustard. For a real French experience, try this dish with a sweet white wine (such as a muscat).

Huîtres: Oysters, served raw any month, are particularly popular at Christmas and on New Year's Eve, when every café seems to have overflowing baskets in their window.

Œuf mayo: A simple hard-boiled egg topped with a dollop of flavorful mayonnaise.

Pâtés **and** *terrines:* Slowly cooked ground meat (usually pork, though game, poultry liver, and rabbit are also common) that is highly seasoned and served in slices with mustard and *cornichons* (little pickles). Pâtés are smoother than the similarly prepared but chunkier *terrines*.

Soupe à l'oignon: Hot, salty, filling—and hard to find in Paris— French onion soup is a beef broth served with a baked cheese-and-bread crust over the top.

Salads (Salades)

With the exception of a *salade mixte* (simple green salad, often difficult to find), the French get creative with their *salades*. Here are some classics:

Salade au chèvre chaud: This mixed-green salad is topped with warm goat cheese on small pieces of toast.

Salade aux gésiers: Though it may not sound appetizing, this salad with chicken gizzards (and often slices of duck) is worth a try.

Salade composée: "Composed" of any number of ingredients, this salad might have *lardons* (bacon), Comté (a Swiss-style cheese), Roquefort (blue cheese), *œuf* (egg), *noix* (walnuts), and *jambon* (ham, generally thinly sliced).

Salade gourmande: The "gourmet" salad varies by region and restaurant but usually features cured and poached meats served on salad greens with a mustard vinaigrette.

Salade niçoise: A specialty from Nice, this tasty salad usually includes greens topped with green beans, boiled potatoes, tomatoes, anchovies, olives, hard-boiled eggs, and lots of tuna.

Salade paysanne: You'll usually find potatoes *(pommes de terre),* walnuts *(noix),* tomatoes, ham, and egg in this salad.

Main Course *(Plat Principal)*

Duck, lamb, and rabbit are popular in France, and each is prepared in a variety of ways. You'll also encounter various stew-like dishes that vary by region. The most common regional specialties are described here.

Bœuf bourguignon: A Burgundian specialty, this classy beef stew is cooked slowly in red wine, then served with onions, potatoes, and mushrooms.

Confit de canard: A favorite from the southwest Dordogne region is duck that has been preserved in its own fat, then cooked in its fat, and often served with potatoes (cooked in the same fat). Not for dieters. (Note that *magret de canard* is sliced duck breast and very different in taste.)

Coq au vin: This Burgundian dish is rooster marinated ever so slowly in red wine, then cooked until it melts in your mouth. It's served (often family-style) with vegetables.

Daube: Generally made with beef, but sometimes lamb, this is a long and slowly simmered dish, typically paired with noodles or other pasta.

Escalope normande: This specialty of Normandy features turkey or veal in a cream sauce.

Gigot d'agneau: A specialty of Provence, this is a leg of lamb often grilled and served with white beans. The best lamb is *pré salé,* which means the lamb has been raised in salt-marsh lands (like at Mont St-Michel).

Le hamburger: This American import is all the rage in France. Cafés and restaurants serve it using local sauces, breads, and cheeses. It's fun to see their interpretation of our classic dish.

Poulet rôti: Roasted chicken on the bone—French comfort food.

Saumon and *truite:* You'll see salmon and trout *(truite)* dishes served in various styles. The salmon usually comes from the North Sea and is always served with sauce, most commonly a sorrel *(oseille)* sauce.

Steak: Referred to as *pavé* (thick hunk of prime steak), *bavette* (skirt steak), *faux filet* (sirloin), or *entrecôte* (rib steak), French steak is usually thinner and tougher than American steak and is always served with sauces (*au poivre* is a pepper sauce, *une sauce roquefort* is a blue-cheese sauce). Because steak is usually better in North America, I generally avoid it in France (unless the sauce sounds good). You will also see *steak haché,* which is a lean, gourmet hamburger patty served *sans* bun. When it's served as *steak haché à cheval,* it comes with a fried egg on top.

By American standards, the French undercook meats: Their version of rare, *saignant* (seh-nyahn), means "bloody" and is close to raw. What they consider medium, *à point* (ah pwan), is what an American would call rare. Their term for well-done, or *bien cuit* (bee-yehn kwee), would translate as medium for Americans.

Steak tartare: This wonderfully French dish is for adventurous types only. It's very lean, raw hamburger served with savory seasonings (usually Tabasco, capers, raw onions, salt, and pepper on the side) and topped with a raw egg yolk. This is not hamburger as we know it, but freshly ground beef.

Cheese Course *(Le Fromage)*

The cheese course is served just before (or instead of) dessert. It not only helps with digestion, it gives you a great opportunity to sample the tasty regional cheeses—and time to finish up your wine. Between cow, goat, and sheep cheeses, there are more than 350 different ones to try in France. Some restaurants will offer a cheese platter, from which you select a few different kinds. A good platter has at least four cheeses: a hard cheese (such as Cantal), a flowery cheese (such as Brie or Camembert), a blue or Roquefort cheese, and a goat cheese.

To sample several types of cheese from the cheese plate, say, *"Un assortiment, s'il vous plaît"* (uhn ah-sor-tee-mahn, see voo play). You'll either be served a selection of several cheeses or choose from a large selection offered on a cheese tray. If you serve yourself from the cheese tray, observe French etiquette and keep the shape of the cheese: Shave off a slice from the side or cut small wedges.

A glass of good red wine is a heavenly complement to your cheese course.

Dessert *(Le Dessert)*

If you order espresso, it will always come after dessert. To have coffee with dessert, ask for *"café avec le dessert"* (kah-fay ah-vehk luh day-sayr). See the list of coffee terms on page 1077. Here are the types of treats you'll see:

Baba au rhum: Pound cake drenched in rum, served with whipped cream.

Café gourmand: An assortment of small desserts selected by the restaurant, served with an espresso—a great way to sample several desserts and learn your favorite.

Crème brûlée: A rich, creamy, dense, caramelized custard.

Crème caramel: Flan in a caramel sauce.

Fondant au chocolat: A molten chocolate cake with a runny (not totally cooked) center. Also known as *moelleux* (meh-leh) *au chocolat.*

Fromage blanc: A light dessert similar to plain yogurt (yet different), served with sugar or herbs.

Glace: Ice cream—typically vanilla, chocolate, or strawberry.

Ile flottante: A light dessert consisting of islands of meringue floating on a pond of custard sauce.

Mousse au chocolat: Chocolate mousse.

Profiteroles: Cream puffs filled with vanilla ice cream, smothered in warm chocolate sauce.

Riz au lait: Rice pudding.

Sorbets: Light, flavorful, and fruity ices, sometimes laced with brandy.

Tartes: Open-face pie, often filled with fruit.

Tarte tatin: Apple pie like grandma never made, with caramelized apples, cooked upside down, but served upright.

BEVERAGES

In stores, unrefrigerated soft drinks, bottled water, and beer are one-third the price of cold drinks. Bottled water and boxed fruit juice are the cheapest drinks. Avoid buying drinks to-go at street-side stands; you'll pay far less in a shop.

In bars and at eateries, be clear when ordering drinks—you can easily pay €10 for an oversized Coke and €15 for a supersized beer at some cafés. When you order a drink, state the size in centiliters (don't say "small," "medium," or "large," because the waiter might bring a bigger drink than you want). For something small, ask for 25 *centilitres* (vant-sank sahn-tee-lee-truh; about 8 ounces); for a medium drink, order 33 cl (trahnte-twah; about 12 ounces—a normal can of soda); a large is 50 cl (san-kahnt; about 16 ounces); and a super-size is one liter (lee-truh; about a quart—which is more than I would ever order in France). The ice cubes melted after the last Yankee tour group left.

Water, Juice, and Soft Drinks

The French are willing to pay for bottled water with their meal (*eau minérale;* oh mee-nay-rahl) because they prefer the taste over tap water. Badoit is my favorite carbonated water (*l'eau gazeuse;* loh gah-zuhz) and is commonly available. To get a free pitcher of tap water, ask for *une carafe d'eau* (ewn kah-rahf doh). Otherwise, you may unwittingly buy bottled water.

In France *limonade* (lee-moh-nahd) is Sprite or 7-Up. For a fun, bright, nonalcoholic drink of 7-Up with mint syrup, order *un diabolo menthe* (uhn dee-ah-boh-loh mahnt). For 7-Up with fruit syrup, order *un diabolo grenadine* (think Shirley Temple). Kids love the local orange drink, Orangina, a carbonated orange juice with pulp (though it can be pricey). They also like *sirop à l'eau* (see-roh ah loh), flavored syrup mixed with bottled water.

For keeping hydrated on the go, hang on to the half-liter mineral-water bottles (sold everywhere for about €1-2) and refill. Buy juice in cheap liter boxes, then drink some and store the extra in your water bottle. Of course, water quenches your thirst better and cheaper than anything you'll find in a store or café. I drink tap water throughout France, filling up my bottle in hotel rooms.

Coffee and Tea

The French define various types of espresso drinks by how much milk is added. To the French, milk is a delicate form of nutrition: You need it in the morning, but as the day goes on, too much can upset your digestion. Therefore, the amount of milk that's added to coffee decreases as the day goes on. The average French person thinks a *café au lait* is exclusively for breakfast, and a *café crème* is only appropriate through midday. You're welcome to order a milkier coffee drink later in the day, but don't be surprised if you get a funny look.

By law, a waiter must give you a glass of tap water with your coffee or tea if you request it; ask for *"un verre d'eau, s'il vous plaît"* (uhn vayr doh, see voo play).

Here are some common coffee and tea drinks:

Café (kah-fay): Shot of espresso

Café allongé, a.k.a. *café longue* (kah-fay ah-lohn-zhay; kah-fay lohn): Espresso topped up with hot water—like an Americano

Noisette (nwah-zeht): Espresso with a dollop of milk (best value for adding milk to your coffee)

Café au lait (kah-fay oh lay): Espresso mixed with lots of warm milk (used mostly for coffee made at home; in a café, order *café crème*)

Café crème (kah-fay krehm): Espresso with a sizable pour of steamed milk (closest thing you'll get to an American-style latte)

Grand crème (grahn krehm): Double shot of espresso with a bit more steamed milk (and often twice the price)

Décaféiné (day-kah-fee-nay): Decaf—available for any of the above

PRACTICALITIES

French Wine-Tasting 101

France is peppered with wineries and wine-tasting opportunities. Trying to make sense of the vast range of French wines can be overwhelming, particularly when faced with a no-nonsense wine-maker or sommelier. Take a deep breath, do your best to follow my guidance, and don't linger where you don't feel welcome.

Visit several private wineries or stop by a *cave cooperative* or a *caveau*—an excellent opportunity to taste wines from a number of local vintners in a single, less intimidating setting. (Throughout this book, I've tried to identify which vineyards are most accepting of wine novices.) You'll have a better experience if you call ahead to let the winery know you're coming—even if it's open all day, it's good form to announce your visit (ask your hotelier for help). Avoid visiting places between noon and 14:00—many wineries are closed then, and those that aren't are staffed by people who would rather be at lunch.

Winemakers and sommeliers are usually happy to work with you...especially if they can figure out what you want. It helps to know what you like (drier or sweeter, lighter or full-bodied, fruity or more tannic, and so on). The people serving you may know those words in English, but you're wise to learn the key words in French (see the "French Wine Lingo" section).

French wines usually have a lower alcohol level than American or Australian wines. While Americans commonly like a big, full-bodied wine, most French prefer subtler flavors. They judge a wine by how well it pairs with a meal—and a big, oaky wine would overwhelm most French cuisine. The French enjoy sampling younger wines and divining how they will taste in a few years, allowing them to buy bottles at cheaper prices and stash them in their cellars. Americans want it now—for today's picnic.

At wine tastings, remember that vintners and wine shops hope you'll buy a bottle or two. If you don't buy, you may be asked to pay a small fee for a tasting. They understand that North Americans can't take much wine with them, but they do hope you'll look for their wines in the US. Some places will ship your purchase home—ask.

Thé nature (tay nah-tour): Plain tea
Thé au lait (tay oh lay): Tea with milk
Thé citron (tay see-trohn): Tea with lemon
Infusion (an-few-see-yohn): Herbal tea

Alcoholic Beverages

The legal drinking age is 16 for beer and wine and 18 for the hard stuff—at restaurants it's *normale* for wine to be served with dinner to teens.

Wine: Wines are often listed in a separate *carte des vins*. House

French Wine Lingo

Here are some phrases to get you started when wine-tasting:

Hello, madam/sir.
Bonjour, madame/monsieur.
(bohn-zhoor, mah-dahm/muhs-yur)

We would like to taste a few wines.
Nous voudrions déguster quelques vins.
(noo voo-dree-ohn day-goo-stay kehl-kuh van)

We would like a wine that is ____ and ____.
Nous voudrions un vin ____ et ____.
(noo voo-dree-ohn uhn van ____ ay ____)

Fill in the blanks with your favorites from this list:

English	French
wine	*vin* (van)
red	*rouge* (roozh)
white	*blanc* (blahn)
rosé	*rosé* (roh-zay)
light	*léger* (lay-zhay)
full-bodied	*robuste* (roh-bewst)
fruity	*fruité* (frwee-tay)
sweet	*doux* (doo)
tannic	*tannique* (tah-neek)
fine	*fin, avec finesse* (fan, ah-vehk fee-nehs)
ready to drink (mature)	*prêt à boire* (preh tah bwar)
not ready to drink	*fermé* (fair-may)
oaky	*goût du fût de la chêne* (goo duh foo duh lah sheh-nuh)
from old vines	*de vieille vignes* (duh vee-yay-ee veen-yah)
sparkling	*pétillant* (pay-tee-yahn)

wine at the bar is generally cheap and good (about €3-6/glass). At a restaurant, a bottle or carafe of house wine costs €10-20. To order inexpensive wine at a restaurant, ask for table wine in a pitcher (only available when seated and when ordering food), rather than a bottle. Finer restaurants usually offer only bottles of wine.

Here are some important wine terms:

Vin du pays (van duh pay): Table wine
Verre de vin rouge (vehr duh van roozh): Glass of red wine
Verre de vin blanc (vehr duh van blahn): Glass of white wine
Pichet (pee-shay): Pitcher

Demi-pichet (duh-mee pee-shay): Half-carafe
Quart (kar): Quarter-carafe (ideal for one)
Bouteille (boo-teh-ee): Bottle
Demi-bouteille (duh-mee boo-teh-ee): Half-bottle

Beer: Local *bière* (bee-ehr) costs about €5 at a restaurant and is cheaper on tap (*une pression;* ewn pres-yohn) than in the bottle. France's best-known beers are Alsatian; try Kronenbourg or the heavier Pelfort (one of your author's favorites). Brittany produces some fine microbrews, worth asking about if you travel there. *Une panaché* (ewn pah-nah-shay) is a tasty French shandy (beer and lemon soda). *Un Monaco* is a red drink made with beer, grenadine, and lemonade.

Aperitifs: Champagne is a popular way to start your evening in France. For a refreshing before-dinner drink, order a *kir* (pronounced "keer")—a thumb's level of *crème de cassis* (black currant liqueur) topped with white wine (upgrade to a *kir royale* if you'd like it made with Champagne). Also consider a glass of Lillet, a sweet, flowery fortified wine from Bordeaux.

After Dinner: If you like brandy, try a *marc* (regional brandy—e.g., *marc de Bourgogne*) or an Armagnac, cognac's cheaper twin brother. *Pastis,* the standard southern France aperitif, is a sweet anise (licorice) drink that comes on the rocks with a glass of water. Cut it to taste with lots of water.

Staying Connected

One of the most common questions I hear from travelers is, "How can I stay connected in Europe?" The short answer is: more easily and cheaply than you might think. For a very practical one-hour lecture covering tech issues for travelers, see www.ricksteves.com/travel-talks.

The simplest solution is to bring your own device—mobile phone, tablet, or laptop—and use it just as you would at home (following the tips below, such as connecting to free Wi-Fi whenever possible). Another option is to buy a European SIM card for your mobile phone—either your US phone or one you buy in Europe. Or you can travel without a mobile device and use European landlines and computers to connect. Each of these options is described below, and you'll find even more details at www.ricksteves.com/phoning.

USING YOUR OWN MOBILE DEVICE IN EUROPE

Without an international plan, typical rates from major service providers (AT&T, Verizon, etc.) for using your device abroad are about $1.70/minute for voice calls, 50 cents to send text messages, 5 cents to receive them, and $10 to download one megabyte of data.

At these rates, costs can add up quickly. Here are some budget tips and options.

Use free Wi-Fi whenever possible. Unless you have an un-limited-data plan, you're best off saving most of your online tasks for Wi-Fi (pronounced *wee-fee* in French). You can access the Internet, send texts, and make voice calls over Wi-Fi.

Many cafés (including Starbucks and McDonald's) have free hotspots for customers; look for signs offering it and ask for the Wi-Fi password when you buy something. You'll also often find Wi-Fi at TIs, city squares, major museums, public-transit hubs, important train stations, airports, aboard trains and buses, and at some autoroute (highway) rest stops.

Sign up for an international plan. Most providers offer a global calling plan that cuts the per-minute cost of phone calls and texts, and a flat-fee data plan. Your normal plan may already include international coverage (T-Mobile's does).

Before your trip, call your provider or check online to confirm that your phone will work in Europe, and research your provider's international rates. Activate the plan a day or two before you leave, then remember to cancel it when your trip's over.

Minimize the use of your cellular network. When you can't find Wi-Fi, you can use your cellular network to connect to the Internet, text, or make voice calls. When you're done, avoid further charges by manually switching off "data roaming" or "cellular data" (in your device's Settings menu; for help, ask your service provider or Google it). Another way to make sure you're not accidentally using data roaming is to put your device in "airplane" or "flight" mode (which also disables phone calls and texts), and then turn on Wi-Fi as needed.

Don't use your cellular network for bandwidth-gobbling tasks, such as Skyping, downloading apps, and watching YouTube: Save these for when you're on Wi-Fi. Using a navigation app such as Google Maps over a cellular network can take lots of data, so do this sparingly or use it offline.

Limit automatic updates. By default, your device constantly checks for a data connection and updates apps. It's smart to disable these features so your apps will only update when you're on Wi-Fi, and to change your device's email settings from "auto-retrieve" to "manual" (or from "push" to "fetch").

It's also a good idea to keep track of your data usage. On your device's menu, look for "cellular data usage" or "mobile data" and reset the counter at the start of your trip.

Use Skype or other calling/messaging apps for cheaper calls and texts. Certain apps let you make voice or video calls or send texts over the Internet for free or cheap. If you're bringing a tab-let or laptop, you can also use them for voice calls and texts. All

How to Dial

International Calls

Whether phoning from a US landline or mobile phone, or from a number in another European country, here's how to make an international call. I've used one of my recommended Paris hotels as an example (tel. 01 47 05 25 45).

Initial Zero: Drop the initial zero from international phone numbers—except when calling Italy.

Mobile Tip: If using a mobile phone, the "+" sign can replace the international access code (for a "+" sign, press and hold "0").

US/Canada to Europe

Dial 011 (US/Canada international access code), country code (33 for France), and phone number.

▶ To call the Paris hotel from home, dial 011 33 1 47 05 25 45.

Country to Country Within Europe

Dial 00 (Europe international access code), country code, and phone number.

▶ To call the Paris hotel from Spain, dial 00 33 1 47 05 25 45.

Europe to the US/Canada

Dial 00, country code (1 for US/Canada), and phone number.

▶ To call from Europe to my office in Edmonds, Washington, dial 00-1-425-771-8303.

Domestic Calls

To call within France (from one French landline or mobile phone to another), simply dial the phone number, including the initial 0 if there is one.

▶ To call the Paris hotel from Nice, dial 01 47 05 25 45.

More Dialing Tips

French Phone Prefixes: France doesn't use area codes. French phone prefixes vary by region or type of call. For instance, all Paris landline numbers start with 01, and all landlines in Provence and the Riviera begin with 04.

you have to do is log on to a Wi-Fi network, then contact any of your friends or family members who are also online and signed into the same service. You can make voice and video calls using Skype, Viber, FaceTime, and Google+ Hangouts. If the connection is bad, try making an audio-only call. You can also make voice calls from your device to telephones worldwide for just a few cents per minute using Skype, Viber, or Hangouts if you buy credit first.

To text for free over Wi-Fi, try apps like Google+ Hangouts,

Any number beginning with 06 or 07 is a mobile phone, and costs more to dial.

Toll and Toll-Free Calls: France's toll-free numbers start with 0800 and are called *numéro vert* (green number); they work only from French phones. Any 08 number without a 00 directly following is a toll call (generally €0.10-0.50/minute; cost announced in French; you can hang up before being billed). International rates apply to US toll-free numbers dialed from France—they're not free.

More Phoning Help: See www.howtocallabroad.com.

European Country Codes			
Austria	43	Italy	39
Belgium	32	Latvia	371
Bosnia-Herzegovina	387	Montenegro	382
Croatia	385	Morocco	212
Czech Republic	420	Netherlands	31
Denmark	45	Norway	47
Estonia	372	Poland	48
Finland	358	Portugal	351
France	33	Russia	7
Germany	49	Slovakia	421
Gibraltar	350	Slovenia	386
Great Britain	44	Spain	34
Greece	30	Sweden	46
Hungary	36	Switzerland	41
Ireland & N. Ireland	353 / 44	Turkey	90

WhatsApp, Viber, Facebook Messenger, and iMessage. Make sure you're on Wi-Fi to avoid data charges.

USING A EUROPEAN SIM CARD IN A MOBILE PHONE

This option works well for those who want to make a lot of voice calls at cheap local rates, and those who need faster connection speeds than their US carrier provides. Either buy a basic cell phone in Europe (as little as $40 from mobile-phone shops anywhere), or bring an "unlocked" US phone (check with your carrier about un-locking it). With an unlocked phone, you can replace the original SIM card (the microchip that stores info about the phone) with one that will work with a European provider.

In Europe, buy a European SIM card. Inserted into your phone, this card gives you a European phone number—and European rates. SIM cards are sold at mobile-phone shops, department-store electronics counters, newsstands, and vending machines. Costing about $5-10, they usually include about that much prepaid calling credit, with no contract and no commitment. A SIM card that also includes data costs (including roaming) will cost $20-40 more for one month of data within the country you bought it. This can be faster than data roaming through your home provider. To get the best rates, buy a new SIM card whenever you arrive in a new country.

I like to buy SIM cards at a mobile-phone shop where there's a clerk to help explain the options and brands. Certain brands—including Lebara and Lycamobile, both of which operate in multiple European countries—are reliable and economical. Ask the clerk to help you insert your SIM card, set it up, and show you how to use it. In some countries you'll be required to register the SIM card with your passport as an antiterrorism measure (which may mean you can't use the phone for the first hour or two).

Find out how to check your credit balance. When you run out of credit, you can top it up at newsstands, tobacco shops, mobile-phone stores, or many other businesses (look for your SIM card's logo in the window), or online.

UNTETHERED TRAVEL: PUBLIC PHONES AND COMPUTERS

It's possible to travel in Europe without a mobile device. You can check email or browse websites using public computers and Internet cafés, and make calls from your hotel room.

Phones in your **hotel room** generally charge a fee for placing local and "toll-free" calls, as well as long-distance or international calls—ask for the rates before you dial. Since you're never charged for receiving calls, it's better to have someone from the US call you in your room.

If these fees are low, hotel phones can be used inexpensively for calls made with cheap international phone cards (*carte international*). These cards are not widely used in France, but they can be found at some newsstands, street kiosks, tobacco shops, and train stations. You'll either get a prepaid card with a toll-free number and a scratch-to-reveal PIN code, or a code printed on a receipt.

Public computers are not always easy to find. Some hotels have one in their lobby for guests to use; otherwise you might find

Tips on Internet Security

Using the Internet while traveling brings added security risks, whether you're accessing the Internet with your own device or at a public terminal using a shared network. Here are some tips for securing your data:

First, make sure that your device is running the latest version of its operating system and security software, and that your apps are up-to-date. Next, ensure that your device is password- or passcode-protected so thieves can't access it if your device is stolen. For extra security, set passwords on apps that access key info (such as email or Facebook).

On the road, use only legitimate Wi-Fi hotspots. Ask the hotel or café staff for the specific name of their Wi-Fi network, and make sure you log on to that exact one. Hackers sometimes create a bogus hotspot with a similar or vague name (such as "Hotel Europa Free Wi-Fi"). The best Wi-Fi networks require a password. If you're not actively using a hotspot, turn off your device's Wi-Fi connection so it's not visible to others.

Be especially cautious when accessing financial information online. Experts say it's best to use a banking app rather than sign in to your bank's website via a browser (the app is less likely to get hacked). Even if you're using your own mobile device at a password-protected hotspot, there's a remote chance that a hacker who's logged on to the same network could see what you're doing. It's safest to use a hard-wired connection (such as an Ethernet cable in your hotel room). If that's not possible, a cellular network is safer than a Wi-Fi connection, and a password-protected Wi-Fi network is safer than public Wi-Fi. Refrain from logging in to any personal finance sites on a public computer.

Never share your credit-card number (or any other sensitive information) online unless you know that the site is secure. A secure site displays a little padlock icon, and the URL begins with *https* (instead of the usual *http*).

one at an Internet café or public library (ask your hotelier or the TI for the nearest location). If typing on a European keyboard, use the "Alt Gr" key to the right of the space bar to insert the extra symbol that appears on some keys. To type an @ symbol on French keyboards, press the "Alt Gr" and "à/0" key. If you can't locate a special character, simply copy it from a Web page and paste it into your email message.

MAIL

You can mail one package per day to yourself worth up to $200 duty-free from Europe to the US (mark it "personal purchases"). If you're sending a gift to someone, mark it "unsolicited gift." For details, visit www.cbp.gov, select "Travel," and search for "Know

Before You Go." The French postal service works fine, but for quick transatlantic delivery (in either direction), consider services such as DHL (www.dhl.com). French post offices are referred to as *La Poste* or sometimes the old-fashioned PTT, for "Post, Telegraph, and Telephone." Hours vary, though most are open weekdays 8:00-19:00 and Saturday morning 8:00-12:00. Stamps and phone cards are also sold at *tabacs*. It costs about €1 to mail a postcard to the US. One convenient, if expensive, way to send packages home is to use the post office's Colissimo XL postage-paid mailing box. It costs €50-90 to ship boxes weighing 5-7 kilos (about 11-15 pounds).

Transportation

If you're debating between using public transportation, renting a car, or flying between destinations in Europe, consider these factors: Cars are best for three or more traveling together (especially families with small kids), those packing heavy, and those delving into the countryside. Trains and buses are best for solo travelers, blitz tourists, city-to-city travelers, and those who don't want to drive. Intra-European flights are an increasingly inexpensive option. While a car gives you more freedom, trains and buses zip you effortlessly and scenically from city to city, usually dropping you in the center, often near a TI. For more detailed information on transportation throughout Europe, including trains, flying, renting a car, and driving, see www.ricksteves.com/transportation.

In cities, arriving by train in the middle of town makes hotel-hunting and sightseeing easy. But in France, many destinations are small, remote places far from a station, such as Honfleur, Mont St-Michel, D-Day beaches, Loire Valley châteaux, Dordogne caves, and villages in Provence and Burgundy. In such places, taking trains and buses can require great patience, planning, and time. If you'll be relying on public transportation, focus on fewer destinations, or hire one of the excellent minivan tour guides I recommend.

I've included two sample itineraries—by car and by public transportation—to help you explore France smoothly; you'll find these in the Introduction.

TRAINS

France's SNCF rail system (short for Société Nationale Chemins de Fer) sets the pace in Europe. Its super TGV (tay zhay vay; Train à Grande Vitesse) system has inspired bullet trains throughout the world. The TGV, which requires a reservation, runs at 170-220 mph. Its rails are fused into one long, continuous track for a faster and smoother ride. The TGV has changed commuting patterns

French Train Terms and Abbreviations

SNCF (Société Nationale Chemins de Fer): This is the Amtrak of France, operating all national train lines that link cities and towns.

TGV (Train à Grande Vitesse): SNCF's network of high-speed trains (twice as fast as regular trains) that connect major cities in France. These trains always require a reservation.

Intercité: These trains are the next best to the TGV in terms of speed and comfort.

TER (Transport Express Régional): These trains serve smaller stops within a region. For example, you'll find trains called TER Provence (Provence-only trains) and TER de Bourgogne (trains operating only in Burgundy).

Paris Region

For more on Paris transit, see page 26.

RATP (Réseau Autonome de Transports Parisiens): This company operates subways and buses within Paris.

Le Métro: This network of subway lines serves central Paris.

RER (Réseau Express Régional): This commuter rail and subway system links central Paris with suburban destinations.

Transilien: It's similar to the RER system, but travels farther afield, serving the Ile-de-France region around Paris. Rail passes cover these lines.

throughout France by putting most of the country within day-trip distance of Paris.

Any staffed train station has schedule information, can make reservations, and can sell tickets for any destination. For more on train travel, see www.ricksteves.com/rail.

Schedules

Schedules change by season, weekday, and weekend. Verify train times shown in this book—online, check www.bahn.com (Germany's excellent all-Europe schedule site), or check locally at train stations. The French rail website is www.sncf.com; for online sales, go to http://en.voyages-sncf.com. If you'll be traveling on one or two long-distance trains without a rail pass, it's worth looking online, as advance-purchase discounts can be a great deal.

Bigger stations may have helpful information agents roaming the station (usually in bright red or blue vests) and at *Accueil* offices or booths. Make use of their help; don't stand in a ticket line if all you need is a train schedule.

Rail Passes

Long-distance travelers may save money with a **France Rail Pass,** sold only outside Europe (through travel agents or Rick Steves'

France's Rail System

Europe). For roughly the cost of a full-fare Paris-Avignon-Paris ticket, the France Rail Pass offers three days of travel (within a month) anywhere in France. You can add up to six more days, each for the cost of a two-hour ride. You'll save money with the second-class version, but first class gives you more options when reserving popular TGV routes. A first-class pass grants you access to lounges in railway stations at Paris Est, Paris Nord, Paris Montparnasse, Paris Gare de Lyon, Strasbourg, Bordeaux, Marseille, Nantes, Rennes, Lille Flandres, Lille Europe, and Lyon Part-Dieu. The France Rail Pass plus regular seat reservation fee (up to €35) also covers you beyond national borders on direct TGV or Thalys fast trains to Amsterdam, Brussels, Cologne, Barcelona, Madrid (from Marseille), Turin, Milan, and Basel.

Each day of use allows you to take as many trips as you want on one calendar day (you could go from Paris to Beaune in Burgundy, enjoy wine tasting, then continue to Avignon, stay a few hours, and end in Nice—though I wouldn't recommend it). Buy second-class tickets in France for shorter trips, and save your valuable pass days for longer trips. Note that if you're connecting the French Alps with Alsace, you might travel through Switzerland, a route that requires France Rail Pass holders to buy a ticket for that segment (about €50).

A **Global Pass** can work well throughout most of Europe, but it's a bad value for travel exclusively in France. A cheaper version, the **Select Pass,** allows you to tailor a pass to your trip, provided you're traveling in two to four adjacent countries directly connected by rail or ferry. For instance, with a three-country pass allowing 10 days of train travel within a two-month period (about $630 for a single adult in 2016), you could choose France-Switzerland-Italy or Germany-France-Spain. The saver pass version of any pass gives two or more people traveling together a 15 percent discount.

Note that France's TGV trains require advance seat reservations, which are limited for pass holders. Reserving these fast trains at least several weeks in advance is recommended (for strategies, see "Reservations," later).

Buying Tickets

Online: While there's no deadline to buy any train ticket, the fast, reserved TGV trains get booked up. Buy well ahead for any TGV you cannot afford to miss. Tickets go on sale 90 to 120 days in advance, with a wide range of prices on any one route. The cheapest tickets sell out early and reservations for rail-pass holders also go particularly fast.

To buy the cheapest advance-discount tickets (up to 60 percent less than full fare), visit http://en.voyages-sncf.com, three to four months ahead of your travel date. (A pop-up window may ask you to choose between being sent to the Rail Europe website or staying on the SNCF page—click "Stay.") Next, choose "Train," then "TGV." Under "Book your train tickets," pick your travel dates, and choose "France" as your ticket collection country. The cheapest (nonrefundable) tickets are called "Prems"; be sure it also says "TGV" (avoid iDTGV trains—they're very cheap, but this SNCF subsidiary doesn't accept PayPal). Choose the eticket delivery option (which allows you to print at home), and pay with your PayPal account to avoid credit-card approval issues. These low-rate tickets may not be available from Rail Europe or other US agents.

After the "Prems" rates are sold out, you can buy other fare types on the French site with a US credit card if it has been set up for the "Verified by Visa," "MasterCard SecureCode," or "American Express SafeKey" program. For a credit-card purchase, choose "USA" as your ticket collection country.

Otherwise, US customers can order through a US agency, such as at www.ricksteves.com/rail, which offers both etickets and home delivery, but may not have access to all the cheapest rates; or Capitaine Train (www.captaintrain.com), which sells the "Prems" fare and iDTGV tickets.

Travelers with smartphones have the option of saving tickets and reservations directly to their phones (choose "m-ticket"). For more details, see http://en.voyages-sncf.com/en/mobile.

In France: You can buy train tickets in person at SNCF Boutiques or at any train station, either from a staffed ticket window or from a machine. You can buy tickets on the train for a €4-10 surcharge depending on the length of your trip, but you must find the conductor immediately upon boarding; otherwise it's a €35 minimum charge.

The ticket machines available at most stations are great time savers when other lines are long. But the machines probably won't accept your American credit card even if it has a chip, so be prepared with euro coins and bills. Some machines have English instructions, but for those that don't, here are the prompts. (Turn the dial or move the cursor to your choice, and press *"Validez"* to agree to each step.)

1. *Quelle est votre destination?* (What's your destination?)
2. *Billet Plein Tarif* (Full-fare ticket—yes for most.)
3. *1ère ou 2ème* (First or second class; normally second is fine.)
4. *Aller simple ou aller-retour?* (One-way or round-trip?)
5. *Prix en Euro* (The price should be shown if you get this far.)

Reservations

Reservations are required for any TGV train, *couchettes* (sleeping berths) on night trains, and some other trains where indicated in timetables. You can reserve any train at any station anytime be-

Coping with Strikes

Going on strike (en grève) is a popular pastime in this revolution-happy country. Because bargaining between management and employees is not standard procedure, workers strike to get attention. Trucks and tractors block main roads and autoroutes (they call it Opération Escargot—"Operation Snail's Pace"), baggage handlers bring airports to their knees, and museum workers make artwork off-limits to tourists. Métro and train personnel seem to strike every year—probably during your trip. What does the traveler do? You could jeter l'éponge (throw in the sponge) and go somewhere less strike-prone (Switzerland's nice), or learn to accept certain events as out of your control. Strikes in France generally last no longer than a day or two, and if you're aware of them, you can usually plan around them. Your hotelier will know the latest (or can find out). Make a habit of asking your hotel receptionist about strikes and checking with the TI. This website gives up to date information on train disruptions: www.sncf.com/en/news/timetables-traffic-updates.

fore your departure or through SNCF Boutiques. If you're buying a point-to-point ticket for a TGV train, you'll reserve your seat when you purchase your ticket.

Popular TGV routes usually fill up quickly, making it a challenge to get reservations (particularly for rail-pass holders, who are allocated a very limited number of seats). It's wise to book well ahead for any TGV, especially on the busy Paris-Avignon-Nice line. If the TGV trains you want are fully booked, ask about TER trains serving the same destination, as these don't require reservations.

If you're using a rail pass, reservations cost €9-18 to for domestic travel, depending on the kind of train they're for and where you buy them. Seat reservations on Thalys, Artesia, and international TGV trains range from €10 to €35, but the price also depends on class of service (they can cost up to €50 in first class on TGV trains to Swiss destinations). Eurostar trains to London don't accept rail passes but do offer pass holders some ticket discounts.

Rail-pass holders can book TGV reservations directly at French stations up to the departure; reservations, if still available, can also be booked anytime as etickets at www.raileurope.com (if lower-priced pass-holder reservations are sold out, try for the "Easy Access" rate). Given the possible difficulty of getting TGV reservations with a rail pass, make those reservations online before you leave home.

If you're taking one of the rare overnight trains in France and need a *couchette*, it can be booked in advance through a US agent (such as www.raileurope.com).

Reservations are generally unnecessary for non-TGV trains (verify ahead, as some Intercité trains require reservations, like the Nice-Bordeaux train), but they are advisable during busy times (for example, Friday and Sunday afternoons, Saturday mornings, weekday rush hours, and holiday weekends; see "Holidays and Festivals" on page 1114).

Baggage Check

Baggage check (*Consigne* or *Espaces Bagages*) is available only at a handful of the biggest train stations (about €5-10/bag per day depending on size), and is noted where available (which can depend on current security concerns, so be prepared to keep your bag). For security reasons, all luggage should carry a tag with the traveler's first and last name and current address (though it's not enforced). This applies to hand luggage as well as bigger bags that are stowed. Free tags are available at train stations in France.

Other baggage-check options in cities are becoming more common, often near train stations (also noted in this book). Here's a tip: Major museums and monuments usually have free baggage check for visitors. Even if the sight is not particularly interesting to you, the entry fee may be worth it if you need to stow your bags for a few hours.

At the Station

- Arrive at the station with plenty of time before your departure to find your platform (platform numbers are posted about 15 minutes prior to departure), confirm connections, and so on. Large stations have separate information *(accueil)* windows; at small stations the ticket office gives information.
- Small stations are minimally staffed; if there is no agent at the station, go directly to the tracks and look for the overhead sign that confirms your train stops at that track.
- Larger stations have platforms with monitors showing TGV layouts (numbered forward or backward) so you can figure out where your car *(voiture)* will stop on the long platform and where to board each car.

Validating Tickets, Reservations, and Rail Passes

- You're required to activate (*composter*, kohm-poh-stay) all train tickets and reservations (when printed on official ticket stock) before boarding any SNCF train. Look for a yellow machine near the platform or waiting area to stamp your ticket or reservation. Reserved tickets that are printed at home on plain paper don't need validation (and won't fit in the machine). You also don't need to activate etickets on your phone.

Rail Passes

Prices listed are for 2016 and are subject to change. For the latest prices, details, and train schedules (and easy online ordering), see www.ricksteves.com/rail.

"Saver" prices are per person for two or more people traveling together. "Youth" means under age 26. Up to two kids age 4-11 travel free with each adult. Additional kids pay the youth rate. Kids under age 4 travel free.

FRANCE PASS FLEXI
Seniors age 60 and up pay prices similar to Saver, even if traveling alone!

	1st Class Indiv.	2nd Class Indiv.	1st Class Saver	2nd Class Saver	1st Class Youth	2nd Class Youth
1 day in 1 month	$139	$113	$124	$100	$100	$85
2 days in 1 month	198	161	175	142	143	121
3 days in 1 month	260	211	231	187	187	160
4 days in 1 month	297	242	264	213	215	181
5 days in 1 month	334	272	296	241	240	206
6 days in 1 month	371	301	327	267	267	228
7 days in 1 month	406	328	359	290	295	253
8 days in 1 month	442	356	388	316	320	275
9 days in 1 month	478	382	423	339	346	298
15 days in 1 month	623	499	552	442	451	389

FRANCE PASS CONSECUTIVE
Seniors age 60 and up pay prices similar to Saver, even if traveling alone!

	1st Class Indiv.	2nd Class Indiv.	1st Class Saver	2nd Class Saver	1st Class Youth	2nd Class Youth
2 days consecutive	$158	$128	$140	$114	$114	$96
4 days consecutive	237	193	211	170	171	145
5 days consecutive	268	218	237	193	192	165
8 days consecutive	353	285	310	253	256	220
15 days consecutive	499	399	442	353	362	311

International Coverage: The single-country France Rail Pass also covers direct TGV or Thalys service to Amsterdam, Barcelona, Brussels, Cologne, Turin, Milan, and Madrid (one train per day from southern France) with normal $10–50 reservation fees (coverage varies with multi-country Eurail passes).

Any pass for France also covers you through France to/from the official Swiss border towns of Basel and Geneva, but TGV Lyria seat reservations are expensive (up to $30 in second class or $70 in first, in addition to a pass).

Paris-Italy night trains do not accept rail passes, but offer a 25% discount off full fare. The same applies for Thello's daytime Milan–Genova–Nice–Marseille service.

EURAIL SELECT PASS–UPPER PRICE RANGE PASS

3 Countries	1st Class Indiv.	1st Class Saver	1st Class Youth	2nd Class Youth
5 days in 2 months	$440	$375	$354	$289
6 days in 2 months	485	413	389	318
8 days in 2 months	567	483	455	372
10 days in 2 months	638	543	512	417

2 Countries	1st Class Indiv.	1st Class Saver	1st Class Youth	2nd Class Indiv.	2nd Class Saver	2nd Class Youth
4 days in 1 month	$362	$308	$291	$291	$248	$238
5 days in 1 month	408	348	328	328	280	268
6 days in 1 month	451	384	362	362	309	296
8 days in 1 month	525	447	421	421	359	344
10 days in 1 month	591	504	474	474	404	387

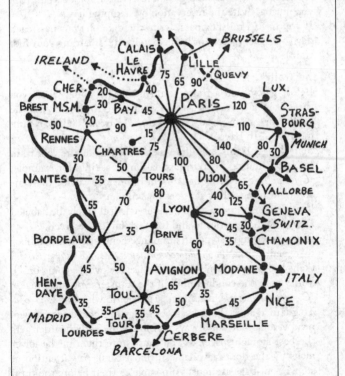

Map key:
Approximate point-to-point one-way second-class rail fares in US dollars. First class costs 50 percent more. Advance purchase ticket discounts also available. Add up fares for your itinerary to see if a rail pass will save you money.

Train-Ticket French

Hello, madam/sir, do you speak English?
Bonjour, madame/monsieur, parlez-vous anglais?
bohn-zhoor, mah-dahm/muhs-yur, par-lay-voo ahn-glay

I would like a departure for Avignon, on 10 May, about 9:00, the most direct way possible.
Je voudrais un train pour Avignon, pour le 10 Mai, vers 9:00, la plus direct possible.
zhuh voo-dray uhn tran poor ah-veen-yohn, poor luh dees may, vehr nuhf ur, lah plew dee-rehk poh-see-bluh

- If you have a rail pass, activate it at a ticket window before using it the first time (don't stamp it in the machine). If you're traveling with a pass and have a reservation for a certain trip, you must activate the reservation by stamping it.
- If you have a rail flexipass, write the date on your pass each day you travel (before or immediately after boarding your first train).

On the Train

- Before getting on a train, confirm that it's going where you think it is. For example, if you want to go to Bayeux, ask the conductor or any local passenger, *"A Bayeux?"* (ah bah-yuh; meaning, "To Bayeux?").
- Some longer trains split off cars en route. Make sure your train car is continuing to your destination by asking, for example, *"Cette voiture va à Avignon?"* (seht vwah-toor vah ah ah-veen-yohn; meaning, "This car goes to Avignon?").
- If a non-TGV train seat is reserved, it'll likely be labeled *réservé*, with the cities to and from which it is reserved.
- If you don't understand an announcement, ask your neighbor to explain: *"Pardon madame/monsieur, qu'est-ce qui se passe?"* (kehs kee suh pahs; meaning, "Excuse me, what's going on?").
- Verify with the conductor all of the transfers you must make: *"Correspondance à?";* meaning, "Transfer to where?"
- To guard against theft, keep your bags in sight (directly overhead is ideal but not always possible—the early boarder gets the best storage space). If you must store them in the lower racks by the doors (available in most cars), pay attention at stops. Your bags are most vulnerable to theft before the train takes off and whenever it stops.
- Note your arrival time, so you'll be ready to get off.
- Use the train's free WCs before you get off (but not while the train is stopped in a station).

BUSES

Regional buses work well for many destinations not served by trains. Buses are almost always comfortable and air-conditioned.

A few bus lines are run by the SNCF rail system and are covered by your rail pass (show rail pass at station to get free bus ticket), but most bus lines are not covered. Bus stations *(gare routière)* are usually located next to train stations. Train stations usually have bus information where train-to-bus connections are important—and vice versa for bus companies.

Bus Tips

- Read the train tips described earlier, and use those that apply (check schedules in advance, arrive at the station early, confirm the destination before you board, find out if you need to transfer, etc.).
- The bus company websites I've listed in this book are usually in French only. Here are some key phrases you'll see: *horaires* (schedules), *en semaine* (Monday through Saturday), *dimanche* (Sunday), *jours fériés* (holidays), *année* (bus runs all year on the days listed), *vac* (runs only during summer vacations), *scol/scolaire* (runs only when school is in session), *ligne* (route or bus line), and *réseau* (network—usually all routes).
- Use TIs to help plan your trip and verify times (TIs have regional bus schedules).
- Be aware that service is sparse or nonexistent on Sunday. Wednesday bus schedules often are different during the school year, because school is out this day (and regional buses generally operate school service).
- Confirm a bus stop's location in advance (rural stops are often not signed) and be at bus stops at least five minutes early.

Regional Minivan Excursions

Worthwhile day tours are generally available in regions where bus and train service is sparse. For the D-Day beaches, Loire Valley châteaux, Dordogne Valley villages and caves, Cathar castles near Carcassonne, Provence's villages and vineyards, the Route du Vin (Wine Road) in Alsace, Brittany sights (including Mont St-Michel), and wine tasting in Burgundy, I list reliable companies that provide this helpful service at fair rates. Some of these minivan excursions just offer transportation between the sights; others add a running commentary and information on regional history.

RIDE-SHARING

You'll find Uber only in bigger cities in France. It works like it does in the US. In general, Uber works better than taxis. Drivers are nicer and more flexible, it's cheaper, and you can generally get a car

PRACTICALITIES

within five minutes. The app from the US works here if you have a US Uber account. They can find you on a map and pick you up anywhere so you don't have to track down a taxi stand, and you can text them if you can't find them.

RENTING A CAR

Rental companies require you to be at least 21 years old and to have held your license for one year. Drivers under the age of 25 may incur a young-driver surcharge, and some rental companies do not rent to anyone 75 or older. If you're considered too young or old, look into leasing (covered later), which has less-stringent age restrictions.

Research car rentals before you go. It's cheaper to arrange car rentals from the US. Consider several companies to compare rates. Most of the major US rental agencies (including Avis, Budget, Enterprise, Hertz, and Thrifty) have offices throughout Europe. Also consider the two major Europe-based agencies, Europcar and Sixt, and the French agency, ADA (www.ada.fr). It can be cheaper to use a consolidator, such as Auto Europe/Kemwel (www.autoeurope.com—or the often cheaper www.autoeurope.eu) or Europe by Car (www.europebycar.com), which compares rates at several companies to get you the best deal—but because you're working with a middleman, it's especially important to ask in advance about add-on fees and restrictions.

Always read the fine print carefully for add-on charges—such as one-way drop-off fees, airport surcharges, or mandatory insurance policies—that aren't included in the "total price." You may need to query rental agents pointedly to find out your actual cost.

For the best deal, rent by the week with unlimited mileage. I normally rent the smallest, least-expensive model with a stick shift (generally cheaper than an automatic). This size works well for two people; I'd go up a size for more than two (e.g. equivalent to a Renault Mégane in size). Almost all rentals are manual by default, so if you need an automatic, request one in advance and be warned that these cars are usually larger models. Roads and parking spaces are narrow in France, so you'll do yourself a favor by renting the smallest car that meets your needs.

Figure on paying roughly $260 for a midsize, one-week rental during busy seasons. Allow extra for supplemental insurance, fuel, tolls, and parking. For trips of three weeks or more, leasing can save you money on insurance and taxes.

Picking Up Your Car: Big companies have offices in most cities (train stations, airports, and downtown), but small local rental companies can be cheaper.

Compare pick-up costs (downtown can be less expensive than the airport or train station) and explore drop-off options. Verify the hours of the location you choose: Most close on Sunday and at lunch (about 12:00-13:30). At major locations like rail stations, you can usually drop off a car after-hours (put keys in lockbox).

When selecting a location, don't trust the agency's description of "downtown" or "city center." In some cases, a "downtown" branch can be on the outskirts of the city—a long, costly taxi ride from the center. Before choosing, plug the addresses into a mapping website. You may find that the "train station" location is handier. But returning a car at a big-city train station or downtown agency can be tricky; get precise details on the car drop-off location and hours, and allow ample time to find it.

If you want a car for only a day or two (e.g., for the Côtes du Rhône wine route, Luberon villages, D-Day beaches, or Loire Valley châteaux), you'll likely find it easy to rent on the spot just about anywhere in France. In many cases, this is a worthwhile splurge. All you need is your American driver's license and a major credit card (figure €60-90/day; some include unlimited mileage, others give you 100 kilometers—about 60 miles—for free).

When you pick up the rental car, check it thoroughly and make sure any damage is noted on your rental agreement. Rental agencies in Europe are very strict when it comes to charging for even minor damage, so be sure to mark everything. Before driving off, find out how your car's gearshift, lights, turn signals, wipers, radio, and fuel cap function, and know what kind of fuel the car takes (diesel vs. unleaded). When you return the car, make sure the agent verifies its condition with you. Some drivers take pictures of the returned vehicle as proof of its condition.

Car Insurance Options

When you rent a car, you are liable for a very high deductible, sometimes equal to the entire value of the car. Limit your financial risk with one of these options: Buy Collision Damage Waiver (CDW) coverage with a low or zero deductible from the car-rental company, get coverage through your credit card (free, if your card automatically includes zero-deductible coverage), or get collision insurance as part of a larger travel-insurance policy.

Basic **CDW** includes a very high deductible (typically $1,000-1,500), costs $10-30 a day (figure roughly 30 percent extra), and reduces your liability, but does not eliminate it. When you reserve or pick up the car, you'll be offered the chance to "buy down" the basic deductible to zero (for an additional $10-30/day; this is sometimes called "super CDW" or "zero-deductible coverage").

If you opt for **credit-card coverage,** you'll technically have to decline all coverage offered by the car-rental company, which means they can place a hold on your card (which can be up to the full value of the car). In case of damage, it can be time-consuming to resolve the charges with your credit-card company. Before you decide on this option, quiz your credit-card company about how it works.

If you're already purchasing a **travel-insurance policy** for your trip, adding collision coverage can be an economical option. For example, Travel Guard (www.travelguard.com) sells affordable renter's collision insurance as an add-on to its other policies; it's valid everywhere in Europe except the Republic of Ireland, and some Italian car-rental companies refuse to honor it, as it doesn't cover you in case of theft.

For more on car-rental insurance, see www.ricksteves.com/cdw.

Leasing

For trips of three weeks or more, consider leasing (which automatically includes zero-deductible collision and theft insurance). By technically buying and then selling back the car, you save lots of money on tax and insurance. Leasing provides you a brand-new car with unlimited mileage and a 24-hour emergency assistance program. Pick-up and drop-off locations are limited to a few major cities (listed on websites). You can lease for as little as 21 days to as long as five and a half months; Idea Merge offers two-week leases. Car leases must be arranged from the US; some companies allow drop off in different countries.

These reliable companies offer 21-day lease packages:

Auto France (Peugeot cars only, US tel. 800-572-9655, www.autofrance.net)

Europe by Car (Citroën and Renault cars, US tel. 800-223-1516, www.ebctravel.com)

Idea Merge (ask about two-week leases; Volkswagen, Citroën, Renault, and Peugeot, US tel. 503-715-5810, www.ideamerge.com)

Kemwel (Peugeot cars only, US tel. 877-820-0668, www.kemwel.com)

RV and Campervan Rental

Even given the extra fuel costs, renting your own rolling hotel can be a great way to save money, especially if you're sticking mainly to rural areas. Keep in mind that RVs in France are much smaller than those you see at home. Companies to consider:

Van It (rents pop-top VW Eurovan campers that are easy to maneuver on small roads, mobile 06 70 43 11 86, www.van-it.com)

Idea Merge (best resource for small RV rental, see listing above)

Origin (current-model Volkswagen vans fully equipped for 2-3 people, rates less than RVs, mobile 06 80 01 72 77, www.origin-campervans.com)

Navigation Options

If you'll be navigating using your phone or a GPS unit from home, remember to bring a car charger and device mount.

Your Mobile Device: The mapping app on your mobile phone works fine for navigation in Europe, but for real-time turn-by-turn directions and traffic updates, you'll generally need access to a cellular network. A helpful exception is Google Maps, which provides turn-by-turn directions and recalibrates even when it's offline.

To use Google Maps offline, you must have a Google account and download your map while you have a data connection. Later—even when offline—you can call up that map, enter your destination, and get directions. View maps in standard view (not satellite view) to limit data demands.

GPS Devices: If you prefer the convenience of a dedicated GPS unit, consider renting one with your car ($10-30/day). These units offer real-time turn-by-turn directions and traffic without the data requirements of a smartphone mapping app. Note that the unit may only come loaded with maps for its home country; if you need additional maps, ask. Also make sure your device's language is set to English before you drive off.

A less expensive option is to bring a GPS device from home. Be aware that you'll need to buy and download European maps before your trip.

Maps and Atlases: Even when navigating primarily with a mobile app or GPS, I always make it a point to have a paper map. The free maps you get from your car-rental company usually don't have enough detail. It's smart to buy a better map before you go, or pick one up at European gas stations, bookshops, newsstands, and tourist shops.

Michelin maps are available throughout France at bookstores, newsstands, and gas stations (about €6 each, cheaper than in the US). The Michelin #721 France map (1:1,000,000 scale) covers this book's destinations with good detail for drivers. Drivers should also consider the soft-cover Michelin France atlas (the entire country at 1:200,000, well-organized in a €20 book with an index and maps of major cities). Spend a few minutes learning the Michelin key to get the most sightseeing value out of these maps.

DRIVING

It's a pleasure to explore France by car, but you need to know the rules.

Road Rules: Seat belts are mandatory for all, and children under age 10 must be in the back seat. In city and town centers, traffic merging from the right (even from tiny side streets) may have the right-of-way *(priorité à droite)*. So even when you're driving on a major road, pay attention to cars merging from the right.

PRACTICALITIES

In contrast, cars entering the many suburban roundabouts must yield *(cédez le passage)*. You can't turn right on a red light, U-turns are illegal, and on expressways it's illegal to pass drivers on the right.

Be aware of typical European road rules; for example, many countries require headlights to be turned on at all times (in France, they must be used in any case of poor visibility), and nearly all forbid talking on a mobile phone without a hands-free headset. Ask your car-rental company about these rules, or check the US State Department website (www.travel. state.gov, search for your country in the "Learn about your destination" box, then click "Travel and Transportation").

STOP AND LEARN THESE ROAD SIGNS

Speed Limit (km/hr) · Yield · No Passing · End of No Passing Zone · One Way · Intersection · Main Road · Expressway · Roundabout Ahead · Danger · No Entry · All Vehicles Prohibited · No Through Road · Restrictions No Longer Apply · Yield to Oncoming Traffic · No Stopping · Parking · No Parking · Customs or Toll Road · Peace

Speed Limits: Because speed limits are by road type, they typically aren't posted, so it's best to memorize them:
- Two-lane D and N routes outside cities and towns: 90 km/hour
- Two-lane roads in villages: 50 km/hour (unless posted at 30 km/hour)
- Divided highways outside cities and towns: 110 km/hour

- Autoroutes (toll roads): 130 km/hour (unless otherwise posted)

If it's raining, subtract 10 km/hour on D and N routes and 20 km/hour on divided highways and autoroutes. Speed-limit signs are a red circle around a number; when you see that same number again in gray with a broken line diagonally across it, this means that limit no longer applies. Speed limits drop to 30-50 km/hour in villages (always posted) and must be respected.

Road speeds are monitored

Driving in France

m = miles
h = hours

ENGLAND
To London
Dover
Calais
BELGIUM
Lille
English Channel
Arromanches (D-Day Beaches)
20m .5h
Honfleur
45m .75h
180m 2.75h
140m 2.25h
GERMANY
LUX.
Bayeux
Mont St-Michel
20m .5h
55m 1h
80m 1.5h
Rouen
Reims
Verdun
90m 1.5h
75m 1.25h
150m 2.75h
Caen
80m 1.5h
Paris
55m 1h
305m 4.5h
Strasbourg
Dinan
195m 3h
Chartres
55m 1h
285m 5.5h
Colmar
50m 1h
40m .75h
85m 2h
140m 2.25h
155m 2.5h
Amboise
Semur-en-Auxois
50m 1.25h
50m .75h
165m 2.5h
Chinon
270m 5.5h
250m 4h
Beaune
135m 3h
145m 2.5h
FRANCE
SWITZ.
Oradour-sur-Glane
360m 5.25h
220m 4.5h
95m 1.5h
55m 1h
Atlantic Ocean
260m 5h
85m 1.5h
Lyon
Annecy
Chamonix
St. Emilion
200m 4h
80m 2h
30m 1.25h
140m 2h
235m 4.5h
ITALY
Sarlat-la-Canéda
Rocamadour
155m 2.5h
225m 4h
Monaco
St. Jean-de-Luz
210m 4.75h
170m 3h
Albi
25m .5h
Avignon
10m .5h
160m 2.5h
20m .5h
70m 1.75h
Arles
80m 1.25h
Nice
San Sebastian
250m 3.5h
Carcassonne
150m 2.25h
105m 1.5h
10m .5h
SPAIN
ANDORRA
95m 1.5h
165m 2.5h
Cassis
Antibes
Collioure
Mediterranean Sea

Note: Travel times may vary based on traffic, construction and road conditions.

regularly with cameras—a mere two kilometers over the limit yields a pricey ticket (a minimum of about €68). The good news is that signs warn drivers a few hundred yards before the camera and show the proper speed (see image above). Look for a sign with a radar graphic that says *Pour votre sécurité, contrôles automatiques.* The French use these cameras not to make money but to slow down traffic—and it works.

Don't Drink and Drive: The French are serious about curbing drunk driving. All motorists, including those in rental cars, are required to have a self-test Breathalyzer on hand so they can tell if they're over the legal blood-alcohol limit (0.05mg/ml—which is lower than in the US—drinker beware). When you pick up your rental car, ask if it has a kit.

Tire Pressure: In Europe, tire pressure is measured in *bars* of pressure. To convert to PSI (pounds per square inch) the formula is: *bar* × 14.5 = PSI (so 2 *bars* would be 2 × 14.5, or 29 PSI). To convert

PRACTICALITIES

French Road Signs

Signs You Must Obey

Allumez vos feux	Turn on your lights
Cédez le Passage	Yield
Déviation	Detour
Doublage Interdit	No passing
Parking Interdit/Stationnement Interdit	No parking
Priorité à Droite	Right-of-way is for cars coming from the right
Rappel	Remember to obey the sign
Vous n'avez pas la priorité	You don't have the right of way (when merging)

Signs for Your Information

Autres Directions	Other directions (follow when leaving a city)
Centre Commercial	Shopping center (not city center)
Centre-Ville	City center
Feux	Traffic signal

to *bar* pressures from PSI, the formula is: $PSI \times 0.07 = bar$ (so 30 PSI $\times 0.07$ would be 2.1 *bar*). Your car's recommended tire pressure is usually found on a sticker mounted on the driver-side doorframe.

Pulling to the Side of the Road: All rental cars are equipped with a yellow safety vest and triangle. You must wear the vest and display the triangle whenever you pull over on the side of the road (say, to fix a flat tire). If you don't, you could be fined.

Fuel: Gas *(essence)* is expensive—about $6 per gallon. Diesel *(gazole)* costs less—about $5 per gallon. Know what type of fuel your car takes before you fill up. Many Americans get marooned by filling with unleaded in a diesel car. Most rentals are diesel; if yours is one of them, use the yellow pump. Fuel is most expensive on autoroutes and cheapest at big supermarkets. Your US credit and debit cards without a chip won't work at self-serve pumps—so you'll need to find gas stations with attendants, or get a chip-and-PIN card before your trip (see page 1045).

Plan ahead for Sundays, as most gas stations in town are closed. I fill my tank every Saturday. If stuck on a Sunday, use an autoroute, where the gas stations are always staffed.

Autoroutes and Tolls: Autoroute tolls are pricey, but the al-

Horodateur	Ticket-vending machine for parking
Parc de Stationnement/Parking	Parking lot
Route Barrée	Road blocked
Rue Piétonne	Pedestrian-only street
Sauf Riverains	Local access only
Sortie des Camions	Work truck exit
Suivre... (e.g., Pont du Gard, suivre Nîmes)	Follow... (e.g., for Pont du Gard, follow signs for Nîmes)
Toutes Directions	All directions (follow when leaving a city)

Signs Unique to Autoroutes

Aire	Rest stop with WCs, telephones, and sometimes gas stations
Bouchon	Traffic jam ahead
Fluide	No traffic ahead
Péage	Toll
Par Temps de Pluie	When raining (modifies speed limit signs)
Télépéage	Automated tollbooths

ternative to these super-"feeways" usually means being marooned in countryside traffic—especially near the Riviera. Autoroutes save enough time, gas, and nausea to justify the cost. Mix high-speed "autorouting" with scenic country-road rambling.

You'll usually take a ticket when entering an autoroute and pay when you leave. Figure roughly €1 in tolls for every 15 kilometers driven on the autoroute (or about €15 for two hours). Cash (coins or bills under €50) is your best payment option as most US credit cards won't work (for more on paying at tollbooths, see the sidebar on page 1108).

Autoroute gas stations are open on Sundays and usually come with well-stocked minimarts, clean restrooms, sandwiches, maps, local products, cheap vending-machine coffee, and Wi-Fi. Many have small cafés or more elaborate cafeterias with reasonable prices. For more information, see www.autoroutes.fr.

Highways: Roads are classified into departmental (D), national (N), and autoroutes (A). D routes (usually yellow lines on maps) are often slower but the most scenic. N routes and important D routes (red lines) are the fastest after autoroutes (orange lines on maps). Green road signs are for national routes; blue are for autoroutes. Some roads in France have had route-number changes (mostly N roads converting to D roads). If you're using an older map, the actual route name may differ from what's on your map. Navigate by destination rather than road name...or buy a new map. There are plenty of good facilities, gas stations (most closed Sun), and rest stops along most French roads.

Parking: Finding a parking place can be a headache in larger cities. Ask your hotelier for ideas, and pay to park at well-patrolled lots (blue *P* signs direct you to parking lots in French cities). Parking garages require that you take a ticket with you and pay at a machine (called a *caisse*) on your way back to the car. US credit cards won't work in these machines, but euro coins will (some accept bills too). If you don't have enough coins to pay the fee, find the garage's *accueil* office, where the attendant can help or direct you to a nearby shop where you can change bills into coins. Overnight parking in garages (usually 19:00-8:00) is generally reasonable (priciest in cities like Paris, Nice, Avignon, and Antibes).

Curbside metered parking also works (usually free 12:00-14:00 & 19:00-9:00, and all day and night in Aug). Look for a small machine selling time (called an *horodateur*, usually one per block), plug in a few coins (€1.50-2 buys about an hour, varies by city), push the button, get a receipt showing the amount of time you have, and display it inside your windshield. (Avoid spaces outlined in blue, as they require a special permit.) For cheap overnight parking until the next afternoon, buy three hours' worth of time after 19:00. This gets you until noon the next day, after which two more hours are usually free (12:00-14:00), so you're good until 14:00.

Theft: Theft is a problem, particularly in southern France. Thieves easily recognize rental cars and assume they are filled with a tourist's gear. Try to make your car look locally owned by hiding the "tourist-owned" rental-company decals and putting a French newspaper in your back window. Be sure all of your valuables are out of sight and locked in the trunk—or, even better, with you or in your room. And don't assume that just because you're parked on a main street that you'll be fine. Thieves work fast.

Driving Tips

- France is riddled with roundabouts—navigating them is an art. The key is to know your direction and be ready for your turnoff. If you miss it, take another lap (or two). See the diagram on page 1107.
- At intersections and roundabouts, French road signs use the name of an upcoming destination for directions—the highway number is usually missing. That upcoming destination could be a major city, or it could be the next minor town up the road. Check your map ahead of time and get familiar with the

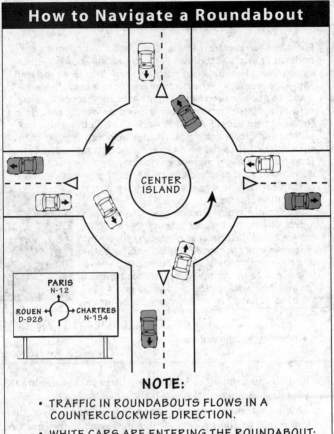

How to Navigate a Roundabout

NOTE:

- TRAFFIC IN ROUNDABOUTS FLOWS IN A COUNTERCLOCKWISE DIRECTION.
- WHITE CARS ARE ENTERING THE ROUNDABOUT; GRAY CARS ARE EXITING.
- VEHICLES ENTERING A ROUNDABOUT MUST YIELD TO VEHICLES IN THE ROUNDABOUT.
- LOOK TO YOUR LEFT AS YOU MERGE! ☺

names of towns and cities along your route—and even major cities on the same road beyond your destination.

- When navigating into cities, approach intersections cautiously, stow the map, and follow the signs to *Centre-Ville* (city center). From there, head to the TI *(Office de Tourisme)* or your hotel.
- When leaving or just passing through cities, follow the signs for *Toutes Directions* or *Autres Directions* (meaning "anywhere else") until you see a sign for your specific destination. Look also for *Suivre* signs telling you to follow *(suivre)* signs for the

French Tollbooths

For American drivers, getting through the toll payment stations on France's autoroutes is mostly about knowing which lanes to avoid—and having cash on hand. Skip lanes marked with a lowercase "*t*"—they're reserved for cars using the automatic Télépéage payment system. A pictograph of a credit card (usually a blue sign) means credit or debit cards only (your US card very likely won't work, so avoid this line). Look instead for green arrows above the tollbooth and/or icons showing bills or coins, which indicate booths accepting cash (booths often allow more than one payment method). Slow down as you approach tollbooths to study your options, and pull off to the side if you aren't positive of the tollbooth to choose.

Exits are entirely automated (if you have a problem at the tollbooth, press the red button for help). Have smaller bills ready (payment machines won't accept €50 bills). Shorter autoroute sections have periodic tollbooths, where you can pay by dropping coins into a basket (change is given for bills, but keep a good supply of coins handy to avoid waiting for an attendant).

To estimate how much cash to have on hand for tolls, use the planning tool at ViaMichelin.com.

(usually more important) destination listed to continue toward your destination.

- Driving on any roads but autoroutes will take longer than you think, so allow plenty of time for slower traffic (tractors, trucks, and hard-to-decipher signs all deserve blame). First-timers should estimate how long they think a drive will take... then double it. I pretend that kilometers are miles (for distances) and base my time estimates accordingly.

- While locals are eating lunch (12:00-14:00), many sights (and gas stations) are closed, so you can make great time driving—but keep it slow when passing through villages.

- Be very careful when driving on smaller roads—many are narrow and flanked by little ditches that lure inattentive drivers. I've met several readers who "ditched" their cars (and had to be pulled out by local farmers).

- On autoroutes, keep to the right lanes to let fast drivers by, and be careful when merging into a left lane, as cars can be coming at high speeds.

- Motorcycles will scream between cars in traffic. Be ready—they expect you to make space so that they can pass.

- Keep a stash of coins handy for parking and small autoroute tolls.

BIKING

You'll find areas in France where public transportation is limited and bicycle touring might be a good idea. For many, biking is a romantic notion, and the novelty wears off after the first hill or headwind. Realistically evaluate your physical condition, be clear on the limitations bikes present, and consider an electric bike. Start with an easy pedal, then decide how ambitious you feel. Most find that one hour on a narrow, hard seat is enough. I've listed bike-rental shops where appropriate (TIs can also guide you), and I've suggested a few of my favorite rides. For a good touring bike, figure about €14 for a half-day and €20 for a full day. You'll pay more for better equipment; generally the best is available through bike shops, not at train stations or other outlets. French cyclists often do not wear helmets, though most rental outfits have them (for a small fee).

FLIGHTS

The best comparison search engine for both international and intra-European flights is www.kayak.com. For inexpensive flights within Europe, try www.skyscanner.com.

Flying to Europe: Start looking for international flights at least four to six months before your trip, especially for peak-season travel. Off-season tickets can usually be purchased a month or so in advance. Depending on your itinerary, it can be efficient to fly into one city and out of another. If your flight requires a connection in Europe, see our hints on navigating Europe's top hub airports at www.ricksteves.com/hub-airports.

Flying Within Europe: If you're visiting one or more French cities on a longer European trip—or linking up far-flung French cities (such as Paris and Nice)—a flight can save both time and money. When comparing your options, factor in the time it takes to get to the airport and how early you'll need to arrive to check in.

Well-known cheapo airlines include easyJet (www.easyjet.com) and Ryanair (www.ryanair.com). Also check Air France for specials. But be aware of the potential drawbacks of flying with a discount airline: nonrefundable and nonchangeable tickets, minimal or nonexistent customer service, pricey and time-consuming treks to secondary airports, and stingy baggage allowances with steep overage fees. If you're traveling with lots of luggage, a cheap flight can quickly become a bad deal. To avoid unpleasant surprises, read the small print before you book. These days you can also fly within Europe on major airlines affordably—and without all the aggressive restrictions—for around $100 a flight.

Flying to the US and Canada: Because security is extra tight for flights to the US, be sure to give yourself plenty of time at the airport. It's also important to charge your electronic devices before you board because security checks may require you to turn them on (see www.tsa.gov for latest rules).

Resources from Rick Steves

Begin your trip at www.ricksteves.com: My mobile-friendly **website** is *the* place to explore Europe. You'll find thousands of fun articles, videos, photos, and radio interviews organized by country; a wealth of money-saving tips for planning your dream trip; monthly travel news dispatches; a collection of over 30 hours of practical travel talks; my travel blog; my latest guidebook updates (www.ricksteves.com/update); and my free Rick Steves Audio Europe app. You can also follow me on Facebook and Twitter.

Our **Travel Forum** is an immense yet well-groomed collection of message boards, where our travel-savvy community answers questions and shares their personal travel experiences—and our well-traveled staff chimes in when they can be helpful (www.ricksteves.com/forums).

Our **online Travel Store** offers travel bags and accessories that I've designed specifically to help you travel smarter and lighter. These include my popular bags (rolling carry-on and backpack versions, which I helped design...and live out of four months a year), money belts, totes, toiletries kits, adapters, other accessories, and a wide selection of guidebooks and planning maps.

Choosing the right **rail pass** for your trip—amid hundreds of options—can drive you nutty. Our website will help you find the perfect fit for your itinerary and your budget: We offer easy, one-stop shopping for rail passes, seat reservations, and point-to-point tickets.

Tours: Want to travel with greater efficiency and less stress? We organize tours with more than three dozen itineraries and more than 900 departures reaching the best destinations in this book...and beyond. We offer an 11-day Paris and the Heart of France tour (focusing on the best of the north), a 13-day Loire to the South of France tour, a 14-day Best of Eastern France tour, a 7-day in-depth Paris city tour, and a 13-day My Way France tour. You'll enjoy great guides, a fun bunch of travel partners (with small groups of around 24 to 28 travelers), and plenty of room to spread out in a big, comfy bus when touring between towns. You'll find European adventures to fit every vacation length. For all the details, and to get our Tour Catalog, visit www.ricksteves.com or call us at 425/608-4217.

Books: *Rick Steves France 2017* is one of many books in my

Rick Steves &
Gene Openshaw

series on European travel, which includes country guidebooks; city guidebooks (Paris, Rome, Florence, London, etc.); Snapshot guidebooks (excerpted chapters from my country guides); Pocket guidebooks (full-color little books on big cities, including Paris); "Best Of" guidebooks (condensed country guidebooks in a full-color, easy-to-scan format); and my budget-travel skills handbook, *Rick Steves Europe Through the Back Door*. Most of my titles are available as ebooks.

My phrase books—for French, Italian, German, Spanish, and Portuguese—are practical and budget-oriented. My other books include *Europe 101* (a crash course on art and history designed for travelers); *Mediterranean Cruise Ports* and *Northern European Cruise Ports* (how to make the most of your time in port); and *Travel as a Political Act* (a travelogue sprinkled with tips for bringing home a global perspective). A more complete list of my titles appears near the end of this book.

TV Shows: My public television series, *Rick Steves' Europe*, covers Europe from top to bottom with over 100 half-hour episodes. To watch full episodes online for free, see www.ricksteves.com/tv.

Travel Talks on Video: You can raise your travel I.Q. with video versions of our popular classes (including my talks on travel skills, packing smart, cruising, tech for travelers, European art for travelers, travel as a political act, and individual talks covering most European countries, including France). See www.ricksteves.com/travel-talks.

Audio: My weekly public radio show, *Travel with Rick Steves*, features interviews with travel experts from around the world. A complete archive of 10 years of programs (over 400 in all) is available at www.ricksteves.com/radio. Most of this audio content is available for free through my **Rick Steves Audio Europe** app (see page 14).

APPENDIX

Useful Contacts 1113
Holidays and Festivals 1114
Recommended Books and Films 1116
Conversions and Climate 1120
Packing Checklist 1123
Pronunciation Guide for
  Place Names 1124
French Survival Phrases 1129

Useful Contacts

For tips on making calls, including specifics on dialing toll-free service numbers, see "How to Dial" on page 1082.

Emergency Needs

Operators at emergency numbers may speak English, but it's not guaranteed. Calls to 112 and 114 are received by either the Emergency Medical Assistance Service (called "SAMU") or the fire brigade, who will reroute the call if necessary.

Police: Tel. 17
Fire and Accident: Tel. 18
Emergency Medical Assistance/Ambulance (SAMU): Tel. 15
SOS All Services: Tel. 112
SOS Médicins (SOS Doctors): Tel. 3624, most speak some English, house calls to hotels or homes (€120 and up, www.sosmedecins.fr)
American Hospital in Paris (English-speaking staff): Tel. 01 46

41 25 25, 63 Boulevard Victor Hugo, in Neuilly suburb, Mo: Port Maillot, then bus #82 {www.american-hospital.org)
Hearing-Assisted SOS All Services: Tel. 114
Collect Calls to the US: Tel. 00 00 11

Embassies and Consulates

In most cities, you'll be directed to the Paris consulate and embassy for passport and other consular issues.

US Consulate and Embassy in Paris: Tel. 01 43 12 22 22 (4 Avenue Gabriel, to the left as you face Hôtel Crillon, Mo: Concorde, http://france.usembassy.gov)

Canadian Consulate and Embassy in Paris: Tel. 01 44 43 29 02 (35 Avenue Montaigne, Mo: Franklin D. Roosevelt, www.amb-canada.fr). For 24/7 emergency assistance call collect to 613/996-8885 or email sos@international.gc.ca.

US Consulate in Marseille: Tel. 01 43 12 48 85 (Place Varian Fry, http://marseille.usconsulate.gov). After hours, call the Paris office.

Canadian Consulate in Nice: Tel. 04 93 92 93 22 (10 Rue Lamartine, nice@international.gc.ca)

Holidays and Festivals

This list includes selected festivals in major cities, plus national holidays observed throughout France. Many sights and banks close on national holidays—keep this in mind when planning your itinerary. Before planning a trip around a festival, verify its dates by checking with the festival's website or France's national tourism website (http://us.france.fr). Hotels get booked up on Easter weekend, Labor Day, Ascension Day, Pentecost, Bastille Day, and the winter holidays.

Here is a sampling of events and holidays in 2017:

Jan 1	New Year's Day
Feb-March	Carnival (Mardi Gras) parades and fireworks, Nice (www.nicecarnaval.com)
April 16-17	Easter Sunday/Monday
April-Oct	International Garden Festival, Chaumont-sur-Loire (www.domaine-chaumont.fr)
May 1	Labor Day
May 8	VE (Victory in Europe) Day
Mid-May	Monaco Grand Prix auto race (www.grand-prix-monaco.com)
May 17-28	Cannes Film Festival, Cannes (www.festival-cannes.fr)
May 25	Ascension

June 4-5	Pentecost Sunday/Monday
June 6	Anniversary of D-Day Landing, Normandy
Mid-June	Le Mans Auto Race, Le Mans—near Loire Valley (www.lemans.org)
June 21	Fête de la Musique (music festival), free concerts and dancing in the streets throughout France
June-July	Nights of Fourvière, Lyon (theater and music in a Roman theater, www.nuitsdefourviere.com)
July	Nice Jazz Festival (www.nicejazzfestival.fr); Avignon Festival, theater, dance, music (www.festival-avignon.com); Beaune International Music Festival; Chorégies d'Orange, Orange (performed in Roman theater, www.choregies.fr); "Jazz à Juan" International Jazz Festival, Antibes/Juan-les-Pins (www.jazzajuan.com); Jousting matches and medieval festivities, Carcassonne; Colmar International Music Festival (www.festival-colmar.com); International Music and Opera Festival, Aix-en-Provence (www.festival-aix.com)
July 1-23	Tour de France, national bicycle race culminating on the Champs-Elysées in Paris (www.letour.fr)
July 14	Bastille Day (fireworks, dancing, and revelry all over France)
July-Aug	International Fireworks Festival, Cannes (www.festival-pyrotechnique-cannes.com)
Aug 15	Assumption
Sept	Jazz at La Villette Festival, Paris (www.jazzalavillette.com)
Sept	Fall Arts Festival (Fête d'Automne), Paris; Wine harvest festivals in many towns
Early-Mid-Oct	Grape Harvest Festival in Montmartre, Paris (www.fetedesvendangesdemontmartre.com)
Nov 1	All Saints' Day
Early Nov	Dijon International and Gastronomic Fair, Dijon, Burgundy (www.foirededijon.com)
Nov 11	Armistice Day
Late Nov	Wine Auction and Festival (Les Trois Glorieuses), Beaune
Late Nov-Dec 24	Christmas Markets, Strasbourg, Colmar, and Sarlat-la-Canéda
Early Dec	Festival of Lights (celebration of Virgin Mary, candlelit windows), Lyon
Dec 25	Christmas Day
Dec 31	New Year's Eve

Recommended Books and Films

To learn more about France past and present, check out a few of these books and films. To learn what's making news in France, you'll find *France 24 News* online at www.France24.com/en.

Nonfiction

A to Z of French Food, a French to English Dictionary of Culinary Terms (G. de Temmerman, 1995). This is the most complete (and priciest) menu reader around—and it's beloved by foodies.

Almost French: Love and a New Life in Paris (Sarah Turnbull, 2003). Turnball takes an amusing look at adopting a famously frosty city.

The Course of French History (Pierre Goubert, 1988). Goubert provides a basic summary of French history.

Culture Shock! France (Sally Adamson Taylor, 1991). Demystify French culture and the French people with this good introduction.

D-Day, June 6, 1944: The Battle for the Normandy Beaches (Stephen E. Ambrose, 1994). Relying on 1,400 interviews with war veterans, Ambrose spins a detailed history of this fateful day.

A Distant Mirror (Barbara Tuchman, 1987). Respected historian Barbara Tuchman paints a portrait of 14th-century France.

French or Foe? (Polly Platt, 1994). This best seller, along with its follow-up, *Savoir-Flair!*, is an essential aid for interacting with the French and navigating the intricacies of their culture.

I'll Always Have Paris (Art Buchwald, 1996). The American humorist recounts life as a Paris correspondent during the 1940s and 1950s.

Is Paris Burning? (Larry Collins and Dominique Lapierre, 1964). Set in the last days of the Nazi occupation, this book tells the story of the French resistance and how a German general disobeyed Hitler's order to destroy Paris.

La Seduction: How the French Play the Game of Life (Elaine Sciolino, 2011). Sciolino, former Paris bureau chief of the *New York Times*, gives travelers a fun, insightful, and tantalizing peek into how seduction is used in all aspects of French life—from small villages to the halls of national government.

The Longest Day: The Classic Epic of D-Day (Cornelius Ryan, 1959). Ryan's classic recounts the hours before and after the D-Day Normandy invasion.

Marling Menu-Master for France (William E. Marling, 1971). A compact guide for navigating French cuisine and restaurant terminology.

A Moveable Feast (Ernest Hemingway, 1964). Paris in the 1920s is recalled by Hemingway.

My Life in France (Julia Child, 1996). The inimitably zesty chef recounts her early days in Paris.

Paris to the Moon (Adam Gopnik, 2000). This collection of essays and journal entries explores the idiosyncrasies of life in France from a New Yorker's point of view. His literary anthology, *Americans in Paris*, is also recommended.

Portraits of France (Robert Daley, 1991). Part memoir, part travelogue, this is a charming reminiscence of the writer's lifelong relationship with France, including marrying a French girl on his first trip there.

The Road from the Past: Traveling Through History in France (Ina Caro, 1994). Caro's enjoyable travel essays take you on a chronological journey through France's historical sights.

Sixty Million Frenchmen Can't Be Wrong (Jean-Benoit Nadeau and Julie Barlow, 2003). This is a must-read for anyone serious about understanding French culture, contemporary politics, and what makes the French tick.

The Sweet Life in Paris (David Lebovitz, 2009). Funny and articulate, pastry chef and cookbook author Lebovitz delivers oodles of food suggestions for travelers in Paris.

Travelers Tales: Paris and *Travelers' Tales: France* (edited by James O'Reilly, Larry Habegger, and Sean O'Reilly, 2002). Notable writers explore Parisian and French culture.

Two Towns in Provence (M. F. K. Fisher, 1964). Aix-en-Provence and Marseille are the subjects of these two stories by the celebrated American food writer. She also writes about her life in France in *Long Ago in France: The Years in Dijon* (1929).

Wine & War: The French, the Nazis, and the Battle for France's Greatest Treasure (Don and Petie Kladstrup, 2001). This compelling story details how French vintners preserved their valuable wine amidst the chaos of World War II.

A Year in Provence and *Toujours Provence* (Peter Mayle, 1989/1991). Mayle's memoirs include humorous anecdotes about restoring and living in a 200-year-old farmhouse in a remote area of the Lubéron.

Fiction

All the Light We Cannot See (Anthony Doerr, 2014). A moving tale of occupied France seen through the experiences of a blind French girl and a lonely German boy whose paths cross in war-torn St-Malo.

Birdsong: A Novel of Love and War (Sebastian Faulks, 1993). This novel follows a 20-year-old Englishman into WWI France, and into the romance that follows.

APPENDIX

Chocolat (Joanne Harris, 1999). A woman and her daughter stir up tradition in a small French town by opening a chocolate shop two days before Lent (also a movie starring Juliette Binoche and filmed in the Dordogne region).

City of Darkness, City of Light (Marge Piercy, 1996). Three French women play pivotal roles behind the scenes during the French Revolution.

The Hotel Majestic (Georges Simenon, 1942). Ernest Hemingway was a fan of Simenon, a Belgian writer who often set his Inspector Maigret detective books, including this one, in Paris.

Labyrinth (Kate Mosse, 2005). This thriller set in Carcassonne jumps back and forth between present-day archaeological intrigue and the medieval Cathar crusade.

Madame Bovary (Gustave Flaubert, 1886). Emma Bovary's yearning for luxury and passion ultimately lead to her demise in this literary classic.

Murder in the Marais (Cara Black, 1999). Set in Vichy-era Paris, private investigator Aimée Leduc finds herself at the center of a murder mystery.

A Place of Greater Safety (Hilary Mantel, 1992). Three young men come to Paris in 1789—Maximilien Robespierre, Camille Desmoulins, and George-Jacques Danton—and the rest is history.

Suite Française (Irène Némirovsky, 2004). Némirovsky, a Russian Jew who was living in France and died at Auschwitz in 1942, plunges readers into the chaotic WWII evacuation of Paris, as well as daily life in a small rural town during the ensuing German occupation.

A Tale of Two Cities (Charles Dickens, 1859). Dickens' gripping tale shows the pathos and horror of the French Revolution.

A Very Long Engagement (Sebastien Japrisot, 1991). A woman searches for her fiancé, supposedly killed in the line of duty during World War I (also a movie starring Audrey Tautou).

Film and TV

Amélie (2001). A charming young waitress searches for love in Paris.

Before Sunset (2004). Nine years after meeting on a train to Vienna, Jesse and Celine (played by Ethan Hawke and Julie Delpy) are reunited in Paris.

Breathless (1960). A Parisian petty thief (Jean-Paul Belmondo) persuades an American student (Jean Seberg) to run away with him in this groundbreaking classic of French New Wave cinema.

Cyrano de Bergerac (1990). A homely, romantic poet woos his love with the help of another, better-looking man (look for scenes filmed at the Abbey of Fontenay).

Dangerous Liaisons (1988). This inside look at sex, intrigue, and revenge takes place in the last days of the French aristocracy in pre-Revolutionary Paris.

Dirty Rotten Scoundrels (1988). Steve Martin and Michael Caine star in this hilarious flick, filmed in and around Villefranche-sur-Mer.

The Gleaners & I (2000). Working-class men and women gather sustenance from what's been thrown away in this quiet, meditative film by Agnès Varda.

Grand Illusion (1937). French WWI prisoners hatch a plan to escape a German POW camp. Considered a masterpiece of French film, the movie was later banned by the Nazis for its anti-fascism message.

The Intouchables (2011). A quadriplegic Parisian aristocrat hires a personal caregiver from the projects, and an unusual and touching friendship ensues.

Jean de Florette (1986). This marvelous tale of greed and intolerance follows a hunchback as he fights for the property he inherited in rural France. Its sequel, *Manon of the Spring* (1986), continues with his daughter's story.

Jules and Jim (1962). François Truffaut, the master of the French New Wave, explores a decades-long love triangle in this classic.

La Grande Bouffe (1973). In this hilarious comedy about French food, French sex, and French masculinity, Marcello Mastroianni leads a rat pack of middle-aged men in a quest to eat themselves to death.

La Haine (1995). An Arab boy is critically wounded and a police gun finds its way into the hands of a young Jewish skinhead in this intense examination of ethnic divisions in France.

La Vie en Rose (2007). Marion Cotillard won the Best Actress Oscar for this film about the glamorous and turbulent life of singer Edith Piaf, who famously regretted nothing (many scenes were shot in Paris).

Les Misérables (2012). A Frenchman trying to escape his criminal past becomes wrapped up in Revolutionary intrigues (based on Victor Hugo's 1862 novel).

The Longest Day (1962). This meticulous re-creation of the D-Day invasion won two Oscars and features an all-star cast including John Wayne, Richard Burton, Robert Mitchum, and Henry Fonda.

Marie Antoinette (2006). Kirsten Dunst stars as the infamous French queen (with a Californian accent) at Versailles in this delicate little bonbon of a film about the misunderstood queen.

Midnight in Paris (2011). Woody Allen's sharp comedy shifts between today's Paris and the 1920s mecca of Picasso, Hemingway, and Fitzgerald.

Paths of Glory (1957). Stanley Kubrick directed this WWI story about the futility and irony of war.

The Red Balloon (1956). A small boy chases his balloon through the streets of Paris, showing how beauty can be found even in the simplest toy.

The Return of Martin Guerre (1982). A man returns to his village in southwestern France from the Hundred Years' War—but is he really who he claims to be?

Ridicule (1996). A nobleman navigates the opulent court of Louis XVI on his wits alone.

Ronin (1998). Robert De Niro stars in this crime caper, which includes a car chase through Paris and scenes filmed in Nice, Villefranche-sur-Mer, and Arles.

Saving Private Ryan (1998). This intense and brilliant story of the D-Day landings and their aftermath won Steven Spielberg an Oscar for Best Director.

The Silence of the Sea (1949). A Frenchman and his niece, forced to house a German officer in Nazi-occupied France, resist through silent protest.

The Sorrow and the Pity (1969). This award-winning documentary about the Nazi occupation doesn't pull any punches about French collaboration, which is why it was banned by French TV.

Three Colors trilogy (1990s). Krzysztof Kieślowski's stylish trilogy (*Blue, White,* and *Red*) is based on France's national motto— "Liberty, Equality, and Fraternity." Each features a famous French actress as the lead (*Blue,* with Juliette Binoche, is the best).

Welcome (2009). A young Kurdish refugee in Calais, France faces the harsh realities of illegal immigration as he tries to join his girlfriend in England.

Conversions and Climate

NUMBERS AND STUMBLERS
- Europeans write a few of their numbers differently than we do: 1 = 1, 4 = 4, 7 = 7.
- In Europe, dates appear as day/month/year, so Christmas 2017 is 25/12/17.
- Commas are decimal points and decimals are commas. A dollar and a half is $1,50, one thousand is 1.000, and there are 5.280 feet in a mile.
- When counting with fingers, start with your thumb. If you

hold up your first finger to request one item, you'll probably get
two.
- What Americans call the second floor of a building is the first
floor in Europe.
- On escalators and moving sidewalks, Europeans keep the left
"lane" open for passing. Keep to the right.

METRIC CONVERSIONS

A kilogram is 2.2 pounds, and 1 liter is about a quart, or almost four
to a gallon. A kilometer is six-tenths of a mile. I figure kilometers
to miles by cutting them in half and adding back 10 percent of
the original (120 km: 60 + 12 = 72 miles, 300 km: 150 + 30 = 180
miles).

1 foot = 0.3 meter	1 square yard = 0.8 square meter
1 yard = 0.9 meter	1 square mile = 2.6 square kilometers
1 mile = 1.6 kilometers	1 hectare = 2.47 acres
1 ounce = 28 grams	1 centimeter = 0.4 inch
1 quart = 0.95 liter	1 meter = 39.4 inches
1 kilogram = 2.2 pounds	1 kilometer = 0.62 mile
32°F = 0°C	

FRANCE'S CLIMATE

First line, average daily high; second line, average daily low; third
line, average days without rain. For more detailed weather statistics
for destinations in this book (as well as the rest of the world), check
www.wunderground.com.

	J	F	M	A	M	J	J	A	S	O	N	D
Paris												
	43°	45°	54°	60°	68°	73°	76°	75°	70°	60°	50°	44°
	34°	34°	39°	43°	49°	55°	58°	58°	53°	46°	40°	36°
	14	14	19	17	19	18	19	18	17	18	15	15
Nice												
	50°	53°	59°	64°	71°	79°	84°	83°	77°	68°	58°	52°
	35°	36°	41°	46°	52°	58°	63°	63°	58°	51°	43°	37°
	23	22	24	23	23	26	29	26	24	23	21	21

APPENDIX

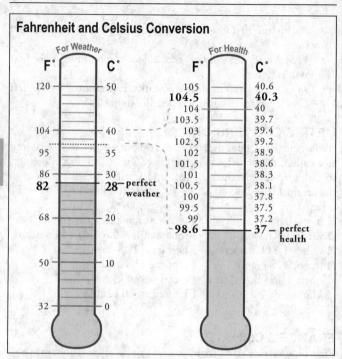

Fahrenheit and Celsius Conversion

Europe takes its temperature using the Celsius scale, whereas we opt for Fahrenheit. For a rough conversion from Celsius to Fahrenheit, double the number and add 30. For weather, remember that 28°C is 82°F—perfect. For health, 37°C is just right. At a launderette, 30°C is cold, 40°C is warm (usually the default setting), 60°C is hot, and 95°C is boiling.

CLOTHING SIZES

When shopping for clothing, use these US-to-European comparisons as general guidelines (but note that no conversion is perfect).

Women: For clothing or shoe sizes, add 30 (US shirt size 10 = European size 40; US shoe size 8 = European size 38-39).

Men: For shirts, multiply by 2 and add about 8 (US size 15 = European size 38). For jackets and suits, add 10. For shoes, add 32-34.

Children: For clothing, subtract 1-2 sizes for small children and subtract 4 for juniors. For shoes up to size 13, add 16-18, and for sizes 1 and up, add 30-32.

Packing Checklist

Whether you're traveling for five days or five weeks, you won't need more than this. Pack light to enjoy the sweet freedom of true mobility.

Clothing

☐ 5 shirts: long- & short-sleeve
☐ 2 pairs pants (or skirts/capris)
☐ 1 pair shorts
☐ 5 pairs underwear & socks
☐ 1 pair walking shoes
☐ Sweater or warm layer
☐ Rainproof jacket with hood
☐ Tie, scarf, belt, and/or hat
☐ Swimsuit
☐ Sleepwear/loungewear

Money

☐ Debit card(s)
☐ Credit card(s)
☐ Hard cash ($100-200 in US dollars)
☐ Money belt

Documents

☐ Passport
☐ Tickets & confirmations: flights, hotels, trains, rail pass, car rental, sight entries
☐ Driver's license
☐ Student ID, hostel card, etc.
☐ Photocopies of important documents
☐ Insurance details
☐ Guidebooks & maps
☐ Notepad & pen
☐ Journal

Toiletries Kit

☐ Basics: soap, shampoo, toothbrush, toothpaste, floss, deodorant, sunscreen, brush/comb, etc.
☐ Medicines & vitamins
☐ First-aid kit
☐ Glasses/contacts/sunglasses
☐ Sewing kit
☐ Packet of tissues (for WC)
☐ Earplugs

Electronics

☐ Mobile phone
☐ Camera & related gear
☐ Tablet/ebook reader/media player
☐ Laptop & flash drive
☐ Headphones
☐ Chargers & batteries
☐ Smartphone car charger & mount (or GPS device)
☐ Plug adapters

Miscellaneous

☐ Daypack
☐ Sealable plastic baggies
☐ Laundry supplies: soap, laundry bag, clothesline, spot remover
☐ Small umbrella
☐ Travel alarm/watch

Optional Extras

☐ Second pair of shoes (flip-flops, sandals, tennis shoes, boots)
☐ Travel hairdryer
☐ Picnic supplies
☐ Water bottle
☐ Fold-up tote bag
☐ Small flashlight
☐ Mini binoculars
☐ Small towel or washcloth
☐ Inflatable pillow/neck rest
☐ Tiny lock
☐ Address list (to mail postcards)
☐ Extra passport photos

PRONUNCIATION GUIDE FOR PLACE NAMES

When using the phonetics: Try to nasalize the n sound (let the sound come through your nose). Note that the "ahn" combination uses the "ah" sound in "father," but the "an" combination uses the "a" sound in "sack." Pronounce the "ī" as the long "i" in "light." If your best attempt at pronunciation meets with a puzzled look, just point to the place name on the list.

In Paris

Arc de Triomphe ark duh tree-ohnf

arrondissement ah-rohn-dees-mohn

Bateaux-Mouches bah-toh moosh

Bon Marché bohn mar-shay

Carnavalet kar-nah-vah-lay

Champ de Mars shahn duh mar

Champs-Elysées shahn-zay-lee-zay

Conciergerie kon-see-ehr-zhuh-ree

Ecole Militaire eh-kohl mee-lee-tehr

Egouts ay-goo

Fauchon foh-shohn

Galeries Lafayette gah-luh-ree lah-fay-yet

gare gar

Gare d'Austerlitz gar doh-stehr-leets

Gare de l'Est gar duh less

Gare de Lyon gar duh lee-ohn

Gare du Nord gar dew nor

Gare St. Lazare gar san lah-zar

Garnier gar-nee-ay

Grand Palais grahn pah-lay

Grande Arche de la Défense grahnd arsh duh lah day-fahns

Ile de la Cité eel duh lah see-tay

Ile St. Louis eel san loo-ee

Jacquemart-André zhahk-mar-ahn-dray

Jardin des Plantes zhar-dan day plahnt

Jeu de Paume juh duh pohm

La Madeleine lah mah-duh-lehn

Le Hameau luh ah-moh

Les Halles lay ahl

Les Invalides lay-zan-vah-leed

Orangerie oh-rahn-zhuh-ree

Louvre loov-ruh

Marais mah-ray

marché aux puces mar-shay oh poos

Marmottan mar-moh-tahn

Métro may-troh

Monge mohnzh

Montmartre mohn-mart

Montparnasse mohn-par-nahs

Moulin Rouge moo-lan roozh

Musée d'Orsay mew-zay dor-say

Musée de l'Armée mew-zay duh lar-may

Notre-Dame noh-truh-dahm

Opéra Garnier oh-pay-rah gar-nee-ay

Orsay or-say

palais pah-lay

Palais de Justice pah-lay duh zhew-stees

Palais Royal pah-lay roh-yahl

Parc de la Villette park duh la vee-leht

Parc Monceau park mohn-soh

Père Lachaise pehr lah-shehz

Petit Palais puh-tee pah-lay

Pigalle pee-gahl

Place Dauphine plahs doh-feen

Place de la Bastille plahs duh lah bah-steel

Place de la Concorde plahs duh lah kohn-kord

Place de la République plahs duh lah ray-poo-bleek

Place des Vosges plahs day vohzh

Place du Tertre plahs dew tehr-truh

Place St. André-des-Arts plahs san tahn-dray day-zart

Place Vendôme plahs vahn-dohm

Pompidou pohn-pee-doo

pont pohn

Pont Alexandre III pohn ah-

leks-ahn-druh twah
Pont Neuf pohn nuhf
Promenade Plantée proh-mehn-ahd plahn-tay
quai kay
Rive Droite reeve dwaht
Rive Gauche reeve gohsh
Rodin roh-dan
rue rew
Rue Cler rew klehr
Rue Daguerre rew dah-gehr
Rue de Rivoli rew duh ree-voh-lee
Rue des Rosiers rew day roz-ee-ay
Rue Montorgueil rew mohn-tor-goy
Rue Mouffetard rew moof-tar
Sacré-Cœur sah-kray-koor
Sainte-Chapelle sant-shah-pehl
Seine sehn
Sèvres-Babylone seh-vruh-bah-bee-lohn
Sorbonne sor-buhn
St. Germain-des-Prés san zhehr-man-day-pray
St. Julien-le-Pauvre san zhew-lee-ehn-luh-poh-vruh
St. Séverin sahn say-vuh-ran
St. Sulpice sahn sool-pees
Tour Eiffel toor ee-fehl
Trianon tree-ahn-ohn
Trocadéro troh-kah-day-roh
Tuileries twee-lay-ree
Venus de Milo vuh-news duh mee-loh

Outside Paris

Abri du Cap Blanc ah-bree dew cah blahn
Aiguille du Midi ah-gwee dew mee-dee
Aïnhoa an-oh-ah
Albi ahl-bee
Alet ah-lay
Alise Ste-Reine ah-leez sant-rehn
Aloxe-Corton ah-lohx kor-tohn
Alsace ahl-sahs
Amboise ahm-bwahz
Annecy ahn-see
Antibes ahn-teeb
Aosta (Italy) ay-oh-stah

Apt ahp
Aquitaine ah-kee-tehn
Arles arl
Arromanches ah-roh-mahnsh
Autoire oh-twahr
Auvergne oh-vehrn
Avignon ah-veen-yohn
Azay-le-Rideau ah-zay luh ree-doh
Bayeux bī-yuh
Bayonne bī-yuhn
Beaucaire boh-kehr
Beaujolais boh-zhoh-lay
Beaune bohn
Bedoin buh-dwan
Bennwihr behn-veer
Beynac bay-nak
Biarritz bee-ah-reetz
Blois blwah
Bonnieux bohn-yuh
Bordeaux bor-doh
Brancion brahn-see-ohn
Brittany bree-tah-nee
Bruniquel brew-nee-kehl
Caen kahn
Cahors kah-or
Cajarc kah-zhark
Calais kah-lay
Camargue kah-marg
Cambord kahn-bor
Cancale kahn-kahl
Carcassonne kar-kah-suhn
Carennac kah-rehn-ahk
Carsac kar-sahk
Castelnaud kah-stehl-noh
Castelnau-de-Montmiral kah-stehl-noh-duh-mohn-mee-rahl
Caussade koh-sahd
Cavaillon kah-vī-ohn
Cénac say-nahk
Céret say-ray
Chambord shahn-bor
Chamonix shah-moh-nee
Champagne shahn-pahn-yuh
Chapaize shah-pehz
Chartres shart
Château de Rivau shah-toh duh ree-voh
Château du Haut-Kœnigsbourg shah-toh dew oh-koh-neegs-boorg
Châteauneuf-du-Pape shah-toh-nuhf-dew-pahp
Châteauneuf-en-Auxois shah-

toh-nuhf-ehn-ohx-wah

Chaumont-sur-Loire shoh-mohn-sewr-lwahr

Chenonceau shuh-nohn-soh

Chenonceaux shuh-nohn-soh

Cherbourg shehr-boor

Cheverny shuh-vehr-nee

Chinon shee-nohn

Cluny klew-nee

Colleville kohl-veel

Collioure kohl-yoor

Collonges-la-Rouge koh-lohnzh-lah-roozh

Colmar kohl-mar

Cordes-sur-Ciel kord-sewr-see-yehl

Côte d'Azur koht dah-zewr

Cougnac koon-yahk

Courseulles-sur-Mer koor-suhl-sewr-mehr

Coustellet koo-stuh-lay

Digne deen-yuh

Dijon dee-zhohn

Dinan dee-nahn

Dinard dee-nar

Domme dohm

Dordogne dor-dohn-yuh

Eguisheim eh-geh-shīm

Entrevaux ahn-truh-voh

Epernay ay-pehr-nay

Espelette eh-speh-leht

Eze-Bord-de-Mer ehz-bor-duh-mehr

Eze-le-Village ehz-luh-vee-lahzh

Faucon foh-kohn

Flavigny-sur-Ozerain flah-veen-yee-sewr-oh-zuh-ran

Font-de-Gaume fohn-duh-gohm

Fontenay fohn-tuh-nay

Fontevraud fohn-tuh-vroh

Fontvieille fohn-vee-yeh-ee

Fougères foo-zher

Fougères-sur-Bièvre foo-zher-sewr-bee-ehv

Gaillac gī-yahk

Gigondas zhee-gohn-dahs

Giverny zhee-vehr-nee

Gordes gord

Gorges de l'Ardèche gorzh duh lar-dehsh

Grenoble gruh-noh-bluh

Grouin groo-an

Guédelon gway-duh-lohn

Hautes Corbières oht kor-bee-yehr

Hendaye ehn-dī

Honfleur ohn-flur

Huisnes-sur-Mer ween-sewr-mehr

Hunawihr uhn-ah-veer

Ile Besnard eel bay-nar

Isle-sur-la-Sorgue eel-sewr-lah-sorg

Juan-les-Pins zhwan-lay-pan

Kaysersberg kī-zehrs-behrg

Kientzheim keentz-īm

La Charente lah shah-rahnt

Lacoste lah-kohst

Langeais lahn-zhay

Languedoc-Roussillon long-dohk roo-see-yohn

La Rhune lah rewn

La Rochepot lah rohsh-poh

La Roque St-Christophe lah rohk san-kree-stohf

La Roque-Gageac lah rohk-gah-zhahk

Lascaux lah-skoh

Lastours lahs-toor

La Trophée des Alpes lah troh-fay dayz ahlp

La Turbie lah tewr-bee

Le Bugue luh bewg

Le Crestet luh kruh-stay

Le Havre luh hah-vruh

Lémeré lay-muh-ray

Le Ruquet luh rew-kay

Les Baux lay boh

Les Eyzies-de-Tayac lay zay-zee-duh-tī-yahk

Les Praz lay prah

Les Vosges lay vohzh

Limoges lee-mohzh

Loches lohsh

Loire lwahr

Longues-sur-Mer long-sewr-mehr

Loubressac loo-bruh-sahk

Lourmarin loo-mah-ran

Luberon lew-beh-rohn

Lyon lee-ohn

Malaucène mah-loh-sehn

Marne-la-Vallée-Chessy marn-lah-vah-lay-shuh-see

Marseille mar-say

Martel mar-tehl

Mausanne moh-sahn

Ménerbes may-nehrb

Millau mee-yoh

Minerve mee-nerv

Mirabel mee-rah-behl

Modreuc mohd-rewk

Mont Blanc mohn blahn

Mont St-Michel mohn san-mee-shehl

Mont Ventoux mohn vehn-too

Montenvers mohn-tuh-vehr

Montfort mohn-for

Montignac mohn-teen-yahk

Mortemart mort-mar

Munster mewn-stehr

Nantes nahnt

Nice nees

Normandy nor-mahn-dee

Nyons nee-yohns

Oradour-sur-Glane oh-rah-door-sewr-glahn

Orange oh-rahnzh

Padirac pah-dee-rahk

Paris pah-ree

Pech Merle pehsh mehrl

Peyrepertuse pay-ruh-per-tewz

Pointe du Hoc pwant dew ohk

Pont du Gard pohn dew gahr

Pontorson pohn-tor-sohn

Provence proh-vahns

Puycelsi pwee-suhl-cee

Puyméras pwee-may-rahs

Queribus kehr-ee-bews

Reims rans (rhymes with France)

Remoulins ruh-moo-lan

Rennes rehn

Ribeauvillé ree-boh-vee-yay

Riquewihr reek-veer

Rocamadour roh-kah-mah-door

Rouen roo-ahn

Rouffignac roo-feen-yahk

Roussillon roo-see-yohn

Route du Vin root dew van

Sablet sah-blay

Sare sahr

Sarlat-la-Canéda sar-lah lah cah-nay-duh

Savigny-les-Beaune sah-veen-yee-lay-bohn

Savoie sah-vwah

Séguret say-goo-ray

Semur-en-Auxois suh-moor-ehn-ohx-wah

Sigolsheim see-gohl-shīm

Souillac soo-ee-yahk

St-Cirq-Lapopie san-seerk lah-poh-pee

St-Cyprien san-seep-ree-ehn

St-Emilion san-tay-meel-yohn

St-Geniès san-zhuh-nyehs

St-Jean-de-Luz san-zhahn-duh-looz

St-Jean-Pied-de-Port san-zhahn-pee-yay-duh-por

St-Malo san-mah-loh

St-Marcellin-lès-Vaison san-mar-suh-lan-lay-vay-zohn

St-Rémy san-ray-mee

St-Romain-en-Viennois san-roh-man-ehn-vee-ehn-nwah

St-Suliac san-soo-lee-ahk

St-Paul-de-Vence san-pohl-duh-vahns

Ste-Mère Eglise sant-mehr ay-gleez

Stes-Maries-de-la-Mer sant-mah-ree-duh-lah-mehr

Strasbourg strahs-boorg

Suzette soo-zeht

Taizé teh-zay

Tarascon tah-rah-skohn

Tours toor

Turckheim tewrk-hīm

Ussé oo-say

Uzès oo-zehs

Vacqueyras vah-kee-rahs

Vaison-la-Romaine vay-zohn lah roh-mehn

Valançay vah-lahn-say

Valréas vahl-ray-ahs

Vence vahns

Verdun vehr-duhn

Versailles vehr-sī

Veynes vay-nuh

Vézelay vay-zuh-lay

Vierville-sur-Mer vee-yehr-veel-sewr-mehr

Villandry vee-lahn-dry

Villefranche-de-Rouergue veel-frahnsh-duh-roo-ehrg

Villefranche-sur-Mer veel-frahnsh-sewr-mehr

Villeneuve-lès-Avignon veel-nuhv-lay-zah-veeh-yohn

Vitrac vee-trahk

Vouvray voo-vray

Villedieu vee-luh-dyuh

French Survival Phrases

When using the phonetics, try to nasalize the n sound.

English	French	Pronunciation
Good day.	*Bonjour.*	bohn-zhoor
Mrs. / Mr.	*Madame / Monsieur*	mah-dahm / muhs-yuh
Do you speak English?	*Parlez-vous anglais?*	par-lay-voo ahn-glay
Yes. / No.	*Oui. / Non.*	wee / nohn
I understand.	*Je comprends.*	zhuh kohn-prahn
I don't understand.	*Je ne comprends pas.*	zhuh nuh kohn-prahn pah
Please.	*S'il vous plaît.*	see voo play
Thank you.	*Merci.*	mehr-see
I'm sorry.	*Désolé.*	day-zoh-lay
Excuse me.	*Pardon.*	par-dohn
(No) problem.	*(Pas de) problème.*	(pah duh) proh-blehm
It's good.	*C'est bon.*	say bohn
Goodbye.	*Au revoir.*	oh ruh-vwahr
one / two	*un / deux*	uhn / duh
three / four	*trois / quatre*	trwah / kah-truh
five / six	*cinq / six*	sank / sees
seven / eight	*sept / huit*	seht / weet
nine / ten	*neuf / dix*	nuhf / dees
How much is it?	*Combien?*	kohn-bee-an
Write it?	*Ecrivez?*	ay-kree-vay
Is it free?	*C'est gratuit?*	say grah-twee
Included?	*Inclus?*	an-klew
Where can I buy / find...?	*Où puis-je acheter / trouver...?*	oo pwee-zhuh ah-shuh-tay / troo-vay
I'd like / We'd like...	*Je voudrais / Nous voudrions...*	zhuh voo-dray / noo voo-dree-ohn
...a room.	*...une chambre.*	ewn shahn-bruh
...a ticket to ___.	*...un billet pour ___.*	uhn bee-yay poor ___
Is it possible?	*C'est possible?*	say poh-see-bluh
Where is...?	*Où est...?*	oo ay
...the train station	*...la gare*	lah gar
...the bus station	*...la gare routière*	lah gar root-yehr
...tourist information	*...l'office du tourisme*	loh-fees dew too-reez-muh
Where are the toilets?	*Où sont les toilettes?*	oo sohn lay twah-leht
men	*hommes*	ohm
women	*dames*	dahm
left / right	*à gauche / à droite*	ah gohsh / ah drwaht
straight	*tout droit*	too drwah
When does this open / close?	*Ça ouvre / ferme à quelle heure?*	sah oo-vruh / fehrm ah kehl ur
At what time?	*À quelle heure?*	ah kehl ur
Just a moment.	*Un moment.*	uhn moh-mahn
now / soon / later	*maintenant / bientôt / plus tard*	man-tuh-nahn / bee-an-toh / plew tar
today / tomorrow	*aujourd'hui / demain*	oh-zhoor-dwee / duh-man

In a French Restaurant

APPENDIX

English	French	Pronunciation
I'd like / We'd like...	Je voudrais / Nous voudrions...	zhuh voo-dray / noo voo-dree-ohn
...to reserve...	...réserver...	ray-zehr-vay
...a table for one / two.	...une table pour un / deux.	ewn tah-bluh poor uhn / duh
Is this seat free?	C'est libre?	say lee-bruh
The menu (in English), please.	La carte (en anglais), s'il vous plaît.	lah kart (ahn ahn-glay) see voo play
service (not) included	service (non) compris	sehr-vees (nohn) kohn-pree
to go	à emporter	ah ahn-por-tay
with / without	avec / sans	ah-vehk / sahn
and / or	et / ou	ay / oo
special of the day	plat du jour	plah dew zhoor
specialty of the house	spécialité de la maison	spay-see-ah-lee-tay duh lah may-zohn
appetizers	hors d'oeuvre	or duh-vruh
first course (soup, salad)	entrée	ahn-tray
main course (meat, fish)	plat principal	plah pran-see-pahl
bread	pain	pan
cheese	fromage	froh-mahzh
sandwich	sandwich	sahnd-weech
soup	soupe	soop
salad	salade	sah-lahd
meat	viande	vee-ahnd
chicken	poulet	poo-lay
fish	poisson	pwah-sohn
seafood	fruits de mer	frwee duh mehr
fruit	fruit	frwee
vegetables	légumes	lay-gewm
dessert	dessert	day-sehr
mineral water	eau minérale	oh mee-nay-rahl
tap water	l'eau du robinet	loh dew roh-bee-nay
milk	lait	lay
(orange) juice	jus (d'orange)	zhew (doh-rahnzh)
coffee / tea	café / thé	kah-fay / tay
wine	vin	van
red / white	rouge / blanc	roozh / blahn
glass / bottle	verre / bouteille	vehr / boo-tay
beer	bière	bee-ehr
Cheers!	Santé!	sahn-tay
More. / Another.	Plus. / Un autre.	plew / uhn oh-truh
The same.	La même chose.	lah mehm shohz
The bill, please.	L'addition, s'il vous plaît.	lah-dee-see-ohn see voo play
Do you accept credit cards?	Vous prenez les cartes?	voo pruh-nay lay kart
tip	pourboire	poor-bwahr
Delicious!	Délicieux!	day-lee-see-uh

For more user-friendly French phrases, check out *Rick Steves' French Phrase Book and Dictionary* or *Rick Steves' French, Italian & German Phrase Book*.

INDEX

A

Abbeys: Cluny, 889–890; Fontenay, 869–871; Fontevraud, 423–425; Jumièges, 228; Mont St-Michel, 303–308; Notre-Dame de Sénanque, 660; St. Georges de Boscherville, 228

Abri du Cap Blanc: 472, 478

Acccommodations: See Sleeping; and specific destinations

Aiguille du Dru (Alps): 798–799

Aiguille du Midi Gondola (Alps): 791, 794–798

Airbnb: 1059

Airborne Museum (Utah Beach): 291

Airlines (airfares): 12, 1109–1110

Airports: Geneva, 770, 785, 819–820; Lyon, 897; Nice, 709–710; Paris, 152–16; Strasbourg, 982

Aître St. Maclou (Rouen): 225–226

À l'Aise Breizh (Dinan): 322

Albert I Park (Nice): 684

Albert, Prince of Monaco: 732, 738

Albert Schweitzer Museum (Kaysersberg): 974–975

Albi: 507–519; eating, 517–518; helpful hints, 509; map, 508; sights/activities, 509–516; sleeping, 516–517; tourist information, 507; transportation, 509, 518–519

Alésia MuséoParc (Alise-Ste-Reine): 866

Alet: 332, 337–338

Alise Ste-Reine: 865–868, 872

Allen, Paul: 680

All the Light We Cannot See (Doerr): 332, 1117

Almanac: xviii–xix

Aloxe-Corton: 853–854, 860

Alpilles Mountains: 574–575, 625

Alpine Museum (Chamonix): 812

Alps (Alpes-Savoie): 764–820; cuisine, 766; geology, 800–801; map, 765; planning tips, 764–766; transportation, 766. See also Annecy; Chamonix

Alsace: 928–989; cuisine, 931; map, 929; planning tips, 930; transportation, 930–931. See also specific destinations

Alsatian folk dancing and music: 950, 986

Alsatian Museum (Strasbourg): 985

Alsatian wines: 932, 934–935, 950, 955–964, 968, 974, 978; map, 957; tours, 958–960; wines overview, 960–961

Amboise: 355–379; eating, 374–376; helpful hints, 356–357, 360; maps, 358–359, 376–377; self-guided walk, 360–362; sights/activities, 362–369; sleeping, 369–374; tourist information, 356; transportation, 356, 377–379

Amboise City Hall Museum: 361–362

Amboise Royal Castle (Château): 351, 362–364, 365

American Cemetery and Memorial (Omaha Beach): 277–280

American Cemetery and Memorial (Thiaucourt): 1030

American Church (Paris): 57, 112

American Hospital (Paris): 25, 1113–1114

Amphithéâtre (Arles): 573–574

Amsterdam: train travel, 165

Angoville-au-Plain Church: 288–289

Anis candies: 868

Annecy: 767–783; map, 768–769

Annecy Château Museum: 774

Annecy, Lake: 767, 770–772, 774–779; map, 776

Annecy Museum: 772, 774

Antibes: 743–757; eating, 755–756; helpful hints, 745, 748; map, 746–747; self-guided walk, 748–750; sights/activities, 748–754; sleeping, 754–755; tourist information, 744; transportation, 744–745, 748, 757

Antibes History and Archaeology Museum: 750, 752

Anybody's Tombstone (Dinan): 321–322

Aosta, Italy: 813

Apartment rentals: 1060–1061; Paris, 132–133; Riviera, 666

Apt: market, 565

Aquarium, in Monaco: 739–740
Aqueduct (Pont du Gard): 620, 623–625
"Arc de Triomphe" (Orange): 636
Arc de Triomphe (Paris): 45, 94, 113
Archaeological museums: Alise Ste-Reine, 866; Antibes, 750, 752; Arles, 582–584; Cluny, 890; Colmar, 946–947; Les Eyzies-de-Tayac, 472, 474–475; Lyon, 906–908; Nice, 695; Paris, 54, 87–88; Pont du Gard, 624; Strasbourg, 985
Archaeological sites: *See* Cro-Magnon caves; Roman sites
Argentière: 811
Arles: 557, 565–596; eating, 592–595; helpful hints, 567, 570; maps, 568–569, 586, 590–591; planning tips, 565–566; self-guided walk, 570–582; sights/activities, 582–588; sleeping, 588–592; tourist information, 566; transportation, 566–567, 570, 595–596
Arles Ancient History Museum: 582–584
Arles Roman Arena: 573–574
Arles Roman Theater: 575–576
Army Museum (Paris): 44–45, 85–86
Arpentis Château: 372–373
Arromanches: 269–275; map, 270
Arromanches 360° Theater: 272
Art: of the Riviera, 671. *See also* Cro-Magnon caves; Impressionism; *and specific artists*
Art museums: general tips, 1050–1051. *See also specific art museums*
Arve River: 791, 793, 808
Atelier de la Soierie (Lyon): 903, 912–913
Atlantic Wall: 279, 289–290, 296
ATMs: 1043–1044. *See also specific destinations*
Attitude, French: 16–17
Aude River: 531–532
Audio Europe, Rick Steves: 14, 17, 1111
Aure River: 247, 255
Autoire: 492
Avenue de la République (Beaune): 838, 839
Avenue Jean Médecin (Nice): 688
Avignon: 557, 596–620; eating, 616–619; helpful hints, 598–599, 602; maps, 600–601, 612–613;
self-guided walk, 602–611; sights/activities, 602–611; sleeping, 611–615; tourist information, 597; tours, 599, 602; transportation, 597–598, 619–620
Avignon City Hall: 603
Avignon Ramparts: 605
Avignon Synagogue: 608
Aÿ: 1013–1014
Azay-le-Rideau: 415–418
Azay-le-Rideau Château: 351, 415–418

B

Back Door travel philosophy: 19
Baeckeoffe: 931, 954
Baie des Anges (Nice): 683
Ballooning: 353, 431, 457
Bartholdi, Frédéric-Auguste: 912, 913, 934, 937, 941; Museum (Colmar), 942, 948–950
Basilica of Ste. Madeleine (Vézelay): 876–879
Basse Corniche: 721–723; map, 722
Bastides: 519–521
Bastille Opera (Paris): 112
Bateaux-Mouches (Paris): 38
Bateaux Parisiens (Paris): 38–39
Baths of Constantine (Arles): 584
Batobus (Paris): 39
Battle of Hastings: overview, 253
Battle of Normandy Memorial Museum (Bayeux): 256–257
Baubigny: 858
Bayeux: 210, 247–261; eating, 259–260; helpful hints, 249; map, 250–251; sights, 252–257; sleeping, 257–259; tourist information, 248; tours, 249; transportation, 248, 261
Bayeux Cathedral: 254–255
Bayeux Tapestry: 252–254
Bay of Angels (Nice): 683
Bay of Mont St-Michel: 297, 300–302
"Bayonet Trench" (Verdun): 1028–1029
Beaches: Annecy, 774; Antibes, 748–749, 752; Cap Ferrat, 726; Cap Fréhel, 340–341; Collioure, 544, 546, 547; Dinard, 337; Dunes de Chevrêts, 343; Etrétat, 242; Juan-les-Pins, 754; Nice, 673, 677, 681, 683, 684, 685; Paris, 63; Pont du Gard, 623; Sables-d'Or-les-

Pins, 340; St-Malo, 332. *See also* D-Day beaches

Beaujolais: 894, 926–927

Beaulieu-sur-Mer: 727

Beaune: 826–848; eating, 845–847; helpful hints, 827–829; maps, 830–831, 842–843; sights/activities, 832–840; sleeping, 840–845; tourist information, 826–827; tours, 829, 832; transportation, 827, 847–848

Beaune Ramparts: 839

Beaune region: 848–864

Beauvais Airport (Paris): 159–160

Bed-and-breakfasts *(chambres d'hôtes):* 1057; Paris, 133. *See also specific destinations*

Belvès: market, 434

Bennwihr: 962

Berthillon (Paris): 149

Beverages: 1076–1080. *See also* Wine and vineyards

Beynac: 450, 452, 453, 459–463; market, 434, 460

Beynac Château: 460

Bibliothèque Carnegie: 1005

Bibliothèque Carnegie (Reims): 1005–1006

Big Red One Museum (Colleville-sur-Mer): 277

Biking (bike rentals): 1109; Tour de France, 1115; Alsace, 959, 963, 965, 969; Amboise, 357, 368; Annecy, 770–771, 774, 775–777; Antibes, 748; Arles, 567; Avignon, 599; Bayeux, 249; Blois, 387, 390; Burgundy, 832, 848, 860; Carcassonne, 526; Chambord, 394; Chamonix, 789; Chinon, 403, 411; Colmar, 935; Dinan, 319; Dordogne, 431; Eguisheim, 965, 969; Giverny, 200; Isle-sur-la-Sorgue, 655; Kaysersberg, 975; Loire Valley, 352–353, 368, 387, 390, 394, 403, 411; Luberon, 653, 655; Lyon, 901, 902; Nice, 677, 681; Paris, 34–35, 41; Rance River Valley, 326; Reims, 995; Ribeauvillé, 963; St-Emilion, 487–488; St-Malo, 334; St-Rémy, 559; Sarlat, 437; Strasbourg, 983; Vaison-la-Romaine, 640, 643–644; Versailles, 185; Villefranche-sur-Mer, 712

Black Virgins: 496, 498

Bléré: sleeping, 373

Blois: 386–393

Blois Royal Castle (Château): 350, 387–389

Blues clubs, in Paris: 110–111

Boat cruises: Annecy, 775; Avignon, 599; Beynac, 461; Carcassonne, 532; Chinon, 404; Colmar, 936; Dinan, 326–327; Honfleur, 242; La Roque-Gageac, 457; Nice, 679, 680; Paris, 38–39, 111, 167–168; Riviera, 671, 679, 680, 710–711, 721, 743; Strasbourg, 986; Villefranche-sur-Mer, 717

Boating: Annecy, 770–771, 774; Antibes, 748; Chenonceaux, 381; hotel barges, overview, 1061; Lyon, 901; Nice, 683; Villefranche-sur-Mer, 717. *See also* Canoeing

Bocuse, Paul: 925, 1039

Bonaparte Bridge (Lyon): 903–904

Bonaparte, Napoleon: *See* Napoleon Bonaparte

Bon Marché (Paris): 107, 109

Bonnieux: 653, 659; eating, 661

Books, recommended: 1116–1118

Bordeaux: 487–489

Boudin (Eugène) Museum (Honfleur): 238–240

Boules: 117, 561, 570, 713, 758

Boulevard Malesherbes (Paris): 108–109

Bourges: 881–885

Bourges Cathedral: 882–884

Bourges Medieval Quarter: 884

Bouzy: 1012–1013

Braille, Louis: 90

Brancion: 886–887

Brancusi, Constantin: 103

Brayer (Yves) Museum (Les Baux): 629

Breakfast: overview, 1063–1064

British Military Cemetery (Bayeux): 257

Brittany: 314–344; cuisine, 316–317; map, 316; planning tips, 315; tours, 315; transportation, 315. *See also specific destinations*

Bruniquel: 520

Brussels: train travel, 165

Budgeting: 12–13

Bullgames, in Arles: 587–588

Burgundy: 821–892; at a glance, 823; cuisine, 823–824; maps, 822, 873;

planning tips, 821–823; transportation, 823. *See also specific destinations*

Burgundy Canal: 864, 865

Burgundy wines: 824–825, 828, 838, 839, 847, 848–864; maps, 857, 859; museum, in Beaune, 837; savoring tactics, 1078; shipping home, 840–841; tours, 829, 832, 848–849; transportation, 848–849

Buses (bus travel): 1097; best three-week trip, 10–11; Paris, 30–32, 33, 36–37, 118–119, 125, 128, 167; airports, 155, 158; tours, 35, 38, 113, 116. *See also specific destinations*

Business hours: 1043

Butterfly Exhibit (Hunawihr): 963

C

Caen: 293–296

Caen Memorial Museum: 293–296

Café de la Mairie (Paris): 109

Café de la Paix (Paris): 97

Cafés (brasseries): 1069–1071; tipping, 1047. *See also specific destinations*

Cahors: 502–503; market, 434

Calvados: 211, 249, 281, 284

Calvet Museum (Avignon): 610

Camarguais Museum: 585

Camargue, the: 585–587; map, 586

Camembert cheese: 211

Campervan rentals: 1100

Camping (campgrounds): overview, 1062

Canadian Cemetery (Juno Beach): 293

Canadian D-Day sites: 292–294

Canal de Bourgogne: 864, 865

Canal du Midi (Carcassonne): 532

Cancale: 342, 343–344

Candes-St-Martin: 411

Cannes Film Festival: 666, 698, 1114

Canoeing: Chinon, 403, 411; Dinan, 319; Dordogne River, 430–431, 450–454; Loire River, 368, 403, 411; Pont du Gard, 622–623

Cap d'Ail: 733

Cap d'Antibes: 750, 752–754

Cap Ferrat: 723–727; cruises, 680, 717; map, 724

Cap Fréhel: 340–341

Carcassonne: 521–539; eating, 537–538; helpful hints, 526–527;

maps, 524–525, 529; nightlife, 533; self-guided walk, 527–531; sights/activities, 531–533; sleeping, 533–537; tourist information, 522–523; transportation, 523, 526, 539

Carennac: 490–491

Car insurance: 12, 1099–1100

Car leasing: 1100

Carnavalet Museum (Paris): 99

Carnegie Library (Reims): 999, 1005–1006

Carnival (Nice): 666, 698

Car rentals: 1098–1099. *See also specific destinations*

Carrières de Lumières (Les Baux): 630

Car travel (driving): 1101–1109; best three-week trip, 8–9; distances and time, 1103; driving tips, 1106–1109; road signs, 1102, 1104–1105. *See also specific destinations*

Casinos: Monte Carlo, 740–741; Nice, 684

Castelnau-Bretenoux Château: 491–492

Castelnaud: 450, 453; sleeping, 459

Castelnaud Château: 458–459

Castelnau-de-Montmiral: 521

Castle Hill (Nice): 682, 692, 696–697

Castles: *See Châteaux*

Catacombs of Paris: 91

Cathars: overview, 512

Cathédrale de Monaco: 739

Cathédrale Notre-Dame: *See Notre-Dame Cathedral*

Cathédrale Russe (Nice): 682, 696

Caunes-Minervois: sleeping, 536–537

Caussade: 506

Cavaillon: 598, 620

Cave art: *See Cro-Magnon caves*

Caveau de Puligny-Montrachet: 850, 856–857

Caveau des Vignerons (Amboise): 368

Caveau des Vignerons (Morey-St-Denis): 863

Cell (mobile) phones: 17, 1080–1084

Cénac: 454; market, 434

Centre de Réintroduction (Hunawihr): 963

Centre d'Histoire de la Résistance et de la Déportation (Lyon): 902, 915–916

Centre International du Vitrail (Chartres): 197

Centre Pompidou (Paris): 45, 102–103

Ceramics, Museum of (Rouen): 227

Céret: 551

Cézanne, Paul: 77, 79, 610

Chagall, Marc: 96, 102–103, 551, 1003–1004; Museum (Nice), 682, 692–694

Chagny: 853, 858

Chalet de la Floria (Alps): 808

Chalon-sur-Saône: 856

Chambolle-Musigny: 862–863

Chambord Château: 350, 393–397

Chamonix: 783–820; at a glance, 791; eating, 817–819; helpful hints, 785, 788; history timeline, 785; maps, 786–787, 790, 806–807; planning tips, 783–784; self-guided walk, 791–794; sights/activities, 791–813; sleeping, 813–816; tourist information, 784; transportation, 784–785, 788–791, 819–820

Chamonix City Hall: 792

Chamonix Protestant Church: 793–794

Champagne: 990, 1007–1015; about, 1011

Champagne G. Tribaut (Hautvillers): 1014

Champagne Herbert Beaufort (Bouzy): 1012–1013

Champagne region: 990–1019; cuisine, 991–992; maps, 992–993, 1013; planning tips, 990; tours, 1007–1008; transportation, 990–991

Champ de Mars (Paris): 83

Champs-Elysées (Paris): 22, 44, 91–94, 113; map, 92–93

Changing of the Guard (Monaco): 738

Chapaize: 887

Chapelle Cocteau (Villefranche): 716

Chapelle du Rosaire (Vence): 761

Chapelle et Phare de la Garoupe (Antibes): 753

Chapel of Penitents (Les Baux): 630

Chapel of St. Leo IX (Eguisheim): 968

Chapel of St. Pierre (Villefranche): 716

Chapel of the Rosary (Vence): 761

Charlemagne: 221, 498, 522, 1005, 1031, 1038

Charles de Cazanove (Reims): 1009

Charles de Gaulle Airport (Paris): 152–157, 159–160; map, 153; sleeping, 132

Chartres: 188–198; map, 190–191

Chartres Cathedral: 191–196; map, 193

Chassagne-Montrachet Château: 850–851, 857

Châteauneuf-en-Auxois: 864, 874

Châteaux (castles): architecture, 1033; history, 366–367; Amboise, 351, 362–364, 365; Annecy, 774; Arpentis, 372–373; Azay-le-Rideau, 351, 415–418; Beynac, 460; Blois, 350, 387–389; Castelnau-Bretenoux, 491–492; Castelnaud, 458–459; Chambord, 350, 393–397; Châteauneuf-en-Auxois, 864; Chaumont-sur-Loire, 350, 399–402; Chenonceau, 350, 379–384; Cheverny, 350, 397–399; Chinon, 408–409; Clos de Vougeot, 862; Clos-Lucé (Amboise), 351, 362–363; Collioure, 547; Commarque, 479; Comtal (Carcassonne), 530–531, 532; Eza, 729; Fayrac, 453; Grimaldi (Antibes), 750; Guédelon, 879–881; Hautes Corbières, 539–542; Haut-Kœnigsbourg, 963–964; Husseren Les Cinq, 968–969; La Fleunie, 482; Langeais, 351, 418–420; La Rochepot, 852–853, 858; Lastours, 542; Montfort, 450, 454; Nazelles, 373; Perreux, 372; Peyrepertuse, 540, 541; Pray, 372, 376; Quéribus, 541; Rivau, 411–412; Rocamadour, 495; Savigny, 855; Ussé, 412; Villandry, 351, 420–422; Villeneuve (Vence), 760. *See also* Versailles Château

Chaumont-sur-Loire Château: 350, 399–402

Cheeses: 144, 211, 354, 432, 564, 766, 824, 894, 931, 991, 1075

Chemin de la Croix (Rocamadour): 493, 495

Chemin des Fontaines (St-Cirq Lapopie): 643

Chemin du Fauvisme (Collioure): 547

Chemins de Fer de Provence: 697

Chemins de Lumières Light Show (Beaune): 837
Chénas: 926
Chenonceau Château: 350, 379–384
Chenonceaux: 379–385
Cher River: 352, 379; canoeing, 368
Cheverny Château: 350, 397–399
Child, Julia: 219
Chinon: 403–415; eating, 413–414; helpful hints, 403–404; maps, 406–407, 416–417; self-guided walk, 404–405, 408; sights/activities, 408–412; sleeping, 412–413; tourist information, 403; transportation, 414–415
Chinon Château: 408–409
Chiroubles: 926
Chisseaux: eating, 385
Chocolat (movie): 456, 868, 1118
Chocolate: 108, 109, 219, 360, 578–579, 689, 1076
Christmas markets: 767, 933, 987
Churches (eglises): architecture, 1032. *See also specific churches*
Church of the Holy Cross (Kaysersberg): 973
Church of the Immaculate Conception (Antibes): 750
Cimetière du Père Lachaise (Paris): 45, 103–104
Citadelle Souterraine (Verdun): 1021
Classical theaters: *See* Théâtre Antique
Climate: 13–14, 1121–1122
Clos de Vougeot Château: 862
Clos-Lucé Château (Amboise): 351, 362–363
Clothing sizes: 1121
Cluny: 888–891
Cluny Abbey: 889–890
Cluny Museum (Paris): 45, 57, 87–88
Cluny Museum of Art and Archaeology: 888
Cocteau (Jean) Chapel (Villefranche): 716
Coffee: 1077–1078
Col de Balme: 809
Col de Banyuls: 551
Col de la Forclaz: 779
Collection Lambert (Avignon): 611
Collégiale Notre-Dame (Beaune): 836–837
Colleville-sur-Mer: 277, 278

Colline du Château (Nice): 682, 696–697
Collioure: 544–554; eating, 553–554; helpful hints, 545; map, 548–549; sights/activities, 546–551; sleeping, 551–553; tourist information, 545; transportation, 545, 554
Collioure Royal Castle (Château): 547
Colmar: 932–955; eating, 952–955; helpful hints, 934–935; map, 938–939; nightlife, 950; self-guided walk, 936–944; sights/activities, 944–950; sleeping, 950–952; tourist information, 933; tours, 935–936; transportation, 933–934, 955
Colmar Dominican Church: 943, 947–948
"Colmar Pocket" Museum (Turckheim): 962
Commarque Château: 479
Comtal Château (Carcassonne): 530–531, 532
Conciergerie (Paris): 61–62
Concoeur: 862
Condat-sur-Vézère: sleeping, 482
Confit de canard: 354, 431, 433, 1074
Confluence (Lyon): 903, 917
Connery, Sean: 680
Conservatoire de Dentelles (Bayeux): 256
Constant, Christian: 140
Consulates: 1114
Cooking classes: Beaune, 828–829; Nice, 680; Paris, 144–145; Vaison-la-Romaine, 641
Cordes-sur-Ciel: 519–520
Costs of trip: 12–13
Côte d'Azur: *See* Riviera; *and specific destinations*
Côte de Grâce (Honfleur): 241
Côte d'Emeraude: 340–343
Côtes du Rhône: 637–651
Côtes du Rhône Wine Road: 647–651; map, 649
Cougnac Cave: 473, 484–485
Courbet, Gustave: 75
Courses camarguaises, in Arles: 587–588
Courseulles-sur-Mer: 292–293
Cours Jean Jaurès (Avignon): 597
Cours Saleya (Nice): 689–690; eating, 703–704

Cousteau Aquarium (Monaco): 739–740

Créancey: 874

Credit cards: 15, 1045–1047

Crêpes: about, 1068

Crépon: sleeping, 273–274

Crestet: 643, 647, 648–649

Cro-Magnon caves: 465–485; at a glance, 472–473; helpful hints, 471–474; map, 466–467; overview, 465, 468–471; planning tips, 471; reservations, 16–17, 471–473

Crown of Thorns: 49, 58, 60

Cruise ships, on the Riviera: 710–711, 721, 743. *See also* Boat cruises

Cryptoporticos (Arles): 576

Cryptoportique (Reims): 1006

Crystal Museum (Chamonix): 812

Cuisine: xv–xvi, 1072–1076; Alsace, 931; Brittany, 316–317; Burgundy, 823–824; Champagne region, 991–992; Dordogne, 431–432; Languedoc-Roussillon, 506; Loire Valley, 354; Lyon, 894, 920; Normandy, 210–211, 311; picnics, 1064–1067; Provence, 563–564; Riviera, 671–672; Savoie, 766; to-go foods, 1067–1068

Curie, Marie: 90

Currency and exchange: 1043–1044

Customs House (Colmar): 936–937

Customs regulations: 1048

Cycling: *See* Biking

D

Dalí, Salvador: 103; Theater-Museum (Figueres), 551

Daumier, Honoré: 74–75

David, Jacques-Louis: 69–70, 610

Da Vinci Code: 877

Da Vinci, Leonardo: 68–69, 355, 361–362, 364–365; *Mona Lisa,* 69

D-Day beaches (Normandy): 261–293; American sites, 275–292; Canadian sites, 292–293; helpful hints, 268–269; history timeline, 266–267; map, 264–265; planning tips, 262–263; tours, 263–268; transportation, 263

D-Day Experience (Utah Beach): 291–292

D-Day Landing Museum (Arromanches): 272–273

Debit cards: 15, 1045–1047

Degas, Edgar: 76, 226, 610

De Gaulle Airport (Paris): *See* Charles de Gaulle Airport

De Gaulle, Charles: 45, 85, 94, 255, 257, 293, 296, 1039

Déjeuner sur l'Herbe (Manet): 75–76

Delacroix, Eugène: 70–71, 89, 227, 256

Dentelles de Montmirail: 647, 650

Department stores, in Paris: 107

Deportation Memorial (Paris): 54–55

Dietary restrictions: 1070

Digne: 697

Dinan: 317–332; eating, 329–331; helpful hints, 318–319; map, 320–321; self-guided walk, 319–325; sights/activities, 325–327; sleeping, 327–329; tourist information, 318; transportation, 318, 331–332

Dinan Clock Tower: 322

Dinan Old Port: 325, 326–327, 331

Dinan Ramparts: 324

Dinard: 337

Dining: *See* Eating; *and specific destinations*

Discounts: *See* Money-saving tips

Disneyland Paris: 204–206

Dizy: 1014

Doerr, Anthony: 332, 1117

Dolder Museum (Riquewihr): 977

Domaine Comte Senard (Aloxe-Corton): 853–854, 860

Domaine de Balme (Alps): 808–809, 811

Domaine de Coyeux Winery: 650

Domaine de la Chevalerie (Chinon): 410

Domaine de Marie-Antoinette (Versailles): 170–171, 175, 183–186; map, 184

Domaine de Mourchon Winery: 648

Domaine Lejeune (Pommard): 849

Domaine Naudin-Ferrand (Magny-les-Villers): 854, 861

Domaine René LeClerc (Gevrey-Chambertin): 863–864

Domaines d'Aloxe-Corton: 853

Dominican Church (Colmar): 943, 947–948

Domme: 450, 452, 455; market, 434, 455

Dordogne: 426–503; at a glance, 427; cuisine, 431–432; map, 429; markets, 432–434; planning tips,

426–428; transportation, 428–431. *See also specific destinations*

Dordogne River: 426, 449; canoeing, 430–431, 450–454; cruises, 457, 461; map, 452–453

Dordogne River Valley: 449–465

Douaumont Ossuary (Verdun): 1027–1028

Driving: *See* Car travel; *and specific destinations*

Ducal Palace (Nice): 690

Duclair: 228

Duingt: 776, 777

Dumas, Alexandre: 90

Dunes de Chevrêts: 343

E

Eastern Dordogne: 490–500; map, 491

Eating: 1062–1076; budgeting, 12; ordering tips, 1071–1072; restaurant phrases, 1130; restaurant pricing, 1063; tipping, 1047, 1069. *See also* Cuisine; Markets; *and specific destinations*

Economy: xix, 1035–1037

Eglise de Carsac: 450

Eglise des Dominicains (Colmar): 943, 947–948

Eglise Jeanne d'Arc (Rouen): 215, 219

Eglise St-Jacques (Nice): 691

Eglise St-Pierre (Mont St-Michel): 303

Eglise Ste. Catherine (Honfleur): 237–238

Egouts de Paris: 83–84

Eguisheim: 961, 964–970; map, 966–967

Eguisheim Castle: 968

Eiffel Tower (Paris): 16, 44, 80–83, 112–113

Eleanor of Aquitaine: 403, 408, 424, 882, 1034, 1038

Electricity: 1043

Elevage du Bouyssou (Sarlat): 464

Embassies: 1114

Emerald Coast: 340–344

Emergencies: 1042, 1113–1114; Paris, 25

Entrevaux: 697

Epernay: 1015

Equestrian Performance Academy (Versailles): 174

Espace Alpinisme (Chamonix): 812

Espace Tairraz (Chamonix): 812

Etang de Vaccarès: 585

Etrétat: 242–243

Euro currency: 1043–1044

Eurostar: 165–166

Evelles: 858

Exchange rate: 1045

Eza Château: 729

Eze-Bord-de-Mer: 728, 730

Eze Church: 730

Eze-le-Village: 728–730

F

Faience: 224, 227

Fashion, in Paris: 108–109

Fauchon (Paris): 108

Fayencerie Augy (Rouen): 224

Fayrac Château: 453

Fenocchio (Nice): 692, 705

Ferris Wheel (Paris): 94

Festivals: 1114–1115. *See also specific festivals*

Films, recommended: 1118–1120

Flavigny-sur-Ozerain: 868–869, 874

Fleurie: 926

Flower markets: Nice, 690; Paris, 61

Flowers, blooming season: 14–15

Foie gras: 431, 433, 441, 462–464, 1073

Fondation Maeght (St-Paul-de-Vence): 758–759

Fondation Van Gogh (Arles): 579–580

Font-de-Gaume Cave: 472, 477–478

Fontenay Abbey (Burgundy): 869–871

Fontevraud Royal Abbey: 423–425

Fontvieille: sleeping, 592

Fontvieille (Monaco): 732, 739

Food: *See* Cheeses; Chocolate; Cuisine; Eating; Foie gras; Markets; Olive oil; Truffles

Food allergies: 1070

Food tours: Avignon, 602; Nice, 680; Paris, 144

Fort Carré (Antibes): 748, 752

Fort de Douaumont (Verdun): 1028–1029

Forteresse Royale de Chinon: 408–409

Fort la Latte: 341–342

Fort St. Elme (Collioure): 550

Forum Square (Arles): *See* Place du Forum

Fougères: 344

Fouquet's (Paris): 93

Fourvière Hill (Lyon): 895, 904–908; eating, 921, 924

Fragonard Perfume Factory (Eze): 730

French Alps: *See* Alps

French attitude: 16–17

French language: *See* Language

French Riviera: *See* Riviera

French Riviera Pass: 665–666

Fuissé: 926

G

Gadagne Museums (Lyon): 903, 911–912

Gaillac: 506

Galamus Gorges: 539–540

Galerie Mario Colonel (Chamonix): 812

Galeries Lafayette (Paris): 97, 107, 111–112

Gare d'Austerlitz (Paris): 164

Gare de Bercy (Paris): 165

Gare de l'Est (Paris): 163–164

Gare de Lyon (Paris): 152, 162–163

Gare du Nord (Paris): 161–162

Gare Montparnasse (Paris): 162

Gare St. Lazare (Paris): 164

Garnier Opera (Paris): 45, 96–97, 112

Gauguin, Paul: 78, 87, 581

Gauls: 636, 821, 866, 867, 874, 906, 907, 915, 1031

Gay nightlife, in Paris: 124–125

Geneva Airport: 770, 785, 819–820

Geography: xviii

Gérard Sion Galerie (Carcassonne): 533

Géricault, Théodore: 70, 226, 610

German Military Cemeteries (Normandy): 286–287, 308

Gevrey-Chambertin: 863–864

Gigondas: 650–651

Gîtes: 1057–1058

Giverny: 198–204; map, 199

Gondolas, in Chamonix: 789, 791, 799–802; map, 790

Gordes: 659–660

Gorges de Galamus: 539–540

Gouffre de Padirac: 499

Government: xix, 1035–1037, 1040

Governor's Tower (Dinan): 324

Gramat: sleeping, 499–500

Grand Balcon Nord (Alps): 803–804

Grand Balcon Sud (Alps): 791, 804–805

Grande Allée des Promenades (Reims): 998

Grande Corniche: 722–723; map, 722

Grand Prix of Monaco: 666, 698, 732, 738, 1114

Grimaldi Château (Antibes): 750

Gros Horloge (Rouen): 220–221

Grotte de Font-de-Gaume: 472, 477–478

Grotte de Rouffignac: 473, 482–484

Grotte du Pech Merle: 473, 502

Grotte Préhistorique des Merveilles: 495

Grottes de Cougnac: 473, 484–485

Grünewald, Matthias, *Isenheim Altarpiece:* 945–946

Guédelon Château: 879–881

Guidebooks, Rick Steves: 1110–1111; updates, 3, 18

Guy de Chassey (Louvois): 1012

H

Halles Boulingrin (Reims): 1006–1007

Hanggliding: 779, 808, 809

Hartmannswillerkopf (Eguisheim): 961

Haussmann, Baron Georges-Eugène: 98

Hautes Corbières Château: 539–542

Haut-Kœnigsbourg Château: 963–964

Hautvillers: 1014–1015

Hédiard (Paris): 108

Helbronner: 789, 794, 797, 813

Henri de Villamont (Savigny): 854, 861

Hermès (Paris): 109

High Corniche: 722–723; map, 722

Hiking (walking): Alet, 338; Alsace, 959–960; Annecy, 771–772; Antibes, 752–754; Avignon, 605; Bayeux, 255; Beaune, 832, 838–839; Beynac, 460–461; Bourges, 884; Burgundy, 832, 838–839; Cap Ferrat, 726–727; Cap Fréhel, 340–341; Carcassonne, 531–532; Chamonix, 802–809; map, 806–807; Collioure, 548–551; Dinan, 325–326; Duingt, 777; Eguisheim, 965–967; Etrétat,

242; Eze, 729, 730; Fort la Latte, 341–342; Giverny, 200; Honfleur, 241–242; Kaysersberg, 975; Lastours, 542; Mont St-Michel, 302–303; Pont du Gard, 622, 624; Rance River Valley, 325–326; Ribeauvillé, 963; Roussillon, 657; Strasbourg, 982; Vaison-la-Romaine, 643; Villefranche-sur-Mer, 717–718

Hill towns of the Luberon: 652–662; map, 654–655

History: 1031–1035

Holidays: 1114–1115

Holocaust Memorial (Paris): 102

Honfleur: 210, 231–247; eating, 245–246; helpful hints, 233; map, 234–235; sights/activities, 233–243; sleeping, 243–244; tourist information, 232; transportation, 232, 246–247

Horseback shows: 395, 891

Hospices de Beaune: 832–836

Hospitals: 1042, 1113–1114; Paris, 25

Hostels (auberge de jeunesse): 1061–1062. See also specific destinations

Hot-air ballooning: 353, 431, 457

Hotels: 1053–1057; modern chains, 1056–1057; rates and deals, 1052–1053; reservations, 15, 1058–1059. See also Sleeping; and specific destinations

Hotel barges, overview: 1061

Hôtel de la Cité (Carcassonne): 530

Hôtel Dieu des Hospices de Beaune: 832–836

Hôtel La Mirande (Avignon): 607

Hôtel Negresco (Nice): 681, 697, 701–702

Houdini, Harry (Jean-Eugène Robert-Houdin): 389

House of Etienne de la Boëtie (Sarlat): 438–439

"House of Heads" (Colmar): 943–944

House of Magic (Blois): 389

Hugo, Victor: 54, 84, 90, 99, 307, 1119

Huisnes-sur-Mer: 308

Hunawihr: 963

Hundred Years' War: 220, 1034

Hurepel de Minerve: 543

Husseren Les Cinq Château: 968–969

I

Ile Besnard: 343

Ile de la Cité (Paris): 22, 48–55; map, 50–51

Ile St. Louis (Paris): 45, 55, 113, 131; eating, 147–149; map, 50–51; sleeping, 131–132

Ill River: cruises, 986

Illuminated Lyon: 900

Impressionism: 75–77, 79–80, 86–87, 198–199, 201–202, 236

Ingres, Jean-Auguste-Dominique: 70, 74, 226

International Center for Cave Art (Lascaux): 472–473, 481–482

International Stained Glass Center (Chartres): 197

Internet security: 1085

Isenheim Altarpiece (Grünewald): 945–946

Isle-sur-la-Sorgue: 653–656

Italy: 797, 813

J

Jardin Anglais (Dinan): 319

Jardin Botanique (Monaco): 739

Jardin des Papillons (Hunawihr): 963

Jardin des Plantes (Paris): 89

Jardin d'Eze: 730

Jardin du Luxembourg (Paris): 89

Jardin du Rocher des Doms (Avignon): 604–605

Jardin Exotique (Monaco): 740

Jazz clubs, in Paris: 110–111

Jewish Art and History Museum (Paris): 45, 101

Jewish Quarter (Paris): 101–102; eating, 146–147

Joan of Arc: 212, 215, 219, 227, 884, 1034; biographical sketch, 218; Museum (Rouen), 224

Joan of Arc Church (Rouen): 215, 219

Joan of Arc Tower (Rouen): 227

John, Elton: 680

Joucas: sleeping, 658–659

Juan-les-Pins: 754

Juliénas: 926

Julien Bridge: 661–662

Jumièges Abbey: 228–229

Juno Beach: 292–293; map, 264–265

Juno Beach Centre (Courseulles): 292–293

K

Kayaking: *See* Canoeing
Kaysersberg: 962, 970–975
Kaysersberg History Museum: 973
Kientzheim: 975, 978–979
Koïfhus (Colmar): 936–937

L

La Basoche (Lyon): 909
La Belle Iloise (Dinan): 323
La Cambe: 286–287
La Capelière: 585–586
Lac Blanc (Alps): 805
Lace Conservatory (Bayeux): 256
La Cité (Carcassonne): 522, 527–531;
    eating, 537–538; map, 529; sleep-
    ing, 533–534
La Cité Médiévale (Rocamadour):
    493, 498
La Cité Religieuse (Rocamadour):
    493, 497–498
La Cohue (Dinan): 323
La Condamine (Monaco): 733
La Confluence (Lyon): 903, 917
Lacoste: 661
La Craquanterie (Dinan): 322
La Croix-Rousse (Lyon): 896, 903,
    914–915
La Défense (Paris): 94–95
La Digue de la Mer: 586–587
Ladurée (Paris): 109
Lady and the Unicorn tapestries: 45,
    57, 87–88
La Ferme de la Sapinière (Omaha
    Beach): 281
La Flégère Lift (Alps): 791, 799,
    801–802, 804–805
La Fleunie Château: 482
La Grande Arche (Paris): 94–95
La Maison de la Truffe (Paris): 108
La Marmite de l'Abbaye: 326
Langeais Château: 351, 418–420
Langrolay: sleeping, 329
Language: barrier and French at-
    titude, 16–17; coffee and tea lingo,
    1077–1078; hotel tip, 1055;
    online translation tip, 1043; Paris
    Métro, 29; picnic terms, 1065;
    pronunciation guide, 1124–1127;
    restaurant phrases, 1130; road
    signs, 1104–1105; survival phrases,
    1129; train terms, 1087; wine lingo,
    1079

Languedoc-Roussillon: 504–554; cui-
    sine, 506; map, 505; transportation,
    506. *See also specific destinations*
Lantern of the Dead (Sarlat): 439
La Petite France (Strasbourg):
    985–986
La Rochepot Château: 852–853, 858
La Roque-Gageac: 450, 452, 456–458
La Roque St-Christophe: 473,
    480–481
La Roquette (Arles): 582, 584
La Route des Anciennes Abbayes:
    228–229
La Route Napoléon: 666–667
Lascaux: 472–473, 481–482
Lastours Châteaux: 542
L'Atelier (Arles): 578, 594–595
Latin Quarter (Paris): 56–58
La Tour Eiffel (Paris): 16, 44, 80–83,
    112–113
La Turbie: 731–732
Lebrec Calvados (Omaha Beach):
    284
Le Brévent Gondola (Alps): 791,
    799–801
Le Bugue: market, 434
Le Caveau des Musignys: 862–863
Le Déjeuner sur l'Herbe (Manet):
    75–76
Left Bank (Paris): 21, 22, 87–91; eat-
    ing, 150–151; guided tours, 39–40;
    maps, 88, 149
Le Hameau Duboeuf (Romanèche-
    Thorins): 926–927
Le Havre: 167–168
Léhon: 326, 330
Le Mans Auto Race: 1115
Le Mémorial de Caen: 293–296
Le Mistral: 564
Le Musée Lapidaire (Avignon): 610
Leonardo da Vinci Park (Amboise):
    364–365
Le Paradou: sleeping, 631
Le Saut aux Loups: 425
Les Baux: 557, 625–632; map, 627
Les Baux Castle Ruins: 626, 628–629
Les Berges du Seine (Paris): 84
Les Bossons: sleeping, 815
Les Chemins de Lumières Light
    Show (Beaune): 837
Les Egouts de Paris: 83–84
Le Semnoz: 778–779

Les Eyzies-de-Tayac: 474–485; caves near, 477–484; market, 434; sleeping, 476

Les Grandes Eaux Musicales (Versailles): 177

Les Grands Montets: 811

Les Haras Nationaux (Cluny): 891

Les Houches: skiing, 811; sleeping, 815–816

Les Larmes de Jeanne d'Arc (Rouen): 219

Les Nuits de Fourvière (Lyon): 900, 908, 1115

Le Somail: sleeping, 537

Les Praz: 799, 801, 802, 804, 805, 808; sleeping, 815

Le Trophée des Alpes: 731–732

L'Hospitalet (Rocamadour): 493, 495

Liberty Leading the People (Delacroix): 70–71

Liberty Tree (Bayeux): 255

Lido (Paris): 93

Ligré: sleeping, 413

Limeray: sleeping, 373

L'Index Lift (Alps): 801–802, 805

Loire River: 345; biking along, 352–353, 368, 387, 390, 394; canoeing, 368

Loire Valley: 345–425; châteaux at a glance, 350–351; châteaux history, 366–367; cuisine, 354; home base, 345–348; map, 346–347; planning tips, 348–349; tours, 353–354; transportation, 349–353; wines, 354–355, 368–369, 390, 399, 405, 409–410. *See also* specific destinations

London: train travel, 165–166

Longest Day, The (movie): 269, 288, 290, 295, 1119

Longues-sur-Mer Gun Battery: 275–277

L'Orangerie (Paris): 44, 79–80

L'Ossuaire de Douaumont (Verdun): 1027–1028

Lot River Valley: 500–503

Loubressac: 492

Louis Vuitton (Paris): 93

Louis XIV (Sun King): 178–179, 1038; Versailles, 178–186

Lourmarin: market, 565

Louvois: 1012

Louvre Museum (Paris): 44, 63–71; map, 66

Low Corniche: 721–723; map, 722

Lower Town (Les Baux): 629–630

Luberon hill towns: 652–662; map, 654–655

Luge: 778, 802, 809

Lumière Museum (Lyon): 902, 916–917

Luncheon on the Grass (Manet): 75–76

Luxembourg Garden (Paris): 89

Lyon: 893–925, 896–897; at a glance, 902–903; cuisine, 894; eating, 920–925; helpful hints, 897, 900–901; maps, 898–899, 910, 922–923; money-saving tips, 896; nightlife, 917–918; orientation, 895; planning tips, 893–894; self-guided walk, 903–904; shopping, 914; sights/activities, 903–917; sleeping, 918–920; tourist information, 895–896; tours, 896; transportation, 901–902, 925

Lyon Airport: 897

Lyon City Card: 896, 912

Lyon History Museum: 911–912

Lyon Museum of Fine Arts: 902, 913

Lyon traboules: 909, 911

M

Madeloc Tower: 550–551

Maeght Foundation (St-Paul-de-Vence): 758–759

Magic, House of (Blois): 389

Maginot Monument (Verdun): 1026

Magny-les-Villers: 854, 861

MAHB (Bayeux): 256

Mail: 1085–1086. *See also specific destinations*

Maison de la Magie (Blois): 389

Maison de la Montagne (Chamonix): 792

Maison des Têtes (Colmar): 943–944

Maison du Chocolat (Paris): 109

Maison Forte de Reignac: 480

Maison Herzer (Kaysersberg): 974

Maison Pfister (Colmar): 941–942

Maisons Satie (Honfleur): 240–241

Malaucène: 638, 647

Manet, Edouard: 75, 610

Manoir de Gisson (Sarlat): 441

Manville Mansion City Hall (Les Baux): 629

Maps: legend, 2. *See also* Map Index

Marais (Paris): 22, 98–103, 124–125, 128; eating, 140–147; guided tours,

39–40; maps, 126–127, 142–143;
shopping, 108; sleeping, 128–131
Marie-Antoinette: 61, 62, 177, 179–
180, 183–184, 186, 1038–1039
Markets: 1066–1067; Albi, 509,
516; Amboise, 357; Annecy, 770;
Antibes, 745, 749–750; Arles, 567,
587; Avignon, 609, 619; Bayeux,
249; Beaune, 827; Beynac, 434,
460; Bourges, 882; Carcassonne,
526; Chamonix, 788; Chinon,
403; Cluny, 888; Collioure, 545;
Colmar, 934, 940; Dinan, 318–319;
Dinard, 337, 340; Domme, 434,
455; Dordogne, 432–434, 434;
Honfleur, 233; Isle-sur-la-Sorgue,
653, 654–655; Kaysersberg, 971;
Lyon, 897, 900; Martel, 490; Nice,
676, 689–690; Orange, 632–633;
Paris, 61, 84–85; Reims, 999,
1006–1007, 1018; Rouen, 214, 226;
Sarlat, 434, 435, 437, 440–441;
Strasbourg, 987; Vaison-la-Ro-
maine, 639; Vence, 760; Versailles,
188; Villefranche-sur-Mer, 712
Marmottan Museum (Paris): 45,
86–87
Martel (Reims): 1010
Martel (town): 490
Martigny, Switzerland: 791, 812
Mary Magdalene: 874, 877, 878
Masséna Museum (Nice): 682,
695–696
Massif Fortifié de Souville (Verdun):
1025–1026
Matisse, Henri: 102–103, 547,
551, 913; Chapel of the Rosary
(Vence), 761; Museum (Nice), 682,
694–695
Matterhorn: 796, 801, 803
Maussane: 631; eating, 632; sleeping,
631
Mayle, Peter: 564, 652, 661, 1117
Medical help: 1042, 1113–1114;
Paris, 25
Medieval Quarter (Bourges): 881, 884
Mémorial de Caen: 293–296
Mémorial de la Déportation (Paris):
54–55
Mémorial de la Shoah (Paris): 102
Mémorial de Verdun: 1026–1027
Mémorial Musée de Fleury (Verdun):
1027
Mémorial 39/45 Museum (Alet): 337

Ménerbes: 661
Menthon-St-Bernard: 778
Menton: 732
Mercedes-Benz (Paris): 93
Mer de Glace (Alps): 791, 798–799,
803–804
Merveilles Cave: 495
Meter Man (Colmar): 942
Metric system: 1120–1121
Métro (Paris): 26–29, 118, 125; Cité
"Metropolitain" stop, 61
Meursault: 850, 856
Middle Corniche: 722–723; map, 722
Minerve: 542–543
Mini-Châteaux (Amboise): 365, 368
Mirabel: 643
Miró, Joan: 95, 551, 759
Mistral, Frédéric: 580–581
Mistral winds: 564
Mobile phones: 17, 1080–1084
Modern and Contemporary Art
Museum (Nice): 682, 695
Modern-Art Museum (Céret): 551
Moët et Chandon (Epernay): 1015
Monaco: 732–743; eating, 742; help-
ful hints, 736–737; map, 734–735;
self-guided walk, 737–740; sights/
activities, 737–741; sleeping,
741–742; tourist information, 733;
transportation, 733, 736, 742–743
Monaco Cathedral: 739
Monaco Grand Prix: 666, 698, 732,
738, 1114
Monaco Philharmonic Orchestra: 736
Monaco-Ville: 733, 737–740, 743
Mona Lisa (da Vinci): 69
Monet, Claude: 76, 221, 226, 236,
913, 947, 1039; Giverny, 198–199,
201–202; Marmottan Museum
(Paris), 45, 86–87; Orangerie
Museum (Paris), 44, 79–80
Money: 1043–1048; budgeting,
12–13
Money-saving tips: 1043; Arles, 567;
Avignon, 597; Lyon, 896; Paris,
42–43, 46, 56–57, 133; Riviera,
665–666; sleeping, 1052–1053;
Strasbourg, 980–981
Mont-Alban Fort: 718
Mont Blanc: 764, 791
Monte Carlo: *See* Monaco
Monte Carlo Ballet: 736
Monte Carlo Casino: 740–741

Montenvers: 791, 798–799, 803–804, 816

Montfort: 450, 454

Montignac: 481; eating, 482; market, 434

Montmartre (Paris): 22, 45, 104–106; eating, 151–152; map, 105

Montmartre Museum (Paris): 106

Montparnasse Tower (Paris): 90–91

Mont Rouge: 657

Mont St-Michel: 210, 296–313; eating, 311–312; helpful hints, 300; maps, 299, 301; sights/activities, 300–308; sleeping, 309–311; tourist information, 297; transportation, 297–299, 312–313

Mont St-Michel Abbey: 303–308

Mont St-Michel Bay: 297, 300–302

Mont St-Michel Ramparts: 308

Montsec Monument (St-Mihiel): 1030

Mont Ventoux: 604–605, 637

Monument to the Dying Lion (Verdun): 1026

Morey-St-Denis: 863

Morrison, Jim: 103

Mortemart: 487

Mountaineering Center (Chamonix): 812

Moutarderie Fallot (Beaune): 838

Movies, recommended: 1118–1120

Moyenne Corniche: 722–723; map, 722

Mumm (Reims): 1008

Musée Alpin (Chamonix): 812

Musée Angladon (Avignon): 610

Musée Animé du Vin (Chinon): 405, 410, 414

Musée Archéologique: See Archaeological museums

Musée Calvet (Avignon): 610

Musée Carnavalet (Paris): 99

Musée-Château d'Annecy: 774

Musée d'Art et d'Histoire Baron Gérard (Bayeux): 256

Musée d'Art et d'Histoire du Judaïsme (Paris): 45, 101

Musée d'Art Moderne de Céret: 551

Musée d'Art Moderne et d'Art Contemporain (Nice): 682, 695

Musée de la Communication (Riquewihr): 978

Musée de la Reddition (Reims): 999, 1007

Musée de l'Armée (Paris): 44–45, 85–86

Musée de l'Hôtel de Ville (Amboise): 361–362

Musée de l'Orangerie (Paris): 44, 79–80

Musée de Montmartre (Paris): 106

Musée Départemental Arles Antiques: 582–584

Musée des Beaux-Arts: Lyon, 902, 913; Nice, 682, 695; Rouen, 226–227; Strasbourg, 985

Musée des Confluences (Lyon): 917

Musée des Cristaux (Chamonix): 812

Musée d'Ethnographie et d'Art Populaire Normand (Honfleur): 241

Musée d'Histoire et d'Archéologie (Antibes): 750, 752

Musée d'Orsay (Paris): 44, 72–79; map, 73

Musée du Débarquement (Arromanches): 272–273

Musée du Débarquement (Utah Beach): 289–290

Musée du Louvre (Paris): 44, 63–71; map, 66

Musée du Petit Palais (Avignon): 604

Musée du Vin de Bourgogne (Beaune): 837

Musée Lapidaire (Avignon): 610

Musée le Secq des Tournelles (Rouen): 227

Musée Lumière (Lyon): 902, 916–917

Musée Marmottan Monet (Paris): 45, 86–87

Musée Masséna (Nice): 682, 695–696

Musée Matisse (Nice): 682, 694–695

Musée Mémorial de la Bataille de Normandie (Bayeux): 256–257

Musée Mémorial d'Omaha Beach: 281

Musée National d'Art Moderne (Paris): 102–103

Musée National de Préhistoire (Les Eyzies): 472, 475–476

Musée National du Moyen Age (Paris): 45, 57, 87–88

Musée National March Chagall (Nice): 682, 692–694

Musée Océanographique (Monaco): 739–740

Musée Picasso (Antibes): 751–752

Musée Picasso (Paris): 44, 99–101

Musée Réattu (Arles): 584–585

Musée Rodin (Paris): 45, 86

Musées des Tissus et des Arts Décoratifs (Lyon): 903, 913–914

Musées Gadagne (Lyon): 903, 911–912

Musée Toulouse-Lautrec (Albi): 513–515

Musée Yves Brayer (Les Baux): 629

MuséoParc Alésia (Alise-Ste-Reine): 866

Museums: sightseeing tips, 1050–1051. *See also specific museums*

Museum of Annecy: 772, 774

Museum of Ceramics (Rouen): 227

Museum of Decorative Arts (Strasbourg): 985

Museum of Ethnography (Honfleur): 241

Museum of Impressionisms (Giverny): 202

Museum of Ironworks (Rouen): 227

Museum of Santons (Les Baux): 630

Museum of the Sea (Honfleur): 241

Museum of the Surrender (Reims): 999, 1007

Museum of the Wine of Burgundy (Beaune): 837

Museum Pass (Paris): 42–43, 46, 56

Museums of Textiles and Decorative Arts (Lyon): 903, 913–914

Mushroom caves: 425

Mustard Mill (Beaune): 838

N

Napoleon Bonaparte: 69–70, 94, 186, 688, 722, 891, 1034, 1039; Tomb (Paris), 44–45, 85–86

Narbonne Gate (Carcassonne): 527

National Guard Memorial (Omaha Beach): 283–284

National Museum of Prehistory (Les Eyzies): 472, 475–476

National Stud Farm (Cluny): 891

Nazelles-Négron: sleeping, 373

Nice: 672–711; at a glance, 682; arrival in, 673, 676; eating, 703–708; helpful hints, 676–677; maps, 674–675, 686–687, 699, 706; nightlife, 697; orientation, 673; self-guided walk, 681–692; sights/activities, 681–697; sleeping, 697–703; tourist information, 673; tours, 679–680; transportation, 673, 676, 677–679, 708–711

Nice Airport: 709–710; sleeping near, 703

Nice Archaeological Museum: 695

Nice Carnival: 666, 698

Nice Fine Arts Museum: 682, 695

Nice Jazz Festival: 1115

Nice Modern and Contemporary Art Museum: 682, 695

Nightlife: budgeting, 12–13. *See also specific destinations*

Normandy: 207–313, 209–210; at a glance, 210; cuisine, 210–211; map, 208–209; planning tips, 207–208. *See also* D-Day beaches

Normandy American Cemetery and Memorial (Omaha Beach): 277–280

Normandy Bridge: 209, 228–229, 242

Normandy Memorial Museum (Bayeux): 256–257

Norman Popular Arts (Honfleur): 241

Notre-Dame Cathedral (Chartres): 191–196; map, 193

Notre-Dame Cathedral (Paris): 44, 48–49, 52–54, 113

Notre-Dame Cathedral (Reims): 1000–1004

Notre-Dame Cathedral (Rouen): 214, 221–224

Notre-Dame Cathedral (Strasbourg): 983–984

Notre-Dame Church (Semur-en-Auxois): 871

Notre-Dame de Fourvière (Lyon): 902, 904–906

Notre-Dame de Grâce Chapel (Honfleur): 241

Notre-Dame de l'Annonciation (Nice): 691

Notre-Dame des Anges (Collioure): 547

Notre-Dame des Anges Church (Isle-sur-la-Sorgue): 654

Notre-Dame de Sénanque Abbey: 660

Nuits de Fourvière (Lyon): 900, 908, 1115

Nuits-St-Georges: 861

Nyons: market, 565

O

Oceanography Museum (Monaco): 739–740

Ochre Cliffs Trail (Roussillon): 657

Ochre Conservatory (Roussillon): 657–658

Old Lyon: *See* Vieux Lyon

Old Market Hall (Colmar): 940

Old Nice: *See* Vieux Nice

Old Town (Colmar): 932, 936–944; eating, 954–955; map, 938–939

Olive oil: 433, 546, 689, 705

Omaha Beach: 275–288; map, 264–265, 276; sleeping near, 287–288

Omaha Beach Memorial Museum: 281

Open Sky Museum (Utah Beach): 291

Opéra Bastille (Paris): 112

Opéra Garnier (Paris): 45, 96–97, 112

Opera, in Paris: 45, 96–97, 112

Oppède-le-Vieux: 660–661

Oradour-sur-Glane: 485–487

Orange: 557, 632–637; map, 633

Orange City Hall: 636

Orangerie Museum (Paris): 44, 79–80

Orange Roman Theater: 634–636

Orches: 858

Orly Airport (Paris): 157–158; sleeping, 132

Orsay Museum (Paris): 44, 72–79; map, 73

Our Lady of Rocamadour: 497–498

Overlord Museum (Omaha Beach): 280–281

P

Packing checklist: 1123

Padirac Cave: 499

Palace of the Popes (Avignon): 604, 606–607

Palace Square (Avignon): 603–604

Palace Square (Monaco): 737–738

Palais de Justice (Paris): 60

Palais de Justice (Rouen): 221

Palais de la Méditerranée (Nice): 684

Palais de l'Isle (Annecy): 774

Palais des Papes (Avignon): 604, 606–607

Palais du Tau (Reims): 1004–1005

Palais Jacques Cœur (Bourges): 884

Palais Jean de Bourbon (Cluny): 890

Palais Lascaris (Nice): 691

Palais Princier (Monaco): 738

Palais Rohan (Strasbourg): 984, 985

Palais Royal (Paris): 71

Panthéon (Paris): 45, 89–90

Paradou: sleeping, 631

Paragliding: 779, 808, 809

Parc de la Bouzaize (Beaune): 838

Parc de la Tête d'Or (Lyon): 901, 906

Parc de Loisirs des Planards (Chamonix): 789, 802, 809

Parc de Merlet (Chamonix): 802

Parc des Buttes-Chaumont (Paris): 89

Parc des Cigognes (Hunawihr): 963

Parc Monceau (Paris): 89

Paris: 20–168; at a glance, 44–45; arrondisements, 21–22; eating, 133–152; entertainment, 110–116; excursion areas, 169–206; helpful hints, 24–26; money-saving tips, 42–43, 46, 56–57, 133; nightlife, 110–116; orientation, 21–22; planning tips, 20–21; self-guided walks, 48–63, 92–94, 112–113; shopping, 97–98, 106–109; sights, 63–106; sightseeing strategies, 42–43, 46–48; sleeping, 116–133; tourist information, 22–23; tours, 35–42, 113, 116; transportation, 26–35, 152–168. *See also specific neighborhoods*

Paris Archaeological Crypt: 54

Paris Catacombs: 91

Pariscope: 23, 110, 111

Paris Ferris Wheel: 94

Paris Métro: *See* Métro

Paris Museum Pass: 42–43, 46, 56

Paris Plages: 63

Paris Sewers: 83–84

Park Couttet (Chamonix): 793

Parthenon Friezes: 67

Passports: 15, 1042

Path of Fauvism (Collioure): 547

Patriarche Père et Fils (Beaune): 839

Pech Merle Cave: 473, 502

Penitents Chapel (Les Baux): 630

Père Lachaise Cemetery (Paris): 45, 103–104

Perfume: 107, 730

Pernand-Vergelesses: 860–861

Perreux Château: 372

Petit Balcon Sud (Alps): 805, 808

Petite Venise (Colmar): 940, 950; eating, 953

Petit Palais Museum (Avignon): 604

Peugeot (Paris): 93

Peyrepertuse Château: 540, 541
Pfister House (Colmar): 941–942
Philip the Fair Tower (Villeneuve): 611
Phone numbers, useful: 1113–1114
Phones: 1080–1084
Piaf, Edith: 103
Picasso, Pablo: 102–103, 551, 913, 947; Museum (Antibes), 751–752; Museum (Paris), 44, 99–101
Pickpockets: *See* Theft alerts
Picnics: 1064–1067; vocabulary, 1065. *See also* Markets
Pigalle (Paris): 106
Piscine du Centre Sportif Richard Bozon (Chamonix): 802
Place Albert I (Antibes): 744, 750
Place Balmat (Chamonix): 793
Place Benjamin Zix (Strasbourg): 986
Place Charles de Gaulle (Bayeux): 255
Place d'Armes (Monaco): 737
Place de la Liberté (Sarlat): 440–441
Place de la Madeleine (Paris): 97–98, 108
Place de la Mairie (Roussillon): 657
Place de la République (Arles): 576
Place de l'Horloge (Avignon): 602–603
Place de l'Opéra (Paris): 109
Place des Châtaignes (Avignon): 608, 618
Place des Merciers (Dinan): 322–323
Place des Oies (Sarlat): 441
Place des Terreaux (Lyon): 912–913
Place des Vosges (Paris): 99, 128; eating, 141
Place Drouet d'Erlon (Reims): 998–999, 1017
Place du Centenaire (Eze): 729
Place du Change (Lyon): 911
Place du Forum (Arles): 580–581, 592–593
Place du Forum (Reims): 999, 1006; eating, 1017–1018
Place du Général de Gaulle (Chinon): 405
Place du Grand Puits (Carcassonne): 531
Place du Guesclin (Dinan): 319–320
Place du Palais (Avignon): 603–604
Place du Palais (Monaco): 737–738
Place du Peyrou (Sarlat): 438
Place du Tertre (Paris): 106

Place du Trocadéro (Paris): 81, 112–113
Place du Vieux Marché (Rouen): 215
Place Louis Lépine (Paris): 61
Place Masséna (Nice): 673, 688–689
Place Nautique (Lyon): 917
Place Rossetti (Nice): 692
Place Ste. Cécile (Albi): 510
Place St. Marc (Rouen): 214, 226
Place St. Michel (Paris): 57–58
Place Vendôme (Paris): 98, 109
Plage d'Albigny (Annecy): 774
Plage de la Gravette (Antibes): 748–749, 752
Plage de la Paloma (Cap Ferrat): 726, 727
Plage de la Salis (Antibes): 752, 753
Plage de Passable (Cap Ferrat): 726, 727
Plage d'Imperial (Annecy): 774
Plage Municipal de Sevrier (Annecy): 774
Plague Cemetery (Rouen): 225–226
Plan de l'Aiguille (Alps): 797–798, 799, 803–804
Planpraz (Alps): 791, 800–801, 804–805
Poilâne (Paris): 109
Pointe du Chevet: 342
Pointe du Grouin: 343
Pointe du Hoc: 285–286
Pointe Helbronner: 789, 794, 797, 813
Pôle International de la Préhistoire (Les Eyzies): 472, 474–475
Politics: 1035–1037, 1040
Pommard: 849
Pompidou Center (Paris): 45, 102–103
Pont Bonaparte (Lyon): 903–904
Pont d'Avignon (pont St. Bénezet): 605–606
Pont de Normandie: 209, 228–229, 242
Pont des Arts (Paris): 63
Pont du Gard: 557, 620–625; map, 621
Pont Julien: 661–662
Pont Neuf (Paris): 63
Pont Valentré (Cahors): 502–503
Pont Vieux (Carcassonne): 531–532
Population: xviii
Port de Lyvet: 326, 327
Porte de Dinan (St-Malo): 336

Porte de Mars (Reims): 999, 1006
Porte des Champs (St-Malo): 336
Port-en-Bessin: 277
Porte St. Pierre (St-Malo): 336
Port Winston Artificial Harbor (Arromanches): 271–272
Post offices: 1085–1086. *See also specific destinations*
Pouilly: 926
Pouilly-en-Auxois: 874
Pouilly-Fuissé: 825, 850
Pray Château: 372, 376
Prehistoric caves: *See* Cro-Magnon caves
Prehistory Welcome Center (Les Eyzies-de-Tayac): 472, 474–475
Presqu'île (Lyon): 895, 914, 917; eating, 914, 924–925; map, 922–923; nightlife, 918; sleeping, 918–920
Prince's Palace (Monaco): 738
Printemps (Paris): 107
Printemps de Bourges: 882
Promenade des Anglais (Nice): 673, 681, 682, 683–685, 697; sleeping, 701–703
Promenade du Paillon (Nice): 688–689
Pronunciation guide: 1124–1127
Provence: 555–662; at a glance, 557; cuisine, 563–564; maps, 556, 557; market days, 565; planning tips, 555–557; tours, 559–561; transportation, 557–559. *See also specific destinations*
Puligny-Montrachet: 850–851, 856–857
Puppets of the World Museum (Lyon): 911–912
Puycelsi: 520–521
Puyméras: 644
Puymin: 641–642

Q
Quai de la Bruche (Strasbourg): 986
Quai de l'Horloge (Paris): 62
Quartier Latin (Paris): *See* Latin Quarter
Quéribus: 541–542

R
Rabanel, Jean-Luc: 594–595
Rabelais, François: 404–405, 410
Rail passes: 12, 15, 1087, 1090, 1093–1096, 1110

Rail travel: *See* Train travel
Rance River: cruises, 326–327
Rance River Valley: 325–326
Reader feedback: 15
Réattu Museum (Arles): 584–585
Refuge-Grand Hôtel du Montenvers: 799, 816
Refuge-Hôtel La Flégère: 791, 816
Refuge-Plan de l'Aiguille: 797–798, 816
Reims: 992–1019; cuisine, 991–992; eating, 1017–1018; helpful hints, 995; map, 996–997; planning tips, 992–993; sights/activities, 998–1015; sleeping, 1015–1017; tourist information, 994; transportation, 990–991, 994–995, 998, 1019
Reims Cathedral: 999, 1000–1004
Renault (Paris): 93
Renoir, Pierre-Auguste: 76–77, 87, 226, 947
Rental properties: *See* Apartment rentals
RER (Réseau Express Régionale): 26–27, 29–30, 155–156, 158, 159, 171, 205
Resistance and Deportation History Center (Lyon): 902, 915–916
Resources from Rick Steves: 1110–1111
Restaurants: *See* Eating; *and specific destinations*
Rhône River: 599, 605–606, 618, 893, 901, 917
Rhône Valley: 926–927
Ribeauvillé: 963
Riquewihr: 962, 975, 976–979
Rivau Château: 411–412
Riviera: 663–763; at a glance, 665; art scene, 671; cuisine, 671–672; helpful hints, 665–667; home base, 663–664; maps, 664, 667; planning tips, 664; transportation, 667–671. *See also specific destinations*
Rocamadour: 492–500; map, 491
Rocamadour Château: 495
Roc de Chère: 777–778
Rodin, Auguste: 78–79, 913; Museum (Paris), 45, 86
RoissyBus: 155
Roman Bridge (Julien): 661–662
Roman Bridge (Vaison-la-Romaine): 639, 642
Romanèche-Thorins: 926–927

Roman sites (ancient Romans): 361, 527, 562–563, 721, 867; Alise Ste-Reine, 865–866; Arles, 565, 573–574, 582–584, 1031; Lyon, 906–908; Orange, 632, 634–636; Paris, 54; Pont du Gard, 620, 623–624; Pont Julien, 661–662; Reims, 1006; Vaison-la-Romaine, 641–642

Roman theaters: See Théâtre Antique

Roque St-Christophe: 473, 480–481

Rosary, Chapel of the (Vence): 761

Rothéneuf: 342–343

Roue de Paris (Paris): 94

Rouen: 210, 212–231; eating, 230–231; helpful hints, 214; map, 216–217; planning tips, 212; self-guided walk, 215–226; sights/activities, 226–229; sleeping, 229; tourist information, 213; transportation, 213–214, 231

Rouen Great Clock: 220–221

Rouen Museum of Fine Arts: 226–227

Rouffignac Cave: 473, 482–484

Rousseau, Jean-Jacques: 90, 383, 773

Roussillon: 657–659

Route de la Champagne (Reims): 1010, 1012–1015; map, 1013

Route des Anciennes Abbayes: 228–229

Route des Bastides Albigeoises: 519–521

Route des Grands Crus: 855, 861–864; map, 857

Route du Beaujolais: 926–927

Route du Vin (Alsace): 955–964; map, 957

Route Napoléon: 666–667

Route of the Ancient Abbeys: 228–229

Route of the Bastides: 519–521

Royal Abbey of Fontevraud: 423–425

Rue Cler (Paris): 44, 84–85, 117–119; eating, 134–140; maps, 120–121, 138–139; sleeping, 119–124

Rue Daguerre (Paris): 91

Rue de la Cavalerie (Arles): 572

Rue de la Cordonnerie (Dinan): 323

Rue de la Monnaie (Lyon): 918

Rue de la Paix (Paris): 109

Rue de la Poissonnerie (Nice): 690–691

Rue de la République (Annecy): 772, 774

Rue de la République (Arles): 578–579

Rue de la République (Sarlat): 442

Rue de la Salamandre (Sarlat): 439–440

Rue des Rosiers (Paris): 101; eating, 146–147

Rue des Saules (Paris): 106

Rue des Teinturiers (Avignon): 609, 617

Rue Droite (Nice): 691–692

Rue du Docteur Fanton (Arles): 580, 593–594

Rue du Jerzual (Dinan): 323–324

Rue du Mont Cenis (Paris): 106

Rue Gutenberg (Strasbourg): 985–986

Rue Jeanne d'Arc (Rouen): 219

Rue Masséna (Nice): 697

Rue Nationale (Amboise): 361

Rue Obscure (Villefranche): 716–717

Rue Royale (Paris): 109

Rue St. François de Paule (Nice): 689

Rue St. Honoré (Paris): 109

Rue Voltaire (Chinon): 405

Russian Cathedral (Nice): 682, 696

RV rentals: 1100

Ryes: sleeping, 274

S

Sables-d'Or-les-Pins: 340

Sablet: 648

Sacré-Cœur (Paris): 45, 104–106

St. Aubin: 857

St. Bénezet Bridge (Avignon): 605–606

St. Catherine Church (Honfleur): 237–238

St. Catherine's Tower (Dinan): 324

St-Cirq Lapopie: 500–502

St-Cyprien: market, 433–434

St-Denis Church (Amboise): 361

Ste. Cécile Cathedral (Albi): 510–513

Sainte-Chapelle (Paris): 44, 58–60, 111; map, 59

Ste. Madeleine Basilica (Vézelay): 876–879

Ste-Mère Eglise: 290–291

St-Emilion: 487–489

St. Etienne Cathedral (Bourges): 882–884

St. Francois de Sales Church (Annecy): 772

St. Genest Church (Flavigny): 868

St-Geniès: market, 434

St. Georges de Boscherville Abbey: 228

St-Jacut-de-la-Mer: 342

St-Jean-Cap-Ferrat: 726–727

St. Jean Cathedral (Lyon): 903, 908–909

St-Jeannet: 762

St-Laurent-sur-Mer: 280–281

St. Leo IX Chapel (Eguisheim): 968

St. Louis Cathedral (Blois): 390

St. Maclou Church (Rouen): 224–225

St-Malo: 332–339; map, 335

St-Malo Ramparts: 332, 334, 336

St-Marcellin-lès-Vaison: 644, 646

St. Martin Church (Colmar): 942–943

St. Michael's Chapel (Rocamadour): 497–498

St. Michael's Church (Chamonix): 792

St. Michel Church (Roussillon): 657

St-Mihiel: 1029–1030

St. Nazaire Church (Carcassonne): 530

St. Nicholas Church (Blois): 390

St-Paul-de-Vence: 757–759

St. Peter's Cathedral (Annecy): 772

St. Peter's Church (Mont St-Michel): 303

St. Pierre Chapel (Villefranche): 716

St. Pierre Church (Avignon): 607–608

St. Réparate Cathedral (Nice): 692

St-Romain: 858

St. Sacerdos Cathedral (Sarlat): 439

St. Salvy Church and Cloister (Albi): 516

St. Sauveur Church (Dinan): 324–325

St. Saveur Church (Rocamadour): 498

St-Suliac: 326

St. Sulpice Church (Fougères): 344

St. Sulpice Church (Paris): 88–89

St. Trophime Church (Arles): 576–578

St. Trophime Cloisters (Arles): 578

St. Vincent Church (Les Baux): 629–630

Salin de Giraud: 585

Salvador Dalí Theater-Museum (Figueres): 551

Sanctuary of Our Lady of Rocamadour: 497–498

Santons Museum (Les Baux): 630

Sarlat-la-Canéda: 434–448; eating, 446–448; helpful hints, 435, 437–438; maps, 436, 445; market, 434, 435, 437, 440–441; self-guided walk, 438–442; sleeping, 442–446; tourist information, 435; transportation, 435, 448

Satie (Erik) Museum (Honfleur): 240–241

Savigny-lès-Beaune: 854–855, 861

Savoie: See Alps; Chamonix

Schweitzer, Albert: 962; biographical sketch, 972; Museum (Kaysersberg), 974–975

Seasons: 13–14

Séguret: 647–648

Seine River: 21, 55–56, 63, 84, 228, 241–242, 360; beaches, in Paris, 63; cruises, 38–39, 111

Semur-en-Auxois: 871–872, 874

Sensation Vin (Beaune): 839

Sentier Touristique de Tirepoil: 753–754

Sewers of Paris: 83–84

Shakespeare and Company (Paris): 25–26, 56

Shopping: budgeting, 13; clothing sizes, 1121; hours, 1043; Paris, 97–98, 106–109; VAT refunds, 1047–1048. See also specific destinations

Sightseeing: budgeting, 12–13; planning tips, 1049–1051; priorities, 13; three-week trips, 8–11. See also specific sights and destinations

Sigolsheim: 975

SIM cards: 1083–1084

Skiing, in Chamonix: 810–811

Sleep code: 1052

Sleeping: 1051–1062; air-conditioning, 1056; budgeting, 12; hotel chains, 1056–1057; online reviews, 1060; rates and deals, 1052–1053; reservations, 15, 1058–1059; types of accommodations, 1034–1062. See also specific destinations

Sleeping Beauty castle (Ussé): 412

Smartphones: 17, 1080–1084

Sorbonne (Paris): 57

Sorgue River: 653, 654

Souillac: market, 434

Spain: day trip, 551

Special events: 1114–1115. *See also specific destinations*

Stained Glass Center, International (Chartres): 197

Stein, Gertrude: 103

Steves, Andy: 41

Strasbourg: 979–989; map, 980–981

Strasbourg Archaeological Museum: 985

Strasbourg Cathedral: 983–984

Strasbourg-Entzheim Airport: 982

Strasbourg Museum of Fine Arts: 985

Suzette: 650

Switzerland: 812; car travel, 766; hiking, 808–809; Martigny, 791, 812

Sword of Roland: 497

Synagogue, Avignon: 608

T

Taittinger (Reims): 1009–1010

Taizé: 891–892

Talloires: 777–778

Tanners' Quarter (Colmar): 937, 940

Tapisserie de Bayeux: 252–254

Taxes: VAT refunds, 1047–1048

Taxis: Paris, 32–34, 116; to/from airports, 156–157, 158; tipping, 1047. *See also specific destinations*

Téléphériques: See Gondolas, in Chamonix

Telephone numbers, useful: 1113–1114

Telephones: 1080–1084

Temperatures, average monthly: 1122

TGV trains: 15–16, 165, 1086–1087; map, 1088–1089

Thalys Train: 165

Théâtre Antique (Roman Theater): Arles, 575–576; Lyon, 902, 906–908; Orange, 634–636

Théâtre des Jacobins (Dinan): 320–321

Theft alerts: 1042; Nice, 676; Paris, 24, 82

Thermes de Constantin (Arles): 584

Thiaucourt: 1030

Time zones: 1042–1043

Tintin (comic strip): 399

Tipping: 1047

Tomb of the Unknown Soldier (Paris): 94

Toulouse-Lautrec, Henri: 75, 106; Museum (Albi), 513–515

Tour de France: 1115

Tour de Madeloc: 550–551

Tour Eiffel (Paris): 16, 44, 80–83, 112–113

Tour guides: 17. *See also specific destinations*

Tourist information: 1041–1042. *See also specific destinations*

Tour Jeanne d'Arc (Rouen): 227

Tour Métallique (Lyon): 903–904

Tour Montparnasse (Paris): 90–91

Tour Philippe-le-Bel (Villeneuve): 611

Tours: Rick Steves, 1110. *See also specific destinations*

Tours-sur-Marne: 1013

Traboules: 909, 911

Train stations, in Paris: 160–165; map, 161

Train travel: 1086–1096; best three-week trip, 10–11; general tips, 1093, 1096; glossary of terms, 1087; map, 1088–1089; Paris, 160–166; reservations, 1091–1093; schedules, 1087; tickets, 1090–1091. *See also specific destinations*

Tranchée des Baïonnettes (Verdun): 1028–1029

Trans Côte d'Azur: 671, 679, 680

Transportation: 1086–1110; budgeting, 12. *See also* Boat cruises; Buses; Car travel; Train travel; *and specific destinations*

Travel insurance: 15

Travel smarts: 5, 10–12

Travel tips: 1042–1043

Treverien: 326

Trianon Palaces (Versailles): 170–171, 175, 183–186

Trip costs: 12–13

Trophée des Alpes: 731–732

Truffles: 108, 431, 432, 437, 441, 464–465, 661

Tuileries Garden (Paris): 63, 79

Turckheim: 962

U

Uber: 1097–1098; Nice, 678; Paris, 32, 116, 156–157

Unicorn tapestries: 45, 57, 87–88

Unterlinden Museum (Colmar): 944–947

Ussé Château: 412
Utah Beach: 288–292; map, 264–265
Utah Beach Landing Museum: 289–290
Uzès: market, 565

V

Vaison-la-Romaine: 557, 638–646; eating, 645–646; helpful hints, 639–641; map, 640; sights/activities, 641–644; sleeping, 644–645; tourist information, 639; transportation, 639, 646
Valle d'Aosta, Italy: 813
Vallée Blanche: 811
Vandenesse-en-Auxois: 865
Van der Weyden, Roger: 836
Van Gogh, Vincent: 77–78, 610; in Arles, 565, 570–573, 575, 579–580, 581–582
VAT refunds: 1047–1048
Vedettes du Pont Neuf (Paris): 39
Vegetarians: 1070
Vélib' Bikes (Paris): 34–35
Vence: 760–763
Venus de Milo: 67
Vercingétorix: 866, 867, 1038
Verdun: 1019–1022; transportation, 990–991
Verdun Battlefields: 1019, 1022–1030; background, 1023–1024; driving tour, 1024–1029; map, 1025; tours, 1023; transportation, 1020, 1022–1023
Verdun Memorial Museum: 1026–1027
Vernon: 200, 203
Verrerie d'Art de Kaysersberg: 972
Versailles: 169–188; eating, 188; maps, 172–173, 187; orientation, 174–177; planning tips, 171, 174; self-guided tour, 177–186; sleeping, 186–188; transportation, 171
Versailles Château: 44, 168–169, 174, 177–182; map, 181
Versailles Gardens: 169, 175, 177, 183
Ver-sur-Mer: sleeping, 274
Veuve Clicquot Ponsardin (Reims): 1010
Vézelay: 875–879
Victoire de Samothrace: 67
Victory Monument (Verdun): 1021
Vieil-Armand WWI Memorial (Eguisheim): 961
Vienne River: 403, 404; canoeing, 403, 411; cruises, 404
Vierville-sur-Mer: 284; sleeping, 287–288
Vieux Bassin (Honfleur): 233, 236
Vieux Lyon: 895, 902, 908–912; eating, 920–921, 924; maps, 910, 922–923; sleeping, 918–919
Vieux Nice: 673, 682, 685–692; eating, 703–705; map, 686–687; sleeping, 701
Villa Ephrussi de Rothschild (Cap Ferrat): 725
Village des Martyrs (Oradour-sur-Glane): 485–487
Village Détruit de Fleury (Verdun): 1027
Villa Kérylos: 727
Villa La Leopolda (Villefranche-sur-Mer): 722
Villa Masséna (Nice): 682–683
Villandry: 420–422; eating, 414, 420–422, 422
Villandry Château: 351
Ville Basse (Carcassonne): 522, 525, 527–528, 530, 538
Ville-Basse (Vaison-la-Romaine): 639, 642
Villedieu: 643–644; eating, 646; sleeping, 645
Villefranche-sur-Mer: 711–721; map, 714–715
Villefranche-sur-Mer Citadel: 717
Villefranche-sur-Saône: 926
Ville-Haute (Vaison-la-Romaine): 639, 642–643
Villeneuve Château (Vence): 760
Villeneuve-lès-Avignon: 611
Villers-Bocage: sleeping, 259
Vineyards: *See* Wine and vineyards
Visitor information: 1041–1042. *See also specific destinations*
Vitrac: 451, 452
Volnay: 856
Vosne-Romanée: 862
Vougeot: 862
Vouvray: 355, 368–369

W

Walking: *See* Hiking
Way of the Cross (Rocamadour): 493, 495

INDEX

Weather: 13–14, 1121–1122

Weekend Student Adventures: 41

Western Emerald Coast: 340–344

Wilde, Oscar: 103

Wine and vineyards: 1078–1080; Beaujolais, 894, 926–927; Bordeaux, 487–489; Côtes du Rhône, 637–638, 643, 647–651; Languedoc-Roussillon, 506, 547–548; Loire Valley, 354–355, 368–369, 390, 399, 405, 409–410; Lyon, 894, 900; Paris, 145; Provence, 559–560, 564–565; Riviera, 672; savoring tactics, 1078; vocabulary, 1079. *See also* Alsatian wines; Burgundy wines; Champagne

Wine Road (Alsace): *See* Route du Vin

Winged Victory of Samothrace: 67

World War I: 85, 520, 887, 972–973, 999, 1006, 1035; Verdun Battlefields, 1019, 1022–1030; Vieil-Armand WWI Memorial (Eguisheim), 961

World War II: 85–86, 90, 247, 932, 962, 972–976, 1035; Deportation Memorial (Paris), 54–55; Holocaust Memorial (Paris), 102; Museum of the Surrender (Reims), 999, 1007; Normandy Memorial Museum (Bayeux), 256–257; Resistance and Deportation History Center (Lyon), 902, 915–916; Village des Martyrs (Oradour-sur-Glane), 485–487. *See also* D-Day beaches

WSA Europe: 41

Y

Yves Brayer Museum (Les Baux): 629

Z

Zellenberg: 963

MAP INDEX

Color Maps
France: IV–V
West Paris: VI–VII
East Paris: VIII–IX
Paris Métro: 10

Introduction
Map Legend: 2
Top Destinations in France: 4
Whirlwind Three-Week Tour of
    France by Car: 9

Paris
Paris Arrondisements: 21
Paris Neighborhoods: 23
Scenic Bus Routes: 36-37
Paris : 46–47
Notre-Dame Facade: 49
Historic Paris Walk: 50–51
Sainte-Chapelle: 59
Major Museums Neighborhood: 64
Louvre Overview: 66
Orsay Museum—Ground Floor: 73
Eiffel Tower & Nearby: 81
Left Bank: 88
Champs-Elysées Area: 92–93
Opéra Neighborhood: 97
Montmartre: 105
Floodlit Paris Driving Tour: 114
Rue Cler Hotels: 120–121
Marais Hotels: 126–127
Rue Cler Restaurants: 138–139
Marais Restaurants: 142–143
Restaurants on the Left Bank: 149
Charles de Gaulle Airport: 153
Paris' Train Stations: 161
Eurostar Routes: 166

Near Paris
Near Paris: 170
Versailles: 172–173
Versailles Château—Ground Floor
    & Entrances: 181
Domaine de Marie-Antoinette: 184
Versailles Town Hotels &
    Restaurants: 187
Chartres: 190–191
Chartres Cathedral: 193
Giverny: 199

Normandy
Normandy: 208–209
Rouen: 216–217
Honfleur: 234–235
Bayeux: 250–251
D-Day Beaches: 264–265
Arromanches: 270
Omaha Beach Area: 276
Mont St-Michel Area: 299
Mont St-Michel: 301

Brittany
Brittany: 316
Dinan: 320–321
St-Malo: 335

The Loire
The Loire: 346–347
Amboise: 358–359
Near Amboise: 376–377
Chinon: 406–407
Near Chinon: 416–417

Dordogne
The Dordogne Region: 429
Sarlat-la-Canéda: 436
Greater Sarlat-la-Canéda: 445
Dordogne Canoe Trips & Scenic
    Loop Drive: 452–453
Cro-Magnon Caves near Sarlat-la-
    Canéda: 466–467
Near Rocamadour: 491

Languedoc-Roussillon
Languedoc-Roussillon: 505
Albi: 508
Carcassonne Overview: 524–525
Carcassonne's La Cité: 529
Near Carcassonne: 540
Collioure: 548–549

Provence
Provence: 556
Public Transportation in Provence:
    558
Arles: 568–569
Near Arles: 586
Arles Hotels & Restaurants:
    590–591

Avignon: 600–601
Avignon Hotels & Restaurants:
    612–613
Pont du Gard: 621
Les Baux: 627
Orange: 633
Vaison-la-Romaine: 640
Côtes du Rhône Driving Tour: 649
Luberon: 654–655

The French Riviera
The French Riviera: 664
Public Transportation on the French
    Riviera: 667
Nice: 674–675
Vieux Nice Hotels & Restaurants:
    686–687
Nice Hotels: 699
Nice Restaurants: 706
Villefranche-sur-Mer: 714–715
Between Nice & Monaco: 722
Cap Ferrat: 724
Monaco: 734–735
Antibes: 746–747

The French Alps
French Alps: 765
Annecy: 768–769
Lake Annecy: 776
Chamonix Town: 786–787
Chamonix Valley Overview: 790
Alpine Crossing from France to
    Italy: 795
Chamonix-Area Hikes: 806–807

Burgundy
Burgundy: 822
Beaune: 830–831
Beaune Hotels & Restaurants:
    842–843
South Vineyard Route: 857
North Vineyard Loop & Route des
    Grands Crus: 859
Back-Door Burgundy Drive: 873

Lyon
Lyon: 898–899
Vieux Lyon: 910
Vieux Lyon & Presqu'île: 922–923

Alsace
Alsace: 929
Colmar: 938–939
Alsace's Route du Vin: 957
Eguisheim: 966–967
Strasbourg: 980–981

Reims & Verdun
Reims-Verdun Area: 992–993
Reims: 996–997
Route de la Champagne: 1013
Battlefields of Verdun: 1025

Practicalities
France's Rail System: 1088–1089
Driving in France: 1103
How to Navigate a Roundabout:
    1107

Explore Europe

At ricksteves.com you can browse through thousands of articles, videos, photos and radio interviews, plus find a wealth of money-saving travel tips for planning your dream trip. And with our mobile-friendly website, you can easily access all this great travel information anywhere you go.

TV Shows

Preview the places you'll visit by watching entire half-hour episodes of Rick Steves' Europe (choose from all 100 shows) on-demand, for free.

your travel dreams into affordable reality

Radio Interviews

Enjoy ready access to Rick's vast library of radio interviews covering travel

tips and cultural insights that relate specifically to your Europe travel plans.

Travel Forums

Learn, ask, share! Our online community of savvy travelers is a great resource for first-time travelers to Europe, as well as seasoned pros. You'll find forums on each country, plus travel tips and restaurant/hotel reviews. You can even ask one of our well-traveled staff to chime in with an opinion.

Travel News

Subscribe to our free Travel News e-newsletter, and get monthly updates from Rick on what's happening in Europe.

Rick's Free Travel App

Get your FREE **Rick Steves Audio Europe**™ app to enjoy…

- Dozens of self-guided tours of Europe's top museums, sights and historic walks

- Hundreds of tracks filled with cultural insights and sightseeing tips from Rick's radio interviews

- All organized into handy geographic playlists

- For iPhone, iPad, iPod Touch, Android

With Rick whispering in your ear, Europe gets even better.

Find out more at ricksteves.com

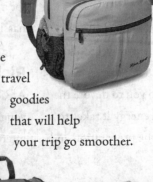

Save time and energy

This guidebook is your independent-travel toolkit. But for all it delivers, it's still up to you to devote the time and energy it takes to manage the preparation and logistics that are essential for a happy trip. If that's a hassle, there's a solution.

Rick Steves Tours

A Rick Steves tour takes you to Europe's most interesting places with great

with minimum stress

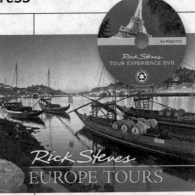

guides and small groups of 28 or less. We follow Rick's favorite itineraries, ride in comfy buses, stay in family-run hotels, and bring you intimately close to the Europe you've traveled so far to see. Most importantly, we take away the logistical headaches so you can focus on the fun.

customers—along with us on 40 different itineraries, from Ireland to Italy to Istanbul. Is a Rick Steves tour the right fit for your travel dreams? Find out at ricksteves.com, where you can also get Rick's latest tour catalog and free Tour Experience DVD.

Join the fun

This year we'll take 18,000 free-spirited travelers—nearly half of them repeat

Europe is best experienced with happy travel partners. We hope you can join us.

See our itineraries at ricksteves.com

BEST OF GUIDES

Best of France
Best of Germany
Best of Ireland
Best of Italy
Best of Spain

EUROPE GUIDES

Best of Europe
Eastern Europe
Europe Through the Back Door
Mediterranean Cruise Ports
Northern European Cruise Ports

COUNTRY GUIDES

Croatia & Slovenia
England
France
Germany
Great Britain
Ireland
Italy
Portugal
Scandinavia
Scotland
Spain
Switzerland

CITY & REGIONAL GUIDES

Amsterdam & the Netherlands
Belgium: Bruges, Brussels, Antwerp &
Barcelona
Budapest
Florence & Tuscany
Greece: Athens & the Peloponnese
Istanbul
London
Paris
Prague & the Czech Republic
Provence & the French Riviera
Rome
Venice
Vienna, Salzburg & Tirol

SNAPSHOT GUIDES

Basque Country: Spain & France
Berlin
Copenhagen & the Best of Denmark
Dublin
Dubrovnik
Edinburgh
Hill Towns of Central Italy
Italy's Cinque Terre
Krakow, Warsaw & Gdansk
Lisbon

Nearly all Rick Steves guides are available as ebooks. Check with your favorite bookseller.

Rick Steves guidebooks are published by Avalon Travel, an imprint of Perseus Books, a Hachette Book Group

Maximize your travel skills
with a good guidebook.

Valley
d & Toledo
& the Italian Lakes District
s & the Amalfi Coast
ern Ireland
ay
a, Granada & Southern Spain
tersburg, Helsinki & Tallinn
holm

KET GUIDES
erdam
ns
lona
nce
on
ch & Salzburg

ue
e
e
a

VEL CULTURE
be 101
pean Christmas
pean Easter
ards from Europe
l as a Political Act

STEVES' EUROPE DVDs
w Shows 2015-2016
ia & the Alps

The Complete Collection 2000-2016
Eastern Europe
England & Wales
European Christmas
European Travel Skills & Specials
France
Germany, BeNeLux & More
Greece, Turkey & Portugal
The Holy Land: Israelis & Palestinians Today
Iran
Ireland & Scotland
Italy's Cities
Italy's Countryside
Scandinavia
Spain
Travel Extras

PHRASE BOOKS & DICTIONARIES
French
French, Italian & German
German
Italian
Portuguese
Spanish

PLANNING MAPS
Britain, Ireland & London
Europe
France & Paris
Germany, Austria & Switzerland
Ireland
Italy
Spain & Portugal

Credits

RESEARCHERS

To help update this book, Rick and Steve relied on...

Mary Bouron

Mary caught the travel bug as a child living in London, and later, as an exchange student in France. Born a Seattleite, Mary now proudly calls herself a Parisian. Deeply in love with a Frenchman, and a mother of three, she occupies her free time hunting for the city's best baguette and studying the delicate difference between our cultures.

Trish Feaster

As a high-school Spanish teacher in San Diego, Trish frequently took her students on summer trips to Europe, sharing her passion for language, history, culture, and cuisine. She later earned a degree in French and now uses her language and teaching skills—along with her love of travel—as a Rick Steves' Europe tour guide and guidebook researcher, and as a travel blogger at thetravelphile.com. Trish enjoys traveling, binge-watching favorite shows, and playing *pétanque* with her partner in their hometown of Edmonds, Washington.

Kristen Michel

Kristen, a native of Seattle, first visited Europe as an exchange student, studying theater. Many years later, she is fluent in French, German, Champagne, and foie gras. Kristen has been leading tours and researching guidebooks for Rick Steves' Europe since 2000. After stays in southern France, Berlin, and Paris, she now lives in Seattle with her husband, Sylvain, and their daughter, Charlotte.

Virginie Moré

After living for 10 years in Los Angeles, Montana, and Florida, Virginie has been back in France for three years. Originally from Brittany, she now lives in Lyon with her husband Olivier, where they fully embrace its title of "food capital of the world." Along with doing book research, she teaches Americans about French culture and history while leading Rick Steves' Europe tours and guiding locally around Lyon.

CONTRIBUTOR

Gene Openshaw

Gene has co-authored a dozen *Rick Steves* books, specializing in writing walks and tours of Europe's cities, museums, and cultural sights. He also contributes to Rick's public television series, produces tours for Rick Steves Audio Europe, and is a regular guest on Rick's public radio show. Outside of the travel world, Gene has co-authored *The Seattle Joke Book*. As a composer, Gene has written a full-length opera called *Matter* (soundtrack available on Amazon), a violin sonata, and dozens of songs. He lives near Seattle with his daughter, enjoys giving presentations on art and history, and roots for the Mariners in good times and bad.

ACKNOWLEDGMENTS

Thanks to Steve's wife, Karen Lewis Smith, for her assistance covering French cuisine, and to Steve's children, Travis and Maria, for help with children's activities. The co-authors would also like to thank David Price, who lives in Avignon and is a fine source of information about key sights in Provence.

Avalon Travel
An imprint of Perseus Books
A Hachette Book Group company
1700 Fourth Street
Berkeley, California 94710

Text © 2017 by Rick Steves and Steve Smith. All rights reserved.
Maps © 2017 by Rick Steves' Europe. All rights reserved.
Paris Métro map © 2017 by La Régie Autonome des Transports Parisiens (RATP).
Used with permission.

Printed in Canada by Friesens. First printing January 2017.
ISBN 978-1-63121-437-0
ISSN 1084-4406

For the latest on Rick's talks, guidebooks, Europe tours, public radio show, free audio
tours, and public television series, contact Rick Steves' Europe, 130 Fourth Avenue
North, Edmonds, WA 98020, 425/771-8303, rick@ricksteves.com, www.ricksteves.com.

Rick Steves' Europe
Managing Editor: Jennifer Madison Davis
Special Publications Manager: Risa Laib
Editors: Glenn Eriksen, Tom Griffin, Katherine Gustafson, Mary Keils, Suzanne
  Kotz, Cathy Lu, John Pierce, Carrie Shepherd
Editorial & Production Assistant: Jessica Shaw
Editorial Intern: Lester Tobias
Researchers: Mary Bouron, Trish Feaster, Kristen Michel, Virginie Moré
Contributor: Gene Openshaw
Graphic Content Director: Sandra Hundacker
Maps & Graphics: David C. Hoerlein, Lauren Mills, Mary Rostad

Avalon Travel
Senior Editor and Series Manager: Madhu Prasher
Editor: Jamie Andrade
Associate Editor: Sierra Machado
Copy Editor: Maggie Ryan
Proofreaders: Jenny Malnick and Patty Mon
Indexer: Stephen Callahan
Production & Typesetting: Rue Flaherty, Sarah Wildfang
Cover Design: Kimberly Glyder Design
Maps & Graphics: Kat Bennett, Mike Morgenfeld

Photo Credits
Front Cover: La Roque-Gageac © Cameron Hewitt
Title Page: Notre-Dame Cathedral, © Dominic Arizona Bonuccelli
  Front Color Matter: p. xii, Collioure, © Dominic Arizona Bonuccelli
Additional Photography: Dominic Arizona Bonuccelli, Abe Bringolf, Mary Ann
  Cameron, Julie Coen, Rich Earl, Barb Geisler, Cameron Hewitt, David C. Hoerlein,
  Michaelanne Jerome, Lauren Mills, Virginie Moré, Gene Openshaw, Paul Orcutt,
  Rhonda Pelikan, Michael Potter, Carol Ries, Steve Smith, Robyn Stencil, Rick
  Steves, Gretchen Strauch, Rob Unck, Laura VanDeventer, Dorian Yates, Wikimedia
  Commons (PD-Art/PD-US). Photos are used by permission and are the property of
  the original copyright owners.

Want more France?
Maximize the experience with Rick Steves as your guide

Guidebooks
Provence and Paris guides make side-trips smooth and affordable

Phrase Books
Rely on Rick's French Phrase Book & Dictionary

Rick's TV Shows
Preview your destinations with 12 shows on France

Free! Rick's Audio Europe™ App
Get free audio tours for Paris' top sights

Small Group Tours
Rick offers several great itineraries through France

For all the details, visit ricksteves.com